JEAN RENOIR

JEAN RENOIR
A BIOGRAPHY

PASCAL MÉRIGEAU

Translated by Bruce Benderson

Foreword by Martin Scorsese

Published by Brett Ratner for Ratpac Press

RATPAC
PRESS

RUNNING PRESS
PHILADELPHIA

Originally published in France by Flammarion © 2012
English-language edition published by RatPac Press in collaboration with Running Press,
An Imprint of Perseus Books, LLC., A Subsidiary of Hachette Book Group, Inc.
All rights reserved under the Pan-American and International Copyright Conventions

Printed in the United States

ISBN 978-0-7624-5596-6

Library of Congress Control Number: 2016957798

E-book ISBN 978-0-7624-5608-6

10   9   8   7   6   5   4   3   2   1
Digit on the right indicates the number of this printing.

Edited by Cindi Rowell and Cindy De La Hoz
Designed by Joshua McDonnell
Typography: Bembo and Brandon

RatPac Press
4000 Warner Blvd.
Burbank, CA 91522

Running Press Book Publishers
2300 Chestnut Street
Philadelphia, PA 19103-4371

Visit us on the web!
www.ratpacentertainment.com
www.runningpress.com

Translator's note: This book was first published in France, where the American title of a film, play, or book first appearing in France had no relevancy for the text. For this edition of the book, I have researched the English-language titles, if different, for works that also appeared in the United States; and these most often appear inserted in parentheses throughout this text.

In memory of Alain Renoir

(October 31, 1921–December 12, 2008)

I was born with the itch to tell stories. When I'd wail in my cradle, it was in hopes of attracting an audience.

—Jean Renoir, December 1972,
Unused epigraph for *My Life and My Films*

Contents

Part II The Legend: January 1, 1941–February 12, 1979

Foreword

By Martin Scorsese

There are very few artists in the history of movies who are undeniable. Jean Renoir is one of those few. If you're dealing with cinema, you're dealing with Renoir. You're seeking out his films, watching them, rewatching them, understanding them. And, inevitably, marveling at them.

Renoir brought something to the art of moviemaking that is still so fresh and surprising that his pictures feel like they were just made, just *invented*. Near the end of his life, D. W. Griffith said, "What's missing from the movies nowadays is the beauty of the *moving wind in the trees*." He was talking about American cinema at the height of the studio system. But, of course, Renoir's cinema *was*—and is—the moving·wind in the trees, the flowing water of a stream, the faces of Jean Gabin and Simone Simon as lovers ashamed of their actions, the eccentric movements of Louis Jouvet as a nobleman reduced to a state of poverty, the red cheeks of a young girl at a social dance, a kite caught in a tree, childish pride on the face of Marcel Dalio as a rich aristocrat, clouds over the skies of Paris. I don't mean to imply that Renoir just strung moments together—he was a storyteller, and a great one. But he was a storyteller of a particular kind. He found and told stories that allowed for life to flow through and over and under the events onscreen—the little surprises and harmonies and beauties of character and atmosphere and light that make up experience. *The River*, which I suppose is my favorite of Renoir's films and one of the greatest pictures I've ever seen, could be described simply as the story of an English girl growing up in India. But the movie is everything that happens *between* the moments of the coming-of-age story. Like every Renoir picture, it's about life, lived moment by moment, every moment coming together and then dissolving in the flow of time.

So much has been written about Renoir over the years. We have his own wonderful book *My Life and My Films*. We have the great André Bazin's book, finished after his death by François Truffaut and his fellow writers and filmmakers-to-be. We have biographies and critical investigations and personal remembrances. And now we have this thorough, probing, exhaustively researched biography, which sets a new standard. Pascal Mérigeau gives us a portrait of Renoir's life that is more recognizably human than any we've previously had. Of course Renoir sanded off the rough edges of his life, as Mérigeau puts it. All of us do the same, I think. And Renoir's imperfections and vanities only bring him closer to us, and to the experience of his extraordinary and eternally wondrous films.

Introduction

The Chameleon on Plaid

Late on the morning of February 20, 1979, Jean Renoir was interred in the family vault in Essoyes cemetery, next to his older brother, Pierre, and their father, Auguste. His mother, Aline, and younger brother, Claude, lay nearby.

It was cold that Tuesday. The ground was frozen, the roads icy; the few faithful who'd come to pay their respects to the memory of the Master worried they'd never make it as far as Essoyes. Driven by Jean Carmet* who voiced his certainty that "the Boss" wouldn't have had it otherwise, the little group swept into a café as soon as arriving and ordered ham and eggs, which were served at the exact moment the funeral procession crossed the square. That same evening in Neuilly, Dido and Alain Renoir, the widow and only son of the director, reminisced about the deceased over a leg of lamb with beans, a specialty of Sébillon, the restaurant Renoir had frequented in the old days.

Jean Renoir had died at lunchtime on February 12, the Monday of the week before, in his house on Leona Drive in Beverly Hills' Benedict Canyon. He was eighty-four years old. On Friday the sixteenth, a mass had been celebrated at the oldest church in Beverly Hills, Church of the Good Shepherd, the same one that had hosted Rudolph Valentino's funeral in 1926 and Gary Cooper's in 1961 as well as the place where George Cukor had staged the funeral scene in the film *A Star Is Born;* and where, a little more than a year after Renoir's service, respects would be paid to Alfred Hitchcock, who would die on April 29, 1980. On the evening of Sunday the twenty-fifth, two thousand people visited the enormous Royce Hall at the University of California, Los Angeles (UCLA) for a ceremony in Renoir's honor, which had been planned some time before but had been transformed into a posthumous tribute at which Cukor, among others, spoke.

On the day after Renoir's death, deep within the part of the country where he'd spent his childhood vacations, he was honored on a scale worthy of his renown, just as would happen in California, where he'd lived the last thirty-eight

---

* *Translator's note:* Jean Carmet, French actor (1920–1994), appeared in Renoir's *Le Caporal epinglé* (*The Elusive Corporal*, 1962) and *Le Petit Théâtre de Jean Renoir* (*The Little Theatre of Jean Renoir*, 1969).

years of his life. That renown was sizable, motivated as it was by admiration for his films, the aura of his personality as the son of a great painter, his reputation for openness to the world and to others, and his extraordinary lust for life and all the pleasures it afforded—among which those of the table ranked high. And so, another leg of lamb serves as a way to begin this story.

Alain Renoir had spent a long time preparing the dish, using a tiny knife to make the incisions into which he inserted slivers of garlic. Unearthing from a cupboard an electric rotisserie whose functioning only he knew, and cursing the appliance without really being annoyed, he finally plugged it in; soon after, it glowed red. He didn't take his eyes from the meat while it cooked, unless to serve himself a glass of champagne. Alain Renoir loved champagne—French brands when he was in France, Californian when he was at home. That evening, or perhaps the day before, or the day before that, he'd discovered one of the two films of his father that he hadn't known: *On purge Bébé*. He'd never see the second, which I'd also brought him, and that's the reason why I've forgotten its title. Ten or so days after this final leg of lamb, he fell ill, spent time in a Sacramento hospital (where the nurses still remember how much this old gentleman made them laugh), and was eventually moved to his house in Esparto. In Paris on a Saturday evening, I heard the voice of his wife, Patricia Renoir, on the telephone, telling me, "Pascal, Alain died yesterday." The date she called: December 13, 2008.

Alain had joined the United States Army and fought in the Pacific during World War II, and had then become a professor of medieval literature at the University of California, Berkeley. He'd laughingly claim that he now never read any text written after the Battle of Hastings, which took place on October 14, 1066. One morning in his arbor (this must have been during my first stay in Esparto), he said to me, "I've talked about my father with dozens of people, but you ask questions nobody ever asked."

The reason for this is simple. Of all the major directors, Jean Renoir was the one who shared the most about himself and his films—both in speech and in writing. He's also one of those to whom the greatest number of works has been devoted worldwide. Works in which all the events related, all the conversations reported, all the characteristics of behavior described, and all the ways of making things known are generally held to be absolutely authentic. And yet, reading between the lines and questioning truths that seem established reveal glaring contradictions, blatant impossibilities, patent expropriations. To understand who Jean Renoir was, we need to restart from zero, drawing from sources that until now were difficult to access, some of which are still unpublished today. We need to take constant care to keep our perspective on his films as they can be read on the screen, and not on this or that rereading of them through a prism of admiration. I quickly understood that reassembling different elements from their sources and observing them with the necessary distance would yield a figure who does not conform to the one commonly described; and as I did this, the various pages of the Renoir legend—one after another—became blurred because they looked too well calibrated to be honest, too carefully drawn. Soon another Renoir began to appear, a more complicated, more original, and considerably more interesting Renoir. Therefore, the story of the fabrication of his legend has become one of the axes of this book that allows us to understand more clearly who this personality really was and how he was transformed at the end of his life into the wise old man he was not. This transformation was accomplished by an overzealous following who were determined he reveal no trait likely to free him from the framework in which they'd judged it convenient to imprison him.

As a matter of fact, how could our perceived image of Renoir, woven from a single cloth, jibe with his films, when this is the same director and same man who envisioned and directed *La Grande Illusion* (*Grand Illusion*) and *La Règle du jeu* (*The Rules of the Game*), films so dissimilar that all they have in common is that both have become classics? The aim of this book, then, was born from the enigma announced by Jacques Lourcelles when he said, "If it's astonishing to have made *Grand Illusion* or *The Rules of the Game*, it's so much more so to have directed both these films, thereby touching *every* stratum of an audience, as if there were a writer capable of creating not only *Les Misérables* but also *The Charterhouse of Parma*."[1]

Before I even had time to share my insight with Alain regarding this fissure between the man as his father is commonly described and his films, Alain in some way corroborated it with his anecdotes and memories as well as his own way of being and considering the world. Alain was as direct as his father had been roundabout, and he called people idiots as easily as Jean had claimed to understand all of them. He hated stupidity as much as Renoir—when he chose to—didn't notice it, or pretended not to. And yet, when the son spoke, it was also Jean you heard—his passions, contradictions, educated guesses, and deficiencies—all of that human complexity. It was something I remarked upon without ever having met Jean Renoir, whose films I discovered like a lot of people of my generation did, on television; and they stayed with me from the start, either because they seemed easily accessible to the child I was—*Grand Illusion*, of course, and *Boudu sauvé des eaux* (*Boudu Saved from Drowning*), obviously—or because I couldn't understand that certain people more intelligent and more cultivated than I thought they were masterpieces. It obviously takes time to realize that claimed imperfections can be more appealing than flaunted virtues, and to understand that a real film is made from the gulf that inevitably opens between the work as imagined by its creator and what he or she manages to accomplish.

I also remember the strange effect near the end of the seventies that *La Chienne* had on me, its uniqueness and beauty, and how I thought the sound seemed to have been recorded in an aquarium holding Michel Simon and the street singers, the pretty girl who is sacrificed, and the sound of automobiles on pavement. Very quickly, I wanted to know who Jean Renoir was, to try to read his identity in his films, to see him appear in his books and in those books about him. Years later, the project of this book came about as a way of fulfilling my wish to draw a portrait with more of a resemblance than those that already existed, whether they were appealing or boring, poorly done or inspiring. All of them offered convincing snapshots when considered in isolation, but mediocrity when combined. And with both admiration and a long-standing affection for this figure, combined with the necessary distance needed for such a subject, I set about trying to relink the fragments, to finally assemble various sequences into a part of the thread of a story that I suspected had never before been told. After five years of this, I had to admit that many of my certainties had fallen apart and that I was actually passing nonstop from surprise to astonishment. Today, my admiration for the director has grown, and my liking for the person has turned into empathy tinged with affection.

Was it the man or the director the articles were honoring the day after his death? The answer is two-sided: homage was paid to the pre-1940 director, but it was the man of his last thirty years who was being saluted. It was as if the young Jean Renoir had only existed through and for his films, as if the only person ever known afterward was an aged, portly gentleman with an incomparable gift for gab, an expert in carefully modulated thoughts. To put it plainly and with very little exaggeration, the Jean Renoir films of the twenties and thirties were the work of a man who wouldn't begin to exist until his career was considered to be over. To the same extent, a gap had been opened between the maker of *The Rules of the Game,* that painter of a society in decline, and Renoir the "Good Papa," sweeping the world with his paternal gaze and on demand uttering the ready-made theories and formulas he was expected to. Meanwhile, a handful of young people had massed under the banner of *Cahiers du cinéma* to spread the news that Renoir had achieved his most authentic masterpieces during and at the end of his Hollywood experience, thereby opening breaches into which he, himself, was delightedly diving, more than happy that someone was still interested in him at a time when his cinema was being labeled outdated in other respects.

On the other hand, as the year 1979 began, some people were actually asking this director for forgiveness.[2] For what? For not having provided him the financial aid that would have allowed him to direct one last film. Those at the source of the decision weren't beating their breasts—no—but ordinary media commentators were taking over the debate; and it was in the name of France that they were asking forgiveness. Forgiveness for having let Renoir leave for California, forgiveness for having "condemned" him to remain an American despite his assurances that he was bearing it admirably. Jean Renoir had left France in 1940 and had never wanted to return and live there. He had a host of reasons for it, and he was quite happy where he was. In February 1979, most of those deploring the fact that Renoir hadn't been able to shoot in France ten years previously weren't exactly fans of the films he'd made after he left that country. That is one of the great paradoxes of a life that has probably produced more of them than anyone else's: Jean Renoir was never more famous than when his films, one by one, were becoming less appealing—all the more so when compared to those films he'd directed in the past, which were being reshown and rereleased. In this way, he found himself confronted by a reality usually experienced by young filmmakers, whose movies are sometimes compared to those of the better of their elders. Peculiarly disorienting as it was, Renoir simultaneously became a present-day director and that director's respected ancestor.

Renoir's films were admired at first because life seemed to proceed naturally in them, without any needless display of cinema. Then, in the second part of his career, they were admired because cinema was being flaunted in every shot. In other words, there was admiration for two diametrically opposed reasons. If he did last and, after Chaplin, became the auteur who incited the most studies, the most reflections, the most analyses, it is probably because his films seemed positioned to work out the answer to a question formulated by someone who wrote the most and best about Renoir, André Bazin—who asked, "What is cinema?" It seems to me that Renoir's unusual personality, his life's trajectory, the swerves in his career, and the analyses inspired by his films all needed to be integrated by reflection. And as the crushing bulk of writing that already existed made me ask what there was about Jean Renoir still to discover, I very quickly came to the conclusion that nearly everything needed to be brought to light.

What kind of man was Jean Renoir in reality? A spoiled brat catapulted into the sophistication of Paris life in the twenties? A well-off bourgeois won over by the Popular Front in the following decade? The director who, like all his colleagues, was fascinated by Hollywood and struggled to bring attention to his films but also had a lifestyle well suited to California? The sage of the mid-fifties, spreading the Good Word to the world, paying his father the most vibrant homage, celebrating the virtues of contemporary cinema and television, delighting all with thoughts about his art, life, humanity, without ever stopping to claim he was a man of the previous century? He was all these people, one after another and sometimes simultaneously. Then what causes that gleam of affection in everyone's eyes—film enthusiast or not—at the mere mention of his name?

"Saint Renoir doesn't exist, and never did," wrote Claude Gauteur, one of the guests at the ham-and-eggs ceremony, the church, and the cemetery on February 20, 1979. And when Gauteur used that sentence to begin his book,[3] he irritated François Truffaut, faithful among the faithful, grand priest of the cult, and most scrupulous guardian of the temple. You could claim that the son of Auguste Renoir was a saint. Of course you could; but he was a secular saint, as members of his Communist family would be quick to point out while remembering their fellow Party traveler in the second half of the thirties. Fine, the sticklers would specify, but take note: he was a secular saint who attended mass every single Sunday it pleased God to offer one in California. So saintly, so secular, in fact, that he even decided to entrust his son's education both to a priest and to a Communist grade-school teacher, which points to someone who is fond of eclipsing antagonisms. Wasn't he at least "the most director-like of all the French as well as the most French of the directors?"[4] Absolutely, as long as we neglect to mention that he hadn't turned fifty before he stopped thinking of himself as French and ceaselessly proclaimed that everything in Hollywood—including the producers, actors, and technicians—was preferable to what he'd known in France.

The genius of Jean Renoir was the way the most implacable adversaries collaborated to justify him without changing their own views. In every circumstance. Perhaps without knowing it, then, they were fine-tuning their behavior to his. Without having to intervene, Renoir comforted them, gave them assurance and confidence, and, in return, received testimonies of their admiration, their tacit accord, and their affection. Such unanimity hadn't always existed. It had taken shape when his films began to count for less, when the man began to speak to all and everyone about nothing and everything, forging the image of himself he intended to project and that he knew was expected, through random interviews and conversations and with a succession of writings. Contrarily, during his period of cinematographic fame in the second half of the thirties, he was a controversial personality, considered difficult and not very trustworthy, as well as opportunistic and generous, but not too generous. Success leads to resentment, it is said; but that not-very-flattering image was already his before his films became a success with the triumph of *Grand Illusion* in 1937.

The year 1940 was his time of exile, a prelude to the wisdom of the fifties that came after a stay in India, which he unhesitatingly proclaimed had changed him completely and had even, well, helped him discover the truth: "Everyone has his reasons." Yes, he insisted without laughing, India had revealed that sentence to him—the same sentence he'd put on paper twenty years earlier and pronounced in *The Rules of the Game*. On that day in 1959, sitting opposite the TV camera filming him, he must have really had great fun coming up with those words, an actor playing himself, pretending to discover a formula he'd invented years ago.

"Everyone has his reasons," rightly says Octave in *The Rules of the Game,* having good reason to deplore that truth peculiar to the human species; and later, he would have been justified in adding that Jean Renoir's reasons were always good ones in the eyes of everyone. This is completely natural for a director whose movies fully take the side of every character, one after another; it is a distinctive feature of his films that contributes to their greatness and probably renders them timelessly unique.

To put all your characters on the same moral level, you have to love them. To love all of them, you have to understand them. To understand all of them, you can't bestow more value on the opinion expressed by one than on the opposite opinion held by another. You cannot choose. Cannot take sides or, at the very least, must pretend not to. Cannot choose between the timorous bank teller in *La Chienne,* the Sunday painter treated sadistically by a cantankerous wife, and the lost woman who is manipulating him and taking advantage of his naïveté and frustrations while all the strings are pulled by her pimp, that bastard who ends up on the gallows, although he's completely innocent of the crime of which he's accused. Cannot choose between Boudu, the tramp, and Lestinguois, the bourgeois. Cannot choose between Inspector Maigret and the beautiful Dane, who is a drug-addicted murderer. Cannot choose—or must, at least, do everything that seems not to—between the cynical huckster masquerading as a man of the cloth and the decent, love-struck boy who kills him in *Le Crime de monsieur Lange* (*The Crime of Monsieur Lange*). Between the king of France and those who will cut off his head. Between the railroad engineer whom women drive crazy and the flirt who uses him to flee justice and save a husband she mistrusts. Between the gamekeeper and the poacher, the marquis and the upstart, the grande dame and the soubrette, the husband and the lover.

To understand all of them that well, you definitely need to see all sides of each, without taking a side yourself; or else, take sides one after the other, which is the same thing. This is the ultimate guarantee of peace of mind, a mind offering to become entirely devoted to the most important cause—his own—whose contours were shaped by chance occurrences of birth and existence. Throughout his entire life, Jean Renoir strove to believe in himself. Convinced that self-confidence can only be acquired in the eyes of others, he made every effort to ensure that others believed in him, the son of a famous artist, born in the shadow of an elder brother who had been hailed as a noble actor and upon whom all qualities of uprightness, rigor, and honesty had been bestowed. Very early, and for a long time, it was up to Renoir alone to find an occupation and create an identity as Jean Renoir. This is how the actor he'd dreamed of becoming interpreted the role he knew best—himself. It was made to his measure, constantly retouched; and it created the most unusual of life paths, which better matched the nature of cinema.

The different incarnations of Jean Renoir's life, like so many others, can be correlated to the women he loved. Three women shaped his three great periods. Catherine Hessling* was both Auguste Renoir's last model and Jean's first wife. She inspired him with her dreams about film and fame. He made an actress out of her at the same time that she made a director out of him. The second woman was Marguerite, a film editor who led him into the world of politics; and the films that they made together carried him to the top. After their separation, the secret of fashioning those films was permanently lost to him; she devoted her expertise, sensibility, and talent to Jacques Becker, Renoir's longtime assistant. Renoir hadn't married Marguerite, but she took his name. Dido, the third woman, was the daughter of a diplomat, and she became secretary to the Great Renoir as well as his spouse and housekeeper, keeping a jealous eye on him, his health, his approach to doing things, and his image. Thus, the gamut of Renoir's women ran from an artist with a wild streak of hedonism, to an unparalleled technician and fervent militant Communist, to, finally, a deeply religious woman who believed in Jean Renoir and God and who devoted her existence to those two idols. Catherine Hessling left Renoir's life just before film discovered sound, and she disappeared from this world seven months after he did.† Marguerite Houllé‡ was his traveling companion during the thirties. Dido Freire became the wife of Renoir the American citizen, world-renowned director, and dispenser of homilies.§

In response to the aspirations of the first woman, to the dreams she expressed to him night and day, Renoir became a producer—he had the money

---

* *Translator's note:* "Catherine Hessling" was the professional name used by the woman born Andrée Heuschling.

† Andrée Heuschling, a.k.a. Catherine Hessling, died on September 28, 1979, in La Celle-Saint-Cloud.

‡ Marguerite Houllé, who went by the name Renoir, died in 1987.

§ Dido Renoir died on May 7, 1990, in Beverly Hills. She is buried in Essoyes, in the same tomb as Pierre-Auguste, Pierre, and Jean Renoir.

for that—and later, a director, because he possessed no shortage of ambition. For the second woman, in 1936, he married the cause to which artists were becoming engaged—something he was well advised to do, because the Communist Party was so powerful at the time it could help him capture an audience. But then, sharing the life of a militant Communist without putting at least one foot into the same boat as she would have to have been a source of conflicts, arguments, questions. The director without recognition he was at that time had to avoid such a predicament, not to mention the man, who wanted such people off his back. He got around more than was usual, played the man of the people and enjoyed it, made guarantees to comrades without ever stopping to associate with their opponents, and never even had to give up claiming he agreed with them. Sometimes he made it seem—first and foremost to himself, probably—that he'd chosen sides. It could be inferred from the words he spoke at meetings and with which he peppered his articles, or supplied to certain journalists; but in his films, no, never, really. His last partner, Dido, was a practicing Catholic, but what need was there to keep questioning the existence of God with her, something he himself wasn't against believing in, or to argue about the importance of religion? It was infinitely more practical to play it smart every Sunday and accompany that woman, whom he addressed using the French formal form of *you*, to mass and confession and to mumble his prayers like a child who had no intention of getting rapped on the knuckles.

All this was how Jean Renoir found freedom. However, those who discovered his films long after hadn't the same luxury to any great extent; and because they loved his films, they decided their choices were his. They believed that he was like them and preferred Boudu to Lestinguois, the revolutionaries to the king. He let them go on, was in complete agreement, when he wasn't impishly scheming to say the same thing before they did. He vindicated them as he did all his characters. Whenever he noticed any resistance to such a routine in anyone to whom he was speaking, he changed his opinion and put as much energy, talent, and genius into it as he had supporting the previous position. He did it with just as much conviction—yes; because everyone seemed to deserve no less than the deepest part of him, he turned his attention to it. With so much sincerity, so much genius. That was how he became the ideal receptacle for all theories, those the most closely related to him as well as those furthest away. Everyone could find something satisfying in his filmmaking and in his personality that reinforced his or her convictions and generated something new about him. It was as if it were enough to invent a method for an admired director who really had none and become his equal—or even, more modestly, his disciple—by conforming to it. In this way, as well, Jean Renoir was a genius at what would eventually be called public relations. The directors of the Nouvelle Vague (the French New Wave) invented a method for him, and he enthusiastically accepted their principles.

Sometimes his attitude toward the world made him talk too much and even write rashly, in circumstances where he had better cause to keep his mouth shut and hold back his pen. But just as actors were flattered by the compliments he lavished on them, those who loved his films approved of him and preferred to throw the veil over his lapses, perhaps dreading that the wrong word might condemn them to the misery of falling out of rank and sect. Meanwhile, adversaries exaggerated, too, and expressed their own abhorrence recklessly by digging up and trotting out things that pinned far too many faults on him than could be believed.

I should point out that Renoir's sincerity is not being cast in doubt. He believed the stories he told and believed even more in the style he'd invented to recount them. Recounting was all he thought of—in words, in films, in books— what did it matter? Recounting: in other words, making you believe. For the span of a conversation, a movie, a book. And the rest? In his eyes, that was less important; there again you might say he had a point.

Jean Renoir played the roles he chose so well—yes, roles, specifically, because he willingly changed parts so that the world, including his adversaries and those who adored him, would see only smoke and mirrors. In that respect, he put as much art into his life as he did into directing his films—reason enough for such a life to be recounted, but by someone other than him, because he did such a thing with acuity, guile, and talent. He was a character constructed, interpreted, and portrayed by himself as much as he was a person, a person whose existence, life trajectory, and work can be unfolded using the many traces he left behind— as if purposely. Before he died, he decided the essentials of his life would be collected in one place on the UCLA campus: 113 jam-packed cardboard boxes, some containing up to fifty or more folders; tens of thousands of letters, personal documents, school notebooks, soldier's notebooks, and breakdowns of film footage; correspondence with producers, actors, technicians; scripts that were filmed or weren't; projects barely sketched out or tracked over several years. And in the depths of other archives—which had been unavailable to some of my predecessors—as well as in some private collections to which I was given access are just as many documents that put to the test evidence that is human, precious, and indispensable—yet so fragile.

In the century that was his, Jean Renoir knew everything and lived almost everything: World War I, the do-it-yourself "art" of the silent cinema, sound;

then politics, Communism, Fascism; exodus, exile, Hollywood, India; the new cinema celebrated and in a sense invented by the Nouvelle Vague, television; writing, finally, and then paralysis. Until his arrival in the United States on December 31, 1940, he took part in history; after that, he became part of legend, part of a Hollywood that barely resembled the one about which he'd always fantasized, and which he then replaced with the legend of himself with the help of several servants whom he had enthralled. And those who reference John Ford by professing that the legend, rather than history, should be printed, will recall that the film from which they're quoting proceeds from precisely the opposite intent: it extinguishes the legend of Ransom Stoddard (James Stewart) as the man who killed Liberty Valance by showing that Tom Doniphon (John Wayne) hid in the shadows that night and shot the villain dead, without letting anyone but the filmmakers catch sight of him.

Along his entire path through the century, Renoir lived in the moment. Pleasure in the moment, as much as a refusal and incapacity to choose, guided him, just as in his films the span of time over which a scene takes place often outweighs the linking of sequences. For this reason, as well, the fragmented portrait drawn of him over the years suits him and corresponds very well to him yet is a poor resemblance. Pursuit of pleasure in the moment required that he quickly find a way to agree with those he was speaking with and keep it up as long as the scene lasted. That he would profess ideas other than those he advanced a few hours earlier was always only for the record. For the record, obviously, but whose? His was rarely held to be lacking; it played with these contradictions, which made him what he was. The part of it that his friends, the people close to him, journalists, and historians retained contained only elements that allowed them to paint a picture of someone essentially decided on in advance. When Renoir said "black" to one and answered "white" to the other, each kept only what he or she had heard, or wanted to hear. This is how he was in his writing as well. In the jungle of his writings, there is always the question of whom he's addressing, what real or imaginary reader he's thinking of, what effect he hopes to produce, what objective he wants to attain, at which precise moment of his life he's writing—which day of the week, even, if not which hour. For the impenitent charmer he was, pleasing mattered, and so did never ceasing to attract attention. In that enterprise, as well, he succeeded.

Jean Renoir made sure that everybody, actors and crew, felt responsible for the film they were working on together. He made each of them believe that the role of director was severely limited. This wasn't a method or even a technique but a way of being. He knew how to give the impression—the illusion—that those who approached him, in his eyes, mattered more than he did himself; as a result, certain accounts more than others ought to be considered from a distance, because their authors ingenuously claim certain merits they didn't possess. Renoir's capacity to "read" character, nature, strength, or weakness at first glance afforded him the ability to adapt instantly to anyone's personality, a principle of attraction that no one could resist. In him, modesty and arrogance formed a partnership, feeding each other to the point of merging. He put all his energy into disguising arrogance, although humility couldn't be counted as one of his cardinal virtues.

His generosity was praised, though expressed little in regard to other directors. The only ones he could not resist praising were the pioneers whose examples had inspired him—Chaplin, Griffith, Stroheim. All three became his close friends. In relation to them, and only them, and especially their fame, he measured himself. The rest—nearly all the rest—seemed of no importance to him. Of the many reasons that made him renounce living in France after the war, the most significant (outside of his happiness in the States) was the fact that only American film would allow him to measure up to the renown of his masters and attain an international reputation on a level with that of his father. All he had to gain from working in France was money; before the war, he was "the" French director and remained so to many people. Only when he understood that American film decidedly had no use for him any longer did he agree to go back to France for the span of one film and then another. In the nation he'd been calling his "ex-country" since the summer of 1941, six months after his arrival in America, he dreamed primarily of the films he wanted to direct in Hollywood and made an Anglo-Saxon audience the priority in his work. Until the end of his days, he insisted—to Americans, especially—that he bore no resentment against Hollywood. He had experienced it as welcoming, he had only friends there, but the movie business was rejecting him in the same way and with the same energy that, he claimed, French producers and distributors had stood in his way earlier. No more, no less.

The story of Jean Renoir is also the story of a divorce—two divorces, actually: the first brutal, the second *glissando*. The first divorce was from the cinema that had made him king and that he thought about leaving as soon as he experienced success, given all its years of indifference toward him in the past. The day after the success of *Grand Illusion*, Renoir began dreaming of Hollywood, of those studios that had enlisted René Clair, Julien Duvivier, Jacques Feyder. Why them and not him? The second was a genteel divorce from his own history at the price of compromises. And so he went about sanding off the rough edges to turn himself, his father, his family into a panorama of pleasantly colored pictures, a gallery of sleek images, a story for good children to teach them that rivalries, jealousies, secret desires, money, ambition, lies, and fakery don't play a part in the lives of exceptional beings. This choice belonged to him, and in that he was justified. The choice of a historian is nonetheless so, and today we must rely on what Renoir decided to leave behind.

Renoir's films are the work of a man who found his identity in his metamorphoses; his cinema was invented as the result of ups and downs, accidents and compromises. Jean Renoir was a chameleon, even—to borrow the term Herbert Hoover inflicted on Franklin D. Roosevelt in 1932—a "chameleon on plaid." What he displayed didn't at all modify his way of seeing, but it strongly affected his way of being seen. In a modest turtleneck or tailor-made sports jacket, Renoir remained Renoir. Did he get to a point of confusion about the nature of his true colors? Maybe, but nobody noticed; and he never imploded. .

By nature, a filmmaker is an opportunist. He takes possession of someone else's book, grabs some emotion from the features of an actress, steals a colleague's idea, borrows his clouds from the sky, his reflections from the river, and from this chaos known as directing a film, from a blend of decisions and luck, intentions and accidental confusions, emerges as the organizer, or pretends to be the authorizer. Renoir was really no more dishonest than anyone else. It's just that the occasions for fibbing and faking were more numerous for him than for most others, and he got immense pleasure from talking about himself and his art.

He'd seize the events of his life and pull out stories to recount just for the pleasure of conversation; and as soon as that door cracked open, an anecdote rushed in, became fable, and quickly became the pretext for a theory. When a man who is asked to talk about himself and his art takes considerable pleasure in it, some theories become necessary, and then it doesn't really matter that in practicing his profession he actually followed none, because he was the polar opposite of a man of system or method.

The story of Jean Renoir teaches us, among other truths, that filmmakers make the films that they can and as they can. Later, when they explain how they made them, they say what makes listeners like them better. Anyone with a genuine desire to understand that film is the process of fabricating truth by starting with what is false and of creating what is false by starting with what is true will see that Renoir, in the events of his own life and with his personality, behaved like a director. He wrote the scenario for, directed, and acted out his persona and his life. Renoir's life, at least as much as his films, provides the answer to the question, "What is cinema?" And what *is* cinema? It is this.

PART I

SEPTEMBER 15, 1894–DECEMBER 31, 1940

1

The Invention of Renoir

Jean Renoir was born on September 15, 1894—just after midnight, he'd write three-quarters of a century later, when he mentioned the event.* Staging this moment in which he plays both star and wailing extra, he'd reference François Rabelais's *Gargantua* and depict his father Auguste Renoir reacting to the arrival that night of such a Grangousier† by exclaiming, "What a mouth! A furnace! He'll have the appetite of a horse!"[1]

A week after Jean Renoir let out his first cry, the son of a Viennese hatter celebrated his ninth birthday. His name? Erich Oswald Stroheim. In the same year, on February 1, John Martin Feeney, who would later change his name to John Ford, had already been born; King Vidor, on the eighth of the same month; Sternberg, on May 29. Charles Chaplin had turned five that April, just as New Yorkers were discovering the first Kinetoscope parlor. At the end of summer, Louis Lumière had filmed the first version of *La Sortie des usines Lumière* (*Workers Leaving the Lumière Factory*), using photographic paper as the medium. In December, in Vienna, Anton and Paula Lang celebrated the fifth birthday of their little Friedrich Christian Anton, better known by the amiable name "Fritz."

Jean Renoir writes that his mother found him horribly ugly on sight and made it known that she wanted him taken away from her as quickly as possible. It's true that the infant's care was entrusted to a teenager from the country: Gabrielle Renard, who was fifteen, and the only one, she herself has said, to find the child born that night attractive. Years later, she was the one who remembered the events he couldn't, thereby becoming scenarist of some of the scenes in his skillfully written book about his father—which was also partly about himself.[2]

* "I was born at Le Château des Brouillards on September 15, 1894, a little after midnight," wrote Jean Renoir. The birth registered three days later at the town council of the Eighteenth Arrondissement lists the date and time as September 15 at 11 p.m.

† *Translator's note:* Grangousier, a character from Rabelais's *Gargantua*, was a punning reference to the term "Big (*Grand*) Gullet (*Gosier*)."

Barely more than one letter exists recounting the impression the birth of his second child produced on Auguste Renoir. The painter wrote to Berthe Morisot and presented the event as "something completely ridiculous . . . the arrival of a son named Jean."[3] Why ridiculous? Because by then Renoir was fifty-three? Because the mother—who, like her son, was in good health—was eighteen years younger than Auguste, a difference that would have obviously counted for more at the end of the nineteenth century than it does in our day? Auguste seems to have been indecisive about the position to take when it came time to announce the news to his friends, as if this birth made him uncomfortable and he felt burdened by this second son from Aline.

Jean came into the world nine years after his older brother, Pierre, who was born in March 1885. When this first birth occurred, Auguste Renoir and Aline Charigot were not married; they waited until 1890 to legitimize a union that, by then, was already around a decade old. Auguste had needed time to decide to found a family, and before that, he suffered months of irresolution before he moved in with Aline, the young woman from Essoyes, a village on the borders of Champagne and Bourgogne in the department of Aube. She was his favorite model, became his companion, and the mother of a first son and then a second; and then, gradually, under the weight of time, this peasant, who was a picture of health, began to thicken and her features collapse to the point that the last photos in which she appears are completely devoid of the fresh, dazzling beauty portrayed in *Le Déjeuner des canotiers* (*Luncheon of the Boating Party*) and dozens of other paintings. While Auguste—eighteen years older—grew so lean he came to resemble the trunk of an olive tree, Aline coarsened and fattened and was stricken with the diabetes that would spell her end.

The birth of Jean marked one of the stages in the life of Renoir the painter; but his union with Aline didn't spell the end of his travels, which he often accomplished alone. His painting sent him to Provence, Normandy, Saintonge, and Brittany. He visited Spain with Paul Gallimard, spent the summer in Pont-Aven, and joined Berthe Morisot not far from Paris. "Renoir isn't made for marriage. He marries every woman he paints . . . with his brush," said Louis-Jacques Samary, a cellist for the orchestra of the Opéra and father of actress Jeanne Samary, whom Renoir painted several times. Renoir himself echoed this remark near the end of his life in answer to a journalist who asked him how he managed to paint with hands crippled by rheumatism: "With my prick!"[4]

He may very well not have been made for marriage, but by 1894 he was well on his way toward accepting the reality of a process, and its completion is illustrated by a highly symbolic picture he painted in spring 1896. To represent "the Artist's Family," in fact, Renoir chose to deck out his own in the trappings of the bourgeoisie, depicting Aline (the same woman he'd painted until then—and would again—as the peasant she had been when he met her) in a matron's hat; Pierre in a sailor suit, which was the uniform of the bourgeois child; and little beribboned Jean in the arms of a crouching servant.

When the school year started in 1894, a few days before Jean was born, Pierre began his education in fourth grade at Notre-Dame de Sainte-Croix, the posh Catholic institution in Neuilly-sur-Seine, just a stone's throw from the Porte des Ternes. Schoolchildren there wore a uniform with a cap, and all of them were the sons of leading families. A more commonplace event perhaps, but definitely part of the same trend, was Renoir's consent to Jean's baptism on July 1, 1895—an "informal" one, as he emphasized to the baby's godfather, Georges Durand-Ruel. Durand-Ruel was the man Aline was dreaming of marrying to Jeanne Baudot, the reason for her choice of that woman as godmother of her son. Georges's father, Paul Durand-Ruel, as well as his two sons, Joseph and Georges, were among those men who expanded the sale of art works to the dimensions of a market. Jeanne Baudot was a painter and daughter of the family doctor, a convinced advocate of Epsom salts. Wasn't all this what Auguste, who understood the impact of such an official birth and found it a ticklish subject to announce to his artist friends, considered in advance "completely ridiculous," an expression that Berthe Morisot, herself a *grande bourgeoise*, was probably one of the least likely even to understand?

Jean was the product of the union of a painter of modest origins and a country girl; but his father became a wealthy, recognized artist, and his mother, a bourgeoise. The setting of his childhood featured a well-off family, a legacy that kept him from ever lacking anything his entire life. He lived, or, more precisely, chose to exist, between two worlds in a way of life similar to Octave's in *The Rules of the Game*, a role Jean would take for himself: a character witnessing the collapse of the class in which life had offered him membership.

In 1894, Auguste Renoir was finally celebrated by critics. Official recognition had come late, but his canvases were selling well and their prices continually climbing. In 1899, for example, Ambroise Vollard observed that a canvas the painter had sold for 150 francs fewer than twenty years before had found a buyer willing to pay 22,100 francs.* To help his wife take care of the new child, Renoir summoned Aline's young cousin Gabrielle from Essoyes. On the morning of her first night in Paris, the girl dashed into the street to play with kids hardly younger than she. After moving in with the Renoirs at the end of

---

* In 1907, Renoir put in a bid of 35,000 francs for a property known as Les Collettes. As a painter, his quoted value had skyrocketed in the meantime so that the sale of a single canvas allowed him to become the owner of a house.

August, a few weeks before the birth of Jean, Gabrielle also began serving as a model, just as some models, at times, were asked to play the role of servants. When Vollard visited the Renoirs for the first time, the year Jean was born, he noticed her in the garden and called her "a maid who looked like a gypsy." The family also took on a cook and laundress, Madame Mathieu. So, the house was filled with women, not all of whom were fully clothed, all of them chatting and laughing under the aloof authority of Madame Renoir as well as the more amused, relaxed manner of "the Boss," as everyone called Renoir.

Because the Boss often seemed willing to let his pockets be plundered, part of the models' job was getting rid of intruders and freeloaders. Jean considered all these women around when he was growing up as family, even though they didn't take their meals with the Renoirs. He would have been surprised to learn that all of them, in fact, were on the payroll, that some people, whom it was tempting to see as willing to serve their masters just by choice, actually needed to make a living. In his book about his father,[5] Jean does not say a word about the battles the painter waged to become recognized and speaks even less about the man's unremitting efforts to be paid—often considerable amounts. Such efforts were only natural, but from Jean's point of view they would have blemished the portrait. The fact that Auguste wasn't against his pockets being rifled (just as Jean would not mind later) more than testifies to his generosity but also shows precisely that pocket money, for him, was always for the record available for the very reason he had no lack of it. If Auguste had been the deeply unselfish man portrayed by his son, would his correspondence so often have involved money issues? Would he have studied with as much doggedness and precision variations in his quoted value with dealers and discovered by working far from Paris the considerable advantage of models in the provinces not asking to be paid for that service?[*]

The house into which the Renoirs moved in 1889, and where Jean was born five years later, owes its right to be called a "chateau," or castle, to its history, built as it was on the location of an "architectural folly" doomed by the French Revolution. Composed of a group of buildings surrounded by gardens and neglected land (part of which would later be intersected by avenue Junot), Le Château des Brouillards ("The Castle of Fog") was located at 13 rue Girardon, near a small square the Parisian town council would in the following century name after the singer Dalida. At first, Jean Renoir's world was a Montmartre not yet dominated

---

[*] "I'm playing peasant in Champagne to get away from those costly Parisian models," he writes to Berthe Morisot in November 1888. (*Correspondance de Berthe Morisot avec sa famille et ses amis* [*Berthe Morisot's Correspondence with Her Family and Friends*], documents collected and furnished by Denis Rouart, Quatre Chemins-Editart, 1950.)

by the shadow of Sacré-Coeur's meringue. Although the building of that church began in 1875, it wasn't finished until 1914. Montmartre was then a world that existed somewhere between country and city and where all kinds of adventures, from snail hunts to the discovery of the social domain, could take place. It was an enclave that had returned to its original state, with rosebushes gone wild, a few lots of nature that a handful of trailblazing yet nostalgic craftsmen were making every effort to domesticate. Pear trees yielded fruits with a never-before-tasted flavor because they'd been grafted, it was said, onto quince trees. In warm weather, the air was impregnated with the perfume of lilacs. "Renoir's studio was there, and that's where Léon Bloy lived, and word had it that Gérard de Nerval had enjoyed coming there to pick grapes," wrote Roland Dorgelès in *Le Château des Brouillards;* and Jules Romains, in *Les Hommes de bonne volonté* (*Men of Good Will*), offered his own portrait of the Montmartre of that time: "The wall plaster is tremendously old and has taken on the color of the old houses on the Butte,* and the color of the eyes of a child from Montmartre can't possibly take in all the poetic experiences that formed his heart. It's a color with a dash of country sun, a bit of provincial humility, shadow thrown by a basilica, wind that has blown across the great Northern plains and mixed with the vapors of Paris, garden lights, the smells of lawns, lilacs, and roses."

The painter's studio was in the attic of the house at 13 rue Girardon. A spiral staircase reached it from the floor for bedrooms, and the ground floor opened on a stairway leading to a garden to which a few steps allowed access. Hallway, dining room, kitchen, and office were at the back, the walls painted white, doors in Trianon gray, as they were in all Renoir's homes. On the floor above slept parents and children, and Gabrielle just above the kitchen.

Gabrielle is the young woman pictured crouching next to the children in *La Famille du peintre* (*The Artist's Family*), painted by Renoir in the garden facing Le Château des Brouillards. This is the same woman Ambroise Vollard, having come unexpectedly one evening, without knowing that Mme. Renoir wasn't home, found in Auguste's bedroom, preparing to read to him while he was in bed. Unfortunately, the book, *La Dame de Monsoreau,* which the painter wanted to hear that evening, couldn't be found.[6]

Gabrielle is also the one who told Jean about the events of his early childhood, and he vividly remembered the division of his affections: "For me, at that time, the world was divided in two. My mother, for the boring things: eat your soup, go to the toilet, 'rub-a-dub-dub,' climb out of that zinc bathtub used for the morning's ablutions. And Bibon, for having fun: walks in the park, games in the sand, and, especially, being carried by her—something my mother absolutely

* *Translator's note:* Butte = the hill on which Montmartre is situated.

refused to do, whereas Gabrielle was only content bent under the burden of my little body."[7] Jean uses the nickname "Bibon" because that's what he called the young woman, whose first name was unpronounceable for him, becoming "Gabibon," then "Bibon" in his mouth. Later on, everyone would call her "Ga." Pierre Renoir, the eldest of the three sons, was the only Renoir child brought up by his mother.

If it's true, as Jean wrote, that Auguste Renoir began drawing his portrait of Aline "thirty years before knowing her," Gabrielle is still the one he represented the most often, sometimes with Jean—an unruly model whom the servants were assigned to keep in place long enough for Auguste to paint *L'Alphabet* (*The Alphabet*, 1898), *Jean au cerceau* (*Jean with a Hoop*, 1898), *Jean lisant* (*Jean Reading*, 1900), and *Jean en chasseur* (*Jean as a Huntsman*, 1901). The child hated his strawberry-blond curls, which made some think he was a girl; the painter liked them, which prevented them from being sacrificed on the grounds that they would protect his skull. Renoir's fear of accidents at home led to his smashing the sharp edges of the fireplaces with a hammer and blunting the corners of tables by sanding. He likewise demanded that the parquet floors not be waxed, fearing that the polish could result in falls. It was something between paternal concern and the precautions of an artist who had no intention of being disturbed, not to mention the fact that his own walk was no steadier than a toddler's. In fact, by the time Jean was born, Auguste Renoir got from place to place with the help of two canes, replaced by crutches when Jean was six.

By July 1896, the Renoirs had left the house on rue Girardon because its dampness was proving harmful to Auguste's joints and moved to an apartment at the bottom of the Butte, on the fifth floor of 33 rue La Rochefoucauld, at the corner of rue La Bruyère. (Auguste's studio was at 64 rue La Rochefoucauld.) When Renoir's legs forced him to abandon stairs altogether in October 1901, the family had to select an apartment located on the second floor of 43 rue Caulaincourt, and the painter rented a studio, at number 73 on the same street, about a third of a mile away from his home and in the same building where writer Yves Mirande and the painter Théophile Steinlein lived.[8] From the rue La Rochefoucauld balcony that Jean had claimed as his domain, the little boy would descend into the tangled bush of Montmartre, which extended right up to the door of the building. He'd become old enough to appreciate the talents of one of his father's favorite models, a certain Marie Dupuy, whose maiden name was Maliverney. She earned the nickname "the Baker's Wife" thanks to an affair with a baker's assistant, and she also made excellent french fries.

The Renoirs held open house every Saturday, a day devoted to the tradition of the pot-au-feu. The rest of the week, Mme. Renoir had the women of the house follow recipes she herself had perfected or collected here and there, several examples of which Jean offers in the book about his father. Bouillabaisse, the art of which had been taught to Renoir and Cézanne by the mayor of L'Estaque in 1895, and sautéed chicken, the great triumph of Aline and her servants, were part of the feast—not to mention the charcoal-grilled meats. One of the many perks for Jean that would come from living in California was the discovery of barbecue, allowing him to reproduce the flavor of his childhood steaks.

The pleasure Auguste found in painting in the country, as well as a need to warm his old bones in the sun, resulted in the family's spending more and more time far from Montmartre. In the past, they had rented a house on the coast of Normandy, where Jean had spent summer nights sleeping in a bed occupied by Oscar Wilde in winter. These days, there were frequent visits to the south, where Auguste had often gone alone over the years and where his family now accompanied him regularly. In January 1900, Auguste, Aline, Gabrielle, Jean, and the Baker's Wife spent some months in a borrowed villa in Magagnosc. The change was accomplished easily, or rather, hastily, because of Mme. Renoir's wish to live again far away from the city, an intention satisfied years before by the buying of a house in Essoyes. Auguste had discovered the village thanks to Aline, who'd been born there. They'd already spent fall 1888 there with Pierre, their eldest son, in a two-room house rented for a few weeks and then used as a pied-à-terre until September 1896. In that month, which was two years after Jean's birth, the painter bought a vintner's house that adjoined a vast barn with a vineyard behind that building. It cost Renoir 4,000 francs, which was exactly what the state had paid four years previously, in 1892, for the purchase of one of the versions of his *Jeunes Filles au piano*[9] (*Young Girls at the Piano*). Aline would give birth on August 4, 1901, at Essoyes, to a boy named Claude, whose nickname became "Coco." Auguste Renoir was old enough by several years to be a grandfather, and there he was—a father yet again.

Fourteen days after Coco was born, the *Journal officiel* reported the appointment of the painter to the rank of Chevalier of the Légion d'honneur. It was a distinction he found anxiety provoking no less than he found it flattering: what were his friends going to think? He wrote to Claude Monet that he'd "allowed myself to be decorated" and hoped that "this bit of ribbon won't stand in the way" of their old friendship; to make a long story short, he "wasn't joking" about whether he'd "done something idiotic or not."[10] On October 20, 1911, he was promoted to the rank of Officer of the Légion d'honneur, then on February 19, 1919, to the higher rank of Commander. In December 1936, at the age of forty-two, Jean would seek the distinction[11]—and get it on January 30, 1937.[12]

During 1903, Renoir spent the summer in Essoyes, the end of autumn and winter in Cagnes-sur-Mer in a house shared with the local post office,* and the last days of spring in Paris. On June 28, 1907, completely won over by Cagnes-sur-Mer and its surroundings, the Renoirs bought a farm there called Les Collettes and moved into it in fall of the following year. The house in Essoyes had cost 4,000 francs; the Collettes property, which was a little less than four and a half acres and planted with 145 olive trees, orange trees, and rosebushes, cost 35,000 francs. It was an enormous house with outbuildings for the models and domestics. A studio for the painter was soon erected among the olive trees, which Jean would film more than a half century later in *Le Déjeuner sur l'herbe* (*Picnic*) and whose luxuriant foliage and gnarled trunks he'd photograph often. The photos were with him all his life, and today they are attached to the walls of the house in the Northern California hills where Alain Renoir, his only child, lived out his last years and died on December 12, 2008.

Jean ended up rolling around on the ground and weeping and moaning that he wanted a Sainte-Croix cap like the one he admired on his brother Pierre's noggin. In September 1902, a year after Coco was born, Jean's wish was granted, and his dream of having his hair cut short achieved. But he hadn't yet reached the age at which his father thought children should start getting an education. Auguste Renoir believed that all forms of education only overtaxed those younger than the age of ten, but it was time for Jean to leave his position in the family to his younger brother. So, he got his cap and a uniform; but as for ending up in boarding school, too, well, that was intolerable. Until then, his life had been spent charging through the woods of Essoyes, playing under olive trees at Les Collettes, staying in Paris among women with generously open bodices and impressive gentlemen of whose growing fame he was unaware, which kept him from imagining that they were destined to enjoy even more notoriety; such men were named Cézanne, Monet, Degas, Pissarro. When it was time for a breath of air, it had come in the form of a Montmartre outing with Gabrielle. Sometimes, as they walked down the Butte, she would stop for a moment to chat with a strange-looking character sitting at a table on the terrace of a café on rue Lepic. The child would tug on the young woman's sleeve because he was impatient for them to go on and impervious to her conversation with this Monsieur de Toulouse-Lautrec. There were so many of these figures that no one knew how to mention all of them. The children of some became Jean's friends; well into her ninetieth year, Aline Cézanne, the painter's granddaughter, still remembered that for Jean and his pals of the time, all children's houses or apartments were cluttered with canvases they never imagined would be declared the works of masters.[13]

* Today, the town hall.

Sometimes Jean felt his older brother Pierre's hint of influence. Pierre, a serious boy whom the age difference made seem even more serious—and more haughty, especially—thought only of the theater and recited verse to please young girls. To the extent that Pierre was a serious student, Jean hated studying. The other little boys at school weren't any fun; he was bored to death and missed Gabrielle. His dream of being one of the big kids was over. Missing his lead soldiers so much undermined the power of the cap and school outfit. Whereas Pierre was almost finished with school and was preparing for his baccalaureate, Jean was discovering a world that repelled him.

In 1902, Jean entered third grade at Sainte-Croix. He spent the following school year at the same establishment, then left to do fifth grade in another school, but came back again to Sainte-Croix in fall 1905. Until then, his academic accomplishments may have fed his ego, backed up as they were by being first in the class for compositional style, history, and Latin translation and by winning several second prizes and certificates of merit. Seventh grade (1906–1907) was less brilliant, if not downright difficult, as much for his teachers as for him, as if he had suddenly given up trying completely. His family's move to the south was his hour of liberation. Beginning in autumn 1907, Sainte-Croix's records no longer show any mention of the name Jean Renoir. All we know of the period, because he touched on it with his son, was that he wasted his time going from day schools to boarding schools.[14]

The trees, the river, the woods at Essoyes, sun and olive trees at Les Collettes—all dominated his time more than school. The dishes cooked by Marie Corot, la Grande Louise, Léontine Baude, and Gabrielle, who took turns at the stove when they weren't working together, made the mundane cuisine of the boarding school detestable. This was how Jean grew up, and it's not surprising that he mentions his studies only for the record in his memoirs under the terse yet telling designation "nebulous school years." Nebulous without a doubt because they left less of an impression on Jean's mind than the fishing trips in Essoyes but contributed to his formation nonetheless, if not scholastically, at least socially, spent as they were in the most highly rated establishments, where only children of polite society were admitted.

In October 1911, the Renoirs, currently living at Les Collettes, rented a pied-à-terre in Nice at 1 rue Palermo, also called place de l'Église-du-Voeu at the time, and today, rue Alfred-Mortier. A secondary school (which was not yet called Masséna) in that city accepted Jean and his younger brother. There Jean became friends with a child named Maurice Jaubert, who in the thirties would compose music for the films of Jean Vigo and Marcel Carné, and whose scores would later be used posthumously on four occasions by François Truffaut.[*] Jean needed a private tutor to prepare for the baccalaureate test and he passed the first part at the beginning of summer. Philosophy was not his forte, but he liked history and could get by in German, a language that a family vacation in Bavaria at the end of summer 1910 allowed him to practice.[†] Auguste Renoir stopped walking after the return from that trip. In fall 1911, the Renoirs moved to 57 *bis* boulevard Rochechouart, into a large apartment with a studio on the same floor.

Armed with his baccalaureate, Jean couldn't decide what to do. He was most content running in the woods and coming home in the evenings covered with dust. His father saw no other future for him but in a manual occupation, such as being a smithy or, better still, a gamekeeper, an ideal occupation for someone who likes nothing better than being aimless—and whose role and costume Jean would assign twenty years later to Gaston Modot, who played Schumacher the gamekeeper in *The Rules of the Game.* Jean's mother had him learn a little piano, but if he was to become a musician, it would be one who had no artistic ambition.

No one asked what his brother Pierre would be. His vocation had been revealed when he was young: he'd become an actor, and he stuck to that course. After debuting at the Théâtre de l'Odéon in October 1908, Pierre left that theater in January 1910 and became part of a production of *Chantecler* by Edmond Rostand on February 6, with Lucien Guitry and Madame Simone, as well as a certain Abel Gance in the role of Poulet Sautillant. By the end of 1910, Gance had directed his first film, *La Digue,* and would claim seventy years later that *Jean* Renoir acted in it. Today, the film is lost and the claim unverifiable. There is no reason, however, that Jean would have participated in a project that in all respects would call for Pierre in the role. At the time, actors barely mentioned their film jobs, because they thought it wasn't acting if it didn't happen on the stage. Pierre was no exception, and for Jean the issue wasn't relevant.

Jean's first encounter with the moving image was in the setting of Dufayel, a department store. He and Gabrielle had gone to that store one day in 1897 with the intention of buying a deal wardrobe for her bedroom, a task Mme. Renoir had delegated to her. In 1865, a Monsieur Dufayel had taken over the Palais des Nouveautés, whose main entrance was located at 26 rue de Clignancourt, and created the first department store with shelves—a store that was the size of an entire block of houses. The dome, which was topped with a beacon, won the admiration of passersby. Customers were impressed by the stained-glass

[*] Maurice Jaubert was killed at the front on June 19, 1940.

[†] Auguste Renoir went to Bavaria regularly at the invitation of the industrialist "Fritz" Thurneyssen. His wife and children, but also Gabrielle and Renée Rivière, the future wife of Paul Cézanne Jr., were usually along for the trip.

windows, the statues by Falguière, and the monumental clock. In obvious accord with the ambition announced by the cluster of sculptures decorating the facade and representing "Progress showing the way to Commerce and Industry," the management featured film screenings, which pleasantly competed with the usual attractions: crocodiles from the Nile and songs for the children. Places like this were where Jean Renoir discovered what was not yet called cinema, and it threw him into a panic. Gabrielle hurried him outside, and that was it for Jean and moving images until he began going every Sunday to showings in the visiting room of the Sainte-Croix high school. He would remember these deliciously burlesque comedy shorts, clowning that the silence—disturbed only by the muffled drone of the machine, the whispers of kindhearted fathers, and the laughter of children—made that much more irresistible. The only title he could later recall, *Les Aventures d'Automaboul,* which perhaps never existed, he probably mistook for a 120-foot reel made by Méliès in 1899 entitled *Automaboulisme et Autorité* (*The Clown and the Automobile*). Two clowns were the diabolically destructive heroes. It's doubtful that the picture inspired a taste for film in Jean Renoir; it's more likely that it instilled an unrestrained passion for automobiles and the obtaining of a driver's license at the age of seventeen.[*]

What he should have been asking himself—not too diligently, but asking all the same—was what he intended to do with his life. The idea soon came to him to walk in the steps of his father—not by having a go with a brush—certainly not—but by joining the cavalry. A lucky drawing of lots had at first exempted Auguste from military service; but in 1870, because a war was on, he had been drafted into the armored cavalry, and later into the regular cavalry, despite the fact that he'd never before "put his ass on a horse." He spent the war in Bordeaux, then in Tarbes, "far from those explosions that made him jump."[15]

For Jean, the army, then. Enlisting in 1913 meant something besides an attraction to the uniform or, as in Jean's case, a love of horses. No one was saying it yet, and the entire world was making every effort to hush it up, but everyone knew that war was threatening. What were Jean's reasons for enlisting before he was drafted? He didn't need the money, and being comfortably well off gave him all the time he needed to think about his future. No one in his family was pressuring him to make a decision, and he had no familiarity with any vocation. Nothing was keeping him from settling in Essoyes, at Les Collettes, or somewhere else, where he could extend his time running through the woods and then maybe make a decision about what studies to take up. But no, he enlisted instead, and in that decision patriotism didn't count for nothing. In

* Driver's license for automobiles, number 4188, issued by the prefect of the Alpes-Maritimes on January 6, 1912.

1969, he described himself as a teenage "spoiled brat, a militarist and nation-alist who distrusted the bourgeois and the worker."[16] He said this four years after describing in his intensely autobiographical novel, *Les Cahiers du capitaine Georges* (*The Notebooks of Captain Georges*), the emotions that motivated people like him to sign up in 1913: "The two groups, England, Russia, and ourselves on one side, and Germany and Austria-Hungary on the other, were just waiting for an excuse to begin the dance. I was close to feeling happy about it. It was truly the occasion to show those German Uhlans how much a French Hussar was worth."[17]

His father had done his duty in 1870, when he was thirty. Jean would do his at an age when he was ten years younger and in the cavalry, like Auguste, because at that point it was the "noble" branch of the army to which only young men of means could aspire. He was not only a soldier but also a cavalier. To which character in *Grand Illusion* was the Jean Renoir of those years closest? To Maréchal (Jean Gabin) or to Boëldieu (Pierre Fresnay)? He liked the style of the first and tried to adopt it himself as well as he could. He liked the latter for his cultivation and sense of belonging to a caste, which took the place of conviction and was bolstered by an asset that Jean had but that Boëldieu lacked: notoriety. Boëldieu's father, if he had existed, would have been unlikely to have received the letter addressed to Auguste Renoir on February 17, 1913, by the commanding officer of the First Regiment of Cavalrymen: "I am very proud that your son has chosen to join my regiment and that you've agreed to entrust him to me."[18]

As Jean Renoir entered adulthood, he knew as much about life as any boy born with a silver spoon in his mouth could reasonably expect. But he was alone. Alone between a too haughty and too remote brother and another sibling who was too young. Alone in his class, because he was different by birth and age from the celebrities and the rich who gravitated toward his family, a group that was a mix of artists and merchants. Alone like any child whose family moves too often for him to keep a friend.

The one he made in Essoyes was called Godefer.* The son of a day laborer, he lived with a dozen brothers and sisters in an old mud-and-straw hut.† Godefer was poor, had no shoes, and when Jean gave a pair of his to him—a brand new pair—Mme. Renoir took them back immediately. Besides, Godefer wasn't used to them, and they hurt his feet. Godefer knew the river, the waterholes where the pike hid, and the secrets of the art of fishing; he had a gift for poaching,

* In reality, Godefert.

† "A dozen," according to Renoir, but in reality five children, who lived not in a mud-and-straw hut, as he writes, but in a house.

and Jean became his apprentice. Until one day, Godefer whistles under his pal's window a little earlier in the morning than usual, the two go off into the blue, and Gabrielle has to send for them. Jean didn't ever see Godefer again. The latter's father has no intention of having a falling-out with Mme. Renoir, a woman who has proved so generous to him. Like all of Jean's captivating stories, this one is a bit embroidered. The Godeferts were well known in Essoyes and actually were poor, but they weren't utterly destitute;* and if this boy actually did initiate Jean into the mysteries of the river and the fields, he was appreciably younger than Jean, despite the fact that the story in the filmmaker's memoirs attempts to produce the opposite impression. As for the anecdote about the shoes, it finds a startling echo in one of Alain Renoir's stories, which recounts how his father made him give his clogs to a child in Essoyes who had none, to show Alain how he might appreciate it if someone did the same for him one day. In Alain's story, that child from Essoyes was named Beysson. He belonged to a family of beggars and had an older sister whose first name was Constance, a girl who was repulsively dirty and with whom Alain, who was about her age, was very much in love. It was to Beysson that Alain tearfully gave his shoes as the way of obeying Jean's order.[19] This means that father and son would have had the same experience, about twenty years apart, in the same village, at nearly the same age, and that the second character in both cases was a child—barefoot and black with dirt—who was a member of a downtrodden family. Perhaps.

In 1913, Jean was alone, still more so because Claude, his younger brother, was getting Gabrielle's attention. She still considered Jean her favorite and the love of her life but had no other choice than to fulfill her function as an employee and care for Coco. Gabrielle soon left her position with the Renoirs, according to what Jean has written, and he gives the following reason for the break: "At the beginning of 1914, she had just married Conrad Slade."[20] It seems surprising that an employee of the Renoir household had the leisure time to get to know an American in a Montparnasse restaurant, Chez Rosalie, to which he'd been attracted by the likelihood of seeing celebrities such as Picasso and Modigliani. Conrad Slade, born March 4, 1871, in Boston, had come to Paris to study at the Beaux-Arts in 1893 and 1894, first as a sculptor and soon after as a painter. Then he had returned to the United States, where he spent two years before moving to Paris in 1896. He'd fallen in love with France and spoke the language without the slightest trace of an accent. He met Gabrielle not in the restaurant on rue Campagne-Première, as Jean suggests, but at the home of the Renoirs.[21]

* Just after the release of *Ma vie et mes films* in 1974, a relative of the Godefert family complained to Flammarion about the image of his family given in the book. (Jean Renoir Papers, Box 30, Folder 6.)

Auguste fascinated Conrad to such an extent that, until the end of his life, he tried to emulate him, with a carefully trimmed beard and smocks and hats identical to the Master's. But the most unsettling detail in Jean's story isn't connected to the occasion of the meeting, which took place in 1913 or 1914 (Conrad and Gabrielle spent a large part of 1915 in Greece). It is that Jean makes an error of more than seven years by placing Gabrielle's marriage in 1914; she actually married Conrad Slade on May 18, 1921, in Cagnes-sur-Mer. Jean served as a witness on that occasion, and on the part of the marriage certificate that asks about his profession are the words "private income."

Even if no one can be expected to remember exact dates, it's still doubtful that Gabrielle, whom Jean endows in his book with "the memory of an elephant," would have been able to forget the day, month, or year of her marriage. And it's just as doubtful that, as their son, Jean Slade, suggests,[22] the revision was introduced to hide the fact that Gabrielle and Conrad's child was born out of wedlock, in December 1920. Even a motive like that doesn't require a falsification of more than seven years.

If Gabrielle really did leave her position with the Renoirs in 1914, her departure had nothing to do with her marriage to Conrad Slade. Recent research[23] reveals that before meeting Aline Charigot, Auguste Renoir had had two children with Lise Tréhot, one of his most celebrated models, about whom Jean says little in his book: a boy, born in Ville-d'Avray on September 14, 1868, and a girl, born in the Tenth Arrondissement of Paris on July 21, 1870. All we know about the first is his birth date and his given name, Pierre, like Pierre Renoir, Auguste and Aline's eldest son. The girl's first name was Jeanne—the feminine form of the name Jean.

Jeanne was baptized on May 23, 1875, in the village of Sainte-Marguerite-de-Carrouges, in the region of Alençon, and was placed there at birth in the care of a nurse. It was the same place where the painter Alfred Sisley had left his last son. Although the baptism certificate mentions the name "Jeanne Marguerite Tréhot," the parish records about the communion and confirmation of the little girl have her appearing as "Jeanne Marguerite Renoir." And in the margin of one certificate the following has been added: "Recognized by Renoir."[24]

In 1893, the year that precedes Jean's birth, when the young Jeanne was twenty-three and wanted to marry a baker named Louis Gabriel Robinet, it was Auguste Renoir who was asked for her hand. The painter responded affirmatively to the request and maintained that his daughter was "a very serious and deeply respectable woman." He contributed to Jeanne's dowry and financed the purchase of a house for the couple in Madré, near Sainte-Marguerite-de-Carrouges. When Jeanne's husband died in 1908, Renoir was anxious to know in whose hands the property would fall if Jeanne were to die as well. So, a will was drawn up, stating that in such a case Gabrielle would inherit the property.[25] As unaccustomed as a man like Renoir was to asking such questions (if we are to believe his son), this precaution is remarkable. And Gabrielle refused to be named sole legatee of the hidden daughter.[26]

Auguste kept helping his daughter by sending her money orders via intermediaries: his art dealer Vollard, the Baker's Wife, and Gabrielle. When Jeanne would go to Paris to see her father, she stayed with the Baker's Wife, and he'd visit her, concealing it from Aline. Therefore, the Boss's female circle knew what his own wife didn't—and all his friends had been told about five years earlier. Gabrielle acted as Renoir's secretary and made the deception possible. Is there, then, anything more to wonder about why Aline Renoir sent her young cousin packing one day at the beginning of 1914, probably after some indiscretion— the discovery of a letter or the rough draft of a will—clued the Master's wife in to the conspiracy of silence around her, with Gabrielle on its front line?

It's certainly a possibility that, before dying, Auguste Renoir revealed his secret to Jean, with whom he was having long conversations that allowed him—as his son put it—"to unbutton." If not, it was at the opening of the will that Auguste's children found out about their half-sister, to whom their father intended to endow an annual life annuity of 450 francs. Pierre wrote to Jeanne on December 17, 1919, two weeks after the death of their father, to inform her of this arrangement. In that letter he mentions mail from Jeanne, which had just been passed to him by Vollard.

Jeanne returned to Sainte-Marguerite after the death of her husband and lived until June 8, 1934. Both Pierre and Jean chose to keep quiet about her existence, and Jean never spoke of Jeanne to his own son, a measure he adopted, no doubt, both out of respect for Aline, his mother, and because he thought the filial love and limitless admiration he bore his father required him to plane down all rough edges in the likeness of him he sculpted. The extra character in the story seemed cumbersome to Jean, and with the cooperation of Gabrielle, his scriptwriter, he decided not to put her in any scene. There could be no blemish on the halo that Jean sketched around the paternal figure, or on his idyllic family portrait. At times, the filmmaker's hagiographers followed the same model.

2

"Other Dogs to Sniff"

The young man who, on February 13, 1913, discovered life in the military, cut quite a figure. The uniform of the First Regiment of Cavalrymen flattered him. His six feet are more noticeable than his extra pounds. His hair is parted right down the middle, his mustache clearly denotes swagger, and his eyes gaze upward. Photos show him posing next to his father, whom an old woman who had been close to Auguste in the past told him he hardly resembled. "We liked Auguste," she added, "because he thought he didn't deserve our affection."[1] Auguste Renoir, who had lived through his time in the military in 1870, undoubtedly saw war on the horizon. He also knew that war would take them by surprise and bring its horror to the young man who stood next to his chair. At that time, the world had just a few more months of peace to enjoy.

Jean had no more time left to grow out of adolescence. After a trip through the barracks in Vincennes, he went back to the First Regiment of Cavalrymen, the base of which was in Joigny, about sixty miles from Essoyes, and got to know the others: first, his comrades in arms, who saw him as a rich kid, a celebrity's son; and then, their commanders, with their disturbing impositions of discipline to which he had to force himself to adapt. The team that they formed was like a new family to him, with coarser, freer ways, and a means of communicating that was more direct, using words that were more daring. Here, Jean Renoir acquired a taste for off-color jokes and developed an appetite for the uncouth. A good education doesn't keep a person from appreciating being dirty; it merely offers a sense of which moments it's appropriate. He was enchanted by the art of the spoonerism, which he had discovered in Rabelais's "Beaumont-le-Vicomte."* Later on, the laugh would be on some of his buddies, to their chagrin.

In fact, since childhood Jean had witnessed the everyday outer reality that surrounded an artist who had taken refuge in his own world and given himself to his art. He had observed the necessary circle of merchants flitting around his

---

* *Translator's note:* Originating in Pantagruel, this is one of Rabelais's most well-known off-color spoonerisms: "Beaumont-le-Vicomte" = "Beaumont the Viscount," slightly mispronounced as "à beau con le vit monte" ("at pretty pussy the dick rises").

father, some of whom were his friends, but all of whose motives and tastes were nonetheless different from his. Sell, buy, appraise, count—the artist is the prisoner of all that. There was nothing like that in the army, which pleased Jean at first. In the barracks, differences of class, education, and economic level were no longer legal tender; or, at least, whoever wanted to ignore them could do so. He expresses this in his first novel,[2] which he wrote about a fictional character—a very convenient ploy when you intend to talk about yourself.

> In my world, I was always on the defensive. Polite society is nothing but an immense commercial enterprise where everybody has something to sell or buy. Here, around the stove in the barracks room, nobody expected anything from anybody other than being there. My few liters of cheap wine didn't count for much. Without me, the evening would have been just the same. All the guys had chipped in, that's all. I felt relaxed, sure of myself. I felt part of a whole, no longer a lost dog unleashed in a deserted street; a dog that was rich, well-fed, but in a despairing quest for other dogs to sniff.[3]

In *The Notebooks of Captain Georges,* Jean Renoir tells the story of the love that unites a hussar and a prostitute. Auguste saw the time before marriage as a period for a man to sow his wild oats. For a woman, too, he claimed, except that it was less commonly acknowledged. Many equated such fooling around with real love. In 1913, men discovered that love at the brothel. We can claim that this isn't real love, that it is more of an individual opinion, that even more it is a sign of a specific historical period. But all that matters is that it was this way and not another; what matters even more is the fact that love for sale was the kind with which Jean Renoir started out. Just as Auguste had met the daughter of his captain in Bordeaux, a girl who wanted to become a painter and whom he encountered again in Tarbes,[4] in the novel Georges is drawn to the daughter of his colonel, but it is in the arms of Agnès, a young peasant who has become a prostitute, that he discovers passionate love.

At the beginning of 1914, Jean wrote his mother to say his departure for Luçon was likely, even though he had just been accepted for the preparatory exam for the school in Saumur. With her he also shared his disappointment about realizing that elite officers weren't being sent to Luçon but to the east of the country, or at least to somewhere near Paris, in expectation of the crisis about to come. "Only the incompetent will be staying,"[5] he wrote, as if he doubted being left out of the confrontation despite the fact that he often presented himself as "having been born yellow-bellied." Placing the First Regiment of Cavalrymen at Luçon was the result of a decision of Georges Clemenceau, who was originally from the region; it would make a fortune for the local brothel, which was called "La Mauresque."* In April, Renoir wrote from the hospital where he'd been sent for an illness, revealing only that it was something contagious.

The fever destined to take over the whole of Europe in just a few weeks was spreading. Auguste Renoir was worried for his sons, and on May 22 he wrote to his biographer and friend Georges Rivière, "We have to take care of Jean's situation before there's a new minister. . . . I'd be very relieved if he weren't so far away from Paris. Explain that to him. Do your best."[6] A few weeks later, Auguste joined Jean in Lagny, where the latter was stationed. The colonel there gave a luncheon in his honor, and, contrary to practice, the sergeant authorized Jean to take part in it. Auguste returned south feeling reassured about leaving his son—whom he saw as a "scatterbrain" who would "stupidly get himself killed"—under the protection of officers he judged to be responsible.

The assassination of an archduke on June 28, 1914, may have still seemed like only an isolated incident, but the epidemic was spreading: Austria-Hungary invaded Serbia on July 25, France mobilized for war on August 1, and, two days later, Germany declared war on France and invaded Belgium.

Jean's regiment, the First Cavalry, left Luçon on August 2. For three centuries, from the time they had been called the "Royal Cavalrymen," their motto had been "In Danger, Action." Now it became "Royal at First—First Always!" And in fact, beginning August 10, with six other regiments combined under the name of the Ninth Division of Cavalry and led by General de L'Épée, Jean took part in the charge at Marville-Maugienne. Nearly fifty years later, he'd receive a letter from one of his long-lost comrades-at-arms reminding him that on that day, "the First Regiment of Cavalrymen charged twice, with our lances."[7] Meanwhile, mobilization continued in the country: the Ninth Division of Cavalry had another battle ten days later, at Neufchâteau in Luxembourg, and then fell into rearguard to cover the retreat to the Marne.

The Renoirs, who were at Les Collettes, came back to Paris in mid-June—Aline by train, Auguste taking a seat in the automobile driven by Baptistin, the Master's chauffeur.† When Aline arrived in Paris, Pierre had already left for his posting, and she found only Véra Sergine, Pierre's companion and partner, as well as their nine-month-old son, who was named Claude after his uncle. On September 3, after the French government had taken refuge in Bordeaux the day before and the Germans were only thirty-one miles from Paris, the

---

* *Translator's note:* "The Moorish Woman."

† Who was replaced a few years later by a young Italian named Bistolfi.

Renoirs went back to Les Collettes, taking their future daughter-in-law and their grandson with them. They were unaware that their oldest son had already paid his tribute in the war.

As a matter of fact, on September 2, near Nancy, at the very beginning of the German offensive on the Grand-Couronné (actually, two days before it officially began), Pierre Renoir the infantryman was wounded and would have to undergo several operations. The surgeons were able to save his right arm, but he lost full usage of it. At Cagnes-sur-Mer, on December 23, he married Véra Sergine. On August 24, 1915, he was demobilized and reclassified as a disabled serviceman, receiving the Military Cross and, by order of the Armed Forces, a military and an Inter-Allied decoration. He would suffer throughout his life from the wounds to his leg and abdomen, the latter forcing him to wear a bandage permanently.

Auguste and Aline Renoir received the news on the same day that both Pierre and Jean had been wounded, although Jean's injuries weren't serious. In reality, Jean's hospitalization at Amiens, then occupied by German troops, probably resulted from his having been "kicked by a horse"—a mare named Venus. "A kick from Venus" was the phrase the patient used to describe his indisposition, wording commonly used for the benefit of mothers of cavalrymen to mean gonorrhea, cheerfully dubbed "hot piss" by the men. This diagnosis can be confirmed in the medical records of soldier Jean Renoir in a paragraph worded "infirmities not resulting in the right to a pension": "firm, indolent nucleate at the top of the left epididymis; residue of gonorrheal orchi-epididymitis."[8]

After a brief stay in Paris, where he was able to meet Vollard, Jean left for Luçon, where he continued convalescing and where his mother, who had gone to Carcassonne to Pierre's bedside, visited him in mid-November. On November 17, Auguste wrote to Paul Durand-Ruel: "My wife leaves Jean tomorrow, to her great regret. He enjoys it for a quarter of an hour and then always becomes impatient to get back to his comrades at the front. But while he waits, he's at the infirmary, more as a patient than as a medic."[9] Meanwhile, throughout September and October, Jean's regiment had been fighting in Picardie, and nearly three-quarters of his comrades had been placed out of combat.

Jean didn't hide from his mother the fact that he'd decided to ask for another type of post. The cavalry's day was over. The war had changed dramatically, dragging the world along with it, and horses would no longer be used. When Renoir rejoined the First Regiment of Cavalrymen, they'd descended into the trenches, and he spent Christmas in those built in the mining villages of Lens. Was this the reason he wanted to change regiments? Maybe. It was also true that the garrison of the unit he'd set his sights on was in Nice, very near Cagnes and family.

Jean's memories of these initial months of war would be dominated by a painful sense of inactivity in contrast to the thrill he got out of maneuvers, revived years later in his first novel and attributed to Captain Georges:

> Our mass swept out with a thundering sound. We no longer belonged to each other. We were the drops of a great wave unfurling on the shore. I have never felt such intoxication dilating my lungs. I no longer existed. I was annihilated in a glorious whole. We weren't on Earth anymore. We weren't even on our horses. The two men at my side were jammed against me, pushed by those next to them. Their legs ground against my legs hard enough to shatter them. Then I felt myself lifted from my saddle. I didn't even wonder if any day would come when I'd be falling back onto my mare. I wasn't wondering anything at all. I no longer existed. I was experiencing the infinite sensual delight that comes from not thinking.[10]

Jean Renoir tried to recover that delight all his life: always eager for adventurous encounters and communal experiences, dreaming of losing all self-possession to the point of feeling like nothing more than one drop among those forming the wave. In 1914, he was a young man empty of desires, projects, ambition, as if his own body, which was already too massive and heavy, was also too much to bear; and for himself, he saw no other community but that of warriors, where personal characteristics, social classes, differences of culture, and disparities of fortune were abolished as a matter of principle. Later, in the twenties and thirties, he allowed himself to be carried along by other waves, which also tossed him back to shore. Still later, his discovery of India would enable him to add a cosmic dimension to his fantasy. That, much more than his past as a cavalryman, to which he would often refer, would be present in his films.

In a country at war, unity is sacred. In the trenches, bourgeois and worker can hardly be distinguished from each other any more than can those like Jean Renoir, who feel displaced because they aren't of any class, or are convinced they aren't. How could he have remained in the stable, when each day thousands of men were getting killed? In February 1915, French and British troops started an operation in the Dardanelles that would end by March in a bloody setback. Simultaneously, General Joffre, who had distinguished himself in the first Battle of the Marne in 1914, launched a series of offensives in Champagne that were equal failures. On the Meuse, thousands of men were massacred at the commune of Les Éparges and in the Bois-le-Prêtre. Everyone became aware that the war would be a long one, that it would seem endless; and as those struggling to survive in the mud of the trenches thought of those hiding far from the battle, resentment took hold.

On February 20, Jean was appointed temporary second lieutenant and sent to the front to the Sixth Mountain Battalion of the Infantry. It was a fate he wanted, and he was proud of his regiment: "Then think about it, Mother, I have the beret."[11] There he stood with a view of the blue line of the Vosges, a stake made sacred by propaganda, and its reality exploded in his face. What did he experience, endure? What war was his? The fact that he kept silent about it means nothing. The spectacle of such horror doesn't lend itself very much to confiding, and even less to eyewitness accounts. In just the period March 6 to 21, 1915, the Sixth Mountain Battalion reported three officers killed, six others wounded, and seven hundred eighty-four noncommissioned officers, first-class privates, and infantrymen killed or wounded.

On April 22, the first poison-gas attack was launched on the Western Front. Five days later, on April 27, 1915, in the region of the Schlucht in Alsace, a bullet from the rifle of a "Bavarian good shot"[12] shattered Jean's left leg, fracturing the neck of the thighbone. Hit during a morning patrol at a place called "the Silver Hollow," on a slope of the Hohneck, the wounded man was forced to wait for nightfall to be evacuated on the back of a mule.* On May 11, he earned a citation on order of the Forty-Seventh Division: "Extremely courageous officer, behaved excellently under fire. Put all his energies into the organization of a defensive position. Led a reconnaissance with goal the demolition of a chapel occupied by the enemy. Succeeded in part in that action and was wounded in thigh."[13]

Transported to the hospital in Gérardmer, he wrote to his family, striving to reassure them, referring to a "slight stiffness in my leg" that he expected the wound would leave him as a memento and suggesting it would add a touch of "the snazzy officer" to his walk. His efforts at playing it down were in vain. Auguste said he was convinced the doctors "are going to cut off his leg";[14] Aline prepared to leave immediately. Once at her son's bedside, she discovered that the wound was more serious than Jean had claimed it was. She was just about to reach the age of fifty-six, suffered from obesity, and had known for two years that she had diabetes. Only a few months before, she had paid a visit to her eldest son, hospitalized in Carcassonne, aware that her younger would have preferred the youthful woman she'd appointed to watch over him. But none of this would stop her astounding decisiveness and lifesaving obstinacy.

With gas gangrene eating away at the wounded man's leg, the doctors were

---

* The official communiqué states that Second Lieutenant Renoir (whose first name is mistaken for the name Léon Georges) had to wait "twenty-four hours between the two lines and has won the admiration of all for his morale and courage in enduring the pain." (*Bulletin des armées de la République réservé à la zone des armées [Report from the Armies of the Republic Reserved for the War Zone]*, vol. 4, Ministère de la Guerre [War Office], 1916.)

inclined to perform a surgical disarticulation. Then, fearing that the infection might reach the thigh, they began talking of an even higher amputation. Aline Renoir was against it, arguing that amputation would kill their wounded patient, whose leg had already begun to turn green. Apparently, back then surgeons weren't authorized to proceed with an amputation without the agreement of the wounded individual—if he was conscious—or of his family—if present.[15] Putting her motherly intuition in service of Jean's cause, and compensating for her ignorance of medical matters with her peasant's stubbornness, Aline Renoir obtained a stay, even though nothing yet indicated it would prove to be lifesaving.

A decree by Georges Clemenceau (who was himself a doctor) automatically made all professors of medicine head doctors of the hospitals in the districts in which they worked. As a result of this, a professor from Lyon named Laroyenne was able to replace the doctor who had been in favor of amputation. Laroyenne had practiced a treatment for gas gangrene involving drainage of the wound and vigorous circulation of distilled water over a period of several days. It was more than time to try the method on Jean.

On May 19, Aline wrote Georges Rivière that Jean had undergone surgery the day before and that he seemed well on the road to recovery. The leg of the wounded man had shortened by four centimeters. A week later, Aline left Gérardmer, and Jean would write to her on June 21, 22, and 26 to let her know about the improvement of his condition and express his worries about her health.

The truth was that Aline Renoir had felt exhausted, ill, and shattered when she got back to Les Collettes and had taken to her bed. A few days later, she was moved to the family apartment in Nice, a better environment for the care that her condition demanded. But Aline Renoir would not read the last letter from her son. She died on June 27, 1915.

Véra Sergine, Pierre's wife, was chosen to bring the news of his mother's death to Jean, who had been moved to Besançon. According to what Jean later depicted in Ma vie et mes films (My Life and My Films), the scene developed as follows. When the visit of the actress—a celebrity in her time—was announced, approximately fifty sick and wounded men who were in the hospital dormitory where Jean was bedded tried to spruce up the place with the help of the nurses. After having been welcomed by the hospital commander, Véra Sergine appeared, her hair shingled and her dress barely covering her knees. The uproar in the room was so extreme that Jean just managed to understand what his sister-in-law had come to tell him. He was surrounded by men who hadn't seen a woman for months—except for those in uniforms or nurses or nuns—and who were discovering with alarm the new look dictated by the changes in fashion. Attempting to recover from the shock, they let it be known that what might be appropriate for an actress was not right for all women—and definitely not for their fiancées or wives. One of them, a peasant from the Vendée, came out with a line that Jean would remember to put in *Grand Illusion:* "If I find my wife like that when I get back, I'll give her a swift kick in the ass!"[16]

Maleck, wife of the painter Albert André, who was an intimate friend of Auguste, would also come to Besançon, and Auguste would thank her for it in a letter dated July 3, followed five days later by a second missive, informing her that Jean was now at the Ritz, where a military hospital had been set up.

Somewhat later, Jean wrote to Auguste. Speaking of his leg, he advised learning "to consider it a piece of useless meat whose ability for movement and whose strength will only return little by little."[17] In 1962, he'd offer up the first sentence of the book dedicated to his father to "the Bavarian good shot [who] gave me a bullet in one leg."[18] His wound and the weeks of convalescence it imposed on him were in fact what allowed him to spend long hours with this father, whom he still didn't know very well, and who had been reduced to immobility by his own paralysis. Although it may have been true, as Jean claimed, that the lame are guaranteed to think about life and see the world differently from the way able-bodied people do and that this was some consolation for his limp, it was also true that for the rest of his life he suffered from that leg, which was prone to recurrent infections because the femur, which had been badly put back together, penetrated his flesh. To heal completely, he would have had to have the bone broken again, an operation suggested by several doctors but one that he stubbornly refused. On December 21, 1935, the Medical Evaluation Board of the Seine had to award him a "permanent pension of 913 francs" following an examination the preceding September 6, which had verified a disability of 25 percent, described in the following words: "Result of a fracture opened by a bullet in area of the left trochanter; four-centimeter shortening of thigh; loss of muscle mass in quadriceps and left gluteus maximus; scars very deep and adherent; suppression of half the abduction of the thigh. Claudication."[19]

During convalescence at Val-de-Grâce in Paris, Jean obtained authorization to spend his days in the apartment on boulevard de Rochechouart, into which his father had moved some time after the death of his wife and where he now lived surrounded by the Baker's Wife and la Grande Louise, one of his former cooks. The son got around with crutches, and the father was confined to a wheelchair. Because family life had been moved to Les Collettes before the death of Aline, and Claude had remained there with the maids, the Parisian apartment had been empty of most of the canvases and drawings since the beginning of the war. Moreover, all social life was a thing of the past and the sound of cannon from afar sometimes disturbed the silence uniting the paralyzed widower and his crippled son.

Jean watched his father paint and listened to him speak as if he'd never before seen or heard him. The fact that one had lost his wife and the other his mother partly obliterated the years that separated father and son. Infirmity brought them closer, and the peaceful and incessant activity of the painter helped the convalescent elude idleness. In those days of intimacy spent with a man who, until then, had been first and foremost the Boss to him and the others, Jean would find material for a book forty years later as well as the elements of a philosophy of existence he would follow his entire life.

Pierre often brought his wife and son to lunch. He had been demobilized since August 24, and on September 25 he returned to the stage to play the Duke de Bligny in *Le Maître de forges* (*The Ironmaster*) at the Nouvel Ambigu theater and then moved on to several other plays, in spite of the restrictions on theaters. During those same weeks, Renoir tried to introduce Jean and Claude to ceramics. When Jean was sent to a hospital in Nice for the rest of his convalescence, the painter went back to Les Collettes.

On November 1, Renoir informed Georges Rivière that Jean had been deemed fit again and that a second army-exemption tribunal had refused to extend his convalescence. The medical inspector at Lorme attested, however, that the wounded man "would do better somewhere else than in the mountain infantry, which necessitates climbing walls and mountains," and Renoir wanted Jean's request "for armored cars to be followed up."[20] On the back of this letter, Jean had added a few lines making it clear that his father had also written to one of his friends, the critic and art historian Élie Faure.

In December 1915, using Faure's name as a reference, Jean applied to a commander whose name has faded away from that letter and become illegible over the passing years. Jean informed him that the request he had made a month before "for the tanks" had received no response; and because his wound rendered him "unfit for any campaign on foot," fifteen days before he had requested to be assigned to aviation. The cavalry, his first corps, had become the initial recruitment pool for aeronautics. He intended "not to sit around vegetating at the depot," considered himself "still able to render some service to the country," and was requesting the support of the commander.[21]

The country had been bled dry. In November, the state had launched the first war bond drive. By February 21, 1916, German troops were instigating their offensive on Verdun. It would last until June.

On January 10, 1916, Jean actually got what he had wanted—an assignment to aviation. He acted as observer and took aerial photos of the fighting from an airplane. By February 4, stationed at Ambérieu-en-Bugey, then at Plessis-Belleville, in Oise, he participated in the capacity of an observer in the preparation of bombings to be carried out by his squadron in Champagne. The aviators were a class apart—not only because they were positioned above the bloody melee but also because they were separated from the hell of the trenches. They took shelter in camps that were as comfortable as circumstances permitted. They took their meals seated at a table and slept in real beds, far from the mud, rats, lice, and corpses. As Jean reported years later, he made some friends, such as the adjutant-major Pinsard, who was also a former cavalryman. However, Jean considered his duties boring, made still more frustrating because of his passion for mechanical things. He adored the Caudron aircraft, which were made completely out of wood, their motors dripping castor oil, which was used as a lubricant. He wanted to fly them himself and not merely carry out topographical surveys. He asked for a training course on several occasions. The request he made on May 1, 1916—also asking to be stationed nearer Paris again so he could pay visits to his father—finally received a favorable response, and he was sent to Ambérieu again, then to Châteauroux, where he got his pilot's license. This wasn't easy because he was at least eleven pounds overweight, a defect that forced him to follow a weeklong low-calorie diet. He was rewarded for the sacrifice, and on August 20, 1916, he was given a license.

On October 28, he joined Squadron C64, based on the Marne. In December, he had his first accident, which he kept from interfering with the fulfillment of his duty in a dazzling enough way to win a second citation on May 13, 1917: "Requested admission to the air force and, despite a dangerous crash, maintained the same enthusiasm and same drive. During the battle of Aisne, accomplished all long-distance photographic missions he was assigned, as well as numerous missions at low altitude that were ordered. Attacked by a fighter plane and effectively confronted it, succeeding in bringing his fully out-of-service plane and its passenger back to the ground."[22] A second accident during a landing put an end to his career as a pilot. He was promoted to lieutenant on September 30, 1917, and left the air force in November of the same year. For him the war was over. From Squadron C64 he was assigned to the Twenty-Eighth Regiment of Cavalrymen and spent some time at the undersecretary's office at the air force base in Versailles. Declared unfit for service, he entered Hôpital de la Pitié to convalesce. He would leave the army officially on November 3, 1919, after a few months of service for the department of press monitoring for the Fifteenth Army Corps in Versailles, then in Nice, from February 23, 1919, until his discharge.

For Jean Renoir, this war was something to be proud of, split as it was among three kinds of military service, two of which, the cavalry and aviation, were looked upon as noble. Jean's body was permanently maimed, having been injured by fighting in the Vosges, but he had known such hell only for a relatively short period of time in comparison to the months of suffering millions of other soldiers experienced. The calm tone in which he relates his war, notably in his memoirs, doubtlessly comes from his education, from that distance at which well-born people are able to observe things, reporting, as if inadvertently, their own misfortunes. However, such flippancy, which almost seems like amusement at times, is also related to a detached position allowed him by circumstances, especially the most terrible of all of them, the wounding of his leg. Those who had fallen but who did not die were considered lucky by their comrades. For them, the war was over, whereas the others were still risking their necks moment to moment. So, yes, within the context of the horrible ordeal that was inflicted on them, Pierre and Jean Renoir had the luck to survive.

In one of those notebooks in which he recorded both fleeting thoughts and projects for books or films appear several lines written in 1946 that are the only traces left of an idea for "a small work [that] has no other pretension than to suggest a few practical recipes for happiness, for the use of my generation and perhaps my [unreadable]," entitled Le Bonheur:*

> The war of 1914 brought my first doubts. Booted out of the cavalry like quite a few others, I got to know the slow torture of the trenches. I'll never forget Christmas 1914 somewhere in the north of France, standing in water. But my belief was unshakeable, and I had no doubt that this was only an exception, a small error in the functioning of the machine. Other problems, including a wound, didn't change the optimism of my position. I navigated civilian life with the same naïve confidence. The harder the blows, the more I enjoyed forgetting them at the wheel of my Bugatti. Nothing less than Hitler could have made me revise my vision of the world.[23]

Jean would not succeed in removing the weight of certain memories, especially those left by expeditions conceived independently by certain members of the staff and that involved machine-gunning the enemy with no other motive than to pass the time. He'd recall them years later and write, "We'd go off hunting down Germans, our hearts as light as if we were on a rabbit hunt. The war had altered our minds to such an extent that we found these disgusting expeditions acceptable. Today, the memory of these monstrous acts turns my stomach."[24]

* Translator's note: "Happiness."

Jean used his weeks of convalescence and days on leave to discover the man who was his father. They also gave him an opportunity to learn to love films. After the comic reels shown by the good fathers of Sainte-Croix came the films of the war years. Many were American, and some were serials. In 1916, films by Cecil B. DeMille, D. W. Griffith, Allan Dwan, and Jacques de Baroncelli were shown in France; and the following year saw productions by Germaine Dulac, Abel Gance, Louis Feuillade, and Thomas Ince. But back then, no one knew who the director was, and even the function of such a figure remained a mystery to the audience. For Jean Renoir and for audiences of the war years, the *stars* were the movies. They included Douglas Fairbanks, Musidora, and Pearl White, heroine of the serials *The Iron Claw* (1916) and *Pearl of the Army* (1916). There was also the serial *Les Vampires* (1916) by Louis Feuillade, which was followed the next year by his *Judex*. During the final year of the war, French screens lit up with the face of Mary Pickford (*The Poor Little Rich Girl*) and Pearl White again, in *The Fatal Ring*. Each afternoon, at the Parisiana on the Grands Boulevards, at the Grand Royal, or in Pigalle, which was very near Jean, on the screen he watched these beautiful young women being pursued by the wicked, into whose clutches they ended up falling—at least until the next installment a week later in that same theater. Pearl White, whom the French audience called "Perle Vite," was his favorite. She was five years older than he, and he'd discovered her in *The Perils of Pauline*, her greatest success, directed in 1914 by the Frenchman Louis Gasnier. She would die at forty-nine of cirrhosis on August 4, 1938, in Neuilly-sur-Seine, three blocks away from Sainte-Croix, when the shooting in Le Havre of *La Bête humaine* had just begun.

And finally, there was Charlie ("Charlot") Chaplin. When one of Jean's friends from the squadron, the son of the 1913 Nobel Prize winner for medicine Charles Richet, mentioned Charlot to Jean, Jean wasn't even familiar with the name. When he got back to Paris on leave, he was just getting ready to check out this Charlot when his brother Pierre, who also hadn't seen any of Chaplin's films, informed him the character had become the idol of audiences and that—even more surprising—his fellow actors considered him equal to the greatest, including Lucien Guitry and Sarah Bernhardt. An actor? OK. What else? The two Renoir brothers discovered Charlot together and were enthralled. One new Charlot film followed another. *Tillie's Punctured Romance* appeared on French screens in 1916, two years after it was made. In 1917, it was *Police,* and the following year was full of smash hits—*The Vagabond, One A.M., The Count,* and *The Rink*. It would take Jean Renoir some time to understand that Charlot didn't exist without Charlie Chaplin and that the close-ups of Mary Pickford that fascinated him owed just as much to D. W. Griffith as they did to the actress.

Jean Renoir had to have known that film was not merely a machine to move and fascinate you, to make you laugh and dream, but also an extraordinary invention that enabled the showing of life and the stopping of time. Between Méliès and Lumière, he very quickly chose, carried away as he was by the memories of afternoons at the puppet shows in the Tuileries and in theaters on the boulevard du Crime,* where he'd tremble at the spectacle of melodramas rendered almost burlesque by their intent to terrify. He had been overwhelmed by the evening at the Théâtre du Chatelet in 1911, where he, his parents, and Gabrielle had witnessed the first production of *Petrushka* from the box of the owner of the newspaper *Le Matin*. In 1968, when Éric Rohmer, backed up by Henri Langlois, insisted on showing him films made by some Lumière cinematographers, they could only elicit a hardly amused indifference on the part of their prestigious guest,[25] an attitude Renoir was barely able to conceal in the conversation they had at the time.[26]

Film had, however, been brought to the Renoirs by a man who intended to offer French audiences images of some of their glorious countrymen. The identity of this man, whom the Renoirs, led by Jean, insisted on looking down upon, may explain why Jean claimed never to have seen *Ceux de chez nous* (*Those of Our Land*), that montage of images that included, among others, Anatole France, Auguste Rodin, Edmond Rostand, Octave Mirbeau, Claude Monet, and Auguste Renoir.

Jean probably didn't attend the premiere, which was given at the Théâtre des Variétés on November 22, 1915. That night, the maker of the film, Sacha Guitry, introduced these slices of life in person, one element of a presentation in which Charlotte Lysès, then his wife, also participated. This was the first public projection of these moving images that show Renoir painting with hands disfigured by rheumatism and that were believed for a long time to be the only ones of him that existed.† The encounter had been negotiated by Gaston Bernheim, and only his "incapacity to refuse anything" had influenced the painter to accept. In the film, a young man is standing next to the Boss, and for years, aficionados of Renoir have claimed it is Jean. And he's even identified as such by Guitry himself in his commentary. But the boy seems much younger than twenty, which was Jean's age in 1915; and he isn't wearing a uniform. Above all, Jean's wound, which he had received in April, would have kept him from standing on the day of the shoot, which happened sometime between June and October

---

* *Translator's note:* "Boulevard du Crime" = nineteenth-century nickname for the boulevard du Temple in Paris because of the many theaters on that street that featured crime melodramas.

† Archive footage from Gaumont equally shows Auguste Renoir, occupied in sculpting, in the company of Ambroise Vollard.

1915. Finally—and perhaps this should have been mentioned first—Ambroise Vollard was there for the shooting of the scene, and he has stated that Claude, who was fourteen at the time, was also present that day, not Jean. Guitry simply mistook sons, or else, in the course of his reediting of *Those of Our Land* and the many changes he made to the presentation, he decided the presence of the great filmmaker near the Master would be more meaningful than that of a boy who was unknown to the public.

In capturing these moments, Guitry was determined to bear witness to the grandeur of the French mind. He was thinking of future generations, just as he often said, but also of the present. As the war became more horrific every day and the outcome of the conflict more uncertain, he actually thought that the superiority of the Arts and Letters of France had to be affirmed. Such a message was of interest to those who were fighting, suffering, and dying, but he was also speaking to the entire world. The same impulse led the government to organize in other countries—Spain, the Netherlands—French exhibitions that emphasized the works of the Impressionists. In January 1914, Renoir had become, along with Monet and Degas, the first painter to be shown at the Louvre while he was still alive, and his fame did not stop increasing.

Since fall 1916, Renoir had been back in Cagnes. The hawkers were elbowing one another for space, the offers flowing in. Each day he set up in the small wood-and-glass studio he'd had built in the garden of Les Collettes to protect himself from the cold. Unfortunately, no camera filmed him working shut up like that, his model posing outside, and only photographs of the scene have survived. For some time, Renoir had been exploring sculpture and had become enchanted by a new model who made him exclaim, "How beautiful she is! I wore out my old eyes on her youthful skin, and then I saw that I was no master—I was a child."[27]

That youthful skin had come from Nice. Sometime before her death, Aline Renoir had posted an ad at the Academy of Painting: "painter seeks model." It was answered by a certain Lucie Heuschling. When the Boss decreed that she was too thin, she informed him she had a sister who was pleasantly plump. Perhaps she'd do the trick? To check her out, Aline went to see her and then suggested she meet the Boss.[28] This is how the family, following Jean's lead, has told the story, placing Andrée's arrival in spring 1915 at the latest. A photograph of the painter and his model—Renoir and the young girl posing in front of *Nu assis* (*Seated Nude*), dated 1915—could be presented as evidence of that version of events. However, taking as certain the date of the canvas, which is in fact only approximate, means also accepting the supposition that the model was only fourteen at the time, something her appearance in the photo renders quite doubtful. Historians agree that Andrée was seventeen when she made her first appearance at Les Collettes. This imprecision makes room for a wholly other version of the events, in which Matisse, who had spent the winter of 1917 in Nice and had met Renoir for the first time then, was the one who sent the Master this young girl because he thought she would appeal to him. The girl already "made a good living posing for the Academy of Painting in Nice."[29]

Her first name was Andrée, and Dédée was her nickname. She had flaming red hair, magnificent blue eyes, was always at ease, and was Auguste Renoir's last important model. She was born in 1900, in Moronvilliers—not far from Reims—on a road where her mother had seen Prussians go by in 1870 and would see Germans pass in 1914. In 1870, when her mother was younger than ten, the village was pillaged by French soldiers in a rout. She remembered eating nothing for several days until a Prussian soldier took her on his knees and gave her a little from his mess tin. In 1914, the village was plundered again by French troops, and Moronvilliers would soon disappear from the map. When those dubbed refugees received authorization to leave, Madame Heuschling headed south with her three daughters: Jeanne, who would always fail at everything that she attempted; Lucie, who always found a way to get something out of every situation; and Andrée, who was fifteen and found a job retouching photographs in Nice.

Therefore, Dédée Heuschling was probably seventeen when she began modeling at Les Collettes. Every morning—or nearly—she took the streetcar from Nice to Cagnes; and once there, she used the full extent of her beauty, her ability to feel at home regardless of the circumstance, her incessant chatter, and her way of leaping about under the olive trees to ravish the old painter. Jean wrote, "She'd go back to Nice every evening, and after she left the house would seem sad. When I was on leave I got into the habit of driving her back home to Nice. My father seemed happy about our mutual affection."[30]

This is how a teenager abruptly found herself placed at the center of a world, a world whose existence she hadn't been aware of even a day earlier, a world where all these fine gentlemen told her what a wonder she was and where reigned an old man who was famous and celebrated and had eyes only for her. The old man had a twenty-three-year-old son, who visited whenever he was on leave, and who came even more often when he was stationed in Nice. He wore a uniform, was forced to limp because of the stiffness in his leg, had been to the firing line, and had seen death close up. He was a hero and the son of one of the luminaries of his time. How can what is about to happen not come to pass?

Returning to life as a civilian, Jean could think only of Dédée. She didn't intend to leave Renoir, so he moved in with his father to be very near her. For the benefit of Claude, whom everyone called Coco and who was now seventeen, the painter had had a kiln built and guided his young son in the creation of his first works. Probably more from idleness than from inclination, Jean started using the kiln, too, and got Dédée involved (unless it was the opposite that occurred).

During summer 1919, the painter went to stay in Essoyes for the last time. That stay was interrupted in August by a trip to Paris for the partial reopening of the Louvre, whose collections had been held in trust during the war. When Renoir got back to Les Collettes, the November cold got the better of him. He recovered poorly from bronchial pneumonia, and, on December 1, the doctors diagnosed congestion of the lungs. During the night of the second to the third of December—at two in the morning—Auguste Renoir passed away. Jean and Claude were at the bedside of the dying man.* The funeral took place on the seventh in Cagnes. The three brothers led the procession. Following the wishes of the deceased, the military honors that gave him the right to the title of Commander of the Légion d'honneur were not mentioned. No speech was made; but the funeral oration of the Abbey Baume, the senior cleric of Cagnes, produced great effect.[31]

Two and a half years later, the remains of the painter and those of his spouse, which until then had rested in the vault of the Roumieux family (the owners of the Renoirs' apartment in Nice), were moved to Essoyes; on June 7, 1922, they were interred in two distinct tombs.

On Saturday, January 24, 1920, at the Cagnes-sur-Mer city hall, Andrée Madeleine Heuschling, born June 22, 1900, became Madame Jean Renoir. The official family record book issued that day names Jean as "landowner."[32]

---

* In a letter to Claude Monet dated December 9, 1919, Pierre Renoir expresses his regret at not having been present at the moment of his father's death.

3

Before He Became Renoir

Catherine (Backbiters)
La Fille de l'eau (The Whirlpool of Fate)

On the morning of his last day alive, Auguste Renoir was painting. For several months, he'd been telling dealers who asked him for canvases that he didn't want to sell any more, that he planned to keep working in order to ensure the future of his children.

In the painter's studio, Pierre, Jean, and Claude found dozens of new canvases in addition to those already placed with Durand-Ruel, Vollard, and Bernheim. Hundreds of drawings, too, not to mention the pastels, bronzes, and terra-cottas. An article that appeared at the end of 1920 in the New York magazine *The Touchstone* described Jean surrounded by his father's work as well as canvases by Pierre Bonnard, Frédéric Bazille, and Berthe Morisot. For her, Jean claimed on the occasion of that interview, Renoir had had a very high regard; and he also very much appreciated Mary Cassatt, who was from the same country as the interviewers though she lived not far from Les Collettes in Grasse.[1] Entitled "Chez Renoir at Cagnes," the article marks the first noteworthy appearance of Jean Renoir in the press of his time. It was written by Harold L. Van Doren. A year younger than Jean, originally coming to France for a series of conferences at the Louvre on the history of art, Harold Livingston Van Doren also penned drawings for the *Chicago Tribune*. He spent the summer of 1924 at Marlotte and appeared in Renoir's film *The Whirlpool of Fate* in the role of Georges Raynal, the lover of the heroine. Back in the United States, he enjoyed a brilliant career as an industrial designer until his death in 1957.

The details of Auguste Renoir's will won't be revealed until 2019, one hundred years after his death. All that is currently known is that Claude inherited Les Collettes and Pierre got the house in Essoyes, but Jean was not forgotten. Because the deceased hadn't revealed his wishes regarding his work, Henry Barbazanges asked several other dealers, notably Durand-Ruel, Georges Bernheim, and Paul Rosenberg, to partner with him in drawing up an offer of 10.5 million francs for the contents of the studio.* They rejected the offering plan, which they thought was too high, and insisted on not going over 7 million. There was no public sale, and the three brothers negotiated the prices in lots.[2]

None of the brothers had to worry about making a living. Although Pierre had long ago begun to carve out a path, at the age of twenty-five Jean's situation was close to Claude's, who was barely out of adolescence. As a result, the two younger brothers teamed up with the sketchy idea of becoming ceramicists. Jean was attracted by the craftsman-like tenor of the project—in theory, at least—especially since Dédée was tempted by the same idea, and Auguste had even considered her as having a talent for it. But, for the moment, Jean was the son of a famous painter and the brother of a great actor who had been treading the boards since leaving the Academy in 1908. Jean was also the husband of a very young woman who was enjoying having money she'd never dreamed possible and which enabled her to support her mother and two sisters. Dédée and Jean's friends were no more in need than they were.

For Jean, his twenties would be a period for socializing. They're marked by the blossoming of his friendship with Albert André, Claude's godfather, and his wife, Maleck. André was an artist as well, had always painted, and was a friend of Renoir. His connection to Jean was deeply sincere; when life separated them, they'd write each other constantly. However, Albert André would not be to Jean what Paul Cézanne, the painter's son, and the two Pierres, Champagne and Lestringuez, were. These three were to become Jean's partners during his first adult ventures.

Pierre Lestringuez, that "friend before I was born," as Jean Renoir describes him, was six years older than Jean. His father, an official at the Ministry of the Interior as well as a writer, was one of the models used by Renoir for *Luncheon of the Boating Party*. The son was massively built and in love with life and all the pleasures it offered those who knew how to take advantage of them. He, too, was a writer. He led a wild social life, primarily composed of compulsive skirt-chasing; and, according to gossip, he was repeatedly successful with the ladies. These involvements had offered him entry into the world of literature and film. He counted Jean Cocteau as well as Jean Giraudoux among his circle. He claimed to be the inventor of a cocktail that he alone appreciated: one part gin, one part whiskey, one part rum, and—"just to smooth it out"—an oyster.[3] He and Pierre Champagne teamed up to drag their friend Jean along on their reckless course to pleasure. A garage mechanic from Nice, Champagne liked to think of himself as a film buff and also loved cars, speed.

* The most reliable historians maintain that there was a total of around 740 canvases, apart from the drawings, sketches, sculptures, etc.

Jean drove a luxurious English model, the Napier, which during that period was the only rival to the Rolls-Royce Silver Ghost. Over time, he'd own dozens of cars, including coupes, convertibles, a Renault, a Ford Spyder, and, of course, a few Bugattis. Starting in the fifties, he'd opt for Jaguars. He adored revamping them, having them outfitted with new features, adding horsepower or leather convertible tops, and couldn't tolerate anyone slamming the doors. Whereas his habit was to climb behind the wheel of his big, blue 2.3-liter Bugatti, which was always breaking down, Dédée stuck to her small Bugatti, which raced like the wind.[4]

On October 31, 1921, at Les Collettes, Dédée gave birth to a son who was named Alain. Seven-year-old Aline Cézanne, Paul and Rénée's daughter and the granddaughter of the painter, became godmother; and Alain was soon after endowed with a godfather considered an eccentric at the time: Philippe Gangnat, the son of Maurice Gangnat, who'd been introduced to Renoir by Gallimard in 1904, and who'd appeared in several of his portraits. Philippe kept a sign on his door that said, "The bell doesn't work, so bang on the door, I'm a masochist."[5] Maurice Gangnat, who'd made a fortune in the steel business and had only begun to be interested in art shortly after meeting the painter, had been "the greatest collector of [Renoir's] recent works over a period of fifteen years."[6] Two years after his death in 1924, his son auctioned off more than two-thirds of his collection, except for the fifty remaining, which he would loan indefinitely in 1938 to the Philadelphia Museum of Art.

Alain's birth lighted no maternal spark in Dédée, who was devoid of such qualities, and the boy was entrusted to the care of Grandma Heuschling. Like Jean, Alain wasn't brought up by his mother, and at the end of his life he'd regret not having understood her. Dédée had found herself catapulted into a fast-moving life of luxury and pleasure, but she was dreaming of becoming an even brighter shining light, on an order of the kind she discovered at the Renoirs'.

A few months after Alain's birth, liberated by Coco's departure to do his military service, the couple moved nearer to Paris. Jean bought some property in Marlotte, not far from Barbizon, on the edge of the Fontainebleau forest. Marlotte was a village of artists. Henry Murger would spend time there, and Honoré Daumier lived in Bourron, which is so close to Marlotte that today the two municipalities have merged. Alfred de Musset had a house there as well. Auguste had visited it quite often to paint; and in his youth he had walked there from Paris in two stints, spending the night in a barn or stable on the way. On May 31, 1922, Jean bought Saint-El, the villa named after its baron, Ludovic de Villée, who'd had that beautiful, white two-story house constructed in 1860. Located on a small hillock at 42 rue Murger, the home was surrounded by high walls and perched haughtily above the village.

Jean, Dédée, their son, and the grandmother hired several servants, including two caretakers as well as a gardener who took over for the caretaker when
he was away. He spent his nights inside the house watching over Renoir's
paintings, which he had forbidden his own son even to look at, because all
those naked women might have had a deleterious effect on him. Soon, Louis
Baude, a potter from Cagnes, moved in to work on his ceramics, because Jean
had had a kiln built as part of a vague plan to establish a factory. Alain was
often put under the care of Marie Tourbe, a woman from Marlotte who would
later become Marie Verrier, who lived in the house in front of which scenes
from *Partie de campagne* (*A Day in the Country*) would be shot. He had a very
difficult childhood, his sleep filled with nightmares punctuated by screams.
Marie was the one to take him to the south for vacations, and by the beginning
of the thirties he got to know Jean Slade, Gabrielle's son, who was a year older
than he was and who became his best friend. Brief visits from Jean, his father,
occurred at the wheel of the blue Bugatti, and he was a man always in a hurry,
always talking at the top of his lungs. Here comes Jean, boasting about having
knocked the policeman down a peg or two for reproaching him about driving
too fast. "You aren't even capable of pulling up those dandelions growing in the
yard at your station!"[7]

That same year, 1922, Paul and Rénée Cézanne bought their own house
in Marlotte and called it La Nicotière, because the diplomat Jean Nicot
(1530–1600), responsible for introducing the French to tobacco, was rumored
to have lived there. The friendship between the Renoirs and the Cézannes was
reinforced by dinners and parties at Saint-El, or at La Nicotière, where Paul and
Rénée kept open house—that is, until Dédée decided she didn't want to hear
another word about Rénée. From that day on, probably around 1928 or 1929,
Alain's grandmother rather than his parents brought him to see his godmother.[8]

Dr. Roesch, the village of Marlotte's physician, put in his own two cents about
the kind of atmosphere dominating Saint-El: "You don't dally at the Renoirs'—
they're always naked as jaybirds!"[9] Maybe not *always,* but certainly more often
than the other inhabitants of the village. It was a party atmosphere. Leprince,
the most popular pastry chef in Fontainebleau, sent mountains of petit-fours
and macarons, which were arranged into pyramids in the ground-floor rooms or,
weather permitting, under the linden tree growing on the back grounds. On one
of the branches of that tree hung the antenna of a radio. An electric wire strung
across the entire length of the grounds enabled it to function in the house, also
equipped with a telephone whose number was Bourron-Marlotte 38.

Alice, Dédée's friend from Nice, came often with her husband, Pierre
Fighiera, to spend a few days. They were rowing on the Loing River when Dédée
launched into an imitation of Lillian Gish, and Jean could not stop laughing, so

he came out with, "That's just too funny—it has to be filmed." Lestringuez was one of the permanent guests at Saint-El, where there was a crush of Parisian friends and their acquaintances on evenings when there was a party. After all, Paris was just a hop, skip, and jump away, especially for people addicted to speed and equipped with comfortable, powerful automobiles. Jean and Dédée often went to the movies in Paris; she had been a film fanatic for a long time. In Nice, "she'd go to the movies after work—every day, and sometimes several times on the same day. She'd see her favorite film a few times in a row."[10]

Back then, films were mostly American. The Renoirs favored them over French films because they had mass appeal, whereas their own country's productions felt stilted, aestheticized, theatrical, cornily patriotic, depressing, colorless. Such an opinion was less about the reality of the films than it was a sign of the times. The war had had a damaging effect on European film, which had held sway before 1914. That year, American films began appearing on screens abandoned by French, German, Italian, and Scandinavian productions for the length of the entire war; but audiences weren't aware of the origins of these films because intertitles were in French and bourgeois dramas were nearly identical whether they came from France, Sweden, or Germany. Those originating on the other side of the Alps were a little different from other European productions: they were stories that took place in the past, and only the Italians were making them. However, audiences rarely noticed the difference between a western filmed in California and a horse opera shot in Camargue, especially because the names of characters in foreign films were Gallicized. The war years contributed to reshuffling the deck, placing America at the top of the game. A poster that plastered the walls of Paris at the beginning of the twenties illustrates the situation. It shows American cannons with the titles of films (American, of course) written on each and includes a foolproof slogan for Mundus, a French corporation combining several companies, including First National, Metro, and Goldwyn: "Mundus is always on target."

In the eyes of Jean and his wife, the only good films were American. Their judgmental attitude toward French cinema of the time seems rash because, although its output was of limited variety, French production was capable of responding to the most dissimilar tastes. Even when that wasn't the case, European films still held up in comparison with American productions. Whereas 1923 saw the release in France of Allan Dwan's *Robin Hood* with Douglas Fairbanks, Flaherty's *Nanook of the North,* Griffith's *Birth of a Nation,* Fred Niblo's *Blood and Sand,* and Stroheim's *Foolish Wives,* European cinema doesn't look bad at all, with its opposing lineup of such historical superproductions as Ernst Lubitsch's *Anna Boleyn* and *Madame DuBarry,* Augusto Genina's *Cyrano de Bergerac,* and the films by the German Lupu-Pick and the Swede Mauritz

Stiller. That same year would see the release of movies by, among others, Jacques Feyder, Abel Gance, Jacques de Baroncelli, Jean Epstein, and Léon Poirier, some of which certainly seem capable of sustaining the attention of audiences as discriminating as Jean and Andrée Renoir.

But it's also true that Dédée was thinking less about the quality of cinema and more about making it big, whereas Jean saw himself less as an artist and more as an entrepreneur. In fact, he was conscious of living in the shadow of Auguste; one of the reasons that prompted him to abandon ceramics, a medium for which he'd shown little aptitude, would come from the fact that he did not accept seeing his creations bought not for their own value but for the market value of the name with which they were signed. His ambition was to pull together the conditions that would allow his wife to make films. Considering that Dédée's dream was less about "making films" than about becoming a star, it was natural enough that Jean would favor those films that pleased audiences the most, and such films were American.

On the other hand, with Jean Renoir, nothing is ever simple. All the more so because he had to reconcile that period with declarations he made years later and with writing he intended for publication. Having become a celebrity, he was naturally concerned about the image he projected. That is what makes it hard to believe that a revelation about the possibility of producing and making works of quality in France coincided with his discovery at the Colisée theater of the film *Le Brasier ardent,* which contains a host of special effects produced by editing, slow-motion sequences, and double exposures to recount the story of a detective who has fallen in love with the wife he's been hired to tail. When Renoir claims that the pleasure he got from this film by Ivan Mozzhukhin (known professionally as Ivan Mosjoukine)—not at all one of those mundane melodramas glutting the domestic market—increased tenfold when he witnessed the indignation of members of the audience who were disgusted by the movie, it becomes difficult to understand how he could imagine being able to act upon his only ambition of the moment, which he himself described, by writing: "I insist on the fact that I gave film a try only in the hope of making my wife a star."[11]

How would Dédée be able to become a star by appearing in films that audiences loathed? Apparently, at the time, her husband was refusing to face his own artistic ambitions, and he even quite adeptly insisted upon silencing them later. At the very least, we can't take every assertion as the gospel truth; we've got to listen to certain other divergent voices. Andrée's, especially, when she declared in 1961, "I never wanted to be a film star—ever; Renoir's the one who'd say that if he had to, he'd exercise his marital rights to make me act in a film."[12] The husband forcing his wife to make movies? Seems strange; but in any case, by 1961 relations between the two had deteriorated so much and for so long a time that the claims of either can't be taken very seriously. There are so many contradictions. Rather than be surprised by them, it's better to concede that Jean Renoir found himself placed from the very beginning in a context that favored filmmaking, the only art requiring a layout of funds as a prerequisite. But that is exactly what makes it an impure art, according to André Bazin's formula.

Jean would experience more contradictions very soon. Once he and Dédée had found a professional name for her in films—Catherine Hessling—the next step was to decide upon a movie they wanted to produce. *Produce,* in fact, because, for the moment, Jean did not envision directing. Such wasn't the case for Albert Dieudonné, who had just directed three films: *Sous la griffe** with Harry Baur, *Son crime,* and *Gloire rouge,* all of which he'd also produced and wrote. The last production was an adaptation of his own play, *Une lâche,*† which he performed onstage opposite Véra Sergine, Jean's sister-in-law. Author, producer, director, actor—Dieudonné exhibited the ambition Jean lacked at the time; on the other hand, Jean had no money problems and also had a wife who, contrary to what she later claimed, dreamed of becoming a star. Dieudonné's meeting with the Renoirs, organized by Véra Sergine, allowed him to anticipate a partnership with nothing but advantages.

In those years, Véra Sergine, as a result of her fame, occupied an important place in the life of the Renoirs, and not only in Pierre's. This can be gleaned from a letter Pierre wrote to the director of the Beaux-Arts, Paul Léon, on February 23, 1923, informing him that he was canceling the gift of one of his father's canvases to the state. The letter's author made it public following a conversation his wife the actress had had with a Monsieur d'Estournelles de Constant, the director of the National Museums, who had approached Véra Sergine during intermission at a performance. D'Estournelles de Constant, writes Pierre Renoir, "doesn't like paintings from my father's late period. It's his right and makes no difference to me; and besides, he's part of that crowd whose unfavorable opinion can only bring joy in my case."[13] In a letter dated April 10, Jean confides to Claude that this d'Estournelles de Constant, whom he designates in passing as "some kind of fairy," had revealed to Véra Sergine his intention to banish the canvas to Luxembourg and had "made his innuendo very clear: they'd chuck it in the toilets and keep it there." In the same message, Jean informs his brother on some progress made by his wife: "Dédé [*sic*] is beginning to ride horseback."[14]

In fact, by saddling up, Catherine/Dédée wasn't wasting time. Her pretext

* *Translator's note:* "In the Clutches."

† *Translator's note:* "A Coward."

for it involved a scenario that Albert Dieudonné would soon claim full ownership of, which was developed from an idea furnished by Jean, who had recalled the content of *Le Journal d'une femme de chambre* (*The Diary of a Chambermaid*). Jean would try for years to bring that novel by Mirbeau—an author he'd briefly met at his father's—to the screen, and he finally accomplished it in 1945, in Hollywood. But for the time being, it was natural for Jean to call on his friend Lestringuez as scenarist and actor, just as he'd taken on Albert Dieudonné as both director and actor.

*Catherine** was filmed using exteriors in Cagnes, Nice, and Saint-Paul-de-Venice, and its interiors were filmed at studios in Boulogne. Catherine is the focus of the film, whose title is identical to the professional name she had taken. But if the film *Catherine* is actually Catherine Hessling's first, it's only partly Jean Renoir's. Partly and—more importantly—accidentally his film. Jean couldn't manage to keep his distance from the production intended to showcase the woman he loved. He couldn't prevent himself from intervening and soon didn't even try but instead began correcting motivations, suggesting modifications. His links with the principal actress but also his friendship with Lestringuez, who plays under the name of Pierre Philippe the role of Adolphe, a pimp, seemed to endow his voice with more weight than Dieudonné's. And for the entire crew, he was the one who signed the checks at the end of each week. In such conditions, how much authority is available to a director?

The end of the shoot, which Renoir doesn't yet call "the *tournaison*,"† didn't put an end to the quarrels, which took a new turn when it came to the editing. Director and producer continued to confront each other ever more violently because, at the very least, Renoir had forced his way in as codirector of the film and because, in circumstances as turbulent as these, the notion of codirection had very little significance.

Renoir organized a screening of *Catherine* intended for his friends and relatives, probably in early 1924. It's unlikely that Dieudonné was invited, but he knew enough about the event to feel shut out and to oppose the distribution of the film in that form. Years later, when asked if he really did direct *Catherine*, Renoir would answer, "Of course, but I'd made an agreement with Dieudonné

* *Translator's note:* Original title = *Une vie sans joie*.

† *Translator's note:* As explained to me by the author, Renoir had reasons for purposely deforming the word *tournage* ("film shoot") and dubbing it *tournaison*. Some French verbs can be transformed into nouns using a limited variety of endings: -age, -ation, -aison. By choosing *tournaison* to describe the work of shooting, rather than the correct contemporary substantive *tournage*, he was emphasizing the artisanal nature of the activity—even associating it with the peasantry's farming. Because technique was essential to filmmaking, Renoir devalued the creative claims of cinema by focusing on its more primitive, hands-on dimensions.

that he'd be credited as the only director."[15] All of those who participated in the venture *Catherine*, except possibly Dieudonné, would say one by one that they had failed. For Jean Renoir, it was because "his" film was never shown to audiences, because the version finally presented in 1927 wasn't his. For Catherine Hessling, the failure of the film was the fault of its official director: "But what an idea to film such a thing, especially using that Dieudonné, who wasn't a very reliable guy.... It was all Renoir!"[16]

In fact, *Catherine* falls within the career of Jean Renoir as a false start, which nevertheless points out a direction. Hence the abundance of scenes filmed in natural locations, some of which are exceedingly beautiful and immediately distinguish the film from the standard production of the period, which in most cases was confined to the studio. The viewer first discovers the character Catherine Ferrand, a young maid, at the washtub; and a later title card presents her as "sweet, sensitive, and intelligent" but suffering "from the moral isolation in which her social condition forces her to live." The alleys of the small subprefecture Varance, the streets of old Nice, a cemetery on the hillside, avenues drenched with rain, country roads bordered by trees, and olive orchards all give the film its tonality, a feature demonstrating the notion that the search for inner truths is accomplished by way of the depiction of exterior truths, made possible only by placing those characters in the framework of their lives, in their landscape. In order to film, Renoir cedes to "observations of the natural world," thereby imposing on film the same sense of motion that the Impressionists introduced in painting. It is this dimension—throughout—that today remains the most striking thing about the entire film, which in other respects seems to vacillate between a certain French tradition connected to the theater and an American influence, noticeable especially in the last scenes, which take place precisely in the spirit of a serial, overflowing with plot reversals and episodes. Moreover, such duality seems to follow the twin paths of the work, which also suffers from the artificiality of its script, a melodrama with a happy ending.

Catherine Hessling's inexperience doesn't do justice to the character Catherine. However, the actress's debut exhibits relative restraint in comparison with the roles to come and the performances of the other players, who give free rein to a sometimes-awkward expressivity because they can't rely on words. The actress, on the other hand, embodies Renoir's expressed preference for the "American acting style, more inspired by the observation of nature" than the "far from natural" performances of French actors.[17] Catherine Hessling will be in a hurry to forget the lesson, but in this first film she valiantly maintains the course, especially in comparison to Albert Dieudonné, who is stiff and starchy in his role as a young man of means with a heart condition whom his mother has been trying in vain to marry off for several years. The character dies while dancing with Catherine as the carnival outside reaches its climax. This death provides the occasion for a rather startling montage that alternates in a series of close-ups of the dying man's face and Catherine's, which on this occasion as on several others recalls the face of Gloria Swanson, one of Dédée's idols. Such effects seem less likely to be attributable to Dieudonné's direction, the principles of which barely differed from the canons of theatrical cinema, than to Renoir's, who may have been expressing his fascination for *Le Brasier ardent,* something he himself maintained a posteriori. The rarity, and especially the relative lack of exaggeration, of the special effects leaves us supposing that Renoir wasn't able to give in to his penchant for experimentation, which the shoot may have helped him discover.

On the other hand, Renoir's interest in acting, which would never fade, is obvious, seeing how much he enjoyed playing the character of the simpering subprefect with a monocle, a mediocre would-be poet and hypocritical seducer. This film also affords us a glimpse of elements of themes inherent in his future works, such as the relations between masters and servants, sustained by an indistinct and possibly even unconscious desire to act as a moralist. But what is definitely essential about this first experience—as unsatisfying and frustrating as it turned out—is the fact that it awoke in Jean an interest in film. It brought Renoir to the conclusion that he had found his way, and without delay he decided to explore the path more thoroughly.

When the editing of *Catherine* was barely completed, Renoir began shooting a new film, *The Whirlpool of Fate,* for which he served as both producer and director. The scenario was by Lestringuez, a fact that was of only secondary interest to Renoir, who exploited it primarily as a pretext for experimenting within a context in strong contrast to the atmosphere of the filming of *Catherine.* For this occasion, the town of Marlotte and principally Cézanne's property, La Nicotière, provided the exteriors, shot during the summer of 1924, after which a small part of the company also went to studios in Boulogne. It was lovely summer weather, and Renoir had brought in all his friends, including his wife, who, it goes without saying, was part of the project and also shared responsibility for the costumes with Pierre Champagne's wife, Mimi. The director took on managing the locations. Pierre Renoir stopped by, too; he was the only professional on the shoot aside from the two cinematographers—the veteran Alphonse Gibory, who'd later distinguish himself with lighting *Madame Bovary,* and the beginner Jean Bachelet, who'd already participated in *Catherine* and would shoot a total of eleven films for Renoir. The painter André Derain was to play a small role, and so would Charlotte Clasis, one of Auguste's former models whom Jean would use again in *La Bête humaine* as the aunt of the character Jacques Lantier. A team was being put together, and with it one of the essential prerequisites of a Renoir film: Jean Renoir at the head of the gang, whose members constituted a kind of family, producing a self-organizing system. In this system, a certain hedonism, as well as the leader's natural charm, was no less important than his talents as an artist and technician. The master of ceremonies would collect all opinions—even ask for them—and show respect for them all. Everyone put in his or her word, which counted as much as that of any other, and everyone was able to feel a part of the decision making. However, the film achieved collectively resembled the one the foreman wanted. Renoir at work liked to have a good time, feel part of the group, and detested being taken seriously. Film had begun to be what it always would, an adventure whose first goal was to give pleasure.

As for having fun, that is just what happened during the shooting of *The Whirlpool of Fate*. Lestringuez played a horrible uncle with an insatiable appetite for his role, Pierre Champagne got to pedal down a country road, Catherine rang at the entrance to her own home. She even had the occasion to smile at her son, who was spending the better part of his time far from her. With painted lips and eyes like coals, she endures the shocks and jolts of a laborious plot, which suddenly makes her tumble down into a quarry. This trauma experienced by poor Virginie (or Gudule, according to certain versions of the film) becomes a pretext for a bit of bravura in the nightmare scene. Renoir directed the scene in a studio where he had had a cylinder built and painted completely black so that a camera placed on a dolly permitted a 360-degree panoramic view and could follow a horse at a gallop. On the same roll of film, he next shot superimposed clouds. This special effect interested him on the grounds that such a craftsman-like approach—or, rather, such bricolage—could achieve an "artistic" dimension he felt was missing in a direct recording of reality. The goal of his life's quest may have been film, yet Renoir still was trying to find his way because he hadn't yet fixed on the type of film he wanted to do.

Despite the obvious pleasure brought by the filming of nature—the canal, the fields, the shoreline—and moments from life, such as the toothaches of the bar manager (André Derain), the bourgeoisie's passion for automobiles, and an apprenticeship in poaching, *The Whirlpool of Fate* has trouble holding the viewer's attention. Once past the opening sequence that focuses on the moving current, which has genuine beauty, the film as a whole seems static, and Catherine Hessling is never put in a position to portray the evolution of her character, which is made understandable only by the intertitles. The film would probably have been forgotten a long time ago if it hadn't been made by Jean Renoir, a great filmmaker of the future.

At the end of autumn 1924, Renoir tried desperately to find a distributor for *The Whirlpool of Fate*. Thanks to Lestringuez, a few months earlier he'd gotten to know a plump little gentleman with lively, mischievous eyes and an appealing personality. Renoir had arrived at Café italien on the Rond-Point des Champs-Élysées—not far from the headquarters of the Société des Films Jean Renoir at 15 avenue Matignon—and discovered this "charming scatterbrain straight out of Courteline's *Les Linottes*"*[18] having a drink with Lestringuez. He joined them and their conversation lasted until dawn of the following day without even—according to a legend that sounds a bit exaggerated—any thought of dinner. In some ways, Renoir's life was a series of loves "at first sight." His charm and instant empathy as well as his sudden enthusiasms, conveyed by the unrestrained use of the word *fantastic*, made him endearing—convinced as he so was by his own infatuations.

The "charming scatterbrain," Pierre Braunberger, was barely twenty years old and had just spent about a year in the United States. He had lived in Hollywood, where he claimed to have met Irving Thalberg, F. Scott Fitzgerald's model for the main character in *The Last Tycoon;* and Thalberg had allowed Braunberger to watch Chaplin at work. The night of the premiere of *The Gold Rush*, Braunberger decided to leave California. At least, that's what he claimed, despite the fact that the premiere of Chaplin's masterpiece took place on June 26, 1925. It is a bit hard to see how Braunberger could have viewed it and how the event could have made him decide to return to France when, according to a certificate he asked Renoir to sign in 1976, Braunberger's position at Les Films de Jean Renoir was as "acting commercial manager and director of production from 1923 to 1927."[19] Renoir signed the asked-for certificate, expressing surprise only at the monthly salary it mentioned, which came to "approximately 25,000 francs." Braunberger's claims had a tendency to contradict each other, but when the two men met, his "American" tales of his short-lived emigration were the kind that had fascinated the young director. Back in Europe, nonetheless, Braunberger would become bored by the London offices of Brockliss & Co., an English firm that sold projection equipment and that was involved in importing and exporting films; and he later felt the same way working on the Champs-Élysées in Paramount's publicity department.

When Braunberger told Renoir about mercury-vapor lamps, not yet known in France but seen by him in use on Hollywood sets, where panchromatic film reserved only for exteriors in France was also being put to use, Renoir lost control. He told Braunberger about problems he'd had with Albert Dieudonné

---

* *Translator's note:* Georges Courteline—the pseudonym of Georges-Victor-Marcel Moineau (1858–1929)—was a late nineteenth-century Montmartre satirist of middle- and lower-middle-class French life.

during the filming of *Catherine*, which still hadn't been released, and about the standoff keeping back *The Whirlpool of Fate*. Braunberger promised to see what he could do.

After a private screening on December 12, 1924, *The Whirlpool of Fate* received a few flattering reviews, which essentially focused on the dream sequence, about which the December 20 issue of the newspaper *Le Débat* wrote that "five pages of literature couldn't live up to this part of the film."[20]

Harold Livingston Van Doren, who had become the filmmaker's first American friend, mentioned the newspaper's reaction in a letter he wrote to Renoir from New York on January 6, 1925. The letter discusses the money Van Doren had borrowed from his father to cover the costs incurred by paying US Customs for the importation rights for a copy of the film. It says, "According to letters I'm receiving from friends and newspaper clippings an office in Paris has been forwarding to me, *The Whirlpool of Fate* has been a hit." Although the remark is a bit of an exaggeration, it's coupled with a request that demanded attention: Harold Livingston Van Doren was actually asking that his name, which had been spelled wrong in the film's credits and publicity material, be corrected. "Levinston, to put it bluntly, isn't my name, and what's more, in America it's a Jewish name! (Beware, Mme. Cézanne. This will amuse her given the conversations we've had about the Jews.)"[21]

As the producer of two films—neither of which had been shown to audiences—Renoir was not questioning his involvement in film, despite what he might claim to the contrary, but was wondering which steps to take to avoid experiencing other similar mishaps. He had already developed some rather firm ideas about the issues he encountered with the first two films and confided them to his brother Claude on February 16, 1925:

> The setbacks at the beginning of my career as a film buff won't turn out to be in vain. I now believe I'm capable of such an undertaking with some chances for success. A film's success depends only upon the way it's launched (although I'd be the first to admit that the film I'm talking about was far from a seamless undertaking). You can be sure of having good bookings out of town and good foreign sales if your film shows exclusively at major theaters on the boulevards immediately after being released, along with advertisements proclaiming its real or supposed success. I studied the fate of all the films that came out this winter. Only those that were released under those conditions had interesting results. That's why I've decided to put them into place this summer, and as soon as

The Whirlpool of Fate begins showing, which is on April 3,* I'll start cooking up a scheme that will promise me a theater for the end of the year.

In that same letter, in response to Claude's expressing a desire to try his own hand at cinema, Renoir reveals that he and his brother Pierre had been looking into "a project that could provide us with some great opportunities for easily producing and releasing films that any one of us would want to make." That project, he informs Coco, requires getting the Folies dramatiques, a "wonderfully situated" theater near "other establishments experiencing very high takings," and the place could also be enlarged to become "one of the hugest movie theaters in Paris." From then on, as he would write, Renoir understood that "theater owners are the masters of the situation."[22]

When he sent that letter to Claude, he had already done an interview with *Ciné-miroir,* which appeared that same month of February 1925 and in which he declared, "I was saved by my father. Rummaging through the many mementoes he left us, I discovered a fairly elaborate study of one of the great dance halls of Paris circa 1880. All I then needed was documentation written by Zola and some of his contemporaries to achieve a very exact picture of the scene I'll soon be shooting. You'll see it and also see how the jazz band was already gathering steam in that period in the form of pistols shot off after a certain signal from the orchestra leader!"[23] February 1925 is an important milestone: although *The Whirlpool of Fate* hadn't yet even been shown in public, Renoir was already thinking about *Nana,* proof that he'd chosen a direction that he attributed later to the failure of *The Whirlpool of Fate.*

Braunberger had in fact finally found a theater, Ciné Corso Opéra on boulevard des Italiens, that was willing to show the film, beginning March 20, 1925.† But audiences weren't rushing to the place, and the hit evoked by the young man from Chicago metamorphosed into an irrevocable commercial failure. On April 11, a columnist for the newspaper *Paris-Soir* spoke of a "lovely film," the details of which "certainly made it worthwhile," and said that this Monsieur Jean Renoir, "the son of a very great painter," had presented "a series of country tableaux and sketches of the life of sailors that had some nice touches"; straightaway he ranked Renoir as "one of the directors upon whom young French cinema can count." From all evidence, however, *The Whirlpool of Fate* was "a crushing bore" for audiences. Renoir was already aware that the aesthetic innovations and techniques he found exciting risked leading him into a dead-end if they weren't put at the service of a plot and some solid characterizations. He had available a considerable fortune, which, naturally, he had no

* *The Whirlpool of Fate* would actually be released on March 20, 1925.

† *Le Figaro* for that day announced, "Starting today."

desire to fritter away, but the fact is that he also believed in the popular aspect of film. And all the more so because he'd caught a whiff of success—even if it remained confined to a narrow circle.

September 1924 saw the release of René Clair and Francis Picabia's *Entr'acte*, with music by Erik Satie. A month later, André Breton came out with his *Manifesto of Surrealism*, followed in December by his magazine *La Révolution surréaliste*. Since autumn of that year, Jean Tedesco, a friend of the Renoir family and the director of the Théâtre du Vieux-Colombier (which had served from 1913 to 1922 as the lair of Louis Jouvet, Pierre Renoir's best friend), had been showing films, concerts, and plays at the venue. He screened German Expressionist works as well as Buster Keaton's *Our Hospitality;* but he was also offering programs of assorted works that combined documentaries with scenes from avant-garde cinema. Along with revivals of films that had come out several months or years earlier, including *Le Brasier ardent,* he projected excerpts, such as a scene from Abel Gance's *La Roue* (*The Wheel*) in November 1924; and he exhibited film montages composed of excerpts, such as *Festival d'expressions Mosjoukine* in January 1925, *Sélection d'expressions de Raquel Meller* in February of that year, and, in March, *Études de ralenti** along with *Jeux de ski dans l'Engadine.*

When Renoir learned from Tedesco that he had also inserted the dream sequence from *The Whirlpool of Fate* into one of his fall 1925 programs, Renoir didn't take it well. But, as usual, his annoyance was short-lived, and Tedesco convinced him to come to a showing and decide based on actual evidence. There was applause when the sequence was projected; and after the lights went back on, the audience recognized Catherine, and their clapping intensified. The dream sequence in *The Whirlpool of Fate* rode the wave of several showings in Paris. However, Renoir had no reason to go back upstream to a cinema arrogantly free of all literary influence when the new direction he'd chosen was leading him toward an adaptation. Perhaps he was burning his idols, as he would later write; but consider that the object of his adoration had glittered for him only for the space of a few months and, even then, intermittently.

His change in point of view was probably brought about at least in part by the discovery of *Foolish Wives*. Released in the United States in January 1922, the film, by Erich von Stroheim, was shown in France the following year; but the date on which Renoir discovered it is unknown. Stroheim's fame was such that French newspapers knew of his works-in-progress; and they exploited the rumors of his excesses, passed on to them by the publicity departments at

* *Translator's note:* "Studies in slow motion."

Universal and then at Metro. But the interest wasn't only about the hundreds of spider webs demanded on the set. It also had to do with a long article that appeared in *Le Figaro* on August 22, 1924, about Stroheim's latest film that cited the title as *Convoitise*, literally translated as *Greed*. There was no hiding the fact that the film was an adaptation of the novel *McTeague* by Frank Norris. According to *Le Figaro*, this book was as celebrated in the United States as *Salummbô* or *Le Crime de Sylvestre Bonnard* was in France. The fact that the filmmaker whom Renoir admired the most was basing the content of his film on a literary work had to have affected Renoir, and he may have read Stroheim's position on the subject, expressed in the July 10, 1925, issue of *Le Figaro*: "If a literary masterpiece is to become a cinematic masterpiece, the director's sensibility has to be identical to his author's. Certain screenplays make you ashamed of knowing how to read. A dreadful film based on a preposterous script is a routine occurrence. A mediocre film based on a literary masterpiece is a criminal insult to the human intellect."

In a way, Stroheim's example liberated Renoir from his scruples. Renoir's opening of an art gallery in the summer of 1925 a couple steps away from La Madeleine, which was also close to the apartment in which he stayed when in Paris, bears mentioning. The building that housed the gallery, at 30 rue de Miromesnil, was also the place where the Cézannes and Pierre Renoir (now separated from Véra Sergine) lived. Jean and Catherine soon became aware that their ceramics weren't any more marketable than the stage scenery, canvases, and scarves painted by Maleck André; but they had an endless supply of ideas for movies, and they recorded some of them in writing.

An example is *La Belote*,[*] which was credited to Lestringuez and Renoir and registered at the Société des auteurs de films on March 22, 1925. Its direction, scheduled for the following year, and even its wrap date were announced in the press several times as well as assorted pieces of information precise enough so that "you'd think the filmmaker himself was an ace pinochle player." A contract created on April 24, 1925, between Jean Renoir—who would be acting alone as producer—and Jean Angelo guaranteed that the actor (who would play Vandeuvres in *Nana*) would perform the role of Ramon in exchange for a fee of "18,000 francs per month, payable every fifteen days." The film was never made, nor was another project—*Alice*—which amounted only to three handwritten pages dated "November 1925."[24] Renoir was also considering another adaptation based on *Manon Lescaut*, definite proof that he had overcome his reservations about "literary" films. The strategy he and Braunberger had designed was finally beginning to work; and over time, each partner equipped himself with

* *Translator's note:* "Pinochle."

the tools he would need.

In July 1925, the creation of a distribution company, Aux films Renoir, was announced. Louis Guillaume, the Renoir family's right-hand man,* was named its authorized representative and Pierre Braunberger, its commercial manager. Another company called Films Renoir was incorporated on September 1, 1925. And on August 15, the beginning of a new project, *Nana*, had been announced in the press. It would star Catherine Hessling and "a great German actor." The contract permitting this adaptation of Zola's novel was finalized between Jules Salomon, the lawyer for the writer's family, and Jean Renoir—only. It stipulated payment in full by Renoir of 75,000 francs, and it is dated October 21, 1925.[25]

Chronology establishes that Renoir never thought of abandoning the profession of film and never even thought of going in any other direction. If the idea of doing so did cross his mind—although no evidence allows us to entertain such a notion—he would have found someone to dissuade him.

Catherine was twenty-five. She was spending her nights in the most posh of nightclubs, sometimes with her husband. She dressed head to toe in silk and furs, and her dresses were designed by Paul Poiret especially for her. She loved being seen and made an effort to attract attention; she tried to "turn on" men she encountered in restaurants. She spoke too loud and laughed too much. When she couldn't avoid going out with her son and noticed a man whom she wanted to find her attractive, she either walked faster or slowed down, leaving Alain with his nurse, because she feared being found out as a mother. On those rare occasions when Alain's nurse wasn't there, Alain might have found himself waiting some time by himself in front of the door of a bar his mother had entered on a whim.[26]

But Catherine was waiting, too. She was waiting for America to call, something she admitted to her friend Alice Fighiera when the latter expressed surprise that Catherine was making no effort to learn how to act. "Well," Catherine told her, "if the Americans come calling, it will mean I've got talent. If they don't, none of it's worth the trouble."[27]

Jean had made two films with Catherine and was still crazy about her. He spent money extravagantly on her. Catherine wanted everything and anything, as long as it was shiny; it was enough for some object to appeal to her taste for Jean to decide he thought it was beautiful. He gave in to her fancies, for example, claiming for some time that he had his guests served two lettuce leaves and a hard-boiled egg, after which he rushed away with them to the nearest restaurant.

---

* Paul Guillaume, Louis's father, was an important art collector and also the Cézannes' lawyer.

For the Renoirs, a page was turning. All that was missing were two signatures at the bottom of a contract, and Renoir and Braunberger added them on December 10, 1926,[28] while Jean and Catherine were already deep into the filming of *Nana*. The agreement brought to a close the project *Catherine*, which had endured for two and a half years. Renoir gave Albert Dieudonné complete credit for direction of the film,* the right to show it as he pleased, and, if he thought it necessary, the right to shoot additional scenes. The same document stated that Pierre Braunberger, "having interceded as a nonhostile arbitrator between the two parties," was now the exclusive holder of the world rights for distribution, and it also authorized him to change the title of the film. This is how Renoir found himself completely divested of a film that had never really been his, although he made a commitment "to take full responsibility, on the one hand, for all running costs . . . and on the other, for the total of the various taxes and fees currently existing or accruing in the future."[29]

Catherine, une vie sans joie, was released on November 9, 1927. It left no other noticeable trace of its existence beyond an interview in *Ciné-miroir*, in which Dieudonné stated, "I'm the sole director of a screenplay I wrote based on an idea that Monsieur Jean Renoir conceived with my collaboration. Moreover, Monsieur Jean Renoir was my sponsor and my apprentice. It remains to be seen if his future productions give me reason to be pleased about that." In fact, by that time, six months after the release of Abel Gance's *Napoléon*, Albert Dieudonné was beginning to lose control. The film had carried him away on a cloud from which he was never to descend; it stole his sanity and condemned him to play the emperor for the rest of his life, usually for an audience of one—himself. History does not reveal whether "the future productions" of "Monsieur Jean Renoir" did give him reason to be pleased.

---

* In answer to a letter from Raymond Borde, the curator for the Cinémathèque of Toulouse, who had just discovered a copy of *Une vie sans joie* whose credits attributed the direction to Dieudonné and who wanted to know how responsibility for the film had been shared, Renoir admits, "I don't know how to answer." (Letters of Raymond Borde, January 27, 1965; and from Jean Renoir to Raymond Borde, February 14, 1965, Jean Renoir Papers, Correspondence, Box 20, Folders 6 and 7.)

4

"A Kraut Movie"

Nana

It was mid-November 1925, and the German filming of *Nana* had begun at the studios in Grünewald. Fritz Lang had just put the finishing touches on *Metropolis* in Babelsberg, and during production its budget had climbed from 1.3 million to 5 million reichsmarks, equal to a little more than 30 million francs at the time. In comparison to what represented the highest budget ever put together for a European film, the 1 million francs available to Renoir reduced *Nana* to the dimensions of a modest production. Two years later, Marcel L'Herbier would spend 5 million francs to make *L'Argent*, another adaptation of a Zola novel, with Brigitte Helm, the star of *Metropolis*. But L'Herbier and Lang were successful, prestigious directors, whereas Jean Renoir was still an unknown in the world of film. *Nana* was the project of two independents—virtual beginners—without the support of any group. One of them was paying for the film out of his own pocket, and he wanted it to have an international future.

Pierre Braunberger, second schemer on this project, would claim to be the source of the idea to entrust the role of Count Muffat to Werner Krauss. That great figure of German cinema was forty-one years old at the time. A year before, he had played Orgon in F. W. Murnau's *Tartuffe*, and six years before, he had been Doctor Caligari in the film by Robert Wiene, the manifesto of Expressionist cinema. He was so little known by French audiences that Renoir was asked in an interview for *La Cinématographie française* on September 25 why he had made such a choice. He justified it by pointing out that the actor enjoyed notoriety all over Europe, except in France, and that his work in G. W. Pabst's film *The Joyless Street*—which wasn't yet distributed in France but which Renoir had had the chance to see—had been exceptional. By August 25, a letter of agreement between the two parties had been signed, specifying that the film would be shot in Berlin, and then in Paris. The actor would receive a fee of $6,000 for the role.

Jean Angelo, chosen to play Vandeuvres, was well known by French audiences, especially because of his part in Jacques Feyder's *L'Atlantide*, which four years earlier had set a new record for ticket sales in the history of French film. His contract, signed on September 21, also specified the condition that he was the "star" of the film. Five days later, the day following the publication of statements by Renoir as well as the appearance of four lines in *Le Figaro* mentioning only Catherine Hessling's and Werner Krauss's names, the actor informed the producer by certified mail that he considered the contract null and void. Renoir sent him a letter on September 29 by pneumatic tube that put an end to the misunderstanding by assuring the performer that the agreement would be honored. The contract that included the details of distribution, made on June 16, 1926, specified that "on all copies of the film and in its publicity ... Mr. Angelo's last name, always to be preceded by his first, will have top billing in the film, and no other star's name can appear in larger characters than his."[1]

The paragraph in *Le Figaro* that Angelo had found offensive also made it clear that Jean Renoir, who "was putting off the production of *La Belote* to a later date," "had gone to Berlin himself to hire Werner Krauss." Braunberger gave a more detailed and less stuffy version of the negotiations, none of which can be verified, seeing that any assertion from this producer should be viewed with some skepticism; but at least the account has the advantage of providing information on certain mores of the time and some of the aspects of Renoir and his friends' lifestyle.

> Werner Krauss wasn't very enthusiastic about shooting in France, which he considers a country on the road to ruin, but in the end he accepted. I don't know which of us had the idea of cooking up an outrageous practical joke. Someone who works with us had gone to the Gare de l'Est where Krauss was arriving and brought him to Chez Francis on place de l'Alma, where we were waiting for him. When he arrived, around noon, we had a drink together, and Jean Giraudoux, Louis Jouvet, Pierre Lestringuez, Pierre Renoir, Jean, Werner Krauss, and I were there. Suddenly Jouvet exclaimed, "Oh! Half past noon, time for the whorehouse!" We all went to a brothel on rue Laferrière that also features quality cuisine (there were two or three establishments like that in Paris), and we sat down around a big table. In these places it was customary to take down your pants, and then the girls would duck under the table during the meal. We initiated Werner Krauss into an additional tradition: the one who can't hold back and put the brakes on before it's too late is the one who has to pay the bill. Naturally, the girls were in on it with us and focused all their energies on him, and Werner Krauss had to pay for the meal. We've pulled that joke several times. When he got back to Germany and learned that we'd been having fun at his expense, he resented us deeply for it, and that only made his anti-French feelings worse.[2]

The actor's anti-French feelings would find an outlet several years later, when his nature found fuller expression in joining the ranks of the Nazi Party. He was declared "actor of the State" by Goebbels and played both Rabbi Loew and Levy, Joseph Süss Oppenheimer's secretary, in the film *Jud Süss* (Veit Harlan, 1940), insisting at the time that it be officially acknowledged that he himself was Aryan and had only created these roles for the purpose of service to the State.[3] After the war, forbidden to work and divested of his German citizenship, he became a citizen of Austria for a while. His German citizenship was reestablished in 1951, and he died in 1959.

A Spanish actor was to be added to the cast to increase the project's international dimension and make way for wider distribution on the European continent. For reasons unknown, the agreement signed in September and the contract established in October with a certain Juan Orduña had no outcome, and the role of Georges Hugon, Vandeuvres's nephew, went to Raymond Guérin-Catelin.

The actress Valeska Gert, in the role of Zoé, Nana's chambermaid, raised the German quota. At the time, she was known as a theater actress and cabaret singer and had just appeared in *The Joyless Street* with Krauss. She would write about Catherine Hessling that she was "an authentic Parisian, chic, capricious, [who] used an outrageous amount of makeup, which, at the time, only Gloria Swanson was doing." In 1934, she made a film with Catherine about the British postal system, directed by Alberto Cavalcanti: "Catherine was Pett, and I was Pott. The film was supposed to be funny, but wasn't, and both of us were vapid."[4]

Using two German actors didn't guarantee German distribution for *Nana* to the extent its promoters had imagined. Even so, they had pulled off the first Franco-German production in history. The film would run only belatedly in Berlin in spring 1929, and quite unobtrusively, something that surprised a few critics who were particularly enthusiastic about Catherine Hessling's performance. A critic for *Die Weltbühne* at that time surmised that "Jean Renoir might be Manet's son, or Velasquez's grandson."

Braunberger's principal contribution to the production appears to have been taking advantage of his Berlin contacts to make it possible for Jean and Claude Renoir to sign an agreement on September 3, 1925, with the Delog Film Kommanditgesellschaft, Jacobi & Co. It was the Berlin firm that made the film possible because it absorbed most of the costs incurred in Germany.[5] Braunberger and Renoir's situation in 1925 required such a partnership, and *Nana* had to have been produced—or at least part of it had to have been—in Germany.

Shooting began October 16 in the Bois de Vincennes with the scene showing the return from the racetrack. Jean Bachelet was Renoir's new chief cinematographer and shared responsibility for lighting with the experienced Paul Holzki when they were in Berlin, while a man named Edmund Corwin did the camerawork. Newspapers of the time introduced Corwin as regularly working in American movie studios, and particularly as Chaplin's collaborator, a claim made again years later by Braunberger, who had probably originated the idea; but that name never existed or appeared again in any credits other than those for *Nana*. It's a mystery that only adds to doubts hanging over Braunberger's American experience, about which we'll never know more than this self-serving person chose to say.

Five days later, Renoir finalized the contract for the rights to an adaptation of the novel, paying Denise Leblond-Zola, the author's daughter, 75,000 francs in accordance with their agreement. She also accepted his offer to collaborate on writing the intertitles. This assured the filmmaker that the author's family wouldn't oppose the adaptation that he'd already begun filming and for which only Pierre Lestringuez's name would appear in the credits.

Renoir had seen Zola at his father's home long ago. "There was an odor of leather and fat coming from him. . . . He was especially nice and brought me some candy."[6] It's unlikely, however, that Jean had a chance to meet the writer more than a few times, because Auguste had openly taken Cézanne's side when Cézanne broke off all relations with Zola, whom he resented for having parodied him through the character of the painter in *His Masterpiece* (1886). Moreover, Auguste had come out with a few remarks about Zola, although they certainly are in no way conclusive. For example, he frowned on his habit of having his characters who were workers use the word *merde*. Auguste was also a member of the anti-Dreyfus camp, and had fleetingly justified his position with a reflection that seems very "Renoir": "The same inevitable camps for centuries, with only the names changed—Protestants versus Catholics, Republicans versus Monarchists, Communards versus the Versaillais. . . . The old quarrel is surfacing again. You're either for Dreyfus or against Dreyfus." And he followed up the remark with a phrase that in itself was empty of sense: "Me, I'd quite simply like to try being French."[7] It was a remark that Jean would treat himself to over the years and finally present in completed form in *La Marseillaise*. Under the rubric of being apolitical, Auguste Renoir demonstrated that you could refuse to choose sides . . . and, at the same time, do so.

"Quite simply French," indeed, and like certain of his countrymen and a number of his colleagues, Auguste Renoir consistently expressed anti-Semitic opinions. Take, as an example, this "reflection," from January 15, 1898, retrieved from the journal of Julie Manet, the daughter of Berthe Morisot and Eugène Manet, who was Edouard's brother: "They come to France to earn money, and then when a fight breaks out they'll hide behind a tree; a lot of them are in the army because Jews like strolling where you'll find military braid. Seeing that they're chasing them out of all countries, there must be a reason, and we mustn't let them accumulate to the same extent in France."[8]

Infinitely more propitious is another of Auguste's utterances, this one about the painter J. M. W. Turner, and quoting Oscar Wilde. Auguste even claimed to have heard it directly from his mouth: "Before him, there was no fog in London."[9] It's a sensibility the filmmaker would revive in writing about *Foolish Wives:* "I've seen it many times, but it took me several viewings before I understood that the Monte Carlo shown on the screen was supposed to represent the little city a few kilometers from Nice that I'm so familiar with: a small, ugly place with a ridiculous park that the inhabitants call 'the camembert' and a casino that looks like bad pastry. On the other hand, Stroheim's Monte Carlo was fascinating. Leading me to conclude that it's the real Monte Carlo that is wrong."[10]

For Stroheim, and therefore for Renoir—who at the time saw the American filmmaker as "a kind of god"—it wasn't about representing the world as it is but about capturing the reality of human relations. *Nana* would be a naturalist film because it was an adaptation of a novel by Zola, and Renoir and Lestringuez envisioned the main character as having a face that was quite primitive ("cut with a scythe," in fact, the filmmaker would say, if a bit hastily) as their way of approaching the cinematographic ideal embodied by Stroheim's films. In 1925, Renoir was new to filmmaking. Because of this, he would try to reproduce what he liked and what impressed him in that medium, which included the Expressionist influence, as can be seen in *Nana,* although that element was to fade from his work. Obviously, naturalism fascinated him, and he set himself the goal of transforming the way it was represented by adding an element of Expressionism—but without really having the means—just as Stroheim had tried to transform it by the use of the baroque.

Except for Nana's mansion, which actually does evoke Stroheim's baroque style, the decor of the film, created by the future director Claude Autant-Lara, is startling primarily because of its sparseness, which links it to the Expressionist trend, without revealing whether such simplicity is a result of a deliberate choice or the consequences of budgetary limits. For his first film directed under normal conditions of production, Renoir found himself confronted with the demands of an unwieldy set that included the re-creation of a period as well as a plethora of roles, with some actors playing several. In addition, he had to take on the responsibilities of a producer in a country that wasn't his, even if he did speak the language perfectly. Last but not least, he wasn't sure whether the deepest part of his nature found anything parallel in the films of Stroheim aside from his admiration for him. Between Zola's theses, which he'd envisioned as separate from his from the very start, and Stroheim's approach, which he tried to copy but that proved too unfamiliar, Renoir seemed ill at ease.

As the first important film he directed and the most ambitious of his silent films, *Nana* displayed a certain inflexibility, whose origin grows partly clearer when we consider what his future work would reveal about him. Its characters seem stilted, and the film prevents plot developments from affecting their lives; yet what infuses the masterpieces to come with richness and complexity are the actions, thoughts, and behavior of the people. The view of women, especially, turns out not to be very like Renoir, because they are shown almost exclusively as greedy and duplicitous manipulators, whereas Renoir's great heroines would be distinguished by their spontaneity—even if it is feigned at times—as well as by their inability to plan anything, at least on the surface. In that way, *Nana* can be compared to *La Chienne*, a film in which the male lead finds himself caught between a cantankerous, greedy, suspicious wife and a gold-digging mistress, who uses her sex appeal to trap him. However, the central character in *La Chienne* is the prey, whereas the one in *Nana* is the predator.

Catherine Hessling's acting choices contribute to the confusion. Her interpretation can seem overdone. And it is, which places the character Nana in a situation of permanent hyperactivity, surrounded by often immobile figures, dominated by Count Muffat, who always seems on the brink of a stroke; but the issue isn't whether the actress is correctly interpreting her role. It's knowing whether the character is playing hers well, whether she has chosen a way to play it that is appropriate. Catherine Hessling and Renoir's Nana relentlessly plays at being the child-woman, capricious, full of affected expressions, rolling eyes, smirking just as much when she caresses as when she claws. That last behavioral characteristic might be enough to label her the first cat-woman in a body of work composed of several others, except that the character is always pulling the same string, and it's hard to accept the fact that she makes every man who comes through her door quiver. As a result, her only motive for seduction seems to be the masochism of her partners, causing the film to make us think that it's a common trait of all the film's male characters, who are as fascinated by anticipating their own degradation as by the later spectacle of acting it out. Such a theme belongs more to Stroheim than it does to Zola, and Renoir's very nature doesn't lend itself to the cruelty that the maker of *Foolish Wives* and *Greed* turns to his advantage.

Renoir was thirty when he directed *Nana*. Apart from several months of war and the wound from which he continued to suffer, all he'd known up to then was the easygoing, pleasant life of young people from rich families. Stroheim was only seven years older when he directed *Foolish Wives,* but they were seven years that counted at that age and counted even more for an immigrant struggling first to survive and then to make a place in a world that had distrusted and rejected him from the start. Stroheim began his career in film with menial jobs, and then worked as an assistant director. He played Krauts and Huns, and studio publicity departments turned him into "the man you love to hate," so he was familiar with humiliation, hatred, and cruelty. What could a man of thirty know about cruelty when his life had been a series of euphoric encounters experienced in enthusiastic bursts, when he was someone who felt appreciated by anybody he met?

Nana missed its mark when it came to Stroheim, and Renoir missed the bull's-eye when it came to Zola as well. Let's not forget Stroheim's words: "If a literary masterpiece is to become a cinematic masterpiece, the director's sensibility has to be identical to his author's."[11] In portraying the fall of a class ruined by its belief that it can buy anything, the film offers a poetic vision that isn't without charm but that is also apolitical. The "golden fly" created by the writer to describe Nana was contaminating an entire society; the one indicated by an intertitle in the film only poisons those who touch her, like Muffat, who seems to want that sickness more than life itself, or others, like Vandeuvres and his nephew, who want to take their own life. Beyond what it shows us about the reciprocal attraction that cements the social classes, the vision of the world expressed in *Nana* remains in inspiration and in nature "artistic," which is the same term Renoir said in the early sixties that had made him bristle in 1925.

Just as directors often do end up out of sync with their own film, Renoir hides behind the technical aspect of his, about which he's passionate. Most likely, he was completely taken by the tracking shots that Murnau had just made popular in *The Last Laugh;* and he performs various camera movements that are sometimes successful but often too obvious. In any case, this is a filmmaker not yet in touch with his identity. Cinema lacked a dimension that it would possess four years later, which would allow Renoir to find himself.

Despite all this, the film is not without its beauty. There is the opening scene, which shows Nana climbing a ladder into the flies of the theater, and then suspended over the stage like a puppet with cut strings, held only by a rope that keeps her feet from touching ground, which arouses the men in the audience. Then there is Nana clothed only in a boudoir screen when she first sees Muffat, who's as fascinated by the dirty water in a basin and the grime on a comb as he is by the eyes she rolls and hair she tosses. Or Muffat sitting alone at a table whose other occupants are shown by a slow tracking shot, which gradually pulls back to reveal them as drunken, rowdy, and aggressive, while he sits there frozen and out of place. The Mabille Gardens, which Jean said inspired him to make *Nana,* with its bandleader firing a pistol into the air and its superbly filmed can-can. The shot of Sabine Muffat and Fauchery, her lover (Claude Autant-Lara, under the pseudonym Claude Moore), in the car taking them toward a future of disillusionment. *Nana* is a realistic, fantastic, and melodramatic film, as well as a comedy of manners, and all of this at the same time. It offers audiences chance flashes of self-recognition in the kinds of behavior it depicts, characters caught by the camera in their fundamental animality, and prevents the possibility of labeling any character victim or culprit, instead letting them all take turns at being one and then the other, or both at the same time.

At the start of December 1925, shooting moved to Paris, to the Gaumont studios on rue Carducci, where the great staircase, inspired by the one at the Opéra Garnier, had been built. It was the most impressive of the sets showing Nana's mansion. Journalists were invited to the set and given an opportunity to admire her gigantic courtesan's bed, which actually belonged to Baroness Vaughan, the morganatic spouse of Leopold II, king of Belgium. This was followed by the filming of the scenes at the Théâtre des Variétés, featuring Lestringuez—a.k.a. Pierre Philippe—in the role of Bordenave, the director of the theater. Next came a chance to watch the Mabille Gardens scene, for which the Moulin-Rouge ballet had been hired. At the end of January, the scenes showing horse racing at Longchamp were filmed at the Gaumont Grand Théâtre, and finally, in February, in the Film d'Art studios, the last scene, which occurs in Nana's bedroom. For it, exclusively, Werner Krauss came back from Berlin.

Without waiting for shooting to end, Renoir had begun editing. Strongly convinced that a film has no chance of attracting an audience if it's not actively promoted, he devoted a significant amount of time and money to publicity. Scads of articles appeared in the press; stills were distributed far and wide because the producer had the foresight to hire a set photographer, a practice that was as yet reserved for a few big-budget productions.

On April 27, 1926, a Tuesday, at two o'clock, a first screening was organized for professionals from the press, not in a movie theater but at the Moulin-Rouge, whose orchestra performed some Offenbach tunes. Renoir would remember the evening as "tumultuous,"[12] featuring the vociferations of a woman calling *Nana* "a Kraut movie." The woman was, he'd make clear, the wife of the "most well-known director of the time," whom Braunberger would "expose" as Léonce Perret. Braunberger adds that on the way out after the movie she hit him several times with her umbrella, causing his head, already unprotected from lack of hair, to bleed. The incident is confirmed in the April 30 issue of *Paris-Midi*.

During that first showing, there was also applause. Several reviews were favorable, and Renoir and Braunberger's publicity machine delivered them to the trade journals in an attempt to spawn more. Skillfully orchestrated as such a maneuver was, it still did not produce the desired effect, and no distributor came forward with an offer to present *Nana* to audiences. Because of a heroine who was too one-note and a structure composed of two sections that were too similar—Vandeuvres's decline following Muffat's—the film lacked contrast and strongly risked not pleasing audiences. On June 15, an article appeared in which Renoir responded to critics' attacks against his film, referring the matter to the authority of Madame Leblond-Zola who "has approved our work." "That is our foremost recompense,"[13] he concluded.

It took until June 16 to establish an agreement between Les Films Renoir and the Louis Aubert Corporation, which foresaw a run of a "shorter version" of the film at the Aubert-Palace on boulevard des Italiens, as well as the distribution of *Nana*—"either in a shorter version or in installments," from October 1, 1926, to January 1, 1927.

Of the eight theaters that showed the film, beginning on December 10, 1926, only two were left by the third week. The good results trumpeted in the professional press, which can't be confirmed by ticket sales actually recorded, wouldn't permit an exclusive Parisian run to last beyond nine weeks. Chance saw Catherine Hessling immediately followed on-screen at the Aubert-Palace by her idol, Gloria Swanson, in *The Coast of Folly*, a film by Allan Dwan, one of the directors that Renoir admired.

In the meantime, Renoir went back to the editing room to perfect the shorter version required by the distributor, a version that seems also to have been offered abroad. Consequently, the length of the film was shortened from 3,200 meters to 2,800, a loss of about twenty minutes. In December, after showings that followed its "exclusive" run in Paris, Renoir restored certain scenes, again bringing the film closer to the version that had been presented at the Moulin-Rouge.

Nana was a commercial failure. Charging that he had been left out of the management of costs and receipts, the day-to-day responsibility of which fell to Louis Guillaume, acting directly on behalf of Renoir, Braunberger would contest the truth of this failure and let it be understood that his partner had cautiously kept good news from him, which is a commonplace practice among associates in this industry, meant to encourage and facilitate the implementation of this practice. If it's true that Braunberger's name appeared on no assignment of rights for the film, and that all of these contracts were signed by Jean and

Claude Renoir,[14] it must only mean that Braunberger played a far more minor part in the venture of *Nana* than he later claimed, and that his after-the-fact reaction can be quite simply explained: Braunberer did not lose any money he did not spend. There's no doubt that Renoir paid for *Nana* out of his own pocket, from the first to the last franc. "*The Whirlpool of Fate, Nana, Sur un air de Charleston* [*Charleston Parade*] are the three films for which I think I had no partners,"[15] he writes in 1965. With that bombast characteristic of the rich, Renoir thought of himself for a moment as having been ruined by the failure of *Nana*. It's true that he had to sell a few of his father's canvases, a painful measure that stayed in his memory:

> Every step that Catherine or I took into the profession of filmmaking was marked by a sacrifice that tore me apart. I was living a new version of *La Peau de chagrin** and spent my days brooding over my disgrace. Each sale of a canvas felt like a betrayal to me. At night I'd pace the floor of my house in Marlotte, whose walls were slowly but inexorably becoming bare. I kept the frames. They were like gaping holes into a hostile universe. Never had I felt more connected to the memory of my father. One night I asked Catherine to join me in the living room. I don't remember exactly what happened. All I can say is that, in front of those empty frames we felt like homeless orphans. We decided to abandon film and at any price save the few works of my father that were left. But it was too late. I had to settle up the last bills from *Nana*.[16]

It's an inspired scene, and one of a number that contributes to forging the legend. A brilliant raconteur, Renoir was also its only audience, but he wasn't living alone then and was still entertaining a lot at home. Actually, no one besides him ever recalled the empty frames. Doubtlessly, a very impressive example of his instinct for cinema. The vaults in the Banque nationale de Paris, the branch located on boulevard Haussmann, held at least a hundred paintings, providing a reserve upon which he could have drawn to become free of the expenses of *Nana* or to replace the canvases that had to be removed from Marlotte. The truth is that he was under no obligation to take down those particular paintings he was keeping in his home† and that he seemed to regard as some of the dearest

---

* *Translator's note:* The difficult-to-translate title of a novel by Balzac, because it's a play on words. *Chagrin* means both "grief" and "shagreen," the latter word denoting an untanned type of leather, or rawhide, with a rough surface, formerly made from horse or wild ass but today most often made from sharkskin. The novel tells the story of a young bourgeois who finds a piece of shagreen that magically grants his every wish but that in turn extracts energy from his body, depleting it each time.

† Pierre Renoir would state in private that he had handed over some of his own canvases to Jean to pay the bills for *Nana*.

things to his heart. Perhaps a certain masochistic element in his behavior was beginning to surface; for it is true that those sales and, even more, the memory of them that Renoir chose to conserve, as well as the anecdotes they inspired him to tell, are hints of some grievous identification with his own film.

Just as Count Muffat ruins himself for Nana, Renoir declared himself ruined by his film. Just as Vandeuvres loses his honor, Renoir claimed to have been dishonored by that sale of paintings. He had produced and directed his film for an audience that didn't want it; but above all, he had done it for himself and Catherine Hessling, who had immediately begun to "play" Zola's character the first time that her husband and Lestringuez had spoken about Nana in her presence. For her, he would have been ready to lose his fortune and his honor. Or almost.

5

Poaching

Sur un air de Charleston (Charleston Parade)
Marquitta
La Petite Marchande d'allumettes (The Little Match Girl)

While Renoir was busy in a Berlin studio re-creating the decline of high society in France's Second Empire and chasing signs of German decadence in the cabarets and clubs of the city after nightfall, Parisians were becoming wild about "Negroes" and the music attributed to them.

Since October 2, 1925, the revelation of *La Revue nègre* had made the star of its first act, Josephine Baker, the darling of "tout Paris." Inspired by her body's lines, the fashion designer Paul Poiret was working for her, and by spring 1926, women of fashion were styling their hair with a heavy pomade to plaster it down; the "Bakerfix" had become the hairstyle of the moment. After *La Revue nègre* toured Europe, Josephine Baker returned to Paris and triumphed in *La Folie du jour,* in which she appeared on the stage of the Folies-Bergère surrounded by "savages," accompanied by a cheetah, and wearing a skirt composed of velvet-plush bananas. Paris was packed with blacks whose shows were written, directed, and promoted by whites.

Lew Leslie was one of these white specialists, who would venture the claim that whites understood blacks better than blacks did themselves. The show he produced was called *Blackbirds,* a title that has been revived several times over the years. Presented in Paris at the end of May 1926 at a dinner theater, the Nouveaux Ambassadeurs, *Blackbirds* put Florence Mills, who had already been the star of the show on Broadway, front stage with a certain Johnny Hudgins, who inspired the admiration of a columnist for *Le Figaro* enough for him to write on May 31, "M. Johnny Hudgins achieves extraordinary comic effects by means that appear simple enough. With unusual skill he blends wit and buffoonery, and his poker-faced attitude is just as droll as his antics. The verses he performs in silence (in other words, he mimes them without speaking) while accompanied by the able cornet player M. Johnny Dunn, make even those who don't understand a single word of English laugh until they cry. I should also mention that M. Johnny Hudgins is an excellent dancer."

Nicknamed "the Wah-Wah Man" after this act, Hudgins had discovered when he arrived in Paris that Josephine Baker had become a big hit re-creating the stage business he'd invented when she was performing with him on Broadway in the revue *Chocolate Dandies*. Jean and Catherine, who didn't miss a single Parisian event, were captivated by the quality of his dancing; and Catherine, who loved dance and pantomime, saw a potential ideal partner in him.

The Renoirs did not discover *Blackbirds* solely because they liked to go out and were up on all the trendy entertainment. Actually, for some time, Jean had had a new friend who was crazy about all forms of music loosely classified under the rubric of jazz. Jean described this friend near the end of his life by painting the following endearing portrait:

> He was the epitome of everything I don't like, a French *grand bourgeois* who knew bars, practiced expensive sports. But scratching the surface of this, I found myself face to face with someone who was both fascinating and fascinated. His enthusiasm for the films I loved . . . and especially his attitude toward other beings rid me definitively of any impression that he was a snob. He loved humanity not only theoretically and as a general principle but directly and individually. He had no prejudice when it came to his friends and could get just as close with a plumber as with a famous writer.[1]

Renoir's new friend was Jacques Becker, born on September 15 like Renoir. In 1926 Becker was twenty years old. Jean, who was twelve years older, had met Becker at the Cézannes' in Marlotte in 1921. Becker was fifteen at the time and Jean twenty-seven. They found each other again in 1926 shortly after Becker came back from the United States, where he'd gone at eighteen to get away from his family and the future laid out for him by his father, as well as to get closer to jazz, which he adored, and to see and hear Duke Ellington, who was his idol. One night when Jean came home to rue de Miromesnil, he found Becker and Catherine listening to a record that Becker had just brought over. The experience had the power of a revelation for Jean. "[That music] made you think of animals in a virgin forest. Their cries evoked monster plants and flowers in violent colors. Then the exotic quality gave way to modern life. For me the record was becoming a portrayal of Chicago, the great city out of which it had come. Of course, I'm not talking about the real Chicago but about the Chicago of detective novels, short-skirted streetwalkers, the wooden facades of underground clubs awash in harsh lights; to put it simply, a Chicago that a young Frenchman could imagine after the Great War."[2]

The kind of film Renoir loved was American, and the music Becker recommended to him was American, too. Catherine wanted to dance with that tall black man from America. Jean convinced Johnny Hudgins to work with him. On the basis of an idea by André Cerf—Renoir's assistant, who had also played Nana's butler—Lestringuez pieced together a scenario. Several boxes of blank film left over from the *Nana* shoots would be used for the production of this new film.

Renoir would later write that he directed *Charleston Parade* in fall 1926 "as a way of saying farewell to film."[3] A farewell to a certain kind of film, perhaps: film among friends and with total freedom of choice, with no worries about anything other than the pleasure of the moment. A silent farewell, not only because film at the time didn't have sound but also because the music planned for this film was never recorded. A farewell cut short, finally, because the film was forever to remain incomplete. *Incomplete* is the word Renoir would use to describe it. But why wasn't the film finished? Because, as has been claimed, Johnny Hudgins, its primary reason for being made, jumped ship after only three days, never to return? No proof exists of the probability of such a defection, and the film as it can be seen today seems to be full duration. If certain coverage appearing in the press at the time can be trusted, the shoot was interrupted when Catherine Hessling fell ill, but it began again a few days later. More likely, the incompleteness of *Charleston Parade* has to do with the fact that the music composed by the pianist at the Boeuf sur le toit, Clément Doucet, was never recorded.

Such an absence of music makes it difficult to assess the film. Caught up in the Negro mania sweeping culture at the time, Lestringuez and Renoir had fun turning the cliché upside down by making the black man an explorer in tux and white gloves and the white woman a "savage" living in an advertising column,* a vestige of civilization in the Paris of 2028, "after the next war," when buildings are in ruin and the Eiffel Tower has been smashed. There are a few special effects in the style of Méliès as well as some slow-motion scenes and some shots of the woman who has returned to nature, dancing with a monkey (probably André Cerf in the getup). Also, Catherine Hessling found her way back to the rope ladder from *Nana*'s opening scene and exhibits an impressive magnetism that keeps her on par with Johnny Hudgins, whom the credits cite as "Johnny Huggins." As she wriggles in front of him, he recognizes the Charleston, "the dance of our ancestors," and asks for more of it: "Show me that wonderful dance. Afterward you can kill and eat me." To which the little savage answers, "Eat you? I can't digest black meat!" Conclusion: "And this is how a new fashion went to Africa: the culture of the white aborigines." Several times, angels appear in

---

* *Translator's note:* A tubular structure used outside for advertising bills, often called a "Morris column" after the printer Gabriel Morris, whose company controlled its distribution in Paris in the nineteenth century. But such columns were actually invented by Ernst Litfass and first appeared in Berlin. They are still used today in Paris.

a cardboard heaven, with the faces of Pierre Braunberger, Pierre Lestringuez, André Cerf, and Renoir.

Charleston Parade was originally entitled *Le Charleston;* but because that title had already been reserved for a documentary by a certain company called Erka, Renoir agreed to abandon it. This is a madcap film that mirrors the way it was produced and directed, a quick sketch and an experiment among pals doing their takeoff on a fad, using up the leftovers of the preceding production, which hadn't met their expectations. The film is proof that Renoir is still far from a real commitment and that film is still a pastime for him. The commercial failure of *Nana* had been a costly deviation from such fun and taught him the first rule of producing: never invest your own money. Even *Charleston Parade*'s brief length of barely twenty minutes corresponds to the musical revelation Renoir has just had and that led him once again to follow the dictates of the pleasure of creating.

It makes perfect sense that the film was barely distributed beyond a few showings for film societies, beginning in March 1927 and including the Théâtre du Vieux-Colombier, where it was accompanied on piano by Clément Doucet. One of the few critics to give an account of it at the time observed that "this script could be the point of departure for a great film," but that it was merely "a sketch in which Mme. Catherine Hessling and M. Johnny Hinnea [*sic*] (white and black) indulge in some graceful routines made even more so by the wonder of slow motion."[4] Under its English-language title, *Charleston Parade,* the film was also shown in April as part of a program compiled by Jean Tedesco for the theater Le Pavillon and was accompanied by the dream scene from *The Whirlpool of Fate*. Since the beginning of the year, Tedesco had in fact taken over management of that space, the former "folly" of Marshal de Richelieu located on rue Louis-le-Grand, where Tedesco offered "a permanent exhibition of the film repertoire of the Théâtre du Vieux-Colombier." In 1927, three years after he'd begun, without really wanting to, but without having done anything to avoid it, Renoir was still an avant-garde filmmaker.

A proposition he received before the release of *Charleston Parade* gave him the chance to move closer to a more mainstream type of film. Although his personality and his experience, which at the time was considered limited to his direction of *Nana,* most likely kept producers away, Renoir had already displayed abilities that convinced those who knew him to come calling. Moreover, the day after the commercial failure of *Nana,* he had made a decision that he voiced in one of the first versions of *My Life and My Films:* "As far as I was concerned, I had no intention of giving up directing films, even if it meant accepting work that was the polar opposite of my tastes and temperament. Because of my love of human truth as well as my ambition to achieve material success, I was determined not to hold back and to face the abuse head on."[5] He would delete the second sentence and replace the first with, "As far as I was concerned, I had every intention of getting out of a profession that had brought me nothing but disappointment."[6] Which says the exact opposite.

The proposition he received came from within his circle, from his sister-in-law, the actress Marie-Louise Iribe, who was now Pierre Renoir's second wife. Their wedding had taken place on November 18, 1925, while the groom was acting in *Le Cocu magnifique* (*The Magnificent Cuckold*) by Fernand Crommelynck on the stage of the Théâtre des Mathurins, for which Pierre also served as director. It was a difficult role to endure, seeing that "tout Paris" was reveling in the scandalous affair that Véra Sergine, whom he'd just divorced, had started to have with the actor Henri Rollan. The fact that the newlyweds didn't want to draw up a marriage contract to document the act would prove to be a disastrously flippant decision less than five years later, when Marie-Louise Iribe made off with a number of important paintings and drawings by Renoir from the home of her husband. The Sunday editions of the daily papers put the event on their front pages on October 5, 1930, and it would be revealed a few days later that the wife, her divorce proceedings pending, had acted with the help of two colleagues from the studio where she was working, one of whom was the son of the novelist and playwright Victor Margueritte. The actress would claim that she had done nothing that was not well within her rights, but the court would not rule in her favor, and on January 16, 1933, it dismissed her suit.

That winter of 1925–1926, Marie-Louise Iribe was dreaming of the great role she had not yet been given by the world of film, despite the fact that in 1921 she had appeared in Jacques Feyder's *L'Atlantide* opposite Jean Angelo, who had played Vandeuvres in *Nana*. She was hoping to work with him again in a production she'd inaugurated through Les Artistes réunis, a company she had created and that was asking Lestringuez* to write a script for a film that Jean Renoir would direct in 1925. At the time, the Renoir family was still participating in financing films. In fact, Pierre was the chief silent partner, allowing his brother Jean to participate to a lesser extent, as Jean would confirm nearly forty years later: "I was also supposed to have a stake in *Marquitta*, which in principle was supposed to belong to [Pierre Renoir's son] Claude Jr. since my brother Pierre had financed it."[7] But this time, Jean didn't end up on the front line and was only hired to perform the work of a technician. The shooting took place in the studios of Gaumont in Buttes-Chaumont, and then continued in the vicinity of Nice.

* Pierre Lestringuez was married to Marie-Louise Iribe's sister.

Lestringuez had dreamed up the story of Prince Vlasco de Décarlie (Jean Angelo), a.k.a. Coco, in the Paris of the Roaring Twenties. He falls in love with Marquitta (Marie-Louise Iribe), a street singer whom he tries in vain to turn into a society lady but who becomes a famous chanteuse after he has given her up. The two lovers then meet again on the Côte d'Azur, but in the meantime the principality of Décarlie has become the scene of some terrible events. Vlasco is no longer a prince but a performer of Caucasian dances in a cabaret. He accuses Marquitta of theft, she flees, he regrets it, he wants to die, she dashes in pursuit of him on the Moyenne Corniche highway, she saves him, and they live happily ever after.[*]

A review by Charles de Saint-Cyr in *La Semaine à Paris* on August 19, 1927, categorizes the film as intended for the most mainstream of audiences: "It's clear that the script writer, M. Pierre Lestringuez, and the director, M. Jean Renoir, wanted to make a work that would be a big, ubiquitous hit. And there is absolutely no doubt that they have. But both of them are people with too much taste whose cinematic skills are too perfected to accept stopping there." The critic for the monthly *Cinémagazine* was of a mind to consider it a "nice film, half sad, half funny," but he also deplored some "scenes that are a bit obvious," a little too "slight," giving as one example the part in which Vlasco comes out of his limousine in tails in order to take away the street singer. "Why show the crowd as so respectful," he bluntly states, "whereas there's a very good chance that in 1927, on an evening under the Métro at boulevard de la Villette, the gentleman in tails who makes a monkey out of the working-class big shot by snatching his lady singer would be told where to go, and how!"

The scene mentioned in *Cinémagazine* is one of those that was accomplished by a technique perfected by Renoir using miniature scenery: "The process consisted of filming the miniature scenery by way of a mirror, and the actors had to keep to positions carefully determined beforehand. We scraped off the silvering on the parts of the mirror that corresponded to these positions. Through these holes, the actors' actual size would change to match the miniature scenery placed behind the camera and reflected in the mirror, which was located in front of the camera. In *Marquitta*, the miniature scenery represented the main intersection at Barbès-Rochechouart with its subway columns and trains moving along the overhead bridge. Of course, behind the actors we put up a piece of real normal-sized scenery, linking it to the corresponding piece of scenery in miniature."[8] Another innovation was a cart for tracking shots that cut down on the jolts caused by the system on rails. Renoir had more of a

* A copy of *Marquitta*, a film long considered lost, was presented on February 9, 1975, as part of an extensive retrospective organized in London by the National Film Theatre.

chance to devote himself to his technical enthusiasms because his functions were limited to directing. Therefore, his experience with *Marquitta* was useful in that it allowed him to exhaust his fixation and consider film once again with a fresh eye.

A little more than two months before the premiere of *Marquitta*, at the end of July 1927 at the Empire on avenue de Wagram, Renoir lost an inseparable friend. He had thought of him as a brother, so much so that he had wanted to make him an actor as far back as during the making of *The Whirlpool of Fate*, although the friend showed no disposition for such a profession. In *Marquitta*, Pierre Champagne plays a taxi driver who handles the Moyenne Corniche road at maximum speed. The day after the shoot, Champagne was given the Bugatti he'd been yearning for—a Brescia. On May 7, he invited Jean to try out the racecar with him.

They left Marlotte together on the route to Bourron. The road was bordered by tall trees, it rained, the sides of the road were dry and the middle soaked. After passing another vehicle, the car skidded—on a patch of oil, Jean would report; the driver and his passenger were thrown about sixty feet. According to Alain Renoir, the steering column went through Champagne's chest; as Jean told it, Champagne's head was smashed on a pile of pebbles, whereas Jean landed on a grassy embankment.

Jean would later recount that he came to in a pickup truck loaded with game that some poachers were going to sell at Les Halles. In rerouting to take Jean to the hospital, these good souls were taking the risk of being harassed by the police. Jean would remember them when he wrote his first play, *Orvet*, in 1955.

The newspapers that reported the accident in 1927 made no mention of the poachers but spoke instead of a certain teacher at the high school in Amiens. According to the May 8 edition of *Le Petit Parisien*, the accident had happened the day before "around 7:30 p.m., on the road to Fontainebleau at Nemours, at the foot of the hill with the Cross of Saint Herem. An automobile that had just passed a car belonging to M. Pierre Bellet, teacher at the private school in Amiens, lost control of the road and bumped against the curb where it rolled over several times, violently projecting its two occupants. The driver, M. Pierre Champagne, a resident of Paris at 34, rue Simard, who was vacationing in Marlotte, was killed instantly. His friend, M. Jean Renoir, the son of the well-known painter and living in Marlotte at Villa Saint-El, has been seriously injured and was taken to a private hospital." The same day, which was also the day when Charles Nungesser and François Coli took off from Le Bourget airport aboard their *Oiseau Blanc* at 5:21 a.m., the front page of *Le Matin* reported the details of the accident and said that "M. Pierre Vellet [now no longer "Bellet"], a teacher at the high school in Amiens, had stopped to help the two victims." Champagne, killed immediately, was taken to the Fontainebleau morgue; and Jean Renoir, who was "seriously injured," was taken to a private hospital in that city. On page 4, the daily offers the following specifics: "Jean Renoir is indeed the son of the painter. He is involved in the direction of films. At the home of his brother M. Pierre Renoir, a dramatist living at 28, avenue du Président-Wilson, Mme. Pierre Renoir, whose stage name is Mme. Sergine, told us: 'My brother-in-law left Friday for his villa in Marlotte. He was supposed to try out a sports car, which must have been involved in the accident.'" According to that same source, which turned out to be Marie-Louise Iribe and not Véra Sergine, Pierre Champagne "had left the same morning with his wife to 'shoot' a film with M. Jean Renoir in Marlotte." Two days later, on May 10, *La Croix* gave the same account of the accident, also stating that "M. Pierre Vellet . . . came to help the two victims." Jean Renoir wasn't wild about teachers, and poachers amazed him. His legend about the accident was more appealing than the news item. In the same way as the story about his shoes as a boy and the tale of his empty frames hanging on the walls in Marlotte after *Nana*, his account is his creation.

The same morning as the tragedy, with the intention of promoting his films, Renoir had presented a point of view about cinema for the first time in the professional press. It was part of a survey in *La Critique cinématographique* concerning film professionals' opinions of the triple screen invented by Abel Gance for his film *Napoléon*. Renoir's contribution began with an expression of the fears that the film had inspired in him a priori: "I went to the Opéra with the mindset that I'd be bored, because I detest historical re-creations, military films, all those superproductions with so many extras gesticulating on-screen." Then: "I have to admit that I then felt as if somebody had kicked me in the chest. . . . I was choked with emotion, literally dazzled, and my prejudices against films that are awash in great waves of humanity fell away all at once. I was dumbfounded, captivated!" Then came the moment for him to express his penchant for paradox—and not without a certain brio: "Therefore, I consider the triple screen to be a fantastic invention, but nevertheless I would have preferred it had never existed!" In other words, he feared seeing mediocre filmmakers make use of it "indiscriminately." As a result, he hoped "for the good of Film, as well as for the good of us all, that the triple screen will remain an exceptional method discovered by an exceptional man, only for his use."[9] He'd see his wish granted.

* *In The Rules of the Game, an airplane feat and a car accident will also be associated with each other.*

Marquitta is Jean Renoir's first film without Catherine Hessling and also his last collaboration with Pierre Lestringuez, who appears in it as well under his usual pseudonym, Pierre Philippe. When the press presented a list of the films Renoir directed, Lestringuez was always mentioned, proof that the importance of the writer remained essential, and also indicating that Renoir had not left his mark to the extent that, for example, Feyder, L'Herbier, or René Clair did. During that summer of 1927, Renoir and Lestringuez's friendship endured, but their paths branched in different directions. While Renoir prepared to make a film with Jean Tedesco, Lestringuez kept working for Les Artistes réunis, for which he'd write the two and only productions that were to come, *Chantage* (1927) and *Hara-Kiri* (1928), both directed by Henri Debain, an actor from *Marquitta*. The first film starred Huguette Duflos, and the second was Marie-Louise Iribe's last screen appearance. She would die five years later, on April 12, 1934, at the age of thirty-nine.

In his rundown of the year's films in *Le Figaro* on December 30, 1927, Robert Spa mentioned Abel Gance's *Napoléon*, Raymond Bernard's *Le Joueur d'échecs* (*The Chess Player*), René Clair's *Un Chapeau de paille d'Italie* (*The Italian Straw Hat*), Fritz Lang's *Metropolis*, Murnau's *Faust*, and E. A. Dupont's *Variété*. When it came to American productions, he singled out Fred Niblo's *Ben-Hur*, with Ramon Novarro; Edwin Carewe's *Resurrection*, with Dolores Del Rio; and Victor Fleming's *The Way of All Flesh*, with Emil Jannings. He also labeled Jean Grémillon's *Maldone* (*Misdeal*) and Dreyer's *La Passion de Jeanne d'Arc* (*The Passion of Joan of Arc*)—"which those few in the know are saying is incredible"—the most anticipated films of the year to come. Last, in the category of promising talents to watch, the reporter cited the name Alberto Cavalcanti. An atypical filmmaker in terms of both talent and disposition, this man from Rio would play a role in Jean Renoir's career and would indirectly influence Renoir's life path.

Born in Rio de Janeiro in 1897, Alberto de Almeida Cavalcanti, the child of an eminent Brazilian family, became the youngest student to attend law school when he was fifteen and was subsequently expelled from it after a row with one of his professors. His father next agreed to send him to Geneva, providing that he stay out of law and politics. His architectural studies soon brought him to Paris where, at eighteen, he gave up interior design for the cinema. After collaborating with Marcel L'Herbier on *Eldorado* (1921), for which he designed the costumes, then on *L'Inhumaine* (1921, scenery) and *Feu Mathias Pascal* (*The Late Mathias Pascal*—also known as *The Living Dead Man*—1926, scenery and assistant direction), as well as on Louis Delluc's *L'Inondation* (*The Flood*, 1924), he directed his first film in 1926, *Rien que les heures* (*Nothing but Time*), a forty-five-minute semidocumentary that followed a single day in the life of Paris, in a style resembling Walter Ruttmann's when he would direct *Berlin: Symphony of a Great City*, a few months later. When Renoir met him, Cavalcanti was both a figure of the Parisian avant-garde and enough of a reputed professional—as a result of his experience with L'Herbier, especially—to be entrusted with substantial budgets. Accordingly, in 1928 he would direct *Le Capitaine Fracasse* (*Captain Fracasse*) with Pierre Blanchar and Charles Boyer.

Whether in England, where he settled in 1933 and directed both documentaries and fictional narratives that were equally impressive (and that included the 1945 masterpiece of horror, *Dead of Night*), in Brazil, or just about everywhere else to some extent (see, for example, his 1956 Austrian adaptation of Brecht's play *Mr. Puntila and His Man Matti*), he forged a career that was one of the most unusual in film history, situated somewhere among the avant-garde, documentary, and the commercially produced film. Cavalcanti died in Paris in 1982 and in the last years of his life refused to discuss his history with Renoir, declaring in 1974, "I won't talk to you about Renoir, because I broke with him somewhere along the way. He took his path and I mine, and they didn't coincide."[10] Their rift may have been caused by Renoir and Catherine's separation. Cavalcanti stayed very close to her, calling her "a very beautiful, very elegant woman, a phenomenal actress, . . . a very restless performer, haunted by Chaplin, . . . difficult to 'grasp,' with a tendency to play things 'in the style of'; but in the end the result was fascinating."[11]

His penchant for experimentation, the ease with which he maneuvered "artistic" milieus, as well as the confines of the profession, his flamboyant homosexual behavior that made no attempt to hide his amorous attachments—all contributed to attracting Renoir, who became an actor for him in the summer of 1927 in *La P'tite Lili*, a sketch of about ten minutes presented as a "modern tragedy on burlap," which the critics suggested was lots of fun even though its "backer hadn't had to spend a fortune on it." In it, Renoir portrays a "figure of working-class Paris" opposite Catherine Hessling. Dido Freire, a young Brazilian of twenty* and a friend of Cavalcanti's family, is also in the film; and Marguerite Houllé was involved in the editing. Catherine Hessling, Marguerite Houllé, and Dido Freire turned out to be the three women in Jean Renoir's life.

La P'tite Lili, derived from a song with lyrics by Gravel and Benech and music by Darius Milhaud, was shown at the Studio des Ursulines, which had specialized in avant-garde film more radical than Tedesco's Vieux-Colombier ever since its opening on January 21, 1926; and it was also involved in helping with the production of films.

* Dido Freire was born April 4, 1907, in Belém.

However, it would not be for the Studio des Ursulines but for the Vieux-Colombier that Renoir directed what turned out to be his last film with Catherine Hessling. It was called *La Petite Marchande d'allumettes* (*The Little Match Girl*) and cocredited to Renoir and Jean Tedesco. The scenario for the film was registered at the Société des auteurs de films on February 22, 1927,[12] but shooting took place at the end of summer and in fall of the same year in the makeshift studio that had been thrown together in the theater attic. It is the film that also marks the director's farewell to the kind of film that—barring *Nana*—he had pursued until that moment: film produced in conditions close to dilettantism, made with the aim of amusing himself and to which he had summoned his ingenuity and desire to experiment with the most diverse variety of techniques.* Jean Tedesco drew an endearing portrait of the Renoir of that time: "Making films starts with spending for the shoot, then selling and renting. For the first part of the job, the producer Jean Renoir was in perfect harmony with the director Jean Renoir. But for the second part, things didn't go as well. The rich man, the '*grand seigneur*,' got the better of the film producer. Chewing on a toothpick distractedly, Renoir in conversation with possible buyers, or with those theater owners intending to 'capitalize' on his product, would let his blue eyes wander and think about the next film."[13]

There's no concern about realism in this adaptation of the fairy tale by Andersen, one of Renoir's cherished authors; from the first scene, there is no attempt to hide the fact that the snowy village presented is a scale model. The medium Renoir uses—a panchromatic film stock—was employed only for exteriors. Braunberger was supposed to have taught him that technicians in Hollywood were also using it in the studio, particularly for obtaining a more high-contrast image. In order to use this stock, Renoir worked with several adventurous professionals to perfect a lighting system whose need for tinkering precluded any kind of future; but the effects of it remain visible more than eighty years later. In fact, the images in this film are magnificent and do justice to its inventiveness and the visual discernment that make up the entire design. The ride in the sky, especially, produces quite a beautiful moment in the fantasy film genre. Each of some thirty minutes of the film indicates that Renoir knows his craft perfectly; when he is really doing what he wants in this period of the late twenties, he delivers a set of often magnificent images, which also stem from a rebellion against being directed into any ready-made channels. *The Little Match Girl* is the work of an unfettered talent, an imagination that refuses to be mastered, at the

* Renoir claimed to have developed the film himself in a tub that would be displayed at the Cinémathèque française in 1972.

risk of seeming to lack a certain maturity.

Premiered on March 31, 1928, in Geneva, where Tedesco had some business involvements, the film was then shown exclusively at the Vieux-Colombier the following June 1. Critics appeared enthusiastic. Paul Ramain wrote in *Cinéa* that "if this film stings our sensations, it's in order to mine our emotions," and, mentioning the use of the new film stock, he concludes, "It's new and still unique in the annals of cinematography." The May 26 article in *Le Journal des débats politiques et littéraires*, which came out a week before the film was released publicly, was no more sparing of compliments. "In the film, the little girl, who can't sell her matches in the street while it is snowing and who tries to warm herself by lighting a few bits of her merchandise, clearly remains, but the dream that she has is altered and then embellished, while being attractively dramatized at the same time. Moreover, a slight intrigue is mixed with the main theme. Innocence and the world of the fairy tale are charmingly and movingly presented. Mme. Catherine Hessling, who resembles no other artist, offers a remarkable interpretation of the role of the little match girl whom we see carried off into the skies by a young man who wants to shield her from death. The ride, masterful from a cinematographic point of view, was created by M. Jean Renoir, all of whose direction deserves praise. By very simple means, and probably without having to spend a considerable sum, he has produced a genuine fairy-tale world. For the good reputation of the French cinema, we should want a work like this to succeed; it borrows nothing from anyone, and its sensitivity is a delight. The dramatic dream in the film is followed by a nice ending."

The mention of a work that "borrows nothing from anyone" sounds strange in light of the events that followed the opening of the film. On June 23, 1928, the prints of *The Little Match Girl* were seized by court order as demanded by Mme. Rosemonde Gérard and M. Maurice Rostand. The widow and son of Edmond Rostand were claiming that Renoir and Tedesco's film closely plagiarized the lyrical tale *La Marchande d'allumettes* performed in 1914 and written by them. Having implemented the legal measure of *saisie-contrefaçon* (immediate seizure of a pirated work), they demanded 100,000 francs for damages. In response, Renoir and Tesdesco put together a counterclaim for 100,000 francs for abuse suffered from the seizure of the allegedly pirated work and sought a judgment for the withdrawal of the seizure.

It wasn't an especially serious affair, but it constituted a first in the history of film, at least in France, and would turn out to be catastrophic for the distribution of the film. And it was not especially serious on the grounds that Renoir and Tedesco's only wrong, if you can call it that, was having drawn from the same source as Mme. Gérard and M. Rostand, a source that can be found in the public domain. Moreover, the newspapers championed the filmmakers' cause; neither were they above poking fun at the strategy taken by the pretentious plaintiffs, whose attitudes and greed (such as their claim of having lent a hand to the writing of *Chantecler*) had already been a source of ridicule for several years. As early as May 18, *La Semaine à Paris* devoted not less than three pages to the affair, which included a piece by Charles de Saint-Cyr, who passionately declared himself in favor of the film, and a letter from Jean Renoir contesting the arguments of his adversaries. The introductory paragraph for all of it, in big fat letters, pointed out the danger implied by the proceedings: "An exceptionally serious act. Mme. Rosemonde Gérard and M. Maurice Rostand's stunt was deliberately accomplished in a manner that would lead to the mandatory closing of the Vieux-Colombier. Theater, cinema, literature, and the arts—have they taken into account the unprecedented and appallingly dangerous implications of such an arbitrary act?"

The judges did not hold forth concerning that question. On October 21, 1928, chaired by a certain Monsieur Wattine, the court refused to pass judgment and went back to establishing the facts. The months passed, until the affair experienced a development so unheard of that *Le Figaro* chose to place an account of it on the front page of the May 16, 1929, edition.

The day before, at ten-thirty in the morning, Monsieur Munsch, who presided over the third division, the assistant district attorney Brachet, several judges, the court clerk, and a cohort of lawyers sat down in the theater of the Vieux-Colombier to watch a projection of the offending object. Georges Claretie, hurried to the location by *Le Figaro*, concluded his account of the projection as follows: "It's likely that the court has come to a decision. Both about the value of the film (although it remains silent about that) and the charges of pirating, which will be the object of its ruling. That is the point to which the interpretation of the law will be applied. Hands are shaken, a few moments of friendly chatting; and then, with briefcases under arms, they return to the Palais de Justice in the falling rain for the purpose of argument and judgment—this time in the light, far from that screen and its funereal horsemen carrying corpses through the clouds."

The decision was pronounced on June 21, 1929. The court "recognized that the film contains quite a few injudicious borrowings," but that "there are no legal issues or pirating involved." It considered the demand for *saisie-contrefaçon* to be "an archaic and savage method." Renoir and Tedesco were awarded 15,000 francs for damages, and Tedesco received 5,000 francs more based on his position as director of the theater. Each was given 1 franc on the grounds of having been morally wronged.

The Little Match Girl had another exclusive run in February 1930, at the Colisée theater, in a sound version that included Wagner, Johann Strauss, and Mendelssohn and that didn't refrain from relying upon many cumbersome explanatory intertitles. But by then the only kind of film had sound dialogue, and very few members of the audience had any interest in admiring the face of the young girl who had died of the cold in the last shot of the film—the face of Catherine Hessling.

In the period between Jean Renoir's last film with his wife and the advent of talkies, Catherine appeared in three other films—*En rade* (*Sea Fever*), *Yvette*, and *Le Chaperon rouge* (*Little Red Riding Hood*)—all credited to Alberto Cavalcanti and all shown at the Studio des Ursulines.

Although *Yvette*, a modern adaptation of a story by Maupassant, didn't exactly charm critics, the actress did bring it some flattering comments, especially from the columnist for *La Semaine à Paris*, who on January 25, 1929, wrote, "Mme. Catherine Hessling is unceasingly interesting in it, as well as being truly remarkable at certain moments (such as the suicide attempt). I'm looking forward to seeing her in *The Little Match Girl*, in which I think she will achieve a triumphant success. She deserves it because of the intelligence that she brings to her natural gifts." In *Little Red Riding Hood*, Catherine Hessling is chased by a wolf in a striped jersey and bowler hat who is none other than her husband, who was also the cowriter and producer of this film shot in June 1929 and about which the press had also announced him as the future director. Perrault's fairy tales were patently in line with the current tastes of the times. An adaptation of *Le Chat botté* (*Puss in Boots*) was being attributed to Renoir, and Lestringuez was working on a scenario inspired by *Peau d'âne* (*Donkey Skin*), to be produced under the aegis of Les Artistes réunis. Neither of these two projects would see the light of day.

Sea Fever, finally, was Claude Heymann's first contribution to film, in the role of cowriter; and soon he would become a part of Renoir's career. The film received a favorable review expressing great enthusiasm for its actress in the October 1, 1929, issue of *L'Opinion*. It was written by Henri Clouzot, the uncle of the future filmmaker. "Catherine Hessling is our French Lillian Gish. With her pale eyes and face so white it looks like a Japanese actor's lacquered mask, she is an apparition of mystery and suffering. Impassive, yes, but how much more artificial! She makes her way through the film looking unreal and wraithlike and inflicts the most remarkable denial of realism on her scenes. With her, film no longer chooses nature as its basis. She is better than that, supernatural. Against the black walls of a lowly dive in Marseille, her blank expression, strange, profound, begins to look like a window open to the infinite." This is how the critic put Catherine Hessling back at the center of a kind of acting that talking pictures and the fashion for "realism" imposed by them would banish. This opinion of Cavalcanti's film could also describe the same kind of cinema that both Jean Renoir and Catherine Hessling had been dreaming of.

6

Soup and Grub

Tire-au-flanc (The Sad Sack)
Le Tournoi (The Tournament)
*Le Bled**

When the Renoir divorce was finalized in 1930, their son felt nothing but relief. In fact, for the last three years, when Catherine and Jean did speak, it was almost always to tear each other apart. Alain had witnessed these confrontations, which were so violent that they made him think his parents had never loved each other. He wouldn't be able to correct this impression until a long time after, when he discovered in their former bedroom in Marlotte a collection of poems by Ronsard with notes in the margin of the book by both husband and wife.[†]

Remembering his unpleasant years at private school and faithful to Auguste's principles, Jean decided to entrust Alain's education not to a public or private school but to two tutors. The lessons were given in Marlotte and eventually included a Communist teacher and the village parish priest. It's always better to get both sides of the story.

Alain didn't see his mother very often, only enough time to listen to her predict that he'd never amount to anything, that he'd join the priesthood, and that she'd always be the only woman in his life. Especially enough time, as well, to suffer her "endless list of woes" concerning his father. "I was seven, eight," Alain remembered, "and I couldn't understand a thing she was saying." Recalling a conversation in Marlotte between his father and someone unknown to Alain who was against the imminent arrival of talking pictures, whereas Jean claimed to believe in them, Alain had no doubt that his parents were in fact already separated. "I was spending winter in Paris with my father and summer in Marlotte with my grandmother, and I liked it quite a bit."[1]

---

* *Translator's note:* "*Le bled*" = term derived from an Arabic term meaning "the country," "the land." For Algerian émigrés living in France, it became a reference to the former homeland. Later, it was adapted by some to suggest a "tiny village" or "the middle of nowhere." Its significance for this film by Renoir designates Algeria.

† In *The Elusive Corporal*, Jean-Pierre Cassel reads Ronsard to the dentist's pretty daughter, who wants to learn French.

Although their relationship as a couple ended and each renounced the other, and although Renoir stopped centering his films around Catherine Hessling, the actress still depended on the director. In fact, she appears fleetingly, without being listed in the credits, in two scenes of *Tire-au flanc:* first as a schoolteacher leading her students through the woods where the soldiers are training, and then as a girl keeping watch in front of the barracks.

According to Pierre Braunberger,[2] Jean Renoir's adaptation of the play *Tire-au-flanc* by André Mouëzy-Éon and André Sylvane was the result of his nephew's crush on a young woman with the attractive name Fridette Fatton. Braunberger's assertions, of course, need to be taken with caution; but they do indicate the reigning atmosphere in the world of film of those times and the role it played in the origins of movies—both masterpieces and turkeys.

One day Braunberger's nephew came to see him to confide that, although he was the real love of pretty Fridette, she depended for her living on the generosity of a very rich and important individual, who was ready to spend his money on getting his protégée into the movies. The young woman, whose portrait Édouard Vuillard had painted at least three times between 1923 and 1927,[*] had just appeared in *The Chess Player,* the film by Raymond Bernard, but hadn't received any offers since. Braunberger met the young lady and to her "generous gentleman" submitted several ideas he thought could be of interest to such an investor aroused by Fridette's appeal. The fact that, among the titles mentioned, *Tire-au-flanc* was the one that caught the backer's attention isn't at all surprising, because the play was performed without interruption at the Dejazet on boulevard du Temple from 1904, its date of creation, to 1908 and had also been revived regularly nearly everywhere in France with the same success. In 1928, two months before the release of the film, the Dejazet would announce that it had presented 3,044 performances of the play. Sure of being able to turn the 700,000 francs that had come out of the pocket of the generous donor to good account, Braunberger had already gotten himself a good bargain.

Also according to Braunberger, Renoir visited the next day and expressed the discouragement he'd been overwhelmed by for some time; and Braunberger talked about the project without thinking for an instant, he claims, that the director would be interested. Renoir, however, did ask for time to consider it. That interval came abruptly to an end the day he himself met Fridette.

Although the story is very probably contrived, it is no less an homage to Fridette Fatton, who has the female lead as the maid, Georgette, in *Tire-au-flanc*

---

[*] *Fridette Faton* [sic] *à table* (1923), *Fridette Faton en visite chez Jean Laroche* (1926), *Fridette Faton et le bonze* (1927).

but who faded into anonymity, unfortunately, immediately after. Braunberger and Renoir have each recounted separately that she would appear at the Billancourt studios each morning wearing yet another set of jewels. To the curious enquiring about who was giving them to her, she invariably answered: "That? That's Arthur!" And when she was asked, of course, who this so generous Arthur was, she would burst out laughing and exclaim, "Arthur? That's my fanny!"

Fridette probably got along best with her male lead, Michel Simon, who plays her fiancé in the film and who had amply earned his reputation as a frenzied seducer, thought of as sex-obsessed by some people. From the first scene, which is quite successful, the two of them never stop kissing while setting the dinner table; and throughout the film the desire that brings them together and makes them surmount the barriers that are supposed to keep them apart is like an underground current irrigating the narrative.

Michel Simon was about seven months younger than Renoir, who could have met him through Cavalcanti. Jean had been in contact with the actor during the shooting of his second film, *The Late Mathias Pascal,* most probably through his brother Pierre. During the day, Simon acted in the film directed by Jean in Billancourt; evenings he acted with Pierre in Jean Giraudoux's *Siegfried,* also with Valentine Tessier and Louis Jouvet, on the stage of the Comédie des Champs-Élysées. *Tire-au-flanc* was his sixth film, which he made after Dreyer's *The Passion of Joan of Arc.*

Throughout *Tire-au-flanc,* Michel Simon attracts attention, whether spilling a gravy boat on the colonel's sleeve, embracing his Georgette, fretting about the vaccination awaiting him at the infirmary, or going over the strange dance steps in the corridor of the brig for his drag routine onstage later, in a performance that seems a precursor to the costume ball in *The Rules of the Game.* This is not the only similarity to the 1939 masterpiece that occurs in *Tire-au-flanc.* It's the first Renoir film in which the central character is not an isolated individual—a woman—as in his previous productions, but a social group. According to some, this very characteristic is a handicap. Éric Rohmer expressed such a notion in 1969 when he stated, "What's disappointing, I think, and also what makes the film difficult . . . is not so much the fact that there is no central character; it's that we really don't know which character to focus on. There is no character who can be considered special."[3]

Renoir decided to adapt the play himself, with the help of Claude Heymann. At twenty-one, Heymann was passionate about film, which—like Renoir—he had discovered thanks to those showings at the Dufayel department store. When asked at the age of six what he wanted to do when he grew up, he'd apparently responded, "I'd like to be God, so that I could go to the movies without paying." Later, his wife would say about him that he had to have been the only man in the world to go on his honeymoon alone; he'd been called to a shoot in Egypt.[4] He'd "hung around the set during *Nana*,"[5] and now he had become the cowriter of *Tire-au-flanc* as well as Renoir's assistant for the film. Two years later he'd be Buñuel's for *L'Âge d'or*.

For the role of Jean Dubois d'Ombelles, called alternately "the Poet" and "the Nut," which comes down to precisely the same thing in military logic, Renoir resorted not to an actor but to the dancer and mime Georges Pomiès. The columnist for *Le Figaro* wrote about him in regard to the show he gave in November of that same year 1928 at the Comédie des Champs-Élysées, for which Louis Jouvet served as a director at the time, that he "knew how to create a very personal art that enhanced with an intellectual quality what is purely acrobatic in American dance." Pomiès also launched into impersonations onstage, and the one he did of Maurice Chevalier was considered among the most successful. Renoir's choice of him turned out to be a wise one. Pomiès approached his character with an agility and ease of movement in space that contrasted in a positive way with the intended impassivity of his face.

According to a principle favored by critics and historians of the cinema—that any work brought to the screen by an admired filmmaker is by nature inferior to its adaptation, which is a radical transformation of the original text—writers pointed out[6] that the character of Joseph, played by Michel Simon, didn't appear in the play. This is false. Another daft idea: claiming that *Tire-au-flanc* or, later, *On purge Bébé* was a source unworthy of Renoir, who wouldn't have consented to be involved with either if he hadn't been forced to by circumstances and the situation of that moment. It makes sense to point out that Renoir had to put up with such a reproach when the film was released. Writing for *Le Journal des débats politiques et littéraires* on August 4, 1928, the critic expressed his disappointment: "This is the first time that M. Jean Renoir has created a film little worth analyzing. We won't waste our time on it then. Is this the fault of the subject? The result isn't worth mentioning, but it should be observed that at the showing several people did burst into laughter." In 1928, the film was considered unworthy of the critics, whereas thirty years later it was material that would be judged unworthy of the director.

Opinions like this are indicative of unfamiliarity with an aspect of Renoir's personality: he was a man who adored spoonerisms, lewd remarks, and every kind of scatological joke, a man who certainly didn't shy away from most opportunities for a laugh. Neither the passing years nor the fame he acquired over time in any way wore down this penchant, which he never ceased to give full expression. Accordingly, merely the mention of Dupanloup, that private Catholic school in Boulogne-Billancourt attended by his second wife, Dido, inevitably caused him to mention that the students there had the habit of singing lewd songs "inspired" by the school's founder, Monsignor Félix Antoine Philibert Dupanloup. And, usually, he would next break tirelessly into the refrain, "Ah! Ah! Ah! Yes indeed, th' Father Dupanloup's a dirty pig," which would invariably draw the following response from Dido: "Jean, stop that idiocy!"[7]

The director and adapter, then, wasn't contemptuous of the material he was working on; it was, on the contrary, a source of pleasure. Consequently, *Tire-au-flanc* is a very funny film, remarkably spirited and possessing a freedom of form that may represent the first instance in Renoir's body of work that doesn't revolve around the self-referential and is devoted to character and situation. The astonishing mobility of the camera allowed the director to capture spontaneous bursts of behavior without ever making the spectator lose the main thrust of a scene. This happens from the beginning with an unexpected shift from a racy tapestry in eighteenth-century style to the frisky behavior of two servants performing their duties and drawn simultaneously toward each other by desire, seemingly unconcerned by the swinging of a cord through that shot, which is attached to the service bell reserved for use by the masters. Here, once more, we're reminded of *The Rules of the Game* by this scene. The presence of Pomiès isn't enough to explain the impression produced by the film of veritable choreography, orchestrated by a director who seems to be rejoicing about the realization of his own mastery.

Aside from this, and contrary to what some commentators liked to claim, *Tire-au-flanc* conveys in no way an antimilitarist mission. Renoir doesn't at all indicate that he possesses such feelings—indeed, the very opposite. He merely reveals his faith in the spirit of the comical private, which depends partly upon the foolishness and absurdities of military life, elements that become validated in the process. The adjutant-major is a big bully, the colonel, a hedonist, the recruits behave like morons; but all of it is the stuff of good soldiering, and everything always ends in a marriage. In three marriages, in fact, including that of Georgette (Fridette Fatton) and Joseph (Michel Simon), the most appealing couple in the film in large part as a result of the profound humanity, warmth, and passion exhibited by the actor. The first intertitle for the movie, which maintains, "In the army, it takes a lot to be thought of as an imbecile, but don't go too far with it," ends up holding true.

Tire-au-flanc paves the way for the kind of film considered commercial, or, rather, commercial in the opinion of the commercial world, which is something that Renoir would recall on numerous occasions. In this way, a new apprenticeship comes into play, hampered as it will be by certain difficulties. About this, Claude Heymann remembered two scenes he wrote inspired by his own army memories that Renoir had the most trouble directing. One of them is about a very funny encounter with a group of schoolboys in the woods when the soldiers are on maneuvers with faces covered by gas masks; the other is about a new recruit at the barracks. "The scene was shot in a real barracks," he said, "at the entrance to the Saint Cloud railway tunnel.* The gag was as follows: Dubois d'Ombelles, carefully dressed, his little suitcase in hand, crosses the grounds and several times runs into officers who all salute him. He seems to find such deference perfectly natural, until the camera, pulling back, reveals the colonel walking in the recruit's steps. Well, I don't know how Renoir went about doing it, but it was totally indecipherable, incomprehensible, as if the gag had been filmed in reverse."[8]

This new path had already been attempted by Renoir even before he filmed his vaudeville army scene because he'd previously signed on to direct two films, both produced and written by the historical novel specialist Henry Dupuy-Mazuel. The two films also had in common the fact that they were occasioned by a commemoration: *Le Tournoi* (*The Tournament*), for the two-thousandth-year anniversary of the city of Carcassonne, and *Le Bled* for the hundredth anniversary of the conquest of Algeria. This afforded them multiple advantages, both financial and promotional, which the sensible Dupuy-Mazuel could not reasonably ignore, especially because the Société des films historiques had already made the ramparts of Carcassonne one of the decors for Raymond Bernard's *Le Miracle des loups* (*Miracle of the Wolves*), which was also an adaptation of one of Dupuy-Mazuel's novels. Moreover, Raymond Bernard had been Dupuy-Mazuel's first choice for both *The Tournament* and for *Le Bled;* on August 3, 1927, Raymond Bernard had signed on to direct the first but reneged on the contract after two months. The Société des films historiques had postponed the project and did the same for *Le Bled* on April 23, 1928, forcing Bernard to abandon the project in favor of his film *Tarakanova,* a project that in the meantime had been delayed.[9]

The fact that the bimillenary city had been brutally redesigned by Viollet-le-Duc in the style of Napoleon III hadn't put the directors off; nor was Renoir unfavorably disposed by the fact that his father had detested its architecture (as had most of his contemporaries) to the point that he refused to live on the rue Viollet-le-Duc in Paris.

Organized as a benefit for the public retirement fund of the French press, the celebrations in the town of Carcassonne took place from July 15 to 29, 1928. Commencing in the cathedral by "a *Te Deum* with singers and grand organ,"[10] they were promising, in particular, as stated in the program, what would look

---

* The Cent-Gardes Squadron at Saint-Cloud.

like "a tournament from the sixteenth century as it would have been staged for the inhabitants of the town by Queen Catherine de' Medici, accompanied by young King Charles IX and the Prince of Navarre." Marie Bell, from the Comédie-Française, was supposed to present a "*cour d'amour*" on Tuesday; the rehearsal of the tournament ensemble would take place on Friday the twentieth; and the blessing of lances and arms, as well as the tournament itself, was to be held on Saturday, which was the day before the visit of the president of the Republic, Gaston Doumergue.

This was a godsend for a producer, who had the use of hordes of costumed extras, a number of horses ridden by the elite of the French Cavalry and French National Riding School at Saumur—there by special permission from the minister of defense—as well as all the benefits of nature. For the script, which was coauthored with the playwright André Jaeger-Schmidt, Dupuy-Mazuel was inspired by one of his own short stories. Renoir was in charge of the filming, with the help, it should be noted, of the set designer Robert Mallet-Stevens and the camera operator Joseph-Louis Mundwiller, whose shots for *Le Brasier ardent* Renoir had admired and who would also collaborate with Renoir on the *Bled* project. The interiors were to be filmed at studios in Saint-Maurice, in the Val-de-Marne, and then at the Studios des Réservoirs in Joinville.

The lead who would play François de Baynes, Aldo Nadi, was a celebrity from the world of sports. In 1920, he had won three gold medals as part of the Italian team at the Olympic games in Anvers—for the foil, the sword, and the saber—as well as a silver medal in the solo event for saber, outdone only by his brother Nedo, who had more medals than him but was nevertheless considered a less outstanding swordsman. In January 1929, there was the brief possibility of Aldo Nadi's getting the role of Christopher Columbus in a film that Renoir would direct.[11] A cavalry officer during World War I, Nadi moved to the United States in the thirties, and then to Hollywood in the following decade, where his apparently delicate constitution didn't dissuade Warners from casting him as a bodyguard in *To Have and Have Not* (Howard Hawks, 1944). In Hollywood, he was also employed as a fencing teacher, notably for *Captain from Castille* (Henry King, 1947), starring Tyrone Power. He eventually became one of the regular guests at Renoir's dinner parties.*

Renoir turned his experience acting as the foreman and technician for a film into an occasion for trying out a few experiments, which included shooting with panchromatic film and the perfection of a platform on wheels that allowed

* In March 1947, Nadi suggested to Renoir that he bring to the screen "the story of the courtesan Loulou d'Ermenonville." (Jean Renoir Papers, Part I—Production Files, Series VII: Notebooks, Box 51, Folder 8.)

the camera to move on two different heights, either eye level with the banquet table or looking down on the guests from above. He was compelled to find a way to use his imagination and inventiveness even if he wasn't being asked in any way to make such an effort. For a long time, *The Tournament* was thought to have been lost, and Renoir felt the need on several occasions to say that the loss wasn't a great one. The unearthing and restoration of a copy confirm this in part.

The film isn't unpleasant to follow, a nicely executed entertainment, but there isn't much to be gained in the way of thematics or much that labels the approach Renoirian. It is true that it is a product of the mixture of genres Renoir favored and that certain psychological details of character can be observed; but the presence of the director in it seems minimal, and the most attentive observer would probably not pause to consider who directed it if the film was projected without any credits. He or she would, on the other hand, react to the hero's gesture of wiping the blade that he just used to stab his adversary on his lady's hair.

The two films shot on and under the same ramparts, provide a worthy comparison. *The Tournament* is situated far from those masterpieces of French silent film such as Raymond Bernard's *Miracle of the Wolves* (1924) and Marco de Gastyne's *La Merveilleuse Vie de Jeanne d'Arc* (*Saint Joan the Maid*, 1929). This is something that Renoir probably realized after screening the finished film. The July 1929 issue of the Swiss magazine *Close-Up* contained an article by Jean Lenauer that claimed that after the producers reedited *The Tournament*, Renoir wanted his name removed from the credits for the film.

The film was shown in preview at the Belgian court during the celebrations at the end of 1928, where that evening, according to the press, "King Albert himself was the one to signal applause,"[12] and it was next shown on February 4, 1929, at the Marivaux theater. That evening was announced for several weeks as "one of the social and artistic events of that winter,"[13] but if the film got the responses it was supposed to, they were characterized by a lack of enthusiasm. In that way, also, it seems like the twin of the next film that Renoir had already begun to direct.

One advantage *Le Bled* possesses over *The Tournament* is that it permitted Renoir to become familiar with Algeria, a discovery that his son counted as having played a part in his father's awareness of the failings in the workings of the world. Alain Renoir recalled,

> My father expressed a lot of enthusiasm at the time about what the French had accomplished in Algeria. He'd express just as much about the Algerians kicking them out at the beginning of the sixties, and that is a fairly clear illustration of his tenor of thought. I think his turn of ideas could be traced to the following: he became disgusted by the way the French thought of and treated the Algerians. In the harbor in

Algiers, people were throwing coins from the deck of the boat and little Algerian boys were diving for them. Everyone called them "*les Bicots*,"* but when I asked my father for "some pennies to throw to the Bicots," I got an out-and-out dressing-down.[14]

Alain, who was eight at the time, had in fact spent several days at the film shoot, as had his mother, who'd also come to visit. By this time, spring 1929, Renoir was entering into a professional collaboration as well as an intimate relationship with Marguerite Houllé, the film's editor. His relationship with her would last nearly ten years and would exert a major influence on his career and his work. *Le Bled* is also the first film in which Jacques Becker appears, even if fleetingly, in a scene directed in a studio.

The assignment left no doubt that the film was to create a hymn in praise of colonization. In his book on Auguste, Jean describes the feelings that gave rise to the image of Marshal Bugeaud in 1848 as well as how they evolved:

> Everyone was perfectly willing to treat him like dirt. The inventor of the kepi and hero of the famous song "L'as-tu vu, la casquette, la casquette" was detested. My father later wondered how legend was able to take hold of this figure and endow him with an admired role. In fact, when we were discussing it, in the mind of the French people Bugeaud had become a kind of Bayard-like† sybarite. Somewhere in my library I must still have some *images d'Épinal*‡ in books that Gabrielle would read me to make me keep quiet when I was four or five years old. Bugeaud was depicted in them under the most glorious light, charging with his bayonet and foot soldiers, accepting the surrender of the Arab leaders, tasting the soldiers' soup and always acclaimed, ringed by hats raised, carried in triumph, kissed by comely citizens. Renoir attributed this posthumous popularity to the awakening of the chauvinistic spirit that would later be forced to come about after our defeat in '70. In 1848 we were still very near Napoleon's victories, and most French people distrusted military glories.[15]

In fact, *Le Bled* is entirely infused with the chauvinist spirit, whose "western colonial" qualities are, moreover, rendered pleasantly enough. The gazelles chased in the sands are not devoid of allure, the falconing scenes are quite

---

* *Translator's note:* Pejorative slang denoting an Arab.

† *Translator's note:* A reference to Pierre Terrail, seigneur of Bayard (1473–1524), an exemplary French soldier often called "the knight without fear and beyond reproach," or "the good knight," and considered to be the epitome of chivalry.

‡ *Translator's note:* Popular eighteenth-nineteenth-century print depicting idealized scenes of traditional French life.

spectacular, as is the falconers' clever use of the birds when they set them against the camels of the fleeing evildoers. The rest is summed up well enough by the opinion expressed in *Le Figaro* on May 12, 1929:

> The filmmakers set their sights on Algeria and decided to extol it in our eyes. *Le Bled* offers a "walk" through the plowing fields, an onslaught of peaceful tractors, a certain gazelle hunt whose technological virtuosity achieves a minor sensation. Is that to say that the Algerians will be satisfied? Depending on how lenient they are, they'll thank the filmmakers for their good will. Algeria could be the source of a magnificent documentary, and we would have liked some picturesque and poetic images like those we saw in *Nanook of the North, La Croisière noire* [*Black Journey*], and *Moana*. From shore to plateau, from the industrial activity to the antique ruins, all of it should be of a passionate nature. Let's just say that such a thing is available to a person who knows how to be inspired by it. Jean Renoir has done his job when it comes to directing, and we have no intention of holding it against him. We merely regret that he has been marshaled by a banal and childish script with its timid and reserved young girl whose wicked relatives want to steal her inheritance, and who, at just the right moment, is saved by the young ruined Parisian, who has become a miniature Saint John after spending a few months in the middle of nowhere. We find it impossible to congratulate Messrs. Jaeger-Schmidt and Dupuy-Mazuel for having together worn out their brain cells for the purpose of delivering this noxious soap opera.

In 1948, revisiting the film in *Les Cent Visages du cinéma,* Marcel Lapierre concluded, "It draws to a close with a 'visual fantasy' that simultaneously reminds us both of Father Bugeaud's soldiers and of farm tractors."[16] It would be impossible to say it better than that.

Le Bled was presented in Parisian theaters in May 1929. In June, Renoir appeared in Cavalcanti's *Little Red Riding Hood,* which was filmed at Marlotte and written and produced by him. During the following winter, Catherine and Jean participated as actors in the shooting in the South of France of *Die Jagd nach dem Glück* (*Pursuit of Happiness*), directed by a crew composed mostly of German technicians. Not a trace of its release exists except for the one in Berlin in June 1930, and no print has survived. It was the last film of Rochus Gliese, one of its three screenwriters and directors, who would next focus his career on set designing. The two others involved in the film had been closely involved with Renoir for the last three years.

The two of them—Carl Koch and Lotte Reiniger—had been married since 1921 and had worked for three years on the film *The Adventures of Prince Achmed*. Reiniger, born in June 1899, had written and directed the film. It is generally thought that Renoir met the couple in Berlin on September 3, 1926, at the German premiere of *The Adventures of Prince Achmed*, which was also attended by Bertolt Brecht. They had, however, actually met before in Paris.

When this masterpiece of animation was presented in France in July 1926 at the Théâtre des Champs-Élysées, Jean and Catherine had attended a breakfast organized in a restaurant in the Bois de Boulogne. When Lotte Reiniger asked from the podium that it not be held against her that she wasn't speaking French, she heard an unidentified person sitting in the audience next to her husband exclaim: "What a charmer!"[17] A moment later the introductions were made and Carl Koch and Jean Renoir became the best friends in the world, soon discovering that both had been stationed in the region of Reims in 1916, one commanding an antiaircraft battery and the other flying a plane, which didn't rule out the possibility that they were firing at each other. Born in 1892 in Nümbrecht, Westphalia, Carl Koch had a remarkable mind and had completed some brilliant studies in art history, philosophy, and history. He would become Jean Renoir's closest friend, the one whom a worried Renoir would ask to accompany him when the headmaster of Fontainebleau summoned him for a frank discussion about the torments that the student Alain—Renoir's son—was inflicting on his professors.[18]

Pierre Lestringuez was still a part of the inner circle. It was with him that Renoir spent some time considering the project of directing pornographic films on behalf of the madam of some brothels in Nice. Or at least this is what the director recounted in his memoirs, explaining that the offer from this Madame Régina had come to him when he was preparing to film *Marquitta* in 1927 and that with Lestringuez he had considered bringing a work of Sade to the screen to be shown in Mediterranean brothels. According to Alain Renoir, the story of a certain "Baron sans Pantalon"—an aristocrat whose feats led these ladies to investigate and discover that the chap was using a cardboard member—inspired a vague regret on the part of his father at not having honored the proposition. On the other hand, Pierre Braunberger, never at a loss for a revelation, claimed that Renoir had indeed gone into action, not by adapting *Justine, Juliette,* or *Philosophy in the Bedroom* but by directing several short films destined for private projection. The producer specified that some of the characters in these special reels were played at times by known actors and actresses who were momentarily out of work and money or who were simply interested in the experience for their own reasons. It is to be feared that only Michel Simon, perhaps, would be able to tell of the exact nature of these incunabula by Renoir if they ever existed.

This anecdote offers us the opportunity to recall what film was like before 1930, open as it was to the most diverse adventures and to the least professional of do-it-yourselfers. Putting together a film up to that point could be accomplished in a minimum of time with only a modest investment. Sound recording and the editing of film with sound did not only entail a transformation of technical tools but also contributed to a significant increase in budgets by approximately 25 to 30 percent. Small-scale traditional businesses couldn't withstand such costs, and average companies were often forced into mergers. Naturally, it followed that the very architecture of the studios where shooting took place had to be entirely reconceived, as did the movie theaters.

The advent of talkies put an end to the idea of "amateur film," which had been essential to Renoir's involvement in the profession. This change also spelled the end of the fashion for avant-garde films, despite the fact that in France films by Luis Buñuel—*Un chien andalou*—and Jean Cocteau—*Le Sang d'un poète* (*The Blood of a Poet*)*—were able to produce the impression of the opposite evolution.

In Hollywood, the power shifted from California to New York, from the studios to Wall Street, and from the filmmaker, who was the only one who kept this new art alive, to the producer, who held the writers and stage actors he hired under his power. In France, the very same revolution occurred a few months later. Forced to invest to redesign the theaters to match the requirements of the new form of film, theater owners had to borrow from the banks. Confronted with higher costs of production, the producers as well had no other choice. The time of the adventurer was over.

One of the consequences for Renoir of this upheaval was his having to wait nearly two years before he could make another film. His work failed to make a name for itself among professionals, who didn't consider his reputation sufficient to inspire confidence, and his films had not received enough notice to make his having signed them a guarantee of their quality. Producers were unwilling to grant him a budget. Even so, talkies would turn out to be a blessing. There is hardly any doubt, in fact, that for a man who enjoyed speech—recounting, sharing, and the exchange of words—as much as Renoir did, the absence of words deprived the art of film of an essential dimension closely linked to human nature. What would have become of Jean Renoir if films had not begun to speak?

* Starring Enrique Rivero as the poet, the actor in *The Tournament* and *Le Bled*.

7

Chamber Pots

On purge Bébé (Baby's Laxative)

In response to the March 1929 issue of the magazine *Mon Ciné* in the context of an "Appraisal of Talking Films," Renoir claimed to "distrust this wonderful advance." The reasons for his reservations? "With talking films, we'll see an avalanche of 'sensationalistic' films, whose artistic value will probably be slight, and the highlight of major films, in a few years, will be having the young leads sing the great aria from *Pagliacci*. What need is there for the talking film when the art of the silent film as it is now offers us complete and marvelous satisfaction? Nothing finer than the films of Chaplin or Keaton will be produced."

Yes, but alas, talkies were here, or nearly, and there was no other attitude to take than one of resignation, as Renoir acknowledges. At that moment in history, the question was no longer knowing whether film would have sound—it had already begun to—but whether it should have speech. Renoir suggests this in the same interview when he says, "Sound film could be of some interest when it comes to recording noises and not words. For example, in a comedy, I'd enjoy matching a clown's slipping to a whistling sound or using sound to indicate the noise of a pile of plates falling." Such a breach, expressed Renoirian style by the sound of a toilet flushing in *On purge Bébé*, is also the one into which Abel Gance plunges when he maintains in *Ciné-Miroir* on May 31, 1929, "I'm deliberately excluding filmed dialogue from the future of cinema, but I passionately summon the great visual and sonorous symphony made possible by synchronization that will capture ubiquitous sound and movement to fill our ears and eyes with wonder like a magnificent gift from the gods."

A few months before, in the January 17, 1929, issue of *Mon Ciné*, Marcel L'Herbier endorsed the identical point of view, predicting that "the recording of words will have disastrous consequences" but agreeing that "the recording of sounds, on the other hand, could, without destroying the universality of the art, produce interesting films." In the case in point, Renoir's conceptions therefore match those pronounced in common by his colleagues. But the most pertinent opinion about the matter, which history has confirmed, turned out to be René

Clair's. In 1927, the person who would three years later direct *Sous les toits de Paris* (*Under the Roofs of Paris*) depicted talking film as a "fearsome monster, an unnatural creation, thanks to which the screen would become an impoverished form of theater."[1] It was a statement he would clarify completely the following year with, "It isn't the invention of talking film that terrifies us; it's the deplorable use that our industrialists are bound to put it to."[2]

On January 27, 1929, the Parisian premiere of *The Jazz Singer* took place at the Aubert-Palace, an event made possible by Louis Aubert's trip to the United States to bring back the projectors that could show it. In this film by Alan Crosland starring Al Jolson, there are barely two minutes of speech and the rest of the dialogue is reproduced by means of the usual intertitles. The music and songs, however, electrified the audience, which after the film's exclusive run of forty-eight weeks numbered nearly 550,000 admissions, an incredible figure for the period.

Roger Richebé was one of the first in France who understood that nothing would stop sound film. As the head of several theaters in the South of France, in 1928 he signed a contract with the American company Western Electric for a ten-year rental of a sound projector. At the time it cost him 500,000 francs, which he would earn back within the first two weeks of showing Robert Florey's *La route est belle* (*The Road Is Fine*) in his theater, the Capitole, in Marseille. Richebé, who paid 800,000 francs for the right to show the film in the southern half of the country, began furnishing about fifteen of his theaters with the same equipment.

Like several other French films of the first years of sound film, *The Road Is Fine* was shot in England, which already possessed studios with the correct equipment, notably Elstree in the London suburbs of Borehamwood, whereas in Paris, the studios on rue Francoeur, for example, were still expected to muffle noises by means of screens they called *nègres;* these screens were covered with felt that wasn't dry-cleaned and that was soon infested with lice.

Pierre Braunberger was the producer of *The Road Is Fine.* He came up with the idea of drafting Robert Florey, a young Frenchman who had been living in Hollywood since 1921, for the project. After that stunning success, he joined forces with his lucky partner on June 1, 1930, to form Les Établissements Braunberger-Richebé, a limited liability company with a worth of 12 million francs. *The Road Is Fine* was Braunberger's contribution to the company, a property valued at 2 million francs. Richebé and his partner, Raduet, contributed their share in the form of the two theaters they owned, the Capitole and the Colisée.

Roger Richebé set up his offices in Paris on boulevard Exelmans, but all activities having to do with distribution and operation were located at 1 boulevard Haussmann. This entailed his becoming a producer, a function for which nothing had prepared him. The headquarters of the company were located in Billancourt, next to the studios directed by Richebé and Braunberger and where, thanks to Braunberger, Richebé would get to know artists, directors, and writers. The Prévert brothers and the Allégret brothers were among them, as was Jean Renoir, whom he discovered was a "Bugattiste," as passionate about those cars as he himself was.

Renoir would come to the studio to meet his friend Braunberger, not to work. Later, some people, Richebé being the first among them, would speak of the ostracism Renoir experienced. What could be the reasons for such hostility? What image of Renoir did the film profession possess at the dawn of movies with sound? Not a very serious one, most likely. This man spoke too loudly and liked nothing better than a good laugh. He switched relentlessly from one subject to another, seeming to find it hard to focus on any one thing, and he didn't need much encouragement to launch into bragging. By all evidence, he was careful to appear unconcerned about activities that he flauntingly claimed to exercise merely as a dilettante. And then, no French director found favor in his sight. When conversation at a bar or restaurant table turned to the films of others, he vividly proclaimed his abhorrence. This Jean Renoir was a loudmouth, often entertaining, but his witticisms would backfire, jettisoning any trust in him, which was something he did not know how to inspire. Most important of all, the experience he'd accumulated so far didn't demonstrate his abilities, and rumor claimed that he hadn't known how to "stick to" the budget of his two last films, *The Tournament* and *Le Bled*.

As if that weren't enough, his name was Renoir, which put him at the head of a considerable fortune, exempting him from having to work to make a living; not to mention that his brother was respected as a celebrity both for his talent and for his behavior, whereas Jean was taking forever to establish his reputation. That was also the reason why he talked louder than he should—this young man of means, whose own body was turning against him, forced it into suits in shades of blue bought at La Belle Jardinière* or Au Petit Matelot† on avenue de Wagram—and he kept wearing the clothes he favored not to be fashionable or comfortable but to display his social self-effacement. He was a fat boy of thirty-five, the frustrated husband of an out-of-work actress, who'd always seemed clumsy and who felt himself growing lumpish. He was graceless with women,

* *Translator's note:* La Belle Jardinière, established in Paris in 1824, was an early ready-to-wear department store that provided clothes at a modest price for middle-class people unable to afford custom suits.

† *Translator's note:* Au Petit Matelot was a store that specialized in clothing for service people, such as chauffeurs, footmen, and other types working in livery.

JEAN RENOIR

a seducer who had trouble seducing those who attracted him. Others in the profession didn't see him as belonging; at best they thought of him as a buddy who was loaded, at worst, a flop. Such singularity would become his strength, but for the moment it was preventing his advancement.

Braunberger's business involvements frequently brought him to Germany, and sometimes Jean went with him for pleasure. This was how the two cronies ended up as extras in *Diary of a Lost Girl,* the film that Pabst was shooting in Berlin in 1929. If we can believe Braunberger,[3] they played customers in a nightclub, in the direct gaze of the wonderful Louise Brooks; Renoir confirmed this in 1974 without being able to remember the title of the film.[4] On the other hand, Braunberger was mistaken in claiming that their participation happened during the shooting of *L'amourchante* (*Love Songs*), which Robert Florey actually directed for Braunberger, but in 1930. Renoir could relate to the appeal of life in Berlin, and he traveled there often, with or without Braunberger, sometimes bringing Catherine along.

Braunberger himself didn't appear to be very much in a hurry to hire his friend Renoir. After *The Road Is Fine,* he produced at least six feature sound films on behalf of Les Établissements Braunberger-Richebé. He handed them over to directors with a reputation, such as Robert Florey, who'd directed *Love Songs* and *Le Blanc et le Noir* (*Black and White*), which had been written by Sacha Guitry; or to Marcel L'Herbier, who did *La Femme d'une nuit.** Or else he gave them to his friends or business partners, as a way for them to start their careers: Marc Allégret was Florey's assistant on the film written by Guitry, and he finished the shooting after Florey's departure. He also shared the direction of *Amants de minuit* (*The Lovers of Midnight*) with Augusto Genina. Another beginner, Jean Tarride, codirected *La Femme d'une nuit.* Braunberger had met Marc Allégret in 1927 through André Gide, who wanted the young man to finish the documentary they'd begun together, *Le Voyage au Congo,* for which they needed a professional's help. Jean Tarride, along with Braunberger and Marc Allégret's brother Yves, was the owner of the Panthéon movie theater, bought in 1929, and shortly after of a theater in Toulouse.

As Braunberger would later claim, it's possible that when he suggested Renoir be given a film to direct, he came up against opposition from Richebé, who had little confidence in Renoir. Even though it's difficult to assess what Richebé—who at the time knew not the first thing about producing a film and confirmed as much in his memoirs and who was completely unfamiliar with anyone's character when he moved to Paris—could have found wrong in hiring an experienced director when he had already agreed to entrust a budget to a

* *Translator's note:* Literally, "The One-Night Woman."

beginner like Jean Tarride. It's more likely that in Braunberger's eyes Renoir had all the sought-after qualities of a table or travel companion, but the rapport and friendship they had for each other stopped at the door to Braunberger's studios, which were open to those he did business with and to those who had proved their expertise or flexibility. Hiring Renoir could mean asking for trouble. His persona was, as well, that of a pain in the neck. The complications encountered on several of his first sound films substantiated that reputation, and it was only their success that redeemed him, or would at least convince others to choose to forget. One of many paradoxes was that Renoir rarely held to his ideas, usually preferring instead to let them play out in an improvisational manner, a tendency that also contributed to the impression that he was "not a safe bet" because he was indecisive. Finally, but probably not least importantly, Braunberger had less need of Renoir—who for a long time was the partner he preferred, if not the only one he had—as soon as he found himself in cahoots with Richebé and the business they did flourished.

Though they came from different inspirations and seemingly are different in nature, Renoir's first two "talkies" cannot actually be considered separately. *On purge Bébé* was directed in March 1931 and shown in theaters in June. It was immediately followed by *La Chienne*, made in July 1931, shown privately in September, and released at the beginning of the following year. The trade journals of April 1931 corroborate that Renoir moved from one to the other without delay. The announcement about the end of editing for the first film appeared on May 5, one week after the readers of the April 24 issue of *La Semaine des spectacles* were informed that "Jean Renoir [had] gone to the country for several days to work on the first draft of *La Chienne*."

Braunberger's recollections are in agreement with those of Renoir that the decision to entrust the director with the task of bringing the Georges Feydeau play to the screen was made at the request of Richebé, who required Renoir to prove himself in order to be offered direction of *La Chienne*. Richebé himself never made any mention of such a request. All he remembers is having bought the rights for three plays by Feydeau: *On purge Bébé, Feu la mère de madame,*[*] and *Ne te promène donc pas toute nue.*[†] He'd only produce an adaptation of the first, relinquishing the rights to the two others, which became two short films in 1936, both directed by Arletty. The next thing Richebé wrote was, "Jean Renoir, my 'Bugattiste,' is quite a nice guy. He'll be the director of *On purge Bébé*."[5]

With such a preface, the genesis of Renoir's first sound film materialized

---

* *Translator's note*: Literally, "Madame's Late Mother."

† *Translator's note*: Literally, "Don't Walk Around Bare Naked."

and became a sort of legend that the director sometimes stoked; he supposedly wasn't interested in the Feydeau play except in hopes of securing the right to tackle *La Chienne* next. In other words, he would have held his nose during the entire production of the film, which actually did occupy so little of his time that he could have made it through without breathing. This means that he was in the same state of mind for *On purge Bébé* as he was three years before for *Tire-au-flanc*. In both cases, this fails to consider the situation of a director who would not give in to suggestions, and it also misjudges Renoir's pronounced penchant for farces.

Actually, one of his favorite stories, which he recounted for years, connects *La Chienne* to *On purge Bébé*. It depicts the relationship of a couple that is destroyed by the parakeet Madame owns. The bird stubbornly persists in leaving its droppings in the soup tureen that occupies the center of the dinner table. The husband wrings the neck of the feathered creature that tortures him, and then the deplorable mania of the bird—in the meantime revived—breaks down the second marriage of its female owner.[6] So much for the benefits of scatology. But the conclusion of the story itself brings us directly back to that of *La Chienne,* because the two spouses tortured one after the other by the parakeet come to an agreement to rid themselves definitively of the bird of misfortune. On the basis of only this story, *On purge Bébé* is just as much a film by Jean Renoir as *La Chienne.*

On purge Bébé is actually an excellent film, written, directed, and edited in three weeks, whose breakdown of scenes, which it owes to Renoir, Pierre Prévert, and Claude Heymann, is as faithful as possible to Feydeau's text. When the play was first staged on April 12, 1910, at the Théâtre des Nouveautés, it was applauded by the critics as one of its author's major successes, and in the April 13 issue of *Le Figaro*, Francis Chevassu went so far as to judge it "a small masterpiece" of its genre in this "joyously liberated play, characterized by generous gaiety, and in which Parisian refinement helms the best of the Gallic spirit." The same *Figaro* was to show less sensitivity to the qualities of Renoir's adaptation, publishing in its July 19, 1931, issue an annihilating review, penned by Richard-Pierre Bodin:

> One could have subtitled this film, which was "evacuated" from the late Feydeau through the most natural routes, "Au flanc de vase,"* in the manner of Samain;† or else, parodying Pirandello, it could be called *Five Characters in Search of an Odor*. When all is said and done, the odor—sorry, I meant the author—sacrifices a little too much to the mode of

* *Translator's note:* "On the Side of the Chamber Pot."

† Albert Samain, a Symbolist poet, 1858–1900.

the put-on. He wears out his subject, dare I say. Please allow me not to go on at length about his matter, because that chamber pot, to our great misfortune, wasn't subjected to any fanning. One word . . . would sum up this foul-smelling little story, but decorum and my political convictions prevent me from borrowing it from a marshal of the Empire.*

It's not known whether Renoir learned about this scathing review, but the fact that he would have drawn some satisfaction from it wouldn't be surprising. The jubilation inspired in him by Feydeau's text was too obvious for reactions to his provocations not to have reinforced it.

The film put together a cast remarkable for its appropriateness. Jacques Louvigny, who plays Follavoine, the manufacturer of the chamber pots he claims are unbreakable and with which he intends to benefit the French army, began his film career in 1914 with *Un fil à la patte* (*Tied Down*)—another Feydeau property. Marcel Simon had created the role of Follavoine in 1910 onstage and was one of Feydeau's favorite actors. Simon's wife, Marguerite Pierry, would portray Madame Follavoine in curlers, carrying around the slop pail with outstretched arms, her bathrobe swaying, and her stockings drooping around her ankles. Michel Simon is an amazing Chouilloux, an official at the Ministry of Defense, which makes him the target of Follavoine's commercial enterprise. Just the account alone that he gives of the cures he has taken in Plombières while suffering from a form of "loose" enteritis is an expression of the pure genius of an actor in harmony with the text and, in the same breath, at a distance from it, in the pleasurable grips of it without in any way revealing the effects he is creating, as if they were occurring naturally. Moreover, Chouilloux is a character being cuckolded and quite obviously not clued in to a misfortune known by everyone and caused by his wife's so-called cousin, Horace Truchet.

Jean Renoir's camera offers us a Horace Truchet with the features of Fernandel. On the advice of Marc Allégret, Richebé went to see the comedian at the Concert Mayol, where he was appearing in the revue *Vive le nu!* (*Long Live Nudes!*), and the day after that he had signed a contract with him for a dozen short films. The first of them, directed by Allégret, was the adaptation of a theatrical comedy by Mouëzy-Éon called *La Meilleure Bobonne*. Cast as well in *Black and White*, another Braunberger-Richebé production, Fernandel moved on to *On purge Bébé*. As the story of Fernandel's first steps into film do not at all

* *Translator's note:* A reference to Pierre Jacques Étienne Cambronne (1770–1842), a general of the French Empire. Taken prisoner by the British at Waterloo and ordered to surrender, he replied, according to one account, with the monosyllabic "Merde!" ("Shit!" or perhaps, in this case, "Bug off!")

suggest but which Renoir affirmed, "The studio didn't believe it was possible to use such an unbelievable face. . . . Braunberger had to insist on him."[7] However, if Richebé had hired him and if Braunberger spoke out in favor of him, who at the studio owned by these two had the necessary authority to oppose his presence in the film? Between his arrival in Paris in November 1930 and the filming of *On purge Bébé* in March 1931, the comedian from Marseille made five films, one of which was a feature. How many would he have made if the film world had welcomed him with open arms?

Renoir's obligation to work fast, within the framework of the play, led him toward a style of direction devoid of effects or fancy flourishes. A few subtle reframings, not many insert shots, a conspicuous use of depth of field. Especially in the scene in which Follavoine tests the vaunted solidity of the chamber pots for the benefit of Chouilloux, the film places itself in service to the text, and therefore to the actors. For Renoir, it came close to being a revelation: for the first time, he experienced a lasting interest in the characters and not in the technique. In this way, as well, *On purge Bébé* represented an opportunity to take a decisive step.

Recording the sound fascinated him, and in the engineer Joseph de Bretagne he discovered an essential collaborator. Renoir was one of the rare directors of that time always to insist on recording sound directly. The films he made in the thirties would stand out for the presence of that quality throughout the production. Even when the sound appeared mediocre, as it does in *La Chienne*, *La Nuit du carrefour* (*Night at the Crossroads*), and *Boudu Saved from Drowning*, it was a characteristic feature of the unique atmosphere created by these films.

Renoir especially insisted on the recognizable sounds of the toilet flushing, triggered by Chouilloux hurrying to the toilet after having inadvertently ingested the purgative that Bébé is stubbornly refusing to swallow: "In my concern for realism, I used the flush of a real toilet in the studio. The result produced the sound of a cataract that thrilled the production representatives and elevated me to the level of a great man."[8] Toilets were much in evidence when talkies came along; for example, Buñuel's *L'Âge d'or*, which had been released the preceding autumn, also included the sound of a toilet flush. It was not a matter of the situations in which they occurred but of the effect they produced. And it's true that during screenings of *Les Trois Masques* (*The Three Masks*),* billed in October 1929 as "the first 100 percent talking French film," the audience applauded the sound produced by the water from a faucet hitting a sink.†

---

* Directed by André Hugon.

† The first Russian sound film allowed the audience to hear farts. (*Road to Life*, Nikolai Ekk, 1931.)

It's likely that *On purge Bébé* as it can be seen today does not conform in every detail to the film that audiences discovered in 1931. In fact, in 1975, right before a rerelease, Pierre Braunberger suggested to Renoir that he make certain cuts, especially "on scenes with Louvigny and Marguerite Pierry": "There are repetitions on the chamber pot. It would be interesting to concentrate more on Michel Simon."[9] Renoir stated then that he was "in agreement with the cuts."[10]

Regardless of whether Renoir directed *On purge Bébé* to prove himself, as he claimed, making a studio film that depended on a text and actors profoundly altered his conceptions. He confirmed this development years later by stating, "I didn't see until 1930 how the obligation to write dialogue put my feet on the ground and created a genuine contact between the people I had to make speak and myself. Since silent film only demands dealing with exterior forms, your imagination can allow you to live in a world that absolutely does not exist."[11] With the advent of sound, film discovered the dimension that the director lacked, and from then on he would be able to show what he was made of.

8

Pitiless

La Chienne

On August 29, 1971, in a letter to Charles David, director of production for Renoir's first two talking films, as well as the former administrator of Les Établissements Braunberger-Richebé,* Pierre Braunberger wrote, "For a long time I've known that the dramatics in our profession come from everyone wanting to be, believing he is, or being the sole author of a film, the sole producer, and that everybody thinks he was the one who first had the idea."[1] Indeed. Among its other equally remarkable characteristics, *La Chienne* is distinguished by the determination of its three promoters to claim full responsibility for its paternity.

Renoir, for a start. He locates the beginning of the project at the advent of the talkie. "I got in contact with several producers and proposed a project based on a novel by Georges de La Fouchardière entitled *La Chienne*. My attempts were in vain."[2]

And then, Pierre Braunberger, who declares: "From the newspaper *L'Oeuvre* my brother had clipped a large part of La Fouchardière's *La Chienne*, which was appearing in installments. One day when I was going to the airport at Le Bourget, my brother gave me what he'd collected and told me, 'Hey, this might be a good idea for Renoir.' I left for London and read the serialized installments in the plane. I really liked them. The entire story hadn't appeared yet in the paper. But my brother talked about it with Renoir, who seemed very enthusiastic when I got back and spoke to him."[3] Then Braunberger explains that it took nearly a year to acquire the rights from Mouëzy-Éon, "who wanted to adapt the subject for the stage and owned the film rights."

And finally, Roger Richebé, who writes, "I read Georges de La Fouchardière's *La Chienne*. Mouëzy-Éon was the one who'd adapted the subject for the stage and who owned the film rights. So I dealt with him."[4]

The book had been released by Albin Michel in January 1930. The play in three acts and fifteen scenes adapted by Mouëzy-Éon was performed at the

---

* In the meantime, Charles David and Renoir had reconnected in Hollywood in 1942, during the shoot for *Forever Yours* (later known as *The Amazing Mrs. Holliday*), with Deanna Durbin, who became Mrs. Charles David in 1950.

Théâtre de la Renaissance beginning on December 12 of the same year—apparently without success, because it closed after thirty performances. In neither case were the chances of having at least heard of the thing rare, especially if you add to them the republication of the text by *Les Cahiers de Bravo* in February 1931. It also can't be ruled out that Renoir, Braunberger, and Richebé had the same idea at approximately the same time. Besides, Richebé was already doing business with Mouëzy-Éon, from whom he'd bought, notably, the rights to *La Meilleure Bobonne*. Acquisition of the rights to adapt *La Chienne* was announced in *La Cinématographie française* on April 11, 1931.

The issue of casting the roles turned out no less thorny. Braunberger demanded the lead be given to Michel Simon and would later claim that Renoir was leaning toward Harry Baur. The casting of Simon was announced on May 23, at which time it was made clear that no other role had been cast. Braunberger also put forward the idea that Renoir was thinking of Florelle for the role of the young woman, and this is confirmed by a paragraph that appeared in *La Cinématographie française* on June 13: "Jean Renoir is making some stabs at pulling together the casting of *La Chienne*. . . . There's talk of Florelle in the role of la Chienne." The actress's thirty-two years convinced the producer to consider her too old for the part. Renoir stated that he was thinking of none other than the woman who was still his wife at the time: "The role of the woman would have suited Catherine superbly." Faced with his producers' refusal, he seems to have told Catherine that he, as well, would give up any chance for the film. Not without cruelty he wrote, "She told me not to, hoping that I would insist on giving it up. I didn't."[5] Already in a very sorry state—separated, in fact—the couple would not survive this.

Sometime before, Richebé had signed a three-year contract with a young actress. Braunberger didn't oppose it, proof that the selection of Janie Marèze for *Mam'zelle Nitouche* led to the impression that she would be perfect in *La Chienne*. Begun in May, *Mam'zelle Nitouche*, directed by Marc Allégret, was finished filming when the shooting for Renoir's film had already started, which suggests that the choice of the actress occurred as a result of impressions culled from the soundstage and confirmed by the rushes. It's more likely, however, that the idea of casting Janie Marèze came from Richebé and Allégret and was then picked up by Braunberger and Renoir on the run so that their production would be the first one featuring the young actress. The two films were presented to the press five days apart—*La Chienne* on September 3, 1931, and *Mam'zelle Nitouche* on the eighth (Renoir made a brief appearance as staff sergeant beside the young actress).

Janie Marèze, at twenty-two, blended the manners of a girl from a good family who had been educated in a convent (and she actually had been) with some attitudes that indicated a certain lax moral standard. Her dresses and skirts showed off her legs, generously presented for admiration. She was pretty, full of life and fun, and her innocent appearance was allied with an already admitted experience that endowed her with a charm that still seems modern on today's screen. After several prizes for singing and comic opera at the Paris Conservatory, she continued to appear on the stage (at the Daunou, Marigny, Gaîté-Lyrique, and Ambassadeurs theaters) and had made her film debut in Jean Choux's *Amours viennoises,* released in February 1931.

If Pierre Braunberger is to be believed, however, in the eyes of Renoir she presented an unexpected handicap, the nature of which could have prevented her from interpreting her character correctly: "That girl has never had an orgasm. You can see it, and it's absolutely essential to intuit the opposite in looking at her. The story relies totally on her physical, nearly animal, attachment to her pimp. That's how he has to hold on to her, by pleasure."[6] To compensate for this flaw, the director and producer were said to have organized a weekend at the house in Marlotte to familiarize Janie Marèze with Georges Flamant, who'd previously never appeared onstage except as an amateur and whose name in publicity would remain "Maurice Georges" until after shooting was finished. The encounter between the two turned out to be explosive, and the young actress fell madly in love with the man playing opposite her. Renoir soon became apprised of the situation, and in his memoirs he writes, "Flamant kept a hold on Janie Marèze using methods from the best tradition of that 'milieu.' He would make her undress and stretch out nude on a sofa while he crouched at the foot of it. He'd do this for hours, 'without touching her.' 'You see, pal, I just kept looking at her . . . watching her with devotion, without touching her. After an hour, I could do whatever I wanted with her. . . . Without touching her, which is the important thing.'"[7]

Like most of the actresses of that period, Janie Marèze was connected to a "generous gentleman," a certain Monsieur Léon Volterra, who ran several theaters, a man with savoir faire and a fortune of greater significance than his talents as a lover had a chance of overshadowing—at least if we're to believe Jean Renoir, who exhibited either a very remarkable appraisal of the situation or a refreshing naïveté. Marèze's affair with Georges Flamant, which was public knowledge, did not call into question her dependence on her wealthy protector, but his family took offense at the publicity it brought to his name and made every effort when the time came to prevent journalists from publishing certain information about it.

In the Billancourt studios, on the soundstage of *La Chienne,* Janie Marèze drove men wild, and Michel Simon was the first in line. If there was nothing else about him that resembled the timorous office worker he played—the frustrated painter under the thumb of a horrendous shrew—he nevertheless knew women better than anyone, including the desires they inspired. From their first meeting, he harbored a flame for the young actress that burned as fervently as the one that devoured her the moment she was near her other partner. History doesn't reveal, unfortunately, whether Michel Simon's eagerness was ever sufficient in achieving its intended goal, but as things were, the relationship among the three actors closely matched the contours of that of the three characters. Just as Legrand becomes enamored of Lulu, who swindles him for the benefit of Dédé—the pimp she passionately loves—so did Michel Simon burn for Janie Marèze, who was under the sway of Georges Flamant.

The film carries the imprint of these real-life relationships. Several scenes between Legrand and Lulu were lived by Simon and Marèze, the corridors at Billancourt were full of such comings and goings, and dressing room doors were slammed more brutally than the doors of the rooms on-screen. When Legrand, who has gone mad with the fires of jealousy and been humiliated beyond reason, kills the woman laughing at him and whom he begs in vain to stop, the actor playing him didn't have to look very far for his character's motivations. According to certain witnesses, Michel Simon had to be stopped long after the director called "cut" to signal the end of a scene because he continued wanting to strangle the woman he'd just murdered with a letter opener for not loving him, or not enough, or as much as she loved another—in any case.

Film history does not usually dwell a great deal on the personal circumstances surrounding the direction of films, but in Renoir's case and especially in the case of *La Chienne,* the situation contributes in an important way to the nature of the film. The incredible impression of truthfulness that emanates from *La Chienne* is also the fruit of the heated relationship linking and tearing apart the three characters, exposed as they are to the gazes that fall upon them from the thirty or so people who made up the technical crew. The fact that Renoir, taking his cue from the film he claimed to adore above all others in 1931—Pabst's *The Threepenny Opera*—chooses to open and close his film on a puppet show, which places the characters in the world of marionettes, where lives are decided by fate and by their author, emphasizes the cruelty of the situations and events being described. Putting them in a variety of frames created by the direction—in windows, doors, paintings—enhances the vertiginous quality of their multiple perspectives. Similarly, the tragic nature of the story is complicated by being observed as if at a distance by a director who is fascinated by the way human passions are brought into bloom by society and constrained by it at the same time, all of which he never stops considering without ironic detachment. Renoir did not find a place for himself in society, and he contemplates its functioning like someone who doesn't belong there yet takes part in it nevertheless.

All that exist here are errors, lies, hypocrisy, and pretense. Legrand's paintings, which sell for a fortune in the galleries, are the work of a man crushed by his fate and his own weaknesses. He finds no other world but the streets to survive in as a bum collecting cigarette butts and opening car doors for people. He feels like a millionaire when a bill burns in his hands, and he parts with it lickety-split for a nosh. At the end of *La Chienne*, Michel Simon has become Boudu without ever stopping being Legrand.

As for Lulu, she no longer exists. Nor does her Dédé, condemned to death and executed for a crime he hasn't committed, perhaps the only one he was innocent of. Consequently, both the pimp and the murderer in *La Chienne* appear as the first of the innocents to be punished while the guilty are saved in a work that establishes human justice for what it is—theater. The cad turned out to be innocent, the decent man guilty. Society rids itself of the first; the second survives in the rags of a tramp. He has always been marginal, and now he dresses that way, which makes him easy to identify.

This film is vertiginous, as is its plot, with a complicated beginning and an ending that is no less so. The question must be asked, in fact: Who declared *La Chienne* Jean Renoir's first masterpiece? Certain people answered that question, yet their responses cast some doubt on that determination.

To begin with, Roger Richebé claimed, "As soon as *La Chienne* was edited, I was shown it. I couldn't believe my eyes, and I was crushed. With the greatest pleasure I had watched Renoir shoot, and every evening I came to the rushes. I was convinced of the high quality of the film, and I don't understand how Renoir could have failed to such a point in his editing."[8] Richebé then gives an account of the interview he had with Renoir, during which he claims the director said, "Monsieur Richebé, do you take me for Lubitsch?" The reference to the director from Berlin, who'd been in Hollywood since 1923 and who was working there as director of production for Paramount, prompted Richebé to remind Renoir that in order to offer him the direction of *La Chienne* he had had to overcome the reticence of some of his associates. Renoir refused to hear it and said that he was "withdrawing from the studio." Richebé: "Féjos is preparing *Fantômas* right now. I'll have him contacted and ask him to do the cut on *La Chienne*." Pál Fejös, a talented Hungarian director, had spent several years in the United States, where he'd changed his name to Paul Fejos and codirected *L'Amour à l'américaine* (*American Love*) with Claude Heymann. He was getting ready to shoot *Marie, légende hongroise* with Annabella and would actually end up directing *Fantômas*. According to Roger Richebé's claim, he would become the one who cut *La Chienne*.

In the second volume of his memoirs, Claude Autant-Lara devotes thirty pages to the issue, giving credence to what Richebé maintains. If this is to be believed, Braunberger played no role in the production of *La Chienne,* which was solely accomplished by Richebé, who had to make an effort to interest Renoir in it, principally because the latter feared "antagonizing the profession of art dealers." A fabrication it seems, but it's amusing to spot a trace of it in the otherwise benevolent review of the film in *L'Humanité* on November 27, 1931, which points out one complete and unforgivable "failure": "The satire of the art business, which is currently causing the death of painting. The subject is barely touched upon. It deserves better than a weak sketch."

In the first volume of his memoirs, Autant-Lara delivered such a whacky account of the filming of *Nana*—for which he provided the function of costumer, set designer, and actor—that it isn't even necessary to recall his bitterness and flaunted anti-Semitism to understand that his attacks against Renoir and, even more so, against Braunberger should be assessed with distance. Without excluding the fact that Autant-Lara could very well have been inspired by Richebé's book, there is still one point at which his claims intersect with the memoirs of the producer: the editing of *La Chienne.* For this he summons the aid of Pierre Lestringuez, who supposedly confided his vision of the events he had witnessed to Autant-Lara but who was no longer living to confirm their truth by the time Autant-Lara's book appeared. According to Autant-Lara, Lestringuez saw the projection of the first cut of the film when Richebé and Renoir were there and told Autant-Lara, "Linkage between scenes was no longer there, all of it having become frequently incomprehensible. . . . It was clear that the essential part of it had remained in Jean Renoir's mind—and he thought he'd expressed it."

After Richebé had cautiously intervened, taking care not to offend the director while impressing upon him that the film was not acceptable, Renoir was actually supposed to have remarked, "Come on, then, you . . . do you really take me for Lubitsch?" What follows also conforms to the version of facts presented by Richebé, and the scene concludes with an outraged Renoir's "definitive" departure, but not before he managed to reproach Lestringuez for his attitude. The next day, Renoir is said to have telephoned his friend to inform him that he'd changed his mind. And Lestringuez had answered that he'd gone too far for Richebé to grant him permission to recut the film. Then Renoir is supposed to have exploded, inspiring the following severe corrective from Lestringuez: "Jean, you're just a beginner, after all. You've barely got a foothold in this profession. You could at least consider an opposing opinion without feeling disgraced by it! Especially, let me tell you, when it's justified, when it's well-founded! Especially when, from all our reactions, you know very well that your edit is a failure. And that's what's bothering you." Then Renoir was to have repeated that he "washed his hands" of the affair and hung up.

Sometime after that, Lestringuez received another call. Renoir asked him to come to the screening of "that thing, that film called *La Chienne,* that dared call itself *La Chienne.*" The showing was held in a theater at Barbès, and journalists and other professionals from the business had been invited. Renoir was attending with his brother Claude, and he was intending to provoke "the scandal that was necessary."[9] There's no doubt that such a screening actually did take place at the location indicated; it's confirmed by a full page that appeared in *La Cinématographie française* on September 12 announcing the presentation of the film on September 17, at ten in the morning, at the Palais Rochechouart.

Lestringuez responded to the request and, on the day indicated, in the movie theater, heard Renoir worrying about Richebé's presence and, after being told that Richebé would be represented by Jean Paoli, one of his business associates, Renoir grumbled to the latter about not being invited. When the screening came to an end and the lights went back on, Lestringuez, convinced that he'd seen a masterpiece, tried to prevent Renoir from reacting the way he feared he would but very quickly perceived that the director was accepting the congratulations addressed to him, was responding to the ovations coming from the audience, was smiling, and then soon was beaming and "out of his mind with joy." Autant-Lara supposedly then revealed to Lestringuez what he was yet unaware of and what Autant-Lara claimed to have heard from Fejos himself: the director had accepted Richebé's offer to let him recut the film, on the express condition that no one would ever know a thing about it.

Autant-Lara's memory has too often turned out to be unreliable, not to mention that his resentments, especially, are too consuming and corrupted to permit faith in all his claims. But several coincidences remain troubling. For example, Richebé as well writes that Jean Paoli stood in for him at the screening organized for September 3, to which "Renoir had come . . . with several friends intending to create an uproar,"[10] but that, in the end, "Renoir knew his craft too well not to acknowledge that the editing was excellent." Unlike Autant-Lara, Richebé showed no animosity toward Renoir and used moderation to recount facts he witnessed or was involved in. Yet again, there is a possibility that the director appropriated Richebé's version for his own retelling.

Pierre Braunberger, on the other hand, refutes the hypothesis about Paul Fejos intervening, insisting yet again that he himself—and not Richebé in the least regard—"was involved in the project from the beginning." He confirms the dissatisfaction his partner expressed after seeing the first cut before specifying, "Denise Batcheff, who'd become Denise Tual, was allowed (perhaps because Richebé insisted) to modify a few scenes of Renoir's edit. But after Renoir violently banned her from the editing room, he very quickly replaced her with

Marguerite Renoir [Houllé]. Richebé claims to have put Fejos to work on the editing of the film, and that's not the case."[11]

It remains for us to hear what the most involved person had to say. And to see that Renoir's account contributes less to dispelling doubt than to upholding it. First, it's necessary to note that the following version of the director's account is from 1938, at the zenith of his career:

> During *La Chienne*, I was merciless, and I do mean unbearable. I made this film the way I wanted to, as I intended, without at all taking into account the wishes of the producer. I never showed a single bit of my shooting script, nor more than a snatch of my dialogue, and I arranged to keep the results of the shots almost completely out of sight until the film had been made. That moment resulted in quite a scandal. The producer was expecting a light comedy; and suddenly he was faced with a dark and desperate drama with the added attraction of a murder that wasn't at all in style at the time.[12]

Why does he begin so aggressively at a time when no one was quibbling over Renoir's having authorship of the film? Why "merciless," "unbearable" from the very start? Above all, who can believe that a director was able to make a film without the producer knowing anything about the project? Especially a director who'd been asked a few weeks earlier to prove himself. How could it be possible that such a director would then go ahead and have his rushes screened without the producer present? Both Braunberger and Richebé, whose memories, as well, rarely coincide, agree separately that they were at these screenings, as they very naturally would be. Even a limited knowledge of the functioning of a film studio would be enough to sweep away claims made by Renoir seven years after the facts. Those having to do with the very nature of the film are no more convincing.

Why would the producer have expected a "light comedy"? Because the author of the novel was known for his humor. But it's only necessary to read *La Chienne* to verify that it's an appallingly dark book. The descriptions of the book that appeared when it was released shed further doubt on the possibility of anyone's thinking of it as a light comedy. Take, for example, the review in *Le Journal des débats politiques et littéraires* on February 18, 1930: "In this novel, Georges de La Fouchardière, who speaks of it as his life's work, the only thing that he would like to leave behind, dims and shrouds his usual humor; and all that now emanates from the action is a bitter irony. It's told by the three characters in the book, so different in heart, mind, and way of life, and it's a humble drama of tenderness and weakness, which gradually increases the anguish of the onlooker until the dramatic and unexpected conclusion."

"Bitter irony," "humble drama," "anguish." And what's more, Braunberger and Richebé had read the book, too, and Richebé had become worried about casting Michel Simon "in a dramatic role, since he'd never played one": "Simon had just scored a hit playing Cloclo in *Jean de la lune*. Cloclo is fundamentally a comic character, and there's no doubt that audiences expected Michel Simon to make them laugh for his next performance. Not to mention that La Fouchardière was known for his humor."[13] These lines were written in 1977; perhaps such a demonstration occurred awfully late. The truth is that the nature of *La Chienne* was known before anyone at all could have discovered the film, a fact upheld by two tidbits that appeared in *La Cinématographie française* on July 4 and in *Le Figaro* on July 19, 1931. The first states, "Jean Renoir is still directing the distressing story from *La Chienne*," and the second announces, "After *La Chienne*, which he's currently directing, Jean Renoir will take on another film, a comedy this time, with a script by André Girard,* intended specifically for Michel Simon."† The precise words "a comedy this time" clearly confirm that even though the directing was still going on, the tone of *La Chienne* was already known. Richebé himself couldn't have expected anything else, having learned from the shooting script handed in by Renoir before filming that the screenwriter had "amped up the dramatic nature of the story and . . . merely touched sketchily on the humor."[14]

One could suspect that Renoir's memory was playing tricks on him seven years after the fact. Or that he was trying to embellish the truth. The rest of his account exhibits the same hostility, but this time he endows his adversaries with it: "They chased me out of the studio, and specifically out of my editing room, but since I tried to get back into it every day, they called the police. Then the producer, who'd had an edit done in line with his ideas, realized that it wouldn't stand up and that the lesser of two evils was perhaps letting me do the job."[15] No one but someone blinded by admiration could take this story seriously. But it's significant that Renoir's telling of it substantiates the existence of an edit different from the one he wanted, thus providing serious reasons for the aggressiveness of his assumptions and for his desire to fog up the issue.

That desire never ceased as the years passed. At the beginning of the seventies, Renoir again brought up the idea that Richebé was expecting a comedy. "Seeing that he wasn't going to succeed in transforming the film into a laugh fest, the producer apparently backed down quickly about changing my edit."[16]

Returning to the issue in *My Life and My Films*, Renoir attributes

---

* André Girard is the father of the actor Danièle Delorme.

† It may have been *Baleydier*, with Michel Simon, directed by Jean Mamy from a script by André Girard.

responsibility for this other edit to "the enterprising Madame Batcheff," who did confirm the truth of the conflict between her and the director but limited its extent: "I had some intense discussions with him about the editing of a certain sequence. He pretended not to understand that it wasn't possible to create good continuity when the same sound occurred twice, on either side of a splice. His bad faith was obvious."[17] Denise Batcheff also makes clear that "Renoir was frustrated" because he was "deprived of his two muses" (Marguerite, his editor and companion, and her assistant, Suzanne de Troeye), but she omits explaining why and how these two women were banished from the editing room.

Renoir repeats the legend—created by him in 1938—of Richebé's "expecting a comedy," but this time he mentions Paul Fejos as well: "When he [Fejos] learned that I didn't agree, he refused."[18] He also recounts that certain "witnesses of this burglary" tried to impress upon him that he lacked distance from his film, which is probably a reference to the role he assigns Lestringuez in his story, and remembers that, having come "to the studio to straighten things out," he found "the entrance to the establishment guarded by two policemen who explained to me that their assignment was to keep me from entering." After spending "three days and three nights" wandering "around the bars of Montmartre, having decided romantically to find forgetfulness in drink," he ended up advised by Yves Allégret to summon Braunberger about it, and the latter is supposed to have recommended he inform "Monsieur Monteux."

Marcel Monteux, a fantastically wealthy shoe manufacturer by trade, was the president of Les Établissements Braunberger-Richebé, but about this meeting, Renoir barely reports anything except the intercession of the businessman's girlfriend: "Monteux met with me at the home of his companion, the scrumptious Berthe de Longpré, famous throughout Paris for her perfect breasts. When I told her the story of the trouble surrounding *La Chienne*, she grew indignant and insisted that her boyfriend immediately order Richebé to let me make my film as I intended."[19] Apparently, Renoir told *her*, and not *them*; and *she* was the one who *insisted*. This leads to the conclusion, then, that Berthe de Longpré and her superior mammaries exerted such considerable authority over Monsieur Monteux that he would immediately do her bidding, even within the domain of the professional or financial.

Renoir next confirms that the screening at the Palais Rochechouart did indeed take place and specifies that the viewing of it roused everyone's enthusiasm, especially that of a young noncommissioned hussar officer whose "drawn features"—which made him seem "on the edge of a nervous breakdown"—were those of Jacques Becker. Because Becker had performed his military service in 1926 and 1927, it's rather hard to see how and why, in 1931, he'd be wearing a hussar's uniform. Also, according to Renoir's account, Valentine Tessier, who was Pierre Renoir's mistress at the time, "was unrestrainedly sobbing," while, "in a trembling voice," Pierre was repeating, "That was really wonderful, Jean, that was so wonderful." What film did they see on that day? The one Renoir wanted or the one that was put together without him? The credits for the film with which we are familiar attribute "sound editing" to Denise Batcheff, who always insisted that she had done the definitive edit on *La Chienne* and then had collaborated with Paul Fejos on *Fantômas*.

In 1971, after Richebé's statements about his role in the production of *La Chienne*, Braunberger must have exploded and defended Renoir, who never stopped being his favorite director, equal to Godard starting at the end of the fifties. Thus, each of the two former partners had his say. In a letter to Charles David that has already been cited,[20] Braunberger wrote, "Though it may be clear that Richebé participated in certain films that we produced together, by his choice of actors and screenplay, I don't believe he participated in anything at all for *La Chienne*, until the double-track editing; the same for *On purge Bébé*, which he agreed to let me produce only to prove that Renoir could 'stick to a budget.'"

Another piece to be added to the case is a letter from Richebé to Braunberger, dated October 2, 1971: "I alone was able to sign him [Renoir] as 'director,' despite the opposing opinions around me, which came from the distribution network as well as from our clients. Why would I be unpleasant to Jean Renoir? Recalling forty years later that *La Chienne* was edited by an American director would be rather inelegant on my part. If this film hadn't been a success, there's no doubt that I would have heard talk about my intervening in it."[21] But Braunberger and Richebé don't stop there, and each tries to offer proof of the truth of his claims.

First, on the side of Richebé, who has often been treated poorly by history, partly because his nickname "Pauvre C . . . ,"* given to him by the ruthless Henri Jeanson, stuck: a letter dated November 4, 1971, in which Jean Paoli, in response to one of October 19, "quite gladly" confirms, "Though I may not have been present at the discussions that you had with Jean Renoir about the editing of the film, I did, however, know that you were making efforts to entrust this film to another director."[22] In that letter, Paoli also provides an account of the

---

* *Translator's note:* "Pauvre C . . ." = "*Pauvre Con.*" *Pauvre* means "poor" in French, in playful opposition to the syllable *Riche* (French for "rich") in Richebé's name. *Con* is French slang for the female organ but also used to imply stupidity, and a *pauvre con* translates as a "stupid bastard" or "stupid idiot." In addition, there is a logic in using a letter of the alphabet (*C*) as part of the nickname, because *bé*, the last syllable of Richebé's name, is how the letter *B* of the alphabet is pronounced in French.

screening at the Palais Rochechouart, the essentials of which Richebé adopts in his memoirs. Paoli finishes the story as follows: "He [Renoir] attended the event, made no commotion, and left the theater at the end of the show without sharing his impressions with me. So I concluded that he hadn't been displeased with the film." And another testimony, this one in manuscript, provided by "P. Martin, 18, bd de Grenelle, Paris 15ème": "This is a follow-up to our telephone conversation about the last stage of editing on *La Chienne*, the film directed by Jean Renoir in which I served as assistant editor. I can assure you that the last stage of the editing was supervised by M. Paul Féjos who also was preparing the direction of *Fantômas* at that time."[23]

Pierre Braunberger, on the other hand, appealed to Marguerite Houllé-Renoir, who delivered a handwritten affidavit on December 12, 1971, stating: "I the undersigned, Marguerite Renoir, certify that in my capacity as editor of the film *La Chienne*, directed by Jean Renoir, I was supervised by Pierre Braunberger, as I was for everything concerning the film."[24]

Although the exact truth may never be established, it should be noted that the editing difficulties Renoir experienced on several of his next films give the impression that, on the one hand, he was working as a beginner but that, on the other hand, the conceptions he was inventing at that time were likely to clash with certain conventions. To put it plainly, no one knew how to edit the shots he filmed, and he himself and Marguerite Houllé probably did not yet possess enough mastery for what was needed. In this regard, it should be recalled that eight years later, when people had had ample time to become accustomed to Renoir's ways, several sequences from *The Rules of the Game* were labeled by some as incomprehensible. Renoir was fascinated by a scene, by those instants when the life of the actors merged with that of the characters. His intention was to discover everything on the screen, the words in the room and the song in the street, the interior light and the light outside; and, for him, continuity was still a subsidiary preoccupation. It was at this point that Renoir found a style, and the searing intensity of that discovery allows for a discussion of the existence of a brilliant instinct.

With the assistance of proven technicians, including the great head cameraman Theodor Sparkuhl, who had worked in Germany with Lubitsch and Pabst, and the sound engineer Joseph de Bretagne, Renoir upset procedures that sound film had just established in the same way that his film jubilantly scrambled the playing cards of the game of society. The importance he attached to the direct recording of sound can explain why the studio technicians would insist on privileging certain shots, because they were more audible than the ones the director himself had chosen for their greater truth. Accordingly, Renoir directly recorded the song in the street that accompanies the murder as part of the task of using mixing to associate it with the dialogue between Janie Marèze and Michel Simon. And logically, the soundtrack also contains the noises of the street, the voices of passersby and the hum of car motors, which the technicians were, naturally, forced to reduce but without violating the director's wish to dispense with all effects created by postsynchronization. This despite the fact that the technique prevalent at the time instructed that a song be recorded in a studio and then mixed, or "blended," as it was called then, with the sounds recorded during filming—the dialogue and the noises that came from the movements of actors.

According to Renoir, that scene is also the only one in the film that was edited in contradiction with this principle: "The only big change is that at the moment of Lulu's murder, the song that can be heard is the one that was recorded in the studio, not the one recorded in the street."[25] Renoir had also chosen to film certain scenes using three cameras running simultaneously as a way of permitting the actors to play the entire scene without being interrupted. Because no one was yet accustomed to the requirements of sound film, and the primary concern was to reproduce dialogue audibly, the editing presented a puzzle. The miracle is that *La Chienne,* probably edited by Renoir and Marguerite, then by Denise Batcheff under the direction of Paul Fejos, actually became the masterpiece that we know.

It was a masterpiece that its leading lady would never see. In mid-August 1931, Renoir filmed the last exterior scenes in Paris on avenue Matignon,* but for Janie Marèze shooting had ended several days earlier. On August 15, at around four-thirty in the afternoon, the car in which she was riding went off the cliff road in the Massif de Maures, right at Cap des Sardinaux, a few miles from Sainte-Maxime. The young woman, who was returning from a luncheon in Val d'Esquières and who was expected at Sainte-Maxime to take part in a bathing beauty contest, was killed instantly. The other occupants of the vehicle were the actress's brother, the film journalist Lucie Derain, and "a fourth person" whose identity wasn't stated by most of the newspapers. The accident seemed to have been caused by a careless act on the part of the driver as he was trying to pass another vehicle. That was the information that appeared on the sixteenth in the Sunday editions of *Le Figaro* and *Le Petit Parisien,* among others. The papers also stated that although Janie Marèze's brother's hip had been broken and Lucie Derain was "very seriously injured," the fourth passenger was unharmed.

---

* It was during the shooting of a scene on avenue Matignon that Jacques Becker found Renoir and was able to become his assistant.

Only *Le Matin* gave the name of this mysterious figure on its front page, and he turned out to be the driver of the car. It was Georges Flamant, whose occupation of actor wasn't mentioned, most probably because *La Chienne,* his first film, was still unknown by audiences. The discreet omission observed by most of the papers could have originated with the pressures brought into play by the family of the actress's "generous gentleman."

A week later, on August 22, a detailed account of the accident appeared in *La Cinématographie française,* which reported that the actress's "vertebral column had been broken in two places" and which also confirmed that the car had been driven by Gilbert [*sic*] Flamant, "a new movie actor who had made his debut in *La Chienne.*" Even before that information appeared, everyone in the milieu of cinema knew that Georges Flamant, who'd been offered a magnificent automobile as his initial fee—or, according to another version, insisted on driving the actress's yellow convertible despite his hardly knowing how to drive—was in fact the driver and, without a doubt, was responsible for the incident. Long after, the mere mention of the name Janie Marèze produced the following reaction by Marcel Dalio as he came out of a showing of *La Chienne* in the seventies: "He killed her, he killed her."[26]

The conclusion was shared by Michel Simon, who noticed Flamant back from the South of France in Richebé's office two days later and threw himself on him with the intention of strangling him. But Braunberger claimed that Simon had taken a pistol from his pocket that he was planning to use to kill Renoir, whom he held responsible for the incident. "Kill me if that amuses you," Renoir supposedly responded. "I've made a film!"[27]

As for the film itself, it had to be presented to the public. If what its promoters said was true, theater owners didn't seem to be in a hurry to show it, because the name Renoir made them nervous or because the publicity surrounding Janie Marèze's death had unsettled them. Jean Paoli, in a letter to Richebé already cited, came forth with an unexpected explanation: "We had as much trouble with the distribution agency managers as we did with the theater owners in renting out *La Chienne.* At the time, Jean Renoir in his capacity as a director—and that isn't the only thing I can point to—wasn't very well thought of. *Le* [*sic*] *Chien andalou* hadn't been a success, which may have been the reason for that hostility."[28] Aside from imagining that Paoli thought *Un chien andalou* was the film Renoir made before *La Chienne,* we must assume that canines had a deplorable reputation among theater owners.

After his associate met with a refusal from Léon Belby, the owner of a theater on rue de Réamur whom he'd gone to see at his estate in Biot before screening the film for him at a theater Belby owned in Antibes, Richebé opted for a discreet release outside of Paris for starters. But in Nancy, the city he chose and where his films played at the Éden cinema, audience members protested against the immorality of the film and, according to some,[29] were planning to go to the point of smashing the seats. Or at least that is what Renoir would claim in 1938, identifying the troublemakers using such terms as "groups from the extreme right" and "fascists," in accordance with the terms then being used in the political camp for which he had become one of the standard-bearers.

Actually, *La Chienne* was shown at the Éden, not "for two days" as Renoir claimed because "the noise and tumult in the theater were enough to make the manager decide to take it off the bill,"[30] but from November 13 to 19, 1931, with a frequency of two showings a day.[31] What is more, the local papers made no mention of any kind of protest at all, nor did the professional journals, which were very much on the lookout for this kind of incident. To the contrary, and as had been expected, the film ran from Friday to Thursday. Advertising inserts appeared each day in the papers, calmly announcing that it was a show not meant for every audience. And the film was still playing in Nancy on the day of its Parisian premiere on November 17; the coinciding dates supply evidence that makes it doubtful that the opening in Nancy was done as a test. There's just nothing to nourish the legend complacently reproduced for years that claims that *La Chienne* was the object of scandal in Nancy. In any case, Renoir had left the showing of the film up to Léon Siritzky, a theater owner whom he had met through Marcel Pagnol.

Siritzky was Russian and had come to France in 1923. He had run some movie theaters in Turkey where his two sons, Sam and Jo, were born; but he had never been a "quartermaster in the Turkish navy" as Renoir claimed in his memoirs, stating that he had gotten that information from Pagnol. Contrary to what Renoir says, Siritzky's first French movie theater was not "a tiny place in a faraway suburb" but the Chanteclerc, at 76 avenue de Clichy. Léon Siritzky was also willing to program *La Chienne* in one of his theaters outside of Paris, the Royal Cinema in Biarritz. Renoir writes, "He began a launch of the film that was unusual. Using announcements in newspapers and on posters, he advised families not to go and see it. This horror show, he warned, wasn't for the tender-hearted."[32] From that notion to the idea that Siritzky accompanied the presentation of the film with a "negative" campaign is but a step, which Renoir took in part in his book, as well as in a cheerful manner for a screening of the film in 1956. He would claim the same thing in an interview with *Cahiers du cinéma*,[33] in which he stated that audiences were invited *not* to see *La Chienne:* "Make sure not to go and see this film, which is horrible." The anecdote is an amusing one, which was gallantly accepted to the letter by historians. And it is false.

Jo Siritzky, who was seventeen years old in 1931 and already working with his father, has supplied a follow-up to the legend: "We had only informed the public that the film was different from those to which people were accustomed and that its severity might shock. French cinema of that period was films like *La Bande à Bouboule* [*Bouboule's Gang*], *Le Costaud des P.T.T.*, or *Ma cousine de Varsovie;* and Jean's film had nothing to do with any of that. One of the rules of the profession is that any attempt to trick the audience will come back against the film. We warned the public, but we would have never advised it not to see a film!"[34] A short article by a local reporter for *Pour vous* that appeared several months later gave an account of the premiere of the film in Orléans: "*La Chienne,* which a conscientious management had indicated as too realistic for young people in Orléans, played to a jam-packed house. At any rate, the film is painful to watch, but is it immoral? Less dangerous, certainly, than one in which we see not exactly unshakeable virtue rewarded by marriage to a Prince Charming."[35]

Meanwhile, the success garnered on the Côte Basque, where *La Chienne* "held its own" for several weeks, convinced a movie theater in Paris, the Colisée, to run the film. In his book, Braunberger comes up with his own version of that. According to him, he was the one who "placed" the film at the Colisée, before the success it encountered convinced Richebé of the possibility of a release in the provinces. Whatever the case, *La Chienne* definitely ran at the Colisée beginning on November 17, 1931. In several French cities, the legions of decency protested against its being shown, especially at Saint-Quentin, where it provoked a stir several times. In Arras, the mayor took it upon himself to ban the film "to children and young people"; but according to *Le Croix,* the source of this information, the police did not "seem to have observed the decree with much severity."[36]

Critics as a whole declared themselves to be favorable and hailed Michel Simon's performance. Richard-Pierre Bodin, in *Le Figaro,* was the most lyrical: "Janie Marèze exists there, by miracle, and is murdered there; Simon pierces Janie Marèze's laugh, through her throat, with a letter opener, a laugh that won't end; then are there still more dead that have to be killed? Janie Marèze, a season of spring smashed to pieces just last summer; Janie Marèze, little dead girl of the screen; Janie Marèze, bringing your laugh back to us from the beyond; Janie Marèze *Chienne,* you'll be bringing it back again, from so far away."[37]

9

Fog and Shadow

La Nuit du carrefour (Night at the Crossroads)

In an article entitled "Souvenirs" that appeared in a special issue of the magazine *Le Point* in December 1938, Renoir recalled the months that followed directing *La Chienne* in the following terms: "Unfortunately for me, the battle that I had to undergo to get *La Chienne* on its feet had given me a reputation as a very cantankerous bedfellow, and after this film I had a lot of trouble finding work. I was thought of as impossible, capable of resorting to the worst kind of violence against any producer who didn't agree with me. I lived as well as I could and made a few low-quality films, until the moment came when Marcel Pagnol allowed me to shoot *Toni*."[1]

"A lot of trouble finding work"? Well, even before *La Chienne* was being shown on screens, Renoir had begun to write a new screenplay that he would direct in early 1932. Between *La Chienne* and *Toni,* those "few low-quality films" numbered four in two years: *Night at the Crossroads, Boudu Saved from Drowning, Chotard et Cie,* and *Madame Bovary,* the last of which Renoir made no mention of in 1938. What other highly motivated director exhibited activity of that caliber? It is the case that Renoir never hesitated to complain, often about his producers, and sometimes with reason. To boot, during that period, he seems to have experienced all the problems that a director could possibly encounter, and none of the films just cited were free of them. To the question of why it happened to him rather than to somebody else, there is only one answer: because he wasn't like the others and didn't view the art of film the way they did.

This discussion should start by examining the kind of problems caused for Renoir by the producers of *Night at the Crossroads.* He would write about it (while inexplicably placing it after, rather than before, *Boudu Saved from Drowning*): "After a period of involuntary unemployment, neither the first nor the last of such periods, I gave in to the temptation to produce a film myself. The money was coming to me from private sources that had nothing at all to do with the film industry."[2] If this last claim can give substance to the premise that nobody at the time wanted to give Renoir work, then it damages the legend spread by both Georges Simenon and Renoir about the direction of the film that puts blame on the stupidity of the producers. What producers, then?

The production company for *Night at the Crossroads* is listed in the credits as Europa Films. Created in 1932 by Robert Boulay, who was close to Marcel Pagnol, Europa Films produced only five movies before ceasing all activity in 1934. The first two films were Renoir's and *Direct au Coeur*, based on the play by Pagnol and filmed at Boulay's estate in the region of Sarthe. This means that the link between Pagnol and Renoir could have been established two years before the making of *Toni*. It could also have been that Europa Films was only a name borrowed for *Night at the Crossroads*, a hypothesis that would allow for the fact that Jacques Becker assumed the function of director of production—liaison between producer and film crew. To add to the enigma, the film is the only one ever distributed by the obscure Compagnie franco-coloniale cinématographique.

The source of funding is no less hazy. Renoir mentions "private sources," which Pierre Braunberger has identified as coming from a friend of Bernard Reichenbach's. One of the administrators of Les Établissements Braunberger-Richebé at the time, as well as being Braunberger's cousin and the father of future filmmaker François Reichenbach, Bernard Reichenbach is said to have met the generous donor for *Night at the Crossroads* on a racetrack. The man had a very pretty twenty-seven-year-old girlfriend named Winna Winfried, and he supposedly offered to finance the film if she could star in it. And yet, Winna Winfried had been born in Denmark and spoke French with a strong accent. However, Else Andersen, the character Winfried would play in *Night at the Crossroads*, based on the novel by Simenon, *is* a Dane. But had the meeting of Reichenbach and the generous lover of the beautiful Dane taken place before or after Renoir had made up his mind about making *Night at the Crossroads*? In the first case, it's possible to imagine that the contribution was important enough to jump-start the project for Renoir; but in the second, we are probably only talking about additional funding. It's doubtful we'll ever find out, but there remains a strong possibility that Renoir got hooked on Simenon's novel *after* he'd learned that casting a young Dane endowed with a rich and generous lover would benefit the financing of a film that he would direct.

A spate of coincidences and some good luck—both racetracks and production companies tend to keep things behind closed doors. Enough, in any case, to allow for the hypothesis that Renoir not only produced but also financed the film, at least in part. Thus, the shortcomings in the shooting of the film, which created doubts about the reliability of the producer and the director, not to mention its commercial failure occasioned enough reasons not to admit such involvement.

Renoir and Simenon had known each other for several years already. The author traces their friendship back to 1921, the year of the birth of Alain Renoir, whom Simenon claimed to have gotten to know while he was still in his mother's womb. Alain, on the other hand, pinpoints the meeting between his father and Simenon as being 1923. It's agreed that in the summer of 1931, Simenon sold the adaptation rights for his novel *La Nuit du carrefour* (*Night at the Crossroads*)—written in April of that year and appearing in June—directly to Renoir and not to Europa Films or some other production company. In his Bugatti, Renoir himself drove to Ouistreham, where Simenon was then living. He paid 50,000 francs for the rights, plus an additional half of that amount for the writer to participate in the adaptation.

A few weeks previously, Arthème Fayard, Simenon's publisher, had granted the producer Pierre Calmann-Lévy, the son of another publisher, the rights to *Le Chien jaune*, another Simenon novel with Inspector Maigret.[*] The two projects were developed at the same time—it's likely that their respective promoters began racing against each other to get their film onto the screen first—and Simenon was closely involved with both of them. Jean Tarride, the director of *Le Chien jaune*, communicated with the author about the various states of the screenplay, which was corrected and amended to a large extent by Simenon, who also discussed the progress Renoir was making on his adaptation of *Night at the Crossroads*.

Additionally, Simenon and Renoir worked closely together for several days during the winter, in the writer's villa in Antibes as well as at Les Collettes. The two kindred spirits understood each other so well that together they perfected a propaganda campaign designed to encourage the promotion of the film. For the release of *Night at the Crossroads*, they announced that they'd signed an agreement for the adaptation of nine novels by Simenon, for the sum of nine times 25,000 francs. From it, the writer, who was just beginning to become known, and the director, who outside the milieu of film was still only Auguste Renoir's son, would both gain a considerable amount of exposure; or would on the condition that *Night at the Crossroads* was a success.[3]

Simenon wasn't present during the filming of *Le Chien jaune* but would come to see Renoir during the *tournaison* (the word Renoir used to refer to the filmmaking activity[†]) of *Night at the Crossroads*. Although Jean Tarride's film went into production first, it wasn't released until July 1932, whereas Renoir's had already been released in April of the same year.

[*] *Translator's note: Maigret and the Yellow Dog is the English-language title of the film that would result.*

[†] *Translator's note: For an explanation of tournaison, see Translator's note on page 55.*

The two films were both family affairs. Jean Tarride had cast his father, Abel Tarride, in the role of Maigret; Renoir had cast his brother to play the inspector. As guaranteed by his contract, Simenon participated in the decisions. The film *Night at the Crossroads* became Pierre Renoir's first talkie, and Pierre also became the first Inspector Maigret in the history of film—and definitely the best.* The film was a family affair in another way as well, a family composed also and especially of cronies. Renoir rounded up people from his circle to take part in a project that was obviously financed on a shoestring budget. Jacques Becker as assistant director also doubled as director of production. Pierre Renoir's son Claude, who was only eighteen, was assistant cinematographer. The painter André Dignimont and the playwright and future critic Michel Duran had acting roles. Mimi Champagne, Pierre Champagne's widow, was "script girl." The critic and cinema historian Jean Mitry lent a hand, whereas Marguerite, of course, was responsible for the editing.

As much as this was a film crew, it was also a fun-loving band of friends. After having filmed the interior scenes at the Billancourt studios, they moved in together about twenty miles north of Paris, at the Carrefour de la Croix-Verte in Bouffémont. That month of February 1932 was rainy and cold. The fog rarely lifted before nightfall, which occurred in the middle of the afternoon every day and created nights that felt endless, which they all spent drinking and eating before deciding to go back to their hotel. Their rooms were at a local residence, or—if Renoir can be believed—a barn, where each of them somehow managed to set up some kind of quarters. Unless, that is, the troop leader decreed that the night was good for the *tournaison*, because the story took place mostly after dark. The atmosphere wasn't unlike those first shoots in Marlotte, minus the sun and comfort, and in addition to a few technical and financial imperatives. "I don't think," Renoir would write, "that there's a place on earth more depressing. Those few houses lost in an ocean of fog, rain, and mud are wonderfully described in the novel.† They could have been painted by Vlaminck."[4]

Marcel Lucien's images justify these impressions; *Night at the Crossroads* is a drowned film. The sound seems to have been recorded in an aquarium, to the point at which the dialogue becomes practically inaudible at times. The plot becomes more and more complicated as it follows the investigation led by Maigret after a certain Carl Andersen discovers, in a car belonging to his neighbor but inexplicably parked in Andersen's garage, the corpse of a diamond merchant from Antwerp. The victim's widow is also murdered after she arrives

* In 1957, Renoir would briefly mention a remake of *Night at the Crossroads*, with José Ferrer as Maigret and Leslie Caron as Else Andersen.

† It rains often in Simenon's novels but very little in *Night at the Crossroads*.

on the scene. The action is confined to the area around the crossroads and the mysterious Else Andersen, Carl's sister, who seems to pull all the men into the aura surrounding her. Maigret himself is not immune to the poisonous charms of the beautiful Else.

Pierre Renoir and Winna Winfried share two scenes in particular that are among the most erotic in Renoir's entire oeuvre. The firefly-like mien of the young woman is accentuated as much by the actress's inexperience and her accent as by the towering appearance of the actor and his extraordinary mastery of his art. The turmoil that afflicts Maigret when the beautiful Else attempts to seduce him—clearly visible on Pierre Renoir's face when he's with Winna Winfried—constitutes one of the great moments of the cinema of Renoir. Renoir himself took immense pleasure in choosing Jacques Becker to help the beautiful actress try on various articles of lingerie, those diaphanous negligees and transparent slips in which she appears on-screen. And he took even more pleasure in letting everyone know that he was entrusting his assistant with such a "risqué"[5] assignment.

Renoir indulged in the manipulative aspect of directing on the sidelines as well. As both crew and gang leader, he was excited by the sight of the relationships that were forming, the flirtations, and the marital strife. He played the director as demiurge, feeding on the swerves of the lives of his characters, actors, and partners; and he delayed that moment of climax when everything would suddenly escape his hands.

Renoir made film by giving his actors their freedom because he respected them for a talent and stature that impressed him or because he was discovering them to the extent that they were becoming aware of themselves. He gave his crew the same complete latitude, seizing with delight some of the finds each of them was able to offer. For example, assistant director Jacques Becker was able to use his technical expertise to piece together from an old factory transformer the generator that production wasn't able to provide; he also shot the scenes of night chases by himself from the wheel of a Torpedo—and twenty years later this was what would enthrall future directors of the Nouvelle Vague, Jean-Luc Godard being the first among them.

Renoir's policy as team leader held that ideas that popped into his head weren't automatically worth more than those that came from others. In the case of a number of productions, whether experimental or not, moving the equipment was primarily the concern of the head cinematographer, who usually ended up deciding between a panoramic shot and a tracking shot. But Renoir liked to keep the camera running for a long time and understood the unforeseen shift that a scene could take during the relationship that builds up between a performer and his character or between one actor and another. This is what continued to fascinate him, much more than the linkage of scenes making up the film, something that often was difficult to maintain during editing, even if Marguerite was present at the shoot and was able to attempt, in advance, to form an idea of the whole by seeing the parts.

The very conditions of the shoots and the atmosphere that Renoir tried to create are enough for us to imagine how much *Night at the Crossroads* is a film that was inundated, but not just by rain. It is marked by conflicts similar to those that assailed the editing and the release of *La Chienne*, but it is free of Richebé's and Braunberger's involvement; so, the director let himself go a bit more than usual, enough to lose track at times exactly where he was in his film. Recovering from that would turn out to be brutal.

The first screening of *Night at the Crossroads* was organized in March 1932. Simenon was invited, and a few days later he announced himself charmed.[6] Another guest, Pierre Braunberger, who hadn't participated in the production, found the film incomprehensible at times and suggested that a reel might be missing. Of course not; it's all there, Renoir responded. Shooting script in hand, Braunberger noticed that about a dozen pages hadn't been filmed. A simple oversight? Perhaps.

The question of the incoherence of the plot was broached much more frequently back then than it is today, in any case—and still more so when Simenon's novel, which is also not crystal clear, was referenced. A number of screenwriters would find themselves confronted by this realization, saying that the adaptations required a "dissection" of the books, which brought to the fore gaps in Simenon's narratives, impossibilities, and dramatic dead-ends that weren't noticed while reading. Audiences of 1932 did not see a film by Jean Renoir in *Night at the Crossroads* but a detective film, and they were expecting to grasp each of the turns of plot that today's spectator is able to think of as secondary.

Another explanation of the issue was furnished several years later by Jean Mitry, who remembered having misplaced two reels he'd been given to take to the laboratory.[7] If this is true, it would mean that those two reels alone contained precisely all the shots having to do with the scenes judged missing, the lack of which no one before had been advised. This hypothesis is difficult to believe, as is one that was also advanced that claimed mishandling resulted in loading the camera with reels that had already been shot. Other kinds of negligence during the shoot on the part of the script girl and Marguerite and Renoir seem more plausible. Simenon gave substance to this after the death of Renoir by claiming that the latter was drunk practically morning to evening on the set. But we can decide simply to see in the film what Renoir shot, with its possible faults and its extraordinary qualities, the former mostly the flip side of the latter.

This film of fog and shadow, whose characters are less people than figures come out of a night to which they seem in a hurry to return, celebrates the triumph of the amorphous over the illusory psychological clarity of behavior that film usually claims to document. Renoir's personal situation at that moment in his life and his career, the difficulties he encountered every day and night on the shoot, his entourage's inexperience—all contributed to making a film with the abstract qualities of a beautiful concerto of sound and image. The slant is the same as the one the director followed for *Nana,* one other film on which he wasn't perfectly in his element. This quality, which is essentially Renoirian, is echoed by the other great Simenon adaptation of the period, characterized by an abstract dimension just as gripping: Julien Duvivier's *La Tête d'un homme.* No less so is the kinship of the two films, down to the two directors' habit of leaving the essential action out of the field of the camera, as in that insanely unsettling scene in Duvivier's film where Maigret interrogates a suspect in a car, and the only thing seen on-screen is the car window with the landscape flowing by behind it.

The author, on the other hand, appreciated Duvivier's film no more than he did Renoir's, and certainly no more than *Le Chien jaune,* which also does not entirely deserve its paltry reputation. In fact, Simenon retracted the favorable opinion produced by the initial screening of Renoir's film quickly enough. In September 1932, he stated in *Pour vous,* "*Le Chien jaune* and *Night at the Crossroads* are failed films. It's not the fault of those who made them, but of those who paid them to. Or more specifically: the fault of the rules and the imbeciles who made them." At the time, Simenon had just given up his decision to bring *La Tête d'un homme* to the screen on his own, giving as his reason the fact that "the producers" had paid him with checks that weren't backed up by capital. At the time, he wanted Pierre Renoir to play Maigret again, but Duvivier preferred Harry Baur for the role. So . . . the producers. Always the producers. But once again, who were the producers of *Night at the Crossroads?*

Simenon's opinion would doubtlessly have been different if Renoir's film had been a success. Released on April 21, 1932, in two Paris theaters, the Théâtre Pigalle and the Élysée-Gaumont, *Night at the Crossroads* divided the critics and had mediocre appeal for audiences, who were disoriented by the film and left unsatisfied.

Thirty-two years later, Renoir would declare in *Cahiers du cinéma,* "It's obvious that the result is a film that is rather incoherent; besides, it couldn't be finished for lack of money. But in the end, that incoherence for which it has so been reproached comes particularly, I believe, from the method used to shoot it, that kind of Commedia dell'arte method, I mean."[8] The words *method* and *commedia dell'arte* certainly wouldn't have occurred to him in spring 1932, right after he had just experienced another commercial failure for which he was probably aware he bore most of the blame.

10

Boudu Priapus Simon

Boudu sauvé des eaux (Boudu Saved from Drowning)

"I'm not making up the room of that man with a female monkey!" The lady from Marlotte whose job it was to do the housekeeping in the Saint-El villa would have rather quit her job than agree to do it. And the fact that the man was none other than Michel Simon certainly did not make her change her point of view. The female monkey's name was Zaza. Gossips prattled that there was a relationship between actor and animal that was "against nature," which Michel Simon tried to deny, but which certain snippets gleaned through closed doors substantiated. For example, Alain Renoir remembered a day he was with his father on the stairs to the apartment where the actor was staying, on the last story of a building on Place Jean-Baptiste-Clément, right at the top of the Butte Montmartre. They heard Simon sharply upbraiding Zaza for her incomprehensible unwillingness; what could possibly be the reason for her refusing to give her master, using her feet, the caresses she usually lavished on him using her hands?[1] Zaza's death in 1936 at the age of four and a half left disconsolate the actor who had raised her at the breast (of his dog).[2] Standing behind a camera, the right index (finger—not toe) pointed at her forehead, she appeared on the logo for Les Productions Michel Simon, a company created in January 1932 with offices at 40 rue François-Ier.

To Georges Chaperot, of the magazine *Candide,* whom he received with Jean Renoir in his dressing room at the Théâtre du Gymnase in February 1932, the actor-turned-producer announced that he and Renoir had developed a project for film to be written by Jacques Deval, entitled *Émile;* as well as another based on a subject by Derain, *N'Bongo;* and, finally, an adaptation of *Le Jugment dernier* by Pierre Henri Cami, the delightful humorist from the city of Pau mostly known as the author of the matchless *À lire sous la douche.** The two buddies also had plans for a *Hamlet* derived less from Shakespeare than from Jules Laforgue; but none of these projects would come to be. *Boudu Saved from*

---

* *Translator's note:* Literally, "For Reading under the Shower."

Drowning wasn't yet mentioned, but it would be the only film Michel Simon produced.

Before that, in November 1931, Renoir had been telling Nino Frank about the actor. "We have a superb understanding of each other; he hates the outrageous complications of the world of film as much as I do ... and we really want to remain independent. We have the capital, the screenplays, and we know what we want. You know what a wonderful comic actor Simon is; so we're going to make a comedy every year. I know I'm more successful with dramas; but are you taking into account Simon's phenomenal *vis comica*?"[3] At this moment in Renoir's career, he seemed more enamored of *la politique des acteurs* than *la politique des auteurs* with which critics who came later would associate him.

Michel Simon continued his constant appearances onstage, but he had also just experienced great success in the movies thanks to *Jean de la lune*, the adaptation of a play by Marcel Achard that was released on March 6, 1931. The film is credited to Jean Choux, but the actor, who debuted the role, claimed responsibility for the film, too—and was probably right in doing so. The casting of Madeleine Renaud and René Lefèvre, the two whom Simon played opposite during the tour of the show in North Africa in spring 1930, was the fruit of his efforts. He had very closely collaborated with Achard on the film adaptation, and nothing happened during the shoot without his permission. The experience had endowed him with a conception of film that his reputation and popularity gave him the right to test with a director whom he did not consider an underling but a partner on his level.

Consequently, the influence exercised by the actor isn't reflected solely in the mirror Jean Renoir held out to him. True as it may be that Boudu seems like a possible continuation of Legrand in *La Chienne*, Michel Simon—as much on the stage as on the screen—taps another vein that irrigates the artistic creation of a period whose historical and socioeconomic characteristics abound.

The year 1932 in France is distinguished by the collapse of nearly a third of the country's industrial production, the delayed effect of a financial crisis that had been impacting Europe for several years and that had been having a worse effect on German society since before 1929. By 1932, Germany had six million unemployed, and France, two million.* Although French cinema still produced 157 films in 1932, which supplied the 2,246 theaters that possessed the equipment for sound film, the number of German productions—175 for that same year—had sharply dropped. Between 1929 and 1936, French revenue decreased by 30 percent, but the economic politics of each successive government, which

---

* The official figures were considerably minimized and claim it was four times less.

privileged the interests of the upper classes, continuously created the illusion that, if it was in fact true that France was feeling the crisis, it was suffering less than most of the other countries, victims of the repercussions of flight capital that was arriving and increasing French gold reserves. These amounted to 37 billion francs in 1929 and equaled 56 billion in 1931. The May 1932 elections showed an upsurge in parties on the Left, which were too divided to keep governmental instability from increasing. The financial crisis began appearing in the streets of French cities, on which the disenfranchised became familiar figures.

In 1929, the year of his first talkie, Michel Simon played a tramp in the film *Pivoine* by the avant-garde documentarian André Sauvage. The film was never finished, and only a few rushes survive. They show the actor bearded as he would be when he played Boudu, dragging his cart along the banks of the Seine. That same year, on April 16, Simon played Clotaire, a.k.a. Cloclo, the character in *Jean de la lune*, opposite Louis Jouvet (whose hair had been dyed red for the role of Jeff), Valentine Tessier, and Pierre Renoir. Some critics reproached him for adapting the play, but most of them congratulated him for it and the public fell in love with this brash scrounger. A year after *Boudu* he'd become Papa Jules, the father, in *L'Atalante*, a libertarian bargeman and anarchist covered in tattoos. The history of that period of French film can also be told through the figure of Michel Simon.

To this list of portrayals another needs to be added. In fact, when Simon played Boudu for the first time on March 30, 1925, on the stage of the Théâtre des Mathurins, the play by René Fauchois had already existed for nearly six years, starting at the Théâtre des Célestins in Lyon on July 15, 1919, and already revived in 1923, with Fernand-René playing Boudu in both productions. Actually, Simon played Boudu on the stage only about thirty times, but his performance was a triumph, and the columnist for *Paris-Midi* used such terms to describe him as "a figure out of Tolstoy" and "a cartoon Christ" before concluding, "When he scratches himself, Michel Simon makes the entire audience scratch themselves."[4]

It can't be said for certain that René Fauchois also appreciated the interpretation of an actor whose "cannibalization" of the work pointed to a different direction than Fauchois had established. Fauchois obviously identified with the good bookseller Lestingois, the role that he had reserved for himself—the man who saves Boudu from drowning at the beginning of the play. Like Louis-Ferdinand Céline, Robert Coquillaud (a.k.a. Le Vigan), and Marcel Aymé, who would describe the scene in his story *Avenue Junot* (1950), Fauchois was a regular at the painter Gen Paul's studio, and that made him a denizen of Montmartre like Renoir. But the resemblance between the playwright and the director stopped there. Also, just as Renoir's version of *La Chienne* often deviated from La Fouchardière's novel, Renoir and Simon's *Boudu Saved from Drowning* departed from the play that had inspired it.

The adaptation, which Renoir alone took credit for, but to which the future director Albert Valentin contributed, only retained the two first acts of Fauchois's text, concentrating them and making them denser. The prologue and epilogue were invented by Renoir, although the broad outline of the play seems to have been respected to the letter. On the other hand, particularly when it came to the spirit of the piece, Renoir and Fauchois were almost completely at odds. Most importantly, in Fauchois's eyes, Lestingois saves Boudu not only from drowning but also from the life he was leading; whereas in the film, Boudu turns down his protector's offer to become a member of the middle class. Extremely dissatisfied with the film, which he'd seen at a private screening, Fauchois made haste to put his play on stage again, this time accompanied by a fourth act in which Boudu gets Madame Lestingois pregnant, then prevents her from killing herself in an attempt to escape what only she sees as a disgrace, whereas everyone around her, starting with her husband, adjusts superbly to the situation. This new draft, in which Fauchois would take the role of the bookseller and Fernand-René the part of Boudu, would be shown in November 1932, while *Boudu Saved from Drowning* was still playing on screens. Fauchois's hope was that it would keep his thunder from being stolen and also give him the opportunity to hammer in a point of view that had just been torn down by the film.

One of the necessary conditions for the success of the adaptation was connected to the personality of the performer who would play Lestingois. Opposite the "monstrous" Boudu that Michel Simon was intending to create with total freedom, only a high-powered actor stood a chance; and for that reason the choice of Charles Granval turned out to be all-important. Michel Simon was probably responsible for it. At the time, Granval was the husband of Madeleine Renaud, who was eighteen years younger than he and was also the actress who played opposite Simon in *Jean de la lune*. The fact that *Boudu* was only Granval's fourth appearance in film,[*] and the first in talkies, lends substance to the hypothesis. Madeleine Renaud presented Granval as an "anarchist," whose productions and stagings at the Comédie-Française exhibited a daring that repeatedly earned him boos from the audience of subscribers.[5] Jean-Louis Barrault, Madeleine Renaud's second husband, held Granval to be one of his three major influences, next to Charles Dullin and Antonin Artaud. According to Barrault, he embodied "emotion, mind, and courage, what an artist is."[6] Therefore, this film

---

[*] After *Le Traitement du hoquet* (1917) and *Mademoiselle de la Seiglière* (1920, directed by the theater figure André Antoine) and *Le Coeur magnifique* (1921).

was a chance to witness the confrontation between two "anarchist" actors; but the main issue was balance among the characters, necessary to the mechanics of the comedy and in line with the world according to Renoir: everyone has his reasons, of course, and one person's reasons are worth just as much as another's.

A certain reputation for *Boudu* has been established over the years that suggests that the film is deliberately taking the side of the unconventional dropout against the bookseller, and even that the film can only be understood as a vindication of nonconformity. The thesis has been upheld by numerous commentators, especially American, but on-screen the position doesn't appear to be as clear-cut.

Unlike the bankers and art dealers in *La Chienne,* Lestingois does not in the least belong to the exploitive class. His shop and his apartment, which he almost never leaves, preferring to gaze at the world—and especially its pretty women—with a telescope, are his only field of action. He truly loves books and knows how to behave generously, especially with Boudu, but also with the poor student played by Jean Dasté (who will have the role of the captain in *L'Atalante*), whom he gives a book by Voltaire that the young man can't pay for. If Anne-Marie, the lively maid, appealingly played by Séverine Lerczinska (a young actress whom, it seems, only Renoir will ever cast in films),* allows Lestingois some liberties that her position as employee perhaps keeps her from refusing, she has still adjusted extremely well to an affair with a bookseller whose waning energies too often deprive her of pleasure. Lestingois is not a bad bloke, then. In fact, he might even have all that's required to be a decent fellow. Yes, he is a little ridiculous at times—that can't be denied—but is there anyone who never is? Not to mention how easy it is for anyone watching to tell that Lestingois's wife has lost all attraction for him. As Madame Lestingois, Marcelle Hainia is perfect in this her first role on-screen, which is in line with the fact that the majority of the cast for this film came primarily from the theater. At first she bears a vague resemblance to Madame Legrand in *La Chienne,* and that impression is strengthened by the setup of the initial situation, precisely recalling the one in the earlier film—until Boudu reawakens her sleeping senses. The bookseller's wife never acts truly afraid of her husband's guest, nothing more than expressing the fact that he disturbs her routines—before she soon finds herself aroused by him.

Although Lestingois fantasizes himself as Priapus in the opening scene and makes Anne-Marie his Chloé, to the tune of Bacchus's flute, as soon as the union between Boudu and Anne-Marie is considered sanctified by marriage, the bookseller bestows the name Priapus on the new groom. It's a conclusion

---

* Séverine Lerczinska plays a peasant in *La Marseillaise.*

that is only temporary, but one that Lestingois was anticipating, actually imagining that someday a young shepherd could come and take away his Chloé. No one can resist Priapus, the maid no more than the wife, and even less so today's audience, who are often inclined to applaud from their armchair behavior they would tolerate in their living room with less kindness than Mme. Lestingois does in her apartment. The shiver that runs down the spine of a petit bourgeois confronted from a distance with attitudes that morality and a good education condemn has something to do with the audience's fascination for Boudu, an obnoxious tramp with whom they end up empathizing more easily than with a bookseller they are amused to see ridiculed. But isn't the hold Boudu has on the audience just like the one to which Lestingois submits, as he, too, is bowled over by an absence of principles and a behavioral freedom in which the life he has been given forbids him to indulge? Neglecting the special nature of the relationship Lestingois forms with Boudu leads to assuming previous to the facts that Renoir's sympathy is deliberately bestowed on the latter. It isn't as simple as that.

Like Boudu, Renoir was attracted to water, the ideal vector for abandonment to nature that he professed by often borrowing his father's metaphor as his own: "You have to let yourself go in life as if you were a cork in the current of a brook."[7] Like Boudu, Renoir endowed laziness with the cardinal virtues. In this, however, there is nothing that could lead to seeing him as an anarchist.

The closeness between Renoir and Michel Simon could have been absolute,[8] but that doesn't necessarily mean that all the actor's ideas were in agreement with the director's. As a result, in Simon's eyes, the film didn't go as far as he'd hoped. He came out and said as much in November 1932 even before the movie had been released: "For the movie adaptation, there were some radical revisions, especially in the shifting of the main character, who became Boudu. Personally, I would have liked to have seen the character of the poor wretch made rich. That would have led to some larger-than-life scenes, at a banquet for tramps, for example. Because the man provided with money and not yet aware of its value would very naturally have done things in a big way. I clashed with Renoir about this issue because he didn't share my way of seeing it. But I'm sure that this is a case of the bad leading to the good because that will let us create a sequel someday to the first Boudu, if he becomes a hit."[9]

In 1938, listing his favorite movies, the actor mentioned *La Chienne* and forgot to include *Boudu*, which Renoir as well ignored that same year but which Simon included a year later in his personal honor role. "From Boudu I have learned," he confessed in 1939, "that one of the attitudes to take toward society is to loathe it."[10] Although Renoir might at times have called the social order into question, it doesn't mean that he "loathed" a society he certainly couldn't reproach for not having pampered him. That is the reason why the denunciation of bourgeois humanism in the film may appear sterile and the celebration of nonconformity lacking generosity at times. The man who chose to entrust the education of his only child to two tutors—one a Communist teacher and the other a priest—appreciated the middle way and was looking for a balance, even to the point, at times, of placing himself in the situation of a tightrope walker.

Boudu does not ruin the Lestingois family; the family merely reconfigures itself as a unit after its encounter with disorder. The bookseller ends up in the same situation he was in initially, surrounded by his two women, except that the maid has now become a widow, as it were, and the wife has rediscovered desire. Besides, what kind of disorder are we talking about? Boudu's exploits are, essentially, limited to ransacking the kitchen, spitting in a first edition of Balzac's *The Physiology of Marriage*, eating sardines in oil with his fingers, and polishing his wax-coated shoes with a satin bedspread—the last two stunts had no trouble arousing the intense disapproval of audiences in 1932. The scene in which Boudu screws (off camera) the middle-class woman on the bed in which she sleeps with her husband, on the other hand, received applause on the level with those prompted by the best moments in perfectly choreographed vaudeville. That's what it is, in fact; and we only need put this moment side by side with the one in *L'Atalante* in which Michel Simon simultaneously frightens and melts Dita Parlo, his boss on the barge, to appreciate what Renoir's film owes to boulevard comedies. Renoir's and Simon's desire to play with that tradition—be it by ironic appraisal—is emphasized by the line from the song, "In winter's gentle breeze, all the birds will freeze . . . ,"* chosen deliberately for the purpose of ridicule† and representing its motif in the form of a hackneyed refrain.

Boudu's dominant characteristic, obviously more than the distrust about money that he displays, could be his ingratitude, noted by the maid in passing. It's a quality that is also responsible for his modernity and that links him to other disenfranchised Renoirian characters. At the beginning of the film, when he has just opened the car door for a rich motorist and is getting tired of waiting for a tip that isn't coming, he gives the man the change that a little girl has handed him shortly before; and when the rich fellow wants to know why, he recycles the answer that the kid gave him: "So you can buy some bread." Nothing supplied him by the Lestingois family gives rise to any thank you on his part. He greets the sardines, bread, and butter he asked for with a furious "that didn't come too

---

* *Translator's note:* For the sake of rhyming in English, translation of those lyrics isn't wholly literal. The actual French is *"En hiver, dans les bois, les oiseaux meurent de froid . . . "* ("In winter, in the woods, the birds are dying of cold . . . ").

† At the time, according to Renoir, it was a big hit at the Casino de Paris.

early" and takes little time arriving at the conclusion that if Lestingois has taken him in, "it's because he needed a servant."

The probable and, eventually, minor difference in point of view between Simon and Renoir hinges on the fact that Simon took the "philosophical" dimension of the tale very seriously, whereas Renoir saw *Boudu* as a pretext for directing a joyful, liberated comedy with a brilliant actor, a film whose spirit is closer in this aspect to *On purge Bébé* than it is to *La Chienne*. Such a parallel removes none of the admiration for a film whose greatness is also due to the fact that it doesn't boil down to its analysis, a film that shows the first assertion of a style whose foundations were laid by *La Chienne*. First and foremost, the spirit of *Boudu* as well as the themes it tackles and the characters it brings to life are in harmony more than any previous films with Renoir's style. The very conditions of the film's direction were especially favorable to that style's being discovered.

Renoir plunges this fictional character of pure poetry, this tramp who never existed and never will other than on the screen, into real life as only Legrand was able to do before at moments in the film *La Chienne*. Boudu is first seen by the bookseller from his window. Michel Simon wanders along the quays in front of the secondhand booksellers' racks. To make such a view from the window possible, the bookseller's shop and his apartment had to be located precisely where the Institut de France stands. It's a tampered perspective, therefore, because Lestingois's bookshop is located on the quai Malaquais, which is farther away from the Pont des Arts than the film makes you think. But this is of little importance. Boudu/Simon is caught by the camera in the crowd of passersby, who don't spot him, a moment of infinite grace that Renoir said he was willing to dispense with, because directing it seemed impossible to him, until Jacques Becker suggested filming from a car. Therefore, it was the assistant director who was responsible for this long tracking shot in which film blends with life to the point of being mistaken for it. In the same way, the onlookers crowding the quay and the bridge while Lestingois is saving Boudu from drowning are in all evidence witnessing something that is less a rescue, which would have filled their eyes with fear and excitement and provoked cries and shouts, than it is the sight, still rare at the time, of a film being shot. In this as well, *Boudu* is like no other French film of its time.

Strangely enough, the path through Paris indicated by the film—and by a director who, after this, will no longer film the Paris of his time except for those moments in *The Crime of Monsieur Lange*—corresponds to the evolution of filmmaking in France in the months that would follow.

Boudu begins in the west of Paris in the Bois de Boulogne, where Boudu's dog disappears. A posh neighborhood, in other words, which was the usual setting for bourgeois dramas that were the typical French production of the time. It ends at the outskirts of the city, in the east, next to Nogent-sur-Marne, the land of dance halls and little white wines you gulp down at a café counter, the same place where Marcel Carné made the film *Nogent, Eldorado du dimanche* in 1929, and where Duvivier would place the characters in *La Belle Équipe* (*They Were Five*) in 1936. This is how Renoir, in the same stroke, revived in the space of one scene themes painted by his father and heralded the kind of films that were to come. And if the lady pushing a stroller in the Bois de Boulogne is none other than Geneviève Becker, Jacques's wife, and the child in the car their Sophie, the man at the end of the film rowing a young woman in a little boat while the wedding party leaves and their boat is capsized really is Georges Darnoux,* an assistant on *Boudu* and the future actor in the role of the seducer of Henriette in *A Day in the Country*.

Contrary to what's claimed by a legend, maintained mostly by Michel Simon and Henri Langlois, which Claude Gauteur's research fortunately demolished, *Boudu* did not close after three days at the Colisée, where it had opened on November 11, 1932, but after three weeks, after which it continued its run at the Pagode. At the time, the advertising posters displayed, "The adventure of *Boudu Saved from Drowning:* from poignant, to sentimental, to hilarious." If the film suffered in the press from competition from Julien Duvivier's *Poil de carotte* (*The Red Head*) and *The Champ* (with Wallace Beery and Jackie Cooper), as well as Clarence Brown's *Susan Lenox: Her Fall and Rise* (with Greta Garbo and Clark Gable), which came out at the same time, it wasn't neglected, either.

The legend goes that *Boudu Saved from Drowning* attracted the ire of critics, but the truth is that the opinions covered the spectrum in fairly equal shares. Among the admirers of the work, Jean Marguet, whose review in *Le Petit Parisien* on November 11, 1932, "Where M. Jean Renoir's Style Comes into Its Own," stated,

> M. Jean Renoir has given film a very special place. The son of the great painter Auguste Renoir, he himself is also a subtle artist and is not afraid to dare. Wasn't it he who, in his first film, *The Whirlpool of Fate,* treated a dream in such an original way that it became a classic? After that, it was *Nana,* and his last film, *La Chienne,* in which M. Jean Renoir gave proof of great skill. He's fond of realism, and sometimes, regrettably, his desire for it pushes him into excess. His most recent film, *Boudu Saved from Drowning,* isn't free of this fault but is still marked by very substantial

---

* Under his real name, Georges d'Arnoux, he was the one who jumped into the Seine in place of Boudu/Simon.

progress. . . . There is no doubt about it, M. Jean Renoir is one of our most original directors.

Some of those who didn't like *Boudu* said they regretted their reaction. In the November 20 issue of *Le Figaro*, Jean Laury wrote,

> I sincerely admire the raw talent of Jean Renoir, his realist's interpretation of life, his placid disregard for "what audiences will say." *La Chienne* was a great, grim, human film, which created interest and dislike but left a strong impression. As far away from us as the type of people he presented, we admitted, without being able to put it to the test, that some of their needs could exist, that one or another instinct would come forth. Crime, which is inexcusable, is made understandable. . . . I didn't understand *Boudu.* . . . My incomprehension made me ill at ease; I tried but did not succeed in resolving the problem of the character of M. Lestingois as kindness; but the dominant trait of such a character is more likely to be unconscious sadism, and it's unpleasant to attribute such a thing to his placid persona. In *Boudu Saved from Drowning*, Jean Renoir invites us to fish in troubled waters.

Contrary to what was claimed in the fifties, the film did not cause a scandal in 1932, no more than *La Chienne* did. *Boudu* isn't shocking. It seems absurd, and it isn't understood. Eight years later, several critics of *The Rules of the Game* would express the same incomprehension.

Aside from lamenting over the display of "appalling" morals, several of the attacks leveled against *Boudu* reproached Renoir for snooping in the direction of René Clair, and *À nous la liberté* in particular, which had been released with success in December 1931. Accordingly, Odette Pannetier in *Ric et Rac* wrote on November 19,

> This film would have needed a René Clair with dictatorial powers. I don't know whose job it was to edit and cut the film, but this worthy figure was clearly loathe to delete the slightest section of film, and the whole thing produces the impression of stretching out before us much more than unfolding before us. With this screenplay, one could obtain an excellent film. It can't be said that the result was bad. It's not comedy; it's long, and all we are is impatient for it to come to an end so we can get out of there. I'll add that the entire audience of the Colisée was purely of the same mind as me. Right behind my seat, a gentleman was telling his wife rather ingenuously, "Obviously, luck isn't with us. Yesterday, Pirandello, and today this ridiculous movie. . . ." I'm perfectly happy for Michel Simon and Jean Renoir to consider such a parallel a great compliment, because it's the only one I can give them as well.

The reference to Pirandello is amusing, but the excessively long reproach is surprising, applied as it is to a film that is short (less than ninety minutes) and that actually seems very compressed. Where the supposed "defect" lies, on the other hand, is singled out by several other critics. Jacques Chabannes, for example, writing on November 18 in *La Semaine à Paris*:

> To end the film, which as a whole is entertaining, if a bit long, and which he has adapted from the play by René Fauchois, *Boudu Saved from Drowning*, M. Jean Renoir bore in mind *À nous la liberté*. But if the last few meters of *À nous la liberté*, windswept on the road, could be the best part of this astonishing film, the rehash that Jean Renoir pulled from it, as an epilogue to *Boudu*, goes on too long at the end of this film. There would be no disadvantage in cutting it. A few other lengthy passages could also be pruned from the film here and there.

That is the origin of the hypothesis that there was a second edit of *Boudu*, after the release in November. Evidence supplied belatedly by the director Jean Devaivre gives substance to it. After having said that two years after the filming the studio technicians were still nauseated by the memory of the scene with sardines in oil ("All the props smelled rancid. You could puke."),[11] the future director of *La Dame d'onze heures* (1948) and *La Ferme des sept péchés* (*The Farm of Seven Sins*, 1949) likes to remember having been put to work with the task of severely shortening the film, whose duration he claimed was then two hours: "I also cut nearly six hundred meters, which equals around twenty minutes; no complete sequences, just material from inside some shots or scenes. Films had to play a maximum of an hour and a half for there to be six continuous showings in place of five when it played exclusively at a theater. If I had refused to make the cuts in *Boudu*, someone else would have done it. I don't think I managed to do it too badly because the film, which was not releasable in the state it was in and was recut by me, became a classic." The trouble for Devaivre, whose memoirs are swarming with highly fanciful episodes, is that he places these events in 1934, which is more than a year after this "not-releasable" film came out. And it's not irrelevant to recall that in the trade journals the length listed for *Boudu* was actually not two hours but ninety minutes.[12]

It's also a fact that René Fauchois, who'd detested the film when he first saw it, would state long after that he'd seen it again and liked it: "Renoir very fortunately removed certain images that had disturbed me in the original version of his film and shortened an ending whose current pace is appreciably improved."[13] He specifies in this same discourse about the film that "several years" had passed between the two screenings of *Boudu* he saw. The second, which was the reason for his statement, was shown by a film society in 1956, and he'd been specially invited as the author of the play. The "several years" were actually around thirty, which would suggest that Fauchois's memory of the 1932 screening might not have been completely precise and that the "certain images" that had been removed "very fortunately" had never existed. A second plausible hypothesis is that the film had been cut after being presented to the author of the play and to the press at the Colisée on October 18 at ten-thirty in the morning and therefore before it was officially released, a frequent practice at the time. Had Jean Devaivre been responsible for this new draft? It's not impossible, but that would mean that he was mistaken about the year in speaking of 1934, and that there's a good chance that the *Boudu* we know really is the one that audiences saw in 1932—a film whose mentality and tempo were enough to distinguish it from the other comedies of the period.

Mentality and tempo, which are actually the same thing: the hymn to freedom that constitutes *Boudu* could have only occurred and developed in the framework of a kind of direction stripped of its essential technical contingencies. The freedom that Lestingois grants Boudu in his home is mirrored in the latitude that Renoir gives Michel Simon and the other actors. The duration of shots, made possible particularly by using depth of field and taking advantage of extensive movement on the part of the camera, frees the performers by entrusting them to their own practice of their art and simultaneously frees the characters' inclination to apathy, which is at the heart of their nature. In this way the film gives substance to a theory of existence expressed by Boudu's behavior, to which the bookseller subscribes as a matter of principle and that Renoir makes his own by following in the steps of Michel Simon.

With *Boudu*, Renoir perfected his apprenticeship in freedom, and his filmmaking escaped the strictures of technique. Nevertheless, at the end of that year, 1932, Renoir was no free filmmaker because his projects did not belong to him to the point that—at least on this occasion—the actor who was his lead was also his producer. He paid for his independence with the commercial failures of his personal films, and he had not acquired the reputation and trust that were enough to convince established production companies to seek him out and endow him with a budget. In his way, he was still a director on an ad hoc basis and therefore forced to remain open to offers that may not have all been able to satisfy him but that at least gave him the opportunity for adventure. Although the elemental components of his art had begun to fall into place, the Renoir of 1932 was an artist searching for an identity, and each experience he was able to have was a chance at finding himself. It was by filming that he acquired his style, and it was by filming that he developed a conception of the world expressed by his movies.

Many have given in to the strong temptation to interpret Renoir's trajectory after the fact as a struggle for the independence of the creative person in the face of economic demands, a battle emphasized by a constantly repeated refusal to give in. And yet, the facts surrounding the first half of the thirties—at the very least—completely contradict the pertinence of any such reading. There exists no trace of a serious proposition declined by Renoir during those years. His desire for experimentation and his lack of alternatives led him, in fact, to accept offers that may appear outlandish, like the adaptation of the play *Chotard et Cie* that he became involved with even before the release of *Boudu*.

It's a fact that, in 1932, the cinema of Jean Renoir had no established existence on the French scene. Whether you are surprised by this, lament it, or use it to mock the blindness of the critics and audiences of the time, that is how it is. The results of the yearly poll of readers of the weekly *Pour vous*, whose purpose was to name the best films of 1932, did not include *Boudu*. It is true that the film was handicapped by its release in November; but if it was cited, it was by fewer than twenty readers, whereas Pagnol and Allégret's *Fanny* received 1,227 votes and Raymond Bernard's *Les Croix de bois* (*Wooden Crosses*), which came in second, had 932 votes. A note in *La Cinématographie française,* a weekly read mostly by theater owners and managers, informs us in its way about *Boudu's* effect on the film buffs of the time, who did not think the film needed to be distinguished from the 107 other productions in the nation that year. Mention is made in the weekly of "direction that is on the mark and realistic, but without the least concern for art," with the principal reason that "most of the scenes are comparable to simple, ordinary events of today."[14] To put it briefly, they considered it a "funny, witty comedy," but "without any great pretensions." The notion of the "art film" was in its death throes but continued to muddle the view of film lovers. A formula for the kind of reputation given to Renoir at the beginning of the thirties is perfectly summed up by the words of the critic Lucien Wahl in 1934: "owing to his putting his art too often in service to things in which there is no place for art."[15] This is also why Renoir didn't find himself in a position to get the films he would have liked to direct produced, while the few offers that came to him did not originate with important producers, who preferred to place their confidence in Duvivier, René Clair, Jacques Feyder, Raymond Bernard, and others.

His credo had not changed since he began. He continued to believe in "troupes," as he had claimed in 1927 in an interview entitled "Conversation" that appeared in *La Semaine à Paris:*

I believe that you have to put together a troupe. Seeing good actors going their separate ways depresses me. Specifically, what's true in the theater—the exception isn't the rule—is just as true in film. In film, as well, even more so in film, the troupe—call it "the company"—is imperative. Very often—too often!—the choice of performers is guided by a concern . . . about its indirect result. The choice of one actor over another isn't governed by their distinctive features, or because of the probability that they can adapt to the subject, but because of what they represent, of who they can become. Persisting in these deplorable habits is condemning oneself to getting nowhere. Cohesion is more difficult to accomplish in film than it is in theater, and it's even more indispensable. Only the troupe can make it a certainty.

And then Renoir mentioned Chaplin as a model for this approach, after which his interviewer explained, "By *troupe*, Jean Renoir is referring not only to the performers, but to everyone involved in the collaboration. He's certain that putting a troupe together is guaranteeing him a common spirit and that such a spirit will be ductile and sensitive and capable of adapting to each subject; it is ideal."

When it came to this idea, Renoir would never vary. Five years later, his dreams of independence, which sometimes steered him in unexpected directions, led him to a surprising project, which a news item in *Pour vous* reported on:

Are we witnessing the creation of a studio in Algiers? It has been seriously considered for some time. M. Jean Renoir . . . has just spent quite a long time in Algiers, where he has studied the cinematographic possibilities of our country. An Algerian production enterprise is being set up here, and plans are being discussed for the construction of a shooting lot in the pleasant neighborhood of Fort-de-l'Eau, the large, elegant summer resort in Algiers. With his sharp appraisal of reality and the help of several friends, M. Jean Renoir has been thinking of creating a studio-laboratory at the ports of Algiers for the purpose of aiding the cinematographic arts, by protecting and developing them.[16]

Renoir would think of organizing this project in Spain in the thirties, then in the South of France in the summer of 1940; and there's no doubt at all that he thought of Pagnol as the model for it. The aesthetic model, perhaps; but it's clear that this was above all a model for industrial and commercial success.

If he had not gone so far as creating a structure or gathering a troupe of actors around him, he was making every effort to work as much as possible with the same technicians. Therefore, at the end of 1932, he took on board his usual partners for the filming of *Chotard et Cie*. These included Marguerite and her friend Suzanne de Troeye, who was also an editor and who was inseparable from Marguerite both in life and on set. There were also Jacques Becker; Renoir's nephew Claude Renoir, as the cinematographer; the painter and set designer Jean Castanier; and several others.

11

Adaptations

Chotard et Cie (Chotard and Company)
Madame Bovary

It's obvious that there's more of Renoir and Michel Simon in *Boudu Saved from Drowning* than there is of René Fauchois. On the other hand, similar to the fact that there is more of Feydeau than Renoir in *On purge Bébé*, Roger Ferdinand is the sole influence on *Chotard et Cie*. It would have been difficult for it to be any other way because this fifth sound film by Renoir, coming as it does at the height of a period with an overwhelming number of adaptations from the theater, is no more a Renoir film than, to give just a single example, *Fanny* is a Marc Allégret film. One of the repercussions of the marked increase in play adaptations sparked by the coming of the talkie was a greater unsettling than ever before of the auteur's status. The problem, when it came to *Chotard et Cie*, was that Roger Ferdinand could only be Roger Ferdinand.

To boot, this particular play was one of its author's least successful. The premiere at the Odéon on October 19, 1928, had been entitled *Chotard et Collinet*, with Fernand Charpin in the role of Chotard and the young Pierre Richard-Willm playing Julien Collinet. Charpin reprised his role in the film, after a film debut as Panisse in *Marius* and *Fanny*, seminal hits of the Pagnol trilogy. At forty-five, he had the authority and expertise needed to personify that portly grocer who reigns over his business and family with a benevolent iron hand. If it's a fact that Renoir was not the one who chose this actor—part of an agenda completely controlled by Roger Ferdinand, who was also the producer—there's no doubt that Renoir was the one who cast the actor who would play Collinet, the engaging poet to whom Chotard agrees to give his daughter and who turns out to be a deplorable grocer but a talented writer and wins the Prix Goncourt. No director other than Renoir, in fact, ever had the idea of hiring the dancer Georges Pomiès, who was also the lead of *Tire-au-flanc*. After that film, Pomiès had appeared in nothing else but a Michelin ad in which he played the iconic Michelin Man (1929). A short while after *Chotard*, he could be seen in Claude Autant-Lara's first feature film, *Ciboulette* (1933), and died after surgery in October 1933 at the age of thirty-one.[1]

Renoir was mistaken when he claimed that *Chotard* was undertaken as a way of "exploiting the success of *Boudu Saved from Drowning*."[2] For one thing, the project had first been announced during the summer of 1930,[3] with Raimu in the eponymous lead and no director yet specified. In fact, Renoir began shooting *Chotard* even before *Boudu* was released. The claim comes from his poor opinion of a film that appears convincing only during its first four minutes.

The opening of *Chotard* falls within the lineage of the one in *Tire-au-flanc*. It is one of the most "Renoirian" that exists and even more masterful than that of the earlier film with its wealth of supple camera movements, starting with a crate marked "Chotard Alimentation" ("Chotard Foods") being loaded by an employee into a van, and then following Chotard from the sidewalk in front of his store into its interior, where he is preoccupied with the demands of a customer, answering the phone, berating another employee—female this time—before he returns to his living quarters. The scene lasts more than two minutes and is typically orchestrated by Renoir, one of the few French directors—in fact, the only one at the time—to begin a tracking shot with a close-up and then launch the camera into what feels like a random discovery of elements.

What follows later is also pure Renoir: a window of the living quarters opening onto a studio-created exterior; a panoramic shot starting with a framed photo on a piano followed by the face of Jeanne Boitel, who plays their daughter; a static shot of Chotard and his wife lunching at a table in the background while, in the foreground, the face of their daughter is reflected in a mirror. Here the depth of field seems to want to thwart the banality of the situation, just as, throughout the film, the mobility of the camera makes an effort to disguise the conventions that bog down the plot and characters. Actually, at times the film seems to want to go faster than the play, which never stops dragging along, and on which Renoir must soon renounce imposing his own rhythm. He does what he can, but the film remains a prisoner of its original material and Ferdinand, through his role as original author, producer, and coscreenwriter.

Having already appeared in *Boudu*, Max Dalban, whom Renoir would also cast in *Toni*, comes up with a caricature of a homosexual employee. Georges Darnoux has a walk-on part; and Louis Seigner, his first real role in movies, plays an idiotic police lieutenant. Jeanne Boitel treats viewers with an eye-catching low-cut dress in the long scene of the costume ball, in which Charpin appears dressed as Louis XIV. These are about the only noteworthy events in a movie that gives Charpin the chance to ham it up and Georges Pomiès to display his litheness. *Chotard et Cie* was released in March 1933, dismissed by the critics,* and ignored by audiences.

* In *Pour vous*, Lucien Wahl touches on "attempts at true film that try for wit and don't attain it," and it is his opinion that "M. Pomiès doesn't have a single moment in which he acts well." (*Pour vous*, no. 223, February 23, 1933.)

The press screening of *Chotard et Cie* had been announced for January 30, 1933, but was postponed to February 13, "owing to a delay in the editing."[4] An excuse, perhaps. It's also possible that Jean Renoir, as he would claim years later, was in Berlin on January 30 of that year,* the evening of the day that Hitler became chancellor. This is possible, but in no way a certainty, because Renoir described such a trip belatedly and was, obviously, very influenced by the many accounts that had appeared in the meantime. He declared in 1969,

> It so happens that I was in Berlin the evening of the day Hitler was elected chancellor of the Third Reich and consequently opened the door to atrocities. It was really quite a date in history. And what struck me was the fact that old Berlin was a quiet city with the good bourgeois smoking their pipes and discussing elections like you would normal ones. You wouldn't have thought that the stakes were that high—and there you are, because the day following the election, another part of the population—unless it was the same one—was going wild with rage. I saw things like that happening; for example, I saw the cream of their youth wearing brown shirts and forcing an old Jewish lady to lick the sidewalk while explaining that the Jews were only good at licking side-walks and that it was all they could do in life. When you see things like that, you don't like Hitler and you want to fight against him.[5]

Whether Renoir fought against Hitler isn't the point here. That he saw "things like that" is a possibility. That life in Berlin changed completely in the space of a few hours? Once again, Renoir is acting less like a witness than a director, starting with a situation that has made an impression on him, whether he was actually there or received a report of it, and then staging it—or rather, concentrating it in space and in time, transforming it into a "vision" adapted for the screen. He never tried to hide the fact that he was a storyteller above all. Should he be expected to present his personal experiences, his own life, his insights exactly as they in fact were? Taking Renoir at his word leads sooner or later to misrepresenting him.

Five years after the above statement, in *My Life and My Films*, Renoir places the scene about "the day following the election" at a later time: "Hitler was elected. I decided to stay in Berlin, figuring I'd witness some historic events. And I did, when I witnessed that appalling incident." And then, once again, he describes the sight of that poor woman forced by "young athletes in brown shirts" to get on her knees and lick the sidewalk. It actually is an appalling

---

* But we also know that Renoir went to Switzerland in February 1933 to show *La Chienn*. (*Pour vous*, no. 225, March 1933.)

incident, and Renoir kept silent about it for more than thirty years. In this book he makes it clear that Braunberger had gone with him to Berlin. The producer confirmed that fact and added several details.

According to Braunberger, Renoir had gone to Berlin to get some paintings out of Germany that he'd consigned to an art dealer. Braunberger was taking the trip to recoup some money belonging to Bernard Reichenbach and frozen in a Berlin bank. Someone named Frau Kreutzberg, a "sister-in-law of Himmler,"* he claims, was planning to produce an adaptation of Dostoyevsky's *The Gambler*, which Renoir would direct. By partnering in the production, Braunberger could recover Reichenbach's money. In the bargain, the Kreutzberg woman also agreed to facilitate the repatriation of Renoir's paintings. Braunberger next writes, "After having discussed this with Jean, and despite that fact that I had no personal interests at stake, we decided to go. We arrived in Berlin only a few weeks after Hitler's rise to power."[6]

Both producer and director independently mentioned that Braunberger was getting a kick out of giving the Hitler salute to groups of Nazis encountered in the street while conspicuously hiding his nose with the other hand. "Such heroic buffoonery seemed futile to me," writes Renoir. "I nearly had to drag Braunberger into a Mitropa sleeping car." But, according to the producer, he would not listen to Renoir, who may have been entertained by the salute gag but who was also "worried" and actually did pressure Braunberger to leave.

Braunberger's account continues with a far-fetched story of an assassination attempt against Hitler with a "small pearl-handled revolver" aimed through a hole made in a pocket of his raincoat and his covertly practicing this routine in the forests of Grünewald. The next part is even more gripping: "On the morning of the Big Day, I'm going with Jean to the office. I have my revolver in my pocket and am wearing gloves. I decide to tell Jean what I plan to do. Terrified, he stops the car. 'You're crazy. You're not going to do a stupid thing like that—give me your revolver!' I refuse. He wants to take it, and we come to blows. He opens the car door, and we roll onto the grass near the Spree, the river that cuts through Berlin. As Jean is a lot stronger than me, he ends up on top and gets hold of the revolver, throwing it into the river. It's probably still there."[7] Maybe.

Renoir didn't seem to have any memory of this incident. He preferred to recall riding in a Berlin taxi next to an "enormous open Mercedes," in which Hitler stood, greeting a cheering crowd. But the remembered Berlin journeys of Braunberger and Renoir end up converging: each of them claims to have left

---

* This information has not been confirmed. On the other hand, it's likely that Lola Kreutzberg (or Kreuzberg) had some dependable backing—especially financial—from the Nazi Party.

Berlin after the other. The trains coming from Berlin were, in fact, jam-packed and took nearly sixteen hours to reach Paris.

While Lola Kreutzberg was preparing an adaptation of *The Gambler*, a German-French coproduction that was finally directed in 1938 by Gerhard Lamprecht and Louis Daquin, Germany was losing its creative talents. In spring 1933, the list of German directors exiled to Paris lengthened daily. Already it included, among others, G. W. Pabst, Detlef Sierck (the future Douglas Sirk), Robert Siodmak, Robert Wiene, Leontine Sagan, Kurt Bernhardt, E. A. Dupont, and Fritz Lang. While Lang prepared to shoot *Liliom*, produced at the Gaumont studios by Erich Pommer—who was also in exile—Billy Wilder, another Viennese by birth and a promising screenwriter, was about to do his first film, *Mauvaise Graine* (*Bad Seed*), with fledgling actress Danielle Darrieux. Most of these people were only passing through, but this influx of talent and expertise, augmented by that of a number of other types of film professionals and several actors, contributed to a glut in the market, something that would take little delay in alarming certain people in the world of French film. A lot of the newcomers had a desperate need for work, as well. Take Peter Lorre as a case in point: he barely had enough to pay for his room at the Hotel Ansonia on rue de Saigon.

A short distance from there, on place des États-Unis, composer Kurt Weill had found refuge at the home of the Viscountess of Noailles. When Bertolt Brecht arrived, after leaving Berlin on February 28 and first going to Prague, Vienna, and Switzerland, Weill's hosts got it into their heads to help them reform the partnership that had created *The Threepenny Opera*, at least long enough for one new work. This venture was supported by George Balanchine, Princess Edmond de Polignac (Winnaretta Singer), Count Harry Kessler, and Jean Renoir. Renoir may have met Brecht through Carl Koch during one of his visits to Berlin, but it was in May 1933 that they really got to know each other, although the precise nature of the bonds they formed at that time isn't clear. The premiere of the "ballet with libretto," *Anna-Anna, or the Seven Deadly Sins*, took place on June 7 at the Théâtre des Champs-Élysées and was followed by four other performances, each composed of several ballets, one of which was by André Derain, who was close to Renoir, with music by Darius Milhaud.

When Brecht was leaving Paris at the end of June to move to Denmark (which he'd leave in 1939 for Sweden), he had enough free time to dine in Meudon, where Renoir had been renting a house for some time. From these evenings, he'd draw material for a short story in which the director took the guise of a painter "known as Mountain on account of his girth."* The story "A Question of Taste" concerns a piece of beef being spit-roasted, an incident from the Second Moroccan War, an art dealer reminiscent of Carl Koch, and a conversation about love forcefully initiated by the painter: "For Germans, it's a stirring of the heart! That's about the only motion that occurs. More than anything else, the couples want their union to be *gemütlich*. Love is supposed to be armless [*armlos*]."[8] By *armlos,* Mountain means *harmlos* (harmless); and when he gets carried away with his exposition, he makes some rash movements that draw the following warning from the art dealer: "Jean, you're turning the spit too quickly!"

Renoir took after Carl Koch when it came to the art of roasting. They were the best of friends, and Brecht's short story reproduces the warmth of those evenings in Meudon when everyone communicated in German and the hours went by unnoticed. At the time, Renoir was in no position to launch his own project and was waiting for a proposition to come along; this made him more of a genial host than a director in the eyes of those gathered around him, who saw him more as the son of a greater painter than as an artist in his own right. He was still unaware that he'd soon have to become interested in "that sentimental floozy,"[9] as his father called Emma Bovary when that character was mentioned.

An editor and his mistress were responsible for the origin of the second film adaptation of Flaubert's novel, which had already been done in Hollywood in 1932 under the title *Unholy Love.*† The editor Gaston Gallimard was the most powerful in France and also the son of one of Auguste Renoir's closest friends. His mistress at the time was named Valentine Tessier.

The NSF (Nouvelle Société de films), named in allusion to the NRF (*La Nouvelle Revue Française*), Gallimard's well-known literary magazine, and founded in 1932 by Gallimard and Robert Aron, had produced three short films of about thirty minutes each directed by Robert Capellani. Aron had referred to them as "simple-minded comedies"[10] when he was offering to buy the rights to *Madame Bovary.* The book would soon enter public domain, and the publisher, Fasquelle, which owned the rights, was hoping to get 100,000 francs for them. This sum was increased 50 percent by a go-between whom Aron identified only by his initials, B. D.,‡ and whom he described as "some poor and needy literary

* *Translator's note:* Quotations from the Brecht story are from the translation that appeared in *The Collected Short Stories of Bertolt Brecht,* edited by John Willett and Ralph Manheim (Bloomsbury, 2015); from the original work, *Geschichten,* vol. II of *Gesammelte Werke of Bertolt Brecht* (Suhrkamp Verlag, 1967); English translation (Methuen London, 1983).

† Directed by Albert Ray, with Joyce Compton.

‡ His name was André Bloch Desmorget (*Pour vous,* no. 255, October 5, 1933).

person" who was "donating" the adaptation he himself had written. Gallimard was overjoyed at getting his hands on so prestigious a project, but he didn't feel the same way about the scenario. "B. D." was asked to please take back his adaptation, and the job was entrusted to the novelist Roger Martin du Gard. Martin du Gard accepted the offer, with even greater enthusiasm when he discovered the excellent rapport he felt during his first work sessions with Jacques Feyder, who'd been approached to direct the film.

Feyder had just returned to France after four years in Hollywood, where, among other films, he'd directed Greta Garbo in her first talkie, *Anna Christie*. He had the prestige and power needed to succeed with the project. He had the reputation, wrote Robert Aron, of "having known nothing but success up to then." Marcel Carné, who had not yet directed anything beyond the short documentary *Nogent, Eldorado du dimanche*, met him the day after his arrival in Paris and devoted a page to him in the February 23, 1933, issue of *Pour vous*. Interviewed for the profile, Feyder announced he was getting ready to direct *1940*, which imagines that, with women having been given the right to vote, the Assembly is composed of "three hundred women and only about a hundred men." The film, in which Françoise Rosay, Feyder's wife, was supposed to play a "feminist leader," would not be made. However, when Carné asked him about the rumor concerning *Bovary*, Feyder answered, "Let me make *1940* first. Afterward, I mean next May or June, we'll speak again about the Flaubert adaptation if that's OK with you. In fact, talk about it is actually quite advanced."[11] The director refused, nevertheless, to comment on whether he was going to make Renée Falconetti his Bovary. *The Passion of Joan of Arc* turned out to be this superb actress's last film, as a matter of fact; and before it, she'd only appeared on the screen twice.*

It may be that Feyder had already thought of whom he wanted for the role. That is what Robert Aron has claimed. He remembers that Gallimard tried to convince the director to consider Valentine Tessier as a potential Bovary by organizing a luncheon at a restaurant on place de la Madeleine, Larue, the swankiest restaurant in Paris at that time.

Invited to its private dining room were Gaston Gallimard and Valentine Tessier, Jacques Feyder and Françoise Rosay, and Robert Aron and his wife. Aron recounted the affair: "The woman they intended to star showed off her aptitude for the role by arriving in the most romantic veil she could dream up, with a wide-brimmed hat she thought elegant women of the nineteenth century favored: a perfect restoration. She was this close to wearing a crinoline petticoat."[12] Alas, the effect produced wasn't the one hoped for. Feyder's face "stayed

* *Le Clown* (Maurice de Féraudy) and *La Comtesse de Somerive* (Georges Denola), both 1917.

blank," and his wife acted "sardonic." Two days later, the director informed Aron that he refused to direct Valentine Tessier in the role. Gallimard was furious and took him off the project. When Martin du Gard took Feyder's side,* the choice was either to abandon the project, which Gaston's brother, Raymond Gallimard, wanted them to do, because he'd always been opposed to his brother's interest in producing films, or turn to another director and another scenarist.

Did Feyder have Françoise Rosay in mind for the part? Did she want the role so much that she was willing to oppose her husband directing any other actress? Robert Aron thinks so. The competition between Madame Feyder and Valentine Tessier was actually quite a close one: Madame Feyder had turned forty-two in April 1933, and Tessier would be forty-one in August; neither was the right age for the character. Nor was Falconetti, who'd been born less than three months before Valentine Tessier.

Tessier found the position in which Gallimard had placed her being reinforced. Not only was she the primary reason for the film but also the urgent situation in which the producers had ended up and their lack of experience in films convinced them to go back to the actress to design the project. She herself had little knowledge of the film milieu, having only appeared in five short films thus far, all of them made in 1912, as well as in René Clair's 1928 adaptation of a Eugène Labiche play, *The Italian Straw Hat*, in which she had a small supporting role. In reality, she knew only the Renoir family to any degree; she had played opposite Pierre on the stage and had been his girlfriend. Through him she had met Jean and had gone to the first screening of *La Chienne*. Thus, Renoir, who'd maintain that he considered her to be like a sister to a small degree, would be drafted for the *Madame Bovary* project. It's possible to imagine a less informed choice.

It had to be done quickly, and that is how Renoir did it. He called Carl Koch—who was then in Germany—to the rescue. Together they finished off the adaptation (which would list only Renoir in the credits). At the same time, a distribution plan was established.

Pierre Renoir would play Charles Bovary. In the summer of 1932, he had been preparing to do a play with Valentine, *La Margrave* by Alfred Savoir. The day before rehearsals began, Valentine, at odds with the author who'd written the role for her, suddenly announced her intention to leave the project. The relationship between the two actors, who'd been living together for some time while the divorce between Pierre and Marie-Louise Iribe dragged on, suddenly ended. While Pierre was on the stage of the Comédie des Champs-Élysées,

* Valentine Tessier and Pierre Renoir had acted together in the first production of a play by Martin du Gard, *Un taciturne*, at Théâtre Louis-Jouvet on October 28, 1931.

Charlotte Lysès (the former Madame Guitry), and then Véra Sergine (Pierre's first wife), replaced Valentine in Pierre's affections; and Gaston Gallimard took Pierre's place with Valentine. When the *Madame Bovary* production requested Pierre, he had just gone back to playing in *Knock* (the role of the drum major) opposite Louis Jouvet, whom he chose to confide in by letter: "I did it for my brother, and I'm not thrilled by the idea, especially since it's going to demand more of me than I thought."[13]

How to cast the *Madame Bovary* character Rodolphe Boulanger was a problem for a while, as Robert Aron explained in an article devoted to the NSF and announcing the impending direction of the film, filming of which, however, had already started: "We have offered the role of Rodolphe to a very great actor. He answered that he didn't want to play a character who wasn't eponymous with the film. Which caused Henri Jeanson to remark wittily that the actor in question wanted *Madame Bovary* called *Rodolphe*."[14] Fernand Fabre didn't make such a fuss and took on the role.

Because of circumstances, Renoir would achieve his old dream of a troupe of actors during the span of one film, primarily because the cast of *Madame Bovary* was dominated by actors from the theater—Valentine and Pierre, but also Robert Le Vigan, who'd play Lheureux after having been onstage with Pierre in *Intermezzo* and *Knock;* and Max Dearly, who'd play Monsieur Homais, after coming from the role of Gillenormand in Raymond Bernard's *Les Misérables.* He'd appear first in the credits for Renoir's film, before Valentine Tessier and Pierre Renoir, despite the fact that they were the two leads. Then there was the fact that exterior scenes required actors not to go home evenings and not to work onstage during the filming of *Bovary.* It was everything Renoir loved. Jean Serge, who became Renoir's assistant in the fifties, met him briefly during that time. In Serge's memoirs, he describes the kind of man Renoir was in 1933, and it was probably closer to the truth than the portrait drawn by those close to the director: "To me he seemed like a 'son of' kind of person—refined, decadent, not wanting to forget his father, but wishing he could make others forget that he was that guy's kid."[15]

Gaston Gallimard often spent time with the company, which necessarily included the chief cameraman, Jean Bachelet; his assistant, Claude Renoir; Jacques Becker (just visiting, though); and Marguerite. Their locations were identical to those in Flaubert's novel—in Rouen, Lyons-la-Forêt, and Yonville. In the last week of August, a notice appeared in the papers: "The scene of a farmers' gathering will be enacted next Sunday in Lyons (Eure). The farmers of the region are invited to come and present their best-looking animals and are requested to dress as much as possible in the style of 1850. A costume contest has been planned. The gathering will end, naturally, with dancing. During the entire day, M. Jean Renoir's cameramen will take advantage of the proceedings to film colorful scenes."[16]

Renoir was working in the most comfortable conditions he had ever known up to then, allowing him, he'd claim, at the last moment to rewrite any dialogue he suddenly judged too far from Flaubert's. Because Robert Aron had taken it upon himself to sign a contract with La Compagnie indépendante de distribution, an enterprise recently created by Roger Metzger and Roger Monteux, two ambitious young men who were convinced they had started out by nabbing a surefire success, everyone viewed the Normandy sky as absolutely cloud free. This is a common feeling in the film world, in which people are often ready to wax lyrical on the spot about a film in preparation or one being made. It was stoked even more by Renoir's fondness for sharing, his sense of friendship, the warmth that radiated from him, and the instant exhilaration he felt when surrounded by the people he liked.

Moreover, the film was highly anticipated. People were obviously getting tired of stage adaptations, and they hoped that literature would endow film with some of its luster. More cachet: Raymond Bernard was directing a version of *Les Misérables* at the same time, and he'd asked Arthur Honegger to compose the musical score. Robert Aron suggested Renoir use Darius Milhaud for *Madame Bovary*. The director needed convincing, not because he was averse to the composer's personality—he was one of Renoir's friends—but because he normally used music that already existed. In the end he was persuaded. *Madame Bovary* would become the first of his films to make use of original music, although this doesn't mean that he gave up also using music that was "source-drawn."

At the beginning of September, when the exterior shots were finished, filming moved to the Billancourt studios and started with the scenes in Homais's pharmacy. Benjamin Fainsilber claimed to have watched the filming of the scene of the departure of the *Hirondelle*, the stagecoach that provided transportation between Yonville and Rouen, and he devoted a page to this in *Pour vous* on September 14, 1933. Although the *Hirondelle* would definitely appear several times in the film, to track Emma's travels to and from Léon, the scene in which Emma tosses a coin into the hat of the singing, scrofulous beggar would not appear.

The next shoot recorded the La Vaubyessard ball, and several Gallimard authors were invited. According to the October 7 issue of *La Cinématographie*, also invited were "Léo Larguier, the poet and respected Flaubert expert; the sketch artist Dariel, some prestigious physicians, and a famous lawyer." Reporters also asked to attend the shoot on this Monday, October 2, declared how impressed they were by the setup from the opening and closing shots in the scene: "An ingenious tracking shot directed by Jean Renoir, using a gigantic gantry made of an inclined plane down which the camera slowly descends to the ballroom and then pulls in closer to Emma Bovary, filled the crew with great admiration."

But who really was saying all of this? Reporters from the Paris newspapers, or hired publicists? Two articles devoted to the shoot—one in the October 7 issue of *Le Matin* and the other in *Le Petit Parisien* of the twenty-ninth—raise some doubt because they both contain the same sentence: "Valentine Tessier whirled by in a pink gown, surrendering to the arms of a cavalryman with a monocle." With a monocle but also bearded, the attentive spectator will amend two months later, obviously frustrated about not being in a situation to appreciate the pink color of the gown, which the director had preferred to the saffron-colored dress Flaubert chose. Lucien Wahl, the respected critic for *L'Oeuvre*, was there that day, as well; and he was visibly reticent, something that worried Robert Aron: "I pressured him, insisted, and finally got this unsympathetic critique out of him: 'Sir, do you think women were already plucking their eyebrows during the time of Flaubert?'"[17] No one had actually thought of that; the extras, as well as Valentine Tessier, exhibit plucked eyebrows on-screen.

The studio shots were finished by the first days of October, followed by several additional exterior shots. Renoir could now devote himself to the editing, which had probably already been started by Marguerite. The first official screening of *Madame Bovary* took place on December 28, 1933, at ten o'clock in the morning in the Palais Rochechouart.

There may have been an appreciably longer version of Renoir's *Madame Bovary* than the one that ran exclusively at the Ciné-Opéra, starting January 12, 1934 (and not the fourth, as is commonly stated). According to Robert Aron, the longer version lasted two and a half hours. Renoir mentions an edit lasting three and a quarter—or even three and a half—hours. Both implicate not the film's distributor for the abridgments, but the theater owners, many of whom would have refused to run the film in its original length—be it two and a half, three and a quarter, or three and a half. The circumstances surrounding various claims about this issue, all made several years—actually, several decades—after the fact, make it necessary to return to the period from mid-October to the end of December 1934. So much happened concerning the film over this time that is still difficult to sort out today.

Making an effort to understand requires hacking an improbable path through a jungle of statements of convenience, appraisals complicated by the passing of time, hazy memories, and claims that poorly hide attempts at self-justification. Certain events that happened during filming also need to be accounted for, things seen by people who would have preferred to keep their mouths shut about them. To put it simply, the cinematic Emma found herself in love with Charles Bovary *after* their marriage. Or, more precisely, her passion was rekindled. Valentine Tessier and Pierre Renoir had been in love but had ended their relationship. Their experience of *Madame Bovary* led them to fall in love with each other once again.

Gaston Gallimard was probably the last to become aware of this, but he did discover his misfortune and very much resented it. That his employees on rue Sébastien-Bottin took it into their heads—as has been rumored—to tape back together the pieces of Valentine's letters he had torn to pieces in a rage may be true. That he visited the editing room in person to have a certain "wedding night scene" destroyed—as claimed by a former editorial chief of *Le Figaro* who was Renoir's close friend[18]—could be the stuff of fantasy, not only because the wedding night scene doesn't appear in Flaubert's *Bovary* but also because it is difficult to see why and how it would have appeared in Renoir's.* There is barely any doubt, on the other hand, that for personal reasons, the publisher who'd become a producer found himself less sympathetic to the film in the fall of 1933 than he had been in the spring and summer of that year, also for personal reasons. Before filming ended, clear skies had turned stormy.

Concerning the issue of the editing and the film's length, Robert Aron mentions that the producers asked Renoir to make some cuts to the film before it was shown. Renoir refused. Renoir "could tell," Aron writes, "that I was undermined; but without my knowing so, he also believed I was in on it. And he stuck to his position, which was justified from an artistic point of view but commercially detrimental." Also from Aron: "And the film was presented in its complete version to those who managed the theaters and circuits upon whom its fate depended. It was a disaster, for reasons you can guess. . . . Although the film, whose quality was appreciated by connoisseurs, enjoyed an exclusivity that was fitting, small-minded theater owners, who ruled over most of the houses and tended to be ignorant and tasteless, were put off by its dimensions. They refused to have it on their programs."[19]

Here it makes sense to interrupt Aron's account to ask what he meant by

* Nevertheless, there is a photo from the set showing Pierre Renoir with Valentine Tessier dressed as a bride, face to face in a bedroom near a window.

the word "exclusivity." If he was using the term in its usual sense, which nothing about his personality or his different works as a historian would lead us to doubt, he's indicating that the cuts were made by Renoir *after* the exclusive Parisian run and therefore *before* it was shown in provincial theaters. Aron's account then goes on and ends with, "Aware of the imminent disaster that was about to be caused by his genius, Jean Renoir did—quickly and despairingly—some massive cutting. Max Dearly, who was playing Homais, saw most of his lines lying with the little hare on the cutting room floor.* Shots of the landscapes were deleted and the celebration at the chateau reduced; only the length of Emma Bovary's agony was preserved."[20] The last part of this sentence may actually match the impression produced by the film, which probably did lose about thirty minutes. We may wonder, on the other hand, how interest was created by eliminating the major part of the most spectacular and costly scene in the film—the ball. This couldn't possibly have been the wish of the producer or distributor, even if they were inexperienced promoters of films.

Before examining Renoir's version of this editing "disaster," another parenthesis is warranted. This one concerns a statement in *Le Matin* on the day the film was released. It can be found smack in the middle of the page devoted to the daily's reviews of new films, and it's unsigned by any author: "*Madame Bovary*, the film directed by Jean Renoir and based on the famous novel by Flaubert, was a big hit at its presentation. People were unanimous in remarking that the setting, atmosphere, and characters—in fact, all things—turned out to be scrupulously faithful to the original story. And yet, it remains in every way a film." What "presentation"—in all likelihood reserved for professionals—could they be mentioning? Because it could only have been one of two—either the one on December 28 or the one on January 4 at the Studio des Agriculteurs—who is being concealed behind the term "people" who so enjoyed the show?

The rest of the article is even more surprising, claiming, "After the public screening, M. Queyrel, the head of the Studio des Agriculteurs, the Bonaparte, and the Ciné-Opéra, went to congratulate the distributors of this production by the NSF, Messrs. Metzger and Monteux, and told them he planned to show *Madame Bovary* in exclusivity in his establishment on avenue de l'Opéra starting today."[21] What other meaning could this note have than as a shout-out to provincial theater managers to put the film on their program, despite the fact that most of them seemed not to want to, according to Robert Aron? In any case, it reinforces Aron's claim that a shorter version for provincial theaters had been put forward.

* Aron had previously told how Renoir had spent more than a day waiting for a hare to bolt in order to film it for the scene of the "*baisade*" (the first love-making scene between Emma and Rodolphe in the woods) but dispensed with the image during editing.

One of the rare—if not the only—firsthand accounts of a press screening comes from the journalist Michel Domange, who attended the one on Thursday, December 28, at ten o'clock. Pagnol's assistant at the time, and, as a result, friendly with the editor Suzanne de Troeye, which thereby connected him to Marguerite, Domange described the experience at the Palais Rochechouart[*] in his memoirs. He says he had taken his place in the box reserved for the director, with Suzanne, Marguerite, and Claude.

> We knew that the preceding days had been marked by a conflict between Jean Renoir and his producer. For commercial reasons the producer was intending to make more cuts in the film than the director had agreed to, just as the film was ready to be released. . . . Arguments about rights had been put forth on either side, but they had only made the positions more rigid. And Renoir knew that he had everything to fear because the film cans were in the hands of the producer and were going to be given directly by him to the projectionist. . . . Renoir had made up his mind. He would station himself in the projection room, and at the first improper cut, he would interrupt the showing, leap onto the stage, and appeal to the judgment of the audience.[22]

The projection went on without incident and was hugely applauded, after which Renoir invited those sitting in his box to a restaurant on square d'Anvers for a lunch that Domange writes was "one of the best and most enjoyable" in his life. If this account contributes nothing to clearing up the mystery of the length of *Madame Bovary*, it is reminiscent of a certain screening of *La Chienne* to which Renoir had gone with the advance idea of causing a scandal, although he abandoned it in the end. Domange also seems to indicate that the cut presented on that day corresponded to the director's expectations, which he considered true to the one completed under his direction or at least modified in a way he found acceptable. In any case, there is nothing about it that would seem to support the thesis of the "disaster" that would soon be evoked.

Renoir's story of the circumstances surrounding the editing of his *Bovary* materializes in the course of several reactions—the first of them nearly immediate, the second, long afterward. In an interview that appeared in March 1934 in the daily *Excelsior*, Renoir already expresses the sad fate with which his film had been saddled. To a question about "what these cuts were," he answers, "Everything that could shock or be considered distressing by people in general and by certain people in particular. For example, I had to remove Homais's typically ironic remarks about priests; this film isn't supposed to shock God-fearing folk.

* And not at the Gaîté-Rochechouart, which Domange indicates erroneously.

I also cut some jokes about pharmacists; you can't offend their sensibilities. . . . I had cooked up, for better or worse, a fairly candid roast. . . . The current stew is a boiled beef concoction that smells like a budget restaurant." Thus, Renoir doesn't indulge in finger-pointing at the independent theater owners and, even more significantly, doesn't make mention of a length considered inordinate. His reedit was limited to a few minor cuts, performed out of concern for offending certain provincial mentalities. The fact that one tirade likely to irritate the clergy escaped the massacre is something we can be happy for. It is the moment when Homais declares, "I've known priests who dressed like a bourgeois to go out and watch women jiggle as they danced. They didn't escape me!"

In this same interview, Renoir introduced a piece of information that constitutes the first trace of the track he'd follow for years after. About the original version of the film, he states, "I watched it intact for my own personal satisfaction with a few people I truly like. And there you have it." Nearly thirty years later, most visibly in a conversation he granted Jacques Rivette and François Truffaut for the Christmas 1957 issue of *Cahiers du cinéma*, Renoir finished peeling away the surface he had only discreetly scratched in March 1934:

> The film was destroyed by cutting it; but the producers, who fought to the best of their ability, weren't responsible for that; it was the distributors, who didn't dare put out a film lasting more than three hours. It just wasn't done. It was a time when double features seemed like a good solution to the crisis in film because there already was such a crisis, just as there is now—the same one, in fact. The distributors were saying, "No, we like the film a lot, but you just can't, it isn't possible. . . . It has to be cut." So I cut it. But strange as it sounds, once this was done, there was no end to cutting it. You know, I find the film as it is now a little boring. Well, when it lasted three hours, it wasn't boring at all. I showed it before it was cut. I did, let's say, five or six screenings in the theater at the Billancourt studio, which does have enough room for fifty people, and they were all thrilled. For example, Bert Brecht saw it, and he was completely delighted. Unfortunately, I'm certain that the integral copy disappeared during the edits, when cuts were made in that copy and then on the negative, and everything that fell on the cutting room floor was burned.

In the account given by Renoir in 1934, he recalls cuts performed with the purpose of not shocking audiences, essentially those in provincial France. Those cuts, as a result, are said to be limited to a few lines of dialogue. In his report from 1957, he speaks of a drastic reduction in the length of the film. The two versions are separated by twenty-three years and aren't forced to confront each other. Moreover, Renoir's notion about the tendencies of the time isn't contradicted by the example of the Raymond Bernard film *Les Misérables,* which was released in Paris less than a month after *Madame Bovary* and which had a length of nearly five hours (280 minutes). That film was the result of a very exceptional production financed and distributed by the group Pathé-Natan, which had a strike force infinitely superior to the one composed of the NSF and the Compagnie indépendante de distribution combined. Presented in its integral version with the original continuity at its grand premiere on February 3, the film was divided into three parts for the purpose of distribution. On the other hand, contrary to what Renoir claims, the principle of the double feature was still unknown in French movie theaters in 1934. As to the proposition that a version of more than three hours seems less long than a foreshortened version, repeated experimentation has proved that it is the case, because the experience of film is less about duration than it is a question of cinematographic rhythm.

All that remains is the question that seems the trickiest: the screenings at Billancourt. If we can easily accept the idea that the theater there wasn't jam-packed at every one of those "five or six" showings, it still seems reasonable that at least a hundred people saw the film over the course of the screenings. And yet, Jean Renoir is the only one who remembers them; for more than seventy years, not a soul has surfaced to point at a trace of them. Brecht was one of the audience members? It's not impossible. The playwright had been living in Denmark since the end of the previous June and would have been able to visit France in December 1933, the only period when these screenings could have happened. But on this as well, Jean Renoir has to be taken at his word, although it needs to be kept in mind that he could have also blended his memories of Brecht in Meudon in 1933 with his desire to take advantage of the prestigious backing of the playwright.

We also can imagine that from mid-October to the end of December, barely more than two months, a first edit lasting three hours or more was developed and shown on several occasions to the producers, to begin with, followed by the distributors and then the theater managers who (alone?) rejected it before Renoir could be convinced to go back to the editing room and cut more than an hour of the film. From beginning to end, it was a prodigious feat repeated each day. It must also be acknowledged, however, that, shortly after the film came out in theaters, there had already been talk about a reduction in length: "To completely depict the action and personalities of the characters required five thousand meters. These five thousand meters were shot by Jean Renoir but couldn't be saved by him."[23] Five thousand meters (approximately 16,404 feet): three hours and seven minutes of film, in other words; but there's nothing to prove that—if the film actually was shot—it was also assembled; and the author of these lines, which appeared in a trade magazine, could very well have been inspired by Renoir himself, who was anxious to pin the responsibility for the commercial failure of the film on anyone other than him.

At the present time, and perhaps for a long time after this, we have no choice but to come back to the *Madame Bovary* by Renoir with which we are familiar. And if the film in fact has the appearance of a work edited in a rough-and-ready manner, numerous viewings of it won't tell us whether the original version lasted three and one-quarter hours, a quarter of an hour more, or forty-five minutes less. As it is, the film neglects few passages from the book, aside from those deficits that are almost natural, dictated as they are by the necessity of compressing the action, such as Charles's childhood and the Bovary couple's life in Tostes. In fact, the film invents a scene, which is the invitation to the La Vaubyessard ball, offered by the marquis on a country road. It's a lovely scene as well, for which Renoir collected several expressions from the book and where Valentine Tessier shows a certain kind of authority.

Perhaps the belief in the existence of a longer version and the impression of a great film put in a sorry state can be traced back to its parceling of scenes, which creates the impression less of a constructed narrative than of a piling on of vignettes. Continuity is absent, the movement from one moment to another has an abruptness, and the scenes often seem too short, which accentuates the excessive length of one or two others. Thus, the dialogue between Emma and the parish priest seems justified less by the progression of the film than by the importance given to the face of the actress shot in close-up or by the veiled presence of the novel sensed in the director's mind as well as the viewer's.

The character of Léon is the one that suffers the most. He's absent during the first part of the film, with his imminent departure from Yonville merely alluded to, and appears only in Rouen at the right moment, summoned to seduce an already conquered Emma. The most surprising characteristic of the film, because it's the most foreign to the art of the director, is the lack of intensity of each scene, which contributes to deepening the mystery of this film. Did Renoir have to cut into these scenes in response to commercial requirements or did they quite simply fail? Both hypotheses are equally admissible. It's difficult to decide whether this lack of binder is more disturbing for the reader of Flaubert, who is keeping track of the deficiencies in defining Emma's character and its development, or for someone who doesn't know the book, to whom the character would probably seem quite obscure. Nevertheless, once the film gets going some beautiful things are revealed.

There are, in fact, several wonderful moments hiding in *Madame Bovary*. The shot that follows the quarrel and reconciliation of Emma and her mother-in-law is even one of the most striking in Renoir's works. After the young woman shiftily offers her excuses, she hurries upstairs. The camera is waiting for her in the bedroom, framing a bed whose whiteness is blinding. Then the shot pulls back slowly to the entrance of the room, and Emma enters the frame on the right. Once in the room, she closes the door noisily. Renoir, who detested slamming doors and couldn't bear car doors closed abruptly,[24] uses a single shot to express this emotional violence, the result of a conjugal situation that has become intolerable for Emma and that she is no longer managing to contain except with great difficulty. The moment is all the more impressive because it's followed by Emma's wild run through the countryside, with the film discovering in an instant the movement that it lacks so often elsewhere. The use that Renoir makes of exteriors, all of which are magnificently reproduced, is related to his desire to place Emma in a rural reality that simultaneously oppresses and enflames her wild fantasy life, transferred to the screen by the theatrical acting he wanted.

In this film, Renoir was "trying to wed real backgrounds with the most stylized acting possible." He developed an "absolute realism of setting and family circle" but contrasted it with "a foreground that popped aggressively out of it," while insisting that his actors "remain just that—actors onstage in the theater." He seemed to lose interest in the decor as soon as the characters began speaking. Only their words and way of saying them were important to him; and this balance between the inert force of the land, of the countryside, and the theatricality of the expressions constitutes the material for this film, the dough that director and actors kneaded and shaped.

In that way, Renoir's *Madame Bovary* gives Flaubert his due; Renoir's Emma dies from not knowing how to decide whether she is feeling the emotions that she expresses or whether, by expressing them, she is conforming to the models she has chosen. It matters less that Valentine Tessier was in fact—and especially seems—too old for the role. That impression stops interfering the moment the scenes gain momentum and vanishes in a magnificent finale. One thinks again of Arletty's remark: "Bovary was very Valentine; Valentine was a Bovary!"[25] And whereas Max Dearly is too mechanical, too expected, and therefore a disappointment as Homais—a character that has never been successfully portrayed in film—Le Vigan, honeyed, suave, and cunning as he is, is dazzling as Lheureux. And Pierre Renoir, massive yet fragile, imposing but lost, delivers a Bovary that is unforgettable.

What, then, keeps this film from being totally appealing? Irony in the style of Flaubert is there at times, as is the meanness. However, the flat, literal manner in which it is all laid out—with good reason—by the adaptation, as well as the way it is filmed, deprives it of an essential dimension of the writer's genius: that humor with which he approaches his characters, delves into them, thereby achieving an understanding of them, making them his. Renoir succeeded in bringing his characters to life, but he never managed to love them. Or perhaps he did much too late, when they had ceased to love themselves. Flaubert wrote about Léon and Emma, "She was as disgusted by him as he was tired of her," when Emma could find no other distraction for herself than her agony.

Roger Martin du Gard was one of the people who could find nothing to like in Renoir's adaptation. In February 1934 he wrote, "Indefensible! (How happy I am not to have been involved in that!)."[26]

Looking back a few months later on the release of the film, in a letter to Pierre Gaut, the producer of *Toni*, Renoir would write about Queyrel, the owner of the Ciné-Opéra: "Regarding *Madame Bovary* and its all-time low, he forgets to tell you that with this film he had fuller houses at the Ciné-Opéra than with any of his previous programs except perhaps *La Maternelle*. February 6 was what brought the revenue down, and if Queyrel had had the least idea of life, he would have understood that Parisians had other things to be concerned about and he would have closed shop."[27] On February 6, 1934, thirteen demonstrators and a policeman were killed during confrontations, and about a thousand were wounded. Three days after that, there were new demonstrations, fifteen deaths, and fifteen hundred wounded.

In May 1944, from Los Angeles, in addition to fifty-four volumes of the work of Paul de Kock, Jean Renoir would place an order from the Gerard D. Lipton bookstore in New York for a clothbound edition of *Madame Bovary*.[28]

Two years later, on June 8, 1946, he wrote to the producer Robert Hakim to make clear his intentions regarding a remake of *Madame Bovary* he had been considering. At the time, he insisted on the need for "absolute fidelity" to the book and considered as indispensable an emphasis on Emma's education, a chapter left out of his first adaptation. He then proceeded to say, "I'd like to insist on her dreams, the books she reads, and also, perhaps, the superficial aspect of her religious sentiment. . . . The refusal to confront the facts and to see life as it stands is currently one of the errors of today's young girls. And in America in particular, if so many women go from one divorce to another and end up living an extremely unhappy life, it is because, like Emma Bovary, they are wasting their time in pursuit of an impossible ideal—impossible and inaccessible especially because it only exists in their imagination." And then: "The best slant to take strikes me as the one taken by the author himself, the difference being that everything would have to be seen, or rather *felt*, by Emma from her point of view."[29]

In this letter, Renoir makes no reference to the 1933 *Bovary*, conceived according to markedly different principles he would be prohibited from adopting again because of the necessity in which he now found himself placed, which was the need to appeal to American audiences. The project would stop there, to the great satisfaction of Alain Renoir, who would write to his father, "I'm happy you're not doing *Madame Bovary,* because my opinion of that respectable old biddy with her independent neosuffragette mentality that was ahead of its time is the same as yours was when you left the Hakim tribe and went on the warpath."[30] In 1949, Vincente Minnelli would direct his *Madame Bovary* with Jennifer Jones.

Thirty years after Renoir's film had placed him at the heart of the tumultuous relationship between Valentine Tessier and Gaston Gallimard, the actress would look him up in the context of a lawsuit she'd initiated against her former lover. In fact, the day after his marriage to Jeanne Léonie-Dumont, on July 23, 1930, the publisher had given a house in Neuilly to the woman who was no longer his mistress but who would soon become his mistress again. And yet, in 1963, according to Valentine Tessier, Gallimard refused to authenticate the reality of this gift, although it was warranted (still according to the actress) "by an act written and signed by his hand."[31] Her lawyer, Floriot, then requested she furnish testimonies from friends to "prove that a month after his marriage I became Pierre's mistress, that we were living in an absolutely matrimonial way and that our relationship was known by everyone ... proof that I was not Gallimard's."[32] This last point was essential, "because according to law, a married man cannot make a benefaction to a concubine!!!" Despite the testimony then furnished by Renoir, establishing that he considered her "in personal terms to be [his] sister-in-law,"[33] Valentine Tessier would be dismissed as a plaintiff and would then write to her ex true/false brother-in-law, "I've moved out of Neuilly—which Gaston Gallimard gave me and then took back! Isn't that charming!"[34]

12

Primitive

Toni

Moving to a house at 17 bis rue des Capucins in Meudon, Renoir left the use of his apartment on rue de Miromesnil to the woman who was still his wife. In August 1933, while Jean had just begun directing *Madame Bovary*, the announcement of the production in Hollywood of a new *Nana* became Catherine Hessling's opportunity for a short-lived reappearance. Not on the screen but in the pages of the magazine *Pour vous*. The interview was done at the actress's home, and therefore at her husband's.

"A fifth floor in the heart of Paris. A door opens on a large apartment full of white, light, contrasts. Handsome antique furnishings in the bareness of the modern style. No cat, no flowers, no dog. And there is Catherine Hessling. A shock of red hair. Two piercing blue eyes stretching toward her temples like those of a feline. The arc of a mouth. Lithe hips in a striped dress. 'I never give interviews.'" Rather than Anna Sten, that young Ukrainian whose *Nana* will be her first Hollywood film, directed by Dorothy Arzner, she would have imagined "a Mae West." She herself admits not having any projects, even after she says she has signed for a film with Cavalcanti. "I knew," writes Claude Gaudin, "that Mme. Hessling adores stripes, polka dots, checks, and Negroes."[1] Jean Renoir's name was not pronounced. Years later, she would draw the following portrait of the man who was her husband: "As far back as I can remember, it's Renoir's fear that strikes me, and his instability. . . . Ceramics never really interested him, it takes patience, doesn't it? So . . . so, film, but that took money, and so, fear. . . . Sir, do you know what it's like to see a fat man who's six feet tall trembling with fear, with panic? It's not a pretty thing to see, I can assure you."[2]

In December 1933, Catherine Hessling would appear in a dance gala at the Théâtre des Champs-Élysées, starring Nati Morales and Spadolini.[3] Soon she'd move into an apartment at 56 rue Galilée, with Spadolini occupying the floor below. Alberto Spadolini, an actor in *L'Épervier* (Marcel L'Herbier, 1933), a dancer in *Marinella* (Pierre Caron, 1936), and an actor in *Le Monsieur de 5 heures* (Pierre Caron, 1938), lived with his male lover, Alex, who without the revolution of 1917 would not have been the grand duke who became a servant and who taught Alain Renoir the art of making french fries (with garlic), all the while trying in vain to convert him to the joys of homosexuality. "A woman can go to bed with any man at all," he would argue, "whereas everybody makes fun of a man who takes it up the ass, so the other man owes you something." The theory appealed to Jean Renoir. According to him, among its adherents was Frederick of Prussia, who, apparently, professed that homosexual soldiers fought better than the others because they dreaded passing for cowards in the eyes of their lovers.[4]

Alain visited his mother every two weeks and had no pleasant memories of the short moments spent with her. Jean, on the other hand, had severed all relations with his wife. The link between them was maintained by Dido Freire, who spent a lot of time with Alain, taking him on vacation to Liverpool, where her father was the Brazilian consul. Dido would briefly share the apartment on rue Galilée with Catherine, who couldn't bring herself throughout the thirties to become cut off from the only director, aside from Alberto Cavalcanti, who had ever believed in her.

For the time being, Jean's official companion was his editor, Marguerite Houllé (spelled Margueritte, at times, and also the way she often signed her name). According to her friends, "Marguerite is addicted to Jean."[5] They called her "the Little Lion," referring to her hair. In the editing room, she displayed authority; in her behavior as a militant, a rousing enthusiasm; and in everyday life, an unassuming manner. Denise Tual has provided a pretty portrait of her and her friend Suzanne de Troeye: "They dressed like Renoir's father's models, with long dresses with full sleeves, and around their neck they wore thin black velvet ribbons attached to lockets. They wore their hair pulled back and high on their heads, a few locks and bangs falling over blue eyes, wonderful."[6]

As some saw it, the relationship between Jean and Marguerite was a love story only for the young woman. Jean was sleeping with his editor, like quite a few other directors did, and that was it. That idea is given credence by the short shrift Jean gives Marguerite in his memoirs. However, such reserve can just as well, and quite probably even should, be understood as a mark of respect for Dido, who succeeded Marguerite and who became Madame Jean Renoir. And the fact that his behavior at the time didn't resemble that of a man very much in love doesn't necessarily offer further information about the relationship. According to Geneviève Becker, "He tried his luck with all women, without being concerned whether they happened to belong to his pals." He did it in a rough-and-ready way without burdening himself with seduction strategies and worried no more than that about the success or failure of his undertakings.

"My father," Alain Renoir would recall, "was no Casanova. He certainly had had several adventures, but they were very rare. He was instead the 'pincher' type, an ass-slapper. On the shoots where everybody was sleeping with everybody, he took even more pleasure in watching the show going on before his eyes in which he himself had chosen not to participate."[7]

Until the end of his life, Alain Renoir asked himself, without being able to answer, whether Jean got close to Marguerite because she was a Communist, or whether he became involved with Communism because Marguerite led him in that direction. The young woman perfectly fit the artisanal, corporatist model developing at the time. The daughter of a worker, she was the sister of committed militants and an irreproachable technician, personified as "a worker peasant" by Renoir's assistant André Zwobada, to fit with his love of nature. She had full membership in a family to which Jean had thus far never gotten any closer than the margin. Most of his films had been produced outside of the system, and he preferred traveling with a "gang" made up partly of those who'd started at the same time as him. There's hardly any doubt that Marguerite's influence helped catalyze Renoir's initial movement toward a profession that he had kept apart from up to that time, to the point of having ended up feeling isolated.

When French filmmakers decided to form their union in summer 1933,[*] they appointed three directors—André Berthomieu, Julien Duvivier, and Jean Renoir—to a committee composed of seven members, which included Jacques Feyder. The Syndicat des chefs cinéastes français (the Union of French Filmmakers), a group of "most of the directors," intended to become the required negotiator not only with governmental powers (Department of Labor) but also with already established professional authorities, namely, the producers' union. In a letter addressed to André Berthomieu in May 1934 in which he presented his resignation, Renoir explained one of the reasons for having enlisted: "Frankly, it pains me to leave an association of good friends that it will now be much more difficult for me to encounter. Isn't an advantage of these unions—and not the least—encouraging friendly relations among people who wouldn't ever see one another without it?"[8] But the fact that he had chosen to become involved is also a sign of his wish to be part of the debates that were beginning to trouble the profession. In spring 1934, one of the issues being put forward concerned foreigners, whom some saw as the cause of the unemployment afflicting film crewmembers.

In fact, for the first time in its history, the French film world was declaring a crisis. Ticket receipts were lower; from 1931 to 1935 they decreased from 938 million francs to 750 million, and the number of films produced had also been decreasing since 1933. The influx of foreign film technicians, many coming

* The first general meeting of the Syndicat des chefs cinéastes français was on August 7, 1933, at 85 rue de Vaugirard.

from Germany, focused the anguish resulting from the drop in activity and stirred up by certain professional organizations. A report that appeared on May 26, 1934, in *La Cinématographie française* revealed that numerous French film professionals couldn't find work and that French studios preferred foreigners because they were cheaper. The position affected the most seemed to be that of head camera. While forty-six French remained on unemployment, twenty-six foreigners were working regularly. That same week, in May, five hundred French film crew workers marched from place de l'Étoile to Opéra, and then to République, carrying signs claiming, "French film workers are dying of hunger."

Renoir's resignation was clearly his reaction to the decision of the association to support this demonstration, which was calling for the strict application of an April 23, 1933, decree regulating the hiring of foreign labor in film and specifying the percentage that was acceptable for each category of employee. The issue was a delicate one. Renoir refused to participate in what seemed to him to be a witch hunt. In the same letter to Berthomieu, he announced that he was also resigning from the Association des auteurs de films. His excuse for that decision was based on their meddling interference in a film that was supposed to be directed by André Sauvage so that the producers' choice, Léon Poirier, could take over. However, Renoir made it clear that his tangible motive lay in the fact that because he was no longer a member of the union, which he had represented for the association, he no longer had a legitimate right to attend the association's meetings. Beyond the declaration of support he expressed elsewhere on behalf of Sauvage, who was in fact the victim of a particularly dishonest and damaging deal, Renoir had only a passing interest in the affair.[9]

Renoir's letter to union members on May 23, 1934, was his chance to make his point of view clear. "If I'm leaving the union," he wrote, "it is because the struggle against foreigners in our profession doesn't seem to me to be the right way to improve the situation. I believe that in France an artistic industry can only function if it acquires a certain international influence. Paris isn't a provincial city. It's one of the world capitals, and its influence has always been owing to and the result of the absorption of numerous foreign elements." He added later in the letter: "I believe that film should be French in spirit (just as American and Russian films are and as German film was before the inane behavior of the producers turned it into a dubious commodity), and when it comes to that we should be uncompromising. And yet, that's not what is currently happening. We've obviously allowed ourselves to be infiltrated by the American mentality. That is bad because the Americans will always make better American films than we can. We should be doing French films because these are the films we do better than others can."[10] Such a profession of faith is already remarkable for the assurance and lucidity at its source, and this same position would be expressed in the film he would soon direct. It would turn out to be nearly visionary in light of the six years that were to follow, a period that is obviously the most wonderful in the history of French film, during which Jean Renoir would direct nine films, most of them major works.

In May 1934, however, Renoir was facing more concerns than certitudes. His relations with Gallimard, whom he blamed for the clumsy and offhand manner in which he accomplished the marketing and foreign sale of *Madame Bovary*, had become nil. "I'm positive there's a barricade blocking me from his office and a face-to-face conversation with him,"[11] he wrote to Jacques Mortier, whose novel, *L'Épingle dans la neige*, he was involved in getting Gallimard to read. Mortier was one of his former schoolmates at Sainte-Croix and had shared the role of best man with the Count de Broel Plater* at Renoir and Catherine's wedding. He had become commissioner of police and the author of crime novels under the name Jacques Levert. He'd let Renoir in on the subject of a film about which Renoir, in this same letter, voiced some not very encouraging news: "I've got major problems of every kind, and I'm very afraid that I'm in no position to foist the direction of *Toni* on any company at all. I'd be absolutely thrilled if this was any kind of work that would allow me to make a living. The possibility of choosing to do the screenplay has to be put off to better times."

Although *L'Épingle dans la neige* would only appear in 1948, under the crime novel imprint Le Bandeau noir, Renoir's film *Toni* ended up going into production only a few weeks after he had confided in Mortier how distraught he was. A reference to the project in a letter to Carl Koch dated June 1, 1934, even reveals that the project was relatively old. Renoir speaks of "our Martigues film when we were hoping to make it before *Madame Bovary*." In that same letter, the director told his friend about the existence of a lead for new work: "I've only received a single serious proposition, from someone you know well. It's Carl Einstein, who used to hang out a lot with Wassmuth and Zucki."[12] I've quoted the first sentence to show that although Carl Einstein and Carl Koch, as pointed out in the second sentence, obviously had friends in common—namely, Ewald Wassmuth and his wife, Sophie, nicknamed "Zucki"—it's extremely unlikely that Renoir had met Einstein through Carl Koch; and this contradicts the common and convenient—but improbable—assumption that Renoir's German relations had to have come from his German friend.

Actually, another trail led Einstein to Jean Renoir. And as is often the case with Renoir, that trail began in the context of his family. To explain it, some light must be shed on the unusual personality of Carl Einstein, a "discoverer of

* Constantin de Broel Plater, a diplomat whose family was of Polish origin and who had emigrated to the South of France in the middle of the nineteenth century.

African art, a great theoretician of modern art . . . who was also a key figure of cultural mediation between France and Germany."[13] Having moved to Paris in 1928, he cofounded the review *Documents* with Georges Bataille and Michel Leiris a year later. His position in the Parisian art scenes and his friendship with the art dealer D. H. Kahnweiler would have been enough for him to have met Jean Renoir.

But it happens that Einstein was also connected to Jean Giraudoux, who was also an enthusiast of African art and who drew inspiration for the character Count von Zelten in his novel *Siegfried et le Limousin* and play *Siegfried* from Einstein and his heroic role in an incident in Belgium during 1918. The play opened on May 3, 1928, and was revived several times, with Pierre Renoir in the title role. The fact that Zelten was based on Einstein is confirmed by Pierre Renoir himself in *Entr'acte,* Louis Jouvet's theater revue: "The character Zelten actually exists. He currently lives in Paris and his name is Karl [*sic*] Einstein."[14]

During the next months, Carl Einstein would occupy a very special place for Jean Renoir, in the setting up of a structure of production and in the direction of *Toni*. Renoir would acknowledge that place when he attempted his memoirs, writing at the time,

> The producer of the film, my friend Pierre Gaut, had arranged for another friend to work with me on the screenplay. It was Carl Einstein, the cousin of Albert Einstein and the author of some remarkable works on the Cubist movement. In my career, Einstein would be followed by Carl Koch. It seems that I've needed friends across the Rhine to free my thinking from a too narrow framework. In this story, which depended on authenticity of detail, this German brought me a way of seeing in contrast to that of the South of France, which is so different than his country and that he better understood as a result.[15]

Renoir would choose to delete these lines from the published edition of *My Life and My Films,* thereby eliminating any reference at all to Einstein, who became the victim of the need the director felt at that time to limit as much as possible the role that other screenplay writers had played in the creation of his films.

The second figure who appeared at this moment in the director's career is more enigmatic than Carl Einstein. It was Pierre Gaut, and he remained close to Jean his entire life, also being, according to Alain Renoir, one of the surest friends. In 1972, looking back on the "*Toni* adventure," Gaut would state, "Since 1920, I'd enjoyed close friendships with Braque, Picasso, Derain, Matisse, and Bissière. Through them I got to know Jean Renoir. We became friends during that period, and no cloud ever came to trouble that relationship. Motivated by the desire to make a film with him, I rounded up 500,000 francs, which was half of the estimate we'd calculated."[16] There is no doubt that at least since 1933 Pierre Gaut had been "wanting to make a film," but not necessarily with Jean Renoir. The potential partner he preferred at the time wasn't Renoir, in fact, but Carl Einstein. Renoir himself confirms this in a letter to Carl Koch: "Carl Einstein has a friend who can put a bit of money into a film. He's very reliable and, especially, very intelligent. Unlike Gaston Gallimard, his intelligence hasn't been spoiled by a kind of perpetual anxiety. He's very athletic and does a lot of flying. He's a former officer, who still participates in some patriotic organizations, which doesn't prevent him from having a lot more freedom of mind than certain intellectuals like those we have known at the NRF."

Pierre Gaut, a business investor? He had been the commercial manager of paintings by Lefranc and Bourgeois for a while, and he was also an art collector. A flyer? Gaut himself seemed very interested in making this known, because, if we can believe the special correspondent for *Pour vous* who was on the set of *Toni*, "M. Pierre Gaut has been to war. He brought back some precious souvenirs from it that he takes around with him in his briefcase and that he is never without. Letters from Guynemer and Pinsard,* photos; Gaut was a flyer. . . . He brought back some other souvenirs—wounds, exploits that he never discusses." All of that is true, and Gaut was also an accomplished athlete, a champion lightweight boxer, a rugby player who belonged to the athletics club known as the Racing Club de France, and the winner of the twenty-four-hour race at the Bol d'or automobile and motorcycle competition.[17]

Born on July 4, 1893, in Eaubonne, Pierre Gaut, like Renoir, suffered from a serious leg wound that he had received in 1915. He had begun the war in the infantry in August 1914. His wounds earned him a medical discharge. However, again like Renoir, he had requested to rejoin, with the air force. A pilot until the end of the war, with the rank of lieutenant, he was made Chevalier of the Légion d'honneur in June 1915. In 1916, he served in the same squadron as Armand Pinsard, the future inspiration for the character in *Grand Illusion*. In May 1940, it was this same Pinsard, then a general, who would oppose Gaut's request for a transfer from Fighter Plane Squadron 21, in which he was then serving, to the irregular military: "I have known Lieutenant Gaut since the war of 14–18. . . . Because of his understanding of fighter-plane aviation, it is my opinion that Lieutenant Gaut is currently in the occupation that suits him and that there is no valid reason for his changing branches."[18] Gaut was promoted to the rank of Officer of the Légion d'honneur in May 1939.

Although it's advisable to view with a degree of caution the information

---

* *Translator's note:* Both Armand Pinsard and Georges Guynemer were highly decorated French heroes of the First World War. Both were fighter aces. Guynemer died flying in a battle with Germans in September 1917.

that appears in Renoir's correspondence, in which he doesn't always demonstrate the most exactitude, the manner in which he presents the facts leads to the conclusion that he met Pierre Gaut through Einstein, and not the opposite. Besides, one of the secondary features of the history of *Toni* has to do with the gradual elimination of Carl Einstein's name. Gaut never mentions him, and Renoir refers to him publicly only on a single occasion, following François Truffaut and Jacques Rivette's comment about the screenplay for *Toni* having been written by Jean Renoir and Carl Einstein. "Carl Einstein was my friend and Pierre Gaut's friend,"[19] is what he stated at the time, without offering any further detail.

Renoir wrote again to Carl Koch about Pierre Gaut: "If I don't find any other money to add to what this man [Pierre Gaut] is completely in favor of providing as a base for a deal, it's awfully obvious that I won't be able to make any film. But it's already quite something to have the guts to look, or rather, to help Einstein look, because he has a lot more connections than I do."[20] This last remark is more of an indication of Renoir's confusion at the time than of the reality of an isolation that was never more than moderate.

At the time, Einstein was involved with obtaining French patents for several of the great cinematographer Eugen Schüfftan's camera processes. Responsible for the special effects in Fritz Lang's *Metropolis* and Abel Gance's *Napoléon*, Schüfftan had moved to France and would do the camera work for *Le Quai des Brumes* (*Port of Shadows*), among other French films. Apparently, Einstein had formed a partnership with Pierre Gaut to commercialize these inventions. Thus, in a letter to a Dr. Tobis at Universal on January 25, 1934, Gaut writes, "Schüfftan is being called—justly, I think—the best technician in Europe. His first invention, the Schüfftan Process [in *Metropolis*], has earned him millions; and yet, his new invention is of infinitely greater significance than the first, because it creates a new filming technique destined to replace all others." But Einstein and Gaut were not satisfied with merely marketing a process that saved money in the construction of scenery. They were also planning to produce films.

Beginning in November 1933, they were in fact looking for another partner, with Universal or with the distribution company Societé d'édition de location de films (SELF), and comparing the potential capital gains from each. A document dated November 8, created by Einstein and hand-corrected by Gaut, stated the sums they were expecting from their schemes: "If 200,000, we earn 70,000. If 150,000, we earn 75,000." On the twenty-eighth of the same month, an agreement with Universal was drawn up for the production of a film based on "a French screenplay" with "a French director."[21]

Renoir's name appeared several months later in the context of the formation of a "joint-venture company for the production and release of a film, *The*

Diary of a Chambermaid,"[22] to which Pierre Gaut pledged 300,000 francs. There is no date given, but there is all reason to think that it was established in spring or at the start of summer 1934. In fact, on July 26, Pierre Gaut and Pierre Braunberger wrote to the Société des auteurs et compositeurs dramatiques (SACD) to make a "firm offer" for an option on the adaptation rights to the novel *The Diary of a Chambermaid* and the adaptation for the stage created by André de Lorde and André Heuzé. In the meantime, therefore, Carl Einstein had put Jean Renoir in contact with Pierre Gaut.

From that meeting, a project was born, and aside from Gaut, Einstein, and Renoir, it also included Pierre Braunberger and Pierre Renoir. A document giving evidence of it is entitled "Presentation of the Ideas and Principles That Have Led These People to Believe in the Effectiveness of Their Efforts and to Unite Together." The first idea, or principle: "It is impossible to earn any money from film with the current methods." That was to attract the financiers, who would find in their plans, among other ideas, "a Parisian epic (from 1918 to the present) that will take place in a petit-bourgeois milieu"; "a heated, violent, and very quick-moving drama, among the rich bourgeoisie"; "the game of classifieds for singles"; and "old and young people."

On May 12, 1934, a letter addressed to Pierre and Jean Renoir enumerates two important points: "The screenplay would be sold at an extremely reduced price given the personal relationships between the director and the authors," and "M. Pierre Renoir would receive extremely worthwhile help from actors." Elsewhere is the caveat, "the screenplay is to be chosen by common accord and in one of the subjects that we have already studied together and that are, firstly, a very well-known novel by one of the greatest literary figures of the last century; and, secondly, a modern novel that has recently created a very considerable stir."[23] If *The Diary of a Chambermaid* is hiding under the term "very well-known novel," the "modern novel" may have been Julien Green's *Léviathan*, for which a note dated May 31, 1934, provides a detailed synopsis, a procedure for an estimate, and a sketch for a work plan foreseeing thirteen days of exterior filming, possibly near Paris, and fourteen days in the studio.

The strategy was not devoid of breadth, and Renoir could finally hope to begin to realize one of his old dreams. The "presentation of the ideas and principles" also specified "always working with the same personnel," as well as the assertion of the wish not to allow the dictates of the distributors to rule over issues of production, or, in other words, shape according to their ideas the works themselves.

The first and only film that would be made had not appeared among the subjects mentioned previously. On July 16, 1934, the private limited liability company Les Films d'aujourd'hui was formed for the production of *Toni*, whose estimate at the time was 900,000 francs and for which the first treatment was dated August 14.[24] The first possible trace of this project appears in a five-page synopsis entitled *Pedro,* is dated April 17, 1934,[25] and describes the story of a young man who is "wealthy, stylish, and snobbish" and whom "the sight of a worker or peasant makes uncomfortable"; he is condemned to several months in prison for having fought with a "yokel." "This is where the actual subject starts," wrote Renoir, describing the friendship in prison that unites the man called Pierre and "a cripple" with whom he escapes and who "obtains false Spanish working papers for him," thanks to which Pierre, "actually having become part of the vast class of manual laborers," will lead "the life of one of the same workers that he had such contempt for in the past."

That "wealthy, stylish, and snobbish" young man resembled Renoir himself. The influence of Marguerite and her friends had, perhaps, not been without effect on the character's discovery of the existence of the downtrodden and, especially, on the empathy he develops for them. *Pedro* was inspired by one of the bedside works of Renoir, Jerome K. Jerome's *Three Men in a Boat.* Another project, with no title or date,[26] but probably from the same period, is a twenty-one-page typed description, with abundant annotations and reworkings, of a highly overcomplicated story situated in Aubagne and Cogolin and near Toulon, which reveals an attraction for the South of France and may be a sign of a desire to subscribe to the tradition of Pagnol.

The members of the private limited liability company Les Films d'aujourd'hui were Jean and Pierre Renoir, "Einstein, a man of letters," and Pierre Gaut. Pierre Braunberger had, therefore, jumped ship midstream. But on September 17, the date the company was registered at the clerk's office, there were only two partners left, Jean Renoir and Pierre Gaut, each owning thirteen 1,000-franc shares.[27]

By that date, Renoir and Einstein were already in the South of France. After several days of location scouting in August, the director had settled in Marseille and telegraphed Pierre Gaut from there on August 26 to have him ask Einstein to join him. At the same time, according to Renoir's desires, Gaut was getting into contact with the Société des Films Marcel Pagnol.[28] The filming forecasted for Martigues was the primary reason for this association, because it simplified logistics and reduced the costs of it, whereas Pagnol himself was given an opportunity to "put the shop in gear" by renting his film equipment and making his crew and actors available. Among those whom Renoir recruited was Suzanne de Troeye, who had already worked with him on four films and in the meantime had become Pagnol's editor. The set designer Marius Brouquier and the camera operator Roger Ledru, two Pagnol film regulars, also worked on *Toni.*

Renoir and Pagnol had several traits in common, among which was the desire, which the latter achieved, to break the dependent link between a filmmaker and the production and distribution of the film. Another was an obsession with live sound. This last characteristic is one that differentiates *Toni* from Italian neo-realism; for reasons other than that, Renoir is rightfully considered a precursor of that movement.

In Marseille, Renoir and Einstein moved into the Hôtel de la Canebière. The director began lending a hand to the screenplay that Einstein was supposed to write by himself and for which he would receive 35,000 francs. The October 17 contract specified that Einstein would act as Jean Renoir's "artistic adviser" on the set.[29] An old acquaintance of Renoir's, Georges Flamant, who had played Dédé in *La Chienne*, was staying in the same hotel, having signed for the role of *Toni*. But at the same time, Pierre Gaut was also considering Fernandel, whom Les Films d'aujord'hui had offered 100,000 francs and a percentage identical to Flamant's for the role. Renoir had sanctioned the choice by letter.

Really? Georges Flamant or Fernandel as the Italian émigré Toni? Because of schedule conflicts, Fernandel did not end up accepting the proposition. However, the actor's popularity could have led to modifying the role, something that wasn't justified by the slight amount of fame enjoyed by Flamant, the choice of whom pointed to a possible solution to the problems Gaut was having pulling together the necessary funds. In point of fact, on August 14, the day following a conversation with Flamant, the producer had written to the actor, "Our project is dependent on rounding up the capital and the technical elements we need to direct it. . . . You had said you could get us a sum of 150,000 francs. It is well understood that if this contribution comes by way of you, and if, in addition, we manage to pull together the remainder we need for the direction of the afore-mentioned film, we will reserve the male lead for you."[30] Flamant would as a result receive a fee of 25,000 francs as well as 5 percent of the profits. In this way, the actor would become part of the joint venture for the film, an arrangement that Gaut and Renoir certainly did not see as of secondary importance.

On September 12, the two first casting contracts were signed. One was for Georges Flamant, who at each stage insisted it be indicated he was the lead, a contingency that led Jean Renoir to state in writing, "It is perfectly understood that this pertains to the role of Toni."[31] The second contract was for Andrex, who had also just finished his work in the film *Angèle*. Flamant's engagement was contingent on the filming of *Toni* beginning no later than September 27; and when Pierre Gaut became worried about the screenplay being ready in time, Carl Einstein tried to reassure him before Renoir relayed the message in a letter dated September 25 that the screenplay would soon be finished and that, in any case, Pagnol's crew was still working on *Angèle,* which had fallen behind, and they would all just have to wait anyway. This deferment would preclude Georges Flamant's participation de facto because he was subject to an inflexibly fixed date of September 27 for the start of shooting. However, in the same letter to Pierre Gaut, Renoir supplied some essential information: "As soon as I know what you and Pagnol have decided regarding the lead role . . ."[32] The phrase is revealing on several counts. Renoir no longer intended to choose the actor who would play Toni by himself. The decision would be shared between the titular producer (Pierre Gaut) and Marcel Pagnol, who had, therefore, become party to the production, an indirect blow to Flamant's ambitions, whose potential contribution had lost its interest. It may also be that by relinquishing responsibility for the choice of the male lead, or in pretending to, Renoir was freeing himself of his moral obligations to Flamant.

From that moment, but for a very short time, Pagnol became the acknowledged negotiator for the director. Accordingly, on September 26, Renoir and Einstein read their scenario to him. The next day, Renoir wrote to Gaut, "This screenplay isn't completely finalized, but to me the best idea seemed that Pagnol become aware of it before we supply him with the definitive version. . . . Pagnol was very interested. He thinks it's going to work very well."[33] The issue of Pagnol's part in the production and conception of the film has never been clearly resolved. The caption of a photo showing Celia Montalvan and Charles Blavette and published in *Pour vous* in November 1934 indicates that a certain indeterminacy surrounded *Toni* at the time, which on that occasion was referred to as "a film by Jean Renoir and Marcel Pagnol."[34]

Forty years later, in 1974, Pierre Gaut, in reaction to the publication of *Écrits de cinéma 1926–1971,* complained to Renoir that he thought he had granted too much importance to Pagnol's contribution: "The financing of the film was sabotaged by Pagnol and his team—Corbessas and his brother René. Pagnol had simply believed me when I told him that his dialogue and your images would make a perfect pair. That's when he agreed to provide half the money needed to make the film—with my supplying the other half. He never helped us carry it out for fear of seeing his dialogue stifled by your images, and he undermined us, that's all."[35] That's all? Since *Toni* remained the only film ever produced by Pierre Gaut, he certainly had no intention of losing possession of it. But it's interesting that in his letter he mentioned "*his* dialogue" and "*your* images" twice, points that Renoir doesn't react to in his response, which is dated June 3.[36] It's probable, actually, that because Pagnol was party to the production, he had lent a hand to the dialogue in *Toni.*

In the margin of the letter from Renoir reporting the confidence that the project had inspired in Pagnol, Pierre Gaut had written, "Kova is brilliant," a reference he'd shed light on in 1972: "When Renoir read him his dialogue, Pagnol listened distractedly and concluded, 'It's a very beautiful film. It will be a great success.' Renoir was thrilled, I a lot less so, since I had just heard Pagnol say to an actor that we had cast, 'Kova, you're brilliant!' and to me, 'That Kova has been lousy in every role.'"[37]

On the same September 26, Renoir wrote, "There's just one question left. Will Toni be an Italian, as he was in our first idea, or will we use Flamant's personality by making this character a Parisian who has come to the South of France to work?" He goes on to say that he's partial to the first solution but is also planning to shoot a test with Flamant, all the while knowing that using the actor would require changes to be made to the other characters. He was also worried about what would then happen to Max Dalban, who would play Albert, the "villain" of the film, but whom he was able for a time to imagine in the role of Toni. There's no doubt about it, suddenly Flamant's personality was proving an encumbrance, even before the discovery of the actor's role as the guilty party in swindling a certain Régine Clary, a naïve young woman willing to do anything, including paying Flamant, so she could "be in pictures."*

The rest of the casting had gotten no further along. The female roles, especially, were problematic. On September 20, Gaut wrote to Einstein, "Do you know who could play Josefa and Marie? Down here we haven't found anything up to now. I'm going to take Marcel Pagnol to see Y. de B., but I think she must be awfully old for playing Marie!"[38] If those initials stand for Yvonne de Bray, as is probably the case, his reservation does make sense. The actress had never appeared in a film and had just turned forty-seven in May.

Renoir, on the other hand, was suggesting Line Noro for Marie,[39] and the next day he informed the producer that Pagnol seconded his proposition. For the role of Josefa, he was thinking of Renée Saint-Cyr, Paula Illery (*Under the Roofs of Paris*), or even Tela Tchaï (Tanit Zerga in Pabst's *L'Atlantide*). By letter, Gaut informed Renoir that Line Noro was waiting to see whether her husband, the director André Berthomieu, agreed before she could provide a firm answer. In the same letter, Gaut mentioned, without naming her, "the little Mexican girl," whom he thought would make a perfect Josefa, as long as her strong accent didn't bother Renoir.

"The little Mexican girl" was Celia Montalvan, who was currently in Barcelona. She'd appeared in three unreleased films in France, and she'd provided Gaut with a photo of the Teatro Comico movie theater in Mexico displaying her name in giant letters. It's certain that Renoir had never seen her on the

---

* Régine Clary had been a writer for the weekly *Le Phare de Villefranche* (1924–1928). In a letter to Georges Auric, Jean Cocteau, who called her "Clarynette," wrote that in the fall of 1925 he'd received two manuscripts from her, "one on opium and the other on coke."

screen, but he may have been referring to her in a September 27 letter to Gaut saying, "The only vague possibility is the young girl who came to see us one day. Just in case, I'm going to have her do a small test. My opinion of her hasn't changed. I think she's not as pretty as her initial appearance makes her seem, but it wouldn't surprise me to discover she has a forceful nature and some acting talent." He could have been speaking of her, but it isn't definite, only because at thirty-four Celia Montalvan was, in fact, no longer a "young girl." That same day, Carl Einstein wrote to Gaut that "the Mexican appealed [to him],"[40] proof that he was still a part of all the decisions, as Renoir suggested: "Einstein and I have now made enough headway in our work for me to have her learn a scene that she will play with Flamant."

Pierre Gaut promptly, and seemingly without even waiting for Renoir's agreement, offered the actress a contract, all the terms of which she accepted from Paris on October 3. Two days later, Édouard Delmont, a regular from Les Films Marcel Pagnol, signed a contract with that company guaranteeing him top male billing. Max Dalban signed four days later. Delmont would be Fernand, and Dalban would play Albert.

On October 14, the ousting of Georges Flamant became official. On that day the actor wrote from Paris, "I accept the pure and simple cancellation of our contract, despite the promises to me from M. Pagnol, M. Pierre Gaut, and M. Jean Renoir as contained in their letter of September 12, 1934."[41]

At first, shooting was scheduled as before, to begin absolutely no later than October 12. However, it finally started on the twentieth, only two days after the roles of Marie and Toni had been cast. The first part fell to the Marseillaise Jenny Hélia, who'd been considered before to play Josefa; and the second went to Charles Blavette, a master tinsmith and outstanding cook who'd become an actor solely through the influence of Pagnol. Blavette's name was added to the cast list in handwriting above the name of another actor, Poupon, which had been crossed out with the stroke of a pen. Poupon was another "Pagnolesque" actor who had appeared on all the casting lists and had been considered at one point for the role of Uncle Sebastian. Less a choice made by reflection than a last-minute decision, it would turn out to be a fruitful one.

The same could be said for the entire cast, each of whom would contribute to giving *Toni* a tone that would forever be unique. When Renoir later states, "As for the performances, I was able to do without the big, commercially successful names,"[42] he had forgotten that before Blavette there had been Fernandel, before Celia Montalvan he'd thought of Renée Saint-Cyr, and before Jenny Hélia he'd wanted Line Noro. All it proves is that theories are born from the works and their conditions, and not vice versa.

The conditions themselves for the making of *Toni*—the feeling of urgency that drove it on, the almost exclusively natural locations, and Renoir's obstinate reliance on live sound—were already enough to contribute to its "primitive" quality, about which Renoir would speak years later. It's the story of an Italian worker who marries his landlady and falls in love with another woman, who is married to an odious man, whom she ends up shooting after he catches her trying to take back the money he has stolen from her and beats her with a belt. Like *La Chienne* before it, *Toni* ends with the death of a man who pays for a crime that someone else has committed. This bitter tragedy, inspired by a news item about an incident that occurred four years before and that *The Rules of the Game* would allude to, takes place in landscapes thought of as having enchanting beauty but from which Jean and Claude Renoir purposely expelled everything that was picturesque. Claude was working as director of photography for the first time in his life and would turn twenty the day after a hurried, fast-moving shoot that was partly improvised, mostly because the actors were not very experienced. As always on Renoir's "*tournaisons*," the atmosphere at Martigues was warm and the evenings lively at the Hôtel Pascal, whose "supply of live fish" was appreciated as much as "its wonderful view of the sea."[43] The Palace Cinéma hosted the screening of the early camera tests, and the local merchants and artisans became caterers for the film people, who'd come to make what they called "Pagnol's film." On November 18, the Santasusaca bakery delivered to the hotel two wedding cakes that were going "to act" in the marriage scene.[44]

The reliable Georges d'Arnoux once again fulfilled his function as assistant director, and he was the one who, on October 11, wrote to Pierre Gaut asking him "to please go to Ruggieri, the store on rue Ballu, and bring 10 kg of red-light powder (for nighttime special effects)."[45] Shooting at the Martigues-Caronte train station on the tracks and the Caronte viaduct needed authorizations, which were granted on October 13 by the Compagnie des Chemins de Fer de Paris à Lyon et de la Méditerranée. "Of course, according to the rules, your extras will need to have regular train tickets."

As sometimes happens, before he had taken the step that would turn him into an actor, Renoir gave himself a place in the film. For the "villain" in *Toni*, Albert, the coarse foreman who hounds women, Renoir chose Max Dalban, whom he had already used in six of his previous films. He was someone Renoir certainly got along well with, but Dalban's stature, heaviness, particular kind of clumsiness, roundness of face, and even his thinning hair, the way he spoke, and his Parisian accent made him resemble Renoir more than any other of the director's favorite actors. Whether he wanted it or not—because nothing says that he intended Dalban precisely for this role—the SOB in this film has something of Renoir.

In a letter written at Martigues on November 19, Pierre Gaut informs his mother that the director "is having a lot of trouble with Blavette," "a beginner [who] will be that much better for it in the film";[46] but these difficulties, provided they were real, wouldn't dissuade Renoir from casting the actor on several later occasions. As time went on, Carette's* excesses, as well, would worry Renoir, especially during *La Bête humaine,* but he never reached the point of making up his mind to manage without him. As much as this was out of loyalty, it also definitely had to do with a pronounced affection for the people he'd chosen, regardless of their behavior or, at times, their ideas. Alain Renoir referred to this when he said Pierre Gaut's very "right-wing" opinions had never thrown a shadow on his friendship with Jean, which, carefully maintained, would endure into the seventies. And when Renoir was awarded the Légion d'honneur near the end of his life, he suggested two names "to be promoted to [his] rank, René Clair and Pierre Gaut."[47]

On the set of *Toni,* as well, some went too far. André Kovachevitch, Pagnol's "fabulous Kova," left a surprising trace of this in the form of a note he signed on November 12: "I give my word of honor that I won't drink alcohol for eight days. I give permission to M. Gaut to stick me in the slammer if I don't keep my word."[48]

Carl Einstein's misadventure is depressing. But it's common enough in the film world. Einstein never found a place for himself on the set. For that reason, even though he was attentive to all those who participated with him in the making of the film—or in any case, gave the impression of being so—Renoir had need for an "artistic adviser" less than any other filmmaker, even one, like Einstein, who had written the screenplay with him. Einstein's involvement in the project is not at all doubtful; reading this letter that he sent to the producer on September 27, shortly before the start of filming, is convincing enough:

> I think we'll succeed in forming an ensemble that is completely Mediterranean. This may produce a novel, rather unexpected impression. Acting without any gimmicks. We'll try to give each of the walk-ons a special characteristic and place each scene in a kind of corresponding milieu. In other words, we'll try to make a real film in the open air, where people don't live and act in artificial isolation. Renoir and I studied many of these questions, and it's thanks to these moments that we'll produce something different enough from *Angèle,* which is a success of the first order, but in which it is a matter of people who are separated from an

---

* *Translator's note:* Julien Carette (1897–1966) was a French film actor who appeared in 127 films during his lifetime, including such works by Renoir as *Grand Illusion, La Bête humaine,* and *The Rules of the Game.*

environment. One thing to which I attach a large enough importance is giving each extra an individuality that is more or less concrete. I believe that we have managed to give each player a quality that goes beyond the cliché "wind-up character."[49]

Yes, but, it is one of the intangible laws of film that the movie belongs to those who are making it; and in his capacity as artistic adviser, Einstein, who on top of that was accompanied by his wife, wasn't participating directly in the making of the film. Pierre Gaut hit harshly on the obviousness of it when he said, "The Einsteins are a fifth wheel, and when you're working, you don't like the sight of inactive people. They've been made aware of it, and they've understood that we don't need them."[50] A handwritten note left by the producer in his archives reveals the sums he loaned to Einstein over the span of months, from July 1, 1933, to September 6, 1934, for a grand total of 61,400 francs, a lot more than the fee provided for in the scenarist's contract. The fact that Carl Einstein, the likeable, intriguing, and unique penniless little gentleman, turned into an insufferable sponger in Gaut's eyes may have precipitated his being pushed aside.

Consequently, the adventure of *Toni* was over for Einstein. In a letter dated January 14, 1935, translated and quoted by Liliane Meffre, he wrote to his friend Ewald Wassmuth, "Then I wrote a screenplay with Renoir, really good stuff this film. But I'm not carried away with it. I honestly did everything I could and went to a lot of trouble creating a decent screenplay, and people are saying that it's good. I hope that Renoir is finally going to finish the editing so that it can come out in February in Paris."

In February, as a matter of fact, Renoir would show his film. But the language he uses in *Comoedia* on the eighth of that month is terrible for Einstein and damning to Renoir himself: "I'm looking forward to showing my film *Toni* because I made it completely independently and for once I can claim responsibility for my work. I owe this good fortune to my friendship with Marcel Pagnol and Pierre Gaut, the director of production." Not a word about poor Einstein.

The worst was yet to come, however. Ten days later, Pierre Gaut also wrote, in response to a question about the music and songs used in the film, "I can confirm that it certainly is M. Jean Renoir who wrote the screenplay and the dialogue for the film *Toni*."[51] Nearly thirty years later, having been saddened that Renoir had neglected to mention his name in an article, Gaut would receive this response from the director: "I don't have any power to change *Écrits 1926–1971*, which, as far as *Toni* is concerned, is composed of texts that I wrote in 1938 and 1935. On the other hand, in my autobiography *My Life and My Films*, which is going to come out next, you figure in due form as the producer of *Toni*."[52] It's doubtful that the producer took into account on that day what he'd made the scenarist of *Toni* endure.

Carl Einstein never knew that his name had been removed from the credits for the film when it was rereleased after the war;[*] or that Renoir, in an undated certificate of transfer of all rights to the film to Pierre Gaut and to Les Films Marcel Pagnol, had written, "I, the undersigned Jean Renoir, sole author of the original scenario entitled *Toni* . . ."[53] On returning to France after having taken part in the war in Spain, with neither money nor visa that would allow him to emigrate, and imprisoned for several days in the spring of 1940 in a camp near Bordeaux, Einstein tried to commit suicide by slitting open his veins. He managed to flee the Hôpital de Mont-de-Marsan to which he'd been admitted. To his friend Kahnweiler he's said to have declared, "I know what's going to take place. They'll intern me and the French police will be my guards. One fine day it will be the SS. But that's something I refuse to let happen. I'll jump in the goddamn water first."[54] On July 5, 1940, his body was found in the Gave de Pau.

Marcel Pagnol didn't come to the set. According to Pierre Gaut, he was "traveling," but "we see Pagnol's family quite often, and Marcel's father, mother, and sister are impressed by the way our team functions." Pagnol came back to the scene afterward in response to the agreement signed on October 16 and specifying the commitment of each party, as well as the various fees to be paid. Renoir would receive 100,000 francs, part of which (37,000 francs) he would contribute to their joint venture; and Carl Einstein, 35,000 francs, in his capacity as coauthor, a sum that shows that the importance of his contribution was not considered negligible at the time. Gaut committed to turning over 350,000 francs to the company Les Films d'aujourd'hui, which Renoir and he would manage. Most importantly, *Toni*'s distribution would be awarded to Les Auteurs associés, Marcel Pagnol's company. Therefore, Pagnol had his say regarding the film, which would be developed in his laboratories, a detail that allowed Pierre Braunberger, who had his reasons when it came to *Toni,* to claim that Pagnol very certainly saw the rushes and probably influenced Renoir during the direction. Obviously, the director's statement about having worked on *Toni* for the first time in complete freedom was of a nature to offend the producer in light of several of his previous films.

Marguerite was the credited editor, assisted by Suzanne de Troeye, who had been appointed script girl on the shoot, but who found herself equally occupied by work finishing *Angèle*. A working copy was ready at the very beginning of January 1935, but Renoir had in advance, on December 29—with Pagnol's blessing—refused to show it to Queyrel, who had programed *Madame Bovary*

---

[*] Carl Einstein's name would be restored after that on some copies.

at the Ciné-Opéra, one of his three theaters in Paris. The director intended that only those partners closely associated with the production would lay eyes on the film in the state in which it was at the time. He didn't trust Queyrel, whom he considered "unreliable," and made it clear that Pagnol was far from satisfied with the release of his *Angèle*.

The edit that Renoir screened on January 5, 1935, for Charles Corbessas, Pagnol's vendor, was around 145 minutes, which he was already in the process of reducing to 129 minutes. The screening confirmed for him that the film actually was too long, especially its first part. Corbessas agreed and also thought "certain scenes were a bit downbeat [morally]." There was hardly any doubt, in fact, that *Toni* was not really the "amusing, light, and very lively" film that Pierre Gaut had "sold" Pagnol on, specifying at the time that its "morbid aspect" had been toned down.

Because Pagnol was against organizing a Parisian screening for Pierre Gaut, Renoir tried to reassure his producer in a letter dated January 10: "[Pagnol] hasn't seen the film yet, but the talk that has reached him has obviously convinced him not to rashly risk the commercial campaign that would assure the good course of the film. I dined with him yesterday evening, and he is kind enough to be interested in *Toni*'s success as he would be in his own child." Kindness, no doubt, but kindness that wasn't completely disinterested, seeing that Pagnol was the distributor of the film, a fact that Renoir certainly wasn't neglecting: "Let's not forget that *Toni* doesn't come off as belonging in your usual commercial category: no star and an atmosphere a bit grim for those used to standard productions." At that moment, the director foresaw a duration of 117 minutes, which he described as "respectable"; and then he delivered this surprising piece of information, which, essentially, reveals his desire at that time to reassure the producer: "For the first time since I've been making films, I'm positive of having done the editing exactly right."[55]

After Pierre Gaut finally saw the film in Marseille on January 17, Renoir appeared more than ever convinced that he had to further reduce the length by close to thirty minutes. Charles Tesson, in his essential study of the making of *Toni*, perfectly delineates what was at stake: "Starting with this delicate moment, Renoir is no longer the only master on board since everyone is going to go with his own idea and try to impose it. By everybody, I mean Pierre Gaut, Marcel Pagnol, his vendor [Corbessas], and the theater owner [Queyrel], who will come into the scene. They are going to see the film as it's being edited, and they are going to say what they want to see disappear or remain."[56]

Renoir faced the ordeal in front of him strengthened by the experience he'd painfully acquired with *La Chienne* and, in lesser measure perhaps, *Madame Bovary*. He now knew that the author of a film—a singular creation that can only be made by several—is the one who knows how to prove himself the "strongest." As he stated later, to be correctly marketed and offered to audiences in the proper conditions, a film had to reunite those who were responsible for it, not put them in opposition. He was no longer unaware that consensus was necessary, even more at that moment in the life of a work than during its direction, which nevertheless also required the usually tacit assent of all those whom it employed. In this sense, it is not really out of place to claim that with *Toni* Renoir finished his apprenticeship in the profession of filmmaking.

The scene of the brawl between Toni and Albert was the first thing to be discussed. The moment that Pierre Gaut declared he was in favor of cutting it, at least partially, Renoir removed it; but when Queyrel, seeing the film for the first time in Marseille on January 19, confided he felt something was missing at this precise moment, Renoir saw to it that it was put back in, slightly modified in structure, so that his two negotiators with opposite opinions could both consider themselves satisfied.

Renoir also listened to Pierre Gaut about a criticism leveled by Queyrel:

The scene with Josefa holding a revolver before she shoots Albert really got him into a state, and he asked me to cut it. I don't agree with him at all. For the first time in a French film we have an expressive shot in which the acting skills of the performer allow the suggestion of a murder without showing this murder. In my opinion this means that it would be madness to eliminate it. You can't accuse this shot of being crude because it's just the opposite. It allows us to avoid crudeness and to put in the viewer's mind the idea of a horrible thing, without showing that horrible thing.[57]

The discussion is an important one, because it touches on the very nature of film, while supplying some understanding of what in Renoir's cinema remained generally misunderstood at the time, as well as why it was. Further along, Renoir tells of another request from Queyrel: "He also asked me to remove the shots showing Blavette dragging Albert's corpse into the clump of trees and bushes. There, it's a matter of something material, and it doesn't harm the characterization in any way. That's why I think I should please him. In order to give him satisfaction, I've also filmed a link shot with Blavette, and I'll see it tomorrow."

At the end of January, the last work on editing had brought the film to a length of 112 minutes, credits included. While the conception for the trailer held most of Pagnol's attention, Renoir became alarmed about the delay in finishing, which was endangering the release planned for February 22. The master print, the last step, was scheduled for February 9 and 10, twelve days before the presentation of the film to audiences. Such a schedule may seem outrageous, but it does conform to the practices in force at the time, which may also help explain the conditions of the release of *Madame Bovary*.

Previewed using a copy scratched from beginning to end, the film actually did come out on February 22, in two Parisian theaters, the Bonaparte and the Ciné-Opéra, where it directly followed *Angèle*. *Toni*, which appeared in the listings of the papers as a "Provençal film," was a commercial failure; and the support given it by critics proved to be without important effect. Renoir's comment: "In those days, corpses in films weren't accepted, or else you needed ones that were noble enough. But the murder in *Toni* wasn't accepted as marketable."[58]

There remains one last point to clear up. The article that appeared in *La Semaine à Paris* on February 22 confirms, even if in an approximate way, the length of *Toni*: "One and three-quarter hours of what can be called pure cinema. One and three-quarter hours of life and intelligence. Jean Renoir can be proud of his work: it's a masterpiece." The film that was shown then ran 112 minutes. And yet the *Toni* that has come down to us today lasts eighty-five minutes. What happened to the twenty-seven missing minutes? When and how have they disappeared? The first part of the answer was provided by Jean Renoir, who stated in *Cahiers du cinéma* in June 1966, "I regret the fact that *Toni*, cold-shouldered by the critics when it came out and, let's face it, by audiences, had to be cut. When a film goes badly, you panic and you think everything can be settled by cutting it. You don't settle anything at all. The concessions do nothing but harm."

The panic mentioned by Renoir, who was, perhaps, tricked by his memory when he claimed that the film was cold-shouldered by the critics, caused Marguerite to end up with an assignment, and she gave an account of it to Pierre Gaut in a letter dated March 28, 1935: "Following your instructions, I went to Marseille on Wednesday, March 14, to finalize the negative of *Toni* after the last cuts had been decided in Paris. The reason for this trip was that Suzanne de Troeye, the editor of the negative, was unwell. I carried out this work the best I could. But I wasn't able to match the latest version of the positive, because certain cuts done after orders received from Paris had already modified the negative. I thought that it wasn't up to me to change these instructions that had come from Paris."[59] According to Marguerite's statement, the film had been cut already in Paris, directly on the two copies shown in movie theaters, and then in Marseille, following which the negative would next be used as a matrix for any new copies that would now conform to the film as it would henceforth be projected in Paris.

The principal victim of this ransacking to which Renoir had to consent was the scene called the handcart, which he would describe in 1966: "The scene that had excited us the most in *Toni* and that we strove to reproduce how it had happened in the real-life tragedy was the transporting of the body of the husband on a cart pulled by the wife who had murdered him. This car was loaded with wash hiding the corpse. Corsican coalmen, of whom there still rest several traces in the film, had accompanied this mortuary vehicle in what they took for an innocent walk to the washing place, along paths of the hill that dominates the lake, lavishing the beautiful Spaniard with jokes and encouraging her with their most beautiful songs." Such a description sharpens our sense of loss, but perhaps there's consolation in imagining that several scenes of *The Rules of the Game* would have disappeared forever, too, after being pulled from the film by Renoir in a similar state of panic—they would have disappeared, that is, like in *Toni*, if their original negative hadn't been preserved.

* In a letter to Marcel Pagnol dated October 29, 1934, Pierre Gaut, who had just seen the film for the first time, declared himself particularly impressed by the scene of the cart.

13

In the Courtyard

Le Crime de monsieur Lange (The Crime of Monsieur Lange)

"Jean Renoir, whom we've now given up trying to follow, may have lived down the memory of both *Chotard et Cie* and *Madame Bovary* with this new film, which may be his masterpiece." The sentence, written by Valéry Jahier, appeared in the October 1935 issue of the review *Esprit* and quite succinctly expresses *Toni*'s importance to the director's career. The work's uniqueness in the context of the times and its harshness, in particular, caused by the effects of live sound, not to mention the feeling that such a film was the closest possible match to life's unforgiving brutalities, certainly did prove harmful to its commercial fate. Yet its director came out of the experience larger in stature and higher in repute.

The chaotic course of the film's casting resulted in a movie without stars, from which Renoir hastened to draw a lesson. Consequently, in February 1935, he wrote in his introduction to *Toni*, "No one more admires the talents of our great stars more than I do. But their films need to be conceived strictly for showing off their temperament, so that the expectations of their audiences will not be disappointed. I prefer collaborating with intelligent, sensitive actors who don't yet have a very long career in film. They can avoid the repetition of some well-tried strategies to which artists who are already too stereotyped are likely to resort every time the chance comes along. Without risking their careers, they can be more spontaneous, less artificial, closer to real life."

The statement, especially the part about using stars, something Renoir was going to have good reason not to renounce, requires some caveats; but the thrust of it is definitely essential and was further clarified in the last part of a carefully written passage: "With such actors, it's advisable to replace routine with constant inventiveness and to avoid subjecting them to a strict shooting script for which every gesture and angle have to be decided in advance. I don't believe the actor should be placed at the beck and call of any technique; it's the technique that should remain flexible enough to accommodate the performance of the actor. In exchange for such freedom of behavior, this method requires the performer to be absolutely faithful to the spirit of the scenario as well as to employ a rigorous mental discipline." Beginning with *Toni,* these principles were in place. The only thing that Renoir had to do now was to dishonor them as outrageously as principles deserve.

"This is film, real film," began the review that appeared March 1, 1935, in *L'Humanité,* which had already devoted several enthusiastic lines to *Toni* on February 22. It set the tone. Renoir didn't see it on that day; he was in Moscow.

Probably in response to Mussolini, who had just created Venice's Mostra,* Stalin wanted the Soviet Union to have its own big film festival. The event, which had a budget of 35,000 gold rubles, was chaired by Eisenstein and took place in Moscow from February 21 to March 1, 1935. The films were shown at the Udarnik (Strike Brigade) theater. Of the sixty-four titles selected, twenty-four would receive prizes. They included Georgi Vasiliev's *Chapaev,* which won the Grand Prize. Soviet comrades were told on December 25 of that year that Stalin had watched the film at least twenty-eight times.[1] Also shown were George Cukor's *Little Women,* King Vidor's *Our Daily Bread,* Cecil B. DeMille's *Cleopatra,* and René Clair's *Le Dernier Milliardaire (The Last Billionaire). Toni* wasn't mentioned, despite the fact that Renoir's "delegation" had made the trip to present it. A postcard sent by Renoir from Moscow to Pierre Gaut and showing the ancient cathedral of Saint Basil cleared up the mystery: "The print of *Toni* got lost in customs, and we're looking for it. It will be too late to put it into competition at the Festival. I'll show it to the film people who asked me for it."[2] Not long before,† Pierre Gaut had received another card informing him that everyone had arrived safe and sound in Moscow—"everyone" meaning the four people who'd signed the card: Jean Renoir, "Margueritte," Claude (Renoir), and d'Arnoux.[3]

For Marguerite, of course, the trip to Moscow was a major event, and the very brief time that had separated the finishing of the film and the festival could mean that she was the one who'd been able to get her comrades to obtain *Toni's* invitation. Claude Renoir was there in his capacity as director of cinematography for the film; d'Arnoux because Renoir adored him and intended to have him around all the time.

The intemperate Georges d'Arnoux was described in a measured portrait of him that appeared in *Pour vous:* "After some car racing and wild times at Fouquet's, d'Arnoux has decided that there are other things in life beside bars, and he's now working as an assistant director—the likes of which you don't see often." The Count d'Arnoux, his father, who'd been forced to acknowledge his

---

* *Translator's note:* The Venice International Film Festival.

† The Soviet postmark has been worn away by time and prevents deciphering the day the postcard was sent. Only the month can be made out.

own ruin, had one day basically told him that the only thing he was still in a position to offer was a good marriage. As a result, Georges had wed the fabulously wealthy but far from beautiful heiress of a button manufacturer. His wife's fortune could fuel his passion for horses, cars, and painting the town red, during which he combined alcohol and cocaine. Madame d'Arnoux's paltry attractions freed him from any scruples about chasing after girls, an activity he pursued with frenetic energy. Confident of a virility he proudly flaunted—whether anyone wanted to see it or not—he'd show off a member that apparently did have what it took to feel smug. He was, again, more exhibitionistic than aggressive, and he choreographed temper tantrums that led him on at least one occasion—before witnesses—to demolish his wife's piano with a sledgehammer because her practicing scales got on his nerves. The pianist reacted to her husband's fits with detached resignation and merely had a new instrument delivered as quickly as possible.[4] On June 15 and 16, 1935, the philanderer raced in the twenty-four-hour competition at Le Mans at the wheel of a Type 55 Bugatti in the colors of Count Georges d'Arnoux's team.

Renoir didn't see very much of Moscow and the Soviet Union: a few movies, of course, which he'd describe the following year in an article in *L'Humanité*, as well as mountains of caviar, making him think that the Soviets had succeeded in raising the standard of living of their comrades to a stupendous degree.[5] If this trip had any effect on the positions he'd take in the months to come, it was probably enhanced by the stop the company made in Germany on their way back from Moscow, giving Jean the opportunity to evaluate to what point the "New Order" had changed the country.

In Potsdam, he discovered that the mayor had had a statue of Frederick II taken down, after which an old lady came up to him, peered at the scalp he'd shaved before leaving France, and told him that because he was obviously an officer in the imperial army he ought to make a speech. That was when Renoir went into action and put forward the idea that, on the contrary, Germany needed lots of statues of Frederick of Prussia, as a reminder that it ought to get rid of Hitler as soon as possible. At least, that's the story he told his son when he got home.[6] The fact that the Soviet Union had declared itself Hitlerian Germany's enemy while the European democracies kept on shillyshallying would provide one of Renoir's motives for joining the Party.

For the time being, Jean went back to work. And while he began work on a new screenplay, Marguerite and he attempted to get Pierre Gaut to give them the money he still owed. On January 21, 1935, Renoir wrote to the producer, "I'm afraid I must ask you, aside from the 3,000 francs you are supposed to send me, two more things: an additional 1,200 francs to pay the rent here [in Meudon], because repairing my car has cost me a fortune. And the same amount to M. Guillaume, 105, rue des Dames, to pay my rent on the Paris place. Without it, they're going to kick me out."[7] On April 10, it was Marguerite's turn; she wrote from Meudon, "Sorry to have to insist again, but on the 15th I'll have some big bills to take care of, and I'd truly appreciate getting a little of the money from what remains of my fees. I need approximately 2,000 francs." A new message from Marguerite on May 15 to the tune of, "I'm sorry to have to ask again. I have a bill of 1,000 francs due, and I would like you to do the impossible and send that sum right away.[8] And best wishes to your mother and to Francette [Pierre Gaut's daughter]." People in the film world can relate just as intensely with friendship as with self-interest. And it's rare enough for the former (or the ghost of it) not to survive the latter.

A few months later, near the end of 1935, Renoir moved with Alain into a two-room attic apartment with a kitchen at 93 rue de Rome. At the time, Marguerite was living in a larger apartment on the floor below. Because Jean shared his father's reservations about school, Alain's education, which would now occur at the Lycée Condorcet, had been taken care of until then by his two private tutors from Essoyes.

An artistic success that was praised almost unanimously, *Toni* still became a financial bust in the end—yet another for Renoir, which put an end to his hopes of forming a lasting production company that would have guaranteed his creative independence. While he was working on the editing of *Toni*, Pagnol had mentioned the possibility of Renoir's collaborating on a *Moloch* idea with Jacques de Féraudy, perhaps an adaptation of the book by Marcel Prévost, *Monsieur et Madame Moloch;* but Renoir was still hoping to keep to his course. To Gaut he wrote, "Naturally, working would interest me a lot, but I'd very much prefer starting something immediately with you, if our company has the means to pay for it."[9] He was especially thinking then of *L'Évasion de Pinsard,* the precursor to *Grand Illusion* that would come later, and also about "a subject that would take place on a boat on the Mediterranean, in the world of fishermen—something we could shoot with Blavette and Bozzi." Shortly after the release of *Toni,* the possibility of Renoir and Gaut producing a new film together wouldn't exist.

His opportunity would come from practically a beginner, without the person's desiring it, someone in conflicting circumstances. If the faithful Jacques Becker hadn't taken part in *Toni,* it was because he himself had just begun directing films, a dream he'd fostered for a long time. To produce his first, Becker appealed to André Halley des Fontaines, the wealthy heir of a family of steelwork owners he'd met on a tennis court in Switzerland in 1922. On Becker's suggestion, Halley des Fontaines had created a production house called

Obéron and formed a partnership with Warner Bros. Paris, which was then looking for medium-length films. From this came *Le commissaire est bon enfant* (*Pitiless Gendarme*), the adaptation of a play by Georges Courteline that was forty minutes long. To do the film, Warner had insisted Becker be "covered" by Pierre Prévert, who had just directed *L'affaire est dans le sac* (*It's in the Bag*). Thus, Renoir's assistant was very connected to Prévert, who introduced him to the October group, a band of actors, musicians, and singers who performed on the street and in factories. Several members of the group appeared in *It's in the Bag*, including Lou Bonin and Marcel Duhamel (who'd later create the imprint Série noire at Gallimard). The screenplay was by Becker and Jean Castanier. A painter of Spanish origin, Castanier (or Castanyer) had designed the scenery for *Boudu*. After *Pitiless Gendarme*, which was shot in three days, the duo of Becker and Castanier worked together again to produce *Une tête qui rapporte*, which was forty-two minutes long, before beginning a feature that was to be shot entirely in the streets of Paris but that was never made. The project that followed would enjoy a better fate, but certainly not as far as Becker was concerned.

Becker and Castanier called their new scenario *Sur la cour*. They started writing this story about a cooperative of printers and laundresses early in 1935 and offered it to Halley des Fontaines. He said he was interested but refused to put his trust in Becker, despite the fact that Becker was his friend and also the one who'd introduced him to the idea of the film. The producer would eventually enjoy a very successful career, especially with two later films by Becker, *Dernier atout* and *Falbalas* (*Paris Frills*), before pursuing an ambitious policy as head of the UGC (responsible for several of Becker's films as well as Rossellini's *Germany Year Zero* and Bresson's *Le Journal d'un curé de campagne* [*Diary of a Country Priest*]). But at the end of winter 1934–1935, Halley des Fontaines didn't have enough faith in his friend's talent, or else his partners refused to move on it; and the project ended up in the hands of Renoir, who accepted. A darker version of what happened, rumored in the French film world of the time, maintained that Renoir, learning about what was happening with the screenplay from Becker, muscled in on the deal and obviously met with no reluctance on the part of the producer.

Becker was furious, angry at Halley des Fontaines, Castanier, and Renoir. According to Geneviève Boyer-Becker, then married to Jacques, Renoir was going through a bad patch at the time and had "become easy to irritate, cantankerous."[10] Nothing or no one found favor with him. He'd been making films for more than ten years and still hadn't experienced any real success, and he knew that the critical recognition afforded *Toni* would have no effect on whether his own projects succeeded. The failure of his last independent production company was making him think that he was going to have to start from zero yet again. Beginning at this moment, and until 1938 and the start of *The Rules of the Game,* he stopped thinking of producing his films himself.

Becker's experiencing what had happened as betrayal is easy to comprehend; and the fact that their split only lasted a few months is a rather clear symptom of his attachment to Renoir and his admiration for him. However, those feelings did not prevent him from afterward conceiving of a kind of cinema different from his mentor's in many respects. Renoir's lack of sentiment regarding the affair is surprising when set against the image projected of him by his worshippers years later: a plump, kindly granddad anxious to preserve his friendships even at the price of his personal interests.

The "treatment for a screenplay in collaboration with Castagnié [*sic*]"[11] dated April 15, 1935, makes it possible to evaluate the distance separating *The Crime of Monsieur Lange* from *Sur la cour,* as well as the extent of the work accomplished in a few weeks by Renoir and Castanier. The story begins in a criminal court where a certain Monsieur Pierre is being tried for murder. A proofreader for the magazine *Les Causes célèbres,* he is accused of having killed his boss, a man named Gilbert, who—with the help of his friend Max—had perfected a scheme allowing him to evade his responsibilities by passing for dead. Finding himself on his own to direct the magazine, Monsieur Pierre writes an article about his boss that creates enough stir to attract attention to the publication; and this newfound success plunges the character into high society. When Gilbert reappears, he gets into an argument with Pierre, who kills him. The jury acquits him.

In the margin of the manuscript, in Jean Renoir's handwriting, are four title suggestions in the following order: *Monsieur Lange journaliste, Le Crime de monsieur Lange, L'Ascension de monsieur Lange,* and *Le Règne de monsieur Lange.* As it was presented, the structure of the screenplay clearly foretold that of the film, but the middle part and, especially, the characters are different. Thus, the laundresses who were in *Sur la cour* (if we are to believe Castanier) have disappeared. It wouldn't be long, however, until they turned up again. It should also be noted that Renoir and Castanier had planned at the time to make the main character a married man, but the wife seems to have thrown a wrench into the works, to judge from the following sentence, made even more slapdash by its lack of punctuation: "He neglects his wife who dies and that is fairly unnoticed in the welter of his affairs."

An episode from Auguste Renoir's life, which Jean would recount in his book on his father, may have had something to do with Jean's excitement about the story of a cooperative. Auguste was seventeen at the time and was working in a studio that made porcelain. Frightened off by the success of porcelain and china factories, his boss was considering selling out so he could devote himself to cultivating melons. Jean writes: "With the agreement of his friends, he went to M. Lévy with an incredible offer. . . . [He] was proposing to create a cooperative. They would pay the boss for rental of the premises with their profits. The workers would share the remainder in equal parts. The idea was to take swift action against the machines that were coming to steal their bread and butter."[12]

By May 2, 1935—only two weeks after the first "treatment"—the project had already developed a great deal. Under the title *L'Ascension de monsieur Lange*, the authors began by making their intent clear: "This film project is based on the general idea that every human being who has won an important place in society and who has shown he's worthy of it has the right to hold onto that place and defend it against a thief; even if this thief backs up his action according to legal principles."[13] The use of a flashback in the film remained, but the court had disappeared, replaced by a border checkpoint in the Pyrénées. More importantly, the character of Lange had been brought closer to the one René Lefèvre would play, who "will look like a puny little bureaucrat," but, "as soon as he's given the opportunity to daydream, will think of his favorite heroes—Indians and cowboys of the West—and imagine himself galloping across the prairie beside them. . . . Under his not very impressive outward appearance teems an intense imaginative life." The company where he works is dubbed "Les Publications populaires," "includes three weeklies," *Le Boy-scout . . .*, *La Petite Lisette*, and *L'Hebdomadaire illustré*, and is run by someone named Cathala (who'd become Batala, perhaps so that the minister of agriculture of Laval's government, Pierre Cathala, couldn't take offense about the name).

A note that appears halfway through the treatment provides a few clarifications about the female characters: "We can picture the typist who is sympathetic to Monsieur Lange replaced by a lady who writes stories for girls in a magazine resembling *Semaine de Suzette*. This lady has her hands full dealing with what's happening in the offices near the one where Monsieur Lange works. She'll go through a series of changes similar to Monsieur Lange's, and her character will be different by the end of the film. To create a contrast with this lady, we're imagining a young, very stylish typist who's extremely irritating and who could be the private secretary of the murdered director." The first woman would end up as a laundress and would no longer be named Marion but Valentine, whereas the typist, Édith, played by Sylvia Bataille, would appear less "annoying" than touching.

A treatment in the Jean Renoir archives in Los Angeles further clouds the mystery surrounding the genesis of this film. Lacking any date or author's name, these twenty-one typed pages[14] don't seem to be the work of Renoir himself. Their presentation, which is different from that of the director's usual treatments and synopses, suggests that they are instead a project that was submitted to him. Without any indication why, the document is identified as coming from Jean-Paul Dreyfus. Entitled *Aventures*, the text provides a detailed account of a plot to boost the sales of a magazine published by the "Société nouvelle de publications hebdomadaires." "Our magazine *Aventures* sold very well the first year, and readers who'd become lovers of crime, mysteries, and detective stories were fighting to get hold of copies of our magazine by the second month after it appeared. . . . Then along came the competition." When Georges Moulin, the director of the company, disappears without a trace, sales skyrocket again. He and André Dumas, his nephew and the chief copy editor, have been "pretending not to get along." But when it's discovered that Moulin has been murdered, Dumas is arrested and tried. The trial "reveals the existence of a plot dreamed up by the editorial staff—Moulin, Roche [the editor-in-chief], and him [Dumas]—to give the magazine a powerful boost by creating an enormous scandal based on a colossal travesty of justice." Clues were left on purpose to jeopardize Dumas and get him convicted, following which Moulin is supposed to reappear.

Could this be an early draft of the treatment, perhaps on the part of Castanier? Or a synopsis that the authors of *Lange* took as inspiration? If that's the case, it's hard to believe that its author, Jean-Paul Dreyfus or someone else, didn't speak out after the release of the film.

Rooted in the heart of everyday Parisian life, set in a courtyard that itself becomes a major character as a result, *The Crime of Monsieur Lange* deals with a theme already initiated by Renoir when he set up several "shops" in the courtyard of La Nicotière for *The Whirlpool of Fate*. *Lange* takes place at the junction of two major careers in the history of French film and partly can be traced to Jean Renoir's encounter with Jacques Prévert. Prévert was probably steered to the screenplay by Castanier. Both were members of the October group and had worked together on several occasions. In addition, Pierre Prévert, Jacques's brother, had worked as an assistant on *La Chienne* and *Boudu*.

The encounter between Renoir and Jacques Prévert was meteoric, confined to a few weeks in the summer of 1935 and made possible by the opposite vectors of the two men. The October group entered Renoir's domain to the cadences of Prévert's phrases at the very time when the latter was preparing to leave it, having been disillusioned by what he discovered in the USSR during a trip with the group to the Moscow Theater Festival in June 1933. Renoir came to his experience with Prévert right after a trip to Moscow, where he hadn't seen a thing. And Prévert was lambasting the members of October for joining the ranks of a Communist Party whose praises Renoir was on the verge of singing.

Both the actors of the October group and Prévert were like a fresh breath of air for Renoir—not only for the man but for his filmmaking. For perhaps the first time since he had begun directing, having now escaped the need to prove himself or worry about producing, Renoir felt liberated. And he'd been around long enough to know that being free did not mean doing whatever struck his fancy. In fact, the film he directed between September 19 and the end of October 1935 in the Billancourt studios accurately followed the established shooting script, which is the opposite of what Renoir would claim afterward: "When it comes to *The Crime of Monsieur Lange,* we mustn't forget Jacques Prévert's contribution, which is crucial. We worked together. I asked him to come to the set with me. He was there every day, which was very kind of him; and I would say to him constantly: 'Well, pal, that's where we have to improvise,' and the film was improvised like all my others, but with Prévert's constant cooperation." As is often the case with Renoir, his account is designed to tell less about the facts than about the circumstances in which it happened.

When Renoir spoke that way in 1957, he was talking to François Truffaut and Jacques Rivette, who had begun their war in *Cahiers du cinéma* against French cinema's heavy reliance on scenarios. Renoir told those with whom he was in conversation what they wanted to hear, and his words were not devoid of grandstanding. It was the case with *Lange* as it was for most of Renoir's films, which were often presented as the product of some amazing gut instincts, when they were actually the result of dogged labor, a highly developed sense of culture, an all-consuming interest in human beings, and a very unique tendency for melding these various assets—all elements of what could be called talent. There is nothing less "fantastic" in it, actually; but for these budding directors, a belief in inspiration falling from the skies offered an obviously less awe-inspiring, less icy, and, absurdly enough, more accessible image of the director. It conformed more easily, above all, to the romantic conception of the artist.

In 1957, everyone knew that the French cinema of the thirties was to an important extent a cinema of screenwriters. The fact that Prévert's brilliance was able to overshadow Marcel Carné's talent is evidence of this. Similarly, the influence of a dialogue writer like Henri Jeanson is easily interpreted as a threat to the very notion of the auteur. Renoir was against such a tendency—quite adamantly so at the time—without making a public issue of it. And he was so again, quite ostentatiously, after twenty years had passed and the time had come to join the voices of young critics who'd just established a model of the auteur—while he simultaneously promoted himself as the sole and sovereign auteur of his own films. The fact that he never asked to work with Prévert again after *Lange* strengthens the thesis Maurice Baquet reified when he said, "He laughingly confessed that with a screenplay by Jacques there was no longer a lot to do. Which was false, of course . . . but not entirely. In my opinion, it was very just—and accurate."[15]

Although it's possible that Prévert kept track of the filming of *Lange*, it's unlikely that his day-to-day involvements were as significant as Renoir would claim. The screenwriter's contributions occurred prior to direction, which doesn't make them any less essential. There are many differences between the Renoir-Castanier project and the shooting script, and they can be seen clearly. Most notably, they concerned the female lead, who changed from an employee of the magazine to a laundress; Batala's seduction of Estelle (Nadia Sibirskaïa); and the character of Meunier's son, which was reduced considerably. The concierge, an important and inspired figure, also seems to have been created solely by Prévert. That character's dialogue—some of the most successful Prévert ever wrote because it is less blatantly "poetic"—clearly carries his mark.

Between the shooting script entitled *L'Ascension de monsieur Lange* and the actual film, on the other hand, there is very little noticeable difference. A few short scenes were removed, either during shooting or during editing. These included Lange discovering—thanks to Estelle's lover, Charles (Maurice Baquet)—the advertisements inserted by Batala (Jules Berry) in his *Arizona Jim* (a duplication of the nearly identical scene between Valentine and Lange); a second scene also showing Lange and Charles in the latter's office cubicle; and another scene that takes place at a railway just after the accident, showing Batala already dressed as a priest. On the other hand, the very beautiful shot of Batala's leaving, which shows Édith following the departing train from the platform to shout to her boss and lover, "I'm fond of you, you know, I really am," does not appear in the shooting script.

The changes in dialogue, a more likely reason for Prévert's presence on the set, aren't very numerous. It was Renoir who cut two lines of dialogue between Charles after his accident and Amédée Lange. Lange suggests that Charles should have stayed in the hospital where "you can see trees from the window" and hears him answer, "No, I couldn't, you had to pay for that." Too melodramatically abject from Renoir's point of view? Possibly.

In *Lange*, Jules Berry sticks to the words of Prévert's dialogue for the first time. The actor's reputation for taking liberties with texts, which was only partly justified, fed the legend promoted by Renoir himself about Berry's improvising his lines. One of the rare interviews given by Sylvia Bataille contradicted it: "[Jules Berry] was very, very pleasant to work with. He didn't improvise. He didn't learn his lines, but they were taught to him. Really, he was a wonderful actor. The only thing is that he thought his character was totally cynical, and to make him less cynical, he'd smile a lot in playing him. He told me, 'You know, Renoir wants him to be cynical, but I'm going to lighten him up and give him some smiles.' And the more he made him smile, the more cynical the character became, and that was fantastic."[16] A study of the shooting script refutes the hypothesis about improvisation: Jules Berry performed his lines as was asked of him; he didn't change them. At the most, he changed certain lines on his own initiative or in response to a suggestion from Renoir to produce a more comic effect. For example, after Valentine asks Édith, "Is it the sewing machine that's making you nervous?" Batala was supposed to send his secretary-mistress away with the line, "There's some mail to type," which Berry changed to, "Then go over there to your machine . . . and sew." On the other hand, contrary to what has at times been claimed, Batala's famous reply in response to Lange's question about knowing who would miss him when he was gone, "Well, women, old man!" did come from Prévert, who'd merely written, "Women!" Jules Berry didn't invent the line; he just "interpreted" it and extended it.

One of the screenwriter's lines, which Valentine was supposed to say to Batala,* remained unsaid: "When you're finished speaking between quotation marks . . ." Prévert used it again for *Le jour se lève* (*Daybreak*) and put it into Arletty's mouth. And just as had been intended for Renoir's film, in Carné's, Jules Berry was the one to whom the line was spoken, which is further proof that stars of the time would inspire the screenwriters, not to mention the directors. Moreover, the car swerving in the first scene of the film when Lange tries to avoid a dog, which was specified in the scenario, would be used again by Prévert at the beginning of *Port of Shadows*.

Lange's cast is one of the most perfect that can be imagined. In picking Jules Berry, which probably happened before Prévert's involvement in the project and therefore before the screenplay was finished, Renoir turned to a star of light comedy. Berry's role as a sometimes dastardly liar and seducer who was, nevertheless, desired and loved by women and adored by the public fit like a glove. Berry's popularity gave Renoir the chance to shape one of those "wicked" characters he appreciated who wasn't ever completely detestable. Batala—just like everybody else—had his reasons. The actor had his, as well, and when Renoir (or Marguerite) realized that the shot of Batala dead near the fountain had been accidently left out, Nadia Sibirskaïa's husband (as she would recount years later) ended up being asked to turn himself into a cadaver "because using Berry like that, for a link shot, without paying him . . ."[17]

Opposite Jules Berry was René Lefèvre, who'd begun his career with Jouvet, had scuffled with Michel Simon in *Jean de la lune,* had been a hit in René Clair's *Le Million,* and had just broken his nose at the races in Lille (horses were his

---

* In the shooting script, Batala's first name was Pal, a detail missing from the film and a possible indication that the authors had been thinking of giving the character a Hungarian background or, at any rate, a foreign one.

obsession for the rest of his life). That broken nose was the end of his career as a juvenile lead, little bursts of which can be spotted in his very restrained performance, a mixture of shyness and ardor, which allowed him to put across very gently an unforgettable Amédée Lange.

The alluring Florelle creates a powerful Valentine whose full life has endowed her with a talent for repartee and a perfect understanding of men. She knows just where she wants to go and pulls the tentative Lange along with her. The actress in this role had been a head chorus girl for a revue in the twenties and was also an excellent singer. She'd been Polly in the French version of *The Threepenny Opera*, and that link to Brecht helped attract her to Renoir, who then became fully convinced because of her participation in Fritz Lang's *Liliom*. Playing alongside blonde Florelle were two pretty brunettes who looked enough alike to be the two faces of the feminine feline so admired by both Auguste and Jean Renoir. One was Sylvia Bataille, probably brought in by Prévert, who'd known her since the late twenties;* the other was the tremulous Nadia Sibirskaïa, who wasn't Russian but Breton.† This triptych of women may have been speaking Prévert's lines, but they never stopped being Renoirian. Each of the three characters—Valentine, Édith, and Estelle—loves and desires in her own way. Édith may seem like a tart at first but is certainly not the least moving of the three when she is revealed to be tragically in love with a man for whom she agrees to prostitute herself. The scene in which Batala insists that Édith go to 28 rue du Colisée to "meet" one of his silent partners provides evidence that Sylvia Bataille was chosen for the role after the screenplay was finished. Batala describes the Ranimax pills man as someone who loves life, "women . . . brunettes," while caressing the actress's hair; and yet, the shooting script contains the designation "women . . . (or brunettes) (or blondes)," which establishes the fact that the line was to be adapted to the hair color of whichever actress was cast.

Another standout from the gallery of portraits in this film is the incredible character of the concierge, Monsieur Baisenard, formerly from Tonkin (maybe), who has "no advice to receive from anyone at all nor any person." Every time it gets late and he gets drunk, he sings "C'est la nuit de Noël." Marcel Lévesque, who'd become a Guitry regular, is stupendous in the role of this outrageous fellow who's not afraid to admit, "I talk to myself . . . because I think a lot of myself . . . according to my true value."

In *The Crime of Monsieur Lange,* traditional French theater and film as

* Prévert gave Sylvia Bataille her first role in the short film *La Joie d'une heure* (André Cerf, 1930, also featuring Georges Pomiès, whom Renoir so appreciated).

† Her real name was Germaine Marie Josèphe Lebas.

epitomized by Jules Berry, Florelle, and Marcel Lévesque meet a new wind sweeping through the France of 1935, fanned by Prévert, consumed by the October group, and completely channeled by Renoir. It is what at once makes the film work, and that was a revelation for Renoir, who afterward would use the services of several of the supporting players in *Lange:* Maurice Baquet for *Les Bas-Fonds* (*The Lower Depths*), Jacques-Bernard Brunius on several occasions, Sylvain Itkine (the retired detective) and Jean Dasté (a printer) for *Grand Illusion,* Guy Decomble (a printer) and Claire Gérard (the prostitute) for *La Bête humaine,* Odette Talazac (the concierge) and Claire Gérard again in *The Rules of the Game;* and this is not a complete list, nor does it take into account the many who appeared in *La vie est à nous.*

The fact that Renoir's *Lange* is a film inspired and colored by anarchism does not mean that Renoir had an anarchist soul at the time, just as his film *La Marseillaise* did not turn him into either an anarchist or a royalist. Nevertheless, the spirit of this film is obviously in tune with his nature to a much larger extent than has been admitted. The costume he donned so late in life, the seams of which he sometimes risked bursting, left little room for expressing his penchant for idiotic jokes, puns, spoonerisms, nonsensical humor, and provocation. At this time, Jaroslav Hašek's *The Good Soldier Švejk* was among the books on his bedside table, and he considered Georges Fourest* to be at the top of his personal poetic pantheon. His preferences were focused on "L'Épître falote et testamentaire pour régler l'ordre et la marche des mes funérailles"† (in *La Négresse blonde*), which he knew by heart and from which he'd recite the following verses whenever he had a chance:

> Que mon enterrement soit superb et farouche,
> Que les bourgeois glaireux bâillent d'étonnement
> Et que Sadi-Carnot, ouvrant sa large bouche,
> Se dise: "Nom de Dieu! le Bel enterrement!"‡

---

* *Translator's note:* Georges Fourest (ca. 1867–1945) was a French Decadent and Symbolist writer in the line of Rabelais, who mostly rejected a career in law for a bohemian life in the Latin Quarter and experimented not only with language distortions but at least once with a literary hoax.

† *Translator's note:* "A Drab Bequest to Settle the Order and Course of My Funeral."

‡ *Translator's note:*
I want my funeral to be splendid, raw,
Seen with gaping jaw by the bourgeois slime
And then Sadi-Carnot with his big wide maw,
Thinking, "Name of God! His grave's sublime!"

On June 21, 1941, from Los Angeles, Renoir would ask Pierre Daltour to bring him several records, "'Y'a d'la joie' by Maurice Chevalier (plus two or three others by him) and 'Le Temps des cerises' by Tino Rossi," as well as Pascal's *Les Pensées* and *La Négresse blonde*.[18]

In 1935, Georges Fourest's *Le Géranium ovipare* was released, and the people of France embraced the belief they would soon make themselves heard. *Monsieur Lange*'s courtyard took the place of a sound chamber for them, and the film itself was their megaphone. For it to become such, the filmmaker obviously had to believe in it—at least a little. More than anything, he had to have found the means and the strength to give form to these streams of words, this deluge of ideas, and this profusion of energy—something that would express them without restraining them and that would make them both accessible and appealing at the same time. The tour de force accomplished by Renoir with *Lange* amounted to giving the illusion of improvisation while structuring chaos—without it ever ceasing to be chaos. Which brings us back to the same point, because such a thing is, quite precisely, exactly what directing is.

Renoir had formed a precise idea of the direction of *Lange* from the start. In fact, it had been designed in his mind even before the scenario had materialized. Accordingly, his notes from April 18, 1935, state, "Criminal court, a single circular tracking shot [he used the term *trave*, his abbreviation of *traveling*, the French word for "tracking shot"]." The inspired circular path at the end of the film that allows the eye to follow Lange from the office to the courtyard, and on which André Bazin commented at length, was, therefore, not invented on the morning the scene was shot by holding up a wet finger to the wind but sometime several months before that. This is also true for what follows in that same shot, when the camera moves forward at the moment Lange moves toward Batala, whom he is going to kill. Renoir's conception of it for the opening scene and not for the final sequence before the film returns to the present time isn't insignificant. The fact remains that the filmmaker had predefined the movement of the film, which he described in 1961: "Technically, this is an attempt at linking, linking the background and foreground with the same shot. It's an attempt to use camera movement to unify both what is happening in life behind the actors and what is happening in the mind of the actors, in the foreground. . . . It was like real snakes surrounding the tripod that held the camera, and that camera was going to wander in every direction, moving in search of the actors, following them, traveling up, down."[19]

No more in film than in literature or elsewhere are form and background differentiated; they come into being at the same instant and simultaneously impose their joint and indissociable existence. Renoir does not fix upon the world of work in the film; he films the movements of those who are working, enters among them all, and goes from their world to another. Their ceaseless comings and goings make the camera move, and because the camera is moving, they come and go ceaselessly. The many preparatory notes left by Renoir show that movement appeared essential to him at early stages in the making of the film, a fact supported by the frequency of the use of the expression "dolly moves forward" at the beginning of the description of various scenes.[20]

Through Amédée Lange, a dreamer, a poet, a weakling becomes a hero, following a logic that does not belong to him alone but is one that society imposes on him: he does away with the thief, swindler, wheeler-dealer—the people who make the world turn around them and for them. At the end, the circle is broken. Lange and Valentine disappear into a country landscape. Three men watch them go off into the distance; one version of the screenplay identified these men as two peasants and an old man. On the screen, they remain silent. The screenplay had planned the following exchange:

> One of the Peasants: All the same. . . . It's a funny world in the cities.
> The Old Man: What do you want? . . . There's no sun. . . . There's no trees. . . . No animals. . . . Nothing, you know.
> A Peasant: There is . . . you can't say there's no subway.

Jean Renoir filmed contemporary Paris very sparingly from then on.

Before *The Crime of Monsieur Lange* began its run at the Aubert-Palace on June 24, 1936, word about it had already begun to give it legs. The day after it opened, the press succeeded in providing it with a body and a soul. In *Le Petit Parisien*, Jean Marguet alluded to it as an "intelligent, powerful work, which can't fail to touch you" and did not omit praising the profound originality of a director who understood how to leave his mark: "He isn't satisfied walking a beaten path. He can imagine but, more importantly, he has the courage to *dare*. Oh! Sometimes he is mistaken, but we discover his personality again and again, from *Nana* to *Madame Bovary*." The critic also valued the fact that at last "Renoir's realism has become tempered with fantasy," adding, "And then, there's a character that isn't announced, a silent character: the decor. I'm talking about that old house in the working-class suburb, which the camera delves through from top to bottom, and that is such an odd sight that it seems to take part in the action."

The rest of the reviews had the same tone, and if all of them joined in lamenting the mediocre quality of the sound and the lack of definition of the images, Renoir could at least enjoy the fact that one of his films had finally been understood and appreciated. Such recognition of its merits was not seconded by audience infatuation; the film did not appear in the list of the twenty-five best films of 1936 as chosen by the readers of *La Cinématographie française.**

But *Monsieur Lange* was truly a turning point in Renoir's career, something he would recognize in hindsight. On November 14, 1945, he wrote to Sam Siritzky, "I hope that this film [*The Diary of a Chambermaid*] will to a small extent play the same role as *The Crime of Monsieur Lange* played in my French career. What I mean is that maybe it will open the door to some projects that are more completely personal."[21]

---

* Marcel Pagnol's *César* was at the top of the list, and Renoir's *The Lower Depths* was eighth.

14

Fellow Traveler

La vie est à nous (The People of France; or Life Is Ours!)

On November 20, 1935, the day following the start of filming for *The Crime of Monsieur Lange*, Sacha Guitry's two first films, *Pasteur* and *Bonne chance*, were shown in a double feature at the Colisée. In the second film, Guitry is pictured giving Jacqueline Delubac a small painting of Jean Renoir by his father, purchased for 32,000 francs. The cinema had taken hold of Renoir, and Renoir had taken hold of the cinema.

What was he like from day to day—the Renoir of the mid-thirties who'd just experienced his first real critical success with *Lange*? Long after—in fact, more than forty years—Henri Jeanson drew this portrait of him:

> Friendship with Renoir, when you were with him, was just like being at home with him, talking about whatever came up, having potluck, friends having wine and a little Camembert, and everybody singing his own tune. Friendship—yes—the real kind, which makes you strong. Oh, that Renoir, how I loved him! He could have asked anything of me. Not a week went by that we didn't "have a bite" together, in Montmartre or somewhere else, or in little cafés that only we knew about. So many times I would wake up in the morning in his apartment on avenue Frochot without knowing exactly how I ended up there. And there was Renoir standing at the door in his pajamas, beaming. "Hey, Toto! The java's ready!" What a good-humored mug the guy had!

Right after *The Crime of Monsieur Lange*, Renoir wasn't yet living on avenue Frochot, but the character Jeanson sketched resembled him. "Jean Renoir had already fallen in with the Communist Party," Jeanson goes on, "and I was anti-everything. Nor did I change." It was as if a first wedge had been driven into this beautiful story, without yet causing a crack. Jeanson had loved *Lange*, that "strange thingamajig mined just about everywhere with Prévert's explosives—yep, quite a strange thingamajig! It went bang, was fantastic, blew up the whole works, kicked piles of officials in the butt, toppled statues about as brazenly as you can, and it was god-awful gratifying to watch."

And then, as if by accident, Jeanson lets drop, "In 1936, Renoir shot *La vie est à nous,* a propaganda movie commissioned by the Communist Party, and he also did Maxim Gorky's *The Lower Depths.*"[1] Between those two films, Renoir made *A Day in the Country,* which no one saw. He made three films in one year; wrote articles; took part in conferences, meetings, and film society screenings; and started some projects that were never finished and required weeks of work. That is how Renoir was, many sided, teeming with any number of things, incapable and simultaneously refusing to focus on any one item, getting a kick out of being everywhere at once, by turns claiming one thing and then the opposite.

Such eccentricity, to the extent that it was, such a failing, as some would call it, had been pointed out by other professionals of the film world, often with affection but also tinged with bitterness. Charles Spaak, with whom Renoir would write *The Lower Depths* and *Grand Illusion,* would say to his wife, "He was a Communist. He'd meet a Fascist with nice boots. Well then! Since he loved beautiful leather, he'd forget that Marxism and Nazism weren't synonymous. Maybe Mussolini's son had a heavenly way of preparing spaghetti or of playing polo? Or did he have a colorful collection of lead soldiers?" And Spaak also said, "For me, that's your perfect traitor," before also adding "With Renoir you forgave everything!"[2] Ten years later, French cinema wouldn't let anything Renoir did get by them.

His house in Meudon, and then his apartment in Paris, were buzzing with pals, certain of whom were called comrades at the time. Marguerite's friends became his, and often their ideas meant less to him than their manner, the warmth they gave off, the feeling of belonging and taking part in a movement, which afforded him a sense of direction. He had the chance to know personalities of people who weren't art dealers or of the film world. They had been attracted by the aura around him since *Lange,* a film unusual enough to embrace the contours of the times. It had shown that cinema could also keep stride with, anticipate, and illuminate the aspirations of a class, make the rising wind blow more powerfully. How could Renoir not believe in it, too? This idea of cinema in service to ideas, to a cause, to a Party to which a lot of his friends belonged?

The truth was, he had several reasons for accepting the proposition Louis Aragon brought to him in December 1935, even before the release of *Lange.* Among these reasons, one has often been neglected. The most secret of all, it may also have been the most decisive. One of the first to come out with it was Pierre Braunberger. Renoir had gone to find him one morning on rue de Charonne at his parents' to ask him what he thought of the Party's offer. Braunberger asks, "Why would such an assignment pose any problem for Renoir? In the political scene, his position was rather on the right.... The films he was making and the ideas they conveyed were on the left, but he, personally, wasn't. He was interested in social issues without being a socialist. . . . Nineteen thirty-six was the year of the Popular Front and the war in Spain. In such an atmosphere, Renoir couldn't experience the Communists' proposition as an unrewarding task. I strongly encouraged him to accept, explaining to him that it was finally an opportunity to find a true audience."[3] The role Braunberger claimed to have played is doubtful, but it is true that Renoir actually had no audience and that this venture could offer him an opportunity to earn one. More than anything, he wanted to make films. Not any kind of film at all, of course, but he wanted to work, at any price—or almost any. Those two reasons—getting an audience and working—counted at least as much as all the political motivations put together, which in his case were often positions taken out of convenience.

Behind the project of *La vie est à nous* were the Party, Aragon, Maurice Thorez, who gave his consent, and Renoir's pals. Jacques Becker came back into Renoir's circle. Like Renoir, he was from a wealthy family, but unlike his mentor he had broken with his family. He was madly in love with film, like Renoir, but was penniless ever since he had turned his back on the career he'd been promised to inherit. Left-wing ideas attracted and stimulated him, and in that way he was also drawn to Jean's example. The exact nature of that example and the advice it entailed? Renoir encouraged Becker to join the Party, whereas he was wary of carrying the card. He was an organizer of others' lives—a director, as usual.

Although Jacques Duclos would not be officially in charge of Party propaganda until a few weeks later, he was the de facto figure in charge, and his actions in support of the mass campaigns of 1934 and 1935 had been appreciated. The former baker who became the number two man of the Party was also a film enthusiast, and his various stays in the Soviet Union had taught him the role that films could play in enlightening the masses. On the eve of the Party's eighth Congress, scheduled for Villeurbanne from January 22 to 25, 1936, and with a view to the April 26 elections, he came up with the idea of producing a film and confided the idea to Jean-Paul Dreyfus.

Dreyfus (who'd adopt his mother's name under the Occupation and call himself Le Chanois) had begun as editor of Jean-George Auriol's *La Revue du cinéma,* had become Jacques Prévert's friend, and had broken with the Surrealists at the same time as had Prévert, Aragon, and the film historian Georges Sadoul. In October 1933, he joined the Party, wrote articles on theater for *L'Humanité,* and worked on films as a studio director, assistant, and set director for Pathé. In some way he was the official Party contact in the theater world and, especially, in the cinema. Shortly after his meeting with Duclos, he received a call from Aragon saying that Renoir had accepted the proposal.

However, Renoir's was not the first name the Communist heads suggested, apparently. Marcel Carné's was. Carné tells in his memoirs how he was summoned to 120 rue Lafayette, then the headquarters of the French Communist Party (PCF), where Maurice Thorez, who'd been the first secretary of the Party since 1931, put forward the idea of his directing a film "showing the life and struggles of the people of France, as well as their aspirations." Forced to turn down the offer because he had just signed a contract for what would be his first feature film, *Jenny,* and therefore lacking the time needed, Carné then heard Aragon, who was there at the interview along with Paul Vaillant-Couturier and, notably, Duclos, suggest, "Maybe there's another possibility. Last week I met Jean Renoir at some friends' we have in common on faubourg Saint-Germain. . . . To me he seems totally behind our ideas. . . . Maybe we could . . ."[4] And they could, in fact. Carné did direct *Jenny,* and sometime afterward discovered in *La vie est à nous* certain images he had filmed at the Party's request during the big demonstration on July 14, 1935, which had pleased them and had become the reason for Thorez's proposition.

Per Françoise Giroud, "One evening in 1936, Renoir took me to hear Maurice Thorez. He was spellbinding. Looked like Jean Gabin, then out came the dialectic."[5] Thorez the orator held Françoise Giroud enthralled, and he also fascinated Renoir. The director was impressed by "the actor" in Thorez, who with one sentence was able to make thousands of spectators rise to their feet. Jean was won over by the persona. The Renoirian paradox in this case came from the fact that Thorez passed for a dull person and boring conversationalist in private and his facade lacked warmth.

> There was no longer much remaining of the entertaining, spontaneous young man, who was satisfied with easy and successful speeches and glad to connect. By the start of 1936, the mask had hardened, the bright personality had fled and came back only in outbursts that were briefer and briefer, rarer and rarer. Calculation had taken the place of spontaneity, and straightforwardness had vanished from prolonged contact with the Byzantine ploys of Moscow. Out of adaptability and compliance, in an organization that demanded more each day, there was now something mechanical and frozen in his manner, becoming more and more noticeable. His confidences in boulevard cafés, apparently, were at the end of their days.[6]

If it's natural that François Mauriac's words here about that "soft, bleating voice," which became "almost as tenderly insistent as that of the peasant calling his broods,"[7] pandered to the professed enemies of Thorez's politics, the opinion of Thorez's comrades, even if they were expressed several years later, seem hardly more flattering. Alain Renoir, who at fifteen felt a lot closer to Communist ideas than Jean ever would, confirmed these impressions: "Thorez always seemed to be angry. My father insisted that he was truly a good person, a remarkable man in every aspect. He would tell me that I ought to admire him, but I never managed to."[8]

Jean did "manage to." But his insistence on defending Thorez to those he was close with and who weren't immediately won over also points to the wishful thinking in which his approach originated. Many intellectuals of that time, and for many years after, considered attraction to the Communists, and, even more, attraction to the virtues they made a point of displaying, to be fed by the pathetic spectacle of peers who had already been won over and to be reinforced by the desire to be on the "good side." To truly believe in Communism, or to pretend to, reservations had to be silenced at times to the point of blindness.

Physically, Renoir and Thorez weren't without a certain resemblance—even the impressive stature of both, as well as their sense of being encumbered by their own bodies—not to mention a tendency toward untidiness. But the plumpness of Renoir was a sign of an appetite for life, and it couldn't hide a keen spirit and extreme intelligence. Thorez's physicality was a sign of premature weariness, already almost to the point of disillusionment. It underlined something coarse about him. In Renoir's eyes, as in those of a basic Communist militant, Thorez was a man of the people, and Thorez himself strived to create that very image. *Fils du peuple* (*Son of the People*), a slender autobiography of him that appeared in October 1937, had been drafted by at least two ghostwriters and took two whole years of review, corrections, deletions, and additions to win the imprimatur of the representatives of the Comintern. In it Thorez is depicted as the son of a miner, but he was actually the natural child of a miner's daughter and a rich grocer.

The people fascinated Renoir in the same way that he fascinated those bourgeois people he didn't shock—from a distance—although a fantasy of fraternity kept the impression afloat. The fact that the director considered the aspirations of the people with a kind of instinctive sympathy more than with any profound commitment didn't prevent him from filming and exalting them, perhaps better than anyone else.

And then, there was the fact that Thorez had an audience, a convinced, enthusiastic, rapturous audience. When Renoir met Thorez, the machine of the cult of Thorez had surged into motion. Launched by order of the Kremlin, it would produce an effect that had never been seen in France, nor ever would again. How would Renoir, who'd always dreamed of climbing onstage to be applauded—the secret dream that Octave, his alter ego, confessed in *The Rules of the Game*—resist the ovations rising from those smoky rooms to that lectern where the master orator drenched in sweat ranted and raved, pulled out all the stops? How could the director, who suffered seeing his films misunderstood or ignored by audiences, not himself want to take advantage of the outbursts of popular fervor supporting Thorez, which Renoir did not see—or preferred not to know—had been scripted to order and staged on demand? Seized by an impetus that seemed irresistible at the time, Renoir took the job as director, then as chronicler and standard-bearer in a battle that belonged to the disenfranchised and that he enjoyed making his. He even would become the lay godfather of Jean Thorez, the son of Maurice Thorez and his girlfriend, Jeannette Vermeersch, born February 22, 1936, and would see the Party machine—press, militants, and associations—put to service for him.

There isn't any doubt that an element of opportunism entered into Renoir's decision to work for the Party. The fact that his hunger for recognition and his desire to take part in a moment in history were at play and were aggravated by a fear of finding no place for his own involvement in the great moment is incontestable. But true as that is, it's important to keep in mind that the period, perhaps to a greater extent than any other in the modern history of France, was definitely one of engagement. Very few intellectuals or artists at that time were not taking some position. Some were moving toward the Left; nearly just as many were courting the Right. The deeper motivations of both were not so different: all of them were being carried on the current of decadence flooding French society, and all were in search of energy, that new dynamism seeping in from Moscow and Berlin.

The more the rumor of a new conflict intensified, the more the traumatism of the First World War became enrooted. It caused some to want an alliance with Germany at any price, but led others closer to the Communist Party, even though they nourished no more illusions on the deeper motivations of socialism as it had been established in the Soviet Union. Romain Rolland was among this group, but he was violently opposed to Henri Barbusse.* Renoir played it by ear and sought an improvisational middle path, tempered by reflection and reason, between the two enemies, the author of *Jean-Christopher* and the one who had written *Le Feu*, a path he steered by his intuition, his friendships, and his passions of the moment.

At the time, it wasn't necessary to want revolution to be emotionally and publicly in sympathy with the Marxist movement. André Malraux pulled this

---

* *Translator's note:* Henri Barbusse (1873–1935), French novelist, promoter of Esperanto, and member of the Communist Party, who moved to Moscow in 1918 and joined the Bolsheviks. His hate campaign against writer Panait Istrati and his propagandist activities on behalf of Stalin and the Soviets eventually raised the ire of several former literary supporters on the Left.

off with more aplomb than Renoir, although both were similarly motivated by an essentially individualist temperament. Others, in unanimous agreement about the decline of their country, were led to dreams of boundless skies, something that would cause flyer Antoine de Saint-Exupéry to flee beyond any measurable horizon. By that point, Renoir hardly had his own feet on the ground, and the two would become involved in 1940 on an ocean liner en route to America. The days they spent together afterward in Los Angeles confirmed their sentiment of a community of shared dreams produced by engagement. In spite of this, there was an essential difference between the two. Like Malraux, Saint-Exupéry wanted to become a hero, whereas the son of Auguste Renoir was working to become Jean Renoir.

With the hotheaded spirit of the newly converted, and the thrill of being a militant drunk on audacity, Renoir would abandon all reservations for nearly three years and become the "fellow traveler" of a Party whose slogans he adopted and whose swords he crossed with the enemies of his "comrades," whether they were dictators, writers, or directors. He acted at times as if he'd been blinded by his new fame and popularity. Films then were to be considered first from the point of view of politics; and his were promoted by left-wing newspapers and violently attacked by publications on the Right. For some, he became "the brilliant director for the Left"[9] (Roger Leenhardt), and for others, "that fat kid who raises his fist during meetings"[10] (Bardèche and Brasillach in 1943).

Personal commitment wasn't enough for Renoir, who was determined that all who loved him follow in his footsteps. Nadia Sibirskaïa, who played the adorable Estelle in *The Crime of Monsieur Lange*, offered an example:

Another time, Renoir invited us to the Communist Party Congress. I was a bit reluctant, because I'd never been involved in politics, but Renoir told me to take it or leave it. So I took it—out of friendship for him. All of Renoir's friends were there and also a friendly fat man I didn't know. I went up to him and took hold of the lapel of his jacket and said, "What's your name?" Everybody around me started to laugh, and I didn't know why. And the friendly fat man said to me, "Well, I know you." Really? Finally, someone was kind enough to tell me that I'd just met Maurice Thorez. Thorez had found it all very amusing, and he invited me to sit by him at the podium. Well, I was terrified. . . . I tried to hide but they found me, so I finally accepted the seat of honor. But after that, they wanted me to speak. Can you imagine, with my voice? I refused. That's how I, too, ended up in *La vie est à nous*.[11]

The history of this film made for the Party begins on the sixth floor of a building.

on rue Lepic. That is where Jean-Paul Dreyfus lived. Although Renoir had a hard time climbing stairs—his wounded leg and extra pounds made them feel endless—the view from the windows of the apartment and the fact that the very attractive Madame Dreyfus was there both made up for it Soon someone else, named Pierre Unik, arrived. He was a journalist and poet who belonged to the Surrealist group, and he'd collaborated with Luis Buñuel on the film *Las Hurdes* (*Land without Bread*, 1933), for which he'd supplied the commentary. He'd been a member of the Party since 1927 and was the private secretary of Marcel Cachin, who had directed *L'Humanité,* since 1918.

A little later, André Zwobada, who'd be an assistant director for *La vie est à nous* and then first assistant director for *The Rules of the Game,* arrived with criticisms of the screenplay being written. "He thought there were some things that were a bit silly, and there were," Le Chanois (Dreyfus) would remember, adding, "Jean Renoir brought his talent as a director to *La vie est à nous,* and he had influence in that profession. He also had a crew. When he'd ask actors or crewmembers for their collaboration, they usually accepted in anticipation of future work. They were wrong, because that wasn't Renoir's style. Recognition and Renoir were two different things, even four different things."[12] The reason for that catty remark, which was unjust at least in part, can be found in the political differences that would arise between Dreyfus and Renoir, exacerbated by the interest of the director in his assistant's wife, especially during *La Marseillaise,* a subject that will be touched upon later.

From Renoir, Dreyfus learned that a director's obligations included showing generosity toward his crew. As a result of their daily work sessions, and from dining every evening afterward in the restaurants of Montmartre (including their favorite, La Mascotte, on rue des Abbesses), Dreyfus would get to know a warm individual who actually paid the bill more often than was his turn. The person who has money pays for the ones who don't, and that's a rule that isn't broken.

Speaking of money, the film needed some, too. All crewmembers and actors were lending their skills free of charge, but bookkeepers and contractors didn't share the same volunteer spirit. It was Jacques Duclos who initiated passing the hat around to comrades during meetings. They'd fill it with coins, which were then poured into small bags, emptied in turn into potato sacks that comrades carried to the Dreyfuses' sixth-floor abode. Then, helped by Zwobada, Jean-Paul and Newmi (or Noémie) Dreyfus would count out a tidy sum, although it was certainly not enough to finance a film. The Party would provide, and the film would cost around 70,000 francs, which was about one-tenth the average budget for a feature film of the time.

Through Dreyfus, the Party kept their irons in the fires of the project. Paul

Vaillant-Couturier, editor-in-chief of *L'Humanité* at the time, was another one who kept an eye open for trouble, armed as he was already by information about the basic ideas Thorez would espouse at the Congress in Villeurbanne in January, which the film was responsible for promoting.

As a result, *La vie est à nous* entailed three basic postulates: two hundred families were the primary cause of the crisis in French society and they formed the mask behind which the hideous face of Fascism was hiding; workers, in the largest sense—laborers, peasants, and the middle classes—were the most affected; and only the proposals of the French Communist Party could guarantee a profound and lasting change. The film combined documentary scenes with those played by actors.

Renoir would later distance himself from the film. In 1969, he declared, "It's a very minor film, a short I worked on only briefly, and I'm responsible for less than five minutes of it."[13] In his memoirs he later writes, "*La vie est à nous,* which I supervised, was mostly shot by my young assistants and crew. I directed a few scenes of it and had nothing to do with the editing."[14] Was this the modesty of a master or a desire to get rid of the thing?

Taking into account the controversies that had surrounded the film, it's logical that Le Chanois would opt for evasion: "I insist without beating about the bush and before history that it was Renoir who did all the work. Now he's saying that isn't true: not very good on his part. Jacques Becker did something and so did I. But when Jean Renoir now says, 'Jean-Paul's the one who did all of it,' and he insisted so again recently, he's saying this to wriggle out of it because he's a naturalized American citizen and he's uncomfortable with it. He's the one who did all of it, and all its qualities, including what's good about the film, are due to him."[15]

In fact, Truffaut decided the same thing, saying it discreetly, not out loud, when he wrote, "Even if you see *La vie est à nous* without knowing that it's a film by Jean Renoir, it's easy to recognize his style in the slightest camera movement."[16] As sometimes happened in his case, Truffaut, in a desire to protect Renoir's status, pushed the envelope a bit too far in his unconditional admiration. We know today—and chose to overlook then—that one of the most beautiful camera movements in the film, which follows the bailiff as he inventories a farm about to be put up for auction, is probably the work of Jacques Becker, as is the entire scene in which it appears.

It's true that the young assistants and members of the crew Renoir talked about played a role far more important than that usually reserved for assistants and crewmembers, but this has no bearing on the fact that the film does carry the mark of the director of *The Crime of Monsieur Lange*. The assistants were

Jacques Becker, Pierre Unik, Jean-Paul Dreyfus, André Zwobada, Jacques-Bernard Brunius, and Henri Cartier. Cartier was trying to choose between film and photography at the time and was not yet going by the name Cartier-Bresson.

It's also true that the initial sequence, a montage of archival images illustrating the teacher's (Jean Dasté) course on the riches of France, was the work of Brunius, who recognized his own hand in it[17] and claimed that he'd exhaustively studied the film montages created by Walter Ruttmann, especially his *Melody of the World*. Brunius also maintained that Renoir himself edited the first two reels of the film, at least.

So, in all likelihood, the fantastic sequence of the auction with Gaston Modot, among others, is Becker's, whereas Renoir is responsible for the sequence about the young out-of-work engineer (Julien Bertheau) who almost loses his spirit in the face of the cruelty of his bosses and being exposed to offers from the extreme Right (represented by Marcel Duhamel as the motorist who is a member of the Croix-de-Feu*).

Subsequently, the engineer experiences the warmth of the Party within a chorale of young supporters, thus gaining through understanding and work the means to reunite with his charming fiancée (Nadia Sibirskaïa), who was preparing him a meal of *oeufs à la Portugaise* at the very beginning of the sequence. As for the first episode, which Dreyfus seems to have monitored especially, Renoir once more uses Blavette and Dalban, the immigrant and foreman from *Toni*, establishing a brand of antagonism between them that is almost identical to that in the other film. Blavette is given one of the "powerful" lines in the film: "Look how Russia has managed to shorten the work day and raise salaries thanks to machines."

Each of the three sequences is introduced by a letter received and read by Marcel Cachin in his office at *L'Humanité*; and the last part of the film is dominated by the Party big names, after which the people begin marching to the strains of "The Internationale." This is where several shots appear that directly recall the images in *Boudu*, which some critics thought revealed René Clair's influence.

If the Central Committee actually intended the film to strengthen the Party's hold on voters just before the elections, as has commonly been claimed, it went about doing so awfully late. Obviously, the film was also meant to promote *L'Humanité*, and it does present the Fascists laying into some sellers of that magazine at a market, but they are quickly driven away by the people. And yet,

---

* *Translator's note:* Croix-de-Feu ("Cross of Fire"), a French rightist league between the two world wars, headed by François de la Rocque. It and other similar leagues of 1930s France are usually distinguished from the more extreme ideology of imported revolutionary Fascism.

a main intention of the film was as a vehicle for the new policy initiated by the Party on order of Stalin. As a matter of fact, the strategy in Moscow had altered since Stalin had begun to take the Nazi threat seriously; according to historians, Georgi Dimitrov, who headed the Comintern, had been given the responsibility of letting Thorez know in no uncertain terms that an alliance among socialists was now to be desired.

In February 1934, Thorez was proclaiming his refusal to choose between "cholera"—meaning, bourgeois democracy—and "the plague," or, rather, Fascism; now he had to let go of that discourse. Such a new direction was immediately translated into the words:

> From this moment on, the Bolshevik lexicon is to be diluted by a typically republican semantic. It should be seen as less a struggle among the classes, between "bourgeois" and "proletariat"; less about "workers" and "revolutionaries"; less about "struggle" and "unrest"; and always more about "the people" and "France"; about a "united nation" and "the republic," "democracy," and "freedom." The PCF is abandoning the enlightenments of Marx and Lenin for Voltaire's, Rousseau's, the French Revolution's, and Valmy's. That's the concession that must be made to reassure the middle classes, the radical factions of the Party, and Catholics, to whom the Party is extending a hand.[18]

The discourse upheld by the Communist leaders in the film, especially Duclos's, which draws its inspiration from the revolutionary tradition of French youth, and the imagery and general tone of the film are totally in keeping with this new orientation. In 1935–1936, it could only have suited a Renoir who was preoccupied with the Nazi threat. This straight-grain pattern, which created the path directly to *La Marseillaise*, had already been cut.

Whatever its ambition, and to whatever extent this really was expressed, *La vie est à nous* would be shown by priority to the leadership of the Party as well as to a few dozen permanent and militant members chosen from those who were the most purely committed. According to Le Chanois, who certainly attended the screening but did not give its exact date, the debate that followed was a troubled one. The reproaches were especially critical of the factory sequences, where the absence of references to any specific union authority led to the most violent arguments: "Our father Renoir was brought down a peg before our eyes as he faced such critiques. Maurice Thorez had an excellent understanding of it; he put an end to the criticisms by remarking that the film was going to have a great impact and a lot of success and that nothing can be 100 percent fair. But that evening, when I dined with Renoir, he came close to calling all of them 'assholes.' . . ."[19]

It's difficult to see exactly why Renoir would have appeared so resistant, because he wasn't accustomed to behaving that way when his more personal works were at stake. He had given them a film by an expert director, allowed excellent actors to do their best at expressing ideas to which he felt close, and had satisfied every aspect of his assignment—even going beyond it. He could also feel confident about the usefulness of his work. He had even gone to the point of writing that it was thanks to *La vie est à nous* that he had "truly come to understand film and its role."[20] But had he come to the point of thinking it?

Screened for the press on April 7, 1936, presented on that occasion by Maurice Thorez and Marcel Cachin in person, the film was given only a type of distribution called "noncommercial" (projections by invitation or reserved for subscribers), because it had no distribution visa. In fact, it apparently was not presented to the censor before July 1936 and was therefore not yet banned in any way, contrary to what has sometimes been written. The issue did not come up until government officials of the Popular Front had to answer a request for a visa for it. The request had been addressed to Jean Zay, the minister of public education and art, by the Communist deputy of the Seine, Louis Mercier. What was at stake was important. According to a communiqué written by the minister, it consisted in "determining the policy of the new government regarding the exhibition of films."[21] The response was negative, and thus the film could only be shown in the context of noncommercial exhibition and, on sufferance, as a limited-audience commercial showing. *La vie est à nous* thus found itself in flattering company: the same commission of censorship had confirmed a complete ban of Jean Vigo's *Zéro de conduite* (*Zero for Conduct*).* *La vie est à nous* never really debuted before the sixties.

Whereas 1936 was a year of total upheaval for the country, for Renoir it was a period of hyperactivity whose truly frenetic character is still difficult to apprehend today. In fact, during a period of twelve months, Renoir worked on at least four screenplays (one of which would not be filmed) and directed three films— *La vie est à nous* in January and February, *A Day in the Country* in June–July, and *The Lower Depths* at the end of October. At the same time, he was monitoring the progress of the screenplay for *Grand Illusion*, organizing its production and preparing its direction, while making first steps on *La Marseillaise*. And he was doing all this while stepping up his involvements in politics and the unions, writing articles and other texts, and attending a number of meetings and film society screenings, especially at the Ciné-Liberté.

Created in March 1936 within the framework of the Maison de la Culture,

---

* Vigo died on October 5, 1934, at the age of twenty-nine.

which Aragon, Nizan, and Malraux, among others, had been appointed to manage, the Ciné-Liberté was one offshoot of the Bureau du cinéma and the Association des écrivains et artistes révolutionnaires, founded in 1933 by Aragon, Vaillant-Couturier, and the critic and historian Léon Moussinac. Its activities had then continued under the aegis of the Alliance du cinéma independent, which had come into being in November 1935. Its statutes defined Ciné-Liberté as a "worker's cooperative for variable-capital production." An article that appeared in *La Flèche* on May 23, 1936, listed its objectives: "battling against the ill fate with which film is saddled," organizing "private screenings of forbidden films," producing films "reserved for screening to adherents," and publishing a magazine carrying its name whose "editorial committee will be composed of Henri Jeanson, Léon Moussinac, and Jean Renoir."[22] The association would count as many as twenty thousand members.

Renoir also sat on the administrative board of Ciné-Liberté, for which Gaston Modot, who played the peasant in *La vie est à nous* and who would soon be the gamekeeper in *The Rules of the Game*, served as general secretary, and for which Becker and Dreyfus numbered among the members. Without being registered in the Party, Citizen Renoir was an active militant, and his path did not always merge with that of his identity as a director. At the beginning of 1936, that path crossed André Gide's, right before his departure to the Soviet Union, a trip from which he would draw information that was diametrically opposed to the distracted conclusions Renoir was able to reach when he had gone there a little more than a year before. The writer would rapidly distance himself from the Communism in the arms of which the director had taken refuge.

For the time being, however, Gide and Renoir met and lunched or dined together, often at the Pharamond, a restaurant in Les Halles known for the quality of its *tripes à la mode de Caen*. On the red banquettes of the establishment's second floor, which was more discreet than the ground floor, Gide happened to sit down very near Alain Renoir, whose thighs he could not completely prevent himself from wanting to grope. The adolescent was uncomfortable. The big man frightened him a bit and made him think of "a gorilla escaped from his cage."[23]

Gide and Renoir were also dealing with another cage in the form of a room in a bourgeois apartment in Poitiers, where a father, mother, and brother had shut up an unfortunate young woman who suffered from epilepsy, guilty in their eyes of having given herself to a man other than the one for whom they'd intended her. At Gallimard, under the title *Ne jugez pas* (*Judge Not*), Gide created a collection of two volumes, *L'Affaire Redureau* and *La Séquestrée de Poitiers*. There are three film adaptations of the second book, all of them dated February 1936. According to the scenarist Jean Aurenche, who also worked on the project, the film never saw the light of day because of the overcautiousness of producers afraid of exposing certain provincial morals, when the majority of a film's receipts came precisely from provincial France.[24] Renoir planned to offer the lead to Marianne Oswald, who would have made her first film if she'd done it. The German singer, exiled in Paris since 1931, was performing songs written for her by Jean Cocteau, Henri-Georges Clouzot, and Jacques Prévert, who were enthralled by her husky voice and talent for reciting texts. Sometime later, Yves Allégret became interested in *La Séquestrée de Poitiers*, without any more success.

On June 20, 1936, André Gide spoke in Moscow on Red Square on the occasion of Gorky's funeral, while Renoir was preparing an adaptation of Gorky's *The Lower Depths*. In the fall, Gide's *Retour de l'URSS* (*Return from the USSR*) was published, and a few weeks later he attended a screening of Renoir's *The Lower Depths*, which he detested, calling it "unworthy of Renoir."[25]

15

"Every Night I Remember"

Partie de campagne (A Day in the Country)

On April 16, 1936, on the first round of the legislative elections, the Communist Party won 1.45 million votes (women did not vote at the time). On the evening of the second round, May 3, the Communists showed a gain of 61 seats in the House, which out of 612 seats amounted to 72 Communist deputies, 148 Socialists, and 55 members of several parties on the Left. Léon Blum formed his government on June 4, and the Popular Front was born.

Still monitoring the progress of the screenplays for *The Lower Depths* and what would become *Grand Illusion,* both of which were entrusted to Charles Spaak, the director and fellow traveler of the Party took refuge in the past. From it he would draw the inspiration and the subject for a film that would not be shown until after the war, just when he would, for all practical purposes, have forgotten it or, in any case, written it off as a loss. But by the fifties, this film would be surrounded by an extraordinary aura, becoming the touchstone for an after-the-fact interpretation of the "Renoir approach," under which the director's entire oeuvre would be grouped. The past in which Renoir took refuge was the 1881 of Maupassant and Auguste Renoir—his, in fact, because the film would be shot at Marlotte. Nevertheless, the concerns that would bring *Partie de campagne** into being were primarily very current. Desire would be its raison d'être, and a young woman of twenty-seven would inspire it.

Ever since Renoir had directed Sylvia Bataille in *The Crime of Monsieur Lange,* he had wanted to work with her again. Born Sylvia Maklès, she was twenty-seven at the time, had married the writer Georges Bataille when she was twenty, and had given him a girl two years later. They had separated in 1932. Still married, the Bataille couple had remained on good terms. They would not divorce until 1946, whereas Sylvia had lived with the psychoanalyst Jacques Lacan since 1938. Georges Bataille visited Sylvia on the set of *A Day in the*

---

* Even though the posters and publicity material identified the film as *Une partie de campagne*, the credits present the film as *Partie de campagne de Guy de Maupassant*.

Country, and he appears in the film as one of the four priests who move across the screen from left to right, next to an unknown actor (who is not Jacques Becker, contrary to what some have suggested), Henri Cartier-Bresson, and Pierre Lestringuez.

Apparently, Renoir had already submitted several projects to Sylvia Bataille—sketches of projects, most likely; but she had turned them down. Extremely cultured and very exacting, she did not find it easy to build a career in film, which she seemed to keep at a distance, while consenting to a few of the offers that came her way. She did not hide the fact that these in no way fulfilled her hopes and that she was doing them only for the money. During *The Crime of Monsieur Lange,* she was already close to Pierre Braunberger, who was quite frank about having a passion for her—which she would protest having ever satisfied.

The producer claimed to have met her during production of the film *Ademaï aviateur* (*Skylark,* 1933), with which he said he was vaguely associated. Even stranger, Braunberger claimed to have encountered Sylvia Bataille during the shoot in Biarritz of a Jean Choux film with Arletty, which Bataille doesn't appear in. (However, the director of *Un chien qui rapporte* did complain that his film was considerably reworked, which may mean that Sylvia Bataille was in it but that her scenes were cut.) Nevertheless, the fact remains that—for the first time since 1931 and *La Chienne*—Braunberger's desires matched the wishes of his friend Renoir.

Renoir seems to be the one who had the idea first for this adaptation of a Maupassant story. According to Sylvia Bataille: "We'd thought about two or three screenplays before we hit upon the idea of *A Day in the Country.* The others were original ideas from Renoir. Then he reread Maupassant, had me read it, we talked about it, and we made the film. I liked it a lot more than the screenplays he'd offered me before."[1] Pierre Braunberger specified that the offer had been discussed and accepted during a lunch all three attended in a café at 93 rue de Rome, where Renoir's and Marguerite's apartments were located.

Braunberger had already dealt with Maupassant, producing Alberto Cavalcanti's *Yvette* in 1927 with Catherine Hessling. There is also a puzzling mention of a *Partie de campagne,* a short film from 1929, in some of his filmographies. It's attributed to Alex Strasser, who is identified as the author of the original idea for the film *The Pursuit of Happiness,* also shot in 1929 and containing Jean Renoir and Catherine Hessling in its cast. There's very little doubt that the producer was in any shape financially in 1936 to produce a feature by himself. His last real producing success was in 1932 with *Fanny,* coproduced with Marcel Pagnol.

Moreover, there had never been any question of Renoir's *A Day in the Country* being more than a short film. Renoir confirmed this (at a later date) by stating that shortly after *La vie est à nous*, he conceived of the project of directing "a short film complete enough to stand alone and with the style of a feature."[2] In particular, the contract assigning the rights to the story, signed on May 15, 1936, with Éditions Albin Michel on behalf of Simone de Maupassant, specified "a prefeature opener film no longer than 800 meters." That stipulation occurs again in a letter addressed to the producer on July 27, 1936, that acknowledges receipt of the second payment for movie rights that total 2,650 francs: "If your film has a length greater than 1,000 meters [in other words, thirty-two minutes], but is below 1,400 meters, you will pay us an additional fee of 3,000 francs within the two days following review of the censorship board."[3]

The description given of the film in a contract dated May 15 deals with a second question: *A Day in the Country* would be a "film with spoken dialogue (sound and color)." And on June 11, R. Meyer et Cie wrote to the producer to inform him of the decision not to participate in the financing of this "color film."[4] *A Day in the Country* in color? Was this really the case, and, if so, what color process would have been used? Was it, perhaps, to be the Francita-Realita process, which had just been used in the production of two films by Jean Vallée, *Jeunes filles à marier* (1935) and *La Terre qui meurt* (*The Land That Dies*, 1936)? Or was it a lure cast out by Braunberger to whet the appetite of obviously over-cautious investors? This second hypothesis seems the most likely.

But the producer's efforts were in vain, and the film was financed by Braunberger alone, with the possible support—even if this was concealed—of Renoir himself. Any support, no matter how negligible, obviously mattered. For that reason, Brunius drafted an agreement with Dubonnet having to do with a practice that was not yet termed product placement. In a letter written in May to a Monsieur Guido, at the Volt Publicité company, Brunius wrote, "We're planning to include a Dubonnet sign in the scenery for the inn in the film *A Day in the Country*. . . . In exchange, you will provide us with a fixed sum of 3,000 francs for advertising the name of Dubonnet. In addition, we are asking you to please obtain for us as soon as possible the Dubonnet sign dating from that period."[5]

Renoir wrote the scenario alone, work that took him more than two months. Between the first treatment he delivered to production, probably at the end of April, and the definitive version, supplied on June 20, the project went from a faithful-to-the-letter adaptation of Maupassant's story, with dialogue reproduced practically word for word, to work that appears remarkably close to the finished film except for certain scenes and shots envisioned in the scenario that would never appear in the film. These discrepancies are far from unimportant. If the missing material had been shot, the film's length of probably fifty-six minutes[6] would have violated the terms of the contract. This possibly proves that, as a result of rewrites, the project grew to a scale that Renoir had neither foreseen nor calculated with any precision. Most importantly, this fact would assume importance a few weeks later, in the middle of summer.

As chance would have it, the historical summer of 1936 was also the summer of *A Day in the Country*. Whereas political events during the first months of that year strongly colored the discernible involvements of the director as he became involved in the experience of making *La vie est à nous*, later in the year his filmmaking resumed its own course as the unrest taking hold of the country progressed around it. *The Crime of Monsieur Lange* had been made in 1935 and would only be perceived as Renoir's "Popular Front" film after the fact. What was confusing about this new film was that as Renoir went about adapting Maupassant by directing a film concerned with desire—a film that would "speak" only about that—he was automatically taking part in the controversies of his time.

The fact that Renoir was the only director in sight among the committed artists and intellectuals of that time also contributed to the birth and expansion of the fantasy of a Renoir built from a single block, whereas the man was many sided, more so perhaps than any other artist of his era. At least two Renoirs were living in the same skin. One of them was directing *A Day in the Country*, and the other was standing up for certain issues, writing columns in newspapers; and no proof exists that the two sides were in communication with each other. For his films to produce such a strong feeling of unity, their maker had to have developed a watertight system of compartmentalization inside himself. If there are few films that are as detached from their times as *A Day in the Country* is, there are also few figures who recorded and embraced the jolts and contradictions of a period to the extent that Renoir did. To confront both these paths truthfully, Renoir had to move to and fro incessantly.

From the world of 1881 in which he'd immersed himself, Renoir detected the rumbling of the first sit-down strikes in the factories that exploded on May 11. When the Matignon Agreements were signed on June 7, he was in Marlotte. That same day, the strike included the film studios, delaying the shooting date of his film, which had been scheduled for the twenty-first of that month. While he struggled to find the actors he still needed for *A Day in the Country*, French cinema was petitioning the state to endow it with a new organization. On June 20, one week from filming, which had had to be put off yet again, Renoir published an article in *Ciné-Liberté* "taking full responsibility" for being against nationalizing film the way many were demanding, for the reason that "this measure can only be beneficial in a classless society in a regime that is under the dictatorship of the proletariat." In no way does the sentence indicate that Renoir desired the coming of a "dictatorship of the proletariat." It is merely a demonstration of the way his vocabulary had become permeated with political speak rather than a sign of contamination of his thinking that led him to wish for the repeal of censorship, which "currently allows the worst pornographic material to come out with impunity and holds sway only over the political domain" and to declare himself favorable to "employing foreign workers in France."[7]

At the same time, the young Italian who was designing costumes and collecting various props for *A Day in the Country* had finished those tasks and was waiting, between Marlotte and the Hôtel Castiglione, where he had established his Parisian quarters, to begin work on the shoot as third assistant director. Luchino Visconti probably owed what he himself would describe as a godsend to Gabrielle ["Coco"] Chanel, who was also Renoir's friend, although he could equally have met the director at the home of Marie-Laure de Noailles. He hadn't reached his thirtieth birthday, and Renoir had introduced him to a book whose tone was close to that of *Toni*'s. It was the James M. Cain novel *The Postman Always Rings Twice*, which had come out in the United States in 1934 and appeared in a French translation two years later. Visconti adapted it for the screen in 1942.* He had just seen *La vie est à nous*, which had produced a "strong impression" on him and had "opened his eyes." "I was coming from a Fascist country where you weren't allowed to know anything, read anything, understand anything, nor undergo any particular personal experiment. I was in shock."[8] From Renoir he learned, he would state, "the way to work with others," and then he said that he had been "fascinated by his personality," while refusing to see in *Ossessione* any type of French influence whatsoever.[9]

The son of Duke Giuseppe Visconti di Modrone and the son of Auguste Renoir would form a friendship, provoked as much by a common attraction to the people and their yearning for social justice as by membership in the same world. It wasn't that Renoir felt as comfortable in salons as he was at the bar of a café; it was that, failing to have a sense of himself as a rightful member of the best society, he still happened to frequent it. Most importantly, he enjoyed living around people whose simple and direct manners suited him and promoted the image he wanted to have.

For a long time, Sylvia Bataille was the only certain member of a cast that kept changing as the weeks went by. A version set by May 4 listed Christiane Dor (the mother); Léon Larive (the father); Jean-Pierre Aumont or Jean Servais ("he," meaning Henri); Marcel Duhamel (the friend); Pierre Prévert, Bernard Brunius, or Charbonnier (the fiancé, who'd become Anatole); and Marthe

---

* *Ossessione*, Visconti's first film.

Mellot (the grandmother). Except for Brunius, none of these actors ended up in the film. In a letter dated May 19, Henri Guisol (Amédée in *La Chienne* and the Meunier son in *Lange*) informed Renoir that he regretted not being able to accept the offer because he was expected in Berlin for another film; Louis Eymond and Bernard Geyond-Vital were both offered the part of Rodolphe by pneumatic-tube mail. A wave of panic swept over the production at the very moment Renoir became "housebound" and could only encounter actors he was considering at his home.

Most of the contracts were established around June 24, which was three days from the actual start of shooting that had been postponed several times. In addition to a fixed fee, Braunberger promised the actors and several members of the crew a percentage of the potential profits. Georges d'Arnoux signed an agreement for 2,000 francs and 1 percent; Jane Marken, 1,500 francs and 2 percent; Sylvia Bataille, 1,000 francs and the potential for a postprofit fee of 5,000 francs. Under the same arrangement, André Gabriello, Jacques Becker, and Claude Renoir stood to get 1,500 francs each, and Marguerite 1,000 with perhaps an additional 1,500. As for Visconti, he was hired with the sole promise of a share of 1 percent of the profits and would thus not be paid at all. It was planned that for the screenplay and the direction, Renoir would collect a salary of 15,000 francs (compared to 50,000 francs for *Toni* and 100,000 for *The Lower Depths*).

Successive estimates mentioned a budget of less than 200,000 francs, reduced by nearly half a few days before the shooting because some contributions hoped for from the outside were not received. A series of delays and incidents pushed costs to heights that the producer certainly had not envisioned—the available funds could not in any way have come near the million and a half francs that Braunberger would claim forty years later to have spent between May and September 1936. This would have made the outlay equal to nearly half the cost of *Grand Illusion* the following year. Scheduled for a week of exterior shots and a day at the Billancourt studios, the "*tournaison*" of *A Day in the Country* would actually require the services of crew and actors for part of the summer. And yet, Renoir's calendar did not authorize this excess. The filming of *A Day in the Country* took place within the time cleared by the temporary failure of the *Grand Illusion* production, and Renoir shut shop on it as soon as shooting on *The Lower Depths* became possible.

It's not rare for a shoot to be prey to panic. Film is a propitious medium for such uncontrollable energies, which certain directors aren't averse to arousing. However, there are few films whose direction was as chaotic as that of *A Day in the Country*. From there to spotting the quintessence of Renoir's method—or more precisely, his nonmethod—in such a hectic endeavor is only a single step for many commentators of the Renoir style, and they take it elatedly. Once again, the legend must give way to an attentive study of the facts, which Olivier Curchod was the first to accomplish.[10]

Actually, production of *A Day in the Country* was prepared as meticulously as required with respect to the rules in effect in the profession, most of which have hardly varied since that time. Jacques B. Brunius, who also played Rodolphe, was the great organizer in his role as director of production, but he was working under the control of a filmmaker who, as much in Marlotte as from Paris, had created a growing accumulation of notes, recommendations, opinions, requests, and advice. Moving the story from Bezons-sur-Seine, where Maupassant had located it, to the region of Marlotte gave Renoir the opportunity to be located on "his land," in scenes and among people that he'd known for fifteen years or so.

La Gravine, a home in the forest on the banks of the Loing, a few miles from Marlotte where the exteriors would be filmed, was rented at the time to Marie Verrier, a "local" whom Renoir had appointed housekeeper and given the responsibility of watching over his son. All the material from Paris had to be delivered directly to the villa Saint-El before being transported to the filming site. The Ermitage movie theater, in Fontainebleau, was reserved for watching rushes at the cost of seventy francs an hour. The craftspeople of the village were hired to make swing seats, a boathouse, and other elements indispensable to the decor. A friend rented his van to the filmmakers, and Paul Cézanne began looking for props. Part of the team stayed at the villa and another part at the Hôtel de la Renaissance, which was opposite it. Auguste had done a painting of that building in 1866 when it was still only Mother Antoni's* Inn, and Alain Renoir had broken one of its windows one day while practicing launching tennis balls with a "cannon" he had just perfected.

Preparations began in Marlotte in mid-May. A month later came the movable scenery for the interior of the inn, consisting of fake doors, windows, and partitions made in the Billancourt studios. The poster with the title *Une partie de campagne* had already been drawn, and a copy of it appeared in *La Cinématographie française* on June 27 with mention of the shoot's having begun. Such information was both precise and premature.

Two days before, actually, Renoir had filmed Sylvia Bataille and Georges d'Arnoux, probably in Marlotte, but it was only a rehearsal, putting together two actors who hardly knew each other and whose roles required them to get

---

* And not "Anthony," as is often cited.

along. The purpose also included tests designed to determine certain lighting techniques and camera angles. Two or three days before that, a first session of tests, done in a courtyard at the Billancourt studios, had allowed the director to assess the other actors in their characters' costumes. This points to the fact that, before filming, Renoir had chosen to isolate Bataille and d'Arnoux—Henriette and Henri—from the rest of the troupe. Their meeting and the love scene on the island are the raison d'être of the film.

Thanks to these miraculously preserved tests, we're able to discover that the troupe was still not definitively cast, if only because the role of the grandmother, described in the screenplay as being "like some Negro idol," was performed by Sylvain Itkine. This member of the October group, who was a friend of Paul Éluard and close to the Surrealists, had already appeared in several films by Renoir. He'd also play the professor who is "madly in love" with Pindare in *Grand Illusion*. In 1940, he created the self-managing cooperative of "Croque-Fruits" in Marseille, dedicated to producing and commercializing "bronze fruit," a sweet with a base of dates and marzipan. Their intention was to offer work to those in need of it and pay each a monthly salary of eighty francs. Among those who frequented the cooperative were Pierre Brasseur, the Prévert brothers, Benjamin Péret, Loleh Bellon, and Sylvia Bataille. Jean Malaquais put references to the "Croque-Fruits" in the novel *Planète sans visa* (*World without Visa*). Forced to flee Marseille for Lyon, where he directed an information network for the Resistance, Itkine was arrested in July 1944 and tortured and executed by Klaus Barbie's henchmen. It is unknown why Sylvain Itkine did not end up playing the grandmother in *A Day in the Country*. As a last resort, the role was given to the experienced Gabrielle Fontan, who was sixty-three at the time.

It was coming down in buckets on June 27. As well as on the days that followed. Every morning, upon rising, eyes would turn toward the sky . . . no, it won't be today, either. Or would be very little—just a few shots stolen between two rain showers, which wouldn't match the ones that would be filmed once the sun came back, given that it was too blindingly bright. The work schedule had to be changed every hour, even more often after several shots had been finished in the house using the movable scenery and when there were only exterior scenes to film. On July 3 and 4, the epilogue on the island was filmed on a shore, under a black sky that suited the gloominess of the scene. To Henri, who admits to coming there often because it recalls "his best memories," the young woman, now married to a simpleton, sighs, "Every night I remember."

The days passed, but not the bad weather, which left only enough time to film some secondary fragments. Thus, given the fact that the exterior filming had been stopped for several days, only a few shots were in the can. The crew had to wait; there was nothing else to do. For those who thought they had arrived for a short and relatively simple film, seeing that it had been perfectly prepared and would thus be quickly shot, the idleness was unbearable, the boredom intolerable. It was barely masked by the visits of friends—Coco Chanel, Georges Bataille, Pierre Lestringuez—all of whom left quickly to get out of the rain. Claude Renoir, the new director of cinematography after his uncle had tried in vain to contact Marcel Lucien (*Night at the Crossroads* and *Boudu*), and Pierre Levent loaded the camera on board a boat on the Loing to film some ripples in the water, images that no one knew as of yet whether they would be used. The trip to Marlotte of the man still married to Sylvia Bataille had led to a few outbursts because the good intentions of the separated spouses weren't able to eclipse all the resentments and jealousies.

Visconti smoked a brand of cigarettes called Congo, a detail that didn't go unnoticed by a fourteen-year-old boy. Alain Renoir was part of the shoot and held the clapboard. He also made an appearance as an angler who claims that if, in fact, "there are fish," "you've got to know how to catch them"; and then he went and had his head shaved, a whim that would lead to his being forbidden to appear again in front of the camera. Alain's most vivid experiences came from observing the gambol of the adults whose games of desire were being reproduced by the film. His father had moved him into the Hôtel de la Renaissance with part of the team, just opposite the villa Saint-El, where Renoir himself was living. Alain shared a room with his cousin Claude, the head cameraman of the film, who only stayed in the room at the end of each week.

When Claude remarked that Pierre Braunberger was arriving in Marlotte on Friday evening and would be leaving by Sunday at the end of the afternoon, several slyly exchanged looks and certain partly concealed gestures were enough to convince Alain that Claude and Sylvia Bataille had had an encounter. At the peak of the adolescent know-it-all syndrome, Alain felt a kind of pride about his conclusions every Sunday when the company would come together around the table of the restaurant in the Hôtel de la Paix in Bourron. He was certain that he was the only one who knew. The day he caught the actress and Georges d'Arnoux—her seducer in the film—in each other's arms, he'd pretend to accept their excuse, voiced in unison: they were rehearsing their scene.[11]

In a version of the screenplay dated June 20, Renoir has handwritten two words in the margin, "Dites donc" (meaning "hey!" or "sure is!"), as if to be certain to call attention to a line—his attention, as a start. It's the innkeeper's line as he points out the mother and daughter from Paris to Henri and Rodolphe, two friends about to become Lotharios. The innkeeper is saying, "Me, I don't have the time, but if I were in your shoes, I certainly know what I'd do." It's actually Renoir himself speaking that line in the film, because he's playing the innkeeper, Père Poulain. Next to Poulain in that scene is his servant, who is also his mistress, and she's played by Marguerite, Renoir's editor and girlfriend in real life. The director Renoir gave the actor Renoir the role of a kind of director who clues in the actors about the direction he expects to see them take, and he does this after having welcomed them into his home. The actual director is first and foremost an innkeeper. In fact, Renoir "certainly knows what he'd do if he had the time," and he makes the woman who shared his life at the time witness the desire inspiring him, and leads her into this adventure, but then seems resigned to the fact that another is going to experience it, although it is someone he has chosen and appointed.

What happens on the screen is what the scenarist and director wanted to have happen. In Marlotte, during these rainy summer nights, another film played out off camera, without the presence of the auteur, who understood that direction surpassed him, just as the jumble of events in *The Rules of the Game* would outstrip Octave, a prisoner of his bear getup. On the screen, the images of the film to come are double-exposed on this one.

Interrupted from July 13 to 15, the shoot resumed on the sixteenth, and three days later, about thirty shots had been filmed. On the eighteenth, they returned to the epilogue with a sense of urgency and sadness—urgency and sadness motivated by the decision made by Braunberger to put a stop to the filming. There was no more money, and no one could do anything about it. The images, as well, are imprinted by all of this. The company separated without having finished what they had come together for. The gloom is augmented by bitter frustration, colored with resentment, the annoyance that accumulated day by day finally overflowing. If no one wants anything more to do with this film, well, they can all go home.

The fact that no one wanted anything more to do with this film wasn't yet established on the day everyone left. Brunius stayed alone in Marlotte to keep an eye on the materials left behind, as a token of good faith for the creditors. In the end, he had to bring everything back to Paris. While Renoir remained silent and was already involved with another project, Braunberger took action and started looking for solutions. A film that had begun had to be finished or all the money that had been invested would be lost forever. Assignment of rights would be declared invalid if the film was not released within three years. On July 24, he signed a contribution agreement with Roger Woog, the director of production for *On purge Bébé* and *La Chienne*, for a total of 15,000 francs, which would be returned to Woog at the first receipts. The shoot could then continue.

Filming began again on August 6, a Thursday. But the next day, Renoir left once more for Paris. He'd signed a director's contract with Les Films de l'Albatros for the screenplay and casting of *The Lower Depths*, on which he had already been working for several weeks. The actors' contracts had been signed at the end of July. Renoir's was dated August 3, as was the letter appointing Jacques Becker, who on that day began working as first assistant director. The filming of *The Lower Depths* began on August 24 at the Épinay studios.

The actors on the banks of the Loing felt they'd been abandoned. The mood was horrible. Sylvia Bataille spoke later of an "atmosphere of hate."[12] Although Renoir's desire to do this film would remain, he was so much in the habit of avoiding and escaping conflicts that he just couldn't accept working in those conditions, regardless of his philosophy. Brunius did his damnedest, and the loyal Claude Heymann came to the rescue.

Renoir had left directives and other information, but there were so many shots left to do, not to mention those for the scene showing the family leaving, which had to be filmed in a studio. What did they think of this film abandoned by its director? They could tell themselves, of course, that Renoir had signed a new contract that prevented him from being with them; but when they learned from the papers on Monday, August 10, that the previous day the director had joined—along with four hundred thousand other people, according to *L'Humanité*—the great march for peace in Vincennes, they wondered a little, all the same, for whom and for what reason they had spent their Sunday working without Renoir on a Renoir film.

Today it is known that several shots on the water were filmed while the director was absent, as was that of the ladies boarding the boat and Rodolphe's dance of the faun as he played Romeo for his tititlated Juliet, a ballet that Brunius improvised. These can be broken down into twenty-three shots, not counting the additional linking shots, and it is now clear that Renoir did not direct them. Nevertheless, *A Day in the Country* is a Jean Renoir film, certainly one of his greatest; and the fact that it can be seen as a result of all those paradoxes associated with Renoir is of definite significance.

Renoir finished working on *A Day in the Country* on the evening of July 18. Probably around August 20—although the exact date remains unknown—he appeared at the set for the last time. It was a lightning-quick visit, and it left Sylvia Bataille, whom he'd forbidden to go to Paris to sign a contract (for the film *Ramuntcho*), just enough time to get what was on her mind off her chest: "One day they tell me he's back. We were at the hotel, and his house was very near, so I dashed over there. I arrived like a fury: 'You were gone for eight days!' 'Yes, I went to sign for *The Lower Depths*.' I tell him, 'You left for eight days and you wouldn't let me leave for twenty-four hours? You're really despicable, a coward!' 'Fine, then, you won't be appearing in *The Lower Depths*!' I answered, 'As if I could give a damn!' And in fact, I wasn't in that movie."[13]

Another incident has been established, but it, as well, has no precise date. Georges d'Arnoux was wounded by turning a hand crank while he was fairly drunk and trying to start his car. A split lip and broken teeth meant that it was impossible for him to be filmed. A letter written by Jacques Becker to the producers describes this injury, which had to be reported to the insurers of the film. Unfortunately, the letter isn't dated. It also contains a second doctor's certificate concerning Renoir. Does this mean that to keep from finishing his film the director reported in sick? Perhaps.

Several photos prove that Renoir was present at the filming on August 15, when a shot of Sylvia Bataille on the swing was taken that would not make the final edit. In it, her expression is one of unbelievable, seemingly endless sadness. The staggering beauty of this image grips you with overwhelming fascination. To whom is such an absent, lost, unmoored look directed? To whom else but the audience, into whose eyes she is already gazing after Henriette has been deflowered. And perhaps to Renoir, standing near the camera on that day, as well. He could have been the one who asked the actress for this strange expression, who wanted it, who perhaps already knew how *A Day in the Country* was going to end up. And what if Renoir had only wanted this film for the scene on the island, if he'd only been dreaming of this look, the chance to catch it on camera, something every director usually avoids and eliminates? The end was written: there's nothing unfinished about *A Day in the Country*, and everything about it is never-ending.

In Renoir's eyes, *A Day in the Country* ceased to exist at the very moment when the camera captured Sylvia Bataille's expression. He no longer wanted to talk about it with anyone, and for years he would not even mention the title. Now the history of it would be written without him.

Renoir's behavior has led to the hypothesis that he'd personally financed the production, or at least financed it in part, and/or refused to pay for the extensions made necessary by the vagaries of filming. The suggestion isn't borne out by any document. One thing is certain, however: Braunberger remained the only one to fight for the film; and he did so even more, quite naturally, after he'd called a halt to production. First of all, when did he make such a decision? According to him, "After two months, the team was furious, and one evening, when Sylvia Bataille and Jean Renoir were in an especially bad mood and seemed to hold it against me for having involved the film in such conditions, I said, 'You don't like the rain, you're bored, we'll stop everything.' The next day, I called everyone together, while telling myself that no one had ever had the nerve to stop a film out of love or friendship."[14] The statement makes it clear that the producer made his decision in the month of August, in the presence of Sylvia Bataille and

Renoir. Probably, in fact, around August 20, after the actress said what she did to the director. It's possible. But then, Renoir had already given up on the shoot. Braunberger's account goes on: "For some time I'd been thinking of myself as quite a wonderful man, but fifteen days later I was wondering how I was going to recuperate the million and a half that the film had cost me. A month later, I was desperate. I then asked Renoir to go back to the film, which from the beginning was supposed to have been of medium length. He did a preedit of it, and I immediately saw that it would be a masterpiece. Renoir wasn't very enthusiastic about reworking the film. He'd just signed with Alexandre Kamenka to direct *The Lower Depths*."

It should be noted that, while they were working on the film, both Renoir and Marguerite would decide, separately, to deny their involvement in any edit or preedit of it. As for the rest of the story, Braunberger so jumbled its chronology that there's no sense in trying to reestablish the sequence of events through his statements. It makes more sense to point out that, on August 19, the bracelets worn in the film by Henriette and her mother were returned to Bénet at 104 rue du Bac, along with a request that the jewelry not be resold immediately so that it could be used again if the film were resumed. Apparently, Muelle, at 59 rue du Faubourg-Poissonnière, waited longer before getting back the costumes it had rented out.

Therefore, although filming did in fact stop during the last week of August at the latest, and even though Renoir had already begun filming *The Lower Depths*, the producer had not given up thinking about finishing a film whose release he had announced in the press as September 26, a maneuver meant to reassure the profession of the health of his company. On October 13, he wrote to Sylvia Bataille, "This film in which you play the lead . . . not having been stopped, we are reminding you that you are at our disposal to finish filming. We are planning to do this between the end of November and beginning of December."[15] The same letter announces that the filming that has been planned would last for three to five days.

On that date, October 13, Braunberger had also just asked Jacques Prévert to write a screenplay likely to "complete" the film that had already been shot. It would be a feature-length film this time, in contradiction with the terms of the contract assigning rights, which he then agreed to negotiate anew. Renoir gave his permission, as explained by Olivier Curchod, who untangled the strands of this episode:

> Apparently, Renoir actively collaborated in getting this scenario under-way; it would consist primarily in framing the material already filmed with two additional parts that would be written and that took place in the Dufour hardware store before and after the trip to the country.

Brunius's archives contain a record of conversations between Renoir and Prévert [one of them is dated November 18, a month and a half after the end of filming for *The Lower Depths*] during which the screenwriter completes and comments upon the ideas brought to the table by Renoir. Renoir was imagining a scene at a cabaret, "La Fourmi" ["The Ant"], conversations between the parents about plans for the marriage of Anatole and Henriette, Dufour's schemes for ruining his neighbor the dairyman and taking over his shop. The leaving of the country is then organized to show the two young people, who don't really love each other, together. The last part of the film examines the consequences of the preceding elements: Dufour's business expanding, Henriette getting engaged, while Rodolphe and Henri resurface and join the little community on rue des Martyrs.[16]

Prévert had a good time, drawing as much as he wrote, creating caricatures and sketches, and giving free rein to his imagination. He invents the role of a dressmaker's apprentice for Jacqueline Laurent, with whom he was in love and whom he'd make the little flower girl in *Le jour se lève,* and imagines a homosexual baker named Patenôtre whose role could be played by Michel Simon. Prévert did Prévert, which only he could do. And to the same extent that Prévert's manner and tone served to enrich *The Crime of Monsieur Lange,* they distance *A Day in the Country* from the film that Renoir imagined, which he had partly shot and from which Prévert cut more than half—nearly eighteen minutes from the thirty-eight-minute edit that exists, not counting the credits and the inserts extracted from Maupassant's text.[17] The main victims of this hatchet job: most of the scenes between Dufour and Anatole, several between Henri and Rodolphe, and the conclusion.[18] It's difficult to imagine Renoir accepting to return to work on a film that he no longer wanted, was no longer excited by, had completely cooled off about, and was being asked, to boot, to revamp its spirit. Why would Renoir turn his *Day in the Country* into a film by Jacques Prévert?

Although the question probably wasn't termed as such, after Prévert read his screenplay to Renoir, Sylvia Bataille, and Braunberger at the end of December in a café a few steps from Salle Pleyel, the answer was given: no. But, according to Braunberger, Renoir was supposed to have claimed "to love the screenplay"—probably in front of Prévert—before lowering the boom once they reached the street: "I've already directed *The Crime of Monsieur Lange.* I'm not going to start working on some Prévert all over again."

Sylvia Bataille's version of what happened is only slightly different: "[Prévert] had changed everything.... Renoir wasn't happy about it, and neither was I."[19] The actress bemoaned the importance given to the character Prévert had designed for Jacqueline Laurent and the fact that he was quite likely to relegate hers to playing second fiddle.

Much later, Renoir would have two different reactions in succession. In 1957, he told Jacques Rivette and François Truffaut: "Braunberger was very happy with the result, so happy that he was imagining doing a feature-length film with it. He had even asked Prévert to write a screenplay. But that's very difficult, you know, doing a patch-up job, turning something conceived as a short film into a long one. So he wasn't happy when Prévert turned it into a small project."[20] In 1974, Renoir wrote that he'd been opposed to the very principle of a long film: "I didn't agree. It was going against the spirit of Maupassant and against the spirit of my screenplay." That was certainly an incontestable fact, but Renoir went on to say, "Jacques Prévert, who was consulted, sided with me. But I had to abandon the film to go and shoot *The Lower Depths*."[21] In this case, his memory was faulty. There's no doubt about the fact that Prévert accepted the commission and did it, and his screenplay was delivered *after* the filming of *The Lower Depths*, right before Renoir started *Grand Illusion*, which he had been preparing for the last several weeks. "The truth," Marguerite maintained, "is that he [Renoir] no longer wanted to finish the film. He was losing interest quickly. It was too late."[22]

A sample line of dialogue from Prévert's work demonstrates the tone of the film he was imagining. To Madame Dufour, who complains about the smell, a cesspool emptier retorts, "Then you mustn't shit, Madame, mustn't shit!" Perhaps it wasn't very *Day in the Country*, in fact.

Thirty years later, Renoir would state that, although he carried on with his plans and despite the fact that it didn't show, the hope remained fixed in his mind of finding the time to finish his film someday. Braunberger went on with his superhuman efforts, primarily by forming relationships with several directors. Among them was Detlef Sierck, who had passed through France in 1938, on his way from Germany to Hollywood, where he'd adopt the name Douglas Sirk. The future director of *Imitation of Life* would call Braunberger's proposition "wonderful" and "impossible," adding, "I was asked to turn it into a feature-length film. I came up with the craziest ideas for finishing it. I tried to write a second part. I also thought of inserting what Renoir had made into a new film to create a film within a film, and I don't remember what else I thought of. Even if I was under the impression that the film was perfect as it was, I was fleetingly tempted."[23]

Yes, "perfect." But that remained enclosed in parentheses until December 26, 1944, which is the date the producer wrote to Jean Painlevé, the governmental director of cinematography for France: "Given the absence of Jean Renoir and the fact that the actors have changed in the meantime, I have preferred not to film these [missing] scenes and to replace them with a spoken text inspired by Guy de Maupassant, illustrated by a certain number of engravings of Paris from the time. . . . I asked Pierre Lestringuez if he might like to work Guy de Maupassant's text into the film."[24]

As early as the end of 1939, Braunberger had offered this work to Lestringuez, and Renoir seems to have given his verbal assent to "let him adapt the parts of the film that we shot into a new version."[25] In his letter to Jean Painlevé, the object of which was to get hold of some supplies of virgin film stock, Braunberger made it clear that the edit would be done by Marguerite, who had taken Renoir as her last name. Painlevé's answer took a long time in coming. It was dated April 9, 1945, and it was negative: "It doesn't seem advisable to me, with the difficulties in film supplies still happening, to finish a production by doing without the director and actors." In this same letter, Painlevé explains, "Moreover, according to certain information I've received, Madame Marguerite Renoir would refuse to do the edit, which means that without any of the original collaborators, you would strongly risk distorting the work begun."[26] After having stated on November 10, 1945, that he intended to make use of this "short film of much less than 1,000 meters, similar to a prefeature opener," Braunberger would finally win his cause, and Marguerite would in fact edit the film, for which Joseph Kosma composed music. The synchronization took place in March 1946 at the studios in Neuilly. *Une partie de campagne,* now called *Partie de campagne,* was presented in September at the first Cannes Film Festival and then to general audiences on December 18, 1946, at the César movie theater.

While Sylvia Bataille was beginning a new life in which film had no place, in the process giving up on the idea of being paid by the producer the 5,000 francs she considered she was owed and that she was still demanding in 1938, Georges d'Arnoux was tumbling down a slope he himself had made slippery. In August 1938, he wrote to Braunberger, "Your letter finds me in the hospital, where I've been for the last ten days (but it's not serious, and you couldn't care less, anyway). I'm here getting detoxed from alcohol."[27] Shortly before the release of the film, the producer received a second letter: "I'm no longer hoping to be in the credits, but if you've decided I can be and it isn't too late, I'd like to be called Georges Saint-Saens (which is also my name)."[28] As for Brunius, he'd appear in the credits under the name Jacques Borel, which was his pseudonym while at Radio-Londres.

On June 7, 1947, Paul Temps, who had played Anatole, wrote to Renoir to tell him that he'd seen this film, which its auteur was unaware of.[29]

On March 24, 1949, Pierre Braunberger sent a request to Films Traders, 167 Oxford Street, London: "It is our pleasure to inform you that Monsieur

Jean Renoir will be in London for a few days at the Hotel Claridge and would very much like to see the film *A Day in the Country*, which he has never seen."[30] The answer from the manager of the Academy Cinema on March 31 was that the copy of *A Day in the Country* wouldn't be available until April 11.

Finally, in a letter to Louis Guillaume dated July 15, 1950, Dido Renoir wrote, "Yesterday, Jean showed *A Day in the Country* for the Slades, but first he eliminated the credits, which he found a bit too indecent." What was there about the credits that could disturb Gabrielle and Conrad Slade? Did Renoir find the lead-in saying, "Pierre Braunberger presents" unwarranted?

16

The Russian Way

Les Bas-Fonds (The Lower Depths)

On July 24, 1936, an article by Jean Renoir appeared in *L'Humanité* to mark the Parisian premiere of Grigori Kozintsev and Leonid Trauberg's film, *The Youth of Maxim*. The text shares the page with an ad for the film paid for by Pierre Braunberger, who was responsible for its showing exclusively at the Panthéon, the theater that belonged to him.

Renoir had discovered *The Youth of Maxim* during his stay in Moscow in March 1935. He began by describing the circumstances of his find, which included a grueling awakening on a morning following a short night with little sleep "spent celebrating the anniversary of the Jewish Theater and talking with its talented performers." Then, a trip to the theater, and finally, his succinct description of the film they did see—*The Youth of Maxim*—preceded by his praise of the speaking style of the actors: "Best of all, the actors did without their usual bombast and spoke simply, the way you do in everyday life—like people."

However, by that time buttering up already required tact, or at least it did in the pages of *L'Humanité* as much as it did anywhere. So, Renoir went about correcting the impression he feared he'd produced by writing the following: "Please don't mistakenly think I'm looking down on the romantic bombast of the first Russian sound films. It was a necessary stage, and Soviet artists have so much sincerity that they've always managed to give us a true impression of humanity even through such a theatrical form." *The Youth of Maxim,* he went on, "is a big step forward. It is progress, and it is the truth." Then: "It's possible that in the USSR all our comrades don't realize the true importance of this film, but that's not important. The tree has been planted, it will bear fruit and Stalin knew what he was doing when he awarded the directors of this film the Medal of Lenin." No doubt, but since when and in what way are political leaders justified in judging something artistic?

The article moves on to a lyrical celebration of the authenticity of the film, which "people of all opinions and all sympathies can sense. . . . This film is truly a Russian Communist film. It could not exist if there had been no revolution, and the men whom it introduces to us are the ones who made it. Those in charge of the great republic at the current time are their brothers. *The Youth of Maxim* is to Communism what the little flowers of Saint Francis of Assisi are to Catholicism." Just like a number of his fellow citizens, the Catholic in Jean Renoir could only, in fact, dream of the impossible marriage of the two religions. The article ends, "That matinee at the 'Red Front' was a total success, and these are marvelous moments that won't ever be forgotten." The editor of *L'Humanité* in charge of the article's headline didn't have to look much further for a title, even if it did require a mild distortion: "*The Youth of Maxim:* A Film That Won't Ever Be Forgotten."

Of those impossible unions taking place at the time, the least unexpected was certainly not the one that brought together White Russians, driven out by the October Revolution, and diehard Communists. According to Alain Renoir, his father "distrusted people from the East, giving as reason the fact that he didn't like it when someone abandoned his country."[1] That perspective would be one reason for the uneasiness Renoir sometimes felt during his American exile. But such a feeling didn't in the slightest provide a reason for him to refuse an offer brought to him by Alexandre Kamenka.

Kamenka was a member of a troupe of actors, film technicians, and directors forming inside the group that producer Joseph Ermolieff had created. At the time, Ermolieff was in charge of the Russian branch of Pathé. Shortly after the revolution, Ermolieff and his troupe moved to Montreuil, into an old stable that had been transformed into a movie studio. The actress Nathalie Lissenko, the actor Ivan Mosjoukine, the director Alexandre Volkoff, and, of course, the producers Alexandre Kamenka and Ermolieff created the company Ermolieff-Cinéma, which would become Les Films Albatros in 1922 and be run by Kamenka alone. Les Films Albatros was most notably responsible for the film *Le Brasier ardent* by Mosjoukine and Volkoff, which had so impressed "Dédée" and Jean Renoir that, according to Renoir, it had led to the choice of his vocation. Although the studio didn't survive the arrival of sound, the production company Albatros continued its activities under Kamenka's reins. Kamenka had become adept at maintaining some privileged links with the Russians, and this made possible their proposition to Renoir that he direct an adaptation of Gorky's work.

In the mid-thirties, as a result to some extent of the advent of the Popular Front, Russia was fashionable in France. Quite a few films with a "Russian" ambience were produced in Parisian film studios, some of which were made by émigré directors such as Alexis Granowsky or Victor Tourjansky, and many of which were by French directors. At the top of the list were *Les Nuits moscovites*

(*Moscow Nights,* 1934) and *Tarass Boulba* (*Taras Bulba,* 1936). Following these were such films as *Volga en flammes* (*Volga in Flames,* 1934), Maurice Tourneur's *Le Patriote* (*The Mad Emperor,* 1938), Jean Dréville's *Les Nuits blanches de Saint-Pétersbourg* (*Kreutzer Sonata,* 1937), and Marcel L'Herbier's *La Tragédie impériale,* shot a few days after *The Lower Depths* under the title *Raspoutine* (*Rasputin*) in December 1936. Back then, actor Harry Baur was the preeminent "Russian," playing the "czar of all the Russias" as well as he did a grain seller, and he starred in all the films just cited except for Tourjansky's and Dréville's. The actor had also played Porphyre, the judge in *Crime et Châtiment* (*Crime and Punishment*) in the 1935 adaptation directed by Pierre Chenal, a film in which Catherine Hessling played Elisabeth—her last appearance.

The Communist press had a good time mocking these productions and did so with even more verve when they were directed by a turncoat. For example, in its February 7, 1936, issue, *L'Humanité* laid into Alexis Granoff (Granowsky), who'd been born in Russia but who was a product of German education and culture. It ridiculed the happenings on the set of *Taras Bulba* in an article entitled "Some White Russians Make a French Film." A little more than a year later, *L'Humanité* announced the deaths of Granoff and "the Soviet writer Yevgeny Zamyatin," who had died on the same day, March 12, 1937. The obituary mentioned two of Granoff's films, but none of Zamyatin's works were cited, proof, probably, that death had cleansed Granowsky of his sins, whereas Zamyatin's were still unredeemable. *L'Humanité* might have recalled, however, that Zamyatin had played a far from minor role in the success of *The Lower Depths,* a film that paper had praised enthusiastically just a few weeks before.

A far from minor role, without a doubt; but what, precisely, did he do for that film? In 1921, when he was thirty-five, in the tradition of Wells he was putting the finishing touches on his futuristic dystopian novel *We,* which would influence such well-known writers as Huxley and Orwell. When an English translation appeared in 1925, the book was still banned in the Soviet Union. The irony in *We* directed at the Soviets was devastating for that regime, seeing that it came from a writer who'd been a victim of czarist censorship, had been forced into exile on two occasions before the Revolution, and then had left the Party in 1917. The notoriety enjoyed by the book in other countries resulted in Soviet authorities' prohibiting its author from being published, and on several occasions Zamyatin directly petitioned Stalin for authorization to leave the country. In a June 1931 letter, he said, "For a writer such as myself, being deprived of the possibility of writing is equivalent to a death sentence. Things have reached the point at which it has become impossible for me to practice my profession, because the act of creation is unthinkable if you are obliged to work in an atmosphere of systematic persecution that worsens every year."[2] Authorization was finally granted him, after a personal intervention by Gorky, whose disciple and close associate Zamyatin was. After a brief stay in Berlin, the author of *We* moved to Paris at the end of 1931, the year the French translation of his book appeared.

It's possible that the idea for an adaptation of *The Lower Depths* came from him. The project languished for several months in the files of Les Films Albatros; the producer considered giving the lead to Charles Vanel, then Paul Azaïs or Albert Préjean. According to what set designer Eugène Lourié has written, he also vacillated about choosing a director. Lourié, whose background was Russian and who had worked for Les Films Albatros since 1933 as its artistic director, would become one of Renoir's closest collaborators and most loyal friends. In his memoirs, he recounts Kamenka speaking to him about an adaptation of the Gorky play and presenting a list of possible directors. Lourié had seen Renoir at work in the Billancourt studios when he was directing *Madame Bovary* and had been impressed by "his quiet authority and his approach to working with the actors."[3] Although Kamenka was leaning toward Victor Tourjansky, Lourié put forward Renoir's name and learned a few weeks later that the director had accepted the project. It's certain that Renoir, still eager to find a way to direct his story about soldiers' escapes, saw Kamenka's production as a chance to work with Jean Gabin, whose name alone would be enough to induce the necessary financial backing for what would become *Grand Illusion*.

Kamenka chose Zamyatin to write the adaptation. A document dated August 3, 1936, confirms this and specifies that the scenario would be the work of Zamyatin, with dialogue written by Charles Spaak and direction by Jean Renoir, who'd be paid a fee of 100,000 francs.[4] Another document, undated but probably written earlier, mentions Jacques Companeez, who also collaborated on the screenplay. The contracts for Zamyatin and Companeez were signed on the same day, July 9, 1936; but it's likely that by that date they'd already handed in their screenplay, which Spaak and Renoir attempted to further revise. The director would characterize the Zamyatin-Companeez version as "very poetic, but absolutely impossible to film."[5]

Apparently, after that, Zamyatin acted essentially as an adviser, whose role was to oversee the development of the screenplay through the eyes of a Russian familiar with Gorky and his work. The archives of Les Films Albatros retain traces of this contribution, mostly in the form of "observations" made by the writer about the various subsequent versions delivered by Spaak and Companeez. Things such as "too many scenes with the baron playing cards," "Anna's death scene too morbid," "we don't understand why [Pepel has no gun]," or even "the audience won't understand." Renoir worked on the same documents, as evidenced by several notes in his handwriting, including one in which he asks,

"Don't you think that this passage has a style that's too 'revolutionary' for this baron?" The question had to do with a speech on the part of the character: "Don't forget that this veal was stolen from the butcher . . . who'd stolen it from the breeder . . . who'd refused to pay the price . . . to the landowner who was cheating the State. From top to bottom, and increasingly more and more, everybody is stealing." The passage "who'd refused to pay the price . . . to the landowner who was cheating the State" has been crossed out, probably by Renoir. That dialogue was absent from the film.

Another remark by the director draws attention to one of the important aspects of this project. It is written in the margin of a scene taking place at the gambling club: "Since we don't want to specify any particular country, it would be better to get rid of the gambling chips." Although surviving documents do show characters' names the same way as they appeared on-screen, it seems that the film's semi-"Russification" must have been accomplished at the last minute.

In a text from November 1936, Renoir makes clear the different possible perspectives for an adaptation: "an exact reconstruction of the atmosphere of the period—in other words, the Russia of 1902";[6] or "placing the action in our times"; and finally, "not situating it in any precise time or place [and] leaving it in an indeterminate environment." He states having been tempted by the first option but writes, "We lacked the material means, and the exteriors would have been fake." For this reason, he adds, he considered, "the idea of setting the film in Paris in the present and replacing the Russian names with suitable French names, while mentioning francs and centimes instead of rubles; in other words, transposing it completely." The second option was scuttled, "mostly to keep from shocking a large proportion of the audience, the ones who are familiar with Gorky's work, who would be thinking of the Russian play when *The Lower Depths* was shown and might see such a radical transposition as a lack of respect for the memory of the great writer."

As a result, the third solution became imperative—"making the environment absolutely indeterminate." And, in the end, Renoir would "hope, as a result, to have better served the memory of Gorky" by conveying "the spirit of his work in this film." Renoir considered this approach superior to having "created a parade of historical costumes and so-called Russian characters." The characters in Renoir's *The Lower Depths* are not Russian, obviously; but nevertheless their names are Vassilissa, Natacha, Nastia, or Kostylev, and they count in rubles. This was something that Jean Gabin would recall learning about very late, after having read the first screenplay and making it known that he wasn't "dying to play a Russian character because [I don't think I'd be] convincing or believable." "My name [in the film] was Jean, and I was in love with a girl named Marie. Everything in it was French. By the time we started filming, suddenly

I was called Pepel, they were talking about 'kopecks' or 'rubles' when it came to money, and there were samovars all over the place. I didn't get it at all, but I trusted Renoir."[7]

Gabin wasn't the only one who no longer understood a thing. Charles Spaak, despite his ringside seat, also seems not to have grasped the entire situation and has presented two versions of it that not only differ but are contradictory. If we're to believe Roger Viry-Babel, who claimed to have heard it from Spaak's mouth, the Communist Party intervened, in the person of Aragon, to keep the film from being perceived as "Russian," because associating Russians and Communism with poverty had to be avoided. The audience, in fact, might forget that the poverty depicted in *The Lower Depths* was caused by the old regime and that the world being pictured was precisely the one before the revolution. However, the version of the story Spaak gives in his memoirs and that his wife repeats in her own book is radically opposed to the one about the Party intervening: their version has their more evolved Soviet brothers objecting to the "Gallicizing" of Gorky's work. In fact, Renoir was supposed to have begun by telling Spaak, "Since Gorky depicts poverty and poverty is international, why not locate the action in an unspecified place?"[8] That orientation is the one indicated by Eugène Lourié in his early conversations with Renoir: "I remember having said to Jean that I didn't take *The Lower Depths* for a fundamentally Russian play, since class struggle is a universal, accessible theme anywhere at all in the world. Such a battle could occur equally in any large city, whether Berlin, Moscow, or Paris. And I began to recall those terrifying images of London in the nineteenth century created by Gustave Doré."[9]

Renoir's adopting the same point of view as the art director's is in line with his assertions; and, according to Spaak, Renoir was forced to "Russianize" his film at the last moment because the Communists wouldn't accept the work of the great Gorky presented as anything other than Russian. "I know that this is the opposite of what I said, but I can't do otherwise," Renoir is purported to have claimed to Spaak. "So I'm giving you a choice: either we do the corrections together, right away, or else I go to a hospital and get my appendix taken out." Such behavior is actually very much like Renoir: he couldn't stand conflict, and he would give in or flee. In this particular case, because he wasn't the only one who had to decide, he didn't insist on choosing but relinquished being the one to decide and fantasized hiding out. Be that as it may, making films remained his strongest desire. That is the way he had always been, and it was not going to change. Spaak blamed himself afterward for lacking "sangfroid and humor." "Imagine," he said to his wife, "a lawyer doing his utmost for three hours to prove the innocence of his client, then sitting down exhausted and wiping the perspiration from his brow, just to hear the accused stand up and proclaim, 'I'm guilty and I admit everything!' . . . I should have opposed the changes just to see Renoir pull the stunt of a sudden attack of appendicitis, grabbing hold of his stomach, and howling with pain in front of the producer, Kamenka, and the insurance company agents and finding himself condemned to a starvation diet for weeks."[10]

Renoir wouldn't see himself reduced to such an extremity. He and Spaak began working; in a few days they had made the requested corrections to the screenplay. Gorky, who died on June 18, probably couldn't have learned about these, despite the fact that Renoir claimed the opposite, insisting that the writer, "to my great surprise," warmly approved the project.[11] He'd maintain the same version of facts even in his personal correspondence. In 1965, when he began hoping to make *The Lower Depths* again in Hollywood with Tony Curtis, he wrote, "Gorky had just died when the film was produced. However, he'd seen the first version of the screenplay and had approved it."[12] Although there is no proof that the first version of the screenplay, credited to Zamyatin and Companeez, wasn't submitted to Gorky, the final version of the script by Renoir and Spaak was "approved by Baroness Budberg and M. Léon Bystritsky."[13] Léon Bystritsky had negotiated the adaptation rights. As for Baroness Budberg, she was one of the most remarkable figures of her time. Nina Berberova devoted a book to her.[14]

In 1911, Maria Ignatievna Zakrevskaya, called "Moura," married Count Benckendorff, a diplomat at the court of the czar who'd been shot in 1919 on his Estonian estate. Later married briefly to Baron Nikolai von Budberg-Bönningshausen, Moura became the mistress of such celebrities as Sir Robert Hamilton Bruce-Lockhart, a diplomat and secret agent who was posted to Moscow at the time; the American writer H. G. Wells; and Maxim Gorky. A double, triple, and perhaps quadruple agent, she had been living in London since 1936, where she worked, among many other activities, as a special adviser for the "Russian" films of producer Alexander Korda. During the war, she'd perform an ambiguous but highly active function for the French who were living in London, for whom she'd correct texts. She'd stun them with the outrageous quantities of gin and vodka she was capable of consuming (when she went out, she always carried her flasks in a bag whose strap was slung across her shoulder). She carefully maintained her relationship with Gorky until his death, which placed her in the privileged position of intermediary. She was the person to whom he demanded sums due him be handed over in full. She also kept a jealous eye on the fate of his works. That included the scenario for *The Lower Depths* on which Zamyatin had been the first to try his hand. At the time, the writer had only a few months more to live. Zamyatin died from an attack of angina on March 10, 1937, at the age of fifty-three, in a furnished house on rue Raffet, in the Sixteenth Arrondissement. A month and a half after his funeral at the cemetery of Thiais, during an evening organized by the writer's friends in homage to him, Renoir gave a short speech.

During the last days of June 1936, the director was busy simultaneously organizing the casting of both *The Lower Depths* and *A Day in the Country*, despite the fact that an illness had forced him to stay at home. Although he saw some of the supporting actors he had planned to use for his adaptation of Maupassant, his meetings with the stars suggested by the producers for his adaptation of Gorky had to be postponed. According to plans, he was supposed to have met with Pierre Richard-Willm, who was the first choice for the role of Pepel; Jules Berry, in line to play the baron; and Danielle Darrieux, whom Kamenka envisioned as Natacha. A note from the producer also mentions Elvire Popesco: "We have to see her and talk to her about the project."[15] However, there was still the question of which role the fiery Romanian could take on—probably that of Vassilissa, the head of the homeless shelter. Numerous preparatory lists that were drawn up show that the leading stars of the time were being considered singly or together. *The Lower Depths* was considered a prestigious production, which called for some big names. Jules Berry had held the inside track for the role of the baron for quite some time, as had Sylvia Bataille for Nastia, a role she'd claim to have lost because she had opposed Renoir on the nonshoot of *A Day in the Country*. Being considered as well were Pierre Blanchar as Pepel (or the baron); Valentine Tessier, Tania Fedor, or Olga Chekhova as Vassilissa; and Raimu or André Luguet as the baron.

The first contract to be signed on July 21 was Jean Gabin's. Renoir had already been in touch with the actor for several weeks, not for *The Lower Depths*, a project that was relatively new for him, but for what would become *Grand Illusion*. The difficulties director and screenwriter had faced in their attempts to finance this film nobody wanted had led them to approach Gabin, who was likely to activate his connections and get the ball rolling just by becoming a part of the project.

Jean Gabin was at the center of a network, receiving around thirty screenplays a year, among which he chose wisely. At the time, he was as much a celebrity as an actor. When he accepted to do a film not for a role in which he had little faith but for a director he trusted, he would approach his part by finding characteristics in it that matched his. Consequently, before he would don Pontius Pilate's toga in Duvivier's *Golgotha* (*Behold the Man*), he was careful to point out that the governor of Judea was a man of the people, whose valor in combat alone had allowed him to attain the high offices he occupied. Between

1935, the year when Duvivier's *Maria Chapdelaine* (released December 1934) made Gabin a star, and 1939, he would appear in twelve films, nine of which could be considered major works. When he signed for *The Lower Depths,* he'd just had an enormous hit with *La Bandera* (*Escape from Yesterday*), released in September 1935. It was the film that for the first time allowed Renoir to see him as the hero in *Grand Illusion.* After *Escape from Yesterday,* Gabin appeared in *They Were Five,* also directed by Duvivier and released in September 1936. (Spaak served as screenwriter for these two last films.) With his July 21 contract with Renoir, Gabin began a series of performances in Renoir films that would make him the only other actor besides Michel Simon to have worked four times with Jean Renoir. In at least the first three of these films, he became, as Pierre Billard has written, "part of a collective he personified but simultaneously felt different from and hoped only to escape."[16] Does this not echo the way in which Alain Renoir was so willing to portray his father? "If he'd been an Eskimo, he would have been the most Eskimo of all the Eskimos. But he'd also have never stopped criticizing Eskimo society from within its ranks."[17]

In 1936, France wanted to believe in the collective effort extolled by *The Crime of Monsieur Lange* or *They Were Five,* and a majority of French people saw themselves as members of a collective on the march toward a better tomorrow. Gabin was one of these people, the displaced individual from *The Lower Depths* who at the end of the film goes off toward a radiant future, the prisoner of war in *Grand Illusion* who crosses the border into freedom, the railway man in *La Bête humaine* whose dream is brutally terminated in blood. Between the first two films and the third, society had changed; and the world was about to collapse.

The meeting between the two Jeans—one called "le Jean" and the other nicknamed "le Gros"—was as you would expect: an actor going crazy for a director with whom "you never felt like you were working," and a director falling overboard for an actor who "didn't act in front of the camera." It would be necessary to wait for *La Bête humaine* for the fate that weighs on Gabin's shoulders in Duvivier's, Carné's, and Grémillon's films to waylay him again in a Renoir film. But it's true as well that in both *The Lower Depths* and *Grand Illusion* the person playing the most opposite Gabin was no romantic leading lady but a male actor—first Louis Jouvet, and then Pierre Fresnay and Marcel Dalio. In the collective of the rejected, among the prisoners, Renoir and Spaak installed a masculine tandem to fill in for the traditional couple that was about to be—or never could be—formed.*

The encounter between Jean Gabin and Louis Jouvet was a priori as

* See also Olivier Curchod, "Le Jean et le Gros, Gabin chez Renoir," *Positif,* n. 573, November 2008.

improbable as that between Pepel and the baron, except that both figures—each in his own way—seem to be losers. Each of the two actors had a past that separated them. Gabin came from the music hall; film had made him king. Jouvet lived only for the theater and had little regard for film. He would turn thirty-nine at the end of the year. *The Lower Depths* was only his fifth film, and the first two, adaptations of *Topaze* and *Knock,* owed more to the theater than to film. The fourth, *Mister Flow,* was not the kind that could restore his confidence after it had possibly been unsettled by his third, *La Kermesse héroïque* (*Carnival in Flanders*). What is more, whereas Gabin was a man of the people, Jouvet was a man of the Left. When the former grew alarmed about rumors claiming the Communists were planning to go after private property, the latter made a fool of him by assuring him that he would not lose anything he'd suffer from no longer being able to enjoy.[18]

That day, on the banks of the Marne, the two actors were chatting as they waited for the crew to announce that they were ready for the moment in the film Renoir would later call "the key scene": the scene in which Pepel speaks of his hopes of escaping the dregs of society with the woman he loves, and then in which the baron recounts his life by describing each outfit he wore during each stage of it. "While speaking, the baron catches sight of a little snail climbing a blade of grass. He picks up the snail and places it on his finger and makes it inch along it." I went to several showings of *The Lower Depths* with an audience. It never failed: when the snail began to inch its way along Jouvet's finger, the room was put at ease. You could sense that mass of spectators ardently following the movements of the snail. The baron was becoming familiar to them and they were identifying with Gabin as they listened to that story."[19]

Renoir would speak of *The Lower Depths* as one of the films whose screenplay he most closely followed. "It was easy, enjoyable work," he would say when talking about a production that had benefited from the expertise of technicians with studio experience. The production reports still exist, and they reveal the efficiency of the crews. For example, the description of September 9: arrival of Jean Gabin on the set at 12:25 p.m.; rehearsal from 12:25 to 12:45; lighting adjustments from 12:45 to 1:00 p.m.; shooting from 1:05 p.m. to 1:30 p.m. The slightest incident was scrupulously recorded. Setbacks were rare, as unremarkable as Suzy Prim making news by arriving late on September 12 and "not knowing her lines."

In an article entitled "French Productions Want to Live, Don't Kill Them Off," in which Renoir expresses his uneasiness at seeing French producers deciding

---

* Actually, the little snail is seen on-screen when it is already on Louis Jouvet's hand.

to have their films directed in other countries out of "fear that the new labor laws could lead to a waste of time in French studios," Renoir goes back to an on-the-spot report of his experience making *The Lower Depths:* "I never enjoyed such a regularity in any of my preceding films. . . . Do you believe—even given their experience and talent—that producers could pull off staying within the precise limits of their budget and shooting schedule if working conditions in French studios were so bad?"[20]

Actually, and very logically, the impression produced by the film matches what you'd expect under such conditions. *The Lower Depths* lies somewhere within the average range of French productions of the period. Perhaps the higher end of average? Maybe. In any case, the first half hour of the film gives that impression. This is the most successful portion and also maintains only a distant connection to Gorky's play. The opening scene is especially magnificent, with its panoramic shots moving in two directions, from right to left and then from left to right, framing Louis Jouvet before the reflection in the mirror makes the viewer understand that the camera angle is from the perspective of the character lecturing the baron. Throughout the entire film, Jouvet dazzles with his mastery, humor, and detachment, opposite a Gabin obviously never more at ease than in the scenes he plays with Jouvet. On the other hand, the scenes in the homeless shelter seem banal at best, most often extremely flat, bogged down by the studio aesthetic, deadened by the actors' attempt to "seem Russian," all the while not seeming it, and certain lines go over like lead balloons.

Renoir was the kind of director who fed on excitement, was nourished by accidents and the unforeseen. He liked nothing better than shaking up both his own ideas and principles and those of others, seizing a detail that went unnoticed until that moment and turning it into an intrinsic motif. He had the ability, in a word, never to take anything for granted. In the context of a production as weighty as this one, about a subject that he hadn't chosen and whose approach had been imposed on him late in the day, he seems cramped, and his directing style becomes one of feeling ill at ease.

And—although such a deficiency is rare in his films—the casting isn't up to his usual standard. Junie Astor is enormously insipid in the role of Natacha, which keeps her from holding on to the position that should have been hers, thereby accentuating an imbalance with the masculine tandem to the point that makes you begin to wonder whether Pepel is more in love with the baron than with Natacha. According to Renoir, Kamenka had asked him to cast Junie Astor as a favor, and Renoir couldn't succeed in drawing from her what the character required.[21]

But Junie Astor is not the only problem. Gabriello, excellent in *A Day in the Country,* delivers a disappointing portrayal in the role of the inspector. His performance is uselessly overelaborated without ever becoming comical, as the actor seems to hope it will be. Paul Temps is another actor from *A Day in the Country* who doesn't manage to make his mark, lost as he is in the middle of a sea of other hairy, bearded men, distinguished only by René Génin. As for Maurice Baquet, he seems to have jumped directly off the screen from *The Crime of Monsieur Lange* into *The Lower Depths*, as he hops about banging out accordion tunes, while flubbing one of the most "Popular Front" lines in the film: "What is a boss? A simple misunderstanding!"

It wasn't by chance that the actor in the group who seemed the most in tune was exactly the one whom Renoir had consciously intended to give "a lyrical way of speaking, a language a second away from being fake." Robert Le Vigan, who had already been excellent as Lheureux in *Madame Bovary*, brought his character to heights that the rest of the film was far from reaching. The actor's suicide scene, which was going to happen as he recited Shakespearean verses that Le Vigan and Renoir had agreed upon, was the object of a conflict that pitted the producer against the distributor and theater owners.

The theater owners took the position that the film was unconvincing and blamed this on certain scenes that dragged, and the distributors seemed to make use of such reluctance to justify their decision to cut down on the number of theaters where the film would be shown and to force the producer to accept limitations in the guarantee of lengths of exclusivity. In an undated draft of a letter intended for a representative of Les Distributeurs français, an official at Les Films Albatros broached the question of "theater owners' apparent refusal of the film." He was referring to an offer from the Gaumont distribution network concerning a release of the film in three of its Parisian theaters, and he expressed surprise about a request to cut some "outstanding scenes with Le Vigan," before he suggested a test screening "to see how audiences react." His conclusion: "It is therefore obvious that if you object to the film showing in some theater or another, it has nothing to do with the scenes you are calling into question but with this kind of film."[22] Jo Siritzky confirms today that, in fact, "no theater wanted the film."[23] The scenes being called into question were, to be exact, those "in the car," the "Actor's rant near the wall," the one "among the baron, Nastia, and Satine up to the point of the scene with the Actor," "the scenes of the Actor in the courtyard," and "the feet of the Actor." Only this last shot would be sacrificed, because the producer emphasized that eliminating the scene of the car would be "harmful to the rhythm of the film." The producer also expressed his regret that such demands had been made after editing, when they could have been carried out "in the cut."

The controversy broadened to such an extent that, a month before the film's release, Renoir sent a letter to the distributors Lehman, Aciman, and Saason that was also signed by Spaak and in which he suggested the possibility of two versions: "The first version made to the entire satisfaction of the theater owners sounded out by you and in which we'll do all the cuts necessary provided that the title of the film is changed and that neither Spaak's nor my name is mentioned. . . . The second left in the state we showed it at the end of last week on rue Francoeur and representing our work for better or worse. It will be shown, to the extent possible, in certain specialized theaters for certain groups."[24] It wouldn't be necessary to go to such extremes, and the film would open at the Max-Linder, the theater that Léon Siritzky had acquired the year before and that would guarantee an exclusive run of four weeks, rather than at the eight that had been planned initially.

Jo Siritzky did not forget the film's premiere:

> After the dinner, we went to the Max-Linder with Gabin. Back then, the entrance to the theater was next to the screen, so we saw a few minutes of the film. Gabin was perfect, but you've no idea of the effect Jouvet produced on the audience. We left without attracting attention and, in front of the theater, Gabin, who was the talkative type at the time and could on occasion come on quite "strong," pointed at his name next to Jouvet's on the facade and said to us, "Get ready to receive a formal complaint." He did nothing of the sort, but he was used to audiences, he came from the music hall; and just from their reactions to the film, he'd understood that Jouvet was going to "grab" all of it. And, in fact, that is what happened.[25]

As far as the press went, this wasn't a question of two opposing conceptions of film—two sides confronting each other—but a matter of two conceptions of society and politics. On the one hand, the papers stigmatized what God-fearing types considered to be unfortunate excesses, and while recognizing that the film "lacked neither power nor atmosphere," *La Croix* reproached it for being "in many places a paraphrase of 'religion is the opium of the masses,'" and advanced the notion that its "treachery goes as far as making the most disgusting character, the hotel-keeper, a religious man."[26] The opposite side had decided on principle that an adaptation of the great Gorky by a filmmaker who was a friend of the Party, who was loved by it, who had directed *La vie est à nous*, who was close to Maurice Thorez, and who had participated in demonstrations and meetings could only be seen as a major event. *L'Humanité* said as much on three occasions. Under the title "*The Lower Depths* Must Be Seen," Jean Kress wrote, "Jean Renoir isn't concerned about making a film or two a year.* He has his

---

* Actually, *The Lower Depths* was Renoir's third film for 1936.

subject, and he treats it the way he feels it." For Kress, this was a "laudable film," "in which there's nothing missing, and where everything has its place." And he said this after having classified Renoir in the category of "naturalist" directors, and not in the "proletarian"[27] category. Less than a month later, Georges Sadoul saw in Pepel "a pathetic example of a man who wants to tear himself away from the dregs of the lower depths and become a man again by becoming a worker," before maintaining that "the people of our country deeply love Jean Renoir, because they know*that this great artist is their profound, sincere, devoted supporter."[28]

Thus, Pepel had gone from being a thief to being a potential worker. The transformation enchanted Georges Sadoul, but it could not have come about except at the price of modifying Gorky's play, which ends with the suicide of the Actor. The film, on the other hand, ends under a sweeping sky, in the open air, as Pepel and Natacha walk toward a future implied to be wonderful. This last image is in homage to the finale of *Modern Times*, released in France on September 24 but seen by Renoir at a private screening.* The image expresses the spirit of the Popular Front, bearer at the time of all hope; and it is heir to the lineage established by *The Crime of Monsieur Lange*, a film that also develops around the murder of a profiteer that is "collectively assumed and morally excused by the tale's author."[29] As part of the same impetus, *The Lower Depths* heralds the wave of dark realism about to sweep through French cinema, a vehicle for the disillusionment that will follow the crazes of the early months of the Popular Front, announcing the storm to come. And soon, Georges Sadoul will use Renoir as an example to discredit the cinema of Carné and Duvivier and to proclaim the division of French film into two opposing camps—not the mediocre directors but those labeled wicked and the good ones.

On December 14, 1936, *The Lower Depths* was in first place for the Prix Louis-Delluc, created a few days before by the efforts of two editors of the weekly *Cinémonde* on behalf of a group of journalists in the field who were all less than forty years old. They presented themselves as "the young independent critics" and ambitiously vaunted their opposition to the Grand Prix of French cinema. Each year since 1933, a coterie of its bigwigs—who for the most part were as remote from film as could be—had awarded the Grand Prix to a film they considered prestigious. After appropriately honoring *Carnival in Flanders* in 1936, they had voted for *L'appel du silence* (*The Call*) by Léon Poirier in 1938 and Maurice Gleize's *Légions d'honneur* (*Legions of Honor*) the following year. The Delluc judges, who numbered twenty-three and included Henri Jeanson

* Renoir had devoted an article to the Chaplin film, which appeared in the first issue of *Ciné-Liberté* on May 20, 1936.

and Georges Charensol, were split between Marcel Carné's first film, *Jenny,* which received nine votes, and *The Lower Depths,* which finally won on the fourth round with twelve votes. Strangely, *The Crime of Monsieur Lange* was considered a candidate despite the fact that it had come out in December of the preceding year. It obtained two votes, putting two Renoir films on the charts that year. The fact that a weak adaptation of a Gorky play had been preferred to the boldness of *Monsieur Lange* seems to imply that "political" criteria were of overpowering import. However, another argument for this was put forward, possibly to conceal such motives, and it was expounded by Georges Charensol a few weeks later: "You would have hoped that the prize would go to *The Crime of Monsieur Lange,* which was unquestionably the most original work our cinema had produced in a long time. But in the end, another Jean Renoir movie was preferred to the one we stood up for. Those supporting it pointed out to us that *The Crime of Monsieur Lange* had ended his career whereas *The Lower Depths* was beginning it, and that argument won over the majority of our comrades."[30]

On several occasions, a remake of *The Lower Depths* was considered. In 1943, one of the film's distributors who owned shares in the production demanded $100,000 for the rights.[31] No action was taken. In 1956, bereft of any serious plans, Renoir wrote to Charles Spaak,

> If they ask me to direct a film here, why don't I propose *The Lower Depths,* which I could adapt to a run-down neighborhood in Los Angeles. It would be a way of using part of our old screenplay and making a little money from it. In order to make such a proposal, I need to be sure not to have any later difficulties with the producers of the film and the original adapter. . . . Our buddy Kamenka probably wouldn't cause any trouble and we could give him a small remuneration. As for the other one, whose name I've forgotten, there's nothing he could get from *The Lower Depths.*[32]

Who in Renoir's mind was this "original adapter," this "other one"? Zamyatin, not only whose name but also whose death he could have forgotten? If Renoir was talking about Jacques Companeez, the coincidence in dates is macabre: the screenwriter died on September 9, 1956, the very same day on which Renoir wrote to Spaak. In 1977, when Renoir would discover Kurosawa's version of *The Lower Depths* (1957), he'd judge the film "ever so much more important" than his.[33]

On December 30, 1936, the executive secretary at the Ministry of State Education and Fine Arts acknowledged receipt of the candidature of Jean Renoir, dramatic artist, for the Cross of Chevalier of the Légion d'honneur.[34] A month later to the day, the minister himself, Jean Zay, informed the director that the president had just granted him the honor.[35] Renoir was forty-two years old and not only the most well-known director in French film but—in the words of producer Jacques Schwob d'Héricourt—"that man who makes films where people spit on the ground."[36]

17

Between Two Wars

La Grande Illusion (Grand Illusion)

Pineapple with kirsch, a fine old recipe from the land of Alsace? Alain Renoir would have been of a mind to agree when he discovered this dessert in November 1936. It was just the thing to gratify the ego of an adolescent finally being allowed to taste alcohol, eight years after his seventh birthday when Pierre Lestringuez had given him a glass of wine to drink. Accompanying son and father in their trip to scout locations were Eugène Lourié, in charge of decor; Jacques Becker; Carl Koch; Charles Spaak; and four new people to the world of Renoir: director of photography Christian Matras, producer Frank Rollmer and his gofer Albert Pinkovitch, and director of production Raymond Blondy.[1]

Renoir later told of how three years of setbacks and rebuffs had gotten them to this point. The wait certainly had been a long one, but the director hadn't been idle—he had directed four films in the meantime. About a year after he'd had his first thought about *Grand Illusion* in autumn 1934, while filming *Toni*, he'd singled out Jean Gabin in the film *Escape from Yesterday* as the actor he wanted for his lead. From December 1935 until January 1936, Alexandre Kamenka had tried to organize the production and then, failing to put together the financing, had chosen to entrust the direction of *The Lower Depths* to Renoir while, in the meantime, Charles Spaak also became part of that production. Then, finally, the film found a producer.

To write this story of military escape, Renoir summoned his memories of war and barracks life; but perhaps more crucial was his reliance on the recollections of a French ace pilot with a tally of twenty-seven official victories. He'd probably met this man, Armand Pinsard, in 1916 when the latter was an adjutant-major. Like Renoir, Pinsard was a former member of the cavalry and—Renoir would write—had saved his life. From the SPAD plane Pinsard was flying, he had machine-gunned the Fokker attacking Jean's airplane while Jean was on an observation mission accompanied by a captain from the Hussars. "I admired [Pinsard] with all my heart. . . . I could spend hours listening to him ramble on about the horses he had broken in. One day, my squadron received orders to decamp. That's when I lost contact with him."[2]

Pinsard came back into Renoir's life in 1934 while the latter was filming *Toni*. Disturbed by the training exercises of a group of pilots in the sky over Martigues, the director and his producer Pierre Gaut went looking for the aviators. Renoir and Gaut—who was also a former aviator—were surprised to recognize their friend, who now wore the uniform of a general. Shortly after the reunion, Pinsard recounted how he'd been shot down by the Germans and sent to prison camps seven times, managing to escape on every occasion. General Pinsard's tales led to a collection of notes entitled *L'Évasion de Pinsard* (*Pinsard Escapes*), entrusted to Charles Spaak in the fall of 1935 as the material for a screenplay.

In April 1917, the magazine *La Guerre aérienne* helped establish Pinsard's notoriety by presenting the story of his escapes. His victories had begun accumulating on November 1, 1916. Among the many episodes recounted in that early publication were several incidents that would appear in *Grand Illusion*: "His reconnaissance mission with an aristocrat, his forced landing and capture by the Germans, his repeated desire to escape and time spent in solitary confinement (thirty-five days mellowed by the letters from his family his jailer passed to him), his emergence from solitary to the tears of his comrades, a series of internments in Germany, his escape from a fortress with a Captain Ménard and their 217-mile walk to the Swiss border (slowed down by Ménard's sprain), with nothing but their provisions and a map."[3]

The process of escape as it's shown in the film is based loosely on an article in *Le Figaro* that appeared on May 23, 1918, marking the occasion on which a certain Lieutenant de Villelume was presented with the Légion d'honneur by the president of the committee: "During his long captivity, he had only one thought, to go back to serving his country. But before he himself left the camp in which he was imprisoned, he made sure that two of his seniors, Commander Ménard and Captain Pinsard, well-known aviators, would succeed in escaping because he considered their return to France more useful than his. All three of them had planned their escape together. But at the last moment, it was apparent that only two men could escape. Quite simply, Lieutenant Villelume sacrificed himself."

But unlike the character Boëldieu in the film, Villelume didn't lose his life there. "After four dangerous attempts, [he], as well, succeeded in reaching the border." Renoir's inspiration for Boëldieu's personality was probably Captain Louis Bossut, whom he'd met in the First Regiment of Cavalrymen, in Joigny, then in Luçon, and finally on a campaign that began in August 1914. An outstanding cavalryman and holder of numerous horse exhibition awards, Bossut also ran a racing stable; but he'd had to give up on the naval career he'd been dreaming of because of poor eyesight, for which he'd taken to wearing a monocle. On April 16, 1917, he was killed in combat.

Pinsard's memories formed the framework of the screenplay, filled out by the recollections of Renoir and Spaak, who'd been too young to go to war because he had been born in 1903 but who brought the account of his brother Paul-Henri, a future minister of Belgium and eminent architect of European unity. Paul-Henri had once caused a scandal when he broke into the Belgian national anthem at the end of a stage show. The director and screenwriter also drew from a great number of works, especially from memoirs of prisoners of war, to the point that quite a few former soldiers felt justified in claiming that *Grand Illusion* was based on their story.

One of the many examples of such an intrigue is the note Marcel Diamant-Berger wrote in 1973 to the permanent secretary of the Académie française applying to occupy the chair that had been vacated by the late Jules Romains: "Captured in Bavaria, I was imprisoned successively in two forts in Ingolstadt and then in October 1917 in the castle of Hirschberg, from which I escaped at the end of November with a renowned aviator, the commander Goÿs de Mézeyrac. Several comrades participated in that escape, and among them was Captain Charles de Gaulle, who on that occasion exhibited great courage and much humor. Fifteen years later, our escape provided the theme for the celebrated film by Jean Renoir and Charles Spaak, *Grand Illusion*." The film's renown was so great that actually all prisoners who had experienced the German camps of the First World War claimed to recognize themselves in it. Most of those who escaped said they were honored by the film, but one man took offense and brought an action against the filmmakers, to which it is worth returning later.

In January 1935, a first estimate of 1,504,000 francs, about average for production budgets of that period, was established by Les Films Albatros for a film initially entitled *L'Évasion* (*The Escape*), then *Les Évasions du capitaine Maréchal*, and, finally, at least as a working title, *La Grande Illusion*. Alexandre Kamenka agreed to produce it. At the time, a four-week shoot was planned, beginning in May and allowing delivery of a master print in July. However, Les Films Albatros bowed out because Kamenka hadn't succeeded in finding any distributor willing to commit financially, apparently for the reason that the absence of a love story seemed insurmountable. One wanted Renoir and Spaak to invent the character of a nurse played, preferably, by Annabella. "When we asked [this distributor] if he'd seen such appealing individuals in the camp where he'd been interred for three years, he admitted that such distraction had been lacking."[4]

At the time, the screenwriter was also working for Gabin on what was still entitled *Jour de Pâques* but that would become *La Belle Équipe* (*They Were Five*). Renoir was aware of the project, having gotten to the point of suggesting to Julien Duvivier that they exchange films. He'd direct *They Were Five* and

Duvivier, *Les Évasions du capitaine Maréchal*. According to Renoir, he was only joking, but the proposition may have been more serious than he would let on: Spaak stated that Renoir "was taken by such a flight of enthusiasm for this subject [*They Were Five*]" that in autumn 1935 he told Spaak to rush to Prague, where Duvivier was directing *Le Gôlem*, in order to "negotiate a strange agreement: he would give him the screenplay of *Grand Illusion* in exchange for the subject of *They Were Five*."[5] An offer that "Dudu" did not pursue: "Duvivier listened carefully to me. 'Your story about soldiers doesn't interest me at all. . . . Have you lost your mind?' I went back to Renoir a little sheepishly. He'd understood quite well what aspects of my screenplay for *They Were Five* had to do with the Popular Front. 'Well then . . . let's keep going, we'll do *Grand Illusion*.'"[6] According to Janine Spaak, Duvivier refused with the excuse that "a story about prisoners of war isn't going to appeal to anyone!"[7] It remains to be said that Spaak's statements about this hypothetical exchange plan shouldn't be given a great deal of credence.

Jean Gabin's involvement enabled this story of escape to bypass the dead end at which it had been left by Les Films Albatros by arousing the interest of producer Frank Rollmer and his company Les Réalisations d'art cinématographique (RAC). RAC had been created in 1934 for *L'Homme à l'oreille cassée* (*The Man with a Broken Ear*) and had just produced *Jenny*, Marcel Carné's first film. Rollmer came forward with a budget of 3 million francs, which was twice Kamenka's estimates. The increase was justified by the significant inflation of production costs during the course of the year 1936. RAC was also to take charge of the distribution. In the end, the film would cost 2.75 million francs and bring in 120 million. The contract signed by Renoir is dated November 9, 1936. In fact, the director had fewer dealings with Rollmer himself, whose involvement was for the most part financial, than he did with the funny little fellow Rollmer had appointed as his right-hand man.

Renoir would write that Albert Pinkovitch was "a born negotiator, convincing each competitor that he'd managed to extract some important concessions from the other side," whereas "he was actually sidestepping the question." This little "dark-haired, pudgy type of Jewish guy . . . had the advantage of possessing soulful eyes" that "misted over with tears when he implored someone," and "he was impossible to resist."[8] He was the son of a Romanian engineer who'd built oil wells for the benefit of the Rothschild family. Baron Philippe Rothschild, as was his habit, had brought the boy to Paris to enter rabbinical school; but studying the Talmud left fifteen-year-old Albert cold. After a few weeks of it, he chose running wild instead, opting for freedom over the baron's allowance, even if it meant panhandling. Off to adventure in the streets of Paris, he went from selling shoelaces on the sidewalk in front of the Gare du Nord to hawking wind-up toys on the median strips of the outer boulevards, mapping a trajectory rich with Parisian slang that led him into the world of finance. There he discovered a passion for the trader's game and soon became the right-hand man for the renowned piker Frank Rollmer, whom he would convince to invest in films. Marcel Carné would state in his memoirs that he suggested Renoir to "M. Albert" when the latter was looking for a director he could trust. Carné also eagerly championed the *Grand Illusion* project on the grounds that it obviously deserved consideration because such men of high standing as Renoir and Spaak were behind it.

Pinkovitch was always pulling on a pipe that never seemed lit and spoke with the strong accent of a Parisian guttersnipe that was spiked with echoes of his Romanian childhood. He could cite the Talmud as well as he could launch into saucy improvisations good enough to perform in Parisian cabarets.[9] The contribution to *Grand Illusion* of the man his friends called "Pink" and whom the crews referred to as Monsieur Albert wasn't limited to bringing finances to filmmaking, the role he'd been assigned. His witticisms, jokes, energy, and joie de vivre were what led Renoir and Spaak to the character the actor Julien Carette would play, who was originally conceived as a "cheeky Parisian." Pink also influenced their creation of the character Rosenthal (played by Marcel Dalio), who hadn't existed in definitive form in early versions of the screenplay.*

In point of fact, Maréchal originally escapes with someone named Dolette, "a slight, lean boy with the attractive face of an intelligent man and wonderful eyes," "an intellectual" whom Robert Le Vigan was supposed to have played. Each of the two men is supposed to have an affair with the German woman farmer who offers them refuge, and they agree to meet at Maxim's on December 25, 1918. The film ends showing the celebration at Maxim's with the table reserved for Maréchal and Dolette empty.

In November 1936, Renoir found himself in Alsace. A decision had been made to film the exteriors of the fortress at the castle of Haut Koenigsbourg, in Orschwiller, about twelve miles from Colmar. The interiors would be shot in a studio. In a letter to his wife, Carl Koch explained that Colonel Didier of the Eighth Artillery Regiment in Colmar, whose men he and Renoir were asking to participate, had showed them a message from Édouard Daladier, the minister of national defense at the time, forbidding the colonel from lending his soldiers to the filmmakers. Colonel Didier is then supposed to have torn up the letter from the minister and promised that his troops would participate in the film.[10] The

---

* Rosenthal was born from the confusion of two characters, "the Jew" and "Dolette," who were combined after Marcel Dalio was cast in the first role.

company, which had set up its quarters in Strasbourg, was there for only a few days before reuniting in Paris, where the director had to do more work on the screenplay and finish casting because some of the roles were still in flux.

In addition to Jean Gabin and Le Vigan, they had been planning for quite a while to use Louis Jouvet (Boëldieu) and Pierre Renoir (the commander of the fortress), who'd just made six films in eight months. Work on the Jean Giraudoux play *Supplément au voyage de Cook* (*The Virtuous Island*) was keeping the two actors from participating in the film, so Renoir offered the role of Boëldieu to Pierre Richard-Willm, who refused it with the excuse that the character wasn't meaty enough and that he wasn't "made of the same stuff" as him. In that same letter,[11] Richard-Willm also noted, "In reading this synopsis, there is a role that appears developed, and it's Gabin's—which makes perfect sense to me—but the other role has to match it in interest and importance, and he has to confront and be more involved with the other." As a result, Renoir and Spaak appealed to Pierre Fresnay, who agreed to play the role. Although it is not known with whom Renoir was planning to replace his brother, it is apparent that the role of the German commander he'd promised Pierre ended up being cast at the last moment and quite by chance.

The initiative for it can be traced back to Raymond Blondy, the director of production. A rumor running through the world of French film about the impression produced by a certain actor on the set of Raymond Bernard's *Marthe Richard au service de la France* reached Blondy. It wasn't so much the actor's interpretation of the role of Baron Erich von Ludow* as it was his day-to-day behavior that had caused a stir in the profession. He was a figure that stood out everywhere because of the quantity of whiskey he ingested as well as his whims and the demands he made. For example, each morning he required a fresh pair of gloves be delivered to him.

One evening in January 1937 at a party, Raymond Blondy, warmed from imbibing several cocktails, met the man. There was no doubt about it: this Erich von Stroheim would definitely fill the bill. Blondy signed him on the spot with a vaguely worded note and gave him an appointment for the next day at the offices of production on rue Saint-Denis, where he arranged for a first check to be made out to Stroheim. In the morning, Blondy telephoned Jacques Becker to inform him of his action. A few moments later, Renoir learned from his assistant that he was going to direct the filmmaker whose works had so counted in the discovery of his own vocation, the very same man he had declared on several occasions to be his "god." According to Becker, Renoir's reaction at that moment was, "But what a damn fool that Blondy is! What a damn fool!"[12]

---

* The film would play theaters only during the month of April 1937.

The German commander for which Blondy had cast Stroheim was supposed to appear in just a single scene, at the officers' mess, and the role was limited to a half-dozen lines at most. Renoir's assistant suggested to the distraught director that the only course of action was to show up at the meeting arranged for Stroheim by Blondy and to impress upon the former that the director of production had made a mistake.*

When he left Hollywood for Paris in response to the offer to do *Marthe Richard*, in whose credits he would appear fifth, Stroheim had already been compelled to abandon his career as a director after 1932's *Walking Down Broadway*, a movie from which he'd been ousted after filming only a few scenes. As an actor, he hadn't appeared in any major film since *As You Desire Me* with Greta Garbo (1932). Having come to France for a single film, he'd leave it again in November 1939, after taking part in seventeen productions in less than three years. After visiting Renoir several times in Marlotte, he'd rent a white house there for a certain period of time. It was the house closest to the edge of the forest, and he would sometimes visit it with Dita Parlo.[13]

Several versions of the story purport to tell what happened in that morning meeting with Stroheim in January 1937 and exactly how it ended with Renoir changing his attitude. Jacques Becker's account, one of the few that comes firsthand, is worth repeating.

Stroheim saw an imposing figure of a man, a man whose existence—and still less, whose films—he'd known nothing about until the day before. The man was coming toward Stroheim with the obvious intention of throwing his arms around him. Heart in mouth, Renoir had just forgotten his German, a language that Stroheim hadn't spoken for the last quarter of a century, anyway; and Becker took it upon himself to translate the director's answer into English when the actor asked about the role intended for him. However, before Becker did, he asked Renoir to repeat something: did he really want to let Stroheim know that the role was a wonderful one, the role of a magnificent officer commanding a prison camp during the war? Yes. But we'll talk about all that later, Renoir added. I'm leaving for Alsace the day after tomorrow, we're close to shooting, and the top priority is making your uniforms. All that was left for Becker to do was to take Stroheim to a tailor.

Two days later, Renoir and Becker were in Colmar. Stroheim, who'd signed for a maximum of four weeks, remained in Paris. His role didn't require his immediate presence on the set because the first few days were being devoted

---

* Raymond Blondy would also serve as director of production on *L'Alibi*, also with Erich von Stroheim, and which Pierre Chenal would begin directing in June 1937.

to the scenes with the extras. He discussed his role in more detail with Carl Koch, whom Renoir had the producers hire as a historical adviser, a title that doesn't do justice to the contribution of his "German friend." Koch would write that a study of the screenplay had provoked nothing less than "dread" in him, a feeling caused by "a French portrayal of prisoners of war in Germany that was very biased." "I had no desire to collaborate on it," he added, "and I set down as a first requirement that a parity between the French and German points of view be observed."[14] Koch must have also made known his certainty that nothing but a German presence in the cast would be enough to allow the film to attain an "international" dimension, and he would claim that Stroheim's hiring had been prompted by such an observation.

On January 21, Koch wrote to his wife that he'd spent all night talking with Stroheim. On the following days, he informed her that they were working relentlessly on the screenplay, for which, he stated on the twenty-ninth, there was still a lot more to do. Carl Koch's reports during this specific period have the quality of having been written and delivered from day to day, at a time when nothing indicated that the film in question was going to become *Grand Illusion*, the major artistic achievement and immense popular success we know today. A few months later, and even to a greater extent as the years passed, each new account would reveal every author's more or less buried desire to draw from this venture the share of glory he felt was rightfully his.

The fact is that, in the days right before filming, certain points were reworked to an important extent in parts of the screenplay, especially those that concerned the character played by Stroheim. But whose idea was it to make the officer who meets Maréchal and Boëldieu at the beginning of the film after their plane is shot down and the commander of the fortress the same character? Did the idea arise from the work sessions between Stroheim and Carl Koch? Or from those sessions among Renoir, Becker, Koch, and (occasionally) Spaak, because they were determined to accommodate their script to this new phenomenon represented by the arrival of Stroheim? Or was it the result of conversations between Renoir and Stroheim?

On September 14, 1942, Stroheim would write to Renoir in French, telling him he hoped he would discover at RKO, with whom he had just signed, "the climate and atmosphere of collaboration (I don't like that word) . . . of cooperation needed to achieve a masterpiece in the genre of *Grand Illusion*." He then added, "If you will remember, when you wanted me for *Grand Illusion* back then, the script had two little bits of a role, which a combination of your brain and mine stimulated by a few whiskeys managed to weld into a single and unique role that was, by far, the best of my career in France."[15] Stroheim did not intend his letter for publication, so the strong possibility exists that the decision to merge the two characters into one was probably made by Renoir and Stroheim together. But exactly when? Doubtlessly before the director left for Alsace, the day after that first encounter.

Koch's letters to his wife attest that the actor arrived in Colmar on the evening of February 2. Probably in the company of someone pleasant, as Renoir would remember nearly nine years later. "Stroheim was constantly with his secretary, nurse, and more—a French woman who spent all her time during filming drumming lines into him, not only at the studio but at home as well."[16]

Stroheim himself recounted in detail his search for an orthopedist who could make him the leather-and-steel surgical collar intended for Rauffenstein, whose wounds to the vertebral column justified his switch from aviator to commander of a prison camp. Stroheim claimed to have arrived in Alsace late in the afternoon on a Saturday and after "a long search" in Colmar finally to have come upon the workshop of a German Jew who must not have respected the Sabbath, and whom he required on the spot to make him the device because he had to film that Sunday.[17] But February 2, 1937, the day Stroheim did arrive, was actually a Tuesday, and Stroheim shot his first scene a week later, which gave him seven days to have unearthed a craftsman and order what he wanted.

It is possible that following this, as he tells it, he came to the set to show Renoir how he looked in dress uniform and full regalia. From there, the story comes for the most part from Françoise Giroud, who worked as the script girl under her real name, Gourdji. According to Françoise, Stroheim appeared each morning on the set dressed from tip to toe to be told that the schedule didn't require him on that day.[18] Having been a director and actor after a period as an assistant director, Stroheim had wide experience with the way shoots were organized, and better than anyone he knew what a call sheet was. It's therefore extremely doubtful that he behaved in such a way on *Grand Illusion*.

Every evening, Renoir, Becker, Koch, and sometimes Spaak, who would be summoned when it was urgent, shut themselves up to make adjustments to the screenplay, while Françoise Giroud filled the function of secretary. Unlike what could be pleasant to imagine, their work had to do with scenes to be shot in Paris, in a studio, not the exteriors they were filming during the day. The screenplay for *Grand Illusion* was obviously not written "from day to day" as has been claimed, a myth that research carried out by Olivier Curchod[19] has put to rest.

In his presentation of the first version of the screenplay—a version that was undated but definitely finished before the end of December 1935—François Truffaut thought he could cast doubt on Charles Spaak's participation in the working out of this "provisional treatment,"[20] which Spaak, moreover, had claimed to have written entirely by himself after his conversations with Renoir. And yet, two other versions of the screenplay have survived, both dating to a time before Stroheim was cast. Like the "provisional treatment," they are not signed, and only the second is dated November–December 1936. Dated, it needs to be said, in Spaak's handwriting. And whereas that one is typed, the one before is handwritten, and also in Spaak's handwriting.[21]

A study of the document dated November–December, the only one of the three that appears to be a script breakdown, reveals its differences from the finished film. Not counting several scenes totally abandoned during shooting (mostly an air battle and a German girl provoking the prisoners) and further character development of Rosenthal, the changes have mostly to do with Rauffenstein. The decisive nature of these changes is unambiguous. It's especially clear that the melding of the two roles of the German officer gave the film a central structure that was definitely lacking. Stroheim's contribution to his own character was significant, and as a result, it was almost logical that Rauffenstein would take on an importance that Renoir and Spaak hadn't envisioned.

According to Renoir, he asked Jean Gabin to wear the jacket Renoir himself had saved from the war, but Stroheim chose his own costumes, which were an all-consuming passion for him. He didn't worry about historical veracity, which left him unimpressed; and despite what he claimed, he'd never been an officer in the imperial army and had left Europe in 1909. All of that suited Renoir just fine.

Eugène Lourié has told of Stroheim's handing him a list in Colmar of the props he wanted to see in the officer's room, which would be reconstructed in a Parisian studio. Three typed pages long, it mentioned, among other things, six pairs of white gloves, a collection of riding crops, five photographs of blond Wagnerian singers in silver frames, and a copy of Casanova's memoirs. All of these can be spotted in the film. Lourié, on the other hand, was responsible for the decision to place an immense crucifix in the room, justified by the location of Rauffenstein's quarters in the fortress's chapel. Because crucifixes were a recurrent motif in scenery for Stroheim's films, the art director was probably trying to please the actor. Lourié also has taken credit for the geranium, "to offer a little color,"[22] as he remarked. In a black-and-white film he couldn't possibly have expected a very striking effect. And yet, the geranium is another element that often appears in Stroheim's films.

Was the idea for showing Rauffenstein cutting the geranium off the stem after Boëldieu's death, and thereby depriving himself of what was presented as the sole trace of life in a colorless world, Lourié's idea, as he has claimed, or Stroheim's, or Renoir's? Not Spaak's, in any case. After the war, and with good reason, he deplored the banal sentimentality* of this moment in the film, the result of the "flirtation between the German officer and the French officer," which turned out to be "the most applauded moment in this new version . . . a really bad scene, it certainly needs to be said, but it's in the nature of a flirt to affect such precious gestures."[23]

It is also a possibility that the screenwriter had to some extent felt excluded from his duties by Stroheim's arrival and the changes it occasioned, forcing him to compare their worth to his contributions to the project when it was assigned to him by Renoir in 1935. The balance of power among the characters had, in fact, been altered. The relationship between the two aristocrats Boëldieu and Rauffenstein was developing to the detriment of the one between the proletarian and aristocrat Maréchal and Boëldieu—a switch that contributed to modifying the very tone of the film. Still evident were Spaak's skills, especially his always-visible talent for depicting human groups in their diversity and unity at the same time, and such an element needed to be considered essential to the success of the film.

Naturally inclined to compromise, hating conflict, enriched by the contributions of all members of a group, the "big fat bird looking hit-or-miss for nibbles in the orchard"[24] found himself face to face with the film world figure he had for years admired above all others, except for Chaplin. Then how could he ever oppose Stroheim's desires? Why would he want to? Stroheim would first have to push the envelope a bit too far—for example, by suggesting there be prostitutes in the mess hall scene, an idea that made Renoir, whose back was against the wall, find the nerve to confront his idol. And because the idol had ended up face to face with a director, one whose primary trait was an interest in consensus (connected though it may have been to a hidden obstinacy), and because that director also respected and admired his idol, Renoir proposed that Stroheim become the director for the span of the film.

Or rather, Renoir did nothing to prevent such an illusion from being encouraged. Stroheim's scenes in *Grand Illusion* were a precipitate of Renoir methodology. Every element of the decor and costume, every word, every intonation— each of Rauffenstein's gestures obviously arises from the actor's choices and is his responsibility—but without the whole of it ever ceasing to appear as pure Renoir style. And this is all the more obvious because Renoir's style is directly opposed to Stroheim's. Whereas Stroheim would have filmed every detail of the decor and every expression in close-up and cut up the scene into a great number of shots, Renoir filmed all of it within the context of continuous action, fashioning

* The cut geranium in *Grand Illusion* bears a likeness to the shot of the drainpipe in *La Bête humaine* as it gushes water into a pail while Séverine and Lantier make love for the first time in the cabin.

scenes made of shots whose length regularly exceeds one minute.

Whether certain theorists of the Renoir approach like it or not, *Grand Illusion* is, in this regard, precise and tangible evidence of Renoir's method, provided there ever was a method in what he did. Equally redolent of Renoir's methodology is an unconventional adaptive ability for circumventing obstacles and following unforeseen paths that reveal possibilities that were not in the slightest suggested in earlier versions of the screenplay. An example is the scene in which Stroheim wanted prostitutes to be present. It had originally been envisioned as located in an abandoned French chateau. After production restrictions prevented shooting in a chateau, the scene in the German mess hall was shifted to the same prefabricated building that served as the setting for a scene showing the French canteen directly preceding it. The parallel between the two situations, two armies, two countries at war, was thereby implied without being emphasized, or even claimed.

Such observations, on the other hand, depend upon small discrepancies noticed by several critics—headed by André Bazin and François Truffaut—who relied upon them to feed Renoir's reputation as a fanatical improviser. It was an image they manufactured in the fifties with the active and benevolent cooperation of Renoir himself. Such revisionism by the party most interested in it—Renoir—found expression in Renoir's account of the scene in which Maréchal first leaves Rosenthal behind, when a sprained ankle keeps the latter from walking, and then returns after derisively warbling the song "Il était un petit navire."* Renoir:

> I was very proud of the scene I'd written. Unfortunately, when we began rehearsing, the actors turned out to be incapable of saying their lines. The physical ordeal to which I'd submitted them was paralyzing them. I had to give up on the scene I'd so counted on. To think about the situation, we took refuge in a house in the middle of nowhere. After a while, one of us, I don't remember who anymore, suggested we replace my dialogue with the song "Le Petit Navire" and change the tone in which it was sung. That song had furnished the sound for an earlier scene and was symbolic of escape.[†25]

---

* *Translator's note:* Literally, "There Was a Little Ship." The strangely morbid nature of this well-known French children's song about cannibalism bears explanation if the import of Renoir's use of it is to be understood. It is a story of shipwrecked sailors who decide to cook and eat the youngest, going into some detail about aspects of preparation, such as the sauce to use with the "dish." In the end the young sailor saves himself by appealing to the Virgin Mary.

† Eight years before his memoirs were published, Renoir had already delivered an identical account, practically every word of it (though in English), in an interview he gave to the BBC in 1966.

A lot of people have wanted to claim the identity of this "one of us" to which Renoir referred. Françoise Giroud[26] and Dalio have both taken credit for it, and the director himself claimed on the day after Gabin died, "He's the one who had the fabulous idea of singing 'Il était un petit navire.'"[27] It's doubtful that the real "savior" of that now-legendary scene will ever be established. On the other hand, it's at least certain that whomever it was had read the script, in which the song is written in full, and that is something that Olivier Curchod has demonstrated.[28] The scene itself excludes any possibility of a last-minute stroke of inspiration: when Rosenthal breaks into "Le Petit Navire," he purposely pronounces the words to it derisively, and when Maréchal begins to sing, he picks up the text at the exact verse that corresponds closely to their current situation: the provisions are running out, and former friends start thinking of devouring one among them. This is obviously a screenwriter's idea. Whether it was Renoir or Spaak, that person would have had to possess a perfect knowledge of the film in its entirety and all of its motifs, to the most minute of their buried implications.

Inspired filmmaker that he was, Renoir was also a matchless improviser, but he certainly did not eschew a scenario, even if he did enjoy at times appearing on the set with his hands in his pockets "without a screenplay, no shooting script."[29] The fact that he had no need to refer ceaselessly to the shooting script merely demonstrates that he possessed a perfect knowledge of it and knew exactly what he was going for, even when he tried to produce the opposite impression, the expression of a kind of suaveness that was related to the wish for self-assertion. Renoir the orchestra conductor recognized the merits of all others and used them gradually to reduce the contribution of the first in line chronologically—the original author of the score. As we have seen, this was someone whose existence Renoir might even have taken pains not to remember, resulting in such language as "the scene I wrote," "my scene," or "my dialogue." By supplying proof that the pride "his" scene would have inspired had been displaced, by hammering in the idea that the reason the actors couldn't perform the scene was also because of "the physical ordeal" he'd imposed upon them, and then by bragging about the merit of an anonymous author (who never existed), Renoir concealed his ego and displayed the appropriate humility, a perfect pedestal for the statue of him the hurried reader would make haste to erect.

Such a way of acting and behaving possessed the merit (and gave Renoir the valuable advantage) of allowing each actor and collaborator to feel like a full participant, a feeling they all expressed. Consequently, Marcel Dalio said, "It was one of Renoir's talents to take into consideration—or pretend to, maybe—what actors said. Any other director would have brushed me off with, 'Would you mind letting me do my job!' Not him. He was so good at putting actors at ease, especially the ones like me who had stage fright, that even from the back, you could be magnificent!"[30]

And, accordingly, Dalio has claimed to be the one who suggested that Maréchal and Rosenthal's rapport turn sour for a moment during the "Le Petit Navire" scene—the same thing that Françoise Giroud claims to have thought of—and that his character's Jewishness be what comes into question. The transformation of Dolette the engineer into Rosenthal the fashion designer was actually influenced by the personality of the actor, hired by Raymond Blondy, he claimed. Blondy had spoken to him at first about the possibility of "playing a Jewish character in the first part of the film," before telling him a little later, "Le Vigan was supposed to play a peasant [sic] who escapes with Gabin, but he didn't think the role was good enough. So we're thinking that Gabin can escape with the pint-sized Jewish guy"—evidence that the role of the "little Jew" had become larger when Le Vigan was no longer part of the film.

Stroheim shot his final exterior scene on February 16, which was after only one week of work. Immediately after, he left for Paris. The remainder of the team stayed in Alsace for ten or so more days in order to film the scenes in the countryside. These included Maréchal and Rosenthal in the fields and on the roads as well as in the surroundings of the German farm, whose interiors would be filmed in Paris. Dita Parlo was cast to play the peasant. At twenty-eight, the German actress was a star in her own country but had already experienced failure in Hollywood. In France, to which she had moved permanently in 1934, her most important work had been with Duvivier (*Au Bonheur des Dames,* 1930) and Jean Vigo (*L'Atalante,* 1934) as the female lead in both films.* In a letter to his brother on March 23, 1945, Claude Renoir would write, "Pinkovitch is in the South of France. Arrested by the Germans, but protected by Dita Parlo."[31] During the Occupation, the actress was for several months the mistress of Henri Lafont, one of the two chiefs—with Pierre Bonny—of the French Gestapo.

Beginning March 1, the Tobis studios, at first, and then those of Éclair, also located in Épinay, opened their doors to the crew and actors so they could make use of the scenery built while they had been filming in Alsace. Contrary to his reputation, Renoir valued working in a studio, and he went back to his resolution to film all interiors for *Grand Illusion* using this method, as Eugène Lourié has confirmed. Lourié had made sure tiling was installed in the Tobis studios for the fortress scenes so that Renoir's reliable sound engineer, Joseph de Bretagne, would be able to record footsteps "live," something the usual soundproof surface

* In *Au Bonheur des Dames*, Dita Parlo plays Denise Baudu, whose cousin Geneviève is played by Nadia Sibirskaïa (*The Crime of Monsieur Lange, La vie est à nous*).

would have made impossible. It had also been Lourié's idea to make the nativity scene out of materials that were likely to be found on a farm, using a turnip for Jesus and a leek decorated with a root to serve as the beard for Joseph. For the last scene, Maréchal and Rosenthal's crossing of the Swiss border, a snowy decor was produced using bath salts and the trunk of a fir tree placed in the foreground of the close-ups of Gabin and Dalio. The exteriors that couldn't be filmed in Alsace would be accomplished after the shoot in the studio. They'd do them near Chamonix, without Dalio or Gabin; the latter had been involved in another film since April.* Finally, Lourié managed to adjust the scenery of the barracks in the first prison camp in a way that allowed Renoir to reveal in one shot the room, the actors, and—through the windows—the courtyard in the background.

It was in the group scenes that the director's "style" proved most creative. Lourié has left us a satisfying description of it: after an initial run-through in telephone-book fashion with actors and director seated around a table, the dialogue achieved an almost natural, friendly conversational tone, personalities opened up, the relationships among characters became apparent, and the scene took shape. The lines were modified as necessary, and the various movements of actors worked harmoniously. They dictated where to place the camera, the choice of lenses, and camera movements.

Julien Carette was one of those performers who, by nature, contributed more than others did. When he tackled his character Cartier, a wisecracking actor in whom he injected his joie de vivre, energy, and puns, he hadn't yet turned forty and had already made around thirty sound films, which came to an average of five a year. When Yvonne Printemps joined the team at dinners, he let loose his verve without worrying about going beyond the limits of decorum, drawing reprimands from Renoir, who, yet, was far from a stickler about it. On the other hand, Pierre Fresnay, the singer-actress's suffering boyfriend at the time, would shoot him the same black looks Boëldieu sometimes throws at Cartier in the film.[32] Carette obviously remembered what Fresnay was hoping people would forget: the fact that Yvonne Printemps had gotten her start at fourteen in the operetta *Nue Cocotte*.† And although Carette did pinch the breasts of the queen of operetta as he imitated the sound of a horn, he was just being mischievous, perhaps, by recalling that she'd had her first success in the revue *Ah! Les beaux nichons!*‡ (1911), starring Maurice Chevalier.

---

* *Le Messager* (*The Messenger*), based on the play by Henry Bernstein, adapted by Marcel Achard, and directed by Raymond Rouleau.

† *Translator's note: Literally, Naked Tart.*

‡ *Translator's note: Literally, Oh! Those Beautiful Boobs!*

Fresnay would confirm that Renoir wanted him to push Boëldieu in the direction of caricature, drawing that impression, on the one hand, from the fact that Renoir had initially chosen Jouvet for the role, and on the other, from the directions he received on the set: "Renoir encouraged me to go that way; he would insist that I take all possible advantage of the white gloves, monocle, and formal language he used with mother and wife. Well, I did my best. . . . As a favor, but it was no fun for me to do because I wanted to defend Boëldieu, but it's clear that the director's intention was to push these qualities to their excessive limit."[33]

Like the characters they play, actors come from a variety of worlds. They all start out with their own experience and habits resulting from the stage, the music hall, the roles of classical repertory, or the idiotic comedies in which they happened to have played. They also have their own particular status as actors, whether they are stars, supporting players, or walk-ons. Film is sustained by this variety, by the relationships that are hatched on the set or at the canteen, all of which the audience watches evolve and become complicated and transformed. The atmosphere Renoir created naturally around him allowed the situations established by the screenplay to blossom and people to open up into all their complexity, producing a lucid experience on-screen without losing any of its inherent features. The characters are frequently considered in tandem, the dialogue's essential configuration; but also, the group remains as often as possible, withdrawing as soon as, for example, two characters such as Maréchal and Dalio escape or Boëldieu and Rauffenstein have a conversation.

Without being distanced from the central device set up by the screenplay, during the filming Maréchal lost his status as Boëldieu's conversational partner, and Gabin did not fail to notice it, grumbling that "for Renoir it's all about the Kraut."[34] This shift and some others led to a palpable modification of the film's meaning. "As for the Marxist conception and opposition between the classes, it was known that Renoir and Spaak's original mission was to increase Maréchal's standing to the detriment of the aristocrat, in order to illustrate Renoir's pet idea of a world divided 'horizontally,' and not 'vertically,' into classes. . . . This is the element of the film that evolved the most from genesis to completion, to the extent to which the result surprised Renoir himself—and most likely also made him a little worried about the reactions the film would entail."[35] On that account, *Grand Illusion* was a chance to plunge into the heart of Jean Renoir's nature. Just as his films are changed—and often for the better—by the friction against realities that come into play while filming, so are his ideas altered when his convictions come into contact with others'—and sometimes for the worse.

JEAN RENOIR

Gabin's and Spaak's reactions in 1937, after a showing of the film was organized on their behalf, helped to arouse Renoir's fears about the film's reception. What the actor saw on-screen was a confirmation of his feeling during filming, that "for Renoir it's all about the Kraut"; and he also saw how impressive Pierre Fresnay was. Essentially, he felt he had been ousted from a film in which his character was nevertheless the most present, even if in a way that was less central than had originally been planned. But Gabin was also aware that without him Renoir probably wouldn't have been able to make *Grand Illusion*. As for the screenwriter, he saw his intentions as having disappeared, and he even began to consider having his name pulled from the credits. On June 9, Renoir wrote to Spaak:

> You have a perfect understanding of that invincible force that during a film compels me to turn everything upside down. Keep in mind that I don't accomplish such reshufflings on my own. I'm incapable of working without collaborators. Unfortunately, that's how things are done, so that even when you think you can do it differently—as was the case for this film—your collaboration with the author of the screenplay ceases at the first turn of the crank. And I'm sure that doesn't have to happen. You need to look at things in another way and consider that there are two directors: one who is more preoccupied with literary tasks, and the other with technical issues. But neither functions without the other.[36]

Neither Spaak nor Gabin was at the premiere of the film on June 8, 1937, at the Marivaux theater. The theater had just been reacquired by Léon Siritzky, and the showing of *Grand Illusion*, whose release had been announced for weeks with large display ads, was the pretext for a celebration of the event, which just happened to favorably coincide with the opening of the World's Fair in Paris. Whereas Françoise Giroud would mention "general consternation" when speaking of that gala night—"tout Paris" promising one of the gloomiest commercial fates for this war film without war—Renoir would call the "extremely fashionable" audience "cold" and warmed up only by "the effects . . . you add to a film blushingly and believe are reserved for illiterate audiences."[37] The morning screening, organized for the press, had been more encouraging.

Jo Siritzky was more interested in preserving the memory of lines in front of the theater of people who had been waiting to get in since the day before: "That's my Proustian madeleine. We'd decided to show the film only at the Marivaux, despite the fact that every theater wanted it. The publicity campaign had brought theater owners to a fever pitch. The evening of the premiere, Jean was there with his wife [Marguerite], and we hadn't slept all night. Neither before or after have I ever seen such enthusiastic audiences. The place was sold out every night for five or six months."[38]

Two hundred thousand spectators, a sizable figure at the time, saw *Grand Illusion* at the Marivaux. The film was distributed to fifty-two cities outside Paris beginning on the symbolic date of November 11, Armistice Day. A few weeks later, *Pour vous* readers' choices for the best French film of the year resulted in the following: 5,603 votes in favor of *Grand Illusion*—3,600 more votes than for the film that took second place.

Enthusiasm was widespread, in fact, and it included the press. Everyone found something gratifying about the film, whether they were on the Left or the Right, regardless of how extreme their position was. It was a stunning phenomenon, coming as it did at a time when political factions dictated aesthetic choices, enough to induce certain newspaper columnists to express their astonishment. For example, Lucien Rebatet, writing under the name François Vinneuil, was carried away with the "simple, virile tone" of a film he'd gone to see "armed to the teeth, ready to start shooting," because he was certain of being confronted with "the teary sentimentality of the overblown style of Judeo-Parisian film." Rebatet went along with many others who, independently, questioned the meaning of a title that appeared to be "an enigma."

> What is this grand illusion? Country? But this film is extremely patri-
> otic in its way. The fraternity of human beings? Theoretically, we'd agree
> completely with M. Jean Renoir. But on a real and individual level, he
> shows us the opposite, the splendid solidarity of beings as different as
> can be in blood, language, rank, all reunited by the same misfortune.
> That is something I don't see as "illusory," thanks be to God! Would the
> illusion still be seeing the war of 1914–1918 as having to be the last? If
> M. Renoir is thinking bitterly that this was incredibly naïve to think, we
> couldn't agree more.[39]

Renoir himself never seemed especially interested in dispelling the mystery, at best providing a semblance of an explanation that grew hazier as the years went by. A possible answer may lie in the following statement made while the film was being directed: "What is the grand illusion? War! With its hopes never fulfilled and its promises never kept."[40] It certainly may have been inspired by a theory the Englishman Norman Angell developed in his 1909 book, revised and expanded by the author in 1933, the year he won the Nobel Prize. The French title of that work, a best seller in its field at the time? *La Grande Illusion.**

It's amusing as well to recall that a young author wrote a poem in 1918 that was violently opposed to war and that was entitled, word for word, "La

* *Translator's note:* The original English title of Angell's book was *The Great Illusion*.

Grande Illusion."[41] His name was René Chomette, and he later called himself René Clair. Moreover, three days after Renoir had registered the screenplay with the Société des auteurs de films, he received a letter from the secretary of the society acknowledging reception of the manuscript and stating, "But we can't keep the title *La Grande Illusion,* because it's already the title of a three-act play by Messrs. Elie Sachs and G. Lambeau,"[42] a play that had been presented on February 26, 1927, at the Théâtre du Vieux-Colombier. Renoir had answered the letter on December 13. He and Charles Spaak had changed their title to "Relation des tentatives d'évasion d'un prisonnier français en Allemagne pendant la guerre 1914–18."*[43]

Most of the films Renoir made in the thirties more or less obviously trace the currents of their times. *Grand Illusion* is no exception, sometimes presenting them as contradictory, and following them with a precision in which can be read some of the reasons for its enormous popular success. In 1937 in France, the fighters who'd experienced the First World War actually felt close to the Germans of that time, whom they'd begun to see less as enemies than as comrades-in-arms, a sensibility that attracted the confirmed Germanophile in Renoir. "Defeat had corrupted Germany," he wrote long after, "but not more than so-called victory had done to France. I now realize that, victory or not, nations don't escape the decline engendered by war. Wars destroy in a few months what a slowly assimilated culture took centuries to build."[44]

In their own way, all of the Germans in *Grand Illusion* are "decent people." He stated in 1946 that in his film, "the French are good Frenchmen and the Germans good Germans. Germans before the war of '39. . . ." And so, in fact, they are. "I strove to show that in France Germans aren't hated,"[45] he explained in 1938. On the other hand, the French aren't wild about the English, or at least don't trust them. And such prejudice is also implied in the film, where the only behavior that flatters the British is their launching spontaneously into "La Marseillaise." However, when it comes to passing information to the British prisoners about a tunnel that has been cut into the floor of the hut they'll be kept in, instinctive distrust is enough to make Boëldieu "forget" that he speaks English fluently. In that respect, *Grand Illusion* is not an exception to the French productions of the period; and even in a film like *Double crime sur la ligne Maginot* (*Double Crime in the Maginot Line*), released in 1937 and about a geographical location indicating an enemy to be feared, all efforts were made to pass over the German threat in silence—to pass over the German *presence* in point of fact. As Vincent Lowy has written, "During all the years leading to

* *Translator's note:* Literally, "Account of the Escape Attempts of a French Prisoner in Germany during the War of 1914–18."

the German occupation, it was fear of war that motivated French people and their governments: for a lot of them, such a feeling involved a pure and simple acceptance of National Socialism, including its racial and cultural atrocities."[46] The Munich Agreement would soon result from such a climate. Renoir would oppose it publicly with the same fierceness and courage that he had used for several years to fight National Socialism.

Renoir's internationalist desires did not eliminate the chauvinist dimension of *Grand Illusion*. The French character in the film is depicted as true to his reputation as a seducer. He is also sardonic and resourceful, in addition to being a patriot, when the fancy strikes him. Everything different about these characters counts for nothing in comparison to what they have in common and what makes them those excellent Frenchmen about whom Maurice Chevalier would sing in another two years.*

In 1937, the France of the common people was lulled by the promise of change, the effects of which they had glimpsed but which was still in the future. Léon Blum heard Montéhus, the anarchist who'd converted to socialism, coming to his rescue and, now past sixty-five, singing "Vas-y Léon" at the top of his lungs. Although the Popular Front may not yet have become the other Grand Illusion, whatever its fate was to be, History had begun to be turned upside down. Unequivocally involved with the Left, and because of its working for a radical change in society toward a higher level of justice, Renoir must have understood with a certain melancholy that the ruling classes of the past were going to have to step aside for the bourgeoisie. Nor was he devoid of nostalgia for the world before World War I, which he had come from and which was becoming more distant. Such nostalgia is echoed in the film. It even reaches a distressing cadence when Boëldieu and Rauffenstein, who are in reality social and historical stand-ins for Renoir, acknowledge that their time is ending and that they are on the road to extinction. Soon, even workers will have the right to die of cancer. The young man who proudly chose the cavalry in 1913 had little to do with Maréchal. Boëldieu resembled him better. *Grand Illusion* is located at the junction of its author's quest for identity at the basis of his personality and the identity crisis sweeping through his country.

The film also comments on another aspect of France in the thirties. In light of the following decades, after the revelation of the Holocaust and the discovery of the role the Vichy regime played in the perpetration of genocide,

* *Translator's note:* A reference to "Ça fait d'excellènts français" ("That Makes Some Excellent Frenchmen"), a song performed by Maurice Chevalier in 1939, with music by Georges van Parys and lyrics by Jean Boyer. Its purpose was to encourage the morale of French soldiers recruited from every walk of life and from opposing political orientations so that all would fight together on behalf of the republic.

the image of Jews portrayed in certain French films seems appalling. However, in approximately the same proportions, antiracist counterattacks were being leveled against such bigoted excesses. "In the thirties, jokes about Jews were told just as jokes about Belgians would be in 1980. Those who laughed at them and were not Jewish weren't necessarily racist in the style of Drumont.* When André Hugon created the series *Lévy et Cie* [*The Levy Department Stores*], it was no example of militant anti-Semitism."[47] The dialogue for *The Levy Department Stores* (1930), the first in the series, was written by Roger Ferdinand, who also went on to *Chotard et Cie*. The fourth in the *Lévy* series, *Les Mariages de Mlle Lévy*, was released in Paris in October 1936.

If these weren't anti-Semitic, then what about an editorial written by Gaston Thierry entitled "Qu'est-ce qu'un film français?":† "We've learned that in a Parisian studio a film is currently being shot whose title and subject matter are 'very French.' . . . And yet, the producer of this film is M. Apfelbaum; the director, M. Hexenstrasse; the first assistant director, M. Rosen; the scenery designer, M. Sussfrucht; the cameraman, M. Atchoum; the director, M. Doppelkuh; the screenplay writer, M. Weisskopf; the composer, M. Armermann; the sound engineer, M. Etelross; the costume designer, M. Arlekin; and the pianist, M. Epuizut."[48] Then, was French film controlled by Jews? Oh, no, by foreigners. Who all happened to be Jewish. No need to write the word, to say it out loud, because everyone understood. Three years later, Renoir as well would let himself be sucked into the same abyss. But for the time being, he remained irreproachable.

It is of note that beginning in the mid-thirties, Jewish characters rarely appeared in French films, in keeping with the prevailing attitude. Not counting the expressions of militant anti-Semitism, it came from the prevailing discourse, the assertion of an escalating xenophobia that avoided referring directly to Jewishness. In this context, *Les Mariages de Mlle Lévy* can be seen as the expression of a bygone period, and the *Lévy* series did indeed come to an end with this film. The rare exceptions from then on stand out: Pagnol's *Le Schpountz* (*Heartbeat*), released in April 1938, in which Léon Bélières (who'd been Moses in the *Lévy* films) as the producer Meyerboom comes off as an inexcusably anti-Semitic caricature; and Marcel Dalio's Rosenthal in *Grand Illusion* and his marquis in *The Rules of the Game*.

When Jean and Alain Renoir took Pinkovitch to spend a few days with them in Essoyes, Renoir insisted Alain be careful not to say around "Pink" that

<hr/>

* *Translator's note:* Édouard Drumont (1844–1917): A French journalist and essayist who founded the Anti-Semitic League of France in 1889, published a newspaper attacking the Jewish presence in France, and vigorously supported the campaign against Dreyfus.

† *Translator's note:* Literally, "What Is a French Film?"

the latter was Jewish.[49] But in this particular situation, was he intending to protect his friend "Pink" from the threat of unpleasant looks, or did he want to guarantee that he himself would not be faced with accusations of compromise? Maybe both. His personality and his past placed Renoir at the juncture of two specific currents that sustained antiracism in the thirties: "For the Right and former soldiers, the exaltation of 'the brotherhood of the trenches' that united soldiers from every background and faith during the First World War; and for the Left and the workers' movement, the denouncement of racism as a criminal diversion meant to alienate the proletariat from class struggle and the fight for revolution."[50] The fact that this "brotherhood of the trenches" probably materialized well after the end of hostilities, during which the two opposed camps had hated their enemy in a similar way,[51] could only have intensified this essentially fantasized sentiment of universal fraternity. *Grand Illusion* links its voice naturally to an antiracist movement that had begun in the early thirties to "launch its first appeals, engage in its first jousts, and muster its first partisans."[52] Renoir, who was a former soldier, a Germanophile, and "on the Left," had a spontaneous rapport with the movement.

One of Renoir and Spaak's novel creations for *Grand Illusion*, if you compare it to the various sources then available on the subject, was Rosenthal, identified in early versions of the screenplay as "the Jew."* In the film, he does display the principles characteristic of these "foreigners" who were being attacked at the time by a fringe of French society. Although he is a clothing designer, a profession considered effeminate—at least—in France at that time, his family is in banking and has come to France recently. The packages he receives, which he generously shares with his comrades, confirm his privileged situation, the result of a fortune acquired and accumulated in their chosen country in just a few years. Consequently, the film relies upon a set of clichés to create an archetype of a character who when first seen is wearing clothing with a Middle Eastern connotation, "betraying" his origins and displaying how he stands out from the group.

Rosenthal's humane qualities are revealed through the course of the plot and by the dialogue. At a later point in the film, the racial slur that pops out of Maréchal's mouth ("I've never been able to stomach Jews!") sparks a feeling of shame in him, and, with the help of the song "Le Petit Navire," makes him come back to the partner in escape he intended to leave by the side of the road. In this way the audience could share Maréchal's (Gabin's) bad conscience, given the

* *Translator's note:* It should be kept in mind that "the Jew" (*le juif*) potentially sounds harsher and less innocent to Anglophone (specifically, American Anglophone) ears than it might have sounded in French. It's meaning is closer to "the Jewish man." To understand this, consider that, in the United States, "He's Jewish" generally has a milder connotation than "He's a Jew." The use of the French term in this case is closer to "Jewish."

occasion to think that their opinion of Jews risked resembling that character's. There's no reason to doubt the fact that Dalio—as he has claimed—did in some way participate in defining the character of Rosenthal, and at the very least, his contribution completed and perfected a creation that was outstandingly deft. A deftness, among other features, with which everyone in 1937 could identify. One person, however, wasn't taken in by it.

In December 1937, Louis-Ferdinand Céline's *Bagatelles pour un massacre* (*Trifles for a Massacre*) was released. In it, he vilified two facets of French decadence, alcohol and film, "from Jewish Hollywood to Moscow the Yid." The pamphlet sold well in bookstores, unlike *Death on the Installment Plan,* whose advance excerpts *L'Humanité* had published. Just as he did for his other projects of the time, Céline attributed the book's failure to the influence of Jews on the press. His attack against *Grand Illusion,* to which he devoted an entire chapter, was unbelievably vicious:

> Usually pro-Jewish films (and all of them are) maneuver, tamper, and monkey with public opinion by means of innuendoes, suggestions, comparisons, gibberish, and barely present the Jew as he is, as downright Jewish, in his role as a warlike "sozial" activist. *Grand Illusion* has given things a push forward . . . reached a turning point. It has brought the Jew out into the open, pulled off his disguise, and placed him in his "sozial" foreground as a Jew, clearly a Jew. *Grand Illusion* is an admirable finish to the exposure of the Jew, the great Yiddicade* of 1937. The advent of the little Jew in the role of official messiah. A perfect millionaire, our little Rosenthal. . . . But so perfectly "of the people." . . . Ah! But "of the people" so much more than being a millionaire! He is rich! Rolling in it . . . take a good look at this little Yid. At the beginning, this little nabob had everything against him when it came to playing redeemer: his profile, his prattle, his puss. . . . A total "stinker" . . . a perfect high-density product of the atrocious class. . . . Everything contemptible that makes the people want to hiss and hang him on the spot. A total parasite, a shifty SuperJew, this is Stavisky's child and a cousin of Barmat.† He

* *Translator's note:* Céline invents the word *Youstricade* from *youtre,* a pejorative term for "Jew," and *-cade,* a suffix usually referring to a public procession, as in "cavalcade."

† *Translator's note:* References to two financial scandals of the period: the Stavisky Affair in France, involving financier and embezzler Serge Alexandre Stavisky, and the Barmat Scandal of 1924–1925 in the Weimar Republic, during which the two Barmat brothers, who were closely aligned with the Social Democratic Party, were accused of food profiteering, bribery, and other crimes. All three individuals were Jewish and provided fodder for right-wing anti-Semitic groups.

represents the totally despicable gallows bird [around those corpses that hung from the streetlamps during the Revolution.][*53]

Renoir, whose name is not mentioned in the pamphlet, was a director and close to the Communists. His film was pro-Jewish. How could Céline not detest it? Yet other aspects of *Grand Illusion* bothered Céline more.

Louis Destouches[†] joined the Twelfth Cavalry for three years on September 28, 1912, about four months before Renoir, which was precisely their difference in ages. Like Renoir's service, Destouches's was for the cavalry, but the heavy, armored cavalry, the more prestigious branch. On October 27, 1914, near Poelkapelle in Belgium, he volunteered for a mission leading a small platoon. Two days later, his brilliant feat earned him a citation of the Order of the Regiment and the opportunity to be awarded a decoration on November 29. But, perhaps more importantly, he also received a wound in his right arm that would bother him all his life. In addition, a concussion he suffered would afflict him with vertigo and permanent ringing in his ears.

In September 1936, Céline visited Leningrad for three weeks, where he witnessed the utter destitution that Renoir hadn't noticed in Moscow, and he became convinced that in creating a privileged class, the Soviet regime had only deepened the pit of inequality, an observation that increased his abhorrence of the Communists and that was first expressed in the thirty pages of *Mea culpa*, which appeared in 1936. Years had passed since Céline and Aragon had been close and since Aragon's wife, Elsa Triolet, had taken credit for the 1934 Russian translation of *Journey to the End of the Night*, the first copy to appear outside of France. It was, however, an abbreviated version, and when the author discovered this during his trip to Russia, it would end up alienating him from the couple. The Soviets had detested *Death on the Installment Plan*, and in Germany, Nazi diatribes associated Jews and Soviets.

The intersection of the life paths of Céline and Renoir is of interest, especially because it's accompanied by another fact: both writer and director had made names for themselves as leading figures of their generation after each had broken with tradition in his art. Céline had done it more spectacularly, by flaying literary language alive; and Renoir had accomplished it by, most visibly, switching the rules in force concerning sound recording and film editing. Whereas the former had experienced immediate success, the latter had been misunderstood for a long time; but both of them were innovators.

* *Translator's note:* What Céline really says is *"gibier de réverbère,"* a variation of *"gibier de potence,"* meaning "gallows bird." But because the enemies of the Revolution were hung in the streets, Céline changes *"potence"* ("gallows") to *"réverbère"* ("streetlamp").

† *Translator's note:* Céline's real name.

There was an essential issue that they could not reconcile: Céline viewed war as an all-consuming horror, inundating the fertile ground of his thinking about the nature of human beings, whereas some of the characters in *Grand Illusion* see war as an obligation that they cannot shirk[*] and others, as a pure product of destiny[†]—twin propositions that Céline's rabid pacifism couldn't accept. In 1932, the Communists invited him to succeed Henri Barbusse, recently deceased, as their official writer. Or at least, that is what he claimed and inevitably began to believe.[54] Renoir, on the other hand, really was the official filmmaker of the Party, for his direction of *La vie est à nous*. In spring 1937, the writer suggested some projects, including a ballet, for the upcoming World's Fair, and learned they had been turned down. Renoir, on the other hand, was becoming a household name, close to the power Céline thought of himself as rejecting. And *Grand Illusion* managed to be presented for a while as if it were associated with the World's Fair. Not to mention that Renoir could boast a famous father, whereas the child of Courbevoie had grown up in a humble milieu, which his memory enjoyed recasting with the colorlessness of poverty. With all of this taken into account, Céline had every reason to detest Renoir.

Bagatelles pour un massacre appeared as Renoir was close to the top. The chapter Céline had devoted to *Grand Illusion* cast a shadow on the aura of good fortune unanimously surrounding the director for the first time in his career; and he could not tolerate such a stain, especially because it was caused by a writer whom he respected and admired. Renoir certainly had the habit of wanting to explain himself or, failing that, smoothing things over. This time he may have been motivated by the certainty that there could only have been some kind of misunderstanding between the famous author of *Journey to the End of the Night* and the undisputed master of French film.

As a result, one day at the beginning of January 1938, Renoir told his son that he wanted him along on a special kind of visit: "I want to meet a writer whom I admire but whose ideas are the opposite of mine. Actually, we don't agree on anything, and the conversation will probably be a very difficult one. You'll come with me, and keep in mind that it might go badly; but whatever happens, don't say anything."[55]

Céline lived at 98 rue Lepic, just a few steps away from Le Moulin de la Galette across the street from him, and, it seems, he went there almost every day. Since 1934, it had been a dance hall on Saturdays and Sundays, but its bar was open afternoons, despite the fact that it was usually empty. The furnishings

---

[*] "We just got to go finish this goddamn war!" says Maréchal to Rosenthal in the last scene of the film.

[†] Boëldieu to Rauffenstein: "For a man of the people, it's terrible to die at war. For you and me, it's a good solution."

screamed poverty, and the bare lamp bulbs had no shades. Céline only had to cross the street to get to it, and Jean and Alain Renoir were merely a few minutes' walk away, but Jean, handicapped by his weight, dragging his wounded leg, had a hard time climbing the hill of rue Lepic to reach the establishment that his father had immortalized sixty-one years before, in 1876, before it was moved in 1924 to the place where it now stood, the corner of Lepic and Girardon. Had the director and writer arranged to see each other? Was Renoir the one who had suggested it? It's more likely that Renoir knew he'd find Céline at the Moulin that day as well as any other.

When the Renoirs arrived, Céline was the only one in the main room. The visit would be brief. Renoir told the writer how much he admired his books; Céline griped, grumbled, insulted. Renoir became insistent and said *Journey to the End of the Night* was a brilliant book, a major work, and that *Death on the Installment Plan* was a wonderful, misunderstood novel. Céline got on his high horse, spluttered, spit venom, persisted in what may have been an act, but played it too well to give the impression that he didn't mean it. Céline wasn't listening, wasn't interested, had flown into a rage. The greatest French writer was nuts. And he climaxed his furious, hateful tirade by sinking his fangs one last time into the greatest French director—to the point of drawing blood: "I promise you that . . . the Germans are going to come and take care of all of that . . . they'll put your back to the wall . . . and that day . . . you can be sure about it . . . I'll be the one commanding the squad!" Renoir turned his back on him and walked off, taking along his son. Once they were in the street, Alain asked him how it could be possible to admire a man who hated him to such a point. The answer: "If you do without admiring someone because he wants to have you shot, you'll quickly end up without any people to admire."[56]

Why had Céline made no mention of the philo-Semitism in *Grand Illusion*—according to Alain Renoir's memory of the encounter, in any case? After all, pro-Jewishness was the touchstone of the abhorrence he expressed in *Bagatelles pour un massacre.* The fact that he didn't support the thesis about war promoted by the vision of the film was the primary cause for his rage. By some mechanism of ricochet, it foreshadowed his postwar attempts at justifying the anti-Semitism in the pamphlets he had written in wartime. This is what finally led to his "promise" about the Germans coming again, which would make no sense otherwise. Yet again, Céline had read the film better than all those after him who persisted in seeing *Grand Illusion* as a pacifist manifesto.

Renoir fashioned his reply to Céline a few days later. In the column he wrote every Tuesday for the Communist daily *Ce soir,* he revealed how Céline's book *Bagatelles pour un massacre* had irritated his friends. He claimed that he himself had stopped reading after four pages, which were enough to let him understand. "Stuff that was like rain, dismal and incessant. M. Céline reminds me very much of a lady with menstrual problems; something has given her a stomachache, so she starts shrieking and accusing her husband. The intensity of her wailing and the colorful quality of her language are amusing at first. By the second time, you yawn a little. After that, whenever it happens, you take off and let her cry all alone." The parallel lacks refinement and comes close to being misogynistic, but it's on the mark.

Next, Renoir brings up "a comrade who's very fond of me and whom I like a great deal" and who insisted on reading the entire thing in order to get an idea of Céline's criticisms of *Grand Illusion*. The report, supposedly created by Renoir after this friend finished reading, went as follows: "To more or less sum it up, Céline has merely maintained that *Grand Illusion* is a Jewish propaganda project. His proof is that in the film I dared to show a real Jewish person and make him sympathetic." The director's friends brought up wanting to give the writer a smack on the bottom in a public place, but Renoir persuaded them to give up their plan, preferring to conclude, "In service to the Jewish people there are also such people as Cézanne, Racine, and many others.* Therefore, we're in good company . . . and should be proud of ourselves. M. Céline doesn't like Racine. How terrible for Racine. Well, I don't like imbeciles, and I don't think that's terrible for M. Céline, because the only opinion that should matter to this Gaudissart† of anti-Semitism is his own."[57]

Renoir's article appeared on January 20, 1938, which was only a week after *Le Canard enchaîné* had given a favorable, as well as one of the first, review of *Bagatelles pour un massacre*. Therefore, one month at most had passed between the appearance of the book and the publication of Renoir's response, which is proof that it hadn't taken him much time to find out about the thing, encounter Céline, and compose his reply. By feistily declaring himself the adversary of a well-known figure who'd attacked him and whose stardom to him seemed greater than his own—because literature enjoyed a higher status among intellectuals than film did—he was putting himself on the same footing as his opponent and making a gesture to the mostly Communist readers of *Ce soir* that would be much more appreciated in the face of Céline's violently attacking them with *Mea culpa*. As a result, Renoir had run off with the ante.

Jean des Vallières's grievances about Renoir were of a different nature. The writer

---

* In *Bagatelles pour un massacre*, Céline also claims that Stendhal and Picasso are Jewish.

† *Translator's note*: A reference to a short work of Balzac entitled *L'Illustre Gaudissart*, about a traveling salesman who can sell anything to anyone—almost—until he meets his match in a very surprising way.

had complained that the screenplay for *Grand Illusion* plagiarized his book without citing it. *Kavalier Scharnhorst* had been published by Albin Michel in 1931. In it, des Vallières gives an account of his captivity in Germany. Exactly like Renoir, he'd begun the war in the cavalry before joining a fighter squadron. *Kavalier Scharnhorst* was the first volume of his autobiographical trilogy *Tendre Allemagne,* which was completed by *Spartakus Parade* (1932) and *L'Escadrille des anges* (1953). Less a true account than a novel, which is also how the author presented it, the book described an experience not unlike that of a number of flyers who'd been imprisoned after their plane had been shot down, had been taken from one camp to another, had tried to escape several times, and had ended up incarcerated in a fortress. The fact that the structure of *Grand Illusion* was identical to his was not in itself very unusual, but there was no doubt that Renoir or Spaak or both had read the book and been inspired by it.

Although it would have been easy for the director and screenwriter to claim that digging tunnels was a natural activity of anyone planning to escape a prison camp or that the barracks generally brought together prisoners from various backgrounds representing different levels of society, the writer would not accept rediscovering in the film a Prussian officer who extended the royal treatment to his prisoners by inviting them to his table and who permitted a French officer to get to know a German who'd worked as an engineer in France or that the prisoners of a fortress organized a disturbance. Des Vallières had even described the show given by the British prisoners in drag: "Likeable, reserved, obedient, they answer 'yes' with the timid voices of 'girls,' they remove their dresses and spend some bright mornings. Fine embroidered lingerie, silk stockings, elastic girdles, garters, and even a lace brassiere leave nothing of their true gender. Sometimes the illusion is disturbing for us because we've never seen them without their pretty blond wigs."[58] The Germans' use of the term *streng verboten* made him prick up his ears, and the actors' reprise of the song "Le Petit Navire," which had been sung in his book "along with an impromptu orchestra beaten out on old cookie tins," put him up in arms.

The writer's wrath was probably intensified by his deep-rooted anti-Communism, which would cause his career to take a surprising turn a few years later. Appointed subprefect in Arles in 1940, as a result of his father's friendship with Pétain, he abandoned the post in 1943, his hatred of the Germans having led to his joining the Resistance. Imprisoned after he hijacked thousands of gallons of gasoline from Gestapo tanks, he was released only as a result of Marshal Pétain's intervention on his behalf with the German embassy, after which he went into hiding in Auvergne using false papers, before moving to Switzerland seven months after the end of the war. A member of the Resistance becoming a refugee in Switzerland, just like a number of former collaborators?

"The problem came mostly from his having been behind the arrest of certain Communists during the war. They'd been deported to Buchenwald and had come back from it. . . ."[59] Des Vallières's son, Pierre, who was born in 1919, would become an excellent film critic under the name Michel Aubriant.

Des Vallières wasn't the only one to see a link between his book and *Grand Illusion*. In an article about the film entitled "Toute la vérité, rien que la vérité" ("All the Truth, Nothing But the Truth"), Francis Carco went so far as to write,

> Since this film was released, no matter how we were taken in, how grabbed by its masculine nature, its breadth, the vigor of its approach, we still must come abruptly to a point at which we have to tell ourselves that *Grand Illusion*'s identical success in France and in Germany may make it an excellent material endeavor, but also that, sad to say, the truth to which it claims to adhere is not all the Truth. In this regard, read the account of captivity entitled *Kavalier Scharnhorst* by M. Jean des Vallières, which has just been published.* That author has not merely told part of what really happened. He has combined the burlesque with the tragic, the pleasant with the disgusting, and this simple reason is enough to endow his book with extraordinary strength. The screen would have trouble accommodating certain scenes described by M. des Vallières. They would quickly assume appalling contours, and would falsify and reverse the meaning of the expression of it all.[60]

It is possible that Carco, the author of *Jésus la Caille*, had gotten wind of the affair when it found its way into two articles by Jean Fayard, the first appearing in *Gringoire* on June 17 and the second in *Candide* on June 25. But it's particularly interesting to think how much the differences emphasized by Carco between *Grand Illusion* and *Kavalier Scharnhorst* provided des Vallières with arguments for attacking the film but also offered the director the weapons to defend himself.

Henri Jeanson would next claim that he'd seen Charles Spaak working on the screenplay with des Vallières's book on the table and that Erich von Stroheim mentioned it also. It's possible, but this adds nothing to an already abundant file. Was *Grand Illusion* copied from *Kavalier Scharnhorst*? Renoir went to great lengths to prove the contrary by responding point by point to Albin Michel and Jean des Vallières in a letter written at the end of June 1937.

Some of his responses are not lacking in humor. For example, to the reproach from des Vallières that he stole from his book "an actor from the Odéon [theater], a civil engineer . . . [and] a typical Parisian," Renoir retorted that, for the

---

* Six years before.

actor, he and Spaak had not been able "personally to use our comrade Maurice Chevalier." Further on, about the betrayed husband that the writer thought he recognized, Renoir wrote, "I'd rather believe, for the honor of French wives, that such a very rare exception had to have been invented by both M. des Vallières and ourselves." On several occasions, Renoir mentions the personal memories of one or another of his collaborators and makes use of his own memories. Thus, when it comes to the French and German officers discovering that they had worked in the same factory, Renoir ends up telling a previously unrevealed episode from his own life: "I must say that a number of similar facts have been reported to me, and also that when I myself was a prisoner of the Germans for three weeks during the Battle of the Marne, in the hospital ward in Amiens where I was being treated, I saw two former engineers, one French and the other German, sharing memories they had in common and realizing they had worked in the same factory in France without knowing each other."[61] Renoir had indeed been treated at the hospital in Amiens, for gonorrhea, but it hadn't been known that he'd been made a prisoner by the Germans, who actually did hold the city for several days in September 1914. When Rivette and Truffaut asked him in 1957 if he himself had been a prisoner, Renoir's answer was no.[62]

At the conclusion of his presentation, Renoir admitted that he and Spaak had "double-checked" the book, which had been brought to their attention by one of the members of the Ligue des évadés (League of Escapees), a group to which des Vallières also belonged. On June 27, he wrote to Aragon to tell him about his worries, arguing in passing that des Vallières was supported by "his friends at *Candide, Gringoire, L'Action française*," and that for them, "it's a matter of insinuating that everything that is national ('La Marseillaise,' the unknown soldier, and prisoners of war, as a case in point) belongs solely to the Fascists."[63] The lawyer defending Renoir for the affair was a counselor named Rappoport; des Vallières's lawyer was Maurice Garçon.

For his defense, Renoir appealed quite naturally to Pinsard. Unfortunately, he didn't succeed in contacting the general, as he wrote to Counselor Rappoport to explain, and added that, on the other hand, he'd be able to count on the testimony of "M. Gaut, the former officer who introduced me to him and who witnessed our conversations."[64] As a result, without having wanted it, Renoir had provoked a new development: if Pierre Gaut, whom Renoir had met in 1934, was the one who "introduced" him to Pinsard, it would mean that he had never met the aviator before. In such a case, the "reunions" while *Toni* was being shot weren't reunions at all. And furthermore, the ace fighter must not have described his escapes and other exploits to the director until long after they had been known by all. Finally, the hero of air warfare had never saved the life of Renoir the aviator. This argument may seem forced, but its merit might

18

"People We'd Like to Be Friends With"

La Marseillaise

A war movie with no fighting, no explosions, no flags flapping in the wind or wounded dying in the mud of the trenches. A war movie without the war. No one would be interested in a film like that, the producers argued to Renoir, Charles Spaak, and Jean Gabin for months. *Grand Illusion* had become, all the same, Jean Renoir's first—and only—hit. A colossal, international hit. Precisely because it was a war movie without fighting, explosions, flags flapping in the wind, the wounded dying in the mud of the trenches. Because it was a war movie without the war. And thus just the sort to distance the traumatism of past horrors, perfect for blurring the vision of the horror that was on its way.

A commercial *and* critical success, *Grand Illusion* fulfilled the dream of every director and put Jean Renoir in center place. It brought him the opportunity to become more discriminating about projects and to hang on to those that really mattered; but his appetite for making films didn't diminish as a result. Renoir was the type who in the course of a meal could reel off four, five, six ideas for a screenplay, and three more between the coffee and the pomace brandy. His ability to become enthusiastic was phenomenal. He'd developed infatuation to the point of its becoming a reflex, and he was familiar with the rules of a profession that often called for launching five projects to open the field to the chance that a sixth might happen someday. And then, every day he was being invited to express himself, to speak, to write; and behind such an increase in calls for interviews, proposals for articles, and offers to write columns were people well aware that his voice mattered from now on. At times he took too much advantage of such a widening of opportunities, because that was the way he was, in line with the frustrations caused by his personal failures and his birthright as the son of a towering artist and the brother of a great actor.

Pierre Renoir was a regular at the dinners on rue de Rome for a small world he couldn't help viewing in a manner that might have seemed condescending. He played the role of an important figure who intended to give such company the impression that he had stronger opinions than he'd ever want to let on, a big brother who couldn't resist seeing his younger sibling as a bit of an immature fool. Henri Cartier-Bresson was often invited, as were André Zwobada, Marc Maurette, and Jean's assistants. But no one came more often than Jacques Becker and Carl Koch, who was requested on certain evenings to practice his rotisserie skills. Marguerite didn't speak much, except when the conversation turned to politics. The ingenuousness of Pierre's new girlfriend, the young actress Elisa Ruis, made her the number one target of the men at the table, who got a kick out of her naïveté and ignorance of classical culture, which left her out of their games.

One of the favorite pastimes of the director and his German friend consisted of placing a Roman emperor within a political situation that would be completely novel for him, inspired as it would be by current events. How would Caesar have reacted to the fall of Blum's government? And what commentaries would Cicero have used to shed light on the situation? Cartography, another of Koch's fetishes, was also an opportunity to remake the world without really touching it. It merely needed to be considered from a different angle—for example, with the North at the bottom of the map and the East on the left—and then move the mountains, reverse the directions in which the rivers flowed, and imagine what it would all entail.[1]

Alain didn't miss a whit at these banquets, and the teachers at the school he attended inattentively, whose job it was to cram his brain with facts in the shortest possible time, thought of him as a dunce. This didn't prevent him from being adored in Siritzky's office, where he played gofer and stock boy four hours a day and where everybody called him by the nickname "Carrot-Top."[2] Alain developed a passion for motorcycles. Jean still loved cars just as much, and new ones appeared often. After a Ford 19 CV came a Packard from the US embassy, then a four-door Delage convertible, and soon a Delahaye. Marguerite drove to the meetings of her cell behind the wheel of a Lancia V4. Life seemed easy for everybody.

The presence of Pierre Lestringuez, who was also a regular guest at these evening gatherings, brought unneeded proof to these forty-somethings that they could, because it appealed to them, still behave like scamps. One evening, their lifelong friend rang the doorbell and was discovered standing on the landing with a small lobster in each hand. Behind him was a delivery man with a case of cognac on his shoulder. "The lobsters are for the record. With lobsters à l'Américaine only the sauce matters," Lestringuez explained.[3] On April 12, 1938, he'd just had the good fortune of seeing his first (and only) play accepted by the Comédie-Française. It had opened on October 13, 1938, at the same time as Giraudoux's Cantique des cantiques (Song of Songs), which had also been directed by Louis Jouvet. Lestringuez's play, *Tricolore*, would have seventeen performances and draw some caustic reviews, such as the one by Pierre Brisson, who described the performance as "innervating with boredom, flatness, and pointlessness."[4] Some people were surprised to see such an opportunity given to a beginner when Labiche's acceptance into the Comédie-Française was still causing a stir. So, it was a good thing to be the close friend of the director of *Grand Illusion*.

Although the ideas of most of Renoir's friends were on the left side of the political chessboard, he himself had no intention of allowing his connection with anyone to be extended in a way that would include that person's political engagement.

> When I would hear my father speak with the same warmth and identical enthusiasm about a comrade of the Party and a militant of the Croix-de-Feu, I wondered whether he was thoughtless or even underhanded. It took me some time to understand that, for him, ideas had little meaning in themselves, and that all that mattered in his eyes was the personality of the individual expressing them. The attachment he felt for Maurice Thorez was the same as the affection he had for the very "right-wing" Pierre Gaut. In all sincerity, he enjoyed lunching with one just as much as dining with the other.[5]

We should not conclude from this in any definitive way that the opinions Renoir expressed were always based on convenience or that they were brought to his lips or pen by the current climate. His films also preclude such a reading. If he remained close to the Party at that time, it was also because the Communists seemed to him to have erected the sole bastion against the rise of totalitarianism, a feeling that was only reinforced by his blindness toward the real nature of a Soviet regime, which he didn't know or didn't want to understand was also a dictatorship. Others who were better equipped because they were more in touch with the facts and more involved than he ever would be gave no better sign of clear-sightedness.

Between 1936 and 1938, Renoir wrote at least sixty-four articles for newspapers and magazines, as tallied by Claude Gauteur, who has rediscovered them and ensured their republication.[6] The director's most important journalistic contribution was the articles he wrote for the Communist daily *Ce soir*, which was first published on March 1, 1937, and a few months later printed an average of 120,000 copies every day, which increased to 260,000 by March 1939. Its market was 80 percent Parisian, and it was the sixth largest daily with a national circulation. *L'Humanité* was in fourth position, with an average number of sold copies of more than 300,000. Coedited by Aragon and Jean-Richard Bloch, *Ce soir* invited prestigious figures to write columns. Accordingly, the Monday issue had one by Jean Cocteau; Thursdays, it was Yvette Guilbert, followed by Elsa Triolet; and Wednesdays, Jean Renoir. Between March 4, 1937, and October 7, 1938, therefore, Renoir supplied the publication with fifty-five articles, during the course of which he managed not only to create a eulogy in praise of laziness and to offer his reflections as much on film as on politics or daily life but also to keep the reader informed about his film projects in progress. As a whole, these articles afforded the considerable advantage of drawing a kind of self-portrait of the director week after week, with a series of snapshots that were often truer and deeper than the thoughts he provided several decades later, especially in *My Life and My Films*.

The joy of living and the impulse to share burst from the prose in these columns, whose author described his reasons for writing them just at a time when the coming direction of *La Bête humaine* would keep him from writing more for several weeks: "When you witness something that annoys you or gives you a laugh, you feel an irresistible impulse to share your annoyance or fun with your friends. That is what I can do with you. And that's really something. . . . I'm not a writer. I'm quite simply a guy who doesn't know how to resist the desire to tell a good one. Except, I swear to you that when I tell it to people I can see or touch, it's a lot better. I sense how it's affecting them, can tell what works, I focus on what I figure is interesting or amusing." In response to a claim that he would have had the opportunity to prepare some of his columns in advance, he delivered one of his typical remarks: "When I have something to tell you, I have to do it right away. If I wait, the story begins to seem stupid to me and out the window it goes."[7]

In April 1937, in remarkably nimble prose, he ridiculed racism in his column, describing the selection in Nazi Germany of "women of pure Aryan race" and the placement of each on "a splendiferous country farm with top-quality animals (of pure race, which goes without saying), on the sole condition that each agrees to assume the position underneath a young German male selected in the same way." The article concludes, "Trustworthy informants have reported to me that there are currently more than ten thousand of such farms."[8] With similar eloquence, on several occasions, he went on the attack against the behavior and style of the dictators of Germany and Italy, relying for such occasions on the verses of his dear friend Georges Fourest,[9] even though many other columnists were using their talents to express jittery neutrality.

In the article he devoted to the *Hindenburg* tragedy,* he begins with his sense of astonishment about the expressions of sympathy from France to Germany, "because, in short, if these people are dead or were horribly wounded, they doubtlessly owe it to the perpetual untruthfulness of the Nazis." He finishes by writing, "But really, how many minutes of silence should we observe in every radio station throughout the world to share in the suffering of families of those other victims of Hitler, the inhabitants of Guernica?"[10]

There is nothing surprising about Renoir's vividly reflecting the ideas of the Party with which he was a fellow traveler. But what compels respect is the fact that every week he abandoned all reserve and stepped up to the front lines, brandishing his sword against dangerous opponents who were far more powerful than his supporters.

Although there is no doubt that Carl Koch remained his best friend, Henri Jeanson was still his comrade-in-arms, the person who appeared with him for the film showings and debates organized by Ciné-Liberté. Renoir fought at his side for a type of cinema rid of industrial encumbrances and the commercial contingencies that were stifling it.

Jeanson had created a portrait of Renoir from the standpoint of the film profession, the way he was before the success of *The Lower Depths* and the triumph of *Grand Illusion*: "They preferred anybody else, no matter whom: L'Herbier, Hugon, Léon Poirier, Machin, Thingamajig, Whatchamacallit, Your Ass. . . . " But then, everything changed for Renoir, as Jeanson explained: "We can be assured, after having seen *Grand Illusion*, that the kind of *La Marseillaise* Jean Renoir will direct for the Popular Front won't be to film what Messrs. Jacques Chabannes, Léon Ruth, and company's show *Liberté* was for the theater: a disgraceful, ridiculous fiasco, a flop devoid of prestige, a festival of failures."[11] *Liberté* had been financed by the CGT† and *La Marseillaise* was being funded by the Party and the CGT. Jeanson, who was associated with the project, maintained his freedom of opinion and expression.

He had no lack of enthusiasm for the *La Marseillaise* project, either. The idea of a film about the French Revolution was discussed jokingly between the two kindred spirits at the beginning—a joke that would turn sour a few months later. In an article that appeared in the monthly *Commune* in July 1936, Renoir and Jeanson explained to readers "How to Make a Film"; and during the meanderings of their discussion, three remarks popped out of their mouths.

* The airship *Hindenburg* caught fire during the approach stage and crashed near Lakehurst, New Jersey, on May 4, 1937. Out of the ninety-seven people on board, thirty-five were killed.

† Confédération générale du travail, a national trade union, strongly allied with the French Communists at the time.

Renoir: Great idea, the Revolution, and so in fashion after the Popular Front's victory!

Jeanson: Actually, these days they're saying the Revolution was very commercial.

Renoir: Let's stage the Revolution! Just one reservation, though! My distributor doesn't like costume dramas. He says costume dramas are finished!

From one exchange to another, the film as they wanted to imagine it proved to be impossible, given the conformism of distributors and the overcautiousness of producers. They were putting on an act, obviously, but it matched the opinion that both had formed of their profession. Renoir had revealed that opinion in a more serious way in an article he wrote two months before, which said, in particular, "Film directors are the sons of the bourgeoisie. They bring the weaknesses of their decadent class to their career. . . . Without further delay, French film has to be restored to the people of France. It has to be snatched away from the profiteers of directing, from the mercantile frauds, from the manufactured stars."[12] *La Marseillaise*, a project that would begin in the last month of the year, would be his response to that profession of faith, whose echoes would sound dubious less than four years later.

"So in fashion." Indeed, the Revolution certainly was; no irony in that. Already, a sequence from *La vie est à nous* had pointed to Jacques Duclos in invoking the spirit of Valmy,* the same spirit that would whip across the France of the Popular Front and carry with it the flaws of a society that was running out of breath. For some time, the militants at their meetings had taken up the refrain of that "Marseillaise" that they had just finished hating, until their leaders had begun breaking into it from the rostrum. In fact, the national anthem had become unofficially associated with the figure of Maurice Thorez. At the Congress of Arles† in December 1937, it constituted "the hallmark of honor reserved for the secretary general, whereas the other major leaders, Cachin, Duclos, Gitton, have to be satisfied, if that can be said, with 'L'Internationale.'"[13]

Who, precisely, thought of the idea for *La Marseillaise* the film? Probably one of the two young women who are seen in the credits, Nicole Vedrès and Noémie Martel Dreyfus. One of them drew Renoir's attention to the book *Les Rouges du Midi* by Félix Gras, which had been serialized in *Le Temps* in 1896, and then was published as a book four years later. Whereas Nicole Vedrès would

* *Translator's note:* The Battle of Valmy (1792) was the French army's first important victory against the Prussians, during the Revolutionary Wars following the French Revolution. Small as it was, it was a huge boost in morale for those who wanted to believe that the goals of the Revolution were indeed being achieved.

† *Translator's note:* The Ninth Congress of the French Communist Party, held at Arles from December 25 to 29, 1937, during which Thorez was undeniably the focus.

end up quickly withdrawing from the project, Jean-Paul Dreyfus's wife became Renoir's close collaborator. Very close, according to several witnesses, who interpreted several trips organized for documentary purposes as excuses for amorous escapades. According to them, Renoir had fallen "madly in love"[14] with the very attractive Noémie (also known as "Newmi") when they met during *La vie est à nous*. Preparations for *La Marseillaise* offered him the right circumstances for taking greater advantage.

Was he really "madly in love"? Not exclusively, at any rate, because his passion for the beautiful Noémie hadn't dissuaded him during the filming of *La Marseillaise* from kneeling before the door of Lotte Reiniger in the middle of the night and begging her to let him in. If we are to believe Geneviève Becker, who was married to Jacques Becker at the time and who was a witness to the situation, the director's wooing of Madame Carl Koch ended up antagonizing her husband enough to settle the matter loudly with his friend, but not to the point of endangering their relationship.[15] Carl Koch's name is listed third in the writing credits for the film.

The first announcements regarding the production of *La Marseillaise* appeared at the very beginning of 1937 in the January 2 issue of *L'Avant-Garde* and in *Le Travailleur du film* on the twenty-sixth of that month. Proclaiming at that time that "today, film's salvation is in the CGT," Renoir cited examples of Soviet directors who were unfamiliar with merchants of film, those "bastards." "In the USSR, filmmakers don't have to put up with the shackles of these mercenaries. They're free. They can make films. And also, they don't have to worry about tomorrow, about being ruined. But we always have to worry about that. We're like the artists of the Renaissance who aren't getting their periodic payments from their patron princes. If such a comparison offends you, consider that such freedom of existence is the guarantee of the new Renaissance happening in the USSR."[16]

On February 11, in an interview given to Georges Cravenne for *Paris-Soir*, Renoir provided some details. He began by associating the project with the World's Fair that would be held in Paris from the end of May until November.

This exhibition may be called "Arts and Technologies," but at the very least French cinema, whose rank among our national arts is well known, must be given a way to demonstrate its vitality. At first we planned to do a film on the life of Jean Jaurès. But although the man is one of the greatest and most distinguished whom France has ever known, his engaging life and worthy views weren't eventful enough to provide a sufficient variety of cinematic incidents. As a result, after much thought over the span of frequent meetings, our minds gradually fixed on the idea of making a film about the first years of the French Revolution. . . . As soon as we'd settled on this theme, we decided that the film would describe the period of French life beginning slightly before the Revolution, in order to reveal conditions in France from that period until Valmy.[17]

That period, in fact, would not be the one chosen for the film. Moreover, they seemed to be going about it a bit late for the film to be shown as part of the World's Fair. Finally, the large publicity campaign for *Grand Illusion* also made wide use of the event of the World's Fair, to the point of being closely associated with it in the eyes of certain audiences of that time. Renoir also announced that "the government will set aside a deposit [for their use] of 50,000 francs to get the project going and for initial publicity."[18] It seems, in fact, that such an arrangement was claimed, putting the film in the category of a state commission, something that was no longer brought up, but that didn't keep opponents on the Right from promptly seizing upon the information and starting to have conniptions. In the weeks to come, the slightest pretext would become an excuse for having them, such as Renoir's mentioning that "the various elements of the screenplay will be pulled together by Charles Spaak." A Belgian to write the film about the French Revolution? There weren't enough talented writers in France? Despite the fact that there was no follow-up to the remark, the Right became apoplectic.

On February 24, while Renoir was filming *Grand Illusion*, the coordination committee in charge of managing the production made an official request in writing for a subsidy from the CGT. The letter would be published on March 10 in *Le Travailleur du film*. On April 9, that magazine would publish the entire screenplay, which had already been provided by Ciné-Liberté on March 12 and had required considerable changes. The wheels had begun to turn.

Henri Jeanson has provided a less detailed account of the launching of the project, but its tone more faithfully re-creates the frame of mind of the two friends at the time. According to him, "a friend of ours who is an impresario" had come to see them to express his surprise that the two were giving talks for Ciné-Liberté and the Popular Front solely out of a love for film when they should have been "taking advantage of those circumstances to make a film on their own." A good idea, perhaps, but with what money? worried Jeanson and Renoir. The well-meaning friend then suggested a potential scheme whose details Jeanson refrains from revealing, but, writes Jeanson, "a few days later, leaflets and posters were making an appeal to the nation" and announcing that "for the first time, a film will be sponsored by the people themselves through a vast subscription drive." The screenwriter went on to say, "'We're going to make a groundbreaking film,' exclaimed Renoir. 'Of course we're all working on a voluntary basis, as a cooperative. We'll receive a part of the profits and invest the remainder in the next film.'"[19]

The next plan was for numerous contributors to be drafted to work on the film, and Renoir announced this in February: "The dialogue that happens in Paris, in the inner suburbs, will be written by Henri Jeanson; Marcel Achard will be in charge of the lines spoken by the French émigrés in Coblenz. A.-P. Antoine, J.-R. Bloch, H.-R. Lenormand will also see to bringing their talents to our film. Finally, I've asked Marcel Pagnol to write the dialogue between Robespierre, the realist, and Brissot, the idealist. I consider that scene to be one of the most important in the entire film, the one that is bound to have the greatest import."[20]

The scene didn't appear in *La Marseillaise;* nor did Brissot, or Robespierre. Seven composers, including Georges Auric, Arthur Honegger, and Darius Milhaud, divided up the music. Louis Jouvet, who "would oversee the performances," played Robespierre. Pierre Renoir was Brissot, and Stroheim had a cameo as "the Austrian officer who commands the international force at the Battle of Valmy" (which wasn't shown in the film). Gabin was a "phenomenal carpenter from Faubourg Saint-Antoine," and the honor of breaking into "La Marseillaise" was bestowed upon Maurice Chevalier. Disappointment was soon to come. Henri Jeanson, according to what he has claimed, was the first to ascertain certain problems in the nature of the project.

During a preliminary meeting at Salle Bonvalet on boulevard du Temple, just a few steps away from place de la République, the director and screenwriter ended up having to explain their plans "in front of three rows of representatives from the Popular Front," which were composed of "a hundred Socialists, a hundred Communists, a hundred Radicals." Jeanson opened the floor and, just as he was inviting Renoir to speak, a listener raised his hand. "Comrades, I don't agree. I accept the principle of a film on the Revolution on the condition that it begins with the reading of the Declaration of the Rights of Man and of the Citizen, by a member of the Comédie-Française, if possible. I'm speaking here on behalf of the Radical Party and Radical Socialism." Then another participant stood up and announced his opposition to the title *La Marseillaise;* after which there was a third, who insisted that the film "end well."

After that, Jeanson spoke:

Comrades, I'm currently writing a film for Julien Duvivier. We have three producers, the three Hakim brothers. That's two too many. If I have to have a hundred of them, good evening. And first of all, what business is it of yours? We're informing you of our plans out of pure kindness, we're not asking for your opinion. Perhaps some of you are pastry chefs, cabinetmakers, or mechanics. If I told you how to make a cake, build a piece of furniture, or build a machine, I'm sure you'd tell me where to go. Well, I'm telling you where to go, too: back to your hammers and sickles.*[21]

After that, Renoir tried to smooth things over and succeeded, but the launching of the *La Marseillaise* cooperative already boded something less idyllic than the perfectly oiled machinery of Monsieur Lange's "co-op."

On Friday, March 12, a large meeting was held at Salle Huyghens in Montparnasse, where the walls had been hung with red, the tricolor combinations of the French flag, and the portraits of revolutionaries from 1793. According to the report in *L'Humanité* the following day, five thousand people came to hear Henri Jeanson; Albert Bayet, who represented the Radical Party; and Marceau Pivert, from the cultural group "May 36." This was followed by the Chorale populaire of Paris performing several songs, after which "Comrade Herman speaking for the Socialist Party," followed by "Comrade Dreyfus," and, finally, "Comrade Germaine Dulac" took the dais. It was then Jean Renoir's turn to come to the mic, and he was "warmly received," before Pierre Renoir said a few words. At last, "our comrade Vaillant-Couturier, in a very well-structured speech, revealed the reasons for being in favor of such a production." To end the proceedings, "Léo Lagrange, undersecretary of state for sports and recreation, announced the support of the government of the Popular Front" and "the meeting resulted enthusiastically in several more songs interpreted by the Chorale populaire of Paris."[22]

In its March 14 issue, the Party's daily reproduced several excerpts of Paul Vaillant-Couturier's speech, chosen mostly to derail reservations against the project that had been advanced by Marceau Pivert, who'd given a short speech at the meeting saying he was against the idea of giving the film the title of "a song whose initial meaning had been twisted, tarnished by the Versaillais."†[23] *L'Humanité* hadn't printed a word about the attack, and Renoir scoffed at the idea that a song "can be reappropriated."[24] "Using the excuse that we're fighting a chauvinism we all hate, would we have to make soldiers in the year II sing the

---

* *Translator's note:* What Jeanson really says relies on a French idiom and an association that is little known today. He tells them that if he were to interfere with the pastry chefs, cabinetmakers, etc., they would "send him packing," expressed as *"envoyer sur les roses"* (literally, "sending someone to the roses"). His rejoinder is that he is sending them out into the sweetbriar (*"envoyer dans les eglantines"*), a clever reference to earlier French Socialists and Communists who wore a red sweetbriar flower in their buttonhole during the period 1900–1910.

† *Translator's note:* The *Versaillais* were the government troops who suppressed the Commune of 1871.

'L'Internationale'? . . . Our film will be called *La Marseillaise,* from the name of the anthem that epitomizes the glorious tradition you just acclaimed."[25] The article with the excerpts of Vaillant-Couturier's speech was accompanied by a photo showing "the actor Pierre Renoir" beside the treasurer of the Parisian region of the Union des syndicats (Workers' Union), Comrade Henri Guiraud, who was chairing the meeting in the absence of Comrade Jouhaux.

The media of the extreme Right reported the meeting as well. As a result, the readers of *Candide* were able to read these words of Lucien Rebatet, the same journalist who'd sing the praises of *Grand Illusion* a few weeks later: "Adding their support to the gathering was an important contingent of frizzy-haired gentlemen [the word *gentlemen* was in English] who preferred the cafés-crème and yogurts of the nearby Dôme and La Coupole to M. Hitler's concentration camps. These gents were lounging in the most visible seats. Real Frenchmen, on the other hand, were kept in check closer to the upper galleries or dark corners of the room."[26] Rebatet also offered the following portrait of the director: "M. Renoir is pink, pudgy, and blond. Wearing a blue turtleneck for a truly proletarian look. He also tries somewhat successfully to affect the accent of M. Gabin. He possesses a delightful modesty: 'French cinema hasn't yet uttered its first word,' a remark found charming by M. Feyder, M. René Clair, and some others. He personifies the Popular Front, which is going to rip French cinema's diaper off. Public honors have turned that head of his white-hot with enthusiasm. He plays it like the purest of the pure." One extra virtue to being members of the left-wing bourgeois is the torrent of wit their existence unleashes; the right-wing bourgeois would be out of work without them.

Shortly after filming *Grand Illusion,* whose editing Renoir was overseeing, he and Jeanson were transformed for the span of several weeks into "traveling salesmen"—as the director put it—whose job it was to bring the good word to comrades and convince them to put their hands in their pockets. From the unions, the CGT would come up with 50,000 francs, and the Union des syndicats, 20,000. Unfortunately, the budget of the new film was more like 3 million, most of which for all intents and purposes had to come from "bills printed to look like banknotes used during the French Revolution, at 2 francs each, which would be sold by union and political groups as well as on the premises of an exhibition on the Revolution, created in Paris. These 2-franc amounts would be deducted from the price of admission when the film played in theaters."[27] It was also announced that *La Marseillaise,* produced by a "production cooperative," would be presented in theaters by a "distribution cooperative." The idea for this "film for the people and by the people," as it was described in widely distributed leaflets, was for it to manage entirely without the capitalists, even if nothing in the plans that had been announced said anything about theaters. As Renoir kept repeating, the film "must not be by a man or a commercial company, it must be the working class's film."[28]

Several weeks later, while *Grand Illusion* triumphed, in the brand new premises of the Maison de la Culture on 27 rue d'Anjou, "the exhibition on the Revolution" was no more successful than the disappointing results registered by the subscription campaign. In *Regards*, Georges Sadoul reported 350,000 subscriptions sold "from the first days of August,"[29] a total that Louis Aragon multiplied by two less than a month later by writing, "There are already 700,000 in circulation as of the end of August."[30] Even if this figure, representing less than half of the 1,550,000 actually in circulation, would have been sold, which it makes sense to doubt, the participation of the people of France would still not have been able to cover half of the planned budget.

The budget itself had a modesty that reeked of optimism, considering that this was a costume drama requiring a significant number of decors and performers, several of whom were stars. As is almost a rule in film, that budget would increase as well in considerable proportions without anyone being able to give a definite opinion about the figure being wielded by Giulio Ceretti, who officiated behind the scenes as the financial go-between for the Comintern and claimed that it was the principal supplier of funds that would allow the film to be made. Ceretti wrote, "We were in need of Jacques Duclos's patience and eloquence to finish *La Marseillaise*. . . . The film's initial estimate was 8 million and ended up costing 18. . . . It was enough for a film to stop for a few days to make the costs become astronomical. That's exactly what happened to *La Marseillaise:* the money needed to keep working without stopping wasn't available."[31] Compared to the budget of 2.5 million for *Grand Illusion*, the sum of 18 million seemed excessive.

On July 31, the following boxed notice appeared in *L'Humanité: "La Marseillaise*, directed by Jean Renoir, and sponsored by Messrs. Chautemps, Zay, Sarraut, Blum, Herriot, Jouhaux, Frachon, Cachin, Paul-Boncour, Thorez, Bracke, Jacques Duclos, Basch, Aragon, etc., will be epoch-making in the history of cinema." It was another attempt to convince readers to subscribe, but the project had already undergone important changes, and the "Société d'exploitations et de productions cinématographiques *La Marseillaise*," LLC, with a fund of 25,000 francs, officially set up in April, was no longer much more than a memory.

It was that same company, represented on that occasion by André Seigneur, with which Renoir had signed a directorial contract guaranteeing him, beginning June 1, "the sum of 5,000 francs per week, plus a 10-percent-share of profits up to 1.5 million francs and 5 percent of the profits above that amount."[32]

However, the initial fantasies of the film's promoters did not withstand the test of reality.

As a member of the limited liability company on the same footing as Jean-Paul Dreyfus, André Zwobada, Louis Joly—the film technician who'd become a journalist—and two representatives from the editorial staff of *Ce soir*, who were also permanent members of the Party, Renoir had quickly understood that the organization would not be able to lead the project toward a satisfactory result. Rightly or wrongly? It was a delicate question to answer, and only Henri Jeanson had the nerve to take it on—with a hatchet.

According to the screenwriter, the turnaround happened "three days" after the meeting at Salle Huyghens, which would mean three days after Renoir blew a gasket:

> We've got to call it quits with these halls on the Champs-Élysées packed with these shameful profiteers of worker comrades. Let's hope that soon somebody throws a bomb at those swine and calls it quits with that privileged class. As for our film, it will be the first film made by the people, for the people, in the name of our people who are our boss, the first in a long series, because the revolution is beginning! And we film-makers will make our own revolution by chasing out of our profession at once and before doing anything else the distributors, the same people whose arrest and death I solemnly pronounce this evening.[33]

By putting his pen in service of his memory more than thirty years after the fact, Jeanson makes use of his own talent as a narrator to put words into Renoir's mouth. It's nevertheless likely that his account respects, if not the letter, then at least the spirit of what the director said that evening. On the other hand, it's very doubtful that the scene he next describes actually took place "three days" later: Renoir telephones Jeanson to ask him to go to dinner that very evening, "eight o'clock, at the little café on rue Lepic," adding, "we absolutely have to talk about the film together, just the two of us." At the agreed-upon hour and place indicated, the screenwriter finds the director with a third dinner companion, a certain Albert, "who sounded like somebody who hawked suspenders." Renoir wants to introduce Jeanson to Albert Pinkovitch, with whom he had made *Grand Illusion* and who reveals having already obtained an advance of a million francs for *La Marseillaise* from European and North African distributors, and who also claims to have entered into relations with the "Yanks."

According to what "Pink" says on that same evening, he has even "made a request to Roosevelt to record a speech to present our flick," a detail that stands out in light of an article that appeared in *La Flèche de Paris* on April

17, in which Jeanson wrote, "President Roosevelt has made it known, merely based on the title, that he himself would present the film of the Popular Front to the American people." In this same article, he also makes clear that "*La Marseillaise* remains *La Marseillaise*. We're working on the screenplay"—proof that his encounter with M. Albert had not been off-putting, which is confirmed in the article in the July 24 issue of *La Flèche,* but that also indicates that claims presented in his memoirs need to be amended. It was not the "day after" the dinner on rue Lepic that he went to the offices of "our cooperative" on rue La Boétie, where a file marked "Estimated Budget for the Film *La Marseillaise*" revealed to him that Renoir had been promised a salary of 400,000 francs for direction. As a talented and experienced screenwriter, Jeanson spruced up the dramatic aspects of his account, especially by condensing its episodes in time, which is something Renoir was wont to do as well.

The sum of 400,000 francs offered to Renoir by Les Réalisations d'art cinématographique (RAC) for *La Marseillaise* may seem extravagant at first, even more so when compared to the fee the director received for *The Lower Depths* less than a year before, which was a quarter of the amount, or the one he'd get for *La Bête humaine* (200,000 francs plus 5 percent of the profits on any amount of revenue up to 100,000 francs). However, to truly understand how Jeanson discovered what he would consider a betrayal on the part of Renoir several weeks after the date he mentions, we must take into account that, bolstered by the triumph of *Grand Illusion,* Frank Rollmer and Albert Pinkovitch's company, RAC, had the use of substantial sums and was able to promise a lot to ensure that they worked with a director whose quoted value had just grown to extraordinary proportions.

This is proved by the agreement Renoir signed on January 15, 1938, whose terms stated that the two parties were agreeing to "two productions written and directed by Jean Renoir, and for which the respective estimates shall not be below 5 million francs." Renoir was to receive "2.5 percent of the sums spent for production of the film that he would direct himself, 10 percent of the profits, reimbursement of all expenses [he] incurred in the context of his work," and "5,000 francs per week, payable every Friday evening,"[34] this last clause spelling out precisely the same terms as the agreement signed on June 1 for *La Marseillaise.* The contract would never be actualized, but the sums mentioned in it suddenly render Jeanson's assertions a bit less outrageous, yet still without clarifying the reasons that motivated the screenwriter to withdraw from *La Marseillaise.* Was the intolerable aspect the fact that Renoir would be paid, and well paid?

It seems likely that if Jeanson had easy access to the budget of the film as he claimed, no one was making a mystery of the fee Renoir wanted or was offered. In fact, Jeanson seemed to have fallen suddenly to earth in discovering that the project possessed a commercial dimension. As someone who would have always been cautious about taking anything at all for granted and who'd unknowingly let himself be carried away on a wave of enthusiasm, he was bound to be quite piqued and to blame himself after the fact for his unaccustomed naïveté and to have felt resentful and bitter. Seemingly more the dreamer of the two, Renoir had come out looking like the one with his feet on the ground.

Jeanson would never forgive what he took for a betrayal, even in hindsight. When the director left for Fascist Italy to direct *Tosca,* the screenwriter would publish an article in which he quoted the figure he'd obtained, according to him, for the direction of *La Marseillaise:* "They sold a Renoir in Italy for 400,000 francs . . . and it's a fake!" Or at least, that's what he claimed. The article in question has never been found. Long after, he'd go on the attack again, against the truth of statements attributed to Renoir while he was staying in Lisbon, just before leaving for the United States. Jeanson's grudge was deep-seated, and it spelled the end of their friendship. Renoir, on the other hand, didn't hesitate a moment to offer Jeanson his support during difficult circumstances, and he did it in terms that warrant consideration.

On December 19, 1939, Renoir wrote to Counselor Pierre Loewel, one of the lawyers of the journalist and screenwriter who was about to go to court. Jeanson was a regular of the law courts, and he had just racked up his seventeenth trial for defamation with a caustic article on the state of French film in the November 3 issue of *Le Merle blanc.* Renoir did not stop merely with expressing the regard he had for his former friend, whom he considered, as he wrote, "a perfectly honorable man for whom I would willingly exchange personal guarantees of morality without fear of disappointment." He also went back, without being asked, to one of the causes of their falling out. "For some time my relationship with Jeanson had been a bit strained. The reason for that 'strain,' I should add, is completely to Jeanson's credit. I was somewhat hoping to resort to a Russian collaboration in case of a 'hard blow,'* and he was adamant about not believing in it. Events separated us, and with this letter, I'm glad I can honorably make amends to him."[35]

The fact that Renoir had received a signal that the wind was blowing differently, mostly as a result of the signing on August 23, 1939, of the German-Soviet Nonaggression Pact, does not compromise the exemplary dignity of the initiative he took in writing his letter. "Exemplary" enough to excite and prolong the hate Jeanson lavished on Renoir until Jeanson's death in November 1970. Renoir would allude to his ex-friend's behavior in a letter in response to Louis Guillaume, who'd been providing him with press clippings about the French

---

* *Translator's note:* Renoir is referring to the possibility of Nazi Germany's attacking France.

release of *The Diary of a Chambermaid.* "What amazes me the most is Jeanson's spitefulness, which he expresses against me every chance he gets. Someone told me he's a friend of Catherine's. He forgets that when he was in prison in 1939, I sent the authorities in charge of deciding his fate a letter pleading his cause, and I did it in spite of the fact that I was in the army, where that kind of expression is in principle prohibited. Such spitefulness amazes me, but it also leaves me completely indifferent."[36]

At the end of July 1937 at the latest, Renoir had therefore become the only master on board a project that, for all practical purposes, kept changing* and interrupting the course of the columns he wrote for *Ce soir*. He still found time for fun, sometimes at others' expense, as Nadia Sibirskaïa recalled:

> One evening we were having dinner together with Marguerite, Lestringuez. . . . Lestringuez said that we should really go and see Cocteau's *Oedipus*. Lady Abdy, who was in it, really wanted to work with Jean. . . . Jean began bellowing, "I can't stand all that shit!" Finally, we all left for Théâtre Antoine. We managed to squeeze into the full house, but all of us were separated. After a moment, we began to understand that we'd been drowning the entire theater with our giggles and remarks. I was sitting in the first row with Marguerite, and I'd pointed out that the soldiers, who were barefoot, had corns. We were already about to lose all control, when Jean Marais, whose first performance it was and who was wearing bands of legging, stamped his foot and caught the cloth ribbon on something, causing it to unroll, to the audience's delight. And above all that, from the other end of the theater you could hear Renoir's gruff voice yelling that it was a shame to bother people with such crap, etc. We had to leave because they were threatening to kick us out.[37]

Oedipus Rex, which had its premiere on July 13, did give Jean Marais a chance to make his debut on stage. However, an especially pleasant part of Nadia Sibirskaïa's account reveals that Lady Iya Abdy, who played Jocasta, and whose "talent" had "not been given the exposure it deserves for a long time" (according to *Le Figaro*), and who "really wanted to work with Jean,"[38] would get her opportunity. A few weeks later, Renoir offered her the role in *La Marseillaise* of an aristocratic émigré. The uninhibited young woman even became the actress of choice at Renoir's parties, which she enlivened with her allure and her humor. Painted by Derain, photographed by Man Ray, extremely wealthy, she'd instill in Alain Renoir some basic rules for dressing elegantly that he wouldn't forget and that he would never entertain the idea of following. Lady Abdy is

---

* The two Marcel dialogue writers, Pagnol and Acard, were no longer on board, either.

also the source of the following expression, flung out at the mention of a rival: "She's so vulgar that she'd be incapable of saying 'Go fuck yourself' without being vulgar."[39] Her social notoriety was enough for her picture to appear in *Le Figaro* wearing the costume of her role as a way of promoting the film, even though her name didn't appear in the credits.[40] Apparently, the portrait wasn't also provided to *L'Humanité*. That was where another kind of advertisement appeared that read, "The people of Coblentz* didn't like 'La Marseillaise.' Their descendants are trying to discredit Jean Renoir's *La Marseillaise*. We French applaud them."[41]

The anecdote about Théâtre Antoine offers proof that success hadn't caused Renoir to stem his rowdy ways. The opposite, in fact, was true; or at least that's the impression his behavior produced. Some—with Jeanson at the top of the list—would accuse him of hyper-megalomania to explain his ways of transgressing the tacit law in his profession that forbids a director from lambasting—publicly, at least—the work of one of his peers. Renoir would flout that law in other ways during this period. This would play more than a slight role in forging a reputation for him in the world of film and theater. It was all still being whispered about at the time. After the war, when his career was hitting an impasse, the whispers would reach a thunderous pitch.

For several weeks, the director was afflicted with another disadvantage. He'd just become enormously successful; and, moreover, it was an entirely personal success because the unparalleled characteristics of *Grand Illusion* were being rightly credited to him. And in the milieu of film more than elsewhere, because it's a more visible and more profitable medium, success provoked a great deal of jealousy.

Finally, it had taken Renoir time to become established, and therefore he'd been a visible part of the landscape for several years, omnipresent, in fact—if not to say invasive—since the time he became a fellow traveler of the Party and began accumulating appearances and commitments. He hadn't turned forty-three yet, but the heaviness of his appearance, his worn suits, his sometimes "populist"-inspired, sometimes natural expressions betrayed a show-off quality and a studied manner, all contributing to make him seem older than he actually was. Jean Renoir was now prominent, a reference, almost an institution, and he lost no chance to give lessons.

In the film world they'd decided to see him as "old." All of it had happened in just a few months. In speaking of *La Marseillaise* years later, Jean-Paul Le Chanois (who, it should not be forgotten, always had a ready supply of vitriol)

* *Translator's note:* Coblentz was the small German town in the electorate of Trèves that had become the main destination for the royalist emigration. They obviously did not like the film *La Marseillaise*.

would declare, "This is really good Renoir, but he didn't feel the big crowd scenes or have the strength to do them; it's not his style. He could be blamed for wanting to jump into something like that at his age! Back then he seemed old to me, the way I'd talk about my old bosses in the past. He was forty-three, and for us, that was 'old.'"[42] An "old" man you addressed using the informal *tu* rather than *vous* during a meal or at a friendly party, but on the set you went back to *vous* and took a respectful distance, which the tradition of that time required.

However, it shouldn't be forgotten that Renoir was one of the only recognized directors of that time who did not behave like a dictator during filming, a quality that might have encouraged his reputation as chronically indecisive. His personality required him to do without the showy trappings of power. This did not make him less of an authority figure when he directed a film; it was, in fact, his way of being "the strongest." Not a dictator, and that's a fact; but his roly-poly appearance and his ability to smooth over all difficulties only made his outbursts more spectacular. At the slightest annoyance, he could dig in his heels; and in the face of it, everybody on the set shrunk without his having to give orders. "On the set you didn't obey him, you were in a state of reverence," remembered Jacques Becker's wife at the time, Geneviève.[43]

On August 4, 1937, which was three weeks from the beginning of filming, Renoir held a press conference to supply certain details. "The grandiose ideas" had had to be abandoned in part. "In fact, the film was already longer than ten thousand meters, which would make it difficult to get shown." One coincidence was being especially savored: "My collaborators and I finished the screenplay once and for all on July 14." Louis XVI would be "the central character in the film," whom "we'll portray by idealizing and not as he was." The people from Marseille would not speak with that accent, "because, whatever you think, Marcel Pagnol, a man of genius, was the one who invented the Marseillaise accent." And finally, for the time being, "casting is still not completely closed," and the only name that could be mentioned was "Pierre Renoir for the role of Louis XVI."[44] The casting of Lise Delamare as Marie-Antoinette would be made public on August 16. And, of course, the people from Marseille in the film would speak with an accent. Because a lot of them were regulars in Pagnol's films? Definitely, according to Renoir's statements in 1937; but definitely not, if you listened to what he'd maintain thirty years later: "In that story about the people from Marseille leaving for Paris to impose the will of the people and right the wrongs of the monarchy, I think the accent was quite important. Because in order to do something like that, you had to be a bit Don Quixote; and yet, Don Quixote certainly had an accent."[45]

Before Aragon took Renoir's place every Wednesday, from August 19 to September 16, in *Ce soir* to report on preparations and shooting of *La Marseillaise,* Renoir used his column to spell out his intentions and to try to become more inclusive. "We've idealized Louis XVI because we want him to explain intelligently and sincerely the ideas of those on his side. We've created a sympathetic character that we would like to see interpreted by a serious actor who has authority with audiences. Along with the king, we'll present the royal family and especially Marie-Antoinette, but we'll avoid the facile polemic that such a character could elicit."[46]

Plainly, the royal couple had great significance for him, and it already seemed a time in the distant past when the director would speak of "that aristocratic spirit that today we call Fascist,"[47] even if it is true that decades later he'd have to protect himself from any association with a monarch "who didn't have the crudeness of the aristocracy of that period."[48] He himself would then provide the reason for such a change in attitude: "I'd read a great deal of documentation on Louis XVI, and I came to the conclusion that he was an extremely likeable figure, and since I'd discovered the same thing in my research, I wanted to portray him that way."

This was something he obviously could not say at the time, but could nevertheless film, sparing the king and depicting the queen as a naïve, naughty little goose whom readings had revealed to him as "an extremely common woman" and "quite simply very stupid." Jean Renoir's Marie-Antoinette is right in line with the one Auguste Renoir labeled a "dumbbell who thought she was clever by playing at being a shepherdess," and whose figure painted on dessert plates brought the beginner artist three pennies as opposed to the two he got for his other plates.[49]

In 1937, it was impossible for him to explain his reasons for depicting Louis XVI in a favorable light: he'd discovered a personality that appealed to him and to whom he even felt a connection. Concerning this, he was following the same trajectory common to historians who were disciples of Jules Michelet and who made a point of recalling that Parisians "have in every period had a weakness for this fat man who had nothing malicious about him and whose portliness radiated blissful, paternal affability, completely disposed to the will of the masses. . . . The fishmongers called him *granddaddy.*"[50] The people's main grudge against Louis XVI had to do with his indecision, a character trait that adversaries most often mistakenly, but sometimes rightly, assigned to Renoir, whom some of his admirers, conversely, wanted to see as just that—a "granddaddy."

The fact that the personality of the king had won him over is not in the slightest bit surprising. All the characters he created were subject to this process of his identifying with them; but, in this case, it happened very naturally given that his own brother would perform the role, thereby boosting and accentuating this tendency. Jean and Pierre Renoir's Louis XVI calls to mind the one Marat in his newspaper *L'Ami du people,*[*] cited by Michelet, said would "cry hot tears at the foolish things that Austrian woman was having done to him,"[51] a remark Alexandre Dumas would reproduce in *La Comtesse de Charny.* At the time, Renoir's reason for drifting away from a revolutionary perspective was the one Aragon privately suggested: it was strategic. But in this regard, at least, the film matched a propensity of his. Renoir hedged, as he often did and as was natural to him, and he was all the more pleased by the fact that he had no other choice when it came to *La Marseillaise.*

This question of the royal couple is one aspect of *La Marseillaise* that offers insight into the extent to which Renoir, during preparations all the way up to filming, saw himself at the mercy of an interplay of powers and pressures. He alone believed that this was enough of an excuse to exaggerate by tenfold his tendency to blame circumstances. He knew he was being watched intently, subject to expectations, surveyed. Should he ever forget, the press would remind him of his obligations. Whereas the Right was worried about the partisan aspect of the project, in the opposite camp, to which the director belonged, there were self-appointed directors of conscience. The terms were different from those employed by the militants a few months before—or at least the way Jeanson reported them—but the mentality remained approximately the same: everyone had an opinion about the subject and intended to promote it. Just as the aristocrats—and to the same extent, the revolutionaries—had their reasons, so did the advisers have theirs, and there was no doubt that Renoir had never felt or endured such a reality to this extent. He'd put its expression into the mouth of La Chesnaye (Marcel Dalio) when he'd make *The Rules of the Game.*

Shooting had been going on for three days when Louis Aragon's column in the August 26 issue of *Ce soir* appeared. In it, Renoir could read that "that fat man," Louis XVI, who was "dull-witted and as mediocre a king as he was a mediocre husband . . . could be the hero of a historical novel, but not of *La Marseillaise.*" When Aragon went on to explain that Renoir "needs to present a likeable Louis XVI," because "if he presented an unsympathetic Louis XVI, it would give the audience the idea that if this king had been different, history would have been changed by it," he was addressing criticisms already expressed within the Party that would not fail to materialize when the film was shown. Near the end of

* *Translator's note: Literally, "The Friend of the People."*

his column, Aragon made it clear that "it would be absurd to see *La Marseillaise* as a documentary about the Revolution" and proclaimed that "above all, this film should be a work of art" and that "the workings of art also include the audience's confidence in the artist as well as his freedom of expression." He then concluded, "I, for one, have confidence in the realist of *Toni, Grand Illusion*, and *La vie est à nous*. And you? . . ."[52]

For the first time in his career, Renoir was working from a crushing amount of historical documentation, and he knew he was also under surveillance; how could he feel free? How could he rely upon that instinct that had always guided him? Moreover, at the end of summer 1937, his situation was very different from how it had been eight months earlier when he took on the project of directing *La Marseillaise:* in the meantime, *Grand Illusion* had made him the most well-known director of his time, a director who certainly no longer needed the Communist Party as a sponsor and who now intended, on the contrary, to direct only films that meant something entirely personal.

To get close to his manner of approach, and perhaps also to avoid inviting too much criticism from diehard specialists and advisers, he would try to depict the historical events with an impersonal eye, as a mere onlooker to history, and downplay as much as he could the historical figures and great events. Taking the point of view of the underling rather than a privileged bird's-eye view would place him on a path more natural for him. It would also expose the film to the disappointment of those who had been waiting for a reenactment of "great" moments. *La Marseillaise* would not be the sweeping historical epic that had been sometimes announced but was a "chronicle of a few facts that contributed to the fall of the monarchy," as its subtitle explained. A series of tableaux, more than a solidly structured narrative, in which life—rather than History—would transpire, haphazardly captured during two summers, 1789 and 1792.

As for the writing of the screenplay, Renoir was essentially able to leave it up to Carl Koch. He'd be criticized for being German, notably by Jeanson, whose sally would look like delayed revenge. Renoir saw Koch as "a very rigorous thinker," a quality that didn't figure among the director's many virtues, and he would state that his friend had been "a fantastic help in our hunt for clichés to destroy wherever we encountered them."[53] He assigned Lotte Reiniger, who was Madame Koch and an animation specialist known worldwide, the task of creating the scenes of the shadow theater.

On the set, Renoir would make use of another special adviser named Antoine Corteggiani, a weapons specialist who had written to him after *Grand Illusion* to point out an error: it was impossible for Rauffenstein (Erich von Stroheim) to be able to kill Boëldieu (Pierre Fresnay) by means of the weapon he had used at the firing distance indicated. So, Renoir enlisted Corteggiani as the person in charge of weapons and the movements of crowds. Corteggiani was also wild about motorcycles, which made him a subject of fascination for Alain Renoir.

In December 1939, Alain, who was then in the army, visited Corteggiani in Montauban, which made it possible for the latter to bring news of his son to Jean, who was in Italy fretting about not having any.[54] On March 23, 1945, Jean received a letter from his brother Claude telling him about the death of Corteggiani, who had been appointed under the Occupation "to the Department of Jewish Affairs."[55] The news was erroneous, and during a visit to Paris in the summer of 1951, Jean would find Corteggiani again.* Corteggiani would also be used again, notably, on Jacques Becker's *Casque d'or.*[56]

On August 28, 1937, the arrival at the Tuileries castle of the federate battalions was reenacted in Fontainebleau, with the help of two to three thousand members of the CGT (the French Trade Union) who'd been enlisted as unpaid extras.

> All over the place, the representatives of the CGT keep their eyes on their men. Because the crowd that is there can be divided into two categories: professional, paid extras, who are all members of the CGT and who come to work every day. They're wearing costumes. But since it's Saturday, there are also volunteer extras who have come "to work for free," after seeing the invitation that appeared in the Party's newspapers. Taking advantage of their day off on Saturday, granted them by the five-day/eight-hour ruling, more than two thousand workers left Paris at seven in the morning and were brought in by special trains to collaborate free of charge on the making of "their film."[57]

Exterior shots went on in Paris in the streets bordering the Panthéon, where the arrival of the Marseillais battalions would be filmed. The scenes with the émigrés were shot near Colmar; the march of the battalion, in Antibes and Tain-l'Hermitage. Then, filming finally moved into the Boulogne studios. There, the most important scenery that had been made represented the dungeons of Fort Saint-Nicolas in Marseille and interiors at the Tuileries.

According to Marc Maurette, who was one of the assistant directors, Jacques Becker directed several of the exterior scenes in Alsace by himself as well as the most important scenes taking place on the route the Marseillais followed on their way up the Rhône Valley. The notion fed certain unfounded rumors that began to circulate in the fifties, according to which Renoir's scenes—the most beautiful,

---

* Corteggiani had written Renoir on November 5, 1947. (Jean Renoir Papers, Correspondence, Box 8, Folder 4.)

whenever possible—had really been filmed by Becker. Marguerite would state that Becker brought in "almost as much footage for the exteriors as Jean Renoir used for the entire film" and explained that Renoir "didn't like repeating the same task twice. He worked a bit like Pagnol did; as long as there was film in the camera he kept the actor in front of it performing. Becker, on the other hand, would work in a more detailed way and shoot things that were eventually cut."[58]

After going back to shooting exteriors in October, Renoir took up his pen again to express his pleasure.

> Down there I was especially happy and had some incredible moments. I experienced the intoxication brought about by work accomplished in common. I even attained that summit of human joy that stems from knowing you've managed to communicate directly with the hearts and brains of some collaborators. It was as if the curtain of flesh separating us from others had suddenly been lifted. The barriers of habit and ego-ism fell, and you achieved (but only for a few seconds) the miracle of direct communication, the miracle that all human progress reaches for, the reason for which people have created speed, invented complicated machines, penetrated the skies, and projected their words through the air in the form of waves.[59]

So ... was the rapture of communal work that had transported him to a state of lyricism all that was needed to make him sing the praises of that very progress he would dub (not only now but also in the future) absolutely appalling? It was more a question of keeping the fire burning beneath the pot if he wanted mil-itants, readers, and audiences on the day the film came out to bubble over with excitement. In this case, Renoir stuck to the score, and he performed it well.

As promoter of the film, Renoir was more interested in exactly how he played that tune. Certainly, *La Marseillaise* had its own way of seeming to be a cautious-enough film, shining its good-natured light on a Revolution carried out by decent people, whose adversaries also had their reasons, which were sometimes as worthy as those of others, and who had reluctantly decided to spill blood only when forced. Renoir was a long way from that meeting in Salle Huyghens where he'd announced, "When it comes to a revolution, it's very dan-gerous not to massacre."[60] And he was also a long way from the conclusion of the speech he gave that same evening: claiming to have seen audience members in a movie theater on the Champs-Élysées standing to give outstretched-arm salutes when Hitler appeared on-screen during a weekly newsreel, he beamingly ended his talk with: "If I'd had a machine gun, I would have fired into the lot!"[61]

The remark released a frenzy of enthusiasm. Such declarations were far from characteristic of him; they'd come out of his mouth in the heat of a meeting, kindled by the crowd, when an evaluation of the consensus showed it corresponded to his and coincided with the ambition of the film's promoters, who were concerned with giving the revolutionaries of the past an image that would allow today's to pursue their struggle without bringing any new enemies out of the woodwork. The people of those times, Renoir claimed back then, "are people we'd like to be friends with."[62]

For Pascal Ory, this was "the key phrase for a cultural world that wants to believe too much in fraternization to keep from seeing artistic creation as any politicizing of fraternity."[63] Ory also thought it right to remark, "Blood flows, and not very much of it, may I add; but it's above all foreign blood. We're talking about the Swiss, about mercenaries, who had, moreover, a strong Alemannic* accent. Essentially, these are the last defenders of the monarchy." But the historian leaves out one fundamental aspect in dealing with the subject of *La Marseillaise:* the time that passed between the beginning of the project and its completion.

If the Revolution shown by *La Marseillaise* lacks any feature suggesting a civil war, it's partly because the spectrum of confrontation between the citizens of France was perturbed by the enemies of the Popular Front. François Truffaut's contention, "[Renoir] is above the fray. He is *giving a report,* and in the end *La Marseillaise* resembles a montage of news items about the French Revolution,"[64] is less a coherent view than the result of an emphasis on voluntarism.

Obviously, an interplay set in motion with "everyone has his reasons" by a film on the French Revolution has little to gain. In the end, what *La Marseillaise* presents could be summed up as a struggle between pleasant people who are merely set against each other by their birth: some were born poor and aren't happy about it, and others were born with a silver spoon in their mouth and can't do anything about it. The reasons of the former are therefore no more laudatory than those of the latter, a situation that is not exactly "revolutionary."

In this aspect as well, *La Marseillaise* is redolent of the spirit of Renoir, whose aristocrats in the film are the ancestors of Rauffenstein and Boëldieu from *Grand Illusion,* left behind by the changes of the time and, for that reason as well, loved by Renoir. Despite this attraction, the film does not hint at any enthrallment with the Ancien Régime. If so, it is certainly of a different nature than that expressed by François Truffaut in his review of the Sacha Guitry film *Si Versailles m'était conté* (*Royal Affairs in Versailles*), in which he identifies "Christian sentiment and a sense of honor, respect for the clergy, and the nobility" as

* *Translator's note: Alemannic* is a family of High German dialects spoken in Alsace, Switzerland, and Germany.

the "keystone of a soundly hierarchical society" that has contributed "for several centuries to the grandeur of France."[65]

The march of time had had just as considerable an effect on the nature of the film as did Renoir's personal inclinations. More than a year had passed between the Party's decision to produce *La Marseillaise* and the film's showing in movie theaters. This was quite a reasonable length of time, especially given the extent of the project. However, the France of January 1938 was not the France of December 1936. During the time between, the stakes had changed.

On June 22, 1937, Léon Blum, who had announced "a hiatus in reforms" in February, presented his resignation after two rounds of Senate votes refused to give him the exceptional financial powers that the Assembly had granted him. Camille Chautemps was selected to replace him. His government would be immobilized while the crisis worsened. The Popular Front remained in power, but the coalition that composed it was gradually disintegrating toward its last breath. For the Communists, the only remedy was handing the baton to Maurice Thorez. While presenting a report of the Party's activities on December 26, "the beloved leader" responded to Mussolini's prophecy that "tomorrow, Europe will be Fascist": "No, Europe will not be Fascist! The democracy of 1789 will triumph!"[66] Democracy, not the Revolution. In *La Marseillaise*, Robespierre certainly had no place.

The wave of enthusiasm that had boosted the project in spring 1937 had definitely begun to ebb, and the militants balked at donating their share, but still the film was made, essentially by committed crewmembers and actors, who had lived together for several weeks more or less cut off from the outside world. As soon as the adventure came to a close, each of them had discovered that the deal had changed. Some of their impassioned evocations of the most glorious story in the world had been drowned in an unbridled search for consensus on the part of the film's promoters, with the director at their head.

In February 1938, audiences were waiting to see the new film of Louis Jouvet, on whom the media was at first concentrating to a much larger extent than on Renoir. Little was said about Renoir in the press until just a few days before the release of *La Marseillaise*. What is more, the publicity for this film was a matter of debate, and it worried the director to see its identity as a "historical film" emphasized.

In a January 31, 1938, letter to Jean Rollmer, who was Frank's son and who worked for his company, Renoir wrote,

> During several meetings with your publicity people, I thought it necessary to stress to those responsible the fact that audiences hate films dubbed "historical," and that any advertising tending to promote the

belief that *La Marseillaise* could be put in that category is advertising I consider to be harmful to the interests of this film. Since the end of shooting, in all my interviews and the various articles I have published, I have constantly defended that point of view. And yet, the very large number of posters I've been seeing today on the walls of Paris reinforce, in my opinion, the idea that *La Marseillaise* will be, as it is termed, a great panorama of history, meaning, in other words, that it will be part of a genre that audiences justly detest.[67]

In defense of RAC's publicity services, however, the Party was really the entity that had been announcing the film in that manner for months. And that was truly the way the film was being viewed, as much by audiences, which it could only very much disappoint, as by the press, which to a large extent was considering it through the prism of political positions.

At nine on the evening of the premiere on February 9, not at the Opéra, as had been planned, but at the Olympia, which had recently been remodeled and which was being advertised as "the most beautiful theater in Europe," the director, wearing a sports jacket and turtleneck, posed for photographers. His friends wanted to see this clothing choice as a mark of independence from convention, a tremendously "proletarian" gesture of superb aloofness. The truth was that only a well-born person who was sure of himself could attempt such an infringement of contemporary codes and do it with a confidence vastly enhanced by knowing he was the center of the event.

The day after the general release of the film on February 10, boxed advertisements in the media trumpeted "An indescribable success."[68] In actuality, it was nothing of the sort. To some, the film seemed biased; to others, its convictions seemed far from assured and were ill-assumed. More than anything, it was too late in coming. The right-wing press flew into a rage, and the left-wing newspapers did a poor job of hiding their lack of enthusiasm behind the expected praise. The most enthusiastic were also the promoters of the film, headed by Aragon. *L'Humanité* and other Party newspapers devoted full columns to preach to the converted, who had other things to worry about and who were more apt to turn to distractions that had no bearing on the situation of the moment.

The timing for *La Marseillaise* was off, and no one could do anything about it. The final proof of this was what film magazines wrote about it—because they were a priori the least subject to partisan influences. Their reviews did not conceal the disappointment they felt about this film by the great director Jean Renoir in the wake of *Grand Illusion*. They paid tribute to Pierre Renoir's performance as Louis XVI, deploring as they did the too minor nature of Louis Jouvet's role; and then, quite often, they allowed themselves to be swept into the vortex of partisan opinions. Accordingly, Serge Veber wrote in *Pour vous*, "Jean

Renoir comes out in no way diminished from this bold adventure," which was a way of making it understood, at the very least, that he'd made a narrow escape. And he concluded, "Too bad that one of the composers of the score for this *Marseillaise* is a German."[69] No kidding.

Having judged it appropriate to make a similar remark, Henri Jeanson then received a letter from composer Vladimir Kosma informing him that he was Hungarian, not German. The screenwriter didn't miss a chance to rant against the film on which he was supposed to have participated and showed particular inspiration to that effect in an article entitled "*La Marseillaise* or the Treachery of Stalin," speaking of a "silent*" and "deadly boring" film by a certain Jean Renoir who was "a prisoner of Moscow," before concluding that "*La Marseillaise* is a victory of Communism over film. A Pyrrhic victory."[70]

Another of the rejected screenwriters, Marcel Achard, restrained his pen, and the review he wrote for *Marianne* was measured. He lamented the fact that the characters didn't speak using Marcel Pagnol's words (or his own, maybe), touched on the fact that he thought the film was a "sad, regrettable vindication of the mad instincts of human beings," but nevertheless admitted that "some of the images are magnificent and equal to those in *Battleship Potemkin*." Finally, he expressed his pleasure that *La Marseillaise*, which, "because of its driving force and Jean Renoir's talent could have been a danger to the public and perhaps become the occasion for fights in the street by setting one French person against another," was "also a boring film."[71] The immediate consequence of the article lost the author his column in the pages of the weekly.

Pierre Brisson was at the time one of the few who stood up against that decision, which directly implicated the very function of criticism. "Before talking about art, know where the artist comes from, what his allegiances are, his leanings and his political patronages. If not, watch out! If such incredible customs spread, they'll quickly spell the ruin of the last vestiges of French democracy. Punishing Marcel Achard for too much precision! . . . Now I've seen everything!"[72]

In that same column, Brisson included a rather lukewarm review of Marcel Achard's new play, *Le Corsaire,* which takes place in a Hollywood studio and had been directed by Louis Jouvet at the Athénée. Pierre Renoir had been intended to play the role of Cristobal, alias One-Eye, and had been rehearsing it for several weeks; but the day after the review of *La Marseillaise* appeared in *Marianne,* the actor dropped out of the role, which was then given to Alexandre Rignault. "None of my articles caused me as many problems," Marcel Achard

---

* *Translator's note:* Jeanson is playing on the term for a "silent film" while also suggesting that the film had nothing whatsoever to say.

would write to Claude Gauteur in 1972.

In Renoir's eyes, the primary responsibility for the failure of *La Marseillaise* belonged to the right-wing press, whereas the distributor turned out to be "incapable of defending" the film, which had been "violently attacked" for motives that lay somewhere between the distributor's "ill will and chickening out."[73] Or at least that is what he announced but probably did not think. For some time yet, he'd remain faithful to his fellow travelers, continuing to serve them with his important public image and his inflammatory declarations. But his head was already elsewhere.

19

"Le P'tit Coeur de Ninon"

La Bête humaine

How could Jean Renoir not be elsewhere in 1938, as his newfound fame resounded throughout the entire world? From then on, when people looked at his calling card, it wasn't so much the name *Renoir* they saw but the title of a film: *Grand Illusion*. From the Soviet East to the great film studios of California, his reputation had grown to unheard-of proportions—at least for a French director. For the period from autumn 1937 to fall 1938, he could count the making and releasing of *La Marseillaise,* the preparation and filming of *La Bête humaine,* and his participation in Joris Ivens's *The Spanish Earth,* not to mention the appearance in Moscow of the first book ever devoted entirely to him, an offer coming from Hollywood, the emergence in France of a rival, and, as a start, the banning of *Grand Illusion* in European dictatorships.

Presented at the Venice Film Festival in August 1937 through the efforts of Minister Jean Zay, the film received "the international jury's award for Best Overall Artistic Contribution." According to Philippe Erlanger, "Hitler and Goebbels were visibly irritated by this. They could not accept the fact that Renoir had shown a German guard refraining from firing on a French prisoner as he was escaping."[1] A favorite in the competition for the Mussolini Cup, the top prize, the film was outflanked in the category of Best Foreign Film by another French production, Julien Duvivier's *Un carnet de bal* (*Dance Program*). Sacha Guitry and Christian-Jaque's *Les Perles de la couronne* (*The Pearls of the Crown*) received the prize for Best Foreign Screenplay. Renoir's award was a consolation prize, which had actually been created for this occasion, something Renoir would pretend to find amusing, attributing it to the "heartthrob" of "a princess" on the jury who'd liked the film.[2] What the director meant isn't easy to decode, but there's very little doubt that he wasn't thrilled seeing himself beaten in a competition by his principal French rival; and he made no attempt to keep from expressing how indifferent Duvivier's film left him: "*Dance Program*? Didn't see it. I wasn't exactly tempted by that story about a woman looking for her former lovers."[3]

Mussolini's government banned *Grand Illusion* in Italy.* A few weeks before, the same decision had been made in Germany; and as it was, Joseph Goebbels is said to have graced the film with the enviable title of "Germany's number one enemy." Recalling these measures in his column for *Ce soir*, Renoir stated that, in contrast to the way the ban had transpired in Italy, the issue had been an object of debate in Germany, in the course of which Goering, who had himself been an ace pilot in the First World War, came out in favor of the film.† It was a remark that would lead to a Portuguese journalist's writing in December 1940 that Erich von Stroheim's performance was the one that had especially "moved and aroused the sincere enthusiasm"[4] of the Reich marshal, who'd been impressed particularly by its "humanity," a quality Goering had already revealed as one of his own cardinal virtues. The film was also banned in Austria after the Anschluss and would also be prohibited in Hungary and Japan.

La Marseillaise, which was also banned in Germany and Austria, was an unequivocal success in the Soviet Union. Although it's impossible to verify, the claim was that seven million people went to see it in Moscow movie theaters over a period of two weeks, and there were supposedly 250 prints in circulation in the country. Renoir's first monograph, a book by the critic and historian Georgy Alexandrovich Avenarius (1903–1958), which appeared in fall 1938, devoted a number of its some seventy pages to the film. In the book, "the realist approach that was used to represent revolutionary events" was considered "unique and unusual for the film genre, which is as a rule profoundly bourgeois, reactionary, degenerate, and hypocritical"; not to mention that "its financing marks a break with the usual commercial practices of the producers/wholesalers of film," because the film had been made "without the participation of capitalist enterprises, relying upon the resources that came by way of hundreds of thousands of subscriptions from French workers." The book then retraced in broad lines Renoir's career; it says he began as a "painter/artist" and moved from avant-garde investigations to "realist" cinema: "During the years leading up to the victory of the Popular Front, Renoir directed a series of realist films whose artistic and political quality place him among the foremost directors in the world."[5] The text is peppered

---

* Or at least that's what Renoir claimed. During his stay in Rome in 1940, it would seem that the issue wasn't actually as cut-and-dried as he'd claimed.

† Perhaps it was his memory of the field marshal's alleged support for *Grand Illusion* that led to the lines in Renoir's play *Carola*, written at the end of the fifties, when Carola tells the German general von Clodius, "I telephoned Berlin. The Führer is on the Eastern Front. I spoke to Goering, who got in contact with the Gestapo. He is terribly sorry about all the problems these blunderers have caused you. He loves the theater and asked me to be sure to tell you that he's one of your admirers."

with citations. Those attributed to Renoir aren't referenced, unlike those coming from Lenin or Stalin.

Although Renoir's rhetoric—and, to a lesser degree, thinking—remained influenced by Communism, he was also dreaming of America, or rather, the American world of film. The offer he received from Samuel Goldwyn at the beginning of 1938 to come and work in Hollywood had only confirmed the validity of his point of view. *Grand Illusion* would not be shown in the United States before September 12, 1938. On October 11, 1938, it would become the first foreign film to be shown at the White House, for Eleanor Roosevelt's forty-fourth birthday. However, by that time, its success and notoriety in Europe had already attracted Goldwyn's attention. Renoir declined Goldwyn's offer, giving as an excuse his "ties with M. Albert Pinkovitch," for whom, he said, "I am also going to begin a film any minute now."[6]

During the release of *La Marseillaise*, "M. Albert" was in New York trying to find some contacts for an English adaptation of *Grand Illusion*. Two days before turning down Goldwyn's offer, Renoir had written to Frank Rollmer, mostly to inform him that Pinkovitch had just telegrammed to ask him to "think of a less extensive project, a drama or comedy," instead of that "seagoing adventure"* he was considering as an excuse for "a screenplay that could serve the cause of peace." "I suppose," he then explained, "that the reason for this change of program has to do with the turn his negotiations in America have taken."[7] There's nothing that confirms the fact that the project had been scheduled to be directed in the United States, but Pinkovitch and Renoir were at the very least thinking about a production financed in part by American capital.

The rumor of Renoir's "American temptation" had already received enough attention for Louis Aragon to choose it as the subject of his September 16, 1937, column: "Jean Renoir . . . asked me to correct some news about him that has appeared in the papers. It's true that, as a result of an agreement with a French film company, he'll go to Hollywood to oversee the direction of the English-language version of *Grand Illusion*. But he won't stay there, and he hasn't been hired there. And that's a fact. We won't lose Renoir."[8] Aragon would soon lose Renoir, but to a place that no one at the time could have foreseen.

These various facts confirm that after the success of *Grand Illusion*, the director had already been thinking of moving in a direction that his repeated statements about the profoundly "national" character of film couldn't in any way have suggested. In fact, at the same moment that Aragon was assuring the public of the director's commitment to France, Renoir himself was writing in a column

---

* Probably *Les Sauveteurs*, a project registered on January 8, 1938, with the Association des auteurs de films.

entitled "Speaking French": "Allow me to finish these few lines with an appeal to our great comrades who have become disgusted with the situation here and gone elsewhere to work. René Clair in England, Feyder in Germany, Duvivier in America. Have they found what they were looking for over there? I doubt it. If possible, I hope they'll come back to us. French film needs them."[9] Those lines can be understood in a different way: why had the careers of the three most prestigious French directors acquired international proportions, whereas Jean Renoir, who'd already been working for ten or so years, and who'd achieved a stunning, celebrated success in the eyes of all, still remained exclusively French?

A few months after that appeal to his "great comrades," the same Renoir would announce what he again called a personal choice and would tell his other "comrades" what they were hoping to hear, disguising his frustration in the trappings of a profession of faith: "What I do know is that I've now begun to understand how you should work. I know that I'm French and that I have to work with a perspective that is absolutely national. But I also know that in doing so, and only in doing so, will I be able to reach the people of other nations and accomplish the endeavor of internationalism."[10] By purposely confusing the causes and the effects, Renoir was obscuring the issue. He was making the best of a bad situation and would continue to operate his shell game in that way until fall 1940. And the ways in which he reoriented the most intimate elements of his personal life would be partly influenced by his desire to point his career in a new direction.

For the time being, Renoir remained "the" director of the Popular Front, or what was left of it. And when Ciné-Liberté decided to distribute *The Spanish Earth*, quite naturally he became the one who was in charge of adapting the Joris Ivens film for French audiences, while writing a commentary that he himself would speak.

Ivens, who was Dutch but who was currently in New York, had originally planned to codirect a film with the editor Helen van Dongen that would be composed of visual archival documents about the Spanish Civil War. When they became aware that most of the images available had been filmed by Franco supporters, the Dutch director decided to go to Spain with the project and then return with a film likely to arouse American consciences to the tragedy taking place in the Spanish Republic. On his way through Paris in January 1937, before boarding a plane for Valencia where the Spanish government had been established, Ivens met various figures, the most important of whom was Luis Buñuel, who at the time represented the Spanish minister of information. He also eventually met Vladimir Pozner, Jacques Prévert, and Renoir.

After four weeks of filming in Spain, he returned to Paris to view the images he'd captured and also showed them to some of the people he'd met in January, probably including Jean-Paul Dreyfus (Le Chanois) and Pierre Unik. During the same stay in Paris, Ivens had several encounters with Ernest Hemingway, who was about to leave for Spain and to whom Ivens tried to make it clear that the war Hemingway was still seeing through rose-colored glasses was in fact a first experiment in Fascism whose inaugural battlefield would be on European soil.[11] Two weeks later, they were in Madrid, and the writer would be in charge of the English-language commentary. According to the director, it was Renoir who expressed his desire to write the French commentary once the film had been finished.

The Spanish Earth came to Paris in April 1938. At the Studio de l'Étoile, the film played on a double bill with Raoul Walsh's *Hitting a New High,* with Lily Pons playing Suzette, a.k.a. Oogahunga the Bird-Girl, who sings arias from *Lucia di Lammermoor, Mignon,* and *Lakmé.* It was an unusual program; but the poster for it was just as surprising, presenting as it did not only direction by Joris Ivens and French commentary by Jean Renoir but also "a report by HEMING WAY [*sic*]." It highlighted a rather unknown figure, mangling his name in the process, and about whom viewers would discover very little because he had contributed nothing to the film other than his very distinguished writing and reading of its commentary in English. This same commentary had originally been recorded by Orson Welles before the diction and vocal tones of the future director were bypassed in favor of the writer's.

As logically would be expected, the right-wing press wrung their hands over Renoir's spoken text as containing "nothing objective."[12] It hadn't been intended as such. *The Spanish Earth* was openly presented as a combat film, a series of often magnificent images that established a parallel between peasants' attempts to farm the arid earth and the war being waged by the Republicans. To the same extent that the commentary of Hemingway, who was personally involved in the armed struggle in Spain, stuck to the facts—achieving a kind of grandeur by its very sobriety—Renoir's seemed detached from the situations being described. It was the director of *Toni* speaking in the lingo of the Communist Party, lauding the "highly primitive" nature of the bread ovens that were "sublimely smoking" as they cooked their "bread of excellent quality." It was the columnist for *Ce soir* describing peasants whose natural impetus is being shackled by "their masters entrenched behind their prejudices and held back by their egotistical sloth"; but now these peasants were being liberated by the Republicans, who "are going to be able to pour the life-giving water into their fallow land that will transform them."

Ivens showed his irritation with this French version, which he didn't discover until 1939: "I appreciated the fact that a great director like Renoir was willing to do something for us and for Spain; but unfortunately, as a director he hadn't understood the value of the images and he talked the entire time. What he said was what the audience was supposed to think as a result of the scenes shown on the screen. Actually, he doubled the imagery with the text and covered with music silences that have great artistic value. I don't like this commentary: it suffocates the film. His goodwill made him too talkative." There's no question about Renoir's goodwill, nor is there any doubt that he showed it with a pronounced tendency to talk too much; but it's equally the case that such a genre of documentary had never "spoken" to him, and that's the precise reason why he spoke too much. Ivens claimed that he had told Renoir, "In my film, there is a dialectical relationship between what is said and what is seen. You approached it from the perspective of fiction, not documentary."[13]

Their difference in perspective would not prevent Renoir from presenting Ivens's Chinese film, *The 400 Million*, to a Parisian audience for a gala organized by the Party at Salle Pleyel on July 8, 1939. Just the same, sixty years later, it would be the cause of an unwarranted attack against Renoir that blamed him not only for having misrepresented *The Spanish Earth* but also for having "mutilated" it, a word employed by historian Kees Bakker in 1999 in calling what Renoir did "the most infamous mutilation."[14] Behind such a charge was the fact that the length of the French version of the film is about twelve minutes shorter than the original American version. And yet, as Ivens himself told it, the copy on which Renoir worked came from Great Britain, where the censor had removed approximately six minutes (out of fifty-five).

Rather than assume that Renoir "mutilated" *The Spanish Earth*, which appears to be a fantasy, it makes sense to think that French censorship, which was very active at the time, also altered the work. The passages sacrificed had to do with the direct implication of Nazi Germany and Fascist Italy for their significant support of Franco, something that was revealed in no uncertain terms in the American version, which was shown for the first time in London in the presence of Joachim von Ribbentrop, then the German ambassador and the man about to become the minister of foreign affairs for the Reich.

Renoir himself had never stopped attacking both Hitler and Mussolini, mostly in his articles for *Ce soir;* and the pair were indicted daily in *L'Humanité* for the role their troops played and the weapons they supplied to Spain. The Communist Party certainly in no way could have influenced Renoir to "mutilate" a work so in agreement with the position of its "comrades" and of Renoir at a moment when the position regarding Spain of the Popular Front's government, like those of the other European democracies, was becoming more unsustainable every day. In her excellent study of the subject, Catherine Vialles correctly writes,

If you compare the two posters for the film, you notice a certain semantic shift: the American version shows an enormous fist risen in the center and in the background three Junkers swooping toward the ground. The French version shows bare earth. In the foreground a horse is pulling a very crude plow pushed by a peasant, and in the distance is a tumbledown hovel. It's probable that the shift was made to quiet the suspicions of censors, but that's not the only reason. *The Spanish Earth* isn't in this case being presented as an evocation of Spain at war, but rather as the daily struggle of the peasants against the aridity of their land and their condition.[15]

Renoir's commentary is obviously in line with the meaning indicated by the French poster. But wasn't the poster decided upon and designed after Renoir provided his commentary? Between the cuts imposed by the British censors and probably the French as well, and Renoir's personal orientation, *The Spanish Earth* obviously lost some of its impact and some of its urgency. But the director certainly did not "mutilate" his colleague's work. In 1975, Ivens decided to record a new French commentary meant to permanently replace Renoir's.*

By spring 1938, the director of *Grand Illusion* was wanted by everyone. While he continued to host screenings at Ciné-Liberté, an organization where he still held the title of secretary, he was also being invited to sit on the greatest variety of juries. For example, with Marcel Achard, André Maurois, Marc Allégret, and G. W. Pabst, he participated in the June 18 competition at the Théâtre Pigalle for the students of Raymond Rouleau and Julien Bertheau. Meanwhile, he was also being requested to exercise his judgment in areas that had very little to do with his art. Along with Marcel Cachin, Francis Jourdain, and the critic and film historian Léon Moussinac, among others, he was asked to sit on a jury to choose among plans for a monument in memory of the former editor-in-chief of *L'Humanité*, Paul Vaillant-Couturier, who had died in 1937. The monument would be erected in the city of Villejuif, where Vaillant-Couturier had served as mayor. The jury rejected, interestingly enough, the plan presented by Le Corbusier.[†]

During the second half of the thirties, no other director, and very few artists, were as visible to the society of that period as Renoir was. The contrast would only become more dramatic in comparison to the life he would eventually lead. Renoir adored giving more and more of himself, wanted to be everywhere at the same time, to talk with each and every one. Not averse either to pontificating,

* To date, no integral version of Renoir's commentary has ever been shown.

† In 1922, Pierre Gaut commissioned Le Corbusier to create a plan for his house on square de Monstouris and also rejected one of the architect's ideas, piquing Le Corbusier's anger and provoking his split with Auguste Perret, whom Gaut had preferred.

he also had trouble resisting puns—even mediocre ones—and jokes, including those that were questionable, counting on the sense of humor of conversationalists or listeners who weren't all that adept at such an art. For example, without the slightest expression of humor on his face he claimed during a debate that film's makeup artists had to be incredible geniuses, given the fact that Shirley Temple, who was ten years old, and the great British actress Dame May Whitty, who'd already seen her seventy-second birthday, were actually the same person made to look younger or older on request.[16] At times someone in the room took him seriously and misreported the joke, helping to concoct a far-from-enviable reputation for the director.

On May 17, 1938, Marcel Carné's *Port of Shadows*, with a screenplay and dialogue by Jacques Prévert, was released in Paris. Audiences went crazy for the film, which was awarded the Prix Louis-Delluc at the end of that year, joining a list of winners that already included *The Lower Depths* in 1936 and Jeff Musso's *Le Puritain* (*The Puritan*), which had received the prize in 1937 after *Grand Illusion* had been classified as out of the competition. At times, it's in the nature of film to bring together extremes on either end of the political spectrum. *Port of Shadows* was attacked by both the Communists and the most hard-line members of the Right for reasons that were remarkably similar. Whereas the critic at *Je suis partout* denounced the work as "morose and spineless" and called it "debased naturalism," Georges Sadoul exploded:

> This has gone beyond any portrait of society; it's a police roundup. And the worst thing about it is the fact that the director (or at least his dialogue writer, Jacques Prévert) obviously has the greatest sympathy for his characters, whom he considers to be genuine heroes. Nevertheless, it shouldn't be forgotten that recruited from such social categories are no real heroes of the people but the henchmen of a Doriot, a Carbone, a Sabiani, the killers of the CSAR,* arms and drug traffickers, and the men of the Tercio, which the author of the novel *Quai des Brumes* [Pierre Mac Orlan] glorified in another of his books, *La Bandera*, dedicated to General Franco.

Demonstrating as a case in point an honesty rare among his colleagues, this same critic and Communist historian would later castigate himself on several occasions for his attacks against *Port of Shadows*, considering them unfounded.

---

* *Translator's note:* CSAR, Comité secret d'action révolutionnaire, dubbed "*La Cagoule*" ("The Hood") by its enemies, was a tiny middle-class radical terrorist group on the Right that existed in secrecy in France from 1936 to 1937. It was responsible for several murders of left-wing supporters.

However, in 1938, he also ended up maintaining that the "entire breadth" of Renoir's "good giant's shoulders tower above the new French school of realism" and that he "alone is worthy of praise. Duvivier, Carné, for example, confuse the people too much with the lumpenproletariat and the steelworker with the ruffian . . . A realist like the great Gorky was right in depicting *The Lower Depths* (as was Renoir after him). But it's important for a realist not to confine himself exclusively to the description of a broken-down class or the remnant of a class." On the other hand, he wrote, "Renoir's art is great, and it is significant, because he does not merely study human beings in their psychological individuality but also in their relationships to a specific group, to a social category, to a class."[17] In the eyes of the Party, Prévert was a renegade, maybe even a Trotskyite; and those with whom he worked found themselves discredited as a result.

Renoir jumped into the debate, too. When asked what he thought of *Port of Shadows,* he answered, "After having seen this film, I'm surprised I never raped my grandmother and my little sister. The French Revolution taught us that man was good."[18] It was a very silly thing to say and fit right in to the groove being dug by the "comrades." Fortunately, Renoir also knew how to be funny; he nicknamed *Port of Shadows* "*le cul des brêmes.*"* Unfortunately, he didn't stop there, and anyone who wished to listen was also told that the film was "Fascist." When Prévert took the bait and threatened Renoir with a thrashing if he didn't stop, Renoir responded, "You know how I am. I merely wanted to say that the characters were Fascist to the core."[19] Fascist to the core? In his memoirs, Carné puts a different remark into Renoir's mouth: "I wanted to say that the characters should have been beaten with sticks by Fascists."[20] Orthographically in French, the difference between the two remarks was fairly subtle: Renoir's use of the word *tripe* in the first version, which accused the characters themselves of being Fascist; and the use of *trique,* in the second version, referring to a beating by Fascists. Which word did Renoir say, *tripe* or *trique*?† He used the word *Fascist,* in any case. Proof that no matter what he happened to say, Renoir would position himself in the line of thinking and language of his political friends.

Actually, Renoir had another, more personal reason to resent *Port of Shadows* and Marcel Carné. The film was described by the press and—most aggravating from his point of view—audiences as signaling the birth of a new kind of cinema that differed from the output of French productions up to that time. Whether true or false, it didn't really matter in this case. The day the film was released, Carné, who claimed to have been born August 18, 1909 (although

* *Translator's note: Brême* means "bream," a type of freshwater fish; so the term translates loosely as "the fish's ass."

† *Translator's note:* "Les personnages avaient la *tripe* fasciste" versus "les personnages appelaient la *trique* fasciste."

the true year was 1906), was able to pass for being under thirty, and Prévert was only thirty-eight, their ages thereby seconding the impression that it was time for a changing of the guard and that the new cinema was already worthy of the highest praise. Renoir was around fourteen years older than Carné; and when he wasn't being referred to as "the Old Man," they were calling him "Fatty." Carné had a nickname as well, "The Kid."* Between Fatty and The Kid, it wasn't a fair fight. To understand this, for once it's enough not to neglect a cardinal principle about the basis of creative personalities: their oversized ego. And this was even more true for a director who had just achieved success after years of work and struggle than it was for all others.

Finally, Marcel Carné was homosexual. This might not have been written about at the time, but it was known, mentioned, and ridiculed. In French society of that period, homosexuals were distrusted. The situation was the same within the Party, where people often appeared to be more prudish than elsewhere. There's no indication that Renoir nourished any homophobic feelings, even if it's true that in some of his columns he grouped together those he claimed were identifiable at first glance as "defrocked priests, homosexuals, drug addicts, and teetotalers,"[21] placing those who were sometimes called inverts in those days in company that was far from flattering in his eyes. Although the presence of caricatured figures like the one in *The Rules of the Game* cannot be used as unconditional proof, there's still no doubt that for Renoir homophobia was the same as it was for most heterosexuals of his time: a vector for expressing revulsion.

An example of this attitude comes from Brunius, who had played one of the two seducers in *A Day in the Country*, had served as Renoir's assistant on several occasions, and had dubbed *The Blood of a Poet* "the menses of a poet," when he expressed concern about having to experience the future output of "the menopause of the *cinéraste*"[†22] Jean Cocteau. Considered in that particular context, Renoir's jibe about the "*cul des brêmes*" can suddenly and rightfully seem less amusing, but that doesn't keep it from appearing innocuous. As a political adversary, or at least considered as such because of his closeness to Prévert, and as a rival for fame, as well as a newcomer and a homosexual, Carné in Renoir's eyes had not a chance.

As The Kid was waiting to work again with Prévert and Gabin on *Le jour se lève* and was about to use Henri Jeanson's dialogue for Arletty and Jouvet in

---

* *Translator's note:* In French, the word was "*le Môme.*"

† *Translator's note: Cinéraste* is Brunius's play on words created by an amalgam of *cinéaste*, the French word for director, and *pédéraste*, the French word for homosexual.

Hôtel du Nord, Fatty had come upon a way to quickly acquire a project. From the perspective of time, it is now clear that it was the next step in a type of composition begun with *The Crime of Monsieur Lange.* At the same time, it represented something else: an unlocked port of entry into a film that was to become his most personal. As chance would have it, this would also be Renoir's second confrontation with the work of Zola, after the adaptation of *Nana* that had marked his beginnings as a "professional" director. Another coincidence was that the film he would make based on *La Bête humaine* was initially supposed to be drawn from a screenplay by Roger Martin du Gard. Martin du Gard had been asked to write the screenplay for *La Bête humaine* in 1933 after just abandoning an adaptation of *Madame Bovary* for Jacques Feyder, before that project became Renoir's. To understand this completely, however, the clock must be turned back several years.

In 1933, a young Marc Allégret—who had begun his career in film with Pierre Braunberger and Roger Richebé—was thinking of directing two adaptations: one based on Vicki Baum's *Lac aux dames* (*Ladies Lake*) and the other on Zola's *La Bête humaine.* Backing for these projects came from Philippe de Rothschild through the influence of Allégret's supporters, André Gide and Roger Martin du Gard. In March, Martin du Gard had tried his hand at adapting Zola's *La Bête humaine* and had delivered the product in July: a screenplay weighing nearly nine pounds. Never again, he swore, would he try to write for the cinema. Eleven months after that, Philippe de Rothschild abandoned plans to produce the film and sold the screenplay to an interested Marcel L'Herbier, before Allégret, who in the meantime had directed *Ladies Lake,* could get back the rights.

This was followed by articles appearing in the press claiming that "Marc Allégret had wanted to direct *La Bête humaine* for months,"[23] but the project would stay packed away until an old acquaintance of Renoir came on the scene: Denise Batcheff, the only editor who'd appeared in the credits for *La Chienne,* and who in the meantime had become Denise Tual. She was also the editor for *Ladies Lake* and was the head of Synops, a film-rights agency she'd created with Gaston Gallimard. In 1937, with Tual acting loosely as broker, the agency helped negotiate a contract between Jean Grémillon and Jean Gabin for a project called *Train d'enfer,* from which Gabin was to realize one of his dreams—driving a locomotive.* Then *Train d'enfer* became the possession of the brothers Robert and Raymond Hakim; and when Grémillon was unable to get along with them, he quit the project and the producers offered it to Marcel Carné. Carné turned

* The project was announced in *La Cinématographie française* on June 3, 1938. To prepare for the role, Jean Gabin drove a locomotive along the Paris–Le Havre line several times, accompanied by Charles Blavette, who had played Toni in Renoir's film.

it down, unwilling to harm Grémillon, and suggested that an adaptation of *La Bête humaine* would also give Gabin an opportunity to operate a locomotive.

The fact that Carné became involved in such a way, as he claims in his memoirs, has not been in any other way established; and his thinking of Zola's novel as a way of giving Gabin the role of locomotive engineer he so coveted had nothing to do with any stroke of inspiration. In addition, because Martin du Gard's adaptation was still the property of Synops, the affair represented a total windfall for them; and it turned into a fairy tale when Raymond Hakim inquired what big American star Carné was imagining in the role of Séverine. The Kid mentioned Simone Simon. The actress, who had been invited to Hollywood following her success in *Ladies Lake,* was none other than the actress that Allégret had wanted to play Séverine.

At the time, Allégret lived in an apartment adjacent to André Gide's.* Gide had created an opening in the wall to make it possible for them to communicate. Gide told Renoir that when he'd awakened one morning he noticed "the smell of a woman" coming from Allégret's room and that he immediately closed up the opening in the wall. The woman whose smell had antagonized the great writer was Simone Simon.[24] Carné, who remains the only one to have shed light upon the role that he is supposed to have played in launching *La Bête humaine,* claims in his memoirs to have been completely unaware at the time of the young actress's bonds with the director and of those that probably existed later between her and Robert Hakim. According to Carné, after he refused this new offer on the grounds that "*La Bête humaine* owes its existence to *Train d'enfer,*" Hakim is supposed to have tried to sway him by shooting back, "If you don't make the film, Renoir will do it instead. . . . He has agreed to it."[25] Gabin was probably the one who'd given Renoir's name to Hakim. It was the case for *La Bête humaine* just as it was for *La Chienne* and most masterpieces: all those who were associated with it in one capacity or another barely interacted except in terms of the energy they spent claiming credit for it.

To direct this new adaptation of a Zola work, Renoir put off the project he'd been considering, *Les Millions d'Arlequin,*† which had been intended to reunite Pierre Renoir, Pierre Fresnay, Yvonne Printemps, Erich von Stroheim, and Louis Jouvet. His description of the genesis of *La Bête humaine,* which seems unusually candid coming from him, may explain why this account remained unpublished. In an undated text, probably written in 1945 or 1946, destination

* The apartment was located at 1 bis rue Vaneau. Pierre Gaut, the producer of *Toni* and Renoir's close friend, would live in the same building.

† Treatments registered on March 24, April 9, and May 9, 1938.

unknown, he confides that after a lecture he'd just given on the subject of *The Crime of Monsieur Lange*, Raymond Hakim approached him to suggest bringing the novel to the screen:

> When I got home, I informed Marguerite about Hakim's proposition. She expressed several doubts about the value of the subject. She'd heard about the novel and knew that it was an important work. But I'd told her so many times that I didn't want to make any more grim dramas that she was taking me at my word and couldn't understand why I would give such a sinister subject the slightest consideration. I spent the night rereading *La Bête humaine*. The next morning, I'd decided to do it. The true reason for that decision was a passion for a young American woman [he means Newmi Dreyfus], who had helped me draft the screenplay for *La Marseillaise*. She made me drop Marguerite, but without consenting to become my mistress. I only got out of that hopeless situation thanks to another love that swept away all my former preoccupations. . . . This American [Newmi] operated exactly like Séverine.[26]

This was the quality that definitively distanced Séverine from the "innocence" with which Renoir would enjoy endowing the character but which every shot in the film would also contradict. At the same time, these lines provide an unembellished account of the deterioration of his relationship with Marguerite. Although he hadn't actually "let go" of his lover—"let go" in the sense of leaving her—the strictures that defined their bond had definitely been "let loose."

As for the real reasons that brought Simone Simon back to France in 1938, they have little to do with film. While she was under contract to Fox, an affair with George Gershwin, whom she'd met in Paris in 1928, was being bandied about by the scandal sheets. It cannot be determined whether the rumor was part of a promotional scheme—an ordinary procedure for Hollywood—or a desire on the part of the composer's circle to dispel certain doubts about his sexual orientation.

However, in 1937, a legal suit brought against Simone Simon by her secretary in Hollywood provoked an investigation that revealed the beautiful French woman had given several of her intimate friends a gold-plated key allowing access to her home. One of these keys, stamped with the initials G. G., had been found among Gershwin's possessions after his death a few months before on July 11. It was time for the actress to disappear from people's minds for a while in Hollywood.

It is an undisputed fact that at the beginning of April 1938, Renoir started working on *La Bête humaine*. On April 14, in fact, he informed the readers of *Ce soir* that the preparations for his "new film" required him to "leave on a trip" and therefore to interrupt his contributions to his columns.[27] According to the terms of a contract dated July 13 between Paris Film Productions and Jean Renoir, he was hired to direct *La Bête humaine* in exchange for a sum of 200,000 francs as well as a percentage of the profits (5 percent, up to a sum of 100,000 francs) and a per diem of 250 francs "contingent on filming in Paris and its regions."[28] Roland Tual, the husband of the former Denise Batcheff, the woman whose role in *La Chienne* had earned her the privilege of being called "the enterprising Madame Batcheff" by Renoir, served as director of production.

Martin du Gard's screenplay was the only element of the undertaking neglected by Renoir. "I won't use it, and I'm sorry about that, because Roger Martin du Gard's shooting script is one of the most beautiful things I've ever read."[29] Had the director really read the writer's screenplay? It's rather unlikely, but at least he must have become familiar with the screenplay by reading a synopsis of it; and he was aware that homage was due du Gard for the fact of his being famous: a year before he'd received the Nobel Prize in Literature. It's also true that the writer had attempted to preserve the bulk of a novel that the director on more than one occasion would rightly maintain could easily be adapted into several films.

The plot of Martin du Gard's adaptation took place in 1914, and Renoir placed his not in 1869, as Zola had, but in 1938. Budgetary concerns weren't the only reason. As he would write once the film was finished, he felt that "such action taking place amidst trains standing on wheels high above the ground and around wooden rail cars would have lost some of its dramatic intensity.... Also, because the France of today isn't that of Napoleon III, because of the way it is now, its qualities as well as its flaws, I believe it deserves to be defended through and through by its children. I'm convinced that the author of *J'accuse* would agree with me on this point."[30]

On the last page of the book, Zola sends "la Lison"* hurtling along the tracks: "A blind and deaf animal let loose among the dead, it sped onward, onward, packed with flesh for the cannon, with these soldiers who were already stupefied by fatigue, drunken, singing." By shifting the action from 1870 to 1914, Martin du Gard had placed it on the same track, the one leading to war. In 1938, there was fear about this happening again, but there had to be hope it wouldn't.

---

* *Translator's note: The name the character gives the locomotive he drives in Zola's* La Bête humaine.

Trains gone wild were already part of contemporary decor. There wasn't a month without an express train derailing, without an engine overturning, without one train crashing into another, whether it was in Angoulême, Calais, the station at Bercy, or Villeneuve-Saint-Georges. It took nine hours to get from Paris to Marseille and two hours forty minutes to reach Brussels. Since January 1, 1938, the operation of the French rail network had been taken over by the Société nationale des chemins de fer (National Railroad Company), just as had been decided the year before on August 31. Trains known as *"michelines,"* considered to be the most modern in the world, were equipped with Bugatti engines and ran on rubber wheels, going back and forth at average speeds of three hundred miles per hour between Paris and Le Havre, where the exteriors for *La Bête humaine* were filmed. "Monsters" of speed that could transform into engines of death, trains were the stuff of dreams and fears. They redesigned the contours of the collective imagination of that time.

The fate of Renoir's new film would be embedded in such a landscape, an element that would up the ante for the film even more. Jean Gabin would meet new star Simone Simon there, in the shadow of Émile Zola and in front of the camera of the director of *Grand Illusion*. All the elements were there to make it a story that the media could tell week after week, enthralling fans of stars, of films, and of trains. Among these, a young adolescent from Montreuil-sous-Bois missed not a crumb of the adventure. He was thirteen and fascinated by trains, and he didn't know yet that one day he would make films. His name was Maurice Pialat.

Renoir finished off his screenplay with a speed unknown even in the time of trains. It took him twelve days, he would claim. This could be the case; the Hakim brothers apparently considered it a bit rushed,[31] which sent Renoir to Denise Leblond-Zola, the author's daughter, to whom he'd already appealed for *Nana,* to secure her approval if not her participation. Whether he did finish it in that span of time depends on what Renoir meant, at that moment, by "the screenplay." There was certainly no question that he meant a shooting script when he stated that "direction begins with the writing of the first line of the screenplay," at most, a document whose purpose was to be "a work plan to follow and to inform the assistant director about the scenery he'll need to put in place."[32]

In reality, Renoir had dictated a treatment, a text outlining the main aspects of the plot and presenting the different characters, a simple preparatory task intended as an initial synopsis for producers that, when approved, was sent to the crew, who could then begin preparing the film while the director wrote what would become the actual scenario. Or, rather, *scenarios*—because there still exist three technical shooting scripts whose corrections and many amendments obviously required more than twelve days of work.

Presenting *La Bête humaine* in 1962,[33] and recalling what he now dubbed "a sportsmanlike feat," which was his way of also saying how little he himself valued that rushed draft (but, if so, then why talk about it?), he played a part of exaggerated modesty as a man of little culture, letting drop, "I have to confess, I hadn't read the novel. I leafed through it very quickly, and it seemed interesting to me." That he must have done before accepting the producers' offer.

Another version he offered Rivette and Truffaut was, "I'd read *La Bête humaine* when I was a kid and haven't reread it for about twenty years."[34] Nevertheless, does it really matter whether—before writing the adaptation—Renoir had read the novel when he "was a kid," or "immediately after the War,"[35] or in the South of France the night following Raymond Hakim's offer, or not at all? All of his versions subjugated a major work to his creative process. They indicate the insignificant nature of a writing task reduced to the dimensions of a performance, during which the only one who suffered was the secretary whose "fingertips were sore from typing."[36]

Throughout the entire preparation for filming, Renoir continued to work on the screenplay. Perhaps an important element of this was his replacing the dialogue he'd imagined putting in his actors' mouths with the actual sentences Zola had written. Evidence of this appears in notes that are undated but presented in a way that is identical to those in documents related to the scenario from August 1938, which are keyed to some exact page numbers in the book: "Second visit to Camy-Lamotte. See Zola, pages 143 and 160. 'People like us don't kill for money.' 'Monsieur, we will obey you, be what you wish, no matter when or where, you need only to demand it, because I belong to you.'"[37]

To justify such a convenient distance—as he admits—from a book to which he paid only distracted attention, Renoir would consult work notes left behind by the author, which were communicated to him by Maurice Leblond, Zola's son-in-law. Renoir was certainly aware that the "literati," who were often not very open to the experience of film and who were quite finicky about the classics, were waiting for the opportunity to trip him up and would be prompt to appoint themselves guardians of the temple. He would also confirm having reproduced quite a lot of important lines of dialogue, just as he had done for *Madame Bovary.* These were prudent statements, intended to guard against the critics he feared, as he should have. Beyond that, Jean Renoir's *La Bête humaine,* which was inspired by a great novel, is a great film.

From the wealth of elements in the book, the screenplay basically preserved the plot line around Jacques Lantier and Séverine, the love story and the account of the crime. As Renoir declared at the time, he had "*churned out* a screenplay inspired by the great writer." He did not pass himself off as an "adapter, nor as a transcriber, but as an author of films," and also stated that whether they were good or bad, his films only had value when he was excited about making them.[38] So much for the irrelevant question of "accuracy" when it came to an adaptation. By relocating most, or nearly all, of the scenes to the railroad tracks, to the train, and to railway stations, or very near them, Renoir was obeying the logic of dramatic poetics and aesthetics. This strengthened the impact of the film but estranged it from Zola's work. The film would never have been anything but a collection of details if such a shift had not precisely matched the direction in which Renoir had begun going with *La Bête humaine*. This approach would reach its peak with *The Rules of the Game*, his next film.

In keeping with statements Renoir successively made, his adaptation found its way from a fundamental point of reference toward certain pet ideas; from its anchoring in Zola, the film took flight toward other climes. Such is the case with all adaptations, but the director's personality has kept us from coolly assessing the goals he stated he had. Then how did he envision the characters and their fates? As follows: "The weighty legacy of the Rougon-Macquart* makes *La Bête humaine* a natural successor to the great tragedies of Antiquity. Jacques Lantier holds as much interest as Oedipus Rex. This train engineer brings with him a context that is as heavy as that of any son of Atreus."[39] Giving birth to such an association may have been so cumbersome it required a pair of forceps, but the link nonetheless is an extremely convenient one. However, concurrent with such claims, an interview with Renoir appeared in which he said, "It's a revolutionary topic because it can lead to the conclusion that individuals living in better conditions would act better and would manage to avoid similar tragedies. It's a refutation of the facile, reactionary theory relying on the convention that people are eternally the same, destined to act in a certain way, and that it's useless to attempt anything to better their lives."[40] Then was this about Oedipus and the Atreidae, or about people oppressed by social injustice? The readers of *Cinémonde* would understand it as the former, whereas those who read *Cahiers de la jeunesse* preferred to hear it as if Renoir were talking about the second idea.

Renoir knew what he was saying and to whom he was saying it. He also knew what he wanted: "An idea came to me to which I still subscribe, and that is that the so-called realist or naturalist element in Zola isn't very important, and that above all Zola is a poet, a great poet."[41] When he made that statement in 1957, such a thesis was on the way to becoming central in the critical approach

---

* *Translator's note:* Rougon-Macquart is the collective title given to a cycle of twenty novels by Zola that were confined to a fictional history of two interrelated families, the Rougons and the Macquarts, their lives presented strictly from the point of view of naturalism.

333

to Zola; but in 1938, Renoir was already claiming it, in addition to other ideas: "I really should admit that [the film] is somewhat outside the domain of my customary thinking, because, out of fidelity to Zola's novel, I extol characters who are individualists, something with which I'm barely familiar."[42]

Finally, Renoir knew how to get what he wanted: "Therefore, I've given the cinematography more importance, attempting to draw expressions from my actors more often seen in silent films than in sound films with dialogue, and I award Kosma's music a place equal to that of the dialogue, which itself is quite copious."[43]

For direction of the cinematography, he relied on the German Curt Courant, whereas Claude Renoir filled the role of the camera operator. Having worked as director of photography for Fritz Lang (*Woman in the Moon*, 1934) and Alfred Hitchcock (*The Man Who Knew Too Much*, 1934), among other filmmakers, Courant created cinematography for Renoir's film that tied it to the German Expressionist tradition and placed it in the same sphere of influence as *Port of Shadows*, the 1938 film that had been shot by Eugen Schüfftan, another great cinematographer who had also worked for Fritz Lang. The images in *La Bête humaine* can be considered even more impressionistic than those in the Marcel Carné film as well as those celebrated so highly in Carné's *Le jour se lève*, which was also the work of Courant and was released in 1939.

The extreme care with which Courant endowed the composition of his shots at a time when the director of photography and the screenwriter were often considered to be at least as important as the director would, in addition, be the basis of some friction. This was something that Jean Gabin wouldn't forget: "One of the rare occasions that I saw Fatty have a tantrum—a gigantic one this time—was when I was at the engine in *La Bête humaine*. The head cameraman asked me to move more to the left 'because it was better for the light.' So Renoir exploded and he started to yell, 'Monsieur Courant, Monsieur Gabin isn't supposed to move to make your work easier. It's you who's supposed to adapt to what he's doing. If he's comfortable where he is now, it's your job to change your lighting. You're working for him, for the character. . . . Stop screwing the actors with your UFA photo crap. . . . Monsieur Gabin isn't going to move.'"[44]

After *La Marseillaise*, a "militant" experiment that had left him with a bitter taste in his mouth, Renoir again became the artist he had always been. Some prefer to say this was a poet, but the place he occupied on the chessboard of public life forced him to put on a mask at times, and he was a master when it came to such maneuvers. His film, which was free of any reference to current events, would nevertheless flaunt the darkness of the time in which he was living without ever ceasing to locate itself in the tradition of classical tragedy.

On several occasions, Renoir would claim that one of Zola's sentences made him decide to accept the offer of *La Bête humaine*, even though it was an offer there was no reason to refuse. It's the moment when Séverine remarks to Jacques Lantier, "Don't look at me like that, you'll wear out your eyes." It's a line delivered by a flirt pretending to be an unsophisticated innocent, whose presence in that public park is dictated by necessity. She and her husband need to make Lantier fall in love with her in order for the crime they've both committed to remain undiscovered. The trap that has been set is disguised as a lover's rendezvous. To work, it requires all the naïveté of a man who fears women, a man in whom they must awaken an impulse for death.

Similarly, Renoir needed to let out the unsophisticated innocent sleeping in him in order to give his readers in *Ce soir* a detailed account of his meeting Simone Simon, whom he'd come to wait for on the quay at the port in Le Havre where the *Normandie* would dock, bringing back from America the woman whom *Ladies Lake* had made a star. Yes, he was a bit of an unsophisticated innocent, but one who loved to come on like a strapping lad. He knew the meaning of the words he was using too well to think he was saying something else when he wrote, "some reporters tell me to climb onto the star." And to make sure his joke had been well understood, he had to add between parentheses, "I mean the star of the sea, which is a kind of big flat boat."*[45]

Photos appeared in the newspapers the next day, showing the director and his star on the deck of the *Normandie*—except that standing right beside the director was his actor Gabin. Fatty had brought along "Jean," the ladies' heartthrob. In the game of seduction, what do we imagine will happen? To which of the two Jeans will "la Simone" (as Renoir calls her in his column) immediately succumb? Renoir in the guise of good buddy and handicapped lover, who dreams of conquests without end and is so convinced of their impossibility that they naturally turn out that way? That day on the quay in Le Havre, Renoir and Octave, the character he would play in *The Rules of the Game*, were already the same person. The director, who'd saved the role of the simpleton and fall guy for himself in *La Bête humaine*, was fully aware of everything.

Gabin was dreaming of driving a locomotive, and Renoir, of being an actor. The film offered each the chance to satisfy his passion. The director had already worked as an actor in his first film as well as in small parts in others. In *A Day*

---

* *Translator's note:* The play on words I've tried to reproduce is much more succinct in French. In both sentences, Renoir uses the word *vedette*, which can mean "movie star" or "gun boat." Thus, he first makes a sexual innuendo about the star who is arriving and then plays on the other meaning of *vedette* ("boat") by mischievously confusing "climbing onto the star" ("*grimper la vedette*") with "climbing onto the boat."

in the Country, he'd played an innkeeper, but that film didn't exist yet, so no one knew he was also a performer. After *La Bête humaine*, everybody would know it. It was one way—possibly one of many—to come out from under the shadow of his father by following in the footsteps of an older brother who'd had vast experience with the giddy world of audiences, stages, costumes, and applause, something with which Renoir was still almost completely unfamiliar. A few months later, on January 3, 1939, Jean would apply for admission to the Union des artistes, to which his brother already belonged.[46] For someone else, it's doubtful such a step would have been necessary. But when it came to belonging, being part of the troupe, he couldn't resist.*

The role he found for himself in Zola's work was as Cabuche, a somewhat inane but tender-hearted fellow living in a cave. He is also repressed and, as a result, sentimental, a touching character condemned by his very innocence for a crime he would have been incapable of committing. Zola's Cabuche is all those things, but Renoir's version is not a total match. Zola's is a worker, a quarryman, whereas Renoir's is a vagrant, an outsider who carts his belongings along the railroad tracks and takes advantage of empty night trains to get some undisturbed shut-eye. The fact that Renoir was not inclined toward wearing the costume of a worker is understandable. On the screen he wouldn't ever play any character who wasn't living "between two worlds"—a county clerk, true, but a ridiculous one; and an innkeeper, of course, but one who was a dilettante version of it. And then, there was also his role as a music critic,[†] but that was truly an example of an occupation that produced nothing useful and therefore wasn't a real one. The fact that Renoir advertised his attraction to outsiders, bums, poachers also makes just as much sense. It's what he partly implies by writing in 1974 about not remembering the reason for the transformation of the character Cabuche into a poacher. This was due, quite probably, he said to a "romantic conception insisting that a man who lives in the woods must be a poacher";[47] and it was something that caused him, he added, "to fall into the trap of a cliché."[‡]

Nevertheless, in the construction Zola develops, Cabuche doesn't lack importance. Revolt is brewing in him. He roars, accuses, is the only one to

---

* The direction of *The Rules of the Game* would prevent Renoir from taking part in the dinner given in his honor for *La Bête humaine* at the restaurant Ruc on Sunday, March 12, 1939. Those who participated in the celebration sent the director a menu signed by them that he saved in his archives. The menu read, "*Panachée d'huitres, Filets de sole Grand Vatel, Poularde à la broche aux primeurs, Fois gras au porto, Salade M.C.B., Fromages, Bombe glacée, Corbeille de fruits, Café, Liqueurs, Pouilly-Fuissé, Fleurie 1938, Hospices de Beaune (Dames hospitalières) 1924, Champagne de St. Marceaux 1928.*" (Jean Renoir Papers, Production Files, Box 53, Folder 12.)

† In *The Rules of the Game*, this detail is indicated in the screenplay, but it doesn't appear in the film.

‡ "I fell victim of the cliché," he wrote in English.

speak about it; and these are the real reasons he ends up in the position of the accused. The rages of Zola's Cabuche are a danger to society. Renoir's Cabuche doesn't scare anybody. He's amusing in a kindly way, rather touching. No one is afraid of him, and nothing he can say really resonates. He's likeable, and his only fault is being found at the wrong place at the wrong time and speaking without thinking, without worrying what others—who in this case happen not to be friendly—hear. The innocent condemned man in *La Chienne* was a prick. What happens to him happens, or should happen, to pricks like him. Too bad—or, rather, just desserts. The innocent condemned man in *La Bête humaine*, although not at all evil and never harming anyone, gets more than his due; yet, as soon as the film is finished with him, it abandons him to his fate without a word of protest or any image that shouts at such injustice.[*]

Cabuche has fulfilled his purpose, the film can continue, and Renoir goes back to his lovers, his murderers. He created his "poetic" vagrant in whom no serious audience member can really believe. What is more, the words of this man-of-the-people have been undercut by the intonations, cadences, and the cautiousness of an actor who gives an exaggerated performance because of so much restraint, making Cabuche less of a character than a bewigged fantasy.[†] This is what Renoir wanted, and he did it. Perhaps without knowing it, the shift he set in motion from Zola's book to his film left its mark on the kind of films he would make, changing them from the past machine of a war that wasn't really his to examples of art accomplished in freedom. And by placing himself in *La Bête humaine,* he set fire to his own cinema.

That fire was also simmering in the eyes of Simone Simon. Renoir would later maintain that the producers would have preferred an actress playing Séverine who had more of the femme fatale about her. According to Renoir's memoirs, they had suggested he cast Gina Manès. Perhaps, but Manès, who had played Joséphine in Abel Gance's *Napoléon,* was forty-five in 1938, an age that didn't make her especially eligible to be cast as a young woman under the thumb of an aging godfather. Perhaps more importantly, Simone Simon was originally part of the project when Marc Allégret was intending to do it; and, supposedly, Carné had wanted her as well. The Hakim brothers had no reason to reject her—quite the contrary. After all, this was Simone Simon, a woman of twenty-eight with a pussycat mien, coquettish airs, and hair dyed black.

In her role as the stationmaster's wife, she wore outfits designed by

---

[*] One version of the screenplay planned for Cabuche to reappear where Lantier's body is found in the last scene of the film.

[†] In this regard, you can read an essential study by François Poulle, *Renoir 1938 ou Renoir pour rien?* (Cerf, 1969).

Mademoiselle Chanel, cut very simply but trimmed with pheasant feather and fox. Renoir wanted to pretend he didn't notice what was behind this full deck of charms, all of which can be read on the screen. Even better, by depicting Séverine as a cat-woman and showing her for the first time in the film with a cat in her arms, and by having Pecqueux mention later that this woman was like a cat, animals that don't like to get their feet wet, the director immediately abandoned hiding his character's true nature under a mask of innocence. In his book, Renoir quotes his father as saying, "Cats are the only women that count, the most fun to paint." Renoir was also looking for fun, and he enjoyed placing himself in the shoes of the great painter at the risk of sacrificing a small part of his character's mystery, surprise, ambiguity, and substance.

On the other hand, are we really talking about the Simone Simon of *La Bête humaine,* one of those "sweet, smiling little women with a completely inoffensive appearance" who are the "heroines of dreadful tearjerkers" whom Renoir "happened to come into contact with in the course of his life"?[48] The truth is that the filmmaker, like all directors who find themselves in the same situation, was trying to justify a choice that he was presenting as his own despite the fact that it was not. A motivation that led him to consider it "rather strange . . . that at the same time as my certainty that Simone Simon was the only performer worthy of playing Séverine, she herself, in America, and without having any idea of my intentions, was thinking of this role and dreaming of playing it."[49] "Rather strange"? Really? The actress had known for the last five years that one director, at least, and several producers were thinking of her for the role.

Séverine also undoubtedly "has her reasons," but the film hardly takes them into account and, when it comes to her, has no intention of fogging the issue. Nor does it spare Roubaud, who murders Séverine's godfather and lover, and then throws her into the arms of another. Such a husband, whose jealousy has pushed him to commit murder and whose crime has made him a willing cuckold, couldn't have been played better by anyone other than Fernand Ledoux, the perfect actor for making audiences accept the jolts of a plot honed razor-sharp. To create it, Renoir was dead right in not according the screenplay for *La Bête humaine* any more importance than he had when he'd prepared it, concentrating his attention less on the structure than on certain "moments" of pure cinema.

You had to be Jacques Lantier and not know much about women in order not to understand at first sight what Séverine/Simon was hiding so little of, and so poorly. Or was that the very thing about her that so irresistibly attracted a boy incapable of having a loving relationship, something that is revealed in a previous scene with his childhood girlfriend, Flore? For that scene, Renoir spent a long time looking for a certain slope of ground he may have spotted during the filming of *Madame Bovary.* It was a location that would make it possible to film the two characters as a train rushed around a curve in the background. In the vicinity of a house André Gide owned not far from Cuverville, everyone had set out looking for this famous embankment. Gide was the one who pointed out a curve in the Ferté–Beuzeville line, where the scene was shot, although it disappeared during the editing of the film.[50] It was the only scene where Flore appears. In Zola's version of the story, she's important—essential, in fact; she's only of secondary interest to the film. Played by the attractive Blanchette Brunoy, she looks extremely fragile, and Alain Renoir would remember her always smelling pleasantly of soap.

Alain Renoir, who was seventeen at the time, worked as an assistant on the film. He remembered having heard Gabin utter in a voice distorted like an animal's, "I'm the one who's the human beast!" When Alain told his father about that interpretation, Renoir advised him not to try to disabuse the actor of that idea, to prevent destroying the personal reference points he'd created for himself. There's something in Gabin's performance as Lantier that seems miraculous. What happened between the actor and his character, and between the actor and the director, to make his performance as Lantier seem so perfect, something that years later still appears so modern? Modern to the extent that it resembles an element of Marlon Brando's work in theater and film in the next decade. It seems as if no actor before Gabin, and very few after, have ever so naturally achieved his mumbling, those hesitations that collide into an explosion of words, those gestures and implications of meaning, those unexpected static poses, the stares and gesticulations that blend insensibility with sudden resolve. One could go so far as to say that *La Bête humaine is* Gabin.

And it's also Julien Carette, because Gabin is never as great as he is in the scenes in which he appears with that actor most associated with the streets of Paris.* Carette's character, Pecqueux, who works as la Lison's stoker, may be the most beautiful in the film, the distillate of Renoir's entire genius. We see Pecqueux (Carette) asking Lantier (Gabin) for that slice of ham to go with the eggs he's beating into an omelet; and Lantier, who's thinking of something else, sighs, "You're making yourself some ham and eggs." Pecqueux studies the face of a friend tortured by an absurd, corrosive passion for a flirt, observes that impassive face, unmoving body, the cigarette butt frozen at his fingertips. We watch Lantier tell his friend what happened, what he has done, which he won't be able to bear, and which he knows he'll die of. It's a certainty that Renoir directed the film for such moments.

---

* Carette was born in Saint-Germain-en-Laye on December 27, 1897. He would die in the most macabre circumstances, burned alive on July 20, 1966, in the wheelchair he needed after having become paralyzed.

The same for the scene with the song "Le P'tit Coeur de Ninon," words by Georges Millandy and music by Becucci: Séverine dancing, Lantier watching her, Pecqueux watching Lantier, the music of the orchestra of the National Rail Company in the background of the scene, the movements of dancers intercut with the eyes of those who aren't dancing—Pecqueux because he doesn't know how to, Lantier because he just can't. There is all the tenderness in the world and the cruelty of unrequited love, the violence of deceit and the obscenity of betrayal, everything that words can't say and that film can, because that is exactly what it is made for.

Speaking of Renoir, Brunius would write, "I saw him passionately polish the scenes that interested him and hurry through those that were just as important but bored him as if they were a chore."[51] The scene of "Le P'tit Coeur de Ninon" enthralled Renoir. It's one of those that contributed to making him the greatest director in the world.

Bernard Blier is said to have stated that Renoir offered him the role of Pecqueux in front of Gabin, the Hakim brothers, and the cinematographer Armand Thirard, although it's not known why the latter would have been there. The actor was certainly a bit young in comparison to Gabin. He was only twenty-two, and Gabin was twelve years older; but despite this, the deal seemed on the way to materializing until Renoir changed his mind and decided to choose Carette. Later, it seems that Roland Tual contacted Blier from Le Havre. Carette had been drunk from morning to night, and Renoir had had enough and wanted to replace him. Blier was shooting the film *Place de la Concorde,* an RAC* film, and the director of production refused to release him. This is what the actor recounted; and he also willingly added (to make his story more interesting) that the film preventing him from working for Renoir never ended up being made.[52]

During the shooting of Renoir's film, Carette became a millionaire. It being his first million, he drank to it generously—Carette drank to everything, in every circumstance. And when there was nothing to drink to, it also became an excuse to drink. He also talked a lot; for example, about a cousin of his wife who lived with them for some time and who was really a riot and had some unusual habits. Imagine, Carette had come home the night before and discovered a ruler in his hand; he was measuring the furniture. Two days later, wifey's cousin had split, and so had the furniture and wifey.[53] That, as well, was true, apparently.

What was definitely the case is that in Le Havre in summer 1938, boats were unloading illegal passengers that the French police would usher to the station:

---

* Translator's note: Réalisations d'art cinématographique, also the producer of *Grand Illusion.*

young Americans who'd come to join the ranks of the international brigades fighting in Spain. Most of them went back on the first ship, but some managed to get past the police nets and begin a long trip to besieged Madrid. In his memoirs, Eugène Lourié recalled the strange atmosphere of the city at the time, rumors about the presence of mysterious agents, some in the pay of Franco supporters and others working for the Republicans, without the locals, being able to tell which was which.

Le Havre had become a hub and in its own way was at the heart of the turmoil. All the crewmembers or actors had to do was open a window in their hotel, which was directly opposite the train station, or walk out of the restaurant La Grosse Tonne, where they took their meals, to notice this incessant movement and hear the rumors. Renoir wouldn't say a word about it in his columns, in the interviews he gave to journalists who visited the set, or later on. Had he decided to see nothing, completely focused as he was on this film, which would not contain an image or sound betraying the unusual circumstances of its direction? Did he wish to cut himself off from a world and a period in which he was a conspicuous figure, thereby asserting, without a word, those artistic desires he'd been repressing for so long out of fear, practicality, discretion, and taste?

Of all the films directed by Renoir in the thirties, *La Bête humaine* is the one that could be said to resemble a film by Renoir the least, and it's also the one that's most attuned to the cinema of its time. In choosing to ascribe Lantier's wound to heredity, as announced by a quotation from the Zola novel at the beginning of the film, the director evokes a fate that at the time would stick to Gabin's roles on-screen, condemning to certain death some of the characters he played. Stretching from Pepel in *The Lower Depths* to Jacques Lantier in *La Bête humaine* are all the hopes born of the Popular Front and abandoned along the way, and everything Renoir liked to believe, or pretended to want to believe.

That dark fate is shared with the other main characters. Séverine and Roubaud are also aware of being doomed. Séverine has obviously known since childhood that she wasn't meant to find happiness. Roubaud tries to conceal his inferiority behind petit-bourgeois values and betrays them constantly, without ever ceasing to believe in them. He's too insipid to escape the common lot and can't even succeed as a murderer. Never in Renoir's work has fate had such crushing weight. Lantier cannot stand it, and he kills himself by throwing himself off the top of la Lison as it is running at top speed, whereas in the novel Pecqueux and he kill each other. "They'll be found without heads or feet, two bloody trunks still pressed together, as if to suffocate each other."

La Bête humaine seems suggestive of *Port of Shadows*, which possesses a nearly identical aesthetic and a related set of themes. However, the film is decidedly different in its depictions of very minor characters and walk-ons, the people whose sense of understanding and community could have saved Lantier, perhaps in other times. And then, of course, there are the images of trains, tracks, stations, this nearly documentary dimension that by way of rhythms, repetitions, and visual and aural echoes transports the film to lyricism and carries it along.* In this aspect, as well, Curt Courant and Claude Renoir's cinematography is exemplary, and Eugène Lourié's sets are entirely keyed to this goal. The cramped interiors are jammed with bodies that reveal the confusion of thoughts and the impediments to impulse. They are spaces cut up by shadow, illuminated in rain, which seem like vistas without future for tormented humans whose only option is to follow the path traced out for them, just as Zola's la Lison must follow the rails, puffing and spitting, wailing as it dives into tunnel after tunnel without end.

The shots filmed by Claude Renoir between Le Havre and Évreux find a natural place within a collection of scenes mostly filmed at the Joinville studios, the majority of whose sound stages had been reserved by Paris Film. Like *The Lower Depths* before it, the film is an example of the expertise and efficiency of French production, which made it possible to finish the project in a little more than two months. At the beginning of October 1938, filming was over, and editing had already begun. The film would be shown on December 23 at the Le Madeleine theater, attended that Friday by "several ministers, the most famous names in law, letters, diplomacy, business, and the arts—in other words, the elite of Parisian society."[54]

What imagery showing the death of Séverine did the audience see during that screening? The question has been asked since a recent edition of the movie on DVD[55] revealed that Renoir had filmed Lantier stabbing her, shots missing from the version that had been known until then, in which the action happens offscreen and is communicated to the spectator only by sound. So that the reality of the young woman's death would not be mistaken, this montage included a shot of her corpse on the bed, eyes wide open and a gaping wound in her throat. A study of the various shooting scripts clearly shows that originally Renoir had no intention of showing the murder but that he changed his views as he was writing and therefore ended up filming the shot, which in the end was left out of the edit, thus returning to his first idea.

But this doesn't answer any question about the existence of these two edits. Olivier Curchod, who brought up the issue, suggests that there was a

---

* In 1976, Renoir would sign a request from Suzanne de Troeye in the context of reestablishing her career, verifying that she had worked as second assistant on the direction of *La Bête humaine* and as the "head editor for the railway scenes." (Jean Renoir Papers, Correspondence, Box 32, Folder 1.)

still unrevealed intervention on the part of the censor or some producers that resulted in their rejection of the image of a corpse, the sight of which certainly would be startling. Nonetheless, at the time the film was released, the very same image was reproduced on a lobby card and intended for display in theaters—in other words, to be used by the press. Although it is the case that the censor applied regulations to films, but not systematically to publicity material, the mystery remains almost entirely unsolved.

Regardless of the answer to such questions, there isn't any doubt that *La Bête humaine* was a success. In the press, the lion's share fell to Zola's name rather than to Renoir's. Catholic newspapers accused the film of all the sins attributed to the author of the book, describing what they saw as "very damaged goods" and stigmatizing "such alcoholic pathology and degeneracy, these murders, suicides, this stifling display of lowness, vices, fatalities."[56] Somewhat more moderately, but more hypocritically, Jean Fayard in *Candide* and François Vinneuil (Lucien Rebatet) in *L'Action française* halfheartedly sang the praises of the technical expertise of the director Jean Renoir, to make it easier to deplore the fact that he had had the fantasy of using it for a second-rate, appalling work.

The critics who were on the Left also made the author of the book the touchstone of their reflections. Georges Sadoul went so far as to write, "Perhaps international film now has its Zola," a conjecture he based on recalling Renoir's earlier films, envisioned as so many volumes of a plan with the ambition to construct—to paraphrase Zola—a natural and social history of France in the thirties. And he concluded with the observation that with *La Bête humaine*, "the names and talents of Émile Zola and Jean Renoir were encountering and comparing each other."[57]

It's not very probable that the audience of that time had interpreted the Jacques Lantier in this film as the character in Zola, which he was not. They had come to see Gabin, and Gabin is whom they saw. They recognized Gabin's fate-struck romanticism, something that had little to do with Zola. It was the quality that made Gabin the great star of his time, and he had just unseated Fernandel as France's favorite actor in the voting of those who owned and managed movie theaters. With Renoir, Duvivier, Carné, and Grémillon, Gabin was Gabin, even if not expressly the same. Sometimes the history of film is written more by actors than by auteurs.

In the fall, to a reporter from *Le Figaro* who had come to interview him on the set and who asked him about his plans, Renoir said, "I want a change of milieu, atmosphere, and period. I'd like to make a light-hearted, clever film that will allow me to live around rare paintings and precious crystal. I want to be intoxicated by wit and beauty."[58] Less than a week before the appearance of this interview, he'd provided the readers of *Ce soir* with his opinion on the Munich Agreement, which had been concluded on September 30, about two weeks before the end of shooting *La Bête humaine*. A photograph taken on that day had brought together the team for the film in front of his camera.

> This four-party pact has a little something of the "white slave trade" about it that would be something to celebrate if it weren't for the consequences. . . . So, the Germans are entering the cities of the Sudetenland. Will our newspapers, as they did for Vienna, publish photographs of those choice pranks that Hitler's men won't fail to play on the Jews in these regions? Will we again see old men on their knees in the mud washing the sidewalks? Women forced to walk holding signs meant to mortify them? In brief, will we again be the indirect, removed witnesses of those filthy Nazi jokes that are so readily and nimbly pulled on the defeated?[59]

Less than a month earlier, he had written to Édouard Daladier, the prime minister who would soon sign the perfidious pact, to "request to be admitted into the film services of the army." In that letter, he said he feared his age and physical condition wouldn't permit his being assigned to a military depot, where he might not be able to offer his country anything beyond "some rather inadequate services."[60] A month later, his request was accepted.

Who really would hold it against him for entertaining the idea of making a "light-hearted, clever" film and for hoping to be "intoxicated by wit and beauty"? Who would have trouble understanding that he intended to distance himself even more from Zola's world? The characters in *La Bête humaine* were trampled by a destiny that was also weighing on the world in 1938.

Like many young people of that time, Jean Renoir's son would have liked to fight in Spain. Still sixteen, he was forbidden even to dream about it. With other members of the crew, he'd put coins on the rails that passing trains would smash to bits, cutting them like razors, and they got a kick out of it. His uncle Claude was one of the director's assistants, his cousin Claude was cameraman. To distinguish one from the other, they called them "Claude Senior" and "Claude Junior." Marguerite was there as well. On the credits she'd have Renoir's name added to her own, which had inexplicably been spelled "Houlet." She adopted Renoir's name permanently a few years later. Of the three women in Jean Renoir's life, she was the only one he didn't marry, but she took his name regardless.

When Alain wanted to buy a motorcycle, Marguerite loaned him some money. As soon as Monsieur Guillaume, who still kept an eye on the family's affairs, heard that news, he came down on the teenager for it. A few months later, Alain became aware of what the family's devoted right-hand man already knew: Jean and Marguerite were no longer in love.[61] Yes, Renoir was moving on to other things.

The wind had begun to blow in a new direction in Jean's life, and Marguerite's as well. They were living at 7 avenue Frochot. It was a private street, right in the middle of the hustle and bustle of Paris but also isolated from it, a peaceful haven in a world gone mad. During the shoot at the Joinville studios, each evening the company gathered at a restaurant in Montmartre or Pigalle, usually at Chez Marianne on boulevard de Clichy. On either side of Gabin on the banquette would be Marguerite and Suzanne de Troeye, with Renoir facing them. They'd talk about the film, the day they'd just spent, the work for tomorrow.

After dinner, they'd walk to avenue Frochot, a few steps away, and sit around a polished table in a room lit only by a hanging lamp. In the shadows, hanging on the walls or merely leaning against them, were dozens of paintings, drawings, landscapes, and portraits, a prominent spot reserved for the one of Jean dressed as a hunter, wearing a cap and a butterfly-knotted ascot, his left hand on his hip, his right holding the barrel of a gun with the butt resting on the ground and a dog at his feet. It was his favorite canvas, painted by his father in 1910. The children of painters would express surprise when their friends at school told them there were no paintings at their house.[62] Jean Renoir had always lived surrounded by these canvases that were rare for others and that he now never wanted to be without, even when he was making a film.

20

Octave or Losing Balance

La Règle du jeu (The Rules of the Game)

Grand Illusion had become an international hit. A sentence written by an American journalist singling out the film as one that had to be seen by every democrat in the world ended up attributed to President Roosevelt, whom history would continue to hold to be its author. *La Bête humaine* had promised to be a commercial success, and it was. An exclusive run in Paris would last for thirteen weeks, and Renoir knew that he could finally do anything he wanted to. But to accomplish such a thing, he first had to dare to do what he'd refused to do since 1934 and *Toni,* which was still something rare in those days: become his own producer. And then, he would have to pull together the 2.5 million francs for his new film, an average budget for productions of that period.

French film wasn't doing well. In comparison to former years, its health was even alarming. Fewer than two out of ten French people regularly went to the movies. The yearly number of films produced had fallen from more than 150 productions annually during the first half of the thirties to 125 in 1938. Even worse, the number of tickets sold continued to diminish, while the costs of production exploded and foreign films played on three-quarters of the country's screens. None of that was the kind of thing that could curb Renoir's ambition. On November 4, 1938, he created the Nouvelle Édition française (NEF), which intended to engage in the "production and distribution of the films of Jean Renoir." His partners were his brother Claude, songwriter and childhood friend Camille François, and André Zwobada, who was one of his assistants. Each contributed 10,000 francs, and in January, Olivier Billiou, who had been working until then for the Hakim brothers, joined them. During shooting of *The Rules of the Game,* and after the rushes had been shown, Gaumont, represented by its director, Jean Jay, would contribute a total of around 2 million francs, which would bring the budget to a sum rarely attained in that period. The offices of the NEF, at 18 rue de la Grange-Batalière in the Ninth Arrondissement, were being sublet to Marcel Pagnol. In December, Renoir and Pagnol became owners of a theater where their films would be shown. The director of *Grand Illusion* was seeking a kind of independence that only Pagnol had known the way to achieve thus far.

This time, another daring move was to decide to do without a screenwriter. Renoir wrote alone, which for him meant collecting opinions, getting help from a few people who were close to him, especially Carl Koch. He was one of the few directors then, along with Guitry and Pagnol (but they were also playwrights), to take sole responsibility for the screenplay and dialogues in his films. Finally, but far from being of least importance, he chose to cast himself in an important role. Like Guitry, perhaps, except that Guitry, who'd always been an actor, had really never played anyone but himself, whether he was being Pasteur, Louis XV, or Napoléon III—an important difference. With Renoir's new film, all the eyes, and perhaps all the blame, would be focused on him; and as if that weren't enough, he was going to put more of himself into his character than any actor, and perhaps any director, had ever done before.

On October 10, 1938, news about his next film he had provided from the set of *La Bête humaine* began appearing in *Le Figaro*. His next film would be inspired by *Les Caprices de Marianne* (*The Moods of Marianne*). The initial treatment, registered on October 11, still had the same title as the Musset play. Another title, *Les femmes sont comme ça*, was changed almost as soon as it appeared to *La Règle du jeu*, just as it was announced that Simone Simon would star in the film. Married to a lawyer, a role intended for Claude Dauphin, and the lover of a pilot, for which Fernand Gravey was being considered, the character was named Aline, after having first been quite naturally called Marianne. These were only the first twists and turns of an intrigue that was so complicated that an entire book was barely enough to reconstruct its course, an astounding feat that has been accomplished, however, by Olivier Curchod and Christopher Faulkner[1] and that must now be followed by an attempt to explain this absolutely insane course of events.

It's especially important to keep in mind that, as Renoir was writing four synopses of *The Rules of the Game*, followed by a first attempt at a continuity script with dialogue, he was also absorbed in editing, performing several other tasks needed to completely finish *La Bête humaine*, and working at creating his production house. Added to this were his efforts at writing a screenplay based on a novel by Albert t'Serstevens for a film that was called *Français de Chicago*, and then *L'Évadé de Chicago*, before becoming *L'Or du Cristobal* (*Cristobal's Gold*). He'd agreed to supervise its direction for Jacques Becker if the case arose, because Becker was being offered the film to allow him to make his grand debut as a director. In a letter dated September 20, 1938, he asked Raymond Blondy, who was the production head for *Grand Illusion*, to maintain confidentiality regarding the conditions of his remuneration for work on Becker's film, because they "obviously don't correspond to those usually given me by producers." They would amount to 50,000 francs for the screenplay only—half of it in cash, half in installments—and in the case of "a basic supervision of the film,"[2] 25,000 francs in cash. Becker began directing in January 1939 in Nice, before giving up after four weeks of it when the producers appeared unwilling to honor their commitment. *Cristobal's Gold* would be finished by Jean Stelli, with scenery by Eugène Lourié and editing by Marguerite. Renoir received credit for the dialogue.

The screenplay for Becker's film, which was registered by Renoir on February 15, 1939,[3] made no mention of Carl Koch, who had indeed collaborated on it, as well as on *The Rules of the Game*, for which he would be credited and on which Zwobada and probably Camille François had also worked. Renoir would do the writing, but would do so by taking advantage of the conversations he had with his partners in the same way he did on his sets, where everyone had the opportunity to speak his or her mind and some chance to see it taken into consideration. He had always functioned in that way and often by passing from one idea for a film to another, well aware that any project could end up stopped at the last minute.

That very thing came to pass at the end of November, when he announced in the press that the shooting for *The Rules of the Game* had been postponed and that he would first adapt *The Diary of a Chambermaid*, which he had not stopped thinking about making. Approximately at the same time, the information arrived that Simone Simon would make Raymond Bernard's *Cavalcade d'amour* (*Cavalcade of Love*) in December and that Fernand Gravey had just signed to do *Le Dernier Tournant* (*The Last Turn*), the first adaptation of the James M. Cain novel *The Postman Always Rings Twice*, to be directed by Pierre Chenal. Renoir had lost the two stars of his film. In a letter to the actress dated November 15, he took formal note of the hitch in plans: "It seems that you're not free before the end of the month of March because of Raymond Bernard's film. This is irksome because I have to shoot before there are leaves on the trees. Well, never mind." "Tell me where I can find *Gone to Earth*?"[4] he also asked her, which suggests that Simone Simon was thinking about acting in an adaptation of Mary Webb's novel. Several years later, Renoir would be planning an adaptation of another book by the same author, *Precious Bane*, with Ingrid Bergman.*

Why did Simone Simon prefer Raymond Bernard's project to Renoir's,

---

* *Gone to Earth* would be adapted into a film with Jennifer Jones by Michael Powell and Emeric Pressburger in 1950.

after he had just given her a magnificent role in *La Bête humaine,* a film that was already being confidently described as a major event? For financial reasons, some have claimed. The actress, or in any case, her agent, was asking for 800,000 francs, which the budget as planned would not allow Renoir to grant. Jean Gabin supposedly declined the role of the pilot for the same reason, a hypothesis that the thinness of the part makes seem doubtful, even if there's no way to know how Jurieux could have been developed if Gabin had played him. Simone Simon's refusal could also have had something to do with what she told Claude Gauteur: that she'd hated Renoir's performance as Cabuche in *La Bête humaine.*[5] Such an argument seems flimsy, especially because, at that moment, Renoir was still claiming to be thinking of having his brother play Octave, all the while secretly hoping, as he'd later confess, that Pierre would say no and suggest he keep the role for himself. Which is exactly what Pierre would, in fact, do, with the excuse that he didn't want to be so far away from Paris and the theater for all those weeks of shooting they were planning to do in Sologne. Less officially, Simone Simon would put forward the idea that Renoir's behavior on the shoot for *La Bête humaine* had displeased her. To put it plainly, the director had wandering hands. His overinterest in hanging around her had antagonized her a great deal.[6] It could be that none of these reasons is the real one; but combined, they form a possible motive for her refusal. In addition, one outstanding feature of *The Rules of the Game* is its refusal to appoint one character as the lead. If such a choice has to be made, it would be Octave, and that is something that can appreciably cool off stars well used to the light of projectors concentrating on them.

Nevertheless, a few days later, the project was definitively launched.

Renoir then actually knew who would replace Simone Simon and Fernand Gravey. For the role of the pilot, whom Gravey was supposed to play before Gérard Landry (Dauvergne in *La Bête humaine*) was considered for the part, he chose the bouncy Roland Toutain, who'd played the part of Rouletabille at the dawn of sound films and who'd also acted in the role of a pilot on several previous occasions, something he was well suited for. Toutain also had the sense of camaraderie needed for the part of André Jurieux (the pilot). Finally, Toutain was close to Georges d'Arnoux. Among their many escapades was one in which Toutain had played at being Tarzan, substituting the chandeliers at the Hôtel Negresco in Nice for the vines, before improvising a bowling party in which they used crystal ashtrays for balls.[7] That connection to d'Arnoux, whom Renoir adored, must have been the principal reason why Renoir asked for Toutain. Toutain's career was on the decline at the time, and his fame would be brief; but at least his name wasn't unknown by French audiences.

On the other hand, when it came to the actress Nora Gregor, Renoir had no such excuse. However, although she was a virtual unknown in film, those French people who followed the society pages knew she was Princess Starhemberg. The marriage between "one of the most prominent actresses of the Burgtheater" and Prince Starhemberg, the former vice-chancellor of Austria who had recently gone public with his opposition to Hitler, had been announced on the front page of *Le Figaro*.[8] Fans of pretty females had even had the chance to enjoy a photo of "the great actress and wife of Prince Starhemberg in her exile from Austria," walking down the Champs-Élysées.[9] And on March 5, 1938, the same daily paper, reporting an anti-Nazi demonstration in Vienna the day before, also informed its readers that "in front of the Hôtel de Ville, fifteen thousand women come to solemnly swear to defend Austria. Urged on by Princess Starhemberg, they pledge themselves to the independent Austria, the expression of which is henceforth, 'red, white, red' until death."[10]

Renoir had gone to the Théâtre du Gymnase to see a new play by Marcel Achard called *Adam*, perhaps to check out Michèle Alfa, a young lead who was being called promising; and to see Claude Dauphin, whom he had cast in the role he thought would be a lawyer at the time. Michèle Alfa wouldn't become part of *The Rules of the Game*, and neither would Claude Dauphin, who would join Simone Simon in making *Cavalcade of Love*. Nora Gregor/Princess Starhemberg, on the other hand, would end up in Renoir's film. During the play's intermission, Henry Bernstein introduced them and, in his capacity as director of the play and owner of the Gymnase, invited them to have a glass of champagne. Renoir and the actress then had a conversation in German. For him, it was love at first sight. She was anti-Nazi; she was a princess, and thus an object of fascination for a *grand bourgeois* like him; and she was charming, a well-respected actress in her country, especially in the theater. She had also acted in twenty-two films, among them *Michael*, directed by Carl Dreyer in Germany in 1924, and three Hollywood productions, the first directed by Jacques Feyder (*Olympia*, 1930), but none since 1933. She had also been in *What Women Dream*, whose screenplay had been written by Billy Wilder before his exile.

She was a bit old for the part in Renoir's film—turning thirty-eight shortly before shooting, which was ten years older than Simone Simon—and she spoke little French. Never mind. The heroine of *The Rules of the Game* would be Austrian in background and would be called Christine. Rounding out her qualifications was that her first and very temporary husband had been a pianist and conductor, and Christine's would be a conductor, too. As a result, the "original screenplay," consisting of three typed pages and dated November 12, 1938, was amended by hand by Renoir, who noted "Christine is Austrian" and replaced an "unhappy childhood spent in a convent" with "a dreamland: the former Austria."[11]

Renoir may have seen this dramatic turn of events, which felt like an answer to his situation, as a good omen. What if Nora Gregor brought luck to *The Rules of the Game* like Stroheim, who was also Austrian and who had arrived late on the scene like her, had brought to *Grand Illusion*? Film also fed itself with superstitions. Renoir's decision can truly be viewed as a kind of crush on his part. Although the exact date on which he hired the actress isn't known, he made up his mind in a very few days, literally right after November 16, the date of the premiere of Marcel Achard's play. The director forced the decision on his various partners, who were all opposed to it, or who at least said they had been a posteriori. The resulting modifications to the screenplay in a version dated December 1938 were accompanied by a list of the main actors and their characters. Nora Gregor (Princesse Starhemberg [*sic*]) headed the list, followed by Jean Renoir, Roland Toutain, Claude Dauphin (the husband), Carette, and Ledoux (the gamekeeper).

Marcel Dalio took over for Claude Dauphin in the role of the husband, who was changed from a lawyer to the Baron de Monteux (in memory of the silent partner in the financing of *La Chienne* and his big-bosomed mistress?) and then to the Marquis de La Chesnaye, because an actress-princess couldn't properly be married to a baron. And that is the way Dalio ended up having to play a marquis, which would arouse the anger of anti-Semites and "real" French people. This time, Renoir's phenomenal talent for adaptation found expression in creating an extraordinary game of mirrors. As for the most faithful friend of the beautiful woman in the film, that character's name would be Octave, and he would be played by Jean Renoir.

Except for the fact that Fernand Ledoux (who had played Roubaud in *La Bête humaine*) was still expected to play the gamekeeper Schumacher, casting was practically finished by December. It included Carette as a poacher, a role that Renoir had already thought about offering the actor for another film, as evidenced by a list of actors intended for a project dating to 1935 and called, successively, *Ida, Tibi, Artus,* and *Le Crime de la Gloire-Dieu.** With the addition of Paulette Dubost and Gaston Modot, for the roles of Mme. and M. Schumacher, the cast for *The Rules of the Game* would be complete by the beginning of February, less than three weeks before shooting started.

* Planned to be cast as well were Yvonne de Bray, Orane Demazis, Séverine, or Héléna Manson to play Marie Tibi, Gaby Morlay as "the princess," and Pierre Fresnay in the role of the "*débauché*." A "girl of the woods" called Bourgogne or Lulu (Yvette Lebon and Jenny Hélia were the performers he was considering) also figured in this project, which contained elements suggesting it was a foreshadowing of the play *Orvet*. (Jean Renoir Papers, Production Files, Box 49, Folder 7.)

It then seemed possible, or at least desirable, to begin shooting in mid-February. About a month before that date, Renoir had gone to Marlotte with Zwobada and Yvonne Bénézech, his secretary, to create a fourth continuity script, then a fifth with dialogue. He did them on the double because his commitments would call him back to Paris on January 21 for the first broadcast of *Club des Vedettes,* a radio program launched by the magazine *Pour vous.* Six days later he had to go to London, where he was giving a lecture and where he met Robert Flaherty. The importance of that encounter with the director of *Nanook of the North* and *Man of Aran* would be revealed a few months later. It was probably during this period that he wrote a new version of the screenplay of seventy manuscript pages, in which the heroine was actually named Christine but her husband was still called Monteux.

There is no way of knowing all the day-to-day details of Renoir's apparently overcrowded schedule during this period of preparation for *The Rules of the Game,* yet nothing seems to have happened in the course of it that left the director particularly impressed. It would not even be much of an exaggeration to think that the film had not yet undergone any bolt from the blue as enormous as the one caused by Stroheim's inclusion in *Grand Illusion,* despite the fact that Simone Simon's defection had been an enormous upset. Renoir was working then as he'd always worked, and liked to work, from all evidence, in a style of great haste that emphasized the urgency of everything he undertook, for which he drew upon an enormous supply of energy and a staggering talent for bouncing over obstacles. He was one of those very rare filmmakers for whom directing did not entail a series of renouncements but a process of adaptation, enrichment, and intensification of depth. Nevertheless, none of his films, before or after, would experience so many shocks, setbacks, or necessary withdrawals as *The Rules of the Game* would, and the memory of it would fill him with a bitterness that cannot be explained away solely by the commercial failure of the undertaking.

During the beginning of 1939, Renoir was able to write as he had always written, beginning with the drafting of several synopses, and then establishing a continuity script with dialogue, which was the last step before compiling a shooting script that he could follow or not during filming, but which he needed and on which the crew depended to establish a shooting schedule and especially to plan and order the construction of scenery. As circumstances would have it, he wouldn't be able to complete this third step before shooting began. As a result, he would have to work on it rather than being able to rely on the usual process of moving on to the next stage, which consisted of adapting the shooting script to the locations and the actors. He had to accomplish both processes simultaneously, and everything else around them.

Directing a film in such a way is an undertaking of unbelievable complexity, an insane enterprise. Renoir was the first to understand this, quite logically, and shortly before the end of filming on June 1, 1939, he'd write to Camille François, "The only error I think I can point to comes from me. It was agreeing to write the screenplay for *Cristobal's Gold*, which delayed the screenplay for *The Rules of the Game* and forced us to start out with an incomplete shooting script. It wasn't a good shooting script; I had to restore several elements of it while we were filming; and if *The Rules of the Game* isn't well received by audiences, I think we can attribute it only to that. It's a lesson for next time: never again to start out without rigorous preparation."[12] Even before it existed, *The Rules of the Game* merited the slogan joined to it as part of its marketing campaign, which its opponents would use to poke fun at it: "A film not like the others."

Before leaving for Marlotte, Renoir gave an interview to the magazine *Pour vous* in which he clearly described the film that was in his head: "An exact description of the bourgeois living in our time. I want to show that, for every game, there is a rule. If you play differently, you start to lose."[13] This is to say that Renoir's ambition was to describe his own milieu, knowledge of which came naturally. The approach to it was completely personal, but it fell within a trend in French film of the time. What is more, the organization of the film around an ensemble of characters from which none clearly stood out was familiar to audiences of that period. Films like that that audiences had seen or would see included Julien Duvivier's *Dance Program*, Yves Mirande's *Café de Paris* and *Derrière la façade*, and Sacha Guitry's *Ils etaient neuf célibataires* (*Nine Bachelors*). And the fact that some of these films were variety sketches didn't rule out their membership in the same genre as *The Rules of the Game*, with which they also shared an attraction to abrupt changes in tone, a tendency for developing the story in multiple directions, and basically the same pessimism.

Even more significant was the fact that Yves Mirande, who'd been famous in his time and then became unknown, when not unjustly scorned, had made a film in 1936 with several similarities to Renoir's masterpiece:* *Sept hommes, une femme* (*Seven Men, One Woman*). Still considered to be one of Mirande's least successful films, it tells the story of Countess Lucie de Kéradec (Véra Korène) who is visited in her chateau in Loir-et-Cher by seven suitors and who intends to choose one. She finally gives up on the plan as each reveals how

---

* The parallel characteristics of the two films have been pointed out by Jacques Lourcelles, among others.

disappointing he is. The plot itself is not so surprising when compared with *The Rules of the Game;* what is astonishing is how similar some of the situations are. These include parallels that hold all the way through the film and include the relationship between the world of the servants and that of their masters, certain amorous intrigues going on in the hallways of the castle, guests in pajamas and a jealous valet, and, especially, a long hunting scene in which several shots come close to foreshadowing those in *The Rules of the Game.*

The issue is not whether Renoir saw *Seven Men, One Woman;* it's highly probable that he did. Even less is the issue whether he was consciously inspired by it. There is barely any doubt that Yves Mirande's film influenced certain choices Renoir made. The truth is that the similarities between the two films—between a very ordinary entertainment and an absolute masterpiece—is a reason to place *The Rules of the Game* in a current that fed French film during the second half of the thirties and that often scathingly analyzed relationships among the classes, the decay of values, the follies and ignorance of the bourgeois milieu, and the cynicism of the rich. More or less precisely, these films present the last days of a certain world.

Was Renoir conscious of this aspect of his film, emphasized by the sources he claimed to have used for it, which first and especially cites Musset and then Beaumarchais, both listed in the credits and both invoking a French mentality that quite clearly seems to have ceased to influence France in 1939? In a confused way he was quite aware; and what he said nearly thirty years later in 1966 merits belief: "What may be interesting about this film is the moment when I made it. I made it between the Munich Agreement and the war; and I was totally overwhelmed when I did, totally disturbed by the state of mind of a part of French society, a part of English society, a part of world society. And I felt that one way of interpreting that state of mind of the world at that moment was precisely not to talk about the situation and to tell a light-hearted story, and I sought my inspiration in Beaumarchais, in Marivaux, in classical authors, in comedy."[14]

Although the "first crank of the camera,"* as it was then called, had been announced in the press for February 15 in Sologne, shooting actually began a week later, in the studios in Joinville, with the direction of the Parisian interiors inside La Chesnaye's mansion.[15] Out of the seven sets created, four showed Christine's suites, the anteroom, dressing room, bedroom, and morning room. The costumes had been designed by Mademoiselle Chanel. The list of them had been completed on February 8, and for years afterward, for important occasions, Paulette Dubost would wear the very simple little dress created especially for Lisette the chambermaid.[16]

---

* Translator's note: "Premier tour de manivelle."

During this time, part of the team had already moved in near Berry and Sologne, between Lamotte-Beuvron and Aubigny-sur-Nère, in preparation for the exterior scenes, which had been planned to last fifteen days. Gaston Modot and Julien Carette were part of that advance group, soaking up the customs and habits of the region in its sunken lanes and café, with Modot wearing his gamekeeper's uniform and Carette in the costume of Raboliot, the local hero of the region immortalized by Maurice Genevoix, winner of the Prix Goncourt in 1925. When a stray motorist asked directions of the pair, he received an answer from Carette in a Parisian accent so purposely exaggerated you could cut it with a knife. "Oh that, my boy. Better ask one of the country bumpkins from here!" Carette would later confide that he'd done three weeks of training in Sologne as a poacher.[17]

The "movie people" established their quarters in Brinon-sur-Sauldre or, more precisely, at La Solognote, the village inn. An article by Pierre Ducroq, special correspondent for *Le Figaro*, described the atmosphere of the area. He'd witnessed the initial scenes filmed in Sologne around March 10, especially the poacher's arrest and his hiring by the marquis.[18] In the village hall in Brinon, a screen had been set up in front of the same platform where young couples danced to an orchestra on Saturdays and Sundays. A projection booth had been cobbled together out of rugs and a mattress, and benches were arranged for those invited to see the rushes at the end of each afternoon.

It was also near Brinon that the long hunting scene was shot before the crew moved to La Ferté-Saint-Aubin, ten or so miles away, where a chateau would represent La Colinière in the film. In April they returned to Joinville, where three soundstages had been reserved for the production for the purpose of filming all the interior scenes at La Colinière. Filming would go on from May 11 to 13 near Fontainebleau, where the car accident would be completed as quickly as possible because Roland Toutain had to leave for Morocco* on Monday the fifteenth. Then, on May 19 would come the scene in the greenhouse, for which Toutain and, for the last shots, Nora Gregor would be replaced by doubles.

The journalists invited to witness the shooting for two days in Sologne didn't miss a chance to extol the harmony that characterized mealtime as much as it did filming. All articles about film productions are alike, regardless of the film, the director, the actors, or the context. However, Renoir had his own way, and it had a tendency to arouse enthusiasm. Having already worked together, often for Renoir, the crew were very familiar with one another and got along

* To act in the Jean-Paul Paulin film *Le Chemin de l'honneur*.

easily. The actors were happy, first of all because they were working with Renoir, then because the atmosphere was excellent, and, finally, because a director who declared himself blown away by their performances and asked for an extra take only for the pleasure of admiring them at least one more time was a big exception.

You had a good time when you were making a movie with Renoir. You ate and drank better than on any other film, and you were glad to be part of a film that you knew in advance would not be one more piece of crap. In bringing Roland Toutain and Carette along especially, Renoir had two hearty lads who loved a joke of any caliber, and Dalio would willingly jump right in if it had the potential of shocking the ladies. The two rascals understood each other equally when it came to raising a glass, but Carette had brought his wife, Ninette, with him, who would dog him not to drink. Various people tried in vain to pull the wool over Ninette's eyes. If need be, they'd discreetly leave in the chateau's most cramped room—the toilet—the glasses of Pernod the actor had no intention of going without. Ninette was well aware that her man went often to the restroom but still couldn't do anything to stop him.[19]

The reporter from *Le Figaro* observed that the weather wasn't what it should have been. During his stay in Brinon, it had even snowed, but Renoir kept from getting aggravated by that as well: "Lousy weather for filming, he tells us. Snow; now that's too much, obviously; but sun: look at that sky! . . . I need clouds. I don't like Sologne when it's playing at being the South of France. I'm my own producer for the first time. I've suffered enough from others. They adapt the circumstances to the weather. Well, I do the opposite. I'm waiting for my own personal light."[20] He was telling the truth but also trying to put on a good face, respecting the tacit agreement between directors and journalists. Everything—rain, bad weather, sun at the worst moment—had cost days of filming. The film was behind schedule, and delays in that world are costly.

The situation was, on the other hand, less disastrous than it had been for the making of *A Day in the Country*, although the reasons were the same. Their stay in Sologne, which had begun several days late because of certain complications in Joinville, would go on for five weeks, whereas only two had been scheduled. When they started filming again in Joinville on April 11, four days after the team had returned to Paris, the film would be in its eighth week, which was the total length of time envisioned from the start by the work schedule; and all the interior shots for La Colinière were still left to film, especially the long scene of the party, which would be unbelievably complex but which Renoir would nevertheless finish in barely more than fifteen days.

In April and May, the effects of a lack of preparation, the day-to-day writing corrections, the complications stemming from the weather, and the fact that they'd gone beyond the budget all swept crazily through the filming of *The Rules of the Game*. This may have helped infuse it with an even more impressive energy than usual but also prevented Renoir from taking the necessary distance from his film.

And then, as is the case for all the films in the world, and even more so for those made by crewmembers and actors who don't go home each evening over a period of several weeks, there was that important consequence so rarely discussed and never, or almost never, written about, having to do with games of love and with chance encounters. Unknown starlets sometimes appeared in places to which they hadn't been invited, attracted by the presence of some actor. And one of these women, at the wheel of a handsome automobile, was asking Alain Renoir, the assistant cameraman—"whose striking red hair, tousled like his mother's, left a touch of fire as he went by"[21]—and Sam Levin, the still photographer, where she could find Marcel Dalio, whom she wanted to meet to discuss . . . well, did it matter? As it happened, Dalio was there, too, but the lady was Sam Levin's type, and she wouldn't get a chance to meet Dalio. Alain, whose room directly adjoined the photographer's, would give up on counting the number of his conquests.

The director's situation was more complicated. To begin with, his partner Marguerite was also his most important collaborator, the editor who also worked as script girl on the shoot, for which she wasn't credited. The official script girl wasn't exactly an experienced one, but Renoir had known her for years. Brazilian by background, she was called Dido Freire. She was a friend of Cavalcanti and had spent a lot of time with Alain, watching over his studies as well as she was able and taking him on vacation several times. The woman's connection to Jean's son was therefore closer than it was to the director.

Alain's mother was responsible for Dido's presence on the set of *The Rules of the Game*. Since Catherine's separation from Jean, she'd remained close to Dido, imagining that Dido might make it possible for her to go back to her husband. Although Catherine had long ago said good-bye to their love affair, she hadn't given up her acting career, and in her mind, the only person who would agree to be interested in it now was her ex-husband.[22] Dido herself was also thinking about writing for film, as proven by a screenplay project that is undated but that must have originated before 1939 and was called *Le Tonneau du clergyman*, a story that took place in England.[23]

The problem for Catherine, and soon for Marguerite, was that Dido was about to discover in Jean Renoir a different man from the one his ex-wife had spent years accusing of every sin in the world. Renoir had the benefit of an irresistible image in the eyes of a woman who'd been encountering the film milieu yet who couldn't seem to become a part of it. Renoir was also clearly aware that the young girl he'd met ten years before had changed. Dido would be thirty-two that April 4, spoke several languages fluently, had nothing to attach her to France, and didn't belong to the profession. She saw Renoir as a star director to whom she wanted to devote herself completely, working for his comfort and laboring for his glory. Her personality made her the exact opposite of Marguerite, who'd met Jean when he was still only a little-known director. She'd worked side by side with him and had helped him become what he was, both through her work as an editor and through her militancy. For her, Renoir was still "Jean." Physically, the two women couldn't have resembled each other less. Marguerite was as cheerful-looking as Dido appeared hard; the latter had none of the feminine appeal that Renoir enjoyed celebrating. Marguerite was the daughter of the people, and Dido was the daughter of a great Brazilian family. Marguerite was deeply attached to France, and Dido was a citizen of café society. Marguerite's manner was simple, direct, and generous, whereas Dido's was marked by class confidence. Catherine had been Jean Renoir's first love and first actress. Marguerite had been his editor and his companion. Dido would be his secretary and his wife.

There was also the fact that Renoir understood that his efforts in seducing Nora Gregor were hopeless. Jacques Becker, who wasn't there during filming, would have had much better luck with the princess;[24] but much more important is the fact that, in losing interest in a woman who was rejecting him, Renoir fell out of love with an actress he'd realized was a poor match for the character she was playing, one whose lack of expertise with the French language had become a handicap he felt was too difficult to surmount. It is true that no element of the screenplay or shooting schedule attests to this. Only Renoir's remarks afterward suggest it. "Keep in mind," he wrote years later to Dido, "that Nora Gregor's clumsiness almost killed the film."[25] It's an unjust judgment, obviously, or in any case an extreme one, but it substantiates after the fact that Christine may have suddenly become less interesting to him. And each day he drew a little more apart from Marguerite, who watched him draw close to the woman whom he'd appointed her assistant.

As director and producer of *The Rules of the Game,* Renoir carried the film on his own shoulders. And the collapse of his relationship with Nora Gregor made the character he'd chosen to play himself even more essential. It's a character who has ended up a guest there just by chance, in a world that isn't his, a good buddy to both the husbands and the lovers, the confidant of ladies he wished he knew how to make love to, a very inoffensive fondler of maids, a music critic[†] who

---

* Dido Freire was born on April 4, 1907, in Belém, Brazil.

† Octave's profession is only mentioned in the screenplay.

wishes he were the conductor, a puppet of his own demons who enjoys playing director for one evening, an actor who is incapable of taking off the bear getup he has chosen to wear. Octave *is* Jean. Octave is Renoir on the set of *The Rules of the Game*.

Nevertheless, he has to try to keep his feet on the ground and not give in to losing his balance. Accept having to eliminate certain key scenes, move others—from a golf course to an apartment, for example—adjust sequences accordingly, factor in the absence of actors working on another film, and soon end up having to keep from being chased off the soundstages in Joinville, which for months had been reserved for other productions. The money had run out several weeks earlier. It's true that Gaumont had become part of the production, but that contribution had the reverse value of putting Renoir under surveillance. If Jean Jay, the Gaumont official, saw something in the film he didn't like, he had the right to assert his point of view. In fact, Jean Jay wouldn't get carried away. It was Renoir's performance that irritated him the most. That rumor would spawn another about Renoir offering to have every scene reshot with Michel Simon in the role of Octave. How such a thing would have been possible is far from understandable, and when Claude Gauteur asked him what he really intended by such a suggestion, Renoir answered that if he could have, he would have put Michel Simon in all of his films.[26] So much for the historian—as far as that can take us. But one sentence can sum up the state of mind of the director better than a description, precise and scholarly as it is. Renoir wrote such a sentence on August 18, 1942, in a letter to his brother Claude, and the circumstances surrounding the text are as important as the text itself.

At the time, Renoir had just been discharged from directing a film he'd begun for Universal, *Forever Yours* (which would become *The Amazing Mrs. Holliday*). He was very happy about this, because he claimed to be "disgusted by this kind of improvising in sugar syrup," adding that although he "very well understands improvisation...you nonetheless need some kind of basic structure; you nonetheless have to have already written the scenes at least once, even badly, even if that means changing them when you find yourself facing the realities of filming." Next came that striking sentence: "This feels like *The Rules of the Game* starting all over again, minus even its confrontational aspect, which could endow this production with some quality, and without the hope of a piece like the hunt upon which you can build something even without a screenplay."[27]

The fact that the disaster with which he'd just been associated, and which he claimed to be more than happy to be able to turn his back on, evoked the memory of his last French film, considered today to be his masterpiece, actually tells us less about *The Amazing Mrs. Holliday*—a film that meant nothing to him when he wrote to his brother—than it does about *The Rules of the Game*, which had been everything for him a little more than three years previously. The anecdote sheds unexpected light on the vision a director can have of the film to which he becomes dedicated. The fact that Renoir's vision was in this case affected by the failure of *The Rules of the Game* does not entirely challenge the impression produced by this sentence. The memory he kept of the making and release of *The Rules of the Game* was so painful that three years later he still hadn't recovered a sense of clarity.

The scene of the hunt as the film's touchstone, then. Renoir named it the "documentary" sequence, the equivalent of the "railroad" sections in *La Bête humaine*. When he'd finished the hunt scene, around March 20, all the shots of animals without actors still remained to be filmed. This would be accomplished at the beginning of April under the direction of Zwobada and cameraman Jacques Lemare, because Renoir and head cameraman Jean Bachelet were needed in Joinville. Filming the animals would require a complicated setup and the sacrifice of several hundred pheasants, hares, and bred rabbits. The accumulated delays in filming had prevented Renoir from participating in the direction of these shots, and his son said that in different circumstances Renoir wouldn't have witnessed it either, because the sight of the death of animals was unbearable to him.[28] Nothing is less certain, because in Renoir's eyes as in those of any director, only the film counted, and consequently, no other option would have been possible other than bending to the requirements of what his own imagination had caused him to think up. Renoir liked to describe himself as fascinated by poachers. Would he really forget that their primary activity, their raison d'être, consists precisely in killing animals?

Renoir is not the only director, but one of many, who had trouble concluding a shoot, difficulty making up his mind to be finished with a film, because all the work he'd have to do next would be solely concerned with what was already "in the can." But with Renoir, this fever took on insane proportions, consonant with the changes he imposed on his own projects, which were inspired by a kind of voracity and perhaps also to some degree an inability to make decisions, which some have described as a lack of confidence, whereas its primary motive was his wish to make the film a part of life as long as possible.

As was the case for Carette and some others, Paulette Dubost, whom the crew had nicknamed "busy breasts,"*[29] would later mention that her role had been fleshed out a great deal during filming. This would happen when Renoir, for example, would casually ask them to move through the background of a

---

* *Translator's note:* In French, this is nearly a play on words, as explained to me by the author: "*seins animés*" ("busy [or animated] breasts") sounds like "*dessins animés*" ("cartoons").

shot, just to see what it was like. Dubost wrote, "We could have gone on filming for months. There was no end to his ideas. If money hadn't been a problem, I believe we'd still be at it."[30] There's not the slightest doubt that Renoir would still be at it, which is a sign of "the genuine artist-director . . . who attempts to recount a story; and as he films it, there comes a point at which he is taken by an innate desire to materialize all reality . . . and so he ventures always further ahead into the jungle of material phenomena in which he is in danger of becoming irremediably lost unless he sacrifices great effort to get back to the major pathways from which he has strayed."[31]

Among these "major pathways" are those that must be taken by the work of the director if he intends the film to resemble one likely to be shown to paying audiences. When the need to finish the work arrives, the director discovers that certain shots haven't turned out; and in the majority of cases, the only option he can choose is resignation and the creation of a composition with these elements missing. But when it came to *The Rules of the Game,* Renoir felt that the sacrifice of entire scenes, to which he'd consented in the madness of a badly prepared shooting schedule, was preventing him from bringing the process to a satisfying conclusion. A screening of a first edit on May 26 showed that three scenes in particular were necessary if the viewer was to understand the plot. The film in such a state "wasn't presentable,"[32] he wrote on May 30 in a confidential note to production.

Therefore, it was imperative that these scenes be filmed, and they would be during the first half of June when Renoir took advantage of a trip Roland Toutain made to Paris. During this time, he filmed the Le Bourget airport scene (in exteriors, but not at Le Bourget); and during a brief spell of free time that had been granted Mila Parely, Dalio, and Pierre Nay from their respective shoots, he filmed in succession the scenes he'd planned to shoot on a golf course and in a tearoom, moving the location of the latter to the home of Geneviève (Mila Parely). He did this not only when a first cut had been delivered but while the sound mixing was being done, to be finished in the final days of June. At the time, Carl Koch wrote to his wife that he and Renoir and the crew were working an average of nineteen hours a day. Renoir's German friend was also in charge of writing the English subtitles intended for the copy that was supposed to be shown at the Colisée movie theater. They'd be written but not placed on the film.

Renoir threw his project into the furnace of filming without enough time to bring it to a point of incandescence. He didn't abandon it or destroy it; he shaped and forged it. In addition, he found himself impelled by the desire to take possession of the role of Octave and was soon led onto a path as unknown to him as it was to all, led by that brilliant intuition that had influenced him to make Octave his double, his alter ego—but that had even taken him to the point of making Jean Renoir *become* that character. It wasn't the actor off on an encounter with the character, not even the character coming forth ahead of the actor, as sometimes happens, but the director putting himself in the scene, not the way a filmmaker directs a performer but actually the way an author places himself at the center of his creation, as painters have done for centuries. Octave, everyone's friend, the buddy of the decent guy whom he has invited into a world that isn't his, the confidant of these ladies and their maids. Octave, who understands everybody's reasons, whether it be the wife, the husband, the mistress, the lover, the poacher, the marquis, the gamekeeper, the cook, the old fogey, or a poor girl who is so foolishly in love that no one notices her. Octave, like a director who has to make the motivations of all the characters his. Jean Renoir, who shares everyone's views, whether they're Party comrades or friends on the Right; something he does during the shoot because he's in control and it has to move forward, and in life because that's the way he is, always trying to smooth things over, dreaming that everybody agrees with one another, that conflicts are worked out at the café before they've even broken out. Jean Renoir, who in that spring of 1939, because he had experienced what he had experienced, and because the history of the world had arrived at the point of no return, understood in making *The Rules of the Game* that life would be easier, in fact, if everybody did not have his reasons, if all of them were not equal. Which is when he began to choose his side, which consisted precisely in not choosing a side.

The fate of the film was still in the future. It would only strengthen Renoir's confused resolve. Whatever he may have to claim later, the failure of *The Rules of the Game* wouldn't surprise him. He knew what his film was, and he knew audiences. "My father never imagined that this film would be a success to the same extent as *Grand Illusion*,"[33] Alain said. Never, really? Once the film was finished, obviously. But actually, it was the virulence of its reception that would provoke Renoir's bitterness, which was intensified by the fact that he was also the producer and was sharpened by the feeling that the entire responsibility for it was on his shoulders.

On June 28, which was barely two weeks after the actual end of shooting, a private screening of the film aroused divisive reactions. The next day, *The Rules of the Game* was presented to the officials who were in charge of choosing the national Grand Prix for French film. It was a prestigious award, and it was also big money (a million francs). It would be given on July 7 to *Port of Shadows*, ahead of two films that were tied, Julien Duvivier's *La Fin du jour* (*The End of the Day*) and Jean Benoît-Lévy's *Le Feu de paille* (*Fire in the Straw*). The snubbing of Renoir's film was actually a confirmation of the overcautious opinions and fears already nourished for several weeks by the distributor and especially by theater owners, who seemed to be resigned to it already: *The Rules of the Game* would not experience any success comparable to that just achieved by *Grand Illusion* and *La Bête humaine.*

This hunch was born out by the change in release strategy that had gone into effect by mid-June: there was no longer any question of presenting the film at the Madeleine, the Gaumont-Théâtre, the Rex, and the Gaumont-Palace. Those two last theaters alone accounted for ten thousand tickets. It would play instead at the Colisée and the Aubert-Palace, which between the two counted for 1,450 seats. As for the film's distribution outside of Paris, first envisioned as a simultaneous release to the entire Gaumont circuit, it was postponed to November 15. The page purchased by Gaumont in *La Cinématographie française* to announce this on June 17 didn't fool anyone, despite the claim that these arrangements were being made "in view of the importance of Jean Renoir's new film."

It is difficult to determine whether the publicity campaign was also cut back, but the many advertisements inserted in various newspapers attest to the film's importance. One promotion scheme even imagined a crossword puzzle competition, in which a "certain number of winners" could carry off "two tickets to see the film" after a drawing. Among the suggested clues were "Princess and foreign star who has just achieved a magnificent performance with a great deal of emotion" and "Son of a great painter who has himself won fame in the art of directing."[34]

Set for July 8, the release was preceded by several screenings, one for friends (July 4), a few others for the press (July 5 and 6), and climaxing in two gala evenings on July 7 at the Colisée and the Aubert-Palace. There again, the reactions were mixed. It seems even uproars organized in advance were to occur. The choice of the Colisée was in itself rather dicey because that theater on the Champs-Élysées was "known for its snobbery."[35] That same night, the film was also presented at Pierre Braunberger's Panthéon, and the screening was followed by a very lively debate.

On July 8 at eight-thirty, Renoir introduced Joris Ivens's *The 400 Million*, during an evening gala organized at Salle Pleyel by the association of the "Friends of the Chinese People," during which Jacques Duclos also spoke. On the ninth, news came that Roland Toutain had been "quite seriously hurt" in a car accident near Nice the night before, which was the same day when the first paying audience members saw the scene of the accident in *The Rules of the Game*. But before they could get to that, they'd had to swallow a poorly chosen first part of the evening composed mostly of the documentary *L'Empire français,* directed by the African specialist Philippe Este and designed to sing the praises of French colonization. Nothing could beat this, of course, in arousing the sympathies of Far Right viewers who'd come to "pull the chain" of a director friend of the Communists, who was depicting his own milieu for the first time in his film: in their eyes, never had Renoir better deserved being called a renegade.

Heckling was de rigueur, especially because everybody knew that the film had encountered numerous obstacles. It was applied particularly to Nora Gregor, whom people enjoyed not understanding a word she said, to the Jewish Dalio playing a marquis, and of course to Renoir himself; each actor's on-screen appearances triggered jeers. However, in a letter to his wife dated July 10, Carl Koch spoke of the enthusiasm of many audience members, making clear that he and Renoir had very much been hoping to reach the popular audiences; some seats were being offered at only twenty-five francs.

Moreover, *The Rules of the Game* isn't a simple film. In such hostile conditions, how would viewers who were neutral—people who were neither particularly well disposed to the film nor malicious toward it a priori—supposed to be able to appreciate its complexity?

When the first reviews appeared in the papers, the harm was already done. All the same, as Claude Gauteur demonstrated in 1980,[36] opinions were evenly distributed among inflammatory articles, cautious inventories, and passionate speeches for the defense. Most of the right-wing publications were in the first category, headed by *Le Figaro,* in which James de Coquet wrote that "*The Rules of the Game* is nothing but a long series of mistakes," called the film a "laborious fantasy served by fuzzy dialogue," and indicated that "these characters belong to no known social species."[37] There were few laudatory articles that didn't rely on the economy of holding back, but contrary to a certain legend about the film, it was certainly not badly received by the press as a whole.

And although *The Rules of the Game* did disconcert, certain opinions attempting to be peremptory were able just as well to arouse curiosity. For example, Gilbert Bernard, the reviewer for *Le Matin,* described a film that "seemed to have been staged sometimes by Pierre Dac, sometimes by Charlie Chaplin, sometimes by Marivaux, and even, on occasions too rare, by Jean Renoir." But the main reproach leveled at the director had to do with his pretension in meddling with everything: "We do wonder, once again, if M. Jean Renoir really did wish to prove something other than that it is difficult to write, direct, and act in your own film."[38]

It is more difficult to know what the audience thought. Apparently, some had been shocked to find out that a French marquis could have a Jewish father who came from Frankfurt, and was called Rosenthal (a wink aimed at *Grand Illusion*), and whose wife spoke with a strong German accent. Others, and sometimes the same people, may not have been able to tolerate the spectacle of a society of masters and valets mixing that also exhibited so much weakness and lack of concern. However, the ways such opinions have come down to us through the reports of a few witnesses have an after-the-fact odor to them, at least partly composed as they are by the fetid emanations generated by the right-wing press, which didn't miss the chance to remark in passing that the image of the Jew produced by the film could please anti-Semites just as well as it could reassure their adversaries.

In order to agree with François Truffaut and say that *The Rules of the Game* was "the film the most hated when it came out,"[39] we need to confine ourselves to the judgments expressed by Renoir's sworn enemies and forget that attacks of that time were of a violence unequaled today. Doing so risks hiding that essential truth about the film being judged incomprehensible, especially the last part, precisely because the director's intentions aren't clearly revealed in it.

In addition, the end of the film always posed a problem in the eyes of Renoir and Koch, who opened up about it several times in his letters to his wife. "Not as strong as the rest," because it was filmed too quickly and "badly edited," which he would write on July 7. But several reasons contribute to an inability to understand the film.

Social caricature marked by cynicism was familiar to audiences in 1939, but certain shifts into intimate confession in *The Rules of the Game* were a lot less so. Mixing tone often proves to be a dangerous exercise. Today's audiences are no more comfortable than those of the past with not being asked to choose between laughter and unease. Neither wants to face associating the two emotions with each other. What is more, Renoir the actor's performance was off-putting, and the character Octave made people feel ill at ease. Above all, if the harm had already been done even before the appearance of the first reviews, it was because the various screenings organized before the release of the film, as well as the first showings of it—marked as they were, it must be remembered, by preplanned heckling campaigns—had stirred panic among Gaumont's shareholders and quite probably also among those of the NEF. The fact that these people had no understanding of the film merely worked to exaggerate the panic, until Renoir himself was suddenly unable to resist it. In such circumstances, the mantra is always the same: cut. And no one then seemed to care about the fact that, when it comes to cinematic entertainment, the film's length has little bearing on its tempo, which is the deciding factor involved in the impression that a film is too long. So, just as had happened several times in the past, Renoir began slashing up his own film.

At the time, it was still the practice to make the cuts directly on copies of the film in circulation. Therefore, Marguerite went to the Colisée and the

Aubert-Palace to carry out a savage "reedit." Marguerite—who'd just witnessed the man she loved abandoning her for another woman; no one failed to see the cruelty of the situation. After two, or perhaps three, days, everything was settled: on July 8, *The Rules of the Game* was ninety-eight minutes long; the day after, as indicated in a letter from Carl Koch to his wife, the film had been reduced to eighty minutes. Also, according to Koch, on the ninth the film was shown "without any incident and with applause during it and when it ended." It was shorter by around eighteen minutes, which is approximately a quarter of the entire length. Compared to the version of the film we know today, which lasts one hundred ten minutes, the loss is staggering, a total of thirty minutes.[40]

And should we be surprised, as Renoir would pretend to be later, that audiences in 1939 hadn't understood *The Rules of the Game,* a quite complex film that was ahead of its time by at least two decades? It's like accusing them on principle as more uncultivated and less intelligent than those of today, and why should we?

Panic. It certainly isn't surprising that the shareholders felt it. Nor is Renoir's panic hardly any more remarkable. There's no need to recall certain episodes from the past, because they would only partially illuminate the state of mind of a director who had changed, if only because he'd finally experienced success. For months Renoir had worked under incredibly complicated conditions, subject to pressure from financial backers as well as the pressure he'd placed on himself by taking on an essential role in the film. It was Renoir who was responsible for Octave's stating that he'd always dreamed of having contact with the public, that he saw himself as a failure—which was precisely how Renoir himself felt at the pinnacle of his fame. He had just broken up with the woman who'd been his partner for years and who now found herself having to work at his side, hand in hand with the woman who had succeeded her.

Just as Carl Koch had mentioned disagreements between Renoir and Zwobada in a letter, he revealed the tensions occurring between Renoir and Marguerite. How could it have been any different? Renoir was experiencing doubts about having chosen Nora Gregor as the right actress to play Christine, and everyone was saying that he'd been wrong in doing so. He'd taken the role of Octave in pursuit of his long-standing dream of being an actor; and now, all around him, even in the movie theaters, people were proclaiming his mistake, saying that he wasn't good, that the failure of the film—because it certainly was going to be a failure—was entirely owing to him. Not only because he had written all of it, decided everything, but also because he had wanted to be in it. He had thrown himself to the lions.

At that moment in his life, which had come along as a page of world history was turning, Renoir was less sure of himself than ever. He knew no more about what to think about this new track he'd taken with *The Rules of the Game* than he had about his past undertakings. Most importantly, he found no one who seemed to be willing to get him out of the bearskin with which he'd weighed down Octave for the evening when he had turned him into the director of the party given by the guests at La Colinière.

Of all the characters in *The Rules of the Game*, Octave is the only real loser. André Jurieux is dead, brought down like a rabbit, the fate common to daredevils who discover too late that the greatest of dangers is being in love. Christine, her husband, her husband's mistress—all the others, in fact—preserve their place in the world. Each has their own, and each knows how to hold onto it. This includes the two professional enemies and rivals in love, the gamekeeper and the poacher, as it does Lisette, the maid, for whom her husband mistakes her employer, Christine.

Octave, on the other hand, has a choice that the others don't possess, something they accept quite comfortably. He has the choice to remain there or to leave, the choice to continue his life as a failure in a world of the affluent or to make a break from that society, to see it for what it is and to try finally to accept himself and stop taking himself for what he is not and will never be. Here, Octave loses, from the very fact that he has a choice and must decide. Rid of his bearskin, which did inhibit him, preventing him from moving around, from breathing, he no longer has anything. His only real friend was killed, his impossible love dead. From the experience, he has drawn the most unbearable of virtues, lucidity. The time of illusion is over for him, and now "he knows that cost of letting everyone have his reasons."[41]

Renoir, as well, was through with illusions. His past involvements had left a bitter taste in his mouth. He clearly saw that the world was on the road to ruin, that upstairs the dizzy whirl continued and no one would stop dancing even though the fire had already begun to lay waste to the floor below. A new woman had come into his life. She was thirty-two, the daughter of a diplomat, spoke several languages, had no attachments to France, and wasn't accepted by the members of the fantasized family of French film. He was already gone before the history of *The Rules of the Game* was finished. It was a solution that he had planned for several months already, yet the failure of his film, to which he'd later find it convenient to point as the reason for everything, counted very little. Even not at all, it is quite likely.

The film would close at the Colisée on August 2, 1939. It would last at the Aubert-Palace until August 24. Its commercial failure was patently obvious, but not as glaring as has often been claimed. However, the project had been extremely expensive. It was primarily the declaration of war that would prevent it from having the provincial run that its promoters would have been able to arrange for it. In its August 12 issue, *La Cinématographie française* provided the list of cities where the film had been shown. They numbered fifty-two, but the publicity for the film kept things vague. Was *The Rules of the Game* currently playing or was it a coming attraction?

Was the film banned by military censorship because it was "demoralizing," which is what historians headed by Georges Sadoul have written? Yes. Like so many others, some of which were by Renoir. The measure was actually not aimed specifically at *The Rules of the Game*. And the interdiction would last only a few months, from September 1939 to February 1940, when it was lifted.

Is *The Rules of the Game* demoralizing? Renoir thought the opposite. The day before its release, in an article about his future plans, he wrote,

> The film I have just finished . . . is a first attempt toward a genre that is less "morbid" than the one that some proven successes are currently imposing on French filmmaking. Nothing lasts forever. Down-in-the-dumps, fog-ridden films have had their obvious usefulness,* and they've helped attract worldwide attention to film. But I feel that audiences may now want to become interested in heroes who are less destitute and degenerate than the films I'm referring to have shown us.[42]

The tone of this passage oddly matches that of an article in the corporatist press that appeared the day after the banning of *The Rules of the Game* and several other films under the title "Attention, Producers! Make Healthy, Optimistic Films!" "A certain number of great films, including some that have even won important prizes, have been banned. This is because at the current time films that undermine should no longer be made. We have to make films that are healthy and optimistic, constructive works. Carné, Chenal, Renoir† must change genres. French producers and directors will know how to follow our leaders onto that rectifying path. They will give us films full of light, courage, and happiness."[43]

Renoir's mind also harbored another anxiety, which he revealed on June 1, and therefore before the release of the film: "I think at my age of the fact that I am no longer a young man still capable of beginning projects with the hope of making money, but a man who has been working for fifteen years and who is being obliged to turn the results of his past work into cash. Nothing lasts

---

* Clearly, Renoir is taking particular aim at Carné's films. Using the adjective "fog-ridden" gives him the opportunity to point to a film without naming it, *Port of Shadows*, whose success he'd found it hard to accept.

† Meaning, the Renoir of *La Bête humaine*.

forever, and I am no longer in a period of life when you should bank on the future. Because of that, in my next film, I will need to make money."[44]

Like the history of *A Day in the Country*, that of *The Rules of the Game* would resume years later; and like the adaptation of Maupassant, the misunderstood "merry tragedy" would come back to life. It's not an exaggeration to write that two essential films of Jean Renoir remained still unknown by spectators at the moment their director chose to commit to the last path his friends were expecting to see him take. Moreover, nothing says that Renoir himself wouldn't have been the most surprised if he hadn't been the actor and director of his own life but had instead been the spectator.

21

Tosca and Il Duce

On August 1, 1939, a telegram was sent from Los Angeles to Paris. It was addressed to Jean Renoir from Joris Ivens: "American press publishes your leaving to work Italy. No one here can believe or understand. Please cable refutation we all have so much faith in you. All the best."[1] Renoir's answer hasn't been found, and it probably never existed. It couldn't contain any form of "refutation."

By the time of the telegram, Renoir's imminent departure for Italy had been known since July 14, the day the information appeared in *Le Matin, Le Jour,* and *Paris-Soir,* among others. A venomous article appeared in *Match* on August 17, composed in part of supposedly collected statements that it is preferable to examine with distance. The title of the article already signaled the tone: "Jean Renoir, Anti-Fascist Director, to Shoot a Detective Film in Italy: *La Tosca.*" The fact that the director was accompanied by his German friend, referred to as his assistant under the name of "Kohr," offered the author, who remained anonymous, a point of focus; and he didn't miss the chance to caricature Koch's German accent and endow him with a series of "*ach*'s" to serve as punctuation for a conversation with Renoir that apparently occurred at the brasserie Viel on place de la Madeleine.

The rest is in keeping with this, close to insulting, written with enough skill so that readers can tell themselves that Renoir is getting what he deserves. The details about the negotiations with the Italian producers demand to be taken at face value, and the article makes sure to make it clear that the director has already received "600,000 francs, handed over in Paris," that "his expenses for the stay and those of his assistants in Italy are covered for six months," and that "accompanied by the faithful Kohr [*sic*] and his secretary, he has moved to . . . Monte Catini Alto [*sic*], into a charming hotel, the Palazzo Paradiso."

A description of Renoir's days serves as the grand finale of the indictment: "Each day, in the morning, at noon, and in the evening, he receives fifty-one Fascist salutes, which is three times seventeen. They come from the staff of the hotel (owner, director, maître d', concierge, bellhop, valets, etc.). He receives them gently and patiently. He cashes them in. With the rest."[2] If Renoir actually did stop in Montecatini, a small city in Tuscany located about twenty-five miles from Florence, his stay there couldn't have been more than a few days, and certainly less than a week. Also, it's probable that the behavior of the hotel employees wasn't particularly meant for him. The anonymous journalist got carried away by his wish for satire and his desire to "pull the chain" of the director.

Several jibes drew a portrait of this "bad lot": "Jean Renoir is the sweetest and most patient man in the world. He shows that unfailing patience, that will to please, that fear of displeasing that you'd think was the privilege of certain courtesans. With them, it's a necessity, but with him, it's a vice."[3] It's harsh for no reason, obviously excessive, but there is nevertheless a real basis to it. Those who had neglected to take into account that failing in his personality were the ones who then became—in all logic—the most astonished and the most disappointed. In terms of Renoir's statements throughout the thirties, and even more so in terms of his writings, this departure for Mussolini's Italy really did seem incomprehensible.

Because it certainly was the same person who wrote in *Ce soir* concerning Goering's and Mussolini's fashion choices, "Where the hell did they dig up those jackets as tight as sausage casings and those boots that yawn with boredom every step they take? If I were the hotel manager and I had bellboys wearing those rags, I wouldn't let them keep their jobs for another second. I'd be much too afraid that they were going to drive away the clientele. And Mussolini's hat, with that unbelievable cotton acorn bonnet falling over his eyes? . . . If the worker who made that outrageous headgear had the least sense of humor, I swear to you that he must have had quite a laugh."[4] Amusing, without any doubt, but not very serious, one might say. Then what to think of this statement made to L.-R. Dauven in response to the banning of *Grand Illusion* in Italy? "M. Mussolini accepts very well being treated as a crook and a murderer. His supporters as well don't see any drawback to it. But Il Duce goes completely red with rage when it's said that his bulging stomach is less photogenic than he imagines it is, or that he wears ridiculous hats and doesn't know how to dress."[5]

The "crook and murderer" wasn't the direct cause of Renoir's going to Italy. But his son was, and forty-five years later that son would declare, "One of my desires has always been to form some contacts with the French. It wasn't a disinterested impulse. I was trying to have it be admitted that we weren't those Fascist monsters that a lot of people were imagining but serious individuals who were producing and shooting films, that Italy wasn't a country where intolerance reigned and where everything was gray."[6]

Vittorio Mussolini was interested particularly in Julien Duvivier, and even more in Renoir: "You can say anything about Renoir, except that he's

Fascist. . . . I wanted him to come to Italy, to know Italy, and to leave it with an opinion of it that was less terrible than the one he had to have had before coming."[7] He stated in his memoirs, which appeared in 1957, that he had to overcome the opposition of the minister of popular culture to taking on Renoir[8] for this production entrusted to ERA Film, a division of Scalera, one of the companies in which he had a stake and which was directed by Angelo Rizzoli, who was also the editor of the review *Cinema,* of which Il Duce's son was the editor-in-chief. It was with Rizzoli that Vittorio Mussolini went "to Cannes in 1939"[9] (it could have been Cagnes instead) to convince Renoir to come and work for him in Italy.

In 1939 it was, yes, but was it before directing *The Rules of the Game,* or well after? If it was before, the meeting could only have taken place in January; but there's no evidence that Renoir had gone south at that time, and his schedule during that period is quite well known. If it was after, everything must have gone extremely fast. Renoir was held up in Paris until July 11, at least, finishing the film, and then by its release, and yet his contract for *Tosca* is dated the day after. In reality, all the evidence points to the assumption that it was before *The Rules of the Game* that Renoir and Vittorio Mussolini made their agreement. If Carl Heil's* account is true, *Tosca* had already been agreed to at the time of the filming of *Grand Illusion,* meaning by the end of winter and the beginning of spring 1937. Carl Koch would have then "advised Renoir not to go and make this film in a Fascist country."[10] It's likely that, this time as well, Renoir found the words to convince his friend to change his opinion about everything.

Furthermore, Scalera had an office in Paris,† an arrangement suitable to facilitate relations with the milieu of French film. It's also from that address that Renoir's contract was sent. Dated July 12, 1939, the contract specifies that Renoir would receive "a fixed sum of 600,000 francs net after Italian taxes"[11] for the making of *Tosca* "in a French version," "based on a screenplay adapted from the novel by Victorien Sardou," and for the "dramatic and technical shooting script and dialogues" and the direction. This was three times his total salary for *La Bête humaine,* apart from money earned through profit sharing.

* A radio announcer and militant anti-Nazi, Carl Heil was driven out of Germany in 1933, and from January 1937 he served as the speaker in German for anti-Nazi broadcasts originating from Paris. He played two roles in *Grand Illusion,* the sentry Carette calls Arthur and the officer who snatches Sylvain Itkine's copy of Pindar out of his hands. Arrested and interned in France in 1940, Heil was sent to Buchenwald in 1943. When Liberation arrived, he became the newscaster for German-language broadcasts on Radiodiffusion française under the name Charles Hébert. He died on November 17, 1983.

† At 20 rue de Berri, and then at 3 rue Godot-de-Mauroy.

The adaptation of *Tosca,* a project reserved to "bring over" Renoir, had first been announced as to be directed by Carmine Gallone. The actors in mind for the film were Viviane Romance and Georges Flamant. The supposition that the presence of Dédé from *La Chienne* could have given rise to Renoir's commitment, a hypothesis perpetuated by the article in *Match* and repeated occasionally in various other places, is far from likely—something that would later be confirmed. As Vittorio Mussolini would have to admit, "coming to Italy" was still "like taking a political position."[12]

Jean Renoir didn't hesitate. Was it because the project excited him and nothing could have dissuaded him from it, as his son would claim? Without a doubt. Because he was dreaming of seeing Italy? Absolutely. Because his goal was to make a lot of money? Yes. Because for months he'd been wanting to leave, place his career on a new path, start a new life? That's it, exactly. For that, the offer of *Tosca* had come just at the right moment. The world of French film was beginning to feel stifling to him. The global success of *Grand Illusion* and, to a lesser degree, the fact that *La Bête humaine* was a hit in France was giving him confidence about his capacity to break through borders. Having his new love at his side increased his desires to be elsewhere. Dido Freire's personality intensified these feelings and made them more accessible. She was a woman who was open to the world and spoke several languages fluently but who wasn't very appreciated by the French film circles in which his former lover Marguerite was a recognized figure. On the other hand, everything else—and it amounted to no small thing—made this moment the worst he could have chosen.

On May 22, in Berlin, Hitler and Mussolini had signed the Pact of Steel. On August 23, the German-Soviet Molotov-Ribbentrop Pact (i.e., the German-Soviet Pact) would be concluded and would send the French Communists into total disarray. One of their highest-ranking members, Louis Aragon, directly addressed Jean Renoir as a way of concluding an article on André Malraux's film *Espoir:* "I'm writing this for you, as well, Jean Renoir, you who have left Paris without wanting to bid me farewell. . . . [I am writing this] for those who are weak or cowardly . . . for those who have given up hope in France too soon and whom, perhaps, I'll no longer be able to view calmly."[13]

Renoir, Dido, and Koch left Paris by car on August 4,[14] the day after a breakfast with the Kochs at Claude Renoir's.[15] After having spent a few days at Montecatini (if we can believe the article in *Match*), they arrived in Rome on August 13, the day after Aragon's article. They moved into the Hotel Excelsior, and Luchino Visconti became their guide. Visconti hadn't worked on a film since he'd served as the prop man for *A Day in the Country.* In San Remo he had just created the scenery for Henry Bernstein's play *Le Voyage* and had been living in Rome since April. On August 10, Carl Koch wrote to Lotte Reiniger that the synopsis for *Tosca*, which he'd been working on in July, was finished.

Planned to last, their stay was over less than two weeks later, in the crises of conscience created by the German-Soviet Pact. On August 27, just when *La Bête humaine* was being presented out of the competition in Venice, Renoir was at Les Collettes, where he wrote to Commander Calvet* of the army's film service, putting himself at his disposal. Renoir also described the "atmosphere of absolute calm" that reigned in Italy and the population's "very friendly" attitude: "During the journey I made to Rome, I heard no offensive remarks about France. It was very much the opposite."[16] From Cagnes, where he was staying on September 1 as German troops invaded Poland, he returned to Paris, still accompanied by Dido; and on September 2 was assigned to a post in the map service of the army. On September 3, Great Britain declared war on Germany, followed on September 4 by France.

At the time, his first Italian trip seemed like a failed escapade, and it truly was a false start that Renoir would choose to keep silent about, preferring to place his decision to film *Tosca* after war with Germany had been declared. Friends he had had in the past had suddenly been plunged into a sinister state of confusion, and Renoir would make use of time to reconsider the question of an opportunity for exile in Italy. His friends no longer knew what their position was because their mortal enemy had become an ally of the Soviet Union overnight, but that didn't prevent them from criticizing Renoir for the choice he was making. In the eyes of the director, the very existence of the German-Soviet Pact definitively divested his Communist friends of the primary virtue he had seen in them, which was to form a bastion against Nazism. But did such a conclusion justify his rushing to be with Hitler's most important ally? He probably didn't ask himself that question.

For the time being, Reserve Lieutenant Jean Renoir naturally found himself assigned to the film service of the army, for which he had completed the obligatory ten days of military instruction on June 5.[17] On September 2, he went to his post in Alsace, where he began spending his time writing reports. One of these, seven pages long, is entitled "Report on a Presentation Concerning the

---

* Commander Calvet, who later became a colonel, served as head of the army's film service from 1926 until June 1940. He was the one who had represented the French army on the censorship board. According to Marcel Carné, he required that the word *deserter* never be pronounced in *Port of Shadows*, that the actor drafted for the role "not look like a hood," and that he carefully fold his military clothing before placing it on a chair.

Composition of Film Crews in Times of War."[18] A second (four pages) is called "Report on the Opportunity to Direct Certain Informational Films for the Use of Families of Those Mobilized";[19] a third (twelve pages) is presented under the rubric "Report on the French Film Production in Times of War."[20] One more (three pages), dated September 18, 1939, is on "La Cinémathèque française."[21] It was also at this time that Renoir and Henri Chomette* endeavored to have the films at the Cinémathèque placed under the protection of Colonel Calvet of the army's film service, who would have them stored in a safe place.

On October 8, when Renoir wrote to Flaherty from Wangenbourg, which was near Strasbourg, to say he was going "to make films that will fascinate me—not with actors anymore but with men, real men,"[22] he wasn't referring to his thoughts about the next stage in his career but about the missions the army had assigned him. This was confirmed in a letter Dido wrote the same day to Flaherty, which informed him that Jean was most often in Paris, that he was "probably going to make a propaganda film," and that he was "currently working on the screenplay," which she considered to be "a good story."[23] But before that, he also produced (two pages) an "Account of the Visit of Noël-Noël† Regarding the Possibility of Organizing Some Cabaret Tours for the Army,"[24] dated October 9.

His mission was close to his heart, certainly, as demonstrated by the interview he granted *Pour vous* in which he claimed, "In times of peace, we directors have the mission of educating or entertaining; in times of war, we assist with information. It's a new discipline for us that has to do with current events. I've already toured the military zone. The spirit of the men is wonderful."[25] By that date, he had filmed various "sights" intended for the *Journal de guerre* of the army's film division. Among these images were some of a cathedral in Strasbourg that he admitted he had always refused to visit because of "snobbery" during trips he'd taken before, especially when he and his friend Champagne went to the Bugatti factory, which was located a few miles from the city.

In his memoirs, he'd also recall that a mistake in directions during an expedition to film some scenes in a school not far from the front had taken him behind enemy lines. No mention of this misadventure was made in the little

---

* A very minor director, the younger brother of René Clair, nicknamed "Clair-the-Obscure" by Henri Jeanson, was a "reactionary, anti-Semite and probably pro-Nazi" (Pierre Billard, *Le Mystère René Clair*). In January 1940, he'd be named head of the film service for its North African headquarters, a "surprising appointment that some interpret as a method of distancing an officer whose pro-Nazi sympathies would be disturbing" (ibid.). He would die on August 12, 1941, of a sudden case of meningitis (polio) at the age of forty-one.

† *Translator's note:* Noël-Noël, born Lucien Noël (1897–1989), an actor, director, writer, and cabaret performer who appeared in more than forty films between 1931 and 1966.

black notebooks in which he kept track of his daily movements and activities. However, some of the thoughts found therein illuminate his ambitions at the time. For example, this desire: "If the wounded captain, with his monocle, could recount what he did, it would be a hit in movie theaters." Or this plan: "Capture in sound all the French accents and dialects under the same uniform." And, finally, this do-it-yourself idea: "Produce a device with fake lenses in front, but at the side a viewfinder [*unreadable*] makes it possible to film people while seeming to be pointing the camera elsewhere."

It was during a trip that went through Paris between September 30 and October 13 that he encountered the journalist for *Pour vous*. He next left for the region of Metz and arrived on Saturday, October 14, around noon, to meet with Captain Bousquet, followed by a "walk in the forest with General Delâtre" (probably de Lattre de Tassigny). In the evening, after a dinner in Saverne, he wrote in his notebook, "Main directive: exalt the individual. We are fighting for the individual against the madreporic* civilizations. Conclusion. Above all, try to capture a human expression in all the shots and portray everything registered in it by the personality of the individual [*underlined*] we are depicting."

Although he had met Jean Loubignac, future director of *Ah! Les belles bacchantes* (*Peek-a-boo*, 1954) and *Coup dur chez les mous* (1956), who like him was on location, he was working from now on with two cameramen: "Very advisable for Méjat and Missir:† close-ups; be discreet; look for a natural expression; don't destroy it by talking to the subject: come forward . . . to the left . . . into the light. Operate as if you were invisible, hidden, silent in any case. For large extensive groups, too. Repeated all day that the actor must be respected, especially if he's an amateur. Heartfelt search for a flash of sincerity on a face."

On October 18, Renoir met Joseph Kessel, who told him "that he can attract attention to the usefulness of film for the army." On the nineteenth, he was in Boulay (Moselle), where he noted that Pierre Fresnay had preceded him by a few days and learned that the meeting with "the general" the director had been requesting for a long time was to happen the next day. On Friday, the morning of the twentieth, in fact, General de La Porte du Theil, commander of the Forty-Second Division of the Infantry (DI), arranged for him to visit the camps. In the afternoon, Renoir filmed floods, and Saturday morning, "the general entering the area."

---

* Referring to a hard coral as found in the tropical seas.

† Raymond Méjat and Hervé Missir were two of the directors in 1938 who worked on the "colonial" documentary *La France est un empire*, which was edited by Jean Loubignac.

"Lots of autograph signings,"[26] he'd also note that day. Jean Renoir was a star, something that General de La Porte du Theil was slow to become aware of. In a letter written on October 20 to his wife, the general wrote, "Yesterday, when I went to Noettingers'... at his home I found a rather fat man: wearing a rather fanciful military uniform, with a black lieutenant's kepi, white braiding, red turban; and a second individual, a short and skinny younger man, wearing the uniform of an officer of the artillery in cut and material, with no braiding." The general didn't know Jean Renoir, and they had to tell him at mess that he'd been dealing with the person who "with Duvivier" was "the best French director and certainly one of the best in the world."

The fact that the general neither knew the "short and skinny" man who was with Renoir and who answered to the name Tiquet is less surprising. The "rather fat man" explained to the general that this "excellent cameraman, very well known," was the head of the army's film service, Henri Tiquet, who was twenty-six at the time and who would become a great cameraman, especially in his work on films by Jean Cocteau and on *French Cancan*. The general's letter allows us to discover that Renoir owed his post to General de Lattre de Tassigny: "He'd remembered him from peace time and put together the deal. Because when it comes to publicity, he knows what he's doing. He had Renoir come to him every day—told him where he had to go the day after, what he should film, created special scenes."[27]

De La Porte du Theil took Renoir into the field, showed him some "incredible landscapes," some scenes "to deal with." The director declared himself "blown away" and asserted that the general had "wasted [his] life," that he was "made to be a director," and then left to "film a scheduled scene because it would have 'the floods' as background." The general expected the man of art to translate to the screen that "double idea: the strictest discipline and the most rigid bearing, with that total ease of spirit and all that sincere affection that dazzles." Founder in 1940 of Marshal Pétain's Chantiers de la jeunesse, General de La Porte du Theil would become its general commissioner until January 1944.

The scenes Renoir filmed for the military were thought to be lost until Stéphane Launey discovered them:

First, the maneuvers of the infantrymen and the artillerymen in the flooded plains of the Moselle presented in the *Journal de guerre* no. 6 are unequivocally shots that were made under the direction of Lieutenant Renoir. . . . The other subjects that have been preserved relate to a visit of [de] La Porte du Theil to the 151st Regiment of the Infantry (RI), the cleaning of cannons, and the grooming of horses in the courtyard of a chateau, a series of shots showing the path taken by a letter from its arrival at the army post office, or else detailing the delivery of provisions and leading up to the soldiers' meals. To that are added two projects, footage filmed at the Eightieth Regiment of the Infantry, attached to the Forty-Second DI, signs of which can be spotted. At the very start, on October 21, the director films scenes within the First Battalion, described by the historian and then Captain Georges Mongrédien in these terms: "One day, the major general arrived at the camp with a lieutenant that we thought was an aide-de-camp. Not at all. This is the famous Jean Renoir, maker of *Grand Illusion*, who today is serving as one of the kingpins of the SCA [the army's film service] and who is on mission. It's about a documentary to be made. . . . Jean Renoir arrives with his crew, there's a bit of direction and 'action.' So, to amuse the civilians, the daily life of the camp is captured: the field kitchen, the soup detail, the platoon returning from maneuvers, pinochle played while sitting on bales of hay, and our dogs, some of which are from Germany."[28]

The last pages of Renoir's second notebook show that he wanted to but hadn't filmed "the magnificent mass"[29] at Luppy on October 22. The church had been too dark, and he had asked for the use of a generator and a sound crew for the following Sunday. This plan is confirmed in the campaign journal kept by an officer of the Eightieth Regiment, which reports that during an encounter on the same day at "Bar Luppy," around a "Sunday Pernod," Lieutenant Renoir "reveals his intention to come back, and, at that time, capture a similar ceremony, with a sound recorder. It's bound, he thinks, to produce a very strong impression in countries with Catholic sentiments, Spain and Italy."[30] This happens to be the first sign of Renoir's Mediterranean connection, which in the months to come would orient Renoir's thoughts about the future of film, and which, for the time being, seemed to stem essentially from religious feelings.

Renoir's final remarks in his notebooks are dated Monday, October 23, morning: "left at six o'clock to film presidential trip," and this "personal reflection" as well: "why not organize a trip—with enthusiasm—and a little directing if need be. I have the impression that the Alsatians are asking only to yell, 'Vive la France!'"

In a note of September 1940, Colonel Calvet writes about Renoir: "Having volunteered to take some shots for the army, he directed some in Alsace that were top quality. A valuable technician, very enamored of his art, excellent comrade and soldier who carries himself correctly."[31]

Renoir's army activities may have enthralled him, but they didn't keep him from thinking about two projects that he had registered on May 30, 1939. These were *Amphitryon* and *Romeo and Juliet*. He had especially been considering the latter for several years, and he wanted to transpose it to North Africa. A departure, by all means, a departure . . .

And yet, there was still a film waiting for him in Italy, the *Tosca* he'd been forced to abandon during the summer. In December, a decision was made in the higher echelons of government to allow the film to be directed. Renoir began devoting his time to obtaining the authorizations he would need for his departure. France and Italy were certainly not at war, but the existence of the Pact of Steel was arousing fears that Mussolini would soon join his German ally, and the relations between the two countries became continually more strained.

And then, Renoir was hardly in the dark about the reactions his exile would not fail to provoke. He'd seen the opinion his friends of the past had formed during the summer. He had every reason to act cautiously and, quite naturally, began by ensuring the backing of the French authorities. In a letter dated September 12, 1939, and addressed to Monsieur Ringel, a functionary at the police prefecture, he asked for support in quickly obtaining an exit visa for himself and Dido Freire, whom he presented as his "secretary." At the time he said that he was entrusted with a mission: "It's a matter of establishing artistic contact between the two countries with the help of cinematography, and to do this by employing crews and artists from both nations."[32] The context for this mission? "The company ERA-Film in Rome, whose president is Monsieur Vittorio Mussolini, has already requested me for five weeks to complete a first film that has a very good chance of being followed by many others."

Renoir next reported that André François-Poncet, the French ambassador in Rome, had interceded with the Commission of Information insofar as this was concerned. It was an organization in charge of propaganda to which the ambassador had made it clear that he considered the presence of Renoir in Rome "very useful." Since August 12, 1939, this organization had been directed by Jean Giraudoux, most of whose plays had been staged by Pierre Renoir for the last several years; and Giraudoux was also a friend of Jean's, making it difficult to imagine that he would try to stand in the way of his initiative. Furthermore, Renoir had another ally at the Commission. It was Pierre Lestringuez, who had been appointed to the organization with the rank of captain on November 24, 1939.

Although there's nothing to indicate that Renoir's mission had ever taken on an official nature, what was at stake was a strong source of interest to him; and less than two weeks from the beginning of shooting *Tosca*, he announced the project to André Beucler in a letter, informing the writer, who was then one of the contacts in Paris with whom he communicated the most, that René

Besnard* was going to take advantage of his next trip to Paris at Renoir's request to interview him about "the necessity of that exemplary cinematic connection between Paris and Rome."[33] Beucler, the author of *Gueule d'amour*, was then on the staff of the Commission of Information, and he and Renoir had known each other since 1925.[34]

Placed on special assignment and removed from the jurisdiction of the army's geographical service on December 15, 1939,[35] Renoir was able to receive his visa in a remarkably short time. In summer 1940, when Julien Duvivier and René Clair would leave France for Hollywood, they also would first negotiate with Giraudoux to obtain mission assignments having to do with creating a bogus French production unit in the United States.

According to Renoirian logic, a mission to Rome had been entrusted to Reserve Lieutenant Renoir, whereas Renoir the director found himself at the bid of an Italian producer to direct a film in Rome for which he'd signed a contract several months before. It was a happy coincidence, to say the least, and reversing the sequence of events only changed the proof he needed in a nonessential way. The director had to make a film in Rome, and the lieutenant was assigned to a mission in Rome. Nonessential for history, perhaps, but cardinal for Renoir, who would write, "The French government didn't want to refuse Mussolini anything. The hope was that the power of cordiality would keep Il Duce out of the war. I was part of the military, and my only job was to obey."[36] Thus, when he wrote his memoirs, he had an excellent reason to keep silent about his trip to Italy in summer 1939 and subordinate his second departure to a certain "mission" he had been ordered to make. Clearly, he was in the position of having to make a film in Rome. But the truth is that at the time Renoir had the firm intention to continue to work in Italy after *Tosca*. In the letter that Eugène Lourié had written to Renoir to inform him that the French authorities had refused to allow him to leave for Rome and for *Tosca*, he had added that perhaps this could happen "later, for the third or fourth film in Italy."[37]

Renoir had no lack of Italian projects. The Manenti company was hoping he would be able to direct *Beatrice Cenci*† in July 1940.[38] Renoir himself was thinking about bringing *Madame Sans-Gêne*[39] to the screen and was toying with a certain "Finnish" plan that remained enigmatic and that André Beucler deemed preferable to be "presented in Italy" because currently no one was "keen" on it in France.[40] Moreover, Renoir's Italian exile hadn't discouraged French producers

---

* A politician and diplomat, René Besnard was then high commissioner of the government of the French Republic at the World's Fair in Rome.

† The film would be directed by Guido Brignone in 1941.

from making offers to him. For example, the Société centrale de cinématographie was asking him to consider an adaptation of the Ernest Pérochon book *Les Gardiennes,*⁎ "whose national relevance would make excellent propaganda."[41]

In the eyes of his future acolytes, Renoir was always on the right side in every circumstance, and his reasons were never any other than the best. Accordingly, the guardians of the temple would adopt as their own the highly improbable claim that Renoir was on mission in Rome. However, it is true that the director's enemies showed no better sense of proportion. As to be expected, his former friends flew into a rage, claiming among other things that when Jean-Paul Le Chanois's father expressed surprise at seeing him leaving for a Fascist country, Renoir retorted, "I've had it with the Russians. And as for Mussolini, I like him!"[42]

Sometimes, a taste for provocation merges with a prudent person's daring; if Renoir didn't make that statement, it's certainly not because he wasn't capable of it. And the possibility that he didn't like Mussolini didn't prevent him from doing a pretty good job at acting like he did for several months running. All the same, the diatribes of his former assistant Le Chanois came quite late and were caused more by the years that followed—those of the Occupation—than by Renoir's actual conduct in 1939. When Le Chanois wrote to Renoir in November 1939,[43] it was to thank him for the "postcards" that Renoir had had "the kindness" to send him; and after having deplored the fact that there was no work in Paris, he sent Renoir his "best regards." As if Le Chanois didn't know at the time that Renoir "loved" Mussolini.

Thus, in December 1939, Renoir and Dido traveled across the Alps once again, in a Delahaye convertible, a bold choice for that time of year. Carl Koch had been waiting for them in Rome, and they found him on the twenty-sixth in the offices of the production company Scalera. This scene was shown and dated by Lotte Reiniger in her sketchbook, which also informs us that on the same evening, the party gathered around an *omelette flambée.* A luxurious apartment located at 5 via di Sant'Erasmo, not far from the Coliseum and the Caracalla Thermal Baths, had been reserved for the director and his secretary, and it included a couple of servants. Recalling these living conditions twenty-five years later, Renoir would write to Leslie Caron, "It was quite pleasant and made us think we were waking up every morning in a setting for some fancy tart— know what I am saying? We felt like we were becoming luxurious tarts!"[44] The

---

⁎ A few years later, the same project would be offered to Henri-Georges Clouzot, who was from Niort like Ernest Pérochon. The film would never be made.

fact that in this same letter he situates this stay in Rome "in 1938" could mean that his memory, here too, was playing tricks on him. Or that he didn't consider it necessary to recall that in 1940, on the eve of the war, he found himself in a situation to be envied in Fascist Italy.

In Rome, Renoir experienced what it was like to be the focus of every kind of attention. He was fussed over, paid for, honored by the Fascist regime; but also welcomed, celebrated, surrounded by the Italian film community, including the part of it that was opposed to that regime. Yet again, then, everybody saw what he was doing as right. The admiration arising from his films and the esteem in which he was held by people on the Left as a "fellow traveler" in the French Communist Party were natural sources of such warmth, which the Fascists' banning of *Grand Illusion* greatly helped maintain.

In fact, sometimes secretly but most often just discreetly, the Italian directors organized screenings of the film, which filled them with enthusiasm. Chief among these young cinephiles were Luigi Comencini, who hadn't yet directed, and Alberto Lattuada. Renoir wrote to them at their Milan office address on March 26, 1940:

All our plans have been upset by the fact that Scalera Film has bought *Grand Illusion* for Italy. If this company really is the owner of the film over here, you can't show it without their permission. I'm going to speak with them and will be as eloquent as I can, but I should tell you in advance that they don't seem very anxious to show the film outside of their commercial distributions. They must have spent a certain amount of money for this film, and their fears about harming the release by proceeding rashly can be understood in a certain sense.[45]

That letter gives rise to several questions. First of all, if *Grand Illusion* was banned in Italy, how and with what intention in mind would a production and distribution company acquire the marketing rights for it on Italian territory? Had Renoir and/or Scalera obtained assurances about an eventual lifting of the ban?* Why did Renoir suggest that Scalera had "had to spend a certain amount of money" when the question is unfounded and, especially, when his own association with Scalera made it certain that he would be kept abreast of these negotiations?

---

* It's probable that *Grand Illusion* hadn't been submitted for review to the Italian censor because no distributor shortly after the presentation of the film in Venice had wanted to take the risk of a ban. Moreover, this feature is shared by a number of films reputed to be "prohibited by the censor" (for example, *Paths of Glory* in France). If so, the film wasn't "banned" in Italy but "unauthorized." *Grand Illusion* would not receive approval through a censor's certificate in Italy until 1947, and that is when it would be distributed by Scalera.

Various exchanges also testify to the fact that during this same period Renoir went into action to find an Italian distributor for several of his films, asking to be provided in Rome with copies of *La Chienne, La Bête humaine,* and *The Rules of the Game.*[46] It's also just as likely that he wanted to stop these showings of *Grand Illusion* that risked causing him problems because the film wasn't authorized in Italy. On the other hand, if it did receive the censor's authorization, that might interfere with the commercial distribution of the film. On March 27, which was the day after his message to Comencini and Lattuada, Renoir would let them know through Dido that he had obtained permission from Scalera to show *Grand Illusion* in Milan on April 20, but for that time and place only.[47]

The presence in Rome of such a respected director, with such an incontestable personality, gave young Italian cinephiles and filmmakers a distraction from their feeling of isolation into which politics had plunged them. In return, Renoir felt liked. There, he was the new member of a community with the added benefit of being the most distinguished of them all, both as a director of several masterpieces and as a French person. In France, he had endured the jealousies of colleagues whom he himself hadn't spared, and he'd had to put up with a profession that had become weary of him and in veiled terms reproached him for having left the woman who ensured his link to crewmembers and to politics. In France, he had to answer for everything he said, he who was so nimble with words, so quick to be flippant. He had to face creditors and bill collectors, who'd banded together in defense and were furious about the failure of *The Rules of the Game,* the film he'd produced, written, directed, and acted in. How could Rome seem like anything to him but paradise on earth, whose door he'd merely peeked through in August 1939 but which was now offering itself to him? When he worked again in Europe a little more than eleven years later, he'd end up in Rome rather than Paris.

He didn't speak about his "mission" with the Italian journalists he met. There was no way of making anything of that but a secret. Instead, he claimed to be benefiting from a year's leave from the army, granted because of the wound he'd received during the First World War.[48] He also said he was filled with enthusiasm for Italy, and he laid the foundations of what would become his pet craze all during 1940: the necessity of creating a "Mediterranean cinema" capable of opposing the harmful influence of the "Protestant-Puritan outlook" that had contaminated film production worldwide since its origins, first under the influence of Nordic filmmakers and then American productions. It was an outlook with "cruel and cold" content that had distorted the taste of audiences. "We others, Latin people, are dressing like them, speaking like them, seeing everything around us like them."[49]

In light of the years that followed and the situation at the beginning of this twenty-first century, this analysis is not without interest. The question here, however, is about the opportunity provided by the place and time that Renoir chose to produce such views. And this becomes more apparent in the way Renoir responded to a query about whether he'd already met the Italian workers he was saying he so wanted to film: "The other morning, at Centro Sperimentale," Il Duce was surrounded by the young and fervent. They had come en masse, forming a single block. . . . Tradition could be read on their faces and, more than ever, on Il Duce's face. . . . In seeing Il Duce, I understood why his words for the Italians are synonymous with homeland."[50] The journalists were thrilled at not encountering "the cliché of a Renoir ill with intellectualism, facile refinement tinged with that extreme morbidity characteristic of certain foreign films," before concluding, "In listening to him speak, we understood that our suspicions were unfounded and that the atmosphere some had wanted to create around him was totally arbitrary and superficial."[51] What they discovered, they wrote in the words of propagandists, "isn't a man who is prey to rash enthusiasms, nor one who stays tied down by preconceived notions." He was one who "didn't wait for the rumor of war to change his opinion about Bolshevism, unlike the majority of French."

Not prey to rash enthusiasms, Renoir? The man who on various occasions declared himself ready to direct numerous films in Italy, and as soon as possible films that were profoundly "Italian," proof that he took *Tosca* for a "French" film? From the different interviews published at the time, the upshot was essentially that he had found in Italy the climate—and he wasn't talking about the weather—he'd been dreaming of and that he didn't intend to leave so quickly. In fact, "Italy today is so rich in subjects that it can satisfy the most unrestrained imagination."[52] In a letter addressed to *L'Ambrosiano,* a Milanese newspaper created in 1922 in support of Fascism and lasting until 1944, Renoir revealed his ideas regarding the necessity of an alliance between Italian and French cinemas: "For me, a genuine servant of Latinity, such a collaboration also offers the immense advantage of creating a common front to oppose the invasion of American film, which will devour us all if we don't defend ourselves."[53] Less than ten months later, he'd be living in Hollywood, under contract to Darryl F. Zanuck's Fox.

Several other French directors were also in Rome at the beginning of 1940, but because their names were Jean de Limur or Jean Choux, or even Marcel L'Herbier, their reputation didn't attract any particular attention from

---

* *Translator's note:* Renoir is referring to the Centro Sperimentale di Cinematografia, the Italian national film school that had been established in 1935.

Mussolini's regime, unlike Renoir's, which the regime certainly intended to use to its advantage. Renoir wasn't satisfied in going along with the game; he took part in it with obvious gusto. Not that he had become a convinced partisan of Mussolini's regime, but because his nature influenced him in every circumstance to want to please and to belong. That is one possible definition of opportunism.

Although the hypothesis of journalistic invention can't be ignored, it's still probable that Renoir was present at the inauguration of the Centro Sperimentale by Mussolini on January 16, 1940,* and that this was the occasion on which he appreciated the fervor shown by those gathered around Il Duce. The series of lectures that Renoir delivered, twenty, according to him,[54] gave young future filmmakers like Michelangelo Antonioni, who was then the critic for the review *Cinema*, the chance to come into contact with one of the most renowned directors of his time, at a period when Italy still had few major auteurs. It was precisely this generation, not yet even at the point of taking their first faltering steps, that would make the great films from Italy in the next three decades. It hasn't been proven, as has been said at times, that Renoir met Roberto Rossellini, who was among those who bowed to Fascist demands to make films. This is not to say that these directors demonstrated any more belief in such ideology than that, especially in comparison to a figure like Alessandro Blasetti, who played the role of the state's official filmmaker.

For Luchino Visconti, Renoir's presence in Rome was a chance to enter more deeply into the milieu of film. He was not a familiar figure in that world at the time. Sometimes, encounters with Renoir took place where Renoir was living, but most often they occurred in the house where Carl Koch and Lotte Reiniger were staying, on via Luigi Settembrini, where several teachers from the Centro Sperimentale and some of their students—including the great-director-to-be Giuseppe De Santis—also met. Several of these people wrote for Vittorio Mussolini's aforementioned review *Cinema*, which gave them carte blanche. Visconti collaborated on the screenplay for *Tosca* with Koch and Renoir to an extent that is difficult to determine. He would also serve as an assistant director for that film.

Renoir explained a lot about the project, especially in an interview he gave to the newspaper *Tempo* that appeared on February 8, 1940, in which he specified having had an idea since 1925 for a *Tosca* with Catherine Hessling. He also stated in that interview that he'd "discovered a different point of view than that of my renowned predecessors": viewing the situation from the point of view of a "director of detective films," he'd been "able to discover in the circumstances

* The invitation card with Jean Renoir's name can be found in the archives at ECPAD (Établissement de communication de production audiovisuelle de la Défense).

of the characters some elements that haven't yet been exploited." This vision had led him to "limit the duration of the action to twenty-four hours, from the execution at dawn of a prisoner in Sant'Angelo Castle to Mario's execution and the death of Tosca the following day at the same hour." One of the advantages of such a choice was that it offered the opportunity "to use many exteriors and take maximum advantage of the Roman atmosphere."[55] The aspect of the project that enthused him the most was the integration of documentary film elements into the framework of a historical spectacle.

In 1889, two years after the staging of Sardou's *Tosca* in Paris, Puccini had highly commended Sarah Bernhardt's performance in Milan. After that performance, which was in French, he'd composed an opera whose fame eclipsed the reputation of Sardou's play. Renoir's *Tosca* drew closer to a return to the source.

A few weeks before shooting, several important issues remained unresolved; casting was one of the most problematic. Viviane Romance had been cast as Tosca. Her status as the top female star in France, mostly because of Duvivier's film *They Were Five,* gave her the power to force on the producers her lover, Georges Flamant—limited in talent and poorly appreciated in character as Flamant was. The couple was rumored to make life impossible for their directors, and Flamant had come to Rome for a film by Jean Choux called *Angelica* (or *Rosa di sangue* [*Blood Red Rose*]), which was being produced by the same company as *Tosca* in a double Italian-French version. Difficulties experienced by the director of that film may have started the rumors.

But the gossip could not have had a very decisive effect upon Renoir because he knew Viviane Romance's lover quite well. He had directed Flamant's debut performance in *La Chienne*. Nevertheless, Renoir loathed the idea of working with Flamant. At least, that was the opinion expressed by the director and screenwriter Ivo Perilli, who claimed that "Renoir schemed with the French Ministry to get the actor drafted."[56] The story is more complicated than that and plays out over a series of exchanges between Rome and Paris made possible through the use of the diplomatic pouch.

On the day of his final acceptance of Scalera's offer, Renoir was informed that he would have to work with the couple. Added to his contract, in fact, was a clause stating, "Monsieur Jean Renoir declares to be aware of the engagement of Georges Flamant and Viviane Romance as the leading performers of the film."[57] Apparently, at first the two actors had not been wild about the fact that the project had been entrusted to Renoir. In an undated letter, Renoir's agent had written to him to say that they "had reconsidered their decision and finally expressed the desire to make the film with you."[58]

In reality, it happened that the contract Viviane Romance signed, whose exact terms Renoir discovered belatedly, gave her the right to review the film for approval, a measure that provoked a letter from the director's agent to Scalera: "M. Jean Renoir has become aware of the contract signed by your company with Mlle. Viviane Romance for her performance in the film *La Tosca*. M. Jean Renoir has been able to determine that this contract contains clauses that are incompatible with and in contradiction to the clauses of the contract signed by your company on July 12, 1939, with M. Jean Renoir."[59] As a result, Renoir asked that Viviane Romance's contract be modified; but Scalera maintained that nothing in it allowed "such control of the direction."[60]

Flamant's case turned out to be just as thorny. Renoir wanted to give the role of Scarpia to his brother Pierre, who'd agreed to it, and the only possibility for this that the director's agent could ascertain—offering Flamant the role of the character Mario Cavaradossi[61]—clashed with the terms of the actor's contract, because he had signed for the role of Scarpia. Therefore, it appears that Renoir had not acted, as Ivo Perilli suggested, to get Flamant "drafted." In fact, Flamant was already mobilized and had been "released until April to make the film." What Renoir appears to have really done is to have attempted to keep the necessary authorizations for this from being granted. Alas, Flamant obtained a discharge and straightaway sent a registered letter to Scalera informing the producer that he was therefore in a position to honor his contract.[62] The issue ended up being brought before an arbitration committee, whose conclusions were unfavorable to Scalera;[63] but in the meantime, Renoir had gone into action to find his Tosca and his Mario, because time was close to running out.

Once the doubts about the possibility of his making the film had finally been lifted in Italy, there was still a long wait for needed accord of the French authorities.* Renoir went ahead and offered the roles to Louis Jourdan and Micheline Presle, who were currently in Rome for *La Comédie du bonheur* (*Comedy of Happiness*), another Scalera production. As the actress later recalled writing in 1957 to Renoir:† "For such a long time I've very much wanted to work with you, dear Jean. Well before this lost opportunity for *Tosca*!!!"[64] In an interview published in 1985, Arletty, whom the director had considered for the role of Geneviève in *The Rules of the Game*, revealed that Renoir had also asked for her for *Tosca*, an offer she had been forced to refuse because she was engaged elsewhere.[65]

---

* Using Jean Giraudoux as his intermediary, Pierre Renoir had come up with two precise questions for François-Poncet, the French ambassador to Rome: "Did he consider the presence of Jean Renoir in Rome to be useful? Did he consider the presence of French actors in Rome for the purpose of making the film *Tosca* to be useful?" Answer: "A strong yes." (Letter from Pierre Renoir, April 9, 1940, Jean Renoir Archives, ECPAD.)

† In response to Renoir proposing that she act in his adaptation of the Clifford Odets play *The Big Knife*.

Micheline Presle, Arletty, but also Edwige Feuillère,[66] Michèle Morgan,[67] Marie Déa,[68] and, finally, Michèle Alfa, whom Renoir had already considered for *The Rules of the Game* and who seemed probable for the role of Tosca in April. Because "she would have to be a brunette," Renoir wrote, "I suppose a wig will be necessary, but ideally she'd dye her hair jet black, which worked so successfully with Simone Simon in *La Bête humaine;* not red or with bluish highlights, truly black."[69] It was dyed that color, in fact, and Jean's efforts didn't discourage Pierre from informing him, on the same day "the invasion of Norway and Denmark by the Krauts" was announced, the fact that "we're still flying blind," adding that, according to the Scalera office in Paris, "we can only pull through from all this with the following cast: Tosca—Viviane Romance; Mario—Flamant; Scarpia—me." Finally, in an attempt to reassure his brother, Pierre concluded, "Flamant will always know how to fight at the bottom of a well and how to be tortured."[70] Proof that the Renoirs were far from convinced of the talent of the actor who had played Dédé in *La Chienne.*[*]

Thus, Pierre Renoir ended up with the all-important role of Scarpia. Dated April 17, the contract foresaw seven weeks of shooting, in exchange for a fee of 140,000 francs as well as 35,000 liras, this latter figure being the amount remaining after Italian taxes were deducted. Direction would begin between April 20 and April 30, 1940.[71] The producer also agreed to offer a contract to Lisa, Pierre's wife, and to his brother Claude.[72]

Less than a month from the beginning of shooting, casting finally seemed to have come to an end. Viviane Romance and Flamant were no longer in the film, without anyone knowing exactly how they had been expelled from it. Pierre Renoir would be Scarpia, Fernand Gravey had replaced Louis Jourdan in the role of Mario Cavaradossi, and Raymond Rouleau or Jean-Louis Allibert[†] would play Angelotti.[73] In the role of the queen, Renoir wanted Gabrielle Dorziat. For Schiarrone, he wanted André Alerme, and for Spoletta, Gaston Modot[74] (who had played the gamekeeper in *The Rules of the Game*). Modot would also function as assistant director for *Tosca.*

Renoir, who was being forced by production to work with Italian crewmembers,[75] claimed that he had always been thinking of Modot to play Spoletta, an idea that the latter had acted upon with satisfaction, thanking the director

---

[*] Between 1940 and 1943, Georges Flamant would star in four films, all with Viviane Romance: *Venus aveugle (Blind Venus)* by Abel Gance, *Cartacalha, reine des gitans* by Léon Mathot, *Feu sacré* by Maurice Cloche, and *Une femme dans la nuit (A Woman in the Night)* by Edmond T. Gréville. Afterward, he would make only five films. In homage to Renoir, he was chosen by Truffaut to play Monsieur Bigey in *Les 400 coups (The 400 Blows)*, his last role. Georges Flamant died on July 23, 1990, at the age of eighty-six.

[†] The actor who played Marseillais Moissan in *La Marseillaise.*

at length for his "very detailed, very precise" letter and, as he did, denouncing Viviane Romance's and Flamant's behavior: "The couple's blackmail should be remembered as an example of how boorish they are, and it didn't come with the slightest surprise."[76] However, on April 2, Modot was informed that the role of Spoletta was not to be his. "You know," he wrote to Renoir, "what upset me the most was being told about it by a third party. A few friendly words from you would have softened the blow, which was hard enough given everything I was led to hope. We can tell each other anything without a problem, which is also why I'm writing you this letter."[77]

It would also be the case that Renoir had been pressured to hire Italian actors; or at least that's what he suggested at the time when he explained, "This is another case in which my role as an employee of the French Propaganda machine has to come before that of film Auteur,"[78] but no Italian name would appear in his exchanges with various correspondents.

Rarely had the casting of a film been established with such haste. And at this point even Fernand Gravey as Cavaradossi could not be considered part of the production. Tired of waiting for the contract promised him, the actor took work with the Théâtre de la Madeleine[79] to extend the run of the Armand Salacrou play *Histoire de rire,* in which he would appear with, of all people . . . Pierre Renoir, who was refusing the offer to extend the run.[80] Pierre Blanchar next came on the scene: "I have an enormous amount of work transforming the role for Blanchar,"[81] Renoir had written on April 20.

Eight days later, on April 28, 1940, the second version of the screenplay was finished, but Renoir was still waiting for his actors. He was losing patience, and his brother, who had signed his contract on the eighteenth, attempted to calm him.[82] The international situation, as well as the state of relations between France and Italy, was making the issue of the necessary authorizations for actors very complicated, which, in fact, was the reason that the production company was nearing the point of using those that it already had under contract for *Comedy of Happiness,* L'Herbier's film. L'Herbier had also written to Renoir to assure him that he would proceed in a manner that would not cause any problems for *Tosca.*[83]

Nothing was working out, and by the beginning of May, everything was falling apart. Renoir telegraphed André Beucler: "Receive telegram from Dewalde indicating impossibility for *Tosca* actors to get authorization to leave."[84] Everything was crumbling, but the next day, the evening of May 6, shooting began. Without the actors.

First night in front of the Farnese Palace, among the guardsmen. In live sound, to the great amazement of the journalists who were there and accustomed to standardized Italian methods of postsynchronization. Renoir had always stated he was against such practices, explaining on several occasions that in his opinion such a compulsive habit was the only major fault he'd noticed in Italian films, which he considered, on the other hand, to be generally better lit than French films.[85] May 9: Shooting at night on the bridge of Sant'Angelo Castle. Renoir is particularly insistent about obtaining a crane shot that begins with a stone angel by Bernini and allows the camera to catch a group of horsemen rushing out of Farnese Palace. Description of the director by Gianni Puccini, the future filmmaker and screenwriter for Visconti (*Ossessione*) and De Santis (*Bitter Rice*), among other films: "Absorbed in thought, he paces back and forth as if on a pirate's sailing ship, the back of his flannel trousers carelessly drooping, like an elephant's rear."[86]

But on the day that page appeared in *Cinema*, May 25, 1940, Renoir had finished shooting *Tosca* and had left Italy nearly a week prior. And although the reasons for this departure are understandable, the circumstances surrounding it have remained obscure until this book.

There's no doubt that the atmosphere in Rome had changed several weeks before, to the point of having become hostile to those from countries that were at war with Germany. The agents of Nazi propaganda were spreading the notion that the responsibility for the German-Soviet Nonaggression Pact was placing a burden upon the Allies.[87] Von Ribbentrop's visit to Rome on March 8 and 9 and, even more so, the meeting between Mussolini and Hitler at Brenner Pass on March 18, fed the rumors of a possible rapprochement between Rome and Moscow, the nature of which was certainly not reassuring to the French who were living in Italy. An amusing anecdote reported by Renoir[88] gives an account in its own way of this change in ambiance.

Michel Simon, who was in Rome at the time for L'Herbier's *Comedy of Happiness*, is the hero of this tale. He was spending his evenings and nights in the city's brothels, and in their receiving rooms he'd enjoyed showing his photographs of Roman ceilings to his favorites for their admiration. One evening he found his spot on the couch occupied by German civilians and insisted to the madam it was his right that she restore it to him immediately. However, "Madame" appeared resistant to his demand. He went home to bed and the next day confided in Renoir about his ire, ending his account by thundering, "They bore the fuck outta me, their goddam ceilings!"

On the morning of Thursday, May 10, 1940, when Renoir came back to his rooms after a night of shooting on the Sant'Angelo bridge, German troops mobilized and invaded Belgium, the Netherlands, and Luxembourg. The news was known in Rome later that same day, and Renoir commented on it in a letter written at that same time to his old friend Lestringuez. His reaction shows remarkable sangfroid, because it was only after having asked Lestringuez to deliver the documents that he included with the letter and promising him that André Beucler would provide him with news of him that he came to the real story of the day: "We've just learned of the invasion of Belgium and Holland by the Germans. Personally, I'm presenting that to the Italians as an example of a great victory for the French."[89]

But what aspects of the German attack allowed Renoir to depict it as a great French victory? It's true that, several years later, he'd make the following statement about the Italians, which was just as enigmatic and which was recorded by Bertolt Brecht in his *Journal:* "I truly like working in Italy. The Italians are such ardent anti-Fascists."[90] The same letter to Lestringuez reveals a detail about Il Duce's schedule—or what his schedule would have been if events hadn't caused him to revise his plans: "Tonight, Benito Mussolini himself is going to have *Grand Illusion* shown. I'm very proud of it."[91] Something to be proud of, then. Thus, Renoir's taste for ridiculing Mussolini seems to have melted away in the sun of a very common brand of vanity, but not his certainty that one person's reasons are just as valid as another's: "Until the last moment, I will do everything in my power to keep on friendly terms with a country that I continue to consider as very likeable. Seen from Paris, the articles that appear in Italian newspapers are incredibly unpleasant. But it has to be understood that seen from here the articles appearing in English and French newspapers aren't any less. You ought to tell our Minister that."[92] The Renoirian sense of proportion was close to the point of genius. Rarely was it tripped up.

The next day, *L'Osservatore romano,* the official Vatican publication, was the only important Italian daily to take a position against the German offensive. The opinion was written by its publisher, Count Dalla Torre. Because the article was worded in such vehement terms, which were constantly repeated in the issues of the paper that followed, groups of militant Fascists began attacking those who bought the paper—to the point of its having to be withdrawn from news kiosks on the evening of May 14. "Officially, the newspaper wasn't banned in Italy, but a large number of agents stopped selling it due to the many incidents that occurred between the Black Shirts and people who were buying *L'Osservatore romano.*"[93] Another sign of agitation was the xenophobic demonstrations the Roman Black Shirts had been organizing since the day before, Monday the thirteenth. Two days later, the police would be ordered to disperse them.[94] Lotte Reiniger had done a drawing dated the evening of that same Monday the thirteenth, showing Renoir and Dido opposite their friends, who included an easily recognizable Carl Koch. The caption, written by the same hand that drew the image, was worded, "Jean talking about his accident at the station."[95] What accident was it?

When Renoir described the end of his stay in Italy in his memoirs, he began by recounting how everyone who bought *L'Osservatore romano* ended up "beaten with a club" by thugs hired "by the Nazis" to stand guard near the newspaper kiosks. Next: "When I asked for *L'Osservatore romano* in a restaurant, I was duly thrashed and would have lost my hide if I hadn't invoked the name of Mussolini, who, after all, was the one who'd brought me into this nightmare."[96] Could it be that this "restaurant" scene was the same one that happened "at the station" in the drawing by Lotte Reiniger? If Renoir knew about what had already been inflicted on those who bought *L'Osservatore romano* for the past three days, why would he, one usually so prudent, have chosen to bring the fact of its sale to the attention of the Fascists or the thugs, and even do so in an enclosed place like a restaurant? And does the word Lotte Reiniger used, "accident" ("*Unfall*"), usually signify a "thrashing"? In any case, it's clearly evident that the artist made no attempt to reproduce any traces of a thrashing Renoir's body would have shown.

André Beucler provided an account of the facts that allows us to answer these questions. To start with, the place: in a station, as indicated by Lotte Reiniger, or in a restaurant, according to Renoir's version? Both: Beucler, Dido, and Renoir dined that evening at the station buffet. Accident or attack? Attack: Beucler explains how Renoir, after they had looked at the menu, began to read *L'Osservatore romano*. Then, "three officers suddenly appear, shouting cusses at us; and as we protest, lift up the table and turn it over on top of us, silverware and all—absurd." Beucler showing off his diplomatic passport doesn't make a difference. It's crumpled, thrown to the floor, and then a new litany of insults against the French and government officials. Threatening to complain to the ambassador only increases the rage of the "officers," who order the three people—all three of whom they assume are French—to leave the place. The three then decide to go to the embassy; but Jean, whose jacket is stained with oil, doesn't think he looks presentable and chooses to wait in the taxi, probably with Dido. The ambassador then tells Beucler that he can do nothing to protect them, that "even Mussolini's son, whom Renoir knows well, wouldn't dare come to [their] defense."

Next, Beucler leaves for the station in the same taxi, still with Renoir, and jumps onto the first train for France. The only mystery that still exists has to do with the date: Beucler clearly situates the events *before* the German offensive, whereas Lotte Reiniger's drawing mentions May 13. And yet, the day on which the *L'Osservatore romano* became a target is definitely the day after May 10, and Lotte Reiniger did her drawing as soon as what happened was reported to her, whereas Beucler related his version of it more than forty years after the fact. Nevertheless, one thing about which Beucler cannot have been mistaken was the reason for his trip to Rome: "I was instructed by Giraudoux to require Jean Renoir to interrupt the filming of *La Tosca* without delay and make arrangements to return to France as quickly as possible."[97] This wording may suggest that Renoir at first didn't want to give up a film for which the French government had granted him permission to leave his native soil while he was still involved in active service for the army. Accordingly, the "accident" at the station would have forced him to, before allowing him years later to endow the reasons for his departure from Italy with a more novelistic twist. That evening at the train station buffet in Rome, when he was with others—contrary to what he'd later indicate—he had an experience that was unpleasant and frightening. However, he certainly wasn't "duly thrashed" or saved by mentioning Mussolini's name as a last resort.

When he would write his memoirs, the main purpose of the pages he devoted to *Tosca* would be to depict under a light favorable to him an episode in his life that was actually far from flattering. The place that he accorded the circumstances surrounding his departure from Rome would then have had even more importance. They had to cast him in a positive role as he attempted to thicken the smoke screen he'd created over the reasons that had made him accept working for a Fascist regime. The beating he received—as the reckless reader of an anti-Fascist newspaper in a restaurant to which he'd gone alone—would correlate to the secret mission assigned to Reserve Lieutenant Renoir. Otherwise, he probably wouldn't have chosen to devote lines to a film he didn't even direct, lines he denied certain other films that were important to his work in other ways.*

None of Renoir's casting decisions would be left in the film. Quite logically, the production turned its back on the French actors planned for it, who didn't receive authorization to go to Italy. Michel Simon, who was already in Rome and who was a Swiss citizen, would play Scarpia. Rossano Brazzi, a young actor of twenty-three under contract to Scalera, would play Mario Cavaradossi. Imperio Argentina would slip into the costume first worn by Sarah Bernhardt, for whom Victorien Sardou had created the character. Thus, to portray an Italian heroine, a French theater icon would be replaced by a Spanish star who'd been born in Argentina, who was a queen of the tango, and who had played opposite Carlos Gardel.† And all this would occur under the direction of a German director.

* *Boudu Saved from Drowning*, for example, did not appear in *My Life and My Films* before several readers of the manuscript pointed out to the author that he couldn't choose to overlook this film. Renoir did, however, refuse to make any mention of *The Elusive Corporal*.

† Imperio Argentina would be dubbed by Giovanna Scotto, and the film would be presented in Rome in January 1941.

To this day it's impossible to say whether the cast had been established definitively, with or without Renoir's agreement, before or after his departure from Rome. The fact that Michel Simon stubbornly refused to consider any of Renoir's reasons—regardless of what they were—for leaving in 1940 and considered himself abandoned by Renoir, to the point of holding it against him for years, suggests that Simon joined the project when the director was still in charge of it.[98] But it is also true that the actor was quick to bear grudges. He himself would stay in Rome until 1942, first for *Tosca* and then for two other Scalera films, one of which, *Una signora dell'Ovest* (*Girl of the Golden West*), was based on a novel by Pierre Benoit and written and directed by Carl Koch.

Renoir would state that the French ambassador in Rome, André François-Poncet, had advised him to leave on the first train. In reality, to accomplish this he first needed six days to deal with contractual obligations and possible diplomatic complications. Vittorio Mussolini would write, "Thanks to my interceding with my father, he [Renoir] was able to leave Italy without being harassed a few hours before the start of hostilities."[99] Actually, as proved by another Lotte Reiniger drawing showing "Jean's goodbyes," Renoir left Rome by train on Sunday, May 19, not "a few hours before the start of hostilities" but three weeks before Italy declared war against France on June 10. Behind him he left Dido for a few days, as well as Michel Simon, Carl Koch, Lotte Reiniger, and a *Tosca* that was no longer his. As for his Delahaye convertible, he asked the French embassy to make a gift of it in his name to the Sisters of Saint-Louis-des-Français.[100]

Carl Koch would take care of the direction of the film, which would begin shooting again on June 12, two days after Italy's entrance into the war. The first screening of *Tosca*, a film directed by "Carlo" Koch, would take place on January 30, 1941. A few months later, Claude Renoir would write to his brother that he'd just seen the film, three weeks before its Parisian presentation on October 2, 1942, and that he had found it "very slow-moving and a bit of a pain," with "too many useless documentary shots." But he would add that "Michel Simon is good."[101]

Carl Koch would die on December 1, 1963, at the age of seventy-one, and Renoir would not see Koch's *Tosca* until March 11, 1978,[102] less than a year before his own death, at a screening organized at Renoir's home by Dudley Andrew,* using a copy from the UCLA Film and Television Archive. The only

* Author that same year of the book *André Bazin* (Oxford University Press).

scene Renoir had directed in this film was the first one, and he hadn't been given the opportunity to work with any of its actors. After seeing it, he wrote that he thought it was "excellent," adding that "Koch was a great director who had never gotten a chance to show it."[103] Renoir would describe *La Tosca* to Lotte Reiniger as a "magnificent film."[104]

Near the end of the war, Renoir received a letter in Los Angeles from an Italian soldier, who at the time was a prisoner of the American army in a Texas camp. The man wanted to tell him how much his lectures at the Centro Sperimentale had interested and affected him. The letter took several weeks to reach its addressee, whom the sender had identified as "Pierre Renoir."[105]

22

All at Sea

Renoir's hurried return from Italy was the beginning of the darkest period in his life. France was in the grip of disaster. Emmanuel Berl would write that it "wouldn't really be a disaster if it wasn't blurring our view of it."[1] As the months went by, people better equipped than Jean Renoir would lose their sense of proportion and reality and become incapable of getting their bearings within the shared chaos that had taken hold of minds. When it came exactly to that—bearings—Renoir had far less than anyone, right after the personal failure of *The Rules of the Game*, which also seemed like humiliation for a famous director, not to mention the fact that his stay of more than four months in a foreign country had isolated him still more from those from whom he'd chosen to cut himself off less than a year beforehand.

When he arrived in France on May 20, 1940, first in Nice and then in Paris, the front page of *Le Matin* reported that fierce fighting had taken place in the region of Maubeuge. *Le Figaro* informed readers that General Weygand had just been named generalissimo and that "the enemy hasn't advanced very far." It had been four days since the announcement of the capitulation of the Netherlands. Even the least pessimistic had become aware that the battle had been lost, although everyone hadn't yet given up hoping for a miracle in the form of a new Battle of the Marne. This pipe dream had resulted in the nomination of Weygand instead of Gamelin and, on the same day, May 17, the recall by Paul Reynaud of Marshal Pétain, the Verdun victor, henceforth vice president of the Council of Ministers.

Renoir moved back into his apartment on avenue Frochot, reuniting with his brother Pierre at this address. He had no idea what his future would be. As the child of a diplomat, Dido was even more concerned than her partner about the need to leave France as quickly as possible. As far back as May 2, when shooting on *Tosca* had not even yet begun, she had written to Robert Flaherty about the fact that she "so wanted Jean to go to America."[2] In that same letter, she had also revealed that Jean had received an offer from a big studio to which he had favorably responded, "only asking for a few other little things, such as a round-trip ticket for him and his secretary and a job with the same company for his secretary as well." Without any other information about this offer, the young woman had added, "Jean thinks that the United States is the best place for him to promote his country's propaganda."

Nothing found up to the present day has given the impression that this American offer was any more serious than Lois Jacoby, who was their go-between at the time, had made it seem. A letter from Jacoby dated May 21 and addressed to Rome leads to the conclusion that Renoir expressed worry in his letters about who would pay for Mademoiselle Freire's trip. Jacoby answered that, although she understood how worrisome the situation in Europe was, only the Hollywood firm with which Jean would be under contract could currently consider the question. Then she added, "I continue to think that it's possible to come to a very satisfying agreement with you, but most producers are currently holding back and waiting to see how the situation will turn out. Thus, Mr. Selznick and Mr. Goldwyn, who are very interested in you, have no idea for the time being when they will begin producing again. Mr. Selznick knows that *Joan of Arc* will be a very expensive film and hasn't yet decided when he'll do it. However, RKO and Metro are racing rapidly ahead, and since Metro owns the rights to *Cyrano de Bergerac,* it could be an excellent place for you to end up."[3]

Lois Jacoby also revealed that she had decided to entrust Renoir's interests to a different agent than the one first considered. Because this different agent, Charles Feldman, was Charles Boyer's exclusive representative, the actor would probably have been able to obtain the necessary authorizations from the French authorities. This all seemed to point strongly to the fact that negotiations were still in the embryonic phase.

On the day on which he wrote to Dido, who was still in Rome, Jean himself refused to consider the reality he was facing, or else he decided not to make anything of it, to keep from alarming his future wife. "The way France looks at this moment is incredible. I'm full of hope, and I see people so resolved that I believe we'll pull through."[4]

In a letter that had been sent to Renoir in Rome slightly before his departure, which means that he probably hadn't read it, Laurette Séjourné,[†] whom

---

* A screenwriter for American television in the fifties who was close to the couple Lillian Hellmann and Dashiell Hammett, Lois Jacoby apparently attempted to play the role of agent for Renoir on behalf of the director and producer of documentaries Richard de Rochemont.

† Archaeologist and ethnologist, as well as the wife of Victor Serge, Laurette Séjourné had already visited Renoir in April 1940, as shown by the drawing by Lotte Reiniger dated April 19 of that month.

he'd asked to meet in Italy, described a very different situation: "The atmosphere here is dominated by anguish that's difficult to escape, and the refugees you see everywhere, with their poor, suffering faces, remind us at every moment what is happening far from us."[5]

Renoir's letter to Dido is dated May 30. For two weeks already the officials at the quai d'Orsay had been attempting to burn their archives, and the inhabitants of the cities to the east and north of France were pulling together what they could of their belongings to leave wherever roads might take them. Renoir asked Dido to inform his Italian producers that in any case he was in no position to return to the filming of *Tosca*. He also told her that he was busy trying to get her a visa for France. A few days later, when Dido left Rome for Paris, the mass exodus had begun. On June 10, the day Italy declared war on France, the government left Paris and declared the capital to be an open city. For the last four days it had been emptying of its inhabitants. On the twelfth, German troops crossed the Marne and a generalized order of withdrawal was given to the French army. Two days later, the Germans marched up the Champs-Élysées.

At that time, Jean and Dido were in Marlotte, which they had reached in a rented Peugeot, after a visit of a few minutes with Alain, who had enlisted in the cavalry in October 1939 and had been posted on January 13, 1940, to the Twelfth Regiment of Cavalrymen. There he would soon find he was a cavalryman without a mount, a major without any superiors, but nevertheless expected to command about fifty men whose retreat he'd lead toward the Loire, ending near Saumur. He was demobilized on July 10, 1940, in Fontacq, a district of Soumoulou in the Basses-Pyrénées. The address he gave was Les Collettes, "in order to avoid being sent back to Paris."[6]

For a few days, Renoir's fate was bound up with that of millions of other French people hurled onto roads, not knowing what they were looking for but well aware of what they were fleeing. There was no other witness of his exodus than himself. The single source for it is the account he offers in his memoirs.

Paul and Renée Cézanne climbed into the Citroën "Trèfle," and Renoir sat down at the wheel. Dido, Jean-Pierre Cézanne, and his young wife followed on bicycle. In the car trunk were Cézanne's rolled-up and tied-together canvases. Renoir had entrusted Aline Cézanne with the portrait of him in a hunting outfit that Auguste had painted in 1901. Several years would go by before he got it back.

Apparently, the group had considered going to Bordeaux, temporarily the seat of the French government; but the journey ended in the department of Creuse, in a hamlet some distance from the road. "The inhabitants welcomed us with open arms," Renoir would write. "They were proud of having 'their' refugees. Our being there enhanced their prestige and aroused the jealousy of the neighboring villages."[7] They found refuge in the barn provided them by a farmer, on the walls of which he hung Cézanne's canvases. Beautiful movie scene, which brings together the empty confines of the villa Saint-El the day after the failure of *Nana* and the paintings strewn throughout the straw and hay in the Creuse.

Chance had led the refugees to this hamlet in the Creuse, which Renoir would always remember with emotion. This rough-hewn, simple life suited him to a tee, and wasn't it also where he once again discovered his father's childhood landscapes? But, wait: Chénerailles is the name of this country town in the sleepy district some thirteen miles from Aubusson; and it was not unknown to the Cézannes. In fact, they'd stayed there a few months before, in January 1940. At least one letter, sent by Paul Cézanne from there to Louis Jouvet, provides evidence of it.[8]

At this time, which was the beginning of summer 1940, the postal services still functioned well, a fact that sometimes surprised Renoir when he happened to send letters from Chénerailles. The address he provided his correspondents— Lestringuez, Giraudoux, a few others—was "c/o Dioton (saddler)." This is where he waited for Robert Flaherty, the director of *Nanook of the North*, to let him know about the progress of the steps he was taking to get to the United States.

On July 8, he wrote to Flaherty to tell him about their accommodations "in a baker's oven and haystack, in the heart of Limousin" and expressed his worry about "what will become of European film after these events." On the twenty-seventh, when Flaherty informed him by telegram that he "thinks it's possible to arrange an advance if needed," Renoir and Dido had already left for Les Collettes; and on August 6, they cabled Flaherty that it was impossible to leave France without special authorization, for which Renoir was about to apply.

His decision to go, however, did not yet seem wholehearted, and even the vague desires to leave, which had been visible for several months and which were endlessly stoked by Dido, seemed to be tempered by the situation. A feeling of helplessness had taken hold of everyone, and Renoir was no exception. His character and his current personal situation were already turning into indecisiveness. In fact, two days later, on August 8, he wrote to Flaherty again to tell him that "certain obligations" were keeping him in France. He considered himself still bound to Rome by Scalera Film, which he wanted "to give a chance to offer another assignment before my taking work elsewhere." Most importantly, he was thinking about "film in France, which has been in such a slump since the catastrophe," and considering it his duty to help to the extent he was able, adding, "I'd be ashamed to walk out on my fellow countrymen when everything is going badly." This last sentence is critical because it explains his new reservations about a plan for exile, the memory of which will come in handy a few months later. For the time being, the beginning of August 1940, his desire truly was to "work here somewhat longer."

On August 10, it was Dido's turn to write to Flaherty, using the same sentence to confirm Jean's frame of mind and present her own opinion, which opposed it. "Jean thinks that his duty is to stay here; but in my opinion this is useless since he won't be able to work for a long time, and it's dreadful for him to remain inactive." She herself, as she makes clear, "would like to leave for America" and is convinced that it won't take Jean long to "realize on his own that there's nothing to do here" and that then "he won't refuse a concrete offer from America." The truth was that Dido was involved in relentlessly trying to convince Renoir to leave as quickly as possible.

On August 12, Flaherty cabled from Washington that his approach was close to paying off. Two days later, Dido answered that Jean had written to the director of Radio and Film to ask him for authorization to leave. Thus, he seemed to have made up his mind, influenced, certainly, by the sentiment expressed in a letter by Dido that "there's barely any hope in seeing someone worrying about our cinema while there are so many other more important things, like the problems of getting supplies to our troops, etc."[9]

Obviously, Dido was unaware at the time that there had indeed been "someone" worrying about the future of film in France, and this had been going on for several weeks. In the eyes of the occupying force, it was even a priority and was being called one. In fact, the German desire to seize control as quickly as possible of both the distribution of films and the machinery of their production was also finding a surprising echo within the echelons of the French authorities. Especially surprising, in view of the fact that the thirties, except for the period of the Popular Front, had been blighted precisely by an absence of political volition when it came to film. And yet, as soon as it had moved to Vichy on June 29, the French government—set straight by the example of German commitment—had suddenly become aware of the essential role that film was being summoned to play.

Certain movie theaters had reopened about ten days after the armistice. The machinery of production was essentially at a standstill, but Vichy intended to restore it to its functional state as quickly as possible. One of the major obstacles to this undertaking had to do with the dispersion of talents and experts, whom it was necessary to bring back together. Such a purpose led to the sending out of operatives in search of directors and actors wherever they could be found within France. Many of them had withdrawn to the region around Nice, and some were waiting for a hypothetical departure for Hollywood while they contented themselves with the hope for better days in France.

Accordingly, Renoir tells in his memoirs about being visited at Les Collettes by "two Frenchmen working for Nazi cultural organizations," which was probably not a totally apt description but justified by the narrator's concern with creating a gripping tableau of the situation. The story goes on in like fashion: "They proposed that I work within the framework of the New France, claiming that I'd benefit in every way possible to make films of my choosing. They often came with an attractive Russian lady who looked like an adventuress in a detective novel. She adored Hitler as if he were a living god. When she spoke of the Führer, she'd go into a trance."[10] To make the scene even more striking, Renoir conjured up Lestringuez constantly repeating that "Hitler has pissed on the leg of lamb,"* which was to say that, before, everything had been going fairly well, but now, everything was just plain rotten. Then Renoir concluded that the moment had come for him to disappear.

If he did actually receive emissaries from Vichy—maybe even on several occasions as he claims—the scene he describes still seems excerpted from a Soviet propaganda or Hollywood film, especially in the way it matches just too well the author's wish to justify his departure for Hollywood at the price of his "shame at leaving his countrymen when everything was going badly," a consideration that had been a major impediment a few weeks before. Now his refusal to compromise would become the primary reason for his exile.

This was the same reason he also gave right after the war, which was backed up at the time by the same argument. On October 25, 1945, in response to a questionnaire sent him by a certain Monsieur Bonnard of the news service Pharos with the purpose of drawing up a biography, Renoir filled in the part labeled "reasons for departure" as follows: "A great mistrust of the Germans, despite everything we were being told about their politeness. If I'd worked in a profession that was less conspicuous than film, I would have stayed."[11] It was a claim he reiterated on many occasions—for example, for the 1962 interview he gave *Cinémonde*. Out of the "thousand" reasons that had led to his leaving for America, he had chosen one: "The offers from the German operatives were so tempting and outstanding . . . that they made me anxious. I wasn't willing to accept them. Also, I thought that it was better to leave. Since the American government had let me know that there was a passport waiting for me, I took advantage of it."[12] The French operatives, which they undoubtedly were, turned

* Translator's note: "Hitler a pissé sur le gigot." Variations of this comic tale of a small, willful boy who ruins dinner by insisting on urinating on a leg of lamb appear in at least two French sources: *Affaire du collier: mémoires inédits du comte de Lamotte-Valois sur sa vie et sur son époque* (literally translated as *Affair of the Necklace: Unpublished Memoirs of the Count de Lamotte-Valois on His Life and His Times*, 1858) and *300 Histoires égrillardes pour corser le pot-au-feu conjugal* (literally, *300 Bawdy Tales to Spice Up the Conjugal Pot-au-Feu*, 1900).

into German ones, which they probably were not. It made the scene even more dramatic and Renoir's choice more praiseworthy when the people depicting a golden future were the world masters.

It's hard not to think of the legend Fritz Lang created concerning his departure from Germany and his meeting with Goebbels, who offered to make him the preeminent figure of German cinema. Lang would ceaselessly improve on that fable as the years went by and the account was repeated, embellishing it with a wealth of always new details, whose staggering precision would seem to come to his mind more and more clearly the longer ago they had occurred. Lang's first account of the event was about ten years after the fact, in April 1943, when his film *Hangmen Also Die!* came out. Renoir was in Hollywood, as well, by then, reading those newspapers that described the attitude his Viennese colleague had adopted.

Historical truth is something else. Beginning in mid-August 1940, Renoir tried to gamble on two tables at the same time, striving to make it possible to leave while also preparing for the failure of this plan. There is nothing reproachable in that, but his eagerness to produce evidence of good conduct and sound thinking afterward catches our attention.

Thirty-three-year-old Jean-Louis Tixier-Vignancour, who had been appointed general-assistant secretary of information right after the armistice, was in charge of film and radio. As a member of the Chamber of Deputies for the Basses-Pyrénées, he had already exhibited his attachment to the ideas of the extreme Right, which he had served with remarkable fervor. He owed his appointment to this post to his very active support of Pierre Laval in July 1940, when Laval strategized to obtain the revision of the Constitution that had allowed Pétain the seat of power, which consequently guaranteed Laval's own place. It was toward Tixier-Vignancour that Renoir had to turn; he had no other choice.

Therefore, on August 14, Renoir wrote to him to inform him of his situation: he was being offered the possibility of working in America. He'd been left hanging by his Roman producers as he waited for them to make a decision, "but if there's a chance of doing something quickly in France, it's quite clear that I should stay here." In the same letter, he spoke of a film project. The screenplay was entitled *Magnificat,* and the story followed an expedition of French missionaries into an unexplored region of Brazil. Renoir would return to this on several occasions as the years passed, most markedly with the idea of transposing it to the United States and creating "a great Catholic and American film." But for the time being, he was writing to Tixier-Vignancour: "If you get the chance one day to talk to the marshal about it, I'll be very flattered. I think the project would appeal to him. It would be a mistake to start again in our profession and leave behind thwarted films. And the depiction of religious heroism may be even more timely than the depiction of our military glories."[13] The vocabulary and tone were in shocking contrast to those he had used several months before as the columnist for *Ce soir*. A loss of certain illusions? The isolation of a fighter seeing his fellow strugglers being disbanded? Proclaimed disgust for political ideas in general, regardless of what they were? The influence of Dido, who was a fervent Catholic? A new attraction to spirituality? Submission to the current line of thinking? All of it, most likely. Producing a character whose outlines are a poor match for those of the man his friends thought they knew.

At the end of his letter to Tixier-Vignancour, Renoir finally wrote, "I'm asking you if you think that such a chance exists. You're the official in charge of our profession, and it's up to you to determine my conduct." Thus, he would do with himself what the government decided. And it should probably be taken into account that he preferred others to make decisions for him. That was nothing, however, in comparison to the short paragraph that he decided was necessary to devote to the present situation. Without being asked, he wrote, "Allow me to take the liberty to tell you my feelings about this subject: here on the Côte d'Azur the sight is appalling. Besides certain of my friends, who are true professionals, the riffraff you're familiar with are still hustling. And as of yet I see no way of eliminating them. The only chance of making a film in the proper way is to find a sponsor who isn't part of that crowd. It isn't easy, and even in such a case, the only way to have a studio and the technical means is by way of the undesirables."[14]

How would you actually "eliminate" such "riffraff" who were rendering it impossible to "make a film in the proper way" when "that crowd," those "undesirables," had their hands on all of the instruments of production? And to start with, who were "that crowd" and those "undesirables" who were part of this "riffraff"? It wasn't the first time Renoir had written such a word. It had appeared in one of the reports he'd written in September 1939 while he was mobilized: "There certainly do exist some very honorable [producers]. But among them all, whether French, naturalized, or simply those who are accredited in France—those who've been in charge of the fates of French film—only undesirables!" And farther down in the same document: "A second danger: the background of the producers working in the French market. Their internationalism, which in general is quite connected to Germanicism or Slavism, perhaps doesn't especially designate them to carry one of the torches of French thought in times of war."[15] One is extremely tempted to give the signer of the letter to Tixier-Vignancour the benefit of the doubt, although nothing about it makes that particularly easy. Renoir himself has made such a thing impossible.

At the beginning of September, Renoir went to Vichy, which he'd already visited a few weeks earlier to register his demobilization,[16] but this time in hopes of seeing some progress in his case. His visit left few traces; it would have been preferable for it not to have left any. But Renoir granted an interview to *La Semaine de Vichy-Cusset,* a weekly founded in 1830 that prided itself on having published Mallarmé's first two prose poems in 1864. Renoir's interview appeared in the magazine's September 21 issue. In it the director complained that in the past the authorities had not awarded his plans for organizing productions the attention they deserved. "If they had," he declared, "a lot of films that would have served the French cause could have been directed. But they didn't want to understand the need for such propaganda, nor did they want to finance it. . . . " Obviously, such neglect is regrettable, even considering the worrisome observation that in Renoir's mouth the word *film* was being associated with the word *propaganda.* But such a thing is still nothing in comparison to the sentence in its entirety: " . . . nor did they want to finance it, leaving the care of this to producers who in the majority are foreigners and Jews." When the journalists then remarked that "most of those people have judged it wiser to retire fast . . . ," Renoir spoke his mind and said, "And so much the better; they weren't doing anything for film and kept the profits. All that's needed is to replace them with producers who, it certainly must be said, were doing all the work."[17] What impression does reading these lines give of Pierre Braunberger, Albert Pinkovitch, Léon Siritzky, and a lot of others?

It would be pleasant to be able to say that the journalists for *La Semaine de Vichy-Cusset* put these words in Renoir's mouth. However, when these words are added to those he uses in his letter to Tixier-Vignancour, their effect is devastating.

"Leave-taking, as I see it," writes Emmanuel Berl, "spawned two sentiments, both unexpected: anti-Semitism and Anglophobia."[18] Although the second may not have found a very fertile breeding ground in the milieu of French film, anti-Semitism brazenly took root there. The Jews weren't only held responsible for the disaster in May and June 1940; they were also considered the cause of French film's poor health. Film was, in fact, in very poor health. By 1939, the situation had become catastrophic. Renoir wasn't the only one to make such denouncements. In fact, certain colleagues of his, who weren't among the least prestigious, hadn't even waited for defeat to express their feelings about the issue. When it came to such an attitude, the statements made by the director of *The Rules of the Game* seem moderate, almost tentative, as long as they're compared to those of certain filmmakers.* It's also true that the example influencing French directors originated at the top and was embodied by Jean-Louis Tixier-Vignancour, who was close to Jacques Doriot, and was also influenced by Jean Giraudoux. Since March 20, 1940, Giraudoux had only served as president of the Federal Information Authority that ruled over the Service du cinéma, but in the past he had very clearly voiced his opinion regarding these issues.[†]

Thus, Renoir was also poised to make good use of film's currently alleged liberation and forgot the fact that in less than nine years he had directed fifteen films, some of them produced or distributed by the "undesirables." To start, he sent answers to whoever interviewed him, barely worrying about the pages on which his statements would be read. This time the paper was called *L'Alerte*, a weekly that had been created that very month of September with the publicized plan of supporting the policy of Marshal Pétain. Its pages must have seemed welcoming to Renoir; on two of them he revealed his thoughts about the situation and future of film under the title "What Will French Cinema Be?" Good question—one element of which is answered by the subhead: "The art on our screen will give us more sincere, more human, less egoistic works." The article

---

* Jacques Feyder in 1938: "These scum outsiders (see Trasnaltor's note below) who've temporarily colonized a large part of French productions have a frame of mind, a lack of culture, a palate that completely disrupts our artistic sensibility, our desire for original creation. They intend to impose their own ideas, which we do not and cannot share. Their vision differs from ours, and they cannot represent French taste. I will never, even for millions, make movies in France for one of them. If French film continues to be placed under their supervision, in bondage to this group of producers who are called French and have names with 'itch' or 'er' . . . anyway, I don't need to name a single one, because you know who they all are" (Conversation with Lucie Derain, *Ciné-France* no. 32, March 1938). Marcel Carné, Renoir's great rival, borrowed the same insinuation in September 1940, stigmatizing the "old gentlemen with 'er' or 'itch,' who lived shamelessly [off of film] in the past and who today are talking about going to America to relaunch [it] and would very much like us to follow them there" (*Aujourd'hui*, September 30, 1940, quoted by Pierre Billard in *L'Âge classique du cinéma français*).
Translator's note: Feyder uses a racist term for those whom he considers nonmembers of French society: *métèque*, a word that is basically untranslatable but that is etymologically derived from the ancient Greek term for a foreigner not possessing citizenship (*metoikos*). In France, the word could injuriously refer to those of Mediterranean background and later to anyone considered a foreigner.

† In *Pleins Pouvoirs* (*Full Powers*), a collection of five lectures given by him and published by Gallimard in 1939, the following lines appear in the chapter entitled "La France peuplée" [loosely, "Living in France"]: "All those who have chosen our country come to us not because it is France, but because it is still the only worksite open to speculation and activity. . . . I'm not talking about what they take from our country, but at any rate, they add nothing to it. They change the nature of it by their presence and their actions. Rarely do they make it more attractive by their personal appearance. We find them teeming in each of our arts or industries, both the new ones and the old ones in a spontaneous generation that recalls that of fleas on a dog barely born" (Jean Giraudoux, *Pleins Pouvoirs* [Paris: Gallimard, 1939]).

that followed was nearly devoid of interest. Renoir claimed to have recently seen two French films that were wracked with mediocrity: a comedy that was "the revival of an enormous success, starring a great comic," a show that was "musty, out of date, moth-eaten"; and "a dramatic, sentimental film featuring a famous couple, one of those couples whose photographs end up in the bedrooms of typists and bourgeois ladies, department store salesgirls and their customers, loose women and well-behaved women." Such characters, he wrote, "are never seen working." "Whether they are portrayed as a laborer, a painter, or a peasant, we never once see them hit anything with a hammer or finish one stroke of their brush or push a plow. . . . Our heroes have a lot of other things to do than using their tools. They have to talk about themselves."

This is how Renoir expressed his abhorrence for the old days, remaining faithful to an idea already expressed in 1936 when he denounced "the stupidity of the current rulers of the film world" and insisted that "those people are idiots, they're illiterate and they're dishonest."[19] But he had changed his tone to make it easier to proclaim his faith in a shining future. "Under the sign of the cult of 'me,' we've produced an entire artificial world without any link to reality. And now, the times, goaded by our hardships, have already stepped out of that convention. The times have begun their climb up the great stair-way."[20] At least the text doesn't depart from the tone of a paper billed as "the weekly of French reform," in service to that person who said, "I give France the gift of myself to ease her troubles."‡[21] Perhaps there is nothing disgraceful in Renoir's pledge, but it comes after several others and, alas, before more of them.

In the fall of 1940, was Renoir contemplating taking part in this rebirth of French film he had glimpsed, as he'd claimed in *L'Alerte*? For several weeks, he had been trying to receive authorization from the Vichy government to leave for Hollywood. Tixier-Vignancour finally gave his permission, about which Renoir informed Flaherty on August 24. "M. Tixier-Vignancour has answered that I would be able (for a certain amount of time) to work with you in the United States. Naturally, this was only a matter of an ethical authorization, which is what I wanted to have."[22] At the time, he was referring to an exile of short duration, and it was accompanied by many professions of goodwill. Accordingly, at the end of August, he wrote to M. Dubois, the assistant director of the Sûreté

‡ *Translator's note:* Perhaps Pétain's most well-known "inspirational" statement, from a radio address he made shortly after the start of the Occupation: "J'ai fait à la France le don de ma personne pour atténuer son malheur."

nationale,[*][†] "I've received an answer from Tixier-Vignancour. . . . My idea is to go and make a film over there, earn a few dollars, then get down to a great idea I have with Gabin and Lestringuez. . . . As Gabin says, 'We've just had our ears boxed' . . . we can't show any military triumphs . . . that would crack people up. . . . So, we've got to show some other stuff in our favor."[23]

Obviously, it would have been awkward on Renoir's part to mention leaving without coming back, but leaving to "earn a few dollars" before returning to work for the new France did indeed seem like a less outrageous plan. Of course, as Dido wrote to the same Flaherty on September 4, consent was nothing without that of the minister of the interior. And those very Vichy officials, in fact, did seem hesitant—perhaps, or at least in part—because the director was still only forty-six, whereas the minimum age required for authorizations to leave the country was set at forty-eight for men. That was one of the reasons, and probably the first, that brought Renoir to Vichy in September. There he discovered several people willing to listen attentively.

In September 1940 at Vichy, among the people Renoir may have encountered were Jean Giraudoux,[24] Jacques Feyder, Yves Mirande, Maurice de Cammage, Marcel Pagnol, and Jean-Paul Paulin, all there the same time he was.[25] It was, they thought, the place where the future of film in France was being decided, and therefore its anterooms and hallways were the places they had gone to do business, as so many others were doing. All of them exhibited their goodwill toward the powers that be, in the same way Renoir had, placing their hopes in these new times; but unlike Renoir, they weren't necessarily intending to leave for America.

Jean-Paul Paulin was the son of Paul Paulin, a friend of Auguste Renoir, and he had gotten to know Jean, who was eight years older, when they were children. Without being close friends, they'd stayed in contact, all the more so because Paulin had also chosen film as his occupation. In September 1940, he was preparing to direct *La Nuit merveilleuse,* an adaptation of the Nativity to the time of civilians' flights from the north of France during the Phoney War and the German invasion in 1940, with Fernandel playing a shepherd. Marshal Pétain was highly pleased by it. Although Pétain wasn't the author of the screenplay, as rumor had it, his cabinet was the source of the project,

---

* *Translator's note:* The French criminal investigation department, equivalent to the FBI in the United States.

† Max Dubois, collaborator of Albert Sarraut from 1930 to 1939 and assistant director of the Sûreté nationale beginning in June 1940, a post from which he would be dismissed shortly after because he acted in favor of the departure from France of those victims singled out by the Nazis.

which had been commissioned to benefit the Secours national.* A friend of Jean-Paul Paulin had served as the intermediary for this project. His name was Roger de Saivre, and in 1926 he had been one of the creators of the "Phalanges universitaires."† The marshal would appoint him deputy chief of staff of his civilian cabinet in July 1941; but in 1940, de Saivre already enjoyed influence in Vichy, and he was the one whom Paulin would approach to unblock Renoir's administrative situation. It worked. When he got back to Cagnes on September 19, Renoir wrote to Richard de Rochemont that he'd received the necessary authorizations,[26] and then on October 5, he wrote to Flaherty to tell him that he and Dido had finally obtained their visas.[27]

The logic behind official decisions, if it exists, is tricky to discern. Renoir had just obtained authorization to leave when the Council of Ministers announced on October 30 that it had revoked the French citizenship of twenty-three public personalities accused of having left France. Among these were the actress Véra Korène, the journalist Pierre Lazareff, the diplomat Alexis Léger (known as Saint-John Perse), and René Chomette, a.k.a. René Clair. This decision was accompanied by the confiscation of property and the cancelation of the order of the Légion d'honneur. René Clair had left for the United States on August 6, 1940. Like Julien Duvivier, who had left on July 1, Clair had taken the ocean liner *Excambion*. A Hollywood contract was waiting for both directors. Clair's fellow passengers across the ocean included Man Ray and Salvador and Gala Dalí. Duvivier had crossed with Darius Milhaud, Jules Romains, and Julien Green. Both directors had already worked in Hollywood. The fact that Duvivier's lover and Clair's wife were of Jewish background was among the number of reasons for their leaving Europe.

On January 11, 1941, the day after he arrived in Los Angeles, Renoir would lunch with René Clair at the Universal canteen and would write to Tixier-Vignancour to give him his address, also asking him to "give his best regards to friends in France."[28] In that letter, he mentioned four names: Coupant,‡ Ville-

---

* *Translator's note: Secours national* = "National Security" or, more literally, "National Aid." Created in 1914 and reactivated for the Second World War in 1939, its purpose was to bring aid to soldiers, their families, and civilian victims.

† *Translator's note: Les Phalanges universitaires* = well-trained right-wing students serving as the "shock battalion" for Pierre Taittinger's Jeunesse patriotes (Young Patriots), a group formed in 1924 to back up the anti-Communist Ligue des patriotes, whose members Taittinger believed had become too old and ineffective to oppose left-wing demonstrators. Les Phalanges universitaires were encouraged to use violence (often by wielding canes) against left-wing demonstrators, but only enough to be effective; and they were also cautioned to avoid confrontations with the police.

‡ Probably Jean Coupan, Tixier-Vignancour's principal private secretary and a director who was interested in filming news from Vichy.

Flanked by his brother Claude, born August 4, 1901, and eldest brother, Pierre, soon to be an actor, Jean, at eight, struggles to remain still next to Aline, his mother, and Auguste in the latter's studio at 73 rue Caulaincourt. Faced with the camera lens, it is the painter who cannot keep from moving.

August 1907. Jean has yet to turn thirteen and is photographed on a street in Essoyes next to one of his father's models—Adrienne, perhaps.

1916. The war has crippled Jean, and age has confined Auguste to a wheelchair. In their now nearly empty Parisian apartment, as cannons rumble in the distance, the son gets to know his father.

Gabrielle Renard, Renoir household employee, model for Auguste, and Jean's nurse. She would return to Jean in Los Angeles in 1941 and live near him with her husband and son until her death in 1959. The last words of Renoir's *My Life and My Films* would be for her: "Wait for me, Gabrielle."

Top: Summer 1924. Filming the flow of life and drifting along with the current with the help of friends. On either side of Jean Bachelet—one of two cameramen for *The Whirlpool of Fate*—are Renoir and Pierre Lestringuez, inseparable when it came to writing and partying.

Left: 1925. Andrée Heuschling, Auguste Renoir's last model and Jean Renoir's first wife, is transformed into Catherine Hessling, the actress. She dreams of Hollywood, and American stars fascinate her—especially Gloria Swanson, whose manner and way of posing she has adopted.

Top: Winter 1925. In the Grünewald studios in Berlin, *Nana* is filmed. The intensity of the floodlights demand dark glasses for a director who is more dazzled by the glamor of his wife and star, Catherine Hessling.

Bottom: Summer 1928. Because Jean Renoir's personal projects aren't allowing him to make his mark he has come back down to earth to direct *The Tournament* in Carcassonne with the help of the elite members of the French cavalry. The star of the film, the swordsman Aldo Nadi, would meet up with Renoir once again in Hollywood during the 1940s.

Top: 1929. Teatime in the Sahara during the shoot for *Le Bled*, produced to mark the bicentennial of the French taking of Algiers. Renoir has no qualms about supplying his technical expertise and has begun to consider creating film studios, a dream he'll pursue until his departure for Califnornia.

Left: The beginning of the thirties. Jean and Marguerite Houllé, his lover and editor, who plays an important role in his body of work. Did he become close to her because she was Communist, or did he become a fellow traveler of the Party as a result of sharing her life?

Top: April 1939. Renoir directs Marcel Dalio, Nora Gregor, Marcel Méral, and Paulette Dubost in the La Chesnaye mansion, as it has been re-created at the studio in Joinville.

Bottom: Spring 1939. Alain Renoir, who hasn't yet turned eighteen, is assistant camera for *The Rules of the Game.* In less than two years, he will become a soldier in the American army.

A tour of the canteens for Lieutenant Renoir.

Beginning of 1940. Throughout the thirties, Carl Koch was Renoir's dearest friend and closest collaborator. Here they are shown in Rome shortly before the filming of *Tosca*. Renoir will film the first scene without the actors and leave Koch with the responsibility of directing the film.

Beginning of 1940. Rome, villa Adriana. At location scouting for *Tosca*, Carl Koch appears far left. Luchino Visconti is holding the umbrella. Having already attended the shoot for *A Day in the Country* in 1936, the future Italian director was still working as Renoir's assistant when this picture was taken. He became Koch's assistant for the shooting of this film.

Capitaine LESTRINGUEZ
MINISTÈRE DES INFORMATIONS
    P A R I S .

Mon cher Pierre,

    Veux-tu avoir la gentillesse de distribuer les lettres que je joins à celle-ci. BEUCLER te donnera de mes nouvelles et je suis sûr que vous vous amuserez beaucoup en bavardant ensemble.

    Nous venons d'apprendre l'invasion de la Belgique et de la Hollande par les allemands. Personnellement je présente cela aux italiens comme une grande victoire française.

    Ce soir Benito MUSSOLINI lui-même va se faire projeter "LA GRANDE ILLUSION". J'en suis très fier. Jusqu'au dernier moment je ferai tout mon possible pour conserver des liens amicaux avec un pays que je continue à considérer comme très sympathique. Vus de Paris les articles des journaux italiens sont très désagréables. Mais il faut comprendre que vus d'ici les articles des journaux anglais et français ne le sont pas moins. Tu devrais dire çà à notre Ministre.

    J'étais bien content hier d'entendre ta voix au téléphone.

    En attendant le plaisir de te voir, je t'embrasse affectueusement.

P.S. N'oublie pas mes lettres, elles sont pressées.

May 10, 1940. On the day of the German offensive against the Netherlands, Belgium, and Luxembourg, Renoir writes from Rome to his old friend Lestringuez. "Tonight Benito Mussolini himself is going to screen *Grand Illusion*. I'm very proud of this."

boeuf,* Georges Prade, and Paulin.

But before all that, all Renoir was thinking of was leaving. That is, it seemed to be all he was thinking of; but as is often the case with Renoir, it wasn't that simple. In fact, on October 5, 1940, he had written not one but two letters. One was to Robert Flaherty to inform him that he'd obtained authorization to leave the country. And the second, which remained unpublished until today, provides proof that he continued to care a great degree about the future of French cinema, despite that fact that he was about to leave.

The purpose of this second letter was about a "Cité du cinéma," a plan about which it is worth knowing a bit more. The idea belonged to a fecund movement that may have already been inspired by Pagnol's plan for a "Cité du cinéma," a film center he envisioned establishing in the village of La Treille. But a similar project is also described in Pierre Gaut's archives under the title "Note for the Creation of a Cinematographic Industry in Spain." It "is composed of two main elements: the construction of the film city and production." This involves "acquiring a one-hundred-hectare lot in Madrid, which the town council is offering at a special price," for the production of films whose "distribution will no longer be surrendered, as was usually the case, to networks of foreign contractors, but will be handled by the company itself," with a "publishing company and a literary film review whose purpose will be propaganda." There's no date attached to Gaut's plan, but it was apparently formed before 1939, and he claims it is a response to the desire of the "government of the Spanish Republic [that] has been seeking for a long time to free itself from the yoke of American producers, in order to prevent the exportation of its capital."[29] It isn't signed, either, but Pierre Gaut hadn't been involved in any activities that were film related since 1934 when he'd met Renoir, and it is likely that Renoir was associated with it, even probable that he wrote it.

Likewise, there is another letter, also undated, that testifies to the fact that Gaut had been equally interested in an idea Renoir was contemplating around 1932 to create studios and film laboratories in Algeria. The idea had not in any way originally been inspired by the situation in France, and Renoir's own idea in 1940 was a revised version of a preoccupation he'd had for nearly ten years.

Consequently, in summer 1940, Renoir decided that the moment had come to dust off this already old idea and express his desire for the creation of a "national or European film center" on the Côte d'Azur. Drafting his idea must not have required a lot of work because certain elements already existed in the "Spanish" document. Although we do not know the date for conception of this, we do know that the document was registered on November 26, 1940, at the

---

* Probably the painter and maker of drawings André Villeboeuf.

Service du cinéma to which it had been addressed.[*]

Entitled "Report on the Creation of Studios in Valbonne" and signed by Renoir and his brother Claude, the text tosses out several general considerations, including establishing the need to direct films using live sound. But the heart of the plan involves the creation of a veritable city of film, whose features are designed in a way that inspires wonder about the personalities of its authors. Not a great deal is known about Claude Renoir, the youngest brother who was trying but failing to find his way in the world of film under the shadow of his two older brothers.[†] He had recently served as director of production on *The Rules of the Game*.

We do, however, have inklings about Jean Renoir's character. Alain liked to think that his father hadn't very actively lent a hand to the drafting of the plan, but in this case it's likely that Alain was blinded by a son's love for his father. Whatever the case, there is absolutely no doubt about the fact that Jean Renoir signed the plan as well as explained and supported it. Above all, the use of the first-person singular prevents the reader from wondering about the identity of the author, because Claude Renoir did not have the authority necessary to spell out theories that only his brother's experience and fame could make heard.[‡]

What is learned from reading this "Report"? Jean Renoir was a lover of endless meals shared with friends during which they remade the world and the world of film; and after the table, when minds were even more apt to improvise with the help of a nice little wine, time and place seemed to have melted away. "It's important to keep the crews from splitting up during lunch hour or breaks. That notorious 'lunchtime' has done a lot of harm to French film. Actors benefitting from a certain importance are very attached to it. They love to stretch it out over a small drink. When they come back to the soundstage they're no longer in their roles, have forgotten their lines, and often perform badly. The drawbacks are the same on another level when it comes to the crew and the director. In France, you can consider the two hours following lunch as lost time."

---

[*] Because Renoir was in Lisbon on that date, waiting to leave for the United States, the date the plan was registered probably is not the same as the date it was received. It's also possible that Renoir's brother Claude was the one who delivered it.

[†] In 1942, Claude Renoir codirected *Opéra-Musette* with René Lefèvre and Paulette Dubost, with cinematography by his nephew Claude Renoir and Joseph-Louis Mundwiller (the head cameraman for *Le Brasier ardent*, Abel Gance's *Napoléon*, and Jean Renoir's *Chotard and Company*). After the war, he worked for television but returned to ceramics in the fifties.

[‡] Claude Renoir would actively participate in the Resistance against the German occupation in the South of France. He'd be decorated with the Military Cross 1939–1945 as well as the Resistance Medal.

But it isn't enough for crew and actors to be put on a diet. It's even more important for them to follow the spiritual path, or at least not to forget it. The section called "Setting up the Cité du cinéma" therefore opens with the following sentence: "In the center, a CHURCH and local residents allowing for the practice of different religions." The paragraph that follows finesses the subject of these "different religions," whose nature and diversity we, on the other hand, would have appreciated knowing. "We must not forget that the Cité du cinéma working at full capacity will bring together more than a thousand individuals. Spiritual life is of primary importance in a profession that aspires to guide public opinion. The priest in charge of this special parish will have to be an individual of the first order, a kind of missionary who will sometimes be liable to find himself before some flocks that are as resistant as the most distant Negroes."[30] As a result, film's asserted ambition becomes "guiding public opinion"; converting servants who are among "the most distant Negroes" has been elevated to a priority.

Well before the plan had been registered with the Service du cinéma, it had been subject to certain intermediaries, who had begun to discuss it with the German authorities. In fact, in a letter kept in the archives of the Festival de Cannes, dated October 5, 1940, and signed only by him, Jean Renoir attempted to convince his correspondent of the idea's importance. The message is addressed to Georges Prade.

Born in 1904, Prade was a sports and society reporter for *Le Figaro,* editor-in-chief of *L'Officiel de la couture et de la mode,* member of L'Action française, and he had been elected city councilor in the Twelfth Arrondissement of Paris in 1929 and had served as vice president of the departmental council of the Seine from 1933 to 1934. In the thirties, Prade had become part of Paris's in crowd thanks mostly to his identity as director of the Rigaud perfume factory. He was also a notorious anti-Communist, something—along with Prade's amusing nickname, "Yoyo"—Renoir must have known.

It's quite clear that in 1940 the former fellow traveler of the Party knew whom to go to. For years his friendships had been split between the Communists and the Right—sometimes, the extreme Right, a unique quality that surprised Alain Renoir for a long time. If it's true that Prade's hectic high-society involvements had made it possible for him to meet Renoir, one of the celebrities of his time, it is also possible that the right-leaning connections forged by the director existed in part because of the relationships he'd formed within the community of airmen and former airmen to which not only Pierre Gaut and of course Armand Pinsard,* among others, belonged but also Prade's father, who was called Georges as well. However, another reason Renoir had for writing to Prade in October 1940 was the fact that Prade was active in the South of France. That "great friend of the Riviera"[31] was actually campaigning to create a "biennale of film in Cannes . . . an enterprise [that] would be destined in the minds of those involved in it to replace the one currently being held in Venice."[32] In July 1939, Prade would be part of the first organizing committee. The South of France, film, anti-Communism: Renoir was knocking on the right door.

The first sentence of the letter to Prade contains one essential piece of information: "I have been informed by our friend Gendre about your conversations with M. Greven regarding the opportunity to establish our Studios in Valbonne."[33] "Our friend Gendre," whose first name was Henri, was the father of actor Louis Jourdan, who had just had his on-screen debut. Henri Gendre was also the owner of the Grand Hôtel in Cannes, possessed land in Valbonne, and had attempted to create a film society. Also interested in this plan, which was still very much in the embryonic stage, was the director of *Paris-Soir,* Jean Prouvost, and a group of Jewish producers, whose presence would become the reason for Gendre's "being denounced in Vichy as 'the leader of a group of Yids.'"[34] Gendre appears not to have participated in the working out of the plan for a "Cité du cinéma."

"M. Greven's" first name was Alfred, and he presented himself as "Doktor." He had been a pilot in the German fighter force during the First World War, was chief producer at the UFA, and was the director of the company Terra Films. Since the armistice he was serving as the delegate from the Reich responsible for film affairs in France. In a few weeks, he'd find himself at the head of an empire, composed of a production house known as Continental-Film, a distribution company called L'Alliance cinématographique européenne, a network of movie theaters called the SOGEC, and a studio, Paris-Studio-Cinéma. His actions in France, mostly at Continental, generally were considered beneficial enough because he had succeeded in producing several excellent films free of any motive of direct propaganda.

As it turned out that autumn of 1940, Greven wouldn't declare himself convinced by Renoir's plan for a "Cité du cinéma." Establishing by his letter that

---

* The person who inspired *Grand Illusion* would become one of the people in charge of setting up the sinister Légion des volontaires français contre le bolchevisme (LVF), the chief executive officer of the nonmilitary national services, in charge, in particular, of the recruitment and social services. Brought before the court of justice in Paris on November 2, 1944, he would be granted mitigating circumstances, which would not, however, help him avoid being condemned to hard labor for life and the confiscation of his property. His son Paul, whom he would enlist at eighteen in the LVF, fought in the Charlemagne division under the name Pinsard-Berthaz and the rank of Obersturmführer.

the "doktor" had already been familiarized with his ideas, Renoir began claiming its purpose was to "furnish the arguments that will refute M. Greven's point of view, which appears to be insufficiently informed." Renoir made mention of Marc Allégret, with whom he'd discussed the issue. Then, on three densely typed pages, he offered a long defense of the plan, in which he saw a "wonderful chance to finally get rid of all the schemes having to do with film (black markets for stars, crews, and extras, loans of money to producers, advance sales and all the filth with which French film has been infested)." "All this rubbish," he explained, "is connected to the fact of films being made in Paris; in Valbonne, we'd have longer, more light-filled days, and more of them in the year; we'd gain time there, and we'd also gain physical and moral health." Further on, he writes, "We also know that in Paris our ideas of purity and greatness will be quickly beaten down by the schemers at Fouquet's and other places, who may have decreased in number but whom I cannot believe have completely disappeared."

In reality, the theses that Renoir was developing in 1940 are those he was already supporting during the time of the Popular Front and in the series of reports that he wrote on behalf of the army in September 1939. They contain the same charge against the producers, the same abhorrence of a certain tendency in French film. Only the coloring of the case has changed: red in 1936 and 1937, khaki in 1939, and the grayish-green of the German soldier in 1940. Unfortunately, and obviously in case the receiver of his October 1940 letter hadn't understood who, in fact, these "schemers at Fouquet's" who had "decreased in number" but, alas, hadn't "completely disappeared" were—to be sure that he'd really made himself understood so that the representative of the great Reich would finally know precisely with whom he was dealing and could not in any case doubt the personal convictions of the promoter of the plan— Renoir judged it necessary to add a postscript to his letter: "It is a good idea to point out to M. Greven that in our concern, there cannot and consequently will not be any undesirables and that we want the widest collaboration with all the representatives of European cinematography."[35] This letter addressed to Georges Prade but actually intended for Alfred Greven is dated October 5, 1940. And the word "undesirable," as well, had by then taken on a new coloring—of which we can only hope Renoir was unaware.

On the day he wrote and signed that letter. Renoir knew that he was probably leaving. If he had addressed his letter to the French authorities, it would be possible to understand that he wanted to convince Vichy that he saw his exile only as temporary—enough time to make a film in Hollywood before coming back to his country and taking part in the great revival of French film.* Unfortunately, it was the German authorities with whom Renoir intended to make contact on October 5, 1940, and to do it after having already brought his plans to their attention, undoubtedly by the same intermediary. Was this done with the purpose of attracting their favor in case he returned to France? It's possible.

The author and signer of the appeal to Alfred Greven is the same man who, right after the war and then in his memoirs, portrays himself refusing offers that, supposedly, were being made to him at the same time. The fact that in the summer and fall of 1940 Renoir would have held on, as he did all his life, to the theory of the cork carried along by water isn't surprising. Neither is the fact that he subscribed to the words of others, regardless of how doubtful these words were, motivated as he was by ordinary opportunism, which was often disguised and sometimes hidden by his desire to appear different and to stand out. But in this case, he moved faster than the current was taking him. The truth is that Renoir anticipated what he supposed he could expect from the German occupiers, especially without neglecting to put words into his letter that express—worse than an accord—a community of viewpoints. However, in this as well, it's possible to find excuses for his frenetic desire to make pledges to the German Occupation, even when he was also taking steps to leave France: fear, confusion, uncertainty; his desire—blameful, yes, but common—to conform to the surrounding atmosphere; unfamiliarity with the principles of a regime even though he had opposed it. And there was the ignorance that he shared with everyone at the time, both about what the German Occupation would be for the French and about the atrocious fate of the German machine's first victims—those same "undesirables" he had mentioned to Greven. But such excuses, whether good or bad—as well as those that can't be accepted as excuses, and those additional excuses that remain unknown to us—didn't survive the war years. Knowing what we do today about Jean Renoir, we would have hoped that he'd keep a low profile after.

The "casual" description that he'd give of his motivations then would be just as embarrassed and just as embarrassing. In 1946, writing to a resident of Essoyes, he brazenly put forth a first reason: "I'd left France in 1940 with the

* The long article that L'Alerte devoted in December 1941 to Renoir's first American film, which will be dealt with in the second part of this book, seems to support the hypothesis that Vichy was convinced that the director would quickly return to France.

idea that if I were in America, it would be easier to bring my son over." Even without taking into account the fact that Alain refused for a long time to leave for the United States and that it took Jean nearly a year and a half to convince him to make the trip, the argument still appears to be the product of rather unusual logic. What follows in the same letter is a brief moment of honesty: "I also gave in—why not be frank about it—to a fit of fear. Some of my films and the magazine articles I'd written were clearly anti-Nazi, and I knew I was being watched." That is true, but Renoir next suggests that, as much of an anti-Nazi under surveillance as he may have been, the occupier was also painting him the picture of a rosy future. "On the other hand, I knew that the Germans wanted to offer me films to make under very outstanding conditions." Victim *and* herald, in a way, but Renoir was suggesting another reading: "I was afraid of suddenly being put before a dilemma: being a traitor or being a hero; and, not knowing if I would have had the courage to be the latter, I thought it would be better to accept the offer of the American government that was putting a passport at my disposal."[36]

All of this would have an effect on the negative image that the profession would create for him. For, although these letters, approaches, maneuverings, finaglings remained unknown by historians for a long time, partly because they were actually judged unworthy of the Renoir touch, they did leave traces, arouse suspicions, and feed rumors in the profession and among his former comrades.

Finally confident that he would soon be able to leave, even if none of the details had yet been decided, Renoir went back to the South of France no later than October 19. All those on the Côte d'Azur at that time didn't look like "undesirables" to him. Some were even friends. Jean Gabin was there. Gabin had written to Denise Tual saying that he'd spoken on the telephone with "Cabuche" near the end of August. It was the name he'd used for Renoir since *La Bête humaine*. Renoir, as well, had written to Denise Tual and told her about his plans to leave as well as about an idea for a film with Gabin. Tixier-Vignancour, to whom he'd submitted this idea, hadn't hidden the fact that for the moment it seemed difficult to him to realize.[37] Jean Gabin confirmed that sentiment the next day in a letter written from Saint-Jean-Cap-Ferrat. Although the actor thought the idea for *Magnificat* was "very appealing,"[38] he himself was in a delicate situation, being pressured by Continental to work for them, which he was refusing. "All the others took what they had thought of as the right choice, and when I returned in 1945, I never cast a stone at anyone for choices made. My refusal in that situation had nothing to do with exaggerated patriotism; it was because something inside me said no to it. To put it more simply, let's say that it bugged me."[39] Jean Gabin would leave France for Lisbon in mid-February 1941, by going through Spain, before departing for New York, and then joining the Free French Forces in 1943.

Renoir preceded him by a few weeks. On October 19, he informed Flaherty that he and Dido were in Marseille and asked him to intervene with the US ambassador in Madrid for the purpose of getting the visa needed for them to go through Spain. Changing his mind a few days later, he decided to leave for Tangier by way of Algiers. From Tangier, Renoir flew to Lisbon on November 22,[40] where he moved into the Hotel Métropole. It was during this flight that he met André Perebinossoff* and his wife, Élisabeth, with whom he developed a friendship that would last for several years in Los Angeles. Dido, held back once again by a visa problem, joined him a week later.

Aside from Barcelona, Bilbao, and Vigo, Lisbon was the last of the European ports that still offered passage to America. Since the month of October, Jews were no longer authorized to enter Portugal, which since 1933 had been under the dictatorship of António de Oliveira Salazar. The official reason for this prohibition had to do with the too great number of false identification papers spotted by the authorities, but the hotels of the city were jam-packed and the waiting lines lengthened in front of the offices of the travel agencies. One of the consequences of such an influx of foreigners was a sizable raise in prices. Accordingly, the English pound, which had been worth 180 francs in July 1940 on the international market, was trading in the fall at 1,000 francs for those who wanted to leave Europe, and ocean and air transportation companies were requiring passage to be paid in pounds or dollars. The average price being asked for the trip was close to $400[†] at the time, a price that did not at all guarantee traveling with a cabin. In June, Pierre Lazareff rented the infirmary of the *Quanza* for himself and the five people he was traveling with. It was a Portuguese cargo-passenger ship, the only way for them to get hold of four beds. In November, the great violinist Zino Francescatti could only get a cabin in exchange for a favor his wife did for the wife of the director of the ship company, whose mink Francescatti's wife brought back from Marseille by way of Spain.

During the week the director arrived in Lisbon, gossip columnists were focusing their attention on the presence of Josephine Baker, while Les Petits

---

* André A. Perebinossoff, a specialist in petroleum mapping, was working at that time for the account of Schlumberger and later for Mobil. He was fleeing France with his wife, Élisabeth Roger, the daughter of the mayor of Courbevoie. From Lisbon, where they as well were staying at the Métropole, they would leave for New York aboard the SS *Excalibur*. I'm indebted to their son, Philippe Perebinossoff, for access to his father's diary and various other elements regarding the subject of Renoir's voyage and stay in Lisbon.

† Equal to nearly $6,700 in 2015.

Chanteurs à la croix de bois,* promoted by the success of the Duvivier film *Dance Program* in which they'd appeared, were performing all over Portugal. Among those Renoir met during his stay were the Portuguese producer and director Ayres d'Aghiar and the singer Marie Dubas,[41] known for the song "Mon légionnaire."

On December 2, the review *Animatografo* devoted a long article to Renoir in the course of which he mentioned that "his Brazilian secretary Dido Freire" had arrived in Lisbon "last Saturday," meaning November 30. Renoir's interviewer was one of his colleagues. He was also the publisher, editor-in-chief, and owner of *Animatografo,* as indicated on the masthead of the magazine. A journalist since 1927, under the amusing pseudonym "Retardador," and the author of an enthusiastic critique of *The Little Match Girl* in 1929, António Lopes Ribeiro was director of the leading revue in the country. He had also been a producer and film director since 1928 and in 1940 was one of the most influential figures in Portuguese cinema. Aside from being considered the official filmmaker of the regime from that time to the fall of the dictatorship in 1974, his many involvements also extended to the theater, and he was truly a lover of film, overseeing the early career of several Portuguese directors, including Manoel de Oliveira. It was in such a capacity that he was welcoming—and celebrating—Jean Renoir. In his first letter to Dido from Lisbon, Renoir wrote, "I'm going to dinner with an extremely nice director who has shown me a very well-executed documentary on villages typical of this region."[42]

What the French director actually saw were some of the films produced by the Department of National Propaganda, for which his interviewer worked; and as would be expected, Renoir claimed to particularly appreciate the "authenticity" of these films. Consequently, about the subject of the film called *A aldeia mais portugesa de Portugal,*† he declared, "The greatest, if not the only, claim to fame of our art is authenticity. And *Village* gives us an impression of authenticity, which is something we rarely see respected by the imagination of directors, cinematographers, and editors of films. Moreover, the beauty . . . of your rustic landscapes, clothing, and architecture gives the film a tenor and significance that make it projectable anywhere."[43]

Although *The Rules of the Game* still hadn't been shown in Portugal, Lopes Ribeiro wrote that its production had been carried out "under the form of a

---

* *Translator's note:* "The Little Singers of the Wooden Cross," but today known in English as "The Little Singers of Paris," this children's choir was founded in 1906 by Paul Bertier and Pierre Martin, two students on vacation at the Abbeye de Tamié.

† Literally, *The Most Portuguese Village in Portugal,* a documentary about the village of Monsanto.

cooperative, meaning that all its collaborators had a share of the profits." This detail, according to Ribeiro, was the reason for the rather cold reception the film had received. "It caused a reaction on the part of capitalist producers, as well it should have. And the critics (who can't, apparently, escape their influence) unanimously condemned a work that we haven't seen and that we therefore won't take the risk of judging; but at least it possesses the courageous merit of breaking with the morbid tradition that has recently been plaguing French film."[44]

This was all in keeping with Renoir's declarations at Vichy and before, and in his interview he didn't forget to mention the plan for the "Cité du cinema," whose instigation he ascribed to Marcel Pagnol. Nor did he forget to mention "his confidence in the direction with which Marshal Pétain wanted to endow French film." Finally, once more he proclaimed his faith in the existence of a Latin school of film, which was alone able to demolish Hollywood hegemony, that impregnable bastion that French film had claimed to want to storm during its entire history. The nations being summoned to unite in such an attack were, as Renoir did not neglect to add, France, Italy, Spain, and Portugal—in other words, one country (France) under foreign domination and three others under the heel of dictatorships. Here, as well, Renoir knew what he was saying, to whom he was saying it, and why he was saying it. Others before him or at the same time as him had had the same idea for a Latin cinema, and it's certainly possible that he had simply co-opted the idea.

In fact, a few weeks later, the French government would assign Jules Calamy the responsibility of "studying the possibilities of a closer cinematic relationship with Spain, [so that] the company Hispano Films would be able to accomplish the making of three films directed and performed by French and Spanish directors and artists."[45] What is more, Portuguese and Spanish filmmaking had at the time already begun to establish ties, mostly through the production company Tobis. And it was during that very November 1940 that Tobis was to come to such an agreement with Lisboa Filme. Finally, it just so happened that the first guided visit accorded Renoir under the supervision of Lopes Ribeiro, when he arrived in Lisbon in November, had been to that exact same studio, Tobis, as well as to the laboratories of Lisboa Filme.[46]

Creating a portrait of French film production in this same article, Renoir denounced a certain "tendency for speculation" whose effects created a situation in which "I've never received what I was owed for my work." Another consequence was that "films were directed by silent partners never known by anybody." Then: "The immigrants coming from every latitude characterizing the majority of producers were responsible in large part for this situation. But the crews weren't unaware of the fact that it's partly up to them to keep our home industry from stagnating. These men who in general have nothing to lose were leading the others—timid and overly careful capitalists who had no faith in film—into investing in movie projects. This is how millions were earned, and how millions were lost."[47]

In his conversation with Fernando Fragoso, Renoir once more affirmed his faith in the existence of a "Latin" school. "I'd allowed myself to be influenced by the idea that 'Latins have no gift for film.' After having lived in Italy and France and visiting Spain, and from being in Portugal today, I see it differently. Latins are the great interpreters of tomorrow. For that reason, we need to set up a close commercial and spiritual collaboration, for all the peoples of our race.'"*[48] His claiming to have recently gone to Spain remains hearsay and merely adds more detail to his account, and there's no hard proof that the words really are Renoir's. Similarly, the unfortunate use of the word *race* could be attributable to the journalist.

On December 6, a large party with a screening of *Grand Illusion* was organized by *Animatografo* in Renoir's honor at the São Luiz Teatro, a historic theater on rua Antonio Maria Cardoso. The gala brought together representatives from the worlds of politics and culture. The Department of National Propaganda sent a delegate, José Alvellos, and the French ambassador was there. Lopes Ribeiro introduced the director, who came onto the stage where Duse had performed in 1898 and made a short speech that he preceded by a few verses of *Lusíadas,* the epic poem by Camões (c. 1524–1580). Reporting on the event in the December 9 issue of *Animatografo,* Ribeiro would write that Renoir had expressed his faith in a Portuguese cinema that the current new conditions would allow to surpass all obstacles. As for the production of French films, it could only benefit from a "genuine and indispensable purification,† which would place film between the hands of authentic professionals and sincere enthusiasts."[49]

There's nothing here to support the thesis that the director indulged in anti-Semitic remarks and pro-Hitler declarations that match the claims leveled at him more than a quarter of a century later by his ex-friend-turned-implacable-enemy, Henri Jeanson. Jeanson's accusations were repeated by Renoir's opponents so constantly and furiously that they warrant our stopping for a moment to examine them. They're based on an article in a Portuguese newspaper that to this day has never been found. Jeanson cited the article on several occasions: both in *L'Aurore* and in *Le Canard enchaîné,* and then in his book *Soixante-dix ans d'adolescence.* Each time he did, he made use of the same

---

* "*Entre todos os povos da nossa raça.*"

† "*Depuração.*"

account, to all intents and purposes based on a fake quotation, the words of which are very obviously not Renoir's, and not even those a Portuguese journalist could have attributed to him, but rather those of an experienced screenwriter and enraged polemicist who'd been hounding his former friend since 1937. It is, unfortunately, the case that Renoir claimed to have been victimized by Jewish producers who were preventing him from working and were exploiting French film. But the possibility of Renoir's devising and speaking the specific words Jeanson puts into his mouth is literally inconceivable. This is not to say that he wouldn't have been capable of it, sadly enough. The main reason for not believing it is actually related to his situation at that time. From mid-November to mid-December 1940, he wasn't yet certain he could leave. Passage on ocean liners leaving for America were rare and difficult to obtain. His girlfriend still hadn't resolved all her visa problems. How could a man that unsure of himself—how could a "chicken," which is how he would end up describing himself—employ such words of violence in those circumstances?

In reality, during all the long months preceding his departure, Renoir never missed a chance to give the powers that be the guarantees he felt were needed, consistently using them often enough to forgo any booming declarations. He kept delivering such guarantees in Lisbon and went around repeating that he owed his departure for the United States to the benevolence of Marshal Pétain's government, and that is true. When he granted the same Fernando Fragoso an interview intended for a Spanish publication, which would include his photograph holding the magazine, he began by claiming he had "the most intense admiration and liking for Spain and its leaders."[50] In this case, as well, the possibility that such a remark was invented by his interviewer can't be overlooked.

There's no need to add that Renoir did not become a Nazi in June 1940. His remarks in favor of the Vichy regime didn't make him a hard-line Pétainist. Afterward, he'd try to diminish the importance of such statements. For example, in 1970, after the appearance of a biography of Saint-Exupéry[51] in which Renoir's behavior in 1940 was briefly held to blame and Dido had read him the few passages about it, he would write, "The only truth is that I always refused to drag Marshal Pétain's name through the mud."[52] But that isn't the "only truth." The truth is that in summer and fall 1940 there were few French people who *would* "drag Marshal Pétain's name through the mud." And so, in contradiction

---

* "I was stupid to get mixed up with the Communist Party and the people of the Left. But time is on my side. I'll come back to France. I know how to handle Hitler. I'm sure both of us will understand each other very well because, like all my colleagues, I was a victim of the Jews who kept us from working and exploited us. When I come back, I'll be in a de-Semitized France, where man will have rediscovered his nobility and his reason to live" (Henri Jeanson, *L'Aurore*, November 5, 1968).

to what he wanted to imply, and which he probably ended up convincing himself, Renoir wasn't opposed to the mainstream of that time. He went along with it, expressing himself and behaving like the hard-line Pétainist he probably was not, to benefit the only cause important to him—his own.

On December 11, Renoir gave a lecture on the subject "How I Make a Film" at the French Cultural Institute.[53] His lecture would be followed a few months later by Louis Jouvet's. Among the other figures who'd already been invited to speak were Antoine de Saint-Exupéry, the Abbé Breuil (known as "the pope of prehistory"), and the historian and academician Paul Hazard. Two days before, Renoir had written to Tixier-Vignancour to let him know that he was getting ready to "leave Lisbon any moment now." He also told him that *Grand Illusion* had been shown on December 6, informed him that he had been made "an honorary member of the Portuguese Film Union" and had been the "only foreigner admitted so far," and expounded upon his "ideas on Latin cinema." "We have decided our next step is to form a committee to investigate that issue. We've asked Spanish and Italian figures to become part of this committee." Renoir ended by requesting his correspondent "send my warm regards to Prade and Mme. Prade."[54]

He'd received the honor he referred to in that letter on December 8, during a special ceremony in the offices of the Union; and it had been presided over by Lopes Ribeiro and the head cinematographer and director of short films, Octávio Bobone. In this situation, Renoir might have spoken a sentence likely to provoke Jeanson's extrapolations: "I'm convinced that the power of money will come out of this war weakened."[55] The statement is a ticklish one to interpret, especially given the fact that it's difficult to decide what caused the director to develop such a conviction. From "the purification" of cinema by eliminating the "undesirables"? And, then, exactly what did such words mean in December 1940? How should we understand them today, considering what we know, which we did not know then: the fact that "elimination" was consummate with extermination?

Only a mind as hostile to Renoir as Jeanson's could detect Renoir's statement as an anti-Semitic barb. The screenwriter would claim that when Saint-Exupéry was getting off the boat and mentioned Renoir, with whom he'd just crossed the Atlantic, Pierre Lazareff, who had come for Saint-Exupéry, refused to meet the director because of his anti-Semitic outbursts in Lisbon. However, the aviator-writer must have overcome the reservations of the journalist awfully quickly. There's no trace of that possible quarrel in the correspondence between Lazareff and Renoir. Nonetheless, Lazareff did produce an uncompromising portrait of the director a few weeks after his arrival in New York, which included the observation that "directly after the armistice, Renoir wrote for pro-Fascist and anti-Semitic newspapers, such as Léon Bailby's *L'Alerte*, but only on the subject of film."

That claim, on the other hand, is inexact. Renoir did not write for "newspapers." He wrote *one* article for *one* publication, which was, in fact, only about film. Lazareff also claimed that the Spaniards wouldn't let Renoir travel across Spain "because they considered him to be a Communist, despite the fact that here he's called a Fascist."[56] It's difficult not to wonder whether the journalist may have simply been trying with these lines to please those who were giving him a chance to write one of their columns.

On December 20, 1940, Jean Renoir and Dido Freire climbed aboard the SS *Siboney*, a vessel that had been chartered a few weeks before by the American Export Lines. The *Siboney* would make seven voyages from Jersey City to Lisbon and back, taking a total of 2,534 passengers. During its preceding voyage, which had left Lisbon on November 14, the ship had taken Zino Francescatti and what was left of the Ballets Russes to New York. On December 20, there were 343 passengers waiting to leave, packed onto the deck and jammed into cabins. Whereas Renoir's girlfriend found herself hedged in "with a slew of women in another cabin,"[57] Renoir shared his with Antoine de Saint-Exupéry, whom he'd met briefly in London at the beginning of 1939[58] and again a few days before when Raymond Warnier, director of the French Institute of Lisbon, had introduced them.

The *Siboney* hadn't been designed for transatlantic voyages. Until this time, it had provided transportation between Miami and Cuba. Its equipment and new diesel motors, installed in 1935, allowed it to attain a maximum speed of twenty-one knots. The crossing would take eleven days, one more than had been planned, which included the inspection of the ship on two occasions by the British authorities, who were demanding that all ships making the crossing, including the *Siboney*, submit to a complete search in Bermuda.

Great Britain actually considered France to be an enemy country and was hunting for currencies and foreign assets likely to be used to serve the Nazi cause against the English. Consequently, a few weeks before, the SS *Excalibur*, which had left Lisbon on September 25, had been inspected for the same reason. It was carrying part of the Ambroise Vollard collection. The art seller had died in July 1939, and his brother Lucien had sold off the collection to Martin Fabiani, who had been one of Vollard's collaborators for a number of years. This part of the collection included a total of 635 pieces, including 68 by Cézanne, 13 by Rouault, and 429 paintings, drawings, and watercolors by Renoir. During the search, the works were impounded and transported to Canada, where they had to remain until the end of the war.[59]

The final hours aboard the *Siboney* were difficult ones. There was nothing more to eat and drink other than cookies and water, but Renoir had found a new friend in Saint-Exupéry. The two men had begun by discussing airplanes. The flyer had flown for the first time in Amhérieux, and that was the same place where the director had learned to fly a plane. And then, the conversation had turned to the subject of film. Saint-Exupéry had experience in that domain, most notably as the screenwriter for the film *Anne-Marie* (1935) by Raymond Bernard, with Annabella. He had also written the film adaptation of Pierre Billon's *Courrier sud* (*Southern Carrier,* 1936) whose filming he'd followed in Morocco. Another of his projects, *Igor,* was never to happen. There were, then, certain correspondences between the two men, and despite the differences in their personalities they found ways to get along.

A week after his arrival in Lisbon, on November 21, Saint-Exupéry had learned of the death of Henri Guillaumet, whose four-engine plane on its way to Syria had probably been shot down by an Italian fighter plane on November 27. "Tonight I feel as if I no longer have a friend," Saint-Exupéry would write on December 1, on the evening of his lecture at the French Institute. And later, he wrote, "Here I am, a lonely, toothless old man left to chew over all this by himself."[60] His approach to the situation in France differed from Renoir's: the director acted completely ready to believe in the marshal's policies and the birth of the "new France" if the wind blew in that direction. The pilot refused to listen to any talk of Pétain, Laval, or Vichy. He believed in the necessity of the continuation, or the resumption, of the war, and one of his goals was to convince Americans of the United States' obligation to enter the conflict. The fact that he was well known would be of help to this purpose.

Within a year, 250,000 copies of *Wind, Sand and Stars* (French title: *Terre des hommes*) had been sold in the United States, and the book received the National Book Award in 1939. Renoir hadn't read it, so the author read it aloud to him. After he did, Renoir made it clear that he was crazy about it and was convinced that he'd find people in Hollywood willing to listen to the idea of an adaptation of a best seller like that, seven years after Saint-Exupéry's *Vol de nuit* had been brought to the screen as *Night Flight*[*] by Metro-Goldwyn-Mayer. *Wind, Sand and Stars,* however, wasn't effective material for a film adaptation, broken up as the tale was into isolated stories without unity of time and place or main character instead of a solidly structured plot. Therefore, the writer promised to provide the director with all the elements of the story, most of which were autobiographical and likely to strengthen an adaptation, which Renoir

* Directed by Clarence Brown, with Clark Gable (1933).

would begin working on several months later.

During the entire eleven days of this difficult crossing, each represented for the other the last witness of a life and a time that were gone. Saint-Exupéry was on the way to a world he already knew, because he'd spent time in New York two years before. Renoir knew nothing about the land on which he was about to embark. Saint-Exupéry was hoping to make the return voyage soon, and Renoir had no idea that nearly nine years would pass before he returned to Europe. Each discovered in the other the ultimate point of reference for his own past. A few months later, after several weeks of living together and many conversations, the writer would cut this message onto a record: "Ah! Jean Renoir, I miss Hollywood a lot, not for Hollywood, but for you. Because you're really one of the men on this planet for whom I feel the most friendship and esteem. I so love your way of thinking, of looking at things, of stirring things up. And there we are, I've made a declaration of love."[61]

On December 31, 1940, Jean Renoir, Dido Freire, Antoine de Saint-Exupéry, and the 340 other passengers of the *Siboney* landed at a dock in the port of Jersey City. The reporters who were there rushed to the writer, for whom Pierre Lazareff was waiting, after having received a cable from Saint-Exupéry announcing his arrival. Renoir would recount the scene in his memoirs: the director and his partner were met by Robert Flaherty. As a gesture of welcome, Flaherty put his own wide-brimmed fedora on Renoir's head, after having tossed Renoir's—a model considered out of style in America—into the sea.

PART II

THE LEGEND

JANUARY 1, 1941–FEBRUARY 12, 1979

23

A New World

Swamp Water

The second life of Jean Renoir began on January 10, 1941, at one in the morning, the moment the flight from Washington touched down at Los Angeles.

His first steps on American soil had occurred under the supervision of Robert Flaherty, who lived in New York at the Chelsea Hotel. Flaherty had to leave the next day for Washington and reserved a room for Renoir at the Royalton in New York on West Forty-Fourth Street, between Fifth and Sixth Avenues. On January 5, a Sunday, Renoir joined Saint-Exupéry on a walk through the Manhattan streets. Saint-Exupéry took him to see Bernard Lamotte,[1] one of his schoolmates from the Beaux-Arts, whom he hadn't seen since the beginning of the thirties. Lamotte ordered up some sardines and Veal Marengo from a nearby restaurant, and they drank Byrrh. Lamotte's place was packed with bottles of the stuff, because its parent company wanted to rival Dubonnet on American territory.[2] Renoir also later mentioned an encounter with a taxi driver of about sixty and the long conversation they'd had about the way people live in France. So enchanted had the driver been by the time they spent together that he told them they wouldn't have to pay for the ride and suggested that Dido and Renoir stay with him and his wife in Brooklyn the next time they were traveling through New York.[3]

After a brief visit to Washington at the invitation of Flaherty, who threw a sumptuous banquet in their honor, Jean Renoir and Dido Freire left for Los Angeles, settling at first in the Sunset Tower at 8358 Sunset Boulevard, the same building in which Raymond Chandler had set a scene from *Farewell, My Lovely* the year before. A few weeks later, the couple moved into a house at 8150 Hollywood Boulevard, with a monthly rent of $350 and an option to buy for $40,000.[4] Jean described it to Alain, who was staying at Les Collettes, as "a kind of American Marlotte." In that same letter to his son, he wrote, "We have housekeepers here, Harry and Grace. He's quite black, and she's a curious cross between Negro and Irish, café au lait with freckles, and very pretty. He used to be a bus driver in Pasadena. They're very nice and very informal." From this "big country, imposing and comical at the same time," he wrote again to say, "I like the Americans a lot," and, "we can get along and we can work together." Another detail: "I'd left thinking of making a film and coming back. But I had to sign a contract including an option for a second film."[5]

Renoir signed this contract without hesitation on January 13. It specified he would receive the sum of $50,000. That information was announced in a bulletin from the Fox publicity department two days later. The director's two agents were Hollywood celebrities: Charles Feldman and Ralph Blum, both from Famous Artists Agency, which they had created in 1934. The offer to Renoir, however, came from a Frenchman whose name was André Daven.

In 1932, with Robert Siodmak, Daven had codirected the film *Quick,* with Lilian Harvey and Jules Berry, but he'd worked more extensively as a production supervisor for German-French movies. As a producer for Erich Pommer, he'd created some important relationships in Hollywood, principally with 20th Century Fox. Therefore, it was altogether natural for him to put Renoir in contact with this studio, which had been directed by Darryl F. Zanuck since 1935 in his capacity as vice president in charge of production. Daven was also one of the people who'd lent money to Renoir, whose own funds were still being blocked in Paris.[6] Others who had done the same included Flaherty, Richard de Rochemont (director and producer of the series *The March of Time*), the director Albert Lewin, and Feldman, Renoir's agent. Dido would remind Flaherty of Daven's contribution, telling him that Jean had "no choice but to sign with Zanuck, since Daven, who works with Fox and advanced money for our trip etc. has already arranged everything with Feldman." Dido also mentioned that Daven "wants to become Jean's producer in the Fox outfit."[7]

In its January 14 issue, the *Los Angeles Evening Herald and Express* announced that "the Frank Capra of France" had signed with Fox, claiming that he'd arrived "today in New York."[8] A month later, *La Bête humaine* was released in the United States under the title *Of Human Passions*. It received enthusiastic reviews.

Darryl F. Zanuck was thirty-eight and produced about a dozen films a year under his own name. However, not a single shot of the some fifty films bearing the logo of 20th Century Fox each year left that studio without being approved by him. A few years later, Joseph L. Mankiewicz would dub him "czar of the rushes." Created by a merger between 20th Century and Fox, the company did not possess the kingly resources of a prestigious studio like Metro-Goldwyn-Mayer, and therefore couldn't attract the stars. Its mark of distinction was the care applied to the making of its films, which earned its image as the studio of directors. This reputation was justified by the fact that film was sacred to it but was contradicted by Zanuck's omnipotence. The screenwriter Philip Dunne described how Fox functioned at the time: "At Darryl Zanuck's 20th Century Fox the final script was as sacred as if engraved on tablets of stone. There was one boss, one arbiter of all disputes, and that was Darryl Zanuck himself. A director usually was assigned only after the script had been completed to Zanuck's satisfaction, and while directors could *suggest* changes, they *made* them at their peril."[9] Dunne's account does need amending, because his desire as a screenplay writer to downplay the part taken by directors in the success of these films is fairly obvious. However, it certainly was how things were in general, making it easy to understand that this studio was a poor match for Renoir.

On January 11, 1941, when Renoir went to Universal to have lunch with René Clair,[10] his only idea of Hollywood was based on legend. "In the airplane that took us to Hollywood, our final destination, my wife and I tried to imagine what we could expect. As if in a dream I saw myself settling in this paradise, beside Griffith, Charlie Chaplin, Lubitsch, and all the saints of Hollywood's international cult. Of course, the Hollywood we were imagining was the old Hollywood."[11]

In 1941, Griffith hadn't made a film for ten years, and he survived by working here and there as a second-unit director without his name appearing in the credits. Chaplin was a world unto himself; and his new film, *The Dictator,* had been screened in autumn 1940. Its official release would be March 7. Renoir's mention of Lubitsch was most unexpected by anyone who remembered the remark he had made during a lecture at the Maison de la Culture on rue d'Anjou on July 7, 1938. When someone in the audience asked what he thought of American film, the director of *La Marseillaise* had gone so far as to say, "I'll borrow Stroheim's phrasing and modify it slightly: it's poop. *Bluebird's Eighth Wife* by Lubitsch, in which a secretary is typing with one finger and says 'Come in!' when the typewriter rings to signal the end of a line, is a piece of crap."[12]

On February 8, Renoir arranged to meet with Lubitsch and then canceled by telegram a few hours before for a reason he admitted was "ridiculous," a minor operation.[13] On March 19, he wrote Lubitsch to say how flattered he was to be working for the same studio as him. Lubitsch had signed a three-year contract with Fox in 1938. His answer to Renoir on March 31 was, "Thanks so much for your charming little note, though I do not know who should feel more flattered—you or I, for working on the same lot."[14]

On January 27, Renoir wrote to King Vidor, who'd recall in his memoirs an evening spent at the Renoirs' in Montmartre in the second half of the thirties.[15] The purpose of Renoir's message was to tell him that he would have preferred to have seen Vidor's new film before meeting him but that time was passing.[16]

Vidor's answer, dated February 6, informed Renoir that his new film had nothing about it to make him feel proud and that, although a few scenes might be amusing, his only ambition had been to make a potboiler.* He ended with the excuse that he was going to bed for a cold but would call as soon as he recovered.[17]

There was nothing that wasn't completely natural about Renoir's striving to accumulate contacts among his American colleagues. He'd always lived surrounded by people, and for several years he'd been at the center of such activity. It's likely that in a world about which he knew almost nothing, his first thought was the fear of being isolated. His unfamiliarity with the language made relationships difficult, and although he began taking English lessons, his progress in them was paltry. He could leave this up to Dido, who went everywhere with him, but he himself was extremely disoriented. The distances traveling from one place to another seemed interminable, and the directors were used to limiting their relationships to those friends they'd known for a long time. In addition, they'd grown used to seeing directors arriving from Europe whose films they rarely knew. All of them went to the studio in the morning the way you go to the office and then came back home in the evening. Hollywood was a gigantic factory.

In all capital letters on Renoir's calling card appeared the only film he'd made that was internationally known, *La Grande Illusion*. Over the weeks, that title would come up with increasing regularity in his letters and in his thoughts. For the émigré director he was, it became an absolute reference. Erich von Stroheim set the tone when he sent him a telegram from New York in French to congratulate him for having signed with Zanuck and to ask him, "Have you screenplay already to consider or would you be interested in the story I'm writing at the moment 50 persons [*sic*] in bomb shelter that happens in Paris before the defeat. . . . Am sure could be another *Grand Illusion*."[18] "Another *Grand Illusion*" was what Renoir was looking for, or at least that was how he presented his ideas for films. Describing for Daven a project entitled *Flight South* (*Les Enfants de l'orage*), he wrote "about children in reform schools ordered to be let out as the Germans approach," and he concluded, "I'm also certain that I'm finally holding between my hands a super *Grand Illusion*."[19] Three days later, Zanuck wrote to Daven and Renoir about this project, which the director had worked on with David Flaherty, Robert's younger brother, as well as Charles David, the production director for *La Chienne*. The story of these boys running away from their reform school was interesting, but at the very most only as a pretext.

---

* The film was probably *Comrade X*, with Clark Gable and Hedy Lamarr.

Zanuck didn't believe that a story—whatever it was—could be a commercial success if it wasn't based on a strong, firmly oriented plot, a line of reasoning that he concluded with an emphasis on *The Grapes of Wrath* and *Grand Illusion*.[20]

The adaptation of the Steinbeck novel had been Fox's big hit for 1940, earning more than a million dollars. Originating with Zanuck and personally produced by him, it had won John Ford an Oscar for best director on February 27. Obviously, Ford had then forgotten about the remake of *Grand Illusion* that Zanuck had refused to produce. Ford's idea had been to substitute English prisoners for the French ones, with Victor McLaglen taking Gabin's role, George Sanders playing the Stroheim character, and either David Niven or Cesar Romero in the role Pierre Fresnay had played.[21] At the time Zanuck had emphasized to Ford, "I think that would be a criminal injustice to attempt to remake the picture in English. The most wonderful thing about the picture is the fine background, the authentic atmosphere, and the foreign characters, who actually speak in the language of their nationality. Once you take this away, I believe you have lost 50% of the value of the picture."[22] In that same message Zanuck called *Grand Illusion*, which he'd discovered the day before because Ford had suggested he see it, "the most magnificent picture of its type that I've ever seen."

Of all the film people with whom Renoir had to do business in Hollywood, Zanuck was the one whom he most consistently and spitefully claimed in private to detest. He harped on his excessive sexual appetite and his contempt for women and mocked his "warrior" behavior, of which Zanuck's membership in the Signal Corps seemed proof.[23] On the other hand, Zanuck had a wonderful grasp of film; and his response to Ford concerning *Grand Illusion* was proof enough of it. He just happened to think of the making of films in a way that did not at all correspond to the way Renoir did. During that period, studios at 20th Century Fox were bringing out excellent films, but Fox "was no place for an auteur."[24] Or at least not an auteur like Renoir, who was used to the interventions of producers that were often unbefitting but always happened after the film was finished. Renoir had a need for discussion and exchange with his various collaborators. His unfamiliarity with English prevented this, but he wasn't the first foreign director to suddenly touch down in the world of the studios. The real problem confronting him during these first weeks was dealing with a producer who decided everything and with whom he couldn't converse. Within the space of several months, he met with Zanuck no more than two or three times, and each time for only a few minutes.

As a result, the relationship between Renoir and Zanuck was limited to Zanuck's sending scripts that Renoir had Dido read and translate, while he submitted his ideas to Daven or to his agents. Later, he would maintain that

Zanuck only offered him projects that were set in Europe, whereas he clearly wanted his debut film to be "American." There is no document that sheds light on this difference in viewpoints, but Renoir discussed it to the greatest extent in an interview he gave to *Cahiers du cinéma*.[25] In fact, all the projects that Renoir thought at the time were "European," and all of Zanuck's suggestions, had to do with "American" stories. As for Europe, in 1941, Americans had only a hazy image of the situation over there, particularly in France. Had the French settled into a pro-Nazi position, or were they strongly opposed to the Germans occupying their country? Were some collaborating while others continued to fight? All of this was quite complicated and certainly didn't permit the description of cut-and-dried situations or the immediate evaluation of actions; and American onlookers didn't understand any of it. France in 1941 was not a workable context for a Hollywood film and even less of one for a film by Fox.

From January to April 1941, failing the ability to come to terms with such a basic state of affairs, Renoir focused his efforts mainly on *Flight South;* but his agents ended up discouraging him, stressing that the violence of the situations described and the picture depicted of the social chaos generated by the flight would be considered unacceptable as much by motion picture producers as by American cinema itself.[26] By then, Renoir had already understood that Zanuck wouldn't produce the film, and he had begun tackling the adaptation of Saint-Exupéry's book.

There are three treatments for *Wind, Sand and Stars,* all under that title. None are dated, but they were probably written between March and May 1941 and are coauthored by Renoir and Maximilian Becker, who was the agent of the writer and later of the director.[27] The action takes place on three continents: in Africa, in Southeast Asia, and in South America, following the young Aéropostale pilots who are its heroes. The story includes the outlines of a love affair with the daughter of an Argentine mechanic and climaxes in the Libyan desert, where one of the planes crashes, after which the pilot and the mechanic are taken prisoner by "a warring band of dissident Arabs"[28] in conflict with French colonial forces and are saved by the intervention of a French general. Its dominant theme, the brotherhood of men that transcends frontiers, ties it clearly to the screenplay for *Grand Illusion.*

Although Renoir had been careful to insist to Zanuck* that there would in no way be any question of war in the film,[29] France's situation in the world was at the heart of the project and imparted a political dimension to it that Hollywood was forbidden to consider in the spring of 1941. Renoir would become

---

* Some of the letters between Renoir and Zanuck appeared in *Les Cahiers Jean Renoir* in 2006. All of those cited here came directly from the Jean Renoir Papers at UCLA.

aware of this gradually, writing to Saint-Exupéry that Walter Wanger, to whom he'd submitted the project right after Zanuck's refusal, had remained very vague about the project, as had David O. Selznick's assistant with whom Renoir had lunched and who had given him the impression that "anything touching on France is a no-go for the moment."[30]

Renoir's two other proposals to Zanuck concerned two adaptations: one of the Claude Tillier novel *Mon oncle Benjamin*, about which Renoir professed he'd "dreamed" for several years, mostly because it dealt with the "birth of democratic ideas" in France,[31] and the other based on Knut Hamsun's *Hunger*. All of them, then, were European subjects, contrary to what Renoir would later insist when he needed to claim that he'd only done what he wanted to do in Hollywood. The justification for this came several years after he had directed his first film, the subject of which was American. His desire to maintain that he'd impressed his views on Zanuck required that he contend having fought to be able to shoot American stories and that the producer was insisting on entrusting him with "European" screenplays.

As far as Renoir was concerned, none of the screenplays that Zanuck had sent to him were appealing. Since he and Dido had arrived in Hollywood, they'd created a file of "possible" projects and subjects that included summaries of books that had been sent or suggested to him for adaptation as well as reading notes for others, some of which were drawn from texts published in *Reader's Digest*. These were kept in a binder, with the first dated February 1941 and the last 1948; and most of them were marked "suggested by . . . "[32] As the weeks passed, the situation became awkward. Renoir was well aware that Fox had only hired him and paid him $50,000 in order for him to direct films, and he also knew he was indebted to the studio for its contribution toward his trip and his living expenses as well as its efforts to enable his son to join him.

He'd at first thought that Alain's experience as an assistant cameraman might offer the hope of his being hired. Then he realized that American studios weren't interested in taking on any more immigrant technicians than they already had. Fox seemed willing to hire Alain as an actor, but he wouldn't hear of it; he was an assistant cameraman, not an actor. Léonide Moguy, with whom he'd worked in France and who was also in Hollywood, was ready to put Alain to work; but for the time being, the necessary visas were the main priority, should Alain end up deciding he wanted to come over. Aside from that, in response to a request by Joris Ivens, Renoir was petitioning Fox to make it easier for André Malraux to enter the United States. Drafted on June 21, the request included the following detail: "He has been very close to the Communists, like myself and many sincere Frenchmen, because we felt that this was the only means of resisting Hitler."[33] The answer came two days later, and it was negative.[34]

Renoir was not ready to direct merely any film at all, but he was well aware that he couldn't refuse Zanuck's suggestions indefinitely. Therefore, he made up his mind to finally accept one subject; and almost immediately, he accepted a second. At the end of March and beginning of April, he became determined to direct the two films mentioned in his contract one after the other. In his eyes, it was the only strategy that would allow him to move on to something else, after he'd freed himself of his obligations—even if this then meant looking for another producer should Zanuck persist in turning down his ideas.

Consequently, he said he was interested in the screenplay for the detective story *I Wake Up Screaming,* which the screenwriter Steve Fisher had sent to him in March accompanied by a note from the producer and which supposedly was to star Henry Fonda, Charles Laughton, and Alice Faye. On March 24, Renoir wrote that he really liked it, but the purpose of the remark was to prove his goodwill, and he would have been quite happy if they decided to make it his first assignment.[35] That same day, the papers announced that *I Wake Up Screaming* would be Jean Renoir's first American film.

Zanuck also recommended he do a Nunnally Johnson screenplay entitled *Venezuela.* The prospect of working with the screenwriter for *The Grapes of Wrath* was doubtlessly flattering, and Renoir called the script "remarkable,"[36] then "admirable . . . but even this does not alter the fact that my specialty is not great spectacle films."[37] However, he hastened to suggest to Zanuck that he use Jean Gabin, who had just arrived in Hollywood, for the film. The producer's April 7 answer was final: "I have come to the conclusion that you should not direct his first American film and that you should direct an American cast in your first American film and that he should have an American director for his first American film."[38] Zanuck also specified that if he decided to entrust the role in *Venezuela* to an actor other than Gabin, he'd have Renoir direct the film, proof that he had great confidence in this project.

The next day, Renoir declared himself to be completely in agreement about the question of Gabin and said, "I'm sure that later, when he and I have become more Americanized, our collaboration will bring you everything you have the right to hope from us."[39] If he were to direct *Venezuela,* he said, he would prefer James Cagney to George Raft, who'd been approached for the role. However, refusing to give up trying to convince Zanuck about adapting Saint-Exupéry's book, Renoir prepared a letter, which he seems not to have sent but in which he backed up his demand with the reminder that "*Grand Illusion,* the only film of mine that you know, was considered a crazy idea by all the producers"; and he ended his probably unsent letter with, "To this moment it has been my destiny not to succeed with anything except what's exceptional and difficult."[40]

A week later, he wrote a new letter to Zanuck: although he wasn't intending to say no to *Venezuela*, which could have in fact been a perfect chance for him to adapt to the American mentality, he supposed that Zanuck had "hired Jean Renoir so he would make Jean Renoir films. And, in this case, I believe that *Wind, Sand and Stars* gives me the ideal pretext."[41] Although he obviously was right to think that he was the only director in Hollywood capable of doing justice to this story that he loved with all his heart,[42] and although he wrote to Saint-Exupéry claiming this, Hollywood simply was not interested in this story. He'd come to that conclusion some time later and write to his agent on July 9, "We are going through a time when everything French interests very few people in Hollywood." However, he also pointed out that this wouldn't always be the case and that the moment would come when it would be possible to "recommence a new offensive."[43]

Before Renoir left Europe he'd gotten in contact with David O. Selznick, who at the time was riding on the success of *Gone with the Wind*. In his letter to Daven on January 21, Renoir reported a "meeting" between Dido and "a Selznick collaborator." A few weeks later, Renoir wrote to Saint-Exupéry, "Selznick wants me to work with him. He'd like to buy me from Fox.... His idea is to have me make Kessel's film on the [French Foreign] Legion."[44]

Was there also a possibility for *Joan of Arc*? A rumor about this had reached France and been boosted by a few paragraphs that had appeared in the professional press.[45] Claude Renoir had alluded to it in a letter to his brother,[46] and then Pierre Lestringuez had mentioned the same thing in a message he'd sent to Renoir by way of Jean Gabin. "I've learned through the press that you're going to take on Joan of Arc to make a film. I can see you telling me about the screenplay for Joan of Arc in 1926 ... at Porte des Ternes.... Ah, Jean, old man, I hope you break out of your shell and give, will be able to give, all that is in you. If you do it, we'll feel the wind over here and we'll be thrilled about it, we who love you for yourself, lock, stock, and barrel!"[47] Thus, Lestringuez, one of those who obviously knew Renoir the best, thought his old friend hadn't delivered everything he carried inside him, meaning that he hadn't yet been given free rein in his films to the part of his personality that was the most authentic.

Selznick didn't do business with Renoir, who remained tied to Zanuck as a result and therefore gave him a definite yes regarding the direction of *Venezuela*. (Walter Wanger would produce a film called *Joan of Arc* with Ingrid Bergman in 1948, directed by Victor Fleming.) Delays in establishing the cast for *Venezuela* allowed Renoir to gain a few extra weeks, and the project *I Wake Up Screaming* was reactivated. Renoir agreed to take it in hand, all the while asking Zanuck why he'd need him to direct a film that would be perfectly appropriate for some American director. He was especially asking to be assigned *The Night the World Shook*, another Nunnally Johnson screenplay, adapted from a Stefan Wendt novel, about an earthquake that makes it possible for some convicts to escape prison. He had no real enthusiasm for this project and wanted to finish directing it as soon as possible to settle his debt to Fox. That is what he wrote in a letter to his agent on April 9. Although he would direct both *Venezuela* and *I Wake Up Screaming* with the sole purpose of honoring the contract he'd signed with Fox, he wanted the agent finally to convince Zanuck or an independent producer to become interested in *Wind, Sand and Stars,* which was the only idea at the moment "capable of placing me in the front rank of Hollywood directors, and of giving me in the US the place I occupied in France."[48]

The Night the World Shook and *Venezuela* remained shelved at Fox, but not *I Wake Up Screaming,* which would be directed by H. Bruce Humberstone.

Being steered around from an idea he considered uninspiring to a project he didn't like began to wear on Renoir. Writing to his brother Claude, he described life in Hollywood as follows: "Outside of all the difficulties I've revealed to you in this letter, the country does possess one quality that is undeniable: you get bored to death."[49] But if Gabrielle could write to him on March 15, "I'm happy to know that you're in a country you like,"[50] it was probably in response to his having told her about some satisfactions his new life afforded him.

There was nothing contradictory in these reactions. If Renoir was admitting that he was getting bored, it was essentially because his future in Hollywood remained uncertain, to such a point that on May 26 he wrote to Raymond Warnier, the director of the French Institute who'd hosted him in Lisbon, "I also believe that I got here at a decadent period. Hollywood was very great during the time when its artists worked there in the spirit of pioneers. Now, they're established. They can't go any further. They're even on the decline, because they've started to miss the European market, and that surprises them. If I had the means, I wouldn't stay here. I'd go to New York where I'd try to write, or else I'd go back to France where I'd cultivate the family soil while waiting for things to settle down."[51] By then, however, he'd known the title of his first American film for four days.

On May 27, the day after Renoir wrote these lines, Fox announced that *Swamp Water* would be directed by Jean Renoir, "the gifted megaphonist* who turned out such European success as *Grand Illusion* and *Madame Bovary*." In the questionnaire that Fox used to present every newcomer, the megaphonist had named *La Chienne* his personal favorite,† mentioned that he lived in Paris in the former residence of Alexandre Dumas senior, and finally replaced the potatoes accompanying the beefsteak in his favorite dish with a green salad.[52]

---

* A playful designation for movie directors, who used megaphones to give directives on a set.

† In 1958, Renoir's answer to the same question would be *The River*.

Swamp Water had been adapted from the novel of a young writer from Georgia, Vereen Bell. Fox had acquired this property for $15,000, even before it was published in installments in the *Saturday Evening Post* beginning on November 23, 1940. The adaptation had been assigned to Dudley Nichols, who had read the story before it appeared. Six months younger than Renoir, Nichols had begun his career in Hollywood in 1930 and had since worked on about forty films, having written several screenplays for John Ford that included *The Informer* and *Stagecoach,* as well as Hawks's *Bringing Up Baby.* He had just adapted an English novel called *Rogue Male,* intended at first for Ford but then directed by Fritz Lang and released on June 13, 1941, under the title *Man Hunt.* In it, Walter Pidgeon plays an English hunter on vacation who discovers he has Hitler in his gun sight.

Man Hunt was the third film directed by the German director for 20th Century Fox and could have been followed by *Swamp Water,* but Zanuck had changed his mind and finally given the film to Renoir. Apparently, Lang had declared himself slighted by having been pushed aside;[53] but after a snippet in a corporate publication echoed this discontent, Lang wrote to Renoir on June 28, "About a remark I was supposed to have made about you concerning your assignment on *Swamp Water.* This remark is not only ridiculous but absurd."[54] Renoir would thank him in French with a letter delivered by messenger on July 9, in which he said that he was completely unaware of the article in question and that, moreover, he was "too much of a beginner in English to read anything but the major news about the war in the daily newspapers."[55] Sometimes the press made references to his poor knowledge of English in a way meant to be amusing. For example, the *New York Post* described a recent encounter between Renoir and the screenwriter Garson Kanin, who had tried to speak very slowly, carefully separating each of his words, to express his boundless admiration for the director's work. Renoir is supposed to have then said to Kanin that he could talk faster, because when it came to compliments, he always understood.[56]

Dudley Nichols worked on the adaptation of the novel during March 1941 in New Milford, Connecticut, communicating with the author on several occasions by letter. In the meantime, the complete text had been published in a single volume. It took Nichols about four to five weeks to finish one screenplay, and he sent that version of *Swamp Water* to Fox on April 27. On May 19, Zanuck informed Nichols that he'd have to cut twenty-five pages of his adaptation, mostly from the first part, despite the fact that the screenplay, dated May 1,[57] had already begun to be sent around.

Lang and Renoir were among those who'd received a copy, and both expressed a desire to direct the film. Renoir even saw in it the best offer that he'd received while in Hollywood, making clear to Zanuck on May 23, "This is exactly the subject I would have chosen for myself if I had been my own producer."[58] Three days later, in a letter to his brother Claude,* he labeled the project "a little less idiotic than the others" but described the novel that had been adapted as "magnificent."[59] The difference in judgment can certainly be explained (as is always the case with Renoir) by the personalities of each of his correspondents but also by the discovery he'd made in the meantime that Zanuck wasn't intending the film to be made using natural decor. And so, the main reason for the enthusiasm Renoir had expressed at first was the result of his anticipating filming "in the swamps of Okefenokee, in the middle of crocodiles, different kinds of snakes, stags, foxes, otters, etc."[60] There was no question of this, not for the reason Renoir claimed, that it was customary in Hollywood to prohibit filming in exteriors—several scenes from *The Grapes of Wrath* had been filmed that way—but because Zanuck considered *Swamp Water* no more than a standard production that didn't justify such an approach, which he in fact made clear to the director in a memo dated May 26: "This is a film that must be made for an economical price. It will have a tight budget and a tight shooting schedule. There is nothing sure-fire about it from a commercial standpoint."[61]

On May 27, Renoir did in fact receive permission to go to Georgia to visit locations, not by car, as he'd been hoping, but by plane, in order to find some settings that could then be of use to the studio's set designers. The same day, Fox announced that the director would be working beside a dialogue director, Irving Pichel. In his letter to Zanuck on May 23, Renoir declared himself to be "delighted" by that decision, and he wanted to "study, with him, a plan of work which will permit us not to be separated."

Pichel, who had begun as an actor and still appeared in films from time to time, was one of those men who did various odd jobs for the studio. He'd been a second-unit director, assistant, codirector (*The Most Dangerous Game* with Ernest B. Schoedsack), and occasionally a director. He'd also be appearing as a producer in the credits for *Swamp Water*. In the production system Zanuck had instituted, function was of secondary importance. Joe Mankiewicz liked to claim that his last film for Fox, *5 Fingers*, had been produced by Zanuck's wife's skiing instructor. The fact that Renoir, who neither spoke nor understood English, needed a dialogue director to help him was easy enough to understand;

* At the same time, in France, Claude Renoir Sr. was desperately trying to find work, and some of the descriptions of the trouble he was having did not lack humor. For example, in a letter to Dido, he wrote, "I failed finding work several times. The last promise of work was a documentary on olive oil for [Maurice] Cloche. When everybody was in agreement, there were no more olives." (Letter from Claude Renoir Sr. to Dido Freire, April 30, 1941, Jean Renoir Papers, Correspondence, Box 1, Folder 20.)

but the truth was that Pichel was going to serve on the shoot as Zanuck's special representative, which Renoir had to have known, Zanuck having sent him a copy of his May 21 memo two days before he'd decided to entrust *Swamp Water* to him: "On the first picture that Jean Renoir makes for us, I have decided to assign Irving Pichel as the dialogue director to aid and assist Mr. Renoir. While Mr. Pichel is a full-fledged director in his own right, I know that he will be willing to sacrifice his personal screen credit and serve Mr. Renoir in this capacity."[62]

Zanuck didn't attend the first production meeting, which took place on May 28 and included Renoir, Dudley Nichols (who'd come from Connecticut especially for this), Irving Pichel, and several executives. Their mission was to spread the boss's word (the screenplay had to be cut), to interpret his orders (which scenes would be convenient to slash?), and to come back with a report on the results. Clearly, they made no decisions. Everything would be done according to the wishes of Zanuck, as he would soon enjoy making clear. That day, through the fog of words, some of which he didn't understand, and behind the screen of behavior, which was difficult for him to interpret, Renoir discovered how a studio like Fox functioned. He also got to know Dudley Nichols, with whom he would work with good understanding and soon develop a wonderful rapport. The report concerning this first meeting[63] makes no mention of Renoir's interceding in any way. It should be remembered that his main concern was the language. Evidence of this comes from his handwritten annotations on the screenplay, all of which are about the French meaning of English words or about their pronunciation.[64] Renoir was also equipped with a list of technical terms and slang used in Hollywood studios, such as, "last shot made before returning home in the evening = *the Window Shot*"; or else, "a bad actor = *a Bum Actor* (*beum*)."[65]

There is a general consensus that *Swamp Water* is a film without stars because Renoir wanted it that way. He himself has claimed this, using it to justify his refusal of what he claimed was an offer from Zanuck, who, according to Renoir, had said he "would very much like" to supply Renoir with "the best stars we have." Renoir's answer to this, supposedly, was, "If you give me actors whose success is established, it's exactly like working with ducks: you throw them onto the water, and they don't ever get wet: they're waterproof, rooted in their success. I'd much rather have people who are still indecisive in order to be able to work with them, to be able to orient them."[66] And as a result, according to Renoir, Zanuck allowed him to "take people who weren't known, but gave me people for the supporting roles who are very well known, like Brennan and old man Huston."

The bulletin from the publicity department at Fox for August 5, 1941, reported that it was the director who had chosen to dispense with stars, but that was really a matter of a justification after the fact. In his letter to Zanuck on May 23, Renoir had written, "I am thoroughly happy with the casting which you propose. Permit me, nevertheless, to express one regret, which is not to be making this magnificent production with Tyrone Power, whom I like tremendously, not only as an actor, but also as a man." At that time, Tyrone Power was married to the French actress Annabella, who had been the star of Raymond Bernard's film *Anne-Marie,* written by Saint-Exupéry. Saint-Exupéry was the one responsible for Annabella and Renoir meeting in Hollywood, although they had probably known each other already, and this gave Renoir the chance to appreciate in private the man who was one of Hollywood's foremost stars at the beginning of the forties and who was just enjoying a new hit in Rouben Mamoulian's *The Mark of Zorro,* which had been released in the United States in November 1940. All the same, Zanuck didn't want to hear any talk about Tyrone Power for *Swamp Water.* "In the first place, he is not available, and in the second place, I am sure when you learn more about this work you will realize that he has a voice which would never be adapted to this locale."[67] In reality, the reason had to do with the fact that *Swamp Water* was too humble a project for a star on the scale of Tyrone Power. For the role of Ben, Zanuck suggested Dana Andrews.

At the time, the actor had only six films to his name, including John Ford's *Tobacco Road,* an adaptation of a play by Jack Kirkland,* taken from the Erskine Caldwell novel, which was not without parallels to *Swamp Water.* Both happen in a remote country place, with characters on the margins of the modern world. After having deplored the fact that he couldn't use Tyrone Power, Renoir informed Zanuck, "I do not say this in disparagement of Dana Andrews, whom I know too little through his brief performance in *Tobacco Road,* in which he was excellent."[68] Accordingly, it would be false to say that Renoir "chose" Dana Andrews, and claiming that he deliberately dispensed with having a star is inexact. On the other hand, the choice of the female lead can be attributed to him.

Zanuck wanted to cast Linda Darnell as the female lead and suggested that Renoir see her in the newly released *Blood and Sand,* also directed by Rouben Mamoulian and also starring Tyrone Power. After returning from his first trip to Georgia, Renoir shared his impressions of Darnell with Zanuck. He found the actress to be "still better in it than in *Chad Hannah,* and if the audience near me did not show very much enthusiasm for her, perhaps it was because she is a little too charming in tragic situations." Above all, he considered Linda

---

* Kirkland would collaborate on the screenplay for *Le Carrosse d'or* (*The Golden Coach*).

Darnell "very beautiful, very sympathetic, very sweet—too sweet, in my opinion, to represent a young girl who, at an age when the others are experiencing the joys and the protection of family life, is obliged to earn her own living as a maid-of-all-work in the home of the village grocers." In short, the actress wasn't suitable for "the splendid story that you [meaning Zanuck] have been good enough to assign to me."[69]

He petitioned to make a test with Anne Baxter, whose other screen tests on file he'd come across. Zanuck gave permission to test Anne Baxter ... and Linda Darnell. Unlike Darnell, Anne Baxter was really still a beginner in Hollywood, but she'd appeared on Broadway since the age of thirteen and had just turned eighteen. She was wholly Renoir's choice, then, and this was in perfect agreement with his "theory of the duck." However, he did not win his cause without a struggle, and even while that struggle was still taking place, Fox put out the word that Linda Darnell would be the female lead in *Swamp Water*.

Zanuck was also very attached to the casting of Walter Huston, who wasn't under contract to Fox, something that didn't keep Zanuck from writing in his memo to Renoir on May 24 that he would not do the film without Huston. Apparently, Renoir had considered casting Lillian Gish to play Hannah, an idea he communicated through Dudley Nichols during the May 28 meeting and that was accepted by Zanuck.[70] But in the end, Zanuck considered the actress too old and preferred Mary Howard, who was twenty years younger than Griffith's heroine. Nevertheless, Renoir did manage to use another leading actress from *The Birth of a Nation*, Mae Marsh, who was under contract to Fox, for a small role in *Swamp Water;* but her name would not appear in the credits.

Did Renoir also want to request Chester Conklin, the delightful "Popper" Sieppe from *Greed,* Stroheim's masterpiece and one of Renoir's major references? In any case, that is what he said in writing to the actor on August 22, mentioning that he had asked Fox to consider him, but that, being a newcomer, he perhaps hadn't known how to go about it, and his request had come to nothing. Then he added, "I admire you immensely, and have not forgotten the good moments you made me spend a few years ago watching you on the screen."[71] Renoir's letter was in response to two notes written in green ink, the first note containing the actor's name on letterhead, dated July 21: "I am in need of work. Have you a part or a bit I would do? I thank you."[72] The second note, dated August 1, read, "I need work badly. Have you a part or bit I would do?"[73] Chester Conklin had been an actor since 1913. He'd worked for Mack Sennett and for Chaplin (*Modern Times, The Dictator*) and then survived by appearing from time to time in walk-ons, without being credited. He died forgotten by everyone in 1971.

Two days after his first meeting in Hollywood, Renoir flew to Fort Worth, Texas, with Dido, Irving Pichel, and an assistant director. From there, they took another flight to Atlanta, and then a third to Jacksonville, Florida, where they spent the night, before leaving in the morning by car for Waycross, Georgia. When they got back to Los Angeles on June 4, he was bursting with enthusiasm, which he expressed to his son five days later. He had discovered "a countryside that wasn't picturesque, but that was as fascinating as Sologne," and had met the editor of the local paper in whom he recognized "the perfect kind of Southern gentleman like the type that you see in *Birth of a Nation*." He had taken "unforgettable walks," and "the people of this land completely resembled the people of Essoyes." In short, he was "awfully fond" of "this whistle-stop." Certainly, "we are going to reproduce the Okefenokee swamp in Hollywood," but "since it's a subject that pleases me, I am going to have two very happy months."[74]

The passion that he'd developed in a few days for the place—and even more for its people—resulted in his trying one last time to convince Zanuck to let him film on location.[75] In vain. Similarly, Zanuck turned down point-blank his extended plea in favor of setting the action in the past and not in an unspecified period that could just as well have been the present as the recent past, where both Vereen Bell's novel and Nichols's adaptation had set it.

On the other hand, when Zanuck intended to replace Dana Andrews with John Shepperd, a young actor for whom he was predicting a flattering future, Renoir clung to the Dana Andrews–Anne Baxter duo. At Renoir's request, the producer agreed to have a session of screen tests organized for all of them, which took place on June 17. On that day, appearing one after the other before the studio cameras were John Shepperd and Linda Darnell, followed by Dean Jagger and Linda Darnell, and then John Shepperd and Lynn Bari (according to Zanuck's wishes). Finally came Dana Andrews and Anne Baxter, who were Renoir's choices.[76] In addition, Renoir was able to obtain a change in the way the film ended so that the last scene would echo the first, with Ben seeing his dog run off after a deer. But most importantly of all, Renoir convinced Zanuck to send him to film a few scenes in the swamps. Obviously, Renoir was beginning to get his footing within the system and to find in it the guarantee that a stubborn director could obtain what he wanted. Or nearly.

The truth is that Renoir was hardly laboring under any illusions. The day after that meeting during which he had, in fact, managed to win a few small victories, he wrote to Lestringuez, "I'm beginning to lose hope in doing anything possible here. Tonight I had a meeting with Fox's big boss, Zanuck. It was the in-your-shirt-sleeves type, exactly like a kriegspiel attack designed by an infantry commandant on a 1912 map with a scale of 25/1000! Our story was feasible, more or less. He's managed to turn it into something I find totally stupid!"[77]

That same day, he wrote to André Halley des Fontaines, "The work that I'm doing here offers no artistic value. . . . From time to time, some very strong individuals show up to do something good, despite all opposition. . . . I so terribly miss the time of *The Crime of Monsieur Lange*. Those days were a bit crazy, our ideas weren't very stable, but what beautiful filmmaking! It sure in heck isn't in Hollywood that you can make a film like that!"[78] Then, four days later, to Henri Chomette, René Clair's brother, he wrote, "I can't prevent myself from noticing how desperate our profession has become, at the very least in Hollywood. It's really a factory. . . . It doesn't feel like working in film, but like being in school. We have a very nice, very friendly teacher who, instead of using the right method, which consists in developing the personality of each student, keeps on practicing the bad one, consisting of modeling the mind of each student after his own."[79]

"Professor" Zanuck was overwhelming the "student" Renoir with notes; and in the face of such an avalanche the director was resorting to giving up. Informed by a June 19 memo that the screenplay had to be amended again, he answered the next day that he liked "the screenplay because it has gained a lot in tempo," but he regretted "the loss of certain things in the old screenplay" and was "unable just now to make any suggestions as to how to keep them and at the same time retain the good tempo we now have."[80] In his letter to Henri Chomette, Renoir rejoiced about "returning to Georgia in a week for a few exteriors to be used as back projections and even—something unique in Hollywood—taking a few direct shots with actors, on location."

The actors from *Swamp Water* whom Zanuck authorized to go to Georgia were Dana Andrews and the dog, Trouble. The trip to Waycross was scheduled to be brief, less than a week. When rain prevented the first five days of work, Renoir asked to extend it, and Zanuck answered that he could remain as long as he hadn't finished what he'd come to do. Filming at the studio, for which preparations were rapidly being made, was supposed to begin July 14, 1941. Having arrived in Waycross on June 25, Renoir, Dido, Irving Pichel, the head cinematographer Lucien Ballard, Dana Andrews, the dog Trouble and its master, and several crewmembers returned to Los Angeles on July 6. That meant that they had stayed at that location for eleven days, and during at least five of these, nothing had been shot.[81] Most of the shots that were filmed were the type normally assigned to a second unit, something that Renoir himself acknowledged in a note for his personal use grouped under "Scenes to film in Georgia."[82]

What Renoir had filmed, therefore, were a few images of the swamp without sound and intended for back projections. There were a half dozen of these shots overall, for which the inhabitants of the region had served as stand-ins.

These would be integrated into the opening scene. There were also several close-ups of Dana Andrews and the dog as well as at least one long shot with a female stand-in that would not be used in the film. The scene showing Ben's entrance into the swamp, which the screenplay represented as contained in only two shots, became Renoir's chance to impose his style: he filmed it in twelve shots, using a moving camera for eight of them, for a total time length of five minutes. As William Gilcher has written, "The shots have a vertiginous quality because, unlike the tracking shots in the town, the swamp offers no points of reference. One tree or vine looks very much like another. This is, of course, the point of the sequence. When Ben goes off toward the back of the image at the end of the sequence, he is lost."[83] Far from Zanuck, far from Hollywood.

Filming in the studio began July 14, as planned. A week later, Renoir wrote to his brother Claude, "In Hollywood, there's no pleasure in my trade. It consists of being seated in a comfortable chair, smoking cigarettes, and saying 'action' and 'cut.' I've understood the futility of trying to do something personal. My boss, M. Zanuck, is a kind of Richebé, the unfortunate difference being that he's four to five hundred times more of one."[84] The next day, he wrote to Dudley Nichols that he'd "rather sell peanuts in Mexico than make films at Fox."[85] "I'm not a eunuch, and the joys of the harem do not constitute an idea which can satisfy me," he explained in that same letter. He also complained about the way Dido had been treated, after she "had put in some very hard work in the swamps of Okefenokee." She had been his "interpreter at every moment on the set," and as a result of his insisting, Fox had just suggested paying her "twenty-seven dollars per week for five weeks," whereas "the starting salary for a typist is fifty-two dollars."[86]

Renoir couldn't do without Dido. She was the only one who made it possible for him to communicate with the actors, the crew, and the producers. However, Dido and he lived together without being husband and wife, and presenting her as his secretary didn't always work as a bluff. For example, about a dinner at the home of Elizabeth Meyer and her husband, the producer and director Pare Lorentz, Thomas Mann noted in his journal that he had met "Mr. Renoir and his Portuguese-Brazilian secretary or girlfriend."[87] Consequently, Renoir worried about potential complications and stayed on his guard. Evidence of this is in a letter to "Mr. Koenig*" of "20th Century-Fox Corp.," who the day before had referred to his companion by calling her "your girl": "I have known Dido Freire for a good many years, and her family as well, and the idea that she could be my *petite amie* seems as comical to me as though it had been applied to my

---

* William Koenig, a production director at Fox.

young sister."[88] The letter wasn't sent. Perhaps Renoir thought—as he often did when he felt ill at ease or, on the contrary, very sure of himself—that he was going a little too far.

On the set, in contrast, he wasn't going far enough for his taste, although he was aware that he was learning what seemed to him like a new role, as he explained to his brother Claude. "Going through this is necessary, but it has to be looked at as a kind of graduate school and not like a way to make good films."[89] He appreciated the professionalism and the high degree of competence of Fox's technicians, and he got along well with his actors. However, the efforts he made to yield to Hollywood methods proved insufficient.

The memo Zanuck sent him on July 30, which was two weeks into shooting, was tantamount to a first warning. It also contained a good description of the difficulties Renoir was encountering: "You are going entirely too slow. . . . We have changed the cameraman and now you have a photographer who can keep up to a fast pace, yet we are getting no more film than we did with the other cameraman."[90] What followed was a list of criticisms: too much time spent on nonessential details; camera too mobile (using dolly or crane shots too often); scenes filmed several ways, whereas you should make up your mind before and stick to it; too much importance given to atmosphere; two hours needed to get the shot of the sheriff, who was filmed with the crane, in front of the shop; the director should be concentrating on the scenes with the leads and find a way to film the others more quickly and as efficiently as possible; four different angles to shoot the sheriff in front of the house, whereas two would have been more than enough; what took two days to film should have been done in one. In conclusion, Zanuck was insisting on "a radical change."

Already, in France, Renoir's methodology had sometimes provoked incomprehension. Some technicians hadn't stopped themselves from pointing out what they considered to be a lack of decisiveness on the part of the director. Under Zanuck's authority, these methods were characterized as vices. Already, Renoir had ironically observed that the "czar of the rushes" made every decision, even the shirts and blouses worn by the actors. At the time, he hadn't known how right he was. In fact, the brassiere Anne Baxter wanted to wear became a problem. Zanuck wasn't having it. Renoir took the actress's side and won his case, earning her gratitude.[91] The producer only wanted to see "sexy" actresses. The letters of the word *SEX*, he wrote in a memo, needed to be able to be read on their face. But it was also true that the wild child Baxter was playing was justification for her doing without a brassiere.

Renoir liked to talk. His custom was to engage in long conversations with the actors, to discuss things with the crew, especially the director of cinematography, who is the primary ally of all directors. Replacing Lucien Ballard, the great head cameraman who was of Cheyenne background and then thirty-four,* with the dubious J. Peverell Marley was the result of Zanuck's decision, because he thought filming had been going on forever. The decision didn't come from Renoir, who, in fact, maintained a connection to Ballard and had been invited in the fall of 1941 to visit him in Arizona, the land of his ancestors. J. Peverell Marley's main attribute was working fast, doing strings of shots without giving the lighting or camera placement any more importance than the boss judged necessary. For Renoir, the loss was doubtlessly an important one, and it contributed to isolating him still more. He wasn't given the time to reflect, or discuss things with others, to tell his stories and hear theirs. And even if this had been different, his proficiency with English wouldn't have allowed it. There are exchanges that can't be aided by an interpreter, regardless of how devoted or gifted that person might be.

One anecdote reveals in an amusing way the kind of misunderstandings to which his poor knowledge of the language could lead. Describing his progress in English nearly a year after shooting *Swamp Water*, Renoir told his brother Claude, "I still have a lot of trouble with the verb *wait*, which, depending upon whether it is pronounced with an open or closed vowel (*wet*), means 'attendre' [to wait] or 'mouiller' [to wet]. And over here, 'wet' is a popular way of saying a lot of things that you can guess. It was bound to produce a laugh when I was talking to an actress during a scene and, instead of asking her to wait a little, I was asking her to 'wet.'" [92]

Above and beyond such difficulties and such obstacles, Renoir still had to try to adapt his style of cinema to the one that prevailed in Hollywood. And yet, his own style, as he'd discovered and perfected it ceaselessly all through the thirties, was the polar opposite of the way Hollywood in general—and Zanuck in particular—saw film. Opposed to shots often of very long duration that served the intensity of the scene and the actors' performance—one of the marks of Renoirian construction—was the Hollywood desire for dramatic efficiency based primarily on cutting, which made the rhythm of editing the most important source of intensity, to the detriment of duration. There's no need to prefer one conception over the other to understand how incompatible the two were and to estimate Renoir's helpless confusion and Zanuck's impatience. Without beating around the bush, Renoir explained his confusion in a letter to Zanuck dated August 1, in which, among other points, he explained, "Our association is a mistake, both for you and for me. The fact is, I have been too

---

* Near the end of his career, Lucien Ballard would end up photographing Sam Peckinpah's films.

long in this profession to change the methods in which I have come to believe sincerely, and which, in any case, are adapted to my temperament. You yourself have very definite ideas on the direction of films, and these ideas have stood the test."[93] But Zanuck would not take hold of the line that Renoir was holding out to him, and he pushed stubbornly forward.

In a memo dated August 2 to Len Hammond, the film's associate producer, and with copies provided to Renoir and Irving Pichel, Zanuck reminded Renoir that he expected the director to decide each evening where to place the camera for the shots of the following day, and that he not change his mind in the morning.[94] The next day, Renoir wrote to Charles Boyer that the French would see him as "some kind of storyteller, rather than a director, replacing the sheet of paper with the screen," that he was currently "exasperating Zanuck" with his slowness, and that he was waiting "from one moment to the next for [Zanuck] to do without" his services, which he didn't "blame him for at all."[95] Contrary to what Renoir seemed to fear, unless he more or less desired it secretly, Zanuck wasn't intending to replace him; but Zanuck continued to attempt to impress upon him his views, especially by means of a long memo dated August 8.

After congratulating Renoir for the results he'd obtained with Anne Baxter and Dana Andrews, Zanuck came to his reprimands. The first concerned the mannered and artificial picturesque quality of the minor characters, who "all seem to be trying to act," unlike those in *The Grapes of Wrath*, for example, who "react naturally and honestly."[96] But, he added, there was nothing about all that that couldn't be corrected with a few retakes. Then Zanuck got back to his usual reproaches having to do with Renoir's slowness and indecision, before concluding by assuring Renoir, "I want you to know that I am behind you."

A week later, in a letter to Eugène Lourié, who'd just arrived in New York, Renoir gave vent to his gloom. "Never would I have believed that you could come to detest your profession the way I detest it now." Refusing to "blame this studio," he "simply made note of" his "lack of ability to adapt to these methods." Then he concluded, "After this film I'm doing now and that will be very bad, I'll try to find some corner in the provinces where I can live very cheaply."[97]

A few days more and the bombshell came. Or at least that's what Renoir would describe, claiming that a "minor" supervisor suggested he call in sick and give up the idea of finishing the film. He supposedly then refused the proposition only to hear the next day that he'd been replaced by another director. That very evening Zanuck is said to have called his home to tell him that he certainly was not and that of course he would be expected on the set in the morning. And, to the applause of the entire team, he began filming again, which then took place in a calmer atmosphere.[98] The fact that the incident hasn't left any written trace doesn't mean that it didn't happen, because for all intents and purposes everything occurred in barely forty-eight hours. However, it seems surprising that a decision as essential as replacing a director during filming could have been taken by a subordinate on behalf of his own boss, especially in a studio like Fox, where nothing ever happened except by order of Zanuck. The tone of the exchanges that occurred in the days that followed implies instead that it was Renoir who wanted to be let go from the film, a request that his agents convinced the director to withdraw, or else one that Zanuck refused to grant. By abandoning the film, Renoir would have put his Hollywood career in peril. By dismissing the director, Zanuck would have admitted having been wrong about hiring him and assigning him *Swamp Water*. Thus, both had an interest in working things out, or in acting as if they had. Nevertheless, beginning on the day of his supposed "return" to the set to the sound of applause, Renoir let things slide.

The end of the film posed a problem, especially after Zanuck refused the one filmed by Renoir, which depicted a brawl between Ben and Tom Keefer and the Dorson brothers. This didn't please the director any more than it suited the producer. Renoir suggested another, which was also rejected. He gave up on asserting his point of view and on September 3 was present at the shooting of the scene written by Irving Pichel according to Zanuck's indications. He kept himself from interfering in any way other than influencing the actors, as he reported to Dudley Nichols in a letter dated September 4 in which he acknowledged Zanuck's qualities as a screenwriter but criticized his lack of "sensibility."[99] This was the price Renoir paid to peacefully finish a film that he'd understood would not belong to him.

Filming for *Swamp Water* ended officially on September 8, but four days later Renoir was back in the studio. Zanuck had decided that after the cuts he had himself required, a scene between Ben and Jesse Wick was missing. He wrote it himself on the eleventh, and the director—in name only—filmed it along with Irving Pichel on September 12. Although it seems that the beginning of this scene, a fifty-second shot, could conceivably be attributed to Renoir, the rest, composed of a dozen shots/reverse shots, close-ups, and inserts, was probably the work of Pichel.[100] This is no more than a hypothesis, based less on established facts than on analyses produced by comparing some of these images to those that exist in films from Renoir's French period. It is certainly not possible to know what that scene and that film in its entirety would have been like if the editing had been in Renoir's hands.

The day after shooting had been completed, Renoir would, in fact, discover that he was not expected in the editing room. And not even welcome, necessarily. It was the custom at Fox not to want the definitively edited version to be the jurisdiction of the director. Experienced directors took such a thing into account. They didn't film shots that they didn't want in the film and that they knew the editors or the producer would "naturally" include. For example, in *How Green Was My Valley*, which was personally produced by Zanuck, John Ford was very careful not to film a close-up of Walter Pidgeon at the door of the church where the woman he loves (Maureen O'Hara) has just married another man. He had no doubt that such an image would be expected by the logic of the emotion-manufacturing machine and would have to end up in the film, whereas the figure of Walter Pidgeon in the background of the shot created an infinitely stronger impression. Back then, Renoir had no experience with the Hollywood way and, unlike John Ford, had not yet won any prestige in Zanuck's eyes. Even if he had tried to proceed in a similar way, there would be no doubt that Irving Pichel would take his place and film the shots the boss wanted. Renoir still detested conflict just as much as he had on the other side of the Atlantic.

What is more, what he found out in September 1941 was far from traumatic for him. It's even probable that in some sense it freed him from a burden. Later, he'd write that the final edit, "the work of Zanuck or one of his assistants* . . . was excellent, anyway, perhaps more adroit than I could have done myself, but it wasn't my edit."[101] He'd already expressed a similar attitude in a letter to Dudley Nichols, regarding a scene written by Zanuck that had replaced the one he'd filmed as well as another scene that hadn't been shot. "The scene is good, like all Zanuck's ideas, which are good in themselves, but they destroy the films, bringing them back solely to an ingenious report of events."[102] It was the exact opposite of the cinema of Renoir, who had taken a long time to become interested in factual sequences just enough to award them forced attention. As a result, he already had no doubt that *Swamp Water* would not resemble a film by Renoir.

Consequently, being excluded from the editing occasioned little more than a relative, very subsidiary surprise. In no way did it produce a fresh wound. The way things had turned out only reinforced his resolve to be free of his contract with a company that his faltering English—or rebellious spirit—had one day made him call "15th Century Fox."[103] Later, he'd attribute one part of the responsibility for his severance from Fox to "the presence of André Daven, who's a bit too much of a schemer for me and makes this studio an unpleasant place for me."[104] However, the direction taken by his Hollywood career in 1941 suggests he lacked patience and, perhaps, a certain form of humility, those same qualities that had permitted other directors to become established, even though they had arrived from Europe with a degree of prestige that was at least

---

* The editing of *Swamp Water* was the work of the experienced Walter Thompson, who'd already edited such films as John Ford's *Young Mr. Lincoln* and Fritz Lang's *The Return of Frank James.*

equivalent to his.

The fact that the publicity campaign for *Swamp Water* made no mention of Renoir's name was in no way remarkable. Such an omission conformed to a convention with barely any exceptions beyond those regarding a Ford or a Capra. Presented to the press on October 7 in New York, the film, for which *Variety* predicted a humble future—mostly because it lacked any big names—was released on November 15 at the Globe Theater on Broadway, where it continued to play until a few days before Christmas. A preview of the film had been shown in Waycross on October 23, which had been declared "*Swamp Water* Day" by the governor of Georgia. Vereen Bell, the author of the novel, was the guest of honor of the celebration, because Fox had refused to send any actor in the film to this location. There was a grand "*Swamp Water* Ball," the *Journal-Herald* of Waycross published a "*Swamp Water* Edition," and a Queen of the Okefenokee was chosen. The film would play for eight days in that city, beating *Gone with the Wind*'s record of seventy-five hundred tickets by selling nine thousand.

It was a blockbuster in the South and a hit throughout the country, promoted by aggressive advertising that Eugène Lourié, on his way through New York, described to Renoir: "The front of the theater had been nicely transformed into a sort of jungle that was very '*Foire du Trône*,'" and the ticket booth was defended by a venomous snake that moved and stuck out its tongue. Your young lead, cut out of plywood, with big letters spelling 'She Swamp Girl' and inscriptions of the type 'Two men crossed seven hundred miles of swamp to win her love.'"[105]

Renoir was correct in writing to his brother Claude in 1945 that *Swamp Water* "went unnoticed because it had no big stars but had very good financial results for Fox."[106] The film was actually excellent on the level of business: it had cost $601,928.62, which included Renoir's $54,500 and Irving Pichel's $12,000;[107] and for a film in its category, its receipts were the highest recorded by Fox for that year. It even sold more tickets than several films with much higher budgets, an accomplishment that inspired Zanuck to memo all Fox producers to point at the cost of the film as an example of the importance of understanding that, although stars were useful, they weren't always indispensable.[108]

Although the quality of Renoir's work with the actors was hailed almost unanimously by members of the press, reviews were divided. Some thought that the director had succeeded in his American debut, even better so than his fellow countrymen Clair and Duvivier. Others insisted on saying that this was proof, once more, that a director who was great in Europe could be awkward in

---

* *Translator's note:* An amusement-park fair held annually in Paris in the spring.

Hollywood. Rather than the differences in opinion between Renoir and Zanuck, Zanuck's difficulties with the director were stressed; and *Swamp Water*'s success vindicated the producer. However, Renoir's image came through unscathed. Although the rumor of the director's slowness and indecision had traveled, the fact that the film was a commercial success dampened this echo.

The credits did indeed present *Swamp Water* as a film directed by Jean Renoir, who as a result found himself associated with the production's good fortune, without anyone's bothering to evaluate the part he had played in it. This was also the case when Renoir severed his contract with Fox and continued to receive offers. His goal at that time was to sign with a company that could guarantee him at least a relative degree of freedom, if indeed he couldn't succeed in carrying out the projects he was considering. His experience at Fox had enabled him to discover how Hollywood works and had allowed him to meet Dudley Nichols, an experienced screenwriter with enviable contacts. Even more importantly, the ten months or so that he'd just spent in California had given him a taste of a lifestyle that he was appreciating more and more.

If he ever had had the serious idea of directing a film in America and then returning to France, which is doubtful to say the least, it belonged to the past. By fall 1941, Renoir had already decided to remain in Hollywood, planning to become a good American director, capable of working within the system as much as possible, without emphasizing his own conceptions beyond reason. He understood that he would not be a French director spending some time in Hollywood, and he realized that he had to start almost from zero and give himself time to succeed. The only urgency he felt had to do with organizing his personal life.

24

California Jean

Forever Yours
This Land Is Mine

As a whole, the French colony in Los Angeles wasn't particularly well disposed toward Renoir when he arrived. Jean Lenauer,* who'd offered his services as a "personal assistant" to Renoir on January 19, 1941, hadn't made a mystery of it. After meeting the director, he wrote, "The stories I'd heard about you had filled me with dread. I was greatly relieved when I lunched with you the other day, because I immediately saw that the man and the artist hadn't changed—that I could keep on admiring him."[1] Such reservations, which were certainly very limited, don't explain why Renoir chose to keep his distance from the French in Hollywood.

Charles Boyer's villa on La Cienega Boulevard was one of the meeting places of that community and, to less of a degree, so was the house of Robert Florey, who'd come to Hollywood as a reporter and established himself as a director. Preston Sturges's establishment, The Players, was also valued. Its three stories at 8225 Sunset Boulevard contained a restaurant on each floor, a beauty parlor, and an immense theater and dance hall with a retractable stage operated by a hydraulic system where the maker of *Sullivan's Travels,* who'd studied in France, gave a gigantic party every Sunday.

There were no natural links between the French who'd been living in Los Angeles for several years and the newcomers, who included Renoir, René Clair, and Duvivier. The more long-term residents already had their circle of friends, and the newcomers were creating them based on whom they happened to meet and the affinities they experienced, without caring about nationality. From Hollywood, Europe seemed far away; and news of the war arrived very watered down.

In Charles Boyer's living room, two autographed portraits were on display: one of Philippe Pétain at the time of Verdun, the other of General de Gaulle.

---

* Jean Lenauer was a film critic in France in the thirties and, at the age of seventy-seven, would play the waiter in the Louis Malle film *My Dinner with André* (1981).

A photograph of Marshal Lyautey was on the facing wall. "In the roles of consul, ambassador, confessor, and master of philosophy at the same time,"[2] Boyer offered his guests the use of a vast library of French works. Founder of a crisis center for the French in Hollywood, he'd created an abundance of funds scattered here and there and was their most generous donor. For example, in May 1941, he gave $500 to the Hollywood chapter of the French War Relief fund, whereas Jean Gabin and Claudette Colbert had given $100; Michèle Morgan, $72; Joseph Kessel, $9; Norma Shearer, $50; and Frank Capra and Gary Cooper, $25. Renoir didn't want to be outdone and signed a check for $225,[3] on another occasion explaining the reason for his generosity: "I'm not at all a 'Gaullist,' but I'm going to send him a little money anyway. . . . I believe such a gesture is in line with our ideal, which is to help the French where they are without worrying about their convictions."[4]

Renoir had every intention of staying out of the debates that were agitating the French community to some degree. His attitude was dictated in part by his need to remain on good terms with the Vichy administration, if only to be allowed to have Alain come and join him. Consequently, he didn't miss a chance to affirm the steadfastness of his thinking. For example, in a letter to the French ambassador in Washington having to do with the difficulties the Hollywood chapter of the French War Relief fund was having getting donations from Americans, he included the following comment, which was quite far from the objective of his message: "Personally (since we're in a country where it's fashionable to assert your convictions), I'm taking advantage of the situation to confirm my feelings of total fidelity to Marshal Pétain, the head of our country."[5] In response, the ambassador congratulated him for his "clear and courageous attitude in these difficult times, during which we must all come together behind the noble and great figure of Marshal Pétain and his government."[6]

The rumor had reached Renoir of a possible break in relations between France and the United States; so, on May 21, he wrote,

> I had written to the ambassador to thank him for his actions on behalf of my son. In this same letter, I'm writing again to affirm to him my loyalty to the marshal. I don't like this kind of declaration very much, but it's the style here, and several times at the studio I've been asked to send a telegram to President Roosevelt to tell him that I agree with him (as if that mattered!). They ask everyone to do that, and, of course, I didn't, since American politics have nothing to do with me. But for several days we've been dealing in Hollywood with a climate that is clearly hostile. "The marshal is a Nazi," young typists are saying as they do their nails.[7]

His words were meant to be humorous, but such determination to offer comments without invitation has something about it that might seem a little disturbing. If his only goal was to solicit the goodwill of people who were momentarily powerful, he was doing it just a bit too much.

As the weeks passed and Alain's situation was arranged according to his desires, Renoir revealed what he really thought in a letter to Saint-Exupéry on June 2:

> Since I last saw you I've realized something very important: I hate the French who live in America.... I especially detest the Gaullists. Because the Pétainists at least try to stand up for the modest scraps normally left over for a civil servant. But the others seem to me truly to represent the dregs of the shabby-looking candidates for the aforementioned scraps. ... I am truly happy to break away from all things political concerning my ex-country. I like Mr. Roosevelt, and I don't like either Vichy, which allows things to get into too much of a mess, or de Gaulle, who looks a little too much like a profiteer.[8]

Expressed more bluntly, that was privately worded as, "the representatives of Vichy are ass-kissers, and those of free France are waiting to become ass-kissers."[9] Now France had become his "ex-country"; and "American politics," which had had "nothing" to do with him on May 21, began to matter on June 2.

Among the number of complex feelings that motivated Renoir in his situation as an émigré, there's one that may seem paradoxical: instinctually, he didn't trust people who had fled their country.[10] That was the reason why he wasn't very keen on associating with the French in Hollywood; and above all, that was what colored his view of his own position. The fact was that he himself had also left his country; to accept that reality, it was more convenient for him to project the responsibility for it on those whom he'd left behind and who in his opinion were behaving very badly—decidedly so.

The story of his son offers insight in this regard. Alain ended up choosing to go to the United States but without his reservations about America having completely disappeared. It would take time to obtain the indispensable visas as well as to pull together enough money. Jean and Dido went to Washington at the beginning of November to carry out the last steps, and then to New York to buy a ticket on a ship. Alain had been in Morocco for a while, still working as an assistant camera operator. On November 19, he left Casablanca on the *Serpa Pinto*, which was to stop over in Mexico before docking in New York, where Jean had reserved a room at the Lafayette Hotel for his son.

Alain landed in New York on December 26, 1941, and went to the recruitment office for Free France, where he dealt with "an idiot."[11] Then he jumped onto a train for Los Angeles, which he reached on December 31, 1941, exactly one year to the day after his father had arrived in America. He hadn't changed his mind about enlisting, and there was even a question of his leaving once again for North Africa; but after the December 7 attack of the Japanese on Pearl Harbor, even though Alain was at sea, the situation had changed. The United States was at war with Japan, and Germany and Italy had declared war against it on December 11. The conflict had become global.

On January 6, Alain, his father, and Dido heard Roosevelt's address to Congress and the nation on the radio. In it the president announced that American forces would be fighting everywhere in the world "for security, for progress, and for peace, not only for ourselves but for all men, not only for one generation but for all generations." And then he finished with the following words: "No compromise can end that conflict. There never has been—there never can be—successful compromise between good and evil. Only total victory can reward the champions of tolerance, and decency, and freedom, and faith." Alain was captivated; his father became impassioned and said to him, "We have to admit that we took off. This country has given us a wonderful welcome. The polite thing to do would be to enlist in the American army."[12]

The "polite thing." Alain thought about it for barely two days and then showed up at a recruiting office. He didn't speak a word of English. On February 3, he left for two months of training at Camp Roberts, about seven miles from Paso Robles, to the northwest of Los Angeles. Skilled in artillery, he left for the Pacific, which included New Guinea, the Philippines, and Japan. He'd come back in December 1945.

Veteran of a war that had left him with physical damage and, he would say, traumatized, Renoir strongly suggested to his only child, who had just turned twenty, that he go and sign up. At the time, he had no idea of the hell on earth that Alain would experience in the Pacific and that his son wouldn't return to civilian life until four years later. Even so, Renoir's attitude calls for elucidation.

The fact that Jean, and before Jean, his father, had done his duty and defended his country explains things only somewhat inadequately. Jean hadn't waited to be called up. In 1913, he'd enlisted, and later, he'd had no more choice about the matter than Auguste had had. On the other hand, whereas Auguste had kept out of combat, Jean had fought on his own soil, which the enemy had invaded.

In 1942, the situation was different. Jean was sending Alain to fight for a country that wasn't theirs. His being too old to enlist himself doesn't very well justify his appointing his son in his place. The opinion about Jean's interest in the military that can be formed today is contradicted by several factors that include his reputation as a pacifist, which mostly originates from a partisan reading of *Grand Illusion*, a reading that is very much open to debate and to which

Alain especially always declared himself opposed. In truth, Renoir's behavior consistently demonstrates less of a hatred of war than a far-from-unusual liking of freedom, as well as an attachment to the army and the notion of country.

It may be true that at this moment in his life Alain had no idea what to do with himself. It should also be kept in mind that in 1938 he had wanted to fight in Spain. His desire to reach the United States was essentially motivated by his wanting to serve Free France (strange as such a trajectory was, it was also characteristic of him). Nevertheless and despite these factors, it is quite likely that it was only the firmly expressed initiative of his father that caused him to rally to the ranks of the American army. Alain himself, in fact, has made no mystery of this motive. As proof of his devotion and sincerity, could Renoir have offered anything better than his own son? He would pay for such a gesture with four years of high anxiety, but the story would end well.

Shortly after, Renoir was asked to justify the decision Alain had made. On March 11, 1942, in fact, the French ambassador in Washington wrote to him, "I've learned that your son, whose trip here I did my best to facilitate, was subjected after his arrival to the influence of those who are forsaking the nation in its hard times. I would like you to send me some details about your son's state of mind and his intentions."[13] In his response, Renoir retraced the series of facts that led to Alain's enlisting and emphasized the importance of Roosevelt's speech. He also mentioned "certain comments warning us that foreigners living in the United States would be called up as recruits in the same way American citizens were and urged to defend the country that is providing their daily bread." And he added the following: "When you're twenty years old and French, either you remain in France and share the sufferings of your countrymen and do what you can to help the government in its arduous task of recovery. Or else, if you leave the country, you enlist and you fight. Whatever the case, the idea of enjoying an easy life in Hollywood while his countrymen were miserable seemed untenable to him."[14] This last sentence has a strange ring to it. Renoir was attributing to his son feelings that were his, and there is no evidence that Alain shared them at the time.

Equally according to Jean's account, Alain is supposed to have asked his father whether he saw "any drawback to his going into the American army." Renoir saw none, of course, something that has become that much more certain because of what we know today, thanks to Alain: the idea was coming from his father. In that same letter to the ambassador, Jean expressed pride in his son, a "boy who speaks about his country with respect, and the son of a man who is determined not to sever the links that attach him to the motherland." It was that same "motherland" that he'd call a few weeks later, in the already-cited letter to Saint-Exupéry, his "ex-country."

As for the rest, it isn't difficult to understand that Renoir's situation required him to resort to a few sleights of hand in reasoning of the type that would make the only alternative seem to be "helping the government" of France, which in this case came down to collaborating with the intentions of a foreign occupying power as well as "enlisting and fighting" but without specifying for which army and against which enemy. It wasn't easy, of course, to write to an ambassador that your own son had gone to war against the government the diplomat represented. It is also true that for several weeks at that time Renoir had been pressured by authorities in Vichy, determined to convince French artists who'd emigrated to return to France.

On May 27, 1941, André Halley des Fontaines, the producer of *The Crime of Monsieur Lange,* had sent him a telegram from the Hôtel du Parc in Vichy asking if he could "possibly shoot a film in France."[15] Renoir answered on June 13 that he was under contract for two films at Fox. On June 22, his brother Claude wrote to him, "I know through Raimu that Ploquin* is going to ask you to return to Paris. Apparently, he is supposed to be asking René Clair, Duvivier, and Gabin."[16]

The first official intervention to this account that has been found is dated December 27, and it comes from the French consulate in Los Angeles, signed by Georges Achard: "The French government has asked me through our ambassador in Washington, to insist urgently that you come back to France as soon as possible. I am taking the same step regarding Mlle. Morgan, Messrs. René Clair, Julien Duvivier, and Jean Gabin. All assurances will be accorded you concerning your stay in the two zones and all opportunities will be granted to you to carry out your professional activities."[17] Renoir answered on January 9, "For personal reasons I would be very happy to make a film in France. I am therefore completely willing to examine the offers that would entail creating a truly French-run company for me."[18] It was a show of goodwill of pure convenience because in that same letter he claimed that before he could commit he first had to direct two films specified by his contract with the Feldman-Blum Corporation, which was actually the company of his agents, to whom he was bound by no agreement of that sort. He simply did not want to go back to France, and no one would blame him for it. All the directors and actors who were contacted at the same moment for that purpose reacted as he had.

On June 4, 1942, precisely of whom was he thinking when he wrote, "The French here all represent a certain kind of perfection of the lowest form of sleaziness"?[19] At the top of the list were the people of film, the French in Hollywood

* Raoul Ploquin, the producer of such films as *Le Corbeau* (*The Raven,* 1943) by Henri-Georges Clouzot and *Les Dames du bois de Boulogne* (*The Ladies of the Bois de Boulogne; Ladies of the Park* [title of censored version], 1945) by Robert Bresson.

with whom he had come into contact. Some of the letters he received from France were of a type that supported such hostility, which seemed to be based on nationality just as much as on behavior observed in California. Thus, when his brother Claude wrote to him, "I understand that you must not be having fun with Duvivier and René Clair,"[20] he might not have been having fun with them, but he had been going out to dinner with them from time to time—on December 21, 1941, at the Brown Derby[21] on Wilshire Boulevard, for instance. A few days later, Claude informed him that Jacques Becker had been freed from his prison camp and offered the following disenchanted observation: "Nobody cleverer than us has been managing to work, even Monsieur Sacha Guitry. However, he's been staying in Paris the whole time."[22]

And then, sometimes French newspapers with articles that concerned Renoir were sent to him. For example, a clipping that was saved in a notebook, whose title set the tone of the article by trumpeting, "$5,000 per Week: That Is What Jean Renoir Is Earning in Hollywood." Not bad, the pliant reader must have thought, a reader who was then politely asked to question why the director wouldn't be "satisfied [and would] want to go to Brazil to shoot a film that was a mystical epic about missionaries." Then:

> The "grand illusion" for Jean Renoir was thinking that you could "work" in Hollywood. Already the great director is going out of his mind. Having left at the beginning of winter, he had a contract for $1,000 a week, for six months, to become acclimatized. When he arrived, the reporters made a beeline for him, and that is how it became known that he had come to shoot a film about Joan of Arc. Fine subject for the person who directed *Grand Illusion*! Alas! the stars are the ones who decide. The agreement isn't one between the stars and Renoir, and if *Joan of Arc* is supposed to see the day, it's with another director, a Russian. Right now, in the film capital, Renoir is preparing a film for Fox. This film is an adaptation of a novel by Saint-Exupéry, *Wind, Sand and Stars*. For creating that shooting script—now that the period of acclimatization is over—he is earning $5,000 a week—and he'll receive that weekly fee during the entire period of filming. Soon he'll begin the first crank of the camera. But he's already thinking of making a screenplay whose title is *I Wake Up Screaming*. . . . Then he thinks he'll leave Hollywood for Brazil. Renoir became familiar with the subject through a Brazilian friend. . . . [23]

Everything in this article in *Paris-Soir* was false, or at best inexact, but what was coming from France wasn't exactly the kind of information to make him view the country he'd just left with a kind eye. Perhaps a certain article that appeared in the December 6, 1941, issue of *L'Alerte*, the Pétainist publication to which he had contributed a text in October 1940, was of a nature to restore better feelings; but if he ever saw a copy, which isn't known, he didn't hold on to it. On the front page of *L'Alerte* a photograph showed him hatted and smiling on the set of *Swamp Water*, framed by Anne Baxter and Dana Andrews, with the caption, "Jean Renoir, French, Triumphs in American Film." On a double-page spread entitled "A Great French Success in Hollywood, Jean Renoir Develops a Fine Film in the United States and Discovers a New Star,"[24] Jean Marois described the brilliant future of this production he called *Eau dormante,* the work of a director who preferred "a perfectly comfortable middle-class apartment" to "those blocks of lookalike bungalows in Beverly Hills that all have their swimming pool and garden with pergola in the mass-manufactured Florentine style."

Renoir, the article went on, spent a long time finding a subject that appealed to him, fixated on that "great idea of a wonderful film with sincerity, simplicity, and force, a film devoted to French missionaries who go forth in extremely moving circumstances to conquer and convert a people who are at first resistant." Then he accepted the fact that it is "worth more to begin with a work keyed as closely as possible to a mainstream audience," and he discovered "a screenplay and a performer that made his having hesitated worthwhile." This "new star" was named Mary Howard, and "to impose her on the producer, Jean Renoir had had to make numerous screen tests." The author was confusing Mary Howard—who had a supporting role in the film and who had been chosen by Zanuck—with Anne Baxter, whose name wasn't mentioned; but the legend of the French director's "imposing" his choices in Hollywood was beginning to write itself. And, of course, "we won't have told everything if we forget to mention how much all the crewmembers adore Jean Renoir."

After recalling the article Renoir had given *L'Alerte* a little more than a year before, in which he mentioned "certain cinematic works that, in our country or elsewhere, have perverted the taste of mainstream audiences because of their poor quality and their pretentions," the article closed with the portrait of a director whose exile had not prevented him from continuing to serve his country: "Established by his first success, Jean Renoir continues to furnish for a sensitive and understanding audience laudatory proof of worthwhile propaganda in favor of the French spirit." For the Vichy press, Renoir in Hollywood was more French than ever. Although a possible return hadn't been mentioned in the article, the reasons that had caused him to leave were described in it as solely professional, thereby indicating that his return to France was more or less imminent. At the time, nothing was further from Renoir's thoughts.

* *Translator's note:* "Still Water," or, literally, "Sleeping Water."

It looked like nothing but hatred of the entire profession when Renoir wrote to his sister-in-law, Paulette: "Whatever the problems I've experienced in Hollywood and which I'm still having, I remain convinced those involved in film here are more honest and more open than all those I knew in France."[25] So, it was no longer only about the French in Hollywood and the fact that certain difficulties he'd encountered with producers had perhaps helped to embitter him; yet Jean Renoir's situation in the thirties hadn't been the least desirable of the French directors. In fact, Renoir seemed to have taken a sudden dislike to everything that was French, as if he were looking for further reasons that would justify—to himself, as a start—his decision not to go back to France, and he confirmed this in the same letter to Paulette Renoir: "Of course I'll go back to France, to stroll around, or to make films. But my future is here."[26]

Other letters came from France from people he did not know, and some of them were poignant. For example, the one he received on February 8, 1941, from Albert Lévy, "ex-director and actor of the Grand Guignol . . . French, son of a Frenchman, with a pension awarded for quality of military service, more than two hundred plays and screenplays." He asked Renoir's help in obtaining a work contract for himself and his wife, "maiden name Simone Godard." He'd performed with Pierre in the past and was awaiting Renoir's answer "anxiously," adding by hand as a postscript, "I truly hope that I'm not writing in vain and that you can find it in your heart to do your best to save a countryman."[27] However, what could Renoir do for a poor Jewish actor, "a Peter Lorre, Lon Chaney, etc., type,"[28] and his wife?

Neither could he do anything for a Monsieur de Sainte-Colombe, first name Paul, information about whom didn't reveal whether he was a descendant of the author of *Concerts à deux violes esgales*.* He was sending Renoir a shooting script intended for RKO so that Renoir could evaluate his "possibilities as a writer of films and dialogues." On May 29, the man wrote him a very anguished second letter about having no work. Renoir responded to it when he got back from Georgia, explaining that unfortunately it was not in his power to choose his collaborators. Over the years, Sainte-Colombe continued to send him letters and projects on a regular basis.

Other requests sometimes came from known figures, such as Darius Milhaud, who had composed the music for *Madame Bovary* and was writing Renoir from San Francisco, a city he'd be thrilled to have Renoir visit; "If you make a

* *Translator's note:* Monsieur de Sainte-Colombe (ca. 1640–1700), reclusive French composer and violist who was a virtuoso of the viola da gamba and likely the most prolific French viol composer before Marin Marais. A novel that hypothesized his relationship with Marais, *Tous les matins du monde*, became an Alain Corneau film in 1991.

film, I'd appreciate your thinking of me for the music."[29] This appeal was communicated again five days later by the musician's agent. However, the director couldn't grant the request. For those who were already there and couldn't find work, as well as those who wanted to come but needed a work contract to leave, Renoir did what he could. He lunched with the former and wrote to the latter. His brother Claude was one of these; he, too, was dreaming of being an American director. Between the two a correspondence grew. Jean asked around, went knocking on doors, and ended up finding an offer for Claude from RKO, which Claude would judge too inferior to his talents.[30]

Joseph Kosma, most notably the composer of the music for *Grand Illusion* and *La Bête humaine,* also asked to be rescued, and his cause was soon taken up by the great film historian Siegfried Kracauer, who asked Renoir on several occasions to make it possible for the musician, whose real name was Jozsef Kozma, and his wife to come to Hollywood. Kracauer and Renoir met in New York and continued in vain to try to help the Kosmas, who lived underground during the entire length of the war. Eugène Lourié, on the other hand, would enjoy a brilliant career in Hollywood as a set designer and would remain one of Renoir's favorite collaborators, also directing some B horror films on his own that were just as good as many others. At the same time, he kept working as an art director on such films as Samuel Fuller's. His last film in that capacity was Clint Eastwood's *Bronco Billy.*

Rumors of the war raging in Europe came in snatches to those in exile. One evening, as Renoir was finishing a letter to Saint-Exupéry, news that had just arrived found its way into his postscript: "As I close this letter, Kessel has phoned me with the news that Rudolf Hess has landed in Scotland. It's insane."[31]

Letters and telephone calls aren't enough to re-create a world. Gabrielle was always at the center of Renoir's thoughts. She had seen him grow up, loved, protected, and made a fuss over him as long as he was at an age for it, and she still held that position. She had married Conrad Slade, the American multimillionaire and painter who was fascinated with Auguste Renoir. After the man's death on September 12, 1950, Jean would write that he "was proud of never having sold a single one of his canvases," that he lived as a "pure artist, following his inspiration without ever making any compromise, without allowing himself to be influenced by the opinion of art dealers and critics," and that he "probably had access to personal funds because he didn't live off the sale of his works."[32] In 1920, a year before Alain was born, Conrad and Gabrielle Slade had had a child, Jean, whom they called Jeannot. Suffering from skeletal tuberculosis of the hip, Jeannot spent long months in Berck with his mother, where Jean, Alain, and Carl Koch would sometimes go camping. Jean had filmed the last scene in *The*

Crime of Monsieur Lange on the beach at Berck. However, Gabrielle and Dédée (Catherine) hadn't gotten along. The relationship between Jean and his former nurse had grown distant, and the director's hectic activities had curtailed many attempts at getting together.

In July 1941, Conrad, Gabrielle, and Jean Slade left the South of France for New England, from where Conrad hailed. Aware that American citizens living in France would have problems if the United States went to war with Germany, the Slades had to wait more than six months before they were able to obtain passage on a vessel. They'd gone through Spain to reach Lisbon, where they'd boarded their ship. Conrad was bored by Boston, and Gabrielle even more so, as she wrote to Jean. Moreover, the wine wasn't very good. He answered that in California, on the other hand, you could find wine of good quality and that he even knew a vintner from Beaujolais who'd moved not far from Los Angeles. And then, it wasn't hard finding good bottles (Riesling and Chablis heading the list). He ordered them regularly from the San Francisco Wine Association, whose Los Angeles representative was a Frenchman. "Dear Ga," wrote Renoir, "it often happens that I go to sleep with a terrible desire to be around you. Write me. Maybe that will make me forget the distance that separates us."[33]

On October 3, 1941, Gabrielle left for California with her husband and their son. Jean and Dido had gone to the station to wait for them. Everybody piled into a fantastic Buick convertible and headed for Renoir's house. In the driveway leading to it, Renoir, Duvivier, and René Clair had had a ball installing fantasy signs inspired by the ads for jazz orchestras that flourished along American roadways and that contained names the French were likely to find entertaining. Artie Shaw, which quite expectedly had become "Arti Chaut," and "John Nsaipa" had plunged the neighbors into a state of great perplexity. Whatever Claude Renoir might have maintained, it was sometimes possible to "have fun" with Clair and Duvivier.

After her arrival in California, Gabrielle and Jean would never again part. The Slades first rented an apartment in Westwood; and a few months later, in the summer of 1942, they rented a house located opposite Jean and Dido's before buying another close by. In the meantime, the Renoirs had become the owners of a house that was less spacious but more to their taste than the one on Hollywood Boulevard in which they had lived after arriving in Los Angeles.

Jean and Dido had found this villa at 1615 North Martel Avenue, between Sunset and Hollywood Boulevards, in February 1942, six blocks from the Hollywood Roosevelt Hotel, in which they would stay for the few days necessary to renovate their new home. The house dated back to the beginning of the century. Agnes Ayres, the silent film actress and costar of Rudolf Valentino—according to rumor, she may have had a more intimate relationship with him than that—had lived in it for some time, before the ascendance of talkies and the crash of 1929, which left her without a penny and apparently sent her to work as a demonstrator of cosmetics. She had died at the age of forty-two on December 25, 1940. Bertolt Brecht provided a quick description of the new house from the evening he visited Renoir there: "Everything was absolutely French at his place. He managed to do this by buying an authentic American house (a wooden dwelling like the kind you see in historical films, not an imitation) and there was nothing but old American pieces of furniture. These furnishings were sparse; he'd chopped away some stucco from the fireplace with a few blows of an axe, and he was now living in an environment of a man of culture."[34]

In the backyard, Jean was going to have a vineyard planted as well as a few roses placed very close to the giant avocado tree that was already growing there. "I can walk to quality restaurants for lunch,"[35] he soon wrote to his older brother, less than a month after telling his younger that he had just applied for American citizenship. He also informed him, "In three years I'll be a citizen of this country. This has nothing to do with current circumstances. It's simply because I feel more at ease in this large country than I do in cramped Europe."[36]

Renoir had severed all his romantic, emotional, and professional links and had chosen a partner who made his day-to-day life easy. She relieved him of any concerns about organization, kept his books, did his correspondence, took notes about his thoughts, and acted as an interpreter and translator. She also venerated him and worked for his fame. If he did get bored or regret his decision at times, he barely admitted it. He had left France for Hollywood. Initially, Hollywood had disappointed him, but he enjoyed California.

Only faraway echoes of his life in the thirties reached him now, and they were growing more distant. Finally, they disappeared altogether when the postal service between Europe and the United States was interrupted in November 1942. Marguerite sometimes wrote to him. Her letters were tender and touching, a bit naïve as well, and especially sad, very sad. For example, on February 13, 1941, on paper with the letterhead of the Hôtel des Phocéens in Marseille, she wrote, "With all my heart I wish you good luck, with all my heart I wish you'll have a bit of happiness and work well. As for myself, I don't know if I can still be happy, but I do very well know that I can't work as well as I could for you, with you. Who here works as well as you do?"[37] Later, on March 24, she wrote, while "waiting to be able to make a living," that she was in Portel, in the Corbières mountains, at the home of Pierre Lestringuez, which was "very good" for her, through him she knew that "everything is going well for you." That same day, Pierre took her to Carcassonne "to see Louis Jouvet." She added, "May I tell you, Jean, that it made me miss you a bit?" She ended with, "trying to eat has become the main concern, and since it's difficult, that takes up almost all the time."[38]

One day (although the letter has not been preserved), Jean decided finally to write to her. Marguerite answered him. She was beginning to wonder if she still had "a little importance" for him. And then:

I wanted to write to you to tell you that there are boys and girls who love each other very much, very much. . . . I've given up working in film. The "filmmakers"—what a lovely word—are finished with me. I console myself by seeing what they've done. The idea of trying something else bothers me because I'm not very courageous. My courage is walking through forests, the rivers of America. I made a gift of it to a boy. That wouldn't be important if I hadn't put everything in it that's in me that's fierce, pure, dark, happy, alive, and sad. But I'm going to bore you and you won't write me any longer, and I so much want you to write to me. . . . I'd like you to be happy, to work well, my dear Jean. With all my heart I'd also like to see you again. Across everything that separates us I kiss you gently.[39]

Several letters from Renoir's brother Claude reveal that Jean asked him to help Lestringuez and Marguerite find work. In an August 19 letter, Pierre Renoir informed Jean that he was playing in Jacques de Baroncelli's film *Le pavillon brûle*, and in a postscript he added that "Marguerite is the editor of [that same] film produced by Tual."[40]

Gabrielle's presence gave Renoir the opportunity to turn the last page of a book that he would have perhaps had more trouble closing without her. She also allowed his immersion into his long-ago past, before his marriage and film. For him, it was almost as if a parenthesis were closing, containing all his films, just when his experience at Fox was teaching him that nothing he'd accomplished until the present had any real meaning in Hollywood. He had to learn what seemed like a new profession; and, in that as well, Gabrielle and everything that she represented for him were able to help.

It isn't a complete exaggeration to say that the reappearance in his life of the sturdy Burgundian, who refused to learn the language of the country where she lived, which was also her husband's, triggered his desire to recall the figure of his father. The problem he was having at Fox had made him consider writing rather than making films; but in November 1941, while he was in New York, Maximilian Becker, his new agent, gave him the idea for a book on Auguste Renoir. Jean didn't seem enthusiastic at first, but in January he wrote to Becker to tell him that he'd begun to gather notes on his father. He assured Becker, "I am becoming more and more excited by the idea of writing a book on my father."[41] For that purpose, as well, his conversations with Gabrielle would turn out to be essential. *Pierre-Auguste Renoir, mon père* (*Renoir, My Father*) wouldn't appear until twenty years later, but the time machine had been set in motion. And although Jean Renoir's allusions to Auguste remained rare, they became more and more frequent over the years, equally spurred by the fact that the painter had become more famous in America than in France.

Gabrielle's presence increased his ability to adapt, something he already possessed to a phenomenal degree. This was primarily owing to her help in his closing the second volume of his life dealing with the twenties and thirties, which was also a time before Dido. The private Jean Renoir of autumn 1941 had been seduced by the flora and climate of California, and he was always writing friends that it made Beverly Hills resemble a spot in Provence. Under the benevolent shadow of Dido, he began retracing the footsteps of the little kid and teenager he'd been with Gabrielle. One woman was sixteen years older than him, the other thirteen years younger, and he had just turned forty-seven. Gone were bars and drinking pals, city lights trained on him, and mics held out for him to take. Gone as well were dinners or suppers that went on endlessly, nights spent gabbing and drinking, the flare-ups to which they'd led. Jean Renoir was beginning a new life in the scent of orange trees and the aromas of childhood.

For a time, he toyed with the idea for a book entitled *Gabrielle,* for which he left behind only a few lines in a school notebook dated September 29, 1946, a Sunday:

> She lived in the house next to mine, and evenings she'd often come through the opening in the fence separating our two gardens and sit down for a few moments with my wife and me, and then she was off. . . . The years fade away. I see myself again as a kid posing for my father. She sees herself as a young girl posing, too, or carrying me, or helping my mother do the housework or the cooking. In the shadows of the little garden in Los Angeles, we can make out the trees at Le Château des Brouillards, the slopes of the hill in Montmartre, and all the places to which Renoir's desire to paint would take the entire household.[42]

The Slade family was closely connected to the life of the Renoirs. On nights when guests were received and the Slades weren't invited, after the guests disappeared, Gabrielle would come through the gate in the hedge to help Dido do the dishes. She'd often end up serving at the table, because generally the American help left at nightfall. However, some guests were helpful. For example, Jean Slade remembered having seen Jean Gabin drying washed glasses next to Gabrielle and chatting with her about her youth, while in the living room Marlene Dietrich, Simone Simon, and Dalio lingered. Renoir's friends also invited the Slades to their places. Once, at a dinner given by Katina Paxinou, Aristotle Onassis, who spoke French with a Marseille accent, gave Simone Simon a magnificent pearl necklace. "Want this necklace, little one?" the shipping magnate asked the actress, who accepted the gift but refused the billionaire's marriage offer. The next day he came to the Slades' in person carrying a basket filled with Greek honey and cheeses and several bottles of the retsina that Gabrielle had declared she was wild about the night before.[43]

Before the Slades came to Hollywood, Saint-Exupéry had come for a stay in the house on Hollywood Boulevard from the end of August to the end of September 1941. Although the press suggested that the writer had arrived at the Renoirs' to work on the screenplay for *Wind, Sand and Stars*, which was thought to be in production at Fox,[44] Saint-Exupéry was actually working on his new book, *Pilote de guerre* (*Flight to Arras*), which would appear in 1942; or more likely, *Citadelle*,[45] which he'd begun in 1936 but would not finish. Staying in a room on the second floor, he lived essentially at night and spoke his text out loud into a Dictaphone for a secretary to type. Renoir and he didn't see much of each other, except during the director's breakfast of bacon and eggs, which was also the writer's supper hour. "The only appetite they had in common was for olive oil,"[46] placed in the icebox to thicken before being spread on toast, an odd habit of the writer that the director had discovered while they were crossing the Atlantic.[47] Sometimes Saint-Exupéry would go with Renoir to Fox before coming back to sleep, but their interactions during that period were limited, especially because it was becoming clearer and clearer to them that their project adapting *Wind, Sand and Stars* was at an impasse. Apparently, Saint-Exupéry had realized this more quickly as a result of certain past experiences; but Renoir wanted to keep believing in it, or at least wanted it to seem that he did.*

The truth was that his personal projects barely elicited an echo. He was used to such a thing, but the wall against which he was throwing himself was higher and stronger than those he'd encountered before. He began thinking of writing a book that could then become a film. The idea appears in a news item from August 1941: "Renoir is presently working on a sequel to *Grand Illusion* in the form of a novel."[48] In fact, Renoir had written the same thing to Maximilian Becker: "After a lot of dillydallying, I'm thinking of beginning with a follow-up to *Grand Illusion*. I know my characters well, and I think I've found a good context and a good story for using them fifteen years later, on the eve of

---

* On May 25, Renoir had sent copies of a report on the project in the form of twenty-five typed pages in English, signed only by Saint-Exupéry, to Walter Wanger, David O. Selznick, Alexander Korda, Albert Lewin, Niven Bush, and the offices of Fox and Metro. (Jean Renoir Papers, Production Files, Box 50, Folder 1.)

the current catastrophes. This project offers the added advantage of interesting the studios in a film afterward."[49] A few weeks later, he had gotten down to thinking exclusively of a book, writing again to Becker, "I'm hoping to turn out a funny enough tale that has drama at the same time, maybe one that's too critical to turn into a film. The studios here prefer rather conventional mush."[50]

Before leaving Fox, he had revived the idea for *Flight South*, which he'd abandoned for a while at the suggestion of his agents. In this new version of the screenplay, the character was named Gabriel Renard, "Renard" being Gabrielle's maiden name before she'd married Conrad Slade. Because Renoir's agent had spoken to him about a project with the actress Luise Rainer, the director wrote to her to say that although he had ordered the book she wanted brought to the screen, he was more interested in talking to her regarding a film about which he'd been thinking, which was doubtlessly *Flight South*. "I'm in the exact same state I was in before beginning *Grand Illusion*. I spend my days thinking about this screenplay, writing scenes, conceiving of characters. If this film isn't made, it would be a terrible blow."[51] Pointing out that it was "impossible to think seriously about something else at the moment,'" he stated that he'd "given my word to Steve Pallos to do everything possible for the project we share" and insisted that Rainer be well aware that "making a film with you is also one of my dreams." Unfortunately for her (something she herself claimed), Luise Rainer had won the Oscar for Best Actress for both her second American film (*The Great Ziegfeld*, 1936) and her third (*The Good Earth*, 1937), which meant that from that point on, her career could only decline. As for Steven Pallos, who was Hungarian, his first film wouldn't be produced until 1948.

Contrary to what he had written to Luise Rainer, Renoir was thinking "seriously about something else at the moment" and had begun to jot down a few notes.[*] With the help of Dudley Nichols, it would soon result in the screenplay for his second official American film, *This Land Is Mine*. The reality was that he had to find work, and already the New York office that managed his accounts had informed him that he was going to have to try to spend less and, especially, reduce the volume of donations he was making to various good causes. They were also thinking of the taxes he would soon have to pay.[52] Exactly one year later, he severed his agreement with this office with the excuse that his funds no longer allowed him to pay the seventy-five-dollar monthly fee they charged.[53]

More than actual projects, projects in embryo were crowding in. The producer Pare Lorentz, who was connected to RKO, had spoken to him about a "documentary film"[54] to be shot in South America, although no further information

* The preparatory notes for this project are dated November 19, 20, and 22, 1941.

about it exists. He himself was thinking about proposing his old dream about adapting *The Diary of a Chambermaid* to David O. Selznick; or if not that, *Poultry Meg's Family*, a Hans Christian Andersen fairy tale. Also, Harry Eddington, a producer at RKO, wanted a remake of *La Chienne*. "At RKO, he [Eddington] is rather independent on account of a contract he has with Cary Grant,"* wrote Renoir to Dudley Nichols, before advancing a hypothesis. "I think it is Cary Grant, who, being crazy about *La Chienne*, made him buy the story." In fact, before the war, some information had appeared claiming that an "American version of *La Chienne*, based on the work by La Fouchardière," would be in development and would "star"[55] Cary Grant. *City Streets* was the title that had been mentioned at the time. It is rather difficult to imagine Cary Grant in the role created by Michel Simon. The character Maurice Legrand seemed poorly suited to the actor, and his interest in *La Chienne* hasn't left any other trace. Renoir had always claimed that the producers had "savagely criticized" *La Chienne*, despite its commercial success, before "working in the same direction," proof to him that "*Port of Shadows* was in line with this." He next provided Dudley Nichols with a long outline of his film. This may have given the screenwriter an advantage when he would write his own adaptation of the novel and the play by La Fouchardière for Fritz Lang's *Scarlet Street* (1945).

One of Renoir's agents, Charles Feldman, came up with the suggestion of adapting a light comedy,[56] whose working title was *Faith, Hope and Mary Potter*, but Renoir, it seems, never began writing it. Also never coming to fruition was the screenplay written by Renoir and Dudley Nichols for *The Age of the Fish*, the American title of *Jugend ohne Gott*,[†] a novel by Ödön von Horváth. Nichols had come up with the idea,[57] and the two offered it to producer Walter Wanger, who was involved with United Artists. However, in February 1942, as Renoir was preparing to move into his new house on North Martel Avenue and Gala Dalí was writing him from the St. Regis Hotel in New York to find out whether the old house was available, and if so, at what price, Renoir negotiated a contract with Universal.[58]

Carl Laemmle, the founder of Universal, had died in September 1939 at the age of seventy-two. In 1936, when he'd sold Universal to the Standard Capital Company and retired, his "creation" was at its worst, heavily in debt, living in the memory of yesterday's glory, the 1930 Oscar for *All Quiet on the Western Front*,

---

* In that fall of 1941, Harry E. Eddington was producing the Alfred Hitchcock film *Suspicion* with Cary Grant for RKO. Eddington would not appear in the credits, and *Suspicion* would remain the only film with Cary Grant he produced.

† In 1939, it had been announced in England that Julien Duvivier would direct *The Age of the Fish*.

and the past successes of its *Dracula*'s and *Frankenstein*'s from the beginning of the thirties.* In 1942, it owed its continual existence to fifteen-year-old Deanna Durbin. She was a diminutive Canadian from Winnipeg who'd been passed over at Metro for Judy Garland but whose first film, *Three Smart Girls,* directed by Henry Koster, had brought in record receipts. She may have been only one of the three actresses in those roles, but her singing voice and her natural appeal conquered American audiences. She sang like an angel, whether it was the songs that had been written for her or Schubert's *Ave Maria* (in the film *It's a Date,* 1940). Universal essentially left keeping its head above water up to her, and she had been making two films a year since 1937.

Renoir's choice—if it was a choice—was a wise one. While the productions at Universal did not lack the necessary quality, they remained modest affairs. As a result, there was much less pressure than there was at Fox, and producers were more or less free to do what they wanted, without having any Zanuck perpetually on their back. Renoir still needed one of them to be in agreement regarding a project that was likely to correspond as much to their expectations as to his ambitions. Was he considering a remake of *La Femme du boulanger* (*The Baker's Wife,* 1938) at the time? A telegram he received from Marcel Pagnol in February 1942 suggests this, but not with absolute certainty. It was informing him that it was "impossible to authorize filming *Femme du boulanger* in English," but that Pagnol could "on the other hand give authorization to film *Regain* [*Harvest,* 1937]."[59]

In an interview he gave to the magazine *Pour la Victoire,* Renoir mentioned two projects. "At last I am going to be able to make a film related to current events. I have my eye on two screenplays; one I wrote myself, and its story takes place in France; the other is an adaptation of the new John Steinbeck novel, *The Moon Is Down.* Given the way things currently are, I think I'll end up doing this second screenplay. It will be the first real film about current events made in Hollywood."[60] He also offered his interviewer several impressions about Hollywood. "Here in Hollywood, being a respected director isn't enough. You also need a smooth tongue. You might have an incredible idea for a film, but if you're not capable of 'selling it,' as they say here, to one of the studio heads, nothing will happen. I'd go so far as to say that it's easier to get the ear of a Hollywood producer than it is with a French producer." Answering next a question about the difficulties he'd had at Fox, he expounded, "Everything that happened can

* Carl Laemmle Jr. was behind Universal's initiative to specialize in horror films. Laemmle's son became a close friend of Renoir, who always called him "Junior." Junior was the one who thought of their "virtual" dinners together in the second half of the seventies, when neither Renoir nor he was in a position to "gather around the table" in the flesh. They thought up menus, prepared meals, and chatted over dinner—all by telephone.

be explained by the simple fact that I didn't speak enough English." Then, picking up the Steinbeck book that was lying on the table: "I think I'm going to be able to do it. I know enough English to be able to explain how I want to film *The Moon Is Down* and, having done that, I'll direct my film as I see it." And finally: "It wasn't only the war that made me come here. I would have come anyway, one day or another. In France, after twenty years of work, I only made two or three films I could put my heart into. Now I love my profession for itself. And I've discovered that if I can't make films based on my ideas, I can always put them on paper; that gives me a satisfaction I didn't believe I was capable of having." A nitpicking mind could ask what had happened to him since August 1941, when he declared that he was beginning to "detest" his profession, to make him claim that he "loved" it "for itself" less than a year later, after not at all having worked at it during this intervening period.

At the end of March 1942, Renoir signed a contract with Universal and described its terms to his brother Claude:[61] one film a year, very well paid, free all the rest of the time. It was a form of security. This last aspect of the matter was probably the one that was the most essential to him. He would direct the films that Universal assigned him, without attaching more importance to them than was necessary, and would also have time to work on personal projects. The title of the film Universal announced in April that would be Renoir's first for the firm was enough to indicate that it was far from being original: *Three Smart Girls Join Up*, which as soon as Renoir's participation in it was announced, the title was changed to *The Divine Young Lady*.[62] It would be the eleventh "Deanna Durbin film," making Renoir the fifth filmmaker to direct the star, after Henry Koster (six films), William A. Seiter (two films), and Edward Ludwig and Norman Taurog (one film each).

A few days after the contract took effect in May, a new title, *Forever Yours*, was announced for this production, although in reality that didn't change anything. Deanna Durbin wasn't fifteen anymore. She had turned twenty in December, but the spirit of the film remained the same, and how it could correspond to Jean Renoir was anybody's guess. Moreover, he would soon find himself in a more prickly situation than it at first had seemed. Deanna Durbin's appeal for American audiences had dulled, in fact. The two films she had made in 1941, *It Started with Eve*, in which she had played opposite Charles Laughton, and *Nice Girl*, were her first failures, which led producer Joe Pasternak, who had "made" her, to leave Universal for Metro, soon to be followed by Henry Koster. Durbin herself wanted to go with them; and in October 1941, she instigated a dispute with Universal and didn't show up at the press conference that had been organized to announce the start of production of her next film, *They Live Alone*. She began demanding to choose her own subjects and directors, and her refusal to participate in *They Live Alone* caused her suspension from the studio. An agreement concluded on January 30, 1942, put an end to the conflict, and Deanna Durbin obtained the right to review the subjects and directors of her films.[63]

As Renoir claimed to various correspondents, the youthful appeal and personality of the young actress probably did charm him. Yet the fact that the genre in which he was about to participate was not a very good match is apparent. Was his main purpose in honoring the contract to move on in a few months and devote himself to another project before returning to Universal for the next cash-earning production? Probably, seeing that this other project had already been launched elsewhere.

Despite the fact that the filming of *Forever Yours* was supposed to begin on June 1, the screenplay had not yet been written. Thus, things were already different for Renoir than the way they had been at Fox. However, in one of the rare serious interviews she would give, Deanna Durbin remembered that the director wasn't worried about it, that he told her not to give it another thought, because as the days passed he was sure to end up finding his way.[64] The person chiefly in charge of the operation, who was functioning as both producer and screenwriter, was Bruce Manning, who was forty-two. He had already written eight of Deanna Durbin's ten films.* Therefore, it was logical for Universal to trust that he could take Joe Pasternak's place and attempt to relaunch the young actress's career. And as for the fact that there was no screenplay, well . . . it had almost become common practice at Universal.

Renoir himself was happy. Deanna Durbin was delightful, and probably even "the best companion I've met among the actresses in this profession."[65] The American crew was impeccable. He'd already realized the value of their spirit and expertise at Fox. Although Dido hadn't been hired by production, it was because she and Renoir had considered it preferable for her to devote herself to preparing the other film he was considering.[66] On the set, he had the advantage of the services of an assistant whom he knew already. Charles David had been in charge of production on his first two sound films, *On purge Bébé* and *La Chienne*. A collaboration with producer Alexander Korda had brought him to Hollywood, where he also worked as a dubbing specialist.

The presence of this figure in round glasses, which gave him an owlish look, would turn out to be even more important for the star of the film than it was for the director. Deanna Durbin had been married to an assistant director since

---

* Bruce Manning had also recently collaborated on the screenplay for *Back Street*, with Charles Boyer and Margaret Sullavan.

April 1941. She divorced him in 1943 and married the producer of several of her films in 1945, which was also the year in which Charles David directed her in his next-to-last film, *Lady on a Train* (1945). Then she retired from films, Hollywood, and the United States and moved near Paris, in Neauphle le-Chateau, where she would live the rest of her life; and in December 1950 she became Madame Charles David.

In 1942, Deanna Durbin was no longer a child, and the film was going to have to be informed by that reality. Moreover, since Pearl Harbor, American film had been granted permission to deal with the all-consuming issue of the war. As a result, it was planned that the young actress would play a character named Ruth who adopts a group of children after their mission in China is bombed by the Japanese and who tries to bring them to the United States. Certainly, the goal assigned the film was to promote the figure of Deanna Durbin into the identity of an adult, a few months after she had actually become one. Renoir was obviously aware of this, but he had to wait for the other elements of the film, while shooting it at the same time. As he wrote to his brother Pierre, "I have every chance but one: I have no screenplay."[67]

Consequently, he began by filming Deanna Durbin and the children on the lots Universal had built for the exterior scenes. The work wasn't unpleasant. Directing the star was a positive experience. She was manageable and didn't jockey for flattering positions in front of the camera. Renoir was already even starting to consider "trying some very new things"[68] if he made a second film with her. And, of course, the little children were "very cute," even if "they didn't have any respect for me as a person."[69] They were also the first children Renoir had used in a film since Toto (Sacha Tarride) in *On purge Bébé*, a detail reminiscent of Lisette's line to Christine in *The Rules of the Game:* "Got to take care of them all the time, even if you have money." In this particular case, Renoir hadn't decided to have children in the film, but it's true that children would soon occupy a place in his films that they had never had, perhaps as a result of the extent to which his thoughts were currently occupied by his own son.

On July 4, industry news carried a short report on the shoot describing the direction of what was supposed to become the film's first scene: "Director Jean Renoir shouts 'camera,' and the Japs begin to talk, giving Deanna instructions about how to get herself and her nine little Chinese charges out of town. With tears streaming down her face, she walks over to the bed and falls sobbing to the floor. The camera crane shoots past her to pick up the balance of the room ... an old Chinese seated in a corner and a Jap soldier hanging a bamboo shade over the window to hide out the curious youngsters. When this is taken, the camera comes back and the scene is finished."[70]

On the set of *Forever Yours*, days, then weeks, passed, and nothing changed, if not the mood of the director. Thought of at first as "delightful" and a "very brilliant man,"[71] Bruce Manning was proving to be "very lazy, all the same," and "very weak," faults that were leading to "the dictatorship of administrative personnel."[72] In short, Renoir had had "enough shooting anything at all without knowing where I was going" and was now thinking of "trying to get out of this tight spot."[73] The undertaking wasn't simple, and the director was overcome with impatience, feeling as if being in this film was like "being in a bath of sugar syrup."[74] He doubted that would change. "Aside from the language and the big resolutions, this feels a bit like the Orient pre–Mustapha Kemal," but fortunately, "everybody is sweet, and Deanna deserves better than this and she has enough talent to get out of this kiss-and-cuddle genre."[75] He was careful not to seem overalarmed to his son, who was dealing with different kinds of uncomfortable situations, but the cup of syrup was about to overflow, and the director could not reasonably continue for weeks more filming fragments of scenes with absolutely no idea how they would be linked, if they ever would be.

Made aware of the situation, his agents tried to bring him to his senses: if he quit the shoot, he'd be putting not only producer Bruce Manning's career in danger but also his own future in Hollywood. So, the director attempted to convince Manning that only Manning himself was in a position to create a film he was supposed to write but wasn't writing, because the option of improvising is only possible for the author of the film, who's supposed to be the one who knows where he wants to go. This is what he explained to Dudley Nichols:

> In a film where improvisation plays such a big part, perhaps it is better that the one who improvises hold all strings in his own hand. He will then find himself more or less in the position of a painter who starts on a canvas without a certain definite conception. This canvas may become a masterpiece providing he be alone to follow his instinct, and that the colors shall be put by him on the canvas, in direct relation with his creative dreaming. And the details of his material work will help his imagination and allow him gradually to define his subject. In other words, instead of starting from the screenplay to arrive at the shooting, the artist can start from the shooting to arrive at the screenplay.[76]

Renoir's legendary capacity to charm worked once again, and it worked even faster because the interests of the two parties weren't at cross-purposes. A meeting at Universal on August 6 that included the bigwigs resulted in the director's being authorized to quit the project, for health reasons. He also committed to never publicly denigrate *Forever Yours*. Two days later, however, in a letter to René Clair, he seems not to have factored in the good news. "I'm stuck in horrible shit. I've been shooting for two months, and there's at least that much more. I'm dying of boredom except for the contact I have with Deanna Durbin, who's a nice girl."[77] But the same day, he told his son how satisfied he was. "Everything is going well, even better because I've had the good fortune to be able to interrupt the film I was making at Universal";[78] and to his brother Claude, he wrote, "The official reason for everyone in Hollywood is that I'm having a lot of trouble with my leg, which is true, too. But the real reason is because my producer and writer, who also happens to be the most delightful man, was bringing me dialogue only at the moment I filmed it, and because the story seemed too weak to me and also because, disgusted as I was with this kind of sugar-syrupy improvisation, I advised him to direct the film himself and let me go."[79]

Although it was true that his leg bothered him, the health excuse was for appearance's sake. No one was duped, and the trade journals did not refrain from commenting. The *Hollywood Reporter* announced that, after forty-seven days of filming, Renoir had ended up withdrawing from the direction of *Forever Yours* because his slow pace had been causing friction within the company for some time. The article stated that it had also been reported that Renoir had asked for ten more weeks of shooting to finish the film, whereas the work schedule had planned for forty-nine days total. According to that same article, this had led to Miss Durbin's insisting that Manning take responsibility for the direction after Renoir's departure. Universal announced that Manning, who had been present on the set from the beginning of filming, had taken the direction in hand for several scenes to allow Renoir to rest.[80] The next day, *Variety* stated that the condition of the director's leg had grown worse over the two weeks during which he had to direct some battle scenes,[81] which wouldn't appear in the film.

Thirty years later, Deanna Durbin provided a version of the facts that clarified certain obscurities. According to her, Bruce Manning suggested that Universal consider *Forever Yours* a loss and suggest to Renoir that he direct in its place a modern adaptation of *The Taming of the Shrew*, transposed to a service station in Texas. Therefore, Renoir's request—of "ten more weeks of shooting," according to the press—wouldn't have been referring to *Forever Yours* but to the Shakespeare adaptation, with Deanna Durbin in the role of Catherine. The actress also claimed that Universal gave a green light to this project and that Renoir said he was in favor of it as well; but the very next day he reneged, giving as reason the fact that his wounded leg was plaguing him. The actress said she'd been shocked by the news of Renoir's breaking his contract with Universal and remarked that even in Hollywood, a captain doesn't abandon his sinking ship. Shortly after, she learned that Jean had signed with RKO.[82]

For Renoir, the shooting of *Forever Yours* had lasted forty-seven days, which was exactly two less than specified by the work schedule. He had filmed enough to have a first edit made and shown. The director himself confirmed what happened: "What must have motivated their decision was the projection of the first edit, which bored me to tears and which must have disappointed them highly."[83] "*Their* decision"? This suggests that Renoir didn't give up the film on his own initiative. Perhaps he wanted to leave, and Universal, in any case, wanted him to leave, so everything was fine.

The production of *Forever Yours,* which became *The Amazing Mrs. Holliday* and was released on February 13, 1943, lasted until mid-December, four months after Renoir's departure. The actual shoot was interspersed with long segments filled mostly with newly written scenes. According to the *Hollywood Reporter,* production lasted a total of 132 days,[84] a figure that seems excessive. The children occupied a place in the film that they didn't initially have when they'd been planned for only the first scenes. Bruce Manning did not appear in the credits as a screenwriter.* Apparently, *The Amazing Mrs. Holliday* still has not been studied on any serious level, despite the fact that Renoir worked on it for nearly fifty days, which, for example, is five times as long as he worked on *Tosca,* in which traces of his contribution have been sought and found much more easily because everyone has known since spring 1940 that he filmed only the opening shots. And yet, it is obvious that there is more of Renoir in *The Amazing Mrs. Holliday* than there is in *Tosca.*

The different elements available in the archives, composed mostly of photographs of the shoot and newspaper articles, make it possible to claim that the exteriors that were supposed to be "Chinese" were directed by Renoir. In the finished film, they are integrated with the action using a series of flashbacks. Without their being irrefutably stamped with the director's style, a number of scenes can be distinguished from the whole by the different lighting and especially by the placement of the camera that established a relationship with the actors that contrasts with what was achieved elsewhere. These scenes stand out clearly enough from the rest of the film and deviate from the Hollywood style of the time, especially its regular alternation between shots/reverse shots that characterizes several other moments, such as the scene at the station, which is successful enough and rather amusing in itself, despite its inane shooting style.

Most importantly, although some scenes *could have been* shot by Renoir and then modified by the addition of inserts, several others obviously belong to him. For example, there is the long dialogue between Deanna Durbin and Edmond

* Screenplay by Frank Ryan and John Jacoby, adaptation by Boris Ingster and Leo Townsend, of an original story by Sonya Levien.

O'Brien, both of them filmed from the back as they walk down a hallway. Then a slow forward tracking shot accompanies them to the window. After that, they stop and turn toward the camera, as their exchange is fixedly captured. Then they begin their walk again in the opposite direction, preceded by the camera tracking backward this time, which is exactly the opposite of the first movement. The scene has marvelous fluidity and is filmed without any loss in continuity, as are several other exchanges, one of which shows Edmond O'Brien behind a glass-paned door veiled by a curtain in a manner that is eminently Renoirian.

A number of times, the systematic use of depth of field leaves the director's mark on the film; likewise for a certain close-up of Deanna Durbin, which seems to foreshadow the upside-down face of Françoise Arnoul in *French Cancan*. Contrary to the impression Renoir wanted to give afterward, these scenes are evidence that he was interested in their direction, and this interest was the source of the accusations of slowness leveled against him. He may have also filmed the actress's song in Chinese, whereas nothing suggests that he was the one who recorded her rendition of "Vissi d'arte" from *Tosca*. Nevertheless, beyond any impressions or hypotheses, the fact is that, although the material he was given was in fact far from interesting, the direction of several sequences proved to be profoundly part of his style. In that respect, *The Amazing Mrs. Holliday*, of which Renoir could well have directed more than half, seems like the inverse counterpart of his next film, *This Land Is Mine*, whose subject enthused him but that he directed in an impersonal style.

During that summer of 1942, Renoir was happy about the premature end of his agreement with Universal. For several months, he had already become focused on a track that interested him a lot more, and that interest increased as he became aware that the Deanna Durbin project had taken a turn for the worse. In fact, on June 6, which was five days after the start of filming on *Forever Yours*, a paragraph in the *Los Angeles Times* revealed, "George Sanders assigned to an untitled picture which Dudley Nichols will produce for RKO. Laughton, Nichols, and Jean Renoir, who is to direct, presented the subject to Charles Koerner, in charge of production at RKO. . . . The action takes place in an occupied country, not identified, in Europe."[85]

Under contract to RKO since January 1, although the agreement hadn't been made public until July 4, Dudley Nichols was then the Hollywood figure who was closest to Renoir. Renoir informed him of the ups and downs of his career almost every day. Over the years, the screenwriter and his wife, Esta, would remain very much in touch with Renoir, as evidenced by the abundance of correspondence they exchanged. He was powerfully connected with the studios and expert at the most complex transactions. In the Hollywood of the forties, Nichols was an influential figure, a characteristic doubtlessly more noticeable than any remarkable qualities as a screenwriter; the prestige attached to films such as *Stagecoach* and *Bringing Up Baby* could have contributed to his being overrated. The relations between Renoir and Nichols, who, moreover, proved to be not very sensible as a producer and clumsy as a director, would turn less idyllic on the set of *This Land Is Mine* than their friendship predicted. Nevertheless, the director did not hold it against him. *This Land Is Mine* was an independent production financed and distributed by RKO. Nichols and Renoir were only accountable to RKO, and they worked as freely as could be desired.

This Land Is Mine, which the *Hollywood Reporter* announced as the official title of this film on July 21, 1942, was first called *Monsieur Thomas*, and it was under that name that Renoir had registered its initial treatment[86] with the Screen Writers Guild on April 2. He'd been thinking of the subject since at least the preceding fall when he'd decided to evolve the project entitled *Les Enfants* about refugees into a film describing life in an occupied country. He'd confirm such an evolution when he discussed the film in 1954: "My first idea . . . was to make a film on the exodus of some children from Paris to the South. The truth is that I was thinking of *Jeux interdits* [*Forbidden Games*],* but without the story of the cemetery, of course; and then, I figured having children play it wouldn't work very well abroad; you've got to have French children play in French; so a film about that situation would have to be made using established actors who could artistically—or, in other words, artificially—convert certain emotions into the customs of the American audience."[87] This recollection was in response to Truffaut's or Rivette's suggestion that the film possessed a kinship in subject matter with one of the *Contes du lundi* (*Monday Tales*) in which Alphonse Daudet uses the voice of a "little Alsatian" to tell the story of the final class given by a teacher after "the order has come from Berlin to stop teaching any language except German in the schools of Alsace and Lorraine."[88] Renoir confirmed the hypothesis and explained that during a conversation with Charles Laughton, "it was our retelling Daudet's story one day that gave me the idea for that story, which I wrote."[89] Actually, the conversation to which Renoir refers probably took place in March 1942, which was shortly before he registered the screenplay for *Monsieur Thomas* and when he already had in place the main events and characters of what would become *This Land Is Mine*. This sheds doubt on the possibility that Alphonse Daudet had had any influence on the film.

William Harry Gilcher has cited the play *Somewhere in France* by Carl Zuckmayer and Fritz Kortner as another possible source; and, in fact, Dudley

* François Boyer's book *Les Jeux inconnus* appeared in 1947, so it seems difficult to believe that Renoir was thinking of it in 1941. The author of the book and René Clément adapted it into the film *Jeux interdits* in 1952.

Nichols had revised the text of this play before its premiere in April 1941. However, as Gilcher also points out "the final script shows no plot similarities other than setting and general theme with *This Land Is Mine*."[90] Likewise, the reference Renoir made to the Steinbeck book *The Moon Is Down* is less an expression of his desire to adapt the novel,* which takes place in a small Scandinavian city occupied by the Germans, than it emphasizes his wish to approach a subject close to the one handled by the novelist.

During the entire time he was working on the Deanna Durbin film, Renoir kept researching documentation about occupied Europe with Dido's help, collecting articles about the underground press and the executions of hostages. They saved excerpts from the *Courrier du Pacifique* and from *Pour la Victoire*† ("How They Die"[91] and "Three Dominican Priests Condemned to Death in Paris, Twenty-Seven People Condemned to Death in One Day, and Bombs Continue")[92] and from the *Los Angeles Times*, about the deportation of hostages under the threat of being shot.[93] In *Pour la Victoire*, he also found an underground tract entitled "Advice for the Occupied" that recommended various safety measures, including, "Your suspender seller thought it was a good idea to display '*Man spricht Deutsch*' on his shop. Go to the other one, even if he can't speak the language of Goethe"; and, "Display a placid indifference, but secretly discuss your anger; it can help."[94]

On July 19, Renoir took advantage of the Sunday lull to jot down a few "Notes for *Monsieur Thomas*." More specifically, they concerned a scene showing M. Thomas getting ready in his room to meet Marie, with a pianist playing "La Damnation de Faust" in the background, while Marie can also be glimpsed through the window of her house. "All this scene would be made in only one shot, the camera starting on the pianist, and, through the door which stayed open, going in to M. Thomas, Marie would soon be seen very far in the background of M. Thomas who is in a close shot. A lens requiring very little light and giving great depth should be used." In these same "Notes," Renoir developed the inclination to film certain scenes so that each element is seen by the same set of eyes, "as if a witness remained hidden in the room and was describing the scene from his point of view . . . the movements of the camera and actors prompting the close-ups, and thereby eliminating the destruction known as

---

* Irving Pichel, Renoir's "second" on *Swamp Water*, directed this adaptation for Fox. The film was released on March 14, 1943.

† *Translator's note*: Published daily for San Francisco's French-speaking population, in that language, the *Courrier du Pacifique* also offered such war-related hard facts as the location of internment camps for the Japanese in the United States. *Pour la Victoire* was an eight-page newspaper published by French exiles in New York, covering war news and Free-French activities in every location. Some of France's most well-known writers contributed to it.

editing." Regarding the tone of the film, his desire was that it be "comic": "We should not fear to push most of our characters toward the burlesque. If the public could laugh during the exposition of this tragedy, reserving its tears for some pathetic moments, it would be a wonderful achievement."[95] A month later, Renoir explained his intentions to the person who would be his lead actor: "I believe that we are helping to bring to life a rather amusing character."[96] The letter was written in French, and the word he used for "funny," *rigolo,* had an odd ring to it, considering the subject.

To play M. Thomas, who would become Albert Lory in the film, Renoir was going to use one of the greatest actors in history, Charles Laughton. They had met briefly in October or November 1937 in London on the set of the film *The Beachcomber*.* Renoir had been invited to Elstree Film Studios by the producer and director of the film, Erich Pommer, and there he discovered that Laughton was an art enthusiast and knowledgeable collector. In 1935, he had purchased Auguste Renoir's *Le Jugement de Pâris* (*Judgment of Paris,* 1908) for $36,000, which for him was an expensive sum. The love of painting and the actor's admiration for the director's father could only bring the two men together. Moreover, there was an astonishing physical resemblance between them, to the point that it would be difficult to watch Lory's character develop on-screen without thinking almost as much of Renoir.

However, such a similarity in appearance wasn't able to cover up certain dissimilarities between the two. Although Renoir's baggy trouser seat and the belly bulging above his belt both resembled Laughton's, Renoir's neglect was a studied one, whereas Laughton's was anything but a sign of indifference to his attire. It was instead the result of a genuine hatred of his physical appearance and his own body. Such hatred caused the actor to neglect himself and to revel in grime, the effects of which anyone who approached him experienced. Laughton projected an appalling image of himself, considered himself permanently at the bottom of the heap, doubted his abilities, and indulged in his masochistic tendencies. Such impulses were unfamiliar to a Renoir who could display genuine modesty as the very sign of being rather satisfied with himself.

In 1931, two years after Laughton's marriage to Elsa Lanchester, who played opposite him on-screen on numerous occasions, an incident caused by a young blackmailer had forced Laughton to reveal his homosexuality. It was a revelation that left his young wife deaf for the space of a week. The couple would never separate, although Laughton became exclusively homosexual when he reached his forties, as Elsa Lanchester would reveal in her memoirs.[97]

---

* The original story by Somerset Maugham was actually called "The Vessel of Wrath." The film based on it, *Vessel of Wrath,* would eventually be retitled *The Beachcomber* for US release.

Laughton had left England in early summer 1939, right after the commercial failure of the Hitchcock film *Jamaica Inn*. However, starting several years before that, he'd already been traveling between London and Hollywood. His great "historical" roles in Alexander Korda's British productions, especially the two in which he played Henry VIII and Rembrandt, as well as his performances as Nero (*The Sign of the Cross*), Javert (*Les Misérables*), Captain Bligh (*Mutiny on the Bounty*), and the "gentleman's gentleman" wandering through the American West (*Ruggles of Red Gap*), had made him an international star. Accepting RKO's offer to play Quasimodo in a new adaptation of the Victor Hugo work, to be directed by William Dieterle, he sailed to America on the *Queen Mary* in June 1939 along with the Irish and red-haired Maureen O'Hara, who'd been his protégé since the age of eighteen. After O'Hara won the role of Esmeralda in *The Hunchback of Notre Dame* at Laughton's insistence, she went on to score a hit in John Ford's *How Green Was My Valley* and then returned as Laughton's lead in *This Land Is Mine,* which was filmed on the sets that had been created for *The Hunchback of Notre Dame.*

Since spring 1941, Laughton had been living in Pacific Palisades, having had the garden adjoining his house overlooking the Santa Monica Bay planted with several olive trees. He enjoyed promising guests that at his home, "You'd think we were in France."[98] When it came to making people think they were in France, the house on North Martel Avenue was unparalleled. Laughton adored France and spoke French superbly. Renoir and he had only reasons to get on well together. Dido would write to Claude Renoir, "Charles and Jean love each other tenderly. They're inseparable. Evenings, when work is over, they spend hours 'taking it easy.'"[99] Laughton also declared himself won over by Gabrielle, who nicknamed him the "big tomcat."

The actor had supposedly become aware of the initial version of Renoir's screenplay in rather unusual circumstances. He was in Chicago when an unknown man came up to him and introduced himself, informing him that they were going to work together soon. The man was Walter Slezak, the Austrian actor, who'd recently moved to the United States. He had acted with Nora Gregor in Carl Th. Dreyer's film *Michael,* and RKO had just given him the role of Major von Keller in Renoir's film. His admiration for Laughton was enormous, and it grew even more so when the Englishman took him to the galleries of the Art Institute of Chicago and revealed his love of art and his astounding erudition. In the night train that was taking them to Los Angeles, Slezak lent the screenplay for *This Land Is Mine* to Laughton.

Around one in the morning, Laughton came knocking on the door to his compartment. He was in tears, overwhelmed by what he'd just read, he claimed, and spent the rest of the night rereading the script for Slezak, playing all the roles.[100] This was one of the actor's hobbies: he enjoyed reading aloud Shakespeare's plays or passages of the Bible, always playing all the roles for his friends. Jean and Dido had the privilege of sharing in several of these evenings, which gave the director the opportunity to discover the Bard, with whom he wasn't very familiar. However, during such sessions, Laughton could fly into a rage when his performance was interrupted by a ringing telephone or the barking of one of Renoir's dogs, Tambo or Nénette. (In Laughton's eyes, such behavior justified the names the neighbors had given the animals, Goering and Goebbels.)

When Laughton appeared in Brecht's play *Life of Galileo*, directed by Joseph Losey and produced by Norman Lloyd, who had then become Renoir's good friend, he is said to have dumbfounded the playwright, who wasn't easily impressed. During rehearsals he would deliver six variations of a single line, among which was "a planter trying to convince the natives that he'd created the world" and "a Frenchman like Jean Renoir."[101] On July 7, the morning after he spent the night on the train from Chicago, Laughton sent Renoir the following telegram: "On the train with Walter Slezak just read the script which is truly wonderful but what a challenge for a tired ham Stop Hope I can live up to half of what is in it."[102] The "tired ham," who became "a tired old ham" in the nearly identical telegram he sent the same day from Albuquerque to Charles Koerner at RKO, and in which the "challenge" was qualified by "tremendous," never stopped acting. Walter Slezak received confirmation of that fact when he lunched with Renoir and Nichols the day after his arrival in Los Angeles. He told them the story of Laughton's "discovery" of the screenplay, and the director and screenplay writer burst into laughter. Laughton had received and had read the script eight weeks earlier.[103]

The "tired old ham" had just turned forty-three. Renoir was forty-eight, and he was convinced that the film would mean the launching of his American career. On September 13, 1942, he wrote to his son, "I've finished writing the screenplay that I was doing with Dudley Nichols for Laughton. We're delighted. He is very intense and shows, clearly, I hope, that certain European leaders preferred to see the Nazis go into their country than to grant their workers a few benefits. It's the entire history of collaborationism, consciously or unconsciously, honestly or dishonestly, that we're trying to explain."[104]

Erich von Stroheim also referred to "collaborationism" in the letter he wrote in French to Renoir in response to Renoir's offering him the role of the German officer in the film. In it, he said he hoped that Jean would find in RKO "the atmosphere and the surroundings for collaboration (I don't like that word) . . . for cooperation needed to complete a masterpiece in the genre of *Grand Illusion*."[105] Stroheim was forced to refuse the part. He was working in the play *Arsenic and Old Lace*, replacing Boris Karloff at the Fulton Theater in New York.

Renoir informed him by letter on September 28 that he couldn't wait and that RKO had requested Walter Slezak for the role.[106]

Such a chronology refutes Slezak's version of the circumstances surrounding Laughton's discovery of the screenplay, which is, nevertheless, partly confirmed by Laughton's telegram of July 7. Unless it can be imagined that the director had considered convincing RKO to replace Walter Slezak with Stroheim. Renoir told Stroheim he had gotten the idea for the character of Major von Keller "while remembering a dinner I had with an important German agent in Lisbon. He pretended to be Swiss, but later I learnt he was German, and that he made little mystery about it. During this dinner he recited French poetry with barely an accent. He knew everything concerning French culture, and declared himself a passionate admirer of it. His ideal was a Europe where the Germans would be the organizers and the French the artists. Probably he was sincere. This refined and cultivated man impressed me as being far more dangerous than a brutal Nazi."[107] There is actually a handwritten reference to this German official in the "Notes for *Monsieur Thomas*," recorded by Renoir on June 23, 1942: "Thinking of Monsieur X, Lisbon."[108]

This Land Is Mine demonstrates Renoir's wish to depict in gray tones—rather than the black and white of film propaganda—a reality with which he wasn't, however, very familiar. Both his wish to make the film and his limitations regarding its subject matter distinguish it from productions of that genre and time but also place it in comparison to them. The story of Renoir's film on occupied Europe finds its parallel in a film by Fritz Lang called *Hangmen Also Die!*, which was inspired by the assassination of *Reichsprotektor* Reinhard Heydrich by Czechoslovakian partisans in Prague on May 27, 1942. According to Brecht, who'd arrived in Los Angeles in July of the preceding year, he and Lang were on a Santa Monica beach the day after the assassination when they had the idea for the film. The director, who, like Renoir, had experienced working at Fox, was going through a bad patch. He hadn't directed a film for more than six months and was without offers or serious projects.

Hangmen Also Die! was to be shot that autumn at the same time as *This Land Is Mine*, but it would be released less than a month before Renoir's film. Its producer was Emeric Pressburger, who would later become Michael Powell's filmmaking partner and who had been born in Czechoslovakia and had spent part of his youth in Prague. The film's release also became the occasion on which Lang for the first time publicly recounted the details of his departure from Germany in 1933, after a meeting with Goebbels. A rare feature that characterized his film was its reliance on facts, indicated and contextualized with relative precision, whereas Renoir's remained in the kind of indefinite haze characteristic of most of the productions of those years, a quality that would attract ample, but rather unjustified, criticism.

This Land Is Mine was supposed to refer to a nonexistent country. "This country" might have been "mine,'" but then, exactly what country was it? Certainly a European country, but one that looked like all the "European" sets in Hollywood films. The epigraph "Somewhere in Europe" would replace the one anticipated by the screenplay, in which that intentionally vague indication had been followed by these words: "This town is half the world today; we fight to keep it from being all the world tomorrow." Responsibility for this painfully maintained impression of vagueness—immediately thwarted for French ears by the sounds of the "Chant du depart"† playing on the soundtrack during the opening credits—wasn't Renoir's but RKO's. Apparently, the studio feared American viewers hadn't acquired any sympathy for a country split between obliged submission to its occupiers and resistance that operated from foreign lands. Renoir made up his mind to accept the fact that the various signs and inscriptions, particularly those on the monument to the dead, would be in English, to match the language spoken by the characters; but from the beginning the scenery suggested by RKO was very "French," because it had been built nearly three years before for *The Hunchback of Notre Dame*.

Eugène Lourié, for his third—first important—American film, was put in charge of "modernizing" the medieval streets from *Notre Dame*. It didn't take the artistic director long to realize that his old partner wasn't doing what he wanted to do. He was under the thumb of Dudley Nichols, who sometimes pulled rank in his role as producer and at other times defended what he considered his rights as the screenwriter. Before filming, during a rehearsal, when Renoir was preparing to have a tracking shot set up and deciding to film the opening scene using a crane, Nichols the producer expressed his opposition to the idea, claiming that the budget hadn't anticipated any crane. According to Lourié, Renoir then decided to film everything in static shots, to preserve the stylistic unity of the film.[109] Later, when the director dared to modify a line slightly, he was met with the disapproval of Nichols the screenwriter, who reminded him that every line he had written had been ratified when they had worked together on the screenplay‡ from the end of August to the end of September, during which the

---

* At the time of filming, a short piece appeared in the *Hollywood Reporter* making fun of the fact that Jean Renoir, Charles Laughton, and Maureen O'Hara had taken the necessary steps to become American citizens while making a film called *This Land Is Mine* (November 18, 1942).

† *Translator's note:* "Chant du depart" ("Song of Departure") is a revolutionary song sung by armies fighting against the Prussians in 1793. For the French, it came to characterize the spirit of revolt and the Resistance.

‡ Dudley Nichols is the only one listed for the screenplay in the credits for the film.

character's name had changed from Thomas to Albert Manville, and then to Lory, and he had been given a mother.

Dudley Nichols's interference also explains why *This Land Is Mine* little resembles Jean Renoir's other films. Renoir himself was aware of this: "In the big studios . . . the sole method is one that promises security; for that purpose, they need shots, reverse shots, ensemble shots, medium shots, done in a way that comes close to allowing them to remake another film with a few retakes if the edit doesn't jibe; and yet, I never did that. I did it in *This Land Is Mine* because the stakes were too important."[110] Renoir actually intended to show American audiences that the French were not all subjugated by the German Occupation and that some had decided to fight, including some of the weakest and most cowardly, such as Albert Lory. But he was also making an effort to become an American director, and he wanted to succeed at making good Hollywood films. That intention and that desire led him to give in to the requirements with which he was presented, for which he merely had to follow his natural bent, something he would describe in a passage in his memoirs that was cut from the definitive edition. "Besides, since this book has no other purpose than informing you about my way of making films, I might as well tell you right away that such a way, whether good or bad, has nothing to do with the way of the conqueror. The first thing I always do with the actors (and I behave the same way with the crew or with the backers or with the audience) is to give in."[111]

When dealing with the requirements of the censors, who monitored every screenplay, there was no other position to take, even if the majority of them seemed harebrained. For example: "page 64, the woman surprised during her bath must be covered with a large towel or any other wrapper."[112] As if the director would ever come up with the idea of showing a woman naked. Or, page 145, on which a line spoken by Albert Lory in his monologue, "I'm not afraid to commit a crime," was to be changed to "I'm not afraid to kill." Or, page 72, "the mocking sounds made by the boys shouldn't be 'razzberries.'" And, of course, no explanation of these requirements was to be demanded.

Filming for *This Land Is Mine* began on October 11, 1942, and ended fifty-four workdays later, on December 11. The rumors spread by the press insisted on Renoir's efficiency, as if the point was to stifle the accusation of slowness and indecision that had been leveled at him at Fox and Universal. "He is ABSOLUTELY on schedule,"[113] trumpeted the *Hollywood Reporter*, a few weeks after having announced that the scenes of trains at the start of filming, the only ones to be shot as exteriors, would be completed on a Sunday, which was the only day of the week when the Los Angeles railroad yards were available.[114]

Obviously, the publicity department at RKO was doing its job, but it is true that the shoot did progress without any major clashes, under the direction of a filmmaker who was fully invested for the first time since his arrival in Hollywood and who was claiming that the film was "probably the most difficult that I had ever made."[115] To his son, he described a "peaceful and friendly atmosphere" on the set and insisted, "I like this RKO studio a lot better than all those I've known in France."[116] Ten days before, he had written to Alain: "At the studio all they're talking about is the war, of course. The Americans are really very nice and very thoughtful. If the opposite situation was happening in France, pure patriots wouldn't fail to drag us through the mud. Here, on the other hand, everyone is friendly and pleasant. Every day I congratulate myself a bit more for having changed countries. And after the war I've decided to stay in the New World. Europe disgusts me."[117] It was precisely the same Europe whose agonies he was busy depicting.

On January 3, 1943, Renoir wrote to Flaherty that he had finished *This Land Is Mine*. Editing came next and was scheduled to begin on January 18 and to last less than a month. However, this was a stage that he customarily covered in broad strides, aided as he was by his style of long-lasting shots and scenes filmed continuously. On the other hand, this time he was going to have to change his approach; and most importantly, it wasn't even up to him alone. Dudley Nichols had his own desires as a producer, and Renoir had to share that responsibility with him. In addition, RKO as distributor had its requirements, which the director had only good reasons to heed. "I'd followed very strict guidelines in shooting the film, and I'd planned my shots like a commercial film, to be able to modify it during the edit if necessary and to measure during previews its effects on an audience I wanted to win over."[118] Accordingly, in a letter to his agent, he stated that he had had to return to the edit relentlessly, "when it was necessary to soften some of the too brutal passages and, by contrast, to give more importance to certain parts which we had neglected."[119] Several times he thought he had finished, before the opinion of one person or another forced him to go back to work. In this way, parts of the film gradually escaped Renoir, while he continued with blind trust and a partner whom he spoke of as "the man I admire the most as a film writer in this town."[120] He would remain a faithful friend of this man, but none of the numerous projects he would have with him afterward would succeed.

The process of conventionalizing *This Land Is Mine* was over by March 1943, after a series of previews during which the press spread blatantly enthusiastic reports,* reinforcing the opinion Renoir expressed to Léon Siritzky: "This time I think I've achieved a quality that can be compared to my several successes

---

* The screenwriter Emil Ludwig called it "a new great picture" in the *Los Angeles Times* on February 15, 1943.

in France."[121] The film was shown for the first time on March 12, and reviews were generally positive. Some reviewers merely worried about the large number of films that took place in occupied Europe being announced on screens in the weeks to follow. Several implausible elements were also pointed out, especially the one that allowed the character Albert Lory to give his entire speech at the end of the film. How could it be imagined that the Nazis would let such a fierce opponent express himself publicly without their interfering?

Certain attacks against the film foreshadowed those that the film would receive in France after the war when it was released there under the title of *Vivre libre.* "Laughton, an Englishman, cast as a French schoolteacher, reading United States literature, interrupted by German officers, hands book to Irish Maureen O'Hara, playing French schoolteacher, and continues reading, without interference or inspection by Nazi officers, in their presence," wrote Herb Martin,[122] who thought the screenplay was "overworked," the direction "poor," and acting "good." However, the most severe indictment came from James Agee, who addressed Renoir directly in *The Nation:* "You cannot afford to dislocate or internationalize your occupied country; or to try to sell it to Americans by making your citizens as well-fed, well-dressed, and comfortably idiomatic as Americans; or to treat the show to the corrupted virtuosities of studio lighting and heavy-ballet composition."[123] It isn't known whether Agee was directing his remarks to Charles Laughton, to whom he was close and for whom he would write *The Night of the Hunter,* the only film directed by the actor.

This Land Is Mine was released on May 7, 1943, on seventy-two screens in about fifty cities in Ohio, Kentucky, and Indiana. Its New York premiere took place on May 28. It wasn't a hit, but it was a solid commercial success* that gave Renoir the chance to prove for the second time, after *Swamp Water,* that his films could touch American audiences. He also received impassioned declarations about the film from French friends exiled from France—Geneviève Tabouis, for example, whose words were, "Am having the most intense admiration for your great work,"[124] and Pierre Lazareff, a few months later: "I can't tell you how much this film has moved me. I actually think it's the only film I've gone to see twice since I've been in the United States."[125]

On August 20, the Venezuelan newspaper *La Estera* published a letter from Louis Jouvet. He and his troupe had seen a special screening of the film three days before in Caracas. "In addition to Charlie Chaplin's *The Dictator,* this is the most beautiful film I've seen for such a long time since we left our country. For us French, it is doubly moving because of its exceptional truthfulness."[126]

---

* *This Land Is Mine* would also be adapted into a one-hour radio play broadcast on April 24, 1944, on Lux Radio Theater, with Charles Laughton and Maureen O'Hara.

That "truthfulness" would be judged "exceptional," in fact, by the French who discovered the film in 1946 after four years of German occupation.

For his third Hollywood experience, Renoir blindly depended upon a partner whom he trusted completely and whom he believed, perhaps with reason, had the relationships and the social manner that could make it possible for him to launch his career in America. However, when it came to *This Land Is Mine,* it wasn't the studio that had stood in his way. It was Dudley Nichols himself, who had led him to modify his directorial style. In reality, there was no authority at RKO putting pressure on the director, and Renoir wasn't unaware that it was at RKO that Welles had been able to direct *Citizen Kane,* a film whose directorial principles exhibited a kinship with his films, especially *The Rules of the Game.* Although Renoir's preparatory notes from July were evidence that his intentions were to make that kind of film, the finished project had no relationship to it; and in terms of style, this film was very far from the films he'd made before. *This Land Is Mine* was ten minutes shorter than *The Rules of the Game,* but it contained two hundred fifty-four more shots; and the camera only moved in one out of every six shots, whereas it had moved in one out of every two in *Rules.*[127]

Obviously, Renoir was bowing to the requirements of a partner who knew— or claimed to know—the expectations of American audiences, something about which Renoir, as a Frenchman, had little awareness. Box office results justified Nichols's point of view, just as those for *Swamp Water* had validated Zanuck's way of proceeding. However, Renoir had changed his style, and the new hand he'd been dealt was a mediocre match. It led to a cold film lacking vitality and intensity, which Nichols's dialogues tipped into sermons that even the brilliant Charles Laughton rarely seemed to be able to own, consequently earning himself the often unjust charge of being a ham. Renoir had directed less of the film he had wanted to direct than the film he'd been recommended to make. It was the portrayal of a reality about which he had virtually no knowledge, but he'd strived to produce an image of it that he thought was worthy.

The fact that the result turned out to contain so little of him is not at all surprising. It was something he seemed to become aware of at a later date, judging from a passage in a May 1944 letter he wrote to Edmond Ardisson, the actor whose first movie role had been in *La Marseillaise.* Ardisson was writing from Algiers to suggest that Renoir think of making "films describing what the French are living."[128] Renoir answered, "This experience has taught me that it is very difficult to make a film like that in a country other than France. I believe that, after the war, after I've had a chance to soak in the atmosphere of the country again, I'll be able to conceive of such an undertaking. And yet, I'll lack one important thing, which is having been an actor in this drama myself."[129]

As Renoir struggled in an RKO studio to create a portrait of an occupied country that would catch hold of the American mind, American troops were landing in North Africa on the nights of November 7 and 8, 1942. This sparked a new crisis. Shortly after, the Vichy government broke off diplomatic relations with the United States, and the Germans invaded French territory that had been designated until then as the free zone. Consequently, all postal service with America was halted, and the isolation of French exiles was intensified. The situation remained more or less the same until spring 1945.

After these events, Pierre Lazareff, in his capacity as chief of the French section of the United States Office of War Information (OWI), suggested Renoir participate in a shortwave radio broadcast destined for France. The director wrote the text of a thirteen-minute speech.[130] Just as he was about to record it, he discovered it had been substantially amended by the American censors. So, he gave up the idea of reading it and explained the reasons for this decision in a letter to Lazareff:

> I've noticed that the spirit of my brief piece has been entirely falsified by these changes. Those changes that I've been requested to make have turned it into a unilateral eulogy to Americans, without such a eulogy being identified as a direct response to some common European criticisms of the United States used often by Nazi propaganda. . . . Unfortunately, I'm very aware that the friends I have in France who could like my speech would not understand such new language coming from me. Nor would they understand my avoiding to speak about the poor and the wealthy, slums and malnutrition, since they know very well that this is the kind of language that is currently capable of bringing the French and the Americans together. Nor would they understand my passing over in silence the accusation of imperialism, which is a major linchpin of enemy propaganda.[131]

This misunderstanding would not dissuade Renoir from offering his services on several occasions to official organizations in charge of propaganda, but his requests wouldn't succeed until long after. For the time being, Renoir the director found himself reduced to a state of inactivity, and this period without films or serious projects was the longest he experienced since the transition from silent to sound films.

25

This Land Is Mine

A Salute to France
The Southerner

On October 16, 1942, an item in the *Los Angeles Times* announced that Jean Renoir had just obtained his divorce. Even so, the person placed in the foreground of this affair, both by the article and by the photos illustrating it, wasn't the director, unknown to Americans, just as most of his colleagues were, but Mrs. Gabrielle Slade. Her testimony, in fact—her "brief hearing" with Superior Court Judge Thurmond Clarke—allowed the judge to grant the request to Renoir, who had been separated from Andrée Madeleine Renoir for the last eleven years on the grounds that he could not stand "her extreme and unjustified jealousy" and her "continual threats of suicide." The newspaper article stated, "Now the gray-haired wife of Conrad Slade, American artist, Mrs. Gabrielle Slade, who as Gabrielle Renard posed for some of the elder Renoir's most famous paintings at the turn of the century, told the court she once suffered a cut hand trying to take a knife away from Mrs. Renoir after the latter had threatened suicide."

"The younger Renoir" had confirmed this occurrence: "My wife was extremely jealous of all the actresses I worked with in pictures. . . . She had no reason for such jealousy, but she was continually creating scenes in public and threatening suicide. Once she threatened to burn our house down, another time she threatened to take ether, and a third time she tried to use a knife on herself. Also, she was always going to windows and threatening to jump out."[1] As part of the grounds for its decision, the court termed "the behavior of Mrs. Renoir" to be characterized by "extreme cruelty" and ruled that her countless suicide attempts by car, knife, fire, and gas, as well as her screaming in the presence of third parties, her constant criticisms, and her false accusations of infidelity, had contributed to rendering life in common impossible.[2]

The henceforth former Mrs. Renoir was not in a position to present her defense, of course; and her husband, represented in this case by Charles A. Thomasset, who was also the president of the Alliance Française in Los Angeles, obtained the divorce that he had been requesting since June. Renoir's wish to sever himself from a relationship that had had no meaning for years seemed legitimate. It's likely that Dido found it rather difficult to live not only "in sin" but also under the same roof with a man married to someone else. Jean himself was also acting very receptive to religious sentiments. He went to mass regularly and from time to time visited a community of monks in the valley of San Fernando. He had developed a relationship with one of them in particular, which would take on rather comical proportions.

The first traces of their friendship go back to fall 1942 when a certain Brother Leonard wrote to Renoir in French, "Already your zeal has succeeded in making it possible to collect enough funds for the purchase of a car for our community. As for buying it myself, I will firmly admit to you that this is rather difficult. I have no idea of the proper sum. . . . Allow me to tell you straight out that we would like a four-door car; a Dodge, Chevrolet, or something of that type."[3] Renoir's answer is dated October 9. "The person in charge of cars at RKO has promised to hold onto the first good car that he finds out about. . . . I'm presently in a situation to afford that expense."[4] A little more than a week later, Brother Leonard informed his benefactor that he had found a Chevrolet for $10,300.[5] Renoir's astonished response was, "Given the fact that in times of war one can't drive fast, I was thinking that an older car would be enough for you and I had set the price at $250."[6] Brought back closer to reason, the monk dug up a 1937 Pontiac costing $275; but on January 20, he was talking about a Buick and, more importantly, informing Renoir that he didn't have his driver's license.[7]

The months passed, and on November 27, 1943, Brother Leonard wrote what constitutes his masterpiece, at least in terms of what has been unearthed by research up to now. The monk began by asking Jean to please excuse his silence of the last several weeks ("I'm coming to you almost as a ghost today"). He then recalled that in France the monks of Saint John of God, the brotherhood to which he belonged, were called Brothers of Charity because "they ask for charity as much as they give it." Next, he moved on to the reason for his letter: "I'm focused on my vocation. As Christmas draws ever closer, I'm here to knock on the door to your heart and your pocket; that is, as long as your finances this year allow you to be as open-minded as the other times. Whatever the case, Brother Leonard needs to keep being your protégé. Imagine: I've got it into my head to have a watch on my wrist, which is just the thing for a nurse, and even worse, I've told myself you're the one who's going to get it for me. A monk has all the nerve, don't you think?"[8] Obviously.

Renoir took some time before answering, and then, "I couldn't send the watch you asked me for. Now, I'm happy to be able to offer you this gift. . . . Attached is a check for fifty dollars. I believe you can find a good watch for less than that. It will please me if you put the difference into your charitable organization."[9] Brother Leonard thanked him on January 6 and confided some sad news: he'd had a bad cold for four or five months, and a sore throat had forced him to stay in bed. A doctor was advising a cure in a dry climate. Therefore, he was putting himself "in the hands of Providence, which will know how to make things turn out the best."[10] If there was an answer to that request, it hasn't been found. It's not yet known, then, whether Renoir ever gave Brother Leonard his stay in the desert; but it's likely the monk ended up recovering from his bad cold.

In fact, in May 1945, he would again remind his "*cher monsieur*" and "*bon ami*" of his existence. As a way of introducing his request this time, he chose to recall that "in war, they say, it's always the best ones who get killed," the pertinence of which we can only hope his correspondent appreciated. Then, "Brother Leonard has a few friends, and often he knocks on the door to their heart and their pocket. I'm planning on traveling to Canada to see my family and get a little rest. As always, if you could help me a bit I would be very grateful to you. Also, now that I am driving the car myself, I'd so like to stop and see you at the studio if it can be done without interfering with your work."[11] An answer from the *bon ami* hasn't been found.

If these communications show less about Renoir's piety than about his generosity, it is still absolutely certain that by that time the director, partly because of the influence of Dido, had become appreciably closer to God. The question of Catholicism was close to his heart. Following *Swamp Water,* he had even made it the central focus of his project *Magnificat* and had envisioned transposing that film from Brazil to the United States. "One of the more serious themes of anti–United States propaganda is based on the claim of this country being anti-Catholic. Perhaps it wouldn't lack interest to respond to such propaganda with a great film that is both Catholic and American."[12]

His new country's reputation was just as important to him, and he said he was ready to study any proposition, while asking Flaherty to inform him about the subject of the American government's intention to "influence the cinema of Hollywood toward a better comprehension of the war effort" and about a plan for "pictures made in South America by directors from the United States."[13] Flaherty responded by advising him to keep his distance from Washington and to continue to direct films like *This Land Is Mine,* which he had no doubt was "a real contribution to the war effort—it will be seen by millions of people."[14]

To keep directing films is quite obviously what Renoir desired, and RKO was waiting for him to suggest some new subjects. He had no lack of ideas, which sent him on a path from a "Gabin film project"[15] he'd sketched out in March, in which Jean would play a waiter in a café in a tropical city, to *Villiers,* dated May 1943, in which "Paul Villiers is a pharmacist's assistant in a large laboratory in a provincial city who has two passions in the world: his very young wife and music."[16] Not to mention *The Tempest*, "A Jean Renoir–Dudley Nichols Production," property of RKO, an initial shooting script of seventy-seven pages dated April 10, 1943,[17] with a second marked April 15,[18] which was submitted to Charles Laughton on the seventeenth.[19]

This Land Is Mine had cost him a great deal of energy, and his health wasn't good. In March, he decided to undergo an operation that had been delayed for months for what his doctors had strangely diagnosed as a "chronic appendicitis" but that turned out to be a fistula.

Several offers reached him, but they were too vague for him to consider seriously. Andrès de Segurola, Deanna Durbin's singing teacher and the vocal coach for all her films, offered him direction of a film in Mexico.[20] From England came an offer from Noël Coward, who wanted to entrust him with directing "a film on Free French aviation based on a screenplay by Joseph Kessel."*[21] Perhaps it was his awareness of his isolation that led him in September to change agents. Feldman-Blum was replaced by Berg-Allenberg.

It's also true that life was sweet in California. Renoir's circle was a good one. Thanks to Gabrielle, the past was often the topic. It was lovely weather, his garden was superb, and every day he would "discover new Californian wines, one more interesting than the ones that had come before." Moreover, he would add, "idleness is helping me take too much advantage of them."[22] Such idleness was, however, completely relative; and the year 1943 came to a close for him with another project, dated December and entitled *The Vagabond*. Charles Laughton would star in it; and with the help of Eddie Donahoe, his assistant on *This Land Is Mine*, Renoir established a budget for it totaling $573,000—which didn't account for Laughton's fee and the director's percentage. There was to be nine weeks of shooting, with 20 percent of it in exteriors.[23] Soon, Simon Schiffrin returned to the attack with the project he had suggested a few months earlier, an adaptation of *Le Bataillon du ciel*, a book by Joseph Kessel.† The film needed to be directed in France,‡ which Renoir, if he can be believed, said he "would very much like to do" but which his commitments prevented him from accepting.[24]

The weeks slipped by, punctuated by letters from Alain, sent from somewhere in the Pacific, as well as by parties given by various people. Renoir had always

---

* *Translator's note:* Kessel was also the author of the novel *Belle de jour*, upon which Luis Buñuel's 1967 film of the same name would be based.

† And not an adaptation of *L'Armée des ombres*, as stated erroneously in *Lettres d'Amérique*.

‡ The story was filmed in 1947 by Alexandre Esway.

known how to make friends, and his human qualities and directorial ambitions charmed the actors and crewmembers that he brought into his employ. As a result, Walter Slezak, who invited him to his ranch in Pennsylvania, also wrote to him, "I am still working on the picture with Frank Sinatra and Tim Whelan,* and after McCarey† and you and Hitchcock‡ and Borzage,§ it feels like being in a provincial vaudeville."[25]

Among Renoir's closest connections was Albert Lewin, one of the most unusual personalities in Hollywood. Eight days younger than Renoir, this Brooklyn boy had just produced an adaptation of Erich Maria Remarque's book *Les Exilés* under the title of *So Ends Our Night*. Directed by John Cromwell, it was the story of refugees—one of whom was played by Erich von Stroheim—attempting to flee Vienna while it is occupied by Nazis. Lewin was in partnership with David L. Loew, the son of one of the founders of Metro, for the purpose of creating his own company. The first film under that aegis was *The Moon and Sixpence,* based on the Somerset Maugham novel, with George Sanders in a role inspired by the personality of Paul Gauguin; and Lewin was preparing his adaptation of *The Picture of Dorian Gray,* also to be with George Sanders. A lover of art and artists who was exceptionally erudite, Lewin possessed a deeply original personality that was bound to appeal to Renoir when Flaherty, who had been Lewin's friend since 1927, introduced the two.

In their Richard Neutra–designed house that had been built in 1938 on Ocean Front Avenue in Santa Monica,¶ Albert and Mildred Lewin hosted dinners that delighted the director. He was won over as much by the splendor of the company—which often included Man Ray (one of Lewin's intimate friends), Hanns Eisler, Max Ernst, or Anita Loos—as he was by the quality of the food, "French champagne, Russian caviar, real foie gras, not to mention an unrestrained love for garlic, which is really pleasant,"[26] and their respect for traditions. "I don't really like 'parties,' having stuck with the old idea of a good dinner, with your back end well propped on a good chair before a lovely white tablecloth and with the flunky changing your plates and filling your glass. That's a lot better than being seated on an ottoman trying to balance your plate."[27]

Al Lewin had been a producer at Metro since the end of the twenties, which made him one of the close collaborators of Irving Thalberg until the

* *Step Lively,* an RKO production, directed by Tim Whelan.

† *Once Upon a Honeymoon.*

‡ *Lifeboat.*

§ *Till We Meet Again.*

¶ In 1954, the house became the property of Mae West, who had naked gladiators painted on the curved walls of the hallways, which led to six bedrooms.

latter's death in September 1936. Lewin remained at the center of a Hollywood system from which his tastes and manner made him stand out. That was enough to fascinate Renoir, who was dreaming of being in a similar situation.

Unfortunately for the Frenchman, Hollywood film had changed, exposed as it was to the drying up of European markets. Although box office receipts on American soil had increased (forty million audience members a week in 1940), which compensated a great deal for profits lost up to then in Europe, film production, because it was intended almost exclusively for the North American market, was becoming more cautious. The number of films produced remained stable at first,* but there was less variety. Risks were more strictly calculated, and daring ideas were more closely supervised. The immigrant directors who'd succeeded in leaving their creative mark on Hollywood when they arrived mostly in the thirties were primarily of German background. They were used to working under the big-studio constraints of UFA, the German motion picture production company, which had been designed to compete with American studios.

Renoir's very nature was opposed to this conception, and so was his cinema, which favored the moment to the detriment of the story, thereby preventing it from being easily transposed, as was the case for the cinema of a Lubitsch or a Fritz Lang. If French directors like René Clair or Duvivier, not to mention Jacques Feyder before them,† were comparatively better adapted, it was also because their ambitions as auteurs were humbler and/or their approaches more common. In Hollywood, the cultivated people liked Renoir's films—especially *The Lower Depths, Grand Illusion,* and *La Bête humaine*—and they appreciated the man as the son of Auguste Renoir and as a Frenchman as well as his quick mind, his culture, his humor, and his behavior.

However, the link between the director and the man was difficult to establish, and those who tried collided with misunderstandings that very quickly became insurmountable. Renoir would never direct more than one and a half films for the big studios. He'd do *Swamp Water* at Fox and *Forever Young* (*The Amazing Mrs. Holliday*) for Universal. His not doing more was less the result of a desire on his part than of an inability to adapt his ambitions and ideas.

Fortunately, life in Hollywood was among the most pleasant of lives, and sometimes Renoir forgot that not practicing his profession resulted in boredom. The break in his relations with France helped emphasize an isolation that the absence of his son rendered more painful, although the truly horrible import of the combat in which Alain was engaged would only be fully revealed at a later date. For now, Jean Renoir found himself in an unusual situation. Throughout

* There were 477 films in 1940, 492 in 1941, and 488 in 1942.

† Albert Lewin had produced Feyder's *The Kiss,* which was Greta Garbo's last silent film (1929).

his entire life, he had accumulated projects, some conceived at the end of meals that then never saw the light of day, and others that he worked on for long stretches, went back to several times, and then restarted at various moments. However, during these few months at the end of 1943 and beginning of 1944, he seemed to be working in slow motion, and the person who had always written copiously, blackening loose sheets of paper or school notebooks, seemed satisfied with his conversations with close relations and friends.

He thought seriously of adapting Mary Webb's *Precious Bane*, starring Ingrid Bergman as the protagonist Prue Sarn, but all that would come of this project was his friendship with the actress. She was then under contract to David O. Selznick, who was planning to use her to play Joan of Arc and who would not give a thought to having the star appear on-screen with a harelip. The idea had very little of Hollywood in it and in London received merely a weak response, the only remaining traces of which are a telegram sent to Renoir by the producer Paul Soskin,[28] who was connected to Rank at the time, as well as Renoir's alluding to the fact that he would enjoy directing the film in England with Dudley Nichols.[29] Because Selznick did not want to hear any talk about *Precious Bane*, the director and the actress figured they had to wait until she was freed from her contract with Selznick so that they could mount an independent production.[30] However, the project would never come to be.

In a letter to his agents, Renoir also mentioned a project about which there remains no information and for which there would be no follow-up because of a "problem of rights and other things."[31] Gary Cooper, with whom he had lunched "at Lucy's,'" would have starred in it. Another idea, but one that was pursued more precisely and for a longer time, was for a film inspired by the controversial figure Sister Kenny, the nurse from Australia who had developed a treatment for polio. At first, Renoir thought the theme was fascinating. For him, it brought to mind the memory of that fisherman's wife in Berck who had devised a treatment for the skeletal tuberculosis that Gabrielle's son suffered from. Renoir maintained then that the time had actually come to "extol pure spirituality, self-sacrifice, and renounce the facile pleasures of life."[32] In this subject, he said he could see "the exaltation of the safeguard of one of God's best creations: I speak of the human body."

On May 9, 1944, the Renoirs lunched at RKO with Mary McCarthy, who would write the screenplay. On June 15, Renoir and Dudley Nichols left for Minneapolis with the goal of meeting Sister Kenny. They stayed for two weeks, returning to Los Angeles on the morning of June 29. Out of the visit

* Actually a reference to Lucey's, on Melrose Avenue, opposite the Paramount studios.

and meeting came a short account given by the director in his memoirs as well as the very ordinary film that the screenwriter would direct in 1946 with Rosalind Russell. Apparently, Renoir himself had suggested to Dudley Nichols that he completely take over this project, in which the director probably had lost interest. The truth is, in the meantime, another idea had been proposed to him. After several months and a few complications, it resulted in *The Southerner,* the director's third American film.*

A year had passed since the British victory in El Alamein and the Allied landing in North Africa, when Renoir had shared with his son his "impression that Unc' Hitler has lead in his wings."[33] The exiled French directors met at Julien Duvivier's home at 8620 Hollywood Boulevard. Present were Jean Benoît-Lévy, René Clair, Louis Verneuil, Michel Bernheim, Renoir, and, of course, Duvivier. The purpose of the meeting: envisioning the future of French film.[34] This was, obviously, premature, but everyone already knew that reconstruction would be long and difficult. Other meetings would be organized in the months to come, including one on December 17, 1944, attended by Pierre Blanchar, who at the time was the president of the Comité de libération du cinéma français.

However, at no moment did Renoir feel involved; and in a letter to his brother Claude, he included a dispirited portrait of his colleagues: "There's something sad and shabby attached to them, keeping you from taking them seriously. The Americans who met them were anxious to learn things about the Resistance, about the struggle against the Germans, and the battle of Paris. Instead of that, during a banquet, he [Blanchar†] and Boyer gave long speeches that included their early days as actors in Paris, their years at the Conservatory, and their meals in restaurants in the Latin Quarter."[35] Renoir wouldn't take part in the rebirth of French film and steered clear as much as possible of the "fiery Gaullists," but he did join the National Council of American-Soviet Friendship, which hosted Dmitri Shostakovich in Los Angeles in the fall of 1943.[36]

On Friday, February 4, 1944, in the chamber of a justice of the peace in Westwood, Jean Renoir married Dido Freire. He asked Gabrielle and Dudley Nichols to be his witnesses, but because Charles Laughton had confided his disappointment about not having been chosen, Renoir appointed a third witness, whose most important duty was to carry the wedding rings, which he quickly misplaced, forcing the judge to use his and his wife's.[37] A small celebration at

---

* His third film, with the caveat that *The Amazing Mrs. Holliday* is only partly a film by Jean Renoir.

† The Renoirs invited Pierre Blanchar to dinner on December 29, 1944, along with Charles Laughton. Simon Schiffrin and Dudley Nichols and their wives were also present.

the home of Laughton and Elsa Lanchester was next, and the following Sunday, Jean and Dido Renoir threw a wedding party.[38] The new husband would inform his brother Pierre by telegram, "All in good health. Alain private first class American army. Dido and I married."[39]

The day before the ceremony, Renoir had received a call from the screenwriter Philip Dunne in New York asking him to work on a one-hour film, composed partly of archive footage. Dunne, whom Renoir may have met during his time at Fox, was now head of the production department of the New York office of the OWI's Bureau of Overseas Motion Pictures. Another screenwriter, Robert Riskin, among whose achievements were Frank Capra's highly successful films, directed this official organization. Apparently, the idea to contact Renoir had come from the actor Burgess Meredith, who was then captain of the Air Transport Command and was stationed in England, where he had just produced *A Welcome to Britain,* a film intended for American troops who were being called to sojourn in Great Britain. The new production Meredith had just been assigned would be the French matching piece, *A Salute to France,* the purpose of which would be to enable American soldiers to acquire rudimentary knowledge about the country they would soon have the mission of liberating from Nazi occupation. The focus had been more apparent in the original title chosen for the film, *Know Your Ally: France.* For the making of the film, Meredith was being sent back to New York.

On several occasions in the past, Renoir had applied to the American authorities to participate directly in the war effort, pointing to the films made in this context by John Ford as an example of what he intended to do; but his requests had remained unanswered, and Burgess Meredith's offer had nothing to do with them. The actor had suggested a loose dramatic line that had been accepted by his superiors and approved by the leaders of the Free French Forces. Two versions of the film had to be directed: one in English, which would be the responsibility of Garson Kanin, and one in French, entitled *Salut à la France* and to be directed by Jean Renoir. The first film was supposed to familiarize the Americans with the French, and the purpose of the second was to give French people the opportunity to learn about the mentality and customs of their liberators. In his new role as a "consultant" of the Office of War Information, unsalaried but with all costs defrayed, the director was expected in New York on February 14 at the latest. On that day, Jean and Dido Renoir moved into the Algonquin Hotel, where they would remain until April 17, 1944, except for a brief visit to Philadelphia on April 14.

Renoir began working on the screenplay with Burgess Meredith, part of the time at the actor's estate, about thirty-five miles from New York. Shooting began at the beginning of March at the Fox Movietone studios on Fifty-Fourth Street and Tenth Avenue. Meredith played the part of an American soldier, Philip Bourneuf played a "Tommy," and the role of the Frenchman, who was called Jacques Bonhomme, was given to Claude Dauphin, who at the time was a lieutenant in the Free French Forces and who had been sent over from North Africa for the occasion Although it had been planned that the French version would be directed first, thereby serving as the inspiration for the English-language version,[40] all plans ended up scuttled; and Renoir attributed this to the demanding presence of a certain actress. "The setup was charming and congenial until a lady you know came along and vamped the male elements of the production. I am speaking of Marlene Dietrich,* unemployed because of Gabin's departure. Since she has been around, our young men think only of things not at all connected with the picture. When we arrived in New York, she played the part of the 'distressed widow.' Now she is playing the part of Messaline. For me, I think she will always remain an extremely boring lady."[41]

It is true that Jean Gabin had just joined the Free French Forces, but it cannot be ruled out that in this case Renoir was giving Dietrich shoes too big to fill, because he himself was getting anxious about staying away from Hollywood for too long. Dudley Nichols had just told him about his idea for a film on Sister Kenny and was himself preparing to direct *Thieves Like Us*,† which would have been his first film but which wouldn't be made. "I would like to be back quickly in Hollywood and to try to make a picture myself,"[42] Renoir wrote on April 9, a week after having informed the screenwriter that Garson Kanin had begun the editing and that he himself had just finished shooting.[43] The remark may have meant that Renoir had directed both versions of the film, each scene having been filmed in succession, in French and then in English. Although the credits on the film would list the cinematographer as the "Army Pictorial Service," without mentioning any name, a letter from Eugen Schüfftan suggests that this cinematographer, who was then looking for work in Hollywood and whom Renoir would consider hiring to shoot *The River*, had been approached: "I was supposed to shoot the Renoir film in New York for the OWI. The day we were leaving, I fell down the stairs and broke my leg."[44] In addition, it's certain that Renoir did not participate in the editing, the English version of which was assigned to Helen Van Dongen, the editor who was married to Joris Ivens. The

---

* Renoir's personal appointment book indicates that Dido and he dined several times with Marlene Dietrich during their stay in New York, on March 2, 3, 8, and 27, to be exact, and on at least two of those occasions René Clair joined them.

† Based on the novel by Edward Anderson and brought to the screen in 1974 by Robert Altman.

French version was assigned to the editor and director Marcel Cravenne.[*]

On April 27, which was a week after Renoir's return to Los Angeles on the morning of the twentieth,[†] the first edit was shown to Philip Dunne and Robert Riskin, who asked for cuts. After they were completed, the length of the film was reduced from eight and one-half reels to five, which shortened it by around thirty-seven minutes. On June 11, a long article in the *New York Times* about *A Salute to France* included the claim that several scenes had been filmed secretly in France (although they had really been created from archive shots) and that the undertaking had required more than eight months of work.[45] From the opinions expressed here and there by the various people responsible for the operation, it came out that the finished film had only a distant relationship to the original project.[46] At least the music by Kurt Weill was excellent, according to those who then saw the film. However, they apparently hadn't understood that Weill's contribution was primarily orchestration and not original composition.

Presented in France in fall 1944 as part of a program of "United Films" by the OWI,[‡] the French version has been considered lost for a long time. When Renoir discovered the English version less than a year before his death, he couldn't recognize any of his work. In a letter to Margareta Akermark, who had sent him a copy of the film, Burgess Meredith would write, "The copy of the film *A Salute to France* that we received has nothing to do with the film that he [Renoir] and I made with Garson Kanin. It may be that it has one or two scenes left from the original, that's all."[47] Renoir conserved the copy he received in his personal archives.

A Salute to France begins against the strains of "La Marseillaise," with shots of the landing of the troops who are preparing to cross the English Channel. Then three soldiers become the focus: Joe the American (Burgess Meredith), Tommy the Brit (Philip Bourneuf), and Jacques Bonhomme, the Frenchman (Claude Dauphin). "Three men, three nations, who are fighting for the same cause and against the same enemy, and taking advantage of it to try to understand one another better," proclaims the commentary, after each of the three has been presented preparing for war. The longest sequence is devoted to Jacques, alternately shown as a father playing the accordion with a child on his knees, as a waiter in a Parisian café, as a coal miner cleaning his hands, as a chestnut

* Marcel Cravenne is said to have participated in the editing of *A Day in the Country* as an intern, without appearing in the credits.

† According to Jean Renoir's personal agenda, Dido and he had left New York on Monday, April 17, at 4:20 p.m. and arrived in Los Angeles on Thursday at 9:15 a.m.

‡ In Paris, at the Balzac, la Scala, and Vivienne movie theaters, among others.

vendor, as a peasant, and as a bank employee, but always singing "Le Temps des cerises"* in English.

The commentary next makes it clear that Tommy would have been a doctor, Jacques a scientist, and Joe a professor, a suggestion permitting it to be understood that the discovery made by Louis Pasteur would not have had any future without the successive contributions of an Englishman, a Russian, and an American. "Then are we thinking about nationalities?" asks Jacques, before a German voice drowns his out. Next, Hitler appears, the speech he is giving dubbed in English, followed by images of Doriot, Laval, and Mussolini and English, French, and American Fascists. Following this, the film recalls German aggressions leveled against France over the space of decades, leading to images of the great figures of the First World War—Clemenceau, Foch, Joffre (but not Pétain)—as well as images of workers, peasants, Guynemer, the Tommies, Lloyd George, the American "boys," President Wilson, and General Pershing. Next come images of the German offensive, the exodus, Nazis in Paris.

Then the film portrays Joe parachuting into France. He is met by a village priest, who is already hiding Tommy, who has also arrived by parachute. At the table, the priest tells them about life in his country since it was subjected to the Occupation. About one of Pétain's speeches: "He said we were paying for our sins, that we must learn to collaborate with the Germans." Then we see de Gaulle, then the taking of hostages, and hear the words, "I knew that the marshal was not our father." Then the priest entrusts his guests to members of the Resistance. "This man is the son of the owner of the castle. The other one is the secretary of the Communist cell in the district."

After several shots of Jacques in a prison camp, images of occupied France, the *maquisards*, executions, Jacques is shown with his hands tied, facing Germans who are photographed from behind, in silhouette. A slow lateral tracking shot leaves them in shadow, but Jacques is fully lighted within a tight close-up in an approaching tracking shot, while a German voice announces his condemnation to death, before he begins to speak: "You said I'm alone. I think not. . . . I speak of soldiers of Russia, they are with me, people of China, hundreds of millions of them, the American boys, in the jungles of the Pacific, the men and women of England, Canada, Australia, partisans of Yugoslavia, people of Greece, Norway, Holland, Belgium, Poland, Czechoslovakia. Wherever there are men who believe in liberty, they are with me, against you. . . . " Victory parade on the Champs-Élysées, with insert shots of Joe and Tommy, Allied planes in the sky of France.

* *Translator's note:* "The Time of Cherries," a song written in 1866 that came to be associated with the Paris Commune when verses were added to it, giving it a revolutionary bent.

During all of this last part can be heard "Le Chant des partisans,"* words in English.

The scenes of reenactment, probably the work of Renoir, are very correctly executed. The one showing Jacques being condemned is even rather remarkable. The three actors are very good in all of it; and these qualities make *A Salute to France* clearly different from the ordinary propaganda film. Then, is it a film "by" Renoir? No, but it's a film made by a talented director that attains the objective it was assigned. Renoir himself was unaware of this at the time and asked Jean Benoît-Lévy, "If by chance the film in question is shown to you in New York, could you tell me how it is, because I don't have any news."[48] In that same letter, he described certain conditions under which he directed it and congratulated himself for having been able to "remove a certain whiny tone, an excusing tone that characterized the screenplay that Captain Meredith wanted to make me film," having succeeded in "bringing in Bernard Lamotte who is French to do the sets,"† and thereby "with his help, getting rid of a lot of the grotesque characteristics that a deep-seated tradition lends to the outer aspect of our countrymen in this nation." He was aware that for him it "would be difficult to have any influence over the editing, [and] Dauphin could do it better than me, having as he does the prestige of arriving from Europe," so he jumped "at the first chance, which was also a vital chance for me, something having to do with all my hope of working in Hollywood." *A Salute to France* ended up, in fact, as a compromise between the American ideas on France and those of Renoir, which was not the kind of thing that could satisfy the director and which explains why he let go of it the moment he left New York.

In July 1946, Renoir would take part in a new "propaganda" operation, by directing a radio broadcast called *Displaced Persons* for the program "Friendship Bridge." Its ambition was to draw the attention of the American troops in Europe to the fate of refugees. "There are more than six million of them," the head of a subdepartment of the Armed Services dealing with news and information wrote to him on July 8, "and this series is meant to see to it that the soldiers behave correctly with these people."[49] The broadcast directed by Renoir was recorded on July 12, 1946, starting at eleven-thirty in the morning in a

* *Translator's note:* The song of the French Resistance, put into music in London by Anna Marly in 1943. The French lyrics were written by Joseph Kessel and Maurice Druon.

† Renoir had written the catalogue copy for an exhibition called *Paintings of Paris* by Bernard Lamotte, organized at the Ambassador Hotel in Los Angeles in August 1942. He was one of the sponsors of the exhibition, as was Marlene Dietrich, Antoine de Saint-Exupéry, Jean Gabin, Sir Charles and Lady Mendl, and Charles Boyer. Arthur Miller would devote a long article to the event in the *Los Angeles Times* of August 9, 1942, entitled "Artist Lamotte Limns Paris of Yesterday."

studio at NBC. Robert Preston, Virginia Cregg, and Hy Averback were among the actors in this episode. Six days later, a thank-you letter was sent to Renoir.

Renoir was in a hurry to return to Hollywood in spring 1944, and that sense of hurry became even more urgent while he was still in New York and got wind of the fact that the film he had started to prepare was in danger. From the beginning, the project had been connected to one of his old acquaintances, Robert Hakim, the producer who had entrusted him with the direction of *La Bête humaine* in 1938. Hakim, as well, was now living in Hollywood and was associated with David L. Loew, who was soon going to produce two of Albert Lewin's films and who was currently in cahoots with United Artists. Loew was proposing that Hakim produce an adaptation of the George Sessions Perry novel, *Hold Autumn in Your Hand,* for the screen. Published in 1941, the book had won the National Book Award the following year, which was the first time the prize had been given to a writer from Texas.

Apparently, Hakim had first thought of Julien Duvivier, but the fact remains that in October 1943 he had had Renoir read not the novel but a first adaptation of it, written by the screenwriter Hugo Butler.[50] According to the director, the producer wanted the film to be made on a modest budget and, strangely, hadn't been aware that the adaptation the way Butler had conceived it would cost a fortune. Renoir is supposed to have then asked to read the novel, which he judged to be "appealing" and which he agreed to use as inspiration "on the condition that I can forget the first screenplay and write another one from it."[51] At first, Renoir worked on the new version with Hugo Butler, to the rhythm of daily sessions over several weeks; and Renoir regularly asked the opinion of Dudley Nichols as they went along. Nichols intervened mostly when it came to the dialogue, correcting lines and trying to anticipate the potential interferences of the censors at the Hays Office. Accordingly, in a letter that reproduced the telephone conversation they had just had, Nichols advised Renoir to avoid using the word *bugger,* informing him in the process that it came from the word *Bulgarian* but, in general, was used as a slang substitute for *sodomizer.*[52]

"The main reason why I am making *Hold Autumn in Your Hand,*" wrote Renoir in September 1944, "is my great confidence in everything that can seem of purely American inspiration applied to films made in America. I believe firmly that film's best interest is to remain local; in other words, we only describe well enough what we have before our eyes."[53]

The actors considered for the film at first were Joel McCrea and his wife, Frances Dee, whom the Renoirs invited to dinner several times, for example, on May 24 with Hugo Butler, and on July 7, when Robert Hakim and his wife also attended.[54] According to Renoir, McCrea and Dee expressed enthusiasm about the idea of working with him, until the day when they discovered the screenplay and let it be known that they didn't intend to play such characters. This would suggest that the two actors had accepted only because they wanted to work with Renoir and had known nothing about the film that he was preparing. Perhaps. One thing is certain, and that is the fact that, after having thought of Dana Andrews to replace Joel McCrea, Renoir accepted the offer made by the executive producer Sam Rheiner to cast Zachary Scott—on "loan" for fourteen weeks from Warner—and Betty Field. Scott had just made his film debut in *The Mask of Dimitrios* by Jean Negulesco, and he'd attain stardom with his role opposite Joan Crawford in *Mildred Pierce*. Betty Field was most known for her performance five years before as the character Mae in *Of Mice and Men,* an adaptation by Lewis Milestone of Steinbeck's novel.

According to Renoir, Joel McCrea and Frances Dee's defection had caused United Artists Corporation to want to pull away, but in reality it seems that this impulse had been triggered by a clause in the agreement between the company, which was then in very bad financial health, and David L. Loew, who provided exclusively for the distribution of films produced by United Artists. And yet, *Hold Autumn in Your Hand* (the film adaptation would be named *The Southerner*) was only to be coproduced by Loew, in partnership with the Hakim brothers, and the higher-ups at United were afraid that Loew would not grant the production all the desired attention. This fear was, in fact, not unfounded, and the producer soon ceased to see the project as a priority; but an agreement would be reached between United Artists, on the one hand, and Loew-Hakim Inc., on the other, with financing guaranteed by Bank of America.

The credits for this film are a poor indication of the genesis of the screenplay, which credits Hugo Butler for the adaptation of the George Sessions Perry novel and Renoir for the screenplay and the direction, with the film presented as "A Jean Renoir production." Just as the part of Butler's work that ended up in the final film remains subject to question, the contributions of the various writers invited to pore one after another over the screenplay are difficult to measure. It seems to be the case that the first to intervene was Nunnally Johnson. Renoir had met him at Fox and had expressed a strong desire to work with the screenwriter of *The Grapes of Wrath*. Both the setting and the very nature of the novel *Hold Autumn in Your Hand* offered him the opportunity to realize this desire. (When his book had appeared, several reviewers compared George Sessions Perry to Steinbeck.) Just as naturally, Renoir had asked for another Southern writer who would be capable of writing dialogue for him, because his own knowledge of the language and life of the South was too limited for him to accomplish this with authenticity.

William Faulkner had moved to Hollywood in 1932 and was growing bored. He stayed there as little as possible, and in December he obtained permission from Warner, with which he had signed a seven-year contract in 1942, to spend only six months a year there. He would soon undertake the adaptation of Raymond Chandler's *The Big Sleep,* one of the rare contributions for which he would receive official credit, thanks in part to the admiration and affection for him of Howard Hawks, who'd also succeeded in getting his name in the credits for *To Have and Have Not.* On the other hand, although Faulkner did work on *Mildred Pierce,* which could substantiate the thesis that it was Zachary Scott who requested he work on *Hold Autumn in Your Hand, Mildred Pierce* was released without his participation recognized. This was also the case for Renoir's film, but at least there was a reason for it: his contract with Warner assured them exclusivity when it came to his collaborations.

According to Zachary Scott, it was because Nunnally Johnson wasn't available to make the changes Renoir wanted that they called Faulkner to the rescue. Faulkner considered the director to be a master; and at their first meeting at the end of the summer, he spoke a few words in French. A few days later, the writer handed over to Renoir the screenplay he had reworked, along with some notes and sketches of dialogue. Faulkner is supposed to have said that he'd worked on the scene in which Sam Tucker lights the stove in the house for the first time and had also rewritten another scene that is essential to the story, which shows Sam catching the catfish that his neighbor had coveted for years and named "Lead Pencil." Although Zachary Scott has claimed that Faulkner wrote the entire screenplay,[55] Faulkner's contribution was, then, relatively limited.[56] Using the actor's claims to shore up an otherwise highly contestable thesis about the notion of the film auteur, Gore Vidal would maintain without offering any genesis of proof that Renoir had taken complete credit for a screenplay that he hadn't written,[57] an allegation he was to return to and say, "Renoir was a man who had great trouble speaking English, much less writing it, and the script was written by William Faulkner. According to Zachary Scott, who acted in it, Faulkner really liked the script and would have been pleased to have had the credit. But Renoir so muddled the business that the credit finally read: 'Screenplay by Jean Renoir.' That was a great heist."[58]

In June 1977, in response to a request coming from Missouri for a documentary being made on Faulkner, Renoir would write that he "would have been very proud to collaborate with William Faulkner, but in fact his contribution was limited to the addition of a few Southern expressions."[59] Jean Renoir's 1944 appointment book reveals that the director and the writer met at least four times between July 25 and August 7,* for cocktails or dinner, sometimes with Robert Hakim and Robert Aldrich.[60]

Zachary Scott remained very close to Renoir and dined frequently at his home. In 1945, Renoir would be asked to direct *The Life of Robert Benjamin Masterson*, and would note down at the time that it was about "the life of Zachary Scott's grandfather, pioneer ranchman of the [*sic*] Texas [*these last six words were in English*]."[61] And in 1961, Zachary Scott would write to Renoir to propose that he bring *Light in August* to the screen, Scott having just bought the rights.[62] Clifford Odets, whom Renoir offered the opportunity to write the adaptation, expressed enthusiasm but thought that "if Zachary Scott wants to play the role of Christmas, everything is jeopardized."[63]

After Butler, Renoir, Johnson, and Faulkner, a fifth screenwriter, John Huston (whose involvement is based on the claim of producer Sam Rheiner),[64] was brought in to polish the finished screenplay for *Hold Autumn in Your Hand*. There's no proof to the claim that George Sessions Perry became associated with the project in one way or another. Hired as a war correspondent, he was in Europe at the time and would return traumatized by what he had experienced, especially in regard to what had happened in Salerno. Thanks to the money he earned from his articles, at the end of the forties he would buy some land to create a farm, motivated by his desire to follow in the footsteps of Sam Tucker in *Hold Autumn in Your Hand*. The plan failed, he began to drink, and, by the start of the fifties, the first signs of a mental illness began to emerge. In 1956, two months after he had disappeared, his body was discovered in a Connecticut river. The inquest concluded that he'd been the victim of an accidental drowning.

While Renoir and one or the other of his various temporary collaborators worked on the screenplay, Eugène Lourié was given the responsibility of scouting the locations. His research for this activity was taken from the novel and the first adaptation, which had been turned over to him by Hugo Butler in person,[65] a detail proving that Butler had not withdrawn from the project as soon as Renoir had become involved. During the summer, Lourié drove to Texas equipped with a 16-mm movie camera, which Renoir had asked him to use to film life in Rockdale—the setting for the novel—and especially the Saturday market there. Essentially, he was going to have to decide whether it was possible to shoot the film at that location, and he determined that the house described by the author wasn't going to work. Above all, gas rationing made shooting in Texas close to inconceivable. Called back urgently by production, Lourié arrived in California by plane, where he was informed that the General Service Studios, on Romaine

* On July 25 and 31 and August 3 and 7.

Street between Santa Monica and Las Palmas, had been reserved.

The year before, David Loew had taken control of that dilapidated outfit, which had been created in 1919 by one of Chaplin's collaborators. The year after he took over the place, he would use it to produce *A Night in Casablanca* with the Marx Brothers. For Renoir's film, trucks would unload the "Texan" dust that was required. As for the cotton fields . . . well, rosebushes had been planned, with balls of cotton solidly affixed to their thorns. Lourié began looking for a site, which he discovered near Madera, not far from Fresno in the San Joaquin Valley, on a lot that belonged to a community of Russian descent that was part of a sect that abstained from alcohol, smoking, and shaving. Renoir visited the place on May 30 and 31, and then on July 27 and 29. An agreement was made with the owners for a few handfuls of dollars, and Lourié had Sam Tucker's and his neighbor's houses constructed. It was a difficult undertaking because of the war rations on the use of wood. This led to the purchase and demolition of an old farm near Ventura and the transporting of its wood to the filming site. In addition, for the flood scene, Sam's house had to be able to be moved using tractors to the side of the river. Finally, the set designer oversaw the installation of a twenty-six-tent village for the crew and actors, as well as a large canvas shelter to serve as the canteen, where 120 meals could be prepared each time the company ate.

Offices located at General Service Studios were used to work out the production details and provided a place for the filming of interiors and scenes that took place in the little Texan town.* This was also where Renoir met his actors, including Norman Lloyd, the person who would play the wild and wicked Finlay. Lloyd would become one of Renoir's close friends. He was twenty-nine years old, hailed from Brooklyn, and had begun acting at a very young age, before being summoned to Hollywood after a New York meeting with Alfred Hitchcock when the director was in search of an unknown to play the "villain" who topples from the Statue of Liberty at the end of *Saboteur*. Lloyd would also become close to Hitchcock and ended up directing several episodes for the series *Alfred Hitchcock Presents*. He later became acquainted with Chaplin (and appeared in *Limelight*), produced the play *Life of Galileo* by Brecht (directed by Joseph Losey, with Charles Laughton), and filmed Renoir's play *Carola* for television. These are no more than highlights of an excessively prolific career. About to turn ninety-eight at the time of this writing, he had come no nearer a decision to retire from such activities.

At the start of summer 1944, Renoir introduced himself to Norman Lloyd

---

* In his memoirs, Eugène Lourié mistakenly located the shooting of these scenes in the studios at RKO.

in the guise of "a large Idaho potato farmer," wearing a Stetson and the most informal of outfits composed of linen trousers and an ordinary open-collar shirt.[66] He confided in Lloyd that the character he would play was far from being developed in the screenplay he was reworking. He was willing to let Lloyd read it in its present state but explained that, in any case, he had the firm intention of improvising a great deal. Their second meeting was the pretext for a discussion of the costume, and that was when the two men discovered a number of affinities in common.

For the shoot, which began the last week of September 1944 and ended on November 11, Renoir swapped his Stetson on certain days for a pith helmet. Sam Rheiner had had a screen installed. Each evening, two films were shown on it, a distraction that dissuaded the crew from breaking up as soon as night arrived. Actors and crewmembers played cards or dice. Every weekend David Loew and Robert Hakim visited. Aside from Eugène Lourié, the director had the advantage of the presence of another Frenchman, Lucien Andriot, who was the cinematographer. He had come to Hollywood in 1914 and each year had done the lighting for an average of a dozen films, most of them B pictures. Considered to be a decent technician, one of his claims to fame was having shot Dolores Del Rio in Raoul Walsh's *The Loves of Carmen* (1927). One of the most well-known remarks attributed to a head cameraman came from him: to an actress upset about his filming her less flatteringly than he had five years before, he responded, "My dear, unfortunately I am five years older now."* Renoir would hire him again for his next film. However, the current shoot would also lead to yet another encounter.

At twenty-six, Robert Aldrich was working on the film as first assistant director. Renoir had met him several times over the summer with Robert Hakim and, at least on one occasion, William Faulkner. This experience would serve as a baptism by fire for Aldrich, who until then had never served a more important function than second assistant director, and most often without appearing in the credits. During the shooting of *The Southerner* in October 1944, he would suggest that Renoir read the Dalton Trumbo novel *Johnny Got His Gun*,† which had been published five years before. A short summary of the book appears in the "project file" kept by Dido.[67] Afterward, Aldrich became the regular first assistant director for most of the productions of Enterprise, created after the war by David Loew. Thanks to Norman Lloyd, he would assist Chaplin on

* In France, the line is attributed to Christian Matras lighting Edwige Feuillère about ten years after having already photographed her.

† Dalton Trumbo would himself bring his book to the screen in 1970. The film received the Jury Prize at Cannes in 1971. When the film was released in France in November 1973, Renoir participated in its promotion.

Limelight before distinguishing himself as one of the most original and daring American directors of his generation.

Aldrich discovered an approach to filmmaking: "Renoir truly believed that a transfusion takes place from the physical surroundings to the performances and the picture itself. We would go on location, and he would walk up and down a riverside, for example, where we were to build the set, for two or three days. He would bring the actors there a week early, get them into costumes, and have them walk around barefoot. I found, as I grew older and directed pictures, that I didn't really have to walk barefoot on the land to appreciate how to shoot or not to shoot. But getting the actors there, on location or on the set—or on the stage, for that matter—and having them in costume, in their parts, seemed to me to make great sense."[68] Going further with his attempts at deciphering Renoir's technique, Aldrich also stated, "He's looking for truth in his own framework—but he wouldn't put it that way. On *The Southerner* he took the actors up to Stockton to get used to the country, he said. He was really trying to figure what the story was all about under the guise of having the actors get used to the farmers."[69]

Renoir found himself in nearly ideal conditions, or at least the best that he'd experienced since his arrival in Hollywood. No producer to monitor and direct him, as it had been with Zanuck and *Swamp Water;* material that suited him, unlike that of *The Amazing Mrs. Holliday;* no responsibility as producer, as had been the case with *This Land Is Mine.* The fact that David Lowe had ceased to believe in the film and had distanced himself only increased the director's freedom, all the more so because Sam Rheiner, the producer's representative, had been fighting for Renoir's cause, to the point at which the affair would mark the end of his collaboration and his friendship with Loew. On the other hand, Renoir's relationship with Loew would remain excellent, and the director wrote to his brother Claude that the film "happened under perfect conditions" and was "shot in a rare atmosphere of friendship and collaboration."[70] This was confirmed a few months later, when Renoir referred to *The Southerner* in a letter to Pierre Lestringuez as his "only work of a personal nature carried out in Hollywood," where all his other films "had been made under the worst conditions" with "all the means necessary for carrying them out, except for freedom."[71].

Renoir used the freedom that he was enjoying on American soil for the first time to direct a film that was fundamentally American. On his own he seems to have given up the tracking shots as a fundamental technique that had so enraged Zanuck. Most of the time, the camera was static, and when it did begin to move, it generally did so to accompany the movement of actors. More than in any of his previous films, the editing turned out to have cardinal importance, adopting the role that the director had ordinarily reserved for the camera. Especially in the scenes showing action, a dynamic was created by alternating shots that were of surprising brevity for the maker of *The Rules of the Game*.

The geographical location of the story and the essential thematic and visual elements had led him to an approach that resembled John Ford's for *The Grapes of Wrath* and *Tobacco Road*. Character portrayal was distinguished substantially by a desire for simplification. Conflicts were clearly delineated, and plot reversals were announced in advance. Only Norman Lloyd's portrayal gave rise to a bit of murkiness. All the rest of the characters stuck to their parts, and the director stayed with the specific requirements he had planned in advance. Zachary Scott was made to represent the hero and was filmed that way, and he fulfilled that assignment at all times in his open shirt and flattering lock of hair. His status as an object of desire for every woman he met was clearly displayed and expressed, although as an actor he lacked a bit of the subtlety that Joel McCrea might have been able to bring to the character. Throughout the film, Betty Field was dressed, coiffed, and made up with an impeccable elegance. She would later regret not having been in a good enough state of mind to have given the best of herself.[72]

The film is interesting for its sense of balance, moving from the specific, the "here and now," to the general concept of "all times and all places." It is rooted in a reality that is carefully depicted, even if Texas had to be moved to California, something Renoir intended to exceed, and even to outstrip, by creating a picture of human existence painted with the colors of eternity. These elements—more than any dramatic art—are what sustain the film. Earth, water, wind, and fire are the intricate motifs that punctuate and feed the narrative just like the naïve images of the calendar ticking off the seasons articulate it. Such is the strength of this film, but also its weakness. Renoir distances himself from the reality he has chosen to describe to offer a meditation in the lineage of great silent classics such as Sjöström's *The Wind*, Murnau's *Sunrise* or, even more, *City Girl*, as well as King Vidor's thirties masterpiece, *Our Daily Bread*.

But *The Southerner* is not the product of the same kind of inspiration as these masterpieces, and this brings up the question of whether the choice Renoir made wasn't actually by default. His lack of knowledge of the reality that he was claiming to depict made him ill at ease and, as is often the case in such conditions, led him to depend on abstractions. Whereas he had no very profound knowledge of the life of the immigrants he portrayed in *Toni* and hardly sustained any intimacy with the workers in *The Crime of Monsieur Lange*, those characters developed in a milieu that was relatively familiar to him and expressed themselves in a language that was his. This time it was not the case, and the people in *The Southerner* are less like characters than archetypes, a quality that was present in the novel but accentuated by the film.

This is clearly revealed by the scene between the farmer and the man from the cities. It is reduced to a confrontation resolved by the rather unimaginative claim that each of the two needs the other, mostly on the grounds that "your plow, she sure didn't grow on no tree." The end of the film, which shows the couple victorious despite everything, because they have decided to remain on their land, matches the conclusion of the book; but originally George Sessions Perry had planned for Sam to be forced to abandon his farm and become a worker, a development considered too pessimistic by his editors, who persuaded him to give up the idea.[73]

The makers of the film certainly had no reason to worry about such a change, of which they were probably unaware. However, it allows us to gauge the shift created by the adaptation, from a description anchored in a given reality, the Great Depression, to a meditation on the ancestral facts of the life of human beings. Obviously, *The Southerner* is further away from *Toni*, aside from certain appearances, than it is from *The River*, especially; and that truly does make it a transitional film. When Renoir made *Toni*, *The Crime of Monsieur Lange*, and *Grand Illusion*, attentive and scrupulous study of the particulars allowed him to aspire to and attain the universal, an alchemy that his uprooted situation in 1944 would keep him from doing from then on.* This uprooting entailed an isolation that caused him to turn away from the present and led him to a rather generalized reflection about the nature of the world, in line with what had inspired him when he wrote the commentary for *The Spanish Earth*.

However, this wasn't his intention, at least if we believe the statement he made just before a screening of *The Southerner* at RKO: "In this story, which is more American than everything that has been shown over the last few years, I have tried with all my love for the country that has welcomed me to express the feelings of a Frenchman for a problem that is extremely local."[74] A little less than thirty years later, his description of the project would take on a different coloration, and the issue would change from being "extremely local" to something cosmic: "I was anticipating a story in which every element would fulfill its function brilliantly, in which things and people, animals and nature could come together in an immense homage to the divinity."[75]

His changing the title in the spring of 1945 was going to lead to more confusion. On January 31, David Loew informed Renoir that the people at United Artists, the distributor, were convinced that the film would win the Oscar and that Renoir would be chosen Best Director; but *Hold Autumn in Your Hand* was not a good title to use to market the film.[76] In his answer to this, which is dated February 5, Renoir said that he was convinced that the title, whatever it would

---

* This is a thesis championed most notably by William Harry Gilcher.

be, had to be simple and concise, and that it was advisable to avoid using the word "Texas" at any price. His suggestions were *Fortitude* or *The Tucker Clan*.[77] However, in becoming *The Southerner*, a title that was probably chosen by the distributor, the film ended up being designated as the portrait of a man of the South, which it actually was not claiming to be and could not be. This also produced the impetus to expose it to charges of inauthenticity, the very thing that Renoir thought would happen when he asked that the word "Texas" be banished from the title.

James Agee focused on this issue once again. After hailing the "many good things" in the film, he rather violently exposed what he saw as its failings: "Just as unfortunate and more constantly disappointing, most of the players are wrong, anywhere from a little bit to a whole world wide of the mark. . . . They didn't walk right, stand right, eat right, sound right, or look right, and, as bad or worse, behind the work of each it was clear that the basic understanding and the basic emotional and mental—or merely human—attitudes were wrong, to the point of unintentional insult."[78]

It is true that "Agee's objections to the film are the same ones that Renoir might have made to a similar film had it been made in France ten years earlier or to any American's attempt to come to France and make *Farrebique*."[79] But, even taking that into account, other members of Renoir's profession felt very differently about the film. For example, the Southerner Robert Parrish, who would direct the film *The Wonderful Country* (1959), was among those who thought that no one would have known how to capture the spirit of the South better than Renoir had with *The Southerner*. Parrish also stated that when he later asked Renoir how he had achieved this marvel, Renoir had answered that his knowledge of peasants was the sole cause of it and added that the case had been the same for *The River*.[80] And that is a film in which peasants barely appear at all.

The fact that *The Southerner* was banned in Memphis, Tennessee, doesn't mean that this portrait of the people of the South had offended them. The measure was initiated by one of the wackiest censors in the history of film: Lloyd T. Binford, who ruled over the Memphis Censor Board with an iron hand from 1928 to 1955. He would also ban Chaplin's films, because of the taste displayed by their director for young girls; all productions that mentioned Jesse James;† the films of Ingrid Bergman, because she was living in sin; and *Rebel without*

---

* A semidocumentary film by Georges Rouquier about a family of peasants from Aveyron (1946).

† At the age of sixteen, Lloyd T. Binford had worked for the Illinois Central Railroad, and one of his colleagues had been killed before his eyes by an emulator of the famous gunman.

a Cause, because it sang the praises of juvenile delinquency.[81] Passed in mid-July 1945, the ban was lifted a month later. Because the first decision hadn't been justified, the second didn't have to be. However, apparently, Binford, who had decreed the banning of *Brewster's Millions* (Allan Dwan) and a rerelease of *Imitation of Life* (John M. Stahl, 1934), because both had scenes portraying relationships between whites and blacks, had found fault in Renoir's film especially for its "depiction of poor white Southerners and, more importantly, the cotton's economy reliance on farm tenancy."[82]

The only effect produced by this short-lived ban was that Memphis theaters showing *The Southerner* filled up more quickly than their owners had hoped. But regardless, the film would have been able to surpass this unintentional boost from being under the spotlight, and it rapidly became a hit. Starting on August 25, 1945, the 1,180-seat Globe Theater on Broadway, in New York, where *Swamp Water* had played, was able to keep showing the film for three weeks, a remarkable run for a modest production without stars. For the first time since his arrival in the United States, Renoir had the best reasons to appear satisfied with the development of his career. "If *The Southerner* makes money, it would be a great deal for me, because I worked for a percentage,"[83] he had written a few weeks before. The film was a happy compromise between his personal ambition and his desire to establish himself as an American director, and it earned him the award for Best Director of 1945 from the National Board of Review and received three nominations for an Oscar —Best Director, Best Sound Recording (Jack Whitney), and Best Dramatic or Comedy Score (Werner Janssen). For Best Director, Renoir found himself competing with Clarence Brown (*National Velvet*), Alfred Hitchcock (*Spellbound*), Leo McCarey (*The Bells of St. Mary's*), and Billy Wilder (*The Lost Weekend*), who was the one to carry off the Oscar.*

However, before the granting of these various distinctions, and even before the film had been released to theaters, Renoir had gone back to the studios at General Service, where he was directing one of his oldest projects.

---

* Renoir's own ballot was saved and is blank, indicating that he did not vote for anyone.

26

Endgame

The Diary of a Chambermaid
The Woman on the Beach

In August 1945, the old studios on Romaine Street were filled with echoes heralding the impending end of the war. Taking advantage of a short break, Renoir described the atmosphere for Paul Cézanne: "I'm writing you from the studio, and while my thoughts are with you and yours, my ears are ringing with sound flooding from the radio giving us the latest war news. The workers have set up a radio on the set, and whenever they have the chance, they crowd around it to listen, hoping for good news. Most of them have children or brothers who are fighting far away, and the hope for the imminent return of those dear to them is making everyone, including me, rather nervous."[1]

During the final weeks of 1944, contact with Europe had been partly reestablished, but it could sometimes take several months for communications to make it across the Atlantic, and at first Renoir received little more than a few telegrams and postcards. He complained about it in a letter to his brother Claude, in which he also told about his projects that included "a film on the Resistance fighters," for which he wanted Claude to serve as technical adviser, which would entail his coming to Los Angeles. He also mentioned an adaptation of the Conrad novel *Under Western Eyes,* which he'd been considering since 1943 as a "subject for Charles Boyer and Dudley Nichols,"[2] as well as the most developed of the three ideas, *The Diary of a Chambermaid.*[3]

One of the first letters that reached Renoir from France was from Claude, who was asking "permission to use the *Roméo et Juliette* you worked on with Lestringuez (the story of the heirs of a former actor who must perform *Romeo and Juliet* to receive their inheritance)." However, the bulk of the letter was news about France, tainted with enough bitterness to dissuade Renoir from returning there—that is, if the idea had ever crossed his mind. In his letter, Claude created

* In April 1944, Dudley Nichols would suggest to Renoir that he consider another Conrad novel, *The Secret Agent.*

the following picture of the state of French cinema: "I was wrong to join the Resistance instead of doing business with the Germans the way our pals did, because, in the end, the purge didn't last long, and the producers are the same people they were during the Occupation, meaning they were accepted by the Germans, and the members of the Resistance are barred." This was followed by a remark about Jean's former assistant, who was also one of his dearest friends, but whom Claude had already told his brother had "become an unapproachable pontiff."[4] "As you know, Jacques Becker is the great French director. He deserves it, but his producers are bankrupt, and that includes Desfontaines."[5]

It's difficult to imagine a delayed kick in the pants more magnificent than that one. On two occasions Jean Renoir expressed his feelings about Becker's work. In a letter to his brother Pierre, he claimed to have "really liked" *Goupi Mains rouges* [*It Happened at the Inn*] and admitted that his "only reservation was perhaps concerning a certain colorless, dull, and theoretical aspect,"[6] before writing to Claude that he considered the film to be "very good, but a little boring," explaining that "it seems as childish as what they're doing in Hollywood, but a lot more pretentious."[7] Shortly after the war, he also shared his opinion of the film with Carl Koch: "It wasn't bad, perhaps a bit *deliberate*, something you'd expect from a smart boy."[8]

Whereas Claude, who kept failing at everything he attempted, refused to admit that talented directors were now in the limelight that his brother had been forced, or had chosen, to abandon, Jean couldn't manage to get enthusiastic about the films of a colleague who was younger than he was, especially one who had been his assistant. All of it is very human in the most ordinary way. To Becker, Renoir would write that he had liked his film, "because it's a mournful expression of our defeat."[9] His motive for saying such a thing is hard to unravel.

If it is true what is sometimes said, that no portrait is as accurate as one drawn by a servant or a provider of goods, then, naturally, the relationship between Jean Renoir and his tailor sheds a special light on the personality of the former. Renoir's tailor was Steve Senyi, whose shop and tailoring place were on Fifth Avenue in New York. Each order produced a detailed letter written in French:

> I received your samples and have included with this letter the two I chose. I'd like you to use the cloth with the check pattern to make a jacket only. With the gray cloth, a jacket and two pairs of matching trousers. As my wife explained to you, these are for sportswear, or else something of that type. My idea would be to have the jackets cut like a sack coat—in other words, without any accentuated waist—and the

---

* His name was actually André Halley des Fontaines.

size a little fuller than a business suit. One row of buttons (probably five), whenever possible, not leather ones (leather buttons seem a bit "ready-to-wear" to me), and the turndown collar should close in a way that hides the shirt entirely. In France, that form of jacket is often called a hunting jacket. According to some of his photographs, Stalin appears to use it from time to time. I would like three right pockets with a flap, two large conventional ones and one small, as in a business jacket, not a patch pocket. I'm planning on using this clothing for my work in the studio and for exteriors. As you can see, I'm not talking about a copy of a sports jacket like the kind I could find in one of your *department stores* [*term in English*], but something more individual. I've included a poorly made little drawing that will give you a vague idea. To be honest, I'm counting more on your talent than on my indications.[10]

In this case, the casualness of the Renoirian touch, so highly and willingly vaunted by commentators, suddenly appears appreciably less conspicuous than expected, his *style negligé* nothing less than studied. And, having received the order, Dido didn't fail to question the professional about whether "changing the button" might easily take care of the problem of the "slightly too tight collar" of the sports jacket as well as inform him that "on the other hand we regret that you have forgotten that we like the buttons on the sleeves open, and not fake ones."[11] For someone whom flatterers would claim only the insistence of friends could have converted to tailor-made suits,[12] Renoir exhibits a demanding nature whose functioning is difficult to catch napping. His son allowed himself to be convinced of this fact, too, but only on one occasion, admitting that a salesman had certainly been right in promising that the trousers prepared especially for him would prove long-lasting—but only in the literal sense: they would never leave the closet where they'd been stowed as soon as they were taken from their box.[13]

In the spring, Renoir received a few letters from France. Ingrid Bergman wrote him from Paris, where she had visited Pierre and Claude. Paulette Goddard and Burgess Meredith had also stopped in Paris. The two actors had met on the set of *Second Chorus* in 1940 and had married on May 21, 1944, at the home of Irene and David O. Selznick, whose house was almost opposite Charles Chaplin's, the actress's former husband. On June 4, the young couple dined at Jean and Dido Renoir's, with Eugène Lourié and the director Lewis Milestone. In January 1945, Paulette Goddard had a miscarriage, after five months of pregnancy. The trip to London and Paris had been intended to help her recovery by making it possible for her to devote herself to her favorite activity, shopping. She had all the means necessary to accomplish that. Although her present husband was less rich than the former had been and the third—Erich Maria Remarque—would be, she herself was one of the richest women in Hollywood. The ten-year contract she'd signed with Paramount in May 1942 guaranteed her $85,000 per film, at the rate of one film a year, and permitted her to appear every year in one production of her choice outside of the studio. It was that particular clause that allowed her to work with Renoir.

He was dreaming of making a film with the heroine of *Modern Times* and *The Dictator;* and he had become connected with Burgess Meredith while working on *A Salute to France.* Coming to an agreement with Paulette Goddard turned out to be easy. It concerned one of his oldest projects, an adaptation of *Le Journal d'une femme de chambre.*‥ His desire to portray Célestine on film had never really evaporated since the twenties. It had still been a possibility when he had believed he would have to give up on *The Rules of the Game.* The theory that the idea had occurred to him during a conversation with Stroheim seems like a less convincing scenario.

It does, however, offer the advantage of an anecdote, said to have occurred during a dinner given by the Renoirs in honor of D. W. Griffith; among the more notable guests were Lillian and Dorothy Gish, the great silent film director Rex Ingram and his wife Alice Terry, and Stroheim. During the evening, Renoir is supposed to have asked Stroheim what film he would direct if he were free to choose one. Stroheim, without hesitating, named the novel by Octave Mirbeau, with Myrna Loy playing Célestine; Tully Marshall, the old fetishist; and he himself playing Joseph, the valet.[14] The dinner in question would have taken place in 1944, on November 13,[15] and it is a fact that the Griffiths, the Stroheims, and Lillian Gish were frequent guests of the Renoirs. Nevertheless, it's doubtful that Renoir would have needed Stroheim in order to think of *The Diary of a Chambermaid.*† It remains a fact that in December 1944, Renoir, Meredith, and Goddard were all in agreement concerning an adaptation of the novel by Mirbeau and celebrated their decision with a dinner given by the director at Chasen's,[16] a restaurant on Beverly Boulevard that was famous for its chili.

At first, RKO was going to produce the film, and Renoir and Dudley Nichols began their negotiations with them in February.[17] But Charles Koerner, the head of the studio, for whom Renoir had great regard, wasn't convinced by

---

* *Translator's note: The Diary of a Chambermaid,* Octave Mirbeau's decadent 1900 novel. The book indicts the bourgeoisie as described from the perspective of Célestine, a maid who reports on their perversions and moral foibles. The lower classes come out looking not much better, although Célestine considers them not quite as vile as their "decent" masters.

† A record created by Dido shows that *The Diary of a Chambermaid* had been suggested to Renoir in June 1942. She doesn't mention who made the suggestion and keeps her words to a minimum ("I won't sum up the action since Jean is completely familiar with it.").

the treatment for the film he received and didn't follow up on it. Renoir would write that RKO "suddenly appeared disgusted"[18] by the screenplay; nor would it please Darryl F. Zanuck, who described his opinion of it to Burgess Meredith: "The possibilities of the story are immense. The script is bad. The basic idea is fascinating and has great potentialities. These potentialities are not realized. I get the impression that is an almost literal adaptation from a French film or a French play and I feel that the translation is so completely literal that innumerable opportunities for characterization and humor as seen through American eyes have been lost."[19]

Exposed to the overcautiousness of the studios, the promoters of the project had no recourse but to imagine an independent solution through a company that they created themselves: Camden Productions was formed as an association among Paulette Goddard, Burgess Meredith, Jean Renoir, and Benedict Bogeaus. Although the first two members of this company did not lack money, the actress often seemed not to know what to do with hers and constantly declared that she was looking for investments, even opening an antique store with her husband in Pomona, New York. However, the most important contribution came from Benedict Bogeaus, and Renoir's participation remained symbolic.

Born in Chicago in 1904, Bogeaus had made a fortune in real estate and various other businesses. He had arrived in Hollywood in 1940, where he had purchased General Service Studios, transforming part of it into an arms factory and renting the sound stages to independent productions. In 1943, impressed by the profits that could be made in the movies, he had created his own company and produced *The Bridge of San Luis Rey,* the second adaptation of the Thornton Wilder novel. Two years later, he returned to take back control of General Service, which he had ceded to David Loew for a time. According to William Harry Gilcher, "Bogeaus' interest in *Diary of a Chambermaid* was purely financial; it seemed like an excellent business proposition since he, as one of the owners of Camden Productions, Inc. . . . could rent studio space from himself and thereby assure himself of some profit even if the film lost money in distribution."[20] He would borrow the capital needed for the film from Domestic Industries, a company in Chicago, as well as the First National Bank of Los Angeles. The budget was $900,000. The budget for *The Southerner* had been $612,000.

In his memoirs, Eugène Lourié shares his recollections of working with Renoir on the new adaptation of *Madame Bovary* for the Hakim brothers, producers for whom he was soon going to design the sets for *The Long Night* (the remake of *Le Jour se lève* directed by Anatole Litvak); yet Lourié skips any mention of *The Diary of a Chambermaid,* despite the fact that he was its art director. Nevertheless, he provides a few facts about its filming in other sources: "I wanted to build sets outside because there were a lot of them: there was the village square, a garden of one estate. Jean said to me: 'I don't want to be bothered by the sun, birds, neighbors, or noises. The acting is so important—try to build everything on the stage.'"[21] Renoir is then supposed to have said, "The truth of reality is not the truth of cinema."

Choosing to shoot in the studio, therefore, when scenes happening out-side—especially in gardens—could have been filmed in real gardens, is not a choice of no importance. Once again it confirms the fact that Renoir, contrary to what has often been claimed, actually valued working in such conditions. Production on the film began on July 9, and it ended on September 6.

Although the credits attribute the screenplay solely to Burgess Meredith, the truth is that several contributors participated in it. The only treatment that has been saved, fully 189 pages long, is the work of Renoir alone and is the first version of the film, completed in the early weeks of 1945.[22] It's an adaptation of the novel by Mirbeau and remains relatively close to it, but also borrows from the play based on the book and written by André Heuzé, André de Lordes, and Thiell Nores. It would change considerably. Renoir stated in June 1945 that he had "given up doing the *screenplay* [*term in English*]" and wanted to entrust the adaptation to Anita Loos, whom he claimed to "admire enormously."[23] An experienced screenwriter, Loos was also the best friend of Paulette Goddard, whom she'd indicate was the inspiration for her diamond-loving gold digger Lorelei Lee in *Gentlemen Prefer Blondes*. It's possible that Loos did collaborate on the screenplay for the film with Renoir, and Dudley Nichols—never far away—may have also lent a hand. According to the account Burgess Mere-dith gave years later, his work mostly involved translating the script, adapting Renoir's ideas for dialogues, and suggesting certain developments, always in line with the opinions of the director.[24] On the other hand, there is no doubt that the screenplay was heavily amended to meet the demands of the Production Code Administration (PCA). In her fascinating study of Renoir's American period, Elizabeth Ann Vitanza has established that these modifications, essen-tially having to do with sexuality, went so far as to contribute to transforming the project profoundly. The flashbacks, those evoking Célestine's past, especially, had to be abandoned, which "had the effect of coloring her character and indi-cating that she is hardly more than a cheap prostitute."[25] The fact that certain lines considered "daring" also had to be suppressed is a product of the censor's logic. Nevertheless, there still exists no way of explaining the fact that the end of the film as it was presented in documents submitted to the PCA before filming and apparently accepted at that time, depicting Louise stabbing Joseph in Cherbourg, differs from the ending that now appears on-screen,[26] in which Joseph is killed by the crowd during a Bastille Day celebration. Those diehard believers in improvisation could see this as supporting their theses, except for the rather important fact that Joseph's death scene in the film, particularly because it is full of walk-on performances, obviously required preparation and consequent organization.

The fact that Burgess Meredith was the only screenwriter credited both on-screen and in the different administrative documents that can be consulted reveals nothing about the sharing of responsibilities. It does, however, parallel the central position occupied by the actor, something that he himself does not fail to describe in his memoirs, which appeared when he was eighty-five, about four years before his death in 1997. "I had the privilege of writing a script with Jean Renoir, for *The Diary of a Chambermaid,* which he directed. I coproduced and acted in it and my wife, Paulette Goddard, played the lead." Throughout the entire shoot, either opposite or side by side with the person whom he took for "the greatest film director of all time," Burgess Meredith was going to play the role of the producer forced to remind the director of his obligations while maintaining jealous vigilance over the interests of his wife, the star, and his own. "I had the job of saying, 'We have to get back on schedule, Jean!' 'No,' said Renoir, 'what we have to do is to make a fine picture!'"[27]

What kind of freedom did Renoir have in such conditions? Renoir's official answer: "The film is good or it is bad, but if it's bad, I'm the only one responsible for it."[28] Renoir's less-considered, on-the-spot reaction: "The truth is that the production doesn't correspond altogether to my previous dreams. . . . Perhaps it will open the door to me to productions that are more completely personal."[29] Despite what that last sentence suggests, the film truly does seem as if it is completely personal, and it validates the decision taken by Renoir to direct it entirely in the studio.

With *The Southerner,* Renoir was attempting to manufacture myth by starting with reality. This time he was endeavoring to re-create a reality with the use of all the artifices belonging to film. To accomplish this alchemical process that was in some way the inverse of his prior accomplishment, he made use of the weapons he'd already summoned for *The Rules of the Game,* all of which reappear in *The Diary of a Chambermaid,* not only on the thematic level—servants and masters, decadence of a social class—but also stylistically. The movement of the characters from one room, house, or world to another was one of the film's essential motifs. Naturally, it required a high degree of mobility from the camera. This aspect of the film was probably at the origin of his choice to shoot in the studio, or it was at least as motivating a reason for doing so as those he had expressed and Lourié reported. Thanks to it, the film clearly became a masterwork of great maturity, but it was out of sync with the dominant Hollywood principles of the forties, and Zanuck had become aware of that when he read the screenplay. In terms of its mentality and its construction, *The Diary of a Chambermaid* also most closely resembled the masterpieces that had inspired Renoir's vocation, with the films of Stroheim and Griffith at the top of that list.

Among the American characteristics of the film is its use of a nearly omnipresent musical score, which takes on the quality of a potpourri of old-fashioned standards from the repertoire of the popular French *chanson*, with such familiar titles as "J'ai du bon tabac," "Il pleut, il pleut bergère," "Do l'enfant do," and others, interwoven with "Fascination" in the guise of a ritornello. The score is the work of the French composer of Ukrainian origin, Michel Michelet, who had come to live in Hollywood in 1940. Michelet was yet another member of the French contingent associated with the film, which included Eugène Lourié, the head cameraman Lucien Andriot, and, of course, Renoir. When it came to leading a team, Renoir proved himself to be just as skillful at it in Hollywood as he had been in France. He had the knack of creating an atmosphere of enthusiasm around himself and the film, and it enthralled the American actors and crew, who were used to relating with less warmth. All those who were asked to express themselves about the subject declared their agreement with Burgess Meredith's feelings about it: "Enthusiasm was his main quality. I've never known a man who was so great a teacher; that is to say, his enthusiasm swept you along with whatever he did. He excited everyone. His ideas were always valid and way ahead of anybody. . . . It also was always fun. And the wine and the companionship were as great a part of it as the actual making of the film."[30]

The paradox of *Diary* comes from the fact that Renoir turned away from realism in favor of an assumed theatricality. Starting with a naturalist novel, he could not have been unaware that filming such a thing in Hollywood, in English and with American actors, had to radically disrupt the setup. It's also just as tempting to maintain that Renoir had no other choice than the one upon which he settled, and that the nature of the film is the product of such a contradiction. The adaptation condenses and shifts the episodes in the novel and on occasion modifies the power struggles. Above all, although she remains the narrator, Renoir's Célestine turns out to be infinitely less venomous, dubious, and troubling than Mirbeau's version of her as well as the Célestine that Jeanne Moreau and Luis Buñuel would create together.

Paulette Goddard kept her hair dyed blond, which she had done for her preceding film, *Kitty*, by Mitchell Leisen, in which she had played a girl from the outskirts of London in the eighteenth century who became a society lady after her portrait was painted by Gainsborough. Nor did she shed her reserve as a Hollywood star. Her Célestine forces us to like her because she's a good girl, attentive to others, and an enemy of conventions. Her appearance allows her to capture attention, but her characterization lacks complexity.

Those moving around her are less characters than figures, attitudes. In the role of Mauger, the old rock-throwing captain and eater of the flowers in his garden, Burgess Meredith is constantly hopping up and down and running in every direction, as if he wants to justify the nickname "my baby" given to him by his maid and mistress. The other characters are modeled in the same way, more like types identifiable at first glance than compositions, with the exception of Joseph the valet, whom Célestine calls an undertaker and whom all condemn for his cruel method of executing geese to give their flesh an exceptional and appetizing flavor. Francis Lederer* manages to create a strong characterization of Joseph, which produces a feeling of unease in both the viewer and Célestine that is otherwise lacking for a long time in the film, until the very long, magnificent sequence of Bastille Day, July 14. On that day, which the Lanlaire family† sees as "France's ruin," Joseph puts his cards on the table and Renoir gets back in stride. A mad wind takes hold of the film, ultimately determining the two impressive crane shots, one in front to catch the death of the valet and the other in back to show the crowd that has come together.

But before this dazzling finale, the film seems to have found itself. It is in the scene of the celebration that Burgess Meredith's monkey-like behavior finds its reason for being. The confrontation between the valet and his mistress (Judith Anderson, in a very impressive performance) about the valuables he insists on carrying off, which she defends each and every inch of the way, is, by itself, a stupendous moment. Movements of the characters through a set whose intelligent construction has suddenly become obvious are revealed with astounding virtuosity. The Bastille Day scene in *The Diary of a Chambermaid* constitutes one of the great moments of the cinema of Jean Renoir and may be the highest point of his American period. At that instant, we witness the postponed validation of the perspective of the film's direction, a blazing moment filled with the revelation of the profound wickedness of a film in which all the characters, one by one and also as a whole, with the possible exception of Célestine, reveal how absolutely detestable they are.

The question truly is one of wickedness, and Renoir's view of human nature is as completely devoid of complaisance as it was in several of his films from

* Born November 6, 1899, in Austria-Hungary, František Lederer was best known as one of the actors in Pabst's *Pandora's Box* (1929). He continued to offer classes at the American National Academy of Performing Arts, which he had founded, until his death at age 100 on May 25, 2000.

† *Translator's note:* The family for whom Célestine works as a chambermaid in the film.

the thirties—especially *La Chienne*. The spectacle of living turns grotesque, or at least that is how Renoir chooses to depict it. And this is the same man who spent such a long time hiding how little respect he felt for the behavior of the human species under his image of "regular guy," perfecting that image with the same care he applied to monitoring the tailoring of his suits. The cruelty that he intended to depict with *Nana* was achieved with *The Diary of a Chambermaid*, even if it was expressed in a way that, at first, may appear a bit too "deliberate," sought. It was no way to charm American audiences in 1946, either.

The fact that Renoir wrote to Goddard and Meredith to say he was very satisfied with the screening organized at the beginning of November in a Fox theater in Inglewood doesn't tell us much. It's obvious that at the time the director was addressing his sponsors and could only display confidence. However, even then he had to admit having made a few changes. "After the first preview, I cut a little of Francis and certain other things which caused the public to laugh. They followed the picture so intently that any small mistake becomes grave, and I had to be very severe. Now, they still follow it with passion, but they do not laugh at the wrong moments."[31] The account given by a reporter about a preview organized after reediting appears to show the opposite—that the changes had hardly any effect on the audience's attitude. "There was laughter and kidding applause in unwanted places, while dead silences greeted sequences obviously intended to amuse."[32] Renoir had not attended that screening in January, but Dido had gone with Ingrid Bergman.[33]

Renoir was mistaken when he wrote to Sam Siritzky, "From a commercial point of view, I think that *The Diary of a Chambermaid* will be fantastic." The results, in fact, were only decent. The release of the film was spread out from February 1946 in Chicago to the end of June in Los Angeles and New York. In general, the figures for the second and third weeks did not confirm the good impression produced by those of the first week, which was proof that audiences weren't finding on the screen what they were expecting to see, which the advertising for the film claimed it was selling. Paulette Goddard's bare shoulders on the poster and the slogan having Célestine say, "Men have used me—now I'm going to use men" certainly promised a lot to audiences, who could start out enticed by this story that was "so French." And yet, the film actually offered nothing that was titillating. It was a somber farce in which desire had little place, and its heroine left at the end with a man whose illness would soon condemn him to death, echoing the character Catherine in Renoir's first film. Renoir was also hoping that the film would play a role "in my American career that would be a little like the one *The Crime of Monsieur Lange* had played in my French career."[34] In that sense, as well, it was not the case. A few months of distance caused him to say about the project, "We were all too close as friends, and it didn't at all work as I would have wanted it to."[35]

On the other hand, the film would have a second career on American television, bringing Renoir, as he would state, "a lot of money."[36] Even today, of all Renoir's films, *The Diary of a Chambermaid* is one of those that American channels specializing in such shows air with the most regularity.

In 1946, Renoir had the good luck to be able to go back to work before the release of *Diary*, even if the experience that would come next would put an end to his hopes for America. While this was happening, others like him who had left France in 1940 were thinking only of going back, whereas he was busy laying the foundation of a permanent life in California.

The France of *The Diary of a Chambermaid* wasn't France; yet, in a sense, it was. One of the most interesting readings of the film saw implicit in it a picture of postwar France, with its settling of scores, its resentments, and its rivalries. What Renoir knew about that reality he could only imagine through the letters he received in California, but those from his brother Claude, especially, were certainly the kind to darken his vision. The film is also evidence of the fact that Renoir had remained French, while at the same time no longer being so. He had chosen to become an American, but contrary to what he perhaps thought then, as well as what would be claimed, he was not enjoying double nationality. On October 15, 1944, he had his name, as well as those of Dido and Alain, placed on the list of French people residing in California and wanting to return one day to France.[37] In February 1945, he wrote to Louis Guillaume, "As for me, I'm dying to return to France, because at fifty you can't change your habits." But in that same letter, he also wrote, "It seems to me that since we've lived comfortably in America, it would be out of place for us to compete with comrades who were less fortunate than us during these last few years."[38] Above all, he refused to think about leaving as long as Alain hadn't come back from the war.

In mid-December 1945, Alain would return after two and a half years of war in the Pacific, in the light artillery. Somewhere in the Philippines, he had become an American citizen. Later, he had been recommended to receive the Congressional Medal of Honor. On several occasions, he had thought his hour had come. In New Guinea, he felt it more than anywhere else, and more than ever on that day when he was near a village that amounted to six straw huts on stilts, and was imprisoned in a shell-crater that was too cramped to be able to sit or stand, and isolated among the Japanese. That was when he thought of the book to which his father was so attached, a beautiful edition of *Roland furieux* illustrated by Gustave Doré, which had disappeared from the shelves of the apartment on avenue Frochot. Jean had been convinced that his son had taken it to sell and strongly reprimanded him. Alain, who did have the habit of dipping his hands into his father's perpetually well-stocked pockets, knew that the expensive volume had been stolen by the maid's nephew and had refused to squeal. On that day in New Guinea, with water up to his chest, the thought occurred to him that his father would never know that he hadn't stolen his *Roland furieux*. And, actually, Jean Renoir would never learn that he hadn't, because afterward Alain had chosen to say nothing about it, fearing that his father would interpret the disclosure as a reproach. It was only after Jean's death that he told the story to Dido.[39]

In fall 1945, Renoir received a proposition from Joan Bennett. For the last six years, the actress had been the wife of the producer Walter Wanger, who was her third husband and someone with whom Renoir had been involved on several occasions, mostly through Dudley Nichols. In addition, the two couples—the Renoirs and Bennett and Wanger—had encountered each other from time to time. A few months earlier, Bennett and Wanger had created a production company with Fritz Lang—Diana Production, which was named after Bennett's eldest daughter. The new company's first film, *Scarlett Street*, had been a new adaptation of La Fouchardière's novel *La Chienne*. Fritz Lang admitted having seen Renoir's version in Germany, and he'd purposely avoided seeing the film again before directing his version, for which Dudley Nichols had been one of the authors of the screenplay. Apparently, Lang had tried to get hold of a copy of the Renoir film, but there is no proof that the search for it was successful.[40]

The story of the genesis of the film that Renoir would make with Joan Bennett comes in a variety of versions depending on the different points of view. To start, there is the star's version, or at least the way it has been phrased by Hollywood-style commentators, who by nature are careful to sugarcoat things when it comes to dealing with a legend. According to them, while looking for subjects for Diana Production and for herself, Joan Bennett had read a psychological thriller by Mitchell Wilson entitled *None So Blind* and said that she was sure that it would make a very good film for her and Lang.[41] But Wanger tells it differently. According to him, Bennett appealed to RKO, who bought the rights to the book and then proposed that Renoir direct it; and Renoir stated that he'd be thrilled to work with her and signed a contract for two films with RKO. Unfortunately, only the last phase of the process claimed by that version of the facts conforms to reality.

The RKO archives contain documents making it possible to establish part of the truth. They reveal that the company's interest in the project occurred before the novel was published. In fact, in June 1944, which is even before the first appearance of *None So Blind* on November 18, where it was serialized in *Collier's*, Mitchell Wilson had submitted a first draft of his story to RKO executives, who wanted him to make a certain number of changes.[42] The definitive text of the novel was given to RKO in September. In January 1945, someone named Michael Hogan delivered the first version of an adaptation. The project, which kept the novel's title, was entrusted to one of the most unusual and talented producers in the history of film.

Val Lewton was a longtime collaborator of David O. Selznick, for whom one of his more noteworthy services was the writing of several scenes for *Gone with the Wind*, including the one showing Atlanta burning. Lewton was also one of the rare producers who could legitimately be termed a creator. Born in Yalta in 1904, in 1942 he was thirty-eight when he joined RKO for the purpose of producing horror films. Whether they were billed as having been directed by Jacques Tourneur,[*] Mark Robson,[†] or Robert Wise,[‡] the masterpieces that he produced exhibited his influence at least as much as that of the directors. Lewton watched over every stage of the process, from the writing of the screenplay, whose definitive version was always established by him, to the promotion of the film.

The adaptation of *None So Blind* was signed by an unknown, and this is the only text on record, so it's tempting to come up with an off-the-wall hypothesis regarding its authorship. Although Val Lewton worked on the screenplays for all of his films and always wrote them in collaboration with talented authors, and although he identified himself as a "writer-producer," he would refuse to be listed that way in the credits, on the grounds that a lot of others, who weren't writing a single line, took the same kind of credit to receive the fee. To avoid being associated with them, he would sometimes use a pseudonym that today has been identified as "Carlos Keith." In the twenties and thirties, he had written novels[§] under the name "Cosmo Forbes" or "Herbert Kerkow"; and although there is no proof that he also concealed his identity under the name "J. R. Michael Hogan," nothing has ever been discovered to disprove it. However, it is more than probable that the screenplay was actually the work of several writers, and Lewton himself may have been one of them.

[*] *Cat People*, with Simone Simon; *I Walked with a Zombie*; and *The Leopard Man*.

[†] *The Seventh Victim, The Ghost Ship, Isle of the Dead*, and *Bedlam*.

[‡] *The Curse of the Cat People* and *The Body Snatcher*.

[§] Nine of these novels have been identified and include *The Fateful Star Murder* (1931), *Where the Cobra Sings* (1932), and *No Bed of Her Own* (1932), which became the film *No Man of Her Own*, with Clark Gable and Carole Lombard. Finally, he also wrote a pornographic work called *Yasmina* (also known as *Grushenskaya*) and five essays, two of which were about Casanova and one of which was called *Manual and History of Cosmetics*.

In spring 1945, a decision was made—probably by Val Lewton—to offer Joan Bennett the lead, and it is true that she expressed a desire to have Renoir direct the film. It seems natural enough that the actress, who knew Renoir personally and who had just been involved in the remake of one of his films, had wanted to work with him. However, today we know that Val Lewton was strongly opposed to this desire. In a letter to Charles Koerner, the director of production at RKO, he wrote, "Miss Bennett's heart seems to be set on Renoir," but he put all his energy into trying to convince the actress that Lewis Allen was "from a practical standpoint, much more desirable than Renoir."[43] In addition to Lewis Allen, he would have also thought of Fred Zinnemann, Jacques Tourneur, Robert Wise, and Edward Dmytryk; but four months later, at the end of September, he surrendered to Joan Bennett's perseverance. Renoir would direct the film, which was now entitled *Desirable Woman*. Renoir's enthusiasm, as described to his brother Pierre in writing, seemed far from inflated: "My agents have stuck me with a film, at RKO, a studio where I'm dying of boredom."[44]

Renoir went to work on the screenplay with Lewton in the producer's house on Corsica Drive, which Lewton had bought in 1943 from the actor Jack Holt, taking advantage of a drop in prices on the coast provoked by a wave of panic about the threat of a Japanese attack that swept through the community of property owners.[45] According to the director, Lewton and he understood each other well until the producer decided to focus on "other projects that were more in keeping with his agenda and that obviously interested him more."[46] It's a plausible hypothesis.

Quite possibly, in fact, Lewton lost interest in a project for which he thought he lacked a suitable director. Just as he had not succeeded in making Joan Bennett see what he considered reason, he never managed to develop a rapport with Renoir. Renoir ended up declaring that if RKO didn't come round to his views as they were expressed by his version of the screenplay, he preferred to drop out of the project and was quite sure he could convince Joan Bennett to work with another director.[47] It's rather surprising that the producer gave in to the director, especially after having ceded to the actress's wishes; but during that same month of November 1945, Lewton had begun to suffer from a mild case of heart disease, which forced him to ease up on his previously manic activities. What is more, at the time he shared an office with the director Mark Robson. Lewton's section of that office was on the second floor, and the doctor had recommended that he avoid stairs. A few months later, he'd leave RKO for Paramount. A second cardiac attack, followed by a third two days later, would prove fatal. He died on March 14, 1951, at the age of forty-six.

Renoir no longer had any illusions about what might look like a personal victory but what was in reality only a compromise. A letter on November 22, 1945, to his brother Claude testifies to this. After having asked his brother for information about *La Symphonie pastorale* and *L'École des cocottes*,* two projects he was considering in the context of the independent production company he was thinking of setting up, he pointed out his agent's desire to see him working for the big studios despite the fact that they were places where he felt "too unhappy." He then added, "Even at RKO, which isn't one of the biggest, the slowness of preparation, the discussions regarding the screenplay, and especially the fact that the film isn't my film but the film of an anonymous group, make things very painful for me. I'm accepting this ordeal because it's necessary, but rather than continuing this way, I'd rather give up my profession and try to write books."[48]

The slowness Renoir deplored certainly was real. At the beginning of 1946,† when the upcoming direction of *Desirable Woman* was announced for the spring, it had already been postponed twice. But Renoir's strongest sentiment continued to be a stubbornly rooted certainty that, yet again, he wouldn't succeed in creating a personal work. And yet, as he himself claimed, RKO was a studio of human dimensions, or nearly so. In addition, he had already worked for the company and had the support of department head Charles Koerner, a man he trusted completely. After Val Lewton's defection, the production had been entrusted to Jack J. Gross, an experienced executive who'd come from Universal, whose specialty was horror films, who didn't bother with the creative aspects of production, and who was satisfied just managing issues having to do with organization and administration. With him, Renoir at least had the assurance that he would be free to do as he intended during the shoot. But on February 2, 1946, Charles Koerner died of leukemia, a tragic event that Renoir would blame for all the problems he encountered.

Renoir created a portrait of Koerner that seems at odds with the way others have described the producer's personality. According to Renoir, Koerner had once charmingly quipped, "Right now, every film is making money, even the good ones."[49] Koerner was, Renoir would maintain, "an extraordinary man," and if he had lived, Renoir would have "made twenty films at RKO." He would have "worked all my life at RKO, because he [Koerner] was a man who understood . . . who acknowledged that you could experiment."[50]

* *Translator's note: École des cocottes* ("School for Tarts," or " . . . for Coquettes," literally) is a play written by Paul Armont and Marcel Gerbidon and originally performed in Paris in 1918. It would be adapted twice as a film, in 1935 and in 1958.

† The final script for *Desirable Woman* is dated January 18, 1946. (Jean Renoir Papers, Production Files, Motion Picture Productions, Box 28, Folder 2.)

Appointed head of RKO's production department in 1942, Charles Koerner, who until then had directed the company's chain of movie theaters, immediately implemented a politics that differed radically from that of his predecessor, George Schaefer. Koerner promoted the production of B movies, a genre at which Val Lewton excelled. Putting an end to the studio's most ambitious projects, he quickly got rid of such elements as Orson Welles and his Mercury Theatre, even though Koerner's personal responsibility for the disastrous reedit of *The Magnificent Ambersons* couldn't absolutely be ruled out. One particular anecdote about Koerner provides a sufficient enough clue to his preoccupations. After seeing *Cat People*, he reproached Lewton for having betrayed him because there weren't enough shots showing the panther, which had cost a lot to rent. However, choosing to keep the appearances of the animal in the film rare is exactly what provides its originality and is the source of its effectiveness.

Renoir seems to have overvalued Koerner's importance after the fact, and the truth is that the producer had turned down several of his projects, including *The Diary of a Chambermaid*.[51] However, Renoir pinned the responsibility for the torments he'd endured on Koerner's disappearance, including those well before February 1946, as evidenced especially by the letter to his brother Pierre on November 22 of the preceding year. An incomprehensible slip of the tongue adds more to this mystery regarding the depth of his affections for those who managed RKO. Three times in *My Life and My Films*, Renoir referred to Charles Koerner by the name Jack Gross, a mistake that led him to pinpoint Gross's death as having occurred in February 1946, when in reality Gross lived until 1964.

Even before he began shooting, Renoir knew that he wouldn't be able, as he'd confirm after the project, to "attempt something that I'd wanted to do for a long time: a film about what you'd call sex today . . . but envisioned from the point of view of the purely physical," and that it would be impossible "to tell a story about love in which the reasons for attraction between the different parties were purely physical, a story in which sentiment would play no part at all."[52] Even if he were able to overcome the misgivings of his producers, the Production Code, to which all his projects had to be submitted, would not have allowed it. In the study she devoted to the film,[53] Janet Bergstrom shows that before Renoir's involvement, the adaptation had to have been greatly revised at the request of the Production Code Administration. In a letter to production, the censors had ranted, "Each [of the characters] is guilty of adultery. There are no compensating moral values indicating directly for these crimes, and, further, in the case of the male lead, the adultery is condoned."[54] It was after these interventions that the character who was Peggy's lover disappeared.

Renoir's first treatment, dated January 18, 1946, also had to be seriously amended. These series of redraftings suggest that Renoir had been able to become progressively less concerned with the film. Information confided by Joan Bennett about the director's not seeming very involved in this work and often allowing his assistants to take care of it[55] doesn't go very far in clarifying this issue. The actress was used to methods and behavior of a very different tenor than those exhibited by Renoir, such as Fritz Lang's, which were situated at the very opposite pole. But in addition, Renoir often declared himself "disgusted" with a project that for one reason or another he had originally judged to be "terrific," and in less problematic circumstances he'd been known to let things slide on the set.

There's nothing surprising about the fact that the filming of *Desirable Woman* proceeded peacefully, in an old studio that had been created by Charles Pathé. Part of Renoir's method was the atmosphere that he knew how to sustain on his set. The fact that Joan Bennett had been speaking French fluently since the age of fifteen added to Renoir's rapport with her. In 1935, she'd convinced her mother to let her finish her studies first in Paris and then in Versailles. Renoir enjoyed the fact that the actress "spent her days knitting," and it amused him to observe that "such a stay-at-home lady is thought of by the American leagues of decency to be the most dangerous femme fatale on the screen."[56] Opposite "such a stay-at-home lady," whose husband would shoot her lover in December 1951,* RKO cast Robert Ryan,† who'd been demobilized in November from the marine unit in which he'd served during the war. Also cast was the experienced Charles Bickford and the near-beginner Virginia Huston, who was twenty-one and who would soon play the character Ann Miller in Jacques Tourneur's *Out of the Past*.

Exterior filming was finished by the end of January, and the studio shoot took until March 30. A few days later, Renoir expressed his satisfaction. He had "rarely been so happy as in this production." He'd been "left alone as never before in making a film," even if, obviously, "that doesn't mean that the results will be perfect, because due to contracts with the actors, I had to begin filming without having done enough work on the screenplay."[57] He'd already expressed this misgiving in a letter to his brother Claude.[58] A few mistakes had been caught during filming, he went on, and he hoped "to catch others in the weeks

---

* The actors' agent Jennings Lang, who would survive but lose a testicle. ("And starting then," Norman Lloyd would state ironically, "he was no longer called Jennings Lang, but Jenning Lang.") The incident took place in the parking lot of MCA. Joan Bennett's career wouldn't recover from it.

† In 1956, Renoir would preface the French translation, published by Gallimard, of *La Cité des anges*, a novel by Jessica Ryan, the wife of Robert. In this preface, Renoir would emphasize the "great danger" threatening Hollywood: isolation.

to come, during editing." But regardless, Renoir stuck to his guns. "I can continue to tell you that the only thing I've done here that was worth the trouble was *The Southerner*."[59]

The film received approval from the Production Code on May 22, 1946. Although Renoir was not unaware that he wasn't finished with *Desirable Woman*, which hadn't yet undergone any test screenings, while also searching for a subject for Ingrid Bergman and Walter Wanger,[60] he went right into his project of an adaptation of *Madame Bovary* for Robert Hakim, who had made an agreement with RKO.[61] Aware that Flaubert's novel risked shocking the Production Code, whose meddling had caused important damage as much to *The Diary of a Chambermaid* as to *Desirable Woman*, Renoir met with the administration's director, Joseph Breen, in an attempt to ward off the objections of the censors. Robert Hakim went with him to his meetings and then Renoir wrote a long letter to the producer in which he reviewed the instructions.[62] It is not known whether the conversation during this interview had turned to Tom Breen, the son of Joseph who was trying to become an actor and whom Renoir would cast in his next film. But in this period at the beginning of summer 1946, Renoir had every reason to believe that, when it came to *Desirable Woman*, the most difficult and the longest were now behind him.

Nevertheless, at the end of August, the words Renoir used in speaking to his old friend Lestringuez about the film he had just directed, "which involves an older gentleman, a young man, and a woman," were filled with bitterness: "There was a novel, published and vaguely read, which is what made RKO decide to grant me the direction of a bad plot. I accepted, I don't know why, probably to pay my taxes, and that has added a few kilometers of film to the yearly clutch of our dear city."[63]

Aside from the fact that, during the period between July 26 and August 27, 1946, Renoir abandoned *Madame Bovary*, what else caused him to express such rejection of a film in which he'd only been moderately interested? What happened is that one of the test screenings of *Desirable Woman* became a disaster. Test screenings are often mandatory in Hollywood, and they generally become unpleasant—even painful—experiences for directors; but until then Renoir hadn't suffered very much from them. On August 2, 1946, RKO filled a Santa Barbara theater with an audience composed mostly of students. None of them, of course, according to the formula, knew what film he or she was going to see. A western? A musical comedy? Perhaps a horror film, which was RKO's specialty. It was none of those. Instead, it was the depiction of a trio of lovers composed of a beautiful young woman, a blind* older husband, and a young man traumatized by war. It was a story of confinement and isolation made by a European director, far from the style and principles to which audiences of that day were accustomed, not to mention that the age of the test audience already made them poor candidates for such an offer. The result was snickering, hooting, a spate of mockery, everything that ordinarily consists of turning something into a laughing stock. Consequently, there was panic at RKO, the film was considered not to be presentable in the state it was in and it had to be modified, torn to shreds, rewritten, have new scenes shot. It had to be turned into a film that would no longer have anything to do with the one that had been shown that black Friday. In the accounts Renoir would give of this misadventure, he'd insist that he himself took the initiative to modify the film radically, concerned as he was about turning it into an acceptable product because he was aware of his entire responsibility. Depending upon the various statements he would speak or write, he would describe the directors of RKO as "very happy"[64] about a film that "displeased them completely."[65]

Three weeks later, Renoir wrote to Alain that on the day after the "bad preview in Santa Barbara" that caused him to say the film was "turning into quite a catastrophe," he had "worked like a galley slave to edit and reedit." This new version would still require two weeks of effort; and if it still didn't work, he would ask "RKO to entrust the film to someone else."[66] Actually, "it didn't work," but the film also wouldn't be entrusted to someone else. On the other hand, it would undergo several assessments, including those of John Huston and Mark Robson,[67] as well as Walter Wanger, who would decide that the story was a double bore, certainly clumsy, and that there was no other solution than to rewrite it entirely.

Renoir got down to this task at the end of September 1946. This wasn't a question of making a work that was personal, but of delivering a product likely to suit an American audience. Coming right after the commercial failure of *The Diary of a Chambermaid*, a second setback would seriously endanger a career in which he set off *The Southerner* as "really the only thing that justifies my trip to America."[68] RKO assigned him a screenwriter, at his request, he would claim. His name was Frank Davis, and he was also a friend of Albert Lewin. Davis and Tess Slesinger, his wife, normally collaborated together, and they had recently written the screenplay for Elia Kazan's first film, *A Tree Grows in Brooklyn*. But Tess Slesinger had died on February 21, 1945, at the age of thirty-nine, and Frank Davis hadn't written anything since. In a letter to Robert Flaherty, Renoir

---

* In the novel, Tod pretends to be blind. In the film, a scene shows Scott putting Tod's infirmity to the test and preventing him at the very last moment from falling off a cliff.

stated that in Davis he'd found his "ideal collaborator" and explained how "here in Hollywood it is pretty hard to fight single-handed for the pictures one would like to make." He also said he was certain that "two minds with the same tastes and ideas are better than one." In that same letter, he characterized the subject of his film as "insignificant."[69]

By the end of November, it was time to return to the studio. More than ever, Renoir blamed himself "for having given in to the voices of the sirens (the studio, agents, actors) who, slyly, for more than a year now, were singing the charms to me of a film that was easy to make, didn't need much energy, and should take me only three months of work." He said it was a "ridiculous venture" that would "cost two years" of his life, because "before collecting new ideas, I'll first have to forget these long months of problems."[70]

Beginning November 25, the scenes between Joan Bennett and Robert Ryan were filmed again, and Renoir probably also had to give in for the first time to that dubbing technique against which he had always rebelled. Another important change: Virginia Huston, who played the character Scott's fiancée Eve in the first version, was replaced by Nan Leslie, a twenty-year-old actress who had virtually no experience. This change implied that the dream scene that opens the film either hadn't appeared in the first version or that it had to be filmed a second time. According to what Renoir then claimed, this second filming of *Desirable Woman*, which ended on December 20 and thus lasted four weeks, entailed nearly half of the film.[71] Ten years later, he would change that to "around a third of the film,"[72] but the exact proportion doesn't really matter. *The Woman on the Beach*, the new title of the film, wasn't similar to *Desirable Woman*, which already hadn't corresponded to the film that Renoir had for a very short time thought of being able to make. No copy seems to exist of the original version of the film, which was finished by the director at the end of January 1946. Thus, we must be satisfied with the second attempt, which was presented in Los Angeles in May 1947 and released in New York the following month, more than a year after the end of the first shoot.

The Woman on the Beach was an irrevocable failure in American movie theaters, and the critical reception was hardly less negative. To understand the violence of such a rejection, an attempt must be made to approach the film by forgetting that it is by Jean Renoir. This must be done in a way that resembles how audiences in 1932 had seen the adaptation of the Simenon novel *La Nuit du carrefour*, without having understood any of it. The general atmosphere of *The Woman on the Beach* can, besides, be compared to *Carrefour*, which has the same fog and the same feeling of an aquarium, of sleepwalking. The film opens with a dream sequence, the first for Renoir since *The Whirlpool of Fate*, and the effects of it on the character of Scott are prolonged. There are also reminders of *La Bête humaine:* the wife, husband, and lover, of course, but especially that same incapacity to love in all of them, loneliness, and various forms of powerlessness. In addition, there is a marked tendency toward abstraction, a characteristic Renoir had already exhibited when confronted with material that didn't suit him; and, in this particular film, it's also the product of the successive compromises he was led to make. In any case, there's nothing to please a viewer who may have been attracted to the idea of seeing a film noir. Although it truly is film noir, it contains no crime other than those that might exist in the minds of the characters, who need to get rid of their traumas, obsessions, and fantasies if they are ever to escape their deep, adherent isolation. The film is about ghosts, those that loom up from the past or cloud the present. A painter who has gone blind is a dead man, as the character Tod remarks.

Éric Rohmer would make the film the touchstone for his admiration of Renoir. Truffaut would cite a certain scene showing Joan Bennett crawling on all fours as one of the ten most erotic in the history of film. Jacques Rivette would speak of "pure cinema"; and, with the hindsight of years, he'd call the film "the first in a trilogy of great masterpieces."[73] All such loving protests are also a defensive reaction to the extent of the rejection to which the film was subjected, and all of them are perhaps justified and accurate. However, they would be more convincing if Renoir's name on the credits hadn't contributed to steering the vision of the film and constructing opinions about it. Enigmatic as Renoir's own description of the first edit of *The Woman on the Beach* may seem, it's also the most convincing: "This is a film in which I wanted to proceed more by suggestion than by demonstration: a film of acts never carried out."[74]

The failure of the film signaled the end of Renoir's association with RKO, which freed him from his contract. As a result, the second film they were supposed to produce together never saw the light of day. It was just as had happened regarding his contract with Fox; the second clause was never honored. In 1941, with Fox, Renoir had made this decision; in 1947, it was the studio that chose to put an end to their relationship with him. At that time, there was no way for him to know that he would never again make a film on American soil.

27

Between Two Worlds

At the beginning of 1946, Jean and Dido bought property at 1273 Leona Drive. It was a dead-end road that started at Benedict Canyon Drive and snaked through the hills to the north of Beverly Hills. Lillian Gish had number 1256. The property was approximately twenty-seven thousand square feet. On it grew an old blackberry bush in the form of a bower, a magnificent walnut tree, an avocado tree, and some rosebushes. Renoir had a single-story house built of around three thousand square feet. He drew up the plans himself and planned to plant olive trees and a vineyard. Building and moving would last more than three years. The Renoirs didn't take possession of their new residence until May 1949; but from then on, they were permanently settled on American soil.

Although none of the films he had made during his exile satisfied him, except for *The Southerner,* his "only American work that justified losing an hour and a half to watch,"[1] Renoir hadn't given up the idea of becoming a Hollywood director. The failure of his last two productions hadn't weakened the prestige attached to his name and his French films, but it had rendered his position fragile. The responsibility for both *The Diary of a Chambermaid* and the fiasco *The Woman on the Beach* had been attributed to him, and the Hollywood machine had given up on making Jean Renoir one of theirs.

The characteristics of Renoir's approach to film had made his integration into Hollywood a tricky affair. The system probably suited a lot of other directors no better than it did him, but they more or less knew how to adapt to it without really making any more effort than Renoir had sacrificed to it. The importance he attached to a scene at the cost of giving preference to continuity—sometimes to the detriment of narrative fluidity— labeled him as peculiar, even if he had gradually dispensed with that approach during the thirties and paid increasing attention to the whole structure of his films. On French sets, Renoir spoke to everyone and everyone spoke to him. Each person believed he or she was permitted to contribute a share, and the director was nourished by such contributions, whether he pretended to be listening or actually retained them. The American tradition didn't allow for that. Other French directors had experienced this and had suffered at the sight of the actors retreating to their trailers the moment the clapperboard signaled the end of a scene and not reappearing until after their lighting stand-in had finished the task. Some of these directors also understood and spoke English correctly, which at the time was not the case with Renoir. The presence of French crewmembers, including Lucien Andriot for two films and Eugène Lourié, or actors who spoke French, such as Charles Laughton and Joan Bennett, could have contributed both to distancing others and, to some extent, to encouraging a certain laziness on the part of Renoir, slowing his progress in the practice of English. His windows opened onto a world that wasn't his.

René Clair had come to the United States at the same time as the Renoirs and had bought a house in Beverly Hills after five years spent in various other locations. However, on July 24, he went back to Paris, with expenses paid by RKO. He had signed with that studio in December, shortly after the success of *And Then They Were None*. The contract was as a screenwriter, director, and producer for two films, one in France and in French and the second in Hollywood. The company that was paying him a salary of $25,000 was the same one that would get rid of Renoir a few months later. And although Clair, like Renoir, would never work again in Hollywood, it was because he himself had made that decision.

Julien Duvivier had no lack of offers either. He'd chosen adapting the Simenon novel *Les Fiançailles de M. Hire* (*Mr. Hire's Engagement*), which would be called *Panique* (*Panic*), over *La Symphonie pastorale* (*Pastoral Symphony*), which had also been offered to him. Renoir, too, had considered that same novel by Gide for a short time, hoping that the author would give him an option, "either for nothing if he's in favor of it, or for a reasonable sum, if he's less in favor of it."[2] "Here in Hollywood," he then added, "people lack ideas, and as soon as you have one, whatever it may be, you've got to keep it secret until you have the rights to it."[3] The idea of adapting *La Symphonie pastorale* had been circulating in Paris for several months already. Jean Delannoy would direct the film in 1946.

In July 1945, Duvivier was in Paris, where the Cinémathèque française honored him on the twenty-first. Included were René Clair, who was visiting Paris at the time, and Jean Benoît-Lévy. Only Renoir was absent on that day. A few weeks before, Duvivier, Clair, and he had sent a telegram in response to an article by Henri Diamant-Berger, who had attacked them. The counterattack was violent, accusing Diamant-Berger of having "had himself appointed representative of the Free French in Hollywood by offices that were obviously unaware of his past, and, in return for a substantial salary," he'd "faced the dangers of the Resistance in California."[4] Diamant-Berger responded the following week, calling them "those three lost Frenchmen" and reproaching them for having "played the defeat card."[5]

Clair and Duvivier went back to France. Michèle Morgan returned to Paris in November 1945. Jean Gabin had returned a few weeks before her. Since April 1943 he had been fighting under the flag of Free France, first at sea and then by commanding a tank during the entire end of the Leclerc division's campaign. Demobilized in July 1945, he was decorated and received the Military Cross. Among the "greats" of French film who were in exile, only Jean Renoir chose not to return.

There were several reasons for that decision, and each of them had its importance. Certainly, Alain was back from the war, but his situation wasn't stable. He had decided to live permanently in the United States. While waiting to go back to his studies, he was going from one small job to another. One day he was working as a gas station attendant, the next as a horse breeder in Arizona with an Indian friend. Jean rightfully thought that his son still needed him. The second reason why Renoir stayed in the States had to do with his conjugal situation.

In a letter to M. Guillaume, which never reached him, Renoir told of his marriage to Dido and asked Guillaume, if he were to see Catherine, to tell her that she could be proud of Alain. He added, "I've had my separation from Catherine converted into a divorce. It would be prudent as soon as things get back to normal to go through the same formalities in Paris. If not, my marriage obviously would count for nothing in France."[6] The fact was that the formality to which he was referring didn't exist as such. It wasn't a matter of the marriage with Dido going unrecognized in France but the fact that, according to French law, he was still married to Catherine. His brother Pierre confirmed this to him on November 22, 1944, writing that "there hasn't been a verdict on the divorce from Dédé [sic]."[7] Renoir's transformation of his separation into a 'divorce, which he'd accomplished in California, had no legal standing in France. This put Renoir in the position of potentially being accused of bigamy.

The affair was a thorny one. It interested "everybody, including the judge, lawyer, attorney," because "for them it's far from ordinary, and there's no example of it in the courts."[8] A judgment on July 18, 1935, pronounced by the Third Chamber of the Civil Court of the Seine, had legalized the separation between Jean and Andrée Renoir. On August 31, 1945, through the intermediary of Louis Guillaume and the Prunier offices at 65 rue de la Chaussée-d'Antin, Renoir requested that the separation be converted into a divorce. Hoping to avoid a trial, he acted conciliatory and, on January 24, 1946, wrote, "I accept the arrangement proposed by Catherine and hope that my accepting to pay her approximately 100,000 francs and the attorney 10,000 francs will definitively settle the old issues between us. In a few days, I will send you a more complete letter in which I will relinquish any claim to what she has removed from Marlotte or from the apartment on rue de Miromesnil."[9]

But a few days later, after having received in the meantime a letter from Louis Guillaume dated January 15, Renoir made a complete turnabout:

The new demands Catherine has made have led me to consult an additional lawyer, Mr. Martin Gang. . . . Following his advice, I have therefore decided to offer nothing at all. I am perfectly in order with the State of California. Here my divorce is legal, as is my marriage. If Catherine does not recognize these laws, I do. As regards a scandal, since I feel that I am within my rights, I'm not the slightest bit concerned. If I am attacked in the newspapers in a way that is able to harm me professionally, I have the right to respond with my own attacks, since defamation of character is considered an offense in all the countries of the world. As to the paintings that Catherine has taken without my permission, I have the right to pursue that issue. I'm not doing that for the moment because it takes too much time and because I am against useless wrangling. But if I am put out by this, I may be obliged to act. I am sorry about having gone back on the terms of my previous letter of January 24 in which I said I was ready to accept Catherine's conditions, not because I felt threatened but because I was attributing her bad humor to a situation that is obviously quite difficult. But her change in attitude amply justifies my own.[10]

Both parties declared themselves ready to fight, and the procedure took its course.

In December, Louis Guillaume informed Renoir that the judgment hadn't been favorable to him. A week later, on December 25, 1946, Renoir wrote back to him:[11]

If I understand correctly, the court refused to acknowledge a separation lasting around fifteen years as a divorce. . . . Will I be condemned to a fine or to some other form of indemnity [*and he added by hand:* "or to prison"]? And once that formality has been taken care of, will I be again allowed to reiterate my request for a divorce; or will I actually have to divorce Dido so that I'll end up in circumstances permitted by French law that will give me the right to begin again with the aforementioned request for a divorce? This second process would not only be ridiculous but impractical. In fact, according to the law of the place in which I am living, California, Dido and I have no legitimate reason that would permit us to begin divorce proceedings—whether her against me or me against her.[12]

Top: Fall 1941. Gabrielle Slade has reunited with Renoir in Los Angeles. With her husband and son, she has first moved into an apartment in Westwood. A photographer for *Life* has been invited to record the event.

Bottom: March 1942. Renoir, accompanied by Gabrielle and Conrad Slade, visits Alain, his twenty-year-old son, recently inducted into the American army and now doing basic training in California. Jean Slade is the photographer.

Top: Summer 1941. Filming of *Swamp Water* in the studios at Fox. Renoir did not obtain permission to film in the swamps of Georgia. Opposite him, two of his actors, Walter Huston and Mary Howard.

Bottom: Summer 1941. Still lacking much English, Renoir supplements his words with gestures to explain to Anne Baxter and Dana Andrews what he is expecting of them.

Top: Summer 1942. Renoir directs *Forever Yours* for Universal. After forty-seven days of shooting, he'll pull out of the film, which will become *The Amazing Mrs. Holiday.* Opposite him, Deanna Durbin and Charles David, Renoir's assistant, who will marry the actress.

Bottom: November 1942. Maureen O'Hara, the screenwriter and producer Dudley Nichols, Renoir, and Charles Laughton on the set of *This Land Is Mine.* "I like this RKO studio a lot better than all those I've known in France," Renoir wrote to his son.

Top: At the home of Robert Florey (center), a Frenchman in Hollywood who arrived in California as a reporter and became a director. On the right is the actor Victor Francen.

Bottom: Fall 1944. Filming *The Southerner* in the San Joaquin Valley near Fresno, California. On the left, shirtless and with dark glasses, is Robert Aldrich at twenty-six, one of the assistants of Jean Renoir, who in this photo appears on the right.

August 1945. The art of washing explained to Paulette Goddard by means of an example in the studios on Romaine Street. *The Diary of a Chambermaid*, a project Renoir had been thinking about almost from the beginning of his career, has been produced by Burgess Meredith, the star's husband and also one of the film's performers.

Spring 1946. About Joan Bennett Renoir writes: "Such a stay-at-home lady is thought of by the American leagues of decency to be the most dangerous femme fatale on the screen." *The Woman on the Beach* will be the last of Jean Renoir's Hollywood films.

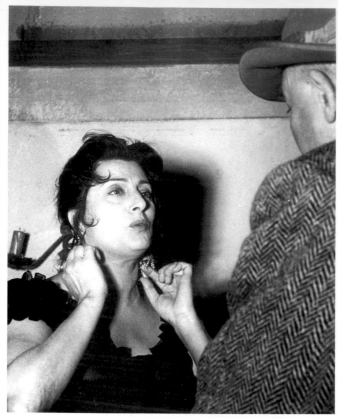

Beginning of 1952. Opposite the "charming and withered" Anna Magnani, whom Renoir is directing in *The Golden Coach* at the Cinecittà studios in Rome. He is "sure the producers never read my screenplay," a situation he considers "fantastic."

July 1954. In the arena at Arles, Renoir prepares for one performance only of *Julius Caesar,* presented to mark the two thousandth anniversary of the creation of the city by the Roman consul. In 1941, Renoir named that play by Shakespeare his favorite of all the works in the classical repertory.

Fall 1954. For his first film in France since 1939 and *The Rules of the Game*, Renoir is directing *French Cancan* in the studios on rue Francoeur. Shown is a meeting of the director, Françoise Arnoul (who plays Nini), and Édith Piaf, one of the stars invited to appear in the film.

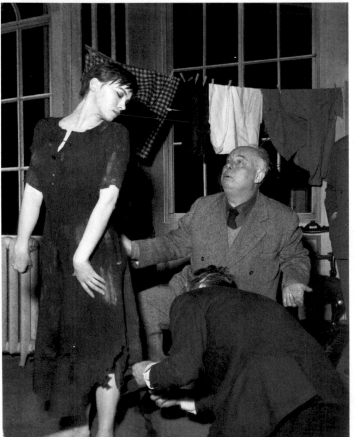

Top: 1955. Presentation of the Louis-Delluc prize to Henri-Georges Clouzot for *Les Diaboliques*. Surrounding the laureate, from left to right, Jacques Tati, Jean Renoir, Jacques Becker, Robert Bresson, Anatole Litvak, Alexander Astruc, André Malraux, and Noël-Noël.

Left: March 1955. Jean Renoir works on the staging of *Orvet* at the Théâtre de la Renaissance. Leslie Caron stars in the play. This will be the only collaboration between the young actress and the director despite the efforts of both to make several film projects come to fruition.

Top: Fall 1955. Since the beginning of the forties, Renoir and Ingrid Bergman had wanted to work together. Thanks to *Elena and Her Men*, it will happen. Here the director is presenting her two co-stars, Jean Marais and Mel Ferrer, to the actress.

Bottom: Between Jean Gabin and Renoir, Ingrid Bergman. The magic of the thirties has vanished, but Gabin and Renoir have worked once again together on *French Cancan* and in front of the photographers are careful to put on their best faces.

Left: June 1958. For the promotion of his book *Pierre-Auguste Renoir, mon père* (*Renoir, My Father*), the director poses for *Paris-Match* next to a portrait of himself painted by his father just before Jean entered private school at Sainte-Croix de Neuilly in September 1902.

Bottom: February 1959. Rehearsals for the ballet Renoir wrote for Ludmilla Tchérina. About that evening's performers he wrote to Gabrielle Slade on February 20: "The girls have pea-brains and the boys are all little flirts."

Summer 1959. For the filming of *Picnic on the Grass* Renoir rediscovers Les Collettes near Cagnes-sur-Mer and the scent of his earlier years. Beside him is the novice actress Catherine Rouvel and the experienced Fernand Sardou.

May 17, 1961. Jean and Dido Renoir arriving at Orly from Los Angeles for the impending *The Elusive Corporal*, which will begin in Vienna at the end of October.

Left: January 7, 1962. On the pont de Tolbiac, Renoir shoots the last scene of *The Elusive Corporal*, filmed mostly in Austria, with Jean-Pierre Cassel in the role of the corporal and Claude Brasseur as Pater.

Bottom: May 1966. The filming of the three-part *Jean Renoir, le patron*, directed by Jacques Rivette for the television series *Cinéastes de notre temps*.

Top: Summer 1969. Filming in Saint-Rémy-de-Provence of "Le Roi d'Yvetot," the last section of *Le Petit Théâtre de Jean Renoir*. Between Fernand Sardou and Jean Carmet stands Ginette Doynel, who was script girl, secretary, and governess during the director's last years in France.

Bottom Left: Dido and Jean Renoir photographed by Jean Slade in their house on Leona Drive in Beverly Hills.

Bottom Right: February 20, 1979. Jean Renoir, having passed away eight days before, is put to rest in the family vault at the cemetery in Essoyes next to his father and his brother Pierre. Sophie, Évangeline, Claude, and Alain Renoir are flanked by Leslie Caron and Dido Renoir.

1968. Jean Renoir at home on avenue Frochot, photographed by Walt Odets.

No progress was made, and on June 12, 1947, Renoir suggested that Louis Guillaume give Catherine a thousand dollars "to be done with it."[13] On October 17, 1949, he learned from Guillaume that "Catherine has decided to lodge an appeal against the judgment that we have obtained."[14] Irreproachably, Renoir's conflict with Catherine would never dissuade him from doing his best to help the Heuschling family, even though they were no longer his. For example, he asked Louis Guillaume to "do what is necessary to ensure that that poor woman goes to her rest in a decent fashion,"* because he understood "very well that Jeanne and Catherine aren't able to do anything to maintain Mme. Heuschling's grave."[15] Before that, at Renoir's request, Louis Guillaume had moved Mme. Heuschling to Fontainebleau, at 72 rue de France, "with a garden, fowl, rabbits, pigeons," along with "her daughter Jeanne, whose Charles is living with another woman."[16] Jeanne had taken care of her mother when she had become infirm and nearly blind.

More than four years after Renoir made the request that his separation be converted into a divorce, nothing had been achieved, and Catherine's appeal suggested that the procedure would be endless. In Renoir's eyes, this was enough of a reason not to return to France.

It was also the case that all the news that reached him from France was far from soothing. Certainly, letters allowed him to reconnect with friends and those to whom he was close. The first of these, from Jacques Becker, was the most touching and was dated Tuesday, May 8, 1945, the same day as the armistice. Becker had just been advised by the American censor that the letter he'd written to Jean on September 15 "on the occasion of both our birthdays" had been held back and would be returned to him. Then, "My dear Jean! If you knew how much I'd like to embrace you, hug you. I'm unimaginably impatient to see you, hear you. If you only knew how much I thought about you since our separation! Aside from the deep affection that connects us, you have played such an important role in my life that your place in my heart and mind tyrannically forces me to think of you nonstop. This is the first time that I've written a love letter to a man, but given the fact that neither of us is queer, it really doesn't matter." Renoir would recall that last sentence for an homage to Becker he gave after the man's death.

In his letter, Becker spoke about Marguerite, who had become his "most valuable collaborator," and to whom Renoir "absolutely had to write" because his "silence is causing her a lot of pain." He mentioned Dido, "a perfect woman who, according to what I've heard from people who have known you in America, has

* Mme. Heuschling, Renoir's former mother-in-law, died on June 29, 1945. Louis Guillaume informed Renoir of this by a letter dated July 3. (Jean Renoir Papers, Correspondence, Box 5, Folder 5.)

succeeded in making you happy, which makes me love her without knowing her." Then he provided some news of those close to him: Geneviève, his wife; his children, thirteen-year-old Sophie and twelve-year-old Jean, the future director; and Étienne, nine, "a terror," who would become a cameraman. Next, Becker described the films he had directed, calling the latest "an odd little film.ʼ . . . It has a host of faults, and the actors aren't what I would have wanted them to be (I'm talking about the two leads, the man and the girl[†]), but it so happens that I prefer this film to the two others. I'm sure you'd like it."[17] The following year, on September 15, Jacques Becker would send Jean Renoir the following telegram: "September 15, 1906, affectionately sends his greetings and best wishes to September 15, 1894."[18]

For a short time, Renoir thought he had lost his best friend and favorite collaborator. He had, in fact, received news that Carl Koch had committed suicide in Berlin. "I'll never find another friend like that,"[19] he wrote at the time. In October, Renoir received a letter from his brother Claude informing him that the news was not true. (The Kochs had written Renoir on September 2, but their letter hadn't arrived.) By the end of 1946, through letters and packages, Renoir and the Kochs reestablished the bonds that had united them for years.

Renoir also received news about Marguerite, but it was because the name of his former girlfriend had appeared in the newspapers in the section having to do with the news of the day. Apparently, it was Duvivier who informed him of the tragedy by handwritten letter. "You must have heard that your ex, Marguerite, has done in her husband, who was kind of a 'bruiser.'"[20] No, Renoir hadn't known about it, but Louis Verneuil later supplied him an article relating the facts. It reported that "the ex-wife of Jean Renoir"[21] had just murdered her husband, Adolphe Mathieu, age thirty-eight, an opera singer. The tragedy had happened one night in an apartment on rue de l'Abbé-de-l'Épée in Paris (Fifth Arrondissement), where the couple, waiting for a divorce, had encountered each other. It appeared that the man had tried to strangle the woman, who defended herself, shooting him five times. Marguerite Mathieu, née Houllé, who went by the name Renoir, was incarcerated for one week at the Roquette prison, before being released. Her defense was justified. "I sincerely feel sorry for her for having been put in a situation that, I'm hoping, was more ridiculous than dangerous,"[22] Renoir wrote about what he would also describe as "quite an upsetting incident."[23]

The large amount of correspondence exchanged in the final months and shortly

---

* *Falbalas* (*Paris Frills*), which would be released in Paris on June 21, 1945.

† Raymond Rouleau and Micheline Presle.

after the war with relatives or friends in France brought to light several feelings, all of which led Renoir not to go back to France. First, he was certain he had not yet succeeded in Hollywood but had a desire to believe that directing a success was still possible, which would allow him to return with his "head held high." "I'm gradually managing to bring together conditions for creation that will allow me to make a film that is absolutely personal. I already had such an opportunity with *The Southerner*, but that was a low-budget film. I would like to have it with a more important film."[24] And: "I don't want to go back to my country without having made the very, very great film that would make it possible for me to hold onto my situation in Hollywood, even if I'm returning to work over there. This is important not only to me but to French film as well. The day when I'll have made a film in Hollywood that corresponds in value and importance to what *Grand Illusion* was for France almost ten years ago, I'll consider the task I assigned myself to be finished and will feel that I have the right to start on something else."[25] If he had to go back someday, it wouldn't be permanent. However, without this "very, very great film," Renoir would have felt that his "time in Hollywood was a stopgap, a sort of refuge for an emigrant."[26]

In the months to come, he began to think that in not getting involved as much as he could and should have, he had perhaps missed his opportunity. From 1941 to 1946, he had thought of himself as passing through, or waiting out something, and now he was beginning to realize that fact. "I lived those war years with the feeling that I was waiting for something, and that everything I was doing was only temporary. Now that the war is over, I've gotten it into my head not to leave Hollywood without having made a film that satisfies me entirely."[27] But when he evaluated the difficulty of that task, "what gives me pause is the problem of pulling together my own ideas in a world and a language that is new for me."[28] He was still unaware of how much his successive failures had contributed to deteriorating his reputation and situation in Hollywood.

To explain further, his perception of the period through which the world was passing left him feeling helpless. Secondly, what he understood about the changes in the art of film was making him feel outmoded and, even more importantly, without any desire to adapt to the new order. "It's strange, but since I've been in exile, the only language I understand is that of the people of my generation or the generations that came before. I've tried to watch a few French films. Aside from one of them—*La Bataille du rail* (*The Battle of the Rails*)—which I thought was incredible, the others bored me. The films being made in Hollywood aren't any better. In fact, they're probably worse but simply and awkwardly trying to make money. In the new French films, each line feels like an ambition to change the world."[29] Or else: "I don't dare to get back in touch with old Europe," he explained to the woman who'd been his Italian teacher in Rome. "The people over there speak a language I don't understand anymore."[30]

These reasons, repeated numerous times to his correspondents, were enough, without adding those objective reasons represented by the situation with Alain and the conflict with Catherine. All of them were complicated by a vague feeling of guilt caused by the discovery of the conditions experienced by those who had remained in France, people whose situations continued to be less desirable than his. No one had endured such guilt more than Marcel Dalio had. Since he'd arrived in Hollywood, he'd been worried for a long time about not knowing what had happened to his mother and his sisters, from whom there was no news. Renoir had tried to help him.[31] However, after arriving in Paris in April 1945, Dalio discovered that his mother, his three sisters, and his father, who had been separated from them for a long time, had all been sent to Auschwitz, probably denounced for not wearing the yellow star. They never came back. "And what was I doing during this time? Playing a fisherman from Brittany in Hollywood,"[32] he would write.

Reassured in November 1944 that his property at Les Collettes hadn't been touched by the bombing ("a single bomb fell in the garden"),[33] Renoir evaluated everything that his exile had permitted him to escape and from it drew some conclusions. "It seems to me that French film belongs first to those who held their own during the Occupation and that before giving productions to do to those who have eaten well in Hollywood, it's perhaps fairer to favor those in the country who starved to death."[34] Over weeks and months, he went back to the same argument on several occasions, often in identical terms. Renoir was truly aware, in fact, that "weekly leg of lamb, steak, and whiskey on the rocks, whether scotch or bourbon, not to mention California pinot, helps you disregard a lot of things."[35]

He also expressed his opinion about those French producers he assumed couldn't have remained active under the Occupation "without more or less reaching an agreement with the Germans." "I have nothing at all against them," he went on. "Everyone is free to save his hide and his money as he wishes, as long as it doesn't lead those chums to the firing squad. But I'm not attached to the idea of going and working with them. I see their names in the papers; they get along with the Americans just as they did with the Nazis.* All of it disgusts me a bit, and I'd like to go and work in France at a time when the world of film is between new hands."[36] On a similar note, the day before introducing Jean Grémillon's film *Le ciel est à vous* (*The Woman Who Dared*) in Hollywood,

---

* An opinion that matches Claude Autant-Lara's, according to whom French film went from the German Occupation to American occupation.

it disturbed him to discover what its producer Raoul Ploquin's involvements had been. According to reports, he "had gone too far in collaborating with the Germans."[37] About his reluctance to rub shoulders with producers who were "compromised," Renoir would say in private, "I don't blame them for what they did. I probably would have collaborated if I'd stayed, but I don't want to deal with someone who collaborated."[38]

At the beginning of summer 1945, Renoir learned that Marlotte had been sold, news that he received without betraying any emotion. Infinitely more important to him was the discovery that Aline Cézanne had succeeded all through the war in hiding his portrait in hunting gear, painted by Auguste. From the time mail had been reestablished between Europe and America, the issue had been one of his great preoccupations. The painting came to him in February 1946,* a few weeks after Alain's return, yet another link reestablished. Along the same lines, he now intended to have the objects and furniture he loved sent to him from France. They'd find a place in the house he would soon begin to design. At this time, inventories, records, remittance statements took up a large part of the voluminous correspondence he had with Louis Guillaume. He was also buying his father's canvases and considering acquiring some by Cézanne.[39] Soon, he was thinking about having constructed "a copy of the dining room fireplace and medallion at Les Collettes";[40] and he asked his brother Claude if that task could be entrusted to "a marble mason in Cagnes or Nice." It was obvious that Renoir was establishing roots in California soil.

By chance he also discovered a branch of the family in America. In August 1942, *Life* published an article entitled "Gabrielle—Renoir's Famous Model Now Lives Quietly in Hollywood."[41] Most noticeable among the illustrations was a photo showing Gabrielle with Jean. A few days later, two women visited the home of Gabrielle Slade, having found her address in the phone book (where Renoir's was not listed). Victoria Charigot was Jean's aunt. The young girl with her was her daughter, Dora. In 1860, Aline Charigot, Jean's mother, had been fifteen months old when her father, Claude (known as Victor), had disappeared. The fellow had taken off for America, probably with a mistress, and settled in North Dakota, after starting out in Canada. From a second marriage, which was really probably his third, he had two children, one of whom was Victoria, making her Jean's mother's half-sister.

Alain gave the following account of their visit: "One day during the war, my

* Reneging on his decision to make a gift of the canvas after his death to the Art Institute of Chicago because his son was "not yet settled down" at the time, Renoir would change his will in 1953 so that the painting would go to Alain. (Letter to Alain Renoir, August 21, 1953, Jean Renoir Papers, Correspondence, Box 12, Folder 8.)

father heard the doorbell, went to the door, and found himself face to face with two ladies. The older had asked him in English if Mr. Jean Renoir was home, and he had answered that he was Jean Renoir. The lady switched from English to French and said to him, 'I'm your aunt, and this girl next to me is your cousin!' And it was true."[42] True, in fact, and Renoir would give in to the pleasure of telling about these exotic family adventures several times while also enjoying the indulgence of adding a number of invented episodes.

For Renoir to decide to go back to France, he also needed to feel wanted, to feel that voices calling for him were not only those of friends.

"Here we talk about you all day, especially with Jouvet and Henri Jeanson," Lestringuez wrote to him, mentioning a dinner where a project having to do with the history of the battleship *Jean-Bart* was being discussed, about which everyone had sighed in agreement, "Only Jean Renoir could make that film!"[43] "You see," added Lestringuez, "if the sirens of Hollywood don't sing too loudly to your ears, you can always do our poor little French film world a damn bit of good." The truth was that Renoir would have had to possess superhuman hearing to be aware of any possible proposition coming from Americans. Hollywood was totally silent, and the fact that he'd crossed the Atlantic dimmed the impact of the calls coming from France.

The real question had to do with knowing how he'd be received over there. "It would really bother me having to deal with people who answered any order I gave them with, 'Shut up, mister. I'm a hero, and during the war you were getting fat in Hollywood.'"[44] That worry was fed by the echoes that reached him concerning reactions to his films in France. He was going through a strange period in which he stubbornly focused on finding a project to direct in Hollywood, where he was no longer an influential player, whereas in Paris his name was being displayed outside theaters and in the papers.

The first Renoir film to appear in Parisian theaters after the war was also his greatest success. But this *Grand Illusion* wasn't exactly the same film as the one audiences had seen in 1937.

At the beginning of 1945, his producer Frank Rollmer's first request had met with a refusal from the censorship committee, which considered it ill-timed to rerelease the film while French prisoners of war were still in German camps. In July, Les Réalisations d'art cinématographique (RAC) drew up a second request. The film was viewed twice—on July 18 and August 1—by the censorship committee, whose members had in the meantime changed. The distributor was insistent, emphasizing that it was impossible to see in *Grand Illusion* the slightest "propaganda regarding the thesis of the good German, because the commandant of the camp (von Rauffenstein/von Stroheim), who had discovered far greater affinities regarding cast and sensibility with his prisoner (Boëldieu/Pierre Fresnay) than he was able to have with a simple *Feldgrau*, still did not hesitate to shoot and kill him."[45] RAC further stated that "this film, which is in no way Vichy-oriented, since it dates to 1937, can't be considered new, since 75 percent of the French population have already seen it before the war." This request, as well, was declined, and the president of the committee explained the decision as follows: "It would be indecent to show this film to an audience among which there could be people repatriated from Buchenwald or Ravensbrück."[46]

A few months later, the censor appeared less finicky and agreed to consider the request, subject to the producer's committing to eliminate three precise scenes. On January 27, 1946, Renoir sent Jean Dewalde, his agent, a telegram meant for the committee: "I grant permission for slight cuts that in no way distort the spirit and direction of *Grand Illusion*, on the condition that they be made by coauthor Charles Spaak."[47] As a result, RAC began eliminating scenes showing the arrival at the first camp of the food parcels, the German expressions of joy at the announcement of the fall of Douaumont, and the kiss between Jean Gabin and Dita Parlo. In addition, the credits, as well as the promotional material, were not to mention the actress's name. On February 27, after viewing this new version, Spaak gave his approval and stated that he had been "very happy about again seeing this film that has kept intact all its qualities."[48] Finally, on March 12, he confirmed to the censorship committee the fact that "the changes the producer has made to *Grand Illusion* on his own initiative, which also happen to be very minor," in no way violate "the spirit of the film and the intentions of its authors."[49]

Grand Illusion was rereleased August 26, 1946, and the Normandie, the large theater on the Champs-Élysées, was always packed. However, the film was seen by some through the prism of the war, the Occupation, and all the dreadful things that had recently happened; and everything that had contributed to making it a hit nine years before turned against it, beginning with Renoir's wish to show "good Germans." In 1946, there couldn't be any good Germans, only Nazis. Similarly, the portrait drawn of Rosenthal the Jew could now be likened to an anti-Semitic caricature. Such a risk led the censors to insist upon the removal of the scene in which Rosenthal shows his generosity, and especially when he remarks that the Germans, as well, "lack everything," before offering a piece of chocolate to a soldier. Most of all, at a moment when accounts were beginning to be settled with collaborationists, any celebration of French-German brotherhood was intolerable.

In addition, *Grand Illusion* was becoming the focus of a controversy whose basic thesis was being established by Georges Altman. He was a journalist, Communist, and important member of the Resistance, who in 1932 had been one of the first to defend *Journey to the End of the Night* and thus for some time had become close to Céline. Altman had written an article for *Franc-Tireur* that was soon reprinted in *L'Écran français:*

> Poor Renoir, and poor some of us, who'd believed ten years ago that you could struggle against the war of Fascism by calling for brotherhood! We have to leave such illusions in the tombs and mass graves they dug. . . . In *Grand Illusion,* by presenting us, sympathetically, of course, with the French soldier Rosenthal, a Jew, but feeling the need to specify, emphasize, that he is one, we very gently bring up the racist issue that climaxed in Auschwitz. That isn't what we wanted, Renoir would say. And all the supporters of that rerelease will swear, I know, with hand over heart, that their intentions are good. But here we are, having learned what Hell is. It was useless and harmful to remind ourselves that Hell is also paved with good intentions.[50]

Soon, *Paris-Matin* began an extensive inquiry, collecting the current opinions of various figures about *Grand Illusion.* When the director Henri Calef was questioned about it, his opinion was that it was "shocking to see on a screen, less than two years after the end of the Occupation, Germans who are so different from those whom we have known."[51] And Paul Éluard suggested that "yesterday's collaborators will make an uncommon show of joining forces against the censor."[52] Renoir's former assistant Claude Heymann, on the other hand, would have a more tempered response and consider the rerelease of the film poorly timed.[53] It is difficult not to agree with him, as well as with Henri Jeanson, who saw the film again and remarked that it "remains a masterpiece," the creation "of a great artist and a man of goodwill," yet concluded his article with the words, "Maybe it's idiotic, but that's the way it is. There are corpses between *Grand Illusion* and us."[54]

The press was not alone in signaling an alarm. The authorities, as well, were disturbed. For example, the director of media in Strasbourg picked up his pen to inform his minister that the rerelease of the film "has aroused some very intense feelings in certain parts of the Alsatian film world" and that "the appropriateness of authorizing this reappearance has been strongly contested by the public."[55] Showing the film again, he explained, "seemed that much more contestable in a province like Alsace that during the four years of its annexation had had a rather different impression of the Germans than that suggested by *Grand Illusion.*" Then: "Several managers of Alsatian theaters . . . have informed me that they are definitely hostile to projecting that film in the three departments of the region.

Moreover, it is not improbable that such a showing, if it were to take place, would be the cause of incidents and demonstrations that would be unfortunate to witness."

In fact, although this new presentation of the film was turning out to be very good business on the bookkeeping level, as much as for the producer and distributors as for the filmmakers,* Renoir couldn't help noticing that he was being violently attacked and unjustly implicated . . . through the only one of his films that had ever created unanimity.

He had no hopes regarding the release of *A Day in the Country,* and he did not hide this from his brother Claude, who had informed him by letter in April 1946 about the existence of this film he had stopped thinking about for a long time and would allude to only briefly for several more years to come. "I don't think the release of this unfinished film can do me any good," he wrote, before musing that Braunberger "will have to resort to some ploys to finish it."[56] Perhaps not to finish it, but to make it presentable. The producer would relate having had the idea of showing the film practically as is while he was swimming in a river in the Lot and saw the SS Panzer Division *Das Reich* passing by. To escape it, he hid out on an island, where he had all the free time he needed to think about *A Day in the Country.*[57] A postcard sent from Cagnes-sur-Mer also made him remember the film. It was from Sylvia Bataille, reminding him that she was still owed 1,700 francs for Marcel L'Herbier's *Forfaiture* (*The Cheat,* 1937) and 5,000 francs for *A Day in the Country.*[58]

In December 1944, the producer shared his intentions with the head of the Centre du cinéma, Jean Painlevé, who was the only person capable of getting his hands on the amount of film that would be needed. "Given Jean Renoir's absence and the fact that the actors have changed since then, I've chosen not to shoot these [missing] scenes and to replace them with a spoken text inspired by Guy de Maupassant, which will be illustrated by some engravings of Paris at the time."[59] Braunberger also explained that he had asked Pierre Lestringuez to write this text and Marguerite to take care of the editing. Painlevé refused the request, first using the excuse of the difficulties of stocking up on film, then pointing out that the director and actors were absent, and, finally, revealing the fact that he'd received "certain information" indicating that "Marguerite Renoir would refuse to do the editing."[60] After Braunberger expressed the desire to distribute *A Day in the Country* as "an opener film"[61] for a main feature, permission was finally granted on January 5, 1946.

---

* In a letter to Louis Guillaume dated November 16, 1947, Renoir mentioned a sum of 468,000 francs. (Jean Renoir Papers, Correspondence, Box 8, Folder 5.)

Contrary to what he had claimed,[62] Braunberger had come to no agreement with Renoir, for the sole reason that he hadn't asked him anything. However, there's very little doubt that Renoir wasn't opposed to the wishes of the producer at least for one reason: the film had ceased to interest him a long time ago. Braunberger had also maintained that the first edit, "in the form of a work print," had been destroyed by the Nazis, but that Henri Langlois had provided him with the negative. According to Marguerite Renoir, who had always denied having collaborated on this first edit, the negative had been hidden in the basement of the Éclair Laboratories in Épinay. This new edit—accomplished without any participation from Jacques Becker and Pierre Lestringuez, according to the editor and her sister, Marinette Cadicqx, her assistant at the time—was completed in January 1946 and based on "everything that had been decided ten years before with Renoir."[63] And as a matter of fact, the film seemed to conform to the director's intentions as they are indicated in the screenplay.

Joseph Kosma, who'd already been approached for the task by Renoir in 1936, was hired to compose the music. For a payment of 10,000 francs, Germaine Montero performed the song that was hummed. The musician and Marguerite supervised the sound mixing at the studios in Neuilly in March 1946. Braunberger organized a screening for his journalist friends and saw to it that the film was presented at the first Cannes Film Festival. On September 21, 1946, *La Partie de campagne** was shown under the short-film category. On December 18, the film began showing at the César on the Champs-Élysées, where it was accompanied by the Gilles Margaritis film *L'Homme* (1946, 20 minutes), produced by Braunberger, as well as the thirty-eight-minute film by Roger Leenhardt, *Naissance du cinéma* (*The Birth of Cinema*, 1946). Although it received excellent reviews as a whole, it wasn't a film that could claim to attract crowds, which have never been particularly attracted to shorts. Braunberger informed Renoir of how it was being received, and Renoir thanked him.[64] A few days later, the producer sent him two press clips, one appearing in *Le Populaire* that was excellent and "the other a savage attack on the part of our friend Jeanson,"[65] and so it was. It was only gradually, thanks in large part to its distribution on the film society circuit, that *A Day in the Country* would gain the reputation with which we are familiar today. In 1946, the film counted no more for audiences than it mattered to the memory of the man who had made it.

It was also in large part thanks to the circuit of film societies that over time *The Rules of the Game* began to elicit admiration. In September 1945, the film had been rereleased in two Parisian theaters with very little success. However,

* The title of the film acquired the definite article (*La*, meaning *The*) it had had in the Maupassant story but that had been left out of the film title until then.

in the October 10 issue of *L'Écran français*, the future director Jean-Charles Tacchella, who was a young critic at the time, published an article that it is possible today to see as the film's first advocate.

None of the reactions provoked by these rereleases or the rerelease of *La Bête humaine* affected Renoir as much as those that occurred when *This Land Is Mine* was shown under the title *Vivre libre*, on July 10, 1946. If the new release of *Grand Illusion* really was untimely, what can be said of the decision to offer French audiences, only a few months after the end of the war, Hollywood's version of an occupied country, filmed by a director in exile, and presented in a dubbed version that everyone judged a disaster? In the eyes of the French, Renoir had gotten it all wrong by pretending to describe a reality he knew almost nothing about. His obvious and incontestable good intentions were drowned in the crossing of the ocean that separated him from his compatriots. In other circumstances, the film's reception would have only been icy. The truth was that the reaction to it was aggressive. For certain people, it even provoked a vague desire for vengeance.

In *France-Soir*, André Lang justified "the irritation of critics and audiences." The "absence of tact" in the film had led to "making the French pay to be inflicted with an offensive, for-profit caricature of the very tragedy in which they themselves were the real-life actors, heroes, traitors, and victims"; whereas "this work of war offering no more than documentary interest" should have "resolutely been written off as a loss." The reviewer in *Le Journal du dimanche* referred to "Germans from a melodrama and talkative members of the Resistance," considered it inexcusable to be "unaware of everything about occupied France and wanting to describe it," "couldn't understand that French people could be unfamiliar at this point with the atmosphere and the details of French life," and understood even less why "one would have the nerve to present these films to French audiences."[66] For Pierre Laroche, although "Jean Renoir is fine" and "hasn't forgotten anything about his profession," "his film is bad" and "even often worse than bad, ridiculous, in other words."[67] In *Le Figaro*, which had been hostile to Renoir for years, Jean-Jacques Gautier deplored the fact that "a Frenchman had even involuntarily created a ridiculously distorted image of suffering and courage."[68]

A few months later, Renoir's "champion" in the thirties, Georges Sadoul, after mockingly relating the plot, would make the judgment that "obviously, it wouldn't be necessary to devote more than ten lines to this film if it hadn't been authored by Jean Renoir, the greatest French director" and would declare "to hold that signature to be a forgery, not because Renoir had never made a bad film, but because this French drinker of red wine, had he wished, wouldn't have painted his country with the colors of cold milk and sang it with the lyricism of a hymn from Presbyterian Minnesota."[69] When it came to expressing his anti-Americanism, Georges Sadoul always found a use for it. However, the harshest attack—partly because it was the most unexpected, made as it was by someone who would soon be positively linked to Renoir—came from André Bazin in an article entertainingly entitled "French Resistance for the Chinese": "It would have been better for everyone—including American film—if we'd been deprived of that work. We would have been able to feign ignorance about 'the rules of the game' to which the maker of *Grand Illusion* has been forced to bow."[70] It should be kept in mind that none of the American films having to do with the Occupation in Europe were kindly received in France right after the war. All of them were judged to be implausible caricatures in the same way as was Lang's *Hangmen Also Die!*

Renoir felt wounded by these attacks, stating that he was "not close to forgetting the profound pain caused me by this lack of leniency on the part of my countrymen."[71] He explained that "this incident only strengthens my desire not to go back to the people whose heroism during this war commands my admiration, but whose touchiness seems regrettable to me."[72] As the days passed, he said he had "returned to a fairer understanding of things" and "found it very natural that the French didn't share his ideas about conciliation, mutual aid, and reciprocal love." "They have reasons for hating one another," he went on, "and it's hard for them to accept the reasons that led me to show all of them in sympathetic colors, which is a reaction against American opinion that was seeing them all in rather dark colors."[73]

Returning to the issue a few months later, he would explain how painful it was for him that the French media had "attacked me personally in such a relentless way" and that they had "blamed me for having brought to the screen a film about the French Resistance without being better informed about its subject." This came down to "having not at all taken into account the way life develops and the way things were in 1942, a situation about which these same film critics could have taken the trouble to find out about before."[74] Given the circumstances, it's difficult not to agree with him, but the wound was an open one, and the reception of his other American films was not going to help close it.

The response of the press and audiences to *Swamp Water*, his first American production, which was shown on French screens on April 23, 1948, was no better than that to *The Diary of a Chambermaid* on June 9, 1948, or *The Woman on the Beach* on the twenty-third of the same month. The most well-meaning columnists seemed scrupulous and offered explanations that included being uprooted, a production system that wasn't suitable for Renoir and his projects, the impossibility of adapting certain topics (the Resistance, Octave Mirbeau); yet despite the excuses they found for the director, they saw only faults in the films. The release of *The Southerner* marked a first turnaround, but that was on May 30, 1950, almost four years since the showing of *Vivre libre*, a film that shouldn't have been shown in France, or at least not so soon, not immediately after the war.

When Ingrid Bergman, on pilgrimage in the lands of Joan of Arc, whom she was preparing to play, sent Jean a postcard showing Domrémy,[75] it was like a wink from fate. Of course, expressions of nostalgia, such as Edmond Ardisson's, still reached the man in exile. The actor who had played the bricklayer in *La Marseillaise* sent him two postcards to say,

> I was in M. Carné's *La Fleur de l'âge*, a film that is currently shut down, probably forever; and it was while shooting that film that I was again able to evaluate your gift as a Director. That man, who nevertheless has managed to have an important name in France, elicits absolutely nothing from his performers. If I received excellent press in *La Marseillaise*, I absolutely owe it all to you, because you'd understood how to draw out the quintessence of my possibilities, whereas M. Carné only knows how to make your blood run cold, bellowing every other minute, without giving you any information, aside from technical indications about where to stand. He's purely an art photographer for whom the emotions to express come into mind after the place you're supposed to occupy and the framing of the camera; whereas you I can still hear: technique is there for the use of the actors, rather than the opposite.[76]

So, Lestringuez was doubtlessly correct in writing that some people in France were lamenting Renoir's absence; but there were others, probably more numerous, for whom Renoir was where he belonged, very far away. His success, the central position that he had occupied at the end of the thirties, and his behavior, which was often that of a loudmouth, had aroused jealousy. Those he overshadowed certainly had no desire to see him come back, and those who had made it in the meantime had no intention of giving him a place they had paid dearly to acquire. French cinema respected Renoir for what he had accomplished. It even often admired him, but it wasn't sure that it liked him. His breakup with Marguerite, which had been as brutal as such events always are, had also fed certain misgivings on the part of crewmembers and other technicians who already didn't value him. Marguerite was a permanent member of a family to which he had never really belonged. And then there were the sides he had taken—first one side and then another. There was his infatuation with

Mussolini's Italy, regardless of the reasons for it, followed by his departure from France; not to mention the fact that his return to that country had been put off for too long. They weren't waiting for him with open arms, and he knew it.

His shady dealings in the fall of 1940 were equally food for rumor. The deprivations endured by those who had stayed made the exile of those who had left seem more golden. That's just the way it was. Consequently, as can be easily imagined, when Renoir received a postcard sent from Gstaad by Simone Simon saying, "Dear Jean, we miss you so much in France. Why don't you come back?"[77] a smile must have come to his face, and perhaps a slight pang, a touch of nostalgia; but life was so sweet in California, and France was so far away. News from his brother Claude wasn't the kind to encourage him to return to a country where "it's impossible to live with 10,000 francs when an egg costs 30 francs and a cabbage, 80," where strikes broke out every day, kindled by the Communist Party, which, according to Claude, was playing indirectly into the hands of de Gaulle, "whose popularity is increasing by leaps and bounds. A large majority of the army is for him and, before long, he'll come out of his silence and become a Franco." In short, the situation was alarming because "both parties are well prepared and well armed."[78]

Renoir certainly claimed to be living an "extremely rustic" existence in California, and he described having "learned to do regularly" what he hadn't done "in Europe, my bed and polishing my shoes."[79] But then, because Claude had told him that his brother Pierre was touring, it had become a matter of dissuading his sister-in-law Lisa from visiting him: Claude had also warned, "To put it charitably, with age, confidence has only increased her bullshit."[80] It was no doubt true that "nowadays the problem is to manage to live without servants," and even if Dido had "managed to get by for years with an old Negress who comes to lend a hand twice a week," it was "exhausting, and she was knocked out" until the arrival of "one of her old friends from England* who stays with us and does a lot of things."[81]

To the needy of Essoyes, through the mayor[82] and the village priest,[83] and to his friends in France, Renoir sent a good number of packages, trying to respond to requests that he hadn't anticipated. Several pages covered with dense writing were sometimes needed to accompany these packages, such as when he had to explain to a recipient the function of the pen cartridges that person claimed wouldn't fit, whereas the manufacturer maintained that there were no other types for it and that those were the ones you were really supposed to use.[84] From Paris for Renoir

---

* The father of that "old friend," Bessie, had been one of Dido's father's servants when he was a consul in Liverpool.

came the larding needle* and the cookbooks,[85] sent by Louis Guillaume; the andirons, the tongs, the fireplace plaque, the oyster knife,[86] and the fish kettle,[87] for which he'd also asked Guillaume. He was also waiting for the truffles and morels from Maison Édouard Gnieu in Aix-en-Provence, which he had sampled at the Slades' and about which he had sent Guillaume a detailed description of the cans that contained them.[88] Finally, there was the Vieux Marc de Pommery obtained thanks to Louis Jouvet, which came across on the cruiser *De Grasse* to New York, where some of their friends took on the task of getting it to him.[89]

Furniture, paintings, and foodstuffs were not the only items to arrive for him from France. Offers came, too. Some were worth thinking about for a moment, and then evaporated. Notably, there was the possibility of a film with Jean Gabin, yet another, a story about a submarine. Renoir wrote to his old partner in crime to tell him that the business with his divorce, which he described as "grotesque," was keeping him from returning.[90] More than a year later, he considered one "very firm" offer from Robert Hakim to be "very interesting." It involved directing "Paulette Goddard in French and in English" in a film that would be called *Casque d'or*.[91] He asked his lawyer, Counselor Masse, his opinion: Was he risking problems if he went to work in France? A little more than two weeks later, he announced that he was pulling out of the project and recommended Julien Duvivier to the producer.[92] In reality, he was determined that his first film in France "be something out of the ordinary." For it, he intended "to write the story and the screenplay," requirements he was now beginning to doubt would be compatible with his position in Hollywood. He was also seeing signs in the changes in American film that he judged unfavorable to him. "There are really two audiences: a kind of elite, on the one hand, and on the other, a crowd composed mainly of kids. If you accept big exploitation, you've got to accept working for twelve-year-old children."[93]

Offers also came from Italy. In Rome, Claude Heymann was working for Universalia, preparing an adaptation of Anouilh's *Eurydice*, which Marcel Carné was supposed to direct under the title *L'Espace d'un matin*, but the affair became muddled, and Renoir's nephew Claude informed him of that fact. In a letter telling Louis Guillaume about refusing the project, Renoir wrote that he had pulled out to avoid getting mixed up with a matter that interested another French director and explained, "They're accusing me of bad things like that in France. It doesn't bother me at all, but to keep that indifference I need to be certain that I really have harmed no one."[94] A week later, his nephew

---

* *Translator's note:* A "larding needle" (*aiguille à larder*) is a needle with a very sharp tip and a usually hollow body that is used to thread thin pieces of fat into a roast to keep it moist and flavorful during cooking.

commented, "People are stupid and jealous, and they were thrillingly getting ready to give your ears a good boxing. 'They' are the pals of the association of authors, whose first step must have been warning an ill-informed colleague. . . . Also, it's thanks to Becker that I've written you, because I hadn't paid any attention to the perils caused by this affair."[95] The affair would have resulted, actually, in Renoir's taking the place of a colleague without meaning any harm, and it didn't stop there. In November, the head of Universalia himself returned to the attack and decided to wait for Renoir, with the agreement and support of Michèle Morgan; and he had already even listed the film, with direction by Jean Renoir, on Universalia's 1949 schedule.[96] Renoir responded by saying he was held back by other projects,[97] but barely a month afterward expressed his worry by telegram about whether the offer of *Eurydice* was still alive.[98] His wait would end when his nephew informed him that arbitration would be announced in Rome but that Carné had no intention of giving up his rights.[99] *Eurydice* would never be made until 2012, under the direction of Alain Resnais, and its title would become *Vous n'avez encore rien vu* (*You Ain't Seen Nothin' Yet*).

The fact that Renoir sometimes gave pause to certain offers coming from Europe did not challenge his desire to favor personal projects and make them his priority. And in the first years following the war, his personal projects were American. Exclusively American. There are also too many of them to create any interest in drawing up a list, but several are still memorable. For example, there was *The Sinner: A Story of Mary Magdalen,* whose time and place were described as "The Present. Lebanon, a desert valley in the American Southwest." It consisted of scenes from the Passion. The first treatment, which was thirty-four pages, was registered with the Screen Writers Guild on April 29, 1946. The treatment makes clear that the excerpts of the Passion were taken from the New Testament and that additional sources of inspiration could be found in the "message of Confucius, Lao-Tse, Lincoln, or any honest man of good will."[100] A second treatment, entitled *The Terror* and coauthored by Charles O'Neill, was sent to Walter Wanger at Universal on July 10, 1946.[101] More than three years later, Renoir, who was then in Calcutta, would come back to that idea and present it under the form of "a Life of Christ in our days in a modern surrounding, with the apostles dressed as modern fishermen and St. Joseph dressed as a modern carpenter. The soldiers surrounding Golgotha would be modern policemen," taking place either in "an American industrial town" or "in a country where people still keep a biblical simplicity," in which case, "India would be great."[102]

The project *Woman of a Hundred Faces,* written by Renoir and Maximilian Ilyin, is the most intriguing, based on an "original story by Louis Bromfield, Thomas Mann, and Maximilian Ilyin."[103] Three versions of it have been preserved, the last signed by Bernard Schubert,* dated January 8, 1948, and labeled as the property of Federal Films.[104] The action takes place in Paris at the end of the twenties, and the "woman of a hundred faces" is an actress or model who in a few months manages to have her features drawn, painted, or sculpted by approximately fifty of the most renowned artists of their time. The basic historical aspects of the story as reproduced by the screenplay had been related in a *Life* article in December 1945. The young woman was named Maria Lani. Since 1941, she had been appearing on the stage of New York's Stage Door Canteen. Now she was hoping that her story would become a Broadway show and a Hollywood film, written as the screenplay was by Thomas Mann, Louis Bromfield, and Maximilian Ilyin.[105] The article didn't mention any actress's or director's name, but it included twelve portraits of Maria Lani, including some by Matisse, Derain, Kisling, Cocteau, Rouault, Léger, Chagall, Lurçat, and Suzanne Valadon.

The real story of Maria Lani and of the project offered Renoir are even more amazing. It reveals that Maximilian Ilyin was not only its promoter but also an actor in it. In spring 1928, Ilyin was called Abramowicz when he arrived in Paris from Russia with his brother. Both of them claimed to be the impresarios of a twenty-year-old woman with an astonishingly changeable face and with an expression that all those who met her described as deeply unsettling. They introduced her as a German actress who had studied with Max Reinhardt. In reality, she was Polish and, to boot, was a stenographer from Prague. She was also the wife of Maximilian Abramowicz. The personality of this unknown star ignited Jean Cocteau's imagination, and he drew her portrait forty times. In a few weeks, Maria Lani had convinced about fifty artists to do her portrait. Apparently, only Picasso and Marie Laurencin refused. Aside from those mentioned in *Life,* the list included at least Picabia, Marquet, Van Dongen, Soutine, Bonnard, Vuillard, and de Chirico. In 1929, the fifty-one works were reproduced in a twenty-page catalogue, *Maria Lani by Bonnard . . .* , accompanied by a preface by Jean Cocteau and texts by Mac Ramo and Waldemar George.[106] The following year, from November 15 to 30, 1930, the portraits were shown at Galerie Georges-Bernheim, on rue du Faubourg-Saint-Honoré.

Maria Lani's fame only served her briefly. Art critics took up their pens to emphasize that the works shown were for the most part sketches. Voices rose to reproach the young woman for being presented as the actress and star that she was not. The enterprise was denounced as a scam. Maria, her husband, and her brother-in-law disappeared sometime after and headed for the United States,

---

* At the time, Bernard Schubert was a screenwriter of B horror films.

but not without Maximilian's signing a contract with Jean Cocteau in September 1935 giving him the exclusive rights to the performance, reproduction, and translation of *La Voix humaine* (*The Human Voice*),* Cocteau's one-act play, which Maximilian would bring out in English in 1944.[†]

In March 1944, in Chicago, Maximilian, whose last name had become Ilyin, told the story of his wife to Louis Bromfield and Thomas Mann, whose daughter had introduced Maximilian to him.[107] It's unlikely that the two writers actually participated in drafting the sixty typed pages that were going to serve as the basis of the project. Neither of them ever mentioned it. However, the fact that both their names were associated with the screenplay gave the project cachet it would have otherwise lacked. On May 16, 1944, Thomas Mann would see Renoir at a dinner given by mutual friends, the Van Leydens,[108] but there's no information about whether the subject of *Woman of a Hundred Faces* was discussed that night. The project wouldn't go any further, and only the producers at Federal Films, William Lebaron and Boris Morros, showed interest for a while. A rumor about it circulated, fed perhaps by Ilyin himself and suggesting a connection with Katharine Hepburn; and a Swedish reporter put forward Renoir's and Greta Garbo's names.[109] That was it. Mme. and M. Ilyin would soon go back to France, where Maximilian would write additional dialogue for the Frank Tuttle film *Gunman in the Streets*, with Simone Signoret, as well as two books about the painters Sevek and Utrillo. Maria Lani would die in Paris on March 11, 1954, at the age of forty-eight.

Renoir also continued to consider the Conrad novel *Under Western Eyes*,[‡] for which there remains the first draft of a treatment about fifteen typed pages in length.[110] He'd also thought about the idea of adapting the Maupassant stories *Ce cochon de Morin* and *La Parure*,[§¶] two projects that foundered because of an issue with the rights. But whether these projects were entirely personal or brought to him, they remained embryonic, and none of them would have allowed him the hope of working freely except within the structure of an independent production that he'd have to organize. Renoir spent many months trying to set up a company that could become involved just as much in theater as in film. It

* Ingrid Bergman would act in it in 1948, and also in 1966, in a film directed for television by Ted Kotcheff.

† In 1956, Maximilian Ilyin would sue Avon Publications, whom he accused of having published an English translation of the play that was not his. The court records of this suit provide proof that Maximilian Ilyin and Maximilian Abramowicz were the same person.

‡ Already adapted for the screen by Marc Allégret in 1936.

§ *Translator's note: La Parure* = "The Set of Diamond Jewelry," or, perhaps, "The Necklace"; *Ce Cochon de Morin* = "That Pig, Morin."

¶ In 1947, Renoir and Henri Troyat exchanged letters about the possibility of adapting *La Parure*.

was proof that although he had not given up the cinema, a certain disillusionment had begun to overcome him, the first signs of which had appeared only a few months after his arrival in Los Angeles. This disappointment probably accounts for, at least in part, his idea of transforming *The Crime of Monsieur Lange* into a Broadway musical with music by Hanns Eisler,[111] with whom he'd worked on *The Woman on the Beach.*

The organization he wanted to create was known at first as "Jean Renoir Productions" but finally ended up being called "Film Group." The films it would produce, four a year at the most, would be distributed by Allied Artists, which was a branch of Monogram, a company that specialized in B films. Forrest Judd, a young screenwriter at Monogram, was helping him accomplish the task.

At the beginning of 1948, the day before a meeting with Steve Broidy, who was then head of Allied Artists, Renoir explained his intentions in a memo written in French and having to do with the production of "films with a budget less than $500,000,"[112] which would require a "long period of preparation and rehearsal with actors and crewmembers to succeed in resolving most of the problems before beginning to shoot." This "would allow reducing the duration of the *speaking scenes* of the shoot to around four weeks, without counting the shots without sound taken on location."[113]

Ideas for film weren't lacking. He was considering a screenplay entitled *Children of Vienna* and several plays by Anouilh—especially his *Roméo et Jeannette** and *Le Voyageur sans bagages*†—but the American rights for these had already been reserved. And then, renewed contact with Georges Simenon was leading to new ideas. The writer had moved to Tucson, Arizona. In spring 1948, he stopped in Los Angeles with his new companion and secretary, Denise. At the end of summer, the Renoirs returned the visit, and the two couples crossed the border into Mexico. The two women waited at a café while their men paid homage to the inhabitants of the local brothel.[114] Jean got carried away immediately by Simenon's novel, *La neige était sale,*‡ which had just appeared, and he was even more taken with *La Fuite de monsieur Monde,*§ which he claimed he intended to make his first completely independent production,¶ a privilege he

---

* Transposed to India, the play would be incarnated in 1952 as *Monsoon*, directed by Rod Amateau from a screenplay by Forrest Judd, Renoir's collaborator and assistant for *The River.*

† After having thought of Charles Boyer for the lead, Renoir was considering Frederic March or Henry Fonda for *Le Voyageur sans bagages.* Jean Anouilh had himself brought his play to the screen in 1944, with Pierre Fresnay, Blanchette Brunoy, and Pierre Renoir.

‡ *Translator's note:* Published in English as *The Stain on the Snow* and, later, as *Dirty Snow.*

§ *Translator's note:* Published in English as *Monsieur Monde Vanishes.*

¶ "I'm hoping to begin shooting the exteriors for *Monsieur Monde* in August in New York and Chicago," he wrote to Simenon on July 4, 1948.

was at the same time according to the Clifford Odets play *Night Music*.

Ideas, yes; but money, no. In September, the loans he was hoping for were refused by the banks that had promised them. Renoir surrendered. "My independent production is a complete failure."[115] "You mustn't save *Monsieur Monde* for me any longer. I've lost hope in setting up my independent production,"[116] he wrote the same day to Clifford Odets and to Simenon, also informing the latter that, although he hadn't been able to see Charles Boyer, he had left him *Le Fond de la bouteille.* For a short time, he thought he would be able to direct *Goya* for the producer B. P. Schulberg, but that plan failed as well.

Renoir had not made a film since the end of 1946 and *The Woman on the Beach*, and he was quite aware that he was at an impasse. Attempting to explain the reason for this series of failures, for these attempts aborted one after another, he wrote to various people about the decay of filmmaking in Hollywood, according to him due mainly to the decline in profits and the increasing fees for stars as well as the incomes of studio bigwigs.[117] He built his case on some disturbing forecasts about the months to come. "At RKO, they made nearly sixty films last year.[†] They're planning on ten for the coming year."[‡118] The next day, he went so far as to suggest "a kind of current of panic sweeping through the city," caused by the fact that, as is the case in Hollywood, where "the studios are practically shut down," "films cost too much, and they're hoping to shoot them at a better profit by making painters and plumbers with their tongues hanging out to accept lower salaries," whereas, "of course, the stars keep getting $300,000 a year and the executives, 400,000."[119]

The fact was that he couldn't find work in Hollywood. Was Renoir the victim of a kind of ostracism? In Hollywood, the year 1947 witnessed the first wave of what would later be known as the witch hunt, and several figures with whom Renoir had ended up associated over the years were being forced to answer questions about their activities on American soil. Among them were Irving Pichel, Renoir's "second" on *Swamp Water*, as well as the first screenwriter for *The Southerner*, Hugo Butler, who would see his name put on the blacklist.

The day after his hearing with the House Un-American Activities Committee on October 30, 1947, Bertolt Brecht jumped onto the first plane headed for Germany. Renoir quite regularly frequented the circle of German émigrés and spoke their language better than he understood English. Hanns Eisler, the composer of the music for *The Woman on the Beach*, was a member of this

---

* Brought to the screen in 1956 by Henry Hathaway as *The Bottom of the Bottle*.

† RKO produced forty films in 1947.

‡ RKO would produce thirty films in 1948.

group, and Brecht had described in his *Journal* seeing Renoir at Eisler's home in October 1943. They were talking about the destruction of Naples, which the director thought couldn't be rebuilt because "it had no style and had simply sprung up among cultured people." And Renoir had gone on, "The age of the hand has been replaced by the age of the brain. The most dangerous animal that exists is the architect. He has wreaked more havoc than war." Brecht had thought that the sight of Renoir eating a sausage was "funny, almost exciting." Then he concluded, "*His* senses are in good shape."[120] On at least one occasion, Brecht and Eisler had spoken of Renoir when he wasn't with them; and on that day in December 1944, it was about the French in Hollywood, and the rumor suggesting that René Clair and Renoir were anti-Semites. Eisler is supposed to have put it right by saying, "Not anti-Semites; it's just that they can't stand Jews."[121]

The composer was the brother of Gerhart Eisler and Ruth Eisler, two important representatives of the Communist International (Comintern) in the United States. On these grounds, because the notion of guilt by association could be brought to bear, Eisler had had to testify before the committee in September 1947. A measure of deportation was taken against him, but in February 1948, he was "granted permission to leave voluntarily" in exchange for the formal promise that he would never attempt to return. Eisler and his wife left the United States for Czechoslovakia on March 26, 1948.[122]

Renoir was aware of all these events, to which he referred in a letter in which he also expressed anxiety about jokes made by his son, "whose ideas are as red as his hair,"[123] and about his son's friends at Santa Barbara College of the University of California:* "A small scandal in my family wouldn't help my own affairs. The film people in Hollywood are more reactionary than the petit bourgeois in Batignolles. Recently Hanns Eisler was insulted in the papers because he's a foreigner and, it seems, a Communist. The same thing could also happen to me, although I keep apart from any kind of politics, not out of fear, but out of disinterest. I don't know anyone more boring than an American Communist."[124] Why would "the same thing" happen to him? Perhaps because his reputation as a man "on the Left," close to the Communists for several years, had preceded him in the United States; and especially because he actually had not abstained since 1941 from any political position.

Nothing compromising, however, seeing that his most memorable intercessions had involved supporting the Soviet Union while it was still an ally of the United States. Renoir had received several offers to make pro-Soviet films—for

---

* *Translator's note:* The school's name from 1944 to 1958, before becoming the University of California, Santa Barbara (UCSB).

example, *Mission to Moscow* in September 1942,[125] which would be directed in 1943 for Warner by Michael Curtiz;* and the month before that, an intriguing *Stalin* written by Emil Ludwig and recorded for their files by Dido using this bizarre description: "Biographical essay that sheds light on the figure of Stalin, and especially the criminal politics of England as represented by Chamberlain, major cause of the current disasters."[126]

The declaration that Renoir recorded on February 25, 1944, did take on a particular tone when related to the "Popular Front" past of its author. On International Women's Day in the Soviet Union, which was celebrated on March 8, he had gone so far as to declare, "Women of Russia, I send you my best wishes. Although these wishes are coming from the United States of America, they are those of a Frenchman who hasn't forgotten the fact that on Red Square, next to Lenin, rests the tricolor flag, the standard of the Commune of Paris. . . . Victory is there, at the end of your machine gun, of your riveters, at the end of your plow, at the end of your darning needles, at the end of your suffering, at the end of your heroism."[127]

He made this statement on behalf of the National Council of American-Soviet Friendship, to which he actively belonged and which would have already been enough reason for his being interrogated three years later. But he was also a member of the directing committee for film of this same council, and in that capacity he was called upon several times to come to the Soviet consulate. On August 12, 1943, with Hanns Eisler and others, he took part in a reception at the Mocambo Café in honor of the director Mikhail Kalatozov,† who would soon become the Soviet consul for Los Angeles. Unknown for a long time, this involvement was revealed by Christopher Faulkner, who obtained a copy of the Jean Renoir file created by the FBI. It is a file that remains mostly suppressed because the majority of the lines on each page were blacked out before the copy was provided, but it still proves that over the years of the war Renoir was an active anti-Fascist.

Also within the framework of the National Council of American-Soviet Friendship, Renoir played an important part in organizing and running a large commemorative party for the tenth anniversary of diplomatic relations between the United States and the Soviet Union. This took place on November 16, 1943, at the Shrine Auditorium in Los Angeles. Walter Huston read a statement from Walt Whitman for the Soviet people. Edward G. Robinson was the narrator for *Song of a Free People,* a cantata composed for the occasion by Bernard

---

* That same month, Renoir also received *Education for Death,* by Gregor Ziemer, which Edward Dmytryk would make for RKO under the title *Hitler's Children.*

† Future director of *The Cranes Are Flying* (1957).

Schoenfeld and Earl Robinson. Olivia de Havilland spoke during the finale. Art direction for the event was by Eugène Lourié, and direction by Jean Renoir, who was equally responsible for a montage of American and Soviet films showing the shared future of the American and the Soviet people in war as in peace and presented as the highlight of the evening.[128]

The National Council of American-Soviet Friendship was classified as a "subversive" organization by ruling no. 9835 on March 21, 1947, as decreed by the Truman administration. In the list that was established and published at that time were two other organizations to which Renoir belonged, the People's Educational Association and the Joint Anti-Fascist Refugee Committee (JAFRC). He was even the codirector, with Dorothy Parker, of the "motion pictures" branch of the latter, and then its honorary president, a position for which he replaced the actor Philip Merivale, who had played Professor Sorel in *This Land Is Mine*. The JAFRC was an umbrella association of several organizations (all of which were declared "subversive" in 1945) whose primary purpose was helping war refugees throughout Europe. This clears up the previously rather enigmatic nature of the two first sentences of a letter from Renoir to Burgess Meredith: "The Varsovie Hospital people are hanging on the phone to proclaim their enthusiasm about your name and Paulette's name printed on the mail paper. I feel the same and hope we will very soon get the necessary money to help these Spanish Partisans who, in the real beginning of the war, were the first defenders of our liberties."[129]

His participation in these various organizations, which apparently was quite an active one, doesn't contradict the sentiment he expressed regarding the American Communist communities, which he judged to be "boring"; but it should also be kept in mind that American law rapidly ended up confusing antiracism with Communism. There's no doubt that Renoir wasn't "invited" to testify before the committee, but that "omission" only signifies that he wasn't denounced by anyone. And if he wasn't denounced, it's probably because his decision to keep such groups at a distance, fed as much by his French experiences as by his observations in Hollywood of Gaullist, Vichy-supporting, or Communist activists, had led him not to take part in meetings attended by people with whom he was also close in other respects. That's the reason why his name didn't appear in any mention of a political meeting whose participants nevertheless counted among his connections. For example, when the screenwriter Bess Taffel was talking about the small group of non-Communists who were still "on the Left" with whom she would associate in Hollywood, she mentioned the names Charles and Oona Chaplin, Hanns and Louisa Eisler, Lion Feuchtwanger, Clifford Odets, and Salka Viertel,[130] who were all friendly with Renoir. It was a fact that Renoir saw them regularly, but in different circumstances.

Renoir's name was never mentioned in any official investigation, but could it have been added to one of those "gray lists" containing the names of crew-members and actors producers were being discreetly advised not to hire? Such lists were never revealed, but apparently they were devised primarily starting in 1951, a time when Renoir was most often in Europe. At any rate, Christopher Faulkner is probably right in suggesting that Renoir had barely a chance to find work at RKO after Howard Hughes took control of the company in 1948. The multimillionaire's fiercely right-wing opinions could only have led to his not hiring a director who had actively and publicly participated in the activities of at least three "subversive" organizations appearing on a list obtainable by anyone.

It could also be the case that in a period when the country was shutting itself off from a part of the world, preference was being awarded American directors rather than those from abroad who had not yet proven themselves. The fact remains that the difficulties Renoir encountered in finding work and financing his personal projects were due to the commercial failure of his most recent productions. Beginning in 1951, when the wave of McCarthyism scoured Hollywood with an intensity never before experienced, making every effort to sweep away anyone who could be associated in one way or another with American Communism, Renoir had stopped working in the United States. He was therefore no longer on the map the Red hunters intended to cleanse.

"I am not seeking a job in Hollywood,"[131] he wrote, after receiving a memo from the Screen Writers Guild concerning the next publication of a list of figures cited in the reports of the Joint Fact-Finding Committee on Un-American Activities of the California Legislature on which his name appeared. He then suggested that he "probably" owed that listing to an article on *Monsieur Verdoux* he'd given *The Screen Writer* in 1947. It was an odd hypothesis, considering his other involvements, which were more "compromising" than his support of Chaplin. He also stated, "I dislike to be mixed up with a bunch of American Communists which I always tried to avoid, and who profess philosophical ideas exactly opposite to mine."[132]

During the entire length of this empty span of time for Renoir, ideas for projects proliferated; but salvation would come from one of the oldest. For a long time he'd thought he would have to abandon it like all the others, because it had come into being when he was still working on *The Woman on the Beach*. In fact, he'd become aware of it in fall 1946 when he'd noticed a summary of a book by Rumer Godden that had appeared in *The New Yorker*. The book was about a brief period in the life of a little girl growing up in India. Its author's sensitivity and subtle wisdom had allowed her to capture the faltering and elusive glimmers of childhood. The article concluded, "This beautifully written long short story may not greatly increase the number of Miss Godden readers, but it will certainly delight the ones she has."[133] As a result, Renoir read *The River* and decided to film that "Story about Children in the Indies,"[134] as was noted on the index card that appeared in his file cabinet of ideas.

On November 19, 1946, he pitched the project to Enterprise Productions, the company of David Loew, the producer of *The Southerner*. That was when he wrote, "I know that few people are going to realize the wonderful possibilities contained in this story, but I feel that it is exactly the type of novel which would give me the best inspiration for my type of work—almost no action, but fascinating characters; very touching relationships between them; the basis for great acting performances; and an unexpressed, subtle, heart-breaking, innocent love story involving a little girl and a physically broken-down, morally sick, but still hopeful, wounded officer."[135]

In that same letter, he claimed he had asked his agents to take an option on the rights for the book and said he was meeting with David Loew the next day. Loew's answer came ten days later. He thought that *The River* would make as good a film as *The Southerner*, but the kind that Enterprise no longer had the liberty to produce. Loew concluded, "In other words, dear Jean, what I'm trying to say is that we are going commercial."[136] Renoir took note: *The River* wasn't suitable for Enterprise Productions.[137] In the weeks that followed, he discovered that "the studios and independent producers do not at all share my enthusiasm." It had become clear to him that "the best place to make it would be in the Indies."[138]

"In the Indies," quite possibly, but for the moment, nowhere. For their adaptation of *Black Narcissus*, Michael Powell and Emeric Pressburger had chosen to re-create the scenery of the convent perched on a summit in the Himalayas in the studios at Pinewood, painting snow-covered mountains on glass. They filmed the exteriors in the subtropical garden of Leonardslee, which is located in Horsham, West Sussex. The author of the book wasn't happy about this; and even though she had probably not seen that film when Renoir approached her through his agents, she was already talking about how disappointed she was in Powell and Pressburger's decisions. After *Black Narcissus* was shown in London in April 1947, she'd say there was nothing in it that was authentic, which is true and exactly what the two filmmakers had assumed and wanted. She'd also claim that it held no interest at all, which is far from the truth. The strongly erotic tenor of the film may have been what had bothered Rumer Godden. She was just as unconvinced by *Enchantment* (Irving Reis, 1948), based on her novel *Take Three Tenses: A Fugue in Time*, which is understandable. However, Renoir was offering to write the screenplay with her, and that was enough to overcome her misgivings. Godden's friends told her that, as a director, Renoir was "simply the finest film director in the world." She herself hadn't seen any of his films and hadn't even known that Auguste Renoir had a son who was a director.[139]

Months passed, and Renoir could not succeed in arousing the interest of a studio or a producer. Later he'd say that because the film takes place in India, everyone had expected that it would at least have some elephants and a tiger hunt, neither of which were part of the story. He had asked Eugène Lourié to read the book. The artistic director was immediately won over. He'd later relate that at that point Renoir had no plans to film in India aside from a few backgrounds, which would be entrusted to a second crew probably directed by Lourié. The film was to be directed in a house specially developed for this project, perhaps located on a bank of the Mississippi.[140] It was true that the first lines of the novel allowed Renoir to imagine filming *The River* without ever leaving the United States: "The river was in Bengal, India, but for the purpose of this book, these thoughts, it might as easily have been a river in America, in Europe, in England, France, New Zealand or Timbuctoo."[141] But at this point, it was more than a question of filming whatever or wherever; the option taken on the rights was expiring without the project's having progressed.

In fall 1948, which was two years since Renoir had become infatuated with the novel, Forrest Judd, who was helping him in his attempt to set up an independent company, put him in touch with a certain Kenneth McEldowney. At forty-two, McEldowney was head of a chain of florist shops in Los Angeles. At one of his branches, just steps from the studios at Fox, he had successfully developed a "drive-in" service operated by pretty young women in short skirts. He was planning to get involved in producing movies, an idea born from his poor opinion of Hollywood films, which he had discovered mostly thanks to the screenings to which he had gone with his wife, Melvina Pumphrey, who worked in publicity at Metro, and whose duties included promoting both Esther Williams's films and the screen siren herself.

McEldowney would recount how the belief that nothing new and interesting could be produced in Hollywood led him to choose a random point on a map of the world. Accuracy demands it be added that he had served in the US Air Force during the war and that he knew India when he left on a first field trip in June 1948 for the double purpose of acquiring partner investors and finding a story to film over there. Then he started negotiating not only with the Indian government but also with princes who wanted to invest in film. Although the princes looked upon such an endeavor as a primarily financial affair, the government was interested in the taxes that would accrue from the direction of an American production, the opportunity for training Indian crews, and the equipment that would be left behind after filming. McEldowney also negotiated with the British National Film Finance Corporation, arguing that the film would be a Commonwealth production because it would be financed with Indian money, even though the Indian government was declaring that India had severed all ties with the British crown.[142]

Apparently, the budding producer had first been tempted by the book *Home to India* by Rama Rau, the daughter of a diplomat, who told him instead to start by reading the Rumer Godden novel, which she thought would be more suitable for film than hers. Taken by *The River*, McEldowney began looking for a director as soon as he got back to California, and those were the circumstances in which Forrest Judd put him in contact with Renoir.

The two new partners went quickly to business. A first draft of a contract made in mid-November with Oriental International Films specified that Renoir's share of the potential profits would be 33 percent. On December 9, 1948, a contract was drawn up between Commonwealth Pictures Corporation and Renoir. The film would not be allowed to exceed the equivalent in rupees of $400,000. For his work, the director would collect the equivalent in rupees of $25,000, to be paid in 1949, plus the identical sum to be paid in 1950; as well as $3,333 for each week of shooting, $1,000 a week for editing in India, and, finally, 20 percent of the profits produced by the film.[143]

For McEldowney, directing the film in India was a matter of absolute necessity upon which the financing of the film depended entirely. Renoir has confirmed this, writing that "the first reason which impelled me to accept McEldowney's proposition to shoot in India was that he was proposing a picture with all the money in the bank, which meant *freedom from fear*."[144] Apparently, the Indian contribution represented around three-quarters of the total budget by the time the film was finished.

An item in an Indian newspaper from April 1956 offers an indication of the funding achieved by the producer. The Maharajah of Gondral, Vikrah Singh, was suing Oriental International Films, United Artists (the film's distributor), and various others, charging that his "late father, who died in 1952, invested $429,707 in the motion picture, which was made in India, but never received any repayment."[145] Consequently, the Maharajah was demanding more than $200,000. Shortly before, McEldowney, who wanted to launch three new productions, had been announcing that *The River* had pulled in $6.5 million in ticket sales throughout the world.[146]

The fact that the producer and director said they were in agreement about not calling upon known actors or actresses resulted less from Renoir's desires than from McEldowney's wish to keep the budget within "reasonable" proportions that were being dictated to him by the conditions for investing. "No star," wrote Renoir in November, but as the film was distributed, on several occasions he would regret not being able to have cast, for example, Charles Laughton or Burgess Meredith,[147] who were too expensive for the film, and he would imagine a number of famous actors in the role of Captain John.*

On the day the contract was made out for *The River*, Renoir was still thinking about first directing the *Goya* that B. P. Schulberg was supposed to produce.[148] A definitive shelving of that project allowed him to take his first trip to India, which he would claim was a prerequisite for signing the contract and which was also something McEldowney would maintain had to be impressed upon Renoir. The first trace of this requirement appears in a letter from Renoir to his agents: "Mr. McEldowney insists that I go now, before Christmas, to India for several weeks in order to meet some useful people, collect documentation for the script, and supervise the filming of a certain elephant round-up, an event which happens only every ten years and which would be incorporated in the picture."[149] In the end, the producer would take it upon himself to cover that elephant hunt, and it is very possible that the director never intended to give it a place in the film.

On January 22, 1949, Renoir informed Louis Guillaume that he was leaving for Calcutta in four days, then to Rome, where it would be possible to write to him at the address of Universalia, before he made a brief visit to Paris—two stop-offs on the way home that he'd finally cancel in order to stop in London and meet Rumer Godden. Dido went with him, as did Forrest Judd. McEldowney, who had arrived weeks earlier, was there, too. Planned to last a bit less than a month, with a return trip scheduled for March 1, this first stay in India, which began February 1, two days after the first anniversary of the assassination of Gandhi, would be extended to mid-April.

Already occurring at a turning point in the director's career, after a period in Hollywood that had left him dissatisfied, this initial Indian visit would turn out to be essential for the life of Renoir. He was fifty-four. For more than eight years he had lived away from his brothers and his lifelong friends. Paul Cézanne, one of the most long-standing, had died on October 6, 1947. Paul was twenty-two years older than Jean, but he had been his first friend. "My father and mother thought of him as their son. . . . If you can consider friendship as an art, Paul held a place in it that was as great as that of his father in the art of painting."[150]

---

* On a list of suggestions created by the William Morris Agency for the role of Captain John in *Eastward in Eden* [*The River*, before the title of the film was changed] appear the names John Dall, Lew Ayres, Richard Hylton, Michael Redgrave, Keith Burt, Scott McKay, James Mason, Glenn Ford, Sam Wanamaker, Robert Walker, Van Heflin, Don Taylor, Roger Livesey, Norman Wooland. (Jean Renoir Papers, Production Files, Box 9, Folder 3.)

The announcement of his death left Jean feeling "very disoriented."[151] It brought his thoughts back to Essoyes, "where he would come almost every summer and we'd go out together on long trips along the river during which the isolation, the narrowness of the little boat, and the snacks we ate on the riverbank brought us intimately together."[152] And these thoughts led to his conclusion that "even in our atomic era, there's no way to go back in time, and the past really is just that."[153]

That reality would be confirmed less than a year after the filming of *The River*, when Pierre Lestringuez, his "friend before childhood,"* would also pass away, on December 18, 1950, at the age of sixty-one. Jean Renoir's first steps in life, his beginnings as a filmmaker, no longer remained, aside from the existence of Catherine Hessling, with whom he had no relationship other than one characterized by conflict, and his brother Pierre. A new Renoir was about to be born, and over the coming years, the legend of him was going to be rewritten.

* *Translator's note:* Meaning that their parents had been friends before they had been born, thus "predetermining" their own friendship.

28

"A Story about Children in the Indies"

The River

From the time of its construction in 1836 to the independence of India in 1947, the Great Eastern Hotel had emerged as the establishment of choice for British officers in Calcutta. Jean and Dido Renoir took possession of the hotel's "royal suite," which was located on the third floor, where they could watch the flurry of red-turbaned employees and could also find Kenneth McEldowney. Four landings had been necessary: the first at Wake Island, "a very small extinct volcano in the middle of the Pacific used for airplane stopovers";[1] the others in Manila, Hong Kong, and Bangkok. The director had to make the most of his stay to decide on locations, meet Indian actors, start pulling together a crew, and film a few test shots. In that period, American films made far from Hollywood were still a rarity, and *The River* would be one of the first to be shot entirely abroad. What is more, the film would be in color, which required extremely heavy equipment to be brought in from London. London was also the place where Eugène Lourié and Claude Renoir Jr., who was director of photography, would receive their training on the use of the Technicolor process.

Because Indian cities and Indian life remain without equivalent today, the impression that they must have produced of another world was probably even more striking in 1949, especially for Renoir, who had not traveled much. The smells, lights, colors, sounds—everything—could have only dumbfounded the director, and the film would convey a trace of that amazement. When he got back from his first trip to Calcutta, he would write that he had found what he considered to be "one of the greatest inspirations in my life," produced by the discovery of "the beauty and the quality of the ancient world," because India "didn't change in four thousand years" and had preserved "an aristocratic style which has about completely disappeared in our mechanized civilization."

"To be confronted every day with boatmen working their oars in the Ganges River who are directly stepping out of an Egyptian bas-relief, or with a girl dressed in a sari just buying in a market, looking like an animated Tanagra statue, believe me, that's exactly the shock I was needing after eight years in Hollywood."[2] Although the rumor of riots between Muslims and Hindus reached his friends in America, who worried about Renoir's being in a city packed with a million refugees since the famine of 1948, he didn't act as if he were affected by it. In Calcutta, on the banks of the Ganges, Renoir felt himself becoming one of those primitives about which he wrote to Georges Sadoul, to thank him for sending his book *Les Pionniers du cinéma:*

"The older I get, the more I believe that in the history of the not entirely original arts, only the primitive period has been able to produce complete masterpieces."[3] He described the shock he felt as comparable to the one caused him by the discovery of sound film.

Another fact about his stay in India, although secondary in comparison to the upheaval occasioned by his revelation, still held significance. Admired and celebrated in France since the middle of the thirties, then having become in Hollywood one among so many others—as well as a figure of controversy in his "ex-country"—Renoir found himself in Calcutta to be the center of attention and thought of as a leading and renowned director who had come to India to direct a great film. He was considered a master by young Indians dreaming of directing films themselves. Because of this, Calcutta was the place where Renoir truly became the great Master, in the exemplary sense that his father had signified for other painters. The particular features defining the relationship between student and master in India increased the importance of this identity, which rekindled the confidence that his adventures and misadventures in Hollywood had caused to wane.

The news of Renoir's arrival—his move into the Great Eastern Hotel had been reported in *The Statesman*—had sped through the community of Bengali apprentice directors, who belonged to the Calcutta Film Society that they had created. All of twenty-seven, Satyajit Ray seemed to be the rashest, appearing one evening at the hotel's reception desk and asking to see Mister Renoir. As soon as he gained access to the royal suite, the questions in his head about film vanished and Ray asked the director what he thought of India. The magic of Renoir came forth instantaneously, and the Bengali master would write about

* Translator's note: Histoire générale du cinema, Vol. 2: Les pionniers du cinéma, Denoël, 1947–1975. Beginning in 1946, Sadoul published six pioneering volumes on the history of world cinema, intended as a response to Maurice Bardèche and Robert Brasillach's Histoire du cinéma, which he judged as too partisan. Sadoul applied a double perspective to the history of film, seeing it as both an art form and an industry, although his own studies were critiqued by some as abounding in factual errors. He was the only film historian of his time to pay detailed attention to the role of film in developing countries and to see it as an effective vehicle of communication among people of different cultures.

him, "Renoir was not only approachable, but so embarrassingly polite and modest that I felt if I wasn't too careful I would probably find myself discoursing on the Future of the Cinema for his benefit."[4] A few days later, the Calcutta Film Society organized an evening during which Renoir would answer questions from budding young directors, encouraging them, among other things, to turn their backs on the American model in order to draw on the Indian reality as material for their films.

A few weeks before his encounter with Renoir, Satyajit Ray had learned that his adaptation of Rabindranath Tagore's novel, *The Home and the World,*[*] would not get off the ground. He began thinking instead of bringing to the screen Bibhutibhushan Bandyopadhyay's *Pather Panchali,* a project that would become his first film in 1955. Contrary to what has sometimes been suggested, Ray didn't participate in the direction of *The River,* because he was involved in his job as a paste-up artist for advertising; yet two of Ray's future close collaborators, the artistic director Bansi Chandragupta and the cinematographer Subrata Mitra, were involved with the filming, although Mitra's services were only in the capacity of a simple observer.

During his first trip to India, Renoir began putting together his crew. He also saw about a hundred female auditioners for a role in the film. To Clifford Odets, he wrote that he had found "an ugly duckling"[5] named Patricia Walters. She was thirteen, Australian in background, and had been found at a school. She would play Harriet, Rumer Godden's alter ego. He had also found an "Anglo-Indian girl who is maybe not a good actress, but who is so nice that I would like to bring her to the States as a wife for an unmarried best friend."[6] This wasn't Radha Sri Ram, who played Melanie, contrary to what has been written.[7] After arriving at the end of January, Renoir had made his two decisions very rapidly, because they were announced on February 15.

Aided in his search primarily by Rumer Godden's two sisters, who were still living in Calcutta, the director also began looking for scenery. Apparently, Satyajit Ray accompanied him at times in these searches, taking advantage of his lunch hours and his Saturdays, but Renoir's main guide was named Hari Das Gupta. Gupta had studied film at the University of Southern California (USC) in 1946 and 1947 and had met the director briefly when Renoir came to speak to the students in his class. Gupta became one of Renoir's assistants. In addition, every evening Chandragupta would give Satyajit Ray an account of the day's work, and Ray would record his friend's observations in a notebook, which he illustrated with photos taken on the set.

---

* Satyajit Ray would direct the film in 1984.

A few days after his arrival in India, in Barrackpore, which is to the north of the city, from a bank of the river Hooghly, which is a tributary of the Ganges, Renoir spotted an unoccupied house belonging to the Maharajah of Gwalior.[8] During the summer of 1949, Eugène Lourié would visit several other residences, before returning definitively to this one. Because a few tufts of grass had yellowed, he had the lawn torn out and sowed a new one to promptly recolor it green, and the street of the village was completely constructed, using the same materials Indians used to build their houses. This solution was suggested by Lourié after weeks of fruitless searching for a "possible" village, and McEldowney was in favor of it, thrilled as he was to be able to reduce the number of workdays. Renoir agreed, too, more than happy to avoid in this way the vagaries of shooting in real exteriors.[9]

This decision is certainly proof enough, if proof is needed, that Renoir had never intended to direct a film purporting to give an account of real India and the life of Indians. Rumer Godden's book, as well, had no such ambition. It was a novel of colonial India in the tradition of many others, and it was very behind the times in comparison to a novel like *A Passage to India* (1924), published more than twenty years earlier. *The River* would be an American film directed in India, not an Indian film, which only an Indian director could make. Satyajit Ray would remember that being reminded of this fact by Renoir during an evening at the Calcutta Film Society had at first disenchanted him. "It was therefore an acute disappointment to hear Renoir declare that *The River* was being made expressly for an American audience, that it contained only one Indian character—a servant in a European household, and that we were not to expect much in the way of authentic India in it. Of course, the background would be authentic, since all the exteriors would be shot in Calcutta. I couldn't help feeling that it was overdoing it a bit, coming all the way from California merely to get the topography right."[10]

Questioned during that same conference about difficulties encountered in Hollywood by the European directors, Renoir indulged in one of those turns of phrase all audiences appreciate, explaining that a film like *Brief Encounter** only existed because London had suffered German air raids and that what Hollywood really needed was a good bombardment.[11]

On their way back to California, Jean and Dido Renoir stopped for a few days in England. That was when Jean telephoned to ask to meet Rumer Godden, who had just moved to Buckinghamshire with her family into a seventeenth-century

* "I call *Brief Encounter* a picture of importance," Ingrid Bergman would write to Renoir, before adding, "(But I forget, we have always had different taste in movies, isn't that right?)" (December 15, 1949, Jean Renoir Papers.)

red brick cottage trimmed in white. As Godden would later write, Renoir, wanting to see her home and meet her family, specified, "*Chez vous,* I 'ear you are ze mozer *de deux petites filles charmantes, et j'espère*—if eet is possible—*d'être en famille.*"

A few days later, a frail brunette with an imposing man appeared at Godden's residence. According to her, Jean was so enormous he barely fit into her cottage, and the children referred to him as Babar the elephant. He was nearly bald, and his shrewd eyes peeked out from rolls of fat that jiggled when he laughed. His "Franglish" was endearing, but he usually expressed himself in a "French, vivid with argot. . . . Our chairs, even the sofa in the sitting room were too small for Jean who eventually, still talking, lay down on the floor to the children's amazement."[12]

Renoir informed the writer, "No one else can write that script." He was intending her to come to Beverly Hills. "Two months, perhaps, to write the script, then casting. . . . Then will come shooting the film, six months, nine months, who can tell?" Naturally, all expenses would be paid by Oriental International Films, with flights in first class, and a stipend of one hundred pounds a week. Rumer Godden said she was won over.

On April 17, 1949, the newspapers reported that an agreement had been concluded between the director and McEldowney specifying four films in Technicolor and in English over the next two years, and the filming of *The River* was to be in October.[13] Two days later, Renoir wrote to Rumer Godden to inform her of the need to find a new title for their project, since *The River* was already taken.[14] He seemed to favor an Indian title, perhaps *Pukha Sahib,* which had been suggested by McEldowney. He also expressed his enthusiasm for Godden's suggestions, *Ganga Nadee* or *Gunga Nahdee.*[15]

Although the first drafts of the screenplay were entitled *Eastward in Eden,* the question of the title would remain hanging for a long time; in March 1951, Renoir wrote to Darryl Zanuck to ask him whether it was true that Fox, which had produced Frank Borzage's *The River,* would only accept the use of the same title on condition that it be preceded by the name of the writer, explaining, "If the name Rumer Godden has to be as big as the title, we must find another title and that would be very bad for the publicity we have already started, and *The River* is undoubtedly the only appropriate."[16] The producer's answer, if there ever was one, hasn't been found.

In Calcutta, Renoir had also made a few test shots that he had screened when he returned to California. In black and white to start with, because Technicolor was refusing to provide a print in color until the distribution of the film in theaters had been decided. He informed Ram Sen Gupta, his cameraman in India, of this hitch and shared with him an important decision he had made. Although Renoir's original idea had been to entrust the role of director of photography to Eugen Schüfftan, the head cinematographer for *Port of Shadows,* among other films, during their stay in London, McEldowney had impressed upon Renoir the fact that hiring an American technician would be likely to thwart certain agreements concerning coproduction. Schüfftan had, in fact, moved to the United States in 1940, where he had changed his name to Shuftan and chose to become an American citizen. As a result, Renoir had contacted a man named Osmond Borradaile (and not "Boradel," as he wrote it then), head cameraman most notably for Robert Flaherty on *Elephant Boy* (1937).* It turned out that he was of Canadian nationality and therefore a member of the Commonwealth.[17] But several days later, with permission from the representative for Technicolor, Renoir offered the film to his nephew Claude, for whom *The River* would constitute his first experience with color and whom Ram Sen Gupta would accompany to London as part of his training in the use of Technicolor.

Among a number of issues still unsolved, the one posed by a certain "description of the Ganges River from the Himalayan Mountains down to the delta" led Renoir to suggest several solutions. He thought that "the best one" consisted in having Claude Renoir shoot "in Switzerland or in the French Alps, where this type of scenery is about the same and where we would find roads, telefarics [*Renoir's attempt at an English spelling of* téléphérique, *which means* "cable car"], funiculars exist, helping us to approach the peaks."[18]

In mid-June, Rumer Godden left London for New York, where a suite had been reserved for her at the Waldorf Astoria. Four days later, she left for Los Angeles. The Renoirs and the McEldowneys met her at the airport. In the car, Dido found the time to tell her discreetly that the producer hadn't been in favor of her coming,[19] stuck as he was on the old Hollywood refrain of wanting writers kept away from the film adaptations of their books.

The Renoirs showed their guest around their house on Leona Drive, where they had been living for a month. The writer would be sharing it with Jean and Dido, as well as Bessie, the English housekeeper, whom Godden would describe as persnickety, and Helen, a black woman who came every morning, left in the evening, and sang in a deep voice. The two dachshunds, Nénette and Tambo,†

---

* Based on the chapter "Toomai of the Elephants" in Rudyard Kipling's *The Jungle Book*. Produced by Alexander Korda and entirely filmed in a London studio.

† Tambo, or *Tambeau*, was derived from the French words *tant beau* ("so beautiful") and was traditional for the dogs in the Renoir family.

were also on the premises. Renoir was surrounded by four women, a re-creation of the world of his childhood; and his adaptation of Godden's book, full of new female characters, echoed it. Two women and a little girl fall in love with a man whose leg has been amputated. The first is named Valérie and resembled Catherine; the second, Melanie, who wasn't completely unlike Dido.

In her memoirs, Rumer Godden offers an account colored by her stay with the Renoirs and insists that, although she got to know personalities such as Esther Williams and Elizabeth Taylor, thanks to the wife of the producer, the Renoirs kept their distance from Hollywood glamour and simply gave her the opportunity to chat with Greta Garbo, to whom she was introduced by Dido when they encountered her at the supermarket.* Because of the Renoirs, she was also treated to the sight of Charles Laughton charging past in Bermudas, a Hawaiian shirt, and straw hat and was invited to dinner regularly at Charles and Oona Chaplin's, Igor and Vera Stravinsky's, Lillian Gish's, the home of Katina Paxinou and her husband, Alexander Minotis, and James and Pamela Mason's, who were always with their little girl, Portland (alias "Porty"), who was seven months old. On the evenings when guests were invited to the Renoirs' house, which was "full of colors, paintings, Mexican rugs, flowers, fruit,"[20] Jean would light the fireplace at five o'clock sharp and place in it four roasting chickens, as well as cuts of beef and lamb. Gabrielle would set the table and lay out the salads, cheeses, and fruits. There were neither hors d'oeuvres, unless they consisted of avocados from the garden, nor dessert, but a single main course; and the master of the house would reckon on one bottle of wine per guest, usually a Burgundy. And if Dido hastened to replace the brand-name bourbon with second-rate whiskey, it meant that Stroheim was coming, and she knew that whatever the quality of the liquid, he'd empty the bottle and waste no time restoring its contents to the toilet.[21] The Masons and the Chaplins were the most frequent guests.

Rumer Godden also recalled that before entering the house, Gabrielle would ask "*où est la dame*" and make an immediate U-turn if "*la dame*" was within earshot. Gabrielle "did not like the hours I spent alone with Jean in the studio, suspecting me of stealing him from Dido whom she adored." She then acknowledged that Dido, as well, began to give her the cold shoulder.[22] Used

* According to Leslie Caron, Greta Garbo and Renoir were considering a project together for some time between 1954 and 1958. At that time, Garbo would come frequently to Leona Drive. Their meetings supposedly ended when Renoir became aware that the star's desire was to play Francis of Assisi. No trace has been found of these meetings or this idea. It is also not known whether Greta Garbo ever got wind of the opinion Renoir expressed about her twenty years earlier in one of his columns for *Ce soir*, in which he described her as a "big beanpole" who gave him "the impression of not having very nice breath" and that he associated her with Marlene Dietrich by stating that he couldn't "stomach them." (*Ce soir*, June 24, 1937.)

to being the only woman closely associated with her husband's projects since they had moved to California, Dido actually did find it hard to see Jean shut up for hours with another woman to adapt her book to film. The truth was that both of Renoir's women, his nanny and his wife, worried about losing him, and given Godden's forty-one years, they took her for a rival. For Gabrielle, this was translated into the mute aggressiveness of a Burgundian peasant, and for Dido, it found outlet in bursts of bad humor.[23] The writer, who at first hadn't been informed that her hosts had put her in Dido's room[†]—therefore, Dido ended up having to spend her nights on the living room couch—recalled several occasions when the two spouses fought viciously about her and in her presence, placing her in an untenable situation.[24]

Renoir declared himself so happy about his collaboration with Rumer Godden that he envisioned writing a play in French with her and soon another screenplay. As for the adaptation of *The River*, the book had been put back on the shelf, just as the director had informed the writer beforehand, and her suggestion to start by drawing up a structure together had been rejected from the start. No, the story would take form by itself, in the course of conversations, with different drafts laid out on large sheets of paper using oversized pencils. Renoir imagined each image visually and indicated in writing its frame and whether it was to be a long shot, medium shot, or close-up. He knew better than anyone that each of these indications never expressed anything but the truth of that moment, but this changed nothing about the way he worked. Renoir's obsession was concerned with authenticity. The Indians would be expressing themselves on the screen with their words, and every gesture would have to be true. That is also the reason he was insisting the writer be present during filming from the first to the last day. He had a deeper knowledge of the text than the author herself possessed at that moment, and when it was a matter of inventing a new line that didn't come from the book, he could sometimes wait up to an hour until the writer found the right words. As for the characters created for the film, what looked like the most insignificant elements of their behavior became the object of long conversations.[25]

The first drafts of the screenplay, under the title *Eastward in Eden*, exhibited a deep reworking of the book, leading especially to the appearance of several new characters. However, the longest part had not been dealt with yet. The screenplay was still a great distance from what the finished film would be like.

* Which was certainly not the first book that he was adapting for the screen, as Rumer Godden would hastily add.

† For at least as far back as their arrival in the United States, Dido and Jean Renoir had separate bedrooms.

No other film he directed, before or after, required so much of Renoir's time, reflection, work. The complications in its preparation, shooting, and editing had an impact of incredible proportions. Of all Renoir's films, *The River* is the one that would change the most as the months passed. It would also be the film that would design a way of making films, giving birth to an ensemble of theories in the context of which the work to come would be considered and the work that came before would be revisited.

But, in reality, the direction of Renoir's *Elena et les hommes* (*Elena and Her Men* or *Paris Does Strange Things*, 1956) or *Le Déjeuner sur l'herbe* (*Picnic on the Grass*, 1959) was just as unlike that of *The River* as *The River* lacked a relationship to the making of *The Crime of Monsieur Lange* or *Grand Illusion*. In the first place, the tumultuous trajectory of the making of *The River* shows that Renoir's films are also born from a series of accidents, obstacles, renouncements, and second choices. His ability to adapt, his phenomenal talent for always landing on his feet, resulted in some astounding successes; but genuine admiration for his films mustn't neglect the enormous amount of insight accumulated along the way and work accomplished throughout the entire process—any more than it should try to construct a universal theory about a method that was less desired than endured.

The importance of *The River* in Renoir's life has as much to do with the violent shock he underwent in discovering India as it has to do with the moment in which he experienced that upheaval. Stroheim and Chaplin, who had always been his idols, were part of the circle of close friends he saw regularly, and they considered him their equal; and on the other side of the world, young directors in the making, starting with Indians and later with the French, were viewing him as an absolute reference. He had become the peer of his masters. From then on he would be faced by disciples.

Rumer Godden left Los Angeles for New York on August 10. The next day Renoir wrote to McEldowney, who was in London, to tell him that James Mason had adored the screenplay but was afraid to leave for India with his little girl. Robert Ryan's opinion was no less flattering, but RKO would probably refuse to free him from his contract with them;[26] and Van Heflin, who also liked the project, was similarly hindered by his agreement with MGM.[27] The search for an actor to play Captain John began and would last for several weeks. The list of names that came up one after another was impressive and included both American and British actors. Glenn Ford, also under consideration for a time, "liked the story, but didn't like the part." In any case, Renoir had only suggested him "for the name" and had found him "very boring" in *Lust for Gold*, which he also hadn't watched all of.[28]

One of the main difficulties had to do with the personality of the captain as Renoir and Rumer Godden had portrayed him. Although the difference between his age and the girls' had to remain great, the character could be young, but "bitter irony, the sarcasm due to his bad wound which made him mature before his time are, as a rule, non-existent in youth."[29] In fact, Captain John was dragging around a leg that had sustained a war injury. Like Renoir. Renoir had auditioned Gar Moore, who appears in the third episode of the Rossellini film *Paisan,* but he had misgivings about him. About the subject in general, Renoir ironically quipped, "This mature state of mind might perhaps be generated by the ablation of somebody's leg, but it wouldn't be so easy to find a young man so overly enthusiastic about his art as to make such a sacrifice."[30] This "idea" that wasn't really one would, however, partly light the way:

> His name is Tom Breen. He is twenty-five and under contract with MGM. He is a little too healthy-looking with his rosy cheeks, and his eyes are not too intelligent. Another thing against him is the fact that he was severely wounded several times during the war, lost an entire leg, and walks sometimes very easily, sometimes quite painfully with an artificial one. A good interpreter must consider the problem from a certain distance in order to have a good perspective. I'm also afraid of the disgusting publicity the distributors would invent about a wounded man playing the part of a wounded man.[31]

A month later, however, the decision was made. Tom Breen would be Captain John. But the letter by which he informed Rumer Godden, who would vainly attempt to convince him to choose another actor, contained an important detail that shows how much the issue of the age of the character turned out to be difficult to resolve. Two characters in the film were named John, the captain and the cousin. For the latter, who had been invented for the film, Renoir had for a moment thought of Charles Laughton or Burgess Meredith and believed, "If they weren't so expensive . . . either would be wonderful."[32] However, as a last resort, he finally opted for Arthur Shields. And yet, he'd also considered this person for the role of the captain.[33] At the time, Arthur Shields was fifty-three, and Tom Breen was twenty-five.

Arthur Shields's name could have been suggested to him by Dudley Nichols, who was also a regular at the dinners on Leona Drive. Like Barry Fitzgerald,* his older brother, Shields appeared often in John Ford films, and Ford used both of them in the same film a number of times,† notably in two films written

---

* Directed by Renoir in *The Amazing Mrs. Holliday.*

† Barry Fitzgerald and Arthur Shields appeared most notably together in two of John Ford's great films, *How Green Was My Valley* (1941) and *The Quiet Man* (1952).

by Dudley Nichols, *The Plough and the Stars* (1936) and *The Long Voyage Home* (1940). Thomas E. Breen, who was the son of the director of the Production Code Administration, Joseph I. Breen, had appeared previously in six films, without being listed in the credits for three of them. Captain John was his first big role, and *The River* would be his last film. Years later, Tom Breen would write to Renoir to tell him that he'd given up film, was all the better for it, and had moved to Phoenix, Arizona. Renoir's answer would contain a postscript: "I saw *The River* again a year ago. In my opinion, you were a talented actor."[34]

There were "no stars"[35] in *The River*, actually, but that fact was less the product of a wish than the consequences of actors turning it down because they weren't dying to spend several months in India. Determining whether this result harmed the film or, on the contrary, benefited it is irrelevant. However, it's likely that the situation affected the project by stressing its experimental character. Similarly, directing a Western film in India under the supervision of a novice producer placed Renoir in a situation that resembled the one he had experienced for *The Rules of the Game:* at the mercy of the most diverse uncertainties yet responsible for everything and on his own when it came to determining the management of operations. During the shoot, Renoir, Lourié, Claude Renoir, and Rumer Godden stayed at the Great Eastern Hotel, unlike McEldowney, who spent his time flooding them with "'memos' which nobody read."[36]

His next departure complicated his relationships with certain people close to him. In a letter dated August 8, 1949, Simenon had asked him to be the godfather of the child whose birth was expected in two weeks.[37] Renoir accepted but added, "If the archdiocese to which you're answerable requires the conditions you're listing,* I'll have to forgo that pleasure that would bring me a little closer to you. You see, I am not receiving the sacraments and my previous divorce had been preceded by a marriage in the Church."[38] When the future father declared that he was "willing to give it a try,"[39] Renoir wrote to the priest of Simenon's parish in Tucson to inform him that he would not be able to take part in the baptism and asked whether there was a possibility to be appointed godfather by proxy.[40] Nearly a year later, in July 1950, he worriedly informed Simenon, "This baptism seems terribly jeopardized to me,"[41] but as it turned out, Jean Denis Chrétien Simenon, called Johnny, and born on September 29, 1949, in Tucson, definitely would have Jean Renoir as a godfather.

"If you don't take part in the film, I'm certain this trip will be an intolerable affair, and if you stay in California, Papa will surely get eaten by the crocodiles,"[42]

---

* The condition to which Renoir was referring specified that it was necessary for the godfather and godmother to be Catholics permitted to receive the sacraments. However, a past divorce was not an obstacle if it had not been preceded by a marriage in the Church.

Alain Renoir wrote to Dido. At the time, he was a student at Harvard and in February 1948 had married Jane Alexander, a young dietitian. After leaving Los Angeles on October 31, 1949, Jean and Dido visited him in Boston, before flying to London, with a stop in New York.

From London, Jean went round-trip to Paris, which he'd left more than nine years ago. He kept his visit discreet, because although he apparently risked nothing—reassured as he was by a letter from Louis Guillaume informing him that a decision of the court of appeals on June 11, 1949, had transformed his separation with Catherine into a divorce[43]—Renoir was still unwilling to attract the attention of his ex-wife and the French legal system.* He took advantage of his trip to make the acquaintance of André Bazin, who came to meet him in the waiting room at the Invalides train station. On that day, Bazin, who "was trembling with emotion at the idea of finally seeing you,"[44] as his wife would write to Renoir, rode with Renoir in the car taking him to Le Bourget airport and collected the information for an interview that Bazin would publish in *L'Écran français* at the end of the month.[45]

While his uncle was working on the screenplay with Rumer Godden and meeting actors, Claude Renoir was in London, too. Nora Swinburne and her husband Esmond Knight† were cast to play Harriet's parents, and the redhead Adrienne Corri, who was nineteen, was cast as Valerie. Her audition for the part took place on a roof at Claridge's.

On November 29, the Renoirs left London for Bombay, then Calcutta, and went back to the Great Eastern Hotel. At the end of the afternoon of December 1, the banquet room of the luxury hotel was full of children, in response to ads placed in the papers stating, "Wanted: an English boy between the ages of five and seven; also three English girls, three to eight, to play roles in an American film to be made near Calcutta during the next four months." About five hundred showed up, many of them accompanied by their parents; although several girls turned out to be appropriate, no boy matched the character of Bogey, the boy killed by the snake. None except Richard Foster, Rumer Godden's nephew and the son of her sister Nancy, who was serving as interpreter for the crew after having helped at the beginning of the year in researching scenery.

The days went by, spent attempting to resolve the technical problems

---

* His fear about this may be able to explain why the marriage of Jean and Dido was not registered in Paris until 1957, records indicating the date of the marriage as August 23, 1957, in Beverly Hills. Catherine Hessling, on the other hand, had in 1955 married Robert Beckers, a close friend of Robert Denoël, whom she had gotten to know in 1940.

† Esmond Knight played the rajah in *Black Narcissus*, a performance that Rumer Godden judged "excessive."

connected primarily to delays in the shipping of equipment and other materials from London, and Renoir still didn't have his Melanie, the character who was the daughter of an Indian and an American, living alone with her father in the neighboring house after the death of her mother. The character, which had been invented for the film, constituted an essential link between West and East, and a few hundred auditions hadn't resulted in finding the person to play her. Renoir decided to go off in search of her. He was headed for Benares (Varanasi), the place from which the photo of a girl had been sent him. The photographer was Raymond Burnier. He was Swiss and had been living in India since 1938, and he was a friend of the philosopher and renowned Indian music specialist Alain Daniélou. Daniélou was close to Rabindranath Tagore and was a professor at the Hindu university of Benares and the director of the school of Indian music. Daniélou invited Jean and Dido to his home on the banks of the Ganges, but not Rumer Godden, on the grounds that he refused to put up an Englishwoman under his roof, until the day when Renoir was able to impress upon him that the writer "*couldn't* be English."[46]

The person in whom Renoir intuited a potential Melanie was Radha Sri Ram. At twenty-six, she was the daughter of Nilakanta Sri Ram, the president of the Theosophical Society. She had a doctorate in Sanskrit and was recognized as an expert in the art of the dance in the Bharatanatyam tradition.* When Renoir saw her dance, he declared himself to be completely won over. Sometime after, McEldowney brought the young woman to Calcutta, where he and his wife tried in vain to convince her to become equipped with a "Hollywood-style" dentition. Radha refused all makeup, and Renoir actively supported it, an outright rebellion against the directives of the Technicolor firm, which, fortunately, had not sent any representative to the shoot.

Filming in Technicolor required extremely heavy equipment, and the type of film used required very substantial lighting. All of the equipment had to be delivered from London. Delays accumulated, and certain materials never arrived. To deal with these circumstances, Claude Renoir repeatedly called for extra generators but wouldn't get them. The camera equipment he was using at first couldn't record live sound. The start of filming had to be put off, and Renoir took advantage of the delays to film some documentary shots, particularly of the Ganges. During this period, his nephew found himself in a situation resembling the one he'd experienced during *A Day in the Country*, when he'd start off on the river while it was raining and film what caught his eye to pass time. During the editing, this partly dormant spell would turn out to have been essential.

---

* Radha Sri Ram would marry Raymond Burnier. The author of a number of works, she would be elected president of the Theosophical Society in 1980.

Renoir also decided to have the dialogue recorded on magnetic tape so that he could hear the actors and appreciate their performances. This was because film that had been shot was sent to London, where it was developed at Technicolor's laboratories and then sent back to Calcutta, making it impossible to see rushes any sooner than at least ten days later. Such a delay made it impossible to refilm any scene considered unsatisfactory. Carl Koch, who was then living in London, saw the rushes first, and the two old friends corresponded by telegram.

Shooting began on December 29, 1949. Every morning at six-thirty, a bus left the Great Eastern Hotel to bring to Barrackpore the crew of Westerners who were staying at the hotel and Indians who lived in the city, the latter group having been told to arrive at the hotel a half hour in advance. Renoir and Dido would make the approximately twenty-five-mile trip in a car driven by a chauffeur named Ram Singh, who would also play the gatekeeper of the house and the children's protector. In the Maharajah of Gwalior's residence, which was the principal shooting location and headquarters for the project, Rumer Godden had organized a dance class. She had taught that art in the past, and most of her students were children. The princes who had financed the greater part of the film were led by Fateh Singh, the Maharajah of Limbdi, who came to the set often and had been nicknamed "Fatty" by the filmmakers. Renoir confided in him his grievances about McEldowney in a long letter in which he enumerated the extravagant personal expenditures of the producer as well as the man's inability to ensure that the shoot would function smoothly. However, Renoir did acknowledge McEldowney's strong talents as a salesman, which actually proved very useful.

Ten weeks of shooting exteriors were dramatically marked, as Renoir would point out, by a group of students invading the set, furious about the profanation of a sacred tree. Renoir responded by inviting them to watch that day's shooting so that they could see for themselves that the film contained nothing offensive. In mid-March, the shoot moved to a studio in Calcutta, where several sets had been built under the direction of Eugène Lourié. The problems created by noises of every kind and by throngs of onlookers, who had contributed appreciably to slowing the pace of direction, were eliminated; but even so, the shoot would last until mid-May, punctuated by the habitual and extremely natural explosions of Renoir's temper.

Editing brought the complicated and eventful vicissitudes of the making of this film into its own and allowed it to take form. Renoir probably did not suspect this was the case when he wrote that he had just directed "the first good one I did since I left France."[47]

After their departure from Calcutta on May 21, Jean and Dido spent some time in Adyar, near Madras, where Radha hosted them at the headquarters of the Theosophical Society and where, thanks to the young woman's mother, they experienced the most authentic Indian cuisine. It was exclusively vegetarian, without a drop of alcohol and without tobacco, except for Dido, who shut herself up in the bathroom to smoke.[48] They next visited Katina Paxinou and her husband, who had returned to Athens, where Renoir was determined to go in order "to see the Parthenon," before stopping in Paris and going back to California.

Renoir began editing *The River* on June 19, in a room reserved for that purpose at the Hal Roach Studios on Santa Monica Boulevard. He worked with George Gale, an editor, for whom this was his first feature film. Before that, McEldowney had tested Gale by assigning him editing of the images McEldowney had brought back from the elephant hunt filmed in December 1949. For both technical and financial reasons, Renoir and Gale had to put together the film using images in black and white. The scope of such an undertaking was revealed by the magnificence of the finished film. They were also confined to the footage that existed, because any new filming was out of the question.

In September, Renoir believed he "had a hold" on his film. "I've just spent three exhausting months cutting it down, making it longer, and turning it inside out in every way possible," he wrote, and "the few people who've seen it really love it."[49] The director Clarence Brown was one of the first to see it. He had asked to see the film for Tom Breen and "had seen only Radha."[50] Nearly two months later, Renoir announced that he was almost finished with it. He was wrong.[51]

Over the course of about ten months of editing, in a process that mainly consisted of progressive distancing from Rumer Godden's novel, the film changed a great deal. It had already profoundly improved during the adaptation and then the shoot. With the agreement of the author, the book—in which India could be said to be absent—gave birth to a film that opened wide the doors of the English enclave to which the action had been confined. The film became fascinating in another way in addition to being vastly superior to the book. This isn't to say that Renoir directed a Bengali film, which only an Indian director could invent, but *The River* still stands as the first film to present India to a Western audience. And in the long trajectory of this film, the audience, in fact, took on a role of prime importance.

Renoir's goal during his first visit to Calcutta was to direct a film intended for American audiences, and for that reason, it makes perfect sense that he listened to what these audiences had to say about the film. His desire for a hit, rendered central by the failure of his previous films and sharpened by the arrangement in his contract that granted him a generous percentage of potential profits, led him to conform to the principle of test screenings, usually detested by directors and the source of the hassles he had endured for *The Woman on the Beach*, which he hadn't forgotten. If he proceeded in this way, organizing no fewer than about fifteen screenings, to which both neighborhood business-people as well as employees of the studios were invited, it was because he knew he was the only one in charge. The producer was allowing him to work as he intended and was sticking to what he knew, promotion. Renoir had the right to consider only those expressed opinions that he thought were pertinent.

It quickly became evident that those he invited to the screening room at the Hal Roach Studios—about twenty for each screening, according to the editor, but around a hundred, according to Renoir—weren't very taken by the character of Captain John, whose motivations remained obscure and whose behavior often seemed incomprehensible, failings that were accentuated by Tom Breen's lack of personality and the blandness of his interpretation. Similarly, the performances of some of the actresses were considered to be not very convincing, a defect that distanced the viewers from the characters and the story. On the other hand, everyone was in agreement when it came to the images of India, even though they were seeing these documentary shots in black and white. They were "poetic" shots, as Renoir would describe them, filmed to while away the days of idle waiting. Making them had also enabled the director to soak up the atmosphere of India, its light and its scent. Doing so may have been influenced by Renoir's discovery in July 1948 of Flaherty's *Louisiana Story*.[52]

One shouldn't assume, however, that the capturing of these images of India was executed only haphazardly. Before filming, Renoir had outlined them precisely and included a note entitled "Instruction for the Second Unit Shooting" that testifies to this. It was a matter, he wrote, of "very precise requirements," which "must be executed according to a very definite style as a contrast with the rest of the picture." For the sequence in spring, this style would be created "by shooting only against two different backgrounds: water and sky"; and it was desirable that "water if possible should be animated by some movement: the current of the river or the circles obtained by throwing a stone in case of a pond." Finally, the sky had to be "blue. A shot with a white sky has great chances to be rejected during the editing unless it represents something very rare like a bird difficult to approach."[53]

In short, a series of screenings revealed that most of the elements coming directly from the novel were boring and that the film became fascinating as soon as it got away from the book. Thus, Renoir found himself being led in a direction that was the opposite of the one that Western producers would indicate, which would have meant following a direction that reinforced the dramatic elements of the story. He also integrated more and more of these "poetic" shots, which ceaselessly affirmed the purely Indian aspect of the film. What it lost in dramatic intensity, it gained in impressions and sensations.

The risk in such a profound transformation lay in dispersing elements of the narrative that the plot, which had become more and more fragmented and hazardous, was no longer capable of reassembling. To remedy this, Renoir or George Gale had the idea of having Harriet tell a story that would be seen entirely through her eyes. This created the need for a text in voice-over, which, after the screening of a version augmented by a temporary commentary, audience members confirmed; they declared that with the voice-over understanding the plot was no longer a problem.

As a result, it was decided to call in a writer. Which writer? There's no mention of this person in the credits; and neither Renoir, the editor, nor the producer of the film have provided any information about him or her. However, based on certain confidential statements collected by Bertrand Tavernier and Pierre Rissient, a hypothesis can be formed. Ellis St. Joseph, who was close to the German colony in Hollywood, who was the author of several plays, stories, and novels, and who was known mostly as the screenwriter of the Douglas Sirk film *A Scandal in Paris* (1948), for which he used the pseudonym "John H. Kneubuhl," has claimed to have collaborated copiously on the screenplay for *The River*. Because he was a man who never showed himself to be inclined to fabrications, and because the text in voice-over corresponds with what is known about his style, it is more than probable that he was in fact the author of these pages, unless future revelations debunk this idea.

His convictions strengthened by the reception that each of his successive edits earned, Renoir went about distancing *The River* even further from Western film traditions. He abandoned the idea of having music composed especially for the film and chose to use the sounds of India that he had had recorded during or on the sidelines of the shoot, as well as some incidental music that was mostly from Mozart. Although certain passages were reworked by M. A. Partha Sarathy, who appeared in the credits as a music adviser, the first notes heard at the beginning of the film are those of a sitar played by Subrata Mitra, a prominent cinematographer in the future and a musician when the fancy took him; Renoir had heard him playing between two shots. From the first image of *The River*, the design traced with rice flour on a floor of ochre to the rhythm of a sitar, the viewer is transported to a world that was completely unknown.

The first showing of the film in Technicolor took place in London on April 17, 1951. Renoir wasn't there. He hadn't seen *The River* in color yet. George Gale and Forrest Judd were present to represent the production. Rumer Godden attended with her sister Rose Mary. The next day, the writer shared her impression with the director in a letter. She began by describing the film as "unusual and magnificent," before saying that Renoir had "caught not only a picture of India, but the spirit of India," and that she was "indeed happy to have been a part in the making of such a picture."[54] She wrote this in spite of the criticisms she intended to express. Except for six lines, these criticisms occupied all of the four typed pages that made up her letter.

What she regretted the most was the impression that the emphasis on India, to some extent, "swamped the story" and produced a picture that was "overloaded with color," so much so that what she had seen was "not a story set in India, but India hung on a not very strong story."* The narrative had seemed "a little sketchy" to her, the family seemed "almost irrelevant," and she thought that when Renoir saw the film in color, he would agree with her that it was "swamped[†] by its very magnificence." The "overabundance of Indian life and colour" was matched by the same quality of the commentary, which she had never liked the use of, even though she understood its necessity. The opening in the form of wanting to welcome you to India on the part of the first film entirely directed there seemed "almost commercial" to her and therefore appalling. George Gale had certainly emphasized to her that the importance accorded Indian life had been decided upon because of Tom Breen's inadequacies. She regretted the loss of the scene of the kite, although she wasn't unaware that her nephew Richard's performance had made it unusable. She deplored the fact that the film didn't make you feel how much Harriet still remained close to childhood. She added, "I do still detest the sentimental little scene with Ned and the children after Bogey's death and wish this could be cut." Finally, although she had appreciated the music and had been touched by "Pat, Radha, Arthur Shields, Bogey, all the Indian people," she could not say that she liked Tommy or Nora Swinburne, "good and beautiful" as she might have been. Her reaction was natural enough, typical of a writer who felt dispossessed of her work. It was also the reaction, just as logical, of an Englishwoman who had lived a delightfully protected existence in India and couldn't accept seeing

---

* In *My Life and My Films*, Renoir would touch on "the rather foolish dignity of an English family living on India like a plum on a peach-tree."

† Rumer Godden used the verb *swamped* twice in the same paragraph.

herself expelled a second time from a world that she wanted to believe hers, when it wasn't in any way.

The letter reached Renoir in New York, where he was staying for a few days to settle some issues having to do with the distribution of *The River*, which he had just seen in its definitive version, before leaving for Paris and then for Italy. He answered the letter on May 2 in typical Renoirian fashion: "I agree 100% with your criticisms about the picture, but I don't believe that I can do anything. It happened that our film was very well received by business people here and I am not sorry to have sacrificed too much to a certain easy, over brilliant side, which I know is against the basic story.... May I add that I had no choice. The many previews we held with small audiences were terrifying. I am convinced that if you had been with me you would have made the same decisions."[55]

As always in such cases, the success of the film would sweep away the reservations of the writer, whose letter demonstrated that she was hardly any more inclined to agree with *The River* than she had been to accept *Black Narcissus*. As for Renoir, he had moved gradually—influenced by the circumstances he'd encountered—away from a book whose potential had initially attracted him; and he had known how to brilliantly exploit accidents and vicissitudes during the production to extract from conventional and rather poor material a work that was remarkable, original, and almost experimental in nature. And the fact that he'd only partly decided, with full consciousness, that it would be like that changes nothing.

At any rate, the film was experimental from the beginning to some extent, because of the fact that it was made by a director and a cinematographer who both had no experience with color and who were working in a country about which they knew nothing. It's also probable that technicians who were accustomed to Technicolor at the time, whose method involved exposing three negatives in black and white simultaneously in the same camera, and adding colors to them later in the developing baths, would have considered it impossible to film in a country like India. Thus, having turned fifty, the director had regained his penchant for that experimentation that had motivated his work during the silent period.

On the first day of shooting *The River*, Jean Renoir and his nephew were beginners who found themselves at the head of a crew of novices, under the distant control of an ephemeral producer. The course of action they took and impressed upon Eugène Lourié, who was responsible for the scenery but also for an important amount of the costumes, was characterized by the greatest simplicity. The decision was equally motivated by the fact that they knew they were being held to the impossibility of seeing their images on a screen before several weeks had passed. Their choices were guided just as much by a kind of wisdom: if the lawn that was there originally was ripped up and the lot sown again, it was because that grass had to be uniformly green and because the potential fields of color were decided and arranged by the filmmakers themselves, who had gone to war against half-tints.

There are many more examples of that approach, but essentially, the point is that *The River* was clearly understood as a film that was by nature artificial. For India to "swamp" the film, as Rumer Godden put it, it was necessary to re-create from India images capable of being captured and then reproduced on the screen. For that same reason, the film couldn't be shot entirely using exteriors, and not many scenes in *The River* were. Some were faked; for example, the terrace of the house was rebuilt on the banks of the river. Many scenes were filmed in the studio. The demands of lighting and the inability of the producer to obtain the necessary sources of energy had also forced Renoir to modify his manner of proceeding, especially when it came to cutting more than was customary and in abandoning the movements of the camera as an essential approach.

The River has a total of about 700 shots, 150 more than *This Land Is Mine*, but it's four minutes shorter, and it has 254 more shots than *The Rules of the Game*, although it is twelve minutes shorter than that film. It's doubtful that this directorial stylistic development was due to any influence on Renoir coming from his American experience. It looks more like the product of a compromise between the slightly insane audacity of undertaking the direction of a Technicolor film in India and the required moderation that governed the accomplishment of that idea—impractical as that idea was from the very start. Here again, it was the filmmaker's ability to adapt that became the issue, both during filming and in the course of editing.

One of the film's great moments seems like a by-product of Renoir's method as it is expressed in *The River*. In the introduction to the death of Bogey, the filmmaker assembled a series of tracking shots, forward-and-backward-moving images of, first, the mother, letting go of her book and dozing off; then, the doorkeeper, the servant Nan, the little girl, the twins, and the baby girl and her rabbit,* all asleep; before Harriet wakes up and calls first to her little brother, and then to his friend Kanu. The back-and-forth swaying motion created by these tracking shots, like a breeze rocking the sleeping humans and watching over them, leads to the little boy, who also looks asleep; but then all the film shows is the pine coffin, and the traces of what has happened left in the characters' minds. It's a magnificent sequence whose measured and quiet order suggests that it was designed prior to editing, each tracking shot obviously having been

---

* According to Rumer Godden, two days of shooting were necessary before the rabbit began to behave the way Renoir had been hoping it would.

decided only after its precise function had been established, as part of the patterns of motion that influence the film.

The very celebrated scene of Melanie's dance, which opens the last movement of the film, works according to the opposite principle. The camera remains immobile, either from the director's choice or from the fact that he lacked enough light; and when the dancer, who until that moment had moved laterally, comes toward the lens, it is she who creates the increasing close-up, a striking effect that resembles the camera's perspective of Sylvia Bataille in *A Day in the Country*. This is one of those moments, like the digression created by the fable of Radha and Krishna written and read by Harriet, into which the narration dissolves, a major characteristic of *The River*, which is actually one of the first examples of the new school of film that came into being around ten years later in the work of such directors as Antonioni and Godard.

The conditions under which *The River* was made, from production to editing—but during the editing more than any other time—imposed on Renoir a filmmaking method that consisted in "destroying the project, forgetting the screenplay, burning the prior text in a blaze of images, inventing a novel cinematic form that is born from the ruin of the words, fertilized by their ashes,"[56] according to the way Alain Fleischer has defined the cinema of Godard. The sole crucial exception to this is that only certain sequences in *The River* were actually conceived that way, and not the entire film.

In Renoir's life, the success of *The River* counted at least as much as his discovery of India and as the film itself. Although McEldowney made no pretense of being a producer, which was obviously a preferred stance because it gave the director free rein, he turned out to be an excellent salesman, a talent for which Renoir was happy to credit him. From the start, he and his wife made every effort to get articles published in different publications reporting on the progress of the project,[57] taking advantage as they did so of the presence of Radha, who had come to spend a few weeks at the Renoirs' at the end of February 1950. McEldowney then insisted that no one be allowed to see the film before the release date had been decided. When he learned that United Artists was preparing to show the film at Radio City Music Hall in New York, he made sure that it would not happen by taking the copy away from his distributor; he understood that a New York release in a large-capacity theater would turn out to be harmful.

He bet on the fact that word of mouth would be highly positive, so he intended to leave the film enough time to take hold as well as to give audiences enough time to decide on their own to see it. Eventually, he opted for the 568 seats of the Paris Theater, on Fifth Avenue and Fifty-Eighth Street, and presented *The River* as a film with prestige—which it actually was—rather than as standard fare. In that undertaking, he was supported by the Theatre Guild, which had recently helped promote two films by Laurence Olivier, *Henry V,* which Renoir considered to be "unbearable,"[58] admitting that he "hadn't understood a single word,"[59] and *Hamlet.* For the occasion of the New York release on September 10, 1951, McEldowney gave the *Saturday Evening Post* an article entitled "We Made a Movie without Hollywood,"[60] which he followed two months later, when the film began to be shown nationwide, with a four-page article in *Life* mostly composed of photos. Under the subtitle "Hollywood-on-Hooghly" in that photo essay, a paragraph stated, "By the time he was ready to shoot the film, real shooting was a daily event in Bengal, where Hindus and Moslems were massacring each other by thousands."[61] As a whole, the reviews were favorable, praising the beauty of the film and lamenting the lack of unity in the plot and the little interest that could be found in the characters.

The River ended its run at the Paris Theater in New York after thirty-four weeks, all tickets having been reserved in advance in the course of the first twenty-six. It remained at Boston's Beacon Hill for eleven weeks, for ten at the Stage Door in San Francisco, for seven in two theaters in Chicago, and for nine at the Fine Arts in Los Angeles. An investigation launched at Renoir's request revealed that United Artists had charged excessively high distribution costs in all these cities and in many others.[62] Years of follow-up and disputes of every sort happened before the relations among the director, the producer, and the distributor quieted down. Renoir blamed McEldowney for not paying him the fees foreseen by his contract. McEldowney accused United Artists of not providing him with reports of the ticket sales and, disappointed with Renoir's behavior, ended up appealing to David Loew:

> I know your great friendship for Jean. Nevertheless, please recognize and accept the facts. Jean has already gained more from this picture than anyone else. He was given a free hand in the production; he received a good salary. A true recognition of the facts would enable you to know that except for the Herculean efforts which were expended by us as well as Jean, on this production, there never would have been any production at all, and except for the enormous time and effort spent by both Melvina and me in the latter stages it would never have been finished or sold, and there would never have been any money to distribute anywhere.[63]

The River would forever remain J. K. McEldowney's* only production.

Beginning on December 19, 1951, the film was shown in Paris at two theaters, the Madeleine and the Biarritz. After the first week, it had sold more

---

* McEldowney died on January 5, 2004, at the age of ninety-seven.

than eleven thousand tickets in each of the two theaters and "the second week promised to be better."[64] At the end of distribution, *The River* was seen by a little more than two million viewers in France, 720,000 of whom were in Paris. For such an unusual production, with no star, it was a triumph, offering Renoir the opportunity to take center stage once more.

Today it is difficult to measure the shock of this film for viewers in 1951. Color film was still a rarity for them; nor had they ever before seen India as *The River* showed it. Great familiarity with color films and other countries of today's audiences has certainly contributed to dating a film whose "cosmic" ambition places it at the heart of the movement the great filmmakers of the period initiated, with a goal to plumb the depths of their characters without ever ceasing to affirm their membership in the world. The influence of the film was enormous, definitely much greater than that of certain other of Renoir's films that can, besides, be considered more completely successful. Although *The River* is located in the sphere of Rossellini's cinematic influence, with which Renoir was probably at best only partially familiar at the time, it was after Rossellini discovered *The River* and after Renoir spoke with him at length about India that the Italian director decided to make the trip. It just so happened that while *The River* was being prepared, Ingrid Bergman, who was a close friend of the Renoirs, found herself with Rossellini, for whom she'd left her husband and with whom she had just made *Stromboli*. Before Rossellini left for India in December 1956, Renoir gave him the names of the technicians with whom he had worked. Among them was Hari Das Gupta, his assistant. The affair that developed between Gupta's wife and Rossellini led to the end of the love story between the director and Ingrid Bergman.

Although every film never expresses anything but the truths that are peculiar to it, there is often a strong temptation to draw lessons of a general nature from a particular experience. Consequently, Renoir would distinguish in what he perceived about Indian life the elements of a philosophy of existence that paralleled a certain wisdom coming from his father. The cork carried by the current of a brook dear to Auguste Renoir, in fact, couldn't dream of any current less inhibiting than the Ganges, and Jean Renoir allowed himself to be carried along by the film's success, inventing for himself a conception of the world perfectly capable of lulling listeners conquered in advance and eliminating with a quick turn of phrase any trace of a possible misunderstanding.

In Calcutta, Renoir had found the truth, which allowed him to love the English colonists in the film as much as their Indian servants, who, to listen to him, were on their way to winning:

The characters in *The River* . . . are intelligent, honest, and capable of mercy. They are cultivated, educated, and convinced that the atmosphere of the "nursery" in which they are living will only disappear with the end of the system. And yet, this system, they believe, is eternal. They're living, working, playing sports, listening to music as they did in London, Paris, or New York. And this in front of millions of the poverty-stricken. The miracle is that, once more, it is the disenfranchised who are winning. Not by the use of weapons, but quite simply because they believe that everything around them is only appearance.[65]

For the British colonial system to collapse, however, it had been necessary for the Indians to fight, for not all of them to be counted among the well-to-do, unlike the Indian members of Renoir's crew, all of whom came from that "group that was the very model of the enlightened Indian bourgeoisie,"[66] deliberately composed by the British to ensure their domination. Above all, it's difficult to see what there is about Renoirian theory that is precisely Indian, and even more difficult to see what distinguishes it from Catholic teachings. God, as well, has his reasons, obviously, which are certainly every bit as good as those of humans.

From then on, it is said, Renoir acquired a passion for all of humanity, strong in his conviction acquired on the bank of the Ganges that it is enough to be patient and wait for everything that tends to overstep to return to an order that knows only how to be what is natural. The time for struggle had passed, and now the time of wisdom, or right-thinking, had come. "The new being I am realizes today that it's no longer the time for sarcasm and that the only thing that I can bring to this illogical, irresponsible, and cruel universe is my 'love.'"[67]

Into the elation of the colors, dancing, the rowers' bodies, enters a share of indifference to the fate reserved for the Indians, expressed all the more freely because they are presented as accepting the principle of it "naturally," an acceptance that the colonialist discourse turns to its advantage and that succeeds in placing *The River* within the tradition of the leading Orientalists. The vision of India is essentially derived from the Western fascination for exoticism, and this makes the film satisfy the purpose given it by the director, to appeal to an American audience. It allows André Bazin to judge such a vision "not false, but a bit superficial, spontaneously optimistic, and implicitly imperial" and to state that "the choice of the point of view is evidence of a certain taking of sides—not in a way that could be considered ridiculous with critical narrowness, on the side of colonialism, but on the side of a code of ethics preferring sociology."[68] And such a moral doctrine, in fact, conforms to a norm in which it is far from finding itself confined, because that norm has been conceived for it and therefore requires no particular adaptation. Thus, when Renoir would claim, without laughter, that India allowed him to understand everybody has his reasons,[69] it would bring up the question of whether he had ever heard of Octave and *The Rules of the Game*.

This detachment from the world that he claimed to have discovered in Calcutta actually goes back at least to 1939, more probably to 1937 and the triumph of *Grand Illusion*. *La Bête humaine* was already expressing such an evolution, marking his break with his years of engagement, indignation, and militancy. Although his humanism had led him in Hollywood to several conscientious actions during the war, for several years already, well before India, he had already been viewing the march of time from a lofty distance, as a voluntary exile who remained far from the fray. Henceforth, he would give in to the desire to please, which had always haunted him but hadn't dissuaded him not so long ago from sometimes striking the first blow and never turning the other cheek. So, without a doubt, there was India, but there was also weariness, fatigue, and a form of disillusionment—all those things that often with age fill the hearts of men.

The River was an important turning point in his work, and its success finally allowed him to perfect his expertise in the art of what was not yet called public relations. Soon the fact that Renoir was a great director wouldn't be enough for his admirers; they would also enjoy depicting him as a great philosopher. To this game as well, he would affably apply his mischievousness and verve—in other words, a kind of genius. Even if it meant sometimes forgetting—not during the exercise of his art but in the comments he was endlessly asked to provide—a thought that had come from his father: "Every great creator issues a kind of message. But at the moment at which he knows he is issuing it, through a strange phenomenon, that message becomes hollow and loses its value."[70]

29

"I'm Bored without You"

The Golden Coach

During his trip to Paris on the way back from India, Renoir stopped at Hotel Lutetia. It was there that he saw Gérard Philipe. Since fall 1949, they'd been writing to each other, after the actor had him sent the book *The Adventures of Till Eulenspiegel,* which Philipe wanted to see adapted for the screen. Philipe explained that in Belgium he'd "been informed of the interest of several investors" and had insisted that Renoir appeared to be the only one "capable of handling the entire direction."[1] Pierre Sicard, a painter about whom Renoir had written in 1950,[2] who'd suggested to him that he adapt Conrad's novel *Almayer's Folly,*[3] had shortly after played messenger, and Renoir thanked Philipe in a letter in which he promised "to reread these adventures about which I remember enough to know that they're fantastic."[4] The message drew an ecstatic response from Gérard Philipe: "I sent you that letter a bit like a little kid would write to Jesus on Christmas. Having your answer was already enough of a reward, but the fact that it's also not a negative response couldn't be better."[5]

It may not have been negative, but a few months later, from "a fishing boat on the Ganges," Renoir took advantage of "preparation for a shot" to deliver his definitive answer. He had, in fact, read "that magnificent book," but although he had remembered "the hardheaded trickster, the fairy-tale Robin Hood," he'd "forgotten the background, the setting full of stakes and executions." "These cruelties terrify me," he went on, without being able to say whether "India and the nearness of Krishna and his flute all around us, even in the horrible streets of Calcutta," were the cause of his new state of mind. He claimed to be going through "a period in which violence doesn't attract me," and added, "Maybe I'm reasoning this way because I've escaped the terrors of the Nazi Occupation. If I had been in Buchenwald, vengeance would certainly seem like a kind of necessary nourishment that was vital to me. I've had the luck only to tremble for those whom I love, and not for myself. But I trembled so much that everything that takes me back to a state of terror frightens me. I'd like to write and film stories that compel men to love." Wishing at the end of his message that their "efforts will be associated in a work of peace," for the actor he touched upon "a monumental idea . . . too difficult to explain" and begged him, if he continued with his project, to make it "with poets," without "too much grand spectacle, which is expensive and doesn't bring happiness."[6]

Gérard Philipe would codirect *The Adventures of Till Eulenspiegel* with Joris Ivens, but for the time being, he turned to another adaptation. The rights to Camus's *The Stranger* were available.[7] The film could be directed in Algiers in spring or fall 1951, and he was "reverently" awaiting Renoir's answer.[8]

Albert Camus's novel had appeared in 1942, and, apparently, after having very vaguely considered bringing *The Plague* to the screen, Renoir did express interest in *The Stranger*. Shortly after their meeting, Gérard Philipe wrote to Max Ophuls to inform him that he wouldn't be able "to make Mozart, same dates as Jean Renoir's film."[9] Even so, despite the fact that the agents of both parties were relying on the strength of the "moral option" Camus had granted Gérard Philipe until August,[10] the path to the project was a long one. The writer agreed to prolong it until October but was disenchanted enough along the way to come up with this clever little observation: "Film is a mountain that can't even give birth to a mouse."[11]

Like all experienced directors, Renoir was not unaware of all the complications that the most straightforward-seeming projects occasioned, and he knew that they could sink such affairs. By the beginning of the year, there was talk of his bringing to the screen *The Madwoman of Chaillot* in two versions, with the French one written by Pierre Lestringuez and the English by Rumer Godden, starring Martita Hunt and Louis Jouvet. The producer was a certain Fritz Bukofzer, under the aegis of Les Films du Tellus. In August, Renoir received this edifying account from Lestringuez:[*]

> Two months ago, I had dinner with Madame Talon[†] and Suzanne Giraudoux,[‡] surrounded by the Rothschilds and other bigwigs of less importance. I have the impression they're not at all keeping us up to date about the sordid and secret little job they're doing for their own benefit on behalf of the film. [*Handwritten note in the margin of the manuscript:* I'm talking of course about Talon and Rothschild. Suzanne herself is the soul of naïveté and is only beginning to become aware of

---

[*] In that same letter, Lestringuez gave Renoir his opinion of *Gone with the Wind*: "It's truly one of the most costly pieces of garbage I've had a chance to see in a long time."

[†] Ninon Talon Karlweiss, a theater agent who was famous for her eccentricity.

[‡] The widow of Jean Giraudoux, who had died in 1944.

what's going on.] No matter how many times Suzanne Giraudoux tells me that she will never accept any other director than you, and that she truly intends the project to be made under your direction, I think that those clever characters don't have the necessary money to do anything suitable and that in their corner they are cooking up a little scheme that is more or less sordid.[12]

Fritz Bukofzer wouldn't produce *The Madwoman of Chaillot** directed by Jean Renoir, with Louis Jouvet, but *Au pays du soleil,* directed by Maurice de Canonge, with Tino Rossi.

In summer 1950, nothing regarding *The Stranger* had yet been settled, and Gérard Philipe's attempts had reached a frantic pitch, proving as the weeks passed that the project was obviously more his than Renoir's. Renoir may have had the excuse of being busy in Hollywood, where he was working on the edit of *The River,* but it was nevertheless clear that his enthusiasm for *The Stranger* was far from overwrought. Less than six days after he had confirmed his decision to "concentrate on Camus's *The Stranger,*"[13] he received a letter from his agent informing him that his last letter "had left our Gérard Philipp [*sic*] feeling completely confused." "You apparently assured him that you had decided to start filming in the spring; as a result, he changed his schedule and put off an important project to fall of 1951. Now he can no longer change his position. He was immensely happy about making *The Stranger* with you, and is terrified that you might change your mind."[14]

It seemed as if all of Paris was buzzing with the rumor, and Renoir's nephew Claude wrote to him to tell him that he had "seen Gérard Philippe [*sic*] yesterday—a disaster if you won't be making *The Stranger* in the spring, since he has incautiously already freed up time for it."[15] Renoir lost no time in writing to the actor. "There's only one thing I want, and that is to make *The Stranger* with you. Whether it's in the spring or fall seems like a very small detail to me."[16] Renoir also insisted to Dewalde, his agent, that he "reassure" Philipe by letting him know that he hadn't "changed" his "mind."[17] Finally, he also asked Dewalde to "think about the issue of transportation, expenses, including those for Dido, who is a great help to me when I'm preparing films."[18]

If Gérard Philipe was so intent on playing Meursault, the main character in *The Stranger,* it was also because the role seemed likely to give his career a new and needed boost. In a few months, on December 4, he'd turn twenty-eight and couldn't keep playing teenagers forever. His portrayal of the scandalous young

* Giraudoux's play would be brought to the screen in 1969 by Bryan Forbes, with Katharine Hepburn and with cinematography by Claude Renoir.

lover of the beautiful married Marthe (Micheline Presle) in *Le Diable au corps* (*Devil in the Flesh*, directed by Claude Autant-Lara, 1947) had scored him a great success in film, and he had gone on to play Fabrice in *La Chartreuse de Parme* (*Charterhouse at Parma*, directed by Christian-Jaque, 1948). He had also played the desperate young man in *Une si jolie petite plage* (*Riptide*, directed by Yves Allégret, 1949), but without much success. *La Beauté du diable* (*Beauty and the Devil*), which he had made in Italy under the direction of René Clair (during which time he also began his correspondence with Renoir from Rome), had been a personal failure for him. Commentators had thought that Michel Simon had stolen his thunder in that film.

Philipe saw Meursault as the character that would finally become his turning point into a mature identity, which he'd already begun building with his portrayal of an unpleasant aristocrat in *La Ronde*, his role as a murderer in one of the sketches in the film *Souvenirs perdus* (*Lost Souvenirs*), and an occasional thief in *Juliette ou la Clef des songes* (*Juliette, or Key of Dreams*). It was while working with Marcel Carné on that film that he wrote to Renoir to tell him that he had spoken about their project with Sacha Gordine, the producer of *Juliette*, after he had found "the two producers I'd already contacted too spineless."[19]

About Gordine, Renoir wrote, "Not knowing this gentleman, I don't see anything inconvenient about it."[20] Quite naturally, however, he asked for information about the man from his agent, who answered, "As a producer he's not unpleasant and offers directors full confidence." However, the agent also considered Gordine "more worrisome when it comes to the financial level." "Although he did end up paying the balance for all his films, he has an unfortunate tendency to count on his cleverness in balancing his budget."[21] It was enough to reassure Renoir, who announced that he also agreed that Jean Aurenche should write the screenplay. Renoir had considered Aurenche's work on *Devil in the Flesh* "delightful,"[22] but he accepted him with the caveat that he also be aware of "that darkly comic aspect of *The Stranger*,"[23] and that he "agrees to consider the story from a point of view that is a bit caricatured."[24]

When Gérard Philipe asked him to allay Gordine's anxieties about the despairing quality of *The Stranger*,[25] Renoir spelled out his intentions in a letter to the actor, stating that, of course, "*The Stranger* will never be a comedy," and that "only the death of the hero of the adventure can create an ending that matches the spirit of the book." However, he did think the project offered "the possibility of drama handled with a kind of dialogue and style that could sometimes achieve burlesque." Furthermore, "after the meeting between our hero and the priest," Renoir wrote, he was thinking of inventing "a type of cinematic and poetic expression of his new, unexpected contact with the world," and "the viewer will be swept into the intoxication of that encounter with a world in which our character had until that point felt like a stranger," thus creating "a sort of 'happy ending.'"[26] No one will ever know what Camus would have thought of such a shift.

The rights for *The Stranger* were free, the letter from the director to the producer "had the desired effect—hooray,"[27] and Renoir wasn't against the actor's choices in entrusting the adaptation to his "favorite"[28] screenwriters, Jean Aurenche and Pierre Bost. The plan was still to start shooting in spring 1951, but the project didn't move forward because Gallimard had begun to demand "ten million for the French rights."[29] Certainly, the editor "understood our objections (a French production would be impossible in such a case, etc.) and brought it down by half, which is still too much,"[30] but a few weeks later, "this wait was driving" Philipe "to distraction," just when "Clouzot seems to have put his hat in the ring." Whereas Philipe was "still hoping," he had conceded that these "constant delays are rather demoralizing."[31] To his brother, Pierre Renoir wrote, "Gaston Gallimard has delusions of grandeur."[32]

In fact, Renoir had understood before Gérard Philipe that the film wouldn't be made because of the "question of rights."[33] His agent had informed him— while simultaneously bringing up the possibility of an association between Braunberger and Halley des Fontaines—that Gallimard was asking for "$30,000, a figure never attained in France," and that "if that pretension were maintained, it's obvious that the affair would become impossible."[34] Consequently, Renoir began thinking of finding another project for the actor, while Philipe was still trying to make the production of *The Stranger* a possibility. After Pierre Braunberger confided his misgivings about Philipe, Renoir wrote to him, "It's because you've seen too many films with him and some of them, like *L'Idiot*,* were rather clumsy. It's the Philipe from *Devil in the Flesh* that attracts me, and I think that if I find the right subject I can make a fine film with him."[35]

Although there's nothing in Renoir's correspondence suggesting that he did not sincerely desire to bring *The Stranger* to the screen, it is certain that he didn't waste much time on the idea. Especially in his correspondence with Braunberger, he expressed more precisely how he felt: "What I'd like to make in France is a swashbuckler. I'm convinced that *La Reine Margot*,† with the Saint Bartholomew's Day massacre and the strange customs of the Valois, made in French and English versions, would be a worldwide hit."[36] Alas, the producer,

---

* Georges Lampin, 1946.

† *Translator's note:* "Queen Margot," a historical novel written in 1845 by Alexandre Dumas, set in Paris in 1572, during the reign of Charles IX.

while wanting "firm information about when you think you'll be getting ready to film in France, what your conditions will be, under what form you want to work, salary, participation, etc.," judged "*Margot* very expensive for my possibilities."[*][37] But when Renoir announced at the end of December that he was "convinced of being able to make a very good film,"[38] his conviction had to do with a new project. "Better than *The Stranger!*"[39] he then enthusiastically claimed, writing on the same day to Gérard Philipe, "Simenon is asking me to film *La neige était sale*. I told him that it would interest me if you were the actor."[40] But Philipe wasn't carried away by the idea, and Renoir moved on to something else: "I think I understand that you aren't very enthusiastic about *La neige était sale*. So I'm suggesting we do *Jézabel*, the play by Jean Anouilh."[41] He wanted to direct the film in French, with perhaps Martita Hunt in the role of Jézabel; but he didn't know whether she spoke French and thought that the film "could have some success in American art movie theaters."[42]

As usual, Renoir was searching in every direction. In fact, although he was thinking more and more seriously of writing, starting with a book about his father, he insisted on considering himself "above all a maker of films."[43] His obstinacy in finding a role for Gérard Philipe continued to surprise his old friend Braunberger, who wrote him in January to inform him that Jean Anouilh "did not wish at any price to have *Jézabel* shown or brought to the screen," and as Braunberger informed him of this, he also slipped in the following commentary: "Obviously I'm mistaken, but I've always thought that your temperament was no match with the homosexual temperament of Gérard Philipe."[44] Renoir answered that perhaps he was wrong to "become involved morally with only one actor in France," but that Gérard Philipe had "changed his work schedule for the year and turned down various things." He couldn't allow himself "not to adjust my standpoint to his."[45] And although the idea had occurred to him that it would be possible to "achieve a worldwide hit by grouping three short stories by Marcel Aymé [or] three good Courtelines,"[†] when Braunberger suggested he adapt *Ondine* by Giraudoux with Gérard Philipe,[46] he considered the suggestion "excellent" . . . although it seemed to him "difficult to imagine *Ondine* without Jouvet."[47]

And because he thought "that the rights for modern French writers were better defended than the sacred papyrus of the Egyptians in their secret tombs,"[48] he started a simultaneous search for English-language projects. As a result, he expressed his interest in the novel *1984* by George Orwell, which had

---

* A *Reine Margot* would appear sometime after as portrayed by Jeanne Moreau, screenplay by Abel Gance, direction by Jean Dréville (1954).

† Something that Max Ophuls had just succeeded in doing with *Le Plaisir* by putting together three short stories by Maupassant.

appeared in 1949, and about which he said he was convinced he "could produce for the screen a beautiful story of love bathed in a perfect atmosphere of horror."[49] Backing up his conviction with "the current demand for a suspense genre based on horror," he imagined "a film in black and white using scale models"[50] that would permit a limited budget.

While he put the finishing touches on the edit of *The River*, for which the printing of color copies would require several weeks of work in the London laboratories, salvation came to him from Italy, by way of France. It took the form of a telegram from producer Robert Dorfmann: "Would you be interested in directing *Carrosse Saint-Sacrement** in Italy in September?"[51] Renoir answered using the same method and inquired what language and with which actress, adding that he intended to reread the play before making a decision.[52] Dorfmann's answer: "French and English, Anna Magnani cast."[53] The next day brought a new telegram from Renoir: "Am very interested in Magnani and *Carrosse*, see Jean Dewalde my agent, letter follows."[54]

The producer's offer is dated March 28, and Renoir's initial agreement, April 3. On that same April 3, Renoir wrote two letters, one to Robert Dorfmann in which he stated his intentions, and not without mentioning "a film to be shot in France"[55] and "conversations concerning a film to do here," which could prevent him from accepting *Le Carrosse*. The second letter was to his agent, in which he informed Dewalde of the "Italian" offer and asked him for information about the intentions of Braunberger, Halley des Fontaines, and Gérard Philipe regarding a project to adapt *La Faute de l'abbé Mouret*,[†] about which he'd received no news for some time.[56]

Ten days later, the decision had been made: filming of *Carrosse* would begin in Rome on September 15, which would be five days after the New York release of *The River*.

Renoir's contract was with Robert Dorfmann, but Dorfmann was the coproducer of a project that had been initiated by Prince Francesco Alliata.[‡] Trained

---

* *Translator's note:* Literally translated, "The Coach of Saint-Sacrament," Prosper Mérimée's witty, ironic playlet, first performed unsuccessfully in 1850, but tardily entering the canon of French Romantic theater in the early twentieth century when revived by Jacques Copeau. Its plot, taking place in Peru, features a viceroy and his mistress, an actress known as "Camilla Périchole."

† *Translator's note:* The fifth novel (published in 1875) in Zola's twenty-volume series *Les Rougon-Macquart*. Translated into English under various titles, including *The Sin of Father Mouret* and *Abbé Mouret's Transgression*.

‡ Born on November 17, 1919, in Palermo as Francesco Giuseppe Felice Immacolata Melchiorre Baldassarre Gaspare Dazio Signoretto Alliata, Principe di Villafranca e del Sacro Romano

in film at the beginning of the forties and director of the first Italian under-water films—which were shorts devoted to the Aeolian Islands—Alliata had met Anna Magnani in 1949 during the filming of *Volcano* on the island of Panarea. The screenplay for the film, which was directed by William Dieterle, was the work of Renzo Avanzo, Roberto Rossellini's cousin. The project had been offered to Rossellini in 1947, and he was largely inspired by it for the film he shot on the nearby island of Stromboli with Ingrid Bergman, for whom he had left Anna Magnani. *Volcano*'s premiere took place on February 1, 1950, to widespread indifference, the day before the birth of Rossellini and Ingrid Berg-man's son, an event that was documented on page one of all the newspapers in Italy, which had been trumpeting what they called the "war of the volcanoes" for months. Through his company Panaria,* Alliata had coproduced *Volcano,* having signed a contract with Magnani for two films. The adaptation of *Le Carrosse du Saint-Sacrement* would be the second, and Luchino Visconti had been working on it for several months.

Actually, La Magnani and Visconti would work together over the sum-mer of 1951, but that was on *Bellissima* and not on *Le Carrosse.* Alliata had turned down the screenplay written by Visconti and Suso Cecchi d'Amico; and according to the producer, "at least twelve or thirteen people"[57] had collaborated on it. These included "Alberto Moravia, Piero Tellini, Antonio Pietrangeli, and Franco Zeffirelli."[58] Alliata's complaint against it was that it was "very far from Mérimée" and, moreover, a "violent lampooning of the Catholic Church."[59] Visconti pretended to accept the need to rewrite it, but that was really the last thing he intended to do. Apparently, the producer then turned to "an American writer who was in Rome and who had written the script for *Quo Vadis*† to write a new screenplay,"[60] which Visconti seems to have rejected haughtily, leading Alliata to decide to call it quits with him.

After having "seen everybody in Italy,"[61] and having come to the conclusion that no filmmaker wanted to take over a project from which Visconti had been fired, Alliata went to France, where, among others, he met with René Clément, who was just about to direct *Forbidden Games,* a Robert Dorfmann‡ produc-tion. Alliata wanted "him to do it" but had found Clément "very cold" and was

---

Impero, Altezza Serenissima, Duca di Salaparuta, Principe di Valguarnera e di Montereale, di Ucria, Trecastagni, Buccheri, Castrorao e Saponara.

* The name was derived from Panarea.

† The credits for *Quo Vadis,* made in Rome by Mervyn LeRoy, list Sonya Levien only as screen-writer.

‡ The filming of *Forbidden Games* began on September 10, 1951. Alliata was mistaken when he told Janet Bergstrom that he'd proposed the project to René Clément the day after a screening of the film.

"afraid of the way he would relate to Anna Magnani who, on the contrary, was a volcano."[62] It's likely that the idea of calling on Renoir came to him from Dorfmann; but it's not impossible that it was inspired by an offer of services from the director's agent, as Alliata has declared.[63] Beholden to the project as a result of her contract with Panaria, Magnani apparently then asked Visconti for advice, who responded by saying, "What are you talking about? ... With Renoir! And you're hesitating?"[64]

In March 1951, the actress was forty-three years old. Her "official" romantic involvements, the last of which had been with Rossellini, as well as her "wild" flings, had been inflaming Italy for years. During the filming of *Bellissima,* she'd gone wild for an electrician on the crew named Lavoretti, whom she'd cloistered away to keep him from visiting his wife and children, with whom he'd been living until then. Her rages were as well known as the endless laments provoked by her fits of jealousy, which were as violent and frequent during friendships as they were during love. When she learned of Ingrid Bergman's arrival in Italy, she publicly vowed to "break all the plates of spaghetti in Rome over her head."[65]

Although there isn't any doubt that the idea of working with Magnani appealed to Renoir, it's no less certain that Robert Dorfmann's offer arrived at the right moment, just when Renoir was desperately searching for a film to direct.

Although there is no evidence, it cannot be ruled out, as Renoir would claim, that he had wanted to adapt *Le Carrosse du Saint-Sacrement** in the past. At the time he said this, he would explain that he had seen the film "as a kind of great adventure story."[66] If we are to believe the statements he made about it later, such a vision is very opposed to the one he came up with as soon as the project was actually offered to him. About that offer, he would say that he had been "convinced that he would be filming in France,"[67] which is surprising, because the first telegram from Dorfmann had expressly mentioned a production to be made "in Italy."

However, his claim that he was unaware "that it was an Italian project" is plausible. Is it true that, at this time, his views "absolutely no longer corresponded"[68] to his ideas during the period of silent films? Now the project interested him because he would like "to make a film with Magnani," because he thought he would "be able to do a good film," and because, since "the film is in two versions, French and English," it would probably be possible for him "to obtain some advantages as far as dollars go," a "last, but not negligible consideration."[69]

---

* It is possible that Renoir had seen Valentine Tessier, his future Bovary, in the role of Périchole in March 1920, on the stage of the Théâtre du Vieux-Colombier.

At first he noticed how similar it was to *Carnival in Flanders* (1935), a film by Jacques Feyder.* Both films take place in a country under Spanish occupation—Feyder's in Flanders, *Le Carrosse* in Peru. "*Le Carrosse* can make an incredible film, a bit in the genre of *Carnival in Flanders,* and can have the same worldwide success as Feyder's film," he wrote to Robert Dorfmann, before explaining, "My ideas are obviously based on the description of the loves of Périchole but also, and especially, on the situation in general. That general situation is the Spanish occupation of an Indian country. From that situation are born habits, obligations, duties, hypocrisies, kindness, and cruelty;† everything needed to make a great film."[70]

It was certainly natural, then, that he considered it "too bad that you wouldn't be shooting the film in a Latin American country," because "streets filled with real Indians would afford the production an extraordinary value,"[71] as would "the style of the churches, bull runs, etc." Thus, he was suggesting that the producer "film some shots for atmosphere in Mexico, for example," which he was also seeking to visit as a "research trip."[72] None of all that would be possible. If it had been, it would have served as a response to the fear expressed by Renoir regarding the flimsiness of the argument in the Mérimée play.

Confined entirely to a Peruvian viceroy's office, *Le Carrosse du Saint-Sacrement,* written in 1828 but performed for the first time without success in 1850, has six characters, only four of whom are of any importance: the viceroy, his secretary, his valet, and his mistress—an actress named Camilla Périchole. She is going to see her lover after the viceroy has been informed of her infidelities, and such behavior is considered scandalous in Lima's fine society. She asks him for the carriage that has arrived for him from Spain, he gives in and the young woman creates a new commotion, which he witnesses from a distance. Quite flimsy, in fact, for a feature-length film. On stage, the play is barely more than an hour long.‡

Starting with his first exchanges with Robert Dorfmann, Renoir began insisting that the film be shot in Technicolor, an already existent element of the Alliata-Visconti project. The director was equally adamant that Claude Renoir be used as director of cinematography, and this demand was granted. On the other hand, he failed in convincing the producer to hire Eugène Lourié as well.

* Written by Charles Spaak, with Françoise Rosay and Louis Jouvet.

† All these elements are already noticeable in *This Land Is Mine* and would also constitute the background in *Carola*.

‡ It was seventy minutes in the production that Jean Vilar would make for the Théâtre National Populaire (TNP) in 1958, with Maria Casarès as Périchole and Georges Wilson as the viceroy.

Having taken up this cause several times, he was met with a refusal, essentially, it seems, because Lourié couldn't be considered to be an American professional, unlike Renoir, who now possessed double nationality—French and American.* That detail about Lourié was capable of thwarting certain agreements regarding coproduction.

Le Carrosse d'or (*The Golden Coach*), as the film would come to be called, was being offered in two languages, French and English; and that meant it required two versions of the dialogue. Renoir suggested using an English or American writer and delivering a rough draft of the screenplay in two weeks, which would be "very imperfect but enough, allowing for the choice of the appropriate actors and writer." It was understood that he would get down to this task as soon as he arrived in Paris, in an office and with a secretary provided him by production.[73]

After a stay of less than two weeks in New York, where he was working with McEldowney on the distribution of *The River*, he arrived in Paris on May 8, with the idea of leaving soon for the United States in order to "convince certain actors" and then make a "quick trip to Mexico"[74] before the shoot. But on May 17, he left for Italy with Dorfmann, met some journalists in Milan, and arrived in Rome on the morning of the nineteenth. He checked in to the Hassler Hotel, the same in which Michel Simon had stayed in 1940.

On May 20, 1951, at a private screening of *Grand Illusion* in the presence of the ambassador of France, Renoir met the "charming and withered"[75] Anna Magnani as well as Renzo Avanzo. Married since 1940 to Visconti's younger sister, Uberta, Avanzo was one of the founders of Panaria† as well as the representative for Technicolor in Italy. In the credits for *The Golden Coach*, he'd be listed as associate producer and writer. It's likely that Renoir was given the adaptation by Visconti and Suso Cecchi d'Amico, which was the property of Panaria; but if not, he at least must have been in possession of the version written by the mysterious American writer of whom Alliata had spoken. This latter was likely the screenplay he alluded to when he claimed that he had not preserved any of it. Apparently, Renoir had not had any chance to make any direct mention of *Coach* with Visconti. In addition to Renzo Avanzo, the writers listed in the credits would include Giulio Macchi, Renoir's assistant for the film; and Jack Kirkland. Kirkland was an American playwright‡ and screenwriter who had

---

* Actually, the question of Renoir's nationality was thornier than that. The issue would come up later.

† Along with Francesco Alliata, Pietro Moncada, and Quintino di Napoli.

‡ His adaptation of Erskine Caldwell's *Tobacco Road* had been a hit on the American stage beginning in 1933 and had been adapted for the screen by John Ford in 1941.

just collaborated on the Henri Diamant-Berger film *Monsieur Fabre* (*Amazing Monsieur Fabre*, 1951), with Pierre Fresnay, the person who had suggested that Renoir call on Kirkland for English dialogue, a task for which Kirkland rapidly outdid himself by "writing another screenplay." Renoir would acknowledge that such work "hasn't been futile because it led me to tighten up and perfect my own screenplay."[76] Kirkland spent several weeks with Renoir "at the beginning, before disappearing in a flash."[77] Lee Kresel, a young American actor who specialized in dubbing and who had appeared in *Quo Vadis* as an extra, turned out to be the real author of the English dialogue.

After dictating the first rough draft of his treatment, Renoir left on June 12 for Sicily for ten or so days, with a stop in Calabria, where his purpose was to visit "a city built by the Spanish."[78] He returned to Rome on the twenty-second and went to Paris on the twenty-fifth, after traveling through Switzerland. As he wrote to McEldowney,[79] he was location hunting in Sicily and Calabria, proof that plans were still to direct the film at least partly using real scenery. But before that, and thanks to Francesco Alliata and his wife, he was granted "an amazing honor"[80] consisting of a private audience with the pope, on June 11 at noon. Encountering Pius XII, who, to him, "seemed in good health, very animated and in appearance younger than he looked in his photographs,"* Renoir was "very moved" and "didn't know how to answer the Holy Father's questions." The pope gave him "a small medal" that he promised to give to Dido.

It was in Paris that the director undertook the organization of the casting of the film. The coproduction stipulated the hiring of French and Italian actors, and the two versions of the shoot required French and English or American actors. Apparently, the producers had played a game of hide-and-seek with the banks to obtain the loans that were needed: in Paris, they talked about a film in French, and in Rome, about a film in Italian.† All the while, they knew very well that the film would first be in English, and even, to put it more precisely, in American English, because its priority was the US market. Renoir was supposed to work with these imperatives, certain as he was at the time of directing the film in two versions, English and French, just as *Volcano* had been shot in English and in Italian (under the title *Vulcano*), the English version having been edited at RKO, which was then owned by Howard Hughes; the other version, in Rome.

Until just before the shoot, he had to resist pressure put on him by production, which for many reasons greatly preferred that the film not be recorded

---

* Eugenio Maria Giuseppe Giovanni Pacelli, elected pope on March 2, 1939, under the name Pius XII, was seventy-five at the time.

† The French poster would present the film as "the first French spectacular in Technicolor." The Italian poster, as "the first Italian production in Technicolor."

using live sound and instead be entirely dubbed later, which was the custom in Italy. "Right or wrong, I've always refused to dub films and I still refuse. Therefore I insisted on confirming to you . . . that if I found myself in a situation in which recording the lead role in the film live was an impossibility, I would be obliged to pull out and I would ask you to please consider another director."[81] Therefore, Anna Magnani, the lead, would be expressing herself in English, a language that she did not speak, and she would learn her dialogue phonetically, as she had done for *Volcano*. It was a worrisome incongruity, but Renoir had no other choice, especially because at this moment of climbing on his high horse he had also suffered a defeat that was about to come into play. However, from such duress he would pull one of the main threads of his screenplay.

Around Camilla, he created a theatrical troupe from Italy, who are arriving in that Spanish colony at the same time as the coach, which has been brought on the same ship. Like the actors in the troupe, Anna Magnani spoke Italian, and like them, she would express herself in a language that was not hers and would play her role in English. And yet, "in English, I can't manage it," Renoir has her say, in substance, thus creating one of the discrepancies from which the film draws its material. *The Golden Coach*'s principal theme is the encounter between two characters, Camilla Périchole and the viceroy, who don't know each other when the film begins, whereas in the Mérimée play they are lovers when the curtain rises. Thus, Renoir associates certain elements of *Le Carrosse du Saint-Sacrement* with a plot that is previous to that of the play and draws his material essentially from the personality of Camilla.

In actuality, the screenplay is situated halfway between the Mérimée play and the libretto by Meilhac and Halévy, on which is based Jacques Offenbach's *La Périchole*, an opéra bouffe in which the coach doesn't appear. The plot centers around the figure of Camilla, inspired for Mérimée by a Pervuian anecdote whose heroine was a celebrated actress of the eighteenth century named Micaëla Villegas. In 1835, the light-comedy writers Desforges and Théaulon made her the heroine of a farce in one act entitled *La Périchole*, who was played by Virginie Déjazet, an interpretation that shifted the anecdote toward burlesque,[82] just as would Renoir's film more than a century later.

Because the plot was decidedly flimsy, and because he wanted to face in advance potential reproaches about "betraying" Mérimée, Renoir distanced himself from the playwright as much as he could, something he would tell Jean Vilar about in writing in 1958. This would be confirmed by Giulio Macchi's complaints to the Italian distributor, whom he held partly responsible for the

---

* The version in two acts was produced on October 6, 1868; the one in three acts, on April 25, 1874.

coolness of the film's critical reception in Italy. Macchi accused the distributor of having accorded too much importance to the literary and dramatic origins of the film. The distributor had "waited for the moment when you [Renoir] left to focus on the things we'd so struggled against, Mérimée, Périchole, Peru, etc."[83]

The search for someone to play the viceroy lasted several weeks. Mérimée's character had gout. By making him younger, Renoir removed a handicap shared by several characters in his films who, like him, were afflicted with a bad leg or foot. This also made casting Pierre Renoir or Louis Jouvet out of the question.* For a while, he considered "a stupid and wonderful [French] southern singer"[84] in whom he saw a possible "young Raimu";† but he abandoned that idea and began to think of Pierre Brasseur, the "only French actor who isn't too old‡ and capable of performing with words and ideas, and of wearing a costume colorfully." Renoir had seen Brasseur in Jean-Paul Sartre's play *Le Diable et le Bon Dieu* (*The Devil and the Good Lord*)§ and received "the biggest kick in the head I've ever gotten, unless it was from Wagner's *The Flying Dutchman* with Koch in Berlin in 1933." By "kick in the head," he meant that he considered the play deadly boring. However, "the dialogue by Sartre is sound and a bit like what I would do for *Le Carrosse*," although the author "repeats himself—is too long—and never forgets that he's a pawn,"[85] pitfalls that he promised himself to avoid. A few days later, Sartre would have Renoir sent, through Brasseur, "a screenplay conceived for Brasseur, Marlene Dietrich, and China, but which would be very suitable for the same Brasseur, and maybe for Radha and India."[86] It was an idea without a future, as was the idea of entrusting Sartre with the dialogue for *The Golden Coach*.

Renoir was still looking for his viceroy. He was convinced that he must have "real actors, capable of the nimble recital of a text that I need to try to write by creating a pastiche of the classics."[87] Soon he began to wax lyrical about "a cabaret singer from the 'Lapin agile' [who] made a stunning tryout" and appeared to be "the first one who attempted to play a character and not just play himself," although the man did display "a certain tendency to overdo it."[88] Jean-Roger Caussimon, whose first film role had been in *François Villon*, directed

---

* Pierre Renoir had played the role with Louis Jouvet and Valentine Tessier in February and March of 1931, during the first European tour (France, Italy, Switzerland, Belgium) of the Compagnie du Théâtre Louis-Jouvet.

† *Translator's note:* Raimu (1883–1946) was a beloved French comic character actor who made a name for himself on the Parisian stage but who was especially admired for his performances from 1931 to 1936 in all three films—*Marius, Fanny,* and *César*—of Marcel Pagnol's trilogy.

‡ Pierre Brasseur was forty-five at the time.

§ Performed on June 7, 1951, at the Théâtre Antoine, with direction by Louis Jouvet.

in 1945 by Renoir's former assistant, André Zwobada,* didn't please Madame Dorfmann, a.k.a. Gisella Mathews,† whom the director spent "three days" trying to convince, deciding to leave Paris only "after having seen Caussimon's contract drawn up and ready to be signed."[89] The casting of Caussimon would be announced by the French press in October.

Renoir left Paris on July 20 to move into the apartment provided for him in Rome at 1 via Jacopo Peri, just steps from the offices of Panaria on via Basento and from the Villa Borghese. The production had also rented a Fiat 1400 for him. His leg had begun to hurt again, and he was using a cane to walk. However, at the end of August, he went to the Venice Film Festival, which took place from August 20 to September 10 and in which *The River* was being shown in competition and as a world premiere on August 30. The film would receive the International Award, along with Robert Bresson's *Diary of a Country Priest* and Billy Wilder's *Ace in the Hole*. The Golden Lion was given to Kurosawa's *Rashomon*. Renoir was back in Rome for Dido's arrival on September 6, after nearly four months of separation.

By that date, it was already out of the question that filming would begin in September. The director's health was worsening; the wound on his leg had become infected, and he had to be hospitalized. If he had delayed having it examined, it was because he was used to the pain caused by the leg. It was also because every new warning sign that had occurred since 1917 had made him dread that the doctors would suggest amputation.[90] In the hospital, he began wondering whether he'd be well enough to direct *Le Carrosse*, a fear he expressed to Clifford Odets in a letter dated October 29 in which he also explained that he had already been bedridden for six weeks. Fifteen days later, he decided to consult a surgeon in Paris and left Rome with Dido on November 19. Professor Robert Merle d'Aubigné, a famous specialist in corrective surgery who practiced at Hôpital Foch in Suresnes, wanted to have him hospitalized, but Renoir chose to go to Hôtel Le Royal Monceau on avenue Hoche, where he stayed until December 1. On the morning of that Saturday, he granted Jacques Doniol-Valcroze an interview that would appear a month later in an issue of *Cahiers du cinéma* devoted to him.

Time passed and was made the most of by preparing sound stage no. 5 at Cinecittà, working on the screenplay, having the costumes created, and bringing over

* "The claim of Zwobada directing *François Villon* totally strikes me as a big joke," Renoir had written to his brother Claude on April 17, 1945. (Jean Renoir Papers, Correspondence, Box 5, Folder 2.)

† In *The Golden Coach*, Gisella Mathews plays the Marquise Altamirano.

the coach that belonged to the Branciforti di Buteras from Palermo. However, the day before the shoot began, Renoir seemed disenchanted, even discouraged. A decision had been made to film exclusively in the studio. According to the producer, the reason for this was because Sicilian and Calabrian scenery had been ransacked by the war. Nevertheless, this wasn't the cause of Renoir's disillusionment. He had always liked working in a studio. Nor was his mood due any more to the concerns caused by some banal questions of precedence, which had led to a letter from his agent to Robert Dorfmann, with a copy to Alliata. Renoir seemed, Jean Dewalde wrote, "rather tormented" by "a new and unexpected situation" having to do with the discovery that the contract signed with "the main star," Anna Magnani, "gave her rights whose effects limited the moral authority of Jean Renoir and that were incompatible with his contract as auteur-director."[91] La Magnani's habit was to rule over her films, and producers would give in to whims that they often chose to anticipate in advance. That was the sum of it. However, the truth was that Renoir had more serious reasons for worry.

To start with, he was dissatisfied with the casting and wanted to replace Riccardo Rialo, who was supposed to play Ramon, with Alexander Knox, the coscreenwriter and actor from *Sister Kenny*, the film Renoir had thought about doing for a while but that was finally directed by Dudley Nichols. Renoir was also complaining that Michael Tor, who had a supporting role but who would not, in the end, appear in the film, "is only concerned with his looks." The scenery was the work of Mario Chiari, who had become part of the project during the time Visconti was working on the film. Renoir had failed to replace him with Eugène Lourié. The costumes were by Maria De Matteis. For Renoir, both "are far from corresponding to a certain visual conception that I have tried to maintain in all my films." Even his work with Anna Magnani was making him hesitate. "I came to make this film in large part because of her. Since that time, I've discovered that her successes are based on last-minute inspiration and not on preparation. Such a thing succeeds wonderfully in her own language. In a foreign language, I'm not sure it could work. In my conversations with her, I've had the impression that Anna didn't understand my screenplay. Moreover, she has had so much work that she wasn't able to work seriously on her English. That represents such a handicap that I feel discouraged about it already." All these "obstacles . . . are so great that often I regret the fact that the doctors have found me in good enough physical shape to continue with my work."[92] The letter to the producer was dated January 28, and the shoot was to start on February 4. However, in his letter Renoir did not mention a major disappointment, the primary cause of his state of mind.

Renoir had had the opportunity to discuss this disappointment with Alliata several times over the last few months, both in Rome and in Paris, but he had to turn the page. That is why he had not mentioned it in his letter. The producer had already committed some very substantial funds, as much during the period when Visconti was involved as recently. Valerio Brosio, the executive producer of the film, had emphasized to him that the potential success of *The Golden Coach*, no matter how considerable, wouldn't allow him to recover his expenses. According to Alliata, responsibility for the budget would be half Panaria's, with funds loaned to them by the Bank of Sicily, and half that of Milanese investors, "the Invernizzis and the Galbanis, large-scale manufacturers who owned the most important cheese companies in Italy."[93] Consequently, this was not, or at least not more than officially, a coproduction with France. And therefore, if no French money was involved, neither would there be a version in French. At least, this was the argument advanced by Alliata, who may also simply have wanted to reduce the budget because, factually, the director was still not working for Panaria but for Hoche Productions, Dorfmann's company, who would pay him the sums stipulated by his contract, a salary of 2 million francs,[94] as well as a bit more than 4 million for royalties (4,238,000 francs).[95] Only his per diem, 20,000 francs a day, as well as a sum of $10,000 as "an advance on the first ticket sales for the film in Anglo-Saxon countries"[96] and payable in the United States during filming, would be handled by the Italian production.[97]

This new factor was the primary cause of Renoir's discouragement. A letter sent by Jean-Roger Caussimon—the actor approached to play the viceroy—to *L'Écran français* confirmed it: "This film will be shot, as planned, in Rome; but as M. Renoir has confided to me in a somewhat sad letter, due to a default regarding the French production, he has had to give up the idea of a French version. And this despite the fact that this was the version he most valued. It was the reason and the purpose of his return to Europe."[98] Nevertheless, it should be kept in mind that Renoir's pretext for returning to Europe was the making of a film intended first and foremost for the American market. Caussimon also confided to the weekly about the letter he had received from Renoir, in which the director had written, "Francesco Alliata, our Italian producer, has only just returned to Rome. He was able partly to save his production of *The Golden Coach* thanks to the help of certain associates in Milan. I use the word 'partly' because, in the half-ruin that occurred, the French version has foundered. I'd suspected it for a week already, but before writing to you I wanted to hear from the mouth of the producer himself that the decision was definitive. I'm heartbroken, first because I had come to Europe with the idea of making a film whose dialogue I'd write myself in my mother tongue. I will have to give up that idea."[99]

---

* At the time, Robert Dorfmann was going through a bad financial patch, which the success of *Forbidden Games* would allow him to escape.

The letter isn't dated, but the decision must have been made either while Renoir was hospitalized in Rome or in semiconvalescence in Paris, probably in November. Renoir and Caussimon would have to wait for *French Cancan* to work together. Duncan Lamont, a thirty-year-old British man who had no significant experience, would be the viceroy in *Coach*, which indicates that the casting for the film had been hastily decided. Jean Debucourt, who'd play the minor role of the bishop, would be the only French actor in the film.*

Although it had no impact on the direction of *Coach*, the plan of action concocted by Alliata and his associates to recoup all or part of their outlay bears mentioning. It consisted in producing two films using the scenery and some of the costumes from Renoir's film—films that were made one after the other on the sidelines of the shooting of *Coach*. Alliata commissioned two screenplays from Age and Scarpelli, a duo who were starting out at the time and who would occupy a central position in Italian film in the years to come. Carlo Ludovico Bragaglia was put in charge of the direction of *At Sword's Edge* and *Secret of Three Points*, which, according to the producer, brought in more money than *The Golden Coach*.[100]

In the past, Renoir had sometimes exhibited a sense of discouragement resembling the kind he expressed in January 1952 and that could have led him to think vaguely of declaring it impossible for him to film. Most directors have endured such reactions close to states of panic. These are just as likely to occur right before beginning a film that has required years of struggle on their part as they are at the moment of carrying out an assignment they accepted for a variety of reasons. Renoir's going so far this time as to deplore the fact that he hadn't been considered physically disabled enough constitutes the first expression of genuine weariness and fatigue. He may not have been any older than fifty-seven, but he had directed about thirty films in twenty-five years, and his wounded leg made moving about that much more difficult when added to his excess weight. Renoir ate like a horse and drank too much, even more so when Dido wasn't there to keep an eye on him; and he had just spent several months without her, among his Parisian friends, with whom he'd been reunited after years of separation, not to mention his Italian acquaintances. "I'm bored without you," he'd written to her, "and—as you know—when I get that way, I eat and I drink."[101] Only filming made him forget his weariness and fatigue, and then he would display a staggering amount of energy, carried away as he was by the pleasure of making films, the enthusiasm of those around him, and his confidence in the

* What happened for *Coach* was the same thing that had happened for *Tosca*: the French actors whom Renoir had chosen had disappeared from the cast.

film he was making.

Such would be the case for *The Golden Coach*, once again. A week before he started to direct, he left it up to "divine Providence, which counts for a lot, even when it comes to films." He also affirmed his faith in his screenplay, which was "now in a good enough form," and was relying upon "the music of the eighteenth century, which will be a revelation outside of Italy."[102] That music was mostly by Vivaldi, which in that period remained practically unknown to mainstream audiences,* and Renoir was correct in writing that the film would permit its "discovery."† He himself owed the discovery of the composer to Giulio Macchi, one of his assistants with the same status for him as his old partner Marc Maurette, whom he had succeeded in having come to Italy. The concertos by the "Red Priest"‡ punctuated the writing of the screenplay just as the works of Musset, Marivaux, Beaumarchais, Mozart, or Saint-Saëns had piloted *The Rules of the Game* years earlier. Renoir would amusingly call Vivaldi his first assistant on *Coach*, delighted to have found a collaborator who never contradicted him. Long after, Maurice Béjart would have a good laugh presenting *The Golden Coach* as "a film directed by Antonio Vivaldi and Jean Renoir."[103]

The music by Vivaldi steered the film in the direction of commedia dell'arte, Renoir would claim, but certainly this was also due to some of Anna Magnani's characteristics, her difficulties with the English language and the lack of interest she showed in rehearsal. Renoir may have wanted to see her pull away from the "realist" register she had mostly exhibited until that point, but his expression of such a desire seems strongly to have been motivated a posteriori, which would refer at that point, without naming them, to Rossellini's films—*Rome, Open City*, obviously, and possibly, *L'Amore*§—but also to Visconti's *Bellissima*, which he may have in fact seen before its official release in Italy.¶ It is more than probable that he had actually seen very little of Magnani in films before directing her.

The actress with whom he became acquainted regularly arrived late on the sound stage. Mornings are difficult for a person who leads an eventful nocturnal existence; and even if Renoir had been able to adopt "French" hours, from noon to seven in the evening, which he'd always preferred, his Camilla's tardy arrivals posed a problem. Especially on the face of a woman who would soon turn

---

* The first authoritative recording of *The Four Seasons* was by I Musici in 1955.

† *Les Enfants terribles*, a film by Jean-Pierre Melville and Jean Cocteau, released in France in March 1950, did contain a few excerpts from two Vivaldi concertos.

‡ *Translator's note:* "il Prete Rosso," Vivaldi's nickname, presumably because of his red hair, after being ordained to the priesthood in 1703.

§ *Translator's note:* Released in the United States at times under three different titles: *Amore, The Miracle*, and *Ways of Love*.

¶ December 27, 1951.

forty-four, the excesses of the night before left their mark, which makeup followed by lighting had trouble erasing. La Magnani was aware of this and didn't intend to be filmed looking that way, but the show had to go on; and the Renoir technique afforded her the time to wake up, as well as liven up. And it helped her master those lines in English, which he began by asking her to say mechanically, without expression or intent, so that little by little they would become hers and soon she could even begin to enjoy them. Like all the other actors in *Coach*, she had to play a scene all the way through, without the potential saving grace of an insert shot that would allow her to repeat a line, to correct an impression.

This film required seasoned professionals as well as actors, and Renoir had known it from the very beginning of the project.[104] His technique, the quality of the screenplay, and the abandonment of natural scenery brought out the theatrical aspect of the work. In the course of rehearsals, which functioned progressively as a kind of vocal warm-up, Anna Magnani passed without being aware of it from life to film, just as Camilla ceases to distinguish the theater from life, a confusion that shapes Renoir's direction. At the beginning of the film, the curtain in the movie theater opens on the curtain in the theater, which itself is opening on the stage, which itself is opening on a representation of life. Colombine or Périchole, Camilla plays her character as it is designed by an author, and as it is determined by her encounters, her crushes, her emotions, her impulses, her flights of enthusiasm or anger, and her exhaustions. Renoir's direction dispels the distinction, eliminates the gaps between the two gambits, those belonging to the theater and those to life. At the end, Camilla—who is both Colombine and Périchole—remains alone on the stage, and the voice of the director in the film indicates that the characters have become spectators. Does she miss them? Yes, a little. That is how it is.

Renoir was happy. "I'm sure the producers never read my screenplay. They have no idea what I'm doing, and that's fantastic."[105] Entirely absorbed by his film and especially by his requirements regarding the treatment of color—which led him to have one set completely repainted several times—as well as by an extreme awareness of how sound was being recorded (a process he'd entrusted to Joseph de Bretagne, his very first engineer), he moved forward his way, saving the technically most complex scenes for the final weeks at the end of April and beginning of May.

At the beginning of March, Claude Renoir had to leave the shoot to travel round-trip to Paris, where his father was about to die. Pierre Renoir passed away on March 11, 1952, from acute uremia, in his home on avenue Frochot. In two more weeks he would have been sixty-seven; and his old friend Louis Jouvet had gone to the grave a few months before him on August 16, 1951. Pierre's funeral took place on March 14 at nine in the morning in the church of Notre-Dame-de-Lorette. That afternoon he was buried in Essoyes. At Cine-città, that same Friday was a day like any other, during which the brother and son of the deceased filmed the shots listed on the call sheet.

Filming of *The Golden Coach* ended on May 10, 1952. On that day the final scene showing Camilla alone on stage was shot.[106] The editing, the recording of the music, and the mixing would be done in Rome. Only the postsynchroni-zation in French, with Anna Magnani dubbing herself, would be accomplished in Paris under the direction of Marc Maurette, without Renoir's taking part in it. Editing was over by the end of July, the first stage of mixing in mid-August. By then it was possible to start organizing some screenings, and the reactions that were collected allowed Renoir to modify those elements audiences thought needed to be.

Going back to the formula of previews that had worked for him for *The River,* Renoir first showed the film in a theater in a Roman suburb to find out the reactions of a mainstream audience, which turned out to be "very positive," according to Alliata.[107] In accordance, Renoir carried out "three or four" sessions of editing changes, but what remained mostly at stake in his eyes and those of the producers was the American market. With this in mind, Panaria organized two screenings of what was still only a preedited state of the film for about a hundred American tourists who happened to be visiting Rome in mid-November.[108] At the end of the month, the film was also shown in London, at a screening that included the Renoirs and Charles and Oona Chaplin; then in Paris, in the screening room of Films Corona, the French distributor of *The Golden Coach.* In both London and Paris, the reactions were unanimous: the film was a masterpiece, in all likelihood destined to become a big hit.

Several days later, the reviews for its Italian release on December 3, 1952, dampened that lovely enthusiasm. Ticket sales in the theaters were mediocre. In a telegram Renoir received from Visconti, who had seen the film that very day, Visconti expressed "all my enthusiasm for *The Golden Coach,*" and appended to his message embraces "full of lots of affection and continual great, great admiration";[109] but getting such a message from the director of *Bellissima* wasn't enough to console Renoir. Alliata attributed the coolness of the critical recep-tion to the influence of the Communists in Italy, who wouldn't have accepted Visconti—one of their own—having been ousted from the project.[110] It was an interpretation that seemed rather fanciful, and Renoir would prefer another that was equally surprising, one that claimed that his "unfaithfulness" to Mérimée was the thing that had caused displeasure. In a report for Unifrance, the orga-nization charged with promoting French film in foreign countries, he would write about the presentation of the film, "Perhaps they were too concerned with the relation between *The Golden Coach* and *Le Carrosse du Saint-Sacrement*. The experience in Italy proves to us that certain Mérimée fans held it against me for having told a different story."[111]

In New York, where he went at the end of the year with Renoir, who was on his way back to California, Alliata was forced to acknowledge that the major American distributors did not want this film that he had conceived for their audiences, already unfavorably impressed as they were by the appalling reviews it had received from American critics in Rome, like the one given by the *Hollywood Reporter* on December 15.[112] And as the days passed, it became obvious to Alliata that less prestigious and less powerful distributors than those to whom he'd shown the film first were no more interested. As a last resort, a company created by Italian producers in the United States, Italian Film Export, would have to take charge of the release of *Coach*. It was a very limited release, starting on January 20, 1954, aided by Renoir's participation between September 30 and October 21, 1953,[113] in several screenings, receptions, and press conferences organized in New York; Williamstown, Massachusetts; and Lakeville, Minnesota. On the last day, October 21, Dido and he would leave for Paris aboard the ocean liner *Liberté*. By then, the French career of *The Golden Coach* had been over for several months, and if the Parisian release of the film was a source of some satisfaction for Renoir, it wasn't enough to ease his disappointment.

Shown in Paris on February 27, 1953, the film would be seen in France by nearly eight hundred thousand viewers. The promoters of a production that had cost less would have judged such a result very satisfactory, but it didn't satisfy those for *Coach*. Renoir himself appeared extremely disappointed with it and placed the responsibility for these results on the distributors, especially Raymond Ventura,* about whom he wrote, "The way he presented *The Golden Coach* proves that he understood nothing about how to present my films."[114]

A few days later, after abandoning a project called *First Love*, based on a novella by Turgenev, which had been transformed into *Les Braconniers*,† and which he was suggesting to the same Ray Ventura, he gave full vent to what would become his leitmotiv throughout the fifties: "The commercial failure of *Coach* and Ventura's impropriety have managed to inspire me with disgust for an occupation that takes too much of my time and brings me too few results. I'm not talking about financial results, which are meager, but about moral results, which are disappointing. Therefore I'm turning more and more to literature."[115]

---

* A star musician under the name Ray Ventura, he was the bandleader of the Collegians. He was also an actor, director, and producer, associated with Robert Dorfmann as part of Hoche Productions and Films Corona. In 1951, he produced and played in *Nous irons à Monte-Carlo* (*Baby Beats the Band*).

† *Translator's note:* "The Poachers."

He continued to seek and to struggle to the same extent, but gave up the idea of moving to Paris and working there, as he had intended. He asked his business manager to take care of everything that needed to be, including canceling the reservation he'd made at the Berkeley* for a place in the garage for his Jaguar.[116]

It was, however, in France that *Coach* received the greatest number of favorable reviews. There were a few unfavorable opinions, but the press as a whole declared itself dazzled by the colors as well as the personality and performance of Anna Magnani, and the pleasure it found in everything that was somewhat reminiscent of the atmosphere of *The Rules of the Game*. Jacques Doniol-Valcroze brought to light this enjoyment in an article he devoted to the film, lamenting as he did the fact that he'd only been able to see the French version. "*The Golden Coach* is the message from *The River* to the rhythm of *The Rules of the Game* expressed through the intermediary of the commedia dell'arte. . . . Whether wishing to or not, Renoir is moving in the direction of the abstract. *The Rules of the Game* and *The River* had social and historical contexts. *Coach* happens nowhere and in a time that only the costumes indicated as being the eighteenth century." He concluded that it was a matter "without a doubt of the first great painterly film."[117] Jacques Rivette would state that he had seen the first showing of the film on the day it came out and hadn't left the theater until the last showing was over. Later, François Truffaut would label *Coach* as "Jean Renoir's masterpiece,"[118] "a finished work that you have to watch without touching, a film that has found its definitive form, a perfect object,"[119] and he would also call it "the noblest and most refined film ever made."[120] But when Truffaut, who'd call his company the "Films du Carrosse," made this remark in 1967, the monument to Renoir had been erected a long time earlier, and the foundations for it had been dug in January 1952, several days before the filming of *The Golden Coach* had begun.

The eighth installment of *Cahiers du cinéma*, with a cover portrait of Adrienne Corri in *The River*, began with an article by Jean Renoir, "On me demande . . ."† Forty-nine of the eighty pages of the issue were devoted to the director, to whom André Bazin paid homage that seemed a little embarrassed at first but soon became lyrical. The magazine creator's "French Renoir" was complemented by the "American Renoir" in which Maurice Schérer, a.k.a. Éric Rohmer, undertook

---

* The Berkeley, on avenue de Matignon, was at the time still a hotel and restaurant. In the thirties, it had been one of Renoir's favorite addresses. It was, for example, the setting in 1938 for the wedding of Marcel Dalio and Madeleine Lebeau, which Renoir and Henri Jeanson attended.

† *Translator's note:* "They Ask Me . . ." Text also published in English as "Personal Notes," in *Sight and Sound* 21, no. 4 (April–June 1952): 152–153.

the rehabilitation of the Hollywood period, which he clearly preferred. Beyond some instances of personal reverence expressed with conviction, especially for *The Diary of a Chambermaid*, to which some brilliant lines were devoted, this text also established the wish to foil the thesis claiming that Renoir in Hollywood enjoyed no creative freedom.*

The truth is that neither Schérer/Rohmer nor the proponents of that thesis were aware of the factual details that would justify their impressions. All of their visions were by nature essentially political. Schérer was pitting himself against the anti-American reading of a press that was strongly left wing. On May 26, 1946, agreements had been concluded between the American secretary of state James F. Byrnes and Léon Blum and Jean Monnet, who represented the French government. They established that in exchange for a loan to France for conditions deemed exceptional, French movie theaters would present American productions three weeks out of each month. It was this agreement that had contributed to radicalizing the positions. The entire profession of cinema had risen against what was called the Blum-Byrnes agreements. Everything that came from Hollywood was henceforth considered harmful, and thus mediocre.

Maurice Schérer did not belong to the world of French cinema. His political beliefs were located on the Right, and his desire to call attention to himself could only result in his defense of Renoir's American films and the need to display his reservations about the French period, the only one that was then being celebrated. Similarly, he rose up against "the myth of a Renoir debased by the diktats of a big company, crushed in the cogs of the mighty Yankee machine," to proclaim that he was not familiar with "any films that are to a more complete degree characterized by improvisation on location than *Swamp Water* or *The Southerner*." It also seemed to him that giving Renoir "the use of the most refined technical tools, far from provoking that stiffness in cutting that everyone deplored, had, on the contrary, facilitated the task of the French director who can handle the dolly or the crane with the most ease." Included in the text was Schérer's guarantee of having had it "from the mouth of André Bazin that *The Woman on the Beach*, far from being due, as was believed, to the whim of a producer, is, on the contrary, one of [Renoir's directions] for which he claimed the greatest authorship, even though it was not completed by his hand."[121]

Schérer knew no more about the conditions in which Renoir had worked in Hollywood than those who were claiming the opposite. On both sides, the supposedly aesthetic choices were made for the most part as the result of political and strategic considerations. If the Renoir of the forties and fifties was

---

* To make his point of view more forceful, the future director took on the French period, touching upon the "too famous and grimacing *Day in the Country* that some people insist on calling one of the high points of Renoir's career."

decreed the greatest by Maurice Schérer and, soon after, by the future directors of what would be established as the Nouvelle Vague, it was, first of all, because the "family" of French cinema and their team in the press considered Renoir as having gone astray and because, in certain eyes, he deserved being called a renegade. It wasn't said, and was written about even less, but even in a text that was as benevolent toward Renoir as Bazin's, the discomfort was obvious in the face of someone who, of course, "had never been 'absorbed' by Hollywood"[122] but "has become an *international* director who is almost as much at ease in Rome, in the Indies, in England, or in America as he is in Paris."[123]

In January 1952, when only the Hollywood and Indian aspects of the director's "international" career could be appreciated, this last proposition was still waiting to be verified; but in this first issue of *Cahiers* devoted to Renoir, there is a strong impression of a passing of the baton from André Bazin to his disciples, voluntary on both sides, but for different reasons. At least as much as the films of Renoir themselves, the way of seeing them was changing.

A year after the appearance of the *Cahiers* Renoir issue, *The Golden Coach* had been filmed and completed. The film had met with commercial failure in Italy and France, and the hopes of seeing it become a hit on the American market, for which it had been conceived, had shrunk considerably. For Renoir the time had come for a sense of disillusionment that was fed as much by the vicissitudes of his career as a director as by the perplexity he felt in his observation from a distance of the evolution of film. Shortly after his return to California, he wrote the following to Clifford Odets: "Since the art of film seems to be disappearing, more than ever we have need of good theater."[124] He was thinking not only of his friend the dramatist but also of himself, who had now decided to write. And although he still believed enough in film to conceive of projects, he did not want "to do something that wouldn't bring any profits."[125] By that it must be understood primarily that he expected to be satisfied financially, which would allow him to spend the greater part of his time in his California home working on his books and his plays.

While he was in Italy, offers had continued to reach him, such as one transmitted to him via letter from Bombay by Forrest Judd, his assistant on *The River*. It proposed that he spend twelve weeks directing an adaptation by the English writer Robert Graves of a story called "Maruf." The work was most likely a tale from *A Thousand and One Nights* or the comic opera it had inspired.* It was to be shot in Technicolor or in new Eastmancolor, in a major studio. The production had "nothing to do with the maharajahs,"[126] Judd added, but was coming

* *Mârouf, savetier du Caire* by Henri Rabaud, libretto by Lucien Népoty (1914).

from a "first class" businessman. Renoir's response was that Eugène Lourié had had that idea first.[*] Renoir had already written a treatment for it.[127] He'd adore filming in Jaipur, but alas, he had "just signed to direct a film in Paris in the spring."[128] It was a polite way of declining an offer that didn't appeal to him.

Another proposition came from Romola Nijinsky about directing a film on the life of her husband, and she was certain that the necessary funds could be easily pulled together, because she had been "offered considerable amounts for this project a good many times."[129] Next came François Gergely, a member of the Syndicat Français des Producteurs et Exportateurs de Films, who was suggesting directing a film in Japan, which could be an adaptation of the novel by Pierre Loti, *Madame Chrysanthème;*[130] then there was Joseph de Bretagne, his sound engineer, who was mentioning the possibility of shooting a film in Panama.[131] At this suggestion, Renoir pulled from his drawers that "story that has been haunting me for a dozen years about some monks lost in the jungle,"[132] which he saw as "a kind of *Grand Illusion* of religion." This possibility seemed to keep his interest to a small extent, and the same day he wrote to his agent to ask him to put him in contact with the producer of the Panama project,[133] but it went no further, nor did one about a screenplay on Hawaii brought to him by "a young man," because "the film had to be ready when Hawaii became an American state," and, moreover, "only a big studio could do it."[134]

Clearly, by that time Renoir understood that he had ceased to interest Hollywood, a sentiment that he would express directly years later, in response to the offer he received about becoming a founding member of the Hollywood Museum. "I don't belong to that institution known as Hollywood, not at all because I don't want Hollywood, but because Hollywood doesn't want me."[135] Had he started to wonder then whether his career as a director was over already? A letter from his son, undated but written in 1953 before the month of June, makes that seem possible. The words Alain used seem to be those one expects will reassure and console. "Whether you remain in film or simply turn to the theater or literature really doesn't have much importance, because had you made only *Grand Illusion* or *The River,* you would still have won your place among those whom Dante shows us around Virgil."[136]

Renoir himself was thinking[137] vaguely of returning to and modernizing the Turgenev story *First Love,*[138] "adapted to an American family living in Europe," and he was finding food for thought from his "memories about poachers, tramps, and beggars in the forest of Fontainebleau"[139] just as much as he was from the novella by Turgenev, but he wanted to combine it with his screenwriter friend Salka Viertel's idea. It was a story that José Ferrer had asked Viertel to tell

---

[*] Lourié makes no mention of this project in his memoirs.

him about. Ferrer had said he was interested, but the only role possible for him was minuscule, and Renoir had little interest in profoundly changing a narrative constructed around a female character, which he was thinking of asking Danièle Delorme to play.* Delorme had apparently agreed in principle, as had Robert Ryan, who had accepted being paid partly in francs.[140] Renoir was planning to entrust Dudley Nichols with the job. All of it was still very fuzzy. Within it can be glimpsed the beginnings of what would become *Orvet,* his first play. The abandoning of that film project seems to coincide with confirmation that *The Golden Coach* had flopped.

News of Chaplin's departure from America, and the fact that he had put his Beverly Hills house up for sale, contributed to a high degree in darkening the vision Renoir had at the time of the world in general and film in particular. He spoke of this departure as a "symbol" and was upset that "not one of the great bosses of the film industry will take it into his head to send him a telegram begging him to come back to our city."[141]

Actually, what seemed the most clearly defined project in that spring of 1953 was by nature theatrical; it was directing a Pirandello play in New York, *Six Characters in Search of an Author,* an undertaking that could be followed by a film.[142] The offer had come from Gabriel Pascal, an English producer[†] and direc- tor[‡] who had been born in Transylvania. Sometime after that, he gave Renoir the choice between Pirandello on stage in New York and a film to direct in Rome and in the Italian Alps that was an adaptation of a long story by Mildred Cram[§] called *The Promise,* which Pascal would produce with Bill Schiffrin.[143] Schiffrin had informed Pascal that Renoir loved the story. Had he really? A week later, there was a new message sent from Rome by Pascal. He was going to try to postpone the staging in New York, thought that they should make *The Promise* together, and was asking whether Claude Renoir would be free for the shoot, estimated to begin in October.[144] Renoir's answer: he wanted to make the film, "not so much because of the story but because of you and also of the financial advantage this job can bring me."[145] It was, he went on, "a very good story, but, as you know, not at all *my* type of story." However, it would still be "a first step

---

* The French press had reported that *Les Braconniers* would be shot in June 1953.

† *Pygmalion,* directed by Anthony Asquith, starring Leslie Howard, 1938.

‡ *Caesar and Cleopatra,* with Vivien Leigh and Claude Rains, 1945.

§ Mildred Cram was one of the screenwriters of the Leo McCarey film *Love Affair* (1939; remade by McCarey as *An Affair to Remember* in 1957). In 1947, Forrest Judd had suggested to Renoir to consider another novel by Mildred Cram, *Forever:* "Story of a great love that begins in the hereafter. Our two lovers are reborn, find each other again in life and will die on the same day to find each other again in the hereafter and be happy 'forever.'" (Notes dictated to Dido, Jean Renoir Papers, Production Files, Box 51, Folder 8.)

in a more important future collaboration" and, most importantly, the money he would earn would allow him to write the book on his father and the two plays about which he was thinking.[146]

Pirandello or Mildred Cram, theater or film, New York or Rome, the two projects seemed so opportune that Renoir gave up the idea of staying in Paris for the summer. Informing Louis Guillaume about his decision, he asked him to have the luggage and packages left at Claude's delivered to the Berkeley and to inquire whether Monsieur de Waelw—who had sold him his Jaguar that had not yet been broken in—would agree to take it back in exchange for money that he would keep as a down payment on another Jaguar, to be delivered in 1954.[147] But alas, Gabriel Pascal's proposals suddenly came to an end.

Summer and fall 1953 were essentially occupied by two projects. It was to them that Renoir alluded when, invited to go to Japan for the project *Madame Chrysanthème*, about which the producer Charles Smadja seemed interested,[148] he responded that although "the idea is very attractive," he could not commit to it for the moment.[149] The first of the projects had come to him from Dowling Productions, a tiny, fledgling Hollywood company and destined to remain so.* It was a suggestion that he bring to the screen the Henrik Ibsen play *The Lady from the Sea*. The film would be directed in Norway and "there would be certain shots of herds of reindeer that could only be captured in September."[150] It would be in English and in Eastmancolor. A few days later, there was talk of preparing for it in February and filming in the studio at the end of March and in April, with exteriors shot at the end of May and in June. Renoir asked his nephew whether he'd be free during that period, all the while adding that nothing was yet signed.[151] But a few days after he had received some photographs of Norway from Dowling Productions,[152] he wrote to Alain, "I have no news from all these fine people and am beginning to think that *The Lady from the Sea* is busy taking a nosedive and disappearing into its natural element."[153]

Confirmation of this came two weeks later in a new letter to Lionello Santi.† "I'm not sure I'm making *The Lady from the Sea* in Norway. I'm afraid that the actress they're suggesting is too unlike the role. I've asked to do some tests with her and think that will be in eight days."[154] The actress's identity remains unknown to this day, and there's a possibility that the truth was that the project didn't progress to the point of establishing a cast, as Renoir was telling Lionello Santi about the offers that other producers were making and telling those other producers about the films that he was planning to make for Lionello Santi. It's

* The only production attributed to Dowling Productions is the Felix Feist film *Donovan's Brain*, based on the novel by Curt Siodmak and released in September 1953.

† Lionello Santi would produce, among other films, *Hands Over the City* (Francesco Rosi, 1963).

natural that he would try to make himself appear very busy and in demand, because he wasn't.

Because he had no prospects, he could consider going to France again, and he asked his agent to introduce him to producers, explaining, "In any case, I'd really like to try to make something in France and in French."[155] Three days later, however, he was writing, "The idea occurred to me of doing something on the life of Van Gogh. I would like to make this film in France and shoot it in the same places where Van Gogh lived and painted. I already have an agreement with the actor Van Heflin, who looks a lot like Van Gogh. I'd like to do the film with a very small budget, but without any concessions you'd call commercial."[156] Although he wanted to direct the film in France, it was still a turnaround on his part, something he explained in a postscript. "Perhaps you'll be struck by the contradiction between my last letter and this one concerning the 'English versions.' I'm very in favor of an English version of *Van Gogh* because it's a film of a special nature with rather strong subject matter that would allow me to dispense with any concessions to the distributor."[157] In Los Angeles, and then in New York, where he went to promote *The Golden Coach,* and then finally in Paris, the project would continue to occupy his mind until the end of February 1954. The day after he returned to France, the papers announced the upcoming filming of *Van Gogh* starring Van Heflin, a film for which Renoir was planning to go next to the Netherlands.[158]

An undated presentation sent to an unknown party, accompanying a fifty-page treatment,[159] reveals a little of what he was planning. "This is the story of Vincent Van Gogh. Today the world considers him to be one of the greatest painters who ever lived. The people of his time, except for a few wonderful exceptions, considered him a failure, a nut. Finding the truth and testifying to it requires an attitude about life that the masses poorly understand. And yet, what is an artist, if not a witness to the truth, and, as the philosopher Kierkegaard has said, 'A witness to truth is a martyr.' Vincent Van Gogh is a martyr."[160] The problem for Renoir—who also touched upon "a documentary method with commentary that turns into acted sequences as it progresses from place to place"[161]—was that he wasn't the only one thinking of Van Gogh.

As early as 1945, in fact, Warner had been interested in the Irving Stone book, *Lust for Life,* a romanticized biography of the artist that had appeared in 1934. They had gone from envisioning Paul Muni to John Garfield for the role, before the producer Arthur Freed got hold of the idea and commissioned a first screenplay from Irving Stone, written in 1947, for a film that was to be directed by Richard Brooks. In 1951, Freed had abandoned the project, which was then taken up again by John Houseman. In France, as well, Van Gogh's fate was inspiring imaginations. Paul Graetz, the producer of Claude Autant-Lara's *Devil in the Flesh,* among other films, had announced a few months before Renoir's idea that he was preparing a *Van Gogh.* He had offered the starring role to Pierre Fresnay, who had refused it.

Renoir's agent informed the director of this fact and told him about an offer from another French producer to direct a film about Eva Peron, in Argentina and according to an agreement with President Peron.[162] "Graetz does not have exclusive rights, nor does anyone,"[163] Renoir answered about the Van Gogh subject. Renoir himself was meeting the following Tuesday, on October 6, with Joseph Schenk and Dore Schary, who, according to him, "aren't planning to make the film," in the hopes of coming to an understanding. He was also seeing the producer Willis Goldbeck, on Van Heflin's suggestion that Renoir plan "to take him on as a partner in this venture."[164]

These different meetings did not fulfill Renoir's expectations, and he informed his agent of that fact from New York. He had "not come to an understanding with Metro for *Lust for Life*" but presented as "certain" his agreement with United Artists (something never mentioned before) and claimed, "The financing for the film will be easy."[165] The failure of negotiations with Metro concerning Irving Stone's best seller obligated him to "back up the project by possessing the rights to a book on Van Gogh"; and he asked his agent to "take an option on Jean de Beucken's *Van Gogh.*" The necessity to depend upon an already existing biography, which he claimed would provide him "with weapons" in what he described as his "conflict with Metro Goldwyn Mayer,"[166] was due in part to the refusal Renoir had encountered on the part of Van Gogh's nephew. The rejection was expressed in French as follows: "Because I'm of the opinion that a film isn't the appropriate medium for establishing a tendency in audiences that might lead to an appreciation of the arts, I am not offering my cooperation."[167] On Saturday, October 21, Renoir and Dido left New York for Paris aboard the ocean liner *Liberté,* which reached Le Havre the following Tuesday.

Renoir's old friend Albert Lewin, a connoisseur of the Hollywood system, was convinced that the chances of having *Van Gogh* produced in Europe were greater than they were in America.[168] Even so, Renoir received proofs of Van Heflin's continued involvement. Heflin had declared, "I'll shoot it in 16 mm, I'll do it in French (and I speak no French), anything you want. The main thing is, we must do this film."[169] Renoir still thought Heflin could play the part because it didn't entail a great deal of dialogue,[170] but he was definitely being forced to acknowledge that the different producers he was meeting in Paris were expressing little interest.

On December 11, which was about ten days after he had declared in an interview for *Radio-Cinéma-Télévision* that he was "very happy about giving up" because he didn't want his producer to "end up at the release in competition with other producers bringing out other films on the same subject,"[171] he registered a forty-eight-page treatment with the Association des auteurs de films. Less than two months later, he resolved to abandon his *Van Gogh,* a decision that he first announced to Van Heflin[172] and then to David Loew, explaining at the time that he was thinking about "an original story to direct in the summer" and that he didn't want to come back to California before he'd collected the notes and reflections he needed for his book on his father.[173]

As for Van Heflin, he continued to stubbornly believe in their film, or to pretend to, and wrote, "If we retain our enthusiasm, I know that nothing can stop this project."[174] In response, Renoir emphasized that he had just finished writing his play, *Orvet,* but that he wasn't yet satisfied with it.[175] In May, he would insist that the actor accept the *Van Gogh* that René Clément appeared to be preparing on behalf of Italian Film Export,[176] the company that had distributed *The Golden Coach* in the United States, certain as Renoir was that there was "no reasonable hope of filming *Van Gogh* in English."[177]

In that same letter, he mentioned the play *Julius Caesar* that he was preparing for July 10, to be performed in the Roman arena at Arles, and spoke of what would be his next film. "As for the rest, I'm very happy with Dido in Paris. Our stay in this old quarter has inspired me with a story, and I'm probably going to make a film about it."[178] He was, and even if *French Cancan* hadn't been "inspired" by his stay in Montmartre, he really was getting ready to make a movie.

* Three years later, Vincente Minnelli would direct *Lust for Life* with Kirk Douglas, a John Houseman production for Metro.

30

Suite Française

French Cancan
Orvet
Elena et les hommes (Elena and Her Men)

André-Paul Antoine was the son of the great figure of Parisian theater André Antoine. He was two years older than Renoir and had been a screenwriter since 1924. He was, in fact, among those authors mentioned when the promoters of *La Marseillaise* were reckoning on assigning its screenplay to an entire gang of writers. Over the course of a career whose regularity, above all, seems remarkable, he had written a few stories that others developed and that resulted in a few successes. He was also responsible for the idea for *Casque d'or,* which Robert Hakim had offered to Renoir in 1947. At the time, Renoir had suggested he give the project to Julien Duvivier, something said to have created a conflict with Jacques Becker when he as well became interested. Intended after that for Yves Allégret, the film finally came back to Becker, who would direct it in September and October 1951.

There's an unproven possibility that the changes imposed by Becker and Jacques Companeez on the treatment by André-Paul Antoine could have led to his recycling certain ideas Becker and Companeez had abandoned for a new screenplay, entitled *French Cancan.* Several situations easily adapted themselves from *Casque d'or*'s Belleville to *French Cancan*'s Montmartre. For example, both films include a scene in which rich gentlemen and beautiful ladies are slumming in a cabaret—called L'Ange Gabriel in *Casque d'or* and La Reine Blanche in *French Cancan.*[*] During the first half of the fifties, French film banked consistently on historical tales, which audiences turned into a trend: *Caroline chérie (Dear Caroline)* was a hit in 1951; *Violettes impériales,* the year following;

---

[*] However, the change from L'Ange Gabriel to La Reine Blanche was Renoir's idea, not André-Paul Antoine's.

La Belle de Cadix* and *Lucrèce Borgia,* in 1953. *Si Versailles m'était conté (Royal Affairs in Versailles)* would be the great success of 1954, and *Nana* one of the events of 1955. Also appearing in 1953 was John Huston's *Moulin Rouge,* with José Ferrer as Toulouse-Lautrec, a film seen by more than four million viewers that struck a "Belle Époque" mother lode, paving the way for films like *La Belle Otero* or *Les Grandes Manoeuvres (The Grand Maneuver). French Cancan* joined this well-fed current.

The screenplay was the property of Franco-London Films, and the film would be produced by Henry Deutschmeister, who had assigned the direction to Yves Allégret. It was the start of 1954, and Deutschmeister was working on *Le Rouge et le Noir (Rouge et Noir [The Red and the Black]),* directed by Claude Autant-Lara, for which shooting was to begin March 24. Deutschmeister had assigned Maurice Aubergé to adapt the screenplay for *French Cancan* by Antoine because he thought it didn't evoke enough "1880s atmosphere" and was in danger of leading to a film that "wasn't sexy," was "without suspense," and wouldn't inspire any empathy on the part of audiences toward any of the characters, whom he considered "too weak."[1]

One of the screenwriters of Jacques Becker's *Falbalas (Paris Frills),* Aubergé worked on the screenplay in the direction indicated by Allégret, who had asked him to adapt the principal role, the creator of the Moulin Rouge—a man named Zidler—to the personality of Charles Boyer,[2] who would play him. However, the producer wasn't won over and went so far as to write, "This work on the film is a lot worse than the first by André-Paul Antoine." Deutschmeister, who had brought Boyer back from Hollywood for Max Ophuls's masterpiece *Madame de . . . (The Earrings of Madame de . . .),* also thought that Zidler was still no more than a "slightly crazy entrepreneur," when the task was to "make him into a more general character, a creator, an artist." Moreover—and this he kept repeating—the film that had been announced was "too long, too expensive." He foresaw "too much scenery,"[3] and he intended to limit the cost to 25 million francs (a little more than $4 million) for that element of the film. In his opinion, the entire budget ought not go beyond 180 million.

It was obvious that the producer was getting impatient. He knew that filming would not be able to begin in May, as had been announced in the press, and he began to think about another option. In the margin of one of the treatments that has been preserved, dated February 1954, is a list of authors the producer was considering contacting.[4] It includes Michel Audiard, Yves Mirande, Francis Carco, and Noël-Noël. But resorting to a new screenwriter—yet another—who,

---

* *Translator's note:* "Cadix" = French spelling of Cádiz, port city in southwestern Spain and capital of the province of the same name.

in addition, would have to get on with Allégret, surely risked delaying even more a project that had been lagging behind for several months. Therefore, the solution was a matter of finding a director who was capable of writing the screenplay himself according to the wishes of the producer, as well as one who could write quickly.

That man existed. For nearly six months he could be found in Paris, waiting for a film to direct. He was one of the most prestigious French directors, and he hadn't worked in France for fifteen years.

On April 18, 1954, the offices of Franco-London Films sent an offer to Jean Renoir's address, following "the verbal conversations"[5] that had occurred between the two parties. The filmmaker was being offered a contract having to do with the direction of *French Cancan*. It stipulated a "work schedule established on the basis of eight weeks of filming, beginning between the first and the thirtieth of September," in exchange for a payment of "7 million francs (500,000 at the end of each week of filming, 1 million at the end of editing, 1 million on the delivery by Technicolor of the first standard copy, and 1 million on the first day of the exclusive release of the film in France). It also guaranteed a 15 percent share of the profits coming from the film." Finally, the agreement specified that "the estimate must not go beyond 180 million francs" and that if it were "impossible to make the film for less than 200 million," the contract would be rescinded.

If hiring Renoir brought nothing but advantages from the producer's point of view, for Renoir Deutschmeister's offer represented a godsend that put him at the head of a project that was already financed, would be written and filmed quickly, and concerned a subject that pleased and suited him. But even though Franco-London Films and Renoir had an understanding, neither Yves Allégret nor, it seems, Charles Boyer had been informed of the fact that the project had changed hands. Proof of this exists in the long letter Allégret sent to the actor on April 24, 1954, which was six days after his contract with the producers had been offered to Renoir instead. In it, he wrote that obviously there wasn't "really anything that could be used to create drama in the story of a gentleman who had 'invented' the Moulin Rouge, meaning, a way to make it entertaining." He thought it appropriate that Zidler be "a lot more colorful, as well as more complex." He thought that the new perspective of the adaptation now depicted him as "a quick-tempered charmer, a stubborn bon vivant, whose way of moving is illustrated mainly by walking." In short, he thought that the project had gained "a liveliness and gaiety that corresponds to what you can rightfully expect trumpeted about a subject whose title is *French Cancan*."[6] At the beginning of May, which was one week after that letter had been written, the set designers working under Max Douy began their task.[7]

While Allégret turned toward other horizons and Renoir attempted to rewrite the screenplay, Charles Boyer disappeared from the project. Perhaps the actor refused the role because firing the director they'd planned to use had displeased him, or perhaps it was because the screenplay and the role had ceased to suit him. Nothing indicates that Renoir had preferred another actor to him. The hypothesis that he did want someone else is, moreover, rather unlikely in the context of Renoir's usual way of operating. He had always accommodated unforeseen complications, whatever they were. Charles Boyer may have grown tired of a project that was continually delayed, and he may also have preferred Christian-Jaque and Martine Carol's *Nana,* in which he was cast as Count Muffat and which began shooting on September 3, a month before Renoir's film started. One fact remains true: at the beginning of summer, news appeared that Jean Gabin would make *French Cancan* in the fall, under the direction of Jean Renoir. However, the circumstances under which Gabin replaced Boyer do become clearer in the context of an event that had left its mark on French cinema shortly before.

On March 17, 1954, *Touchez pas au grisbi,**† directed by Becker and edited by Marguerite Renoir, was released and won over audiences. It was the first success for Jean Gabin since 1939 and *Le Jour se lève.* Max, the gangster in *Grisbi,* has succeeded at what he thinks will be his last "hit," the one that will allow him to retire. That won't be the case, and Max's story takes a tragic turn; but for the first time since the war, the actor was playing a character that was his age. He would be fifty on May 17. For French audiences, it was said, Gabin was back. And yet, Becker hadn't been thinking of him at first. He had wanted Daniel Gélin, who turned down the role, and then François Périer, whom the director was forced to reject in favor of Gabin owing to the necessity of his producing a success commercially after the mediocre results of *Casque d'or* and the failure of *Rue de l'Estrapade* (*Françoise Steps Out*).

Gabin next reunited with one of his prewar directors, Marcel Carné. But the making of their film, *L'Air de Paris* (*Air of Paris*), with Arletty, hadn't gone well, primarily because Carné intended his protégé, Roland Lesaffre, to occupy the foreground of the screen, and that was to Gabin's detriment. Soon Gabin played Marshal Lannes in Sacha Guitry's *Napoléon,* before filming *Le Port du désir* (*House on the Waterfront*) for Edmond T. Gréville, but his schedule was still open for the next few weeks, and the recent success of *Grisbi* had not yet set off an influx of new offers or produced any noticeable effect on the amount

* *Translator's note:* Literally, "Don't Touch the Loot."

† *Touchez pas au grisbi* would eventually sell 4,170,496 tickets in France.

of his fees. Deutschmeister was the first to dive into the gap and make good business of it. At the time, Gabin was less highly rated, and thus less highly paid, than Charles Boyer, who would go on to put the emphasis on his Hollywood career. As a result, the producer succeeded in pulling off an excellent coup, both financially and publicity wise. Jean Gabin, once more one of France's favorite actors, directed by Jean Renoir, auteur of *The Lower Depths, Grand Illusion,* and *La Bête humaine*—now that was quite a nifty idea for a producer.

Although Gabin was aware that the role had originally been offered to Charles Boyer—someone he had never appreciated—he allowed himself to be convinced. And, naturally, Renoir thought all of these arrangements were absolutely super. He had only good reasons for thinking so.

Nevertheless, Renoir still had to interrupt the preparation of this film to respond to the offer that he'd accepted to direct *Julius Caesar*—which in 1941 he'd named as his favorite play.[8] The plan was to stage it in the arena in Arles to mark the celebration of the two thousandth anniversary of the creation of the city by the Roman consul. For this event, he would receive a fee of 500,000 francs, in addition to a per diem of 60,000 francs.[9] The contract had been negotiated by his new agent, the former actress Blanche Montel,* who had become an impresario in 1943 under the aegis of her own company, Cimura.† The only performance would be on July 10, and rehearsals would take place in Paris on the stage of the Théâtre de Paris, which was a "minuscule matchbox in comparison to the arenas."[10] The actors wouldn't catch a glimpse of their costumes until the day of the show. All of them were film actors: Paul Meurisse‡ playing Brutus; Jean-Pierre Aumont, Antony. Henri Vidal was Caesar, and Yves Robert, Cassius. Loleh Bellon would play Portia; Françoise Christophe, Calpurnia. In general, theater people were hardly enthusiastic about seeing "filmmakers" interloping in their territory,§ but even though the show was "expected to trip up," as Paul Meurisse would claim, they didn't take the thing very seriously, convinced as they were that, as was often the case during festive celebrations, the atmosphere would resemble a bullfight. And it actually would be like that, at least as far as the audience was concerned.

As was his habit, Renoir played it blasé. When Jean-Pierre Aumont asked

---

* Wife of Henri Decoin, then Jean-Pierre Aumont, whom she divorced in 1940.

† Cimura would be taken over by Gérard Lebovici in 1965, and five years later he would create Artmédia.

‡ Paul Meurisse became a member of the Comédie-Française after *Julius Caesar*.

§ Two years before, Joseph L. Mankiewicz's choice of Marlon Brando to play Marc Antony in his adaptation of *Julius Caesar* had given rise to protests.

him who had translated and adapted the play for the performance, he answered, "while nodding his head up and down," that it was "this little couple whose name I forgot," who were "really nice" and "seemed like they understood English."[11] And, as always, "abounding in contradictions,"[12] Renoir worked like a beaver in Paris with the actors, where a reading intended for the press was organized, and then in Arles for a few days. Less than a month before the performance, he was worried because "the actors don't know a word of their text."[13] He had a top-quality assistant, Jean Serge,† who, apparently, was the one who had thought of contacting Renoir.[14] He would remain one of Renoir's preferred partners in the years to come. In his memoirs, Jean Serge recalled the reigning atmosphere in Arles in July 1954: "We didn't sleep the last week, replacing it with a bath at dawn. All day, they fueled up with pastis, and me, with white wine."[15] By "they," he mostly meant Henri Vidal and the director.

Renoir has given a vivid account of that performance of *Julius Caesar*, recalling the panic that ripped through a troupe deprived at the last moment of a dress rehearsal, confronted with a breakdown in the sound system. He had spoken to them, it seems, about Brahma, Shiva, Kali, and Krishna to calm their nerves. He also appears to have asked Jean Parédès, who was playing Casca and complaining about his toga being too long, to walk on it and to pretend to stumble as he entered the scene, thereby inciting hilarity in the audience. Five years later, Renoir wrote to his son about what he categorized as a "flash of improvisation": "I took advantage of the assistance of the people who lived there, who furnished me with a Roman crowd '*avé l'assent*,'‡ made up of the *Gardians* of Camargue,§ who were thrilled to be disguised as Roman horsemen and inside an amphitheater that is two thousand years old."[16]

"Renoir handled the situation like a general leads a battle,"[17] remembered Paul Meurisse, who would also write, "If there exists any day in the life of an actor that's more beautiful than the others, that day was it."[18] That evening,

---

* Grisha and Mitsou Dabat were this "little couple" of translators. Grisha Dabat was the screenwriter for Max Pécas's *De quoi tu te mêles Daniela* (*Daniella by Night*, 1961) and for José Bénazéraf's *L'Éternité pour nous* (American titles: *Exercise on the Beach, Romance on the Beach, Sin on the Beach, Sun on the Beach*; 1963). He directed *Et Satan conduit le bal* (*And Satan Calls the Turns*, 1962), written and produced by Roger Vadim.

† Serge Messberg, born in 1916 to Ukrainian immigrants. He adopted the name "Jean Serge" in reference to Victor Serge. He died in 1998.

‡ *Translator's note:* "*avé l'assent*" = Renoir is referring to an accent in the South of France and imitating that accent at the same time, showing how such speakers pronounce "*avec l'accent*" (which means "with the accent").

§ *Translator's note:* "*Gardians* of Camargue" = Camargue (in the vicinity of Arles, where Renoir was at the time) is western Europe's largest river delta, where the *Gardians*, genuine European cowboys, ride horses and raise black bulls for the ring.

finally, Renoir experienced the giddiness caused by applause and ovations, a new sensation for him, something that Octave in *The Rules of the Game* laments never having experienced.

André Bazin produced two ecstatic reports about the show, emphasizing his admiration for "the improvisational genius, the human presence of Jean Renoir."[19] This was because Bazin had, of course, made the trip, had seen the last rehearsals, and had witnessed that the organization of a rosette race in the arena really had prevented holding a dress rehearsal. As a result, none of the lighting effects and details of the staging could be sorted out. He had brought François Truffaut with him.

Truffaut was twenty-two and was writing for *Cahiers du cinéma*. When his article, "Une certain tendance du cinéma français," in which he came down on everything he didn't like with violence and arrogance, appeared in the January issue, it attracted attention; and in the spring he became the film critic for the weekly *Arts*, which was under the direction of Jacques Laurent and brought together some of the most brilliant writers of the French intellectual Right. During the same period, he had written to several directors to inform them of his desire to meet them and to devote articles to them. Renoir was one of these, as was Buñuel, Preston Sturges, Abel Gance, Max Ophuls, Rossellini, Fritz Lang, and Nicholas Ray. Truffaut certainly couldn't miss the chance to approach one of his idols by not being in Arles during this month of July.

A group of other young people felt the same way, and they had driven down from Paris. The group included Alain Cavalier and his wife, the editor Denise de Casabianca; the future director Charles Bitsch; the director of photography Pierre Lhomme; and Jean-Claude Brialy, who would provide a very pleasant account of the jaunt in his memoirs.[20] Their infatuation showed the extent of their admiration for the director and for the man, whose legend had begun to be written.

In April and May 1954, a long, two-issue interview with Renoir by Truffaut and Rivette did indeed appear in *Cahiers*. Never before in France—probably even in the world—had a film director been able to express himself to such an extent regarding his career and his cinema.* As a follow-up, on June 30, *Arts* reproduced long excerpts from the conference Renoir gave at the Institut des hautes écoles cinématographiques (IDHEC), which had been intended particularly for former students. The "official statue" to Renoir was erected in three months and in three publications, its pedestal constructed of what would eventually be called

---

* However, the first long interview in *Cahiers* was devoted to Jacques Becker, in February 1954. But it did not run the length of two issues, as did Renoir's.

"the Renoir method." That method depended on one of the cardinal principles of Truffaut's article, "Une certaine tendance du cinéma français": the refusal of film considered to have been "scripted," which led to the rejection of directors like Clouzot, René Clément, and Autant-Lara, among others. The method was unveiled in the course of the interview in *Cahiers,* and Renoir outlined it as he answered questions, claiming in particular that he had often had recourse to what he called improvisation. However, Truffaut and Rivette took responsibility for defining the method in the form of an assertion: "All in all, you prepare your work with the idea of abandoning all of it on the set," they suggested. "Absolutely," answered Renoir.

That notion of improvisation was essential. Renoir came back to it during his conference at the IDHEC, and his remarks at that time demonstrated remarkable clarity: "I don't think that it's improvisation, exactly. Rather, I think it's adaptation." And later on: "You have to have the line of the film established very firmly in your head, know what each assertion means, each curve, each change that seems to deviate. You have to know how to draw it back to a line that, in the end, will be the main thread of the story and that will allow the telling of a very definite story. And that story must not change." This is not really the same thing, not a question anymore of "abandoning all of it" on the set. Yet, these two sentences excerpted from his conference aren't included in the text by Truffaut published in *Arts.*

The fantasy of the "Renoir method" was actually born in spring 1954 from the encounter between a wish and a will:* Renoir wished to attribute his American failure exclusively to his way of making films, which called for "discovering the content of a film as you go through the process of shooting it," something that was true in part—but only in part—and that especially had no value as a generality. Renoir's wish was bolstered by Truffaut and Rivette's will (especially Truffaut's will) to establish a system for the principles upon which they depended, to be heard and noticed, or to justify the certainty they had acquired that there is only one way to make films: the one that they were planning to put into practice themselves and that they claimed was inspired by their chosen masters. It's not insignificant that the part of Renoir's conference in which he states, "Naturally, you've got to have a very good knowledge of technique," was not given any presence in *Arts.* "Knowledge of technique" means possessing the necessary experience in the practice of filmmaking if you want to attempt making a film. Because Truffaut was at war with the French tradition that preferred beginners be trained for the profession, most usually by serving as an assistant,

* The passages having to do with "the Renoir method" owe a great deal to the work accomplished by Olivier Curchod.

relaying such an idea that contradicted the personal ambitions and the theories he was trying to set up was simply unthinkable. By affirming several times, both during his interview with *Cahiers* and in his conference, the collective nature of cinematic creation, Renoir was actually opening the door through which Truffaut was going to bolt. He was able to insist that nothing that precedes shooting—all of which essentially has to do with the screenplay—is of any importance, because everything happens on the set . . .

When Truffaut himself became a director, he would continually prove by his own experiences how risky such a principle was the moment it was put into practice. However, what was at that time only his truth of the moment, dictated by circumstances and his personal situation, from then on became set in stone. Similarly, indicting certain habits of French production led quite naturally to the principle of prohibiting the very idea of shooting in a studio. As a result, Truffaut was led to insist that the directors he elected only worked in this way when they were forced to.

Thus, Renoir would find himself placed in the driver's seat as the supposedly inflexible defender of directing in natural scenery, despite the fact that only two of his sound films had been directed entirely in exteriors, *Toni* and *A Day in the Country.* This was the same director who, when given the choice—especially when it came to certain scenes in *The Diary of a Chambermaid* and *The River*—had preferred the studio to natural scenery. As a matter of fact, the only known expression of his wish to shoot in exteriors had to do with the direction of *Swamp Water;* and in that case, the producer had been opposed to it. On the pretext that Zanuck had authorized him to go on location to record a few shots, Renoir would claim that he had won a great victory, using it to suggest that the spirit of decisiveness and conviction of which he had given proof had allowed him to overcome the habits and reluctances of a big Hollywood studio. Creating this impression was truly his intention, and in his eyes it had nothing to do with any general truth concerning the superiority of shooting in exteriors.

When he recalled the filming of *Swamp Water* for René Gilson, he remembered having chatted with the owner of an old wooden farm whose dog, although he was called Jerry and not Castillot, Médor, or Tambo, was like those he'd known in Burgundy; and in the process of telling this story, he insisted he'd "managed to shoot this film in Georgia," thereby flouting "all the rules in Hollywood." It didn't require more for some to claim that the splendor of the film came from the fact that it was shot in exteriors, whereas we know today that Renoir never filmed for more than five days in the swamps of Georgia, and only with a single actor. Thus, Jean-Luc Godard would write, "*Swamp Water* can

* This film only because it had remained unfinished.

also pride itself on having, over the long term, revolutionized Hollywood. For the first time, a big studio accepted the idea—quite reasonable, after all—of not shooting exteriors in interiors. *Swamp Water* is in principle *Toni*, with twenty years of experience behind it. Gone is the taste for risk, and present is the certainty of daring."[21] It's a lovely assertion; but the data that have inspired such an analysis are false.

Although the answer seems self-evident, the question must, however, be asked: Why did Truffaut, and after him the future directors of the Nouvelle Vague, make Jean Renoir "the Boss" a half century after the painters had chosen and nominated Auguste Renoir for the same position? The primary reason has the value of being obvious, in fact. They deeply loved his films and sincerely admired the man. But as overwhelming as that reason may seem, it was not the only one.

Because Renoir had become an American director, he wasn't a rival in the eyes of aspiring French directors. Much as they wished to sweep clean the French film landscape, they could still save him without their suffering from it. Renoir wasn't very well liked in the profession, following the Italian episode in his career, his departure in 1940, and the lack of enthusiasm he had exhibited at the idea of returning to work in France. These factors had banished him to the margins of a system he had ruled over during the second half of the thirties, during which time he had aroused jealousies whose effects the passage of time had not dissipated.

But Truffaut and the others were calling for the disappearance of this same system. Because some of his films had been poorly viewed in their time, including *The Rules of the Game* and his American productions, the young critics felt there were injustices to correct and, when necessary, they exaggerated the importance of his rejections, creating subjects for scandal out of works (*La Chienne, Boudu Saved from Drowning*) that had merely been misunderstood. They turned what were little more than ordinary failures, or even modest successes, into commercial disasters. Following such logic, it was also suitable to temper the enthusiasm inspired by certain films (*Grand Illusion, La Bête humaine*) so that they could sing more stridently and more passionately the praises of those films that had disappointed. As a result, the American period was to be proclaimed fruitful, brilliant, dazzling. About it, Jacques Rivette would write in fall 1953 that, along with Hitchcock's films, Howard Hawks's comedies, and the work of Rossellini, it made up "that modern form of cinema that only directors will be able to understand."[22]

And what about audiences? Rivette doesn't say so, but it should be kept in mind that the characteristic of Renoir's films made before 1940 and praised the most unanimously was described in the following terms by Normal Lloyd: "Life flows in them without your ever becoming aware that it's film."[23] Now it was a case of the opposite. The films of the fifties and sixties were brilliant because, rather than showing life, they showed film at work. It is also, however, more than true that the most convenient way for a commentator to become noticed consists in rejecting what others have loved and celebrating what is commonly held to be negligible.

That was the way that Renoir became the high priest of improvisation and the mortal enemy of the screenplay; the most resolute opponent of filming in a studio; the victim throughout his entire career of the stupidity and dishonesty of producers, in particular, and of the profession as a whole; a director to whom Hollywood had offered the chance to blossom by giving him permission to get round the rules that were in force. Seeing himself portrayed in that way as a rebel certainly must have amused him, he who would include a passage in his memoirs (eliminated from the definitive edition) that confessed that his first impulse had always been to give in, just as much when it came to actors as to backers, crew, or audiences.[24] In addition—and perhaps, in particular—Renoir's very personality lent itself better than any other to the designs of budding directors. The French directors most well known in the mid-fifties were Julien Duvivier, René Clément, Henri-Georges Clouzot, and Claude Autant-Lara.* In Truffaut's opinion, all of them placed too much importance on their screenplays. In addition, they shared personality characteristics that were, to say the least, "difficult"—making it likely that any rash and reckless person who came knocking would be in for a stern rebuff. It was the opposite in Renoir's case. His nature tended toward sharing and the desire to charm, the wish to please. That desire and that wish were translated in him into a fanatical need to find grounds for understanding and reasons to be in league with those with whom he talked, regardless of their ideas or their identities.

Leslie Caron, who nevertheless venerated him, would recount in her memoirs how she had often heard him in conversation adopt the opposite opinion of the one with which he had started, merely to win the approval of the person with whom he was speaking. This overwhelming need very naturally led Renoir to declare himself in agreement, whatever the opinion being proposed or even attributed to him. In addition, genuine affection, sincere admiration, and profound respect were now being expressed toward him, whereas in Hollywood no one wanted his ideas, and in most of France, he had already begun to be somewhat forgotten. These compliments aroused a response in him, which it was certainly not in his nature to neglect or even consider with distance. These young

---

* At that time, André Bazin defended Autant-Lara's films (*Le Blé en herbe* [*The Game of Love*], *Rouge et Noir*) against the opinion of Truffaut.

people knew his cinema better than anyone. They loved his films unreservedly. They granted him a place in their publications that would seem enviable in the eyes of any director at all. Why would he oppose their suggestions? Why would he refuse to admit that to him screenplays had always seemed a rather unimportant stage in the process? Or that filming in the studio was unbearable? Or that the boldness of his films and their wish to rise up against ordinary mentality had caused considerable scandal? That his career in Hollywood left him feeling completely satisfied? Renoir was much too shrewd for that. Much too intelligent, as well.

Therefore, during an interview with André S. Labarthe, who would "suppose" that he had "no shooting script on paper," Renoir began by seeming to disagree with him, in order to immediately allow him, and the reader at the same time, to choose the side that they'd decide to take: "I had a shooting script on paper," he answered, "but naturally and, as usual, I couldn't follow it."[25] In the face of such intelligence, such guilefulness, and such an understanding of the gears of the human mind, the man who was surest of himself and of his own theories would seem like a child.

The shooting script was the issue that made it possible for Renoir's personal interests to fall into synch with those with whom he was speaking. By asserting the nearly subsidiary nature of the screenplay, Renoir found a way to renew and pursue his mission of minimizing the contributions of the authors with whom he had collaborated. He had suffered too long from not being recognized not to want to appear alone on the playbill. The importance that had been awarded screenwriters in French film during the thirties was excessive, and the discredit heaped on them became just as exaggerated; but it would have cast no aspersion on the merits of an auteur like Renoir to recognize the part played by Prévert in *The Crime of Monsieur Lange* as well as that played by Charles Spaak in *Grand Illusion*.

Nearly twenty years after their first encounters, when Truffaut had become a celebrated director, he visited Renoir in Beverly Hills as often as he could, and there were bonds of friendship, absolute trust, and genuine profound affection between them. But in 1954, the young Truffaut seemed like one admirer among many to Renoir, even if he was the most eager and most prolific of them all. Truffaut would remember that on the set of *French Cancan* Dido couldn't tell him apart from Rivette, even though the latter was a full-time intern and Truffaut only showed up from time to time. Thus, Dido scared Truffaut a bit, he would confess in a letter to Renoir,[26] including in that letter the old joke about the inseparable duo that went back to the fifties, referring to them as "Truffette and Rivault."

Faced with them and with the journalists who had been invited by the production, as well as with the actors, most of whom knew him only by reputation, Renoir became the actor he had always dreamed of being, playing the role that he knew best—himself. He turned the set of *French Cancan* into his own little theater.

When Renoir got back to Paris the day after his time in Arles, he launched into the preparation of the film, for which he had finished the first draft of a treatment before his departure.[27] As a start, he had to give up the idea of casting Leslie Caron in the role of Nini. Ever since he'd noticed the young dancer and actress on a platform at Victoria Station, during one of his stays in London when he was preparing *The River*, he seems to have placed her at the center of his thoughts, without yet having ever spoken a word to her. Gene Kelly had chosen her to be his partner in *An American in Paris*, and she now lived the most often in the United States. In New York, at the home of the painter Pierre Sicard, Renoir spoke to her for the first time, and they exchanged addresses so that they could see each other again soon in Los Angeles.

Back in Hollywood, she received the following letter from Renoir: "My producer can't wait for you for *French Cancan*. He's suggesting I do another film with you later. I'm going to try to invent a subject suitable to the talent of our dear little Leslie."[28] During fall 1954, Leslie Caron was, in fact, busy filming *Daddy Long Legs* with Fred Astaire, about which she'd informed Renoir in an undated letter in which she said she was certain that *French Cancan* would be "a fascinating film." She was also asking to read "a more advanced script" and was rejoicing at the idea of acting with Gabin. She wondered whether it would be possible to wait for her until November and whether Deutschmeister would be able to "hire [her] out from MGM," although she was fully aware that "in francs, that obviously makes a lot they're asking."[29]

A lot, obviously and absolutely, and too much for Deutschmeister, who, in any case, wanted to assign the female lead in his film to an actress more in fashion than Leslie Caron, with whom few in France were familiar at the time, even if the cover of the *Paris-Match* issue of May 31, 1952, presented Brigitte Bardot as "the new Leslie Caron."[30] Renoir clarified the issue in his letter of July 19. "Françoise Arnoul is the one who'll play the role that I had written entirely for you." And he added, "I'm lucky. She isn't Leslie Caron, but she's an actress of incredible dexterity."

Was the role of Nini "written entirely" for Leslie Caron by Renoir? No, given that the screenplays that had existed before Renoir came onto the project had already begun to give shape to that character. And no, again, because Renoir had first thought of Danièle Delorme, something that Jean Serge specifically confirms in his memoirs.[31] None of these details challenges the fact that the young actress fascinated the director. From their first meetings he had wanted to cast her in every film he thought of. Today, Leslie Caron thinks that Renoir distinguished certain qualities in her that he possessed himself. "To a small extent I was the girl's version of what he'd been as a young man. There was a certain kinship of character. He saw me as intractable and untamable, and particularly liked the fact that I stood up to the studios. Underneath his paternal exterior, he himself was extremely wild, and no one had ever been able to tame him."[32] The young Jean Renoir had indeed been intractable, and with age he had learned how to disguise this trait of character, just as he'd been able to preserve his freedom by giving in to constraints and fleeing conflict. In a letter to her written two years later, in which he turned down her proposition to direct the Giraudoux play *Intermezzo* in London, because he didn't "believe that audiences in 1958 would be inclined to let themselves be deluded by fairy tales, no matter how beautiful," he added, "I also admit that I haven't given up my dream of presenting you as a kind of female Chaplin."[33]

Leslie Caron turned twenty-three on July 1, 1954, and Françoise Arnoul had become the same age on June 3 of that year. On the day on which Renoir had described Arnoul as "an actress of incredible dexterity," he hadn't worked with her yet. He had only met her at his home on avenue Frochot. That day, as she would recount, he had spoken of everything and nothing, as was his habit; and she hadn't said very much, overawed, intimidated, and captivated as she was. The conversation had ended with the following compliment and promise: "You know how to listen, so you can act. You'll be my Nini!"[34]

She certainly would be his Nini, because he hadn't been given a choice. Since her film debut, Françoise Arnoul had already made twenty pictures. In barely five years, this daughter of a general and an actress had established herself as the "sex-kitten" star of French film with her sulky pout, catlike manner, slender legs, and generous décolletage. Her impeccable figure, which she'd exposed in *L'Épave* (*Sin and Desire*, Willy Rozier, 1949), her first film, and the breast she had uncovered opposite Fernandel in *Le Fruit défendu* (*Forbidden Fruit*, Henri Verneuil, 1952) had created a great deal of notoriety that the producer of *French Cancan* hadn't been able to resist. In the history of French film, Françoise Arnoul became the hyphen between "the" French star of the fifties, Martine Carol, and Brigitte Bardot.

Renoir seems to have wanted Arletty to play Lola de Castro de la Fuente de Espramadura, the great coquette who was better known under the name "la Belle Abbesse." She is Nini's love rival and mistress of the principal sponsor of Zidler (Jean Gabin). However, it seems that the meeting between the son of

Auguste Renoir and Léonie de Courbevoie* was never to take place. Arletty's career had hit rock bottom, and Deutschmeister preferred hiring Maria Félix, who at the time (late June 1954) had just started filming *La Belle Otero* at the Joinville studios. That film was being directed by Richard Pottier, and the lighting was by Michel Kelber, who would become the head cameraman for *French Cancan*. The forty-year-old Mexican star would—already—play a tart for her French debut after a time in Spain where there had been a mad run on her records. She'd won her notoriety less by the quality of her films than by her escapades—her unbridled storms of passion for the great toreadors; and Luis Miguel Dominiguín had been at the top of that list. More than an actress, this was a media personality who'd been hired by Deutschmeister to be directed by Renoir in his first production since *The Rules of the Game* that wasn't geared primarily to American audiences.

The director began calling up his actors from the past: Valentine Tessier, who had been his Bovary, would play Nini's mother. Gaston Modot, the gamekeeper in *The Rules of the Game,* would appear as the valet. Max Dalban, the foreman in *Toni,* would be the manager of La Reine Blanche. As a result, the link between yesterday's Renoir and today's was assured. He'd been absent from France for too long to know who the French actors were now. He cast Jean-Roger Caussimon, whom he'd wanted to make the viceroy in *The Golden Coach,* in the role of Baron Walter. For the remaining parts, he summoned newcomers—Michel Piccoli, for one, who would become a marvel as a fop in stripes.

When filming began on October 4, 1954, in the studios on rue Francoeur, Renoir hadn't worked in France for fifteen years. He knew the extent of the failure of his American exile better than anyone. He was also aware that his Italian film hadn't been received as he had hoped. His return to Paris was taking off in the best conditions he could have dreamed, after months of trying vainly to get started on several productions. For Jean Renoir, *French Cancan* became his film of happiness regained. His collaborators and actors spoke the same language he did, and some of them were his friends. Day after day, the newspapers reported on his renewal of ties with Paris, with French film, with the Montmartre of his childhood. Each evening, he went back to his apartment on avenue Frochot with Dido at his side. Once again he was at the center of his game, and it was everything he loved. Moreover, with the screenplay that he'd been given, he was creating an ode to showmanship, a hymn to pleasure, which gave him the opportunity to portray an impresario at the mercy of the goodwill of his sponsors and the caprices of women who were fighting for his attention. And

---

* *Translator's note:* "Léonie de Courbevoie" is a reference to the actress Arletty's birth name, Léonie, and her place of birth, Courbevoie.

he had been able to entrust that role to one of his former partners in crime, the person with whom he'd experienced the greatest success.

As for the screenplay, Renoir began by simplifying it and, especially, ridding it of any cumbersome developments. The story as imagined by Antoine and rewritten by Maurice Aubergé, with the possible help of Jean Ferry,* dealt with two couples, one formed by Zidler and his mistress and the other formed by Céline, the "little gal from Belleville," and Paulo. Renoir turned Céline into Nini, the little laundress, and although he did keep the name Paulo, that character would no longer be the anarchist activist that he was, who wanted to take Céline with him to Spain and who finally ended up surrounded and shot down by the police. He would die in the arms of the young woman, killed by a bullet right to the heart, at the same moment that the Moulin Rouge was opening its doors and the cancan triumphing. All of it was high drama, in fact. As Renoir cut, compressed, and concentrated, the story gained in intensity, recentered on the relationship between Zidler and Nini, wanted by three men—Paulo, Zidler, and a prince fallen from the sky who was a character completely invented by the director. One of the forms of Renoir's genius concerned his capacity for absorption, of making some elements his. The moment he touched them, they seemed never to have belonged to anyone else. The result was a construction that was exceedingly dear to him: a quartet of lovers composed of a woman and three men, a device that can be spotted in several of his films in which, as Truffaut would write, "the three male characters represent the three kinds of men that a woman encounters in her life."[35]

Although Renoir the magician may give the impression that he is pulling out of his hat—or, out of nowhere, one might as well say—the thousand and one elements of his art, he is also busy putting into his pocket all those who come near him. Naturally, the actors are the first to declare themselves won over; and it's not at all difficult for him to make them think that never before has he known any happiness comparable to what they are giving him. He places his performers at the center of his world, flattering them and making a fuss over them. If one of them has just flubbed a line, a wink or elbow thrust in the direction of the cameraman lets him know that he has begun moving the camera an instant too soon or a second too late, and finally, that a new take is necessary, through the fault of the technician, not the actor, who for his part was perfect, perfect as always.

Jean Serge's testimony to this effect may be gently exaggerated but nevertheless contains interest because it comes from someone who deeply admired

---

* One of the versions of the screenplay that has survived carries the name of Jean Ferry, without it being possible to determine whether he received it in the process of a consultation or actually worked on it.

Renoir. It's especially valuable because it indicates the tack chosen by the director with his actors: "First day on the set, first scene, Maria Félix. . . . Action! Renoir is glued to the eyepiece of the camera. Cut! He stops everything, walks up to her, takes her hand, looks deeply into her eyes, and says, 'My dear Maria, you're too beautiful. My text isn't worthy of you. Don't say another word. Your image is enough.'"[36] No actress or actor in similar circumstances would ever think that perhaps the line hadn't been said the way the director wanted it to be. Renoir would reveal the secret of his workmanship without seeming to in the book devoted to his father in which he wrote about horses. "He let them do what they wanted. And finally it was they who were doing what he wanted."[37] Nevertheless, there was one person on the set of *French Cancan* who wasn't taken in.

Gabin knew "his" Renoir better than anyone did, and he knew he'd been hired to play a role that had been intended for Charles Boyer. He also hadn't forgiven the director for having acquired an American nationality, for the son of Auguste Renoir having chosen not to be French anymore. He couldn't accept it. Their reunion was cool, with Renoir opening his arms wide as he always did. "My dear Jean. . . ." Gabin extended a hand to shake. "Hello, Monsieur Renoir." For the actor to relax, Renoir had to ask him a crucial question about how to make *lapin à la moutarde*. Did you put the crème fraîche on the animal before roasting it, or as it is almost finished cooking? Their first conversation during the shooting of *French Cancan* had to do with that recipe. All the actors and crew would claim to have heard it and would report it, although their unanimity doesn't guarantee the truth of it. After that, Gabin behaved the same way as he had in the past; he was always on time and knew his lines and was attentive to his fellow actors and the director. Even so, time had passed since *La Bête humaine,* and a breach had widened between the two of them in which war, America, and the wounding of self-esteem occupied too important a place for rabbit in mustard sauce to be able to distract their minds on any long-term basis. Alain Renoir would claim that the failure of Gabin's American career was the cause of the coldness he showed Renoir, but that suggestion seems dictated more by filial love than by an attentive observation of the facts. But if such a train of thought should be followed, it must be admitted as well that the director's luck in Hollywood was hardly more enviable than that of the actor's.

Françoise Arnoul wasn't laboring under such prejudices and was entirely subject to Renoir's charm. Every morning she found on her makeup table a few verses written in lipstick and signed "the old poet in love," to which the director would add, "don't get the wrong idea,"[38] as well as suggestions and indications regarding her acting that he had noted down in the night on little worn-looking pieces of paper that he pulled from one of his pockets. Before each take, Renoir would offer a generous hats-off to his actors, and when he next required another take, he presented his request as if he were greedy; it was the pure pleasure of seeing them perform again he was seeking, and it was as if reluctantly, and in passing, that he suggested they do it differently; oh, it was far from a big deal, just to find out what doing it that way would be like. And often, he'd get out of them what another director wouldn't even dream of asking, because having been persuaded that the idea had come completely from them, they were that much more delighted to do it for him; it had all been decided on their part.

There was no apparent difference in the way the stars and the supporting actors were treated, nor in the way the extras were. For group scenes, he spoke to each of them discreetly, apart from the others, explaining to one that he'd come to La Reine Blanche that evening for the purpose of seeing that pretty girl over there on the other side of the set, or to another that she'd let herself be convinced by a girlfriend to go with her to the Moulin Rouge and that she was enjoying the show, the atmosphere, the colors more than she'd expected.[39] As a result, everyone felt involved, everyone had a role to play, which seemed essential to the film at the moment when Renoir was speaking to him or her, which it actually was in its way, except that it was the assistants who ordinarily took care of the extras. Jacques Becker would write in 1959 that the "only technical truth" that Renoir had taught him all through the years when he worked as his assistant was that "you don't direct actors with vinegar."[40]

Nevertheless, it can happen that pouring syrup still can't manage to mask the sourness motivated by certain rivalries. For example, on the set of *French Cancan,* in the scene in which Nini had to flick off la Belle Abbesse's hat, Françoise Arnoul involuntarily slapped Maria Félix, sending her into a fury. The volcanic performer retaliated by slapping her coactress twice as hard, then withdrawing to her dressing room, surrounded by the entourage of admirers, lovers, and servants who were perpetually in tow; and she refused to go on shooting. It was nothing but a blunder solely on the part of Françoise Arnoul, which goes without saying. But that didn't stop Gabin, who knew actresses better than anyone, from putting himself close to the camera—which was the best place to see the shock he knew was coming—or from whispering into Michel Piccoli's ear, "I'm going to get me a ringside seat."[41] The flowers the young actress soon brought the offended party were instantly thrown back in her face by Maria Félix, and during what remained of the shoot, she stopped speaking to Arnoul. Renoir had to change the places planned for the two actresses in the scene that followed the prince's suicide attempt. Although reports of these incidents, which were as a whole ordinary, hadn't yet gone beyond the walls of the studio—except to offer something to talk about in a profession quite used to this kind of mishap—the newspapers did not lack for choice tidbits. *French*

Cancan was emerging in all respects as a prestige production, moving onward to the rhythm of Renoir's steps dancing the cancan for his actors, in front of the photographers.

This dimension of the film, which placed it high on the scale of the kind of French production smitten with historical portrayals, was also guaranteed by the fact that the most renowned technicians had been drafted for it. The scenery was the work of Max Douy, who'd already served on *The Rules of the Game* and had become Claude Autant-Lara's art director. The images were created by Michel Kelber, who had just shot Maria Félix in *La Belle Otero*. The costumes were by Rosine Delamare, the younger sister of Lise Delamare, who had played Marie-Antoinette in *La Marseillaise*. These people worked on a regular basis with the producer and therefore hadn't been chosen by Renoir, but all of them were considered masters in their field.

Douy, Kelber, and Delamare had come directly from the sound stage of *Rouge et Noir* to *French Cancan*. This wasn't something that was particularly pleasing to Autant-Lara, who was far from delighted about the return of one of his rivals, especially given Autant-Lara's irritable temperament and the grudge he bore Renoir since *Nana,* both of which had led to his taking a dim view of his colleague's behavior. On Sunday, October 2, two days before shooting on *French Cancan* began, he wrote to Deutschmeister to complain that the day before "Renoir—through a third party—had asked to see some reels from *Rouge et Noir,* whose aesthetic solutions interested him," and he regretted that Renoir hadn't called him himself, "which would have been simple courtesy."[42]

Although altogether different from what it would have become if Yves Allégret had directed it, *French Cancan* conforms no less to the template of Franco production, a quality that still did not prevent Renoir from making work that was personal. The appearance in it of several guest stars, especially Édith Piaf, Patachou, and André Claveau, who'd all been invited to belt out a ditty, strengthened that membership, and it wouldn't be unfair to write that *French Cancan* was *also* a producer's film, with some of the faults inherent in that category but also with some of the value. Deutschmeister's initial reason for his great worry during the preparation of the film, before Renoir joined the project, was that the cost of the scenery determined the pace of a shoot already being slowed down by filming in Technicolor, which requires a heavy and cumbersome camera and lighting that takes a long time to set up. As is the rule, set changes were scheduled long in advance, and all the scenery had to be taken down to make room for what came next. For each scene, Renoir had no more time than had been planned. The scene in the cabaret La Reine Blanche would be among those that suffered the most from these contingencies, but Renoir was well aware that he couldn't expect to enjoy the same freedom he had had on

The Rules of the Game. For a long time, he'd been accustomed to submitting to the same requirements as most film directors. And then, despite the completely personal tone he was able to give the film, because of his ability to incorporate and adapt, he wasn't forgetting that he'd been hired for a specific task and that the conditions under which he carried out this work could determine the direction his career would take.

Some of his letters seem to reflect his awareness of that reality. For example, on December 12, 1954, he wrote to Leslie Caron that he had finished "the *real* scenes" of the film; he had "left two or three days of exteriors with a lot of extras, some close-ups of important but secondary characters"; but, he assured her, "the problems are behind me," and he was going "to be able to focus almost entirely on *Orvet.*"* Then: "After the middle of next week, I'll only give my mornings to *French Cancan* and will be spending them in the editing room."[43] Although he'd devoted all the care needed to the film, he was happy it was finished, because he was in a hurry to move on to something else, which happened to be the play he'd written that he intended to put on as soon as possible.

On the other hand, he was writing to the actress he'd let believe might be the star of *French Cancan;* and she was also the one who'd be in *Orvet,* and to whom, quite naturally, it was important for him to say that she and the project they had together were the only things on his mind. In reality, Renoir had put all his energy and all his faith into *French Cancan,* even if the film in his eyes wasn't the entirely personal work that he dreamed of making for his return to France. He'd especially put that energy and faith into the sumptuous and very long last sequences about the opening of the Moulin Rouge, into its explosion of colors, music, and emotions. It was the ultimate testimony of his extraordinary mastery as a director.

Another facet of his talent was revealed through the lyrics of the song he wrote for the film, with music by Georges Van Parys. "La Complainte de la Butte," sung by Cora Vaucaire, was such a success afterward that a lot of people forgot that it was by Jean Renoir,† who'd written it in Paris on October 28 and November 2, 1954,[44] thinking naturally of the style and tone of the songs he had heard during childhood. It is this same childhood in Montmartre to which the film pays tender homage, and it re-creates an area on the edge of the city that resembles much more what Montmartre might have been like a few years before Renoir's birth. Motivated by the desire to create a tribute to Auguste Renoir and to the great Impressionists, sustained by the wish to evoke that

---

* "*Orvet*" means "slow worm," or "blind worm" (*anguis fragilies*), a small legless lizard that gives birth to live young.

† Jean Serge would collaborate on the writing of "La Complainte de la Butte" without being credited, but he received a share of the royalties.

world of spectacle and pleasure, *French Cancan* is also fed by the nostalgia of a man returning to his world after fifteen years of absence, a man who had become sixty years old two weeks before the beginning of filming. The character of Zidler, who became Danglard in the film because of fear of conflict with the descendants of the creator of the Moulin Rouge, finds himself—like Gabin and like Renoir—at a turning point in his life as both a man and an artist. All three can't avoid the fact they've begun their last hurrah. For Renoir, *French Cancan* was something of a swan song.

Even before he started filming, Renoir did not mince words in a letter to David Loew about the new direction he intended to give his career. He was experiencing the same excitement, the same "apprehension and joy," about his theatrical projects that he'd felt when he was getting ready to direct his first film.[45] For several months, especially since the commercial failure of *The Golden Coach* and the realization forced on him about how difficult it was to find funding for films that were completely personal, he had imperceptibly allowed the world of cinema to move away from him. He had grabbed the opportunity represented by *French Cancan,* and its success would fleetingly reactivate his desire for film; but change was under way, motivated by his desire to write books or plays. Among other things, writing meant staying at home in California, right next to Dido and Gabrielle and not far from his son and grandchildren, without having to struggle to keep practicing a profession he had admitted—already more than a year ago—now brought him too little satisfaction.[46]

French Cancan was an indisputable success, but it nevertheless bore the marks of this exhaustion. Although Françoise Arnoul is excellent as Nini, Maria Félix was limited as an actress and put too much stock in her appearance to make la Belle Abbesse more than two-dimensional; Gabin, although very much at ease most of the time, seemed to be "phoning in" his last great rant about life, love, and spectacle, which had essentially come straight down from *The Golden Coach* and thus seemed a bit starchy. As for the actors in the supporting roles, such as Philippe Clay, who were often very good, they still weren't finding themselves in any situation to make audiences forget about the Carettes or the Dalios of the old days. How could they be blamed? Who could keep anyone from sensing the absence of a Carette or Dalio? As a whole, the impression produced by the casting recalled the experience of watching *The Lower Depths,* a film that was the same from the point of view of production; and Renoir's eternal tendency to offer great attention to certain scenes and be done with those that interested him less was harmful to both films.

Finally, one needed an excessive taste for artifice not to think that certain elements of the scenery—the fake exteriors or La Reine Blanche—didn't somewhat diminish the pleasure in spectacle. Although the cobblestones used for the streets of Montmartre were real, and the staircases were genuine structures, the painted skies, puny trees, and meager traces of vegetation ended up feeling stifling, making the claim that they correspond to their intended impression seem heedless. The truth was that Renoir wasn't very interested in the scenery, and his indifference made his relationship with Max Douy touch and go.[47] Yet the whirl of the cancan, the gracefulness of the women, Gabin's authoritativeness, the colorfulness of the imagery, the love for spectacle, and the taste for pleasure all swept away such reserves—although they did not mask a certain darkness.

The rather inane romanticism of the prince hardly complemented the cynicism in Danglard's behavior, especially the way he related to women. It was as if unselfish love had no place in this world. Darkness and cruelty did instead, such as when Danglard and Nini encounter the aged Prunelle,* who used to be queen of Montmartre and who has become a beggar, and Danglard suggests Nini could end up exactly like her. Renoir's take on his characters sometimes seems detached, almost cold. Disillusioned, at any rate, reaching the point at moments of looking almost as if his heart is no longer in it; as if, by dint of wanting to love everyone and by managing to achieve it, or in seeming as if he has—which is nearly the same thing—he no longer loves anyone. Continuing to peel off the veneer in that way can lead, as well, to judging his homage to the Impressionists as too unimaginative, too obvious, and too forced.

On the sidelines of *French Cancan*'s success in theaters when it was released in May 1955 (nearly four million tickets sold[†‡]), a certain uneasiness began to show. Pierre Kast, one of Renoir's assistants on the shoot, would report it. It was caused by the fact that the legend of Renoir in the process of being established was already starting to rock the boat, because the personality of the director had started to obscure the reality of the work, the fullness of the public personality interrupting the beam of the projector and threatening to block the screen. "There is a Jean Renoir legend, or rather, legends," wrote the future director. "In addition to a recent written tradition, there are several older oral traditions, which are also contradictory. Friends, former friends, collaborators, former collaborators were all deeply affected by their encounters with him, close to being enchanted, in the way that the friends of Merlin were said to have been at the

---

* Played by Pâquerette, who had already appeared in *Casque d'or*.

† A remarkable result, actually, but one that also calls for a comparison. *French Cancan* was number ten in the ratings for films of that year, beneath three other French productions or coproductions: *Le Comte de Monte-Cristo* (*The Count of Monte Cristo*; Robert Vernay), *Napoléon* (Sacha Guitry), and *The Grand Maneuver* (René Clair).

‡ The accounts for *French Cancan* were settled by December 31, 1956, and the figures for ticket sales communicated to Renoir on January 29, 1957, revealed the producer's percentage for France and North Africa as yielding 8,777,990 francs. (Jean Renoir Papers, Box 13, Folder 12.)

Round Table." And he added, "I'd prefer that the continuity of Renoir's work have more importance than his hat, his way of speaking, his humor, the events of his life. . . . For me, Renoir's work is more important than his legend or his behavior, and the continuity of his work as an auteur of film is more important than all the rest."

True—if one takes into consideration that the only events of Renoir's life that were retained were those that he himself chose to reveal. Pierre Kast, who at the time had spent several months on the editorial staff of *Cahiers du cinéma* protesting what he referred to as Truffaut's "critical dogmatism," perfectly evaluated the danger that threatened Renoir's admirers, who were often tempted to forget, above all, that Renoir wasn't claiming to draw any "conclusions for anyone but himself."[48] The lesson in *French Cancan*, if there must be one, is that it's about cinema, as well as about the music hall, music, songs, colors, movement, and feelings. Nothing less, certainly, but also nothing more. Everyone would probably agree about that if the film weren't credited to Jean Renoir. But in the middle of the fifties, a matrix for reading films was manufactured. It may have been convenient, but it was also blinding.

In an article that he devoted in February 1955 to Becker's *Ali Baba et les quarante voleurs* (*Ali Baba and the Forty Thieves*), Truffaut made that film the touchstone of his critical theory: "If *Ali Baba* had been a failure, I would have still defended it by virtue of the *Politique des Auteurs* that my colleagues in criticism and I practice. . . . In spite of ten or twelve people fiddling with his scenario—ten or twelve too many, except for Becker—*Ali Baba* is the film of an *auteur*, an auteur who has achieved an exceptional mastery, an auteur of films. Accordingly, the technical success of *Ali Baba* confirms the validity of our politics, the *Politique des Auteurs*."[49] The reasoning is circular, the better to chase its own tail, but what is especially significant is that in the same article Truffaut energetically rejects any suggestion that a director chosen by him could experience a bad patch or be feeling his age, which anyone would have maintained about "Jean Renoir in his Hollywood period,"[50] especially.

As a result, Truffaut the disciple broke with his mentor André Bazin, for whom critical thought was applied exclusively to the film as it was projected on the screen, the work alone mattering, not the achievements that had come before or the personality of the auteur. Bazin was free to like certain of Renoir's films and others less. Truffaut would not allow himself to do this, and forbid others. A few months before, on the subject of *Touchez pas au grisbi*, by a director whose work he had followed from the beginning, he wrote that, on the other hand, "we haven't experienced Renoir as anything but inspired."[51] The party line was that Renoir was always inspired, that his films to come could only be so many masterpieces.

Until a recent period, studies of Renoir obeyed that law as it had been decreed essentially for the purpose of conquest, and the legislator of it himself moved on without saying so, as soon as his objectives were attained. To conform to this rule, critics and historians would be led to exhibit an admirable adaptability when it came, for example, to *The Golden Coach*. To better celebrate its theatricality, they would forget that Renoir was, according to them, not supposed to like working in the studio, while they simultaneously disregarded the desire he had expressed to direct the film in part in real scenery, in Mexico at first, and then in Calabria. That's certainly one way of creating a false truth at the price of two falsehoods.

The oldest trace of Renoir's interest in writing for the theater appears in the form of a "Project for a one-act play"[52] dated July 18, 19, and 20, 1934, the period in which the company that would make possible the production of *Toni* a few months later was established. It was a sketch, at most, and ended up being delayed permanently. After that, on several occasions, Renoir jotted down some notes, thought about doing an adaptation for musical theater of *The Crime of Monsieur Lange,* and then moved on to other things. In February 1951, as he was putting the finishing touches on the editing of *The River,* a project for a play in three acts came into being. *Les Soeurs Thomas* are the daughters of a millionaire who live in California and who have been together for more than fifty years. The character Jack the Ripper is associated with the story and is a composite of two different people, the wife and the husband. The author was thinking about playing himself in the piece.[53]

In January 1953, after the commercial failure of *The Golden Coach,* Renoir worked on what would become *Orvet* but what was then entitled *The Poachers.*[54] The different treatments that have been preserved show that Renoir spent the entire month of January working on the project.[55] It began as a screenplay,[56] and for a while, the plan was to have Danièle Delorme play the lead in the film, which took place in Burgundy. The first trace of this idea can be found in several treatments for an identical project dating back to 1938. That project was partly inspired by a crime Renoir would also use as material for a novel,* changing titles several times in a succession that included *Tibi* and *Artus.* The story focused primarily on a poacher and his daughter, a "dissolute" man, a princess, and a girl from the forest.[57]

Renoir's meetings with Leslie Caron in Hollywood led to his decision to transform *The Poachers* into a play. Caron may have reminded him of the girl who was with the poachers who'd saved his life, picking him up on the road where he lay unconscious, after the accident on May 7, 1927, that had killed his friend

* Le Crime de l'Anglais (The Englishman's Crime).

Pierre Champagne. Now her character Orvet, which had been a supporting role, became the central figure in the play. Renoir's version of the accident, as has been described, was romanticized, to say the least, and it's even possible that the character had been inspired by his memory of Constance Beysson, the urchin from Essoyes with whom Alain had been in love and had described as being like a little savage. Moreover, Renoir has stated that he'd asked Dudley Nichols for permission to use the name Orvet, which had been invented by the screenwriter when he collaborated on treatments for *The Poachers* entitled *Noblesse oblige.*[58] Renoir had known poachers since childhood, when they'd come to his family's house with venison to sell. Near the end of his life, Alain still remembered some pike fish poachers had sold them.[59] Renoir had already described their world in *The Whirlpool of Fate,* three years before the accident in 1927.

Dressed in rags* and always barefoot, Orvet is also a savage. The daughter of a drunken poacher, she sells not only the mushrooms she finds in the forest but also, at times, her body, always in a spirit of complete innocence. Then she meets Georges, a writer who becomes enamored of her and who tries to give her an education; not only her transformation but especially the act of transplanting her to Paris have disastrous consequences for her.

The spirit of Hans Christian Andersen floats through *Orvet.* Georges is working on a theatrical adaptation of *The Little Mermaid,* and the plot makes one think of *The Little Match Girl.* It's also reminiscent of the figure of Pygmalion, and Pirandello's influence is obvious, without that keeping the work from ever seeming eminently Renoirian. All such references and many others can be easily spotted in the director's films. In the course of several different treatments, Renoir kept modifying his view of the characters, sometimes presenting all of them as products of illusion, sometimes clothing them—or some, in any case— with the trimmings of reality. Just after the performance of *Julius Caesar* in Arles, he also reworked the character of Georges to adapt him to the personality of Paul Meurisse—especially by making him younger.

Although there are inklings of Marceau from *The Rules of the Game* in the father of Orvet, a role played onstage by Raymond Bussières, one of his lines also points to Julien Carette† and was derived from a play on words used by the actor in *Grand Illusion: "À la tienne Étienne et casse pas le bol!"*‡§ To the ears

* The robe worn by Leslie Caron onstage would be created by Givenchy.

† Apparently, Renoir wanted to use Carette in *Orvet.*

‡ *Translator's note:* "Here's to you, Étienne, and don't break the bowl!" However, *"casse pas le bol"* can also mean "don't fret" or "don't worry about it." In addition, *"À la tienne, Etienne,"* is sometimes said playfully just for the repetitive sound of it, even when the person being spoken to is not named Etienne.

§ In *Grand Illusion,* it's *"Casse pas le litre!"*

and eyes of Renoir enthusiasts, the play is swarming with reminiscences, and the Pirandello-like quality of it as a whole is noticeably accentuated by them. This happens all the more because the theater in its specificity offered Renoir the opportunity to exert his prerogatives as an auteur well beyond the limit allowed by film. Whereas in film the moment always comes when the work must be delivered and when its form ends up permanently established, a play is based mainly on the notion of rehearsal and develops naturally. Each rehearsal is different from the others, and the director can continue to exercise his influence, with even more latitude when he himself is the author of the work. Thus, Renoir was experimenting with that freedom offered by the theater, changing things until the last moment, correcting what he deemed necessary from day to day, and enjoying the liberties taken by Jacques Jouanneau, in the role of William, with his text.

With William, Jouanneau let his fantasies run free, in fact, provoking some degree of irritation on the part of his acting partners. Especially Raymond Bussières, who wasn't amused by his excesses, despite the fact that Renoir was constantly enchanted by them.[60] The share of dissatisfaction and indecision Renoir possessed inside himself also exercised its rights, which is something he would indicate in an interview he gave to *Cahiers du cinéma*. He'd attributed the defects he noticed during the preparation of *Julius Caesar* to his own direction, and certainly Shakespeare couldn't be blamed for them. On the other hand, anything wrong with *Orvet* was just as much the responsibility of the author as of the director. This led to his modifying the text of the play on several occasions, provoking Truffaut to utter the heartfelt cry, "It's never completely the same!" The future director stated that he'd seen the performance "five times, each time with renewed pleasure," and observed that "the first week, the text would change every evening to make it easier for the actors." Finally, he called the play "an amazing gallery, characterized by a richness comparable to Balzac."[61] Renoir himself began to show an obvious liking for the thing and was now thinking of adapting his friend Clifford Odets's play *The Big Knife*, as Dido was to inform the author on April 21.[62]

The first performance of *Orvet*, announced in the February 5 issue of *Paris-Match* as well as in other publications, took place on March 12, 1955. On the cover of the magazine was a shot of "the star, Leslie," and inside, seven pages devoted primarily to the "little French girl" who had just become "legendary in America." One photo showed her with Renoir during her arrival at Orly;*

---

* Actually, a good part of the cast of *Orvet* had come as a delegation to Orly. Among them were Paul Meurisse and Raymond Bussières.

another pictured them reading the play together at the home of the author, who was quite visibly in the midst of a fit of laughter.[63] The play was one of the media events of the season, but it still had to face the critics.

That is when the tone turned vindictive. The most diverse influences were spotted in the piece, and they were deplored—from Marcel Aymé's *La Vouivre* to Giraudoux's *The Madwoman of Chaillot*, from *Pygmalion* to *Six Characters in Search of an Author*. Renoir's allusions to his own films delighted Renoir aficionados, but their dramatic and literary remembrances spoiled the pleasure of the "Thespians," who never lack more indulgence than when film people get it into their heads to venture onstage. It was also true that the play, characterized by a certain type of naïveté that was often confused, invited criticism. It was, in any case, a chance for the caricaturists of the press to have a field day. The caption to a drawing by Senep twisted the play's title: "It's not a slow-worm, it's a tapeworm."[64] Cabrol availed himself of a well-known French idiom to show Paul Meurisse, Leslie Caron, and Raymond Bussières "swallowing a garden snake."[†65] Pinatel showed the actress, her male lead, and the author as if drowning in the manuscript and pointed out that "it certainly is characteristic of the author of *The River*."[66] *Orvet* would close at the Théâtre de la Renaissance on June 19, after ninety-five performances.[‡] To the extent that any records show, the play has never been performed since, outside of amateur productions.

The day following a performance of *Orvet* attended by Ingrid Bergman, Renoir told Leslie Caron that he and Dido had invited her to supper, after which the actress had sat down on the sidewalk in tears and declared that she was "penniless and exhausted"[67] now that the films she'd made for Rossellini had become commercial failures. Renoir had then added, "As a result, Leslie, I won't be making the film that I was intending to shoot with you. Or at least not immediately. I've promised Ingrid to help her."[68]

It was also the case that during that spring 1955 Henry Deutschmeister,

---

* *Translator's note:* A reference to the title of the play, *Orvet*, a word that means "slow worm," or "blind worm," but also the name of the character played by Caron.

† *Translator's note:* The French reads "*faire passer la couleuvre.*" It draws its sense from the well-known idiom *avaler des couleuvres* ("swallowing garden snakes"), which means "swallowing an affront." *Faire passer* suggests "getting something down" (for example, when a bitter pill is coated with sugar to make it easier for a child to swallow). So, the actors are dealing with something "hard to swallow." The use of *couleuvre* in this play on words is apt because of the title of the piece, *Orvet*, meaning "slow worm," a serpentine creature (see previous notes).

‡ And not four hundred, as indicated in *Correspondance 1913–1978*, a figure assuming that the play ran for more than a year.

who was satisfied with the experience of *French Cancan*, offered to make a second film with Renoir. There is a possibility—and Renoir confirmed it in writing*—that the producer had asked him to write a screenplay specifically intended for Ingrid Bergman. In fact, "Deutsch," as he was called, was a friend of Rossellini, who was fond of calling him "the only Jew Hitler had to *pay* to make him leave Germany," explaining that the revelation of some prewar real estate deals tying Deutschmeister to certain bigwigs of the Nazi Party risked compromising them.[69] Deutsch was likely to have had a considerable sum transferred to an account in Switzerland in exchange for his silence and his departure. In 1956, Rossellini is said to have convinced the producer to take an interest in the film projects of aspiring directors at *Cahiers du cinéma*.

One of the more noteworthy results of this was Deutschmeister's signing a contract and paying an advance to Truffaut for a film that was then entitled *La Peur de Paris*, a first version of the adventures of Antoine Doinel that would become *Les 400 coups* (*The 400 Blows*) three years later.

Renoir and Ingrid Bergman had been wanting to work together for more than ten years, a factor that would have been enough to justify Renoir responding to Deutschmeister's interest in the project. However, it was also the case that Bergman's career actually was going through a bad patch. *Journey to Italy, Giovanna d'Arco al rogo* (*Joan at the Stake* or *Joan of Arc at the Stake*), and *Fear*, her latest films, were commercial failures that had also been ill received by Italian critics. Sometimes their wrath spared Rossellini, who remained an icon in Italy. Nevertheless, they did accuse him of "betraying" the case of neorealism and focused on the actress as the undeniable cause of all the evils. Nothing was spared: implications on a personal level, reproaches about her luxurious lifestyle, remarks smacking of xenophobia. At the same time, the most recent stagings of *Joan of Arc at the Stake*, in December 1954 and January 1955 in Barcelona, beginning February 17 in Stockholm, and then in Palermo until April 27, weren't a comfort to her. On the contrary—her performance was judged deplorable almost unanimously. The offer from Renoir and Deutschmeister couldn't have come at a better time.

Ingrid Bergman would recall in her memoirs that Renoir's response in Hollywood in the forties to her insisting that he work with her was that she was too big a star for him. He'd told her they'd have to wait until her career was in decline and then, when she was falling, he would be there to catch her. Consequently, in 1955, he'd come to see her in Santa Marinella to tell her that the moment had come. The actress's response? "Roberto will never let me work

* "The producer Deutschmeister had asked me to write a screenplay that could call attention to the exquisite actress Ingrid Bergman." Preliminary notes for *Ma vie et mes films*, November 23, 1970. (Jean Renoir Papers, Production Files, Box 71, Folder 9.)

with someone else."[70] However, Rossellini did accept. Renoir was one of the rare colleagues whom he admired. The change his own career was undergoing was one reason to turn away from his actress. His sexual appetite was creating distance between him and his wife, and inspiration was beckoning in the direction of India, in the footsteps of the director of *The River*.

During the filming of *The Golden Coach* in Rome and, even more frequently, in Santa Marinella, where he and Dido spent several weekends, Renoir had spoken at length with Rossellini about India. Before Rossellini left for that country in December 1956, he asked Renoir for a list of technicians capable of helping him on location. High up on this list was the name Hari Das Gupta, Renoir's assistant for *The River*. Rossellini was going to fall madly in love with Gupta's wife, Sonali Sen Roy, who was twenty-seven and the mother of two sons, a four-year-old and a four-month-old. She would become the director's chief collaborator for all the preparation and shooting of his film *India*. On December 29, 1957, she gave birth to his daughter Raffaella and remained his companion until 1973.

Rossellini described his relationship with Renoir as "much more than a friendship . . . an extraordinary love," adding that "as surprising as it may seem, we have never discussed film together," having as they did "so many other things to tell each other."[71] These feelings were shared to some extent by Renoir, who discovered that Rossellini was an even more effusive friend than he himself was, something that seemed to embarrass him at times. In a letter to Dido, Renoir described an evening in Rome with Ingrid and her son Robertino as follows: "Then Rossellini arrived. I'm supposed to be his brother . . . no less. He was very nice as well."[72]

Renoir was particularly shocked on several occasions by the way Rossellini behaved toward his wife, whom Renoir had known long before he met the Italian director and for whom he felt a true friendship. In June 1951, he wrote to Dido from Rome saying that he didn't believe Ingrid was happy, despite what her friends were claiming. "Rossellini—who is charming—isn't a 'husband.' The truth is that everyone here has the impression that it can't possibly last, given his attitude. He arrived after lunch, making some excuse about business, and he wasn't hungry, having already eaten a sandwich. I'm even wondering whether he could be interested in somebody else already."[73]

Obviously, the situation at hand wasn't easy for the Renoirs. They were close friends with a woman whose husband was behaving like an out-of-control skirt-chaser. In October 1957, Rossellini confided to Renoir about his situation: Sonali was pregnant with his child and hidden away somewhere in Paris; Ingrid was aware of her ill fortune and waiting for their imminent separation. In Renoir's report of it to Dido, he described them as being "in the sorry and ridiculous state that the romantics call passion and that the authors of the Middle Ages saw as subject matter for a joke."[74] Then he added, "Roberto is dreaming of giving up filmmaking, and writing and living in a hovel in the South of France with Sonali. We are swimming through sh . . . ,* but both of them are very unhappy and deserve our sympathy as friends." To this letter, which was typed, Renoir added a handwritten note: "Jean Renoir, who's happy he's not Roberto Rossellini and has Dido."

The performance of *Orvet* seen by Ingrid Bergman was one of the last and happened at the end of May at the earliest. After the final performance of *Joan of Arc at the Stake* in Palermo on April 27, 1955, the actress had spent three weeks in Sicily with Rossellini.[75] Quite probably, Renoir and Deutschmeister had already come to an agreement by then about their new project together, or at least who would star in it. Although she hadn't worked in Hollywood since 1949 and Hitchcock's *Under Capricorn,* her name certainly hadn't been forgotten in the United States; and Renoir had every right to think that the film would relaunch the star's American career as well as his own. Therefore, nothing seemed more logical than making two versions, one in French and the other in English. This made it natural for an American company to participate in the production.

On July 22, Deutschmeister and Franco-London Films had come to an agreement regarding this with Berkshire Pictures Corporation, a company located at 1501 Broadway in New York City. On October 25, the two parties signed a coproducer's contract for the film, which was to be entitled *The Red Carnation.* Berkshire agreed to a "screenplay ready for filming written by Cy Howard" and to the casting of Mel Ferrer as the costar, who would receive equal billing with Ingrid Bergman.[76] But the very existence of such a contract poses a problem: no American coproducer appears in the credits for *Elena and Her Men.*† Instead, three companies are listed. Two of them were French—Deutschmeister's Franco-London Films and Joseph Bercholz's Films Gibé; and one was Italian—Electra Compania Cinematografica. What is equally troubling is the attribution of the "screenplay ready for filming" to Cy Howard. The screenplay for *Elena and Her Men* was actually the work of Renoir alone, and he was cosigning the adaptation of it with Jean Serge. Cy Howard, moreover, was not very well known as a screenwriter and had only written the English dialogue. Actually, everything seemed to have been done merely to give the impression

---

* *Translator's note:* The phrase Renoir actually used was "*Nous nageons en pleine c . . .* [con *nerie*]." ("We're swimming in bloody stupidity.")

† *Translator's note:* The French version was entitled *Elena et les hommes.*

that the production was partly American. In addition, the only traces of any activity at all on the part of Berkshire Pictures Corporation are the contracts for Renoir's film. If this company really had nothing to do with the production, why was it necessary for Deutschmeister to sign these contracts? He never had any production agreement with any American company, neither before nor after *Elena*.

The answer to this is related to Renoir's personal situation and a desire expressed as early as the making of *The Golden Coach* to be paid his salary in the United States and in dollars. In fact, his American nationality prohibited him from "signing any contract keeping him out of the United States for a period lasting beyond the expiration date of his passport"; and he had gone so far as having "suggested that the contract mention that, officially, the editing would be done in the United States."[77] As a result, although the produced film was the property of Franco-London, it was really with Berkshire that Renoir was signing a director's contract on October 31, 1955, which was being figured partly in dollars (a total of $45,000) and partly in francs (450,000), the latter to be paid in Paris between November 15 and December 15.[78] He confirmed this in a letter to one of his French agents whom he reminded that, because his "contract for the directing" was "with [Deutschmeister's] American partner, M. Shapiro,"[79] he was going to ask his American agents to take on the responsibility of recouping the $10,000 still owed him by the producer. In fact, when Renoir worked in New York on the English-language version of the film during the summer and fall of 1956, Irvin Shapiro acted as his contact.

The screenplay Renoir fashioned with the "exquisite Ingrid" in mind was called *L'Oeillet rouge* (*The Red Carnation*), a reference to the carnation worn in their buttonhole by the supporters of General Boulanger, the French minister of defense from January 1886 to 1887. When Boulanger was ousted from the government, a movement in support of him had been born; and in January 1889, he found himself in a position to attempt a coup d'état with a significant chance of success. On the evening of January 27 of that year, Georges Boulanger chose love over politics and returned to his mistress, Céline de Bonnemains, rather than seizing power as his allies were encouraging him to do. While in exile in Belgium, he committed suicide on September 30, 1891, on the grave of Madame de Bonnemains, who had died of tuberculosis two and a half months earlier. No direct reference to this page of history would survive in the film, which did, however, follow the framework of the story fairly closely. Either legal action threatened by the general's daughters[80] or a fear that a reading of the film would be interpreted as an intention on the part of its makers to poke fun at Marshal Juin*[81]—whose current situation some thought closely resembled Boulanger's in 1889—was what forced Renoir to revise his project.

It's not surprising that just before shooting began, Renoir claimed that the decision to distance himself from any historical anecdote was taken for practical reasons. "My producers and I thought that it would be better to stick with pure fiction, that it was more convenient. Moreover, my story is much too fanciful to be endowed with any appearance of reality. It's better to start out by saying that it's not a true story."[82] Seven years later, he would attribute the difficulties met by the film to the disruption caused by abandoning any reference to General Boulanger, which had happened, according to him, as a result of complications caused by the general's heirs. "This last-minute disruption didn't help me make a very good film. I made the kind of film I could . . . I made the kind of film you can make when you're improvising almost completely."[83] At the time, he claimed that he'd managed only to "snatch some situations in which Ingrid was brilliant," as were some of the other actors, especially Jacques Jouanneau and Pierre Bertin.

A fictional story, then, yet one that held onto the themes initially planned, "a general, a conspiracy, a coup d'état,"[84] for which a daisy took the place of the carnation, and on which Renoir worked in collaboration with Jean Serge. To accomplish this, he moved to Saint-Germain-en-Laye, into a hotel called the Pavillon Henri-IV. From there, he wrote to David Loew on July 10 that Louis XIV had been born in one of the establishment's rooms and also stated that he'd finished the first version of a treatment of what he called his "Bergman picture."[85] The treatment, which was twelve pages long, would be registered with the Association des auteurs de films on August 22.[86]

For the time being, he had to be prepared to film two versions simultaneously, one in French and one in English, using the exact same cast for both. The French actors would also speak the English dialogue, and Ingrid Bergman and Mel Ferrer would also have to express themselves in a language that wasn't theirs. The beautiful Elena's heart would vacillate between the brilliant General Rollan, played by Jean Marais, and the seductive Henri de Chevincourt, whom Renoir was thinking of awarding a Basque ethnicity to justify the accent of his actor, who was a native of New Jersey. Adding such a factor wouldn't have been necessary if Gérard Philipe had played the character of Henri de Chevincourt, which had been the plan for a while.

---

* *Translator's note:* Alphonse Pierre Juin (1888–1967), the last living marshal of France, who was a veteran of both world wars and distinguished himself during a North African campaign against the Germans during World War II. The comparison with Boulanger comes from his opposition to de Gaulle's decision to grant independence to Algeria, because of which he was forcibly retired from military service.

Philipe had just worn such a uniform designed by Rosine Delamare, the costume designer for *French Cancan* and *Elena,* in René Clair's *The Grand Maneuver,* which would be one of the big hits of 1955. After the role of Chevincourt had been offered to him, he moved on at the end of July 1955 to the Yves Allégret film *La Meilleure Part* (*The Best Part*), shot primarily on a hydraulic fill dam in Savoy. Then he spent several hours on Sacha Guitry's set in the role of a medieval minstrel for *Si Paris nous était conté* (*If Paris Were Told to Us*) and, finally, after a trip to the USSR and Poland lasting several weeks, filmed *Les Aventures de Till l'Espiègle* (*The Adventures of Till Eulenspiegel*), the film he'd asked Renoir to direct in 1949. Philipe had found himself a codirector, Joris Ivens. The project was all he thought about, and shooting was supposed to begin at the end of the year, which was the same time as *Elena and Her Men.* This obviously explains why the actor, who had so wished to work with Renoir five years previously, declined the offer made to him by the director. A different explanation, no more official than the first, claims that the actor refused because he didn't want to play a character who claims that "fighting for ideas serves nothing." Philipe is supposed to have expressed his opposition to that line during a reading of the screenplay organized at Renoir's on avenue Frochot and to have said, "You'll have to take out that sentence if you want to have me, because I believe the opposite of that."[87]

Although Gérard Philipe truly was the kind of person who wouldn't want to speak a sentence like that, Renoir was the type who would look for another option, at any price. It's doubtful he wouldn't have tried to find one on that occasion, not to mention the fact that the line didn't end up in the film. If a difference in opinion did occur between the director and the actor, Philipe could have been using it as an excuse to turn down an offer that corresponded neither to his desires of that moment nor to his schedule. What is more, the contract established on August 22 by Deutschmeister with Berkshire Pictures Corporation indicated that casting of Mel Ferrer had been decided by that date. It isn't impossible that the participation of a well-known American actor was more attractive than that of a fashionable French actor, especially one who visibly favored a project that had personal meaning for him.* In any case, all this seems enough to justify Renoir and Deutschmeister's lack of tenacity regarding what may have been their original idea. The director's desire for American audiences as his film's first priority would, naturally, lead him to prefer an American actor for the project.

By casting Jean Marais in the role of General Rollan, the producer had the

---

* François Truffaut would call *The Adventures of Till Eulenspiegel* "the worst film of the year." (*Arts,* November 14, 1956.)

insurance of one of the favorite actors of French audiences. In that year, 1955, eight million of them would see *The Count of Monte Cristo,* in which Marais starred, elevating Robert Vernay's film to the top rank of French productions. He had just played François I in *If Paris Were Told to Us,* which was also a Deutschmeister production, and he'd celebrate his forty-third birthday on the set of Renoir's film. Ingrid Bergman said she was delighted to have a leading man and cinematic lover who was homosexual and made no secret of it. "Those people," she observed, "are the only ones who play love scenes perfectly because neither prudery nor sensuality embarrasses them."[88]

For all these reasons, following on *French Cancan, Elena and Her Men* was confirmation that Renoir's return to France had brought him into the world of standard productions of that time. The director was conforming to the norm that characterized prestigious films of the fifties, with their historical retellings and the great stars of the period. An anecdote quite clearly describes behavior that might have also been the sign of a kind of detachment. Conveyed by Jacques Morel, an actor who had a supporting and very secondary role in the film as the character Duchêne, it suggests that, to say the least, a kind of confusion had characterized the casting process.

The actor reported that production, which wanted him in the film, had actually sent him to meet Renoir at a luncheon, during which the director explained the role he intended for him. Shooting came sometime after this, and Jacques Morel was surprised "not to find much similarity between the role I was playing and the one I'd been told about."[89] Aware of the fact that "the filmmaker, after some difficulties with the descendants of the general," had had to rework his screenplay, and having also verified that the number of days of filming and the fee corresponded to that specified in his contract, he hadn't worried about this change. And then, one day when Morel had been filmed "for more than a week," while the setup of a scene was being put in place, Renoir "stopped short" before him, exclaiming, "Oh shit! . . . Oh shit! . . . How stupid!" Then, finally, an explanation issued from the mouth of the director: "I got the role mixed up!"[90]

Was the role he confused with Morel's that of General Rollan, the only role except for the one being played by Mel Ferrer that had any scope? Possibly. But the fact remains that Jacques Morel had "to continue for several weeks and a number of days that ran past schedule to film a role as 'an intelligent walk-on' devoid of interest and without any relationship to the one I'd hoped for." It was that much easier, however, due to the fact that his participation amounted to "the most profitable financial endeavor" of his film career. It is doubtful that Renoir would have gotten "the role mixed up" and more probable that production had pounced on a chance to hire Jean Marais, a star whose presence would further boost the glamour of the film.* Renoir just hadn't found the right moment, the time, or the courage to inform Morel of his ill fortune.

Filming for *Elena and Her Men* began on December 1, 1955, in the Saint-Maurice studios, where the crew responsible for scenery had been working since October 10.[91] The exteriors were to be filmed on the grounds of Ermenonville and in the woods at Saint-Cloud. Ingrid Bergman would remember the experience as "stimulating." Renoir, on the other hand, would speak of it as a horrible ordeal from which he had difficulty recovering. The cold that took over France during the winter of 1955–1956, which was one of the worst that the country had ever known, came close to being insurmountable, but what rapidly brought things to that point were the obstacles created by the simultaneous direction of two versions.

Ingrid Bergman spoke fluent French, but she hadn't had much practice in that language recently, except for *Joan of Arc at the Stake,* onstage and in front of Rossellini's camera, an experience that led her to regret that her husband spoke to her only in Italian. The French distributor of *Joan of Arc at the Stake* had her dubbed by Claude Nollier, which aroused the wrath of Truffaut, to whose ear the actress's Swedish-Italian-English intonations had sounded like "a lovely Burgundian-Lorraine accent."[92] Renoir, on the other hand, had preferred to make Elena a Polish princess, and hearing her speak would prove one of the pleasures offered by the film. Mel Ferrer also got by in French, although he struggled to pass for a Basque gentleman (his voice ended up dubbed). However, it was the recording of the English dialogue that turned into a nightmare. Most of the French actors didn't understand that language. They had to speak their lines based on what they could understand of them phonetically, and Renoir ended up having to simplify the dialogue ceaselessly, and then do the same for the shots, and then the scenes. "I had to do without so many 'necessary precautions,' so many close-ups that could have punctuated the actors' performances; I had to improvise so much to simplify the English text for the French actors, the French text for Ingrid, that it's impossible for me to consider this production as anything but an ordeal."[93]

It was also an ordeal because the money, apparently, began to run out before shooting was over, something that happens at times with the most richly endowed productions. The actors had been paid generously, as Jacques Morel had remembered. However, the comfort they'd worked in was only illusory. The

* A condition that mandates having to accept that Jacques Morel, a robust actor whose looks didn't really lend him to Don Juan roles, could have been a plausible General Rollan. That itself is a hypothesis that could lead to doubts regarding the truth of the facts as they were reported.

sums spent to fill posters and credits with prestigious names didn't benefit the film, and its budget didn't correspond to the requirements of historical reconstruction and the simultaneous direction of two versions. Or, at least, that was how Renoir chose to remember it.

Traces of conditions during filming that match the way he later remembered experiencing them can be found in an undated document written in the context of a conflict that pitted director against producer. The document speaks of Renoir's struggling to obtain the contracted payments promised from the producer and shows each blaming the other for the film's failure. Consequently, these notes must be viewed with a sense of distance. They characterize the film as "poorly prepared and poorly organized," claim that the crew was required to work in unfinished scenery "in the middle of hammer blows, on icy sound stages," and protest that the actors rarely saw the costumes before a scene was shot. The document also claims that Renoir agreed to begin shooting while he was still feverish, poorly recovered from an illness that production had exploited to make their insurance pay for part of the preparation and that he actually saved the film "by an impossible amount of work" applied toward the "abridgment" and "rewriting of the scenes."

The document also specifies to the law firm Sereni & Herzfeld, which was defending Renoir's interests, that the director had indicated to Deutschmeister from the beginning that he was "not eager to make the film" and that he had informed the producer "of the difficulties" he foresaw.[94] Last, the producer is accused of deciding to stop shooting while at least two essential scenes remained to be filmed, forcing Renoir—if it can be believed—to substitute a scene sung by Juliette Gréco, who'd been summoned by production, for a scene with dialogue.

"Why not take advantage of Gréco when you have the pleasure of having her?"[95] Renoir would ask. But in reality, it's highly unlikely that the scene with Juliette Gréco was pieced together off the cuff. The singer-actress remembered being hired and choosing her costumes, accompanied by Sylvia Bataille, in conditions that were completely normal.[96] As for the song, Renoir had written the lyrics in December,[97] three weeks after the start of shooting, and the entire crew was humming the melody well before the scene was in the can, which was the last week of filming, according to Renoir.

Renoir claimed that he'd been informed of Deutschmeister's decision "by an electrician, on the soundstage."[98] At the time, the rumor was circulating in French studios that Claude Autant-Lara, who was preparing to direct *La Traversée de Paris* (*Four Bags Full*) on behalf of this same Deutschmeister, was making every effort to spur on the producer's impatience, causing him to pressure Renoir to finish. On the other hand, Jacques Saulnier, who was the assistant production designer for the film, as he had been for *French Cancan*, had no memory of any hurry at all, and his participation ended on March 7, as his contract predicted.[99]

Ten months after the start of shooting, which ended officially on March 17—although it had actually ended several days later*—Renoir wasn't through with *Elena and Her Men*. He still had to work on the English version of the film, a task he got down to in a room at the Titra Dubbing Corporation, at 235 West Broadway in New York. This was the company where Lee Kresel, who had written the English dialogue for *The Golden Coach*, worked. Kresel would eventually become its director.

Having left Cherbourg on July 13, Renoir stayed at the Waldorf Astoria and then the Royalton Hotel. He planned on staying in New York for three weeks,[100] a time he would take advantage of for some meetings with the press. He wound up staying for nearly three months and didn't leave for Los Angeles until October 13.[101] On August 11, he said he considered it "depressing to spend my days in a projection room trying to accomplish perfect synchronization."[102] The endeavor was made even more difficult because Deutschmeister was refusing to let Warner, which would distribute the film in the United States, learn that *Elena* had been postsynchronized. The producer had "sold" the Americans a film shot with live sound and with actors who spoke their lines in perfect English.

On September 1, Renoir informed Deutsch that synchronization problems encountered during the scene between Olga and Lionel (Olga Valéry and Jean Claudio) at the beginning of the film were forcing him to "contemplate a substantial cut in the American version."[103] At the time, he mentioned approximately fifteen shots. Four days later, there was a new letter: "The scene that opens the film has been spoiled because of the sound. My idea was to establish tension between the piano and the military music coming from the street, punctuated by Bergman's performance. My intention isn't working out. In France, where Bergman is less discussed, we can perhaps keep the scene. In America, I've got to make an impression on audiences from the start. Let me add that I was hoping to improve Olga's performance by dubbing and that I didn't, in fact, succeed. The Lionels that I attempted are a lot worse than our French Lionel."[104] On October 6, in response to Deutschmeister's request that he talk to Jack Warner about the film without saying that it had been dubbed, Renoir opted for a joking tone: "It would seem impossible to me to claim that Jean Marais speaks with a New England accent and Morel and his friends with a Brooklyn accent."[105]

* In a letter to Clifford Odets dated March 19, 1956, Renoir stated that all that remained to be filmed were a few exteriors, without the actors, which included the scene of the balloon taking off.

The truth was that he was living through an ordeal: he'd always opposed, often vehemently, the very notion of dubbing, a principle he'd already reversed for *French Cancan,* in which Anna Amendola "sang" "La Complainte de la Butte" with the voice of Cora Vaucaire. Nevertheless, his communications with Deutschmeister remained cordial, even warm; and when he wrote from New York he still called him "my dear Deutsch." Only after the American release of the film did his relationship with the producer became contentious. This is proof that Renoir wasn't piqued about the conditions under which *Elena* had been produced; and, in any case, he didn't hold Deutschmeister responsible for them. Although he compared the end of the experience to the way Napoléon's armies must have felt after their retreat from Russia in 1812, he insisted on seeing Deutsch as probably the best French producer he could have had and admitted being unable to imagine how things would have turned out with someone less intelligent and toward whom he didn't feel the same sense of friendship.[106]

Renoir, then, couldn't make it to Paris by September 12, the day of the French release of the film. In informing the producer of his unavailability, he didn't use the excuse of the work he was doing in New York. That might have left him enough time for a round-trip across the Atlantic. Instead, he mentioned the need to have surgery, without revealing the nature of the operation. He did, however, explain that he had already waited too long* and then suggested, "Why not ask Sacha Guitry to present *Elena*? If you cable me, I'll send him a letter appealing to a lot of old memories we share. After all, he did know my father."[107]

On that same day, August 28, Jean Marais wrote to him, "It's a wonderful film that makes a person feel happy," before offering in a postscript, "Although Jean Cocteau is ill, I think he'd write a text that I'll say if Sartre can't present the film."[108] Several weeks later, from London, Christian-Jaque wrote Renoir to say, "Sorry about not having been able to present your so delightful film in Marseille," and added that, as a result, he'd been "deprived of the joy of pleasing you and of publicly saying all the good things"[109] he thought about the film.

Everything seemed in league against *Elena.* Renoir was miserable, and Deutschmeister was furious. On the date of the Parisian release, which was the day after the grand premiere, the producer wrote to the director, "Our disappointment was complete yesterday. Not a *single* actor in the film was in the theater. Madame Bergman said that she was too fatigued from her English film† to come to Paris. Messieurs Marais and Mel Ferrer are making a film now

---

* The operation was for a hernia, which necessitated that he lose weight.

† *Anastasia,* a Fox production, in English, directed by Anatole Litvak and filmed primarily in Paris. However, some of the exteriors were directed in Denmark and England.

and weren't able to get away. Even having the film presented by a celebrity like Charlie Chaplin or Jean Cocteau wasn't possible for reasons that you know." Then: "At the Colisée, no one applauded the film while it was being shown, but there was applause at the end."[110] As for the foreign distributors, they had been "irritated" by the film. (In reality, the only ones who actually were irritated were the Italian and the French distributors.)

A week later, there was a new letter. The film was "doing" well at the Colisée, badly at the Marivaux.[111] A week after that and, "The news about the film is quite grave for us. Ticket sales fell by about 30 percent in the second week."[112] Deutschmeister also compared sales for Renoir's film to those for René Clair's *The Grand Maneuver,* which had been released in April 1955. In two weeks, it had drawn nearly twice the amount of viewers as *Elena.* Finally, "the reviews" for *Elena* were "extremely bad, except for the one in *Le Figaro littéraire.*"

Claude Mauriac had in fact called the film "irreplaceable, and Jean Renoir is the only one in the world who could have directed it." It was a work of "commendable grace, sensitivity, color, and rhythm."[113] But Renoir had already understood by then, and in the meantime, he had written to the producer. "My conclusion is that America remains a last hope. . . . I absolutely must change the beginning and end of the film. Its future in America depends upon it."[114]

A few days before finally leaving New York for California, Renoir delivered a first report for the editor of the film, who had also worked on *French Cancan* and most of Deutschmeister's productions. "It feels like I'm coming out of a nightmare. I had some good moments during *Elena,* the work with Ingrid, Jean Marais, Jouanneau, and most of the actors, as well as my collaboration with your team and preparation with Jean Serge. But facing these glowing memories are so many shadows, problems."[115]

It would be important to move on as quickly as possible to something else, but the producer was relentlessly sending him news of the film's distressing fate. "All we have is bad news. Up to now, marketing has been a catastrophe wherever the film has been released. . . . We'd hoped to be able to give you better news, at least for some territories, but unfortunately, we have nothing satisfying to tell you."[116] Although it can't be ruled out that Deutschmeister was painting a black picture, as is almost a habit in the profession of producers, and all the more so when the director's contract specifies an interest in the profits, there is no doubt that the results weren't corresponding to his expectations.

Deutsch was a respected producer who was responsible for several good films. He had the reputation of managing his affairs with an iron hand, while putting sentiment to one side. For example, Renoir reproached him for having paired *Elena* with a twenty-minute opener entitled *L'Album de famille de Jean Renoir,* in which Renoir answered questions from Pierre Desgraupes. Renoir had agreed to participate while he was working on the editing of *Elena,* thinking that the film, directed by Roland Gritti, was being made to be shown on television first. He was less unhappy about the way it had ended up being programmed than he was expecting to be remunerated by Deutschmeister, which Deutschmeister refused.[117]

The American version was released under a title Renoir thought was "indecent":[118] *Paris Does Strange Things.* It would play only in a few art theaters, because Warner had considered its commercial potential insufficient for a wider distribution.[119] This signaled the end of any hopes, which had already been extremely limited for the last several months. "*Elena* is playing in Buffalo,'" wrote Renoir. "Without telling me, they've added a commentary by Mel Ferrer and changed the editing. The reviews are appalling."[120] The American version was twelve minutes shorter than the French version. Because it's a known fact that Renoir himself had already made several cuts he thought the dubbing had necessitated, it's quite likely that Americans had seen a film that was very close to the version seen by French audiences. When he returned to this issue with more distance, he appeared less categorical and stated that the beginning and end of the film had been changed. Various letters he exchanged with the producer from New York reveal that he was the one who made these changes. But again, with distance, there was also no more mention of the commentary Mel Ferrer is said to have recorded. And he added, "I maintain that other changes were made, but I can't judge the extent of the massacre, having refused to see this film that was no longer mine."[121]

In this same interview, which is undated but which occurred before 1960, Renoir claims that *Elena* was well received by audiences in several European countries. Did any "mutilation"[122] of the film at the behest of the distributor really occur, as Renoir claimed? There is some doubt about this. On the other hand, Renoir was correct in writing that the American reviews were "appalling," and Ingrid Bergman didn't escape that massacre. In the *New York Times,* Bosley Crowther compared her to "a chicken with its head cut off."[123] The tone of all the reviews could be summed up by a sentence written by William K. Zinsser in the *New York Herald Tribune:* "Nothing can explain . . . how the great Jean Renoir could have made such a picture, or why, having made it, he didn't throw it in the Seine."

Renoir's wish to direct *Elena and Her Men* in English and in French (stated as early as summer 1955), and his justifiable desire to take into account the American market, afflicted the production with the risk of missing both of the chosen targets. The fact is that *Paris Does Strange Things* was a disaster, whereas

---

* The film was released in New York on March 29, 1957.

Elena et les hommes wasn't a success.

Reviews in France weren't completely scathing, but as a whole they were mediocre. For example, Pierre Billard admitted his "perplexity" and asked whether it was suitable "in the name of the '*politique des auteurs*' ['auteur politics'], which at its most exaggerated would spare us having to see films, to put our faith in Renoir in honor of his past, and to hide the immense disappointment occasioned by his latest manifestation."[124] An answer to this question followed: "The weakness and incoherency of the editing, the pointlessness of the characters, the insufficiency of the acting . . . are more difficult to explain (and excuse) with Renoir than with any other. The greats have less of a right to go wrong than others. Especially at this point."[125]

However, returning to the film nearly forty years later, Billard stated that he was "delighted by the virtuosity of the shell game of the linking of shots" by Renoir the "master manipulator,"[126] thereby demonstrating that time had obviously done its work. Moreover, in 1956, there were some who mistrusted this lack of distance, fearing that they might be making *Elena and Her Men* the victim of the same misunderstanding suffered by *The Rules of the Game*. Georges Sadoul was among them, but he was also one of the few to lay down terms for the comparison by suggesting that *Elena* lacked "the love of mankind that inspired Renoir in the thirties and impelled him to the heights of genius."[127]

Conversely, several months later, Jean-Luc Godard would employ a lengthy love song to salute "the most intelligent film in the world," perceiving in it "art at the same time as the theory of art, beauty at the same time as the secret of beauty, film at the same time as the explanation of film." Although *Elena and Her Men*, he further wrote, "is the most Mozartian film of its auteur," it is "less so by means of its surface appearance, as is *The Rules of the Game*, than it is by its philosophy." *Elena* would be to *French Cancan* what *The Magic Flute* was to *Concerto for Clarinet*, and "as for its content: the same irony and the same disgust. As for its form: the same inspired daring in the context of simplicity." He concluded, "To the question, what is film? *Elena* answers, more than film."[128]

On the level of formulation, Godard was already in possession of consummate artistry. His expression of enthusiasm for *Elena and Her Men* in 1956, beyond any strategic considerations, made some sense. Working in the context of standard European production, Renoir was attempting, daring, risking what the majority of his colleagues were being careful not to do. But more than a half century later, it is also possible to perceive that such daring, intelligence, and mastery were not enough. The only real miracle of the film, in regard to the conditions of its production, resides in the fact that it more or less managed to remain standing. And this feat is probably less the result of Renoir's genius than of the experience he had accumulated over the years, an experience that

Godardian logic attributed to "thirty years of improvisation while shooting."[129]

In 1956, to better celebrate Renoir's merits, it was considered de rigueur to deride *The Grand Maneuver;* and such a comparison was suggested by certain similarities between the two films, which Gérard Philipe's presence in *Elena* would have emphasized. But this was also a way of challenging René Clair, a director who was too famous and too prestigious to escape becoming a designated target. Today, there is a decided resemblance between the two films that encompasses their flaws and their good characteristics. If the question were asked about which of the two, each within the framework of its own logic, ought to be considered the more successful, it's not a certainty that Renoir's would be named.*

Speaking only of Renoir's films, it becomes apparent that the surface aspects of *French Cancan*—its colors, interiors, costumes, action, and overall pacing—are as appealing as those features of *Elena* are disappointing, making one think especially of that other Deutschmeister production, *Rouge et Noir*. The sets for *Elena* were by Jean André, who was Max Douy's assistant for *French Cancan*. That had been André's first job, and, suffering from the fact that Renoir had appeared little concerned with his work, he hadn't felt very confident about his task. This was especially the case after the director made a wounding, ironic remark to him in front of the crew concerning the material André had chosen for curtains (and for good reason, according to his assistant).[130]

It's also true that the cinematography in *Elena and Her Men* isn't among the most successful of Claude Renoir's work. As harmful as it may be to the impression that is produced, such a lack of immediate appeal is, however, not irrevocable. It's just that the "*fantaisie musicale*" announced in the credits is not very convincing. Instead, everything seems like a veneer, laborious, constrained. It has more of an agitation than a rhythm. When it comes to all the echoes of *The Rules of the Game* in the film—Eugène (a very good Jacques Jouanneau) fondling Lolotte the maidservant (Magali Noël) in her kitchen; the general's assistant (an unbearable Jean Richard) endlessly pursuing the same Lolotte through hallways; Claire Gérard's character punctuating the action with the same commonplaces she spouted in *Rules;*† Gaston Modot (the gamekeeper in *Rules*) playing a gypsy—all they inspire is a desire for this film to end.

The casting seems at the very least uneven, something that had never before happened in a film by Renoir. Not to mention that Elena, a new Renoirian figure, confronted by exaggerated interest from three men, seems quite lackluster,

---

* The jury for the Louis-Delluc Prize would make such a choice. In 1955, it would honor *The Grand Maneuver*, and the following year it would ignore *Elena and Her Men.*

† Claire Gérard played Mme. La Bruyère in *Rules* and a traveler in *La Bête humaine.*

compared with her predecessors. Similarly, the reflections on love, showmanship, and life lack brilliance, as if Renoir were reeling off those themes derived from his two previous films without really thinking about it. Ingrid Bergman is radiant at times, but it's totally fruitless, like a fragile icon with worn-out puppets dancing around her.

To tell the truth, all of it seems just out of convenience, and it could actually be that abandoning any precise historical reference was the first renouncement, followed by many others, caused one after another by the difficulties stemming from simultaneously directing two versions, from the lack of time, from a series of simplifications, and from abandoning certain scenes. Today, *Elena and Her Men* produces the effect of a disaster-ridden film. Reading the director's stated opinions between the lines makes it obvious that he thought so, too.

The commercial failure of the film, although relative,* would turn out to be as harmful to Renoir's career as *The Woman on the Beach* had been. However, after that ultimate Hollywood experience, the director still had the will to fight, which had been inspired by his desire to make *The River*. *Elena*, on the other hand, left him feeling helpless. While in New York, he spent time with his old friend Albert Lewin, and together they contemplated pulling together an independent production company.[131] However, the results from the marketing of *Elena*—French, to begin with, and then, especially, American—led them to give up the idea.

During the first months of 1957, Renoir's bitterness focused exclusively on Deutschmeister, whom he couldn't forgive for having made possible, he thought, the massacre of the American version of the film. The person whom he'd described in writing in October 1956 as "probably the best French producer"[132] and a man for whom he harbored "true friendship"[133] had "wrested control of a new edit"[134] from him for this film that required "the most delicate edit of all those I have done."[135] On the other hand, the reproaches he leveled at the producer indirectly in his personal letters were not in any way attached to the conditions of production. He was only concerned with the American fate of the film.

It is true that most of his friends of that time were American or lived in the United States. Therefore, he had to insist that *Paris Does Strange Things*, which they had seen or would be able to see, wasn't his film. The French failure of the film was a disappointment for Renoir, but the American disaster was actually a humiliation. His reaction managed to show that. He was counting on the film

---

* All the same, the film would attract a total of a little over two million viewers by the time its distribution was finished. The twenty most successful films of 1956 were seen by an average of more than four million viewers.

to relaunch his Hollywood career, which was the one that, from all evidence, continued to count the most in his eyes. Ingrid Bergman's career had already taken a new turn, but that was thanks to Anatole Litvak's *Anastasia,* which had brought her the Oscar for best actress on March 27, 1957; and it would be followed by several other prestigious awards. His was at a standstill. "I don't see any film taking shape for me in Hollywood," he wrote. "*Elena* has ruined me,"[136] he wrote on August 9, 1957, thereby confirming the fact he'd put hopes in the project that had now vanished.

Had *Elena* really ruined him? No, because Hollywood had been finished with him after *The Woman on the Beach,* which was already ten years ago. Yes, because an American success would have allowed him to get back into the country's good graces. In Renoir's life and career, *Elena and Her Men* had everything of the fool's bargain about it. And it's not certain that Rossellini's writing to him, "Everything that is alive in modern cinema comes directly or indirectly from you,"[137] was any great consolation at the time.

On February 28, 1957, the Golden Globe for best actress was awarded to Ingrid Bergman for *Anastasia,* a film that Jean and Dido detested.[138] Kirk Douglas received the best actor award for *Lust for Life,* a performance that Renoir judged "grimacing."[139] The actress who had earned mostly sneers under Renoir's direction was now being awarded, as was the film he had dreamed of directing. At that point how could he *not* have thought that the time of film for him was over?

31

Kicked in the Head

Le Testament du docteur Cordelier (Experiment in Evil)
Le Déjeuner sur l'herbe (Picnic on the Grass)

All during the preparation and direction of *Elena and Her Men,* Renoir kept to his habit of continuing to work on other projects. In May, he put down in a notebook some ideas having to do with two projects: *La Lutte contre les conventions* and *Les Cailloux du chemin*[*1]—the second describing the life of a Mexican family that had entered California illegally. Just before finishing the shoot of his "Bergman movie," he also registered a project entitled *Le Feu aux poudres.*[2] But several weeks after he had returned to Los Angeles, in October 1956, no idea for a film seemed to give him pause, or at least not to the point of its having left any traces. It was something that had never happened since he'd become a director. He was working for the theater, preparing the Parisian direction of Clifford Odets's *The Big Knife* from a distance and thinking about his own play, which took place during the Occupation and that would become *Carola.* By January 1957, he had also already written the first chapter of his book about his father.[3]

By now, Gabrielle and Jeannot Slade had moved into their new house, a few steps away from Dido and Jean's. They had been living alone since the death of Gabrielle's husband on September 12, 1950, and in November 1954 the Slades bought one of the two lots still available on Leona Drive.[4] Gabrielle was now seventy-five. Her health was poor, and she rarely left her home anymore.[5] It was partly thanks to her and her memories that Renoir was able to complete the book about his father that he'd decided to write several years ago and had finally gotten down to several weeks before. For the time being, his daily conversations with Gabrielle provided him with notes that he used to compose the chapters he'd begun to "muddle through"[6] as 1957 began. He knew that the moment was coming when the woman who once again had become indispensable to him almost from the beginning of his time in America would be taken from him forever.

* *Translator's note:* Literally, "The Struggle against Conventions" and "The Pebbles on the Path."

Gabrielle, who still saw Renoir as a child, and Dido, who was his wife, friend, and secretary, together formed a duo to watch over Renoir. The two women understood each other perfectly and made every effort to protect Jean from the world, softening aspects of his life by smoothing away upsets and creating an atmosphere of well-being around him. The price for this at times entailed those little white lies that make the existence of those one loves more pleasant. For example, Jean made no secret of the fact that he detested the very principle of frozen food, so Dido and Gabrielle were careful not to mention in front of him that the vegetables they served came from a freezer, thereby allowing him to marvel at the benefits of that California climate that provided fresh peas regardless of the season.[7] And because the world was a decidedly wonderful place, it turned out that Gabrielle was an unparalleled cook, whereas Dido's food preparation skills were limited to opening a can. Guests who came to the Renoirs' often left the house on Leona Drive with a recipe for a dish they'd appreciated in their jacket pocket or handbag. It wasn't unusual for their hosts to receive letters a few days later that were almost as ecstatic as this one:

> Just a word to say that I tried your recipe for "Poulet Gabrielle" yester-day evening for Charlie and Jim Agee and that it was a hit—it was so wonderful!! Charlie had never been so impressed by anything else in his whole life. He kept saying that when we're together again, we'll be able to open a restaurant and serve that dish as our specialty. I think I did everything correctly—I added a lot of garlic, as you'd said—and with the olives and all the rest, it was delicious. I can't tell you to what point—but that's something you know already. I think I'd better put the recipe in our safe![8]

Sent to Dido, the letter is signed Oona. "Jim Agee" was the great writer and critic James Agee, the same person who'd been far from appreciative of *This Land Is Mine* and *The Southerner*. The "Charlie" who "had never been so impressed by anything else in his whole life" was none other than Charlie Chaplin.

In his memoirs, Renoir explains that Clifford Odets was the one who introduced him to Chaplin. Renoir states in that book that his relationship with Odets, which had begun in 1941, was one of the strongest in his life; and his admiration for the playwright's works includes Odets's films. He goes so far as to call Odets's *None but the Lonely Heart* (1944), with Cary Grant, a masterpiece, a distinction that occurs rarely—only once, in fact—in Renoir's written and spoken pronouncements, and especially when it comes to the films of his contemporaries. In 1957, Renoir created a sterling portrait of his friend: "A tall body topped by hair sticking out all over the place and gestures that go to the limit. When he raises his two arms to convince you, there's no end to them.

His fingers stretch toward the heavens as if he wanted to scrape the sky until the clouds burst."[9]

In *My Life and My Films,* Renoir also describes his last dinner at the home of Odets, who Renoir says was hospitalized the next day for supposedly routine tests but who would die less than a month later. Renoir says that Dido and he were the only guests that night. Odets's son, Walt, and daughter, Nora, served them dinner in the garden of the house on Beverly Drive. Odets had been divorced from Bette Grayson since 1952, and she had died of pneumonia on February 22, 1954.[*] At another, unspecified time, Renoir gave a more precise account of this dinner at Odets's, and that description appears in a biography of the playwright.[10] According to Renoir, the dinner took place on July 14, 1963. The garden where it was served had been unusable for several months as had the swimming pool near which the table was set up. Japanese lanterns hidden in the trees illuminated the setting. To the music of Mozart's concertos, Nora and Walt Odets served the dinner, which Clifford himself had prepared. It was accompanied by a Château Lascombes 1953, and Renoir spoke at length about his father painting right up to the point of his demise. Nora Odets was nineteen at the time, and Walt was sixteen.[†]

Today Walt is amused by the fact that Renoir, whom he adored, had indulged in his habit of "staging" his account of that evening. For one thing, Renoir situates it as happening on the evening of July 14; but this last dinner was actually not a farewell meal. It was not given by Clifford Odets the night before his hospitalization, but some three months before, and it certainly wasn't inspired by that occasion. Nothing distinguished it from the other dinners the Renoirs attended at the home of Odets and his children.[11]

Dido and Jean went every day to visit Odets in his room at Cedars Lebanon Hospital, where they also found visiting Shirley MacLaine, Cary Grant, Danny Kaye, and Harold Clurman, the critic and man of the theater.[12] Elia Kazan was often present. He described Renoir as an "enormous loaf of country bread," always focusing on the sick man, leaning over him, and kissing his hands. One day, starting with a discussion of the straw from which Clifford Odets was drinking, conversation focused on details of general ideas that were of little importance in themselves but whose consideration Renoir claimed he had made his rule of thumb. Kazan witnessed their farewells: Dido left the room, and Renoir "leaned over Odets and kissed his forehead. There was compassion in the kiss, but also the most profound humility in the face of suffering and death that

---

[*] Married to Luise Rainer from January 1937 to May 1940, Clifford Odets had wed Bette Grayson in May 1943.

[†] And not "fifteen years old" and "about twelve," as Renoir writes in *My Life and My Films.*

I had ever seen. Saying nothing, Renoir left."[13] Clifford Odets died the next day, on Saturday, August 10, 1963, four days before his fifty-seventh birthday. He'd wanted the Renoirs and Stella and Luther Adler to take legal responsibility for the care of his children. Jean was for it, but Dido refused.[14]

In spring 1956, Renoir began working on his French adaptation of Clifford Odets's play *The Big Knife,* which had been performed in New York with John Garfield in the lead role. Back on March 4, 1956, the author had granted Renoir "production, translation and adaptation rights for all the theaters in France."[15] Less than a month later, Renoir had already "translated two acts" and was saying he was certain that the third wouldn't take him "more than four or five days."[16] Six years later, when Renoir became interested in another Odets play, *Golden Boy,** he described his first experience translating Odets's work as follows: "I'd have to *betray it,* as I did for *The Big Knife,* which I hope he never reads in French. He'd hold it against me forever!"[17] While simultaneously preparing and filming *Elena and Her Men* and while he was working on the postsynchronization of that film in New York he thought about *The Big Knife* constantly.

A year before, Robert Aldrich, who had been Renoir's assistant on *The Southerner,* had adapted the play into a film, with Jack Palance playing Charlie Castle, a Hollywood actor who wants to rediscover the ambition he felt when he started out, partly to please his wife Marion (Ida Lupino). But he succumbs to the pressures—and soon, blackmail attempts—put upon him by his producer, Stanley Hoff (Rod Steiger). Thinking that the existence of this film, which hadn't yet been released, would put an end to Renoir's desire to do an adaptation, Odets had told him about it, but Renoir moved forward with his plans to adapt it for the stage.[18]

Renoir chose Daniel Gélin to play the lead in the stage adaptation. He talked Gélin up to Clifford Odets, promising he'd be "a great Charlie Castle,"[19] and compared him to John Garfield while presenting him as the "number 1 star of French film" whom "no producer could imagine doing without,"[20] a description which was in reality somewhat exaggerated. For the role of the producer, he was planning on casting Michel Simon, who'd already agreed to play the role in July 1956. Performances would begin in the provinces and then move to Paris—probably at the Théâtre des Mathurins—between November 15 and December 10, 1956, at the latest.[21] Jean Parédès, who had played Casca in the production of *Julius Caesar* in Arles, was part of the cast at that time, as was a

---

* Clifford Odets's greatest success, staged in 1937 with Luther Adler and Frances Farmer as the leads and Elia Kazan and John Garfield in supporting roles. It was brought to the screen in 1939 by Rouben Mamoulian, with Barbara Stanwyck and William Holden. Odets also adapted it into a musical, which was staged in 1964, after the death of the author.

young Annie Fargue, to whom Renoir claimed he was "deeply committed,"[22] although Michel Simon was against Micheline Presle's playing Marion.[23] As a result, Jean Serge, who was supposed to direct the play, contacted Nicole Courcel for the part.[24] Renoir thought she was "a great actress" but wondered whether she was "too young for Marion" and kept insisting, "The ace in our hand is having Michel Simon."[25] On August 12, he wrote Clifford Odets from New York, "Danielle Darrieux could play Marion."[26] In the meantime, he gave in to his enthusiasm for the project and began to regret "more and more not directing it"[27] himself. Directing *Elena and Her Men* wouldn't afford him the time, but, in the fall, the production was postponed and preparations were put on the shelf. On October 22, 1956, Gaston Gallimard agreed to Renoir's June request[28] to have the French translation of the play published.[29]

As a result, while in Los Angeles, Renoir went back to preparations for the play, to be called *Le Grand Couteau* in its French production; and it soon became clear that he'd have to rethink the casting completely. Michel Simon "pled that there were impossibilities and began dwelling on his financial problems as a pretext for requesting arrangements with the directors that were stupidly impractical."[30] Renoir wrote to Madame Doynel, "that puts the kibosh on the entire arrangement,"[31] and he didn't have much faith in Jean Serge's suggestion that he possibly entrust the role of Hoff to Charles Laughton or Peter Ustinov, worried as he was that "Charles would have a hard time with the French." Finally, the choice fell to Paul Bernard. He was an experienced actor, but in film as well as in theater his career was on the decline, and he was a lot less well known than Michel Simon. Stanley Hoff would be his last role.* When Michel Simon defected, Micheline Presle could be offered the role of Marion, which she liked a lot.[32] She wouldn't, however, end up being cast, and nor would Nicole Courcel. Claude Génia was chosen. Annie Fargue was out as well, replaced by Vera Norman, who'd discreetly ended her career as a film actress three years before when she'd married Luis Saslavsky, the director of her last film, *La neige était sale* (*Stain on the Snow*). The only cast member left over from the previous year was Daniel Gélin. *Le Grand Couteau* would be staged at the Théâtre des Bouffes-Parisiens, "with Pierre Lazareff contributing to the financing and promotion." "Previews" were to take place between October 1 and 5, 1957. Its sponsors were unhappy with the title, which they "accused of being drastically antipromotional."[33]

Given that both his film and theater projects had become more French than American, Renoir needed a point person in Paris. The death of Louis

---

* Bernard died on May 4, 1958, at the age of fifty-nine.

Guillaume in January 1956 had emphasized the urgency of such a necessity; but it would have been unlikely anyway that the person who had been the Renoir family's right-hand man* for forty years would have had an easy time fulfilling functions that demanded a perfect knowledge of the film milieu. Renoir found that one person in a million in the woman who had begun her career as his script girl on *The Golden Coach,* followed by *French Cancan* and *Elena.* Her name was Anne Marie Georgette Courtois, but she had chosen to keep the name of her husband, Pierre Doynel, whom she'd divorced in 1937 and who had died in 1945 after returning from a concentration camp. To her three first names, she preferred "Ginette" but would readopt "Anne" when she married Claude de Saint-Phalle in 1974. Born in 1900 in Tlemcen, Algeria,† Ginette Doynel was six years younger than Jean Renoir and seven years older than Dido. She and Renoir shared the same infirmity. During the war, on a train trip with her daughter in a cattle car, she had contracted polio. Superhuman efforts had led to her being able to walk again, at first with the aid of crutches, as she crossed the Seine each day by the Pont de l'Alma, one step at a time, to get to work.[34]

Beginning in 1956, Ginette Doynel occupied an essential place in Renoir's life as his contact to the French media, authorized representative, ally, factotum, and passionate admirer. Whether it was a matter of dealing with a distributor, getting back a print, tracking down a bad debtor, suggesting names of technicians to Vincente Minnelli—who was in France for *An American in Paris*—or even sending a gift to California for a birth occurring among Renoir's circle of friends, she took care of everything from her office on avenue Frochot. After Gabrielle's death in 1959, she took her place with Dido as one of the women in the triangle in which Renoir occupied the pivotal point, the reason for the triangle's existence. It was an unusual form of geometry, but it had been a primary source of equilibrium for Renoir the child, when Gabrielle and his mother formed two of the sides. And he had re-created this arrangement as soon as he settled in California, between Gabrielle and Dido, and then between Dido and Ginette. This time, the two women lived fifty-six hundred miles from each other. When Jean was alone in Paris, Ginette looked after him. She monitored his intake of alcohol and his desultory attempts at dieting, reporting all of it to Dido.

This isn't to say that things always proceeded smoothly. Jealousy had its

* Renoir referred to him as his "private secretary."

† In 1974, when Madame Doynel was trying to obtain her birth records for her next marriage, she wrote to Renoir, "Not a single step of progress since 1962. One certainly can't ruffle the feathers of these 'little angels.'" (June 6, 1974, Jean Renoir Papers, Correspondence, Box 30, Folder 6.)

place in their relationship. In Ginette's eyes, Dido sometimes seemed to "forget" that her husband was a genius to whom she ought to submit completely. Dido thought at times that Ginette took liberties that went beyond the sphere of her functions. Signs of their antagonism sometimes appeared in the correspondence they exchanged, and certain letters are rather harsh; but, in general, at least appearances remained intact. This correspondence between the Renoirs and Ginette Doynel is a gold mine of incredible information. Three times a week on average, a letter left Paris for Beverly Hills. It contained a large sheet of paper blackened on both sides by typed single-spaced lines, organized under headings. Dido, or Renoir himself, answered nearly every one of these missives. Mme. Doynel's virulent anti-Communist and anti-Gaullist commentaries on French political life, which also appear in the correspondence, were, on the other hand, rarely dealt with. Mme. Doynel signed her letters "la Joconde" or, more often, "la Gourde."† Jean Renoir's name in them was "the Maestro," and Dido's was "the Maestrotte." Doynel continued to work as a script girl, but very occasionally. After filling that function in 1956 for the filming of Raymond Rouleau's *Les Sorcières de Salem* (*The Crucible*), which was edited by Marguerite Renoir, she did not work at it again until 1963, for Alain Jessua's *La Vie à l'envers* (*Life Upside Down*).

A persistent legend holds that Truffaut not only named his company Films de Carrosse in homage to *The Golden Coach* (a fact) but also called his hero and alter ego Doinel in reference to Ginette Doynel. For one thing, it's improbable that Truffaut had anything to do with Mme. Doynel before Antoine Doinel came into existence. During that time, his relationship with Renoir had been limited to those periods when Renoir was in Paris, and Truffaut therefore would have had no need of her to be in contact with him. If he did meet her, then, it would have been in her capacity as a script girl during the making of a film. Moreover and more convincingly, Claude Gauteur was close to Truffaut at this time, and Truffaut shared his reflections with him regarding his character's name. The director had wanted to base it on the name of a friend of his at *Cahiers du cinéma*, Jacques Doniol-Valcroze. Doniol-Valcroze sometimes wrote for that magazine under the pseudonym "Étienne Loinod," and by considering Loinod in light of its origin, Doniol, Truffaut arrived at Doinel.[35]

Starting in 1956, Renoir had invested Ginette Doynel with the power to represent him officially, and one of her first important missions was to collaborate closely on the rerelease of *Grand Illusion*. On April 17, 1956, Renoir and

* *Translator's note:* "la Gourde" = French for "Dumbbell" or "Dimwit."

† The actor Pierre Olaf (Pierrot in *French Cancan*), a close friend of the Renoirs, referred to Mme. Doynel with the nickname "Durandal" (a reference to the magical sword of the medieval knight Roland).

Charles Spaak had become the sole owners of "worldwide" rights for the film, after having repurchased them following RAC's bankruptcy.[36] For five years, searches throughout Europe had been taking place to recoup a negative of the 1937 version, thought to have been destroyed during a bombardment of Paris in 1942. A copy had been located in Munich in 1945 and was returned to the French authorities in Mayence, but it had been misplaced. In 1956, Ginette Doynel and the editor Renée Lichtig had to work with three incomplete prints to establish a version that was presentable. It was shown for the first time on November 13 for Spaak and his wife, Lucienne Wattier (one of Renoir's agents), Claude Renoir, and Joseph de Bretagne, among others. Dialogue for the scene showing the death of Boëldieu had to be recorded again to prevent parts of it from being inaudible in a large theater.[37]

On November 30, 1956, Renoir wrote to Lucienne Wattier to ask her to seek the help of Pierre Fresnay,[38] as well as Stroheim, who was now living in Maurepas, not far from Versailles.[39] Stroheim's response is dated January 3, 1957. He was happy to redo that scene; but, "Because—there is a but! You see, right now I cannot walk, I can't even move. For a period of four five months I am condemned to remain motionless flat on my back, and there is no truss, or 'mentonnière,' the like of which I wore in the Grande Illusion that can help that poor decalcified spine of mine."[40] With wonderful courage, the sick man suggested recording the dialogue at his home, if it was possible to send a sound engineer to that location. Renoir then let him know that there was no hurry.[41] In reality, Stroheim was suffering from cancer of the spinal tissue, from which he would not recover. At the end of March 1957, dressed in black silk pajamas, he received the medal of the Chevalier of the Légion d'honneur from the hands of René Clair. On April 8, Denise Vernac, Stroheim's last companion, wrote to Renoir, "Your name was on everyone's lips. . . . You definitely hold the largest place among all the friends who had come to share his pride and joy for a brief moment. Ever since Grand Illusion, no one has been able to pronounce Erich's name in France without associating it with yours."[42]

Erich von Stroheim passed away on May 12, 1957, at the age of seventy-one. A week later, Charles Spaak sent an account of the funeral to Renoir. At the church, the violinists from the Monseigneur, the cabaret that the deceased had frequented, played some Viennese melodies. Then, on arrival to the cemetery, about fifty cows had begun following the casket, "an episode worthy of Greed." No one in attendance, among which were "six screenwriters, five directors, and an actor," would mount the little platform to say a few words. "All of us refused, understanding that you don't improvise just anything at all before the coffin of Von Stroheim." Then: "To be honest, I do have to add that a director, detained at the studio for a section that he was adding to his complete works, had sent an enormous wreath bedecked with a violet ribbon on which letters written in gold spelled out: 'To Eric . . . Léonide.'"[43]

All the work searching for a copy of *Grand Illusion* and all the work on restoration using elements that were available would turn out to be unnecessary. In 1957, Renée Lichtig discovered a copy in excellent condition at the Cinémathèque française, on rue d'Ulm. On October 30 of that year, it was shown for Renoir there.[44] At the time, Renoir founded a company with Spaak called "Compagnie R. S." (Renoir Spaak). Ginette Doynel would manage it. Her principal duty was to market the film, which had a third Parisian release on October 6, 1958. When Spaak withdrew from the company in 1959, it became "Compagnie Jean Renoir" and was composed of two associates, Jean Renoir and Ginette Doynel. She became its manager, and each of them became entitled to five hundred parts of a nominal value of one hundred francs. Twenty years later, shortly after the death of Renoir, since "the capital had declined by three-quarters," the value of each part would be no greater than twenty-five francs.[45]

As Renoir himself would remark with a kind of surprised and amused irony, he was becoming a "business man." Although the primary reason for the creation of his "company" remained the marketing of *Grand Illusion* and, soon after, certain additional films he had made, it was also a response to a particular feature of his personal situation. Renoir was living in the United States where, naturally, his revenue was taxed; but he was visiting France regularly, and his stays there were expensive, especially because he was used to living high on the hog. Moreover, the fees he was receiving for work in France were also being taxed. It was natural for him to deduct the costs entailed from his revenue when they involved business expenses, and therefore these were picked up not by the individual Jean Renoir but by the company named after him. The issue of being doubly taxed—in America and in France—would remain crucial until the end of his life, and the situation involved a game of hide-and-seek in which Renoir and his consultants made every effort to represent him officially as making no income in France. For this reason, the fees that he earned—especially for the sale of his books—were paid to a Swiss account.

Although it is commonly believed that a director needs to work, such a fact immediately becomes camouflaged by a kind of obviousness that prevents him from being questioned. And yet, although a director does work in order to exist, he also does so to live. Because the sums that his art generates are considerable, the relationship between a director and money is bound to be a special one. The question isn't whether Renoir needed money to live; it's more about considering

---

* At the time, Léonide Moguy was directing *Donnez-moi ma chance* (or *Piege à filles*; English title: *Give Me My Chance*) in the Billancourt studios.

one truth: during the entire period of preparation, direction, and editing and the period that follows right up to the release of a film, a director/producer is living off the costs of production.* The reasons that motivate a director to become a producer of his own film are many, ranging from the need to compensate for a lack of offers to the wish to remain master of his own creation; but the desire to control financial contributions while benefiting from them in the process, even if this only involves tax exemptions, is not simply for the record. Although the Compagnie Jean Renoir became a coproducer of *Le Testament du docteur Cordelier* (*Experiment in Evil*), its purpose was not to participate directly in the financing of the film but to reap Renoir the advantages he rightfully expected from that arrangement.

The statements regarding that perfectly natural practice are conserved in the account books that reflect each franc drawn from "Maestro's little cashbox," which is how Mme. Doynel termed it: the restaurant dinner with Pierre Gaut, the melba toast and toilet paper, the champagne "with Ingrid," the dress and blouse for "Mme. Freire," the flowers given Marguerite Cassan, the Maestro's Gillette razor blades and shirts, the Nescafé and Nestlé canned milk, the aperitif served to the workers at the Bouffes-Parisiens, the sausage, sardines and oranges, the Christmas presents for the mailman and the tip for the telegraph boy, the daily newspaper and the box of Suponéryl, the stamps, and even "handouts to unidentified parties," such as panhandlers. Everything was recorded. Even documented was the fact that Renoir bought himself "Céline's book" in October 1957. It was probably *D'un château l'autre* (*Castle to Castle*), which had been in bookstores since June.[46]

Although Renoir had "taken three months to regain the strength to go back to work"[47] after *Elena and Her Men,* he wouldn't allow himself to concentrate exclusively on the book about his father and the idea he had for a new play. Film remained his profession, and writing and directing screenplays were his main sources of income. He also suspected that the writing of his book *Renoir* would demand a great deal of time.[48] He briefly considered a new film with Ingrid Bergman, inspired by "a book a bit out of date"[49] whose title he didn't disclose to the actress. It was the novel *Sleeveless Errand* (1929) by Nora James, which had been banned in England in its time; consequently, "the end being a suicide† should be changed."[50]

However, Renoir did his best to think long term. This was what he explained

---

* Although this is no longer always the case today, it was in the times of Renoir, who, naturally, became used to that reality.

† Actually, a double suicide.

after having developed a strategy with his American agents. Its first step entailed the direction "a year from now of a film with Negros for Hecht-Hill-Lancaster."[51] About this project he revealed no other details. Harold Hecht and James Hill had worked with Burt Lancaster to produce Robert Aldrich's films *Apache* and *Vera Cruz* and had just produced Alexander Mackendrick's *Sweet Smell of Success,* with a screenplay by Clifford Odets. According to Renoir's agenda, he would next move on to "producing or directing *Manon* or another film with Leslie, to be shot in France or England, [and then] in two years, *Chair et cuir,** possibly in English and hopefully with Alec Guinness." These two films "would be produced in Europe, probably in Paris."[52]

Informed on March 22 that the rights for *Chair et cuir,*[53] the novel by Felicien Marceau from which he hoped to adapt his "most important film since *The River,*"[54] had already been purchased by an English producer, just as had those for *L'Oeuf,*† the theatrical adaptation of the book, Renoir gave up the project because he found it "too complicated."[55] In the meantime, New York journalist Alice Hughes had been suggesting that Renoir become interested in the Jean Dutourd novel *Doucin* (1955), which had been published in the United States under the title *5 a.m.,* and which he could use to "make a movie for Joan Crawford."[56] Renoir's response was, "I know Jean Dutourd through his book *Au bon beurre,* which I greatly admire. I am sure anything he writes is worthwhile. And the idea of directing Joan Crawford is exciting."[57] Two weeks later, a new letter stated that he and Dido had been filled with enthusiasm by the book and that Miss Crawford, whose talent he admired immensely, would be extraordinary in such a role.[58]

The idea for it would remain there, as would the project to adapt *Manon Lescaut,* which Renoir wanted to propose to Metro and about which he wrote to Leslie Caron. "Clouzot has used the title *Manon* for a very fine film vaguely inspired by *Manon Lescaut.*‡ But his story has nothing to do with the real *Manon,* which remains one of the most powerful stories of the eighteenth century. Manon is a great role in which you would be wonderful because of your innocent look. It would also be a great film if we could get away from the insipidness with which the musicians of the nineteenth century, like Massenet and Puccini, encumbered that daring subject."[59]

* *Translator's note:* Literally, "Flesh and Leather."

† *Translator's note:* "The Egg."

‡ With Cécile Aubry, Serge Reggiani, Michel Auclair (1949).

Very quickly, he turned toward another idea and dwelled on it for a long time. Simenon had insisted that he reread *Trois chambres à Manhattan* (1946),* and he had reserved its film rights for Renoir. Renoir declared that he was taken by the idea: "The role of the woman, which would be modified," he wrote to Leslie Caron, "would be wonderful for you. It's just a matter of making her younger. She's a wreck, but you can be a wreck at the age of twenty."[60] Without waiting, he even pulled together an initial treatment, bolstered as he was by the commitment of the young actress, "who's proving to be remarkably faithful and full of energy and refusing a big production so she can make this with me."[61] Once again, there was the possibility of Metro's being interested, and filming would be in New York the following winter. But a few days later, the first answer came. The new treatment for *Trois chambres à Manhattan* that had been submitted to Metro hadn't been convincing. Renoir concluded from this that he didn't know "how to write treatments."[62] When Leslie Caron suggested to him that he have the screenplay written by Clifford Odets, his response was that "it would be wonderful!"[63] However, the playwright would stubbornly refuse to consider it.[64]

Winter arrived without any of his projects' progressing. The house on Leona Drive was on the way to becoming what it would be until the end of the seventies, an obligatory stopping-off place for French actors and directors staying in California. Accordingly, on April 18, a dinner at the Renoirs' included Micheline Presle, Françoise Arnoul, Gérard Philipe, and Jean Marais, who'd come to take part in the San Francisco International Film Festival.[65] Charming and warm, full of humor, and a master without rival of the art of conversation, Jean Renoir as host was appreciated for his personality and admired by everyone for the films he had directed; but his celebrity itself, combined with his distance from Europe, had reinvented him as a monument. And monuments, as full of vitality as they may be, belong to the past. Renoir the individual and the name were in demand, but film, it was believed, could do without the director's genius. He himself wasn't taken in. He understood that although the promoters of *Le Grand Couteau* wanted him to be in Paris, it was because they were counting on his name to attract the spotlights. "Dido had an idea. If the production is reimbursing me for the costs of travel and my stay, it's in return for a certain kind of publicity that my participation in the direction will bring the play. Despite the 'cinematic' implications of the word *supervision,* I think it should be agreed that the billing credit me with 'Supervision by Jean Renoir.' I don't want to take away the moral benefit of the direction from Jean Serge. Of course, I expect to become completely involved in that direction with Jean Serge."[66]

* Translator's note: Titles of the English translations of the book are *Three Rooms in Manhattan* and *Three Bedrooms in Manhattan.*

On September 10, 1957, Renoir arrived in Paris alone, and the same evening, he went to the theater where he watched the rehearsals and participated until two in the morning in choosing the details for the costumes and scenery.[67] A week later, a piddling little photo of the director appeared on the front page of *Arts*, along with boxed text having him say, "I don't believe in structured theater."[68] The article was composed of statements collected by François Truffaut, who immediately declared that he was furious about the treatment inflicted on his text, and he confided his rage to Renoir: "I have been indignant and miserable about the idea that you could think I was the instigator of that stupidity. . . . The text I handed in was twice as long. 'They' cut some of my questions, a lot of your statements, clumsily connected one fragment to another."[69] With his message, Truffaut included the very virulent letter he had sent to André Parinaud, the editor in chief of the weekly.

The day after his arrival, Renoir lunched with Paul and Micheline Meurisse. Here he was, back in the milieu of Paris for a little less than three months. The letters he wrote to Dido during his entire stay make it possible to follow his activities almost from day to day, and certain details give rise at best to doubt, and at worst to uneasiness. For example, on Saturday, October 26, he informed his wife that he was planning to lunch with "Peck,* Floflo,† Pierre Gaut, Maud‡" the following Tuesday, and this information was followed by the sentence, "We'll be chewing up Israelites."[70] Is it to be concluded from this that to share a meal with friends whose opinions one would like to believe weren't his, Renoir the chameleon would be espousing—at least on the level of humor—their anti-Semitic witticisms, which, moreover, apparently were not offensive to Dido, as if she were accustomed to them? The most alarming thing about the remark, however, in its connection to Renoir resides in the choice of the word "Israelite," which seems to be derived directly from the anti-Semitic diatribes that occurred before the war. Wasn't Jean Renoir aware of what had happened in Europe in the meantime?

Maud and Pierre Gaut attended the premiere of *Le Grand Couteau* on October 5, 1957.[71] That evening, as would all the members of the audience who saw the play through January 26, 1958, which was the last performance, they

---

* Sedley Peck, an American journalist who'd been living in France since World War I, after serving in the Lafayette squadron. By the time of this luncheon, he and his wife were living in California, in the San Gabriel Canyon Valley, but were visiting France.

† Dolores "Floflo" Peck, Sedley Peck's wife.

‡ Pierre Gaut's wife.

also viewed a Jean Renoir film called *Un tigre sur la ville.** It consisted of a single shot lasting around ten seconds, presented as an excerpt from a film with Charlie Castle. A tracking shot showed Daniel Gélin hit by a bullet and collapsing to the ground and ended with a close-up of the actor. Today that reel is considered to have been lost.

"The play ended with a lot of curtain calls," wrote Ginette Doynel to Dido, "and the line, 'I'm putting my money in government bonds' was a big hit, which proves that people forget that this takes place in America and think that in France it would be the same."[72] Renoir had been careful beforehand to win over audiences, writing in the theater program that *Le Grand Couteau* "has found its best milieu in Paris," and even that "this play could only be performed here" since "Parisian audiences have just the right dose of optimism and despair, resentment and generosity to make it possible for them to share the author's preoccupations completely."[73] A few months before, he had depicted the same audiences quite differently, following the failure of the French version of a George Bernard Shaw play starring Valentine Tessier, *Mrs. Warren's Profession:* "We're witnessing the triumph of the grocer. And the grocer wants sentimentality. He also wants some smut and suspense. But above all, he wants to snivel about some fictional situations. It flatters him because he thinks he's a good person, and it makes up for his remorse at having rooked his customers. Tragic situations don't make him cry, because they're beyond him."[74]

To the extent that the preview for *Orvet* had been cold, the one for *Le Grand Couteau* on October 9 was "triumphant,"[75] which was in no way a prediction of how the critics would react, as Renoir advised Clifford Odets: "It's in fashion now to act brutal and try to present every event with a kind of acidic, destructive humor, and Jean Renoir turning up from California and giving a successful performance on the most Parisian of stages is a choice target."[76] Renoir would later maintain that the evening inspired an article whose author claimed that he had "seen someone in the audience who should be invited to all the previews, because he was having such a great time," and that this audience member was none other than Renoir himself, who explained that he always has a good time and that if he didn't, he wouldn't be doing this kind of work.[77] *Le Grand Couteau* wasn't a remarkably amusing play, and it certainly didn't have enough laughs to be attributed to any spectator other than the author of the French text, someone who also can't very willingly be imagined actually taking a seat in the theater. By the following day, Renoir was referring to *Le Grand Couteau* as "perhaps the most wonderful experience that I've ever had, including my own films."[78] It shouldn't be forgotten that his letter was intended for Clifford Odets.

* *Translator's note:* Literally, "A Tiger in the City."

"There's not a minute of boredom,"[79] wrote Jean-Jacques Gautier on October 10, and his review set the tone. During that second half of the fifties, the contemporary English-language theater was triumphing. Marcel Aymé was translating Arthur Miller (*A View from the Bridge*). England was discovering John Osborne and *Look Back in Anger*, and the Parisian production of *Le Grand Couteau* was part of this trend. Above all, the play offered audiences an immersion in the Hollywood jungle, which was still an object of curiosity and fascination. Its revelation of evil and brutality rarely failed to appeal, offering a harsh counterpoint to the sleek images in films and popular magazines. In the play, Clifford Odets was showing the underbelly of a Hollywood that in some way had become a part of the past since the original creation of the play in 1949. In the eyes of Renoir and, probably, the audience—even if they weren't really conscious of it—this increased its attraction. Although the character of the producer was "likeable" to Renoir, as he stated at the time, that character also belonged to a category that had disappeared. "The time of the Hoffs is over. People have no passion any more. Imagine if a man like Thalberg had presented *Elena*. Either he would have destroyed it completely—tossed it into the wastebasket—or else, the opposite. He could have enriched its meaning, asked to add things that matched its spirit. Today, on the other hand, the tendency is to reduce, to create a type of middlebrow product. The tendency is for insipid fare."[80]

The show actually was a success, and that accomplishment could only encourage Renoir along the parallel track that he was following. For several months he'd been working on *Judith*, a play about the theater, taking place during the Occupation. Already on the evening of the preview of *Le Grand Couteau* he'd decided, "This performance has put me back in the 'media spotlight.'" He had also "thought of probably taking advantage of it to find a place for *Judith* after having gotten rid of implausibilities caused by my ignorance of the situation during the war."[81] The first reviews confirmed his good impression. "The reviews aren't raves. But they were so enough to create a positive climate in Paris."[82] Some of them were far from loving, but Renoir claimed that it was of "prime unimportance" to him that Max Favalelli had lamented the fact that he "lacks the lyricism of Bob Aldrich" because "the fuss made about *Le Grand Couteau* definitively classifies me as an auteur of the theater and is preparing the way for *Judith*."[83] Having decided not to go back to Los Angeles before his new play had been staged, he worked relentlessly with Mme. Doynel, asking her to make the press believe that he'd left for a few days for the South, so that he could have more freedom.

At the end of October, Renoir decided that *Judith* was "exact enough from the point of view of 'occupation' to give it to people to read,"[84] despite the fact that it needed "quite a bit more work." By then he seems to have given up the idea of offering it to Ingrid Bergman because he preferred that Carola (the character whose name would later become the title of the piece) have no accent. Soon he was thinking of Danielle Darrieux and intended to have the text read by Jean Meyer, who was the director of the Comédie-Française.

Renoir was becoming as full of nervous energy as he had been in the good old days. For television he recorded the broadcast of *La Joie de vivre*, to be shown on November 2. If Mary Meerson[*] is to be believed, a screening of *The Diary of a Chambermaid* rocked[85] the theater on rue d'Ulm. He had also handed in the initial treatment of the screenplay *Villa de l'extra*,[86] based on a synopsis of *Paris Province*. During the final days of November, Danielle Darrieux signaled her willingness[87] to take the role of Carola in his play, and an enthusiastic Paul Meurisse wrote to Dido, "Danielle Darrieux is carried away by the play, and I will bow out of the Comédie-Française."[88]

In Paris, Renoir also came back into contact with André Daven, who had signed him with Fox in 1941. After returning to France, Daven had just coproduced *The Grand Maneuver* with René Clair; and he also seemed interested in Renoir's new idea for Leslie Caron, a film that was "a thousand times more interesting than *Trois chambres à Manhattan*."[89] "He'd like me to pair Pierre Brasseur with Yves Montand and use Brasseur in the role of an old man," Renoir wrote about the subject, but then Daven made a mistake: "To convince us, he sent Ginette and me to see René Clair's *Porte des Lilas*.[†] . . . We've rarely been that bored by a film, and the enthusiasm of the company Cinédis for their products worries me a little."[90]

On December 3, Renoir left Paris for London, where he met with Leslie Caron. Then he went to visit Dido's mother in Liverpool. On December 10, he boarded the *Sylvania* for New York, arrived a week later, and on the 21st took a plane.[91] By that time, none of the hopes he had for *Judith* had borne fruit, and there was no definite project in view. A little less than a year later, he'd write that the only asset attached to his play was "Martine Carol's good intentions."[92]

Back in Beverly Hills at the end of 1958, he discovered Leona Drive lit up by the immense Christmas tree that Harold Lloyd had had planted in his garden, just opposite the Renoirs' house.[93] Alain, his wife, and their two sons—John, who was turning six on December 27, and Peter, who'd been born on May 31, 1954—were visiting from Berkeley, where Alain was now teaching medieval

* Henri Langlois's lover, who had also attended the premiere of *Le Grand Couteau*.

† With Georges Brassens, Pierre Brasseur, and Dany Carrel.

English literature.* Alain wouldn't speak about his mother to John, Peter, or his daughter, Anne (who would be born in September 1960), for quite some time. None of them would learn that Dido wasn't their grandmother, as their father had made them believe, before they had practically become adults.[94] When the family went to France for a few weeks in the summer and fall of 1967, Alain concealed a visit to his mother, Catherine, from his children.

Renoir's world had become the place where his family lived, much more so than Paris, which for him contained nothing more than an ambience of nostalgia. Now it was France where he felt uprooted, far from Dido, the children, Gabrielle and Jean Slade, and his dachshunds. Nearly all of his letters from France asked for news about the dogs. Tambo had died in September 1956 at an advanced age. All that was left was Nénette, Tambo's daughter. "We're living on our hill in Beverly Hills, about as isolated as monks in a monastery,"[95] he wrote to Pierre Gaut. This was where his life was, where he worked on the book about his father, where he reworked *Judith,* transforming the play into *Carola.* However, when he did at times come down from his hill to direct, it wasn't to do so in American studios or theaters, close as they were. He had to cross the Atlantic.

It wasn't for lack of trying. He asked Dudley Nichols to translate *Carola* into English. At this point, a future for the play seemed more American than French. There was soon a good reason for this: Curd† Jürgens. He was the only German actor of that time who was known outside his country and who was supposed to debut on Broadway. The role of the general in Renoir's play would have been appropriate for him, but he wanted an original creation, not an adaptation of a play that had already been performed elsewhere. That made it preferable that *Carola* not be directed in Paris first.[96] Not to mention the fact that the play hadn't yet attracted much attention in Paris, except among actors, and not among theater directors. Renoir had written to Deborah Kerr, whom he'd seen in *Heaven Knows, Mr. Allison,* directed by John Huston, and told her he was "very impressed" by her "magnificent interpretation." He offered to have her sent a translation of *Carola.*[97] Months, then years, would pass before he'd give up directing *Carola* for the stage because no stage wanted it.

The only performances of the play while Renoir was living took place in

---

* The relationship between father and son was also reflected in their shared love for classic texts, as evidenced by this remark in a letter from Renoir to his secretary: "Alain must be better. His last letter was completely devoted to the analysis of a line in fourteenth-century English that I had mistakenly attributed to Chaucer." (Letter to Ginette Doynel, October 10, 1956, Jean Renoir Papers, Correspondence, Box 13, Folder 9.)

† *Translator's note:* Curd Jürgens (1915–1982) was usually billed in English-speaking countries as "Curt Jurgens."

Berkeley in May 1960. Amateur actors who were all students put on seven performances on the stage of the Wheeler Auditorium. Renoir spoke about his films to his actors, who weren't familiar with them. Several of the films were shown on the same occasions in the context of a retrospective devoted to him. As a result, the students saw *Grand Illusion*, about which Renoir claimed, "Goebbels had ordered all available copies in Europe destroyed."[98] This was followed by *Picnic on the Grass, Swamp Water, The Southerner, Nana, The Golden Coach*, and *The River*. The day before the first dress rehearsal of the play, he explained the disastrous fate of *The Rules of the Game*, pointing out that "the day after its first public showing, the distributors drastically reduced the length."[99] A screening of a restored copy was organized soon after and attended by Dido and Alain Renoir. Several months later, it would be shown in New York, on January 28, 1961.

Carola's premiere took place on May 13, 1960. The eponymous role was played by Deneen Peckinpah, who hadn't yet turned twenty-one. The other actors were also very young, and that experience in theater would remain the only one they would ever have.[100] The student who played Campan was Syd Field, and Renoir impressed him to such a degree that several months later he visited him in Los Angeles and decided to give up studying medicine for film. He would write a number of works on the technique of screenwriting and create a captivating portrait of Renoir in which he mentioned the parallel created by the director between trying on a costume and adjusting the character to the personality of the person playing him or her.[101] It's also thanks to Syd Field that it is known that Aldous Huxley attended one of the performances in May 1960 and that Ray Manzarek, who created the Doors five years later with Jim Morrison, was fascinated by *Grand Illusion* and by everything having to do with Renoir.

After the play had been performed in Berkeley, Renoir finally proposed it to Ingrid Bergman, for whom he'd written it. But she didn't like the role.‡ A more "diplomatic" version of the story claimed that she declined out of consideration for Leslie Caron. At any rate, Bergman claimed to be too busy setting up her new house near Paris. Renoir would next think of Simone Signoret. Burgess Meredith wrote to him that he adored the text, but in the same letter he confessed that he was powerless to get the play produced.[102] Renoir's agents

‡ According to Norman Lloyd, when he directed *Carola* for television, he was so determined to have Leslie Caron for the role that, one day, when Dido Renoir called him to tell him that Ingrid Bergman was at their home and wanted to meet him, he chose not to come because he was certain that the actress wanted to convince him to give her the role of Carola. Norman Lloyd did not know at the time that Ingrid Bergman had made it known in October 1960 that she did not want to play Carola. (Jean Renoir Papers, Correspondence, Box 16, Folder 10.)

would admit the same thing. The people of the theater thought *Carola* was too dated and too European a play to appeal to a New York audience. One of them wrote explaining that Anouilh's *Mademoiselle Colombe* had failed on Broadway, and he didn't see how *Carola* could succeed.[103]

In Renoir's life, the play was something of a work under a curse. When it was suggested in 1972 that he record it for television, his health forced him to decline the offer and to ask Norman Lloyd to produce and direct it in his place. That was how Leslie Caron finally became Carola, acting opposite Mel Ferrer, Albert Paulsen, Michael Sacks, and Anthony Zerbe, among others. It was a very fine cast, but because of its length, the text had to be pruned, with permission of the author. The adaptation was credited to James Bridges.* However, according to Norman Lloyd, Bridges essentially only adapted some of the dialogue, because the translation wasn't considered to be satisfactory,† and insisted on appearing in the credits, eager to see his name associated with Renoir's. Rehearsals began on October 18, 1972, and the play was performed in its theatrical continuity, as would also be done for its recording, in scenery designed by Eugène Lourié that consisted of a dressing room and a corridor. Three cameras, whose movements had been choreographed at length, recorded simultaneously, which allowed the performance to be shot in continuous action in the studios of KCET on Sunset Boulevard, which Monogram had used for its productions, followed by Allied Artists.

PBS broadcast *Carola* on February 6, 1973. In June 1974, Renoir received a letter from someone who wanted to express his "fascination and admiration for the teleplay *Carola*."[104] He wanted to use the text for the courses he was giving at the University of Southern California. His name was John Milius, and he was the author of the screenplays *Jeremiah Johnson* and *The Life and Times of Judge Roy Bean,* among others. At the time, he had begun adapting Conrad's *Heart of Darkness,* which would become Francis Ford Coppola's *Apocalypse Now.* Norman Lloyd offered Renoir a screening of the broadcast on a Sunday morning, January 4, 1976,[105] but there is no evidence that the director went to see it and, thus, he may have never witnessed the televised version of *Carola.*

In 1962, François Truffaut sought permission to present a radio-play version of *Carola* for Europe 1, starring Marie Dubois.[106] All he knew of the play at the time were the excerpts of it that *Cahiers du cinéma* had published. In his

---

* Screenwriter, producer, and director who worked in the theater for a long time. One of his better-known films is *The China Syndrome* (1979).

† The credits list Robert and Angela Goldsby for the translation. They were the authors of several translations for the theater, from Corneille to Victorien Sardou. Dido Renoir also receives a translation credit, although there is no proof that she actually collaborated on it.

answer, Renoir recommended that he begin by reading "the version closest to the English adaptation."[107] To Mme. Doynel, Renoir as well wrote, "Since I have lost hope in seeing *Carola* presented in a theater, maybe this 'radio production' [Truffaut's] will rejuvenate this poor forgotten thing, in which, I must admit, I've lost all interest,"[108] The project wouldn't come to pass. However, Truffaut may have remembered *Carola* when he was writing the screenplay for *Le Dernier Métro* (*The Last Metro*) from winter 1978 to summer 1979, which was just before and after the death of Renoir.

Leslie Caron was one of the first to become aware of the coincidental similarities between Truffaut's film and Renoir's play, which she had performed on American television in 1973. Three years before that, she had loaned Truffaut her personal copy of the text for it to be published by *L'Avant-Scène* in November 1976. Shortly after the release of *The Last Metro* on September 17, 1980, she spoke about it to the director, for whom she had acted in *L'Homme qui aimait les femmes* (*The Man Who Loved Women*):

> My relationship with him was in no way egalitarian. I thought of myself as his student, and so I confessed my astonishment to him with a great deal of respect and caution. To my great surprise, he answered very curtly, cut me short, and refused to talk about it. I was shocked that he'd made no mention of the play, didn't even acknowledge Jean Renoir in the credits, even though it would have been so simple to dedicate the film to him. And while it was playing, he never mentioned *Carola* to journalists. As a result, we didn't see or speak to each other for two years. It was only when he sensed he was close to the end that he called me and that I went to see him.[109]

In addition, the director heard that his film had provoked "disappointment" in Mme. Doynel, who by then had become Mme. de Saint-Phalle, and she'd shared it with Dido: "Don't think I have anything against him for being inspired—oh so much—by *Carola*. What shocked me is the fact that it [the play] wasn't mentioned in the credits for this film. As you are, I'm certain that Jean Renoir would have been thrilled by his success."[110]

Three weeks later, Truffaut wrote to Dido:

> I've cleared up my disagreement with Anne de Saint-Phalle. Contrary to what I was thinking, it wasn't about the election of François Mitterrand* but about *The Last Metro*, which she felt was too close to *Carola*. Part of her reproach has to do with my not mentioning *Carola* in my interviews as a source of inspiration. Her letter left me in shock, and

---

* *Translator's note:* Mme. Doynel was strongly against Mitterrand.

I answered her very quickly, saying that the problem had been about Suzanne Schiffman and I not wanting to be accused of copying the Lubitsch film *To Be or Not to Be,* which deals with the same subject with the same elements, but with a more farcical tone. Moreover, while shooting *La Nuit américaine* [*Day for Night*] or *Baisers volés* (*Stolen Kisses*), every time I show male-female relationships, it's impossible for me not to think of Jean Renoir, impossible not to question myself about the solutions that he would have found to resolve this or that problem. That is what I wanted to express in the Dieppe catalogue when I said, "We will continue to imitate Jean Renoir without ever forgetting that he is impossible to imitate." Anne de Saint-Phalle, I think, was satisfied with my answer, which will allow us to maintain a good relationship. I wanted you to know about that development.[111]

Although *The Last Metro*'s direction would turn out to be as little like Renoir's as possible, there's no doubt that Renoir himself ever wrote a message that was more "Renoirian" than Truffaut's. In return for it, Truffaut would receive a letter from Dido assuring him of her friendship and categorizing her reaction as caused by Anne de Saint-Phalle's reproaches, which had been somewhere between "amusement and indignation."[112] Dido would also send a copy of her response to Leslie Caron, who had spoken to her previously about these borrowings and about Truffaut's behavior. The actress concluded from this that Jean Renoir's widow had no intention of stirring the pot with the maker of *The Last Metro* and had decided to bury the hatchet.[113]

Was it really necessary to revolt against Truffaut's film? The truth is that its resemblances to *Carola* seem quite indistinct and are limited to use of the same scenery—a Parisian theater during the German Occupation. In addition, it would have been easy for Truffaut to ask Dido for the rights to adaptation for *Carola,* and they certainly wouldn't have been denied. The fact that he didn't supports the arguments in defense of him and suggests that in fact this was a question of *Carola*'s unconscious influence. For if he'd become aware of the influence exercised on the screenplay while he was writing, nothing would have prevented him from indicating what *The Last Metro* owed to *Carola,* which, again, boils down to very little.

On April 6, 1958, Renoir left Los Angeles for New York, this time with Dido. On the fourteenth, after a week spent at the Waldorf Astoria, they flew to Paris.[114] The rerelease of *Grand Illusion* was their primary reason for this new stay in Europe, during which Renoir would direct two films.

The treatment for the first film, thirty-two typed pages, was entitled *Le Déjeuner sur l'herbe* (*Picnic on the Grass*) and was registered on June 9 with the

Association des auteurs de films.[115] Renoir understood that, if he wanted to direct a film, he had no other option but to produce it himself, something he had refused to do since *The Rules of the Game*. This time the process would take nearly a year, and another project would intervene. It came from television, and he spoke of it from the beginning as a "TV broadcast."[116] Its title would become *Le Testament du docteur Cordelier*. Thus, Renoir had two films for the year 1958.

However, for the moment he was devoting his time to *Grand Illusion*. After arriving in Paris, he had had his presentation of that work filmed, and soon he would learn that a jury composed of 117 critics from around the world had included it in the twelve best films of all time. Informing Charles Spaak of the news, which could not yet be made public, Renoir explained that he knew "by way of an indiscretion" that the film was the only French one on the list and that he was intending to go to Brussels to attend its October 17 showing as part of the World's Fair.[117] In the end, *Grand Illusion* would be categorized as the fifth best film.* Throughout fall 1958, Renoir traveled through Europe with Dido, stopping, for example, at the Venice Film Festival, to pay homage to Erich von Stroheim, and in Lausanne, where he had heard that some underground screenings were being organized.

The film was released in Paris on October 6 at the Studio Publicis. It played for five months, selling 133,000 tickets, a figure that represents a brilliant success for a revival. It produced the same craze in the provinces, and theater managers brought the news to Renoir. For example, in Roanne, a city of 43,000 inhabitants, 7,068 people saw the film during its first week at the Marivaux theater, and then another 3,027 came during the second week.[118]

Renoir gave his all, racing through France to present his film. He spoke to the newspapers, held forth on the radio, and appeared on television. During these appearances and interviews, these recollections of his own life, he created a character, put on the costume that would be his from then on, and applied the finishing touches to his life as a man and a director. The elements of what would become his legend materialized, and his memoirs would give more substance to them. He took intense pleasure in telling these stories, which were partly invented but more often positioned into cogent narratives. Sometimes he would write them, and they resembled first drafts of the stories he'd recount in *My Life and My Films*. For example, he fashioned an account of the genesis of *Orvet* that would soon be set in stone: after an accident that cost Pierre Champagne his life, some poachers picked him up while he was unconscious. He came to in a pickup truck loaded with game, among which "the dead eyes of a deer were staring at me." His rescuers took him to the hospital in Fontainebleau. A few

---

* After *Battleship Potemkin*, *The Gold Rush*, *The Bicycle Thief*, and *The Passion of Joan of Arc*.

weeks later, in the woods, he met the person who initiated him to the life of "that strange population of woodland tramps."[119]

It was the same for his films. He made recorded presentations for them, becoming the actor he'd always dreamed of being, one who until then had only worked sporadically. He was an actor who gave brilliant performances of the role he knew best, a role he wrote and shaped based on chance encounters and demands they made on him. Jean Renoir was playing Jean Renoir. He'd been forced into this role by the difficulties he encountered in trying to practice his art as well as the indifference shown his works; but he embraced his role with blatant enthusiasm and an aptitude that were only betrayed at times by a nervous glance at the camera or a trace of hesitation in his voice. The course he followed had been determined by circumstances, and it would end with his *Petit Théâtre* (*Little Theatre*).

For the moment, he was thinking equally of *Picnic on the Grass* when he began pursuing "a television broadcast that I have to write and direct,"[120] as well as a "ballet for a delightful girl named Ludmilla Tchérina."[121] A dancer, actress, painter, and sculptor, Ludmilla Tchérina actually was a delightful young woman. So delightful that Renoir was intending to give her the starring female role in *Picnic on the Grass*.[122] She was thirty-four and had asked Renoir to create a short ballet for her. It would be presented on February 19 and 20 as the first part of *Les Amants de Teruel,** which had been written for her by Raymond Rouleau.

As a result, Renoir wrote *Le Feu aux poudres*† for her, about "Strongalia," a country enslaved by the double dictatorship of army and progress that was attempting to conquer another country, "Molivia," which was devoted solely to the pleasure of living. The inhabitants of Molivia respond with smiles and flowers to the armies of Strongalia, and the conflict is resolved by an unusual battle opposing the head of Molivia, that paradise on Earth, to the grand priestess of Strongalia. Molivia wins, which symbolizes "the male conquering the female by his sexual brutality."[123] That was how Renoir described the project to Pablo Picasso,‡ whom he asked to create the scenery for the show. The painter's answer—if there ever was one—has not been found, but the scenery was conceived by Renoir's old partner Jean Castanier. Ludmilla Tchérina danced

---

* Raymond Rouleau would direct *Les Amants de Teruel* (*The Lovers of Teruel*) in 1962, with Ludmilla Tchérina and with cinematography by Claude Renoir. The Cannes Film Festival would select it over Jean Renoir's film *The Elusive Corporal*.

† *Translator's note:* "Making Sparks Fly," or, more literally, "The spark that set off the powder," used metaphorically to describe something that sets off a usually violent incident.

‡ Pierre Gaut was in touch with Picasso. In 1955, Renoir had written Gaut to thank him for having spoken to Picasso about *Orvet*. (Letter to Pierre Gaut, January 19, 1955, Pierre Gaut Collection, Cinémathèque française.)

to music by Mikis Theodorakis. According to the terms of the contract made on October 18, 1958, Renoir would receive "the sum of 1.5 million francs as compensation," and rehearsals would take place between January 20, 1959, and the end of February.[124]

Renoir and Dido had spent Christmas and New Year's in England, dining at Rumer Godden's on December 21, which was the evening they arrived in London and moved into the Savoy.[125] When they got back to Paris, Renoir began the two weeks of rehearsals that preceded the direction of *Le Testament du docteur Cordelier*. Financing for the production came jointly from SOFIRAD, which was a branch of RTF,* and the Compagnie Jean Renoir. It was "the most revolutionary shoot in all of French film,"[126] according to Jean-Luc Godard. In reality, it was in line with the rules and habits of television production. *Cordelier* was a "TV drama," and Renoir would say that from the beginning he had wanted it to be directed and broadcast simultaneously, as was then sometimes the case. Speaking about what he called an "experiment" at the time, he explained that "it consisted in applying to the making of a film, except in a few special cases, the methods used for live TV broadcasts."[127] As it would happen, however, *Cordelier* would not be directed and broadcast simultaneously.

Of the many good reasons that Renoir had for undertaking this adventure, his taste for experimentation most easily comes to mind. The technique of recording complete scenes in uninterrupted order using several cameras was a means to a goal he'd tried to achieve over the years: finding a way to give actors the opportunity to impart and maintain the development of their characters. Using this method, he was essentially hoping to place the actors in a situation that closely resembled the one they experienced on stage but which traditional directorial strategies destroy.

Although there isn't any doubt that such a motivation was essential to him, it cannot be ruled out that his attraction to the experience had originated by default. If he was working for television, it was also, and even firstly, because film wasn't making any offers. Rossellini, with whom he had given an interview to *France Observateur* about this new orientation, which had led both of them to the small screen, was in the exact same situation. The explanations they offered might have been excellent, exact, and pertinent, but this didn't mean they weren't justifications after the fact. Tricky as it may be to distinguish among such explanations, it should be acknowledged that they aren't mutually exclusive. The desire for experimentation and the taste for the contemporary elicit even less credence when you consider that, although the

---

* In 1964, Radiodiffusion-télévision française (RTF) would become the Office de Radiodiffusion-télévision française (ORTF).

first impulse is genuine, the second seems the result of something strongly urged. The fact that Renoir then wanted to convince Clifford Odets to write for the small screen doesn't prove he himself considered television "the medium of the future,"[128] as he claimed at the time. He knew how to pros-elytize when occasions called for it, without necessarily possessing any firm belief himself.* If such a question can be posed, it's also because the results of this first experiment raise questions about the real implications of the direc-tor's involvement in this project.

Describing for his son the conditions of the direction of *Cordelier*, Renoir mentioned that the film had cost 31 million (old) francs, which was nearly four times less than the same thing directed for the cinema. Certain estimations had reported a budget of 61 million, but the figure cited by Renoir already situates the budget at a height that was rarely attained at the time for a "TV drama." The average budget back then had been around 15 million. In that same letter to Alain, he explained that "this method gives the actors the chance to develop their performance based on their own inspiration [and] makes for some moments of genuine intensity."[129] Begun in exteriors, at Marnes-la-Coquette and Pigalle, among others, direction lasted a total of fourteen days during Janu-ary 1959, apart from the necessary rehearsals before recording in the studio, for which up to eight cameras were used. Renoir had written this letter to his son before beginning the editing.

Although Renoir never clearly stated any reason that had led him to be inspired by *The Strange Case of Dr. Jekyll and Mr. Hyde* when he made *Corde-lier*, he had referred to Robert Louis Stevenson's novella several times already, notably in a letter to Leslie Caron about *Orvet:* "There's a little of Dr. Jekyll and Mr. Hide [*sic*] in Georges. Instead of doing what he doesn't dare do under the different appearance of Mr. Hide, Georges gives in to his passion in his imagination. Mr. Hide is his profession as a writer."[130] In his adaptation—or, to be more precise, his "crystallization of a literary reverie,"[131] as Jean-Luc Godard has nicely put it—Jekyll is therefore called Cordelier and Hyde is named Opale. Jean-Louis Barrault plays both roles without the benefit for the second of any effects other than fake teeth and some tufts of hair on his hands. The hair on his head changes from white for Cordelier to black for Opale, and cheeks swollen by the use of cotton balls are enough to accomplish his transformation. Such mea-sures would have prevented the possibility of a "live" TV broadcast simultaneous with Renoir's direction, which he nevertheless would claim he had desired at

---

* Renoir's first impression of television was less flattering, and in 1950 he wrote about it: "Every house in America is topped by an antenna, and every family crowds around a little screen where they're served a diet whose cooks I'm far from envying." (Letter to Raymond Burnier, September 22, 1950, Jean Renoir Papers, Correspondence, Box 10, Folder 13.)

the start of the project. That approach would have also prevented any shooting in exteriors.

In Jean-Louis Barrault's memoirs, *Souvenirs pour demain* (*Memories for Tomorrow*), he makes no mention of his work with Renoir. The theater was his life, and in it film held no importance for a long time. During the fifties, his cinematic appearances were limited to *Royal Affairs in Versailles* and playing Marivaux (*Les Fausses Confidences**) and Anouilh (*La Répétition ou l'Amour puni*†) on television. During the month of January 1959 he was nominated by André Malraux to head the Théâtre de France (Odéon), and in his memory the fourteen days of shooting on *Cordelier* couldn't compete with that life event. It is also the case that his double performance wasn't appreciated, considered almost unanimously to be too hammy and full of grimaces, a judgment that wasn't very fair but that didn't prevent him from speaking of the experience as "one of my best memories."[132] Renoir attributed the failure of *Cordelier* partly to the effect on audiences of a performance that was "too magical for our clodhoppered audiences."[133]

A broadcast: that was how Renoir presented his *Cordelier* on-screen, after he was seen arriving with Dido at the RDF's Centre René-Barthélemy at Buttes-Chaumont and met by his editor Renée Lichtig. He then headed for Studio 14, greeted technicians, removed his hat and coat, sat down behind a table, gave his attention to a few recommendations, did a voice test, and waited for the signal that indicated he could begin speaking. With his image appearing on one of the screens in the control room, he said, "We have all just witnessed the conclusion of a remarkable adventure. So remarkable that to me it seems worth making it the object of tonight's broadcast. Let's begin at the beginning and go back a few months. The story takes place in one of those suburbs to the west of Paris that serve as a place to live rather than work." At that moment, the image of a street filmed with a tracking shot from a car and seen up until then on one of the control screens came into view as the beginning of a tale whose premises Renoir's voice continued to set forth. It was a brilliant introduction that asserted the specialness of the medium of television. It also established the auteur as storyteller. The deference everyone showed him created an aura of prestige, expertly indicating that the story about to follow was true at the same time that it wasn't. There was no doubt about it: the "broadcast" couldn't have begun better.

In this presentation, Renoir displayed a good-guy nonchalance that was

** *Translator's note:* Translated by Timberlake Wertenbaker in 1983 as *False Admissions*.

†* *Translator's note:* Literally, "Repetition or Love Punished."

natural to him, and what followed showed that the same spirit had flourished during the making of the film. From Stevenson's novella, which wasn't credited, he had preserved the theme of a transformation through chemistry, but his intention was to deal with the conflict between Good and Evil in terms of realistic psychology, whereas Stevenson had approached it through the aid of symbolism. In Renoir's work, the inflexible psychiatrist Cordelier frees his repressed impulses through Opale, his double. When a long flashback reveals that Cordelier, who is the lover of his assistant, dismissed her as soon as a bourgeois woman came to ask him to treat her son, a "pervert" who is sleeping with the maid, such triteness coming from Renoir is staggering, and not only because of the many times he has dealt with different degrees of intensity on the subject of affairs with servants, one of his great themes.

What had happened to make a man as smart as he serve up an exposé as stupidly unimaginative as this one? What was worse, none of the characters in *Cordelier* seems worth the sympathy of the viewer. Although Opale fleetingly suggests Boudu, thereby making him seem inoffensive, such as when Opale's "impulses" compel him to pinch the buttocks of nurses, the same cannot be said about his attacking a little girl, killing an old man, or mistreating a disabled person; all those activities redefine this character as monstrous. If the liberation of desires only unleashes forces of destruction, they might as well stay buried. It requires a high degree of kindheartedness toward the director not to see how summary his reflection is. Similarly, the assertion that soul and body are no more than one falls particularly flat, the trivial result of hazy considerations regarding two aspects of scientific thought. Renoir was definitely interested in the issue, and various notes he made testify to it, including those he kept in a notebook during August 1955: "Do animals have a soul? If not, do we have the right to make them suffer? Given the fact that they cannot buy eternal life with their earthly suffering. If that is the case, do we have the right to kill them? Does the soul spread by osmosis? Does a dog acquire a soul through the company of its master? And what about plants?"[134] At least *Cordelier* answers these questions: only human beings possess a soul. Then so be it.

Was Renoir too old now, as some bluntly suggested when the film was shown? No, but he was in a hurry to move on to something else (thinking at the time of *Picnic on the Grass*) and caught up as he always was in a whirl of various activities, working for a medium and a public that—counter to his declarations—he did not view with scorn. He was especially excited about a new technical system, and he had polished off the work for it in advance, thereby breaking with all his habits. And yet, this method of filming called revolutionary hadn't produced any beneficial effect. Renoir had expected it to free him, but it constrained him, stifled his direction. The editing had blown apart the continuity he'd attempted to create for the actors' performances, the benefits of which one would have hoped to see in the rushes.[135] The scenery was bad, the scenes too talky, stilted. On the other hand, the exteriors furnished the ultimate proof of the failure of the technique. They were the only scenes endowed with some life, impelled by a certain freedom. As for the rest, the "broadcast" was your average "TV drama" being produced by French television of the period. For that reason, Jean Serge, who appeared in the credits as an artistic collaborator, seems to have tried to put forward the idea that presenting the film to the public would be a mistake, but "Renoir's entourage was now advising him not to miss the chance to make money, [and] in the end he sided with them." Renoir and Serge's relationship wouldn't survive that misunderstanding and would leave the assistant regretting not "having been more stubborn and better at being so when dealing with all the excesses of Renoir's genius that weren't in his best interests and that I didn't know how to oppose. . . . I was a fanatic admirer," he concluded, "and there was no place for restrictions or reservations when it came to the mysteries of my faith."[136]

Jean Serge also remembered, "Renoir himself was aware that *Cahiers du cinéma* often attributed intentions to him that he had not had." As usual, Godard, Truffaut, and Claude Chabrol, with a certain kind of courage, spoke in defense of the film. Chabrol's reasons for this are worth reporting. In spite of *Cordelier*'s faults—visible to Chabrol as much as they were to others—he continued to like the film nearly fifty years after it had been directed. As he saw it, Renoir had dealt with the thing by making fun of both the project and himself. Chabrol saw the work as an act of derision, which pleased him. The only thing he deplored was the fact that Stevenson had also had to pay the cost of it.[137]

A few of Jean Renoir's ardent supporters continue to insist that *Le Testament du docteur Cordelier* is his consummate masterpiece and claim that time will prove them right. A half century has gone by without their having won over any nonbelievers to their cause, but perhaps this is only the proof that time takes its time. Renoir as well put his trust in the future when it came to this subject. "If *Cordelier* had been made around 1935 and been shown at the Cinémathèque, the same critics, the same colleagues, the same personalities who didn't like this film would have shouted masterpiece."[138] The truth is that since 1961 all have stood their ground.

It was 1961, in fact, because *Cordelier* was delayed for more than two years. For reasons differing from those that have put them in conflict since, film and television were already at war in 1959.* To put it more precisely, film chose to

* Pierre Braunberger displayed a great deal of optimism when he wrote to Renoir on December 31, 1964, "I'm sure you know that, thanks to me, there's no more conflict between film and television." (Jean Renoir Papers, Correspondence, Box 20, Folder 5.)

interpret the experience of *Cordelier* as a declaration of war. It wasn't, but the conflict, whose motives were exceptional and consequently no expression of any general truth, delayed the editing and presentation of the film until June 1961 (outside of Paris) and until November 16 of the same year on television and at a theater in Paris. As a result, audiences had already been able to see another Jean Renoir film, *Picnic on the Grass*.

Shortly after filming *Cordelier*, Renoir dove immediately into the rehearsals for the ballet written for Ludmilla Tchérina. "The girls have pea-brains and the boys are all little flirts," he wrote to Gabrielle Slade, explaining that he hadn't "worked very much on this ballet because I was shooting a small film at the same time," and that "with Tchérina it's hard to do anything at all without getting her angry, and I hate to do that more and more."[139] The director and the dancer actually never did succeed in getting along, and Renoir didn't see any part of his contribution in the show presented at the Théâtre Sarah-Bernhardt on February 19 and 20, 1959. Only a trace of their lack of understanding remains, in the form of a letter by Mme. Doynel in response to Ludmilla Tchérina. Tchérina was enquiring about Renoir's health, after he had had hernia surgery, and Ginette Doynel wrote in answer:

> [Jean Renoir] has asked me to tell you that he highly appreciates your gesture and thanks you for it. He is also very appreciative of the great success of your undertaking. He congratulates you very heartily. He asks you to believe that he was extremely happy about having had the chance to make his modest contribution to your work, it being the case that your wishes and choices led to circumstances that prevent Monsieur Renoir from recognizing anything authentic in the employment of his "argument" other than his name. For that reason, he here repeats his desire that, in return, the most modest usage be made of this name in the future.[140]

From then on, there could be no question of that "delightful girl" starring in *Picnic on the Grass*.

On the same day the letter to Ludmilla Tchérina left the office of the Compagnie Jean Renoir, fifty-six hundred miles from avenue Frochot, Gabrielle Slade passed away at the age of eighty. She had known she had cancer since 1956, and she had visited France for the last time in 1950. It was a "disastrous" stay, according to her son, who had gone with her. She was constantly bothered by the cold, and there seemed nothing left of what had been her country.[141] Renoir received the news of her death from Jean Slade by telegram. The director had lost the person whom he probably cherished the most, and the final words of his memoirs would be addressed to her: "Wait for me, Gabrielle."

"Dido and I keep thinking of Gabrielle," he wrote to Alain sometime after the news of her death. "We're almost happy we weren't there. This way, her parting can stay in the domain of the unreal. Moreover, I believe that she hasn't really left and will stay with us until our turn comes."[142] The next day, Renoir wrote another letter. It was to Reverend Father Diard, from the seminary mission Les Fontaines in Chantilly. "This passing has driven my other preoccupations from my mind for a few days, especially since I sense a tendency in certain journalists to 'romanticize' the relationship between my father and Gabrielle. Our world exists on completely fabricated clichés. The notion of 'painter and model' immediately calls one of them forth. These poor helots of the mind don't realize that with people like my father who were able to come close to certain revelations, relationships with other human beings had been freed of the base complications that are standard among those whose lives are dedicated to commerce."[143]

The fact that these words were addressed to a man of the church doesn't lessen the impression produced. Although it's understandable that Renoir intended to banish any temptation of his correspondent to conceive of the possibility of a sexual relationship between his father and Gabrielle, as some articles in the press may have hinted, and although respect for Gabrielle and Aline Renoir and their memory was the motive for his reaction, why did he express it with such anxiousness and intensity, as the tone suggests? The strapping young man he'd been before the war seemed to have become rather sensitive, one who refused even to imagine that the young, beautiful Gabrielle could have inspired any desires in Auguste Renoir beyond those of the artist. In what way could a love affair, even if it was adulterous, have affected Auguste Renoir's image? Neither Boudu nor Lestingois would have written such a letter, although Cordelier certainly could have.*

Almost since his arrival in California, Jean Renoir had essentially lived surrounded by two women with opposite demeanors, one as closed and tense as the other was exuberant and generous. Whereas the first was his wife, the second, who was his nurse and who had taken on the role of mother and confidante—"both sister and maternal friend,"[144] as Jean Slade put it—embodied the feminine as his father had represented it. Renoir had celebrated it in his films and his writings. According to all those who knew them intimately, Dido protected Jean, kept all day-to-day concerns away from him, and managed his relationships, his affairs, and his bank accounts. As the years progressed, money

* It's likely that revelations about John F. Kennedy's nature would have disturbed Renoir, who had written to Pierre Gaut, "The assassination of Kennedy deeply shocked us. We had 'a prince' for a president, with all the elegance of a prince." (Letter to Pierre Gaut, December 11, 1963, Pierre Gaut Collection, Cinémathèque française.)

had taken on an importance in Renoir's existence that it had not had in the past. Pierre Braunberger, who had known him for such a long time, wasn't the only one to become aware of this, and he wrote to him, "I don't really see that you have any more material needs than you had in the past."[145]

As Jean Slade remembers today, "Gabrielle would claim that if he hadn't had Dido, Jean would have died without a penny. He never would have possessed his own house."[146] Perhaps this is the case, although Jean Renoir had houses throughout his life, and he never lacked money. It is true that his wife controlled the accounts with a firm hand. She would forbid her husband's secretaries to change carbons as long as they still left the slightest impression on a copy.[147] She would lament unceasingly about the servants costing them "a fortune" and feared nothing so much as "footing the bill," beginning with Renoir's.[148] Under Dido's influence, Jean had become calmer, more organized, more sensible, apparently more oriented toward the spiritual than toward life's pleasures. In that, he was the opposite of the man he had been. Happier, perhaps, happy and also constrained—happy in his constraint. However, the fact that he had found his sense of well-being in such submission doesn't prevent evaluating what could have been the consequences of this new deal.

Clifford Odets's son, Walt Odets, who remained close to the Renoirs long after the death of his father and who would become a psychoanalyst, stayed frequently with them in both Beverly Hills and in Paris during the sixties. He has characterized Dido as "the lion at the gates" and explained, "She allowed him to live like a child. And even like a newborn. A newborn of more than two hundred pounds."[149] He was a newborn over whom his nurse kept watch. And she would soon be followed by another guardian, Ginette Doynel. This big baby with blue eyes and pink skin would transform in a flash into a preadolescent with a taste for dirty jokes. As soon as Dido turned her back, into the ear of one of his guests he might whisper some bawdy secret about the good luck he would claim he was still experiencing with certain actresses.[150] Whether it was reality or fantasy didn't really matter. The old Jean Renoir was asleep and only woke up when his wife wasn't in earshot. In a letter to Dido in which he mentioned the various divorces in their social group, he praised "the spiritual intimacy" they had and that he could only succeed in having with her, before coming up with the following sentence: "If it's a matter of a mundane affair, why not have recourse to a professional prostitute who is more skilled at it and often very beautiful."[151] Why not, in fact.

"Mundane affairs" didn't agree very well with spirituality, and Jean Renoir's mentality matched that of the bourgeois of the nineteenth century. Enamored of that same purity, obviously, of which the figure of his father would be divested by the disclosure of some guilty liaison, he took delight in confining himself to a state of infantilism. In a few months more, each of his visits to Europe would arouse the obsessive desire to get back to the cradle that the house on Leona Drive had become for him. It was a house that he and Dido no longer called anything but the childish name "*maïon*."* They used the word without the article that means "the" or "a," how children who are beginning to speak refer to things, by turning them into beings. Moreover, when Mme. Doynel would speak of him in her letters to Dido, she would use the name he had given himself before he learned to pronounce it correctly—"your little Dan."† Few men have as many mothers as Jean Renoir had.

The figure of Gabrielle was at the center of his next film. Her features were those of an unknown, whom Renoir had met in November. That evening, he was presenting *Louisiana Story* at the Cinémathèque on rue d'Ulm as part of the tribute to his friend Robert Flaherty, who had died on July 23, 1951. Among those in the audience were Claude Beylie, an eminent Renoir expert, with his friend and colleague Professor Georges Rouveyre, and Rouveyre's wife, Catherine. Beylie was certain that Renoir would like the young woman and introduced her to him. The director asked the photographer Philippe Rivier, who would be working on the set of *Picnic on the Grass,* to take some photos of her.

Catherine Rouveyre, whose maiden name was Vitale, was from Marseille. A few weeks earlier she had begun her studies at the Centre d'art dramatique on rue Blanche. She had just celebrated her nineteenth birthday on August 31. In December, Renoir asked her to come to avenue Frochot and read a scene "as if it were from the telephone book." Then he asked her to read it as if from a telephone book but also with a Marseille accent. At that moment, he called Dido over from the next room and asked her to take a look at the young actress. A month after that, taking advantage of his direction of *Le Testament du docteur Cordelier,* he asked her to do a test before the cameras at RTF,[152] a simple appearance that was never supposed to be a part of *Cordelier*. In March, when his breach with Ludmilla Tchérina was complete, he asked Catherine Vitale to come to the studio on rue Damrémont for more extensive tests. However, she wasn't the only candidate. At the entrance she ran into Michèle Mercier, whose audition was to follow hers. Mercier was six months older than she and a bit more experienced. Finally, in April, Renoir called Vitale to tell her that "if the film is made," she was going to be its actress. Soon he suggested that

* *Translator's note:* "*maïon*" = the way a French infant would try to pronounce *maison,* meaning house.

† *Translator's note:* As pronounced, its closest transliteration into English might be *Daw,* like the English word *dawn* without the final *n*. It was the way Renoir pronounced his name when he was a small child.

she change her name to Rouvel, a derivative of her husband's name, Rouveyre. Replacing a celebrity like Ludmilla Tchérina with a total unknown cooled some of the Siritzkys' interest in the film.[153] However, Pathé would remain behind the distribution to the same extent, which also later became the case with *Cordelier;* and Renoir would consider the Siritzkys' attitudes toward both films as having been irreproachable. Moreover, one can't help think what would have become of that character if the dancer had been left to play her.

To play the scientist Étienne Alexis, front-runner of the next election for president of the United States of Europe and an advocate of artificial insemination, Renoir first thought of Pierre Blanchar. He was the one who had stood in to play opposite Catherine Rouvel during the tests that had been filmed in March.[154] The actor's stiffness, his starchy acting style, and his image as a man of another time was a convenient match to the character. However, he would be sixty-seven in June 1959, and the nearly fifty years separating him from the woman who would star with him obviously constituted an insurmountable obstacle. Therefore, in the end, Renoir preferred Paul Meurisse, who was forty-six, and with whom he shared a warm friendship that had been expressed in numerous letters since they had worked together on the production of *Julius Caesar* in Arles. A few months previously, the actor had sent to Beverly Hills a recipe and a phial of liquid created by a producer from the South of France that could be used to make pastis.[155] Meurisse's wife, Micheline Gary, had acted in *Cordelier*. She would appear in the production for *Picnic* as well. For that film, Renoir also rounded up Blavette,* who had acted in *Toni;* Paulette Dubost, who had been his Lisette in *The Rules of the Game;* and Jean-Pierre Granval, the son of Madeleine Renaud and Charles Granval, who'd played the bookseller who saves Boudu from drowning.†

The production began in studios on rue Francoeur, where rehearsals had begun in mid-June.[156] This was where the interiors would be filmed for the next three weeks, representing around a quarter of the film. Renoir had actually chosen to reuse the setup for *Cordelier,* as well as the service of several crewmembers, including head cameraman Georges Leclerc. Shooting with several cameras required a long period of preparation blocking out the movements of the actors. On the scenery the actors would again find indications that had been drawn with chalk on the floor of the studio, and they would be constrained to follow them.

* In a letter dated November 22, 1957, Blavette told Renoir about a recent encounter with Jean Giono, who had declared to her "verbatim": "If Jean Renoir likes any at all of my works, he can make use of them." (Jean Renoir Papers, Correspondence, Box 14, Folder 5.)

† Marc Simenon, son of Georges and himself a future director, would work as an assistant on this film.

Speaking seven years later about the subject, Renoir claimed that he "did not like it." He thought it "practical" because it "allowed shooting with a certain security, and not spending too much money." However, he also thought that it "kills something extremely important, which is the actor's surprise at being faced with the scenery." It was quite simple, in fact: if he'd been a "dictator," he would have begun "by forbidding any piece of chalk on a set or stage."[157] But had he become aware of his mistake during direction, during editing, or after the film was released? Although it's true that using color limited the number of cameras, the exteriors in *Picnic* possess a splendor to which Renoir himself rarely came close, even in *The River*. This is even more the case when the art of editing is taken into account, bringing to heights the associations among shots of nature, tall grasses, leaves, and the river, in celebration of the union of the scientist and the young girl.

In general, those involved in the shooting of *Picnic* over a period of about twenty days in July experienced it as a period of happiness. Returning to Les Collettes and his father's house, among the olive trees, on the banks of the river, Renoir recommuned with his youth, rediscovered Gabrielle's former features and soft curves, as well as Dédée's, his first love, in Catherine Rouvel. He had been nine when Auguste became the owner of Les Collettes. It was the age of racing along worn paths and games under the olive trees. This was also the place where he'd met the girl who was going to become his first wife and where he learned about love. Together, the two of them had probably lost themselves in the tall grasses. Later, it had become the place where Andrée and Jean had lived and tried their hand at the art of ceramics. Under this same sky, they had made their first film, *Catherine*.

In directing *Picnic,* Jean completed the circle of his own story and went on with the work of remembering he had begun for his book on Auguste, thereby uniting film and painting; and both Renoirs, son and father, came together beyond the space of years. "The guy who was working here wasn't making a film," whispered a grip to Paul Meurisse, who was amused by the behavior of that "old charmer whose flattery is as thick as a sailor's rigging . . . and who sits next to the camera finding everything 'fantastic.'"[158] Everything is typical Renoir in this film, whose title is borrowed from a painting by Manet.

The "old charmer" was also his own producer, who wagered 50 percent of the takings from *Grand Illusion* as a reimbursement guarantee for the sums invested by the UFIC* and Consortium Pathé, to a limit of 10 million francs.[159] As the months passed, Renoir's memory of the shoot would take on a different complexion, leading him to decide to never again produce one of his films

* Union pour le financement de l'industrie cinématographique.

himself. In that as well Dido would support him. She may even have had the idea before he did. "I had come to this conclusion after *Picnic on the Grass*, about which complaints never stopped and where food was also a crucial issue. Let others take care of it!"[160] The resentments accumulated, sometimes falling on the faithful—for example, Renée Lichtig, the editor for *Cordelier* and *Picnic*, whom Dido confirmed they were "right, alas, to mistrust" and about whom she claimed she was "still shuddering."[161] Renée Lichtig would work on *The Elusive Corporal*, to Renoir's great satisfaction, and this time he would describe her as being "the very soul of devotion."[162]

It is true that Dido had a hard time standing the presence of women around Jean.

Accordingly, Catherine Rouvel, from the wisdom of her nineteen years, didn't neglect to notice that "Renoir was another man on those rare times when Dido wasn't around,"[163] which is not to say that she saw anything in his behavior that could be interpreted ambiguously. The director kept a jealously protective eye on his discovery, so jealously protective that, even before the shoot began, he made her sign an exclusive contract that contained the following lines: "You will not be able to collaborate directly or indirectly with any enterprise during the period of shooting the present film nor during the first year following the release of *Picnic on the Grass*, nor may you enter into any engagement during this period." A year, then; and even three, since the contract also contained the clause: "these arrangements being within the scope of the preemptive right of Les Films R. S. over your engagements for a total period of three years from this day."[164] It clearly signified that for three years Catherine Rouvel would have to consult Renoir before signing any kind of contract at all. As a result, she would be forced to refuse roles offered to her in *La Jument verte* (*The Green Mare*) and in a film by Gérard Oury,* because Renoir claimed that the theater would be more advantageous to her than the cinema. A clause in the same contract established that Renoir was committed "to guaranteeing [her] an engagement in another film in the year following the release" of *Picnic*. Catherine Rouvel signed without thinking about it, too happy to be working for a director whose films she and her husband revered. When she took the role of Fanny in the play *Marius* in the spring of 1962 at the Théâtre des Variétés, Renoir came to applaud her and also told her that he thought the play was quite dated.[165] It took until January 1963 to see Catherine Rouvel again on the screen, in the Claude Chabrol film *Landru* (*Bluebeard*).

Today, *Picnic on the Grass* seems like a film by a young man from another era. In it Renoir rediscovers the child, the adolescent, the boy in love that he

---

* Probably, *La Menace* (*The Menace*).

once was and that he confronts with the questions that are troubling, or that soon will trouble, the modern world: the birth of a united Europe, artificial insemination, nuclear energy, the links between the pharmaceutical industry and government authorities, the creation of dubious icons. Like *Cordelier*, this film opens on a screen of a black-and-white television broadcast, introducing characters in color as they are watching television and talking about what they have just heard and seen. One of the paradoxes comes from the fact that this production, filmed according to techniques that come from television, mutates rapidly toward a kind of cinema whose mentality closely resembles models from the past. While completing the circle of his own history, Renoir rediscovers the tone, rhythm, and mentality of silent film.

More than the work of an elderly man, *Picnic on the Grass* is that of a director who began in the twenties and is equipped with the experience he acquired over the course of a long career. In this way, *Picnic* becomes infused with some of the essence of *A Day in the Country*. This gives birth to the same desires in a Mme. Poignant (Marguerite Cassan)—whose artificially inseminated child has been taken away from her because he is too intelligent—as in the fulsome Mme. Dufour (Jane Marken) and her daughter (Sylvia Bataille) in *Day*.

Another paradox that is eminently Renoirian: the film deals with disturbingly serious subjects using a farcical tone. Renoir takes pleasure in poking fun at a modernity for which he actually has little liking, but without ever forgetting to indicate that all of it, through and through, isn't very important. In that aspect as well, *Picnic on the Grass* is as likeable as *Cordelier* wasn't. It is true that Renoir spent a long time working on and preparing his film. Not less than seven versions of the screenplay exist in his personal archives. He afforded it all the care and all the attention he had denied his television broadcast.

Renoir may have put all of that into *Picnic*, but in 1961, audiences did not seem willing to recognize it. *Picnic*'s only irremediable flaw comes from the fact of its very nature as a Renoirian film, fit only to delight Renoirians. Today it remains more admired by a few attentive or partisan critics than appreciated by audiences in general. A few weeks after its Parisian release on November 11, 1959, nothing was noticeable about the film for Renoir other than the fact that his undertaking had failed. "Now that I am no longer in the maelstrom, I can see the extent to which *Cordelier* [which had not yet been released] and *Picnic* are commercial failures. This fortifies my will to tackle my work in Berkeley, to work on my various plays, and on the book. It gives me a pathological distaste for all the processes relating to film or television. I have the impression that this field is not only foreign but hostile to me and that I'll get kicked in the head in trying to enter it again." And when he tells Ginette Doynel in that same letter that "Nénette has a cold,"[166] he's not talking about the young woman in his film, whom the viewer learns in the last shot is actually named Antoinette, but about his dog.

At the end of summer, Renoir and Dido had gone to Venice for its film festival. *Cordelier* had been shown in a small theater and was a "big success." Also, the August 31 screening of the complete restored version of *The Rules of the Game* "was a kind of triumph."[167] Renoir had discovered this "new" *Rules of the Game* a few days before, during a screening organized especially for him at the Francoeur studios. The resurrection of what is today considered his greatest film was the work of two passionate supporters, Jean Gaborit and Jacques Maréchal, whose company, Les Grands Films classiques, had acquired the rights to distribute the film in May 1958 from Camille François. A few weeks later, in 280 boxes of film that had lain forgotten in the GTC laboratories, Gaborit and Maréchal had identified the scenes that Renoir had edited out of the film just after its release as well as some that had been abandoned by him during editing.

With the help of the editor Jacques Durand, they had reconstructed a version of nearly 106 minutes, which then became and has continued to be the standard. This restored version would first be released commercially in London in September 1960, then in New York in January 1961, and finally in Paris, at the Médicis studios, on April 23, 1965. The scale of the restoration was, naturally, proportionate to the damage that had been caused in 1939, and therefore, audiences in the sixties were witness to a "new" creation at the same time that they were being confronted by Renoir's current output. Undoubtedly, this was a situation unheard of in the history of film. The director of the present moment was being considered through the prism of the stunning modernity of a film directed more than twenty years before. The shadow cast by *The Rules of the Game* and *Grand Illusion,* then later by *La Chienne* and other films, on *Cordelier* and *Picnic,* and soon on *The Elusive Corporal,* could only lessen the splendor of these new productions. The more his past films were celebrated, the more he himself discussed them, the more Renoir was perceived as a director of the past.

As the sixties arrived, he attempted to adopt a new posture. Thus, a few months before, he had cited the "experiments" *Cordelier,* which he had just finished, and *Picnic on the Grass,* not yet directed, as his reasons for accepting an offer from UC Berkeley, and he claimed that he was hoping these films would permit him "to interest the students . . . and tackle the questions to deal with in a less theoretical manner." He also wanted to take advantage of his stay in order to "attempt an experiment of that type."[168] The preoccupations he presented as priorities weren't pretenses, but Renoir was also aware that he owed the offer he'd received, something that had begun on his son's initiative, more to his reputation than to his current identity. And if he was in a position then to accept spending about five months in Berkeley, it was mostly because no film project was taking shape on the horizon.

In November 1957, he had refused an initial offer from the university, giving as reason that he was "too busy with the project for *Judith*."[169] Two and a half years later, his *Judith*, having become *Carola*, would have its first production on May 13, 1960, and the actors would be students. As a Regents' Professor of English and Dramatic Art, Renoir was to receive a salary of $75,000.[170]

32

"It Won't Be Made, It Won't Be Made"

Le Caporal épinglé (The Elusive Corporal)
Pierre-Auguste Renoir, mon père (Renoir, My Father)

From the end of February to the end of June 1960, Jean and Dido Renoir, who'd come back to Beverly Hills on January 13, moved to Berkeley, where Alain Renoir was teaching medieval English literature, and where Anne, his third child, would be born on September 12. During the five months of conferences and workshops that began with the first production of *Carola,* Renoir continued writing the book on his father and tried to get some vague projects for films on their feet. For a while, he was thinking of bringing *Irma la Douce* to the screen with Leslie Caron and Yves Montand, who was then in Hollywood acting in *Let's Make Love* with George Cukor. The idea for *Irma* had been suggested to Renoir by an importer of films, but Renoir had been "thinking about it for a long time,"[1] a reflex response for him. His memory of the play by Alexandre Breffort, produced in Paris in November 1956, was actually quite cloudy, as he had to confess to Yves Montand after Montand informed him that the role envisioned for him did not correspond to the one Renoir had described.[2] Renoir would soon learn that the rights for *Irma la Douce* had been bought by the Americans; and that in any case, although Christine Gouze-Rénal was the one who had acquired them, she intended to cast Brigitte Bardot and have Marcel Camus direct.[3] This information doubly established that Renoir in no way figured on the lists of either Hollywood or French producers. As it turned out, Billy Wilder was the one who directed the film—and not with Montand's costar for the Cukor film, Marilyn Monroe, the actress whom Mme. Doynel[4] believed would get the part of Irma—but with Shirley MacLaine.

Back in his home on Leona Drive at the end of June, Renoir seemed to have understood that the only projects he could consider with any chance of success were those that interested no one but himself. In any case, that was the meaning of the point he made to Mme. Doynel when he asked her to inquire about the rights for the Knut Hamsun novel *Hunger:* "Our chance of getting an option rests on the fact that the elderly Knut Hamsun gave in to his attraction to the Nazis during the occupation of his country in 1940 and that he's 'taboo' in the eyes of a lot of film producers. I've already wanted to film some of his novels and ran up against that obstacle. Now I think it has become water under the bridge, and *Hunger* is such a wonderful subject that we can close our eyes to the shortcomings of a writer who was weakened by age and illness."[5] *Hunger*, which appeared in 1890, actually is a superb book, and it matters little in this case that Renoir was in a hurry to exonerate its author for a "weakness," which led him—among other "excesses"—to offer his 1920 Nobel Prize medal for literature to Joseph Goebbels in 1943, something resulting in his condemnation and obligation to pay a hefty fine in 1948.* Because Hamsun had died in February 1952, Renoir corresponded with his son, Tore, on the subject of this adaptation.

His attempts to direct *Hunger* would last for three years. In September 1961, Tore Hamsun stated that he was sorry that Renoir hadn't yet succeeded in his undertaking and accepted prolonging the option.[6] A few days later, the director put his difficulties down to his refusal to make the film in Norway—for the reason that he didn't speak its language—and said that he now had the idea of directing *Hunger* in the same city where Hamsun had set it.† It would be a silent film accompanied by a commentary that he himself would speak in French, and he would entrust the English version to Charles Laughton.[7] Tore Hamsun thought it was an excellent idea but was doubtful about the possibility of finding a good Norwegian actor.[8]

On March 1, 1962, the project was set in motion again by a telegram from Oskar Werner to Renoir: "*Cher Maître* read in the paper that you're preparing Knut Hamsun's *Hunger* may I offer myself as actor would be very honored if you'd choose me I was Jules in *Jules et Jim* [*Jules and Jim*] and your great admirer."[9] The director, who had written to Dido on March 18 to say that he was having trouble "deriving a potential screenplay from *Hunger* [and had] lost faith,"[10] declared four days later that his "interest was renewed."[11] In the spring of 1963, the screenplay for *Hunger* was sent to the producer of *Le Caporal épinglé* (*The Elusive Corporal*) and Pierre Braunberger,[12] among others. Without success.‡

It was the beginning of the sixties, and Pierre Braunberger was surprised at the lack of eagerness the director showed regarding the ideas for projects he had been sending him. "I understand that you're imagining a film in the United States that will bring you a lot of money, but I don't understand why

---

* The Norwegian government had emphasized Hamsun's age and illness to delay his trial until 1948 because it threatened to endanger the unity of the country.

† Christiania (now called Oslo).

‡ In 1965, *Hunger* was brought to the screen by the Danish director Henning Carlsen. Peer Oscarsson won the best actor award for it at Cannes in 1966.

you're not imagining a French film to do before or after your American film. Your financial concerns can be safeguarded just as well in France. Didn't Truffaut make a considerable amount of money with *The 400 Blows*? . . . I get the impression you haven't viewed the French situation clearly."[13] At the time, the case was probably not that Renoir didn't want to make a film in France but really that he didn't want to work with Braunberger, whose financial situation at that moment made it possible for him to produce only some short films. Moreover, Mme. Doynel had gone on the warpath against the producer. She was contesting his distribution rights to films he was booking and protesting his gifts to the Cinémathèque of copies that did not belong to him. This did not keep Renoir from expressing a genuine attachment to the producer, and they discussed several projects over the course of the decade.

What exactly was that French situation Braunberger had spoken of? It's certainly true that Truffaut had earned "considerable amounts of money." However, the success of *The 400 Blows*, as well as other films released in 1959, such as Chabrol's *Les Cousins* (*The Cousins*) and Resnais's *Hiroshima mon amour* or Godard's 1960 hit *À bout de souffle* (*Breathless*), remained relative. These productions were good business because they had had modest budgets, but they were dwarfed by other profit-makers in a market dominated in 1959 by *La Vache et le Prisonnier* (*The Cow and I*), *The Green Mare*, *Babette s'en va-t-en guerre* (*Babette Goes to War*), and *Les Liaisons dangereuses* (*Dangerous Love Affairs*); and in 1960 by *Le Bossu* (*The Hunchback of Paris* or *The King's Avenger*), *Le Capitan* (*Captain Blood*), *La Vérité* (*The Truth*), and *Les Vieux de la vieille* (*The Old Guard*). For Renoir, the deal hadn't changed. His worth for producers was still being measured by the financial outcomes of his previous films. And the truth was, *Elena and Her Men* and *Picnic on the Grass* had failed at the box office.

At the beginning of 1961, David O. Selznick contacted him regarding rights for another "Indian" novel by Rumer Godden, *Kingfishers Catch Fire* (1953), for which the producer thought Renoir had an option. Renoir wrote to the author to let her know that Selznick was thinking of Jennifer Jones for the role and was considering him as the director. He was expecting to meet with Selznick and the actress, Selznick's wife, as soon as they got back from Mexico in about eight days, and in his letter to Godden, he added, "I'm so used to dreams suddenly falling apart that I'm trying to protect myself against a disappointment by endlessly repeating to myself, 'it won't happen, it won't happen.'"[14] It didn't happen, in fact, for anybody, and such a situation makes one think, relatively speaking, of has-been Norma Desmond in *Sunset Boulevard*, convinced that Cecil B. DeMille has decided to cast her, when the producer-director had merely asked his assistant to get some information about the 1932 Isotta Fraschini automobile belonging to her.

Although Michel Simon expressed his joy in 1961 at the idea of "making *La Communion du pauvre*" with Renoir, because he thought Renoir seemed to be "the only one capable of directing a work that above all calls for the talents of heart with which [Jean Renoir has been] so generously gifted,"[15] that offer, coming from a certain company called Unifilm, does not seem to have left any other trace. In reality, the light would come from another of his former partners.

On February 8, 1961, Charles Spaak wrote to Renoir about *Le Caporal épinglé*, a book that had appeared in 1947 in which "a certain Jacques Perret (a man of the extreme Right) recounts his memories of captivity in Germany." Describing the work as "full of verve, and by a good writer," without "any plot," but rather a "series of short tableaux, often extremely funny in terms of sentiment and expression," the screenwriter added that Guy Lefranc, "a director with average talent, a prisoner himself, wanted to draw a screenplay from it." He also explained that the film was to be produced by Pathé before another company took over the project, "whose advantage is having a vague option with a certain Belmondo, a young (excellent) actor who is very quickly building a career à la Gabin" and was asking Spaak to work on a new adaptation. The fifty pages that Spaak had written had given him the idea that "it would be really fascinating to go back to the subject of *Grand Illusion* with you, twenty years later, 'without any illusions' this time." After confronting Spaak with the fact that Renoir's last film had "not been a success," the producers gradually came around and declared themselves "delighted" with Spaak's work. "Which proves what idiots they are,"[16] the latter commented.

Renoir wasted not a moment in getting back to him. "What you're saying about the subject excites me a great deal, and even before knowing the details of the story, I've decided, if it's possible, to make the film with you."[17] As soon as he knew a bit more, having read Spaak's screenplay and paged through the book, he wrote to René Bézard, the managing director of Consortium Pathé, to say he was "carried away" with the subject, adding that the treatment by Spaak "seemed like an excellent foundation."[18] In that same letter, he mentioned not having "read all of" the book, which is also what he'd say in different words when he claimed to have read it "in one night," because *Caporal épinglé*'s seven hundred pages required more from a reader than a few hours overnight. Finally, he informed his correspondent that he'd already gotten in contact with Les Films du Cyclope, from which he had not yet received any news.

Les Films du Cyclope had been created in 1952 and was on a roll. Among the films it had produced were two French hits, 1957's *Le Triporteur* (*The Tricyclist*) with Darry Cowl and 1959's *The Cow and I*, directed by Henri Verneuil. The success of the André Cayatte film *Le Passage du Rhin* (*Tomorrow Is My Turn*), a production of Franco-London Films released in November 1960 and cited by

Spaak in his letter to Renoir, had just confirmed, right after the Verneuil film with Fernandel, that audiences were interested in stories of prisoners of war. Les Films du Cyclope was being run by the flamboyant Adry de Carbuccia.

Born on August 17, 1900, in Paris, Adrienne Turpin-Rotival, the daughter-in-law of the police prefect Jean Chiappe,[*] had married Horace de Carbuccia on November 20, 1927. Carbuccia had been the deputy of Corsica from 1932 to 1936 and was also the founder and director of *La Revue de France* (1921–1939), Les Éditions de France (1923–1944), and *Gringoire*[†] (1928–1944). In the thirties, the Carbuccia salon on avenue Foch was one of the most frequented rendezvous for artistic and literary Parisian society, whom the couple also received in their summer residence at Grande Pointe, located between Beauvallon and Sainte-Maxime.

Adry de Carbuccia would publish a novel as well as her memoirs, the latter under the title *Du tango à Lily Marlène*. About the novel, which was entitled *Marie-Madeleine*, a copy of which she had given Renoir to read several years before it was published in 1969, he wrote to Dido, "Very deft and surprisingly shameless. *The Rules of the Game* is a pastoral compared to this gullible and sly display of purely physical desires. It takes place in 'the world.' Without realizing it, the author drags her heroes through the mud that she thinks is perfumed. . . . Needless to say it takes place in Saint-Tropez. . . . It's nothing but a shrewd imitation of Françoise Sagan, a *Bonjour tristesse* applied to a middle-aged lady."[19] In the preface to her memoirs, she writes, "I've met a number of writers, novelists or poets, soldiers, corporals or marshals, men of politics of every stature, a few bad boys, a substantial contingent of princes, a handful of dictators and even a king. . . . I've lived one hundred lives in one and have not at all come through it disillusioned."[20]

The fact that the project consisted of adapting a book by an author extremely associated with the political Right into a film that was being produced by a figure of the extreme Right was certainly no reason to refuse it,[‡] especially because it had been brought to Renoir by a screenwriter who had written his triumph, *Grand Illusion,* and one of his successes, *The Lower Depths.* On the other hand,

---

* *Translator's note:* Chiappe was associated with the Right and became one of the figures implicated in the Stavisky affair. His dismissal from his post led to far-right demonstrations that some feared might result in a putsch against the government.

† *Translator's note: Gringoire* was one of the more prominent French interwar newspapers, on the extreme Right, with heavy coverage of politics and a highly respected literary section.

‡ It was for Adry de Carbuccia that Jacques Becker filmed *Ali Baba et les quarante voleurs* (*Ali Baba and the Forty Thieves*) with Fernandel in 1954. Carbuccia was also the one who, in 1961, produced *Un nommé La Rocca* (*A Man Named Rocca*), the first film of Jacques's son, Jean Becker, based on a novel by José Giovanni, starring Jean-Paul Belmondo.

in 1962, when Renoir was thinking of bringing a book by Céline—probably *Journey to the End of the Night*—to the screen, Braunberger did not shy away from warning him, "It would obviously be awkward to use money from *Gringoire** to make the work by Céline you were talking to me about. If we do make it someday, we'll do it without any political ambiguity."[21] When the director insisted, "It's possible that Céline's book is the big thing to do,"[22] the producer answered, "Not yet the moment to do Céline, especially after Perret."[23] This moment wouldn't come.

The Elusive Corporal did signal Pierre Gaut's return into Renoir's professional life. The producer and the director of *Toni* had never lost touch and had continued to correspond and meet frequently when Renoir was in Paris. However, Pierre Gaut had played no role in his friend's career until the film produced by Adry de Carbuccia reinvolved him. He was invited to screenings for the crew, after which his opinion would be asked.

Carried away with Spaak's idea, Renoir wrote to the screenwriter, "If we manage to depict this total don't-give-a-damn we'll have done something that the others haven't yet. It's implied in the works of the Nouvelle Vague but with a slight anarchist aspect that is short of the truth. This calm and ironic approach to destroying those who remain gods for a lot of people of this century goes beyond anarchy. This is the wave that's going to change the world. Even here in America you can feel the drops of spray coming before it."[24]

Four days later, he expressed an even stronger conviction. "It's a great subject. The book can serve as the basis for a unique screenplay. If people would get off my back, I could create a successor to *Grand Illusion* that would cause it no shame." He began pressuring Mme. Doynel, whom he'd appointed negotiator with Cyclope, to get him a profit share of the receipts, as he'd had for most of his films; and he expected no less than "25 million old francs."[25] On April 15, 1961, a contract offer was sent from Cyclope's office, and Renoir accepted it on April 21. As author of the adaptation, he'd receive five installments of 34,000 francs† each, and as director, five installments of 12,000 francs each, beginning with the first public release of the film. He then requested that the producer buy back these installments for a lump sum of 230,000 francs.[26] On April 28, Cyclope declared themselves in agreement and sent him a schedule. On May 16, Jean and Dido flew to Paris.

In the meantime, the thorny question of Guy Lefranc's situation had to be settled. Actually, it was his project, and since April 1958, the shoot had been announced as beginning shortly, "under the direction of Guy Lefranc,"[27] with

* The name "Carbuccia" was added in handwriting.

† These were new francs.

gave him the right to differ. But those modulations could "only remain when collaborating with directors who are not writers (Feyder, Grémillon, Cayette, for example), who aren't changing the text but requiring the actors to respect it exactly instead." With Renoir, it was "completely the opposite."

Yes, Renoir was also a writer. He always had been, had become even more of one, and liked writing more and more. Soon, it would be all he would like doing, in fact. Encountering the rediscovered rushes for *A Day in the Country* was proof of it, as was the lack of enthusiasm he had exhibited in working with Prévert after *The Crime of Monsieur Lange*. Renoir insisted on actors, respecting the text only when he was its author, certain as he was that his dialogue was always better than someone else's. His films bore him out, and the memory of *Grand Illusion* stood as no contradiction to Spaak when Spaak declared the importance, in his eyes, of dramatic continuity. It was Renoir's intention to be the only author of his films, and since the thirties, that wish had led him to fly in the face of the primacy with which French cinema awarded the screenwriter. Now that Renoir knew he had also become a writer, he was certainly not going to back away from such a battle. So, Spaak pulled away from the project—with a smile. "It will always be the case that we'll be able to work together until a certain moment. . . . Since this end-of-the-road moment has always been very exciting, I have no reason to hold it against you."[31]

The screenplay for *The Elusive Corporal* delivered to production was dated September 20, 1961. In it, Renoir set forth a principle that he considered essential, although the film itself is a poor example of it because the producers intervened against the wishes of the director. "The film begins with a documentary image, with no apparent relationship to the story that we are going to tell. And approximately every three hundred meters, a documentary image will interrupt the narrative both to remind faulty memories of the great events of the last war and to create, at the same time, some delightful contrasts. This first image, illustrating a trivial fact from American life (a dance, sports event, parade, it really doesn't matter), will be subtitled 'June 1940,' with the explanation of the fact being related."[32] "Approximately every three hundred meters" would be too much, a great deal too much, for Cyclope, and Renoir's plan would not come to be. The principle consisting of integrating fiction—in other words, personal stories—with images of official history as portrayed by newsreels is also what led Renoir to film in black and white. Passing from one element to the other smoothly, without any immediate visual discrepancy, was one of the component elements of the project—even one of the most essential.

For questions of budget, and although Renoir had claimed he could make *Corporal* in France in less than eight or nine weeks,[33] it was first planned that the film would be shot in Yugoslavia, before Cyclope opted for Austria and the

Rosenhügel studios in Vienna. On October 10, Renoir and Dido moved into their quarters at the Parkhotel Schönbrunn, which was located on the edge of the grounds of the chateau. But two days later, Dido had to leave for Los Angeles because one of their domestic service employees was suddenly too ill to carry out duties. Two days later, Guy Lefranc had to return to France. His seventy-eight-year-old father had had an attack that left him completely paralyzed. Renoir spent Saturday writing the scene in which the corporal escapes into the forest. He wanted to finish it before the arrival in Vienna of Mme. de Carbuccia,[34] whom he'd taken often to calling "Madame Cyclope." She "was still on edge," wrote Renoir on Sunday morning, after he'd received a letter from Jacques Perret informing him that the producer had asked him to work on the screenplay and, moreover, to "redo the dialogue." It happened that the writer was unavailable for that task, but Renoir got huffy and planned to ask Mme. Doynel the next day to announce to Cyclope that he preferred to pull out of the film, the shooting of which was supposed to begin in nine days. "If I don't make a stink, she's going to interfere with the shots and—my biggest fear—monkey with the editing." As happened to him at times just before a shoot, he "wanted to break while the time was appropriate."[35] In return, Dido ranted, "Maybe it's good that there's an ocean between Mme. Cyclope and me. Otherwise I think this would end in a murder. . . . You make YOUR film, and if not send them walking."[36] It wouldn't be necessary, but Renoir had already done more than foresee that the road he was preparing to take would be strewn with pitfalls.

Filming was scheduled to begin on Monday, October 23. The Thursday before, Renoir worked some more for a large part of the night on the screenplay, which he announced was "going well."[37] He again met with the actors, who had just arrived in Vienna. Jacques Jouanneau, who had already worked in *French Cancan, Orvet,* and *Elena and Her Men,* was part of the cast, but most of the others were newcomers. Jean Carmet, the oldest to have a leading role in the film, was forty. He'd been acting for twenty years, and his voice was better known to audiences than his face, thanks to the everlasting radio soap opera *La Famille Duraton,* which had been created in 1937 and finally ended in 1966. In him, Renoir discovered a man dear to his heart, whom Gabrielle "would have adored."[38] Their close relationship would be maintained by letters and by several visits of the actor to Beverly Hills. Carmet would also be the only actor present at Renoir's interment in Essoyes.* Jean-Pierre Cassel, who was twenty-nine, owed the start of his success to his talents as a dancer and to the three films he had made nearly one after another for Philippe de Broca, *Les Jeux de l'amour (The*

---

* Leslie Caron would be at Essoyes. To this day, Françoise Arnoul resents Mme. Doynel for having made her believe that the ceremony would be reserved for the family and that she couldn't attend it.

Love Game), *Le Farceur* (*The Joker*), and *L'Amant de cinq jours* (*Five Day Lover*). The role of "Four-eyes" Ballochet had gone to Claude Rich, who was thirty-one. Claude Brasseur, twenty-five, was playing Pop; and Guy Bedos, twenty-six, would be "the stuttering prisoner." For the role of the dentist's daughter, the production called on a young German star, Cornelia Froboess, who hadn't yet turned twenty. She'd been famous since the age of eight thanks to her singing. Then, in less than ten years, she had acted in about fifteen films that were the equivalent of those Elvis Presley was doing in Hollywood, and these had made her the idol of kids from German-speaking countries.*

It didn't take Renoir at all long to declare himself particularly satisfied with his actors. On the evening of the first day of shooting, he wrote to Dido to tell her, "Cassel and Brasseur are excellent and delightful to work with."[39] On the second day, he refilmed the scene he'd recorded the day before, which hadn't been to his satisfaction. It was the last scene in the film, before the epilogue that took place in Paris, featuring a dyed-in-the-wool Parisian, François Darbon, playing the peasant from Beauce; and Renoir deplored the fact that he wasn't "peasant enough." "He's a 'theater'-style actor, and by that I mean 'bad theater.'"[40] It was a rather unjust judgment of a remarkable theater performer, who would also attract applause in two films by Truffaut.

On the other hand, directing the first scene with Ballochet on October 28 became proof for him that it had been a good idea to cast Claude Rich in the role. Even the other actors declared themselves won over. Jean-Pierre Cassel described how he and Claude Brasseur waited in vain for the word "cut!" at the end of the filming of their first scene. They could see the director seated in his chair, "tears running down his cheeks, until he finally said in an emotional voice, 'All right . . . cut . . . but I wish we didn't have to.'"[41]

As was his habit, Renoir directed his actors without seeming to direct them, letting them discover their positions and gestures on their own. Although such a way of doing this was still unusual, it has become part of the way film has evolved. Lighter cameras are less constraining to the movements of the actors, the pace of filming can be speeded up, and the time of the dictatorial director shouting commands on the set is on the eve of ending. Consequently, the young actors in *Corporal* found themselves working for a director who had made history and whose methods corresponded to those being promoted by the generation to which they belonged. Because Renoir's method essentially consisted of creating a climate of camaraderie and friendship with his actors, he could only have seemed to them as he actually was: the most modern of the classic directors. He

---

* Cornelia Froboess would next pursue a "serious" career in both theater and film and would appear notably in R. W. Fassbinder's *Veronika Voss* (1982).

never looked through the lens of the camera and did not use a viewfinder, which made him seem like someone who paid no attention to the technical aspects of filmmaking. He would place—and, occasionally, shift—the camera as needed, without investigating the framing this obtained, although it always appeared perfect when the footage was screened. The actors appreciated that, as well, and it made them feel that much freer, and even more loved.

Although Renoir said he was "irritated" by "Guy Lefranc's and Gigi's slowness, which unfortunately offset Leclerc† and Picavet's speed,"[42] he also wrote, "The small drawbacks, differences in conception, pigheadedness, etc., are very minor compared to the rigid tyranny of a film in a big American studio,"[43] and filming went forward as harmoniously as one could desire. To the journalists who visited the set, the director claimed he was relentlessly rewriting the screenplay and came out with one of his characteristic barbs: "I'm truly fond of René Clair and full of admiration for him, but when he has finished writing, the film is over. The result is wonderful, too. For me it's the exact opposite: when the film has been written, everything begins."[44] And because, if he could also be believed, nothing for him was ever written, the mystery of Renoir would grow more impenetrable the more he pretended to be interested in clearing it up. In reality, although continually reworking the screenplay did have to do with his desire to reach for a form of perfection, the practice also allowed him to limit the hold of production over the film. By stabbing René Clair in the back, he was displaying his "modernity" and, even more than that, his originality. Renoir judged Clair's most recent film‡ (if not also his others) mediocre; not that there was anyone who would believe that he actually thought the films of a colleague—a rival, in other words—were "wonderful." But his remark was also an expression of a reality that is too often forgotten: there are several ways to make a film, and there's no proof that one of them is preferable to any other.

During this time, in Paris, *Le Testament du docteur Cordelier* was finally being shown to audiences. On November 17, Mme. Doynel went twice to the George V theater for information on the initial takings, and they were far from impressive. Renoir kept saying this lack of success "left me cold," and seemed "natural," because "you don't dawdle for two years with a film made in the enthusiasm of a brief moment."[45] When the results turned out to be clearly catastrophic, he'd acknowledge that he had just "received one of the nastiest slaps in my life."[46] As for Mme. Doynel, she insisted on continuing to think that the failure of the film

* Roland Girard, the director of production.

† Georges Leclerc, the director of photography.

‡ *Porte des Lilas*; see note on page 681.

was due to a "cabal" and was sorry that "the Maestro" hadn't been able to be in Paris, because he knew how to "galvanize the masses." She kept from informing him of Marie Lestringuez's death three days before. "He's getting enough grief from Guy Lefranc without having to hear this sad news. . . . [Lefranc] has really disappointed me. It proves what an idiot and softie he is, and the fact that the Maestro took him on out of kindness makes it that much more disgusting."[47]

It may indeed have been out of kindness, and Mme. Doynel's irritation had to do with the fact that Lefranc intended at the very least to have his contribution acknowledged. Whether he deserved it or not, he wanted his role in the genesis of the project, which he'd worked on for seven years, to be credited in a clear way. Nonetheless, the woman who was now Renoir's agent was uncompromising. "If they don't agree to give Guy Lefranc 50 percent less publicity than the Maestro, I'll threaten that Jean Renoir won't sign the film. Because it's in their interest that he does, I'm not risking anything."[48] Mme. Doynel wasn't reduced to such an extreme measure. *The Elusive Corporal* was indeed presented as Jean Renoir's film, which it truly was. Guy Lefranc appeared in the credits under the puzzling title of "adjunct director." What had become of his adaptation? If we're to believe what Renoir said about it, "nearly nothing at all." And not much more when it came to Jacques Perret's novel, either, which does seem rather excessive. Renoir couldn't keep himself from diminishing the merits of others. Thus, right in the middle of the editing process, he stated, "I think that *Corporal* isn't bad because I've worked on Perret, not to mention on that idiot Guy Lefranc. I kept next to nothing of their work, but that work was there and allowed me to go a little farther."[49] In other words, the only merit of the book and the first attempts at adapting it were that they existed. The truth of the story was really that, and Renoir created an honest vision of it. Even at its most extreme, his behavior betrayed a lack of self-assurance and confidence, channeling as it did that feeling of disquietude characteristic of all humanity whose expression was one of the loftiest achievements of his filmmaking.

On December 6, Renoir was able to cable Dido that shooting was finished. Only one short scene remained to film in Paris and he would leave Vienna the following Saturday. On Sunday the tenth, he returned to avenue Frochot. At first he planned on having the epilogue take place on the grounds in front of Sacré-Coeur,[50] but after more location scouting he decided to rewrite the scene[51] and film on the Pont de Tolbiac on the morning of January 7.[52] In the meantime, he had worked on the editing, a task that had been delayed for several days because he hadn't been able to get hold of a Moviola but that was now being made easier by a "good mixture of *Cordelier* and classic methods"[53] he had managed to devise. During this stay in Paris, Aline Cézanne acted as his chauffeur. She'd always adored driving and, in her spare time, was practicing the art of parallel parking in the garage with the use of buckets and brooms.[54]

The first edit was finished by the end of January. On the twenty-seventh, Ginette Doynel wrote to Dido that when the screening was over, Renoir "had needed several minutes to come back to life." Then she added, "Yet again 'your little Dan' has made a masterpiece. If audiences don't react as they should, it's obviously because they have become completely stupid."[55] To her letter, Renoir added a few handwritten lines declaring himself "very happy" with this first edit to which the newsreel sections hadn't yet been added. The completion of the film had been celebrated at the restaurant Louis XIV on boulevard Saint-Denis.

His good mood didn't last, thwarted as it was by the intentions of the producers regarding the release. Informed that it had been decided that *The Elusive Corporal* would be associated with *The Cow and I* in the trailer, Renoir grew angry.[56] Away from Dido for too long a time and yearning for the country that had now been his for more than twenty years, he began to imagine somber events lurking in the future, caused in part by the trouble they were having in finding someone they could trust to watch their house on Leona Drive during their absence. "If I have to make another film in France, for financial reasons, I'd view that obligation as a catastrophe," he wrote, adding, "I wonder if it wouldn't be a better idea to sell *Le Chasseur* [the painting *Jean as a Huntsman*], *since we can't enjoy it in our home.*"[57] In 1926, he had sold some paintings by his father in order to make *Nana*. In 1962, he was claiming that he was ready to get rid of the painting he held most dear in order *not* to make films. Dido answered him on February 6, the date of their anniversary, calling it in her letter the "happiest day of my life." She told him she would oppose such a sale with all her strength. "We'd really have to be in the soup," she insisted, at the same time admitting having learned just the day before that their friends had a dealer who would be ready to pay $250,000 for *Jean as a Huntsman*. "He can hang onto his high hopes all he wants!" she concluded.[58]

There was no doubt that Renoir was having a hard time withstanding an isolation that was only relative. In reality, he was surrounded by people and very sought after. However, certain evenings weighed heavily on him; for example, those during which he dined on a can of sauerkraut "pepped up" with vinegar and accompanied by a bottle of Muscadet.[59] Far from Dido, despite the fact that Mme. Doynel was watching over him, he ate and drank too much, and what he was beginning to see as a dependence on alcohol worried him. "When I get back, you have to keep me from drinking too much wine. My work depends on it. I'm realizing now that I'm invited out too much and that I don't know how to say no. When I'm with you, it will be easier for me to stay sober."[60]

Throughout his entire time in Paris, he thought about wanting to get back to America and began putting some effort into inventing projects likely to interest Hollywood. One of them he was considering was an adaptation of *Quentin Durward,*[*] which he would ask to be written by Clifford Odets, who "would be spectacular at giving voice to characters as rustic as Louis X, Charles the Bold, the Wild Boar of the Ardennes,[†] and their companions."[61] He had also written to Dido to ask her opinion of Warren Beatty, who might be able to play the Walter Scott hero. She had seen the young actor in *The Roman Spring of Mrs. Stone,* the film adapted from a novel by Tennessee Williams that had not yet been released in France. Renoir had spent the evening before he wrote to Dido with Luise Rainer, Odets's first wife, and her husband, Robert Knittel,[‡] director of the major British publishing house William Collins, which was going to publish *Renoir, My Father* in Great Britain. At the time, Renoir was extremely worried about the English translation of his book. The one submitted to him by Randolph Weaver didn't suit him. "You're right in suspecting that my days are spent worrying over how to find a good solution for the translation of the book *Renoir.*"[62] With that in mind, he left for London as soon as he had finished *Corporal,* without waiting for the release of the film.

Considered—at least for the moment—to be the definitive version, *The Elusive Corporal* was shown in Billancourt on March 15 for the first time. Only the members of Renoir's crew were invited to attend. The second showing occurred the next day in the same location, but this time Renoir's friends were invited. "Pierre Gaut, his young daughter, and Maud were very impressed," wrote Renoir. "Braunberger and Truffaut liked the film a lot." He also noted that the only reservations were expressed by "a nephew of Mme. de Carbuccia named Chiappe, who has technical pretensions and suggested a cut."[63] Mme. Doynel was there as well and "barked" at the aforementioned Chiappe, "'What are you butting in for?'"[64] According to her, *Corporal* was "something incredible" that would "certainly meet with as much success as *Grand Illusion,* maybe even more, if that is possible"; and she added, "After they've seen this film the producers are going to throw themselves on your darling 'little Dan' and insist he make a film, and they'll be right."[65] At that same screening, Marc Maurette, Renoir's assistant again for the shoot, and his wife were also present; and they "didn't like the film," Renoir wrote to Dido, suggesting that *Le Corporal* "isn't in line with

---

[*] *Translator's note:* A historical novel by Walter Scott, published in 1823.

[†] *Translator's note:* William de la Marck (1446–1485).

[‡] Leslie Caron remembers that Luise Rainer would talk nonstop about Clifford Odets to Knittel.

such people's thinking."[66] Maurette was, in fact, a dyed-in-the-wool, militant Communist, whom Renoir had enjoyed goading in the thirties by calling his regular visits to Moscow "pilgrimages."[67]

Pierre Gaut had seen a first edit on February 20. According to Renoir, he'd been "terrorized by the evocation of war and defeat." "It's obvious," Renoir noted on that same evening, "that the comical aspect has now given way to tragedy. I'm very happy about it. We don't have a right to poke fun at such memories."[68] And on April 15, the man who had been Renoir's friend for close to thirty years wrote to Dido, "The film is magnificent. I think that it's even better than *Grand Illusion*."[69] Renoir's intentions in his film were certainly different from those expressed in his greatest success, something that the pundits would soon have a field day pointing out, going so far as to reject any similarities between the two films. This doesn't change the fact that all those who saw *Corporal* then made references to *Grand Illusion*, just as Spaak had when he'd presented the project to Renoir, a point of view that Renoir himself had seconded. And the fact that those who first saw the film in 1962 almost unanimously judged it more successful, more powerful, and more dazzling than the one he'd made in 1937 tells nothing about the nature of the two productions, or even about the real reactions of those who were invited to the screenings. It was just that the makers and promoters of the film found themselves caught in a whirlwind of resounding congratulations and stuttering promises for the future. Their intoxication at that time made their awakening that much more difficult when the results in the theaters turned out not to conform to their expectations.

Renoir himself kept cool. He maintained the impression he'd received during editing, something he communicated to Dido when a screening of the film in that state "for about forty people chosen randomly"[70] had produced some good reactions.

> I like *Corporal* and believe it's a good film. But more than ever I'm blending the comical with the tragic, and that can make it unbearable for audiences used to schmaltz. The new films make me think of kids' entertainment. They think they're being daring because they show promiscuity. It's the kind of daring of twelve-year-old children who are flabbergasted at discovering they have sex organs. Such sex stories have taken over the world. It's all people think about. My *Corporal* is violent and (I hope) very pure. Maybe it will be seen as strange to a timid audience who'd like to be impure.[71]

Even if that analysis is burdened with snap judgments, it is a clear one concerning *Corporal;* and it reveals that Renoir knew how to maintain the necessary distance from his own film.

Although the climate that dominated Paris at the beginning of 1962 seemed to have little effect on his morale, one of its repercussions was going to affect the release of *Corporal*. It's not really possible to draw any conclusions regarding his thoughts about the wave of attacks disrupting France at that time, and he alluded to the situation only to Dido, whom he intended, above all, not to alarm. The day after the demonstration for peace in Algeria and against the OAS,* during which nine people had been killed by the police at the Métro stop Charonne, Renoir reported the account of a female friend to his wife. The woman had been "completely moved by the sight of the crowd in the Métro, so reverent, those masses of flowers," and he predicted that "a lot of people will go to the funerals of the victims of the previous demonstration," but that "this crowd is very calm, very dignified, and isn't looking for a fight." Then he made clear that he was a lot more worried about the floods threatening Los Angeles, which he thought were "as worrisome as the events in Paris." But he put his mind at ease by reflecting that their "house is high enough," even if landslides could always occur.[72] A week later, he begged Dido not to be too affected by the news coming from France and assured her, "People are much too prosperous to attempt any overthrow. These are repercussions of the situation in Algeria, and the French in France couldn't care less about it."[73]

On March 1, on the way back from a dinner at Maud Gaut's, he witnessed the explosion of a "very powerful bomb on the sidewalk in front of a North African restaurant, the Lucky-Sport,"[74] right next to the cabaret Tabarin. There was no victim of the attack, and what had interested him then was "the way people behaved." He went on, "Those passing by stopped, people came out of little bars, from the café on the corner and the tabac, and without panicking they discussed the probable placement of the bomb. It was rather ironic. People thinking 'more idiots.' . . . But you could tell that plastic bombs had become part of Parisian mores in the same way as head colds or stalled elevators."[75]

In the meantime, dramatic events had taken place at the Val-de-Grâce military hospital, and one of the developments would lead to putting off the release of *The Elusive Corporal*. Sent to the hospital after being wounded during an attack in Algiers, Yves Le Tac, the brother of Parisian deputy Joël Le Tac, was targeted on Sunday, February 18, by an OAS operation during which one of the two policemen entrusted with guarding the wounded man was killed. Jacques Perret's son, Jean-Louis, was one of the four suspects of the commando. A search that took place at the home of Jacques Perret, who was himself a member of the propaganda branch of the OAS-Métro, received heavy press

* *Translator's note:* OAS = Organisation de l'armée secrète, a far-right paramilitary organization during the Algerian War. Its goal was to prevent Algeria's independence from France.

commentary. Obviously, a film adaptation of the writer's most well-known book had nothing to gain from such unexpected publicity. During the luncheon that had been their only encounter, Renoir had thought Perret was a "sensitive and reasonable man."[76] The postponement of the film's release was announced on April 1. On the same evening, Renoir and Mme. Doynel left for Le Mans, where the film was to be presented the following day as a benefit for former combatants from the region. In Le Mans and in Lyon, where he would be on April 5, demonstrations against *The Elusive Corporal* had been announced.

Renoir made it clear that he was happy about the April 1 decision. He'd had enough of Paris—and, quite probably, of his film *Corporal*—enough of people buzzing around him. He was in a hurry to leave for London and then Leona Drive. "This April Fool's trick is fine with me. I have no desire to put myself on display. I'm tired of explaining my films and my ideas to the public. And I think people have seen enough of me. So I'm going to be firm and refuse to participate in the postponed release of *Corporal,* will refuse to go and turn on the charm at Cannes and will leave as planned."[77] The management of the Cannes Film Festival had actually expressed its interest in the film, which had been screened on March 23 for the committee in charge of selections. Pierre Braunberger was one of its members. Since the day before, the producer had insisted that Renoir delay his departure and go "turn on the charm at Cannes."[78] But, without waiting, the director had warned him, "I'm not falling for it."[79]

On April 11, while Renoir was in London, he learned that *The Elusive Corporal* would not be shown at Cannes, whereas the films the French were presenting included Agnès Varda's *Cléo de 5 à 7* (*Cleo from 5 to 7*), Robert Bresson's *Procès de Jeanne d'Arc* (*The Trial of Joan of Arc*), and Raymond Rouleau's *The Lovers of Teruel* with Ludmilla Tchérina. On the other hand, the film would be shown in competition at the Berlin International Film Festival, which in those days took place at the end of June. Its reception was rather cool, because it may not have been the best idea seventeen years after the end of war to show audiences in Berlin this story of French prisoners held in Germany. The film found no favor in the eyes of the jury, which was headed by King Vidor. Renoir did not make the journey to Berlin.

In London, where he put the finishing touches on his book and took steps to promote it upon its release, Mme. Doynel, who had come with him, wrote to Dido, "Your 'handsome little Dan' charmed everyone, starting with the journalists."[80] Forced to prolong his London stay by a few more days to attend to additional unexpected corrections on the book, Renoir finally returned to his home on April 26.

On May 2, a preview of *Corporal* was arranged at the Mac-Mahon theater, and Ginette Doynel assured him that it had been "very successful," before

asking him whether he'd agree to a few cuts suggested by Jean-Luc de Carbuccia, Adry's son. These depicted the arrival and the departure of the camp
prisoners, as well as the sequence having to do with the discipline camp.[81] After
having announced his agreement by telegram on May 7, on condition that the
cuts be made by Renée Lichtig and that the balance of the scenes concerned be
taken into account,[82] Renoir revealed what he really thought, molded as it was
by the experiences he'd had in the thirties and for which *The Rules of the Game*
especially had paid the cost: "It is always very dangerous to fiddle with an edit. It
always augurs catastrophe. Either a film works and two or three overlong scenes
can't prevent that from happening, or else it doesn't work and deleting those
overlong scenes won't make it a success. I have too much affection for Jean-Luc
not to let him judge the situation entirely, but he has to be well aware that fiddling with a film can murder it even if it seems innocent and only has to do with
details." At the time, he already knew that the actions of the producers were less
inspired by their claim of feeling it was overlong than by their disappointment
regarding its first public showings in the provinces. In that same letter, he in
fact wrote, "If the results continue to be as awful as they were in Toulouse and
Rennes, it will obviously be the death knell of my career in film."[83]

The worst hadn't come yet. Soon he would learn that Cyclope had hacked
away from the film, and those cuts hadn't even been done by Renée Lichtig.
On May 11, a screening had been organized for the editor, during which she'd
confirmed that the sacrifice "goes way beyond the two or three minuscule cuts"
that had been talked about. For one thing, the newsreels had disappeared, and
the editor was especially shattered by the elimination of the Japanese footage.
What was more, the last reel hadn't been shown that day. The next day there was
a new screening—this time of the complete copy. The airplanes had disappeared
from the final scene, which had been amputated by at least three minutes. Renée
Lichtig added, "Mme. de Carbuccia, I swear, had nothing to do with it. She was
crying on the telephone this morning, furious at M. Girard. She's going to ask
them to restore the cuts tomorrow."[84]

It didn't really matter whether it was the director of production, Mme. de
Carbuccia, her son, or the distributor who was responsible; and before even
receiving the editor's explanations, Renoir had drawn the only conclusion that
made sense to him: "If those people are too stupid to understand that they're
destroying their film, too bad for them. As for me, only one idea makes sense, and
that is to hear no more talk of film. Nor do I want to pull the act of withdrawing
my name. I find this ridiculous. . . . My mistake was to believe that people who
were proud of having produced *The Cow and I* could have a bit of taste."[85]

However, less than a week later, there was a new letter: the most harmful
cut was the one at the end having to do with the airplanes, the one "between the

scene with the peasant and the one with the bridge." "That threat of war lends the separation of the two friends a note of melancholy that can help leave the viewer with a deeper impression. . . . Successful films are made from small things like that, and by destroying them, you destroy films."[86] Renoir's friend Pierre Gaut, who had seen the film in the edit Renoir had wanted and had just reseen it in a theater, declared himself appalled. "We walked out of there shattered. By making imbecilic cuts to your masterful film, that imposing work from which nothing can be subtracted and to which nothing can be added, they've managed to put out a film that could be called *Prisoner Gags*. All that are left are the situations and the repartee."[87]

Shown in Paris beginning May 23, *The Elusive Corporal* was not considered a success,* despite what the first week's results—sixty-five thousand tickets—had led everyone to expect. Renoir was too accustomed to commercial failures to be affected more than was reasonable, but he was particularly displeased by the fact that no one had been able to see his film the way it had been filmed and edited. "The critics judged my film based on the cut version." His conclusion: "Those imbeciles at Cyclope took away my chance to hit the jackpot."[88] Despite this, Renoir's relationship with "those imbeciles" remained warm, as evidenced by the letters he continued to write to Mme. de Carbuccia, such as this one from July: "I don't hold it against Cyclope, because I have too much faith in divine equilibrium. If I missed the mark with *Corporal,* it's probably because I am benefiting from too many advantages in other domains."[89] In October, he declared, "I have to avoid working with Cyclope in the future,"[90] but a few months later he was considering various projects with the producer and her son.

    Contrary to what was maintained, critics had not been unanimously unfavorable. Georges Sadoul in *Les Lettres françaises* had appreciated the simplicity of the film and found its tone "assured and true like a soldier's, an enlisted man's."[91] In *Combat,* Pierre Marcabru hailed "a fraternal and sincere film, a film that hides behind nothing."[92] It's true as well that certain reviews were harsh. For example, in *L'Humanité,* Samuel Lachize called it "a film that certainly needs to be seen as reactionary, with a subject that doesn't seem to be betrayed by its approach." Certainly, the most vicious attack was the work of Françoise Giroud,

* Given the statistics for the film's receipts, the reasons for that observation are rather mysterious. Having sold more than two million tickets, *The Elusive Corporal* would be classed in fifteenth place among the successes of the year and in eighth place among French films, which included *Un singe en hiver* (*A Monkey in Winter,* directed by Henri Verneuil), which the majority held to be a commercial success. The disappointment felt probably resulted from their comparing the film's outcome to the triumph of *The Cow and I* and the prestige of *Grand Illusion.*

the continuity girl for *Grand Illusion,* who ended an article entitled "The Toad in the Soup Tureen" with these words: "'This film isn't my film,' announced Jean Renoir, refusing to participate in an RTF broadcast because certain cuts had been made in *The Elusive Corporal* without his consent. Well, glad he did! He'll never say it enough!" Fourteen years later, when Françoise Giroud had become secretary of state for culture, and shortly after she had presented Renoir with the officer's rank of the Légion d'honneur, Pierre Gaut asked Renoir to get her to have dust removed from the monument to the National Convention at the Panthéon that had covered it since 1920. Gaut's father had erected the monument. Renoir's answer to this was, "I don't know Françoise Giroud personally. Outside of her function on *Grand Illusion,* I've met her twice in my life: at a dinner and when she presented me with the Légion d'honneur."[93]

The run of the film ended on June 12, after only four weeks of exclusive showings, without their reintegrating any of the scenes that had been cut, despite the promises that had been made.[94] The failure of the film may have been relative, but it was still unjust, yet also predictable. Although the discrepancy between *Grand Illusion* and *The Elusive Corporal* was frequently emphasized by the press, the latter film even being represented by *Candide* as "La Petite Illusion"—and it did make sense to expect such a thing—the disparity between the two wars and between the personality of the prisoners in each of the two global conflicts provoked the rejection of *Corporal.* The protagonists in *Grand Illusion* were combatants, and those who did escape were going to win the war. The characters in *Corporal* were defeated and could do nothing about it, even if the corporal and Pop promised each other on the Pont de Tolbiac to rid France of the swastikas that were sullying the country.

The disappearance of the aristocracy mentioned and regretted by Boëldieu and Rauffenstein, not to mention Renoir himself, had become a reality. There is no spirit of chivalry in *The Elusive Corporal.* Although Bailochet is killed during an escape attempt, as is Boëldieu, the latter sacrifices himself to make it possible for Maréchal and Rosenthal to flee; and he is killed by someone like him, whereas Ballochet's action resembles a suicide and is carried out by some anonymous sentry. In that sense, it's not by chance that Renoir chose not to film the death of Ballochet, of which the viewer becomes aware only through sounds and the expressions on the faces of his comrades. Even the rear ends of those who are absent meet different fates. Whereas a prisoner in *Grand Illusion* promises to give his wife a swift kick in hers, the peasant in *Corporal* maintains that his better half can certainly do what she wants with hers as long as the farm remains well maintained. There's nothing glorious about that, and such moments are typical of the film as a whole, which evokes collapse, defeat, and little acts of cowardice among individuals, everything that French audiences in 1962 were refusing to hear discussed. There is clearly an example of fraternization between French and Germans in both films, but the two aristocratic officers candidly discussing the disappearance of their world gave way to two noncommissioned officers discussing the scale of punishments in their respective service branches and finding accord in their paltry schemes. The prisoners in *Grand Illusion* had been caught while fighting, whereas those in *Corporal* didn't even get a chance to fight. If *The Cow and I* and *Tomorrow Is My Turn* were hits during the same period, it was because they emphasized the virtues that the French ascribed to themselves—something that *Grand Illusion* had also done in a less blatant manner—and they did it without any real reference to the shame of defeat and the tragedy of 1940.* In *The Elusive Corporal,* the enlisted man of 1913, the combatant of 1914, the wounded of 1915, and the aviator of 1916 are also given voice, as is the man who cultivates nostalgia.

Renoir cultivated nostalgia nonstop in this period. He gave it free rein in the book on his father, which appeared in bookstores as he was still engaged in that train of thought. It's a wonderful book, a magnificent portrait that is also a self-portrait, carried along by Renoir's memories as well as Gabrielle's. They are redesigned memories, recounted at length and also staged. Pierre-Auguste Renoir emerges as a kind of fictional character, celebrated by a son whose eyes, naturally, have never seen a better father or a greater painter. It's known that the project first came into Renoir's mind shortly after he arrived in the United States, after his agent at the time suggested it to him. Over a period of nearly twenty years, he constantly returned to the project, especially when he began to rely on Gabrielle's memory. She would talk and he would listen while recording the conversation with a tape recorder. However, after Gabrielle died and a whim of Dido led her to listen to the voice of the deceased, she discovered that Jean had reserved the use of the mic for himself, reformulating each sentence his way as he heard it. Dido called him a ham on that day.[95]

All during this period, he was also thinking of writing his memoirs, an undertaking that would require even more time and that would be characterized by several false starts. Although interrupted by his trips and stays in Europe, the writing of his *Renoir* seems to have been done in a less uneven manner. It was fed by a large collection of preparatory notes, mostly handwritten and begun in 1942.

From February to August 1942, Renoir attempted to establish a guiding line for the book and accumulated rough outlines and notes[96] while working

* Released in December 1962, Alex Joffé's film *Les Culottes rouges* (*Red Culottes*), with Bourvil and Laurent Terzieff, substantiated the vogue for escape stories. It was seen by 1.8 million viewers.

from March 1942 to May 1943 on a text that he had entitled *Au temps de mon père.*[97] From then on, he began pulling together press clippings, letters from his father, and his own and Gabrielle's remembrances. To get into stride, he also exploited various lectures given at the request, among others, of the Alliance Française in Los Angeles in January 1942[98] and in Pasadena in March 1943.[99] Although the only part of this preparatory work that exists in his archives is on the order of about a thousand pages, there are only three successive versions of what would become the definitive text, whereas there are more than ten for *My Life and My Films.*

Over the years, Renoir also wrote several articles for American magazines. For example, the May 19, 1952, issue of *Life* contains a ten-page story illustrated with fifteen reproductions under the title "My Memories of Renoir," material the author would use again and develop for several passages in his book. An inattentive proofreader failed to correct the sentence, "I was born in 1893,"[100] a typo that didn't seem to bother Renoir. On the other hand, he asked for a correction regarding the text accompanying the reproduction of *The Judgment of Paris,* which had read, "At Les Collettes my father had a huge studio built for him. There around 1914 he painted this scene of classical gods, which, he once said, were the only deities he really worshiped."[101] Renoir wrote to point out that his explanation about the subject of the painting might have been unclear. His father was a Christian, he emphasized, and his great admiration for Greek mythology was totally intellectual and came from his love of art. Religion was not involved.[102] The date on the letter means that it was written in Rome, where shooting on *The Golden Coach* had just finished.

A great many different reasons led to the decision to write the book. In the first place, Renoir wanted to pay homage to his father. And the isolation in which he lived in California partly created the need to immerse himself once again in his childhood, with his hands pressed in Gabrielle's. The desire to write also counted for something, at a time in his life when film had begun to bring less satisfaction than it had in the past and when he had a better grasp than ever before of the "impure" nature of a form of art in which money had so much importance. As the years passed, the word "purity" turned up more and more frequently in his writing, applied as much to films, stories, and people as it was to ethics.

Part of Renoir's personality began to take on the trappings of the frustrated writer who found transcendence in contact with the great texts and great authors; and throughout his life this was expressed by habits that came close to a kind of graphomania. As a result, beginning at the end of the fifties until the time during which he wrote *Renoir* and even more after the failure of *The*

---

* *Translator's note:* Literally, "In the Time of My Father."

Elusive Corporal, in his eyes writing became the ideal way to express himself; and it also allowed him to stay home alone with Dido, whose company he was finding it more and more difficult to do without. Because his father was tremendously famous in the United States, writing a book about him also enabled Jean to make a name for himself in a country where his films had never been granted much prominence while simultaneously allowing him to hope that his efforts would bring in substantial amounts of money, which turned out to be the case. Finally, creating a dazzling image of this paternal figure could mean coming out of the shadows himself, from the obscurity of his identity as an artist who had refused to present himself as an artist, a creator who had spent a long time wanting to be an artisan, a frustrated actor blotted out by the figure of his brother, the real actor.

Whereas film had not allowed him to compete anywhere but in France with the aura of his father, writing was exactly what it should be, in all its purity. A director's prestige, no matter how celebrated, couldn't really be compared to that of a painter who was known and admired the world over. In celebrating his father, the son's stature grew in his own eyes. Thus, at the age of sixty-five, Jean freed himself from Auguste Renoir. Just a few years later he was able to write, "I've spent my life trying to determine the influence of my father on me, jumping from periods in which I was doing everything I could to escape that influence to other periods in which I overindulged on formulas that I thought were characteristic of him."[103] From its first to its last page, his book is motivated by these two orientations, which appear to be opposites but which are finally reconciled.

At one point he had thought of naming the book *Au jardin de mon père,*[104] a title that occurred to him while he was thinking of the *Fioretti di San Francesco.*[*][105] Dido, however, thought the title was too weak, before coming around to recognizing its virtues. Nevertheless, it was a better idea for the title to mention Jean Renoir's name, and it became *Renoir par Jean Renoir.*[†] Whereas the sales in France, where it was published by Hachette, turned out below what he had hoped for, the 1962 British and American editions, entitled *Renoir, My Father,* had excellent results.[‡] The book earned him a number of

---

* *Translator's note: Au jardin de mon père* translates literally as "In My Father's Garden." The *Fioretti di San Francesco (The Little Flowers of St. Francis)* is a collection of fifty-three excerpts (called *florilegia* in Latin) written at the end of the fourteenth century about the life of Saint Francis of Assisi. Although the text is anonymous, most scholars now suspect it was the work of Ugolino Brunforte.

† *Translator's note:* "Renoir by Jean Renoir."

‡ For the first six months of 1964 alone, Renoir received a check for royalties of $2,164.25, after commissions had been deducted. (Letter from the William Morris Agency, October 2, 1964, Jean Renoir Papers, Correspondence, Box 20, Folder 3.)

admiring gestures, such as the one from the great head cameraman Jack Cardiff, who mentioned in his letter that he was the fortunate owner of a painting by Auguste Renoir, *Andrée assise*.[106]

Renoir saw the discrepancy in appreciation between France and the two Anglophone countries as proof that his "ex-country" was expressing a decided lack of gratitude toward him. He did not take into account the fact that Anglo-Saxons generally evidence a greater interest in biographies than the French do and that admiration for the painter's genius was more widespread in the United States. The book's appearance in America resulted in a number of praise-filled articles, but its release in France was relatively unobtrusive. This was barely changed by its winning the Charles-Blanc Prize—for art history books—from the Académie française the following year.[107]

Before the book even appeared and *Corporal* was released, Renoir knew that his future writings wouldn't benefit from the same a priori advantages.

> The next book I write, if it isn't on Renoir, won't find its place as easily. It's the same as the case of a film on a subject like Ben Hur or the Ten Commandments. It would have to be a major failure to end up like a slap in the face. That's why I'm tempted by the idea of making another film that would allow us to invest a few dollars and perhaps reach a stage where we could live (modestly) with the revenue that comes in. Then I could write without worrying about the future. But being practical in that way won't bring me to the point of accepting something bad. I'll only make a film if, first of all, the subject appeals to me; secondly, if we've solved the problem of someone housesitting at *maïon;* and, thirdly, if you can stay with me during these undertakings.[108]

No doubt about it: what he now wanted to do was to write, and he no longer saw film as anything but a way of making money and living as he intended to. He was not unaware that the chances for him to make films were going to prove rare. The fact that he wasn't in a position of strength led to hesitations about rejecting offers that came his way. For example, when Adry de Carbuccia insisted that he direct *Les Camisards** in autumn 1962, he began by claiming, "I've skimmed through a work about that subject. It was a series of horrors and acts of violence on both sides, and I refuse to show such incitements to murder on a screen."[109] However, little more than a month later, he wrote that he still "found the subject just as appealing" but wanted "at least a year at *maïon* with

---

* *Translator's note:* The Camisards were Protestants from the region of the Cévennes. From 1865 to 1870, they waged war against the state, which had forbidden their religion and which would massacre them.

[Dido]" and was in favor of shooting in the summer of 1963. On the other hand, he felt "very tired" and a "craving for peace and quiet" and, "precisely because of that," felt that this might be his "last opportunity to make a film," but only if Dido could come with him, because "every day without [her] is a day that has been lost." In her company, he saw "my different professional problems a lot more clearly."[110] He spoke the entire afternoon of April 10 with Jean-Luc about another of the Carbuccias' projects but said that the idea "terrorizes everybody except his mother." It concerned the war in Algeria.[111]

Pierre Braunberger also wanted to work with Renoir. They had already been discussing their project as early as before *French Cancan*. "His story—or rather, my story—as a Jew during the exodus,* seems to be gelling and could be good," wrote Renoir. To "figure out the first draft," Renoir had suggested calling in a writer, arguing that "instead of losing their time inventing the events in a story, Shakespeare or Molière drew from the works of their predecessors or from history, keeping the best of their form for what was essential, namely, the structure and the final dialogue, which are the true mark of a genuine auteur."[112] It was Braunberger's idea to entrust the task to Galtier-Boissière,† "a good idea," according to Renoir, who, on the other hand, thought he wouldn't accept and suggested "Boulle, the writer for [*The Bridge on the*] *River Kwai*." A few weeks later, the producer chose "a young writer called Rossi [who] is very good,"[113] and the subject was henceforth "largely based on *his exodus*." Rossi's first name was Jean-Baptiste, and in 1950 he had published a novel, *Les Mal Partis*,‡ the story of passionate love in the summer of 1944 between a schoolboy and a young nun, which he was attempting to have adapted for the cinema. Braunberger had tried to accomplish this, hadn't succeeded, and had delegated the direction of two short films to Rossi. Also in 1962, the young writer adopted the pseudonym "Sébastien Japrisot" and authored his first detective novel, *Compartiment tueurs*.§* In 1975, he would direct *Les Mal Partis* (*Bad Starters*) himself, going back to the name of Jean-Baptiste Rossi for that occasion. In May 1962, Braunberger would ask him to read *Hunger*, which Renoir would, hopefully, also direct and which Braunberger wanted at the time to "set in Paris."[114]

---

* *Translator's note:* The "exodus" being referred to was the flight of French populations from the east and north in 1940 as German troops invaded.

† Jean Galtier-Boissière, writer and creator in 1915 of *Le Crapouillot*, which he would direct until his death in 1966.

‡ *Translator's note:* Published in the United Kingdom and the United States as "The False Start" and "Awakening," respectively.

§ *Translator's note:* Published in English as *The 10:30 from Marseille*, this novel about murder in a train would become Costa-Gavras's first film, *The Sleeping Car Murders*, in 1965.

But in the meantime, *The Elusive Corporal* had been released, and Renoir wrote to the producer, "I owe you an explanation about my hesitations, which are strong enough to lead me to renege temporarily from doing anything at all in Europe. Let me add that the idiotic cuts that Cyclope amputated from *The Elusive Corporal* have made me seriously disgusted with film."[115]

From Paul Graetz, the producer of *Devil in the Flesh,* among other films, Renoir received a letter suggesting he bring to the screen the George Barr book *Épitaphe pour un ennemi.* As Graetz explained, "The hero is a young American soldier who is assigned to evacuate about thirty French civilians onto the Normandy beach the day after the landing."*[116] Graetz then expressed his opinion about Renoir's most recent film: "*The Elusive Corporal* is a wonderful film, but it's obviously a film without any distribution possibilities for all the English-speaking countries, first of all because there is no actor in the credits that would interest them. Therefore it could only play in art theaters."

Renoir, who had also asked Eugène Lourié to help him launch a production of *Quentin Durward* shot in English and in French,[117] answered without delay that Graetz's project did indeed seem a "really great subject."[118] However, after Graetz informed him that Warren Beatty had refused the role in that film and that Graetz was thinking of offering it to George Peppard,[119] Renoir informed the producer† of his decision to devote himself to writing a new book.[120] For the same reason, he also declined an offer to chair the jury at the Venice Film Festival from August 25 to September 18.[121] After several weeks characterized less by hesitation than by expectation, Renoir had returned to his first idea: "All of that doesn't measure up to the joy of writing a good book at *maïon*."[122] From then on, that was the task to which he devoted himself. However, nearly two years would be needed before he could say he had finally begun his book and was working on it every day.[123]

---

* The film would be directed by Robert Parrish as *Up from the Beach* (1965), with Cliff Robertson.

† Paul Graetz died on February 5, 1966, at the age of sixty-four, while producing *Is Paris Burning?*

33

"I've Become a Museum Piece"

Les Cahiers du capitaine Georges (The Notebooks of Captain Georges)
Le Petit Théâtre de Jean Renoir (The Little Theatre of Jean Renoir)

On the night of December 15, 1962, Charles Laughton passed away at the age of sixty-three. Renoir was unaware that his former best friend in Hollywood had been suffering from cancer. They hadn't seen each other for several years, but after Billy Wilder was forced to turn down Elsa Lanchester's request to be one of the pallbearers, she telephoned Renoir. The following Friday, December 20, the deceased was carried from his house on Pacific Palisades by actor Raymond Massey, lawyer Lloyd Wright, agent Taft Schreiber, intimate friend David Roberts, and Jean Renoir. Christopher Isherwood read a few verses from *The Tempest,* and "Dido looked like a Goya painting in her black lace mantilla."[1]

Stroheim had died in 1957, Dudley Nichols in January 1960. Chaplin was now living in Europe, and Albert Lewin spent most of his time in New York. Practically all who were left of their first American friends were Norman Lloyd and David L. Loew. An even more long-term friend, who was French, was Jacques Becker; and he had died on February 21, 1960, at the age of fifty-three; however, life had separated the two friends quite some time ago.

When Becker died, Renoir had dedicated several wonderful texts to him as a tribute to their friendship. In one of them, he alluded to the remark Becker had written to him just after the war: "This is the first time that I've written a love letter to a man, but given the fact that neither of us is queer, it really doesn't matter."[2] In response to this, Renoir wrote about their relationship, "I'd like to call it love, but I'm stopped by the sexual implications with which men of our time have loaded that word. You can't say 'I love a man' without immediately noticing a look of slight surprise in the person to whom you're talking. Deep down inside, he wonders whether it has something to do with homosexuality."[3] All these homages from Renoir to his former assistant deserve to be quoted, except for the fact that they all lack one important element: not for a moment does Renoir discuss the films of Jacques Becker, whom he never identified as anything but his ex-assistant. The only exceptions to this are two short sentences in his memoirs: "He possessed a talent that was as convincing as he was. His film *Casque d'or* will remain a masterpiece of cinema."[4] Even when his tone becomes lyrical, the Master doesn't forget to discuss Becker only as being second to himself. That is the way it would be, right up to and within *My Life and My Films,* which contains a chapter devoted to Becker—or to be more exact, to the nature of their relationship, as exemplified by the following lines: "Jacques Becker, my brother and son, I can't accept the fact that you're rotting in your grave. I'd rather believe that you're waiting for me in some corner of the afterlife, ready to make another film with me."[5] Truly lovely lines, in fact, but through which Renoir would like to believe and suggest that the greatest blessing Becker could hope for from eternity would be working "with" Renoir—for Renoir. But what if, rather than going backward to the supreme joy of being Renoir's assistant, Becker were really dreaming of making his own films?

Renoir wasn't one of those rare directors who celebrated the talent of their colleagues. What made him different from a lot of others was the fact that he tried to make the opposite believed, and even succeeded at it. For example, he saw *Jules and Jim* with Braunberger in Paris on January 23, 1962, which was the day after the film was released. On February 8, he wrote to Truffaut, "Let me take the opportunity to tell you that *Jules and Jim* seems to me to be the most precise expression of contemporary French society I have ever seen on the screen."[6] The phrase brings to mind what he wrote to Becker about *It Happened at the Inn,* which he claimed to like "because it's a distressing expression of our defeat,"[7] whereas he was talking about a film that he had really considered colorless, childish, and pretentious. Renoir's letter to Truffaut continued with a dissertation on ethics, about the passage in a few years from one civilization to another, about the city of Tournus, the Renaissance, and the Knights of the Round Table,* and the letter mentioned that it "is very important for us men to know where we are with women, and equally important for the women to know where they are with men." Truffaut, he added, was helping "to dispel the cloudiness of that issue."[8]

It is easy to understand why the young director kept that letter for a long time "in the inside pocket of his jacket."[9] However, rereading it more coolly suggests more ambivalent reactions, and the appreciation seems less homage to the director's talent and the splendor of his film than an exposition of general considerations about the march of time. Additionally, it's a fact that the question

---

* In one of his last letters to François Truffaut, Renoir mentions the Knights of the Round Table in reference to the directors of the Nouvelle Vague: "You don't need anyone in order to transport your friends into a world in which the inhabitants are genuine knights. The Nouvelle Vague gathers these barons at a roundtable." (Letter to François Truffaut, August 11, 1978, *Correspondance 1913–1978*.)

of the relationship between the sexes interested Renoir to a high degree. His notebooks and pads are blackened with the thoughts the subject inspired, and, clearly, he thought that the big change had happened in 1914, as he indicates in his letter to Truffaut. Aside from that, nothing in his notes suggests that his opinions on this subject define him as empathetic to the moral of *Jules and Jim*.*

Further proof of this occurred the day after Renoir saw the film and confided about it to Dido, singing a far different tune. "Very beautiful, but same feeling of ennui as a lot of new products of French cinema. We're smack in the middle of bourgeois literature at the end of the nineteenth century, with its charm, flimsiness, and emptiness. That kind of modern, subway-entrance style."[10] If the reference to the "subway-entrance style" seems obscure, it can be cleared up by a certain passage from Renoir's book on his father. "When he was teaching us how to do ceramics, he would speak to us about modern art's mistakes in seeking to copy nature without digesting it. He would mention the clumsiness of Parisian subway entrances, inspired directly by lianas or flowers."[11] What could these "new products of cinema" actually be that he discovered in January or February 1962, other than *Jules and Jim*? To Dido he wrote that they make him "think of entertainment for kids" and that they "think they're daring because they represent easy morals."[12]

Although Renoir repeatedly expressed pleasure at the success of his "young friends," especially when *The 400 Blows* triumphed at Cannes, he felt far from the kind of cinema they were practicing. Those filmmakers whose example had convinced him to "enter film"—Chaplin, Stroheim, Griffith—had recognized him as one of theirs and counted him among those close to them. They were the figures against whom he weighed himself. The Satyajit Ray films that he was able to see essentially made him miss the books that inspired them,[13] which he preferred to the films; and the fact that a few talented young French who had erected a statue to him were themselves making a stab at filmmaking with success was all well and good, but there was nothing in that to impress him, nor even to appeal to him on any deep level.

At the beginning of the sixties, Renoir was a lonely old gentleman who was allowing his nostalgia for the old days full rein. Moreover, if there had ever been a god who admired the attempts of his disciples, it wasn't Renoir;

---

* In one of his notebooks appears the following sentence: "Today the use of antibiotics and homosexuality have done away with a lot of risks and have left lovers only with the dull pain of disappointments." It comes as a conclusion to this passage: "The elimination of risk has killed pleasure (of love—of the senses—of doing things badly). In the past, a girl risked the reprobation of her social circle—a child—dishonor. A man—disease—responsibilities—the murderous jealousy of a rival—the wrath of an irate brother." (Notebook manuscript, undated, Jean Renoir Papers, Box 35, Folder 9.)

and since he'd become a director, others' films had, in general, left him cold. As soon as he would acknowledge that his time as a director had passed, he would recover a small amount of interest in the spectacle of film, which was maintained mostly by his affection for François Truffaut. However, most often he would continue to reserve his professions of admiration for the person to whom he was speaking or writing, rarely forgetting to back up such a display by expressing his indifference toward the person whose praises he'd just finished singing. Admiration between creative people only blooms fully after rivalry has disappeared. Such is what Paul Meurisse would give expression to when he'd describe the final years of Renoir's life: "He leaves for America. He's venerated there like a saint in his shrine. The French visiting Los Angeles go to see him. On pilgrimage. With piety and a serene mind. Age is keeping him from working any longer. He isn't a competitor anymore. So, relieved, we bow down before him."[14]

Actually bow down, and some of the faithful have to have icons. For example, film critic Pauline Kael came up with a request she herself labeled "embarrassing." She wanted Renoir to send her a photograph so that she could contemplate his face each day: "The more I think of your films the more I love you," she wrote, and, "I'm beginning to understand that what I love in Truffaut's and Satyajit Ray's cinema is related to yours."[15] Agnès Varda's request was less preposterous and obviously pleasanter: "You were familiar with me as a photographer. Maybe you remember me," wrote the young director. "I've just finished shooting Le Bonheur [Happiness], a film that pays homage to Mozart and your father, Renoir. In addition, I'd like to pay homage to you with a detail and present a color excerpt from Carrosse d'or on a television screen during a family scene. I'm crazy about that film, and the sight of a very short excerpt would give a delightful and moving dimension to the scene."[16] Varda was requesting permission to use thirty to fifty seconds of the film and fifty to eighty seconds of the soundtrack, and because Renoir "seemed to remember that this was a very fine woman,"[17] this posed no problem. In the end, she'd choose to show a passage from Picnic on the Grass in her film.

Confronted as he was by these excesses of veneration, Renoir suffered more than ever by the rare discordant notes he heard. The day after the appearance of a special issue of the review Premier Plan that was entirely devoted to him and in which his career and his work were often treated severely, he was worried about knowing whether their other installments contained authors who were "that biased and ill-meaning,"[18] and he admitted that he had become "a bit touchy now."[19] In addition, the course that he would give to the students at UCLA in 1963 would leave him dissatisfied. "I wonder whether 'direction' can be taught and whether the future director wouldn't do better to acquire culture

in the general sense, get to know a few good books, good paintings, good musical works, understand them, absorb and digest them. Obviously, that is the kind
of thing that would represent good preparation for the profession of film."[20]

Working on the conception of what would become *Les Cahiers du capitaine
Georges* (*The Notebooks of Captain Georges*) went on for nearly three years, but
Renoir only got down to writing it by the beginning of summer 1964, after
having decided to close some doors that had opened since *The Elusive Corporal*.
It was a carefully thought-out decision that was succinctly expressed. "I haven't
done anything for two years except tread water. The honors they're coveting
me with are harming me in the practical domain. I've become a museum piece.
I'm paid big compliments without any offers to work."[21] This was a bit unjust.
For one thing, he wasn't indifferent to those honors and they were allowing his
work to live on. However, "treading water" was costing him time and energy. A
month spent thinking about a film project was a month lost to the book that he
wanted to write. "But at least this book exists; even if it is discussed and certain
publishers don't want it, I know it will still be printed, whereas you never know
whether a film will be shot."[22]

During this period, he was working again on his adaptation of *Hunger* and
was writing a treatment for it under the title *Yladjali*.[23] On the other hand, he
seemed attached only by default to a potential adaptation of *La Célestine* by
Fernando de Rojas (c. 1465–1541), which was both a play and a novel and had
inspired Picasso in 1903. The project was Braunberger's, who talked about it
as "the film I've wanted to make most since 1942."[24] However, Renoir quickly
declared himself "worn out in advance by the difficulties related to shooting in
Spanish,"[25] something that also led him at the same time to refuse to consider
an embryonic proposition having to do with *Don Quixote*.[26] Once he had started
working on his novel, he confided to Braunberger that he preferred to renege on
a subject he did not think "could interest a modern audience," even if "we found
an actress with genius." He added, "I would have had to make *La Célestine* right
after *The Golden Coach*. Obviously, I don't have many films left to make, and
I'd like those that come from my camera to represent a step forward from my
previous works."[27] Then there would be no *Célestine*.*

* At the same time, an Italian producer was also trying to bring the work to the screen by
modernizing it, under the direction of Carlo Lizzani. Also, an adaptation was directed in Spain
by César Ardavin.

Renoir stayed a bit longer with the Vladimir Pozner* novel, *Curtain Raiser,* which had appeared in 1961. Renoir stated he was "very taken with this subject, [which] could serve as a basis not only for an excellent film but also give me the chance to apply certain new ideas that I've been seeking in vain to apply for several years."[28] Renoir and Pozner had crossed paths during their departure from Europe in 1940. The director and writer had taken the same route "from Marseille to Oran and from Oran to Casa, not to mention Tangiers, Lisbon, New York, and Hollywood."[29] At the time, the Pozners' daughter, Catherine, was three, and she was to become "an excellent editor."[30] The heroine of Pozner's novel is a little girl of seven named Diane who is discovering the world of adults. Although the setting is different, a private residence in Paris, the themes are suggestive of those found in *The River*. Encountered in the novel's pages are an actress, a servant, a magician, and an enchanted necklace. For the first character, Renoir naturally thought of Leslie Caron, who wasted no time in saying she was "very interested"[31] in making the film. However, after a meeting with David O. Selznick, Renoir mentioned the name of Jennifer Jones, the producer's wife, whom the director claimed was very eager to work with him. During Renoir's conversation with Selznick, Colette's *Chéri* also came up, "which Jennifer was bursting with a desire to be filmed."[32] Nothing would come to pass of all of that. Nor was Jennifer Jones fortunate enough to appeal to Adry de Carbuccia.[33] It seems that, in spite of his misadventure with *Corporal,* Renoir had offered the product to Cyclope, in addition to offering them *Hunger.* "What a joy to make another film with you," Mme. Cyclope had written to him, certain that "Leslie will be perfect."[34] She was also thinking of Vittorio Gassman, whom she had seen in *Il Sorpasso,* but the role would have to be expanded for him. Renoir hadn't thought of Gassman for this "role of a grotesque cynic,"[35] but he acknowledged that for him he was "one of the best actors of our time."

The weeks passed, weariness set in, and he kept thinking about the project but couldn't succeed in arousing the interest of a producer capable of putting it together. Soon, Pozner was the only one who remained determined, envisioning Danielle Darrieux and Serge Reggiani in the film, but above all bent on working on the adaptation while also mentioning in passing that Jean Delannoy was

* *Translator's note:* The reference is to Vladimir Aleksandrovich Pozner (1908–1975), a Russian Jewish émigré to the United States who had spied for the Soviet Union during World War II while working for the US government. It is not a reference to his son Vladimir Vladimirovich Posner (b. 1934), who was educated partly in the United States and who later became a prominent spokesperson on American television for the Soviet Union during the Cold War. During Renoir's departure for the United States in 1940, when he made the acquaintance of the Pozners, the son would have been six years old.

inquiring about the novel.[36] Renoir's response to that: Delannoy would do it if the mood took him.[37] More than two years later, the writer would renew his efforts and point out that Leslie Caron was still onboard* and that Pierre Braunberger was prepared to produce, but this time—for once—Renoir proved quite firm: "I've decided not to make films anymore. I've become involved in literary work that is taking all my attention and that I wouldn't know how to interrupt."[38] Such firmness appears even more remarkable, actually, because of the fact that at the same moment he wasn't writing anything and was trying to launch other film projects.†

By the beginning of 1964, Renoir had admitted, "*Aspects of Love* is the only project I have left."[39] The truth was that he had only become interested in this novel by David Garnett (the author of *Lady into Fox*) shortly before. *Aspects of Love* had appeared in 1955, and Renoir had himself commissioned a French translation[40] of it for his eyes only.‡ The plot plays out over seventeen years, focusing on a character who is an actress, her passionate admirer, and his nephew and uncle; and it intimately examines the different forms that love can take.§ The project was one of two that Renoir would put on the back burner* while writing *The Notebooks of Captain Georges. Julienne et son amour,*¶ the second, would occupy him for several years. He worked on it starting in spring 1963, and at the beginning of September of that same year he'd attempt to have a treatment read by Brigitte Bardot. The idea of using the actress had occurred to him very early, and the actor who had played the whistling Pierrot in *French Cancan*, Pierre Olaf, had encouraged him along those lines after reading the treatment, certain as he was that Bardot "would be wonderful in the role of Julienne."[41] Olaf thought that Leslie Caron, to whom Renoir had spoken of the project, "would need work in order to play it, whereas Brigitte Bardot would fit into the skin of the character like a hand in a glove."[42] Braunberger sent the screenplay to Olga Ortiz, Bardot's agent. Mme. Doynel, claiming that "until

* The birth of Caron's son had led to her being unavailable for the role, so an agent then suggested replacing her with Bibi Andersson. (Letter to Martin Rosen, July 1, 1964, Jean Renoir Papers, Correspondence, Box 19, Folder 11.)

† *Curtain Raiser* would be adapted for television in 1973, under the title *Le Lever du rideau*, cowritten by the author and Jean-Pierre Marchand.

‡ The book would not appear in France until 1996, with Éditions Christian Bourgois, under its original title.

§ A musical adaptation of *Aspects of Love* would be performed in London in 1989 and then be brought to television in 1993. A film adaptation from the novel would be created for the screen in 2005 by Gale Edwards, with Sarah Brightman and Albert Finney.

¶ *Translator's note:* Literally, "Julienne and Her Love."

now [BB] has always refused to act in costume,"* also voiced herself confident that Bardot "would change her mind to make a film with you."[43] But Mme. Doynel had no confidence in Braunberger, and less than a week later, she had another copy of the screenplay sent to Sami Frey, "who was living with her up to a few days ago."[44]

Julienne is the resident of a brothel, and her lover, a man from high society. Their story resembles that of Agnès and Captain Georges. Among the questions to which the book gives rise, the one of the male character's first name remains unanswered. The first name of the writer in *Orvet*, another alter ego for Renoir, is Georges, as well, as are most of the principal male characters in the various literary and film projects that Renoir began in the fifties. It can't be ruled out— although nothing has yet to prove it to the present time—that Renoir thought of Georges Simenon—the writer closest to him—as he began to write. One of the first drafts of what would become *The Notebooks of Captain Georges* begins with the words, "My name is Georges Anselme," and starts with the landing in Nice of the plane coming from Paris. At that stage the book was called *L'Amour et la Grâce, Mémoires imaginaires*.[45] However, less than a month later, it had become *Le Bonheur, Mesdames*, "a treatment for a film by Jean Renoir," and it goes back to the same situation: Georges goes from Paris to Nice to attend the funeral of a certain Ernest, in response to a telegram† addressed to him by a woman named Blanche Lepic, whose name isn't familiar to him and who, at the church, turns out to be a "full-bosomed" young woman.[46]

On March 19, the project became *Au bonheur, mesdames* and was then presented in the form of a synopsis,[47] thereby confirming its cinematic purpose and providing more proof that Renoir had been juggling his ideas for a long time before diving into the actual writing of a novel. The difficulty in finding one's way through the maze of notebooks and pads is increased by these incessant changes of mind, with Renoir's jumping ceaselessly from an idea for a book to an idea for a film and, moreover, frequently transforming one into the other, or the opposite. He was led only by his desire to tell stories, something that he confirmed often and that his archives evidence in enormous quantity; but for him to get down to writing his novel, his mind had to be drained of his preoccupation with film. "Too much going out—too many honors—and especially too many film projects," he wrote to justify his tardiness. "It's only when I've completely given up making films that I'll be able to write seriously."[48]

---

* There was no bearing to this claim, which was no more than an expression of the ambience of quasi-religious fervor created and maintained by those close to Renoir.

† "It would be a great comfort to have you attend Ernest's funeral."

The close of spring 1964* was the beginning of the period in which he thought only of his novel, but before that, it was the removal of his gallbladder on May 1 at Cedars of Lebanon Hospital that forced him to postpone any idea of film.[49]

"This is about the sexual experiences of a young, rich bourgeois Frenchman at the beginning of the century," he would write after he had completed his novel, remarking at that time that he had been "helped a lot more by my memories than by my imagination."[50] From the beginning, this is how it had existed in his mind; and in response to the German publisher of the book about his father, who wanted to see him write his autobiography, he had clearly stated, "Digging through my memories, I sorted out a few characters, and by changing their identities, I'm trying to use what happened to create a novel."[51] Actually, the early drafts of the book indicate just that, especially these first lines, which are dated summer 1964: "When I think of Georges, of our friendship, which exceeded the limits of what people ordinarily call friendship, I'm completely bowled over by it. . . . I was Renoir's son, but that name didn't have much meaning for him. In Georges's milieu, my father's painting was considered 'garish.'"

Next, the author describes the circumstances of a forty-eight-hour leave:

My parents were in the South of France, too far from the garrison town to go and see them in so little time. They were leaving the apartment in Paris for my use. The Baker's Wife,† my father's model, would come in the morning and stuff me with café au lait and warm croissants. The first day, I was knocking on the door of a few friends. I was thinking of impressing them with my corporal's braids. My unexpected visit messed up their schedule. My rank as a corporal didn't impress them at all. That evening, I was going to the Variétés, where they were offering a revival of *Orphée aux enfers* [*Orpheus in the Underworld*], with the usual

---

* From July to December 1964, there are only three mentions of ideas for films: On July 23, Renoir inquired about the availability of the rights for the Jules Supervielle novel *Le Voleur d'enfants* (appearing in English translation as *The Kidnapper* and adapted to film in 1991). He received an offer from a certain "Goldstein" company through which he had seen a film on Chicago that had excited him. And he mentioned a "story of a child sent to an institution for young delinquents and abandoned children" who escapes to find his mother again. This "illustration of a human group a bit like what I did in *Grand Illusion*" seems to have been presented by his agent to United Artists and to Warner on September 1.

† "The Baker's Wife died the day before yesterday," Pierre Renoir had written to his brother on December 8, 1950. (Jean Renoir Papers, Correspondence, Box 10, Folder 16.)

wonderful theater troupe. Max Dearly's[*] and Diéterle's[†] talent and Offenbach's dazzling music were powerless in making me forget I was alone. I finished my evening in a big café on the boulevard, alone with a beer. For a moment I had the desire to pick up a hooker with the sole purpose of enlightening her on the responsibilities inherent to the rank of corporal. But none of those who approached me seemed worthy of being let in on the secret.[52]

The tenor of the work was quite confessional; and the first lines, written by hand, sometimes in school notebooks and sometimes on loose pages, indicated that at first Renoir had thought of claiming he himself was the possessor of Captain Georges's notebooks, that he was deciding to make them public and have them published. In finally choosing to assign this role to the character of an English gentleman whom he'd name Richard Edmond Hartley, he was able to construct an additional screen between himself and the fiction, thereby giving him the opportunity to invest in the personality of Georges more freely and completely. Although such a decision eliminated his temptation to create an autobiographical narrative on two levels, in which the first narrator (Jean Renoir) would have risked overriding the second (Georges), it did not at all diminish the concertedly intimate dimension of this first novel.

On the eve of the First World War, a young man from a good family, whose sexuality was initiated by the caresses of his English nurse Nancy, the lover of a butler named Corneille,[‡] meets Agnès, a young peasant who has become a prostitute. The "house" where she lives and works is built in the "Arab style." It's a brothel in a "small Western city," located "not very far from Les Sables-d'Olonne." This could be the brothel called la Mauresque that Renoir had frequented when he was stationed in Luçon, a city in the Vendée that actually is only slightly more than thirty miles from Les Sables-d'Olonne. However, it would be a mistake to think of *The Notebooks of Captain Georges* as a roman à clef. The book is infinitely richer than that. It's a story of tragic love that is the fault of a man who didn't know how to understand the woman he loved, and for whom he will spend his entire life weeping.

It will probably never be known whether Renoir had loved one of the women at la Mauresque in Luçon, but on every page the resemblance between Captain Georges and Renoir is striking and heightened by the reminders of the director's films. When Georges makes the observation that he is as "jealous

---

[*] M. Homais in *Madame Bovary*.

[†] Amélie Diéterle (1871–1941), an actress at the Théâtre des Variétés for more than thirty-five years, whose portrait Renoir painted twice.

[‡] Like his counterpart in *The Rules of the Game*.

as a man of the people" and can very well imagine "stabbing my mistress and slowly burning the life out of my rival," the voice we hear is that of Dalio in *The Rules of the Game*. When it's a matter of the way a bourgeois sees the man of the people, it's Jean Renoir before his exile who appears: "The rich man is attracted to the poor. He'd like to love him. He already loves his poetry, his traditions, his daughters, and the way he speaks. He feels attracted by a thought that he can't define completely, by strange ways, and perhaps especially by a lightheartedness that his own caste lost a long time ago. . . . The bourgeois loved the man of the people as long as he stayed in his place."

In retracing the story of that wellborn man who didn't know how to understand a woman from a background of lower status than his, but whom he loved, could Jean Renoir prevent himself from thinking of Catherine, or Marguerite, both of whom were women of the people and could not bring him the stability that Dido—who came from the same world as he—would bring him? However, the reader who knows nothing about Jean Renoir draws the same amount of pleasure from the book as someone who believes he or she knows the author well. The author introduces the book by characterizing it as "another aspect of *Grand Illusion*, a sexual *Grand Illusion*."[53] Jean Renoir's first novel is one of his major works, on the level of his greatest cinematic achievements.

Robert Knittel, who had published *Renoir, My Father*, was the first to receive the book. Renoir had had the manuscript translated into English with him first in mind. The reaction to it came in May 1965; and Renoir, who had feared for a brief spell that "the editors are finding it a bit crude, or rather, indecent,"[54] began by voicing his disagreement with Ned Bradford, the book's editor, who thought "the first third ought to be heavily edited." To Mme. Doynel, Renoir wrote that the book "isn't only the story of a man but also about society, and I shouldn't move on to the captain's individual problems until after having carefully established his relationship with that society in which he feels deprived of human contact."[55] But about ten days later, he wrote, "Examining the translation led me to a revision of the French version. I cut quite a bit, especially in the first third."[56]

A month later, on June 17, Robert Knittel informed Renoir that Gallimard had agreed to publish the book in France.[57] The negotiations with Gallimard would be carried out by the French representative of Helen Strauss, Renoir's agent at the William Morris Agency. Mme. Doynel, on the other hand, was proposing the manuscript to Presses de la Cité, which refused it at the beginning of July, thereby opening the way for an agreement with Gallimard, which had offered a minimum guarantee of only 250,000 francs, but accompanied by some "interesting percentages."[58]

In fall 1965, a little less than a year after he had finished the first draft, Renoir sent Knittel his suggestions for a title and began by expressing a regret: "The best [title] for my book would be *L'Éducation sentimentale* [*Sentimental Education*]. Unfortunately, a certain Flaubert has already used it."[59] There followed a pell-mell list of other titles: *Death of a Horse, La Douceur de vivre* (*The Sweet Life*), *The Constant Prostitute, The Embarkation for Cythera*, but he added that the last two "are a bit too eighteenth century" and admitted that he preferred "something that is simpler, like *Les Amours du capitaine Georges,* or the first title, *The Notebooks of Captain Georges*."[60] The last one stuck.

From October 10 to 20, the Renoirs stayed at the Westbury Hotel in New York so Jean could contribute to the promotion of the book when it was released in America.

At Gallimard, when the title was discussed, *Le Capitaine Georges* was advanced as "more commercial"[61] than *Les Cahiers du capitaine Georges,* which had the "appearance of a true account rather than a novel." Renoir accepted the change, mentioning as he had in similar cases that he'd already thought of this title himself.[62] Then, after having given his OK, he expressed doubts and suggested *La Chair et Dieu,*[*][63] which Claude Gallimard considered "amusing, but on another level, much too allusive and parodic."[64] The publisher would finally decide in favor of *Les Cahiers du capitaine Georges.* For the dust jacket, Renoir had suggested the phrase "The Last of the Grand Bourgeois."[65] The book would come out with the wrapper band,[†] "By the author of *The Rules of the Game*." Although Gaston Gallimard seems not to have taken any part in these various exchanges, Renoir never visited the publishing company without wanting to see him, as Roger Grenier recalled: "He would ask me each time if Gaston was there. I would knock on the door to his office, and I'd see how happy the two men were to see each other again."[66]

Weeks and months passed. Renoir was forced to observe the total lack of interest in his book on the part of French journalists. He asked Mme. Doynel about this, and she suggested that "maybe this collection is one of secondary importance to them" and maintained that "in any case, a novel, no matter how good it is, can't attract as much attention from the critics as a book on your father."[67] In March, an article finally appeared in *Le Figaro,* which managed to convince him that "the way to attract critics' attention to a literary work is by having connections."[68] Then he consoled himself. "The fate of this book, if

---

[*] *Translator's note:* Literally, "Flesh and God."

[†] *Translator's note:* "Wrapper band" (French term: *bande*). In France, some books are wrapped along the bottom of the cover with a usually red, removable band of paper containing information about a prestigious fact associated with the book. This is most often done when the book has won one of France's many varieties of literary prizes.

we're lucky, can perhaps follow that of my book on Renoir, which was more or less ignored in France but a best seller in America and which continues to sell and earn me a lot of letters from people throughout the world."[69] Although *The Notebooks of Captain Georges* would be hailed almost unanimously as a masterpiece, to the point of Renoir's acknowledging "never having had anything like its success with the press,"[70] *Les Cahiers du capitaine Georges* would appear about six months later in a climate of indifference that wasn't even polite.

Such indifference toward a major work is only surprising in light of the fact that journalists and film critics of the same period were celebrating the slightest word Renoir pronounced and covering with ecstatic praise film work that might be considered not always so deserving, or at least not in such proportions. *Le Testament du docteur Cordelier* or *Picnic on the Grass,* and, soon, *Le Petit Théâtre de Jean Renoir* (*The Little Theatre of Jean Renoir*) were the pretext for a hundred analyses that are as scholarly as they are adoring, by the same writers who offered not a single line to *Les Cahiers du capitaine Georges.* The silence in the pages of *Cahiers du cinéma,* especially, is deafening, the only exception being a paltry allusion to the work by Truffaut.

The numerous testimonies to the novel Renoir received remained in the private domain, as if no one dared risk publicly liking the book. *Les Cahiers du capitaine Georges,* François Truffaut wrote to him, "resembles no other novel because it blends things that, as a rule, are never encountered together in even the freest books: the clap and profound faith—that belongs to you, it's a Renoir mix, the great human salmagundi." But very quickly, the young director moved on to what followed, in a hurry to inform Renoir that "Bassiak,* the guitarist in *Jules and Jim,* influenced by a passage from your book on your father, has just written a song about the little cork and Jeanne Moreau sings it on her new record," before concluding, "You've taught me the cinema and quite a few other things as well, but I often think that you—and Bazin†—also taught me how to live."[71] All of this doubtlessly delighted Renoir, but the appreciation of his book might have appeared rushed to him.

Renoir seems not to have thought at first of being able to bring his novel to the screen. The idea would come to him after others contacted him about it. "An actor named Franchot Tone has just offered me an option on *The Notebooks of Captain Georges.* At first it seemed like a good idea. He's refined and likable, and certainly rich enough to be able to launch a production. After considering it, I refused, believing that we ought to see whether there's not some way to make this film in France, in French, and under my direction."[72] That

* Pseudonym of the writer and painter Serge Rezvani.

† André Bazin died on November 11, 1958, at the age of forty.

effort would not go very far; and Pierre Braunberger, his last real friend in the profession, who signed some of his letters, "your friend, your disciple," let him know that he didn't possess the means for a production like that.[73] William Wyler may also have been interested in the book, because his archives contain a project for an adaptation in the form of a forty-seven-page treatment authored by Clarence Marks, who sets the action as taking place entirely before the First World War.[74]

As soon as Renoir had finished writing his novel in December 1964, he began researching film projects again. They would bring him to Europe with Dido the following spring. Over the years, his links with the Hollywood film industry had become so uncertain that he could hardly hope for any offers from it. Now he was sought only by promoters of unusual films, which meant they would be hard to finance, or those who were drawn to him by his fame and/or the memory of his films. Wes Herschensohn was a composite of both types, who had been trying for several months to mount the production of a film about and with Picasso. He was expecting Picasso's principal role in the project to deal with the animation sequences, which would make his drawings and canvases come alive.

After his first visit to Leona Drive, Herschensohn returned a few days later with the screenwriter he had just found, Ray Bradbury. In the course of conversation, Renoir mentioned that although all his films had brought in money, they were more appreciated by critics than by audiences, and Bradbury exclaimed, "Your films are immortal works of art! How much money did Rembrandt make, for God's sake, or van Gogh? If we artists only created to please the money moguls, the whole history of the world would be without one damned work of art!"[75] By the end of their encounter, during which it was established that Renoir would direct the scenes in the film that were to be played by actors— then to be Leslie Caron, Audrey Hepburn, and Gregory Peck—Bradbury took his copy of *Renoir, My Father* out of his pocket and asked the author to sign it. So, Renoir found his copy of *Fahrenheit 451* in his library and handed it to Bradbury to sign.

At the beginning of June 1965, Herschensohn and Renoir met with Lewis Morton, head of the screenwriting department at MGM, who would inform them two weeks later that the project wasn't for Metro. On that day Renoir noticed some young men with long hair in the hallways of the studio and was delighted about the return to a style to which, up to then, only the twentieth century had put an end.

When Wes Herschensohn succeeded in financing his film in the fall of 1965, Renoir was no longer available, and was probably too worn out to become involved in an undertaking like that.[*]

The only American friends Renoir had now who were truly active and enjoying actual notoriety were two young actors whose fame had led him to toy with the idea of a new adaptation of *The Lower Depths*.

The first of these friends to whom Renoir mentioned Gorky's novel was Tony Curtis. Soon to turn forty,[†] Curtis was making film after film, after having played Antoninus in Stanley Kubrick's *Spartacus* and the saxophonist disguised as a woman and in love with the character played by Marilyn Monroe in Billy Wilder's *Some Like It Hot*. Since February 1963, he'd been married to his second wife, Christine Kaufman, a young Austrian actress of eighteen who had played opposite him in *Taras Bulba*. The couple's friendship with Renoir was partly because of the fact that Curtis had a passion for the art of painting. Dido was the godmother of their first daughter, Alexandra Theodora Dido, who had been born on July 19, 1964. As a gift for the girl, the Renoirs had asked Mme. Doynel to find a "very luxurious gift" in the style of 1900, or Napoleon III.[76] The "smart" dress bought at Jones in Paris cost 128 francs,[77] and the dinner organized for the occasion took place at the restaurant Le Bistro in Los Angeles on Saturday, January 9, 1965, formal dress required.[78] The Curtises were regular visitors to Leona Drive as were the Renoirs to Carolwood, the luxurious residence the actor bought after the triumph of *Some Like It Hot*. However, Kaufman and Curtis's separation in 1968 would mark the end of their friendship as a couple with Renoir.[‡] The last letter from Curtis to Renoir is dated February 14, 1967, and in it he confided that the actress[§] with whom he was making a film was becoming so "difficult" that working with her was turning out to be "practically impossible."[79] By then, there had been no more talk for quite some time of remaking *The Lower Depths* with Tony Curtis. It had been two years since Renoir had written to Mme. Doynel, "Every time I'm stopped by the American

---

* *Picasso Summer* would be directed by Serge Bourguignon and Robert Sallin in 1969, with Albert Finney and Yvette Mimieux playing the couple who leave San Francisco for the South of France seeking Picasso. The film would never be shown anywhere but on television. Wes Herschensohn died in 1985.

† Tony Curtis was born Bernard Schwartz on June 3, 1925, in New York City and died September 29, 2010.

‡ Of the two ex-spouses, Christine would remain the more faithful to the Renoirs and would continue to visit them.

§ He is probably referring to Monica Vitti, who played opposite him in Pasquale Festa Campanile's *On My Way to the Crusades, I Met a Girl Who . . .* (1967).

fear of depicting such poverty."[80]

Actually, giving up Gorky hadn't come so easily to Renoir. His desire to do so was reactivated by links with another young actor, fostered by his dear Leslie Caron. Renoir had met Warren Beatty in fall 1960 through Clifford Odets, who had taken on the role of father figure for Beatty after Elia Kazan had served as one. During a party at Odets's home, Beatty had noticed a "fat man" and asked who he was. According to Beatty, the conversation had gone like this: "Jean Renoir? Is he related to the painter? It's his son. Haven't you ever seen *Grand Illusion*? I think I have. And not *The Rules of the Game*? No. You absolutely have to see that film, and you should talk to Renoir."[81] Shortly after that, Beatty saw *The Rules of the Game*, which impressed him to such a degree that he would be inspired by it fifteen years later when he was writing his first screenplay, *Shampoo*, a film directed by Hal Ashby. The influence persisted at least until *Bulworth*, which he would write and direct in 1998. "I got to know Renoir very, very well. And loved him, loved him. If I had to pick someone who I think embodies it all, it probably would be Jean Renoir."[82] Their relationship was not as profound as the actor would have liked it to be, at any rate, and unlike Tony Curtis's, it didn't leave any traces in Renoir's correspondence. It is known, however, that in 1962, the director, who was then in Paris, had asked Dido to see the film *The Roman Spring of Mrs. Stone* in order to decide whether Beatty, whom he had met already, could play Quentin Durward in the film he was vaguely considering. In spring 1962 the friendship between Beatty and Odets came to an end, after the failure of a project to adapt *La Dame aux camélias** in the form of a screenplay by Odets entitled *Fifteen Doves in Flight*, in which Camille was a young black woman. According to Suzanne Finstad, Beatty's biographer, direction of the property would have been offered to Renoir, but the fact that there is no reference to the film on his part suggests that he was probably never informed of the possibility of that undertaking.

In February 1964, during a party at Le Bistro to celebrate Leslie Caron's being nominated for an Oscar,[†] Warren Beatty met the young actress, who left her husband—director and head of the Royal Shakespeare Company Peter Hall—for Beatty a few weeks later. This would nourish the relationship between the actor and Renoir, as would the fact of Beatty's playing opposite a woman closely connected to Truffaut, Alexandra Stewart, in the Arthur Penn film *Mickey One*. Around the same time, Truffaut received an offer to film a story about a gangster couple who had been notorious in the thirties. It was

---

* *Translator's note:* Alexandre Dumas's 1848 novel, *The Lady of the Camellias*, which was then adapted for the stage. The majority of its American adaptations for stage or film are known simply as *Camille*.

† For the role of Jane Fosset in *The L-Shaped Room*, directed by Bryan Forbes.

Bonnie and Clyde. Warren Beatty would produce and act in the film, directed by Arthur Penn after Truffaut had finally rejected the project, which had also been offered to Jean-Luc Godard. In August 1967, right after the appearance in *Esquire* of an article by Rex Reed entitled "Will the Real Warren Beatty Please Shut Up," Beatty organized a prescreening of the film at the Directors Guild in Los Angeles. Among the personal friends invited were Renoir as well as Frank Sinatra, Billy Wilder, William Wyler, and George Stevens, all of whom would celebrate the triumph of the film with applause lasting three minutes.

In September, the actor was in Paris with Leslie Caron, and Renoir asked Mme. Doynel to organize a screening of *The Lower Depths* for him.[83] Thanks to Mary Meerson and the Cinémathèque française, Beatty and Caron saw the film on the morning of September 10, in the theater at the Palais de Chaillot. Both of them stated they were "very impressed,"[84] reported Mme. Doynel, before Leslie Caron wrote, "Warren was filled with admiration for your work."[85] Filled with admiration, indeed, although a detail had surprised the two viewers: Renoir had actually insisted to Ginette Doynel that she draw "Warren's attention to the fact that this role had been a determining factor in Gabin's career,"[86] even though Caron and Beatty had both noticed that the actor's name was listed at the top of the credits. Nevertheless, the faithful secretary kept from seeming flustered. "[Leslie Caron] was surprised by the important place he occupied in the credits, and I told her that they had been redone, which I actually do believe."[87]

According to Leslie Caron, Warren Beatty was the one who had the idea to remake the 1936 film, something Renoir himself wouldn't have really desired, doubting the actor's ability to portray the thief, which would have been a better match for Tony Curtis, who had grown up closer to the streets.[88] The director had vaguely imagined "setting it in a Los Angeles slum."[89] "Warren would unobtrusively burglarize houses in Bel Air. . . . No one would connect it with *The Lower Depths,* but Gorky's work would strengthen it as a whole. It's always a good idea to rely upon a masterpiece, even if you move away from it."[90]

The project for *The Lower Depths* California-style wouldn't develop any further.* Warren Beatty lamented that fact years later, going so far as to identify that failure as one of the regrets of his career.[91] For Leslie Caron, it was less the director than the actor who had wanted them to work together. Renoir had become aware very quickly that it would be difficult to create something with Beatty. He possessed a personality that tended toward the manipulative and deep down was more of a producer than an actor, a characteristic that his future career would reveal quite clearly.[92] Could Renoir have sensed that his

---

* Another of Renoir's films, *Boudu Saved from Drowning,* would be transposed not to Bel Air but to Beverly Hills to become *Down and Out in Beverly Hills* (Paul Mazursky, 1986).

conciliatory behavior wouldn't have allowed him, for once, to come out on top in the end, as had usually been the case? Perhaps. On the other hand, he was also aware that any other offers were arriving infrequently by then.

Even so, he was getting wind of certain ideas. One was an adaptation of . the Carson McCullers novel *The Heart Is a Lonely Hunter*, coming from some "artistic-type producers,"[93] as he wrote to Claude, suggesting he become the director of photography. That same day, in a letter to Mme. Doynel, he claimed that the contract had already been negotiated, despite the fact that the offer, sent to him by Tom Ryan,* was dated July 29, three days previous. "I'm going to dive into the screenplay like a madman in hopes of catching the last rays of summer sun,"[94] Renoir promised. Alas, Oskar Werner, whom Renoir and the producers were considering for the role, was only to "detest the script"[95] and say he preferred "to try to revive our old project, *Hunger*." On August 19, the actor and Renoir dined with the producer and director Stanley Kramer, who offered to present their "old project" to Columbia, but not without warning that "the merchants of film won't understand anything about this subject."[96] Three weeks later, the same Oskar Werner suggested a film "on the life of Han Van Meegten†
. . . brilliant forger," to be shot in Europe.[97] Next, he and Renoir agreed to call the film *The Master Forger*, which was the title of the biography about Van Meegeren by John Godley that had appeared in 1950.

In October, it was Braunberger's turn to suggest an adaptation, this time based on the stories of Maurice Rheims, who had also sent a screenplay by way of Braunberger for Renoir to examine. Two days later, Renoir answered that the stories were excellent, and the screenplay, "a very beautiful story, but not for me."[98] Included with Braunberger's message had been a letter from Jean-Luc Godard he was forwarding about an adaptation of Stendhal's *Lamiel* written by Jean Gruault, which Godard had declined "for emotional reasons [his involvement with Anna Karina]."[99] "I've spoken about it with Gruault," wrote Godard, "who is as thrilled as I at the idea of Renoir perhaps being interested in making *Lamiel*." Renoir answered five days later saying that he'd be "delighted to read Godard's breakdown of scenes for *Lamiel*," and if it "had been endorsed by a man of his value, it must be good." However—and at this point Renoir was putting forward an argument that was the opposite of the one he'd expressed less than ten days before regarding *The Lower Depths*—he "distrusted films based

---

* Tom C. Ryan would actually produce and write the adaptation of *The Heart Is a Lonely Hunter* the following year. It would be directed by Robert Ellis Miller and star Alan Arkin and Sondra Locke.

† The name is actually Han Van Meegeren.

on masterpieces.'" The reason for this brand-new distrust? "I very much want to express my own ideas, good or bad, by way of a book or a film." Then: "Oskar Werner and I have just missed doing an American film because they wouldn't let me have all the authority over the screenplay."[100] What American film could he have been talking about?

Actually, Renoir was still thinking of the novel *Aspects of Love* by David Garnett, a project that "fascinated"[101] him and that he had been claiming was a certainty ever since his agent had said he himself was "enthusiastic" about it and that he would be able to get it financed easily "if Jeanne Moreau agrees to play the main role."[102] Soon he wrote to the actress to tell her that he had wanted to work with her since he had seen her in her first film with Allégret,[†] but until then he hadn't "encountered a purpose 'savage' enough to show you to advantage."[103] At the end of December, Jeanne Moreau, who had just filmed the exteriors in Greece for Tony Richardson's *The Sailor from Gibraltar*, informed Renoir that she "found the beginning of *Aspects of Love* excellent, but Venice a bit conventional."[104] At the beginning of summer 1966, she accepted the role of Rose, adding at the time that she wouldn't be available before the following spring.[105] Although United Artists had definitively pulled out of the film[106] in the meantime, Renoir spent his time creating a cast. He was thinking of entrusting the role of the countess to "Mme. Rex Harrison,"[107] whom he'd met with her husband and thought was "very amusing and very pretty."[‡] The character's becoming an Englishwoman would be enough to make it possible to use her, and he was hoping that casting Rex Harrison's wife would also bring him onboard.[108] Renoir had the screenplay sent to Columbia in London and asked that it be delivered to Cary Grant, who would say that he was flattered but didn't think the story was a good match for him.[109] At the end of winter 1967, Renoir would accept the fact that the project for *Aspects of Love* had failed, and he forced himself to find solace by thinking of his "dream" of having Jeanne Moreau "make a film about a female Boudu"[110] with him, an idea that he would characterize as "exhilarating."[111]

However, in June of the same year, Oscar Lewenstein, who was preparing Truffaut's film *La mariée était en noir* (*The Bride Wore Black*) at the time but who would end up not producing it, was also contacted. Mme. Doynel met with him and in Renoir's name asked for 100,000 francs for the screenplay and

---

[*] *Lamiel* would be directed by Jean Aurel in 1967, using a screenplay adapted by him from the Cécil Saint-Laurent novel *La Fin de Lamiel* (*The End of Lamiel*), which itself had been derived from the work by Stendhal. Anna Karina played Lamiel in the film.

[†] *Julietta* (1953), the seventh film with Jeanne Moreau and the only one she made with Marc Allégret.

[‡] Rachel Roberts, Rex Harrison's third wife.

350,000 francs for the direction of *Aspects of Love*. Lewenstein, on the other hand, wanted a more developed treatment in order to convince the distributors. Jeanne Moreau, who had already worked twice for the producer,* took part in the discussion and accepted forgoing a portion of her fee so that the film could be made.[112] This final attempt failed as well.

These setbacks naturally contributed to Renoir's increasing pessimism, to the point that he began depicting the evolution of the human species in very somber colors. Consequently, in a letter to his friend Pierre Gaut, he wrote, "The dream of a democratic society is crumbling. The world is going back to the divisions of the Middle Ages: small groups of exclusive elite who take refuge in esotericism to defend themselves against the masses, and on the other side, hordes of serfs and villains. They drive cars instead of working their fields with a bit of wood, but they're lower in the spiritual sense than their tenth-century ancestors, who may not have known how to read but knew how to build the cathedral in Tournus."[113] Renoir, a man from another time, never ceased claiming to be one; and he formulated that truth using a variety of expressions, certain of which were unexpected, such as these three sentences about painting that he wrote at the end of his life: "I don't understand the fad for abstract art. Several times I've seen abstract paintings that are very beautiful and extremely pleasant to look at, but they're like riddles. Once you've found the solution, there's very little to get out of them."[114]

Although Renoir was hoping to make *Aspects of Love* in English in 1965, he was also working on a French project. He hadn't given up the ambition of directing for English-speaking audiences but wasn't unaware that he probably had more of a chance of finding financing in France. He favored the first idea, but for several years his reputation with American producers had been deteriorating, whereas in Paris he had the advantage of a few supporters he could still imagine were enough. He also had access to the stars of Europe in a more direct way than through channels leading to the big names in Hollywood, who represented his only way of convincing a studio. French actors, on the other hand, knew him and wanted to work with him, although Renoir's tendency was often to think secondly of the stars of the day and dream more often of the film that he *could* direct with his partners from the past. Accordingly, the project for *La Mort satisfaite*,† dating from spring 1965, whose first treatment he'd just completed, was making him think that he finally "could be on the track of a great film."[115] "Jouvet, if he were alive, would be Death," wrote Renoir. "Michel Simon, if his health

* For two films by Tony Richardson, *Mademoiselle* (1966) and *The Sailor from Gibraltar* (1967).

† *Translator's note:* Literally, "Death Fulfilled."

permitted, would be the old man at the end. Valentine Tessier, from the time when she acted in *Intermezzo* (thirty years ago) would be the general's wife."[116]

He combined six stories under the title *C'est la révolution*, and Braunberger wanted to produce it. He'd written them in June, but at that time there were eight stories, and he'd mentioned the possibility of "adding an Edgar Poe."[117] He said he was aware of the fact that the title was "perhaps a bit flimsy," but, although it was "easy to strengthen," it seemed better to him to "leave it flimsy."[118] Soon he was thinking of the actors he'd like to cast: for the segment called "La Duchesse," Anna Magnani or Elvire Popesco, and Simone Signoret, who'd visited him often on Leona Drive whenever she was in Hollywood, especially when there for Stanley Kramer's *Ship of Fools*. And he wanted Edwige Feuillère, Madeleine Renault, Laurent Terzieff. For the segment "Crème de beauté," Geneviève Page and Michel Piccoli, and, "for the role of Mathilde, the best one in the whole film, I suggest Gisèle."[119] Gisèle Braunberger was the wife of the producer. For "La Grande Cuisine," he wanted Jean Parédès, Léo Joannon as the *maître d'hôtel,* along with Daniel Ivernel or Paul Meurisse. For "Le Roi d'Yvetot," he wanted Michel Simon and Claude Rich. However, after Mme. Doynel had gone to see Simon onstage in what she called *Le vent souffle sur le Sargasses,** she confirmed Braunberger's opinion—that the actor was now "so old and so hideous that it was physically impossible for a woman to be able to desire him and make love with him." So, Renoir eliminated Michel Simon, thought of Gabin to replace him, kept Claude Rich, and began considering Annie Girardot, Marina Vlady, and Emmanuelle Riva. In the segment "La Cireuse électrique,"† he saw Pierre Olaf and Marguerite Cassan, then Philippe Noiret, Marie-José Nat, Anouk Aimée, or, once again, Annie Girardot. And, finally, for "La Guerre,"‡ Oskar Werner and Jean Carmet, if not Mastroianni and, in the role of the corporal, Charles Aznavour. All these casting ideas were sent to Braunberger in two letters at the end of November and end of December 1965.[120] The producer wanted Renoir to write to Gabin himself, but the director was hesitant. "I'm afraid that a letter from me to Gabin would produce the opposite effect." He didn't trust himself to come up with "'the hook' signifying our friendship."[121] He wouldn't decide until February, and only a rough sketch of a letter has survived: "It's obvious that collaborating with you again would be a profound joy for me. But there is one thing I hold even dearer than your collaboration, and that's our friendship, which, although distant remains no

---

* She was referring to René de Obaldia's *Du vent dans les branches de sassafras* (literally, "Wind in the Branches of the Sassafras Tree").

† *Translator's note:* Literally, "The Electric (Floor) Waxer."

‡ *Translator's note:* Literally, "The War," or simply, "War."

less alive. That's why I'm asking you whether this project speaks to you at all. Don't hesitate to refuse."[122] Gabin informed Mme. Doynel that because he was too busy with La Gafer, the production company that he had just created with Fernandel, he couldn't accept.[123]

In the meantime, in November and December 1965, Mme. Doynel visited Leona Drive, having "come to help me write a script."[124] During that same month of December, Renoir met Henry Miller, who sent him a postcard afterward: "Just a little word to say what a pleasure and a privilege it has been to get to know you. It should have happened years ago, but better late than never."[125] A little less than three years older than Renoir, Miller had been living for the last few months in Pacific Palisades. On September 10, 1967, he married for the fifth time, in Beverly Hills, to a twenty-seven-year-old Japanese woman named Hoki (Hiroko) Tokuda and made Renoir one of his two witnesses at the ceremony. Less than two months later, in Paris, during a conversation with the great photographer Brassaï, who was one of Miller's close friends, Miller mentioned a film being shot that was to be called *Henry Miller and His Friends*. "In Los Angeles, the filmmaker shot a magnificent scene with Jean Renoir," he explained. "We had as much fun as a couple of clowns."[126] The writer, who, unfortunately, did not mention the name of the director, spoke next of Renoir as "a wonderful, intelligent, warm and so human man," and insisted that Brassaï read *The Notebooks of Captain Georges*. Five years later, Miller wrote to Renoir after having reread his book. "I think I've already said how much I would have loved to be able to write a book like this myself. And I mean what I say very sincerely. . . . You should have been a writer, in addition to everything that you already are."[127]

Mme. Doynel returned to Paris on December 22, 1965, and learned on January 15 from an anguished call from Pierre Gaut that Jean Renoir had been hospitalized.[128] A kidney infection had caused the hospitalization, an emergency measure, and it had been announced on the radio in the morning. That was how Gaut had learned about it. It was nothing serious,* but the papers repeated the news. Renoir soon received a great many expressions of friendship, a get-well card from the restaurant Sébillon in Neuilly,[129] and a letter from a former waiter at Francis, the brasserie on the place de l'Alma.[130]

Marcel Pagnol wrote to him, too. "We're still talking about you over here, and more than ever. You're the master and example for the new generation of directors, who sometimes do me the honor of citing my name along with yours.

---

* Renoir wrote to Pierre Gaut on February 4, 1966, "My infection didn't require surgery. All that's left of it is a slightly bloated prostate." (Pierre Gaut Collection, Cinémathèque française.)

The only ones that have survived and still play in theaters that are part of the big chains are ours: *Grand Illusion, Toni, The Rules of the Game, Fanny, The Baker's Wife, Jofroi*. If I had a print of *La Chienne*, it could be distributed like a new film. Aren't you ever coming back?"[131] Coming back to live in France? He'd never considered it. Coming back for a few weeks—yes, but only to work, and probably to end up being told (as he wrote to several of his correspondents) that any project he mentioned and that the Americans claimed was a better match for European cinema was, well, the same one the French thought was made for Americans.

He hadn't visited France since spring 1965. Then, after a talk he gave at Harvard on March 5, he flew from New York to Paris on the morning of the seventh. Dido and he visited Essoyes and Cagnes, which gave him the chance to observe that the museum created from Les Collettes "didn't have much meaning" but also that "changing private property into public property offers the enormous advantage of saving the olive trees."[132] Three weeks later they came back to Leona Drive.[133] Slightly more than a year after, there was more travel: New York, first of all, for *The Notebooks of Captain Georges*, from April 23 to 29, and then an arrival in Paris on the thirtieth. In mid-May, Jean and Dido went to London and to Liverpool,* and then returned to Paris on the twenty-first. At that point, Dido went back to California, and Jean, as always, assumed a frenetic pace: the opening ceremony of the Jean Renoir movie theater at 43 du boulevard Clichy and the recording of a broadcast that made up the second section of the three-part *Jean Renoir, le patron*, to be shown in the television series *Cinéastes de notre temps*. It contained extensive interviews with Jacques Rivette; visits to Essoyes and Sologne, where filming had taken place for *The Rules of the Game* (the Parisian release of a restored copy of that film on April 23 became the undisputable proof of its triumph); and reunions with Michel Simon and some others. In this way, several major elements of the Renoir touch were recorded, and more than forty-five years later they remain essential. In April, after Renoir had been informed that Rivette's film *La Religieuse* (*The Nun*) was prohibited by the censor, he had written to the director of the ORTF, which was the producer of *Cinéastes de notre temps*, to ask that the direction of the broadcast be entrusted to the young director.[134]

Renoir was talking to print, radio, and television journalists and going out every evening. He was in stunning form.[135] However, the primary reason for this new stay in Paris had to do with the project for *C'est la révolution*. Renoir was there because, in the first place, Pierre Braunberger thought his presence was

---

* This was Dido's first visit to Liverpool after the death of her mother on January 29, 1966.

necessary and was counting on a possible grant from the Avance sur recettes,* a government service of the CNC that helped with production; and this was something he could not do without. The producer truly thought that the director's notoriety, bolstered by his mentions in the press as a result of his various appearances, would convince the commission responsible for the Avance sur recettes more effectively than a project that was still imperfectly designed. But a few months later, he would acknowledge, "We went too fast by letting Jean Renoir come to Paris too soon and applied while we knew that the screenplays weren't yet in perfect shape."[136]

The decision came on July 8, and, as Braunberger would claim afterward to have foreseen, it was unfavorable. That same day, Renoir lunched with Jeanne Moreau, which, according to Mme. Doynel, helped him to take "this setback from the Centre [CNC] very philosophically."[137] The secretary, as well, put up a good-hearted struggle against the bad luck by imagining that "with Braunberger it would have constantly been a penny-pinching struggle."[138] The producer had been banking on a grant of a million francs, which represented a third of the projected budget, and without that subsidy he wasn't in a position to assemble the financing. A revolt on the part of the press—especially Henry Chapier's articles in *Combat*[139]—led the CNC to react with the reminder that the grants were awarded to projects after the screenplays had been read, and not to screenplay authors. Renoir remained very quiet. The director of the CNC, André Holleaux, wrote to him personally on July 30: "The esteem in which your film work is held and the regard surrounding it throughout the world justify my adding that it is with infinite regret that I'm informing you of such a result."[140] Renoir decided not to answer the letter. The reasons for his discretion at that moment were partly the result of the philosophy of existence he had forged over years of being rebuffed. "I'm accustomed to seeing my film projects rejected for years. . . . This fear of my ideas isn't new for me. I understand it and thank fate for granting me pleasant recompense for this more than one time."[141] Even more than that, however, such discretion was the result of a strategic concern. "Above all we must avoid anything that could seem like criticizing the Centre. We'll need them in case of a Franco-English coproduction of *Aspects of Love*."[142]

For their failure to win the Avance sur recettes, Mme. Doynel blamed the commission less than she did Braunberger, who, "with his relationships at the Centre could have made it work if he'd gone to greater lengths and hadn't slacked off in believing that the commission was meeting eight days later than it was."[143] She particularly resented his having gone to the Berlin International

---

* *Translator's note:* The "Avance sur recettes" (meaning, "advance on contract" or "advance against takings") is a French financial-aid program for films provided by the Centre national du cinéma et de l'image animée (CNC). It was created in 1959 by André Malraux.

Film Festival at the same moment the decision was being made. Nonetheless, that did not change the fact that Jean Renoir's not having received the aid he needed for his production was nothing but appalling.

In reality, the issue was less about the commission's responsibility to evaluate projects than about the system itself. For such a decision—preventing a great director from making a new film—not to have been made, the commission would have had to acknowledge that the grant wasn't for any project but for an auteur with talents so recognized that refusing to help him appeared obscene. Asking a commission to judge from a screenplay in fact laid open the project to whatever rightly or wrongly it declared of no consequence. Evaluating screenplays was the commission's exact responsibility, unless it had been established from the beginning that the reputation of the director took precedence over the project, in which case it wouldn't even have been necessary to submit the screenplay to be read.

And that would have obviously been desirable for the additional reason that any director who was rejected could have taken advantage of the arguments Renoir employed for the occasion: "The only people who can help me are those who believe in me and who know that my screenplays are written with precision but are still only springboards to help me at the start of filming. It is only in the excitement engendered by working with actors and crewmembers that I discover the meaning of a subject. I can only give a form to my creations after I've discovered the quality of the material on which I'm working."[144] Many other directors have taken this risk and still do, in keeping with such theories that, when actually practiced, barely support anything that isn't related to convenience. To be convinced of this, it's enough to compare the project rejected in 1966 to the screenplay for *Julienne et son amour*, which was also not made but in which both meaning and form are clearly visible. The fact that *C'est la révolution* had been submitted before it had been perfected doesn't lessen the offense to Renoir in denying him any aid at all.

Renoir returned to California on August 3, 1966. On the ninth, he wrote to Charles Spaak to tell him he had "come back to America following the impossibility of making a film I was thinking of doing."[145] On September 2, he confided to Paul Meurisse that he "thought that the best way of processing the Centre's refusal was to write another book."[146] Finally, the idea of transforming *C'est la révolution* into a film for television occurred to him. At least such a solution would have one advantage: "I don't think I'd be able to cope with all the long months needed to make a film."[147] That argument also makes it possible to understand why Renoir became interested in directing several short films. The filming necessary for each of them could be followed by a period of rest before he went on to the next. His health was poor, in fact, and although in general his state had gradually improved since his return to Leona Drive, he was suffering from "unpreventable bouts of insomnia that are inevitably claiming a lot of my time."[148]

Such a frame of mind made him attentive to one of two offers coming jointly from Roger Vadim and the screenwriter Claude Brulé. One of those offers was brought to him on behalf of Robert Favre Le Bret: an invitation to preside at the jury for the next film festival at Cannes, but that was something Renoir turned down because, as he said, he was actually "incapable of judging others' films."[149] It was an offer sent by Vadim and Brulé on behalf of Edmond Ténoudji to direct one of the three sketches adapted from some Edgar Allan Poe stories for the film *Histoires extraordinaires** that appealed to Renoir.

He had already been thinking about Poe before he met Vadim and Brulé in Hollywood, and he informed them that he had no intention of faithfully adapting the Poe story he had chosen, "The System of Doctor Tar and Professor Feather." Instead, he wanted to transpose the action and introduce a love story, to the point of using it like a "springboard"[150] in a way that somewhat resembled his approach to the Stevenson novella *The Strange Case of Dr. Jekyll and Mr. Hyde* when he had made *Cordelier*. Renoir presented Ténoudji's offer as a "firm" one, but the producer of the film would be Raymond Eger. Vadim would direct one of the stories himself. The third story was planned for Mario Monicelli; and Mme. Doynel, who was keeping track of the project for Renoir, told him that Alain Delon was the actor they wanted for the lead in that segment. Because the actor and director weren't free at the same time, there was a possibility that Monicelli would be replaced by Fellini;[151] and that was how it turned out.

However, Alain Delon would not play Toby Dammit for Fellini. He was replaced by Terence Stamp. Delon would play William Wilson in a sketch directed by Louis Malle. Thus, the place intended at first for Renoir was taken by Malle. Meanwhile, Renoir had learned that Claude Chabrol had written a treatment for "The System of Dr. Tar and Professor Feather," so Renoir decided, "I wouldn't want him to give up a project on which he'd worked before me and wouldn't want to make my film on this subject unless he sees no possibility of making his."[152] Because Chabrol then worked with Raymond Eger, it seemed likely that the producer had actually made the same offer to at least two directors.†

The day after a televised interview, during which Renoir admitted having

---

* *Translator's note: Spirits of the Dead* (1968), taken from a phrase in an 1827 poem by Poe, was the title of the film for American distribution. In the United Kingdom, the film has appeared under two different titles: *Tales of Mystery* and *Tales of Mystery and Imagination* (for video).

† Claude Chabrol directed *The System of Dr. Tar and Professor Feather* (under the French title *Le Système du docteur Goudron et du professeur Plume*) for television in 1981.

forgotten the name of the author of the phrase "We're dancing on a volcano," quoted in connection with *The Rules of the Game*, Claude Brulé informed him that it came from Monsieur de Salvandy, who'd said it during a ball in 1830.[153] In that same letter, the screenwriter asserted that he'd written the adaptation of *William Wilson*, which would be attributed to Daniel Boulanger in the credits for that film by Louis Malle. It was proof that Jean Renoir wasn't the only one to be handicapped by that capriciousness to which producers devoted themselves. Renoir would never bring Edgar Allan Poe to the screen.

Months went by without anything precise taking shape. Renoir was working, but his mind labored to pause on something lasting. He went from one idea for a film described in a few pages at the very most to a proposal whose wording or author made it seem untenable; from a notebook in which he wrote down his thoughts of the moment to another in which he strung together the sentences of a potential autobiography. Concerning the latter, Roger Grenier had written to him to let him know that Gallimard wanted to publish in France the "book on film"[154] it was rumored he was then writing. Renoir answered that he was still at the note-taking stage and that "quite a bit of time"[155] would be necessary. For the moment, he was motivated by one ambition, and that was to "make a film (at least one) before it was too late."[156]

Soon he would be seventy-three, and he felt burned out by life. "Since I returned from Europe, I've started on a lot of projects but haven't felt up to giving definitive shape to any of them. I blame my health for that.... Mentally I'm doing better, my thoughts are very clear, but the stiffness and weakness in my legs are making my movements difficult."[157] Despite this, he decided to go back to Paris, with or without Dido; and it turned out to be without, because his wife had accepted "the idea of such a temporary separation."[158] He returned in October 1967, after Alain, his wife, and their children had visited France. A vacation of a few weeks had made it possible for Alain to see his mother again, one last time. After that last visit with Catherine, which Alain concealed from his children,[159] he would refuse to read the letters she sent him. Dido confided this to Jean Slade years afterward.[160]

From August 7 to 13, Renoir went to Montreal to take part in the Festival International du Film* where he sat on the jury for judging the Canadian films of that year.† For that occasion, Pierre Rissient had planned for John Ford, Fritz Lang, and Jean Renoir to meet one another. Rissient remembers the meeting as

---

* This was the eighth and last season of that festival, whose acronym was FIFM.

† Thus, Renoir consented to perform the same functions in Montreal he had claimed to be "incapable" of performing in Cannes a few months previously.

"surprisingly devoid of interest." The three directors were satisfied with spouting a few banalities regarding the weather and how happy they were in finding themselves together far from Hollywood. The most important thing for all of them had been not being the first to arrive, each of them making an effort to be the last one introduced.[161]

Renoir's main reason for being in Montreal had to do with the presentation of a restored copy of *La Marseillaise*. A few weeks before, on the morning of Saturday, June 3, Mme. Doynel had organized a screening of it at the Ursulines movie theater on behalf of Pierre Billard and Gilles Jacob, who were "very influential film critics."[162] They "severely criticized [the film], found the beginning too slow, the sound bad," but also announced they were "filled with enthusiasm by the [depiction of the] afternoon of August 10 [and] the performances of your brother and Jouvet."[163] Renoir commented, "Critics' reactions don't surprise us. They only know how to become interested in a film when stars champion it. But they aren't familiar with any of the people who appear at the beginning of *La Marseillaise*."[164] As a portrait of specialists who were benevolent when it came to him, Renoir's words at the very least lacked warmth, not to mention generosity.

Renoir repurchased the rights to *La Marseillaise*. The restored version, relying especially on a copy that had been repatriated from Moscow, was released in Paris on October 27, 1967. On that date Renoir had been in Paris for ten days and was on a tour to present the film that included several provincial cities, Switzerland, and London. At the end of November, *La Marseillaise* was shown at the London Film Festival. After *Grand Illusion* and *The Rules of the Game*, it represented yet another personal triumph, even if it was one of more modest proportions. But yet again it was a triumph resulting from a film that had been directed thirty years previously. Five years had passed since his last production, and he was becoming buried under invitations, requests for interviews, and documentaries about him.* No serious offer came his way. From mid-October 1967 to April 1968, in the provinces of France, in Lausanne, or in London, he spoke about his films and about himself and answered all the questions that those in the audiences wanted to ask. The only questions he dodged were about the future, which would lead to his citing Dante: "Dante reported these words spoken by a man who had arrived in Purgatory and was asking, 'But who are these people?' 'They are,' he was answered, 'those who wanted to predict the

---

* One of them, received in January 1967, had to do with a thirty-minute documentary in color intended primarily for the BBC and Canadian Broadcasting. It came from Mark Peploe, the future screenwriter of *Profession: Reporter*, as well as scripts for Michelangelo Antonioni and for four films by Bernardo Bertolucci. Peploe himself would become a director. (Jean Renoir Papers, Correspondence, Box 22, Folder 4.)

future.'"[165] In Lausanne, he saw Simenon again and couldn't understand why he didn't invite him to stay in his gigantic and luxurious home in Epalinges.* It even vexed Renoir in a certain way,[166] but not enough to make him ever stop imagining that the writer seemed to be one of his only true friends. The following year, Renoir would write him to express his desire to bring *Il y a encore des noisetiers* (*There Are Still Hazelnut Trees*) to the screen and take for himself[167] the role of the lonely banker shut up in his apartment on the place Vendôme, who regains his taste for life by making the child of his granddaughter his own son. It was a project that went no further, seemingly a passing fancy or an idea thrown out to try to please the book's author.

On an afternoon of January 1969, during this stay in Europe, he also gave a brief lesson about how to direct actors to Gisèle Braunberger. According to Mme. Braunberger, who was an actor at the time, it looked like a simple experiment that Renoir very much wanted to conduct in a small studio at the Department of Research of the ORTF. It included a head cameraman, Edmond Richard; a sound engineer, René Forget; a grip and electrician, Maurice Lelièvre and Daniel Mahé; and a table, two chairs, and a green plant. Renoir had excerpted a brief scene from Rumer Godden's *Breakfast at the Nikolides* (1942). The film is entitled *La Direction d'acteurs par Jean Renoir* and lasts twenty-two minutes. The director began by quickly introducing the text and then asked the actress/director to read it without the slightest thought about its meaning, before setting about finding the tone and certain expressions with her. Finally, the time came to record it in a single take, using only the beginning of the text. This resulted in interesting footage, which Renoirian reverence would carry to heights that the film itself had not attained or claimed to attain. In this case, Renoir relied especially on a technique dubbed "rehearsal Italian style," which he repeatedly asserted having learned from Michel Simon during the making of *Boudu Saved from Drowning* and claimed having used regularly since that time. In *My Life and My Films*, he would describe it as follows: "Essentially, it consists in seating the actors for a scene around a table and having them read the scene repeatedly while prohibiting any expression. For the reading to be productive, it must be as flat as one from the telephone book. In practice, every conscientious actor learns his role that way and abstains from all reactions before having explored the possibilities of each phrase, each word, each gesture. Actors who immediately shape their interpretation of a role all have the chance of falling into cliché."[168] Renoir also cites Louis Jouvet as adept at that way of proceeding. And that leads to several questions.

The theater resorts to the principle of "Italian style" rehearsal not at the

---

* On January 11, 1965, Simenon had written to Renoir: Denyse, suffering from a "serious nervous breakdown [*the phrase was in English*]," had entered a clinic and would "never live in that house she dreamed of." (Jean Renoir Papers, Correspondence, Box 20, Folder 6.)

beginning of work but at the *end,* usually before the "run-throughs"; and the definition of this technique applies to the recitation of lines that have already been learned and rehearsed. This technique, then, consists of rememorizing as a whole a text that rehearsals have contributed to splitting into separate pieces. When "*l'italienne*" takes place on the stage, it also presents an opportunity to adjust the lighting and other stage machinery, and in that case it becomes an "*allemande.*"* And that is precisely what it is with Renoir as with a number of other directors: the actors speak the text they've learned and rehearsed as they move in front of the camera so that the technical aspects of filming can be adapted to it. And in this case, despite what Renoir would claim, it wasn't a matter of having the actors sit around a table. It's also reasonable to doubt that Jouvet's conception of "Italian style" was identical to the one presented by Renoir. In addition, rightly or wrongly, it's hard to imagine Michel Simon bothering with that exercise, or Jean Gabin and most of Renoir's actors. Moreover, even the details of some information about Simon reported by Renoir are of a nature to increase one's doubt. After having established that the character Boudu can seem simple, whereas in truth he isn't, Renoir recounted that after they had worked together "Italian style," Michel Simon got up from the table one day and began walking and talking with Boudu's voice and suddenly declared that he was Boudu and that it was enough from then on to follow him.[169] However, in what way was it necessary for Michel Simon to "look for" a character that he had already played onstage, and with success to boot?

Moreover, it turns out that not a single actor has mentioned that way of proceeding, and no trace of it appears in any testimony, interview, or memoir. Similarly, none of those who visited the soundstage of a Renoir film has any memory of that practice. The only mention that can be found comes from Eugène Lourié, who writes in his memoirs that during the filming of *Grand Illusion,* Renoir would ask his actors to sit down with him around a table and say their text as if they were reading from the telephone book. Then: "The next readings were more like friendly conversations, and little by little, the relationships between characters developed, their personalities sharpened, and the scene took shape."[170] This actually corresponds to the description given by Renoir himself, which is unsettlingly expressed in very similar words. Even so, Lourié wrote his memoirs in 1985, which was eleven years after the appearance of those by Renoir, who only began to mention this "Italian style" technique in the fifties, after shooting *The Golden Coach,* in which it's possible that the difficulties he had with Anna Magnani are what led him to this type of "rehearsal," an experiment that he would repeat later, but only in theater.[171]

* *Translator's note:* Literally, "a German."

As for the rest, including what research has discovered up to now, nothing offers irrefutable proof that the "Italian style" for Renoir was not one of those extrapolations with which he enjoyed supplementing his own legend and that was intended for listeners smitten with theories and also convinced in advance by them. The less he filmed, the more he spoke. It was a natural direction, and there is absolutely no doubt that he would have preferred never to have seen it initiated; it put him in the position of the great man whose only right to expression was through words. Audiences were now demanding theories from a famous director who was no longer making films, who enjoyed being the center of attention, and for whom the resulting publicity could help overcome the squeamishness of distributors. Renoir—someone who tried to please his listeners in every circumstance—was willing to give them theories if that is what they wanted. It is important to take them for what they were.

As for the practice of making films, throughout Renoir's entire stay in Europe, he took advantage of the few moments of down time to work, with Mme. Doynel's help, on the last of his surviving projects, a film intended for Jeanne Moreau.

Julienne et son amour is the story of the relationship that forms between an "upper-class" man and a "humble prostitute" living and working in a "third-rate brothel" in Paris before the First World War.[172] Henri asks Julienne to live with him for a month, they begin to fall in love, and the story ends tragically. The interplay of dramatic vectors is reminiscent of *The Notebooks of Captain Georges,* and the themes are characteristic of those throughout Renoir's oeuvre, which are based on his personality. Renoir defines the first of these themes as "about the danger for a fish in going from water to air."[173] Or more precisely: "You have a goldfish living very happily in a bowl with water that is particularly repugnant. You take this fish and put it in a bowl with very clean water. You put it back in the dirty water. It dies."[174] Aside from a few variants, it was the same story that had delighted Alain, whose father told it to him at the beginning of the thirties, one day when they were somewhere on the coast of the English Channel and were walking on a pontoon. The fish then was a herring caught in the sea and placed in a bowl in which the saltwater was gradually replaced, a teaspoon a day, by freshwater. The herring got used to its new environment, but one day when the man was walking on a pontoon, he dropped the bowl in the sea and the fish drowned.[175]

The question asked by Renoir, plaguing him, and which he had examined with his films was in fact that; and he examined its different aspects in the form of three interrogations: "What am I like from the outside? How do people see me? How do they accept me?"[176] And he did so in total honesty. "It's an incredible subject that is part of a set of preoccupations that I've had for such a long time, quite long before having read *Chair et cuir* [*Flesh and Leather*];* it's a subject that is in Camus's *The Stranger* and also in *La Chienne*."[177] *Chair et cuir* and *The Stranger* were two books that he had wanted to adapt, and *La Chienne* was the first of his films that had satisfied him. However, no matter how many others there were, the truer it was that "You make *one* film, you write *one* novel, you paint *one* picture in your life. It's the same film, the same novel, the same painting that you perfect all the time. I have only one thing to say. I don't have thirty-six."[178] Nevertheless, such a description doesn't take into account all of Jean Renoir's work. He also became involved with proposals that had little relationship to him and during which he looked no further than beyond some reason to make the film his on some deep level.

Julienne et son amour, on the other hand, was not a project that came to him by default, one of those films that he accepted because he knew in advance that they would only cost him a minimum of effort. He was much more attached to it than to *Aspects of Love*, as he would write.[179] He was so attached to it that he gave up on that other screenplay he had also intended for Jeanne Moreau, which had been entitled first *La Clocharde* and then *En avant, Rosalie!*† and in which the actress was supposed to play the "female Boudu" that so appealed to him. Speaking of the Boudu film, it should be mentioned that Renoir had considered Michel Simon's possibly playing Portillon, alias Bébé Rose, who would be Julienne's best customer in *Julienne et son amour*. Dirk Bogarde could have been Henri; but Renoir had sent Tony Curtis the screenplay, which hadn't interested Omar Sharif and had elicited no reaction from Mastroianni.[180] And, if necessary, if the distributors decided so, the title could be changed to *Les Millions d'Arlequin, On ne joue pas avec le feu, Chacun chez soi*, or *Le Jeu de l'amour*‡—it didn't matter. What mattered was that *Julienne et son amour* was an expensive film, which required reproducing the world of before 1914, especially the rue Lepic. It was a film whose budget was estimated at 6 million francs, twice as much as the one that had been envisioned for *C'est la révolution*, which Braunberger hadn't succeeded in financing. Once more the producer appealed to the Avance sur recettes. Mme. Doynel delivered the application for it in April 1968.[181] It contained a budget that had been downsized to 5 million francs and that included fees for the author and director and for Jeanne Moreau and the male lead as well.[182]

---

* A novel by Félicien Marceau that appeared in 1951 and from which the author successfully adapted a play, *L'Oeuf* (*The Egg*) in 1956.

† *Translator's note:* Literally, "The Female Bum" and "Forward, Rosalie!"

‡ *Translator's note:* Literally, "Harlequin's Millions," "You Don't Play with Fire," "Each One at Home," and "The Game of Love."

Renoir returned to Leona Drive on April 3. Consequently, it was from Los Angeles that he followed the course of events perturbing the world of French film since the decision taken by André Malraux, the current minister of culture, to oust Henri Langlois as director of the Cinémathèque française. He had taken part in these events when he was still in France. Like hundreds of directors throughout the world, he had notified the new management of the Cinémathèque that it was prohibited from showing his films. On February 16, at Studio-Action, on rue Buffault, he had taken his place on the rostrum for the press conference given by the newly created Comité de défense de la Cinémathèque française, for which he served as the honorary president and Alain Resnais, the president; Jean-Luc Godard and Henri Alekan, the vice presidents; and Truffaut, the treasurer. On March 21, a meeting was organized in Grenoble before six hundred people, during which two recorded speeches were broadcast, one by Pierre Mendès France* and the second by Jean Renoir. The April issue of *Cahiers du cinéma* had a portrait of Henri Langlois drawn by Gabriel Pasqualini[†] on its cover. "The dragon who watches over our treasures," as Jean Cocteau had dubbed him, was shown armed with Étienne-Jules Marey's chronophotographic gun, out of which came a strip of film on which could be made out the faces of seven directors: Renoir's among those of Rivette, Chabrol, Godard, and Rouch, with Truffaut and Pierre Kast beneath them. Renoir, the only director appearing on the cover who hadn't been "born" from *Cahiers*, had also contributed a text to celebrate the two-hundredth issue of the magazine, and it contained the following lines: "When I began to make films, I didn't dare dream of seeing myself mentioned between Griffith and Stroheim. Well, it happened. And *Cahiers* had something to do with it."

Reinstated as the head of the establishment, Langlois wrote to Renoir on April 27 to offer him the honorary presidency of the Cinémathèque.[183] Renoir's response, in which he accepted the appointment and declared himself to be "very honored," would take more than a month.[184]

This happened because he reflected for a long time before answering. And hesitated a great deal. And consulted others. Mme. Doynel to start with. She had firmly discouraged him from accepting, thinking it wiser to wait for the decision from the Avance sur recettes. The reason she gave may have been

---

* *Translator's note:* Pierre Mendès France (1907–1982), a French anticolonialist politician whose efforts resulted in the removal of French forces from Vietnam. Mendès France served as minister of foreign affairs from 1954 to 1955 and minister of state from January to May 1956, before resigning.

† Pseudonym of the painter and director Charles Matton, who the day after his first exhibition, which was very poorly received by the critics, decided to change his name and became principally an illustrator for the press.

dictated by a concern for strategy, but she added others to it, which were the cause of her detesting everything having to do with the Cinémathèque: "They have no money and are willing to try anything to get it, including renting out films that don't belong to them. . . . The most serious thing is that your name will be used by them for publicity and as a cover-up. Not to mention that they'll dip into your pocket."[185] Mme. Doynel deeply believed that the Cinémathèque was closely associated with Pierre Braunberger, who had entrusted the institution with copies of films for which he did not possess the rights. Mme. Doynel had put forth months of struggle to keep these copies from being marketed, and her correspondence with both the Cinémathèque and the producer are riddled with accusations, implications, and legal threats. Certainly, their relationship was a source of conflict, but the extremely vehement tone taken at once by these exchanges seems surprising. In any case, Renoir had been perfectly instructed to see things a certain way by Mme. Doynel's words: "Langlois and Mary Meerson are scoundrels" and Braunberger, a "gangster," whom, she hoped, would not succeed at "softening up" the Maestro.[186]

Renoir had been aware of Braunberger's faults for more than forty years. Their expression had never weakened his real and profound affection for this unusual character, whom legend attributed, among other fantastic acts, with having upon reflection once chewed and swallowed the check that he could not bring himself to hand over to the payee when they were face to face. "The dishonesty in Braunberger making use of my films without informing me about it is obvious,"[187] Renoir wrote. But four days later, as answer to Mme. Doynel's suggestion that he take back the producer's right to market certain films of his, he responded, "[Then] who would distribute silent films today?"[188]

As for Langlois, he was not much of a friend for Dido, either, and she complained about having to host him in Los Angeles, about having to organize meetings, dinners, and parties for him. "I'm beginning to receive some mail for Langlois, which makes me fear that it won't be long before he comes back to get on my nerves again."[189] Thirteen days later, in fact, Dido would go to wait for Langlois at the airport to drive him to Leona Drive, where in the days that followed she would receive those whom he had asked her to invite over. It made no difference whether or not her husband was there.

Renoir's opinion was noticeably more moderate and could be summed up in one sentence: "Whatever there is that you can hold against him, he's the only person I know capable of keeping the Cinémathèque alive."[190] Barely two weeks after the death of the "dragon" at the age of sixty-two, on January 13, 1977, Renoir would come forth with a remarkably balanced opinion of him: "I have no illusions about the friendship Henri Langlois had for me. But nobody is perfect, and, weighing the facts of the issue, I believe that he sincerely cared for me. Of course, that love was fed by his passion for the Cinémathèque. If this had been some other schemer, losing films would have been just as likely. The difference would have been that even more of these films would have been deliberately destroyed by the people of commercial film, who have no interest in conserving such competition to their products."[191]

Renoir found nothing to oppose the arguments advanced by Mme. Doynel to convince him to decline Langlois's offer, a point of view that Dido probably supported more than she opposed, so Renoir hesitated. "What you're telling me is hardly encouraging. On the other hand, I wouldn't want to disappoint the friends who have always stood up for me. I'd like to know what Truffaut thinks about this issue."[192] Truffaut came out "obviously in favor"[193] of it, as did Gérard Lebovici, who "thought there was little [risk] in accepting."[194] Renoir, however, continued to waver, all the while fearing to "seem to be hiding." He also suggested that Mme. Doynel led Langlois to understand that he was waiting "to have had a conversation with him in order to make a decision."[195] In fact, he was intending to leave for Paris on June 6,* but when the situation in France† prevented him from planning this trip, he acknowledged that he had waited too long to answer Langlois and that he had to decide without "having spoken directly with friends in Paris."[196] However, it was only nearly three weeks after having chosen this course of action that he finally decided to write to Langlois to inform him that he had accepted. His letter is dated June 15. He had waited for news he had received that same morning: a telegram from Ginette Doynel informing him that the CNC had just granted *Julienne et son amour* an *Avance sur recettes* for a sum of 500,000 francs.[197]

The news was important, but Renoir barely seemed thrilled by it. Not so much because the sum allocated seemed quite modest in regard to the projected budget but because the situation in France frightened him. Mme. Doynel's letters had informed him that what he himself had categorized as "street fights"[198] were now over, and it wasn't the strikes and the various movements that worried him. It was the position in which he was going to be placed.

This grant is probably going to make my presence in Paris more urgent. However, I'm putting off my return as much as I can because of the

---

* The trip was motivated, as well, by the possible conclusion of an affair that had been going on for several years: the legal suit threatened in 1965 by the heirs of the sculptor Richard Guino, who, since 1913, had been sculpting the works that Renoir conceived and designed. (Renoir's hands had become too disabled by arthritis to do the sculpting himself.) The status of coauthor of the works of Renoir was to be awarded to Guino according to a 1971 judgment of the third division of the civil court of Paris, which was confirmed by the Court of Cassation in 1973.

† *Translator's note:* A reference to the civil unrest in France beginning in May 1968.

political situation. If I'm in Paris, it will be impossible for me to shy away from all the demonstrations with the young people in the world of film. . . . And yet, from what I've read in the papers, the country is going to be more and more cut in two. Reactionaries on one side, revolutionaries on the other. And when it comes to a public profession like film, you have to take sides. It makes me wonder whether I should get involved with directing *Julienne*.[199]

That last sentence indicates the extent to which a feeling of helplessness was paralyzing him. While taking the side of the younger generation, who had been supporting him for years, he wasn't afraid of offending the distributors and producers in a position to affect the financing of his film. In this instance his considerations weren't of a strategic nature; what terrified him was taking sides. Octave was still wide awake inside Renoir.

Spring and summer 1968 were quite clearly a time of great hesitation. In principle, Renoir had accepted going to Venice for its international film festival,[200] where a tribute to him had been organized, but Mme. Doynel had confided her fear about the festival's possibly "being politicized."[201] He was thinking of using the excuse of his health to cancel the trip, while simultaneously accepting the fact that "the Venice International Film Festival is amicable to me." In his opinion, over there, they had "always proved to be favorable to my efforts."[202] His dilemma was solved three days later when he gave up the idea of going to Venice.[203] However, because Mme. Doynel had put forward the idea that using poor health as an excuse risked harming the project for *Julienne et son amour*, Dido and he decided to go to Venice.[204] Unfortunately, less than a week before the opening of the festival, which was scheduled for Saturday, August 24, a low-power bomb exploded at the festival exhibition center, and Renoir learned about it in a paragraph that appeared in the August 19 edition of the *Los Angeles Times*. The attack was reported as a first angry gesture from Communist and Leftist groups against the festival, which they saw as an expression of capitalist interests.[205]

Renoir picked up his pen immediately to write to Mme. Doynel:

My name is associated with the movements on the Left. If my being at the festival can be interpreted as approving of the movements on the Right, I risk passing for a turncoat. I was expecting roundtables with representatives of revolutionary movements, and that I accept. But on no account do I want to be part of the phalanx of the defenders of commercial film. The situation seems unfathomable to me. On the one hand, the producers and distributors are withdrawing their films because the festival is too much on the Left; on the other hand, the Socialists and the Communists are accusing the festival of being capitalist.[206]

Unfathomable, definitely, and an idea Dido had was probably the only one capable of getting them out of this cul-de-sac. Because Renoir, "rightly or wrongly," as he wrote, had accepted being the honorary president of the Cinémathèque, he would rely on that organization's position as his, one he could adopt with all the more confidence because "Langlois has every interest of keeping the honorary president of his organization above the fray."[207] Moreover, having learned from Fritz Lang that Lotte Eisner would bring copies of his films, Renoir—who also inquired about whether Hitchcock would be at the festival—concluded in a postscript also worthy of Octave, "The advantage of consulting Langlois is that the decision will be the Cinémathèque's and not mine."[208] As planned initially, Renoir and Dido would leave Los Angeles on August 29 for Milan, then Venice.

On the Lido, where he would present the Golden Lion for that year to Alexander Kluge for *The Artist in the Circus Dome: Clueless,* Renoir again saw Giulio Macchi, who had been his assistant on *The Golden Coach.* In the meantime, they had kept in contact, especially when Renoir was thinking of bringing to the screen the novel by the great scriptwriter Ennio Flaiano,* *Tempo di uccidere* (1947), under the film title *Short Cut* (1946).†[209] Since 1957, Macchi had been a producer for RAI, and in 1964, he had suggested to Renoir that he direct a series of three 1-hour films on the life of Jacques Offenbach. Renoir had announced that he was "delighted" by the offer. He adored Offenbach's music but claimed to know almost nothing about his life and considered that historical period especially interesting. He had also recommended a young French assistant named Guy Cavagnac‡ to Macchi, declaring that Cavagnac was very erudite and "very proficient in the genre of 'research.'"[210] Finally, he pointed out the existence of an "excellent film" on Offenbach written and directed by Marcel Achard.§ None of these films would be made, but when Renoir spoke to Macchi about *C'est la révolution,* Macchi saw a possibility of having the film produced for television, whose potential he was convinced it was "time to exploit."[211] And as a result, Mme. Doynel would soon write to Dido, when she had returned to California after the festival and left Jean behind in Paris, that the Maestro was "working on a project of sketches for Italian television."[212]

---

* Writer, notably, of Antonioni's *La Notte* and several films by Federico Fellini.

† Directed in 1989 by Giuliano Montaldo (American title: *Time to Kill*), with Nicolas Cage.

‡ Guy Cavagnac would direct *Soldat Laforêt* (*Laforet the Soldier*) in 1971, with Catherine Rouvel in the cast. He was very close to the Renoirs and became one of the best experts on the work of the director, about whom he authored two interesting works.

§ *La Valse de Paris* (*The Paris Waltz* was its informal English title), with Pierre Fresnay and Yvonne Printemps (1950).

Not only Italian television but soon French television, as well—the ORTF—had become involved; and when that happened, there would no longer be any question of shooting in Rome as had been mentioned. The company Son et Lumière was to be the executive producer.* As a result, Renoir would follow in the footsteps of Orson Welles. To mark the arrival in France of color television, the ORTF had produced Welles's adaptation by Louise de Vilmorin of the Isak Dinesen (Karen Blixen) tale "The Immortal Story,"† with Jeanne Moreau.‡ Although the film was supposed to be presented on May 24, 1968, a public service strike had delayed its broadcast. It wasn't until September 30 that television viewers would discover *The Immortal Story*, introduced by Jean Renoir. In it he spoke about the dream pursued by Orson Welles, about the "thoroughly irreproachable" Jeanne Moreau, and about a particular sex scene that had given him qualms but that in the end had "absolutely stupefied and thrilled" him. In conclusion, "It's a beautiful film. And personally, I drew profound pleasure from that brief walk in the secret and enchanted world of Orson Welles."[213]

Renoir would also write to Jeanne Moreau to express his admiration, which was shared by Dido; but this was in 1976, probably after Dido had also seen the film. "Dido and I just saw the film *The Immortal Story*. . . . We walked out bowled over by the caliber of your close-ups. In the milieu of film you've created a series of incredibly beautiful portraits. Usually, we're shocked by the pretension of directors trying to imitate Auguste Renoir, but this time we bow in total admiration for Orson Welles and also for his sense of imagery. But you were the one who was captured by the camera, so it's to you we are addressing these compliments."[214] In the meantime, Welles had sent Renoir an offer to participate in his film *The Other Side of the Wind,* and it was accompanied by three pages of dialogue. If Renoir agreed, Welles "would fly to Hollywood immediately";[215] but the next day Renoir informed Welles that he was ill and "incapable of appearing in your show."[216] Welles never missed any television broadcast of *Grand Illusion,* and the scene with "La Marseillaise" brought tears to his eyes every time, something that during the filming of *The Other Side of the Wind* provoked John Huston to remark, "Oh boy, here we go, he's going to cry again!"[217]

When Renoir died, Welles wrote in the *Los Angeles Times,* "Jean Renoir stands on his own: the greatest of European directors: very probably the greatest of all directors—a gigantic silhouette on the horizon of our waning century."[218]

---

* Son et Lumière would produce Maurice Pialat's *La Maison des bois* (*The House in the Woods*) in 1970, a work that is probably the greatest success in the history of French television.

† *Translator's note:* Produced in France as *Une histoire immortelle.*

‡ The director of production for the film was Marc Maurette, one of Renoir's former partners.

Renoir was busy with the preparation and direction of what would become *Le Petit Théâtre de Jean Renoir* (*The Little Theatre of Jean Renoir*) for most of 1969. Before that, he turned down an offer sent to him by Pierre Rissient to bring to the screen a Jim Thompson story called "This World, Then the Fireworks,"* which was presented to him under the title *Tout feu tout flamme*.† ‡ It was a project that Romy Schneider had already agreed to in advance, but it came to Renoir at a time when he claimed his schedule was too full.[219] Dido and he were filmed in their home by James Frawley as part of the film that he was directing, *The Christian Licorice Store*;§ traveling to Rome and back in March; then leaving again for Paris, where they arrived on April 25.

Dido had gone back to Los Angeles less than three weeks later, leaving Jean in the care of Mme. Doynel. The few days of cohabitation between her and Dido hadn't been free of discord, which reached a point at which they stopped writing each other, something that had never occurred until that moment. After several weeks of silence, Mme. Doynel wrote to Dido, "If I haven't written to you since you left, it's because you upset, even wounded, me deeply. Because of your absence I've abandoned my personal life . . . so that Jean Renoir would be alone as little as possible, and I did that for him and for you. . . . The friendship shared by all three of us was absolutely unequivocal and seemed wonderful to me. Why has it been spoiled? If I didn't react when you were here, it was because I know the extremes I can go to and would have probably said some things that would wound you."[220]

Dido's response came without delay. "Dear Ginette, you have a right to your opinion and I to mine. I hate making a show of my feelings, so why go on about this?"[221] Ginette Doynel was six years younger than Renoir and seven years older than Dido. Both women had only known the director at the height of his glory, and each of them had been enlisted into his service—remaining in the shadows, certainly, but still expecting the light to rebound on them at times. The secretary, who was adding the role of a caretaker to her duties, thought that the Maestro's wife sang his praises with too much restraint. She had trouble understanding that Dido sometimes thought less about serving Renoir's genius

* Directed with that title in 1997 by Michael Oblowitz.

† *Translator's note:* Literally, "all fire, all flame," but used as a metaphor for "burning with enthusiasm."

‡ When the story was first published in French, it was entitled "La Cité des gens merveilleux" (literally, "The Town of Wonderful People"). It appeared a second time in France with the publisher Rivages Noir and was called "Après nous le grabuge" (literally, "After Us, Havoc").

§ With Beau Bridges as a tennis player "corrupted" by life in California. The film's distribution was extremely limited, but afterward its director made four other films, including *The Big Bus* (1976) and *The Muppet Movie* (1979).

than preserving his peace of mind.[222] Dido, on the other hand, couldn't stand the fact that Ginette's behavior made some people take her for a substitute spouse, and she would therefore lose her temper when she discovered any photo of Ginette at Renoir's side.[223] The display of so many professions of affection—all those "my very dear little Ginette"'s from Dido and those "dear Maestrotte"'s from Mme. Doynel—meant just one thing: Renoir's wife and secretary had no affection for each other. No one expected them to go that far, including Renoir, who had a permanent need for a woman around him, from the instant it had become impossible for him to have two.

During the time devoted to directing *The Little Theatre*, which would span several weeks between mid-June and mid-September, Mme. Doynel was that woman, with Dido going back to her role at the end of October 1969 when Renoir returned to Los Angeles. She would hold on to that role from then until the end, far from Ginette. When there was still a possibility of beginning the shoot on June 9, Renoir, whose health was poor, started making an effort to drink less and wanted Dido to do the same, something she accepted. "Of course I'll give up alcohol, since you're asking me to, and I'm sure I'll be able to make this small sacrifice at the same time you are."[224] The measure wouldn't be enough, and in July, when the filming of "La Cireuse électrique" ("The Electric Waxer"), the second sketch in the film, had to be interrupted after his female lead Marguerite Cassan broke her wrist, Renoir noticed that his leg wound was becoming infected.[225] In August, he'd make an appointment at the Hôpital Cochin and be prescribed a course of penicillin.[226]

When French television viewers tuned into *The Little Theatre of Jean Renoir* in 1970, they saw a man whose weight had dwindled and who was visibly exhausted, presenting them his last fantasy. In the studios of Saint-Maurice and Paris-Studios-Cinéma, at the exteriors shot in Versailles, Aix-en-Provence, and Saint-Rémy-de-Provence, Renoir had held his own as best he could, aided by breaking up the work into several sequences separated by some rest periods. However, those who visited the set had been able to catch him on the point of dozing, indifferent to the buzz of conversation, bursts of laughter, shouts—all the hubbub associated with film. He was seventy-five, had never taken it easy, had squeezed every possible drop out of life.

During the preceding months, he had managed to pull together some ideas and compose some stories, and he was worn out. He was also already at the point of having given up the idea of ever directing *Julienne et son amour* but hadn't informed anyone about that except Dido. As a result, she found herself placed in a delicate situation regarding Jeanne Moreau, who was then in Hollywood and whom she encountered often and who was still going to great lengths to make the film possible. "Yesterday with Jeanne Moreau you were the only subject of conversation," Dido wrote to him. "She adores you. No need to tell you that I was in seventh heaven. You're telling me that you won't be making *Julienne*. Maybe Jeanne Moreau should be told because she's struggling to interest someone in your project during her stay in Hollywood (besides, it surprised me because I thought you had an understanding with Warner)."[227] Then, a few days later, when the actress was supposed to have dinner at Leona Drive that same evening: "She seems to have interested Mike Nichols in *Julienne*. I'm taking your advice, not saying anything, and confining myself to congratulating her."[228] Dido and he were the only ones who knew, but even when he was filming Jeanne Moreau singing "Quand l'amour meurt" ("When Love Dies") for *The Little Theatre*, Jean Renoir had decided that he wouldn't be making any more films.

For "Le Dernier Réveillon" ("The Last Christmas Dinner"), the first of the four sketches and one of the two that had not been anticipated by *C'est la revolution* (the second being "When Love Dies"), he remembered an old idea that would make it possible for him to "say everything I think about that horrible Santa Claus."[229] On the same subject, which he had filed among several different projects, Renoir mentioned a "story by Alfred Savoir," about whom he had intended at the time to identify as "the one who gave me it." This was certainly an old idea, because Alfred Savoir—the author, among other works, of *La Margrave*,* which Pierre Renoir had produced in 1932, and *La Huitième Femme de Barbe-Bleue* (*Bluebeard's Eighth Wife*), which had been brought to the screen by Sam Wood and then by Lubitsch—had died in 1934.† Renoir had also written about the personal sentiments that had inspired the "horrible Santa Claus": "Here we now are in that obscene period that the people of our time have the nerve to call Christmas. As if the birth of Christ had any relationship to that display of questionable taste. 'Santa Claus' or 'père Noël'—call him what you will—seems to me to be associated with Galeries Lafayette, or even the Monoprix."[230]

Directed entirely in a studio, "The Last Christmas Dinner" is not a success. The attack on the pagan celebration of Christmas misfires and feels ponderous and banal. The actors, some of whom are dubbed, aren't at ease in their performances, and the only stirring thing about it is the slight tip of the hat Renoir offers to Hans Christian Andersen in his introduction, as well as to a certain little match girl, who also died of hunger and cold in the snow like the two hobos

---

* *Translator's note:* Margrave = the feminine form of a medieval title usually reserved for a military man assigned to defend the border provinces of the Holy Roman Empire. In this case, it's referring to Frederica Sophia Wilhelmina, margrave of Bayreuth, the sister of Frederic the Great.

† For a long time Renoir had remained in contact with Étienne Rey, who had written several plays with Alfred Savoir.

in this later film. "The Electric Waxer" is no more convincing in its inflexible reflection on the way humans are tyrannized by their machines. It is gussied up with moments of singing that lack charm;* and the frantic fidgeting of its actors, Marguerite Cassan and Pierre Olaf, can't claim to make up for the film's absence of rhythm. The actors' talent isn't the issue, but more likely the lack of time and work, which hampered the passage "from fantasy to what is normal," to borrow Éric Rohmer's words.[231] Rohmer also wrote, "In almost all of Renoir's films, you can see the actor's technique, starting with something excessive that at times even appears clumsy, but suddenly emerges into what is natural. . . . When the mechanism of technique breaks down, the natural looms up."[232] Unfortunately, in "The Electric Waxer," excess establishes itself and persists. Reminiscent of *La Chienne,* the portrait of the dead husband watches the man who has replaced him, but this time he is animated, changing in relation to the events. It's a fine Renoirian idea that attests to the director's at least having kept intact his freedom and ability for invention. "Le Roi d'Yvetot" ("The Virtue of Tolerance"), the last sketch of *The Little Theatre,* is a stunning exhibition of those talents, a brilliant set piece on several great Renoirian themes.

Renoir borrows the king, whom Béranger's song†‡ describes as having "taken pleasure as his code,"[233] as a model for his character Edmond Duvallier (played by Fernand Sardou). He is a naval captain who has retired with his young wife, Isabelle (Françoise Arnoul), to a village of Provence. The wife suffers from recurrent migraines that are healed by her relationship with a veterinarian (Jean Carmet), a newcomer to the region. Duvallier provokes his rival—who in the meantime has become his friend—into a duel with pistols that comes close to the veterinarian's suicide (because only Duvallier's arm is loaded); but afterward Duvallier shows up in the village in the company of his wife and her lover, in that way accepting to recast his situation as "a cuckold in luck"§ because of his winning toss on the town's bowling green. "The Virtue of Tolerance" includes

* Lacking charm *purposely*, according to its unquestioning supporters, a bewildering explanation.

† Written in 1813, Pierre Jean de Béranger's song most notably inspired two operas, one by Alphone Adam (1842) and one by Jacques Ibert (1928), as well as a ballet by Joseph Lucien Petipa (1865).

‡ An anecdote reported by Monet holds that Auguste Renoir, dining out, heard someone from the neighboring table say, "Monsieur Renoir, you have quite a fine talent. What a pity that you aren't more well known!" Renoir, then, is said to have smiled and hummed "Le Roi d'Yvetot." (Félix Fénéon, *Oeuvres plus que complètes, Texts Collected by Joan U. Halperin*, Vol. I, Chroniques d'art, Librairie Droz, 1970.)

§ *Translator's note:* The French term is actually the expression *veine de cocu*, which means "luck of the devil," or, more literally, "cuckold's luck" because it is derived from the notion of "lucky in cards, unlucky in love."

several wonderful moments: for example, the shot of Françoise Arnoul seated in the stairway while the veterinarian performs a procedure on her dog made necessary by the animal's having swallowed a large bone.

The actors are all at their best, and they come back at the end to say goodbye to the audience before the last curtain fall. Rarely has the switch from comedy to drama, and even from the burlesque to the tragic, been handled as brilliantly and with as subtle a touch as when the little maid finds herself in a position of having to answer the deceived husband's question about where his wife and friend are, after the two have shut themselves up in the bedroom. It's this employee's embarrassment that clues in the husband, producing a great moment in film superbly handled by Dominique Labourier in the role of Paulette, the lowly domestic who dreams of being a courtesan of quality.

With her, Renoir had the opportunity to turn the last page of his book on maidservants, started during the silent period and highlighting Fridette Fatton (*Tire-au-flanc*), Séverine Lerczinska (*Boudu Saved from Drowning*), Paulette Dubost (*The Rules of the Game*), and Paulette Goddard (*The Diary of a Chambermaid*). Labourier was twenty-six when she met Renoir for the first time at the restaurant Sébillon in Neuilly, having come with Évangéline Renoir, her agent and the wife of his nephew Claude.* She had just played the television role† of the girl with the harelip from Mary Webb's novel, which Renoir had wanted to direct with Ingrid Bergman a quarter of a century before. However, on that day, there was no discussion of *Sarn*. Still in search of a performer for his film, Renoir had asked the advice of Françoise Arnoul, whom he'd already cast, and she had recommended Dominique Labourier, whom she'd seen in the TV movie.[234]

It was planned that Labourier's participation in "The Virtue of Tolerance" would require three days of filming in June, but it would happen that she would spend nine days on the set, because Renoir enjoyed having her appear in the background of scenes where her presence wasn't necessarily required. As she would remember, the screenplay and dialogue were very precisely written and the director intended them to be respected; but the actual direction—actors' movements within the camera field, their positions and gestures—kept evolving in relation to their emotions, reflexes, and manner. Renoir noticed that when Dominique Labourier was speaking with crewmembers or with her fellow actors, she had a tendency to make big gestures with her arms or hop around in place, so he asked her to behave that same way in front of the camera during the takes. "The best female roles are of maids and prostitutes," he'd claimed, thereby uniting the maid Paulette's occupation with the one about which she

* Indiscriminately referred to as Évangéline or Évangèle.
† *Sarn* by Claude Santelli, 1968.

was claiming to aspire. It may also have been a confirmation of the fact that in Renoir's mind as a man of the nineteenth century, surrounded at home from early childhood by maids and discovering sensuality at the brothel, the two roles had merged.

Today, Dominique Labourier speaks of him as radiating the tenderness of a bear, which doesn't mean she is thinking of Octave and the outfit he couldn't shed. Renoir was attentive to others, curious about everything, and prompt to seize upon the slightest exterior detail, which he was as likely to use in a scene as a means of being evasive. For example, one day, just as a reporter covering a story on the set was asking him his opinion about the events of May 1968, Renoir suddenly became aware that the young actress was passing by and hurried to recommend that someone bring her a wrap to cover up, claiming he feared she might catch cold.[235]

Although the three or so minutes of the sketch "When Love Dies," a song by Georges Millandy* with music by Octave Crémieux,† look like a simple transition between "The Electric Waxer" and "The Virtue of Tolerance," they also function as something of a farewell. Jeanne Moreau appears onstage, in front of a painted backdrop, wearing a black-and-gold Belle Époque dress. The shot of her is static at first, until the second verse, when the camera begins to move slowly toward her, only to pull back again until it reaches its initial position, a few seconds before the actress also resumes hers. The song ends with the words "When all is over," after which Renoir reappears, tossing a marble onto the stage of his miniature theater, whereupon the ball becomes a *pétanque*‡ bowling ball instantly appearing on the screen for "The Virtue of Tolerance." All is over, yes, but not really.

Renoir attended the funeral of his brother Claude in Essoyes. He had died at the age of sixty-eight in Antibes on October 9. Now Renoir was the last survivor of the siblings. He had just turned seventy-five. On October 26, 1969, he left Paris for Los Angeles. He would never see France again.

* Also the author of "Le P'tit Coeur de Ninon," which is heard in *La Bête humaine*.

† Most famously, that same song was performed by Marlene Dietrich in Josef von Sternberg's *Morocco* (1931).

‡ *Translator's note: Pétanque* = a form of outdoor bowling, in which both feet stay unmoving on the ground as a hollow metal ball is tossed along gravel or hardened dirt in an attempt to get it as close as possible to a small wooden ball.

34

Big "Snowflasks" Are Falling . . .

Ma vie et mes films (My Life and My Films)

Jean Renoir had entered the winter of his life.

"Here I am at the end of a stage. From now on I won't count any longer on my films to try to make others participate in my joys, my surprises, my admiration, and at times—though rarely—my disgusts."[1] These lines aren't dated, and where the author intended to use them is also unknown, but they convey Renoir's state of mind when he got home after directing his *Little Theatre*. So do these, which follow them:

> I'm not going to make films any longer because I have no understanding of the method that relies on a blueprint. I can only work effectively when the machine is already in motion. But I no longer have the legs I had at sixty, and I'd have to give up hopping around like a rabbit from the camera to the actor, from the actor to the sound engineer. My conception of direction is, above all, as a physical practice. They're opening film schools throughout the world. In them they're studying screenplay writing, use of the camera, directing actors, editing, and set design. I maintain that the most important subject they ought to study is running. It's the director's speed of movement that makes it possible for him to maintain personal contact with the actors and crewmembers charged with transmitting his thought. Therefore, since there is no more running on foot for me, there are no more films. On the other hand, every day I've been discovering a bit more of the intoxication that comes with the discovery of the individual I am. By writing a book, I'm getting to know myself. It isn't always a pleasant discovery. But it's the required path for going off to find out about the world. It's more than probable that what will give me my discovery will be limited to a few obvious truths. The main thing is to eliminate what obviously seems false.[2]

Renoir would devote his last years to writing, but that final period would also be one of immobility. Although his gradually ceasing to walk certainly had to do with the growing handicap of his leg, as well as the various torments that come with age, it was also the result of he himself having given up movement, which is what his doctors confided to Dido. When it was no longer possible for him to run, Renoir gave up walking. And as the months passed, his legs and his entire body underwent a form of paralysis that couldn't be medically explained. It was as if he had seen that immobility in the evening of his life as a last chance to draw closer to his father, whose infirmity had also nailed him to his chair.

To get to know himself better, he undertook the writing of a book of memories. Was this a natural occupation for an aged gentleman who had retired from filmmaking? Doubtlessly, yes, but throughout his life Renoir had accumulated notes and reflections, writing down not only his ideas for films or books but also his thoughts and his considerations about his profession and himself. Therefore, when he finally decided to write this book, he was able to avail himself of an important number of texts, usually handwritten, and running from a few lines to several pages in school notebooks or unbound sheets of paper. Some of these texts are dated; others merely mention the day of the week, very often Sunday. Most of them have no indication of the date, and they eked out a course for him that led to *My Life and My Films*.

Because of this, the idea for his book probably goes as far back as the one in tribute to his father. Both of them can be traced to the first half of the forties and, thus, shortly after his arrival in California. The columns he wrote for *Ce soir*, the article that appeared in *Le Point* in 1938, and the many talks he had given in various locations already express the pleasure he had always experienced in talking about himself, and throughout them is the constant permanent desire characteristic of all authors of memoirs: to create a flattering image of oneself. But his nature inspired another wish that is less shared: he was determined not to hurt anyone. Such was the claim he made in 1964 in response to an offer from the German publisher of *Pierre-Auguste Renoir, mon père,* who had asked him to write his memoirs: "I've been thinking of writing an autobiography for a long time. Each time I get down to it, I'm stopped by the fear of causing pain either to people who are still alive or to their descendants."[3] To these two facts, he added one more: giving his text to Dido and Mme. Doynel to read and asking their opinion, because, quite logically, they cared about the image of him that the book projected. *My Life and My Films* would come into being from these different influences, and it would be resumed again and again and revised a number of times. However, his conception of his book was essentially keyed to that aspect of his identity that he described when asked, after the appearance of *The Notebooks of Captain Georges,* how he had approached the novel: "I'm essentially a storyteller, and any instrument for telling stories suffices, whether it's a camera, a pen, or simply my voice."[4]

The first notes he organized for a project he clearly identified as a book of memoirs date to 1963,[5] just after the failure of *The Elusive Corporal*. Four years later, Renoir reassembled these reflections under the title *Faire des films: considérations, recettes et souvenirs*,[6] which was retitled *Souvenirs d'un faiseur de films*[*] after he actually began writing.[7] At the beginning of February 1968, he wrote:

> I'd also like to entitle this collection *Confessions limitées*. In fact, I'm not claiming to present the public with an autobiography littered with the names of famous figures and characterized by exciting anecdotes. My intention is merely to offer a few viewers who gave me their friendship by watching my films with some interest an account that is as sincere as possible of my life in films. I cannot promise to be absolutely truthful. Years have passed since my first works, and time changes everything, even the memories. . . . My memory is good enough, but that capricious faculty does on occasion play tricks on me. What I can promise is my absolute sincerity as a man of 1968.[8]

In May 1971, more titles appeared: *Souvenirs imaginaires,* followed by *Souvenirs incomplets ou De l'identité*,[9] and finally, *Souvenirs incomplets ou Réflexions d'un metteur en scène*,[†10] which would last as the title for a long time. He also worried quite early in the process about the epigraph he'd write for his book. On December 30, 1972, he wrote these two sentences: "I was born with the itch to tell stories. When I'd wail in my cradle, it was in hopes of attracting an audience." As the months passed, those sentences were preceded by "For me life began with entertainment," or were followed by "I was born a spectator," which wouldn't stick. The first epigraph would remain until just before sending the manuscript to his editors.

Renoir wrote, then dictated, allowing himself to be carried along by the inspiration that came at any moment, which led him to focus on a period of his life that sometimes had occurred before another about which he'd already written. For example, in February 1972, he dictated the chapter "Souvenirs de Berlin après *Nana*"[11] ("Memories of Berlin after *Nana*"), which in the book would become "Berlin—Autres influences" ("Berlin—Other Influences"). By then, his memory was already no longer what it had been in 1968; nor were his capacity for work and ability to concentrate. These factors explain why his book would finally take on a form that he had claimed four years previously he wanted to avoid, a series of portraits and anecdotes intercut with his reflections.

---

* *Translator's note:* Literally, the two titles might be "Making Films: Considerations, Formulas, and Memories" and "Memories of a Maker of Films."

† *Translator's note:* Literally (perhaps), "Imaginary Recollections"; "Incomplete Memories or About Identity"; and "Incomplete Memories or A Director's Reflections."

The essential element concerning what he'd planned to offer on the subject of direction would disappear. For a time, he'd been collecting such material under the title *Petite Grammaire du cinéma*,[12] but it had been supplanted by his wanderings over the years. *My Life and My Films* would be a book of stories, a work of imagination as much as an evocation of events he had lived. It would also be a controlled self-portrait.

The months passed, and he devoted them exclusively to his book with the help of a Frenchwoman who had come to make a twenty-five-minute documentary on Monterey's Cannery Row and take a course at the American Film Institute. Eva Lothar was thirty-eight and had been presented to Renoir by Nick Frangakis, a mutual friend. Renoir and Frangakis had known each other since 1961. After attempting to become an actor, the young man had entered the monastery of Loyola and had taken the name Brother Basil two years later at the monastery of Saint Andrew in Valyermo, which was in the Mojave Desert. At Loyola, he'd participated in the organization of a film festival, inviting among others the directors George Stevens and Mervyn LeRoy, as well as the producer and screenwriter Charles Brackett, who had been Billy Wilder's main collaborator for quite some time. The monks had asked him to repeat the experience, and he had contacted Renoir at the beginning of summer 1961. Having yet seen only his films *Swamp Water* and *The River*, Frangakis had immediately been won over by the director's extreme simplicity. The description Frangakis gives today of Renoir's effect on him provides a certain idea about what such simplicity might have been: "If I'd been familiar with *The Rules of the Game* before meeting him, I never would have dared to knock on his door."[13] After he had left the monastery with the plan of becoming a director, Frangakis remained a fast friend of Renoir, who developed close ties with the monks of Valyermo through him. Father Yang, who was Chinese and came from the Buddhist faith but who had converted to Catholicism, and Father Werner, who had been born in Belgium, were among the frequent visitors to Leona Drive until Renoir's death. It was they who regularly heard his confession. After one of those sessions, Renoir winked at Dido and commented, "Now we really are husband and wife."[14]

In spring 1972, Renoir's health never stopped deteriorating. In May, he "put himself between the hands of a Chinese man who seemed to have a fine understanding of the human body,"[15] but he was becoming weaker and weaker, was constantly worn out, and fell often.[16] The doctors who attended to him followed one after another, expressing their incomprehension. Dido was reduced to summoning a certain "miracle doctor" who would administer a mysterious serum to him each day, but it as well proved ineffective.[17] In August 1972, Renoir had two strokes in the space of eight days. "His paralysis is minimal, and he doesn't suspect anything, at least I hope so. The doctor says that he can recover, but that he'll never come back to what he was before. I don't want strangers to know about it."[18] On the morning of September 5, he had another fall. "For a few days he's been having hallucinations interrupted by moments of lucidity. . . . The doctors no longer seem interested in his condition."[19] One of them, however, suggested they avail themselves of a treatment reputed to be miraculous, perfected by a "Doctor Nihens,'" wrote Dido. It was in Germany and cost a fortune, but they had "some money in Switzerland."[20] To this Mme. Doynel responded that money was no object. The safe on avenue Frochot held "55,000 francs and six kilos of gold."[21]

Mme. Doynel had left avenue Frochot on December 31, 1971, and set up her office a few steps from where she lived at 10 rue Pergolèse in the Sixteenth Arrondissement.[22] Since Renoir had decided to sell his apartment, she spent the weeks that followed taking an inventory of the furniture, moving the archives, and sending some of it to Alexander Sesonske at the University of California at Santa Barbara, because he alone was "capable of writing a book as documented as the one he's devoted to me,"[23] Renoir[†] emphasized. When Renoir sold his apartment on avenue Frochot, he lost his last personal link with France.

During that month of September 1972, he slept nearly all day, while servants and nurses were there to take care of him. He spent his nights awake when Dido was alone with him, forced to call for help when she couldn't get him back up by herself.[24] However, his mental state began to improve, and on September 28, he dictated a letter to Dido for Mme. Doynel in which he explained, "I can gather my ideas easily, but have to struggle against an invincible drowsiness that limits the amount of work I can provide."[25] In the meantime, Dido and Alain had convinced the doctors to have all medications except vitamins stopped. Renoir himself described the state of affairs that settled in then: "My state changes from one day to the next. Sometimes I wake up fresh as a bud; the next day as soon as I climb out of bed I can't take a step."[26] But this didn't keep him from continuing to work on the book that would become *My Life and My Films*.

* This was actually Paul Niehans, the promoter of "live cellular therapy," which used fresh embryonic cells from animals. During the same period, Niehans was caring for Chancellor Adenauer who was one of his patients.

† After the death of Renoir, Mme. Doynel, who had become Anne de Saint-Phalle, rejoiced to Célia Bertin, the only authorized biographer, that Sesonske had abandoned his project. "I'm breathing a sigh of relief thinking that Sesonske has given up that biography of Jean Renoir he was supposedly thinking about." (Letter from Anne de Saint-Phalle to Célia Bertin, April 11, 1984, Jean Renoir Papers, Correspondence, Box 36, Folder 6.)

From then on, the world for him was limited to the house on Leona Drive. From his bedroom he could enjoy the garden, and from the garden he could glimpse Hollywood at the foot of the hill. At him looked the bust of him his father had sculpted. Guests became rare. Jeannot Slade came every day, Professor Alexander Sesonske, often. At the time, Sesonske was the best American connoisseur of Renoir's work. Norman Lloyd visited from time to time, as did Peter Bogdanovich and Nick Frangakis. And then there was Leslie Caron, who was like his adopted daughter and who in October finally began preparing for television the role of Carola in an adaptation of the play by Norman Lloyd. Renoir, whose health had forced him to refuse to direct the work, wearily acknowledged, "It brings a lot of notoriety and few profits."[27] Helen Strauss, his agent, also came to see him sometimes; and one day she presented him with a project by George Cukor to adapt the book about his father for film or television—which of these it would be was still undecided.[28] The film wouldn't be made. In 1959, a project for a film on the life of Auguste Renoir had been rejected. Through the intermediary of a Parisian law firm, Jean and the other members of the family had informed Sidney Harmon, of Security Pictures, that they were opposed to any representation of the painter on the screen.[29]

Jeanne Moreau was among those—who no longer numbered more than barely ten or so—who didn't forget him. The letters she wrote to him were rare but long, and always very beautiful. "I think of you often often [sic], I think of you always. Sometimes with remorse because I never write to you."[30] Otherwise, the news coming from Europe was sad. Renée Cézanne died in October, and Bessie, the Renoirs' former servant, a few weeks later. Katina Paxinou would die in February 1973. On March 25 of that year, David Loew, the oldest American friend of the Renoirs, would pass away at the age of seventy-five.

On December 24, 1972, a telegram arrived at Leona Drive from Pontarlier: "For once it's true we're under the snowflasks and right in the Jura So Merry Christmas and kisses."[31] It was signed Simone and Yves. Since December 1964, not a Christmas had passed without a telegram from Signoret and Montand, and always the French word for *snowflakes* ("*flocons*") had been misspelled by one wrong letter (as "*flacons*").†

---

* "It's the night before Christmas and big snowflasks are falling the angels on wing and off you go and we send you kisses as we love you that is to say fantastically." (Telegram from Yves Montand and Simone Signoret, December 24, 1964, Jean Renoir Papers, Correspondence, Box 20, Folder 4.) [The word for *snowflakes* ("*flocons*") is again misspelled ("*flacons*"). See note below.]

† *Translator's note:* Whereas the French word for *snowflakes* is "*flocons*," in their telegrams to Renoir Signoret and Montand always misspelled it as "*flacons*," the French word for a small bottle or flask, or a normal-sized one that contains wine.

On January 22, 1973, François Truffaut announced he was coming to Los Angeles in June for six weeks. He'd just directed *La Nuit américaine* (*Day for Night*). In his letter he mentioned the impression that Dido produced on him. She made him feel "a little frightened," but now that he had become a director, he was hoping to be less intimidated.[32] This would, in fact, be the case; and Truffaut was going to become the most important figure during the last years of Renoir's life, the most valued friend, almost a second son, who would visit Renoir, often every day, whenever he came to California. Although the affection between them had until then been one-way—Renoir considered the young critic sympathetically but without any special warmth—it established itself more and more strongly and intensely over the months and became just as essential to both of them. In the fifties, Truffaut had needed Renoir, and now the relationship was reversed, because the young director also guaranteed the old master's ultimate link to film. In the meantime, Truffaut had been writing to Renoir, and his letters were often quite beautiful. For example, the following, sent from Toledo on November 13, 1970:

> I've never been able (or never known how) to tell you to what point *The Rules of the Game*, seen and reseen twenty times between the ages of thirteen and fifteen—when my life was going so badly—helped me to cope, to understand the motives of the people in my group of friends; and how it allowed me to go through an appalling adolescence until the precise moment when I met Bazin, who saved me once and for all. . . . I'll always have the feeling that my *life is connected to your work*. All of this is poorly explained in this letter, but would be even worse if I said it in person, the most important being to confide in you to what point it has been necessary to me to feel part of your family in the realest sense of the word; I have the impression of having said too much or too little, but I know that you'll understand everything.[33]

The passage of time had changed both their lives. Renoir was aware that he would not be making any more films. He was worn out and ill, whereas Truffaut's success had produced a calming effect on him. He had put a stop to his habit as a reformer of faults and put away his battery of "shoot-em-up" postulates that had been used to assert his arguments and carve his way through the jungle.

Renoir, who was currently getting acupuncture treatments, was feeling better, and the new year would prove better than the last had been. Dido protected him more than ever, striving to keep annoyances away. As a result, she kept him from finding out about an article that had appeared in the review *Cinéma*[34] in which Catherine Hessling, his first wife, had bombarded him with reproaches.[35]

After being reread and corrected, and then translated into English and made into two copies, the manuscript of *Souvenirs incomplets* was sent directly to Robert Knittel at the beginning of February.[36] The editor made known his reaction to it on March 20. He was enthusiastic, although as a whole it seemed to him to "lack body."[37] Knittel also thought that details about the less-known films were lacking and that the book was "too nice."[38] The author's response was that he agreed and that "actually," he had "already begun that course of revitalizing"[39] it. Michael Bessie, the potential American editor for the book, had a similar reaction. Atheneum Press would publish the book, which Renoir said he had definitely decided to revise into "something more unexpected and with more bite."[40] A few weeks later, during a visit to Leona Drive, Michael Bessie persuaded the author to go back to work in order to touch upon the American part of his career, which was absent from these earlier drafts. So, Renoir promised to "grab the bull by the horns."*[41] The fact that he'd decided to take on his period in Hollywood only after having been encouraged to do so by an editor who realized American readers would probably find such an omission unappealing is an indication of the emotions inspired in him by that period of his professional life.

That spring of 1973 restored a little of his energy and morale, but his daily activities remained limited. "Jean has dived into the rewriting of his book, helped by a secretary that he likes a great deal.† She comes every day from 2 to 7 p.m. When he isn't working in the morning, he sleeps until lunchtime, followed by a siesta . . . and *Souvenirs incomplets*."[42] Nothing motivated him if it didn't have something to do with his book. Dido said she was incapable even of making him sign a letter and was hoping that a "new treatment of electric shock to his head" would be beneficial. The first of such daily sessions had made it possible for him to take a few steps in his bedroom.[43] Soon a hypnotherapist[44] would also be called in, and later a psychologist.[45]

Dido had an uncompromising view of *Souvenirs incomplets* that was encouraged by Mme. Doynel. Both wife and office manager were especially in line about the urgent need they saw to reduce the amount of coverage about Renoir's first wife and first actress. Mme. Doynel expressed her opinion with the words, "I'd like the importance he gives to Catherine Hessling in the first part to be cut back a bit. It almost gives the impression that she's the one who

---

* *Translator's note:* The idiom that Renoir really used was *prendre mon courage à deux mains* (literally, "take my courage in both hands").

† Her name was Nina Simmons, and she was a successor in that role to Eva Lothar. She was charming and youthful enough to cheer up Jean Renoir during the months that she spent with him, just as Andrée Heuschling's charm and youth had brightened the final months of Pierre-Auguste's life. This continued until Dido decided that she "came onto Jean" too much and decided to sack her. (Conversation with Jean Slade.)

did everything. Confidentially, I have to admit that it irritated me a little."[46] This time Dido was on her side: "I agree with you 100 percent and hope that Jean Renoir will speak a bit less about Catherine Hessling and a bit more about the difficulties he encountered in the profession."[47]

In the early versions of the text, Renoir had actually lingered over these difficulties, creating a portrait of himself that resembled and conformed more to what his story had been: a director who had known how to make personal works not by bracing himself with very fixed principles—the fact was, he always possessed very few—but by giving in to counterarguments, retreating from them, in other words. He was terrified of conflict and valued his peace of mind above all. Most of the misunderstandings regarding Renoir's personality would have been cleared up if the final version of *My Life and My Films* had included these all-important lines about his "way of making films": "Such an approach, whether good or bad, has nothing to do with a conqueror's. The first thing I do when it comes to actors (and I do the same thing with crewmembers, financial backers, or even audiences) is always to give in."[48] It's a certainty that such an admission helped give the director an image that was in conflict with the one his supporters expected of him, and it's also amply clear that it called into question the very notion of the auteur as it had been proclaimed by film critics and historians from the fifties to the sixties. That image of him and the notion of the auteur hinged on this very question, and that's exactly what the person or persons responsible for suppressing these lines were thinking. The fact that Renoir hadn't resisted the demand he eliminate those lines is enough to demonstrate that "the first thing" he did actually was to "always give in." However, it's also the case that he was already very impaired at the time.

Years later, Jacques Rivette, one of his most passionate defenders, would remember that on the set of *French Cancan*, "to keep the peace . . . he gave in all the time to the producer, to the actors."[49] And it was precisely by giving in "all the time" that he became the strongest, succeeding the most often in getting what he wanted and, even more, in eliminating what he didn't want. This was less about technique or method than it was about a way of being. Other directors—Maurice Pialat, to cite one example—had adopted the opposite strategy. He never gave in and obtained results that were just as magnificent. Much more than a principle, the difference resulted from a person's nature.

One of the rare suggestions that Renoir resisted and that came from Mme. Doynel was explaining the reasons that led him to become an American citizen. "I'm not going to talk about the issue you're bringing up, but will explain how struck I was by the failure of *The Rules of the Game*. There are a host of reasons that led to my becoming an expatriate, but that one can be counted among them."[50] The reality is that the years had contributed to bringing to the foreground a reason that had been no more than ancillary in 1939 and 1940.

When it came to the coverage accorded to Catherine Hessling, he gave in. It led to the elimination, once again, of certain passages that the first readers of the manuscript had considered of little advantage to him. Especially material having to do with Renoir's state of mind after the failure of *Nana:* "She [Catherine] accepted the fact that audiences had a hard time accepting her but was already planning projects that would provide her with a second round. As for me, I was determined not to give up directing, even if it meant accepting work the least in harmony with my tastes and temperament. Between my love of human truthfulness and ambition for material success, I had definitely decided not to hesitate and was ready to wallow in disgrace."[51] How to accept such a thing? That between his "love of human truthfulness" and his desire to make money, the great man didn't hesitate, even if it meant he necessarily had to "wallow in disgrace"? It has to be the case that in writing this book Jean Renoir had decided to find some form of frankness to which, obviously, he had never been accustomed. Near the end of his life, some of the people who venerated him thought it was preferable for him not to be that way, concerned as they were about protecting his image and shielding him from any potential reproaches.

François Truffaut had read the manuscript of *Souvenirs incomplets* in his room at the Beverly Hills Hotel in 1973, at the beginning of summer and that fall, something he would remind Renoir of when he was filming *L'Histoire d'Adèle H. (The Story of Adèle H.).*[52] Upon his return to Paris, he had written to Mme. Doynel to tell her about the happiness he'd experienced during his visit to the Renoirs', and the secretary announced how taken she, too, was by him. "He is really adorable, and he's one of the few who loves you very sincerely and profoundly, and who has your sensibility and your humanity. His work shows how much your disciple he is."[53] Renoir's answer was, "We completely share your good opinion of him."[54]

Beginning in the summer of 1973, no decision would be made without the issue's having been presented to Truffaut first. And when Jean and his wife had a conflict, the young director would find himself placed in the position of justice of the peace. When Dido maintained that Paolo Barzman, her husband's last secretary, was being paid well enough for the work he was being asked to do,* but Jean disagreed, insisting that his salary be increased or that at least his merits be recognized in one way or another, Renoir in desperation would put an end to the confrontation by saying that he was going to ask Truffaut's opinion.[55]

---

* "What Dido would give me was barely enough to fill up the gas tank of my car," remembers Paolo Barzman.

The rumor had made it all the way to France that Jean Renoir was writing his memoirs, and it was repeated in an article that appeared in *France-Soir*. "In Hollywood Jean Renoir has just finished his *Souvenirs incomplets*."[56] The article prompted Gaston Gallimard to send a telegram to Mme. Doynel, in which the editor said he'd already started negotiations with Knittel. Gallimard would follow that first approach with a letter to the author. "You know that everything having to do with film interests me. I'm therefore awaiting your manuscript with impatience."[57] In the meantime, Renoir had consulted Truffaut, who thought it was a good idea, "providing the book be published in the NRF line with white covers and not in a less prestigious collection like the way *Capitaine Georges* was published."[58] Truffaut also advised Renoir to take advantage of the occasion by having his play *Carola* published.

Mme. Doynel was to take charge of negotiations with Parisian publishers, and these would go on until the end of January 1974.* As a result, no editor was involved in the final changes to the text, which was submitted to a few high-ranking readers, naturally including Truffaut. Actually, the young director was staying in California from September 21[59] to November 1, 1973,[60] mostly in Los Angeles, but also for a few days at the end of October in San Francisco, where he was introducing *Day for Night*. It was during this period, "after a long discussion with Truffaut,"[61] that Renoir changed the title. The book would now be called *Ma vie et mes films*. This was against the opinion of Dido—who preferred *Souvenirs incomplets*, which Truffaut thought was "defeatist"[62]—and that of Mme. Doynel, who claimed to miss the first title "infinitely"[63] and detest the second. Several weeks had been necessary to arrive at this new title. Finding it had been complicated by the emergence of a project by a young, enthusiastic historian who wanted to publish the director's writings with Belfond.

At the beginning of June 1973, Mme. Doynel informed Renoir about Claude Gauteur's idea; and she introduced him a few days later as "one of your great admirers [who] knows your work better than Rivette and Truffaut."[64] For their book, "Belfond and Gauteur are suggesting the title *Le Passé vivant*,† with the subtitle, *Ma vie et mes films*."[65] Renoir gave his approval of the title but wanted "to be able to reserve the suggested subtitle, *Ma vie et mes films*, for *Les Souvenirs incomplets*."[66] For *Le Passé vivant*, he was supposed to receive an advance of 20,000 francs, a sum he wanted them to transfer to "our bank in Lausanne."[67] Pierre Belfond accepted giving up on the title *Ma vie et mes*

---

* The contract with Atheneum for the American edition is dated May 13, 1973. Renoir signed it in December.

† *Translator's note*: Literally, "The Living Past."

films,[*] and then it was a matter of finding someone to write the preface for *Le Passé vivant*. Mme. Doynel suggested François Truffaut, "*the only one* who is really your disciple, and for whom you're not merely a marketing label."[68] Renoir rejected the idea, for the reason that Truffaut "already wrote the preface for the Bazin[†] about me and such a new expression of friendship would be too 'family.'"[69] He explained that his young colleague, who "comes to see us every day and spends a lot of time advising me," feared that Gauteur's book would compete with *Ma vie et mes films* and was putting pressure on him to require by contract "the right to approve the choice of articles [and] the right to review the title and the publication date."

That is how it would be. Renoir, who also wanted to reserve *Le Passé vivant* for himself, approved the title *Écrits de cinéma 1926–1971,*[‡] which Mme. Doynel had first submitted by telephone to Truffaut, who thought that "it's an honest title and clearly states what's inside the book"[70] and would "see the articles in question before the proofs." These many exchanges bear witness to one reality: beginning in fall 1973, in Renoir's eyes Truffaut's opinion took precedence over all others, including Dido's and Mme. Doynel's. Actually, François Truffaut is the editor of *Ma vie et mes films*.

It was also in the fall that Renoir changed the epigraph for that book. On the manuscript, dated October 29, 1973,[71] appears the following sentence for the first time: "I dedicate this book to the auteurs to whom audiences refer using the term Nouvelle Vague and whose concerns are mine." This note is written by hand on the first page, followed on the second by the typed epigraph, "I was born with the itch. . . ." This latter epigraph, which had been present since the first versions of the manuscript, disappeared immediately after. It had been beautiful, profoundly Renoirian, in tune perfectly with the spirit of the book. Suddenly appearing at the last moment, the tribute to the Nouvelle Vague would be all that was left.

As for the rest, the final changes had to do with a few omissions. Mme. Doynel was very upset about the absence of *Boudu Saved from Drowning* ("The hippie before the term existed")[72] and of *Picnic on the Grass* ("That shows how, once again, you gave a young actress her start"),[73] and Truffaut supported her in these opinions. By that time, he was back in Europe and wrote to Renoir from the Hotel Dorchester in London.[74] Becoming aware of other things that were missing, the secretary enquired whether Renoir had intentionally neglected

---

[*] Because Claude Gauteur retains no memory of this exchange, the title idea *Ma vie et mes films* had probably come from Pierre Belfond.

[†] André Bazin, *Jean Renoir*, Champ Libre, 1971.

[‡] *Translator's note: Literally, *Writings on Film 1926–1971*.*

Madame Bovary and *The Diary of a Chambermaid*. "Don't you think that they'll hold it against you because the critique in *Cahiers du cinéma* at the time praised it very highly, if my memory is correct?"[75] His answer: "Following your advice, I mentioned *Madame Bovary*, but I don't see where to fit *Diary*."[76] In the end, he managed to include it.

On December 24, 1973, François Truffaut, who was spending the holidays at the Renoirs', could read the annual telegram that came to Leona Drive: "The rain here is falling in big drops* but even so it's Christmas Eve Kisses."[77] After that, the director flew to New York, where he had to introduce *Day for Night*. A telegram from the Renoirs was waiting for him at the Hotel Pierre, in which they informed him how much they'd enjoyed his film, which they'd seen in their home. A letter would follow: "We're still spellbound by *Day for Night*, moved and amused at the same time by that portrayal of situations that are so familiar to us. What a beautiful film!"[78]

At the beginning of January, Claude Gallimard's reaction after having read the manuscript reached the auteur: "Readers who are less specialized will read your work the way you read a novel, in one sitting."[79] As a postscript, the publisher confirmed that he was in contact with Mme. Doynel to establish a contract. However, the conditions specified by Gallimard weren't agreeable to her.[80] When negotiations were over, Gallimard had raised his offer of an advance of 20,000 francs to 25,000 francs, after Mme. Doynel had demanded 30,000.[81] On January 25, she informed Renoir they had signed with Flammarion, from whom she had obtained 50,000 francs by claiming that Gallimard was willing to offer 45,000.[82] The book's publication date was planned for May, and Thérèse de Saint-Phalle would be his editor at Flammarion.[83]

Mme. Doynel's meeting with Thérèse de Saint-Phalle, a former journalist who had become a novelist and editor, would change her life radically. Through her, she would get to know Thérèse's uncle and godfather, Count Claude de Saint-Phalle. He was eighty years old,† like Jean Renoir, and he had been a widower for forty years. On July 26, he married Ginette Doynel, making her a bride at the age of seventy-four. "All that thanks to Jean Renoir!" she wrote on the day when she officially announced the news to Renoir.[84] Renoir was to soon benefit from Monsieur de Saint-Phalle's advice, since he was a specialist in stock market trading. After he advised the Renoirs not to buy gold in Switzerland, as they'd intended to do,[85] they found themselves the owners of shares of Iowa Beef, Gray Drug, Hydrometal, Levi Strauss, Sheller-Globe, and

---

* *Translator's note:* As always, despite the fact that this time the subject was rain and not snow, *flocons*, which, aside from "snowflakes" can also mean "flecks," was misspelled as *flacons* ("bottles").

† Claude de Saint-Phalle would pass away in 1997 at the age of 103.

others.[86] It is true that "M. de Saint-Phalle spoke about the Stock Exchange very poetically,"[87] as François Truffaut would write. Having become a countess and choosing to have herself called Anne again, Mme. Doynel continued to spend time catering to the interests of the Maestro, and then to those of Dido.

At this point, the publication date of *Ma vie et mes films* was scheduled for the beginning of June. As Henri Flammarion wrote to Renoir, "This house is yours," and now he was expecting a novel from him.[88] But Renoir soon began to have doubts about the title he had chosen for the book he had already finished. Michael Bessie, his American editor, had suggested calling the book *Wait for Me, Gabrielle*, coming from the last sentence in the text, and Renoir loved that idea. He ran it past several people, and all of them were enthusiastic about it.[89] He became determined to call his book *Attends-moi Gabrielle*. On April 29, he wrote to Truffaut to ask him for his opinion.[90] However, on May 3, Mme. Doynel informed him that it was too late to make a change and that, regardless, Flammarion's preference was *Ma vie et mes films*.[91] Probably informed about that situation by Mme. Doynel, Truffaut sent the author a "diplomatic" response: "My reaction to *Attends-moi Gabrielle* would be to tell you that it's 'kaboom!,' but I should add, for the sake of being objective, that *Ma vie et mes films* is just as 'kaboom!'"[92]

Kaboom, then. In English, the title would be *My Life in Film*, at first, and, finally, *My Life and My Films*. The list Renoir sent to his New York publisher directing to whom to send review copies included George Cukor, John Houseman, Lee Strasberg, Roberto Rossellini, Henry Miller, Ingrid Bergman, Katharine Hepburn, and Christopher Isherwood.[93]

Jean Renoir's *Écrits de cinéma 1926–1971* was available in bookstores in April 1974; *Ma vie et mes films,* two months later. The French press expressed its enthusiasm about the latter. *Le Figaro* reviewed it positively two days in a row.[94] *Le Monde* published an article by François Truffaut that began with a quotation from *The Rules of the Game:* "We're here to hunt, goodness gracious saints alive, not to write our memoirs!"[95] Later in the article, Truffaut wrote, "This book, delighting constantly with its style, harmoniously blends the very careful crafting of the memoirists of the nineteenth century with the tone of a Henry Miller."[96] Nevertheless, *Ma vie et mes films* had its detractor. A member of the family of Godefer,* who'd been Jean's childhood buddy in Essoyes, complained to Flammarion about the image of his family members that appeared in the book.[97]

The excitement occasioned by the book, his love for François Truffaut, as well

---

* *Godefert,* according to Bernard Pharisien, the great specialist on the history of Essoyes.

as the warmth, affection, and attention Truffaut gave him, contributed significantly to improvements in Renoir's health; but his return to life's daily woes was brutal. Dido did not hide from Mme. Doynel that Jean sometimes suffered spells of "rambling,"[98] as well as the fact that she was now betting on a "female doctor who seems devoted to [him], and is energetic and not dangerous." The name* had been suggested to her by a friend "who detests drugs and is more of a 'Christian Scientist.'"[99] However, sometime later, Dido added a handwritten note to a letter signed by her husband: "Alas, that 'rare bird' who was against drugs was an illusion. That lady doctor turned out to be more dangerous than the male physicians, but I won't give her the opportunity."[100]

The final months of that year would be very hard. On September 28, Renoir, who had gotten from place to place only by wheelchair since July,[101] was hospitalized for about ten days for a series of tests.[102] Right before this, Dido confessed her feelings of powerlessness. "Jean hasn't been doing well at all for the last week. I don't know what to do anymore."[103] He had "lost the use of his legs," and "his suffering is unbearable."[104] A recent hip fracture, discovered by X-rays, was "inoperable because of an infection in the bone." "Jean probably won't be able to walk anymore, but God willing, he'll still be able to lead a life that's feasible. The doctors have lowered the dosages of the medications that were giving him hallucinations."[105]

When he got back to Leona Drive, he spent his lucid moments wondering about the nature of the writing—a novel or stories—he would do next. He answered various requests from film historians about his works. Signoret and Montand, he realized, hadn't forgotten him. On December 24, they sent him a telegram: "Here it's the rain that's falling in big drops† but even so it's Christmas Eve We kiss you with all our heart."[106] But on December 30, he had to be hospitalized[107] again—this time for polyps and prostate problems.[108] He was sent home on January 25,[109] and a few days later began working again, "one or two hours a day, still trying to find what he wanted to do."[110]

On February 6, 1975, important news reached him, which he hastened to tell Truffaut: "I just found out that the Academy of Motion Pictures gave me a special Oscar. You probably already know about it, but I wanted you to be the first to whom I demonstrate my joy and my pride."[111] That same day *Variety* announced that Howard Hawks was also going to receive an "Honorary Oscar."[112] The ceremony would take place on April 5, and *The Godfather: Part II*

---

* Doctor Sarah Pearl, whom Dido Renoir mentioned in her letter, is probably the practitioner from Beverly Hills who in certain situations is asked to teach actors the art of coughing correctly onstage or before the camera.

† *Translator's note:* The same typo explained in previous notes (*flacons* instead of *flocons*).

would triumph.* Renoir wasn't there, and nor was Truffaut, who'd been nominated that year for best director for *Day for Night,* an award that Francis Ford Coppola was to win. Ingrid Bergman, who won the award for best supporting actress in the film *Murder on the Orient Express,* was in the position of having to present the Oscar to Renoir and receive it on his behalf. As people were filing out of the ceremony, Bergman, having hoped that the standing ovation that greeted her arrival onstage had been intended for Renoir and not her, found herself being questioned by journalists only about her impressions and feelings upon winning an Oscar. As a result, she ended the session rapidly and declared, "I was thinking that you'd be asking me questions about Renoir, but since you're not doing anything about that, good evening."[113] Five days later, the old director received the following telegram: "That you'd been given this [the Oscar is something] we'd [wanted] for a long time. Kissing you with big snowflasks."[114]

Renoir described his existence in the space of these months for Janine Bazin: "I've led a life of waiting recently. I would have liked time to shrink and put me into a physical state that's more acceptable. I've earned one point against my illness, from the fact that I've become familiar with it: it's a thighbone hit by a German bullet in 1917 that very calmly made use of all that time to become infected openly."[115] And then, especially, there was Truffaut, so often present, and always there for him. "His presence during his visit to Beverly Hills came to brighten my life."[116] Still moving about only in a wheelchair, Renoir soon managed to work a little, two hours a day at most, but his most important activity was of another nature. "Dido's and my principal concern is to get hold of 16 mm copies of my past films and to have fun screening them. Outside of that, any effort is too hard for me."[117]

In the living room of Leona Drive, Renoir had a film screening system installed. It consisted of a 16-mm projector behind a small window, which was itself hidden by a painting by Braque,† and a screen that could be rolled down when needed. He often began watching a film at eight o'clock in the evening, usually one of his, and Dido would remember that it sometimes drew tears from him.[118] During the nearly three years that he worked for Renoir, Paolo Barzman can't remember having seen any films but Renoir's on Leona Drive.‡ "The idea

---

* A rare occurrence would be two films by the same director among the five films nominated: Francis Ford Coppola's *The Godfather: Part II* and *The Conversation;* Roman Polanski's *Chinatown;* Bob Fosse's *Lenny;* and Irwin Allen's *The Towering Inferno.*

† Norman Lloyd prefers remembering the painting that opened when needed like a hinged door to reveal the projector as having been painted by Auguste Renoir. In that way, symbolically, the father's work would disappear to permit the son's to exist. Norman Lloyd's memory is, unfortunately, more beautiful than the reality.

‡ Films other than those by Renoir were usually shown Saturdays and Sundays at the end of

would come to him at times from a line in the book he was dictating to me that would remind him of another—in *Toni*, for example—and then he would say it would be nice to see *Toni* again, and so we would."[119]

Having become the cultural attaché to the French consulate in Los Angeles beginning in spring 1976, Christian Tual, the son of Denise Tual, who had edited *La Chienne,* and of Roland Tual, who'd been the director of production for *La Bête humaine,* would be invited regularly to these screenings. The day they first met, Renoir had greeted Christian by immediately mentioning the "enterprising Mme. Batcheff," which is what he had called the former editor in *Ma vie et mes films*. Christian Tual has always been convinced that the director never forgave his mother for her editing changes on *La Chienne*. Truffaut's smiling attempts to improve Renoir's outlook about it failed one after another, and Renoir would become impatient to move on to another subject.[120]

In November 1975, Dido, Jean, and Greg, his nurse, went to a theater that was wheelchair accessible (this detail had determined their choice) to see Woody Allen's *Love and Death,** and they "really loved" it, judging Woody Allen's "work very cinematographic."[121] On the other hand, Bob Fosse's *Cabaret,* which had been out already for three years and which was seen by Renoir at a screening at the studio, inspired no commentary on his part. He said he was "in a bad position to judge this film," because he "was familiar with that period in Berlin."[122] A year later, they'd see *L'Armée des ombres* (*Army of Shadows*) in their living room. It had been released in France seven years earlier but hadn't played in the United States. They then wrote to Simone Signoret, "We're filled with enthusiasm. What a masterpiece! And you are phenomenal!"[123] However, the rule in general was that he preferred copies of his own films to those brought to him by Alexander Sesonske or the professors at UCLA. Those were the films he wanted to show to his guests, and he never tired of seeing them again. Dido wanted his guests to be of male gender. After Christian Tual showed up on several occasions with an attractive friend, Mme. Renoir let him know that she expected him in the future to avoid bringing around her husband young women who were too attractive.[124]

In October, Jean-Claude Brialy came to see Renoir and convinced him to accept being promoted to the rank of Officer of the Légion d'honneur. The young actor's charm had worked, Truffaut confided to Mme. de Saint-Phalle, who wasn't very convinced by the argument that such a distinction "will help the young people in film."[125] The idea had come to Brialy when it had been suggested

---

the afternoon. Norman Lloyd and Todd McCarthy were among the regular guests at these showings.

* An actor from Renoir's *La Marseillaise* and his *Little Theatre*, Edmond Ardisson plays the priest in this Woody Allen film.

to him that he organize the Gala of the Union des artistes in Los Angeles; and he had rushed headlong into what he would describe as the "craziest and most catastrophic gamble"[126] of his career. After Renoir had accepted, he convinced some of the Master's actors to participate in the celebration. Valentine Tessier, Paulette Dubost, and Marcel Dalio; Françoise Arnoul and Michel Piccoli; Jean Marais, Catherine Rouvel, Jean Carmet, Claude Brasseur, and Jean-Pierre Cassel would all make the trip to Los Angeles. To present him with his distinction, Renoir was considering "either René Clair or Pierre Gaut."[127] The honor would finally fall to Françoise Giroud, who was then the junior minister for women's affairs and, beginning in August 1976, the junior minister for culture. She would go on to write that she had "gotten on my knees to say near his ear the few words for the occasion."[128] However, neither those who were there nor any of the cameras remembered or recorded that kneeling gesture.

If Renoir did show any reluctance, it was because he felt rejected by that nation he had been referring to as his "ex-country" since summer 1941, and because he thought France had not afforded him the consideration he believed he deserved. It was a feeling that, especially, the refusal of the Avance sur recettes for his project *Vive la revolution!* had exacerbated. In his eyes, official authorities had exhibited a lack of gratitude toward him. He expressed such a point of view in a letter regarding the problems with the conservation of the copy of *The River*, when he had wanted André Malraux to intervene to "convince the English government to reverse the action"[129] of destroying the Technicolor negative of that film. Malraux "certainly owes me that," he had written at the time. His resentment was fed especially by his correspondence with Pierre Gaut, whose very right-wing opinions were leading to his detesting the Gaullists, hated as well by Mme. Doynel. It may well be that Gaut was also getting down to the task of rejecting everyone to some degree. His response to a letter from Renoir[130] just after the death of Georges Braque, to whom Gaut had been close, is characterized by surprising brutality. "Braque's death didn't affect me. I didn't think much of the man and I didn't like his painting. . . . During at least the last twenty years of his life while he was under Maeght's wing he only went after money and honors and credits and all he put out were paintings of birds. His funeral services were just as expected, orchestrated for commercial and publicity ends by the Maeght, Malraux, and company."[131] An even more essential influence upon Renoir, starting in 1939, can be traced to Dido, who'd never kept her dislike for France any secret.

Renoir's disenchantment with the country of his birth had been born very soon after he arrived in California. In 1975, when he agreed to be promoted to the rank of Officer of the Légion d'honneur, he had been an American citizen for thirty years. In 1945, when that citizenship became official, his French passout had been taken away from him.[132] Renoir was going to have to regain his French nationality in order to accept his promotion to the rank of Officer. The issue could have been handled easily enough; in some cases such government administrations know how to demonstrate a good-hearted approach. However, this time Renoir said he was plagued by worries about it on two levels. On the one hand, he had always distrusted Catherine and feared fresh action on her part if she ever found out that he had become French again, even though the litigation between them had been settled about twenty years earlier.[133] Secondly and especially, he was adamant that the steps toward double nationality be concealed from his fellow Americans.

Similarly, when the consulate, represented by Christian Tual, who'd been contacted by Truffaut, offered to intervene with the ministry to accelerate the request for French citizenship, Renoir insisted in a letter written by Dido that they stick to the current procedure. "Despite Jean's desire to become French again (while still remaining American) we'd be making an error in risking to offend the Americans."[134] The diplomat, then, was being expected to demonstrate tact. "Jean Renoir is concerned about not letting the American press and public opinion get hold of this story, because Americans are fussy nationalists and could hold against him a gesture that they'd interpret as a sign of ingratitude toward them."[135] Therefore, Renoir wanted "the possibility of obtaining this French passport to be accomplished with the greatest discretion, while keeping officials from talking to the press."[136] Although Christian Tual agrees today that Renoir's fears were obviously unfounded—Americans at that time had already completely forgotten about this French director who'd chosen to become one of theirs—the affair would still be accomplished with absolute discretion, to the point that nothing about it would filter out until today. On May 27, Anne de Saint-Phalle could write to Dido, "Jean Renoir is becoming French again. A letter from Christian Tual informed me of that fact this morning."[137] Renoir received his French passport in August.[138]

The decoration was presented to him on Leona Drive on November 20, 1976, four days before the Los Angeles Gala of the Union des artistes. Among the guests at the celebration was Sophie Renoir, Claude and Évangèle's twelve-year-old daughter. Ten years later, she'd receive the César* award as most promising actress for her performance in Éric Rohmer's *L'Amie de mon amie* (*Boyfriends and Girlfriends*). Right now, however, she was the one doing the filming. "She certainly impressed us with her surprising authority. She glided among the journalists and photographers and managed to capture the guests who interested her the most with her own camera."[139] Images from this

* *Translator's note:* César award = France's national film award.

ceremony show a Jean Renoir who is visibly drained, the look in his eyes vague, obviously "elsewhere." It would be his last public appearance. Three weeks later, he wrote to Giulio Macchi, "I'm hanging on by writing and thinking of the good old days when I had two legs."[140]

It was advisable more than ever to protect him. Dido took care of that task on Leona Drive, Mme. de Saint-Phalle in Paris. The devoted secretary's ascension to the rank of countess hadn't blunted her claws. When the director Bernard Paul, who was then Françoise Arnoul's boyfriend, wrote to her to ask permission to use an excerpt from *The Rules of the Game* in one of his films, she didn't bother asking Renoir, to whom she merely stated, "If I wasn't aware of their left-wing tendencies, I'd find no fault in it, but I fear this film may have ultra-left leanings."[141] Therefore, she informed the distributor of the film that it was out of the question to consent to loaning it for free and that she was requiring 3,000 francs a minute for France and 6,000 for the rest of the world. Then she added a note to Dido saying, "I think that's the best way not to say no, because I don't think they will pay such a price. Given that requirement, Françoise Arnoul will probably write to Renoir and turn on the charm, and that's why I'm warning you about it."[142] A few days before that, she blew up in learning that *The Little Theatre* had been shown "with great success"[143] at the Fête de l'Humanité.† Five years after Renoir's death, in July 1984, when Dido agreed to see the special correspondent from *Libération* after *Lettres d'Amérique* had just been released,[144] Mme. de Saint-Phalle went ballistic again. "That's a Communist newspaper! The current Party tactic is to appropriate Jean Renoir (e.g., the Lycée Jean Renoir in Bondy, which is a stronghold of the Communist Party; an interview in *Libération*, a Communist newspaper. What's next, *L'Humanité*?). If I were in your place, I'd be suspicious about requests for interviews and especially about the kinds of questions they'll ask you."[145]

You'd think she had no idea that Renoir was once "the" director for the Party.‡ The detest she expressed for François Mitterrand was just as virulent and provoked another fit of rage in February 1977 after she'd learned that *The Little Theatre* had been shown in one of the theaters directed by Frédéric Mitterrand.

---

* Probably *Dernière sortie avant Roissy* (*Last Exit before Roissy*).

† *Translator's note:* "Festival of Humanity" = annual event organized by the French Communist newspaper *L'Humanité*.

‡ After the funeral of Maurice Thorez, who'd died on July 11, 1964, Mme. Doynel had written to Renoir, "Thorez had a rather extraordinary funeral, in my opinion, given the crowd that was apparently there. Propaganda seized on it to blow the importance of Communism in France out of proportion and for the elections to scare any poor suckers who might happen not to be voting for our dear Joan of Arc [de Gaulle]. When Thorez died, a number of reporters called me wanting your opinion of the man. It's as well you weren't there." (Letter from Ginette Doynel, July 18, 1964, Jean Renoir Papers, Correspondence, Box 19, Folder 11.)

"[The film] was shown in a movie theater belonging to Mitterrand's nephew. Armed with his uncle's protection he doesn't pay what he should."[146] And the threat of being sued, she added, "doesn't seem to bother the young Mitterrand very much."[147] In addition, when selling the film in foreign countries sketch by sketch seemed like a possibility, Renoir, put under pressure, relented and wrote to her, "Besides, I've grown to think that it could happen. I agree, more or less, but reluctantly, that they can only show a part of the film on the condition that they pay almost as much for the film cut as for the film not cut."[148]

The following summer, because she had decided to move to another country soon with her husband, Anne de Saint-Phalle began making arrangements that would allow the Compagnie Jean Renoir to continue to exist post December 31, 1977, after which she only wanted to manage Renoir's personal interests.[149] She would prolong that deadline for a few months, but for the time being was asking Dido to prepare the Maestro for such news. Ten days later, Renoir let her know about his "sadness at losing a link with the past"[150] and about the "deep distress" into which this departure was plunging him. Yet again, François Truffaut, who was in Los Angeles in July, played an important role. To Dido, Anne de Saint-Phalle wrote, "We [Saint-Phalle and Truffaut] talked about the future of the Compagnie Jean Renoir. In any case, he's ready to take charge of the marketing of our films. Aside from that, I think it will be necessary to carry out a destruction en masse of the useless objects.... This alliance with Les Films du Carrosse seems full of promise to me."[151] The parts of Renoir's archives that weren't preserved in Truffaut's offices would end up a few months after Mme. de Saint-Phalle's death in 1989 on a sidewalk on rue Pergolèse. On that day, Alain Renoir would warn Claude Gauteur about it by telephone, and he would hasten to carry off what he could, seeing the rest, all the rest, disappear into the dump truck.

The last handwritten letter from Jean Renoir that has been preserved is dated January 27, 1976. It consists of just a few lines of shaky writing that are barely readable and that are addressed to François Truffaut: "The world is pouring floods of tears—beginning with Dido's and mine—for the story of Adèle's misfortunes. What a beautiful film. Your treatment of it has filled us with enthusiasm."[152] Dido and he had seen *The Story of Adèle H.* about ten days before "in a movie theater with an audience" and Truffaut had been there.[153]

Renoir was losing the use of his hands little by little,[154] but that didn't keep him from writing. Or to be more exact, from speaking while Paolo Barzman wrote. "Jean has become infatuated with this nice boy and listens only to him,"[155] observed Dido nearly a year after Paolo's arrival on Leona Drive, where he had come to replace his sister Luli for Renoir in March 1976. Luli and Paolo were the children of screenwriters Ben and Norma Barzman, who'd been forced by McCarthyism to leave Hollywood for France. Ben was Canadian and had moved to Hollywood in 1942, and Norma was American. Luli and Paolo both spoke French fluently.

When Paolo had taken his sister's place on Leona Drive, he had not yet turned nineteen. He was thinking of staying only two or three months, as Luli had done before him, especially because he'd been informed very early that, whereas Dido had a lower tolerance for young women being near Jean, Jean himself wasn't very enthusiastic about working with boys. In reality, Paolo would "last" until the death of Renoir, a period of nearly three years. Looking back on it, Paolo attributes such longevity in part to the fact that he had a poor idea of the director's fame:

> I certainly knew who he was, but I absolutely didn't view him as one of film's classic directors. In my eyes, Jean Renoir was an old gentleman who was unbelievably kind, someone who radiated his joy for living. Just the mention of his name, nearly forty years later, brings a smile to my lips. I truly think he was happy to find himself face to face with someone who didn't consider him to be a living god and wasn't waiting around for some sacred word to fall from his lips. What was happening on Leona Drive was crazy enough. You had to see Dalio enter the living room, pull off his cashmere overcoat and throw it to the floor, then kneel before Renoir and kiss his hand. Dalio style, of course, with a serving of mockery, but even so. When guests were announced, Jean was made ready for it, washed, dressed, brought out to be shown; but the minute that, according to her, he would start to talk too much, Dido would see to it that he stop. An entire mise en scène was organized around him, an entire farce in which Truffaut participated, refusing to see him in any way but as a brilliant old artist and old sage. I sincerely believe that he himself didn't give a damn about all that, and even all that ceremonial bored him deeply. With me, he talked about cooking, chicks, he loved racy stories and jokes that were a bit off color. He had nothing to do with his reputation, image; all that burdened him more than anything else.[156]

Paolo would show up every day at the beginning of the afternoon. The condition of Renoir's hands no longer allowed him to write, and, in summer 1976, he also lost the ability to read. So, his secretary would read to him what they'd composed the day before, always going back to the beginning of the text; and thus, the more they advanced in the writing, the harder, and more disjointed, the work became. After about twenty pages, Renoir would fall asleep, then soon awaken and then fall asleep again. "At the end, he would often not know which book it was."[157] The great difficulty had to do with the need to channel thought, to find a place for each imagined scene in the narrative, which had been hard to put together, to invent some link points; and that difficulty was that much greater from the fact that he himself didn't really want to find such coherence:

> He would struggle against his mind rambling, but his desire to speak in a disconnected way would ceaselessly get the upper hand; it was what he really wanted, he would have liked to let go. And that was especially what Dido didn't want. Mornings I'd type up good copies of the handwritten pages from the day before. But before being able to read them to Jean, I had to submit them to the office of Brazilian censorship. Then came the shrieks and yelling. Dido would censor everything that seemed to her to come from Jean's "ravings." You were supposed to stay within the exact framework of the story or novel. It was important for it to remain "coherent" in the eyes of the censor. If not, what would "people" say? That Jean Renoir had become senile? No, that wouldn't do, "people didn't need to know," it had to be made "presentable," and that was everything.[158]

When Paolo arrived, Renoir had already dictated a first draft of what was going to become *Le Coeur à l'aise.** That was the book they would work on together at the very beginning and that would appear to be autobiographical. It is organized in sequences that could also stand as short stories and is about a certain Clément Bourdeau, a man recently turned one hundred years old who is recalling his memories. The book was almost entitled "Amis, je viens d'avoir cent ans,"† the character's first words. But the author decided against that title in October 1976.[159] The contract for the book with Flammarion, to which the manuscript had been submitted in May,‡ had been signed in July; and when *Le Coeur à l'aise* would appear in bookstores at the beginning of 1978, Renoir had already finished the next, *Le Crime de l'Anglais,*§ which retraces the triple murder that was committed on the night of January 21–22, 1885, at La Gloire-Dieu, which is very near Essoyes. Gabrielle had told Renoir about this event, which froze the entire region with fright and inspired a lament of sixteen verses during that period. In the thirties, Renoir had created at least four treatments about it

---

* *Translator's note:* Literally, perhaps, as "The Heart at Ease."

† *Translator's note:* "Friends, I've just turned one hundred."

‡ Under the title *Le Voyageur indécis* ("The Indecisive Traveler").

§ *Translator's note:* "The Englishman's Crime."

for a film project.* In the novel, La Gloire-Dieu becomes La Chèze-Dieu, and the title of the book is derived from the nickname given to one of the two murderers, someone named Trancard, whose bowler hat earned him the moniker "the Englishman." Renoir finished writing the book in December 1977, while rereading and correcting the proofs for *Le Coeur à l'aise,* and Truffaut took on the responsibility of bringing them to Paris.[160] In February 1974, in fact, Renoir had asked Truffaut to sign off on the final corrected proof of his books.[161] In February 1978, Mme. de Saint-Phalle had the manuscript of what was still called *L'Assassinat* sent to Truffaut;[162] and that novel would appear the following year as *Le Crime de l'Anglais.*

Finally, Renoir went to work on what would become *Geneviève,* his last book, which would appear after his death. He finished the first version of it in August 1978[163] and consecrated his last reserves of strength to this novel whose main character is a young woman who is condemned to a wheelchair by her paralysis and who experiences a love affair that ends in the most calamitous of manners. It was the final projection of a paralyzed storyteller, who turned his story into a tragic tale about a cripple.

During their working sessions, Renoir at times experienced the whim to dictate letters to Paolo in which he touched upon his memories, his films, his style of doing things and thinking. Paolo Barzman still has the same opinion about that:

> That's really what he wanted to do, much more than to write novels, and I encouraged him to move in that direction, to dictate letters to me meant for his friends, even those who were no longer alive, or to personalities, characters in his film, heroes of books. The idea of writing a letter to Octave, to himself in *The Rules of the Game,* in other words, excited him more than any other project, and that's what he wanted. But when Dido got wind of it, she howled in protest and kept repeating, "What are people going to think?" Jean was there, was looking at me, and he was dying to write such letters. Today I blame myself for not having known how to get around Dido, but I was obviously too young, too naïve.[164]

Jean Renoir would never write his letter to Octave.

Renoir opened up about that tumultuous need of his to recount things, something he had always had but that had become his sole activity after he became infirm. In a letter to Georges Simenon dated December 1, 1977, he wrote, "I

---

* *Ida, Tibi, Artus,* and *Le Crime de La Gloire-Dieu.*

discovered the idol whose religion is even more tyrannical than literature and film. It's simply telling stories. In these years I've produced two books. I hesitated a great deal before diving into this new pastime, and that is partly because of you. When I look at the collection of your books that you've sent me, I feel embarrassed. They take up an entire shelf of my library, and each volume is a masterpiece. Upon reflection, I've told myself that masterpieces were invented precisely to serve as encouragement to their successors."[165] With that last sentence, Renoir discreetly closed one door and opened wide another, wanting the storytellers of today and tomorrow, the directors and writers, to step into it.

And on December 12, 1977, he wrote to the person whose example had affected him more than any other, whose films he had discovered while convalescing from the wound he had received in the war, the one who became his friend years later, to assure him of his affection and offer him his wishes for Christmas and the New Year.[166] Thirteen days later, on December 25, that friend, Charles Chaplin, passed away at his house in Vevey, Switzerland. He was, as Renoir wrote to his widow, "the genius of the century."[167]

Just like his father, Jean Renoir worked until his last day. He was having more and more trouble speaking, and the words in his mouth sounded like gibberish without any meaning to ears other than Paolo Barzman's. Even Dido couldn't understand them most often.[168]

In December 1978, to the numerous torments assailing the old man was added an infection of the leg he had wounded more than sixty-three years before. "They're going to open it up again for him—a little like what happened in Rome—but unfortunately his resistance isn't the same,"[169] wrote Dido to Anne de Saint-Phalle. Truffaut left Los Angeles on December 20. Dido and her sister Dulce, who was visiting at Leona Drive, summoned the monks in Valyermo who were his friends for a final service at the table in the dining room, a last communion.[170] On December 24, Montand and Signoret's annual message reached him: "It's the night of Christmas, we're kissing you with big snowflasks."[171] It would be the last telegram.

All that was left was to wait. Dido endeavored to make Jean "forget the existence"[172] of *Le Coeur à l'aise*. She probably hid from him the death of Paul Meurisse from a heart attack during the night of January 18–19.[173] He insisted on writing to Ingrid Bergman: "March is still far away, but the main thing is that we know that it exists. We won't say the month of March from now on, but the month when Ingrid is coming to see us."[174]

February 12, 1979, was a Monday. That morning resembled every morning. The invalid was in the hands of Greg, his nurse. Paolo Barzman was there at the beginning of the afternoon, as he was every day. At lunchtime, in the house on Leona Drive, Jean Renoir passed away. The sun was shining in California. In France, it was pitch dark.

Notes

The Chameleon on Plaid

1. Jacques Lourcelles, *Dictionnaire du cinéma, les Films*, Robert Laffont, 1992.

2. Pierre Montaigne, "Pardon Jean Renoir!," *Le Figaro*, February 20, 1979.

3. Claude Gauteur, *Jean Renoir: la double méprise*, Éditeurs français réunis, 1980. Updated and augmented edition, *D'un Renoir l'autre*, Le Temps des Cerises, 2005.

4. Pierre Lherminier, *Cinéma d'aujourd'hui*, n° 2, May–June 1975.

1. The Invention of Renoir

1. Jean Renoir, *Renoir*, Librairie Hachette, 1962; then *Pierre-Auguste Renoir, mon père*, Gallimard, Folio, 1981.

2. Ibid.

3. Letter from Auguste Renoir to Berthe Morisot, September 15, 1894.

4. Jean Renoir, *Pierre-Auguste Renoir, mon père*.

5. Ibid.

6. Ambroise Vollard, *En écoutant Cézanne, Degas, Renoir*, Grasset, 1938.

7. Jean Renoir, *Ma vie et mes films*, Flammarion, 1974.

8. Letter to Mme. L. B.-M. Gaumont, May 23, 1974, Jean Renoir Papers, Correspondence, Box 30, Folder 3.

9. Bernard Pharisien, *Renoir, de vigne en vin à Essoyes*, Némont, 2012.

10. Henri Perruchot, *La Vie de Renoir*, Hachette, 1964.

11. Jean Renoir Papers, Correspondence, Box 1, Folder 5.

12. Jean Renoir Papers, Correspondence, Box 1, Folder 6.

13. Conversation with Aline Cézanne.

14. Conversations with Alain Renoir.

15. Jean Renoir, *Pierre-Auguste Renoir, mon père*.

16. Roger Viry-Babel, *Jean Renoir, le Jeu et la Règle*, Denoël, 1986.

17. Jean Renoir, *Les Cahiers du capitaine Georges*, Gallimard, 1966.

18. Jean Renoir Papers, Correspondence, Box 1, Folder 1.

19. Conversations with Alain Renoir.

20. Jean Renoir, *Pierre-Auguste Renoir, mon père*.

21. Conversation with Jean Slade.

22. Ibid.

23. Marc Le Cœur and Jean-Claude Gélineau, *Renoir, O Pintor da Vida*, São Paulo, 2002.

24. Jean-Claude Gélineau, *Jeanne Tréhot, la fille cachée de Pierre-Auguste Renoir*, Éditions du Cadratin, 2007.

25. Bernard Pharisien, *Pierre Renoir*, Némont, 2003.

26. Conversation with Jean Slade.

2. "Other Dogs to Sniff"

1. Jean Renoir, *Pierre-Auguste Renoir, mon père*, Gallimard, Folio, 1981.

2. Jean Renoir, *Les Cahiers du capitaine Georges*, Gallimard, 1966.

3. Ibid.

4. Jean Renoir, *Pierre-Auguste Renoir, mon père.*

5. Letter to Aline Renoir, early 1914, *Correspondance 1913–1978*, Plon, 1998.

6. Letter cited by Barbara Ehrlich White, *Renoir*, Flammarion, 1986.

7. Letter from D. *(for Daniel)* Deschênes (Hôtel Carlton, Lausanne), November 18, 1963, Jean Renoir Papers, Part II, Correspondence, Box 19, Folder 1.

8. "Notification d'un arrêté portant concession d'une pension militaire de retraite," December 7, 1933, Jean Renoir Papers, Box 52, Folder 3.

9. Letter cited by Barbara Ehrlich White, *Renoir.*

10. Jean Renoir, *Les Cahiers du capitaine Georges.*

11. Jean Renoir Papers, Correspondence, Box 1, Folder 1.

12. Jean Renoir, *Pierre-Auguste Renoir, mon père.*

13. Citation du sous-lieutenant Jean Renoir à l'ordre de la 47 division, au QG, May 11, 1915, signé général d'Arnau de Pouydraguin, cited by Stéphane Launey, "Jean Renoir sous l'uniforme," in *La Revue historique des armées*, n° 259, June 2010.

14. Henri Perruchot, *La Vie de Renoir*, Hachette, 1964.

15. See, especially, Georges Duhamel, *Vie des martyrs*, Mercure de France, 1917.

16. Jean Renoir, *Ma vie et mes films*, Flammarion, 1974.

17. Letter to Pierre-Auguste Renoir, undated, *Correspondance 1913–1978.*

18. Jean Renoir, *Pierre-Auguste Renoir, mon père.*

19. Certificate from the Centre de Réforme de la Seine on September 6, 1935, Jean Renoir Papers, Production Files, Box 52, Folder 3.

20. Letter cited by Barbara Ehrlich White, *Renoir.*

21. Jean Renoir, *Correspondance 1913–1978.*

22. BCAAM, citation du sous-lieutenant de cavalerie Renoir à l'ordre de la 5ᵉ armée, au QG, May 13, 1917, signé général Mazel, cited by Stéphane Launey, "Jean Renoir sous l'uniforme."

23. *Le Bonheur*, Autumn 1946, Jean Renoir Papers, Production Files, Box 75, Folder 6.

24. Jean Renoir, *Ma vie et mes films.*

25. Conversation with Éric Rohmer.

26. *Lumière*, in the series *Aller au cinéma*, Institut pédagogique national, Cinémathèque française, Télévision scolaire.

27. Reported by Roux-Champion, cited by Henri Perruchot, *La Vie de Renoir.*

28. Conversations with Alain Renoir.

29. Jean Renoir, earlier draft of *Ma vie et mes films*, June 8, 1971, passage absent from the definitive edition, Jean Renoir Papers, Production Files, Box 71, Folder 6.

30. Ibid.

31. Abbey Baume's entire funeral oration is reprinted in the book by Jeanne Baudot, *Renoir, ses amis, ses modèles*, Éditions littéraires de France, 1949.

32. Jean Renoir's official family record book, Jean Renoir Papers, Production Files, Box 52, Folder 4.

3. Before He Became Renoir

1. Harold L. Van Doren, "Chez Renoir at Cagnes," *The Touchstone* 8, October–December 1920.

2. Anne Distel, *Renoir*, Citadelles & Mazenod, 2009.

3. Conversations with Alain Renoir.

4. Ibid.

5. Ibid.

6. Barbara Ehrlich White, *Renoir*, Flammarion, 1986.

7. Conversation with Jean Slade.

8. Conversations with Alain Renoir.

9. Conversation with Marie-Claude Roesch-Lalance.

10. Jean Renoir, earlier draft of *Ma vie et mes films*, June 8, 1971, passage absent from the definitive edition, Jean Renoir Papers, Production Files, Box 71, Folder 6.

11. Jean Renoir, *Ma vie et mes films*, Flammarion, 1974.

12. Conversation with Pierre Philippe, in *Cinéma 61*, n° 57, June 1961.

13. Letter from Pierre Renoir to Paul Léon, director of Les Beaux-Arts, February 23, 1923, Jean Renoir Papers, Correspondence, Box 1, Folder 2.

14. Letter to Claude Renoir, April 10, 1923, Jean Renoir Papers, ibid.

15. Cited by Alexander Sesonske, *Jean Renoir: The French Films, 1924–1939*, Harvard University Press, 1980.

16. Conversation with Pierre Philippe, in *Cinéma 61*.

17. Jean Renoir, *Ma vie et mes films*.

18. Ibid.

19. Request from Pierre Braunberger for a certificate validating his career, March 1976, Jean Renoir Papers, Correspondence, Box 32, Folder 3.

20. *Le Débat*, December 20, 1924.

21. Letter from Harold Livingston Van Doren, January 6, 1925, Jean Renoir Papers, Correspondence, Box 1, Folder 3.

22. Jean Renoir, *Correspondance 1913–1978*, Plon, 1998.

23. *Ciné-Miroir*, February 1925.

24. Jean Renoir Papers, Production Files, Box 38, Folder 3.

25. Jean Renoir Papers, Correspondence, Box 3, Folder 4.

26. Conversations with Alain Renoir.

27. Ronald Bergan, *Jean Renoir: Projections of Paradise*, Overlook Press, 1994.

28. Jean Renoir Papers, Production Files, Motion Picture Productions, Box 2, Folder 7.

29. Contract for transfer of rights to film *Catherine* between Jean Renoir and Pierre Braunberger, December 10, 1926, Jean Renoir Papers, Production Files, Motion Picture Productions, Box 5, Folder 5.

4. "A Kraut Movie"

1. Jean Renoir Papers, Production Files, Motion Picture Productions, Box 5, Folder 5.

2. Pierre Braunberger, *Cinémamémoire*, interviews by Jacques Gerber, Centre Georges Pompidou/CNC, 1987.

3. David Welch, *Propaganda and the German Cinema 1933–1945*, Oxford University Press, 1983.

4. Valeska Gert, *Je suis une sorcière: kaléidoscope d'une vie dansée*, translation and notes by Philippe Ivernel, Éditions Complexe, 2004.

5. Agreement between les Films Renoir et la Delog Film on September 3, 1925, Jean Renoir Papers, Production Files, Motion Picture Productions, Box 5, Folder 16.

6. Conversation with Michel Ciment, in *Positif*, n° 173, September 1975.

7. Jean Renoir, *Pierre-Auguste Renoir, mon père*, Gallimard, Folio, 1981.

8. Julie Manet, *Journal (1893–1899)*, C. Klincksieck, 1979.

9. Jean Renoir, *Pierre-Auguste Renoir, mon père*.

10. Jean Renoir, *Écrits 1926–1971*, edited by Claude Gauteur, Belfond, 1974.

11. *Le Figaro*, July 10, 1925.

12. Jean Renoir, *Ma vie et mes films*, Flammarion, 1974.

13. *Ciné-Miroir*, n° 100, June 15, 1926.

14. Contracts for transfer of rights of *Nana*, Jean Renoir Papers, Production Files, Box 3, Folder 2.

15. Letter to Ginette Doynel, January 16, 1965, Jean Renoir Papers, Correspondence, Box 20, Folder 6.

16. Jean Renoir, *Ma vie et mes films*.

5. Poaching

1. Jean Renoir, *Ma vie et mes films*, Flammarion, 1974.

2. Ibid.

3. Ibid.

4. *Le Figaro*, March 28, 1927.

5. Earlier draft of *Ma vie et mes films*, Jean Renoir Papers, Production Files, Box 71, Folder 2.

6. Jean Renoir, *Ma vie et mes films*.

7. Letter to Ginette Doynel, January 16, 1965, Jean Renoir Papers, Correspondence, Box 20, Folder 6.

8. Jean Renoir, *Ma vie et mes films*.

9. *La Critique cinématographique*, n° 24, May 7, 1927.

10. *Écran 74*, n° 30, November 1974.

11. Ibid.

12. Jean Renoir Papers, Production Files, Motion Picture Productions, Box 9, Folder 6.

13. Jean Tedesco, "L'Artisan Jean Renoir," in *Ciné-Club*, n° 6, April 1948.

6. Soup and Grub

1. Conversations with Alain Renoir.

2. Pierre Braunberger, *Cinémamémoire*, interviews by Jacques Gerber, Centre Georges Pompidou/CNC, 1987.

3. Éric Rohmer, ORTF, 1969, cited by Roger Viry-Babel, *Jean Renoir, le Jeu et la Règle*, Denoël, 1986.

4. Conversation with Danièle Heymann.

5. Claude Heymann, conversation with Jacques Siclier, *Claude Heymann, Portrait d'un illustre inconnu*, a documentary film by Richard Frances and Philippe Jamont, 1991.

6. Alexander Sesonske, *Jean Renoir: The French Films, 1924–1939*, Harvard University Press, 1980.

7. Conversations with Alain Renoir.

8. Claude Heymann, conversation with Jacques Siclier, *Claude Heymann, Portrait d'un illustre inconnu*, a documentary film by Richard Frances and Philippe Jamont, 1991.

9. Eric Bonnefille, *Raymond Bernard: fresques et miniatures*, L'Harmattan, 2010.

10. *Le Figaro*, June 16, 1928.

11. *La Revue de l'écran*, n° 2, January 5, 1929.

12. *Le Figaro*, January 2, 1929.

13. *Le Figaro*, December 8, 1928.

14. Conversations with Alain Renoir.

15. Jean Renoir, *Pierre-Auguste Renoir, mon père*, Gallimard, Folio, 1981.

16. Marcel Lapierre, *Les Cent visages du cinéma*, Grasset, 1948.

17. *Lotte Reiniger, Carl Koch, Jean Renoir, Die Gemeinsamen Filme, Szenen einer Freundschaft*, CICIM Stadt Tübingen Kulturamt Stadtmuseum, 1994.

18. Conversations with Alain Renoir.

7. Chamber Pots

1. Cited by Pierre Billard, *Le Mystère René Clair*, Plon, 1998.

2. Ibid.

3. Pierre Braunberger, *Cinémamémoire*, interviews by Jacques Gerber, Centre Georges Pompidou/CNC, 1987.

4. Letter to Claude Beylie, August 29, 1974, Jean Renoir Papers, Correspondence, Box 30, Folder 6.

5. Roger Richebé, *Au-delà de l'écran*, Éditions Pastorelly, 1977.

6. Conversations with Alain Renoir.

7. Jean Renoir, *Ma vie et mes films*, Flammarion, 1974.

8. Ibid.

9. Letter from Pierre Braunberger, June 25, 1975, Jean Renoir Papers, Correspondence, Box 31, Folder 5.

10. Letter to Pierre Braunberger, June 30, 1975, Jean Renoir Papers, Correspondence, Box 31, Folder 5.

11. Letter to Mr. Schlamm, April 14, 1949, *Correspondance 1913–1978*, Plon, 1998.

8. Pitiless

1. Archives of Les Films du Jeudi.

2. Jean Renoir, *Ma vie et mes films*, Flammarion, 1974.

3. Pierre Braunberger, *Cinémamémoire*, interviews by Jacques Gerber, Centre Georges Pompidou/CNC, 1987.

4. Roger Richebé, *Au-delà de l'écran*, Éditions Pastorelly, 1977.

5. Jean Renoir, *Ma vie et mes films*.

6. Pierre Braunberger, *Cinémamémoire*.

7. Jean Renoir, *Ma vie et mes films*.

8. Roger Richebé, *Au-delà de l'écran*.

9. Claude Autant-Lara, *La Rage dans le cœur*, Henri Veyrier, 1984.

10. Roger Richebé, *Au-delà de l'écran*.

11. Pierre Braunberger, *Cinémamémoire*.

12. Jean Renoir, "Souvenirs," *Le Point*, December 18, 1938.

13. Roger Richebé, *Au-delà de l'écran*.

14. Ibid.

15. Jean Renoir, "Souvenirs."

16. Letter to Claude Beylie, June 30, 1975, Jean Renoir Papers, Correspondence, Box 5, Folder 31.

17. Denise Tual, *Le Temps dévoré*, Fayard, 1980.

18. Jean Renoir, *Ma vie et mes films*.

19. Ibid.

20. Letter from Pierre Braunberger to Charles David, August 29, 1971, Archives of Les Films du Jeudi.

21. Archives of Les Films du Jeudi.

22. Ibid.

23. Ibid.

24. Ibid.

25. Letter to Claude Beylie, June 30, 1975, Jean Renoir Papers, Correspondence, Box 5, Folder 31.

26. Unpublished conversation with Marcel Dalio.

27. Pierre Braunberger, *Cinémamémoire*.

28. Archives of Les Films du Jeudi.

29. Roger Viry-Babel, *Jean Renoir, le Jeu et la Règle*, Denoël, 1986.

30. Présentation of *La Chienne* to the Congress of "Film Societies," May 1956, republished in *Positif*, n° 173, September 1975, in a translation by Jeannine Ciment.

31. *L'Est républicain*, November 12, 1931.

32. Jean Renoir, *Ma vie et mes films*.

33. Jacques Rivette and François Truffaut, "Nouvel conversation avec Jean Renoir," *Cahiers du cinéma*, n° 78, Noël 1957.

34. Conversation with Jo Siritzky.

35. *Pour vous*, n° 217, January 12, 1933.

36. *La Croix*, May 30, 1932.

37. *Le Figaro*, December 6, 1931.

9. Fog and Shadow

1. Jean Renoir, "Souvenirs," *Le Point*, December 1938.

2. Jean Renoir, *Ma vie et mes films*, Flammarion, 1974.

3. Pierre Assouline, *Simenon*, Julliard, 1992.

4. Jean Renoir, *Ma vie et mes films*.

5. Conversation with Geneviève Boyard-Becker.

6. *Paris-Soir*, April 16, 1932.

7. *Les Cahiers de la cinémathèque*, n° 26–27, 1979.

8. Conversation with Jean-Louis Noames, *Cahiers du cinéma*, n° 155, May 1964.

10. Boudu Priapus Simon

1. Conversations with Alain Renoir.

2. Conversation with Paule Hutzler, *Almanach Ciné-Miroir 1936*.

3. Conversation with Nino Frank, *Pour vous*, n° 157, November 19, 1931.

4. Paul Achard, *Paris-Midi*, March 31, 1925.

5. Broadcast of *Tête d'affiche*, September 20, 1966.

6. Ibid.

7. Jean Renoir, *Pierre-Auguste Renoir, mon père*, Gallimard, Folio, 1981.

8. Jean Renoir, *Ma vie et mes films*, Flammarion, 1974.

9. Conversation with Odile Cambier, *Cinémonde*, October 20, 1932.

10. Conversation with Doringe, *Pour vous*, May 10, 1939.

11. Jean Devaivre, *Action ! Mémoires 1930–1970*, Nicolas Philippe, 2002.

12. *La Cinématographie française*, October 22, 1932.

13. *Cinéma 56*, n° 7, November 1956.

14. *La Cinématographie française*, October 22, 1932.

15. Lucien Wahl, *Pour vous*, n° 270, January 18, 1934.

16. *Pour vous*, n° 217, January 12, 1933.

11. Adaptations

1. *Le Journal des débats*, October 10, 1933.

2. Roger Viry-Babel, *Jean Renoir, le Jeu et la Règle*, Denoël, 1986.

3. *Le Figaro*, August 10, 1930.

4. *Le Figaro*, January 30, 1933.

5. Conversation with Michel Ciment, *Positif*, n° 173, September 1975.

6. Pierre Braunberger, *Cinémamémoire*, interviews by Jacques Gerber, Centre Georges Pompidou/CNC, 1987.

7. Ibid.

8. Bertolt Brecht, *La Vieille Dame indigne et autres histoires, 1928–1948*, translated by Bernard Lortholary, L'Arche, 1988.

9. Jean Renoir, *Pierre-Auguste Renoir, mon père*, Gallimard, Folio, 1981.

10. Robert Aron, *Fragments d'une vie*, Plon, 1981.

11. *Pour vous*, February 23, 1933.

12. Robert Aron, *Fragments d'une vie*.

13. Cited by Bernard Pharisien, *Pierre Renoir*, Némont, 2003.

14. *Pour vous*, n° 249, August 24, 1933.

15. Jean Serge, *Le temps n'est plus de la bohème*, Stock/Kian, 1991.

16. *Le Journal des débats*, August 23, 1933.

17. Robert Aron, *Fragments d'une vie*.

18. Jean Griot, Letter to Ronald Bergan, *Jean Renoir, Projections of Paradise*, Overlook Press, 1994.

19. Robert Aron, *Fragments d'une vie*.

20. Ibid.

21. *Le Matin*, January 12, 1934.

22. Michel Domange, *Ah! Mes aïeux . . . (1830–1945)*, Les Éditions du Nant d'enfer, 1990.

23. André de Masini, *La Revue de l'écran*, n° 115, February 20, 1934.

24. Conversations with Alain Renoir.

25. Conversation with Emmanuel Decaux et Bruno Villien, *Cinématographe, n° 108, March 1985*.

26. Letter to Gilles Margaritis, February 18, 1934, cited by Claude Sicard, "Roger Martin du Gard et Gustave Flaubert," in *Voix de l'écrivain: mélanges offerts à Guy Sagnes*, edited by Jean-Louis Cabanis, Presses Universitaires du Mirail, 1996.

27. Fonds Pierre Gaut, Cinémathèque française.

28. Letter of May 11, 1944, Jean Renoir Papers.

29. *Jean Renoir: Correspondance 1913–1978*, Plon, 1998.

30. Letter from Alain Renoir, undated (circa 1946), Jean Renoir Papers, Correspondence, Box 10, Folder 2.

31. Letter from Valentine Tessier, December 1963, Jean Renoir Papers, Correspondence, Box 19, Folder 4.

32. Ibid.

33. Letter to Valentine Tessier, December 30, 1963, Jean Renoir Papers, Correspondence, Box 19, Folder 4.

34. Letter from Valentine Tessier, April 1965, Jean Renoir Papers, Correspondence, Box 20, Folder 10.

12. Primitive

1. *Pour vous*, August 10, 1933.

2. Conversation with Pierre Philippe, *Cinéma 61*, n° 57, June 1961.

3. *Le Figaro*, December 1, 1933.

4. Conversations with Alain Renoir.

5. Conversation with Geneviève Boyard-Becker.

6. Denise Tual, *Le Temps dévoré*, Fayard, 1980.

7. Conversations with Alain Renoir.

8. Jean Renoir, *Correspondance 1913–1978*, Plon, 1998.

9. See Isabelle Marinone, *André Sauvage, un cinéaste oublié*, l'Harmattan, 2008.

10. Jean Renoir, *Correspondance 1913–1978*.

11. Ibid.

12. Ibid.

13. Liliane Meffre, *Carl Einstein, 1885–1940, Itinéraires d'une pensée moderne*, Presses de l'université de Paris-Sorbonne, 2002.

14. Ibid.

15. Earlier draft of *Ma vie et mes films*, Jean Renoir Papers, Production Files, Box 70, Folder 1.

16. Pierre Gaut, excerpted from a conference at the Institut d'Art et d'Archéologie, Université de Paris I, cited in "Spécial Renoir," *L'Avant-Scène* n° 251, July 1–15, 1980.

17. Letter from Pierre Gaut to the Minister of National Defense, undated, 1940 (April or early May), file on the career of Lieutenant Pierre Gaut, SHDAI 1P29 914/1.

18. General Pinsard, May 25, 1940, file on the career of Lieutenant Pierre Gaut, SHDAI 1P29 914/1.

19. *Cahiers du cinéma*, n° 78, Noël 1957.

20. Letter to Carl Koch, June 1, 1934, *Correspondance 1913–1978*.

21. Fonds Pierre Gaut, Cinémathèque française.

22. Ibid.

23. Ibid.

24. Jean Renoir Papers, Production Files, Box 12, Folder 3.

25. Jean Renoir Papers, Production Files, Box 48, Folder 2.

26. Ibid.

27. Jean Renoir Papers, Production Files, Box 12, Folder 3.

28. Fonds Pierre Gaut, Cinémathèque française.

29. Jean Renoir Papers, Production Files, Box 12, Folder 3.

30. Ibid.

31. Ibid.

32. Fonds Pierre Gaut, Cinémathèque française.

33. Ibid.

34. *Pour vous*, n° 315, November 29, 1934.

35. Letter from Pierre Gaut, May 27, 1974, Jean Renoir Papers, Correspondence, Box 30, Folder 4.

36. Letter to Pierre Gaut, June 3, 1974, Fonds Pierre Gaut, Cinémathèque française.

37. Pierre Gaut, excerpted from a conference at the Institut d'Art et d'Archéologie, Université de Paris I, cited in "Spécial Renoir," *L'Avant-Scène*.

38. Fonds Pierre Gaut, Cinémathèque française.

39. Telegram to Pierre Gaut, September 26, 1934, Fonds Pierre Gaut, Cinémathèque française.

40. Fonds Pierre Gaut, Cinémathèque française.

41. Ibid.

42. Jean Renoir, *Comoedia*, February 8, 1935, reprinted in *Écrits 1926–1971*, edited by Claude Gauteur, Belfond, 1974.

43. Advertisement for the hôtel Pascal, Fonds Pierre Gaut, Cinémathèque française.

44. Fonds Pierre Gaut, Cinémathèque française.

45. Ibid.

46. Ibid.

47. Letter to Ginette Doynel, January 19, 1976, Jean Renoir Papers, Correspondence, Box 32, Folder 1.

48. Fonds Pierre Gaut, Cinémathèque française.

49. Cited by Liliane Meffre, *Carl Einstein, 1885–1940*.

50. Letter from Pierre Gaut, June 3, 1974, Fonds Pierre Gaut, Cinémathèque française.

51. Ibid.

52. Fonds Pierre Gaut, Cinémathèque française.

53. Ibid.

54. Cited by Liliane Meffre, *Carl Einstein.*

55. Letter to Pierre Gaut, January 10, 1935, Fonds Pierre Gaut, Cinémathèque française.

56. Charles Tesson, *La Production de Toni: la règle et l'esprit, Cinémathèque,* n° 1, 2, and 3, 1992 and 1993.

57. Fonds Pierre Gaut, Cinémathèque française.

58. Conversation with Jacques Rivette and François Truffaut, *Cahiers du cinéma.*

59. Fonds Pierre Gaut, Cinémathèque française.

13. In the Courtyard

1. *L'Encyclopédie du cinéma soviétique et russe.*

2. Postcard addressed to Pierre Gaut, March 1935, Fonds Pierre Gaut, Cinémathèque française.

3. Ibid.

4. Conversations with Alain Renoir.

5. Ibid.

6. Ibid.

7. Fonds Pierre Gaut, Cinémathèque française.

8. Ibid.

9. Letter to Pierre Gaut on December 27, 1934.

10. Conversation with Geneviève Boyer-Becker.

11. Fonds Jean Renoir, Cinémathèque française.

12. Jean Renoir, *Pierre-Auguste Renoir, mon père,* Gallimard, Folio, 1981.

13. Fonds Jean Renoir, Cinémathèque française.

14. Jean Renoir Papers, Box 49, Folder 3.

15. *CinémAction,* n° 98.

16. Conversation with Jean-Pierre Pagliano, *Positif,* n° 408, February 1995.

17. Conversation with Pierre Philippe, in *Cinéma 61,* n° 60, October 1961.

18. Letter to Pierre Dalfour, June 21, 1941, Jean Renoir Papers, Correspondence, Box 2, Folder 2.

19. Broadcast of *Jean Renoir vous parle de son art,* August 1961, reprinted in *Jean Renoir, conversations et propos, Cahiers du cinéma,* 1979.

20. See, in particular, Jean Renoir Papers, Production Files, Box 2, Folder 8.

21. *Jean Renoir: Correspondance 1913–1978,* Plon, 1998.

14. Fellow Traveler

1. Henri Jeanson, *Soixante-dix ans d'adolescence,* Stock, 1971.

2. Janine Spaak, *Charles Spaak, mon mari, Éditions France-Empire, 1977.*

3. Pierre Braunberger, *Cinémamémoire,* interviews by Jacques Gerber, Centre Georges Pompidou/CNC, 1987.

4. Marcel Carné, *La Vie à belles dents, Éditions Jean-Pierre Ollivier, 1975.*

5. Françoise Giroud, *Si je mens . . . ,* Stock, 1972.

6. Philippe Robrieux, *Maurice Thorez, vie secrète et vie publique,* Fayard, 1975.

7. *Le Figaro,* April 22, 1936.

8. Conversations with Alain Renoir.

9. *Esprit,* February 1937.

10. Maurice Bardèche and Robert Brasillach, *Histoire du cinéma, Volume 2, Le Cinéma parlant,* 1943.

11. Conversation with Pierre Philippe, in *Cinéma 61,* n° 60, October 1961.

12. Jean-Paul Le Chanois, *Le Temps des cerises, Conversations with Philippe Esnault*, Institut Lumière/Actes Sud, 1996.

13. Roger Viry-Babel, *Jean Renoir, le Jeu et la Règle*, Denoël, 1986.

14. Jean Renoir, *Ma vie et mes films*, Flammarion, 1974.

15. Jean-Paul Le Chanois, *Le Temps des cerises*.

16. François Truffaut, in André Bazin, *Jean Renoir, Éditions Champ Libre, 1971*.

17. Jacques-Bernard Brunius, *En marge du cinéma français, Éditions Arcanes, 1954*.

18. Christian Delporte, *Une histoire de la langue de bois*, Flammarion, 2009.

19. Jean-Paul Le Chanois, *Le Temps des cerises*.

20. *L'Avant-Garde*, January 1937, cited by Pascal Ory, *La Belle Illusion, Culture et Politique sous le signe du Front populaire 1935–1939*, Plon, 1994.

21. Pascal Ory, *La Belle Illusion*.

22. Cited by Francis Courtade, *Les Malédictions du cinéma français*, Alain Moreau Editeur, 1978.

23. Conversations with Alain Renoir.

24. Jean Aurenche, *La Suite à l'écran, Entretiens*, afterword by Bernard Chardère, Institut Lumière/Actes Sud, 1993.

25. André Gide, *Journal (1889–1939)*, Collection Bibliothèque de la Pléiade (n° 54), Gallimard, 1939, p. 1261.

15. "Every Night I Remember"

1. Conversation with Jean-Pierre Pagliano, *Positif*, n° 408, February 1995.

2. Cited by Olivier Curchod, *Partie de campagne, Jean Renoir: étude critique*, Nathan, 1995.

3. Cinémathèque française.

4. Letter from R. Meyer & Cie, June 11, 1936, Fonds Jacques-Bernard Brunius, Cinémathèque française.

5. Fonds Jacques-Bernard Brunius, Cinémathèque française.

6. Olivier Curchod, *Partie de campagne, Jean Renoir*.

7. *Ciné-Liberté*, n° 2, June 20, 1936, reprinted in *Écrits 1926–1971*, edited by Claude Gauteur, Belfond, 1974.

8. Giuseppe Ferrara, *Luchino Visconti*, Paris, 1963.

9. Conversation with Jacques Doniol-Valcroze and Jean Domarchi, *Cahiers du cinéma*, n° 147, September 1963.

10. Olivier Curchod, *Partie de campagne, Jean Renoir*.

11. Conversations with Alain Renoir.

12. Conversation with Jean-Pierre Pagliano, *Positif*.

13. Ibid.

14. Pierre Braunberger, *Cinémamémoire*, interviews by Jacques Gerber, Centre Georges Pompidou/CNC, 1987.

15. Archives of Les Films du Jeudi.

16. Olivier Curchod, *Partie de campagne, Jean Renoir*.

17. Jean-Pierre Berthomé, *Positif*, n° 408.

18. Carole Aurouet, *Les Scénarios détournés de Jacques Prévert*, Dreamland Editeur, 2003.

19. Conversation with Jean-Pierre Pagliano, *Positif*.

20. *Cahiers du cinéma*, n° 78, Noël 1957.

21. Jean Renoir, *Ma vie et mes films*, Flammarion, 1974.

22. Conversation with Marguerite Renoir et Marinette Cadicqx, *Télérama*, n° 661, September 16, 1962.

23. Jon Halliday, *Conversations avec Douglas Sirk*, Éditions Cahiers du cinéma, 1997.

24. Archives of Les Films du Jeudi.

25. Letter from Pierre Braunberger to Jean Painlevé, January 15, 1940, ECPAD.

26. Letter from Jean Painlevé to Pierre Braunberger, April 9, 1945, Archives of Les Films du Jeudi.

27. Letter from Georges d'Arnoux to Pierre Braunberger, August 1938, Archives of Les Films du Jeudi.

28. Letter from Georges d'Arnoux to Pierre Braunberger, undated, Archives of Les Films du Jeudi.

29. Letter from Paul Temps, June 7, 1947, Jean Renoir Papers, Correspondence, Box 7, Folder 9.

30. Letter from Pierre Braunberger to Films Traders, March 24, 1949, Jean Renoir Papers, Correspondence, Box 9, Folder 6.

16. The Russian Way

1. Conversations with Alain Renoir.

2. Cited by Jorge Semprun, preface to Eugène Zamiatine, *Nous autres,* Gallimard, 1979.

3. Eugène Lourié, *My Work in Films,* Harcourt, Brace, Jovanovich, 1985.

4. Fonds Films Albatros, Cinémathèque française.

5. Roger Viry-Babel, *Jean Renoir, le Jeu et la Règle,* Denoël, 1986.

6. Jean Renoir, *Écrits 1926-1971,* edited by Claude Gauteur, Belfond, 1974.

7. André G. Brunelin, *Jean Gabin,* Laffont, 1987.

8. Janine Spaak, *Charles Spaak, mon mari,* Éditions France-Empire, 1977.

9. Eugène Lourié, *My Work in Films.*

10. Janine Spaak, *Charles Spaak, mon mari.*

11. *Jean Renoir vous présente,* Les Bas-Fonds, directed by Jean-Marie Coldefy, January 1, 1962.

12. Letter to Ginette Doynel, January 20, 1965, Jean Renoir Papers, Correspondence, Box 20, Folder 6.

13. Archives Kamenka.

14. Nina Berberova, *Histoire de la baronne Boudberg,* Actes Sud, 1988.

15. Archives Films Albatros, Cinémathèque française.

16. Pierre Billard, *L'Âge classique du cinéma français,* Flammarion, 1995.

17. Conversations with Alain Renoir.

18. Ibid.

19. Jean Renoir, *Ma vie et mes films,* Flammarion, 1974.

20. *Regards,* n° 147, November 5, 1936.

21. Alexander Sesonske, *Jean Renoir: The French Films, 1924-1939,* Harvard University Press, 1980.

22. Archives Films Albatros, Cinémathèque française.

23. Conversation with Jo Siritzky.

24. Letter from Jean Renoir and Charles Spaak to Messieurs Lehman, Aciman, and Saason, November 10, 1936, Jean Renoir Papers, Correspondence, Box 1, Folder 5.

25. Conversation with Jo Siritzky.

26. *La Croix,* December 13-14, 1936.

27. *L'Humanité,* December 19, 1936.

28. *L'Humanité,* December 24, 1936.

29. Pascal Ory, *La Belle Illusion, Culture et Politique sous le signe du Front populaire 1935-1939,* Plon, 1994.

30. Georges Charensol, *La Femme de France,* January 31, 1937.

31. Letter from William Saason, March 1943, Jean Renoir Papers, Correspondence, Box 3, Folder 15.

32. *Jean Renoir: Correspondance 1913-1978,* Plon, 1998.

33. Alexander Sesonske, *Jean Renoir.*

34. Jean Renoir Papers, Correspondence, Box 1, Folder 5.

35. Jean Renoir Papers, Correspondence, Box 1, Folder 6.

36. Charles Spaak, "Mes 31 mariages, Jean Renoir vu par Charles Spaak," *Paris-Cinéma,* n° 10, December 12, 1945.

17. Between Two Wars

1. Conversations with Alain Renoir.

2. Jean Renoir, *Ma vie et mes films*, Flammarion, 1974.

3. Olivier Curchod, *La Grande Illusion*, Nathan, 1994.

4. Charles Spaak, "Mes 31 mariages, Jean Renoir vu par Charles Spaak," *Paris-Cinéma*, n° 10, December 12, 1945.

5. Ibid.

6. Charles Spaak and Jean Renoir, *La grande illusion*, Paris, 1971.

7. Janine Spaak, *Charles Spaak, mon mari*, Éditions France-Empire, 1977.

8. Jean Renoir, *Ma vie et mes films*.

9. Conversations with Alain Renoir.

10. *Lotte Reiniger, Carl Koch, Jean Renoir, Die Gemeinsamen Filme, Szenen einer Freundschaft*, CICIM Stadt Tübingen Kulturamt Stadtmuseum, 1994.

11. Cited by Frank Priot, "*La Grande Illusion:* histoire du film en dix chapitres," in "*La Grande Illusion:* le film d'un siècle," *Archives*, n° 70, February 1997, Institut Jean Vigo Perpignan–Cinémathèque de Toulouse.

12. André G. Brunelin, *Jean Gabin*, Laffont, 1987.

13. Marie-Claude Roesch-Lalance, *Dans l'intimité de la communauté artistique de Bourron-Marlotte, si les maisons nous racontaient . . .*, edited by the Association des Amis de Bourron-Marlotte, 1986.

14. *Lotte Reiniger, Carl Koch, Jean Renoir, Die Gemeinsamen Filme, Szenen einer Freundschaft*.

15. Jean Renoir Papers, 1915–1927 (Collection 105), Performing Arts Special Collections, Young Research Library, University of California, Los Angeles, Part II, Correspondence, Box 3, Folder 9.

16. Letter to Claude Renoir, May 11, 1946, *Lettres d'amérique*, Presses de la Renaissance, 1984.

17. Letter from Erich von Stroheim, cited by Arthur Lennig, *Stroheim*, University Press of Kentucky, 2000.

18. Françoise Giroud, *Si je mens . . .*, Stock, 1972.

19. Olivier Curchod, *La Grande Illusion*.

20. François Truffaut, in André Bazin, *Jean Renoir*, Éditions Champ Libre, 1971.

21. Olivier Curchod, *La Grande Illusion*.

22. Eugène Lourié, *My Work in Films*, Harcourt, Brace, Jovanovich, 1985.

23. Charles Spaak, "Mes 31 mariages."

24. Jean Renoir, conversation with Danièle Heymann, *Le Monde*, September 14, 1974.

25. Jean Renoir, *Ma vie et mes films*.

26. Françoise Giroud, *Leçons particulières*, Fayard, 1990.

27. "Adieu à Gabin. Renoir: Nous étions de la même race," interviews by Pierre Montaigne, *Le Figaro*, November 18, 1976.

28. Olivier Curchod, *La Grande Illusion*.

29. Georges Fronval, *Cinémonde*, February 25, 1937, cited by Olivier Curchod, *La Grande Illusion*.

30. Marcel Dalio, *Mes années folles*, J.-C. Lattès, 1976.

31. Jean Renoir Papers, 1915–1927 (Collection 105), Box 5, Folder 2.

32. Marcel Dalio, *Mes années folles*.

33. Pierre Fresnay and Pierre Possot, *Pierre Fresnay par Fresnay et Possot*, La Table Ronde, 1975.

34. André G. Brunelin, *Jean Gabin*.

35. Olivier Curchod, *La Grande Illusion*.

36. Jean Renoir, Letter to Charles Spaak, June 9, 1937, cited in *Archives*, n° 70, February 1997, Institut Jean Vigo Perpignan–Cinémathèque de Toulouse.

37. Ibid.

38. Conversation with Jo Siritzky.

39. *L'Action française*, June 11, 1937.

40. *Cinémonde*, February 4, 1937.

41. Pierre Billard, *Le Mystère René Clair*, Plon, 1998.

42. Letter from the Association des auteurs de films, December 9, 1935, Jean Renoir Papers, Correspondence, Box 5, Folder 9.

43. Letter to the Association des auteurs de films, December 13, 1935, Jean Renoir Papers, Correspondence, Box 5, Folder 9.

44. Jean Renoir, *Ma vie et mes films*.

45. Jean Renoir, *Écrits 1926–1971*, edited by Claude Gauteur, Belfond, 1974.

46. Vincent Lowy, *Guère à la guerre*, L'Harmattan, 2006.

47. Jean-Pierre Jeancolas, *15 ans d'années trente*, Stock, 1983.

48. *Paris-Midi*, May 25, 1935, cited by Jean-Pierre Jeancolas, ibid.

49. Conversations with Alain Renoir.

50. Simon Epstein, *Un paradoxe français: Antiracistes dans la Collaboration, antisémites dans la Résistance*, Albin Michel, 2008.

51. See, especially, Stéphane Audoin-Rouzeau, *14–18, Les combattants des tranchées*, Armand Colin, 1987.

52. Simon Epstein, *Un paradoxe français*.

53. Céline, *Bugatelles pour un massacre*, Denoël, 1937.

54. Henri Godard, *Céline*, Gallimard, 2011.

55. Conversations with Alain Renoir.

56. Ibid.

57. *Ce soir*, January 20, 1938, in *Écrits 1926–1971*.

58. Jean des Vallières, *Kavalier Scharnhorst*, Albin Michel, 1931.

59. Luc van Dongen, *Un purgatoire très discret, la transition "helvétique" d'anciens nazis, fascistes et collaborateurs après 1945*, Perrin/Société d'histoire de la Suisse romande, 2008.

60. Francis Carco, *Le Figaro*, June 28, 1937.

61. *Jean Renoir: Correspondance 1913–1978*, Plon, 1998.

62. *Cahiers du cinéma*, n° 78, Noël 1957.

63. Ibid.

64. Jean Renoir, July 10, 1937, ibid.

65. Janine Spaak, *Charles Spaak, mon mari*, France-Empire, 1975.

66. Letter to Thomas Curtiss, August 2, 1974, Jean Renoir Papers, Correspondence, Box 30, Folder 6.

67. Archives of the Société des auteurs.

68. *Les Cahiers de la cinémathèque*, n° 18–19, 1976.

69. Jean Renoir, March 5, 1938, *Correspondance 1913–1978*.

70. Conversation with Jean Slade.

18. "People We'd Like to Be Friends With"

1. Conversations with Alain Renoir.

2. Conversation with Jo Siritzky.

3. Conversations with Alain Renoir.

4. Pierre Brisson, *Le Figaro*, October 23, 1938.

5. Conversations with Alain Renoir.

6. Jean Renoir, *Écrits 1926–1971*, edited by Claude Gauteur, Belfond, 1974.

7. *Ce soir*, April 14, 1938.

8. *Ce soir*, April 29, 1937.

9. *Ce soir*, December 16, 1937.

10. *Ce soir*, May 20, 1937.

11. *La Flèche de Paris*, July 24, 1937.

12. *La Flèche de Paris*, May 30, 1936.

13. Philippe Robrieux, *Maurice Thorez, vie secrète et vie publique*, Fayard, 1975.

14. Emma Le Chanois, in Jean-Paul Le Chanois, *Le Temps des cerises, Conversations with Philippe Esnault*, Institut Lumière/Actes Sud, 1996.

15. Conversation with Geneviève Boyard-Becker.

16. Conversation with Léon Weissleib, *L'Avant-Garde*, January 2, 1937, reprinted in *La Revue du cinéma, Image et Son*, n° 315, March 1977.

17. *Paris-Soir*, February 11, 1937.

18. Ibid.

19. Henri Jeanson, *Soixante-dix ans d'adolescence*, Stock, 1971.

20. *Paris-Soir*, February 11, 1937.

21. Henri Jeanson, *Soixante-dix ans d'adolescence*.

22. *L'Humanité*, March 13, 1937.

23. *Le Figaro*, March 13, 1937.

24. Ibid.

25. *L'Humanité*, March 14, 1937.

26. Lucien Rebatet, *Candide*, March 18, 1937.

27. *La Cinématographie française*, March 19, 1937.

28. *Commune*, n° 44, April 1937.

29. *Regards*, August 19, 1937.

30. *Ce soir*, September 2, 1937.

31. Giulio Ceretti, *À l'ombre des deux T., 40 ans with Maurice Thorez et Palmiro Togliatti*, Julliard, 1973.

32. Copies of the excerpts from the contract on June 1, 1937, Jean Renoir Papers, Correspondence, Box 1, Folder 6.

33. Henri Jeanson, *Soixante-dix ans d'adolescence*.

34. Contract for January 15, 1938, Jean Renoir Papers, Correspondence, Box 1, Folder 7.

35. *Jean Renoir: Correspondance 1913–1978*, Plon, 1998.

36. Letter to Louis Guillaume, July 4, 1948, Jean Renoir Papers, Correspondence, Box 8, Folder 12.

37. Conversation with Pierre Philippe, in *Cinéma 61*, n° 60, October 1961.

38. *Le Figaro*, July 14, 1937.

39. Conversations with Alain Renoir.

40. *Le Figaro*, February 11, 1938.

41. *L'Humanité*, April 7, 1938.

42. Jean-Paul Le Chanois, *Le Temps des cerises*.

43. Conversation with Geneviève Boyard-Becker.

44. *Le Figaro*, August 5, 1938.

45. Conversation with Michel Delahaye and Jean Narboni, *Cahiers du cinéma*, n° 196, December 1967.

46. *Ce soir*, August 9, 1938.

47. *L'Avant-Garde*, February 12, 1937, cited by Pascal Ory.

48. Conversation with Michel Delahaye and Jean Narboni, *Cahiers du cinéma*, n° 196, December 1967.

49. Jean Renoir, *Pierre-Auguste Renoir, mon père*, Gallimard, Folio, 1981.

50. Jules Michelet, *Histoire de la Révolution française*, vol. II, chap. X, 1847.

51. Ibid., vol. IV, chap. VI, 1847.

52. *Ce soir*, August 26, 1937.

53. *Cahiers du cinéma*, n° 78.

54. Letter from Antoine Corteggiani, December 31, 1939, Archives Jean Renoir, ECPAD.

55. Letter from brother Claude Renoir, March 23, 1945, Jean Renoir Papers, Correspondence, Box 5, Folder 2.

56. Letter to Dido Renoir, July 1, 1951, *Correspondance 1913–1978*.

57. Pierre Autre, *Ciné-France*, September 24, 1937.

58. Valérie Vignaux, *Jacques Becker ou l'exercice de la liberté*, Éditions du Céfal, 2000.

59. *Ce soir*, October 28, 1937.

60. *Le Figaro*, March 13, 1937.

61. *L'Étudiant français*, monthly publication of la Fédération nationale des étudiants d'Action française, April 10, 1937.

62. *Regards*, February 10, 1938, cited by Pascal Ory.

63. Pascal Ory, *La Belle Illusion, Culture et Politique sous le signe du Front populaire 1935–1939*, Plon, 1994.

64. Notes for edited texts of André Bazin, *Jean Renoir*, Éditions Champ Libre, 1971.

65. *Cahiers du cinéma*, n° 34, April 1954.

66. Philippe Robrieux, *Maurice Thorez*.

67. Jean Renoir, *Correspondance 1913–1978*.

68. *Le Figaro*, February 13, 1938.

69. Serge Veber, *Pour vous*, February 16, 1938.

70. *La Flèche de Paris*, February 19, 1932.

71. *Marianne*, February 16, 1938.

72. *Le Figaro*, March 27, 1938.

73. Telegram to Albert Pinkévitch, February 19, 1938, *Correspondance 1913–1978*.

19. Le P'tit Cœur de Ninon

1. Philippe Erlanger, *La France sans étoile: souvenirs de l'avant-guerre et de l'Occupation*, Plon, 1974.

2. Conférence given at the Maison de la Culture de la rue d'Anjou, July 7, 1938, cited by Claude Gauteur, *D'un Renoir l'autre*, Le Temps des Cerises, 2005.

3. Ibid.

4. António Lopes Ribeiro, "O grande realizador francês Jean Renoir esta em Lisboa," *Animatògrafo*, December 2, 1940.

5. Avenarius, *Jean Renoir*, Moscou, 1938 (privately translated for the author by Christian Rozeboom).

6. March 7, 1938, *Correspondance 1913–1978*, Plon, 1998.

7. March 5, 1938, *Correspondance 1913–1978*.

8. *Ce soir*, September 16, 1937.

9. *Ce soir*, February 17, 1938.

10. Jean Renoir, "Souvenir," *Le Point*, December 1938.

11. Joris Ivens, *The Camera and I*, Seven Seas Books, 1969.

12. *La Croix*, May 1, 1938.

13. *Les Cahiers de la Cinémathèque*, "La guerre d'Espagne vue by le Cinéma," n° 21, January 1977.

14. Kees Bakker, "*The Spanish Earth*, the Spanish, and *Terre d'Espagne*," Catalogue of the Yamagata International Documentary Film Festival, "A Joris Ivens Retrospective," 1999.

15. Catherine Vialles, *Jean Renoir and The Spanish Earth*, European Foundation Joris Ivens Newsmagazine, n° 10, November 2004.

16. Conversations with Alain Renoir.

17. Georges Sadoul, "Récents progrès du cinéma français," *Cahiers du bolchevisme*, n° 8, August 1938.

18. Conference given at la Maison de la Culture de la rue d'Anjou, on July 7, 1938, cited by Claude Gauteur, *D'un Renoir l'aut*.

19. Marcel Carné, *Les Cahiers de la cinémathèque*, n° 5, winter 1972.

20. Marcel Carné, *La Vie à belles dents*, Éditions Jean-Pierre Ollivier, 1975.

21. *Ce soir*, January 27, 1938.

22. Jacques-Bernard Brunius, *En marge du cinéma français, Éditions Arcanes, 1954.*

23. Claude Vermorel, "Émile Zola au cinéma," *Pour vous,* n° 314, November 15, 1934.

24. Conversations with Alain Renoir.

25. Marcel Carné, *La Vie à belles dents.*

26. "À propos de *La Bête humaine*," Jean Renoir Papers, Production Files, Box 13, Folder 43.

27. *Ce soir,* April 14, 1938.

28. Confirmation of contract on July 13, 1938, Jean Renoir Papers, Correspondence, Box 1, Folder 7.

29. *Cinémonde,* August 4, 1938.

30. *Cinémonde,* December 7, 1938.

31. Roger Viry-Babel, *La Vie de Jean Renoir.*

32. *Cinémonde,* August 4, 1938.

33. *Jean Renoir vous présente . . . ,* Radiodiffusion-Télévision française, direction by Jean-Marie Coldefy, January 1962.

34. *Cahiers du cinéma,* n° 78, Noël 1957.

35. *Cinémonde,* December 7, 1938.

36. *Jean Renoir vous présente . . . .*

37. Jean Renoir Papers, Production Files, Box 1, Folder 7.

38. *Ce soir,* July 24, 1938.

39. *Cinémonde,* December 7, 1938.

40. *Les Cahiers de la jeunesse,* n° 38, December 15, 1938.

41. *Cahiers du cinéma,* n° 78, Noël 1957.

42. *Ce soir,* October 7, 1938.

43. Ibid.

44. Edited by Bertrand Tavernier (unpublished).

45. *Ce soir,* September 3, 1938.

46. Application for admission to the Union des Artistes and Letter to M. Martinelli, January 3, 1939, documents furnished by Bernard Pharisien.

47. Letter to Alexander Sesonske, November 27, 1974, Jean Renoir Papers, Correspondence, Box 30, Folder 9.

48. *Cinémonde,* December 7, 1938.

49. Ibid.

50. Denise Tual, *Le Temps dévoré,* Fayard, 1980.

51. Jacques-Bernard Brunius, *En marge du cinéma français.*

52. Conversation with Bertrand Blier.

53. Conversations with Alain Renoir.

54. *Le Matin,* December 25, 1938.

55. Studio Canal.

56. *La Croix,* January 15, 1939.

57. *Regards,* January 5, 1939.

58. *Le Figaro,* October 13, 1938.

59. *Ce soir,* October 7, 1938.

60. Letter of September 14, 1938, *Correspondance 1913–1978.*

61. Conversations with Alain Renoir.

62. Conversation with Aline Cézanne.

20. Octave or Losing Balance

1. Olivier Curchod, Christopher Faulkner, *La Règle du jeu, Scénario original de Jean Renoir*, Nathan Cinéma, 1999.

2. *Correspondance 1913-1978*, Plon, 1998.

3. Jean Renoir Papers, Projects, Box 47, Folder 17.

4. Letter to Simone Simon, November 15, 1938, private collection.

5. Conversation with Claude Gauteur.

6. Conversation with Dominique Lebrun.

7. Conversation with Isabelle d'Arnoux-Tournade.

8. *Le Figaro*, December 3, 1937.

9. *Le Figaro*, July 8, 1937.

10. *Le Figaro*, March 5, 1938.

11. Jean Renoir Papers, Production Files, Box 9, Folder 9.

12. Letter to Camille François, June 1, 1939, *Correspondance 1913-1978*.

13. *Pour vous*, January 25, 1939.

14. *Jean Renoir, le Patron, Conversations et Propos*, Éditions de l'Étoile/Cahiers du cinéma, 1979.

15. For a precise chronology of the filming, see Olivier Curchod, Christopher Faulkner, *La Règle du jeu*.

16. François Arnoul, *Animal doué de bonheur*, Belfond, 1995.

17. *Le Petit Parisien*, July 15, 1939.

18. *Le Figaro*, March 25, 1939.

19. Paulette Dubost, *C'est court, la vie*, Flammarion, 1992.

20. *Le Figaro*, March 25, 1939.

21. Odile Cambier, *Jean Renoir et le graphophone, petite histoire en marge de* La Règle du jeu, *Cinémonde*, n° 543, March 15, 1939.

22. Conversations with Alain Renoir.

23. Screenplay by Dido Freire, 38, rue de l'Exposition to Paris, 7ème, 9 typed pages, undated, Jean Renoir Papers, Production Files, Box 49, Folder 8.

24. Conversation with Geneviève Boyard-Becker.

25. Letter of July 8, 1951, *Correspondance 1913-1978*.

26. Conversation with Claude Gauteur.

27. *Lettres d'amérique*, Presses de la Renaissance, 1984.

28. Conversations with Alain Renoir.

29. Ibid.

30. Paulette Dubost, *C'est court, la vie*.

31. Siegfried Kracauer, *Théorie du film, la rédemption de la réalité matérielle*, Flammarion, 2010.

32. "Note de Jean Renoir pour la direction de la production de *La Règle du jeu*," May 30, 1939, Jean Renoir Papers, Production Files, Box 9, Folder 10.

33. Conversations with Alain Renoir.

34. *Le Figaro*, July 4, 1939.

35. *Le Matin*, July 10, 1939.

36. Claude Gauteur, *Jean Renoir, la double méprise*, Les Éditeurs français réunis, 1980.

37. *Le Figaro*, July 12, 1939.

38. *Le Matin*, July 10, 1939.

39. François Truffaut, *Les Films de ma vie*, Flammarion, 1975.

40. For a precise account of the cuts made, see Olivier Curchod and Christopher Faulkner, *La Règle du jeu*.

41. François Poulle, *Renoir 1938 ou Jean Renoir pour rien? Enquête sur un cinéaste*, Éditions du Cerf, 1969.

42. *Paris-Spectacles*, July 1939, republished in Jean Renoir, *Écrits 1926-1971*, edited by Claude Gauteur, Belfond, 1974.

43. Marcel Colin-Reval, *La Cinématographie française*, September 2, 1939, cited by Jean-Pierre Jeancolas, *15 ans d'années trente*, Stock, 1983.

44. Letter to Camille François, June 1, 1939, *Correspondance 1913–1978*.

21. Tosca and Il Duce

1. Jean Renoir Papers, Correspondence, Box 1, Folder 12.

2. *Match*, August 17, 1939.

3. Ibid.

4. *Ce soir*, March 25, 1937.

5. *Ce soir*, December 16, 1937.

6. Vittorio Mussolini, in *Le Cinéma italien à l'ombre des faisceaux (1922–1945)*, by Jean A. Gili, Institut Jean Vigo, 1990.

7. Ibid.

8. Vittorio Mussolini, *Vita con mio padre*, Mondadori, 1957.

9. Maurizio Giammusso, *Vita di Rossellini*, Elleu, 2004.

10. Eveline and Yvan Brès, *Carl Heil, speaker contre Hitler*, les Éditions de Paris, 1994.

11. Contract from Scalera Film for the direction of *Tosca*, July 12, 1939, ECPAD.

12. Vittorio Mussolini, in *Le Cinéma italien à l'ombre des faisceaux*.

13. *Ce soir*, August 12, 1939.

14. The journal of Lotte Reiniger 1939–1940, in *Lotte Reiniger, Carl Koch, Jean Renoir, Die Gemeinsamen Filme, Szenen einer Freundschaft*, CICIM Stadt Tübingen Kulturamt Stadtmuseum, 1994.

15. Ibid.

16. *Correspondance 1913–1978*, Plon, 1998.

17. Jean Renoir Papers, Production Files, Series XII: Personal Items, Box 52, Folder 3.

18. ECPAD.

19. Ibid.

20. Ibid.

21. Ibid.

22. *Correspondance 1913–1978*.

23. Letter from Dido Freire to Robert Flaherty, cited by William Harry Gilcher, *Jean Renoir in America: A Critical Analysis of His Major Films from* Swamp Water *to* The River, University of Iowa, 1979.

24. ECPAD.

25. *Pour vous*, October 18, 1939.

26. Jean Renoir Papers, Part I, Production Files, Series VII: Notebooks, Box 53, Folder 4.

27. Letter from général La Porte du Theil to his wife, October 20, 1939, cited by Stéphane Launey, "Jean Renoir sous l'uniforme," in *La Revue historique des armées*, n° 259, June 2010.

28. Stéphane Launey, "Jean Renoir sous l'uniforme."

29. Jean Renoir Papers, Part I, Production Files, Series VII: Notebooks, Box 53, Folder 4.

30. Campaign journal of the 80th regiment of infantry, October 22, 1939, SHGDR 34N93, provided by Stéphane Launey.

31. SHD/DAT, 8 Ye 9 912, Stéphane Launey, "Jean Renoir sous l'uniforme."

32. *Correspondance 1913–1978*.

33. Letter to André Beucler, April 22, 1940, private collection.

34. Letter from André Beucler, December 7, 1976, Jean Renoir Papers, Part II, Correspondence, Box 32, Folder 12.

35. Jean Renoir's military file, Jean Renoir Papers, Part I, Production Files, Series XII: Personal Items, Box 52, Folder 3.

36. Jean Renoir, *Ma vie et mes films*, Flammarion, 1974.

37. Letter from Eugène Lourié, January 14, 1940, Archives Jean Renoir, ECPAD.

38. Letter from Giulio Manenti, November 26, 1939, private collection.

39. Letter from André Beucler, February 25, 1940, Archives Jean Renoir, ECPAD.

40. Ibid.

41. Letter from S. Landsman, March 30, 1940, private collection.

42. Jean-Paul Le Chanois, *Le Temps des cerises, Conversations avec Philippe Esnault,* Institut Lumière/Actes Sud, 1996.

43. Letter from Jean-Paul Dreyfus (Le Chanois), November 8, 1939, Archives Jean Renoir, ECPAD.

44. Letter to Leslie Caron, July 5, 1975, Jean Renoir Papers, Part II, Correspondence, Box 31, Folder 5.

45. Letter to Messieurs Comencini and Lattuada, March 26, 1940, Archives Jean Renoir, ECPAD.

46. Letter from André Beucler, March 14, 1940, Archives Jean Renoir, ECPAD.

47. Letter from Dido Freire to Messieurs Comencini and Lattuada, March 26 1940, Archives Jean Renoir, ECPAD.

48. *Film*, A. III, n° 6, February 10, 1940.

49. Giuseppe Isani, *Cinema*, February 10, 1940.

50. *Film*, A. III, n° 6, February 10, 1940.

51. Giuseppe Isani, *Cinema*.

52. *Film*, A. III, n° 6, February 10, 1940.

53. "Une lettera di Jean Renoir sulla collaborazione italo-francese," *L'Ambrosiano*, March 16, 1940.

54. Alexander Sesonske, *Jean Renoir: The French Films, 1924–1939*, Harvard University Press, 1980.

55. *Tempo*, IV, n° 37, February 8, 1940.

56. In Jean A. Gili, *Le Cinéma italien à l'ombre des faisceaux (1922–1945)*.

57. Contract from Scalera Film for the direction of *Tosca*, July 12, 1939, ECPAD.

58. Letter from Jean Dewalde, undated, Archives Jean Renoir, ECPAD.

59. Letter from Jean Dewalde to Scalera, February 2, 1940, Archives Jean Renoir, ECPAD.

60. Letter from Jean Dewalde, February 3, 1940, Archives Jean Renoir, ECPAD.

61. Letter from Jean Dewalde, undated, Archives Jean Renoir, ECPAD.

62. Letter from Louis Guillaume, February 10, 1940, Archives Jean Renoir, ECPAD.

63. Letter from Pierre Renoir, April 9, 1940, Archives Jean Renoir, ECPAD.

64. Letter from Micheline Presle, June 3, 1957, Jean Renoir Papers, Correspondence, Box 13, Folder 17.

65. Interview by Emmanuel Decaux et Bruno Villien, in *Cinématographe*, n° 108, March 1985.

66. Letter from Jean Dewalde, March 20, 1940, Archives Jean Renoir, ECPAD.

67. Telegram to Denise Batcheff, April 1940, Archives Jean Renoir, ECPAD.

68. Telegram from Jean Dewalde, March 23, 1940, Archives Jean Renoir, ECPAD.

69. Letter to Suzy Berthon, April 11, 1940, Archives Jean Renoir, ECPAD.

70. Letter from Pierre Renoir, April 9, 1940, Archives Jean Renoir, ECPAD.

71. Contract of April 17, 1940, Collection Jacques Renoir.

72. Letter to Jean Dewalde, April 5, 1940, Archives Jean Renoir, ECPAD.

73. Letter to Suzy Berthon, April 11, 1940, Archives Jean Renoir, ECPAD.

74. Letter to M. Barattolo, April 20, 1940, Archives Jean Renoir, ECPAD.

75. Letter to M. Barattolo, April 20, 1940, Archives Jean Renoir, ECPAD.

76. Letter from Gaston Modot, April 11, 1940, Archives Jean Renoir, ECPAD.

77. Letter from Gaston Modot, April 3, 1940, Archives Jean Renoir, ECPAD.

78. Letter to Jean Dewalde, April 5, 1940, Archives Jean Renoir, ECPAD.

79. Letter from Fernand Gravey, April 9, 1940, Archives Jean Renoir, ECPAD.

80. Letter from Pierre Renoir, April 9, 1940, Archives Jean Renoir, ECPAD.

81. Letter to M. Barattolo, April 20, 1940, Archives Jean Renoir, ECPAD.

82. Letter from Pierre Renoir, April 23, 1940, Archives Jean Renoir, ECPAD.

83. Letter from Marcel L'Herbier, April 1940, Archives Jean Renoir, ECPAD.

84. Telegram to André Beucler, May 5, 1940, Archives Jean Renoir, ECPAD.

85. *Film*, A. III, n° 6, February 10 1940.

86. Gianni Puccini, in *Cinema*, n° 94, May 25, 1940.

87. *Le Figaro*, February 24, 1940.

88. Jean Renoir, *Ma vie et mes films*.

89. Letter to Captain Lestringuez, May 10, 1940, private collection.

90. Bertolt Brecht, June 29, 1942, *Arbeitsjournal*, edited by Werner Hecht, Suhrkamp Verlag, 1973 (privately translated for the author by Bernard Lortholary).

91. Ibid.

92. Ibid.

93. Released by the Havas Agency, *Le Figaro*, May 15, 1940.

94. *Le Matin*, May 15, 1940.

95. *Lotte Reiniger, Carl Koch, Jean Renoir, Die Gemeinsamen Filme, Szenen einer Freundschaft*.

96. Jean Renoir, *Ma vie et mes films*.

97. André Beucler, *Plaisirs de mémoire, de Saint-Pétersbourg à Saint-Germain-des-Prés, Tome 2*, Gallimard, 1982.

98. Conversation with Freddy Buache.

99. Vittorio Mussolini, *Vita con mio padre*.

100. Letter to Louis Guillaume, August 8, 1947, *Lettres d'amérique*, Presses de la Renaissance, 1984.

101. Letter from Claude Renoir, September 22, 1942, Jean Renoir Papers, Correspondence, Box 3, Folder 9.

102. Letter to Ginette Doynel, March 11, 1978, Jean Renoir Papers, Correspondence, Box 34, Folder 2.

103. Letter to Ginette Doynel, April 2, 1978, Jean Renoir Papers, Correspondence, Box 34, Folder 2.

104. Letter to Lotte Reiniger, March 29, 1978, Jean Renoir Papers, Correspondence, Box 34, Folder 2.

105. Jean Renoir Papers, Correspondence, Box 9, Folder 16.

22. All at Sea

1. Emmanuel Berl, *La Fin de la IIIème République*, Gallimard, 1968.

2. *Correspondance 1913–1978*, Plon, 1998.

3. Letter from Lois Jacoby, May 21, 1940, Archives Jean Renoir, ECPAD.

4. *Correspondance 1913–1978*.

5. Letter from Laurette Séjourné, May 20, 1940, Archives Jean Renoir, ECPAD.

6. Letter from Alain Renoir, March 1957, in answer to a query about his father having to do with his military situation in France, Jean Renoir Papers, Correspondence, Box 13, Folder 14.

7. Jean Renoir, *Ma vie et mes films*, Flammarion, 1974.

8. Cited by Bernard Pharisien, in *Pierre Renoir*, Némont, 2003.

9. *Correspondance 1913–1978*.

10. Jean Renoir, *Ma vie et mes films*.

11. Jean Renoir Papers, Correspondence, Box 5, Folder 8.

12. Conversation with Hervé Le Boterf, *Cinémonde*, n° 1435, February 6, 1962.

13. Letter to M. le Directeur de la Radio et du Cinéma, August 24, 1940, Renoir, *Correspondance 1913–1978*.

14. Renoir, *Correspondance 1913–1978*.

15. Jean Renoir, "Rapport sur la production cinématographique française en temps de guerre," Archives Jean Renoir, ECPAD.

16. Centre de démobilisation du canton de Cusset, July 30, 1940, Jean Renoir Papers, Part I—Production Files, Series XII: Personal Items, Box 52, Folder 3.

17. Louis F. Fournier and Jean-Henri Guillaumet, *Avec Jean Renoir, La Semaine de Vichy-Cusset,* September 21, 1940.

18. Emmanuel Berl, *La Fin de la IIIème République.*

19. *Ciné-Liberté,* n° 2, June 20, 1936.

20. *L'Alerte,* September 24, 1940.

21. Speech by Philippe Pétain, June 17, 1940.

22. *Correspondance 1913–1978.*

23. Letter to M. Dubois, August 24, 1940, Jean Renoir Papers, Correspondence, Box 1, Folder 2.

24. Letter to Monique Lauer, June 3, 1946, *Lettres d'amérique,* Presses de la Renaissance, 1984.

25. Fournier and Guillaumet, *Avec Jean Renoir.*

26. Letter to Richard de Rochemont, September 19, 1940, *Letters,* edited by Lorraine Lo Bianco and David Thompson, Faber and Faber, 1994.

27. Letter to Robert Flaherty, October 5, 1940, *Correspondance 1913–1978.*

28. Letter to Jean-Louis Tixier-Vignancour, January 11, 1941, Jean Renoir Papers, Correspondence, Box 1, Folder 17.

29. Fonds Pierre Gaut, Cinémathèque française.

30. *Rapport de Jean Renoir et Claude Renoir sur la création de studios à Valbonne,* registered with the Service du Cinéma on November 26, 1940, cited by Jean-Pierre Bertin-Maghit, *Le Cinéma sous l'Occupation,* Olivier Orban, 1989.

31. Gaston Thierry, "Le Festival international du film aura lieu à Cannes, Paris-Soir," June 17, 1939, cited by Loredana Latil, *Le Festival de Cannes, écho des relations internationales,* doctoral dissertation, 2002.

32. Letter to Georges Prade to Jean Zay, national Minister of Education, October 26, 1938, cited by Loredana Latil, *Le Festival de Cannes.*

33. Letter to Georges Prade, October 5, 1940, Private archives of the Festival International du Film.

34. Pierre Billard, *Le Mystère René Clair,* Plon, 1998.

35. Letter to Georges Prade, October 5, 1940, Private archives of the Festival International du Film.

36. Letter to Louise Chevalier-Munier, May 15, 1946, *Correspondance 1913–1978.*

37. Letter to Denise Tual on August 24, 1940, cited by Denise Tual, *Le Temps dévoré,* Fayard, 1980.

38. Letter from Jean Gabin to Denise Tual on August 25, 1940, cited by Denise Tual, *Le Temps dévoré.*

39. André G. Brunelin, *Jean Gabin,* Laffont, 1987.

40. The journal of André A. Perebinossoff, courtesy Philippe Perebinossoff.

41. Preparatory notes for *Ma vie et mes films,* undated, Jean Renoir Papers, Production Files, Box 71, Folder 7.

42. Letter to Dido Freire, undated, circa November 1940, *Correspondance 1913–1978.*

43. *Animatògrafo,* December 2, 1940.

44. Ibid.

45. *Primer Plano,* March 9, 1941.

46. *Tobis, 75 anos em 2007* ("O realizador francês Jean Renoir visita os estúdios da Tobis e o laboratório da Lisboa Filme, durante a sua passagem por Lisboa").

47. Interviews during November 1940 by Fernando Fragoso, reprinted in *Hollywood em Lisboa,* translated by Walter Salles, Vida Mundial Editora, 1942.

48. Conversation with Fernando Fragoso, *Hollywood em Lisboa.*

49. *Animatògrafo,* December 9, 1940, translated by Walter Salles.

50. Conversation with Fernando Fragoso, *Primer Plano,* December 1940.

51. Curtis Cate, *Saint-Exupéry, Laboureur du ciel,* translated from the English by Pierre Rocheron and Marcel Schneider, Grasset, 1973.

52. Letter to Ginette Doynel, November 21, 1970, Jean Renoir Papers, Correspondence, Box 26, Folder 1.

53. *Bulletin des Etudes portugaises et de l'Institut français du Portugal* 8, n° 1.

54. *Correspondance 1913–1978.*

55. Maria Irene Soeiro, *Lisbonne, plaque tournante pendant la 2ème Guerre Mondiale—Le sort de quatre illustres Français (Jean Renoir, Joseph Kessel, Antoine de Saint-Exupéry, Pierre Lazareff)*, Universidade de Aveiro, 2002.

56. Pierre Lazareff and Waverly Root, "Nazis Don't Trust Own Fliers, Send Them Out Blindly on Raids," *Daily Mirror*, January 1, 1941.

57. Preparatory notes for *Ma vie et mes films*, undated, Jean Renoir Papers, Production Files, Box 71, Folder 7.

58. Emmanuel Chadeau, *Saint-Exupéry*, Perrin, 2000.

59. Lynn H. Nicholas, *Le Pillage de l'Europe, les œuvres d'art volées par les nazis,* translated by Paul Chemla, Le Seuil, 1995.

60. Pierre Chevrier, *Antoine de Saint-Exupéry*, Gallimard, 1949.

61. *Cher Jean Renoir*, Gallimard, 1999.

23. A New World*

1. Renoir will meet up again with Bernard Lamotte in Los Angeles and will have him work on *A Salute to France* (1944).

2. Curtis Cate, *Saint-Exupéry, laboureur du ciel,* translated by Pierre Rocheron and Marcel Schneider, Grasset, 1973.

3. Jean Renoir, text for radio that was not broadcast, December 1942, Jean Renoir Papers, Production Files, Box 12, Folder 14.

4. Lease signed on January 22, 1941, Jean Renoir Papers, Box 52, Folder 9.

5. Letter to Alain Renoir, March 8, 1941, *Correspondance 1913–1978*, Plon, 1998.

6. Letter from Dido Freire to Robert Flaherty, September 4, 1940, cited by William Harry Gilcher, *Jean Renoir in America: A Critical Analysis of His Major Films from* Swamp Water to The River, University of Iowa, 1979.

7. Letter from Dido Freire to Robert Flaherty, January 11, 1940, cited by William Harry Gilcher, *Jean Renoir in America.*

8. Jimmy Starr, "Zanuck Signs French Director Renoir to Long Term," *Los Angeles Evening Herald and Express*, January 14, 1941.

9. Philip Dunne, *Take Two: A Life in Movies and Politics,* McGraw-Hill, 1980.

10. Letter from Dido Freire to Robert Flaherty, January 11, 1940, *Correspondance 1913–1978*.

11. Jean Renoir, *Ma vie et mes films,* Flammarion, 1974.

12. Cited by Claude Gauteur, *D'un Renoir l'autre,* Le Temps des Cerises, 2005.

13. Jean Renoir Papers, Part II, Correspondence, Box 1, Folder 18.

14. Ibid., Folder 19.

15. King Vidor, *A Tree Is a Tree: An Autobiography,* Samuel French Edition, 1953.

16. Jean Renoir Papers, Part II, Correspondence, Box 1, Folder 17.

17. Ibid., Folder 18.

18. Telegram, January 15, 1941, ibid., Folder 17.

19. Letter to André Daven, January 21, 1941. Jean Renoir Papers Part II, Correspondence, Box 1, Folder 17.

* *Translator's note:* Jean Renoir wrote correspondence in both French and English, especially after moving to the United States. Letters written in English were, of course, translated into French by the author of the original French edition of this book, and it became my task, with the help of the author, to reinstate the original English. For the sake of consistency of source, in Part II of this book, for certain short quotations from letters originally written in English, I have used the collection *Letters: Jean Renoir* (Faber, 1994) edited by Lorraine Lo Bianco and David Thompson and also gratefully borrowed brief sentences from translations of French letters into English in that book by Craig Carlson, Natasha Arnoldi, and Michael Wells.

20. Letter from Darryl F. Zanuck to André Daven and Jean Renoir, January 24, 1941, ibid.

21. Joseph McBride, *À la recherche de John Ford*, translated by Jean-Pierre Coursodon, Institut Lumière/ Actes Sud, 2007.

22. Memo from Darryl F. Zanuck to John Ford on March 2, 1938, Rudy Behlmer, *Memo from Darryl F. Zanuck: The Golden Years at Twentieth Century Fox*, Grove Press, 1993.

23. Conversations with Alain Renoir.

24. Philip Dunne, *Take Two*.

25. Conversation with Jacques Rivette and François Truffaut, *Cahiers du cinéma*, n° 34, April 1954.

26. Letter from William Dover to Jean Renoir on March 28, 1941, cited by Alexander Sesonske, "Jean Renoir in Georgia: Swamp Water," *Georgia Review*, spring 1982.

27. *Wind, Sand and Stars*, treatments by Jean Renoir and Maximilian Becker, 25, 27, and 28 pages, Jean Renoir Papers, Production Files, Box 50, Folder 1.

28. Ibid. Cited by Elizabeth Ann Vitanza, *Rewriting the Rules of the Game: Jean Renoir in America, 1941-1947*, doctoral dissertation, University of California, Los Angeles, 2007.

29. Letter to Darryl F. Zanuck, March 29, 1941, Jean Renoir Papers, Correspondence, Box 1, Folder 19.

30. Letter to Antoine de Saint-Exupéry, June 11, 1941, Jean Renoir Papers, Correspondence, Box 2, Folder 2.

31. Letter to Darryl F. Zanuck, March 24, 1941, Jean Renoir Papers, Correspondence, Box 1, Folder 19.

32. Jean Renoir Papers, Part I, Production Files, Series VII: Notebooks, Box 51, Folder 8.

33. Letter to Darryl F. Zanuck, June 21, 1941, Jean Renoir Papers, Correspondence, Box 2, Folder 2.

34. Letter from Darryl F. Zanuck, June 23, 1941, Jean Renoir Papers, Correspondence, Box 2, Folder 2.

35. Letter to Darryl F. Zanuck, March 24, 1941, Jean Renoir Papers, Correspondence, Box 1, Folder 19.

36. Letter to Charles Feldman on April 5, 1941, *Correspondance 1913-1978*.

37. Letter to Charles Feldman on May 14, 1941, *Correspondance 1913-1978*.

38. Letter from Darryl F. Zanuck, April 7, 1941, Jean Renoir Papers, Correspondence, Box 1, Folder 20.

39. Letter to Darryl F. Zanuck, April 8, 1941, Jean Renoir Papers, Correspondence, Box 1, Folder 20.

40. Draft of Letter to Darryl F. Zanuck, April 9, 1941, Jean Renoir Papers, Correspondence, Box 1, Folder 20.

41. Letter to Darryl F. Zanuck, April 16, 1941, Jean Renoir Papers, Correspondence, Box 1, Folder 20.

42. Letter to Antoine de Saint-Exupéry, April 2, 1941, Jean Renoir Papers, Correspondence, Box 1, Folder 20.

43. Letter to Maximilian Becker, July 9, 1941, Jean Renoir Papers, Correspondence, Box 2, Folder 3.

44. Letter on April 29, 1941, *Lettres d'amérique*, Presses de la Renaissance, 1984.

45. *La Revue de l'écran*, January 30, 1941.

46. Letter from Claude Renoir, January 24, 1941, Jean Renoir Papers, Correspondence, Box 1, Folder 17.

47. Undated letter from Pierre Lestringuez, Jean Renoir Papers, Correspondence, Box 9, Folder 16.

48. Letter to Charles Feldman, April 9, 1941, *Correspondance 1913-1978*.

49. Letter on April 15, 1941, *Lettres d'amérique*.

50. Letter from Gabrielle Slade, March 15, 1941, Jean Renoir Papers.

51. Letter on May 26, 1941, *Lettres d'amérique*.

52. Questionnaire from Fox, January 25, 1941, Jean Renoir Papers, Production Files, Box 53, Folder 1.

53. Letter from Dudley Nichols to Theresa Helburn on June 3, 1944, cited by Harry William Gilcher, *Jean Renoir in America*.

54. Letter from Fritz Lang, June 28, 1941, Jean Renoir Papers, Correspondence, Box 2, Folder 2.

55. Jean Renoir, *Correspondance 1913-1978*.

56. *New York Post*, March 5, 1941.

57. *Swamp Water*, First Draft Continuity, Jean Renoir Papers, Production Files, Box 11, Folders 1 and 2.

58. Letter to Darryl F. Zanuck on May 23, 1941, *Correspondance 1913-1978*.

59. Letter to Claude Renoir on May 26, 1941, *Lettres d'amérique*.

60. Memo from Darryl F. Zanuck, May 26, 1941, Rudy Behlmer, *Memo from Darryl F. Zanuck.*

61. Memo from Darryl F. Zanuck, Colonel Jason Joy, director of public relations for Fox, May 21, 1941, Rudy Behlmer, *Memo from Darryl F. Zanuck.*

62. Conference with Mr. Zanuck (on First Draft Continuity of May 1, 1941), Jean Renoir Papers, Production Files, Box 11, Folder 4.

63. *Swamp Water,* annotated screenplay, Jean Renoir Papers, Production Files, Box 11, Folder 6.

64. English translation of Studio Terms for Jean Renoir, Jean Renoir Papers, Production Files, Box 11, Folder 7.

65. Conversation with Jean-Louis Noames, *Cahiers du cinéma,* n° 155, May 1964.

66. Memo from Darryl F. Zanuck, May 26, 1941, Rudy Behlmer, *Memo from Darryl F. Zanuck.*

67. Letter to Darryl F. Zanuck, May 23, 1941, in *Correspondance 1913–1978,* and *Jean Renoir: Letters,* edited by Lorraine Lo Bianco and David Thompson, Faber and Faber, 1994.

68. Letter to Darryl F. Zanuck, June 7, 1941, in *Correspondance 1913–1978.*

69. Conference with Mr. Zanuck (on First Draft Continuity of May 1, 1941), Jean Renoir Papers, Production Files, Box 11, Folder 4.

70. Letter to Chester Conklin, August 22, 1941, Jean Renoir Papers, Correspondence, Box 2, Folder 4.

71. Letter from Chester Conklin, July 21, 1941, Jean Renoir Papers, Correspondence, Box 2, Folder 3.

72. Letter from Chester Conklin, August 1, 1941, Jean Renoir Papers, Correspondence, Box 2, Folder 4.

73. Letter from Jean to Alain Renoir, June 9, 1941, *Lettres d'amérique.*

74. Jean Renoir's notes regarding *Swamp Water,* June 5, 1941, Jean Renoir Papers, Box 11, Folder 7.

75. Letter from Lew Schreiber to Mr. Koenig, with copy to Jean Renoir, June 16, 1941, Jean Renoir Papers, Correspondence, Box 2, Folder 2.

76. Letter to Pierre Lestringuez, June 13, 1941, *Lettres d'amérique.*

77. Letter to André Halley des Fontaines, June 13, 1941, Jean Renoir Papers, Correspondence, Box 2, Folder 2.

78. Letter to Henri Chomette, June 17, 1941, *Lettres d'amérique.*

79. Memo to Darryl F. Zanuck, June 20, 1941, Jean Renoir Papers, Box 11, Folder 7.

80. *Swamp Water:* Georgia Location, 20th Century Fox Film Corp., Jean Renoir Papers, Production Files, Box 11, Folder 7.

81. Jean Renoir Papers, Production Files, Box 11, Folder 7.

82. William Harry Gilcher, *Jean Renoir in America.*

83. Letter to Claude Renoir, July 20, 1941, *Lettres d'amérique.*

84. Letter to Claude Renoir, July 20, 1941, *Lettres d'amérique.*

85. Letter to Dudley Nichols, July 21, 1941, *Correspondance 1913–1978.*

86. Thomas Mann, *Tagebücher,* September 29, 1941.

87. Letter to Mr. Koenig, July 12, 1941 (unsent), Jean Renoir Papers, Correspondence, Box 2, Folder 3.

88. Letter to Claude Renoir, July 20, 1941, *Lettres d'amérique.*

89. Memo from Darryl F. Zanuck, July 30, 1941, Rudy Behlmer, *Memo from Darryl F. Zanuck.*

90. English translation of Studio Terms for Jean Renoir, Jean Renoir Papers, Box 11, Folder 7.

91. Conversations with Alain Renoir.

92. Letter to Claude Renoir, July 6, 1942, *Lettres d'amérique.*

93. Letter to Darryl F. Zanuck, August 1, 1941, *Correspondance 1913–1978.*

94. Memo from Darryl F. Zanuck to Len Hammond on August 2, 1941, Rudy Behlmer, *Memo from Darryl F. Zanuck.*

95. Letter to Charles Boyer, August 3, 1941, *Lettres d'amérique.*

96. Memo from Darryl F. Zanuck, August 8, 1941, Rudy Behlmer, *Memo from Darryl F. Zanuck.*

97. Letter to Eugène Lourié, August 17, 1941, *Lettres d'amérique.*

98. Conversations with Alexander Sesonske, "Jean Renoir in Georgia: Swamp Water"; conversation with Jacques Rivette and François Truffaut, *Cahiers du cinéma,* n° 34, April 1954.

99. Letter from Jean Renoir cited by Alexander Sesonske, "Jean Renoir in Georgia: Swamp Water."

100. Ibid.

101. Jean Renoir, *Ma vie et mes films*.

102. Letter to Dudley Nichols, September 13, 1941, *Correspondance 1913–1978*.

103. Jean Renoir, *Ma vie et mes films*.

104. Letter to Claude Renoir, May 18, 1945, *Lettres d'amérique*.

105. Letter from Eugène Lourié, November 30, 1941, Jean Renoir Papers, Correspondence, Box 2, Folder 7.

106. Letter to Claude Renoir, May 18, 1945, Jean Renoir Papers, Correspondence, Box 5, Folder 3.

107. Jean Renoir Papers, Production Files, Box 11, Folder 6.

108. Memo from Darryl F. Zanuck, December 3, 1941, cited by Alexander Sesonske, "Jean Renoir in Georgia: Swamp Water."

24. California Jean

1. Letter from Jean Lenauer, February 3, 1941, Jean Renoir Papers, Correspondence, Box 1, Folder 18.

2. Jean-Pierre Aumont, *Le Soleil et les Ombres*, Opera Mundi, 1976.

3. Jean Renoir Papers, Correspondence, Box 2, Folder 1.

4. Letter to Charles Boyer on July 6, 1941, Jean Renoir Papers, Correspondence, Box 2, Folder 3.

5. Letter to G. Henry-Haye, French ambassador in Washington, April 21, 1941, Jean Renoir Papers, Correspondence, Box 1, Folder 20.

6. Letter from G. Henry-Haye, French ambassador in Washington, May 23, 1941, Jean Renoir Papers, Correspondence, Box 2, Folder 1.

7. Letter to the Baron James de Bayens, French ambassador in Washington, May 21, 1941, *Lettres d'amérique*, Presses de la Renaissance, 1984.

8. Letter to Antoine de Saint-Exupéry, June 2, 1942, *Jean Renoir: Correspondance 1913–1978*, Plon, 1998.

9. Conversations with Alain Renoir.

10. Ibid.

11. Ibid.

12. Ibid.

13. Letter from G. Henry-Haye, March 11, 1942, Jean Renoir Papers, Correspondence, Box 3, Folder 3.

14. Letter to G. Henry-Haye, March 23, 1942, *Lettres d'amérique*.

15. Telegram from André Halley des Fontaines, May 27, 1941, Jean Renoir Papers, Correspondence, Box 2, Folder 1.

16. Letter from Claude Renoir, June 22, 1941, Jean Renoir Papers, Correspondence, Box 2, Folder 2.

17. Letter from Georges Achard, December 27, 1941, Jean Renoir Papers, Correspondence, Box 2, Folder 1.

18. Letter to Georges Achard, January 9, 1942, *Lettres d'amérique*.

19. Letter to Estrella Boissevain, June 4, 1942, *Lettres d'amérique*.

20. Letter from Claude Renoir, May 4, 1941, Jean Renoir Papers, Correspondence, Box 2, Folder 1.

21. Journal of André A. Perebinossoff, courtesy Philippe Perebinossoff.

22. Letter from Claude Renoir, May 20, 1941, Jean Renoir Papers, Correspondence, Box 2, Folder 1.

23. "5.000 dollars par semaine: c'est ce que gagne Jean Renoir à Hollywood," *Paris-Soir*, July 24, 1941.

24. *L'Alerte*, n° 64, December 6, 1941.

25. Letter to Paulette Renoir, February 27, 1942, *Lettres d'amérique*.

26. Ibid.

27. Letter from Albert Lévy, February 8, 1941, Jean Renoir Papers, Correspondence, Box 1, Folder 18.

28. Ibid.

29. Letter from Darius Milhaud, May 1, 1941, Jean Renoir Papers, Correspondence, Box 2, Folder 1.

30. Conversations with Alain Renoir.

31. Letter to Antoine de Saint-Exupéry, May 20, 1941, Jean Renoir Papers, Correspondence, Box 2, Folder 1.

32. Letter to Mrs. Floyd S. Chalmers, Toronto, July 8, 1964, in answer to a request for information for a book being planned, Jean Renoir Papers, Corresppondence, Box 19, Folder 11.

33. Letter to Gabrielle Slade, June 20, 1941, Jean Renoir Papers, Correspondence, Box 2, Folder 2.

34. Bertolt Brecht, June 29, 1942, *Arbeitsjournal*, edited by Werner Hecht, Suhrkamp Verlag, 1973 (privately translated for the author by Bernard Lortholary).

35. Letter to Pierre Renoir, June 17, 1942, *Lettres d'amérique*.

36. Letter to Claude Renoir, May 28, 1942, *Lettres d'amérique*.

37. Letter from Marguerite Renoir, February 13, 1941, Jean Renoir Papers, Correspondence, Box 1, Folder 18.

38. Letter from Marguerite Renoir, March 24, 1941, Jean Renoir Papers, Correspondence, Box 9, Folder 16.

39. Letter from Marguerite Renoir, undated, probably beginning of 1941, Jean Renoir Papers, Correspondence, Box 9, Folder 16.

40. Letter from Pierre Renoir, August 19, 1941, Jean Renoir Papers, Correspondence, Box 2, Folder 4.

41. Letter to Maximilian Becker, January 28, 1942, Jean Renoir Papers, Correspondence, Box 1, Folder 17.

42. *Projet Gabrielle*, September 29, 1946, Jean Renoir Papers, Production Files, Box 75, Folder 6.

43. Conversation with Jean Slade.

44. "Renoir Writer Coming," in *The Reporter*, August 4, 1941.

45. Emmanuel Chadeau, *Saint-Exupéry*, Perrin, 2000.

46. Curtis Cate, *Saint-Exupéry, Laboureur du ciel*, translated from the English by Pierre Rocheron and Marcel Schneider, Grasset, 1973.

47. Preparatory notes for *Ma vie et mes films*, undated, Jean Renoir Papers, Production Files, Box 71, Folder 7.

48. "20th-Fox Options Renoir's Sequel to Grand Illusion," *Los Angeles Herald Express*, August 7, 1941.

49. Letter to Maximilian Becker, August 10, 1941, Jean Renoir Papers, Correspondence, Box 2, Folder 4.

50. Letter to Maximilian Becker, September 4, 1941, *Lettres d'amérique*.

51. Letter to Luise Rainer, November 18, 1941, *Lettres d'amérique*.

52. Letter from Noel Singer, CPA, Business Management Tax Consultant, October 8, 1941, Jean Renoir Papers, Correspondence, Box 2, Folder 6.

53. Letter to Noel Singer, October 8, 1942, Jean Renoir Papers, Correspondence, Box 3, Folder 10.

54. Letter to Dudley Nichols, September 17, 1941, *Correspondance 1913–1978*.

55. *Le Figaro*, March 26, 1939.

56. Letter from Maximilian Becker, January 19, 1942, *Lettres d'amérique*.

57. November 1941, Jean Renoir Papers, Part I, Production Files, Series VII: Notebooks, Box 51, Folder 8.

58. Letter to Alain Renoir, February 13, 1942, *Lettres d'amérique*.

59. Telegram from Marcel Pagnol, February 29, 1942, Jean Renoir Papers, Correspondence, Box 3, Folder 2.

60. G. L. George, "Les Projets de Jean Renoir," *Pour la Victoire*, n° 17, May 2, 1942.

61. Letter to Claude Renoir, March 30, 1942, Jean Renoir Papers, Correspondence, Box 3, Folder 3.

62. "Lady Next for Durbin," *The Reporter*, April 15, 1942.

63. *American Film Institute Catalogue, Within Our Gates: Ethnicity in American Feature Films, 1911–1960*, University of California Press, 1997.

64. William K. Everson, "Deanna Durbin and Jean Renoir, an Unravelled Mystery," *Films in Review*, October 1985.

65. Letter to Antoine de Saint-Exupéry, June 2, 1942, *Correspondance 1913–1978*.

66. Ibid.

67. Letter to Pierre Renoir, June 17, 1942, *Lettres d'amérique*.

68. Ibid.

69. Letter to Alain Renoir, June 6, 1942, *Correspondance 1913–1978*.

70. "Mrs. Showman Goes Studio Strolling," by Ann Lewis, *Showmen's Trade Review*, July 4, 1942.

71. Letter to Pierre Renoir, June 17, 1942, *Lettres d'amérique*.

72. Letter to Claude Renoir Sr., July 12, 1942, *Lettres d'amérique*, 73.

73. Ibid.

74. Letter to Alain Renoir, July 27, 1942, *Lettres d'amérique*.

75. Ibid.

76. Letter to Dudley Nichols, July 26, 1942, *Correspondance 1913–1978*.

77. Letter to René Clair, August 8, 1942, Jean Renoir Papers, Correspondence, Folder 8.

78. Letter to Alain Renoir, August 8, 1942, *Lettres d'amérique*.

79. Letter to Claude Renoir, August 8, 1942, *Lettres d'amérique*.

80. "Renoir Removed from Durbin Pic. Manning Directs," *Hollywood Reporter*, August 7, 1942.

81. "Renoir Quits U Feature Due to Old Wound," *Variety*, August 8, 1942.

82. William K. Everson, "Deanna Durbin and Jean Renoir."

83. Letter to Claude Renoir Sr., August 7, 1942, *Correspondance 1913–1978*.

84. "*Forever Yours*' Ends after 132 Days Work," *Hollywood Reporter*, December 1, 1942.

85. Edwin Schallert, *Los Angeles Times*, June 6, 1942.

86. Jean Renoir Papers, Production Files, Box 12, Folder 2.

87. Conversation with Jacques Rivette and François Truffaut, *Cahiers du cinéma*.

88. Alphonse Daudet, *La Dernière Classe*, 1872.

89. Conversation with Jacques Rivette and François Truffaut, *Cahiers du cinéma*.

90. William Harry Gilcher, *Jean Renoir in America: A Critical Analysis of His Major Films from* Swamp Water to The River, University of Iowa, 1979.

91. *Pour la Victoire*, June 13, 1942, Jean Renoir Papers, Production Files, Box 12, Folder 6.

92. *Pour la Victoire*, July 18, 1942, ibid.

93. *Los Angeles Times*, July 2, 1942, ibid.

94. *Pour la Victoire*, July 18, 1942, ibid.

95. "Notes for *Monsieur Thomas*," July 19, 1942, in French with translation in English, Jean Renoir Papers, Box 2, Folder 2.

96. Letter to Charles Laughton, August 24, 1942, *Correspondance 1913–1978*.

97. Elsa Lanchester, *Herself*, Michael Joseph Limited, 1983.

98. Ibid.

99. Letter from Dido Freire to Claude Renoir, November 17, 1942, Jean Renoir Papers, Correspondence, Box 3, Folder 11.

100. Walter Slezak, *What Time's the Next Swan?* Doubleday & Co., 1962.

101. Bertolt Brecht, *Journal*, May 3, 1945.

102. Telegram from Charles Laughton, July 7, 1942, Jean Renoir Papers.

103. Walter Slezak, *What Time's the Next Swan?*

104. Letter to Alain Renoir on September 13, 1942, *Lettres d'amérique*.

105. Letter (in French) from Erich von Stroheim, September 14, 1942, Jean Renoir Papers, Correspondence, Box 3, Folder 9.

106. Letter to Erich von Stroheim, September 28, 1942, *Correspondance 1913–1978*.

107. Letter (in English) to Erich von Stroheim, August 27, 1942, *Correspondance 1913–1978*.

108. "Notes for *Monsieur Thomas*," June 23, 1942, Jean Renoir Papers, Production Files, Box 12, Folder 5.

109. Eugène Lourié, *My Work in Films*, Harcourt, Brace, Jovanovich, 1985.

110. Conversation with Jacques Rivette and François Truffaut, *Cahiers du cinéma*.

111. *Souvenirs incomplets*, 163 typed pages, annotated and corrected, January–July 1972, Jean Renoir Papers, Production Files, Box 71, Folder 2.

112. Production Code, Jos, I. Breen, October 6, 1942, Jean Renoir Papers, Production Files, Box 12, Folder 7.

113. *Hollywood Reporter*, December 4, 1942.

114. Ibid., October 12, 1942.

115. Letter to Siegfried Kracauer, November 16, 1942, *Lettres d'amérique*.

116. Letter to Alain Renoir, November 26, 1942, *Lettres d'amérique*.

117. Letter to Alain Renoir, November 16, 1942, *Lettres d'amérique*.

118. Conversation with Jacques Rivette and François Truffaut, *Cahiers du cinéma*.

119. Letter to Maximilian Becker, March 15, 1943, *Correspondance 1913–1978*.

120. Letter to John B. L. Goodwin, January 18, 1944, Jean Renoir Papers, Correspondence, Box 3, Folder 3.

121. Letter to Léon Siritzky, April 1943, Jean Renoir Papers, Correspondence, Box 3, Folder 16.

122. *Time*, April 26, 1943.

123. Translation by Jean-Paul Török, *Pour en finir with le maccarthysme, Lumières sur la Liste Noire à Hollywood*, L'Harmattan, 1999.

124. Telegram from Geneviève Tabouis, June 3, 1943, Jean Renoir Papers, Correspondence, Box 4, Folder 1.

125. Letter from Pierre Lazareff, November 23, 1943, Jean Renoir Papers, Correspondence, Box 4, Folder 2.

126. Cited in *Lettres d'amérique*.

127. Alexander Sesonske, *This Land Is Mine*, unpublished text.

128. Letter from Edmond Ardisson, May 1944, Jean Renoir Papers, Correspondence, Box 4, Folder 7.

129. Letter to Edmond Ardisson, May 23, 1944, *Lettres d'amérique*.

130. Text in French, Jean Renoir Papers, Production Files, Box 12, Folder 14.

131. Letter to Pierre Lazareff, December 20, 1942, *Lettres d'amérique*.

25. This Land Is Mine

1. "Film Director Granted Divorce, Jean Renoir, Son of Artist, Helped in Case by Father's Model," *Los Angeles Times*, October 16, 1942.

2. Judgment of divorce on October 13, 1942, Jean Renoir Papers, Correspondence, Box 3, Folder 10.

3. Letter from Brother Leonard, undated, fall 1942, Jean Renoir Papers, Correspondence, Box 9, Folder 17.

4. Letter to Brother Leonard, October 9, 1942, Jean Renoir Papers, Correspondence, Box 3, Folder 10.

5. Letter from Brother Leonard, October 15, 1942, Jean Renoir Papers, Correspondence, Box 3, Folder 10.

6. Letter to Brother Leonard, October 19, 1942, Jean Renoir Papers, Correspondence, Box 3, Folder 10.

7. Letter from Brother Leonard, January 20, 1943, Jean Renoir Papers, Correspondence, Box 3, Folder 13.

8. Letter from Brother Leonard, November 27, 1943, Jean Renoir Papers, Correspondence, Box 4, Folder 2.

9. Letter to Brother Leonard, January 2, 1944, Jean Renoir Papers, Correspondence, Box 4, Folder 3.

10. Letter from Brother Leonard, January 6, 1944, Jean Renoir Papers, Correspondence, Box 4, Folder 3.

11. Letter from Brother Leonard, May 23, 1945, Jean Renoir Papers, Correspondence, Box 5, Folder 3.

12. Cited by Claude Gauteur, in Jean Renoir, *Écrits 1926–1971*, edited by Claude Gauteur, Belfond, 1974.

13. Letter to Robert Flaherty, March 15, 1943, *Correspondance 1913–1978*, Plon, 1998.

14. Letter from Robert Flaherty, March 23, 1943, *Correspondance 1913–1978*.

15. Two typed pages, 11 pages, and 2 pages, March 19, 24, and 26, 1943, Jean Renoir Papers, Production Files, Box 50, Folder 9.

16. Jean Renoir Papers, Production Files, Box 49, Folder 16.

17. Jean Renoir Papers, Production Files, Box 48, Folder 31.

18. Jean Renoir Papers, Production Files, Box 49, Folder 1.

19. UCLA, Charles Laughton Papers, Box 21, Folder 6.

20. Telegram from Andrès de Segurola, May 22, 1943, Jean Renoir Papers, Correspondence, Box 3, Folder 17.

21. Telegram from Simon Schiffrin, July 13, 1943, Jean Renoir Papers, Correspondence, Box 4, Folder 1.

22. Letter to Pierre Lazareff, January 11, 1944, Lettres d'amérique, Presses de la Renaissance, 1984.

23. Letter to Charles Koerner, January 3, 1944, Jean Renoir Papers, Correspondence, Box 49, Folder 13.

24. Letter to Simon Schiffrin, June 30, 1944, Lettres d'amérique.

25. Letter from Walter Slezak, end of March 1944, Jean Renoir Papers, Correspondence, Box 4, Folder 5.

26. Letter to Albert André, October 25, 1946, Lettres d'amérique.

27. Ibid.

28. Telegram from Paul Soskin, February 1944, Jean Renoir Papers, Correspondence, Box 4, Folder 4.

29. Letter to Dudley Nichols, April 9, 1944, Correspondance 1913–1978.

30. Letter to Olwen Vaughn, January 11, 1944, Lettres d'amérique.

31. Letter to Feldman-Blum, September 12, 1943, Jean Renoir Papers, Correspondence, Box 4, Folder 2.

32. Letter to Dudley Nichols, April 2, 1944, Jean Renoir: Letters, edited by Lorraine Lo Bianco and David Thompson, Faber and Faber, 1994.

33. Letter to Alain Renoir, November 16, 1942, Lettres d'Amérique.

34. Meeting of November 14, 1943, Jean Renoir Papers, Correspondence, Box 4, Folder 2.

35. Letter to Claude Renoir, April 17, 1945, Jean Renoir Papers, Correspondence, Box 5, Folder 2.

36. Letter from Sigmund Thomas L. Harris, September 22, 1943, Jean Renoir Papers, Correspondence, Box 4, Folder 2.

37. Conversation with Jean Slade.

38. 1944 Agenda of Jean Renoir.

39. Telegram to Pierre Renoir, undated, Jean Renoir Papers, Correspondence, Box 10, Folder 1.

40. Conversation with Burgess Meredith, William Harry Gilcher, Jean Renoir in America: A Critical Analysis of His Major Films from Swamp Water to The River, University of Iowa, 1979.

41. Letter to Dudley Nichols, March 24, 1944, Correspondance 1913–1978.

42. Letter to Dudley Nichols, April 9, 1944, Correspondance 1913–1978.

43. Letter to Dudley Nichols, April 2, 1944, Jean Renoir: Letters.

44. Letter to Siegfried Kracauer, April 15, 1944, in Helmut G. Asper (ed.), Nachrichten aus Hollywood der Briefwechsel Eugen und Marlise Schüfftan mit Siegfried und Lili Kracauer, Wissenschaftlicher Verlag, Trier 2003. Translated from the German by Eithne O'Neill, Positif, n° 598, December 2010.

45. Jean Renoir Papers, Production Files, Motion Picture Productions, Box 25, Folder 4.

46. Letters from Simon Schiffrin, mid-June 1944, and from Alan Antik to Jean Renoir, August 1944, Jean Renoir Papers, Correspondence, Box 4, Folder 8.

47. Letter from Burgess Meredith to Margareta Akermark, July 21, 1978, cited by William Harry Gilcher, Jean Renoir in America.

48. Letter to Jean Benoît-Lévy, May 26, 1944, Lettres d'amérique.

49. Letter from David E. Friedkin, Chief Troop Information Sub-Section, July 8, 1946, Jean Renoir Papers, Production Files, Box 12, Folder 7.

50. Jean Renoir Papers, Part I, Production Files, Series VII: Notebooks, Box 51, Folder 8.

51. Conversation with Jacques Rivette and François Truffaut, Cahiers du cinéma.

52. Letter from Dudley Nichols, September 13, 1944, Jean Renoir Papers, Correspondence, Box 4, Folder 9.

53. Letter to Denise Ravage, September 19, 1944, Lettres d'amérique.

54. 1944 Agenda of Jean Renoir.

55. Tom Dardis, Some Time in the Sun: The Hollywood Years of Fitzgerald, Faulkner, Nathanael West, Aldous Huxley and James Agee, Charles Scribner's Sons, 1976.

56. Joseph Blotner, *Faulkner: A Biography*, Random House, 1974.

57. Gore Vidal, "Who Makes the Movies?, " *New York Review of Books*, November 25, 1976.

58. Gore Vidal, *Artistes et Barbares*, L'Âge d'homme, 1985.

59. Letter to Walt Lowe (Mississippi Authority for Educational Television), June 5, 1977, Jean Renoir Papers, Correspondence, Box 33, Folder 3.

60. Elizabeth Ann Vitanza, *Rewriting the Rules of the Game: Jean Renoir in America, 1941–1947*, doctoral dissertation, University of California, Los Angeles, 2007.

61. Notes dictated to Dido, Jean Renoir Papers, Production Files, Box 51, Folder 8.

62. Letter from Zachary Scott, October 20, 1961, Jean Renoir Papers, Correspondence, Box 17, Folder 3.

63. Letter from Dido Renoir, December 21, 1961, *Correspondance 1913–1978*.

64. William Harry Gilcher, *Jean Renoir in America*.

65. Eugène Lourié, *My Work in Films*, Harcourt, Brace, Jovanovich, 1985.

66. Norman Lloyd, *Stages of Life in Theatre, Film and Television*, Limelight Editions, 1993.

67. Notes dictated to Dido, Jean Renoir Papers, Production Files, Box 51, Folder 8.

68. Eugene L. Miller and Edwin R. Arnold, *Robert Aldrich: Conversations*, University Press of Mississippi, 2003.

69. Ibid.

70. Letter to Claude Renoir, January 16, 1945, *Lettres d'Amérique*.

71. Lettre to Pierre Lestringuez, November 22, 1945, *Lettres d'Amérique*.

72. Letter from Betty Field, December 18, 1945, *Correspondance 1913–1978*.

73. Maxine C. Hairston, afterword to *Hold Autumn in Your Hand*, University of New Mexico Press, 1969.

74. René Gilson, "Jean Renoir à Hollywood," *L'Écran français*, n° 7, August 15, 1945.

75. Jean Renoir, *Ma vie et mes films*, Flammarion, 1974.

76. Telegram from David Loew, January 31, 1945, Jean Renoir Papers, Correspondence, Box 5, Folder 1.

77. Letter to David Loew, February 5, 1945, Jean Renoir Papers, Correspondence, Box 5, Folder 1.

78. James Agee, *The Nation*, June 9, 1945, republished in *Agee on Film*, Grosset & Dunlap, 1969. French translation by Brice Matthieussent, James Agee, *Sur le cinéma*, éditions des Cahiers du cinéma, 1991.

79. William Harry Gilcher, *Jean Renoir in America*, 965.

80. *Mississippi Blues*, by Robert Parrish and Bertrand Tavernier (1983).

81. Michael Finger, "Banned in Memphis," *Memphis Flyer*, May 8, 2008.

82. Laurie B. Green, *Battling the Plantation Mentality: Memphis and the Black Freedom Struggle*, University of North Carolina Press, 2007.

83. Letter to Claude Renoir, May 18, 1945, *Lettres d'amérique*.

26. Endgame

1. Letter to Paul Cézanne, August 13, 1945, *Lettres d'amérique*, Presses de la Renaissance, 1984.

2. Jean Renoir Papers, Part I, Production Files, Series VII: Notebooks, Box 51, Folder 8.

3. Letter to Claude Renoir, February 17, 1945, *Lettres d'amérique*.

4. Letter from Claude Renoir, May 11, 1945, Jean Renoir Papers, Correspondence, Box 5, Folder 3.

5. Letter from Claude Renoir, March 23, 1945, Jean Renoir Papers, Correspondence, Box 5, Folder 2.

6. Letter to Pierre Renoir, April 12, 1945, Jean Renoir Papers, Correspondence, Box 5, Folder 2.

7. Letter to Claude Renoir, April 17, 1945, Jean Renoir Papers, Correspondence, Box 5, Folder 2.

8. Letter to Carl Koch, December 14, 1947, Jean Renoir Papers, Correspondence, Box 8, Folder 5.

9. Letter to Jacques Becker, October 21, 1946, Jean Renoir Papers, Correspondence, Box 7, Folder 1.

10. Letter to Steve Senyi, June 17, 1945, Jean Renoir Papers, Correspondence, Box 5, Folder 4.

11. Letter from Dido Renoir to Steve Senyi, August 8, 1945, Jean Renoir Papers, Correspondence, Box 5, Folder 6.

12. Célia Bertin, *Jean Renoir,* Éditions du Rocher, 1994.

13. Conversations with Alain Renoir.

14. Thomas Quinn Curtis, *Erich von Stroheim,* uncredited French translation, prefaces by René Clair and Jean Renoir, Éditions France-Empire, 1970.

15. 1944 Agenda of Jean Renoir, supplied by Elizabeth Ann Vitanza.

16. Ibid.

17. Letter to Claude Renoir, February 17, 1945, *Lettres d'amérique.*

18. Letter to Sam Siritzky, November 14, 1945, *Lettres d'amérique.*

19. Letter from Darryl F. Zanuck to Burgess Meredith, May 25, 1945, Jean Renoir Papers, Correspondence, Box 5, Folder 3.

20. William Harry Gilcher, *Jean Renoir in America: A Critical Analysis of His Major Films from* Swamp Water *to* The River, University of Iowa, 1979.

21. Telephone conversation with William Harry Gilcher; William Harry Gilcher, *Jean Renoir in America.*

22. Jean Renoir Papers, Production Files, Box 4, Folder 9.

23. Letter to Claude Renoir, June 22, 1945, *Lettres d'amérique.*

24. Burgess Meredith, *So Far, So Good: A Memoir,* Little, Brown, 1994. And conversation with William Harry Gilcher, *Jean Renoir in America.*

25. "PCA Correspondence regarding changes to Diary," Margaret Herrick Library, cited by Elizabeth Ann Vitanza, *Rewriting the Rules of the Game: Jean Renoir in America, 1941–1947,* doctoral dissertation, University of California, Los Angeles, 2007.

26. Ibid.

27. Burgess Meredith, *So Far, So Good.*

28. Conversation with Jacques Rivette and François Truffaut, *Cahiers du cinéma.*

29. Letter to Sam Siritzky, November 14, 1945, *Lettres d'amérique.*

30. Conversation with William Harry Gilcher, in William Harry Gilcher, *Jean Renoir in America: A Critical Analysis of His Major Films from* Swamp Water *to* The River, University of Iowa, 1979.

31. Letter to Paulette Goddard and Burgess Meredith, November 7, 1945, *Jean Renoir: Letters,* edited by Lorraine Lo Bianco and David Thompson, Faber and Faber, 1994.

32. *The Hollywood Reporter,* January 28, 1946, cited by Elizabeth Ann Vitanza, *Rewriting the Rules of the Game.*

33. Letter to Claude Renoir, January 26, 1946, *Correspondance 1913–1978,* Plon, 1998.

34. Letter to Sam Siritzky, November 14, 1945, *Lettres d'amérique.*

35. Letter to Monique Lauer, April 10, 1946, *Lettres d'amérique.*

36. André Bazin, "Cinéma et télévision with Jean Renoir et Roberto Rossel," *France Observateur,* n° 442, October 23, 1958.

37. Jean Renoir Papers, Correspondence, Box 4, Folder 10.

38. Letter to Louis Guillaume, February 24, 1945, *Lettres d'amérique.*

39. Conversations with Alain Renoir.

40. Patrick McGilligan, *Fritz Lang: The Nature of the Beast,* St. Martin's Press, 1997.

41. Brian Kellow, *The Bennetts: An Acting Family,* University Press of Kentucky, 2004.

42. Janet Bergstrom, *Le Compromis du rêve, Renoir et La Femme sur la plage,* translated from the English by Pierre Rusch, *Trafic,* n° 24, Winter 1994.

43. Letter from Val Lewton to Charles Koerner, May 14, 1945, cited by Janet Bergstrom, *Le Compromis du rêve.*

44. Letter to Pierre Renoir, November 22, 1945, *Lettres d'amérique.*

45. Joel E. Siegel, *Val Lewton: The Reality of Terror,* Secker and Warburg/British Film Institute, 1972.

46. Conversation with Jacques Rivette and François Truffaut, *Cahiers du cinéma.*

47. Letter to Mark Robson, November 15, 1945, cited by Janet Bergstrom, *Le Compromis du rêve.*

48. Letter to Claude Renoir, November 22, 1945, *Lettres d'amérique.*

49. Conversation with Jacques Rivette and François Truffaut, *Cahiers du cinéma.*

50. Ibid.

51. Letter to Claude Renoir, May 18, 1945, *Lettres d'amérique.*

52. Conversation with Jacques Rivette and François Truffaut, *Cahiers du cinéma.*

53. Janet Bergstrom, *Le Compromis du rêve.*

54. Letter from Joseph Breen to William Gordon, March 28, 1945, Production Code Administration Collection, Margaret Herrick Library, cited by Elizabeth Ann Vitanza, *Rewriting the Rules of the Game.*

55. Conversation with William Harry Gilcher.

56. Letter to Paul Cézanne, April 5, 1946, *Lettres d'amérique.*

57. Letter to Louis Guillaume, April 5, 1946, Jean Renoir Papers, Correspondence, Box 6, Folder 4.

58. Letter to Claude Renoir, January 26, 1946, *Correspondance 1913–1978.*

59. Letter to Pierre Renoir, May 8, 1946, *Lettres d'amérique.*

60. Ibid.

61. Letter to Claude Renoir, July 26, 1946, *Lettres d'amérique.*

62. Letter to Robert Hakim, June 8, 1946, *Correspondance 1913–1978.*

63. Letter to Pierre Lestringuez, August 27, 1946, *Lettres d'amérique.*

64. Conversation with Jacques Rivette and François Truffaut, *Cahiers du cinéma.*

65. *Ma vie et mes films*, Flammarion, 1974.

66. Letter to Alain Renoir, August 23, 1946, *Correspondance 1913–1978.*

67. Janet Bergstrom, *Le Compromis du rêve.*

68. Letter to Jean Lauer, October 2, 1946, Jean Renoir Papers, Correspondence, Box 7, Folder 1.

69. Letter to Robert Flaherty, December 21, 1946, *Correspondance 1913–1978.*

70. Letter to Claude Renoir, November 4, 1946, Jean Renoir Papers, Correspondence, Box 7, Folder 2.

71. Letter to Pierre Lestringuez, December 26, 1946, Jean Renoir Papers, cited by Janet Bergstrom, *Le Compromis du rêve.*

72. Conversation with Jacques Rivette and François Truffaut, *Cahiers du cinéma.*

73. In André Bazin, *Jean Renoir*, Éditions Champ Libre, 1971.

74. Jean Renoir, "Hollywood découvre la simplicité," interviews by Paul Gilson, *L'Écran français*, n° 58, August 1946, 5.

27. Between Two Worlds

1. Letter to Fernand Bercher, November 9, 1946, *Lettres d'amérique,* Presses de la Renaissance, 1984.

2. Letter to Claude Renoir, September 25, 1945, Jean Renoir Papers, Correspondence, Box 5, Folder 7.

3. Ibid.

4. *Carrefour*, February 3, 1945.

5. *Carrefour*, February 10, 1945.

6. Letter to Louis Guillaume, September 10, 1944, *Lettres d'amérique.*

7. Postcard from Pierre Renoir, November 22, 1944, Jean Renoir Papers, Correspondence, Box 4, Folder 10.

8. Letter from Louis Guillaume, July 27, 1947, Jean Renoir Papers, Correspondence, Box 7, Folder 10.

9. Letter to Louis Guillaume, January 24, 1946, Jean Renoir Papers, Correspondence, Box 6, Folder 1.

10. Letter to Louis Guillaume, February 2, 1946, Jean Renoir Papers, Correspondence, Box 6, Folder 2.

11. Letter from Louis Guillaume, December 18, 1946, Jean Renoir Papers, Correspondence, Box 7, Folder 3.

12. Letter to Louis Guillaume, December 25, 1946, Jean Renoir Papers, Correspondence, Box 7, Folder 3.

13. Jean Renoir Papers, Correspondence, Box 7, Folder 9.

14. Jean Renoir Papers, Correspondence, Box 9, Folder 13.

15. Letter to Louis Guillaume, October 4, 1947, *Lettres d'amérique.*

16. Letter to Louis Guillaume, May 8, 1945, Jean Renoir Papers, Correspondence, Box 5, Folder 3.

17. Letter from Jacques Becker, May 8, 1945, Jean Renoir Papers, Correspondence, Box 5, Folder 3.

18. Telegram from Jacques Becker to Jean Renoir, September 15, 1946, Jean Renoir Papers, Correspondence, Box 6, Folder 9.

19. Letter to Claude Renoir, April 17, 1945, *Lettres d'amérique.*

20. Letter from Julien Duvivier, October 24, 1948, Jean Renoir Papers, Correspondence, Box 9, Folder 1.

21. *L'Aurore–France libre,* October 20, 1948.

22. Letter to Louis Guillaume, November 12, 1948, Jean Renoir Papers, Correspondence, Box 9, Folder 1.

23. Letter to Julien Duvivier, December 15, 1948, Jean Renoir Papers, Correspondence, Box 9, Folder 3.

24. Letter to Monique Lauer, April 10, 1946, *Lettres d'amérique.*

25. Letter to Sam Siritzky, February 14, 1946, *Lettres d'amérique.*

26. Letter to Monique Lauer, April 10, 1946, *Lettres d'amérique.*

27. Letter to Pierre Braunberger, January 14, 1947, *Correspondance 1913–1978,* Plon, 1998.

28. Ibid.

29. Letter to Albert André, October 25, 1946, *Lettres d'amérique.*

30. Letter to Maria Cupelli, October 1, 1946, *Lettres d'amérique.*

31. Letter to Emil Ludwig, November 1, 1944, *Lettres d'amérique.*

32. Marcel Dalio, *Mes années folles,* J.-C. Lattès, 1976.

33. Letter from Claude Renoir, November 24, 1944, *Lettres d'amérique.*

34. Letter to Louis Guillaume, January 16, 1945, *Lettres d'amérique.*

35. Letter to Pierre Renoir, November 22, 1945, *Lettres d'amérique.*

36. Letter to Louis Guillaume, July 2, 1945, *Lettres d'amérique.*

37. Letter to Claude Renoir, September 12, 1945, *Lettres d'amérique.*

38. Conversations with Alain Renoir.

39. Letter to Renée Cézanne, May 25, 1946, *Lettres d'amérique.*

40. Letter to Claude Renoir, February 28, 1947, *Lettres d'amérique.*

41. "Gabrielle—Renoir's Famous Model Now Lives Quietly in Hollywood," *Life,* August 3, 1942.

42. Pierre Chartrand and Bernard Pharisien, *Victor Charigot, son grand-père,* Némont, 2007.

43. Letter from Pierre Lestringuez to Jean Renoir, June 20, 1946, Jean Renoir Papers, Correspondence, Box 6, Folder 6.

44. Letter to Louis Guillaume, July 27, 1946, *Lettres d'amérique.*

45. Letter from Henry Cayla, director of general distribution of Réalisations d'art cinématographique (RAC), to Captain Lhéritier, director of Les services de la Censure cinématographique, July 19, 1945, Archives du Centre national de la cinématographie.

46. *Paris-Matin,* September 10, 1946, cited by Sylvie Lindeperg, *Les Écrans de l'ombre, la Seconde Guerre mondiale dans le cinéma français (1944–1969),* CNRS Éditions, 1997.

47. Telegram of January 27, 1946, Archives of Le Centre national de la cinématographie.

48. Letter from Charles Spaak to Frank Rollmer, February 27, 1946, Archives of the Centre national de la cinématographie.

49. Letter from Charles Spaak to the President of la Commission de Censure, March 9, 1946, Archives du Centre national de la cinématographie.

50. Georges Altman, "La Grande Illusion de 1937," *L'Écran français,* n° 62, September 4, 1946.

51. *Paris-Matin,* September 10, 1946, cited by Sylvie Lindeperg, *Les Écrans de l'ombre.*

52. Ibid.

53. *Paris-Cinéma,* August 27, 1946, cited by Sylvie Lindeperg, *Les Écrans de l'ombre.*

54. Henri Jeanson, "Les Grandes Illusions perdues," *Le Canard enchaîné,* September 18, 1946.

55. Letter from the director of media in Strasbourg, J. Billmann, to the undersecretary of State at the Directorship of the Council and to the Department of Information, September 26, 1939, Archives du Centre national de la cinématographie.

56. Letter to Claude Renoir, May 14, 1946, *Lettres d'amérique*.

57. Pierre Braunberger, *Cinémamémoire*, interviewed by Jacques Gerber, Centre Georges Pompidou/CNC, 1987.

58. Postcard from Sylvia Bataille to Pierre Braunberger, September 15, 1942, Archives of Les Films du Jeudi.

59. Letter from Pierre Braunberger to Jean Painlevé, December 26, 1944, Archives of Les Films du Jeudi.

60. Letter from Jean Painlevé to Pierre Braunberger, April 9, 1945, Archives of Les Films du Jeudi.

61. November 20, 1945, Archives of Les Films du Jeudi.

62. Pierre Braunberger, *Cinémamémoire*.

63. Conversation with Marguerite Renoir and Marinette Cadicqx, *Télérama*, n° 661, September 16, 1962.

64. Letter to Pjerre Braunberger, January 14, 1947, *Lettres d'amérique*.

65. Letter from Pierre Braunberger to Jean Renoir, January 20, 1947, Jean Renoir Papers, Correspondence, Box 7, Folder 4.

66. *Le Journal du dimanche*, July 28, 1946.

67. *Franc-Tireur*, July 13, 1946.

68. *Le Figaro*, July 17, 1946.

69. *Les Lettres françaises*.

70. *L'Écran français*, n° 55, July 1946.

71. Letter to Claude Renoir, July 26, 1946, *Lettres d'amérique*.

72. Ibid.

73. Letter to Louis Guillaume, August 8, 1946, *Lettres d'amérique*.

74. Conversation with Kira Appel, *Paris-Presse*, December 4, 1946, republished in *La Revue du Cinéma, Image et Son*, n° 315, March 1977.

75. Undated postcard, probably spring 1948, Jean Renoir Papers, Correspondence, Box 10, Folder 4.

76. Two postcards from Edmond Ardisson, August 27, 1947, Jean Renoir Papers, Correspondence, Box 8, Folder 1.

77. Postcard from Simone Simon, May 12, 1948, Jean Renoir Papers, Correspondence, Box 8, Folder 10.

78. Letter from Claude Renoir, December 5, 1947, Jean Renoir Papers, Correspondence, Box 8, Folder 5.

79. Letter to Pierre Renoir, December 31, 1947, Jean Renoir Papers, Correspondence, Box 8, Folder 5.

80. Letter from Claude Renoir, December 17, 1947, Jean Renoir Papers, Correspondence, Box 8, Folder 5.

81. Letter to Pierre Renoir, December 27, 1947, *Lettres d'amérique*.

82. Letter to Étienne Decesse, November 12, 1946, Jean Renoir Papers, Correspondence, Box 8, Folder 4.

83. Letter to the parish priest of Essoyes, November 12, 1946, Jean Renoir Papers, Correspondence, Box 7, Folder 2.

84. Letter to Louis Guillaume, March 27, 1948, Jean Renoir Papers, Correspondence, Box 8, Folder 8.

85. Letter to Louis Guillaume, December 12, 1947, Jean Renoir Papers, Correspondence, Box 8, Folder 5.

86. Letter to Louis Guillaume, February 14, 1948, Jean Renoir Papers, Correspondence, Box 8, Folder 7.

87. Letter to Louis Guillaume, November 12, 1948, Jean Renoir Papers, Correspondence, Box 9, Folder 2.

88. Letter to Louis Guillaume, January 2, 1949, Jean Renoir Papers, Correspondence, Box 9, Folder 4.

89. Letter to Joseph Lucachevìch, January 26, 1949, Jean Renoir Papers, Correspondence, Box 9, Folder 4.

90. Letter to Jean Gabin, July 3, 1947, *Lettres d'amérique*.

91. Letter to Louis Guillaume, September 3, 1948, Jean Renoir Papers, Correspondence, Box 8, Folder 14.

92. Letter to Louis Guillaume, September 20, 1948, *Lettres d'amérique*.

93. Letter to Pierre Braunberger, January 3, 1949, *Correspondance 1913–1978*.

94. Letter to Louis Guillaume, September 20, 1948, *Lettres d'amérique*.

95. Letter from Claude Renoir Jr., September 27, 1948, Jean Renoir Papers, Correspondence, Box 8, Folder 14.

96. Letter from Salvo d'Angelo, November 27, 1948, Jean Renoir Papers, Correspondence, Box 9, Folder 2.

97. Letter to Salvo d'Angelo, December 9, 1948, Jean Renoir Papers, Correspondence, Box 9, Folder 3.

98. Telegram to Joseph Lucachevitch, January 14, 1949, Jean Renoir Papers, Correspondence, Box 9, Folder 4.

99. Letter from Claude Renoir Jr., January 19, 1949, Jean Renoir Papers, Correspondence, Box 9, Folder 4.

100. Jean Renoir Papers, Production Files, Box 48, Folder 23.

101. Ibid.

102. Letter to Dudley Nichols, March 24, 1950, *Correspondance 1913–1978*.

103. Jean Renoir Papers, Production Files, Box 50, Folder 4.

104. Jean Renoir Papers, Production Files, Box 50, Folder 7.

105. "Speaking of Pictures . . . These Are the Faces of Parisian Model Maria Lani," *Life*, December 3, 1945.

106. *Éditions des Quatre Chemins*, 1929.

107. Gert Heine and Paul Schommer, *Thomas Mann Chronik*, Verlag Vittorio Klostermann, 2004.

108. Thomas Mann, *Journal 1940–1945*, edited by Peter de Mendelssohn and Inge Jens, French edition introduced and annotated by Christoph Schwerin, translated from the German by Robert Simon, Gallimard, 2000.

109. *Dagens Nyheter*, September 18, 1947.

110. *Under Western Eyes*, June 11, 1948, Jean Renoir Papers, Box 49, Folder 11.

111. Letter to André Halley des Fontaines, November 16, 1946, *Lettres d'amérique*.

112. "Memo pour meeting Broidy," February 4, 1948, Jean Renoir Papers, Correspondence, Box 8, Folder 7.

113. Ibid.

114. Célia Bertin, *Jean Renoir*, Éditions du Rocher, 1994.

115. Letter to Clifford Odets, October 1, 1948, *Correspondance 1913–1978*.

116. Letter to Georges Simenon, October 1, 1948, *Lettres d'amérique*.

117. Letter to Louis Guillaume, October 4, 1957, *Lettres d'amérique*.

118. Letter to Pierre Renoir, December 27, 1947, *Lettres d'amérique*.

119. Letter to Pierre Lestringuez, December 28, 1947, *Correspondance 1913–1978*.

120. Bertolt Brecht, October 2, 1943, *Arbeitsjournal*, edited by Werner Hecht, Suhrkamp Verlag, 1973 (privately translated for the author by Bernard Lortholary).

121. Bertolt Brecht, December 12, 1944, *Arbeitsjournal*.

122. Larry Ceplair and Steven Englund, *The Inquisition in Hollywood: Politics in the Film Community, 1930–1960*, University of California Press, 1979.

123. Letter to Robert Flaherty, December 21, 1946, *Correspondance 1913–1978*.

124. Letter to Alain Renoir, January 31, 1947, *Lettres d'amérique*.

125. Jean Renoir Papers, Production Files, Box 51, Folder 8.

126. Ibid.

127. "Recorded greetings for the Annual Women's Day of the Soviet Union, March 8, 1944," text in French, Jean Renoir Papers, Production Files, Box 13, Folder 35.

128. Christopher Faulkner, "An Archive of the (Political) Unconscious," *Canadian Journal of Communication* 26, n° 2, 2001.

129. Letter to Burgess Meredith, October 27, 1945, *Letters*, edited by Lorraine Lo Bianco and David Thompson, Faber and Faber, 1994.

130. Larry Ceplair and Steven Englund, *The Inquisition in Hollywood*.

131. Letter to Dudley Nichols addressed from Paris, January 12, 1954, *Correspondance 1913–1978*.

132. Ibid.

133. *The New Yorker*, October 19, 1946.

134. Jean Renoir Papers, Part I, Production Files, Series VII: Notebooks, Box 51, Folder 8.

135. Letter to Charles Einfeld, November 19, 1946, *Correspondance 1913–1978*.

136. Letter from David Loew, November 29, 1946, Jean Renoir Papers, Correspondence, Box 7, Folder 2.

137. Letter to David Loew, December 1, 1946, *Correspondance 1913–1978*.

138. Letter to Claude Renoir Jr., February 4, 1947, *Correspondance 1913–1978*.

139. Rumer Godden, *A House with Four Rooms*, William Morrow, 1989.

140. Eugène Lourié, *My Work in Films*, Harcourt, Brace, Jovanovich, 1985.

141. Rumer Godden, *Le Fleuve*, translated by Bertrand de La Salle, Albin Michel, 1949.

142. Harry William Gilcher, *Jean Renoir in America: A Critical Analysis of His Major Films from* Swamp Water *to* The River, University of Iowa, 1979.

143. Contract of December 9, 1948, Jean Renoir Papers, Correspondence, Box 9, Folder 3.

144. Letter to Mr. Schlamm, April 14, 1949, *Correspondance 1913–1978*.

145. Press clip transmitted by David Loew to Jean Renoir on April 20, 1956, Jean Renoir Papers, Correspondence, Box 13, Folder 14.

146. *Film Daily*, April 11, 1956.

147. Letter to Rumer Godden, September 21, 1949, Jean Renoir Papers, Correspondence, Box 9, Folder 3.

148. Letter to Salvo d'Angelo (Universalia), December 9, 1948, Jean Renoir Papers, Correspondence, Box 13, Folder 14.

149. Letter to Bert Allenberg, November 16, 1948, *Correspondance 1913–1978*.

150. Letter to Louis Guillaume, October 28, 1947, *Lettres d'amérique*.

151. Ibid.

152. Letter to Marie Lestringuez, November 6, 1947, *Lettres d'amérique*.

153. Ibid.

28. "A Story about Children in the Indies"

1. Letter to Louis Guillaume, undated, on paper with the letterhead Pan American World Airways System, Jean Renoir Papers, Correspondence, Box 10, Folder 3.

2. Letter to Mr. Schlamm, April 14, 1949, *Correspondance 1913–1978*, Plon, 1998.

3. Letter to Georges Sadoul, January 28, 1948, *Lettres d'amérique*, Presses de la Renaissance, 1984.

4. Satyajit Ray, "Renoir in Calcutta," *Sequence*, n° 10, January 1950, republished in Marie Seton, *Portrait of a Director: Satyajit Ray*, Dobson Books, 1971.

5. Letter to Clifford Odets, February 15, 1949, *Correspondance 1913–1978*.

6. Ibid.

7. *Correspondance 1913–1978*.

8. Letter to Eugène Lourié, February 11, 1949, *Lettres d'amérique*.

9. Eugène Lourié, *My Work in Films*, Harcourt, Brace, Jovanovich, 1985.

10. Satyajit Ray, "Renoir in Calcutta."

11. Ibid.

12. Rumer Godden, *A House with Four Rooms*, William Morrow, 1989.

13. A. H. Weiler, "By Way of Report," *New York Times*, April 17, 1949, cited by William Harry Gilcher, *Jean Renoir in America: A Critical Analysis of His Major Films from* Swamp Water *to* The River, University of Iowa, 1979.

14. Letter to Rumer Godden, April 19, 1949, *Correspondance 1913–1978*.

15. Letter to Rumer Godden, April 29, 1949, *Correspondance 1913–1978*.

16. Letter to Darryl Zanuck, March 29, 1951, Jean Renoir Papers, Box 11, Folder 3.

17. Letter to Ram Sen Gupta, June 7, 1949, *Correspondance 1913–1978*.

18. Letter to J. K. McEldowney, July 1, 1949, *Correspondance 1913–1978*.

19. Rumer Godden, *A House with Four Rooms*.

20. Ibid.

21. Conversations with Alain Renoir.

22. Rumer Godden, *A House with Four Rooms.*

23. Conversations with Alain Renoir.

24. Interviews by Ronald Bergan, *Jean Renoir: Projections of Paradise*, Overlook Press, 1994.

25. Rumer Godden, *A House with Four Rooms.*

26. Letter to J. K. McEldowney, August 11, 1949, *Correspondance 1913–1978.*

27. Letter to Rumer Godden, August 22, 1949, *Correspondance 1913–1978.*

28. Letter to Rumer Godden, September 20, 1949, Jean Renoir Papers, Correspondence, Box 9, Folder 12.

29. Letter to Rumer Godden, August 22, 1949, *Correspondance 1913–1978.*

30. Ibid.

31. Letter to Rumer Godden, September 20, 1949, Jean Renoir Papers, Correspondence, Box 9, Folder 12.

32. Ibid.

33. Letter to Rumer Godden, October 25, 1949, *Correspondance 1913–1978.*

34. Letter to Thomas E. Breen, December 20, 1965, Jean Renoir Papers, Correspondence, Box 21, Folder 3.

35. Letter to Bert Allenberg, November 16, 1948, *Correspondance 1913–1978.*

36. Rumer Godden, *A House with Four Rooms.*

37. Letter from Georges Simenon, August 8, 1949, Jean Renoir Papers, Correspondence, Box 9, Folder 11.

38. Letter to Georges Simenon, August 13, 1949, Jean Renoir Papers, Correspondence, Box 9, Folder 11.

39. Letter from Georges Simenon, August 15, 1949, Jean Renoir Papers, Correspondence, Box 9, Folder 11.

40. Letter to Claude Renoir Sr., October 31, 1949, Jean Renoir Papers, Correspondence, Box 9, Folder 13.

41. Letter to Georges Simenon, July 30, 1950, Jean Renoir Papers, Correspondence, Box 10, Folder 11.

42. Letter from Alain Renoir to Dido Renoir, undated, Jean Renoir Papers, Correspondence, Box 10, Folder 3.

43. Letter from Louis Guillaume, June 15, 1949, Jean Renoir Papers, Correspondence, Box 9, Folder 10.

44. Letter from Janine Bazin, April 28, 1974, Jean Renoir Papers, Correspondence, Box 30, Folder 2.

45. André Bazin, "L'auteur de *La Grande Illusion* n'a pas perdu confiance dans la liberté de création," *L'Écran français*, n° 230, November 28, 1949.

46. Rumer Godden, *A House with Four Rooms.*

47. Letter to Robert Coryell, May 7, 1950, *Correspondance 1913–1978.*

48. Jean Renoir, *Ma vie et mes films,* Flammarion, 1974.

49. Letter to Raymond Burnier, September 1, 1950, Jean Renoir Papers, Correspondence, Box 10, Folder 13.

50. Ibid.

51. Letter to Pierre Braunberger, October 21, 1950, *Correspondance 1913–1978.*

52. Letter to Robert Flaherty, July 26, 1948, *Correspondance 1913–1978.*

53. "Instruction for the second unit shooting," undated, Jean Renoir Papers, Production Files, Box 9, Folder 4.

54. Letter from Rumer Godden, April 18, 1951, Jean Renoir Papers, Box 11, Folder 4.

55. Letter to Rumer Godden, May 2, 1951, Jean Renoir Papers, Box 11, Folder 4.

56. Alain Fleischer, *Réponse du muet au parlant, en retour à Jean-Luc Godard,* Le Seuil, 2011.

57. Melvina Pumphrey, "Cameras Finally Roll on *The River* in India," and W. Gordon Graham, "The Making of *The River,*" *Christian Science Monitor*, June 10, 1950, cited by Harry William Gilcher, *Jean Renoir in America.*

58. Letter to Jacques Becker, October 21, 1946, Jean Renoir Papers, Correspondence, Box 7, Folder 1.

59. Ibid.

60. Harry William Gilcher, *Jean Renoir in America*.

61. "Pageant of India, the Exotic Colour of an Ancient Land Animates *The River*," *Life*, November 5, 1951.

62. Letter from Julius Lefkowitz and Company, January 5, 1952, Jean Renoir Papers, Correspondence, Box 11, Folder 13.

63. Letter from J. K. McEldowney to David L. Loew, September 6, 1954, Jean Renoir Papers, Correspondence, Box 12, Folder 21.

64. Letter from Charles Smadja, United Artists, December 28, 1951, Jean Renoir Papers, Box 11, Folder 12.

65. Letter of December 4, 1971, published in *Écran 72*, n° 1, January 1972.

66. Jean Renoir, *Ma vie et mes films*.

67. *Cahiers du cinéma*, n° 8, January 1952.

68. André Bazin, "Un pur chef-d'œuvre, *Le Fleuve*," in Bazin, *Jean Renoir*, Éditions Champ Libre, 1971.

69. *Jean Renoir vous présente . . .* Radiodiffusion-Télévision Française, direction by Jean-Marie Coldefy, January 1962.

70. Jean Renoir, *Pierre-Auguste Renoir, mon père*, Gallimard, Folio, 1981.

29. "I'm Bored without You"

1. Letter from Gérard Philipe, undated, Jean Renoir Papers, Correspondence, Box 15, Folder 18.

2. "Pierre Sicard," translation by Jeannine Ciment, in *Positif*, n° 173, September 1975, reprinted in *Jean Renoir, le Passé vivant*, éditions Cahiers du cinéma, 1989.

3. Jean Renoir Papers, Production Files, Box 51, Folder 8.

4. Letter to Gérard Philipe, October 1, 1949, Cinémathèque française, Fonds Anne et Gérard Philipe, AGP 134.

5. Letter from Gérard Philipe, October 14, 1949, Jean Renoir Papers, Correspondence, Box 9, Folder 13.

6. Letter to Gérard Philipe, January 3, 1950, Cinémathèque française, Fonds Anne et Gérard Philipe, AGP 134.

7. Letter from Gérard Philipe, June 8, 1950, Jean Renoir Papers, Correspondence, Box 10, Folder 10.

8. Letter from Gérard Philipe, undated, Cinémathèque française, Fonds Anne et Gérard Philipe, AGP 134.

9. Letter from Gérard Philipe to Max Ophuls, June 14, 1950, Cinémathèque française, Fonds Anne et Gérard Philipe, AGP 134.

10. Letter from Gérard Philipe, undated, Jean Renoir Papers, Correspondence, Box 15, Folder 18.

11. Letter from Albert Camus to Gérard Philipe, August 14, 1950, Cinémathèque française, Fonds Anne et Gérard Philipe, AGP 134.

12. Letter from Pierre Lestringuez, August 16, 1950, Jean Renoir Papers, Correspondence, Box 10, Folder 12.

13. Letter to Louis Guillaume, June 17, 1950, Jean Renoir Papers, Correspondence, Box 10, Folder 10.

14. Letter from Jean Dewalde, June 26, 1950, Jean Renoir Papers, Correspondence, Box 10, Folder 10.

15. Letter from Claude Renoir Jr., June 28, 1950, Jean Renoir Papers, Correspondence, Box 10, Folder 10.

16. Letter to Gérard Philipe, July 2, 1950, Jean Renoir Papers, Correspondence, Box 10, Folder 11.

17. Letter to Jean Dewalde, July 2, 1950, *Correspondance 1913-1978*, Plon, 1998.

18. Ibid.

19. Letter from Gérard Philipe, September 16, 1950, Jean Renoir Papers, Correspondence, Box 10, Folder 13.

20. Letter to Claude Renoir Sr., September 22, 1950, Jean Renoir Papers, Correspondence, Box 10, Folder 13.

21. Letter from Jean Dewalde, September 27, 1950, Jean Renoir Papers, Correspondence, Box 10, Folder 13.

22. Letter to Gérard Philipe, September 30, 1950, Cinémathèque française, Fonds Anne et Gérard Philipe, AGP 134.

23. Ibid.

24. Letter from Jean Dewalde, October 6, 1950, Jean Renoir Papers, Correspondence, Box 10, Folder 14.

25. Letter from Gérard Philipe, September 16, 1950, Jean Renoir Papers, Correspondence, Box 10, Folder 13.

26. Letter to Gérard Philipe, September 21, 1950, *Correspondance 1913–1978*.

27. Letter from Gérard Philipe, September 25, 1950, Jean Renoir Papers, Correspondence, Box 10, Folder 13.

28. Ibid.

29. Letter from Gérard Philipe, November 4, 1950, Jean Renoir Papers, Correspondence, Box 10, Folder 15.

30. Ibid.

31. Letter from Gérard Philipe, undated, probably end of December 1950 or beginning of January 1951, Jean Renoir Papers, Correspondence, Box 15, Folder 18.

32. Letter from Pierre Renoir, November 2, 1950, Jean Renoir Papers, Correspondence, Box 10, Folder 15.

33. Letter to Pierre Braunberger, October 21, 1950, *Correspondance 1913–1978*.

34. Letter from Jean Dewalde, October 14, 1950, Jean Renoir Papers, Correspondence, Box 10, Folder 14.

35. Ibid.

36. Letter to Pierre Braunberger, November 20, 1950, Jean Renoir Papers, Correspondence, Box 10, Folder 15.

37. Ibid.

38. Letter to Jean Dewalde, December 30, 1952, Jean Renoir Papers, Correspondence, Box 10, Folder 16.

39. Ibid.

40. Letter to Gérard Philipe, December 30, 1950, Jean Renoir Papers, Correspondence, Box 10, Folder 16.

41. Letter to Gérard Philipe, February 2, 1951, Cinémathèque française, Fonds Anne et Gérard Philipe, AGP 134.

42. Ibid.

43. Letter to Jean Dewalde, July 2, 1950, *Correspondance 1913–1978*.

44. Letter from Pierre Braunberger, February 17, 1951, Jean Renoir Papers, Correspondence, Box 11, Folder 2.

45. Letter to Pierre Braunberger, February 24, 1951, Jean Renoir Papers, Correspondence, Box 11, Folder 2.

46. Letter from Pierre Braunberger, February 23, 1951, Jean Renoir Papers, Correspondence, Box 11, Folder 2.

47. Letter from Jean Renoir, March 1, 1951, Jean Renoir Papers, Correspondence, Box 11, Folder 3.

48. Letter from Jean Renoir, February 24, 1951, Jean Renoir Papers, Correspondence, Box 11, Folder 2.

49. Letter to Christopher Mann Ltd., January 11, 1951, Jean Renoir Papers, Correspondence, Box 11, Folder 1.

50. Ibid.

51. Telegram from Robert Dorfmann, March 28, 1951, *Correspondance 1913–1978*.

52. Telegram to Robert Dorfmann, March 30, 1951, *Correspondance 1913–1978*.

53. Telegram from Robert Dorfmann, April 2, 1951, *Correspondance 1913–1978*.

54. Telegram to Robert Dorfmann, April 3, 1951, *Correspondance 1913–1978*.

55. Letter to Robert Dorfmann, April 3, 1951, *Correspondance 1913–1978*.

56. Letter to Jean Dewalde, April 3, 1951, *Correspondance 1913–1978*.

57. Conversation with Janet Bergstrom, in "Généalogie du *Carrosse d'or* de Jean Renoir," *1895*, n° 62, December 2010.

58. Ibid.

59. Francesco Alliata, conversation with Matthieu Orléan, *Renoir/Renoir*, Éditions de La Martinière/ Cinémathèque française, 2005.

60. Conversation with Janet Bergstrom, "Généalogie du *Carrosse d'or* de Jean Renoir."

61. Ibid.

62. Ibid.

63. Ibid.

64. Laurence Schifano, *Visconti*, Librairie Académique Perrin, 1987.

65. John Kobler, "Tempest on the Tiber," *Life*, February 13, 1950.

66. Conversation with Jacques Rivette and François Truffaut, *Cahiers du cinéma*.

67. Ibid.

68. Ibid.

69. Letter to Jean Dewalde, April 3, 1951, *Correspondance 1913–1978*.

70. Letter to Robert Dorfmann, April 3, 1951, *Correspondance 1913–1978*.

71. Ibid.

72. Letter to Jean Dewalde, April 10, 1951, *Correspondance 1913–1978*.

73. Letter to Robert Dorfmann, April 13, 1951, *Correspondance 1913–1978*.

74. Ibid.

75. Letter to Dido Renoir, May 21, 1951, *Correspondance 1913–1978*.

76. Letter to Prince Francesco Alliata, January 28, 1952, *Correspondence 1913–1978*.

77. Letter to Clifford Odets, October 5, 1952, *Correspondance 1913–1978*.

78. Letter to Dido Renoir, June 7, 1951, *Correspondance 1913–1978*.

79. Letter to Kenneth J. McEldowney, June 8, 1951, Jean Renoir Papers, Correspondence, Box 11, Folder 6.

80. Letter to Dido Renoir, June 12, 1951, *Correspondance 1913–1978*.

81. Letter to M. Brosio, Panaria Film, January 30, 1952, *Correspondance 1913–1978*.

82. Laurent Fraison, "La Périchole, Genèse et analyse de la version primitive," *L'Avant-Scène Opéra*, n° 66, August 1984.

83. Letter from Giulio Macchi, July 12, 1952, Jean Renoir Papers, Correspondence, Box 11, Folder 19.

84. Letter to Dido Renoir, June 29, 1951, *Correspondance 1913–1978*.

85. Letter to Dido Renoir, July 8, 1951, *Correspondance 1913–1978*.

86. Letter to Dido Renoir, July 20, 1951, *Correspondance 1913–1978*.

87. Letter to Dido Renoir, July 8, 1951, *Correspondance 1913–1978*.

88. Letter to Dido Renoir, July 14, 1951, *Correspondance 1913–1978*.

89. Letter to Dido Renoir, July 20, 1951, *Correspondance 1913–1978*.

90. Conversations with Alain Renoir.

91. Letter from Jean Dewalde to Robert Dorfmann, September 17, 1951, Jean Renoir Papers, Box 11, Folder 9.

92. Letter to Prince Francesco Alliata, January 28, 1952, *Correspondance 1913–1978*.

93. Francesco Alliata, Conversation with Janet Bergstrom, "Généalogie du *Carrosse d'or* de Jean Renoir."

94. Letter from Louis Guillaume, May 4, 1953, Jean Renoir Papers, Correspondence, Box 12, Folder 5.

95. Ibid.

96. Letter from Jean Dewalde to Francesco Alliata, December 4, 1952, Jean Renoir Papers, Correspondence, Box 11, Folder 24.

97. Renoir will inform Louis Guillaume of the payment of that sum by a letter dated January 7, 1953, Jean Renoir Papers, Correspondence, Box 12, Folder 1.

98. "Jean Renoir ne pourra pas réaliser *Le Carrosse d'or* (d'après Mérimée) dans sa langue maternelle," *L'Écran français*, n° 359, January 9–15, 1952.

99. Ibid.

100. Francesco Alliata, conversation with Janet Bergstrom, "Généalogie du *Carrosse d'or* de Jean Renoir."

101. Letter to Dido Renoir, August 21, 1951, *Correspondance 1913–1978*.

102. Letter to Prince Francesco Alliata, January 28, 1952, *Correspondance 1913–1978*.

103. Maurice Béjart, *Un instant dans la vie d'autrui, Mémoires*, Flammarion, 1979.

104. Letter to Dido Renoir, July 8, 1951, *Correspondance 1913–1978*.

105. Letter to Clifford Odets, May 4, 1952, *Correspondance 1913–1978*.

106. Jean Renoir Papers, Production Files, Box 3, Folder 1.

107. Francesco Alliata, conversation with Janet Bergstrom, "Généalogie du *Carrosse d'or* de Jean Renoir."

108. Ibid.

109. Telegram from Luchino Visconti, December 10, 1952, Jean Renoir Papers, Correspondence, Box 11, Folder 24.

110. Francesco Alliata, conversation with Janet Bergstrom, "Généalogie du *Carrosse d'or* de Jean Renoir."

111. Letter to Harold J. Salemson, January 3, 1953, Jean Renoir Papers, Correspondence, Box 12, Folder 1.

112. Letter from Harold J. Salemson, December 18, 1952, Jean Renoir Papers, Correspondence, Box 11, Folder 24.

113. Program for Jean Renoir created by l'Italian Film Export, Jean Renoir Papers, Motion Picture Production, Box 3, Folder 2.

114. Letter to Louis Guillaume, May 5, 1953, Jean Renoir Papers, Correspondence, Box 12, Folder 5.

115. Letter to Louis Guillaume, May 13, 1953, Jean Renoir Papers, Correspondence, Box 12, Folder 5.

116. Ibid.

117. Jacques Doniol-Valcroze, "Camilla et le don," *Cahiers du cinéma*, n° 21, March 1953.

118. Presentation of a Renoir festival at the Maison de la Culture de Vidauban in 1967, represented in *Les Films de ma vie*, Flammarion, 1975.

119. Ibid.

120. Ibid.

121. Maurice Schérer, "Renoir américain," *Cahiers du cinéma*, n° 8, January 1952.

122. André Bazin, "Renoir français," *Cahiers du cinéma*, n° 8, January 1952.

123. Ibid.

124. Letter to Clifford Odets, February 17, 1953, *Correspondance 1913–1978*.

125. Letter to Ram Sen Gupta, March 31, 1953, *Correspondance 1913–1978*.

126. Letter from Forrest E. Judd, December 15, 1952, Jean Renoir Papers, Correspondence, Box 11, Folder 24.

127. *Marouf: The Cobbler of Cairo*, Jean Renoir Papers, Production Files, Box 47, Folder 2.

128. Letter to Forrest E. Judd, December 23, 1952, Jean Renoir Papers, Correspondence, Box 11, Folder 24.

129. Letter from Romola Nijinski, January 3, 1953, Jean Renoir Papers, Correspondence, Box 12, Folder 1.

130. Letter from François Gergely, January 12, 1953, Jean Renoir Papers, Correspondence, Box 12, Folder 1.

131. Letter from Joseph de Bretagne, February 1, 1953, Jean Renoir Papers, Correspondence, Box 12, Folder 2.

132. Letter to Joseph de Bretagne, March 3, 1953, Jean Renoir Papers, Correspondence, Box 12, Folder 3.

133. Letter to Jean Dewalde, March 3, 1953, Jean Renoir Papers, Correspondence, Box 12, Folder 3.

134. Letter to Jean Dewalde, March 31, 1953, Jean Renoir Papers, Correspondence, Box 12, Folder 3.

135. Letter to Sol Lesser, Hollywood Museum Associates, December 10, 1962, Jean Renoir Papers, Correspondence, Box 18, Folder 5.

136. Letter from Alain Renoir, 1953, Jean Renoir Papers, Correspondence, Box 15, Folder 18.

137. Letter to Lee Kresel, February 25, 1953, Jean Renoir Papers, Correspondence, Box 12, Folder 2.

138. Treatment dated June 25, 1952, registered with the Société des auteurs de films on July 3, 1952, Jean Renoir Papers, Production Files, Box 48, Folder 5.

139. Ibid.

140. Telegram to Raymond Ventura, Hoche Production, February 15, 1953, Jean Renoir Papers, Correspondence, Box 12, Folder 2.

141. Letter to Clifford Odets, February 17, 1953, *Correspondance 1913–1978*.

142. Letters to nephew Claude Renoir, June 14, 1953, and to Louis Guillaume, June 16, 1953, Jean Renoir Papers, Correspondence, Box 12, Folder 6.

143. Letter from Gabriel Pascal, July 16, 1953, Jean Renoir Papers, Correspondence, Box 12, Folder 7.

144. Letter from Gabriel Pascal, July 23, 1953, Jean Renoir Papers, Correspondence, Box 12, Folder 7.

145. Letter to Gabriel Pascal, July 28, 1953, Jean Renoir Papers, Correspondence, Box 12, Folder 7.

146. Ibid.

147. Letter to Louis Guillaume, June 16, 1953, Jean Renoir Papers, Correspondence, Box 12, Folder 6.

148. Letter from François Gergely, September 12, 1953, Jean Renoir Papers, Correspondence, Box 12, Folder 9.

149. Letter to François Gergely, September 21, 1953, Jean Renoir Papers, Correspondence, Box 12, Folder 9.

150. Letter to Lionello Santi, August 7, 1953, Jean Renoir Papers, Correspondence, Box 12, Folder 8.

151. Letter to Claude Renoir, August 9, 1953, Jean Renoir Papers, Correspondence, Box 12, Folder 8.

152. Letter from Dowling Productions, August 18, 1953, Jean Renoir Papers, Correspondence, Box 12, Folder 8.

153. Letter to Alain Renoir, August 21, 1953, Jean Renoir Papers, Correspondence, Box 12, Folder 8.

154. Letter to Lionello Santi, September 4, 1953, Jean Renoir Papers, Correspondence, Box 12, Folder 9.

155. Letter to Jean Dewalde, September 18, 1953, Jean Renoir Papers, Correspondence, Box 12, Folder 9.

156. Letter to Jean Dewalde, September 21, 1953, *Correspondance 1913–1978*.

157. Ibid.

158. "Jean Renoir va tourner en France un *Van Gogh*," *Paris-Presse*, November 5, 1953.

159. Jean Renoir, *Œuvres de cinéma inédites*, edited by Claude Gauteur, Gallimard, 1991.

160. Jean Renoir Papers, Production Files, Box 49, Folder 17.

161. Conversation with André Bazin, *Radio-Cinéma-Télévision*, November 29, 1953.

162. Letter from Jean Dewalde, September 29, 1953, Jean Renoir Papers, Correspondence, Box 12, Folder 9.

163. Letter to Jean Dewalde, October 2, 1953, Jean Renoir Papers, Correspondence, Box 12, Folder 10.

164. Ibid.

165. Letter to Jean Dewalde, October 18, 1953, Jean Renoir Papers, Correspondence, Box 12, Folder 10.

166. Letter to Louis Guillaume, October 18, 1953, Jean Renoir Papers, Correspondence, Box 12, Folder 10.

167. Letter from V. W. VanGogh, October 23, 1953, Jean Renoir Papers, Correspondence, Box 12, Folder 10.

168. Letter from Albert Lewin, November 3, 1953, Jean Renoir Papers, Correspondence, Box 12, Folder 11.

169. Handwritten letter from Van Heflin, undated, Jean Renoir Papers, Correspondence, Box 15, Folder 18.

170. Letter to Jean Dewalde, Jean Renoir Papers, Correspondence, Box 12, Folder 11.

171. *Radio-Cinéma-Télévision*, November 29, 1953.

172. Letter to Van Heflin, February 12, 1954, *Correspondance 1913–1978*.

173. Letter to David Loew, February 24, 1954, *Correspondance 1913–1978*.

174. Handwritten letter from Van Heflin, February 1954, Jean Renoir Papers, Correspondence, Box 12, Folder 14.

175. Letter to Van Heflin, March 29, 1954, *Correspondance 1913–1978*.

176. Letter from Van Heflin, April 1954, Jean Renoir Papers, Correspondence, Box 12, Folder 16.

177. Letter to Van Heflin, May 3, 1954, *Correspondance 1913–1978*.

178. Ibid.

30. Suite Française

1. Note from Henry Deutschmeister on February 15, 1954, Fonds Meunier 02, Cinémathèque française.

2. Letter from Yves Allégret to Charles Boyer, April 24, 1954, Fonds Meunier 02, Cinémathèque française.

3. Note from Henry Deutschmeister on February 15, 1954, Fonds Meunier 02, Cinémathèque française.

4. Fonds Meunier 02, Cinémathèque française.

5. Letter from Franco-London Films to Jean Renoir, April 18, 1954, Jean Renoir Papers, Correspondence, Box 12, Folder 18.

6. Letter from Yves Allégret to Charles Boyer, April 24, 1954, Fonds Meunier 02, Cinémathèque française.

7. Conversation with Jacques Saulnier.

8. Fox Questionnaire, January 25, 1941, Jean Renoir Papers, Production Files, Box 53, Folder 1.

9. Letter from Cimura, July 30, 1954, Jean Renoir Papers, Correspondence, Box 12, Folder 19.

10. Paul Meurisse, *Les Éperons de la liberté*, Robert Laffont, 1979.

11. Jean-Pierre Aumont, *Le Soleil et les Ombres*, Opera Mundi, 1976.

12. Ibid.

13. Letter to David Loew, June 13, 1954, *Jean Renoir: Letters*, edited by Lorraine Lo Bianco and David Thompson, Faber and Faber, 1994.

14. Jean Renoir, *Ma vie et mes films*, Flammarion, 1974.

15. Jean Serge, *Le temps n'est plus de la bohème*, Stock/Kian, 1991.

16. Letter to Alain Renoir, September 9, 1959, Jean Renoir Papers, Correspondence, Box 15, Folder 14.

17. Paul Meurisse, *Lès Éperons de la liberté*.

18. Ibid.

19. André Bazin, *Jean Renoir*, Éditions Champ Libre, 1971.

20. Jean-Claude Brialy, *Le Ruisseau des singes*, Robert Laffont, 2000.

21. Jean-Luc Godard, "*Swamp Water*," in "Spécial Renoir," *Cahiers du cinéma*, n° 78, December 1957.

22. Jacques Rivette, "L'Art de la fugue," *Cahiers du cinéma*, n° 26, August–September 1953.

23. Conversation with Norman Lloyd.

24. Jean Renoir Papers, Production Files, Box 71, Folder 2.

25. André S. Labarthe, "La Règle et l'Exception," *Jean Renoir, Conversations et Propos*, Éditions de l'Étoile, 1979.

26. Letter from François Truffaut, January 22, 1973, Jean Renoir Papers, Correspondence, Box 29, Folder 9.

27. Letter to David Loew, June 13, 1954, *Jean Renoir: Letters*, edited by Lorraine Lo Bianco and David Thompson, Faber and Faber, 1994.

28. Letter to Leslie Caron, July 19, 1954, *Correspondance 1913–1978*, Plon, 1998.

29. Letter from Leslie Caron, undated, before July 1954, Jean Renoir Papers, Correspondence, Box 15, Folder 18.

30. *Paris-Match*, n° 168, May 31, 1952.

31. Jean Serge, *Le temps n'est plus de la bohème*.

32. Conversation with Leslie Caron.

33. Letter to Leslie Caron, October 7, 1956, Jean Renoir Papers, Correspondence, Box 13, Folder 9.

34. Françoise Arnoul, *Animal doué de bonheur*, Belfond, 1995.

35. François Truffaut, *Les Films de ma vie*, Flammarion, 1975.

36. Jean Serge, *Le temps n'est plus de la bohème*.

37. Jean Renoir, *Pierre-Auguste Renoir, mon père*, Gallimard, Folio, 1981.

38. Conversation with Françoise Arnoul.

39. Conversation with Gisèle Braunberger. The future wife of Pierre Braunberger was still called Gisèle Hauchecorne and at eighteen years old was an extra in *French Cancan*.

40. Jacques Becker, "Le cinéma a besoin d'amants," *Arts*, November 1959.

41. Conversation with Michel Piccoli.

42. Archives Claude Autant-Lara, Cinémathèque de Lausanne (information supplied by Jean-Pierre Bleys).

43. Letter to Leslie Caron, December 12, 1954, *Correspondance 1913–1978*.

44. Jean Renoir Papers, Production Files, Box 3, Folder 23.

45. Letter to David Loew, August 30, 1954, Jean Renoir Papers, Correspondence, Box 12, Folder 20.

46. Letter to Louis Guillaume, May 13, 1953, Jean Renoir Papers, Correspondence, Box 12, Folder 5.

47. Conversation with Jacques Saulnier.

48. Pierre Kast, "Le Nez de la Belle Abbesse," *Cinéma 55*, n° 2, December 1955.

49. *Cahiers du cinéma*, n° 43, February 1955.

50. Ibid.

51. *Cahiers du cinéma*, n° 34, April 1954.

52. Jean Renoir Papers, Production Files, Box 50, Folder 8.

53. Jean Renoir Papers, Production Files, Box 48, Folder 24.

54. Jean Renoir Papers, Production Files, Box 35, Folder 11.

55. *The Poachers*, synopsis, January 31, 1953, Jean Renoir Papers, Production Files, Box 35, Folder 10.

56. *Les Braconniers*, "Projet de film de Jean Renoir," 31 typed pages, 5 handwritten pages, Jean Renoir Papers, Production Files, Box 52, Folder 11.

57. Jean Renoir Papers, Production Files, Box 49, Folder 7.

58. Conversation with Jacques Rivette and François Truffaut, *Cahiers du cinéma*, n° 78, Noël 195.

59. Conversation with Alain Renoir.

60. Conversation with Leslie Caron.

61. François Truffaut, "*Orvet*, mon amour," *Cahiers du cinéma*, n° 47, May 1955.

62. Letter from Dido Renoir, April 21, 1955, *Correspondance 1913–1978*.

63. *Paris-Match*, n° 306, February 5–12, 1955.

64. *Le Figaro*, March 21, 1955.

65. *Franc-Tireur*, March 23, 1955.

66. *Dimanche-Matin*, March 27, 1955.

67. Leslie Caron, *Une Française à Hollywood*, translated by Anne-Marie Hussein, Baker Street, 2011.

68. Ibid.

69. Jean Gruault, *Ce que dit l'autre*, Julliard, 1992.

70. Ingrid Bergman and Alan Burgess, *Ma vie*, translated by Eric Diacon, Fayard, 1980.

71. Roberto Rossellini, *Fragments d'une autobiographie*, Ramsay, 1987.

72. Letter to Dido Renoir, May 28, 1951, *Correspondance 1913–1978*.

73. Letter to Dido Renoir, June 7, 1951, *Correspondance 1913–1978*.

74. Letter to Dido Renoir, October 23, 1957, *Correspondance 1913–1978*.

75. Tag Gallagher, *Les Aventures de Roberto Rossellini*, translated by Jean-Pierre Coursodon, Éditions Léo Scheer, 2005.

76. Jean Renoir Papers, Production Files, Box 3, Folder 8.

77. "À toucher pour Ellena [sic]," note from Dido Renoir, undated, Jean Renoir Papers, Production Files, Box 3, Folder 8.

78. Jean Renoir Papers, Production Files, Box 3, Folder 8.

79. Letter to Lucienne Wattier, CI-MU-RA, January 28, 1957, *Correspondence 1913–1978*.

80. *Jean Renoir vous présente . . .*, Radiodiffusion-Télévision française, directed by Jean-Marie Coldefy, January 1962.

81. Jean Serge, *Le temps n'est plus de la bohème*.

82. *Arts*, n° 544, November 30, 1955, in Jean Renoir, *Écrits 1926–1971*, edited by Claude Gauteur, Belfond, 1974.

83. *Jean Renoir vous présente . . .* , Radiodiffusion-Télévision française.

84. Ibid.

85. Letter to David Loew, July 10, 1955, Jean Renoir Papers, Correspondence, Box 12, Folder 30.

86. Jean Renoir Papers, Production Files, Box 4, Folder 10.

87. Jean Serge, *Le temps n'est plus de la bohème.*

88. Ibid.

89. Jacques Morel, *Regards en coulisses*, Guy Authier, 1978.

90. Ibid.

91. Conversation with Jacques Saulnier.

92. Published under the name of Robert Lachenay, *Cahiers du cinéma*, n° 48, June 1955.

93. Letter to Blanche Montel and Lucienne Wattier, September 24, 1956, *Correspondance 1913–1978.*

94. "Notes to Deutschmeister," undated, Jean Renoir Papers, Production Files, Box 5, Folder 4.

95. Conversation with Jacques Rivette and François Truffaut, in "Spécial Renoir," *Cahiers du cinéma,* n° 78, December 1957.

96. Juliette Gréco, *Je suis faite comme ça, Mémoires,* Flammarion, 2012.

97. "Chansons sur six thèmes musicaux de Joseph Kosma," December 22, 1955, Jean Renoir Papers, Production Files, Box 5, Folder 3.

98. "Notes to Deutschmeister," undated, Jean Renoir Papers, Production Files, Box 5, Folder 4.

99. Conversation with Jacques Saulnier.

100. Letter to Charles Spaak, September 9, 1956, *Correspondance 1913–1978.*

101. Letter to Borys Lewin, October 9, 1956, *Correspondance 1913–1978.*

102. Letter to Ginette Doynel, August 11, 1956, Jean Renoir Papers, Correspondence, Box 13, Folder 7.

103. Letter to Franco-London Films, September 1, 1956, Jean Renoir Papers, Correspondence, Box 13, Folder 8.

104. Letter to Mlle. Deutschmeister, September 5, 1956, Jean Renoir Papers, Correspondence, Box 13, Folder 8.

105. Letter to Henry Deutschmeister, October 6, 1956, Jean Renoir Papers, Correspondence, Box 13, Folder 9.

106. Letter to Lucienne Wattier, September 14, 1956, Jean Renoir Papers, Correspondence, Box 13, Folder 8.

107. Letter to Henry Deutschmeister, August 28, 1956, Jean Renoir Papers, Correspondence, Box 13, Folder 7.

108. Letter from Jean Marais, August 28, 1956, ibid.

109. Letter from Christian-Jaque, undated, Jean Renoir Papers, Correspondence, Box 15, Folder 18.

110. Letter from Henry Deutschmeister, September 12, 1956, Jean Renoir Papers, Correspondence, Box 13, Folder 8.

111. Letter to Henry Deutschmeister, September 19, 1956, Jean Renoir Papers, Correspondence, Box 13, Folder 8.

112. Letter from Henry Deutschmeister, September 26, 1956, Jean Renoir Papers, Correspondence, Box 13, Folder 8.

113. Claude Mauriac, "*Elena et les hommes,*" *Le Figaro littéraire,* September 22, 1956.

114. Letter to Henry Deutschmeister, September 15, 1956, Jean Renoir Papers, Correspondence, Box 13, Folder 8.

115. Letter to Borys Lewin, October 9, 1956, *Correspondance 1913–1978.*

116. Letter from Franco-London Films (signature unreadable), January 4, 1957, Jean Renoir Papers, Correspondence, Box 13, Folder 12.

117. Letter to Blanche Montel et Lucienne Wattier, September 24, 1956, *Correspondance 1913–1978.*

118. Letter to Ingrid Bergman, February 25, 1957, *Correspondance 1913–1978.*

119. Letter to Lucienne Wattier, January 28, 1957, *Correspondance 1918–1978.*

120. Letter to Ginette Doynel, February 27, 1957, Jean Renoir Papers, Correspondence, Box 13, Folder 13.

121. Collectif, "The Situation of the Serious Filmaker," *Film Book* 1, 1959, reprinted in Harry M. Geduld, *Film Makers on Film Making: Statements on Their Art by Thirty Directors*, Indiana University Press, 1967.

122. Ibid.

123. Bosley Crowthers, "Screen: French Import; Parisian Film Shown at the Paramount," *New York Times*, March 30, 1957.

124. Pierre Billard, *Cinéma 56*, n° 12, December 1956.

125. Ibid.

126. Pierre Billard, *L'Âge classique du cinéma français*, Flammarion, 1995.

127. Cited in "Jean Renoir," *Premier Plan*, n° 22–23–24, edited by Bernard Chardère, May 1962.

128. Jean-Luc Godard, *Elena et les hommes*, in "Spécial Renoir," *Cahiers du cinéma*, n° 78, December 1957.

129. Ibid.

130. Conversation with Jacques Saulnier.

131. Letters to Leslie Caron, October 11, 1956, and to Ginette Doynel, October 8, 1956, Jean Renoir Papers, Correspondence, Box 13, Folder 9.

132. Letter to Lucienne Wattier, January 28, 1957, *Correspondance 1913–1978*.

133. Ibid.

134. Letter to Ingrid Bergman, February 25, 1957, *Correspondance 1913–1978*.

135. Ibid.

136. Letter to Ginette Doynel, August 9, 1957, Jean Renoir Papers, Correspondence, Box 14, Folder 2.

137. Letter from Roberto Rossellini, January 22, 1957, Jean Renoir Papers, Correspondence, Box 13, Folder 12.

138. Conversation with Leslie Caron.

139. Letter to Dudley Nichols, September 1958, *Jean Renoir: Letters*, edited by Lorraine Lo Bianco and David Thompson, Faber and Faber, 1994.

31. Kicked in the Head

1. *La Lutte contre les conventions* and *Les Cailloux du chemin*, notebook, May 2, 1956, Jean Renoir Papers, Production Files, Box 5, Folder 6.

2. Registered with the Société des auteurs de films, October 15, 1955, 12 and 15 pages, in French with English translation, Jean Renoir Papers, Production Files, Box 35, Folders 1 and 2.

3. Letter to Jean Serge, January 22, 1957, *Correspondance 1913–1978*, Plon, 1998.

4. Letter from Jean Slade, November 5, 1954, Jean Renoir Papers, Correspondence, Box 12, Folder 23.

5. Letter to Pierre Gaut, January 14, 1957, *Correspondance 1913–1978*.

6. Ibid.

7. Conversations with Alain Renoir.

8. Letter from Oona Chaplin to Dido Renoir, undated, circa 1950, Jean Renoir Papers, Correspondence, Box 15, Folder 18.

9. Jean Renoir, "Clifford Odets," *Programme du Théâtre des Bouffes-Parisiens*, 1957, reprinted in *Le Passé vivant*, Éditions Cahiers du cinéma, 1989.

10. Margaret Brenman-Gibson, *Clifford Odets: American Playwright, the Years from 1906 to 1940*, Atheneum, 1982.

11. Conversation with Walt Odets.

12. Harold Clurman, *All People Are Famous (Instead of an Autobiography)*, Harcourt, Brace, Jovanovich, 1974.

13. Ibid.

14. Conversation with Walt Odets.

15. Letter from Clifford Odets, March 4, 1956, Jean Renoir Papers, Correspondence, Box 13, Folder 3.

16. Letter to Clifford Odets, April 9, 1956, Jean Renoir Papers, Correspondence, Box 13, Folder 4.

17. Letter to Dido Renoir, March 5, 1962, Jean Renoir Papers, Correspondence, Box 17, Folder 8.

18. Letter from Clifford Odets, May 18, 1955, *Correspondance 1913–1978*.

19. Letter to Clifford Odets, April 9, 1956, Jean Renoir Papers, Correspondence, Box 13, Folder 4.

20. Letter to Clifford Odets, March 19, 1956, *Jean Renoir: Letters*, edited by Lorraine Lo Bianco and David Thompson, Faber and Faber, 1994.

21. Letter from Jean Serge to Ginette Doynel, July 1956, Jean Renoir Papers, Correspondence, Box 13, Folder 6.

22. Letter to Jean Serge, July 11, 1956, Jean Renoir Papers, Correspondence, Box 13, Folder 6.

23. Letter from Jean Serge to Ginette Doynel, July 1956, Jean Renoir Papers, Correspondence, Box 13, Folder 6.

24. Letter from Jean Serge to Ginette Doynel, July 1956, Jean Renoir Papers, Correspondence, Box 13, Folder 6.

25. Letter to Jean Serge, July 11, 1956, Jean Renoir Papers, Correspondence, Box 13, Folder 6.

26. Letter to Clifford Odets, August 12, 1956, Jean Renoir Papers, Correspondence, Box 13, Folder 7.

27. Letter to Ginette Doynel, July 24, 1956, Jean Renoir Papers, Correspondence, Box 13, Folder 6.

28. Letter to Gaston Gallimard, June 12, 1956, Jean Renoir Papers, Correspondence, Box 13, Folder 5.

29. Letter from Gaston Gallimard, October 22, 1956, Jean Renoir Papers, Correspondence, Box 13, Folder 9.

30. Letter from Jean Serge, February 9, 1957, Jean Renoir Papers, Correspondence, Box 13, Folder 13.

31. Letter to Ginette Doynel, February 15, 1957, Jean Renoir Papers, Correspondence, Box 13, Folder 13.

32. Letter from Micheline Presle, June 3, 1957, Jean Renoir Papers, Correspondence, Box 13, Folder 17.

33. Letter from Jean Serge, August 8, 1957, Jean Renoir Papers, Correspondence, Box 14, Folder 2.

34. Conversation with Leslie Caron.

35. Conversation with Claude Gauteur.

36. *France Film International,* June 5, 1956.

37. Letter from Ginette Doynel, November 14, 1956, Jean Renoir Papers, Correspondence, Box 13, Folder 10.

38. Letter to Lucienne Wattier, November 30, 1956, *Correspondance 1913–1978*.

39. Letter to Erich von Stroheim, November 30, 1956, *Correspondance 1913–1978*.

40. Letter from Erich von Stroheim, January 3, 1957, Jean Renoir Papers, Correspondence, Box 13, Folder 12.

41. Letter to Erich von Stroheim, January 15, 1957, *Correspondance 1913–1978*.

42. Letter from Denise Vernac, April 8, 1957, Jean Renoir Papers, Correspondence, Box 13, Folder 15.

43. Letter from Charles Spaak, May 20, 1957, Jean Renoir Papers, Correspondence, Box 13, Folder 16.

44. Letter to Dido Renoir, October 30, 1957, *Letters*.

45. Letter from Anne de Saint-Phalle to Dido Renoir, March 26, 1979, Jean Renoir Papers, Correspondence, Box 34, Folder 15.

46. "Dépenses petite caisse depuis arrivée du Maestro," Jean Renoir Papers, Motion Picture Production, Box 11, Folder 10.

47. Letter to Lee Kresel, April 4, 1957, *Correspondance 1913–1978*.

48. Letter to Ginette Doynel, May 5, 1957, Jean Renoir Papers, Correspondence, Box 13, Folder 16.

49. Letter to Ingrid Bergman, February 8, 1957, *Correspondance 1913–1978*.

50. Letter to Katharine Brown, February 9, 1957, Jean Renoir Papers, Correspondence, Box 13, Folder 13.

51. Letter to Ginette Doynel, February 27, 1957, Jean Renoir Papers, Correspondence, Box 13, Folder 13.

52. Ibid.

53. Letter from Ginette Doynel, March 22, 1957, Jean Renoir Papers, Correspondence, Box 13, Folder 14.

54. Letter to Ginette Doynel, January 27, 1957, Jean Renoir Papers, Correspondence, Box 13, Folder 12.

55. Letter to Ginette Doynel, March 31, 1957, Jean Renoir Papers, Correspondence, Box 13, Folder 14.

56. Letter from Alice Hughes, March 18, 1957, Jean Renoir Papers, Correspondence, Box 13, Folder 14.

57. Letter to Alice Hughes, March 22, 1957, Jean Renoir Papers, Correspondence, Box 13, Folder 14.

58. Letter to Alice Hughes, April 11, 1957, Jean Renoir Papers, Correspondence, Box 13, Folder 15.

59. Letter to Leslie Caron, February 6, 1957, Jean Renoir Papers, Correspondence, Box 13, Folder 13.

60. Letter to Leslie Caron, April 26, 1957, Jean Renoir Papers, Correspondence, Box 13, Folder 15.

61. Letter to Ginette Doynel, May 5, 1957, Jean Renoir Papers, Correspondence, Box 13, Folder 16.

62. Letter to Leslie Caron, May 23, 1957, Jean Renoir Papers, Correspondence, Box 13, Folder 16.

63. Letter to Dido Renoir, September 20, 1957, Jean Renoir Papers, Correspondence, Box 14, Folder 3.

64. Conversation with Leslie Caron.

65. Letter to Jean Serge, April 18, 1957, Jean Renoir Papers, Correspondence, Box 13, Folder 15.

66. Letter to Ginette Doynel, September 5, 1957, Jean Renoir Papers, Correspondence, Box 14, Folder 3.

67. Letter to Dido Renoir, September 11, 1957, *Correspondance 1913–1978*.

68. *Arts*, n° 636, September 18–24, 1957.

69. Letter from François Truffaut, September 1957, Jean Renoir Papers, Correspondence, Box 14, Folder 3.

70. Letter to Dido Renoir, October 26, 1957, *Correspondance 1913–1978*.

71. Letter from Ginette Doynel to Dido Renoir, October 6, 1957, Jean Renoir Papers, Correspondence, Box 14, Folder 4.

72. Ibid.

73. *Paris-Presse*, September 15, 1957.

74. Letter to Valentine Tessier, February 7, 1957, Jean Renoir Papers, Correspondence, Box 13, Folder 13.

75. Letter to Dido Renoir, October 9, 1957, *Correspondance 1913–1978*.

76. Letter to Clifford Odets, October 10, 1957, *Correspondance 1913–1978*.

77. Conversation with Jacques Rivette and François Truffaut, *Cahiers du cinéma*, n° 78, Noël 1957.

78. Letter to Clifford Odets, October 10, 1957, *Correspondance 1913–1978*.

79. *Le Figaro*, October 10, 1957.

80. Conversation with Jacques Rivette and François Truffaut, *Cahiers du cinéma*, n° 78, Noël 1957.

81. Letter to Dido Renoir, October 9, 1957, *Correspondance 1913–1978*.

82. Letter to Dido Renoir, October 18, 1957, *Correspondance 1913–1978*.

83. Letter to Dido Renoir, October 10, 1957, *Correspondance 1913–1978*.

84. Letter to Dido Renoir, October 26, 1957, *Correspondance 1913–1978*.

85. Letter to Dido Renoir, November 4, 1957, *Correspondance 1913–1978*.

86. Twenty typed pages, submitted during November 1957, Jean Renoir Papers, Production Files, Box 49, Folder 15, and Jean Renoir, *Œuvres de cinéma inédites*, edited by Claude Gauteur, Gallimard, 1991.

87. Letter to Dido Renoir, November 14, 1957, Jean Renoir Papers, Correspondence, Box 14, Folder 5.

88. Letter from Paul Meurisse to Dido Renoir, November 29, 1957, Jean Renoir Papers, Correspondence, Box 14, Folder 5.

89. Ibid.

90. Letter to Dido Renoir, November 27, 1957, Jean Renoir Papers, Correspondence, Box 14, Folder 5.

91. Letter to Dido Renoir, November 14, 1957, Jean Renoir Papers, Correspondence, Box 14, Folder 5.

92. Letter to Yves Bonnat, November 28, 1958, Jean Renoir Papers, Correspondence, Box 15, Folder 4.

93. Célia Bertin, *Jean Renoir*, Éditions du Rocher, 1994.

94. Conversation with Peter Renoir.

95. Letter to Pierre Gaut, January 14, 1957, *Correspondance 1913–1978*.

96. Letter to Dudley Nichols, August 7, 1958, *Correspondance 1913–1978*.

97. Letter to Deborah Kerr, March 1, 1958, Jean Renoir Papers, Correspondence, Box 14, Folder 9.

98. Syd Field, *Going to the Movies: A Personal Journey through Four Decades of Modern Film*, Bantam Dell, 2001.

99. Ibid.

100. About that experience, see, especially, Ernest Callenbach and Roberta Schuldenfrei, "The Presence of Jean Renoir," *Film Quarterly,* n°2, winter 1960, and Virginia Maynard, "A Rehearsal with Jean Renoir," *Educational Theatre Journal,* n° 2, May 1961.

101. Ibid.

102. Letter from Burgess Meredith, September 14, 1963, Jean Renoir Papers, Correspondence, Box 19, Folder 1.

103. Letter from Michael Shurtleff to Mardette Perkins, transmitted by Perkins to Jean Renoir, August 15, 1960, Jean Renoir Papers, Correspondence, Box 16, Folder 8.

104. Letter from John Milius, June 5, 1974, Jean Renoir Papers, Correspondence, Box 30, Folder 5.

105. Letter from Norman Lloyd, December 22, 1975, Jean Renoir Papers, Correspondence, Box 31, Folder 11.

106. Letter from François Truffaut, October 23, 1962, *Correspondance 1913–1978.*

107. Letter to François Truffaut, October 26, 1962, *Correspondance 1913–1978.*

108. Letter to Ginette Doynel, October 28, 1962, Jean Renoir Papers, Correspondence, Box 18, Folder 3.

109. Conversation with Leslie Caron.

110. Letter from Anne de Saint-Phalle to Dido Renoir, January 19, 1982, Jean Renoir Papers, Correspondence, Box 36, Folder 1.

111. Letter from François Truffaut to Dido Renoir, February 7, 1982, Jean Renoir Papers, Correspondence, Box 36, Folder 1.

112. Letter from Dido Renoir to François Truffaut, February 22, 1982, supplied by Leslie Caron.

113. Conversation with Leslie Caron.

114. Letter to Ginette Doynel, April 1957, Jean Renoir Papers, Correspondence, Box 14, Folder 9.

115. Registration receipt on June 9, 1958, Jean Renoir Papers, Production Files, Box 4, Folder 1.

116. Letter to Clifford Odets, November 10, 1958, *Correspondance 1913–1978.*

117. Letter to Charles Spaak, October 22, 1958, *Correspondance 1913–1978.*

118. Letter from M. Anglade, le Marivaux, November 3, 1958, Jean Renoir Papers, Correspondence, Box 15, Folder 4.

119. Letter to Jean Gilhem, administrator of the Festival de Théâtre Amateur de Cahors, April 21, 1959, *Correspondance 1913–1978.*

120. Letter to Clifford Odets, November 10, 1958, *Correspondance 1913–1978.*

121. Ibid.

122. Conversation with Jo Siritzky.

123. Letter to Pablo Picasso, November 28, 1958, *Correspondance 1913–1978.*

124. Letter from H. Baché, Monarch, October 18, 1958, Jean Renoir Papers, Production Files, Box 15, Folder 3.

125. Letter to Leslie Caron, December 8, 1958, Jean Renoir Papers, Correspondence, Box 15, Folder 5.

126. Jean-Luc Godard, *Arts,* n° 718, April 15, 1959.

127. Letter to Alain Renoir, March 16, 1959, *Correspondance 1913–1978.*

128. William W. Demastes, *Clifford Odets: A Research and Production Sourcebook,* Greenwood Press, 1991.

129. Letter to Alain Renoir, March 16, 1959, *Correspondance 1913–1978.*

130. Letter to Leslie Caron, December 12, 1954, *Correspondance 1913–1978.*

131. Jean-Luc Godard, *Arts,* n° 718, April 15, 1959.

132. Conversation with Célia Bertin, in Célia Bertin, *Jean Renoir.*

133. Letter to Dido Renoir, December 8, 1961, *Correspondance 1913–1978.*

134. Notebook, "Réflexions," Paris, August 20, 1955, Jean Renoir Papers, Production Files, Notebooks, Box 35, Folder 9.

135. Letter to Alain Renoir, March 16, 1959, *Correspondance 1913–1978.*

136. Jean Serge, *Le temps n'est plus de la bohème,* Stock/Kian, 1991.

137. Conversation with Claude Chabrol.

138. Jean Renoir, December 23, 1961, *Écrits 1926–1971,* edited by Claude Gauteur, Belfond, 1974.

139. Letter to Gabrielle Slade, February 20, 1959, cited by Célia Bertin, *Jean Renoir*.

140. Letter from Ginette Doynel to Ludmilla Tchérina, February 26, 1959, Jean Renoir Papers, Correspondence, Box 15, Folder 17.

141. Conversation with Jean Slade.

142. Letter to Alain Renoir, March 16, 1959, *Correspondance 1913–1978*.

143. Letter to Révérend Père Diard, March 17, [1959], Jean Renoir Papers, Correspondence, Box 15, Folder 18.

144. Conversation with Jean Slade.

145. Letter from Pierre Braunberger, December 23, 1960, Jean Renoir Papers, Correspondence, Box 16, Folder 12.

146. Conversation with Jean Slade.

147. Conversation with Paolo Barzman.

148. Conversation with Walt Odets.

149. Ibid.

150. Conversation with Jean-Jacques Annaud.

151. Letter to Dido Renoir, November 28, 1961, *Correspondance 1913–1978*.

152. Conversation with Catherine Rouvel.

153. Conversation with Jo Siritzky.

154. Conversation with Catherine Rouvel.

155. Letter from Paul Meurisse, undated [before 1959], Jean Renoir Papers, Correspondence, Box 15, Folder 18.

156. Letter to Leslie Caron, June 14, 1959, Jean Renoir Papers, Correspondence, Box 14, Folder 13.

157. Conversation with Jacques Rivette, *Jean Renoir le Patron*, part 1, *La Recherche du relatif*, May and June 1966, program *Cinéastes de notre temps* by Janine Bazin and André S. Labarthe, reprinted in *Jean Renoir, conversations et propos*, *Cahiers du cinéma*, 1979.

158. Paul Meurisse, *Les Éperons de la liberté*, Robert Laffont, 1979.

159. Letter from the Compagnie Jean Renoir to the director of the Union pour le Financement de l'Industrie Cinématographique, July 28, 1959, Jean Renoir Papers, Correspondence, Box 15, Folder 12.

160. Letter from Dido Renoir, December 4, 1961, Jean Renoir Papers, Correspondence, Box 15, Folder 12.

161. Letter from Dido Renoir, January 17, 1962, Jean Renoir Papers, Correspondence, Box 17, Folder 6.

162. Letter to Dido Renoir, January 31, 1962, Jean Renoir Papers, Correspondence, Box 17, Folder 6.

163. Conversation with Catherine Rouvel.

164. Contract of June 19, 1960, cited by Alain Desvignes, *Catherine Rouvel*, Éditions Autres Temps, 1997.

165. Conversation with Catherine Rouvel.

166. Letter to Ginette Doynel, January 22, 1960, *Correspondance 1913–1978*.

167. Letter to Alain Renoir, September 9, 1959, Jean Renoir Papers, Correspondence, Box 15, Folder 14.

168. Letter to Alain Renoir, March 16, 1959, *Correspondance 1913–1978*.

169. Letter to Henry Nash Smith, University of California, Berkeley, November 6, 1957, Jean Renoir Papers, Correspondence, Box 14, Folder 5.

170. Letter from Clark Kerr, president of the University of California, May 22, 1959, Jean Renoir Papers, Correspondence, Box 15, Folder 10.

32. "It Won't Be Made, It Won't Be Made"

1. Letter to Yves Montand, February 8, 1960, *Correspondance 1913–1978*, Plon, 1998.

2. Letter from Yves Montand, February 19, 1960, *Correspondance 1913–1978*.

3. Letter from Ginette Doynel, May 6, 1960, Jean Renoir Papers, Correspondence, Box 16, Folder 5.

4. Letter from Ginette Doynel, June 15, 1960, Jean Renoir Papers, Correspondence, Box 16, Folder 6.

5. Letter to Ginette Doynel, August 27, 1960, Jean Renoir Papers, Correspondence, Box 16, Folder 8.

6. Letter from Tore Hamsun to Ginette Doynel, September 21, 1961, Jean Renoir Papers, Correspondence, Box 17, Folder 2.

7. Letter to Tore Hamsun, October 1, 1961, Jean Renoir Papers, Correspondence, Box 17, Folder 3.

8. Letter from Tore Hamsun, October 11, 1961, Jean Renoir Papers, Correspondence, Box 17, Folder 3.

9. Telegram from Oskar Werner, March 1, 1962, Jean Renoir Papers, Correspondence, Box 17, Folder 8.

10. Letter to Dido Renoir, March 18, 1962, Jean Renoir Papers, Correspondence, Box 17, Folder 8.

11. Letter to Dido Renoir, March 22, 1962, Jean Renoir Papers, Correspondence, Box 17, Folder 8.

12. Letter from Ginette Doynel, May 30, 1963, Jean Renoir Papers, Correspondence, Box 18, Folder 10.

13. Letter from Pierre Braunberger, December 23, 1960, Jean Renoir Papers, Correspondence, Box 16, Folder 12.

14. Letter to Rumer Godden, February 7, 1961, *Correspondance 1913–1978*.

15. Letter from Michel Simon, January 1961, Jean Renoir Papers, Correspondence, Box 16, Folder 12.

16. Letter from Charles Spaak, February 8, 1961, Jean Renoir Papers, Correspondence, Box 16, Folder 14.

17. Letter to Charles Spaak, February 18, 1961, Jean Renoir Papers, Correspondence, Box 16, Folder 14.

18. Letter to René Bézard, February 27, 1961, *Correspondance 1913–1978*.

19. Letter to Dido Renoir, January 1, 1962, Jean Renoir Papers, Correspondence, Box 17, Folder 6.

20. Adry de Carbuccia, *Du tango à Lily Marlene, 1900–1940*, Éditions France-Empire, 1987.

21. Letter from Pierre Braunberger, June 9, 1962, Jean Renoir Papers, Correspondence, Box 17, Folder 11.

22. Letter to Pierre Braunberger, July 9, 1962, Jean Renoir Papers, Correspondence, Box 17, Folder 12.

23. Letter from Pierre Braunberger, July 13, 1962, Jean Renoir Papers, Correspondence, Box 17, Folder 12.

24. Letter to Charles Spaak, March 3, 1961, *Correspondance 1913–1978*.

25. Letter to Ginette Doynel, March 7, 1961, *Correspondance 1913–1978*.

26. Letter to Les Films du Cyclope, April 21, 1961, Jean Renoir Papers, Correspondence, Box 16, Folder 16.

27. *La Nouvelle Nouvelle Revue française*, n° 64, April 1, 1958.

28. Michel Boujut, *Conversations with Claude Sautet*, Institut Lumière/Actes Sud, 1994.

29. Letter to Ginette Doynel, March 7, 1961, *Correspondance 1913–1978*.

30. "Propos rompus," conversation between Jean Renoir and Jean-Louis Noames, *Cahiers du cinéma*, n° 155, May 1964.

31. Letter from Charles Spaak, August 5, 1961, Jean Renoir Papers, Correspondence, Box 17, Folder 3.

32. *Le Caporal épinglé*, September 20, 1961, Jean Renoir Papers, Production Files, Box 1, Folder 9.

33. Letter to Ginette Doynel, March 7, 1961, *Correspondance 1913–1978*.

34. Letter to Dido Renoir, October 12, 1961, Jean Renoir Papers, Correspondence, Box 17, Folder 3.

35. Letter to Dido Renoir, October 15, 1961, Jean Renoir Papers, Correspondence, Box 17, Folder 3.

36. Letter from Dido Renoir, October 18, 1961, Jean Renoir Papers, Correspondence, Box 17, Folder 3.

37. Letter to Dido Renoir, October 19, 1961, Jean Renoir Papers, Correspondence, Box 17, Folder 3.

38. Letter to Dido Renoir, November 29, 1961, *Correspondance 1913–1978*.

39. Letter to Dido Renoir, October 24, 1961, Jean Renoir Papers, Correspondence, Box 17, Folder 3.

40. Letter to Dido Renoir, October 27, 1961, Jean Renoir Papers, Correspondence, Box 17, Folder 3.

41. Pierre Billard, *Le Nouveau Candide*, cited in *Premier Plan*, n° 22–24, edited by Bernard Chardère, May 1962.

42. Letter to Dido Renoir, October 25, 1961, Jean Renoir Papers, Correspondence, Box 17, Folder 3.

43. Letter to Dido Renoir, October 29, 1961, Jean Renoir Papers, Correspondence, Box 17, Folder 3.

44. Pierre Billard, *Le Nouveau Candide*, cited in *Premier Plan*.

45. Letter to Dido Renoir, November 22, 1961, Jean Renoir Papers, Correspondence, Box 17, Folder 4.

46. Letter to Dido Renoir, November 26, 1961, Jean Renoir Papers, Correspondence, Box 17, Folder 4.

47. Letter from Ginette Doynel to Dido Renoir, November 18, 1961, Jean Renoir Papers, Correspondence, Box 17, Folder 4.

48. Letter from Ginette Doynel to Dido Renoir, November 25, 1961, Jean Renoir Papers, Correspondence, Box 17, Folder 4.

49. Letter to Dido Renoir, February 18, 1962, Jean Renoir Papers, Correspondence, Box 17, Folder 7.

50. Letter to Dido Renoir, December 20, 1961, Jean Renoir Papers, Correspondence, Box 17, Folder 5.

51. Letter to Dido Renoir, December 22, 1961, Jean Renoir Papers, Correspondence, Box 17, Folder 5.

52. Letter to Dido Renoir, January 6, 1962, Jean Renoir Papers, Correspondence, Box 17, Folder 6.

53. Letter to Dido Renoir, January 31, 1962, Jean Renoir Papers, Correspondence, Box 17, Folder 6.

54. Conversation with Aline Cézanne.

55. Letter from Ginette Doynel to Dido Renoir, January 27, 1962, Jean Renoir Papers, Correspondence, Box 17, Folder 6.

56. Letter to Dido Renoir, January 31, 1962, Jean Renoir Papers, Correspondence, Box 17, Folder 6.

57. Letter to Dido Renoir, February 2, 1962, *Correspondance 1913–1978*.

58. Letter from Dido Renoir, February 6, 1962, Jean Renoir Papers, Correspondence, Box 17, Folder 7.

59. Letter to Dido Renoir, February 5, 1962, Jean Renoir Papers, Correspondence, Box 17, Folder 7.

60. Letter to Dido Renoir, April 7, 1962, Jean Renoir Papers, Correspondence, Box 17, Folder 9.

61. Letter to Dido Renoir, March 14, 1962, Jean Renoir Papers, Correspondence, Box 17, Folder 8.

62. Letter to Dido Renoir, January 20, 1962, Jean Renoir Papers, Correspondence, Box 17, Folder 6.

63. Letter to Dido Renoir, March 17, 1962, *Correspondance 1913–1978*.

64. Ibid.

65. Letter from Ginette Doynel to Dido Renoir, March 17, 1962, Jean Renoir Papers, Correspondence, Box 17, Folder 8.

66. Letter to Dido Renoir, March 16, 1962, Jean Renoir Papers, Correspondence, Box 17, Folder 8.

67. Conversations with Alain Renoir.

68. Letter to Dido Renoir, February 20, 1962, Jean Renoir Papers, Correspondence, Box 17, Folder 7.

69. Letter from Pierre Gaut to Dido Renoir, April 5, 1962, Jean Renoir Papers, Correspondence, Box 17, Folder 9.

70. Letter to Dido Renoir, February 23, 1962, Jean Renoir Papers, Correspondence, Box 17, Folder 7.

71. Letter to Dido Renoir, February 22, 1962, Jean Renoir Papers, Correspondence, Box 17, Folder 7.

72. Letter to Dido Renoir, February 9, 1962, Jean Renoir Papers, Correspondence, Box 17, Folder 7.

73. Letter to Dido Renoir, February 15, 1962, Jean Renoir Papers, Correspondence, Box 17, Folder 7.

74. *Le Figaro,* March 2, 1962.

75. Letter to Dido Renoir, March 2, 1962, Jean Renoir Papers, Correspondence, Box 17, Folder 8.

76. Letter to Dido Renoir, April 1, 1962, Jean Renoir Papers, Box 17, Folder 9.

77. Ibid.

78. Letter to Dido Renoir, March 24, 1962, Jean Renoir Papers, Correspondence, Box 17, Folder 8.

79. Ibid.

80. Letter from Ginette Doynel to Dido Renoir, April 13, 1962, Jean Renoir Papers, Correspondence, Box 17, Folder 9.

81. Letter from Ginette Doynel, May 4, 1962, Jean Renoir Papers, Correspondence, Box 17, Folder 10.

82. Telegram to Ginette Doynel, May 7, 1957, Jean Renoir Papers, Correspondence, Box 17, Folder 10.

83. Letter to Ginette Doynel, May 8, 1962, Jean Renoir Papers, Correspondence, Box 17, Folder 10.

84. Letter from Renée Lichtig, May 27, 1962, Jean Renoir Papers, Correspondence, Box 17, Folder 10.

85. Letter to Ginette Doynel, May 21, 1962, Jean Renoir Papers, Correspondence, Box 17, Folder 10.

86. Letter to Ginette Doynel, May 29, 1962, Jean Renoir Papers, Correspondence, Box 17, Folder 10.

87. Letter from Pierre Gaut, May 28, 1962, Fonds Pierre Gaut, Cinémathèque française.

88. Letter to Ginette Doynel, June 7, 1962, Jean Renoir Papers, Correspondence, Box 17, Folder 11.

89. Letter to Adry de Carbuccia, July 14, 1962, *Correspondance 1913–1978*.

90. Letter to Ginette Doynel, October 28, 1962, *Correspondance 1913–1978*.

91. *Les Lettres françaises*, June 5, 1962.

92. *Combat*, May 30, 1962.

93. Letter to Pierre Gaut, December 15, 1976, Jean Renoir Papers, Correspondence, Box 32, Folder 12.

94. Letter from Ginette Doynel, June 12, 1962, Jean Renoir Papers, Correspondence, Box 17, Folder 11.

95. Conversation with Jean Slade.

96. Jean Renoir Papers, Series V, Box 76, Folder 3.

97. "Various drafts and reworkings of *Au temps de mon père*," March 18, 1942–November 11, 1943, Jean Renoir Papers, Series V, Box 76, Folder 4.

98. Jean Renoir Papers, Series V, Box 76, Folder 8.

99. Jean Renoir Papers, Series V, Box 76, Folder 3.

100. *Life* 32, n° 20, May 19, 1952.

101. Ibid.

102. *Life* 32, n° 26, June 30, 1952.

103. Jean Renior, *Ma vie et mes films*, Flammarion, 1974.

104. Letter to Dido Renoir, March 2, 1962, Jean Renoir Papers, Correspondence, Box 17, Folder 8.

105. Letter to Dido Renoir, March 23, 1962, Jean Renoir Papers, Correspondence, Box 17, Folder 8.

106. Letter from Jack Cardiff, February 25, 1964, Jean Renoir Papers, Correspondence, Box 19, Folder 4.

107. Telegram from Ginette Doynel, June 16, 1963, Jean Renoir Papers, Correspondence, Box 18, Folder 12.

108. Letter to Dido Renoir, March 23, 1962, Jean Renoir Papers, Correspondence, Box 17, Folder 8.

109. Letter to Dido Renoir, February 15, 1962, *Correspondance 1913–1978*.

110. Letter to Dido Renoir, March 23, 1962, Jean Renoir Papers, Correspondence, Box 17, Folder 6.

111. Letter to Dido Renoir, April 10, 1962, Jean Renoir Papers, Correspondence, Box 17, Folder 7.

112. Letter to Dido Renoir, March 18, 1962, Jean Renoir Papers, Correspondence, Box 17, Folder 8.

113. Letter to Dido Renoir, April 3, 1962, Jean Renoir Papers, Correspondence, Box 17, Folder 9.

114. Letter from Pierre Braunberger, May 14, 1962, Jean Renoir Papers, Correspondence, Box 17, Folder 10.

115. Letter to Pierre Braunberger, June 5, 1962, Jean Renoir Papers, Correspondence, Box 17, Folder 11.

116. Letter from Paul Graetz, May 7, 1962, Jean Renoir Papers, Correspondence, Box 17, Folder 10.

117. Letter to Ginette Doynel, May 13, 1962, Jean Renoir Papers, Correspondence, Box 17, Folder 10.

118. Letter to Paul Graetz, May 13, 1962, Jean Renoir Papers, Correspondence, Box 17, Folder 10.

119. Letter from Paul Graetz, June 22, 1962, Jean Renoir Papers, Correspondence, Box 17, Folder 11.

120. Letter to Paul Graetz, July 14, 1962, Jean Renoir Papers, Correspondence, Box 17, Folder 12.

121. Letter to la Mostra de Venise, July 29, 1962, Jean Renoir Papers, Correspondence, Box 17, Folder 12.

122. Letter to Dido Renoir, March 16, 1962, Jean Renoir Papers, Correspondence, Box 17, Folder 8.

123. Letter to Ginette Doynel, July 3, 1964, Jean Renoir Papers, Correspondence, Box 19, Folder 11.

33. "I've Become a Museum Piece"

1. Elsa Lanchester, *Herself*, Michael Joseph Limited, 1983.

2. Letter from Jacques Becker, May 8, 1945, Jean Renoir Papers, Correspondence, Box 5, Folder 3.

3. Jean Renoir, "Jacques Becker ou une amitié," in Jean Queval, *Jacques Becker*, Seghers 1962, reprinted in *Le Passé vivant*, éditions Cahiers du cinéma, 1989.

4. Jean Renoir, *Ma vie et mes films*, Flammarion, 1974.

5. Ibid.

6. Letter to François Truffaut, *Correspondance 1913–1978*, Plon, 1998.

7. Letter to Jacques Becker, October 21, 1946, Jean Renoir Papers.

8. Letter to François Truffaut, *Correspondance 1913–1978*.

9. Antoine de Baecque and Serge Toubiana, *François Truffaut*, Gallimard, 1996.

10. Letter to Dido Renoir, January 24, 1962, *Correspondance 1913–1978*.

11. Jean Renoir, *Renoir*, Librairie Haohette, 1962; then *Pierre-Auguste Renoir, mon père*, Gallimard, Folio, 1981.

12. Letter to Dido Renoir, February 22, 1962, Jean Renoir Papers, Correspondence, Box 17, Folder 7.

13. Letter to Christine Burnier, December 2, 1963, *Correspondance 1913–1978*.

14. Paul Meurisse, *Les Éperons de la liberté*, Robert Laffont, 1979.

15. Letter from Pauline Kael, October 21, 1962, Jean Renoir Papers, Correspondence, Box 18, Folder 3.

16. Letter from Agnès Varda, October 7, 1964, Jean Renoir Papers, Correspondence, Box 20, Folder 3.

17. Letter from Dido Renoir to Ginette Doynel, October 24, 1964, Jean Renoir Papers, Correspondence, Box 17, Folder 12.

18. Letter to Ginette Doynel, July 21, 1962, Jean Renoir Papers, Correspondence, Box 17, Folder 12.

19. Letter to Ginette Doynel, July 27, 1962, Jean Renoir Papers, Correspondence, Box 17, Folder 12.

20. Letter to Christine Burnier, December 2, 1963, *Correspondance 1913–1978*.

21. Letter to Ginette Doynel, July 20, 1964, Jean Renoir Papers, Correspondence, Box 19, Folder 11.

22. Ibid.

23. Jean Renoir, *Œuvres de cinéma inédites*, edited by Claude Gauteur, Gallimard, 1991.

24. Letter from Pierre Braunberger, July 30, 1964, Jean Renoir Papers, Correspondence, Box 19, Folder 11.

25. Letter to Ginette Doynel, June 12, 1964, Jean Renoir Papers, Correspondence, Box 19, Folder 5.

26. Ibid.

27. Letter to Pierre Braunberger, July 20, 1964, Jean Renoir Papers, Correspondence, Box 19, Folder 11.

28. Letter to Ginette Doynel, June 12, 1963, Jean Renoir Papers, Correspondence, Box 18, Folder 11.

29. Letter from Vladimir Pozner, September 20, 1964, Jean Renoir Papers, Correspondence, Box 20, Folder 2.

30. Ibid.

31. Letter from Leslie Caron to Ginette Doynel, August 15, 1963, Jean Renoir Papers, Correspondence, Box 18, Folder 13.

32. Letter to Ginette Doynel, November 17, 1963, Jean Renoir Papers, Correspondence, Box 19, Folder 3.

33. Letter from Ginette Doynel, November 25, 1963, Jean Renoir Papers, Correspondence, Box 19, Folder 3.

34. Letter from Adry de Carbuccia, September 12, 1963, Jean Renoir Papers, Correspondence, Box 19, Folder 1.

35. Letter to Adry de Carbuccia, October 7, 1963, Jean Renoir Papers, Correspondence, Box 19, Folder 2.

36. Letter from Ginette Doynel, January 7, 1964, Jean Renoir Papers, Correspondence, Box 19, Folder 5.

37. Letter to Ginette Doynel, February 3, 1964, Jean Renoir Papers, Correspondence, Box 19, Folder 6.

38. Letter to Vladimir Pozner, September 26, 1966, Jean Renoir Papers, Correspondence, Box 21, Folder 12.

39. Letter to Ginette Doynel, February 3, 1964, Jean Renoir Papers, Correspondence, Box 19, Folder 6.

40. *Aspects of Love,* 57 pages, Jean Renoir Papers, Production Files, Box 39, Folder 4.

41. Letter from Jean Renoir to Ginette Doynel, May 23, 1963, Jean Renoir Papers, Correspondence, Box 18, Folder 10.

42. Ibid.

43. Letter from Ginette Doynel, September 7, 1963, Jean Renoir Papers, Correspondence, Box 19, Folder 1.

44. Letter from Ginette Doynel, September 14, 1963, Jean Renoir Papers, Correspondence, Box 19, Folder 1.

45. *L'Amour et la Grâce, Mémoires imaginaires,* December 7, 1952, Jean Renoir Papers, Production Files, Box 58, Folder 3.

46. *Le Bonheur, Mesdames,* 3 pages, incomplete, January 5, 1963, Jean Renoir Papers, Production Files, Box 58, Folder 1.

47. *Au bonheur, Mesdames,* synopsis, 18 pages, March 18 19, 1963, Jean Renoir Papers, Production Files, Box 58, Folder 1.

48. Letter to Ginette Doynel, February 22, 1964, *Correspondance 1913-1978.*

49. Letter to Ginette Doynel, April 27, 1964, *Correspondance 1913-1978.* Letter from Dido Renoir to Virginia Rowe (Austin Riggs Center), May 6, 1964, Jean Renoir Papers, Correspondence, Box 19, Folder 9.

50. Letter to Randolph Weaver, December 29, 1964, Jean Renoir Papers, Correspondence, Box 20, Folder 5.

51. Letter to Klaus Piper, R. Piper & Co., Munich, September 22, 1964, *Correspondance 1913-1978.*

52. *Georges,* 39 handwritten pages, together with 174 handwritten pages dated summer 1964, Jean Renoir Papers, Production Files, Box 58, Folder 4.

53. Conversation with Hugues Desalle, phonograph record *Français de notre temps, Hommes d'aujourd'hui,* n° 52.

54. Letter to Randolph Weaver, December 29, 1964, Jean Renoir Papers, Correspondence, Box 20, Folder 5.

55. Letter to Ginette Doynel, May 7, 1965, Jean Renoir Papers, Correspondence, Box 20, Folder 10.

56. Letter to Ginette Doynel, May 18, 1965, Jean Renoir Papers, Correspondence, Box 20, Folder 10.

57. Letter from Robert Knittel, June 17, 1965, Jean Renoir Papers, Correspondence, Box 20, Folder 11.

58. Letter from Ginette Doynel, July 12, 1965, Jean Renoir Papers, Correspondence, Box 20, Folder 12.

59. Letter to Robert Knittel, September 21, 1965, Jean Renoir Papers, Correspondence, Box 20, Folder 14.

60. Ibid.

61. Letter from Thérèse Léon, service de presse Gallimard, November 2, 1965, Jean Renoir Papers, Correspondence, Box 21, Folder 2.

62. Letter to Thérèse Léon, November 6, 1965, Jean Renoir Papers, Correspondence, Box 21, Folder 2.

63. Letter to Claude Gallimard, December 22, 1965, Jean Renoir Papers, Correspondence, Box 21, Folder 3.

64. Letter from Claude Gallimard, December 22, 1965, Jean Renoir Papers, Correspondence, Box 21, Folder 3.

65. Letter to Thérèse Léon, November 29, 1965, Jean Renoir Papers, Correspondence, Box 21, Folder 2.

66. Roger Grenier, *Instantanés,* Gallimard, 2007.

67. Letter from Ginette Doynel, March 15, 1966, Jean Renoir Papers, Correspondence, Box 21, Folder 6.

68. Letter to Ginette Doynel, March 28, 1966, Jean Renoir Papers, Correspondence, Box 21, Folder 6.

69. Letter to Ginette Doynel, April 7, 1966, Jean Renoir Papers, Correspondence, Box 21, Folder 7.

70. Letter to Ginette Doynel, November 15, 1966, Jean Renoir Papers, Correspondence, Box 22, Folder 2.

71. Letter from François Truffaut, June 30, 1966, Jean Renoir Papers, Correspondence, Box 21, Folder 9.

72. Letter to Ginette Doynel, May 18, 1967, Jean Renoir Papers, Correspondence, Box 22, Folder 8.

73. Letter to Ginette Doynel, May 24, 1967, Jean Renoir Papers, Correspondence, Box 22, Folder 8.

74. *The Notebooks of Captain Jones* by Jean Renoir, Screenplay by Clarence Marks, 47 pages, William Wyler Papers, Box 35, Folder 5.

75. Wes Herschensohn, *Resurrection in Cannes, the Making of* The Picasso Summer, A. S. Barnes and Co., Thomas Yoseloff Ltd., 1979.

76. Letter to Ginette Doynel, November 20, 1964, Jean Renoir Papers, Correspondence, Box 20, Folder 4.

77. Letter from Ginette Doynel, November 30, 1964, Jean Renoir Papers, Correspondence, Box 20, Folder 4.

78. Letter from Tony Curtis, December 30, 1964, Jean Renoir Papers, Correspondence, Box 20, Folder 5.

79. Letter from Tony Curtis, February 14, 1967, Jean Renoir Papers, Correspondence, Box 22, Folder 4.

80. Letter to Ginette Doynel, February 1, 1965, Jean Renoir Papers, Correspondence, Box 20, Folder 7.

81. Conversations with Warren Beatty, BFI, in Suzanne Finstad, *Warren Beatty: A Private Man,* Aurum, 2005.

82. Ibid.

83. Letter to Ginette Doynel, August 27, 1965, *Correspondance 1913–1978*.

84. Letter from Ginette Doynel, September 11, 1965, Jean Renoir Papers, Correspondence, Box 20, Folder 14.

85. Letter from Leslie Caron, September 20, 1965, Jean Renoir Papers, Correspondence, Box 20, Folder 14.

86. Letter to Ginette Doynel, August 27, 1965, *Correspondance 1913–1978*.

87. Letter from Ginette Doynel, September 23, 1965, Jean Renoir Papers, Correspondence, Box 20, Folder 14.

88. Conversation with Leslie Caron.

89. Letter to Leslie Caron, September 30, 1965, Jean Renoir Papers, Correspondence, Box 20, Folder 14.

90. Ibid.

91. Warren Beatty Transcript, October 15, 1990, Brunetti Collection, Margaret Herrick Library, Academy of Motion Picture Arts and Science, Beverly Hills, in Suzanne Finstad, *Warren Beatty: A Private Man.*

92. Conversation with Leslie Caron.

93. Letter to Claude Renoir, August 3, 1965, Jean Renoir Papers, Correspondence, Box 20, Folder 13.

94. Letter to Ginette Doynel, August 3, 1965, Jean Renoir Papers, Correspondence, Box 20, Folder 13.

95. Letter to Ginette Doynel, August 12, 1965, Jean Renoir Papers, Correspondence, Box 20, Folder 13.

96. Letter to Ginette Doynel, August 20, 1965, *Correspondance 1913–1978*.

97. Letter to Ginette Doynel, September 8, 1965, Jean Renoir Papers, Correspondence, Box 20, Folder 14.

98. Letter to Pierre Braunberger, October 15, 1965, Jean Renoir Papers, Correspondence, Box 21, Folder 1.

99. Letter from Pierre Braunberger, October 4, 1965, Jean Renoir Papers, Correspondence, Box 21, Folder 1.

100. Letter to Pierre Braunberger, October 9, 1965, Jean Renoir Papers, Correspondence, Box 21, Folder 1.

101. Letter to Ginette Doynel, October 12, 1965, Jean Renoir Papers, Correspondence, Box 21, Folder 1.

102. Letter to Ginette Doynel, October 15, 1965, Jean Renoir Papers, Correspondence, Box 21, Folder 1.

103. Letter to Micheline Rozan, November 18, 1965, Jean Renoir Papers, Correspondence, Box 21, Folder 2.

104. Letter to Ginette Doynel, December 28, 1965, Jean Renoir Papers, Correspondence, Box 21, Folder 3.

105. Letter to Charles Sachs, July 13, 1967, Jean Renoir Papers, Correspondence, Box 21, Folder 3.

106. Letter from Ginette Doynel, March 22, 1967, Jean Renoir Papers, Correspondence, Box 22, Folder 6.

107. Letter to Ginette Doynel, August 8, 1966, Jean Renoir Papers, Correspondence, Box 21, Folder 11.

108. Letter from Ginette Doynel, August 13, 1966, Jean Renoir Papers, Correspondence, Box 21, Folder 11.

109. Letter from John Van Eyssen, September 12, 1966, Jean Renoir Papers, Correspondence, Box 21, Folder 12.

110. Letter from Ginette Doynel, March 3, 1967, Jean Renoir Papers, Correspondence, Box 22, Folder 6.

111. Letter to Ginette Doynel, March 8, 1967, Jean Renoir Papers, Correspondence, Box 22, Folder 6.

112. Letter to Ginette Doynel, June 30, 1967, Jean Renoir Papers, Correspondence, Box 22, Folder 9.

113. Letter to Pierre Gaut, October 26, 1965, Fonds Pierre Gaut, Cinémathèque française.

114. Letter to Pierre Gaut, May 30, 1976, Jean Renoir Papers, Correspondence, Box 32, Folder 2.

115. Letter to Ginette Doynel, April 24, 1965, Jean Renoir Papers, Correspondence, Box 20, Folder 9.

116. Letter to Ginette Doynel, April 28, 1965, Jean Renoir Papers, Correspondence, Box 20, Folder 9.

117. Letter to Ginette Doynel, June 21, 1965, Jean Renoir Papers, Correspondence, Box 20, Folder 11.

118. Letter to Ginette Doynel, June 23, 1965, Jean Renoir Papers, Correspondence, Box 20, Folder 11.

119. Letter to Pierre Braunberger, December 28, 1965, Jean Renoir Papers, Correspondence, Box 21, Folder 3.

120. Letters to Pierre Braunberger on November 29 and December 28, 1965, Jean Renoir Papers, Correspondence, Box 21, Folders 2 and 3.

121. Letter to Ginette Doynel, January 2, 1966, Jean Renoir Papers, Correspondence, Box 22, Folder 5.

122. Draft of a letter to Jean Gabin, February 17, 1966, Jean Renoir Papers, Correspondence, Box 21, Folder 5.

123. Letter from Ginette Doynel, March 2, 1966, Jean Renoir Papers, Correspondence, Box 21, Folder 6.

124. Letter to B. Reed, December 20, 1965, Jean Renoir Papers, Correspondence, Box 21, Folder 3.

125. Postcard from Henry Miller, December 1965, Jean Renoir Papers, Correspondence, Box 21, Folder 3.

126. Brassaï, *Henry Miller, rocher heureux,* Gallimard, 1978.

127. Letter from Henry Miller, May 26, 1972, *Jean Renoir: Letters,* edited by Lorraine Lo Bianco and David Thompson, Faber and Faber, 1994.

128. Telegram from Ginette Doynel, January 15, 1966, Jean Renoir Papers, Correspondence, Box 21, Folder 4.

129. Menu from the restaurant Sébillon, January 17, 1966, Jean Renoir Papers, Correspondence, Box 21, Folder 4.

130. Letter of January 19, 1966, Jean Renoir Papers, Correspondence, Box 21, Folder 4.

131. Handwritten letter from Marcel Pagnol, February 17, 1966, Jean Renoir Papers, Correspondence, Box 21, Folder 5.

132. Letter to Randolph Weaver, May 24, 1965, *Correspondance 1913–1978.*

133. Letter to Ginette Doynel, April 1, 1965, Jean Renoir Papers, Correspondence, Box 20, Folder 9.

134. Letter to Claude Condamine, April 15, 1966, Jean Renoir Papers, Correspondence, Box 20, Folder 9.

135. Letter from Ginette Doynel to Dido Renoir, July 6, 1966, Jean Renoir Papers, Correspondence, Box 21, Folder 10.

136. Letter from Pierre Braunberger to Ginette Doynel, September 12, 1966, Jean Renoir Papers, Correspondence, Box 21, Folder 12.

137. Letter from Ginette Doynel to Dido Renoir, July 9, 1966, Jean Renoir Papers, Correspondence, Box 21, Folder 10.

138. Ibid.

139. Henry Chapier, "La France renvoie scandaleusement Jean Renoir aux États-Unis," *Combat,* August 1, 1966.

140. Letter from André Holleaux, July 30, 1966, Jean Renoir Papers, Correspondence, Box 21, Folder 10.

141. Letter to Ginette Doynel, August 8, 1966, Jean Renoir Papers, Correspondence, Box 21, Folder 11.

142. Ibid.

143. Letter from Ginette Doynel, August 13, 1966, Jean Renoir Papers, Correspondence, Box 21, Folder 11.

144. Letter to Maurice-Jacques Keller, September 6, 1966, *Correspondance 1913–1978.*

145. Letter to Charles Spaak, August 9, 1966, Jean Renoir Papers, Correspondence, Box 21, Folder 11.

146. Letter to Paul Meurisse, September 2, 1966, Jean Renoir Papers, Correspondence, Box 21, Folder 11.

147. Letter to Ginette Doynel, September 26, 1966, Jean Renoir Papers, Correspondence, Box 21, Folder 11.

148. Letter to Randolph Weaver, September 22, 1966, Jean Renoir Papers, Correspondence, Box 21, Folder 11.

149. Letter from Ginette Doynel, December 9, 1966, Jean Renoir Papers, Correspondence, Box 22, Folder 3.

150. Ibid.

151. Letter from Ginette Doynel, December 16, 1966, Jean Renoir Papers, Correspondence, Box 22, Folder 3.

152. Letter from Ginette Doynel, January 13, 1967, Jean Renoir Papers, Correspondence, Box 22, Folder 4.

153. Letter from Claude Brulé, February 13, 1967, Jean Renoir Papers, Correspondence, Box 22, Folder 4.

154. Letter from Roger Grenier, April 21, 1967, Jean Renoir Papers, Correspondence, Box 22, Folder 7.

155. Letter to Roger Grenier, May 2, 1967, Jean Renoir Papers, Correspondence, Box 22, Folder 7.

156. Letter to Ginette Doynel, August 31, 1967, Jean Renoir Papers, Correspondence, Box 22, Folder 10.

157. Ibid.

158. Ibid.

159. Conversation with Peter Renoir.

160. Conversation with Jean Slade.

161. Conversation with Pierre Rissient.

162. Letter from Ginette Doynel, June 5, 1967, Jean Renoir Papers, Correspondence, Box 22, Folder 10.

163. Ibid.

164. Letter to Ginette Doynel, June 9, 1967, Jean Renoir Papers, Correspondence, Box 22, Folder 10.

165. Interviewed by Alain Liatard, *La Vie Lyonnaise*, n° 160, March 15, 1968.

166. Conversation with Freddy Buache.

167. Letter to Georges Simenon, May 12, 1969, Fonds Simenon de l'université de Liège, cited by Pierre Assouline, *Simenon*, Julliard, 1992.

168. Jean Renoir, *Ma vie et mes films*.

169. *Jean Renoir: An Interview*, introduction by Nick Frankagis, Green Integer Books, 1998.

170. Eugène Lourié, *My Work in Films*, Harcourt, Brace, Jovanovich, 1985.

171. Conversation with Leslie Caron.

172. *Jean Renoir: Julienne et son amour*, edited by Claude Gauteur, Henri Veyrier, 1978.

173. Conversation with Jean-Pierre Mithois, *Le Figaro*, July 17, 1968, cited by Claude Gauteur, *Jean Renoir: Julienne et son amour*.

174. Conversation with Guy Braucourt, *Les Lettres françaises*, October 8, 1969, cited by Claude Gauteur, *Jean Renoir: Julienne et son amour*.

175. Conversations with Alain Renoir.

176. Conversation with Jacques Rivette and François Truffaut, *Cahiers du cinéma*, n° 78, Noël 1957.

177. Ibid.

178. Conversation with Hugues Desalle, phonograph record *Français de notre temps, Hommes d'aujourd'hui*, n° 52.

179. Letter to Ginette Doynel, May 16, 1968, *Correspondance 1913–1978*.

180. Letter to Ginette Doynel, May 9, 1968, *Correspondance 1913–1978*.

181. Letter from Ginette Doynel, April 26, 1968, Jean Renoir Papers, Correspondence, Box 23, Folder 7.

182. Letter from Ginette Doynel, June 17, 1968, Jean Renoir Papers, Correspondence, Box 23, Folder 9.

183. Letter from Henri Langlois, April 27, 1968, Jean Renoir Papers, Correspondence, Box 23, Folder 7.

184. Letter to Henri Langlois, June 15, 1968, *Correspondance 1913–1978*.

185. Letter from Ginette Doynel, May 7, 1968, Jean Renoir Papers, Correspondence, Box 23, Folder 8.

186. Letter from Ginette Doynel, December 31, 1964, Jean Renoir Papers, Correspondence, Box 20, Folder 5.

187. Letter to Ginette Doynel, January 12, 1965, Jean Renoir Papers, Correspondence, Box 20, Folder 6.

188. Letter to Ginette Doynel, January 16, 1965, Jean Renoir Papers, Correspondence, Box 20, Folder 6.

189. Letter from Dido Renoir, January 13, 1962, Jean Renoir Papers, Correspondence, Box 17, Folder 6.

190. Letter to Ginette Doynel, March 8, 1973, Jean Renoir Papers, Correspondence, Box 28, Folder 11.

191. Letter to Ginette Doynel, February 4, 1977, Jean Renoir Papers, Correspondence, Box 33, Folder 1.

192. Letter to Ginette Doynel, May 9, 1968, *Correspondance 1913–1978*.

193. Letter from Ginette Doynel, May 9, 1968, Jean Renoir Papers, Correspondence, Box 23, Folder 8.

194. Ibid.

195. Letter to Ginette Doynel, May 15, 1968, *Correspondance 1913–1978*.

196. Letter to Ginette Doynel, May 20, 1968, *Correspondance 1913–1978.*

197. Telegram from Ginette Doynel, June 14, 1968, Jean Renoir Papers, Correspondence, Box 23, Folder 9.

198. Letter to Ginette Doynel, May 20, 1968, *Correspondance 1913–1978.*

199. Letter to Ginette Doynel, June 16, 1968, *Correspondance 1913–1978.*

200. Ibid.

201. Letter from Ginette Doynel, July 17, 1968, Jean Renoir Papers, Correspondence, Box 23, Folder 10.

202. Letter to Ginette Doynel, July 19, 1968, Jean Renoir Papers, Correspondence, Box 23, Folder 10.

203. Letter to Ginette Doynel, July 22, 1968, Jean Renoir Papers, Correspondence, Box 23, Folder 10.

204. Letter to Ginette Doynel, July 30, 1968, Jean Renoir Papers, Correspondence, Box 23, Folder 10.

205. *Los Angeles Times,* August 19, 1968.

206. Letter to Ginette Doynel, August 19, 1968, *Correspondance 1913–1978.*

207. Ibid.

208. Ibid.

209. Letter to Giulio Macchi, February 25, 1958, Cinémathèque française.

210. Letter to Giulio Macchi, March 1964, Cinémathèque française.

211. Letter from Giulio Macchi, March 3, 1964, Cinémathèque française.

212. Letter from Ginette Doynel to Dido Renoir, September 22, 1968, Jean Renoir Papers, Correspondence, Box 23, Folder 12.

213. Jean Renoir, *"Une histoire immortelle,"* 1968, reprinted in *Le Passé vivant,* Éditions Cahiers du cinéma, 1989.

214. Letter to Jeanne Moreau, March 2, 1976, Jean Renoir Papers, Correspondence, Box 32, Folder 3.

215. Letter from Orson Welles, May 7, 1971, Jean Renoir Papers, Correspondence, Box 26, Folder 8.

216. Letter to Orson Welles, May 8, 1971, Jean Renoir Papers, Correspondence, Box 26, Folder 8.

217. Conversation with Françoise Widhoff.

218. Orson Welles, "Jean Renoir, the Greatest of All Directors," *Los Angeles Times,* February 16, 1979.

219. Letter to Pierre Rissient, February 12, 1969, Jean Renoir Papers, Correspondence, Box 24, Folder 2.

220. Letter from Ginette Doynel to Dido Renoir, July 18, 1969, Jean Renoir Papers, Correspondence, Box 24, Folder 7.

221. Letter from Dido Renoir to Ginette Doynel, July 24, 1969, Jean Renoir Papers, Correspondence, Box 24, Folder 7.

222. Conversation with Claude Gauteur.

223. Conversation with Jean Slade.

224. Letter from Dido Renoir, May 16, 1969, Jean Renoir Papers, Correspondence, Box 24, Folder 5.

225. Letter from Ginette Doynel to Dido Renoir, July 18, 1969, Jean Renoir Papers, Correspondence, Box 24, Folder 7.

226. Letter from Ginette Doynel to Dido Renoir, August 20, 1969, Jean Renoir Papers, Correspondence, Box 24, Folder 8.

227. Letter from Dido Renoir, August 1, 1969, Jean Renoir Papers, Correspondence, Box 24, Folder 8.

228. Letter from Dido Renoir, August 9, 1969, Jean Renoir Papers, Correspondence, Box 24, Folder 8.

229. "Projets divers," undated, Jean Renoir Papers, Production Files, Box 51, Folder 13.

230. Letter to Pierre Gaut, December 16, 1966, Fonds Pierre Gaut, Cinémathèque française.

231. Éric Rohmer, *"Le Petit Théâtre de Jean Renoir,"* *Cinéma 79,* n° 244, April 1979, reprinted in Éric Rohmer, *Le Goût de la beauté,* texts collected and presented by Jean Narboni, Petite Bibliothèque des Cahiers du cinéma, 1984.

232. Ibid.

233. *Le Roi d'Yvetot,* song by Pierre Jean de Béranger (1813).

234. Conversation with Françoise Arnoul.

235. Conversation with Dominique Labourier.

34. Big "Snowflasks" Are Falling . . .

1. Untitled, undated, Jean Renoir Papers, Production Files, Box 71, Folder 7.

2. Ibid.

3. Letter to Klaus Piper, R. Piper & Co., Munich, September 22, 1964, *Correspondance 1913–1978*, Plon, 1998.

4. Letter to Ginette Doynel, January 3, 1966, Jean Renoir Papers, Correspondence, Box 21, Folder 4.

5. *Comment faire un film*, 8 pages, May 5, 1963, Jean Renoir Papers, Production Files, Box 72, Folder 8.

6. One hundred ten handwritten pages, September 5, 1967, Jean Renoir Papers, Production Files, Box 72, Folder 3.

7. Notebook of handwritten notes, January 5, 1970, Jean Renoir Papers, Production Files, Box 71, Folder 12.

8. Notebook, *Réflexions, souvenirs d'un faiseur de films*, Sunday, February 24, 1968, Jean Renoir Papers, Production Files, Box 51, Folder 20.

9. Jean Renoir Papers, Production Files, Box 69, Folders 2, 3, 4.

10. May 14, 1973, Jean Renoir Papers, Production Files, Box 69, Folder 5.

11. Five pages, February 22, 1972, Jean Renoir Papers, Production Files, Box 72, Folder 10.

12. Jean Renoir Papers, Production Files, Box 72, Folder 8.

13. Conversation with Nick Frangakis.

14. Ibid.

15. Letter from Ginette Doynel, May 13, 1972, Jean Renoir Papers, Correspondence, Box 27, Folder 10.

16. Letter from Dido Renoir to Ginette Doynel, July 25, 1972, Jean Renoir Papers, Correspondence, Box 28, Folder 2.

17. Letter from Dido Renoir to Ginette Doynel, August 8, 1973, Jean Renoir Papers, Correspondence, Box 28, Folder 3.

18. Letter from Dido Renoir to Ginette Doynel, August 20, 1972, Jean Renoir Papers, Correspondence, Box 28, Folder 3.

19. Letter from Dido Renoir to Ginette Doynel, September 5, 1972, Jean Renoir Papers, Correspondence, Box 28, Folder 4.

20. Letter from Dido Renoir to Ginette Doynel, September 11, 1972, Jean Renoir Papers, Correspondence, Box 28, Folder 4.

21. Letter from Ginette Doynel to Dido Renoir, September 19, 1972, Jean Renoir Papers, Correspondence, Box 28, Folder 4.

22. Letter from Ginette Doynel, December 23, 1971, Jean Renoir Papers, Correspondence, Box 27, Folder 4.

23. Letter to Ginette Doynel, April 17, 1972, Jean Renoir Papers, Correspondence, Box 27, Folder 9.

24. Letter from Dido Renoir to Ginette Doynel, September 10, 1972, Jean Renoir Papers, Correspondence, Box 28, Folder 4.

25. Letter to Ginette Doynel, September 28, 1972, Jean Renoir Papers, Correspondence, Box 28, Folder 4.

26. Letter to Ginette Doynel, October 19, 1972, Jean Renoir Papers, Correspondence, Box 28, Folder 5.

27. Ibid.

28. Letter from Dido Renoir to Ginette Doynel, September 29, 1972, Jean Renoir Papers, Correspondence, Box 28, Folder 4.

29. Letter from Coudert Frères to Sidney Harmon, January 6, 1959, Jean Renoir Papers, Correspondence, Box 15, Folder 6.

30. Letter from Jeanne Moreau, August 21, 1972 at 6:00 p.m., Jean Renoir Papers, Correspondence, Box 28, Folder 3.

31. Telegram from Simone Signoret and Yves Montand, December 24, 1972, Jean Renoir Papers, Correspondence, Box 28, Folder 7.

32. Letter from François Truffaut, January 22, 1973, Jean Renoir Papers, Correspondence, Box 28, Folder 9.

33. Letter from François Truffaut, November 13, 1970, Jean Renoir Papers, Correspondence, Box 24, Folder 11.

34. Conversation with Pierre Philippe, in *Cinéma 61*, n° 57, June 1961.

35. Letter from Dido Renoir to Ginette Doynel, February 1973, Jean Renoir Papers, Correspondence, Box 28, Folder 10.

36. Letter to Ginette Doynel, February 3, 1973, Jean Renoir Papers, Correspondence, Box 28, Folder 10.

37. Letter from Robert Knittel, March 20, 1973, Jean Renoir Papers, Correspondence, Box 28, Folder 11.

38. Letter to Ginette Doynel, March 14, 1973, Jean Renoir Papers, Correspondence, Box 28, Folder 11.

39. Letter to Robert Knittel, March 24, 1973, Jean Renoir Papers, Correspondence, Box 28, Folder 11.

40. Letter to Ginette Doynel, March 19, 1973, Jean Renoir Papers, Correspondence, Box 28, Folder 11.

41. Letter to Ginette Doynel, June 8, 1973, *Correspondance 1913–1978*.

42. Letter from Dido Renoir to Ginette Doynel, April 7, 1973, Jean Renoir Papers, Correspondence, Box 29, Folder 1.

43. Letter from Dido Renoir to Ginette Doynel, April 11, 1973, Jean Renoir Papers, Correspondence, Box 29, Folder 1.

44. Ibid.

45. Letter from Dido Renoir to Ginette Doynel, August 1973, Jean Renoir Papers, Correspondence, Box 29, Folder 5.

46. Letter from Ginette Doynel to Dido Renoir, April 30, 1973, Jean Renoir Papers, Correspondence, Box 29, Folder 1.

47. Letter from Dido Renoir to Ginette Doynel, April 19, 1973, Jean Renoir Papers, Correspondence, Box 29, Folder 1.

48. *Souvenirs incomplets*, 163 typed pages, annotated and corrected, January–July 1972, Jean Renoir Papers, Production Files, Box 71, Folder 2.

49. Louis Skorecki, "Rivette and Renoir vont en bateau," *Libération*, September 19, 1994.

50. Letter to Ginette Doynel, June 22, 1973, *Correspondance 1913–1978*.

51. *Souvenirs incomplets*.

52. Letter from François Truffaut, March 1–3, 1975, *Correspondance 1913–1978*.

53. Letter from François Truffaut to Ginette Doynel, July 6, 1973, Jean Renoir Papers, Correspondence, Box 29, Folder 4.

54. Letter to Ginette Doynel, July 6, 1973, Jean Renoir Papers, Correspondence, Box 29, Folder 4.

55. Conversation with Paolo Barzman.

56. Kira Appel, *France-Soir*, July 30, 1973.

57. Letter from Gaston Gallimard, September 12, 1973, Jean Renoir Papers, Correspondence, Box 29, Folder 6.

58. Letter to Ginette Doynel, August 10, 1973, Jean Renoir Papers, Correspondence, Box 29, Folder 5.

59. Letter from François Truffaut, September 13, 1973, Jean Renoir Papers, Correspondence, Box 29, Folder 6.

60. Letter to Ginette Doynel, November 1, 1973, Jean Renoir Papers, Correspondence, Box 29, Folder 8.

61. Letter to Ginette Doynel, October 20, 1973, Jean Renoir Papers, Correspondence, Box 29, Folder 7.

62. Ibid.

63. Letter from Ginette Doynel, October 25, 1973, Jean Renoir Papers, Correspondence, Box 29, Folder 7.

64. Letter from Ginette Doynel, June 15, 1973, Jean Renoir Papers, Correspondence, Box 29, Folder 3.

65. Letter from Ginette Doynel, September 21, 1973, Jean Renoir Papers, Correspondence, Box 29, Folder 6.

66. Letter to Ginette Doynel, September 27, 1973, Jean Renoir Papers, Correspondence, Box 29, Folder 6.

67. Ibid.

68. Letter from Ginette Doynel, October 3, 1973, Jean Renoir Papers, Correspondence, Box 29, Folder 7.

69. Letter to Ginette Doynel, October 20, 1973, Jean Renoir Papers, Correspondence, Box 29, Folder 7.

70. Letter from Ginette Doynel, November 8, 1973, Jean Renoir Papers, Correspondence, Box 29, Folder 8.

71. *Souvenirs incomplets*, typed treatment, in French, Jean Renoir Papers, Production Files, Box 68, Folder 1.

72. Letter from Ginette Doynel, November 8, 1973, Jean Renoir Papers, Correspondence, Box 29, Folder 8.

73. Letter from Ginette Doynel, November 16, 1973, Jean Renoir Papers, Correspondence, Box 29, Folder 8.

74. Letter from François Truffaut, December 1, 1973, Jean Renoir Papers, Correspondence, Box 29, Folder 9.

75. Letter from Ginette Doynel, December 6, 1973, Jean Renoir Papers, Correspondence, Box 29, Folder 9.

76. Letter to Ginette Doynel, December 17, 1973, Jean Renoir Papers, Correspondence, Box 29, Folder 9.

77. Telegram from Yves Montand and Simone Signoret, December 24, 1973, Jean Renoir Papers, Correspondence, Box 29, Folder 9.

78. Letter to François Truffaut, February 27, 1974, *Correspondance 1913–1978*.

79. Letter from Claude Gallimard, January 7, 1974, Jean Renoir Papers, Correspondence, Box 29, Folder 10.

80. Letter from Ginette Doynel, January 12, 1974, Jean Renoir Papers, Correspondence, Box 29, Folder 10.

81. Letter from Ginette Doynel, January 23, 1974, Jean Renoir Papers, Correspondence, Box 29, Folder 10.

82. Letter from Ginette Doynel, January 25, 1974, Jean Renoir Papers, Correspondence, Box 29, Folder 10.

83. Letter from Ginette Doynel, February 22, 1974, Jean Renoir Papers, Correspondence, Box 30, Folder 1.

84. Letter from Ginette Doynel, June 11, 1974, Jean Renoir Papers, Correspondence, Box 30, Folder 5.

85. Letter from Ginette Doynel, July 11, 1974, Jean Renoir Papers, Correspondence, Box 30, Folder 6.

86. Letter from Ginette Doynel, June 30, 1976, Jean Renoir Papers, Correspondence, Box 32, Folder 4.

87. Letter from François Truffaut, November 13, 1975, Jean Renoir Papers, Correspondence, Box 31, Folder 9.

88. Letter from Henri Flammarion, March 29, 1974, Jean Renoir Papers, Correspondence, Box 30, Folder 2.

89. Letter to Ginette Doynel, April 28, 1974, Jean Renoir Papers, Correspondence, Box 30, Folder 3.

90. Letter to François Truffaut, April 29, 1974, Jean Renoir Papers, Correspondence, Box 30, Folder 3.

91. Letter from Ginette Doynel, May 3, 1974, Jean Renoir Papers, Correspondence, Box 30, Folder 4.

92. Letter from François Truffaut, May 7, 1974, Jean Renoir Papers, Correspondence, Box 30, Folder 4.

93. Letter to Michael Bessie, June 13, 1974, Jean Renoir Papers, Correspondence, Box 30, Folder 4.

94. *Le Figaro*, June 4 and 5, 1974.

95. François Truffaut, "Les Cinémémoires de Jean Renoir," *Le Monde*, June 13, 1974.

96. Ibid.

97. Letter from Ginette Doynel, June 6, 1974, Jean Renoir Papers, Correspondence, Box 30, Folder 6.

98. Letter from Dido Renoir to Ginette Doynel, April 24, 1974, Jean Renoir Papers, Correspondence, Box 30, Folder 3.

99. Ibid.

100. Letter from Dido Renoir to Ginette Doynel, undated, circa May or June 1974, Jean Renoir Papers, Correspondence, Box 30, Folder 4.

101. Letter to Norman Denny, July 28, 1974, Jean Renoir Papers, Correspondence, Box 30, Folder 8.

102. Letter from Dido Renoir to Anne de Saint-Phalle, September 29, 1974, Jean Renoir Papers, Correspondence, Box 30, Folder 8.

103. Letter from Dido Renoir to Anne de Saint-Phalle, September 27, 1974, Jean Renoir Papers, Correspondence, Box 30, Folder 8.

104. Letter from Dido Renoir to Anne de Saint-Phalle, September 29, 1974, Jean Renoir Papers, Correspondence, Box 30, Folder 8.

105. Letter from Dido Renoir to Anne de Saint-Phalle, October 5, 1974, Jean Renoir Papers, Correspondence, Box 30, Folder 9.

106. Telegram from Simone Signoret and Yves Montand, December 24, 1974, Jean Renoir Papers, Correspondence, Box 30, Folder 11.

107. Letter from Dido Renoir to Herman G. Weinberg, January 9, 1975, Jean Renoir Papers, Correspondence, Box 30, Folder 13.

108. Letter from Dido Renoir to Alexander Sesonske, January 24, 1975, Jean Renoir Papers, Correspondence, Box 30, Folder 13.

109. Letter from Dido Renoir to Anne de Saint-Phalle, January 27, 1975, Jean Renoir Papers, Correspondence, Box 30, Folder 13.

110. Letter from Dido Renoir to Robert Knittel, February 5, 1975, Jean Renoir Papers, Correspondence, Box 31, Folder 1.

111. Letter to François Truffaut, February 6, 1975, Jean Renoir Papers, Correspondence, Box 31, Folder 1.

112. "Special Oscars to Renoir, Hawks and *Earthquake*," *Variety*, February 6, 1975.

113. Mason Wiley and Damien Bona, *Inside Oscar: The Unofficial History of the Academy Awards*, Ballantine Books, 1986.

114. Telegram from Simone Signoret and Yves Montand, April 10, 1975, Jean Renoir Papers, Correspondence, Box 31, Folder 3.

115. Letter to Janine Bazin, July 1, 1975, Jean Renoir Papers, Correspondence, Box 31, Folder 6.

116. Ibid.

117. Letter to Claude and Évangèle Renoir, October 21, 1975, Jean Renoir Papers, Correspondence, Box 31, Folder 9.

118. Jean-Pierre Thibaudat, "Dans la maison de Jean," *Libération*, July 16, 1984.

119. Conversation with Paolo Barzman.

120. Conversation with Christian Tual.

121. Letter to François Truffaut, November 19, 1975, Jean Renoir Papers, Correspondence, Box 31, Folder 10.

122. Ibid.

123. Letter to Simone Signoret, November 7, 1976, Jean Renoir Papers, Correspondence, Box 32, Folder 11.

124. Conversation with Christian Tual.

125. Letter from Anne de Saint-Phalle, October 29, 1975, Jean Renoir Papers, Correspondence, Box 31, Folder 9.

126. Jean-Claude Brialy, *Le Ruisseau des singes*, Robert Laffont, 2000.

127. Letter to Anne de Saint-Phalle, January 19, 1976, Jean Renoir Papers, Correspondence, Box 32, Folder 1.

128. Françoise Giroud, *Leçons particulières*, Fayard, 1990.

129. Letter to Ginette Doynel, August 19, 1966, Jean Renoir Papers, Correspondence, Box 21, Folder 11.

130. Letter to Pierre Gaut, December 11, 1963, Fonds Pierre Gaut, Cinémathèque française.

131. Letter from Pierre Gaut, January 7, 1964, Jean Renoir Papers, Correspondence, Box 19, Folder 5.

132. Letter from Christian Tual to Dido Renoir, April 27, 1976, Jean Renoir Papers, Correspondence, Box 32, Folder 4.

133. Conversation with Christian Tual.

134. Letter from Dido Renoir to Anne de Saint-Phalle, March 22, 1976, Jean Renoir Papers, Correspondence, Box 32, Folder 3.

135. Letter from Christian Tual, April 27, 1976, Jean Renoir Papers, Correspondence, Box 32, Folder 4.

136. Ibid.

137. Letter from Anne de Saint-Phalle to Dido Renoir, May 27, 1976, Jean Renoir Papers, Correspondence, Box 32, Folder 5.

138. Letter to Anne de Saint-Phalle, August 5, 1976, Jean Renoir Papers, Correspondence, Box 32, Folder 8.

139. Letter to Claude Renoir, January 14, 1977, Jean Renoir Papers, Correspondence, Box 32, Folder 14.

140. Letter to Giulio Macchi, December 15, 1976, Fonds Jean Renoir, Cinémathèque française.

141. Letter from Anne de Saint-Phalle, June 30, 1976, Jean Renoir Papers, Correspondence, Box 32, Folder 6.

142. Ibid.

143. Letter from Anne de Saint-Phalle, June 14, 1976, Jean Renoir Papers, Correspondence, Box 32, Folder 6.

144. Jean-Pierre Thibaudat, "Dans la maison de Jean," *Libération*, July 16, 1984.

145. Letter from Anne de Saint-Phalle to Dido Renoir, July 11, 1984, Jean Renoir Papers, Correspondence, Box 36, Folder 6.

146. Letter from Anne de Saint-Phalle, February 23, 1977, Jean Renoir Papers, Correspondence, Box 33, Folder 1.

147. Ibid.

148. Letter to Anne de Saint-Phalle, January 21, 1977, Jean Renoir Papers, Correspondence, Box 32, Folder 14.

149. Letter from Anne de Saint-Phalle to Dido Renoir, June 7, 1977, Jean Renoir Papers, Correspondence, Box 33, Folder 5.

150. Letter from Anne de Saint-Phalle to Dido Renoir, June 17, 1977, Jean Renoir Papers, Correspondence, Box 33, Folder 5.

151. Letter from Anne de Saint-Phalle to Dido Renoir, July 25, 1977, Jean Renoir Papers, Correspondence, Box 33, Folder 6.

152. Letter to François Truffaut, January 27, 1976, Jean Renoir Papers, Correspondence, Box 32, Folder 1.

153. Letter to Anne de Saint-Phalle, January 7, 1976, Jean Renoir Papers, Correspondence, Box 32, Folder 1.

154. Letter from Dido Renoir to Lotte Reiniger, March 30, 1976, Jean Renoir Papers, Correspondence, Box 32, Folder 3.

155. Letter from Dido Renoir to Anne de Saint-Phalle, February 5, 1977, Jean Renoir Papers, Correspondence, Box 33, Folder 1.

156. Conversation with Paolo Barzman.

157. Ibid.

158. Ibid.

159. Letter to Anne de Saint-Phalle, October 21, 1976, Jean Renoir Papers, Correspondence, Box 32, Folder 10.

160. Letter to Anne de Saint-Phalle, December 3, 1977, Jean Renoir Papers, Correspondence, Box 33, Folder 11.

161. Letter to Ginette Doynel, February 27, 1974, Jean Renoir Papers, Correspondence, Box 30, Folder 1.

162. Letter from Anne de Saint-Phalle, February 17, 1978, Jean Renoir Papers, Correspondence, Box 34, Folder 1.

163. Letter from Dido Renoir to Anne de Saint-Phalle, February 5, 1977, Jean Renoir Papers, Correspondence, Box 33, Folder 1.

164. Conversation with Paolo Barzman.

165. Letter to Georges Simenon, August 13, 1977, Jean Renoir Papers, Correspondence, Box 33, Folder 11.

166. Letter to Charles and Oona Chaplin, December 12, 1977, *Correspondence 1913–1978*.

167. Letter to Oona Chaplin, December 28, 1977, *Correspondance 1913–1978*.

168. Conversation with Leslie Caron.

169. Letter from Dido Renoir to Anne de Saint-Phalle, Jean Renoir Papers, Correspondence, Box 34, Folder 11.

170. Célia Bertin, *Jean Renoir*, Éditions du Rocher, 1994.

171. Telegram from Simone Signoret and Yves Montand, December 24, 1978, Jean Renoir Papers, Correspondence, Box 34, Folder 11.

172. Letter from Dido Renoir to Anne de Saint-Phalle, January 9, 1979, Jean Renoir Papers, Correspondence, Box 34, Folder 13.

173. Letter from Anne de Saint-Phalle to Dido Renoir, January 25, 1979, Jean Renoir Papers, Correspondence, Box 34, Folder 13.

174. Letter to Ingrid Bergman, January 22, 1979, Jean Renoir Papers, Correspondence, Box 34, Folder 13.

Films

Catherine [Une vie sans joie] (Backbiters)
　　Production: Films Jean Renoir.
　　Producer: Jean Renoir.
　　Directors: Albert Dieudonné, Jean Renoir.
　　Screenplay by Jean Renoir.
　　Adaptation by Jean Renoir, Pierre Lestringuez.
　　Intertitles by Jean Renoir.
　　Cinematography: Jean Bachelet, Alphonse Gibory.
　　With: Catherine Hessling (Catherine Ferrand), Louis Gauthier (Georges Mallet), Eugénie Naud (Mme. Laisné), Albert Dieudonné (Maurice Laisné), Georges Térof (Gédéon Grave), Pierre Philippe [Pierre Lestringuez] (Adolphe), Oléo (une prostituée), Jean Renoir (le sous-préfet), Pierre Champagne.
　　Filmed: March–May 1924. 55 minutes. Black and white.
　　Distribution: Films Jean Renoir; Pierre Braunberger (1927).
　　Released: November 9, 1927.

La Fille de l'eau (The Whirlpool of Fate)
　　Production: Films Jean Renoir.
　　Producer: Jean Renoir.
　　Screenplay by Pierre Lestringuez.
　　Cinematography: Jean Bachelet, Alphonse Gibory.
　　Set Direction: Jean Renoir.
　　Costumes: Mimi Champagne, Catherine Hessling.
　　Assistant Director: Pierre Champagne.
　　With: Catherine Hessling (Virginie [Gudule] Rosaert), Pierre Philippe [Pierre Lestringuez] (Oncle Jef), Pierre Champagne (Justin Crépoix), Harold Livingston (Georges Raynal), Georges Térof (M. Raynal), Fockenberghe (Mme. Raynal), Maurice Touzé (La Fouine), Henriette Moret (La Roussette), Charlotte Clasis (Mme. Maubien), André Derain (un paysan), Van Doren (le patron du Bon Coin).

Filmed: Summer 1924. 89 minutes. Black and white.

Distribution: Maurice Rouhier, Studio Films.

Released: March 20, 1925.

Nana

Production: Films Jean Renoir.

Producer: Jean Renoir.

Screenplay by Pierre Lestringuez, based on the novel by Émile Zola.

Adaptation by Jean Renoir.

Intertitles by Denise Leblond-Zola and Jean Renoir.

Cinematography: Edmund Corwin, Jean Bachelet.

Camera: Alphonse Gibory, Raleigh, Holski, Asselin, Perie.

Art Direction: Claude Autant-Lara, André Cerf.

Set Direction: Robert-Jules Garnier.

Music: Maurice Jaubert, Offenbach.

Editing: Jean Renoir.

Production director: R. Turgy.

With: Catherine Hessling (Nana), Werner Krauss (le comte Muffat), Jean Angelo (le comte de Vandeuvres), Raymond Guérin-Catelain (Georges Hugon), Pierre Philippe [Pierre Lestringuez] (Bordenave), Pierre Champagne (La Faloise), Valeska Gert (Zoë), Jacqueline Forzane (la comtesse Sabine Muffat), Claude Moore [Claude Autant-Lara] (Fauchery), Harbacher (Francis), Jacqueline Ford (Rose Mignon), Nita Romani (Satin), Marie Prévost (Gaga), René Koval (Fontan), André Cerf (Le Tigre), Pierre Braunberger (un spectateur au théâtre), R. Turgy (un spectateur au théâtre), Catherine Hessling (une spectatrice au théâtre).

Filmed: October 1925–February 1926. 10,499 feet, then 9,186 feet. Black and white.

Distribution: Aubert–Pierre Braunberger.

Released: April 27, 1926.

Sur un air de Charleston [Charleston; Charleston-Parade] (Charleston Parade)

Production: Films Jean Renoir.

Producer: Jean Renoir.

Screenplay by Pierre Lestringuez, based on an idea by André Cerf.

Cinematography: Jean Bachelet.

Music: Clément Doucet.

Editing: Jean Renoir.

Assistant Directors: André Cerf, Claude Heymann.

With: Catherine Hessling (la danseuse), Johnny Hudgins (l'explorateur), Pierre Braunberger, Pierre Lestringuez, and Jean Renoir (les trois anges).

Filmed: Fall 1926. 25 minutes. Black and white.

Distribution: Néo-film (Pierre Braunberger).

Released: March 19, 1927.

Marquitta

Production: La Société des artistes réunis.

Producer: M. Gargour.

Screenplay by Pierre Lestringuez.

Adaptation by Jean Renoir.

Cinematography: Jean Bachelet, Raymond Agnel.

Set Direction: Robert-Jules Garnier.

With: Marie-Louise Iribe (Marquitta), Jean Angelo (Prince Vlasco), Henri Debain (le comte Dimitrieff), Lucien Mancini (le beau-père), Pierre Philippe [Pierre Lestringuez] (le gérant du casino), Pierre Champagne (un chauffeur de taxi), Simone Cerdan.

Filmed: Winter 1927–May 1927. 120 minutes. Black and white.

Distribution: Jean de Merly.

Released: September 13, 1927.

La Petite Marchande d'allumettes (The Little Match Girl)

Directors: Jean Renoir, Jean Tedesco.

Producers: Jean Renoir, Jean Tedesco.

Screenplay by Jean Renoir, based on a story by Hans Christian Andersen.

Cinematography: Jean Bachelet.

Set Direction: Erik Aaes.

Music: Manuel Rosenthal, Michael Grant.

Editing: Jean Renoir.

Assistant Directors: Claude Heymann, Simone Hamiguet.

With: Catherine Hessling (Karen, la petite marchande d'allumettes), Jean Storm (le jeune homme, le soldat), Manuel Raaby [Rabinovitch] (le policier), Amy Wells [Aimée Tedesco] (la poupée mécanique).

Filmed: August 1927–January 1928. 29 minutes. Black and white.

Distribution: Films SOFAR.

Released: June 1, 1928.

Tire-au-flanc (The Sad Sack)
  Production: Néo-Film.
  Producer: Pierre Braunberger.
  Screenplay by Jean Renoir, Claude Heymann, André Cerf, based on the play by A. Mouëzy-Éon and A. Sylvane
  Intertitles: d'André Rigaud.
  Cinematography: Jean Bachelet, P. Engsburg.
  Set Direction: Erik Aaes.
  With: Georges Pomiès (Jean Dubois d'Ombelles), Michel Simon (Joseph Turlot), Maryanne (Mme. Blandin), Jeanne Helbling (Solange Blandin), Kinny (Lily Blandin), Fridette Fatton (Georgette), Félix Oudart (le colonel Brochard), Jean Storm (le lieutenant Daumel), Paul Velsa (le caporal Bourrache), Manual Raaby [Rabinovitch] (l'adjudant), Esther Kiss (Mme. Fléchais), Zellas (Muflot), André Cerf (un soldat), Max Dalban (un soldat), Catherine Hessling (une fille qui se tient devant la caserne).
  Filmed: Summer 1928. 120 minutes. Black and white.
  Distribution: Films Armor, Éditions Pierre Braunberger.
  Released: July 18, 1928.

Le Tournoi dans la cité [Le Tournoi] (The Tournament)
  Production: Société des films historiques.
  Producer: Henri Dupuy-Mazuel.
  Screenplay by Henri Dupuy-Mazuel, André Jaeger-Schmidt, based on the novel by Henry Dupuy-Mazuel.
  Adaptation by Jean Renoir.
  Cinematography: Marcel Lucien, Maurice Desfassiaux.
  Camera: J.-L. Mundwiller.
  Set Direction: Robert Mallet-Stevens.
  Costumes: Georges Barbier.
  Editing: André Cerf.
  Assistant Director: André Cerf.
  Direction of the Production: M. de Maroussem, François Harispuru.
  With: Aldo Nadi (François de Baynes), Jackie Monnier (Isabelle Ginori), Enrique Rivero (Henri de Rogier), Suzanne Desprès (la comtesse de Baynes), Manuel Raaby [Rabinovitch] (le comte Ginori), Blanche Bernis (Catherine de Médicis), Gérard Mock (Charles IX), Viviane Clarens (Lucrece Pazzi), William Aguet (le maître de cavalerie), January (un officier de la Garde), Narval (Antonio), Max Dalban (le capitaine des veilleurs).
  Filmed: Summer–fall 1928. 120 minutes. Black and white.

Distribution: Jean de Merly, Fernand Weil.

Released: February 9, 1929.

Le Bled

Production: Société des films historiques.

Producer: Henri Dupuy-Mazuel.

Screenplay by Henri Dupuy-Mazuel, André Jaeger-Schmidt.

Intertitles: André Rigaud.

Cinematography: Marcel Lucien, Léon Morizet.

Camera: André Bac, Boissey.

Set Direction: William Aguet.

Editing: Marguerite Houllé.

Assistant Directors: André Cerf, René Arcy-Hennery.

Direction of the Production: François Harispuru.

With: Alexandre Arquillère (Christian Hoffer), Enrique Rivero (Pierre Hoffer, son neveu), Jackie Monnier (Claudie Duvernet), Diana Hart (Diane Duvernet), Manuel Raaby [Rabinovitch] (Manuel Duvernet), Berardi Aissa (Zoubir), Mme. Rozier (Marie-Jeanne), M. Martin (Ahmed, le maître-fauconnier), Hadj Ben Yasmina (le chauffeur), Jacques Becker (l'ouvrier agricole des Hoffer).

Filmed: February–March 1929. 102 minutes. Black and white.

Distribution: Mappemonde Film.

Released: May 11, 1929.

On purge Bébé (Baby's Laxative)

Production: Braunberger-Richebé.

Producer: Charles David.

Screenplay by Jean Renoir, Pierre Prévert, based on the play by Georges Feydeau.

Cinematography: Théodore Sparkhul, Roger Hubert.

Set Direction: Gabriel Scognamillo.

Sound: Joseph de Bretagne, D. F. Scanlon, Bugnon.

Editing: Jean Mamy.

Assistant Directors: Claude Heymann, Pierre Schwab.

Production Director: Gaillard.

With: Marguerite Pierry (Julie Follavoine), Jacques Louvigny (M. Follavoine), Michel Simon (M. Chouilloux), Olga Valéry (Clémence Chouilloux), Nicole Fernandez (Rose), Fernandel (Truchet), Sacha Tarride (Toto).

Filmed: March 1931. 62 minutes. Black and white.

Distribution: Braunberger-Richebé.
Released: June 1931.

La Chienne
Production: Braunberger-Richebé.
Producer: Charles David
Screenplay by Jean Renoir, André Girard, based on the novel by Georges de la Fouchardière.
Cinematography: Théodore Sparkhul.
Camera: Roger Hubert.
Art Direction: Marcel Courme.
Set Direction: Gabriel Scognamillo.
Sound: Joseph de Bretagne, Marcel Courme.
Editing: Denise Batcheff, Marguerite Houllé, Jean Renoir.
Assistant Directors: Pierre Prévert, Pierre Schwab, Claude Heymann.
With: Michel Simon (Legrand), Janie Marèze (Lucienne Pelletier) [Lulu], Georges Flamant (André Jaugin) [Dédé], Magdelaine Bérubet (Adèle Legrand), Gaillard (Alexis Godard), Lucien Mancini (Wallstein), Jean Gehret (Dagodet), Alexandre Rignault (Langelard), Max Dalban (Bonnard), Romain Bouquet (Henriot), Pierre Desty (Gustave), Marcel Courme (le colonel), Henri Guisol (Amédée), Sylvain Itkine (l'avocat), Christian Argentin (le magistrat), Marthe Doryans (Yvonne), Jane Pierson (la concierge).
Filmed: Summer 1931. 100 minutes. Black and white.
Distribution: Braunberger-Richebé, Europa-Film (CSC).
Released: November 17, 1931.

La Nuit du carrefour (Night at the Crossroads)
Production: Europa-Films.
Screenplay by Jean Renoir, based on the novel by Georges Simenon.
Cinematography: Marcel Lucien, Asselin.
Camera: Paul Fabian, Claude Renoir.
Set Direction: William Aguet.
Sound: Joseph de Bretagne, Bugnon.
Editing: Marguerite Houllé.
Assistant Directors: Jacques Becker, Maurice Blondeau.
Production Directors: Jacques Becker, Gaillard.
With: Pierre Renoir (Maigret), Georges Térof (Lucas), Winna Winfried (Elsa Andersen), Georges Koudria (Carl Andersen), Dignimont (Oscar), Lucie Vallat (Mme. Oscar), G. A. Martin (Grandjean), Jean Gehret (Émile

Michonnet), Jane Pierson (Mme. Michonnet), Jean Mitry (Arsène), Michel Duran (Jojo), Max Dalban (le docteur), Gaillard (le boucher), Boulicot (le policier), Manuel Raaby [Rabinovitch] (Guido).

Filmed: January–February 1932. 75 minutes. Black and white.

Distribution: Comptoir français cinématographique.

Released: April 21, 1932.

Boudu sauvé des eaux (Boudu Saved from Drowning)

Production: Société Sirius.

Producers: Michel Simon, Jean Gehret, Le Pelletier.

Screenplay by Jean Renoir, Albert Valentin, based on the play by René Fauchois.

Cinematography: Marcel Lucien.

Camera: Jean-Paul Alphen, Asselin.

Set Direction: Jean Castanier, Hugues Laurent.

Sound: Kalinowski.

Music: Raphaël, Johann Strauss.

Editing: Marguerite Houllé, Suzanne de Troeye.

Assistant Directors: Jacques Becker, Georges Darnoux.

Direction of the Production: Clément Olivier.

With: Michel Simon (Boudu), Charles Granval (M. Lestingois), Marcelle Hainia (Mme. Lestingois), Séverine Lerczinska (Anne-Marie), Max Dalban (Godin), Jean Gehret (Vigour), Jean Dasté (l'étudiant), Jacques Becker (le poète sur le banc), Jane Pierson (Rose), Georges Darnoux (un invité du mariage).

Filmed: Summer 1932. 87 minutes. Black and white.

Distribution: Établissements Jacques Haïk.

Released: November 11, 1932.

Chotard et Cie (Chotard and Company)

Production: Société des Films Roger Ferdinand.

Producer: Roger Ferdinand.

Screenplay by Jean Renoir, Roger Ferdinand, based on the play by Roger Ferdinand.

Cinematography: J.-L. Mundwiller.

Camera: Claude Renoir, René Ribault.

Set Direction: Jean Castanier.

Sound: Kalinowski, Roger Handjian.

Editing: Marguerite Houllé, Suzanne de Troeye.

Assistant Director: Jacques Becker.

With: Fernand Charpin (François Chotard), Jeanne Lory (Marie Chotard), Georges Pomiès (Julien Collinet), Jeanne Boitel (Reine Chotard, then Collinet), Malou Trekin (Augustine), Dignimont (Parpaillon), Max Dalban (Émile, un employé), Louis Tunc (le sous-préfet), Louis Seigner (le capitaine de la police), Robert Seller (le chef de la police), Fabien Loris (un invité du bal), Freddie Johnson (le musicien de jazz).

Filmed: November–December 1932. 83 minutes. Black and white.

Distribution: Universal.

Released: March 1933.

Madame Bovary

Production: La Nouvelle Société de films.

Producer: Gaston Gallimard, Robert Aron.

Screenplay by Jean Renoir, based on the novel by Gustave Flaubert.

Cinematography: Jean Bachelet.

Camera: Alphonse Gibory, Claude Renoir.

Set Direction: Robert Gys, Georges Wakhévitch, Eugène Lourié.

Costumes: Lazare Medgyès.

Sound: Joseph de Bretagne, Marcel Courmes.

Music: Darius Milhaud ("Le Printemps dans la plaine"), Donizetti (*Lucia di Lammermoor*).

Editing: Marguerite Houllé.

Assistant Director: Pierre Desouches.

Direction of the Production: René Jaspard.

With: Valentine Tessier (Emma Bovary), Pierre Renoir (Charles Bovary), Alice Tissot (Mme. Bovary), Max Dearly (Homais), Daniel Lecourtois (Léon), Fernand Fabre (Rodolphe), Pierre Larquey (Hippolyte), Robert Le Vigan (Lheureux), Helena Manson (Héloïse), Léon Larive (le préfet), Florencie (l'abbé Bournisien), Romain Bouquet (M. Guillaumin), Georges Cahuzac (Rouault), Alain Dhurtal (le chirurgien), Maryanne (Mme. Homais), André Fouché (Justin), Edmond Beauchamp (Binet), Georges de Neubourg (le marquis de la Vaubyessard), Henri Vilbert (Canivet), Robert Moor (l'huissier), Marthe Mellot (Nicaise), Monette Dinay (Félicité), Christiane Dor (Mme. Lefrançois), Odette Dynes (Mlle. Musette), René Bloch (le chauffeur de taxi), Paulette Élambert (Berthe Bovary), Max Tréjean, Albert Malbert, Pierre Bost.

Filmed: Fall 1933. 120 minutes. Black and white.

Distribution: Compagnie Indépendante de Distribution.

Released: January 12, 1934.

Toni

    Production: Films d'aujourd'hui.

    Producer: Pierre Gaut.

    Screenplay by Jean Renoir, Carl Einstein, based on the account of a crime of passion by Jacques Levert (Jacques Mortier).

    Cinematography: Claude Renoir.

    Camera: Roger Ledru.

    Set Direction: Marius Brouquier, Léon Bourelly.

    Sound: Barbishanian.

    Music: Paul Bozzi.

    Editing: Marguerite Houllé, Suzanne de Troeye.

    Assistant Directors: Georges Darnoux, Antonio Canor.

    Direction of the Production: E. Boyer.

    With: Charles Blavette (Antonia Canova) [Toni], Celia Montalvan (Josepha), Jenny Hélia (Marie), Max Dalban (Albert), Édouard Delmont (Fernand), Andrex (Gaby), André Kovachevitch (Sebastian), Paul Bozzi (Jacques, le guitariste).

    Filmed: Summer 1934. 90 minutes. Black and white.

    Distribution: Les Films Marcel Pagnol.

    Released: February 22, 1935.

Le Crime de monsieur Lange (The Crime of Monsieur Lange)

    Production: Obéron.

    Producer: André Halley des Fontaines.

    Screenplay by Jacques Prévert, Jean Renoir, based on an idea by Jean Castanier.

    Cinematography: Jean Bachelet.

    Camera: Champion.

    Set Direction: Jean Castanier, Robert Gys.

    Sound: Moreau, Louis Boge, Roger Loisel, Robert Teisseire.

    Music: Jean Wiener.

    Editing: Marguerite Houllé, Marthe Huguet.

    Assistant Directors: Georges Darnoux, Jean Castanier.

    Direction of the Production: Geneviève Blondeau.

    With: René Lefèvre (Amédée Lange), Jules Berry (Batala), Florelle (Valentine), Nadia Sibirskaïa (Estelle), Sylvia Bataille (Édith), Henri Guisol (Meunier), Maurice Baquet (Charles), Marcel Levesque (le concierge), Odette Talazac (sa femme), Jacques Brunius (Baigneur), Jean Dasté, Marcel Duhamel, Paul Grimault, and Guy Decomble (les imprimeurs), Edmond Beauchamp (le curé), Sylvain Itkine (l'inspecteur de police retraité), Claire Gérard (la prostituée), Paul Demange (le créancier), Fabien Loris, Janine Loris, Jean Brémaud, Henri Saint-Isles, Pierre Huchet, Marcel Lupovici, Charbonnier, Max Morise, René Génin.

Filmed: October–November 1935. 84 minutes. Black and white.

Distribution: Minerva.

Released: January 24, 1936.

La vie est à nous (The People of France; Life Is Ours!)

Directors: Jean Renoir, Jean-Paul Dreyfus [Le Chanois], Jacques Becker, Jacques Brunius, André Zwobada, Henri Cartier-Bresson, Pierre Unik, Maurice Lime.

Production: Parti communiste français.

Screenplay by Jean-Paul Dreyfus [J.-P. Le Chanois], Pierre Unik, Jean Renoir.

Cinematography: Claude Renoir, Jean-Serge Bourgoin, Jean Isnard, Alain Douarinou.

Sound: Robert Teisseire.

Music: "L'Internationale," "Ronde des Saint-Simoniens," "Song of the Komsomols," "Auprès de ma blonde," "La Cucaracha."

Editing: Marguerite Houllé, Jacques Brunius.

With: Jean Dasté (le professeur), Jacques Brunius (le président du conseil d'administration), Pierre Unik (le secrétaire de Marcel Cachin), Max Dalban (Brochard, le contremaître), Madeleine Sologne (une ouvrière spécialisée), Fabien Loris (un ouvrier), Simone Guisin (la femme dans le casino), Teddy Michaux (un fasciste), Charles Blavette (Tonin), Émile Drain (Gustave Bertin), Jean Renoir (le gardien de la salle), Madeleine Dax (une secrétaire), Sylvain Itkine (le comptable), Roger Blin (un forgeron), Georges Spanelly (le chef de l'usine), Fernand Bercher (le secrétaire), Eddy Debray (l'huissier), Henri Pons (M. Lecocq), Gabrielle Fontan (Mme. Lecocq), Gaston Modot (Philippe), Léon Larive (un client de la vente aux enchères), Pierre Ferval (un client de la vente aux enchères), Julien Bertheau (René, un ouvrier au chômage), Nadia Sibirskaïa (Ninette, sa petite amie), Marcel Lesieur (le propriétaire du garage), Frédéric O'Brady (Mohammed, le laveur de voitures), Marcel Duhamel (le volontaire du service national), Tristan Sévère (un ouvrier au chômage), Guy Favières (un vieil ouvrier au chômage), Jacques Becker (un jeune ouvrier au chômage), Muse Dalbray (une femme au chômage), Claire Gérard (la bourgeoise dans la rue), Jean-Paul Dreyfus (P'tit Louis), Charles Charras (un chanteur), Francis Lemarque (un chanteur), Vladimir Sokoloff, Yolande Oliviero, François

Viguier, Madeleine Sylvain, Marcel Cachin (lui-même), Martha Desrumeaux (elle-même), Jacques Duclos (lui-même), Marcel Gitton (lui-même), André Marty (lui-même), Renaud Jean (lui-même), Maurice Thorez (lui-même), Paul Vaillant-Couturier (lui-même).

    Filmed: February–March 1936. 66 minutes. Black and white.

    Distribution: Ciné-liberté.

    Released: April 7, 1936.

Partie de campagne (A Day in the Country)

    Production: Films du Panthéon.

    Producer: Pierre Braunberger.

    Screenplay by Jean Renoir, based on the story by Guy de Maupassant.

    Cinematography: Claude Renoir.

    Camera: Jean-Serge Bourgoin.

    Set Direction: Robert Gys.

    Props and Costumes: Luchino Visconti.

    Sound: Joseph de Bretagne.

    Music: Joseph Kosma.

    Hummed song performed by Germaine Montero.

    Editing: Marguerite Houllé, Marinette Cadicqx, Georges Cravenne (1946).

    Assistant Directors: Jacques Brunius, Jacques Becker, Yves Allégret, Henri Cartier[-Bresson], Claude Heymann.

    Direction of the Production: Roger Woog.

    With: Sylvia Bataille (Henriette Dufour), Jane Marken (Mme. Juliette Dufour), Georges Saint-Saëns [Georges Darnoux] (Henri), Jacques Borel [Jacques Brunius] (Rodolphe), André Gabriello (M. Cyprien Dufour), Paul Temps (Anatole), Gabrielle Fontan (la grand-mère), Jean Renoir (le père Poulain, l'aubergiste), Marguerite Houllé (la servante), Henri Cartier (le premier séminariste), Georges Bataille (le deuxième séminariste), Pierre Lestringuez (le curé le plus âgé), Alain Renoir (le garçon qui pêche).

    Filmed: June 27–end of August 1936. 37 minutes. Black and white.

    Distribution: Films de la Pléiade, Panthéon.

    Released: December 18, 1946.

Les Bas-Fonds (The Lower Depths)

    Production: Albatros Films.

    Producer: Alexandre Kamenka.

    Screenplay by Yevgeny Zamyatin, Jacques Companeez, based on the play by Maxim Gorky.

Adaptation by Jean Renoir, Charles Spaak.

Cinematography: Jean Bachelet, Fedote Bourgassoff.

Camera: Jacques Mercanton.

Art Direction: Alexandre Kamenka.

Set Direction: Eugène Lourié, Hugues Laurent.

Sound: Robert Ivonnet.

Music: Jean Wiener, Roger Désormière.

Editing: Marguerite Houllé.

Assistant Directors: Jacques Becker, Joseph Soiffer.

Direction of the Production: Vladimir Zederbaum.

With: Jean Gabin (Pepel), Louis Jouvet (le baron), Suzy Prim (Vassilissa), Junie Astor (Natacha), Vladimir Sokoloff (Kostilev), Robert Le Vigan (l'Acteur), André Gabriello (l'inspecteur de police), Camille Bert (le comte), Léon Larive (Félix), Jany Holt (Nastia, la prostituée), Maurice Baquet (Luka, l'accordéoniste), René Génin (le vieil homme), Lucien Mancini (le restaurateur), Paul Temps, Sylvain Itkine, Henri Saint-Isles, René Stern, Robert Ozenne, Alex Allin, Fernand Bercher, Annie Cérès, Nathalie Alexeiev, Jacques Becker.

Filmed: September 5–October 3, 1936. 89 minutes. Black and white.

Distribution: Les Distributeurs français, S. A.

Released: December 10, 1936.

La Grande Illusion (Grand Illusion)

Production: Réalisations d'art cinématographique (RAC).

Producers: Frank Rollmer, Albert Pinkovitch.

Screenplay by Charles Spaak, Jean Renoir.

Cinematography: Christian Matras.

Camera: Claude Renoir.

Set Direction: Eugène Lourié, assisted by Georges Wakhévitch.

Costumes: René Decrais.

Dresser: Suzy Berton.

Sound: Joseph de Bretagne.

Music: Joseph Kosma.

Editing: Marguerite Houllé, assisted by Marthe Huguet.

Assistant Director: Jacques Becker.

Technical Adviser: Carl Koch.

Script Girl: Gourdji (Françoise Giroud).

Direction of the Production: Raymond Blondy.

With: Jean Gabin (le lieutenant Maréchal), Pierre Fresnay (le capitaine de Boëldieu), Marcel Dalio (le lieutenant Rosenthal), Erich von Stroheim (le capitaine, puis commandant von Rauffenstein), Dita Parlo (Elsa), Julien Carette (Cartier, l'acteur), Gaston Modot (l'ingénieur au cadastre), Jean Dasté (l'instituteur), Carl Heil (Krantz, dit "Arthur," et l'officier dirigeant la fouille de la chambrée), Sylvain Itkine (le lieutenant Demolder, dit "Pindare"), Georges Péclet (Charpentier), Habib Benglia (le Sénégalais), Claude Sainval (le capitaine Ringis), Roger Forster (Maisonneuve), Jacques Becker (l'officier anglais qui casse sa montre), Carl Koch (le "gendarme de campagne"), Albert Brouett (le prisonnier russe barbu), Werner Florian, Michel Salina, Georges Fronval.

Filmed: February–May 1937. 113 minutes. Black and white.

Distribution: RAC.

Released: June 9, 1937.

La Marseillaise

Production: Société de production et d'exploitation du film *La Marseillaise*.

Producers: André Zwobada, A. Seigneur.

Screenplay by Jean Renoir, Carl Koch.

Cinematography: Jean-Serge Bourgoin, Alain Douarinou, Jean-Marie Maillois.

Camera: Jean-Paul Alphen, Jean Louis.

Set Direction: Léon Barsacq, Georges Wakhévitch, Jean Périer.

Costumes: Louis Granier.

Sound: Joseph de Bretagne, Jean-Roger Bertrand, J. Demède.

Music: Joseph Kosma, Sauveplane, Rameau, Mozart, Bach, Rouget de l'Isle, Lalande, Grétry.

Editing: Marguerite Houllé.

Assistant Directors: Jacques Becker, Carl Koch, Claude Renoir Sr., Jean-Paul Dreyfus, Marc Maurette, Tony Corteggiani, Louis Demasure.

With: Pierre Renoir (Louis XVI), Lise Delamare (Marie-Antoinette), William Aguet (La Rochefoucauld), Léon Larive (Picard), Elisa Ruis (Mme. de Lamballe), Georgette Lefebvre (Mme. Élisabeth), Marie-Pierre Sordet-Dantès (la dauphine), Yveline Auriol (la dauphine), Pamela Stirling (une courtisane), Génia Vaury (une courtisane), Louis Jouvet (Roederer), Jean Aquistapace (le maire du village), Jaque-Catelain (le capitaine Langlade), Georges Spanelly (La Chesnaye), Pierre Nay (Dubouchage), Edmond Castel (Leroux), Werner Florian (Westerman), Aimé Clariond (M. de Saint-Laurent), André Zibral (M. de Saint-Méry), Maurice Escande (le seigneur du village), Jean Ayme (de Fougerolles), Irène Joachim (Mme. de Saint-Laurent), Andrex (Honoré Arnaud), Charles Blavette (un Marseillais), Edmond Ardisson (Jean-Joseph Bomier), Fernand Flament (Ardisson), Alex Truchy (Cuculière), Paul Dullac

(Javel), Jean-Louis Allibert (Moissan), Georges Péclet (le lieutenant Pignatel), Géo Lastry (le capitaine Massugue), Adolphe Autran (le batteur), Édouard Delmont (Cabri), Nadia Sibirskaïa (Louison), Jenny Hélia (l'interpellatrice), Gaston Modot (un volontaire), Julien Carette (un volontaire), Séverine Lerczinska (une paysanne), Marthe Marty (la mère de Bomier), Odette Cazau (Thérèse), Edmond Beauchamp (le curé), Blanche Destournelles (Clémence), Pierre Ferval, Roger Prégor, Fernand Bellon, Jean Boissemond, Lucy Kieffer.

Filmed: August 28–November 3, 1937. 135 minutes. Black and white.

Distribution: RAC.

Released: February 9, 1938.

La Bête humaine

Production: Paris Film Production.

Producers: Robert and Raymond Hakim.

Screenplay by Jean Renoir, based on the novel by Émile Zola.

Cinematography: Curt Courant.

Camera: Claude Renoir Jr.

Set Direction: Eugène Lourié.

Sound: Robert Teisseire.

Music: Joseph Kosma.

Editing: Marguerite Houllé, Suzanne de Troeye.

Assistant Directors: Claude Renoir Sr., Suzanne de Troeye.

Direction of the Production: Roland Tual.

With: Jean Gabin (Jacques Lantier), Simone Simon (Séverine Roubaud), Fernand Ledoux (M. Roubaud), Julien Carette (Pecqueux), Colette Régis (Victoire), Jenny Hélia (Philomène), Blanchette Brunoy (Flore), Jacques Berlioz (M. Grandmorin), Georges Spannelly (Camy-Lamotte), Léon Larive (le valet de Grandmorin), Gérard Landry (Dauvergne), Jean Renoir (Cabuche), Charlotte Clasis (Tante Phasie), Jacques Brunius (un ouvrier agricole), Émile Genevois (un ouvrier agricole), Tony Corteggiani (le chef de section), Marcel Pérez (un éclaireur), Claire Gérard (une voyageuse), Marceau (un mécanicien), Georges Péclet (un cheminot), Guy Decomble (un patrouilleur), André Tavernier (le magistrat), Jacques Roussel.

Filmed: August–September 30, 1938. 100 minutes. Black and white.

Distribution: Paris Film.

Released: December 23, 1938.

La Règle du jeu (The Rules of the Game)

Production: La Nouvelle Édition française.

Producer: Claude Renoir Sr.

Screenplay by Jean Renoir, Carl Koch.

Cinematography: Jean Bachelet.

Camera: Jacques Lemare, assisted by Jean-Paul Alphen and Alain Renoir.

Set Direction: Eugène Lourié, assisted by Max Douy.

Costumes: Coco Chanel.

Sound: Joseph de Bretagne.

Music: Mozart ("Ouverture" from *The Marriage of Figaro*, "Danse alle-mande"); Chopin; Strauss (*Die Fledermaus*); G. Claret et Camille François ("C'est la guinguette"; "En revenant d'la pêche au bas Meudon"; "En revenant d'la revue"); Monsigny (*Le Déserteur*); Rosi ("Tout le long de la Tamise"); Saint-Saëns ("Danse macabre"); Salabert ("Nous avons l'vé l'pied"); Scotto ("À Barbizon").

Assistant Directors: André Zwobada, Henri Cartier-Bresson, Carl Koch.

Script Girl: Dido Freire.

Editing: Marguerite Houllé, assisted by Marthe Huguet.

With: Marcel Dalio (Robert de La Chesnaye), Nora Gregor (Christine de La Chesnaye), Roland Toutain (André Jurieux), Mila Parély (Geneviève de Marras), Jean Renoir (Octave), Paulette Dubost (Lisette), Gaston Modot (Schumacher), Julien Carette (Marceau), Pierre Nay (de Saint-Aubin), Odette Talazac (Charlotte de La Plante), Pierre Magnier (le général), Richard Francoeur (M. La Bruyère), Claire Gérard (Mme. La Bruyère), Roger Forster (l'homosexuel), Anne Mayen (Jackie), Eddy Debray (Corneille), Léon Larive (le chef), Tony Corteggiani (Berthelin), Nicolas Ameto (le Sud-Américain), Lise Elina (la reporter radio), Jenny Hélia (la domestique), André Zwobada (l'ingénieur Caudron), Henri Cartier-Bresson (William, le domestique anglais), Célestin (le domestique), Camille François (la voix du présentateur radio).

Filmed: February 22–May 19, 1939. 112 minutes. Black and white.

Distribution: La Nouvelle Édition française, Gaumont.

Released: July 8, 1939.

Tosca

(Film uncredited to Jean Renoir, who directed only the opening scene, without any of the actors.)

Direction: Carl Koch.

Production: ERA-Scalera Films.

Producer: Arturo Ambrosio.

Screenplay by Alessandro de Stefani, Carl Koch, Luchino Visconti, Jean Renoir, based on the play by Victorien Sardou.

Cinematography: Ubaldo Arata.

Set Direction: Gustavo Abel, Amleto Bonetti.

Costumes: Gino. C. Sensani, Rosi Gori.

Sound: Piero Cavazzuti.

Music: Giacomo Puccini.

Editing: Gino Betrone.

With: Imperio Argentina (Floria Tosca), Michel Simon (Scarpia), Rossano Brazzi (Mario Cavaradossi), Carla Candiani (Marchesa Attavanti), Adriano Rimoldi (Angelotti), Nicolas Perchicot (Sciarrone), Juan Calvo (Spoletta), Armando Petroni (Cecco), Massimo Girotti, Vanda Capodaglio, Olga Gentilli, Nicola Maldacea.

Filmed: Spring–summer 1940. 105 minutes. Black and white.

Distribution: Scalera (Italy).

Released: January 1941 (Rome), October 2, 1942 (Paris).

Swamp Water

Production: 20th Century Fox.

Producer: Irving Pichel.

Screenplay by Dudley Nichols, based on the novel by Vereen Bell.

Cinematography: Peverell Marley, Lucien Ballard.

Art Direction: Richard Day.

Set Direction: Thomas Little.

Costumes: Gwen Wakeling.

Music: David Buttolph.

Editing: Walter Thompson.

With: Dana Andrews (Ben Ragan), Anne Baxter (Julie Keefer), Walter Brennan (Tom Keefer), Walter Huston (Thursday Ragan), John Carradine (Jesse Wick), Mary Howard (Hannah Ragan), Virginia Gilmore (Mabel MacKenzie), Ward Bond (Jim Dorson), Guinn Williams (Bud Dorson), Eugene Pallette (Sheriff Jeb McKane), Russell Simpson (Marty McCord), Joseph Sawyer (Hardy Ragan), Paul Burns (Tulle MacKenzie), Frank Austin (Fred Ulm), Matt Willis (Miles Tonkin), Dave Morris (the barber).

Filmed: July 26–September 6, 1941. 86 minutes. Black and white.

Distribution: 20th Century Fox.

Released: October 23, 1941 (Waycross, Georgia); November 16, 1941 (New York); April 23, 1948 (France).

Forever Yours [The Amazing Mrs. Holliday]

(Film uncredited to Jean Renoir, who withdrew as director after forty-seven days of filming.)

Direction: Bruce Manning.

Production: Universal.

Producer: Bruce Manning.

Associate Producer: Frank Shaw.

Screenplay by Frank Ryan, Hans Jacoby, based on an original story by Sonya Levien. Adapted by Boris Ingster, Leo Townsend.

Cinematography: Woody Bredell.

Art Direction: Jack Otterson.

Set Direction: R. A. Gausman.

Costumes: Vera West.

Music: H. J. Salter, Frank Skinner.

Editing: Ted Kent.

With: Deanna Durbin (Ruth Kirke), Edmond O'Brien (Tom Holliday), Barry Fitzgerald (Timothy Blake), Arthur Treacher (Henderson), Harry Davenport (Commodore Thomas Spencer Holliday), Grant Mitchell (Edgar Holliday), Frieda Inescort (Karen Holliday), Élisabeth Risdon (Louise Holliday), Jonathan Hale (Ferguson), Esther Dale (Lucy), Gus Schilling (Jeff Adams), J. Frank Hamilton (Dr. Kirke), Christopher Severn, Vido Rich, Mila Rich, Teddy Infuhr, Linda Bieber, Diane DuBois (the children), Charles Trowbridge (immigration officer), Philip Ahn (Major Ching), Irving Bacon.

Filmed: June 1–August 5, 1942 [Jean Renoir]. 96 minutes. Black and white.

Distribution: Universal.

Released: February 19, 1943 (United States).

This Land Is Mine (Vivre libre)

Production: RKO.

Producers: Jean Renoir, Dudley Nichols.

Screenplay by Dudley Nichols, Jean Renoir.

Cinematography: Frank Redman.

Set Direction: Darrell Silvera, Al Fields.

Costumes: Renié.

Sound: John E. Tribby, James G. Stewart.

Music: Lothar Perl.

Editing: Frederic Knudtson.

With: Charles Laughton (Albert Lory), Maureen O'Hara (Louise Martin), George Sanders (Georges Lambert), Walter Slezak (Major von Keller), Kent Smith (Paul Martin), Una O'Connor (Mrs. Lory), Philip Merivale (Professor Sorel), Thurston Hall (Henry Manville), Nancy Gates (Julie Grant), John Donat (Edmond Lorraine), Wheaton Chambers (Mr. Lorraine), Cecile Weston (Mrs.

Lorraine), Georges Coulouris (the prosecutor), Ivan Simpson (the judge), Frank Alten (Captain Schwartz), Leo Bulgakov (little fat man).

Filmed: October 24–December 20, 1942. 103 minutes. Black and white.

Distribution: RKO.

Released: May 7, 1943 (United States); July 10, 1946 (France).

A Salute to France (Salut à la France)

Directors: Jean Renoir, Garson Kanin.

Production: Office of War Information.

Screenplay by Philip Dunne, Jean Renoir, Burgess Meredith.

Cinematography: Army Pictorial Service.

Editing: Marcel Cohen, Maria Reyto, Jean Oser.

Music: Kurt Weill.

With: Claude Dauphin (Jacques Bonhomme, the French soldier), Garson Kanin (Joe, the American soldier), Burgess Meredith (Tommy, the British soldier).

Filmed: March–April 1944. 34 minutes. Black and white.

Distribution: United Artists.

Released: October 13, 1944 (Paris).

The Southerner

Production: Producing Artists Inc.

Producers: David Loew, Robert Hakim.

Screenplay by Jean Renoir, based on the novel *Hold Autumn in Your Hand* by George Sessions Perry.

Adaptation by Hugo Butler.

Cinematography: Lucien Andriot.

Set Direction: Eugène Lourié.

Sound: Frank Webster.

Music: Werner Janssen.

Editing: Gregg Tallas.

Direction of the Production: Sam Rheiner.

With: Zachary Scott (Sam Tucker), Betty Field (Nona Tucker), J. Carroll Naish (Henry Devers), Beulah Bondi (Grandma Tucker), Jay Gilpin (Jot Tucker), Jean Vanderwilt (Daisy Tucker), Paul Burns (Uncle Peter Tucker), Charles Kemper (Tim), Norman Lloyd (Finley Hewitt), Percy Kilbride (Harmie Jenkins), Blanche Yurka (Mama Tucker), Noreen Nash (Becky), Estelle Taylor (Lizzie), Paul Harvey (Ruston), Jack Norworth (the doctor), Nestor Paiva (the bartender), Dorothy Granger (party girl), Earl Hodgkins (wedding guest),

Almira Sessions (store customer), Rex (Zoonie, the dog).

    Filmed: September 16–November 11, 1944. 92 minutes. Black and white.

    Distribution: United Artists.

    Released: April 30, 1945 (United States); May 30, 1950 (France).

The Diary of a Chambermaid

    Production: Production Camden Inc.

    Producers: Benedict Bogeaus, Burgess Meredith.

    Screenplay by Burgess Meredith, Jean Renoir, based on the novel *Le Journal d'une femme de chambre* by Octave Mirbeau and the play by André Heuse, André de Lorde, Thielly Nores.

    Cinematography: Lucien Andriot.

    Set Direction: Eugène Lourié.

    Costumes: Barbara Karinska.

    Sound: William Lynch.

    Music: Michel Michelet.

    Editing: James Smith.

    With: Paulette Goddard (Célestine), Burgess Meredith (Captain Mauger), Francis Lederer (Joseph), Hurd Hatfield (Georges Lanlaire), Reginald Owen (M. Lanlaire), Judith Anderson (Mme. Lanlaire), Irene Ryan (Louise), Florence Bates (Rose), Almira Sessions (Marianne).

    Filmed: July 21–September 15, 1945. 86 minutes. Black and white.

    Distribution: United Artists.

    Released: February 15, 1946 (United States); June 9, 1948 (France).

The Woman on the Beach

    Production: RKO.

    Producer: Jack Gross.

    Screenplay by Jean Renoir, Frank Davis, J. R. Michael Hogan, based on the novel *None So Blind* by Mitchell Wilson.

    Cinematography: Leo Tover, Harry Wild.

    Art Direction: Albert S. d'Agostino, Walter E. Keller.

    Set Direction: Darrell Silvera, John Sturtevant.

    Sound: Jean Speak, Clem Portman.

    Music: Hanns Eisler.

    Editing: Ronald Gross, Lyle Boyer.

    With: Joan Bennett (Peggy Butler), Robert Ryan (Lieutenant Scott Burnett), Charles Bickford (Tod Butler), Nan Leslie (Eve Geddes), Walter Scande (Otto Wernecke), Irene Ryan (Mrs. Wernecke), Glenn Vernon (Kirk), Frank

Darien (Lars), Jay Norris (Jimmy).

    Filmed: February 2–April 13, 1946. 71 minutes. Black and white.

    Distribution: RKO.

    Released: June 2, 1947 (United States); June 23, 1948 (France).

The River

    Production: Oriental International Films Inc.

    Producer: Kenneth McEldowney.

    Screenplay by Rumer Godden, Jean Renoir, based on the novel by Rumer Godden.

    Cinematography: Claude Renoir.

    Camera: Ramananda Sen Gupta.

    Set Direction: Eugène Lourié, Bansi Chandra Gupta.

    Sound: Charles Poulton, Charles Knott.

    Music: Classical Indian music, Schumann, Mozart, Weber (*Invitation to the Dance*, op. 65).

    Editing: George Gale.

    Assistant Directors: Harishadhan J. Das Gupta, Sukhamoy Sen, Bansi Ashe.

    Direction of the Production: Kalyan Gupta.

    With: Patricia Walters (Harriet), Radha Sri Ram (Melanie), Adrienne Corri (Valerie), Thomas Breen (Captain John), Nora Swinburne (the mother), Esmond Knight (the father), Richard Foster (Bogey), Arthur Shields (Mr. John), Suprova Mukerjee (Nan), Penelope Wilkinson (Elizabeth), Jane Harris (Muffie), Sajjan Singh (Ram Singh), Cecilia Wood (Victoria), Jennifer Harris (Mouse), Nimai Barik (Kanu), Trilak Jetley (Anil), June Hillman (the narrator).

    Filmed: December 29, 1949–April 1950. 99 minutes. Color.

    Distribution: United Artists.

    Released: December 19, 1951.

The Golden Coach (Le Carrosse d'or)

    Production: Panaria Films, Delphinus & Hoche Productions.

    Producer: Francesco Alliata.

    Screenplay by Jean Renoir, Renzo Avanzo, Jack Kirkland, Giulio Macchi, Ginette Doynel, based on the play *Le Carrosse du Saint-Sacrement* by Prosper Mérimée.

    Cinematography: Claude Renoir, Joan Bridge (color consultant).

    Camera: Rodolfo Lombardi.

    Set Direction: Mario Chiari.

Costumes: Maria de Mattéïs.

Sound: Joseph de Bretagne, Ovidio del Grande.

Music: Antonio Vivaldi, Arcangelo Corelli, Olivier Metra.

Editing: David Hawkins.

Assistant Directors: Marc Maurette, Giulio Macchi, Vito Pandolfi.

Direction of the Production: Valentino Brosio, Giuseppe Bordogni.

With: Anna Magnani (Camilla), Duncan Lamont (Ferdinand, the viceroy), Paul Campbell (Felipe), Riccardo Rioli (Ramon, the bullfighter), Odoardo Spadaro (Don Antonio), Nada Fiorelli (Isabelle), George Higgins (Martinez), Gisella Mathews (Marquise Irene Altamirano), Ralph Truman (Duke de Castro), Elena Altieri (Duchess de Castro), Dante (Harlequin), Renato Chiantoni (Captain Fracasse), Giulio Tedeschi (Balthazar, the barber), Alfredo Kolner (Florindo), Alfredo Medini (Polichinelle), the Medini brothers (the four brother acrobats), William C. Tubbs (the innkeeper), John Pasetti (the captain of the guards), Cecil Mathews (the baron), Fedo Keeling (the viscount), Jean Debucourt (the bishop), Rino (Doctor Balanzon), Lina Marengo (the old actress), Raf de la Torre (the chief justice).

Filmed: February 4–April 19, 1952. 100 minutes. Color.

Distribution: Corona.

Released: December 3, 1952 (Rome); February 27, 1953 (Paris).

French Cancan

Production: Franco-London Films, Jolly Film.

Producer: Louis Wipf.

Screenplay by Jean Renoir, based on an idea by André-Paul Antoine.

Cinematography: Michel Kelber.

Camera: Henri Tiquet.

Set Direction: Max Douy.

Costumes: Rosine Delamare.

Sound: Antoine Petitjean.

Music: George Van Parys.

Editing: Borys Lewin.

Assistant Directors: Serge Vallin, Pierre Kast, Jacques Rivette.

With: Jean Gabin (Danglard), Françoise Arnoul (Nini), Maria Félix (la Belle Abbesse), Jean-Roger Caussimon (le baron Walter), Gianni Esposito (le prince Alexandre), Philippe Clay (Casimir), Max Dalban (le propriétaire de La Reine Blanche), Valentine Tessier (Mme. Olympe), Michel Piccoli (Valorgueil), Jean Parédès (Coudrier), Jacques Jouanneau (Bidon), Gaston Modot (le domestique de Danglard), Dora Doll (la Génisse), Franco Pastorino (Paulo), Michèle

Philippe (Éléonore), Jean-Marc Tennbcrg (Savate), Anna Amendola (Esther Georges), Hubert Deschamps (Isidore), Lydia Johnson (Guibole), Albert Rémy (Barjolin), Annik Morice (Thérèse), France Roche (Béatrix), Édith Piaf (Eugénie Buffet), Léo Campion (le commandant), Michèle Nadal (Bigoudi), Jean Raymond (Paulus), Sylvinne Delannoy (Titine), Pierre Olaf (le siffleur, Pierrot), Anne-Marie Mersen (Paquita), Pâquerette (Mimi Prunelle), André Claveau (Paul Delmet), Patachou (Yvette Guilbert), Jaque-Catelain (le ministre), André Numès Fils (le voisin), Jean Mortier (le gérant de l'hôtel), R. J. Chauffard (l'inspecteur de police), Jacques Hilling (Le chirurgien), Jean Sylvère (le groom), Pierre Moncorbier (l'huissier), Robert Auboyneau (le liftier), Palmyre Levasseur (une blanchisseuse), Laurence Bataille (la pygmée), Jedlinska (la Gigolette), Jacques Ciron (un dandy), Claude Arnay (un dandy), Martine Alexis, Bruno Balp, H. R. Herce, Corinne Jansen, Maya Jusanova, Jacques Marin, René Pascal, André Philip.

Filmed: October 4–December 20, 1954. 97 minutes. Color.

Distribution: Gaumont.

Released: April 27, 1955.

Elena et les hommes (Elena and Her Men)

Production: Franco-London Films, Les Films Gibé, Electra Compania Cinematografica.

Producer: Louis Wipf.

Screenplay by Jean Renoir.

Adaptation by Jean Renoir, Jean Serge, Cy Howard.

Cinematography: Claude Renoir.

Camera: Gilbert Chain.

Set Direction: Jean André.

Costumes: Rosine Delamare, Monique Plotin.

Sound: William Robert Sivel.

Music: Joseph Kosma.

Editing: Borys Lewin.

Assistant Director: Serge Vallin.

With: Ingrid Bergman (la princesse Elena Sorokovska), Jean Marais (le général Rollan), Mel Ferrer (Henri de Chevincourt), Jean Richard (Hector), Juliette Gréco (Miarka), Pierre Bertin (Martin-Michaud), Magali Noël (Lolotte), Jean Castanier (Isnard), Jacques Jouanneau (Eugène Godin), Gaston Modot (le chef des gitans), Jean Claudio (Lionel), Elina Labourdette (Paulette), Frédéric Duvallès (Godin), Dora Doll (Rosa la Rose), Mirko Ellis (Marbeau), Jacques Hilling (Lisbonne), Jacques Morel (Duchêne), Michèle Nadal (Denise

Godin), Olga Valéry (Olga), Renaud Mary (Fleury), Albert Rémy (Buchez), Léon Larive (le domestique d'Henri), Grégory Chmara (le domestique d'Elena), Léo Marjane (le chanteur de rue), Robert Le Béal (le docteur), Jim Gerald (le propriétaire du café), Paul Demange (un spectateur), Claire Gérard (une femme dans la rue), Yves Thomas, René Berthier, Gérard Buhr, Jaque-Catelain, Lyne Carrel, Corinne Jansen, Liliane Ernout, Pierre Duverger, Hubert de Lapparent, Palmyre Levasseur, Jean Ozenne, Louisette Rousseau, Simone Sylvestre, Les Zavattas, Les Chanteurs du Lapin à Gil.

    Filmed: December 1, 1955–March 1956. 98 minutes. Color.

    Distribution: Cinédis.

    Released: September 12, 1956.

Un tigre sur la ville

    Direction of the Production: Jean Renoir.

    With: Daniel Gélin (Charles Castle).

    Filmed: End of September 1957. 15 seconds. Black and white.

    Premiere: October 30, 1957.

Le Testament du docteur Cordelier (Experiment in Evil; The Testament of Dr. Cordelier)

    Production: Compagnie Jean Renoir, Radio-Télévision française, SOFIRAD.

    Screenplay by Jean Renoir.

    Cinematography: Georges Leclerc.

    Camera: Bernard Giraux, Jean Graglia, Pierre Guéguen, Pierre Lebon, Gilbert Perrot-Minot, Artur Raymond, Gilbert Sandoz.

    Set Direction: Marcel-Louis Dieulot.

    Costumes: Monique Dunand.

    Sound: Joseph Richard.

    Music: Joseph Kosma.

    Editing: Renée Lichtig.

    Assistant Directors: Maurice Beuchey, Jean-Pierre Spiero.

    Direction of the Production: Albert Hollebecke.

    With: Jean-Louis Barrault (le docteur Cordelier/Opale), Michel Vitold (Dr. Séverin), Teddy Bilis (M. Joly), Jean Topart (Désiré), Micheline Gary (Marguerite), Jacques Dannonville (le policier-chef Lardout), André Certes (l'inspecteur Salbris), Jacqueline Morane (Alberte), Ghislaine Dumont (Suzy), Jean-Pierre Granval (le propriétaire de l'hôtel), Madeleine Marion (Juliette), Gaston Modot (Blaise, le jardinier), Jaque-Catelain (l'ambassadeur), Didier d'Yd (Georges), Primerose Perret (Mary), Régine Blaess (la femme de l'ambassadeur), Raymond Jourdan (l'infirme), Raymone (Mme. des Essarts), Sylvianne Margolle (la petite fille), Dominique Dangon (la mère), Annick Allières (la voisine), Claudie Bourlon (Lise), Jacqueline Frot (Isabelle), Françoise Boyer (Françoise), Monique Theffo (Annie), Céline Soles (une fille), Jean Bertho (un passant), Jacques Ciron (un passant), Jean Renoir (lui-même).

Filmed: January 1959 (14 days). 95 minutes. Black and white.

Distribution: Pathé.

Released: November 16, 1961.

Le Déjeuner sur l'herbe (Picnic on the Grass)

Production: Compagnie Jean Renoir.

Screenplay by Jean Renoir.

Cinematography: Georges Leclerc.

Camera: Jean-Louis Picavet, Andréas Winding.

Set Direction: Marcel-Louis Dieulot.

Costumes: Monique Dunand.

Sound: Joseph de Bretagne.

Music: Joseph Kosma.

Editing: Renée Lichtig.

Assistant Directors: Maurice Beuchey, Francis Morane, Jean-Pierre Spiero, Hedy Naka, Jean de Nesles.

Direction of the Production: Ginette Doynel.

With: Paul Meurisse (professeur Étienne Alexis), Catherine Rouvel (Antoinette, dite Nénette), Fernand Sardou (Nino, son père), Jacqueline Morane (Titine, sa soeur), Jean-Pierre Granval (Ritou, son beau-père), Charles Blavette (Gaspard), Robert Chandeau (Laurent), Micheline Gary (Madeleine, sa femme), Ingrid Nordine (Marie-Charlotte), Frédéric O'Brady (Rudolf), Ghislaine Dumont (Madga, sa femme), Hélène Duc (Isabelle), André Brunot (le vieux prêtre), Jacques Dannonville (M. Poignant), Marguerite Cassan (Mme. Poignant), Raymond Jourdan (Eustache), Jean Claudio (Rousseau), François Miège (Barthélemy), Régine Blaess (Claire), Pierre Leproux (Bailly), Michel Herbault (Montet), Paulette Dubost (Mlle. Forestier), Jacqueline Fontel (Mlle. Michelet), M. You (Chapuis, le contremaître), Roland Thierry (un annonceur), Michel Pericart (un annonceur), Lucas (un annonceur), Dupraz (un annonceur).

Filmed: July–August 1959. 92 minutes. Color.

Distribution: Pathé.

Released: November 11, 1959.

Le Caporal épinglé (The Elusive Corporal)
Production: Films du Cyclope.
Screenplay by Jean Renoir, based on the novel by Jacques Perret.
Producer: G. W. Beyer.
Adjunct Director: Guy Lefranc.
Cinematography: Georges Leclerc.
Camera: Jean-Louis Picavet, Gilbert Chain, Antoine Georgakis, Robert Fraisse.
Set Direction: Eugène Herrly.
Costumes: Wolf Witzmann.
Sound: Antoine Petitjean.
Music: Joseph Kosma.
Editing: Renée Lichtig.
Assistant Directors: Marc Maurette, J. E. Kieffer.
Direction of the Production: René G. Vuattoux.
With: Jean-Pierre Cassel (le caporal), Claude Brasseur (Pater), Claude Rich (Ballochet), Jean Carmet (Émile), Jacques Jouanneau (Penche-à-gauche), Conny Froboess (Erika), Mario David (Caruso), Raymond Jourdan (Dupieu), Philippe Castelli (l'électricien), Guy Bedos (le bègue), Gérard Darrieu (l'homme au strabisme), Sacha Briquet (l'évadé déguisé en femme), O. E. Hasse (le voyageur ivre dans le train), Lucien Raimbourg (le garde, à la gare), François Darbon (le fermier français), Élisabeth Marcus, Élisabeth Stiepel, Helmut Janatsch.
Filmed: Winter 1961–1962. 105 minutes. Black and white.
Distribution: Pathé.
Released: May 23, 1962.

Le Petit Théâtre de Jean Renoir (The Little Theatre of Jean Renoir)
Production: RAI, Son et Lumière, ORTF.
Screenplay by Jean Renoir.
Cinematography: Georges Leclerc.
Camera: Henri Martin, Claude Amiot.
Set Direction: Gilbert Margerie.
Sound: Guy Rophe.
Musique: Jean Wiener ("Le Dernier Réveillon," "Le Roi d'Yvetot"), Joseph Kosma ("La Cireuse électrique").
Editing: Geneviève Winding.
Assistant Director: Denis Epstein.
Direction of the Production: Robert Paillardon.
With: Jean Renoir (lui-même). "Le Dernier Réveillon": Nino Formicola (le

clochard), Milly Monti (la clocharde), Roger Trapp (Max), Robert Lombard (le maître d'hôtel), André Dumas (le gérant de l'hôtel), Roland Bertin (Gontrand), Paul Bisciglia (un clochard), Frédéric Santaya, Pierre Gualdi, Jean-Michel Mole, Poucette Devaison, Tom Clark, G. Taillade, Daniel Sursain, Sébastien Floche, Gilbert Caron, Sabine Hermosa, E. Braconnier, Lolita Soler, Alain Peron. "La Cireuse électrique": Marguerite Cassan (Émilie), Pierre Olaf (Gustave, son mari), Jacques Dynam (Jules, son second mari), Jean-Louis Tristan (le représentant), Claude Guillaume (un jeune amoureux), Denis de Gunsberg (un jeune amoureux). "Quand l'amour meurt": Jeanne Moreau (la chanteuse). "Le Roi d'Yvetot": Fernand Sardou (Duvallier), Françoise Arnoul (Isabelle Duvallier), Jean Carmet (Féraud), Dominique Labourier (Paulette), Andrex (Blanc), Edmond Ardisson (César), Roger Prégor (M. Jolly).

Filmed: June–mid-September 1969. 100 minutes. Color.

Released: December 15, 1970.

Collaborations

La P'tite Lili

1927.

Production: Néo-Film.

Producer: Pierre Braunberger.

Screenplay by Alberto Cavalcanti, based on the song "La Barrière" by Eugène Gavel and F.-L. Benech.

Cinematography: Jimmy Rogers.

Set Direction: Erik Aaes.

Editing: Marguerite Houllé.

With: Catherine Hessling (la P'tite Lili), Guy Ferrand (le proxénète), Jean Renoir (le passant), Roland Cailloux (un concierge), Erik Aaes (un marin ivre), Jimmy Rogers (le policier), Dido Freire (la couturière), Jean Storm (le ministre), Alain Renoir (l'intrus).

Filmed: Summer 1927. 115 minutes. Black and white.

Distribution: Néo-Film.

Released: October 1, 1927.

Le Petit Chaperon rouge [Le Chaperon rouge] (Little Red Riding Hood)

1930.

Direction: Alberto Cavalcanti.

Producer: Jean Renoir.

Screenplay by Alberto Cavalcanti, Jean Renoir, based on the story by Charles Perrault.

Cinematography: Marcel Lucien.

Camera: Jimmy Rogers.

Editing: Marguerite Houllé.

Assistant Directors: Pierre Prévert, André Cerf.

Direction of the Production: M. Guillaume.

With: Catherine Hessling (le petit chaperon rouge), Jean Renoir (le loup), Mme. Neskrassof (la grand-mère), Amy Wells [Aimée Tedesco] (la mère, la journaliste, une jeune fille), André Cerf (le notaire), Pablo Quevedo (le jeune garçon), Pierre Prévert (la petite fille à la tête chauve, la femme un peu vieille, le parrain), La Montagne (un fermier), Odette Talazac (la femme du fermier), William Aguet (une vieille femme anglaise), Viviane Clarens (une jeune fille), Pola Illery (une jeune fille), Raymond Guérin-Catelain.

Filmed: Summer 1929. 60 minutes (?). Black and white.

Released: May 14, 1930.

Vous verrez la semaine prochaine

1929.

Direction: Alberto Cavalcanti.

Screenplay by Alberto Cavalcanti.

Cinematography: Elli Lotar.

Editing: Alberto Cavalcanti.

With: Catherine Hessling (l'actrice principale), Alain Renoir (le Grand Druide), Jean Renoir, Pablo Quevedo.

Filmed: Summer 1929. A few minutes.

Die Jagd nach dem Glück (The Pursuit of Happiness)

1929–1930.

Director: Rochus Gliese.

Production: Comenius-Film, Berlin.

Producers: Lotte Reiniger, Carl Koch.

Screenplay by Lotte Reiniger, Carl Koch, Rochus Glies, based on an idea by Lotte Reiniger and Alex Strasser.

Cinematography: Fritz Arno Richter.

Set Direction: Rochus Gliese, Arno Richter.

Sound: Lotte Reiniger, Carl Koch.

Music: Théo Mackeben.

With: Alexander Murski (Marquand, a hog vendor), Berthold Bartosch (Mario, his assistant), Amy Wells [Aimée Tedesco] (Jeanne, his daughter), Jean Renoir (Robert, a businessman), Catherine Hessling.

Filmed: Winter 1929–1930. 144 minutes. Black and white.

Distribution: Deutscher Werkfilm Gmbh.

Released: May 27, 1930 (Germany).

The Spanish Earth (Terre d'Espagne)

1938.

Director: Joris Ivens.

French commentary written and spoken by Jean Renoir.

Production: Contemporary Historians Inc.

Screenplay by Joris Ivens.

Cinematography: John Ferno (Fernhout), Joris Ivens.

Sound: Irving Reis.

Music: Marc Blitzstein, Virgil Thomson, based on Spanish folk music.

Editing: Helen Van Dongen.

Filmed: Spring 1937. 54 minutes. Black and white.

Distribution: Ciné-liberté.

Released: April 1938 (Paris).

L'Album de famille de Jean Renoir

1956.

Director: Roland Gritti.

Production: Paris-Télévision.

Screenplay by Pierre Desgraupes.

Cinematography: Jean Tournier.

With: Jean Renoir, Pierre Desgraupes.

Filmed: 1956. 26 minutes. Color.

Distribution: Cinédis.

Released: September 12, 1956.

La Direction d'acteurs par Jean Renoir

1968.

Director: Gisèle Braunberger.

Production: Les Films de la Pléiade.

Producer: Pierre Braunberger.

Screenplay by Gisèle Braunberger, Jean Renoir.

Cinematography: Edmond Richard.

Sound: René Forget.

Editing: Mireille Mauberna.

Direction of the Production: Roger Fleytoux.

With: Jean Renoir (himself), Gisèle Braunberger (herself).

Filmed: 1968 (one afternoon). 22 minutes. Color.

Distribution: Les Films de la Pléiade.

Released: October 16, 1970.

The Christian Licorice Store

1969.

Director: James Frawley.

Production: National General Pictures.

Producers: Michael S. Laughlin, Floyd Mutrux.

Screenplay by Floyd Mutrux.

Cinematography: David Butler.

Art Director: Dale Hennessy.

Sound: Bill Randall.

Music: Lalo Schifrin.

Editing: Richard Harris.

With: Beau Bridges (Franklin Cane), Maud Adams (Cynthia Vicstrom), Gilbert Roland (Jonathan Carruthers), Jean Renoir (himself), Dido Renoir (herself).

Filmed: 1969. 90 minutes. Color.

Distribution: Cinema Center Films.

Released: November 1971 (United States).

Plays

Jules César (Julius Caesar)

By William Shakespeare.

Direction: Jean Renoir.

Translated into French and adapted by Grisha Dabat, Mitsou Dabat.

Producer: Philippe Decharte.

Sound: Philips Company.

Music: Beethoven (Symphony no. 5).

Direction of the Production: Jean Serge.

With: Paul Meurisse (Brutus), Jean-Pierre Aumont (Antony), Henri Vidal (Julius Caesar), Yves Robert (Cassius), Loleh Bellon (Portia), Françoise Christophe (Calpurnia), Jean Parédès (Casca), Jean Topart (Octavius), Gaston Modot (Ligarius), Henri-Jacques Huet (Flavius), Jaque-Catelain (Decius), François Vibert (the soothsayer).

Only performance, Arles, July 10, 1954.

Orvet

By Jean Renoir.

Directed by the author.

Producer: Jean Dercante.

Set Direction: Georges Wakhévitch.

Costumes: Barbara Karinska, Givenchy.

Music: Joseph Kosma.

With: Leslie Caron (Orvet), Paul Meurisse (Georges), Michel Herbault (Olivier), Catherine Le Couey (Mme. Camus), Raymond Bussières (Coutant), Jacques Jouanneau (William), Marguerite Cassan (Clotilde), Yorick Royan (Berthe), Suzanne Courtal (Mère Vipère), Pierre Olaf (Philippe-le-pied-bot), Georges Saillard (le docteur), Georges Hubert (le premier chasseur), Henry Charret (le second chasseur).

Premiere (Paris): March 12, 1955.

Le Grand Couteau (The Big Knife)

By Clifford Odets.

Translated and adapted by Jean Renoir.

Direction: Jean Serge.

Set Direction: Hughes Pinneux.

With: Daniel Gélin (Charles Castle), Claude Génia (Marion Castle), Paul Bernard (Marcus Hoff), Paul Cambo (Smiley Coy), France Delahalle (Patty Benedict), Vera Norman (Dixie Evans), Teddy Bilis (Nat), Andrea Parisy (Connie Bliss), François Marie (Buddy Bliss), Robert Moncade (Hank Teagle), Andrès Wheatley (Russell), Jacques Dannonville (le jardinière [the gardener]).

Premiere (Paris): October 30, 1957.

Carola

By Jean Renoir.

Adaptation by Jean Renoir, Robert Goldsby, Angela Goldsby.

Set Direction: John T. Dreier.

Costumes: Shan Slattery.

Sound: Susan Brewer, Larry Belling.

Assistant: Robert Goldsby.

With: Deneen Peckinpah (Carola Janssen), Robert Martinson (le général von Clodius), Eileen Coltrell (Mireille), Carolyn Rosqui (Josette), Sydney Field (Campan), Dan Moore (Henri), David Grimsted (le colonel Kroll), James Tripp (Parmentier), Duke Stroud (Camille), Malcom Green (le lieutenant Keller), Robert Phalen (le premier gestapiste français), Charles Head (le second gestapiste français), David Vilner (le premier policier militaire allemand), Dan Rich (le second policier militaire allemand), Tony Loeb and Cliff Ghames (les gestapistes), Jim Mantell and Lewis Brown (les soldats allemands), Wendy Goodman (une actrice), Sheila Ryan (une actrice), Susan Brewer (une actrice), Miles Snyder (un acteur), Stephen Vause (un acteur).

Premiere (Berkeley, California): May 13, 1960.

Selected Bibliography

Works

Carola, theater, *L'Avant Scène Théâtre*, no. 597, November 1976.

Geneviève, novel, Flammarion, 1980.

Le Cœur à l'aise, novel, Flammarion, 1978.

Le Crime de l'Anglais, novel, Flammarion, 1979.

Les Cahiers du capitaine Georges, novel, Gallimard, 1966; Folio no. 2548, 1994.

Ma vie et mes films, Flammarion, 1974; Champs Contre-Champs, Flammarion, 1987; Champs Arts, Flammarion, 2005.

Orvet, theater, Gallimard, collection Le Manteau d'Arlequin, 1955.

Renoir, Hachette, 1962; then *Pierre-Auguste Renoir, mon père*, Gallimard, Folio no. 1292, 1981 and 1999.

Various Writings

Écrits 1926–1971, edited by Claude Gauteur. Belfond, 1974; Ramsay Poche, 1989 and 2006.

Julienne et son amour, introduction by Claude Gauteur, Henri Veyrier, 1989.

Le Passé vivant, edited by Claude Gauteur, Éditions de l'Étoile–Cahiers du cinéma, 1989.

Œuvres de cinéma inédites, edited and introduction by Claude Gauteur. Cahiers du cinéma–Gallimard, 1981.

Correspondence

Antoine de Saint-Exupéry, *Cher Jean Renoir*, Gallimard, 1999.

Correspondance 1913–1978, edited by David Thompson and Lorraine Lo Bianco, adapted for the French edition and translation of English-language letters by Édith Ochs, Plon, 1998.

Letters, edited by David Thompson and Lorraine Lo Bianco, preface by Bernardo Bertolucci, afterword by Henri Cartier-Bresson, Faber and Faber, 1984.

Lettres d'Amérique, edited by Dido Renoir and Alexander Sesonske, Presses de la Renaissance, 1984.

Bibliographies

Christopher Faulkner, *Jean Renoir: A Guide to References and Resources*, G. K. Hall, 1979.

Roger Viry-Babel, *Jean Renoir, Films, Textes, Références*, Presses universitaires de Nancy, 1989.

Screenplays

French Cancan, *L'Avant-Scène du cinéma*, no. 544, September 2005.

Julienne et son amour, followed by *En avant, Rosalie!*, texts redacted by and preface by Claude Gauteur, Henri Veyrier, 1979.

La Chienne, *L'Avant-Scène du cinéma*, no. 162, October 1975.

La Marseillaise, *L'Avant-Scène du cinéma*, no. 162, October 1975.

La Petite Marchande d'allumettes, *L'Avant-Scène du cinéma*, nos. 383–384, July–August 1989.

Le Testament du docteur Cordelier, *L'Avant-Scène du cinéma*, no. 6, July 1961.

Toni (and shooting script for *La Direction d'acteurs par Jean Renoir*), in "Spécial Renoir," *L'Avant-Scène du cinéma*, no. 251, July 1–15, 1980.

And Charles Spaak, *La Grande Illusion*, La Nouvelle Édition, 1949; *L'Avant-Scène du cinéma*, no. 44, January 1965; Bibliothèque des classiques du cinéma, Balland, 1974.

Biographies and Essays

G. A. Avenarius, *Jean Renoir*, Moscow, 1938.

André Bazin, *Jean Renoir*, edited by François Truffaut, Champ libre, 1971.

Ronald Bergan, *Jean Renoir: Projections of Paradise, A Biography*, Bloomsbury, 1992.

Célia Bertin, *Jean Renoir*, Perrin, 1986.

Célia Bertin, *Jean Renoir, cinéaste*, Gallimard, 1994.

Maurice Bessy and Claude Beylie, *Jean Renoir*, Pygmalion/Watelet, 1989.

Claude Beylie, *Jean Renoir (1894–1979)*, Anthologie du cinéma; Avant-Scène, no. 106, 1980.

Claude Beylie, *Jean Renoir: le spectacle, la vie*, Seghers, collection Cinéma d'aujourd'hui, 1975.

Armand-Jean Cauliez, *Jean Renoir*, Éditions universitaires, 1962.

Guy Cavagnac, *Jean Renoir, le désir du monde*, Henri Berger, 1994.

Bernard Chardère (ed.), *Jean Renoir*, *Premier Plan*, nos. 22–24, May 1962.

Collection, *Lotte Reiniger, Carl Koch, Jean Renoir, Die Gemeinsamen Filme, Szenen einer Freundschaft* (with contributions by Heiner Gassen, Claudine Pachnicke, Alfred Happ), Stadt Tübingen Kulturamt Stadtmuseum, 1994.

Collection, *Renoir/Renoir*, La Martinière–Cinémathèque française, 2005.

Olivier Curchod, *La Grande Illusion*, Nathan, 1994.

Olivier Curchod, *Partie de campagne, Jean Renoir: étude critique*, Nathan, 1995.

Olivier Curchod and Christopher Faulkner, *La Règle du jeu*, Nathan Cinéma, 1999.

Frank Curot, *Jean Renoir, l'Eau et la Terre*, Minard, 1990.

Frank Curot (ed.), *Nouvelles Approches de l'œuvre de Jean Renoir*, Université Paul-Valéry Montpellier III, 1995.

Giorgio Di Vincenti, *Jean Renoir, la vita, I film*, Marsilio, 1996.

Raymond Durgnat, *Jean Renoir*, University of California Press, 1974.

Christopher Faulkner, *The Social Cinema of Jean Renoir*, Princeton University Press, 1986.

Christopher Faulkner and Paul Duncan (eds.), *Jean Renoir: A Conversation with His Films*, Taschen, 2007.

Nick Frangakis (introduction by), *Jean Renoir: An Interview*, Green Integer Books, 1998.

Claude Gauteur, *D'un Renoir l'autre*, Le Temps des cerises, 2005.

Claude Gauteur, *Jean Renoir: La Double Méprise (1925–1939)*, Les Éditeurs français réunis, 1980.

William Harry Gilcher, *Jean Renoir in America: A Critical Analysis of His Major Films from Swamp Water to The River*, University of Iowa, 1979.

Penelope Gilliatt, *Jean Renoir: Essays, Conversations, Reviews*, McGraw-Hill, 1975.

Ulrich Gregor, *Jean Renoir und seine Filme: eine Dokumentation*, Eine Gemeinschaftspublikation des CICIM und der Stadt Tübingen, mit Unterstützung der französischen Filmtage Tübingen, 1970.

Pierre Haffner, *Jean Renoir*, Rivages cinéma, 1988.

Pierre Leprohon, *Jean Renoir*, Seghers, collection Cinéma d'aujourd'hui, 1967.

Martin O'Shaughnessy, *Jean Renoir*, Manchester University Press, 2000.

François Poulle, *Renoir 1938 ou Jean Renoir pour rien? Enquête sur un cinéaste*, Cerf, 1969.

Frank Priot, "*La Grande Illusion:* histoire du film en dix chapitres," in "*La Grande Illusion:* le film d'un siècle," *Archives*, no. 70, February 1997, Institut Jean Vigo Perpignan–Cinémathèque de Toulouse.

Daniel Serceau, *Jean Renoir, la Sagesse du plaisir*, Cerf, 1985.

Daniel Serceau, *Jean Renoir, l'Insurgé*, Le Sycomore, 1981.

Alexander Sesonske, *Jean Renoir: The French Films, 1924–1939*, Harvard University Press, 1980.

Carlo Felice Venegoni, *Jean Renoir*, La Nuova Italia, 1975.

Roger Viry-Babel, *Jean Renoir, le Jeu et la Règle*, Denoël, 1986.

Elizabeth Ann Vitanza, *Rewriting the Rules of the Game, Jean Renoir in America, 1941–1947*, University of California Los Angeles, 2007.

Conversations with Jean Renoir

Patrick Bureau, "Un entretien avec Jean Renoir," *Les Lettres françaises*, no. 1145, August 25, 1966.

Bert Cardullo, *Renoir on Renoir: Interviews*, Cambridge University Press, 1989.

Michel Ciment, "Entretien avec Jean Renoir," *Positif*, no. 173, September 1975.

Michel Ciment and Bernard Cohn, "Entretien à propos de *La Marseillaise*," *Positif*, no. 93, March 1968.

Michel Delahaye, "Renoir: Théâtre + Cinéma = T.V.," *Cinéma 59*, no. 38, July 1959.

Michel Delahaye and Jean Narboni, "La marche de l'idée," *Cahiers du cinéma*, no. 193, December 1967.

Jacques Doniol-Valcroze, "Entretien avec Jean Renoir," *France-Observateur*, November 19, 1959.

Jacques Doniol-Valcroze and Jean Domarchi, "Entretien avec Jean Renoir," *Cahiers du cinéma*, no. 147, September 1963.

Jean Douchet, "Jean Renoir: *Le Déjeuner sur l'herbe*, une farce sur la science," *Arts*, no. 736, August 19, 1959.

Harry M. Geduld, *Film Makers on Film Making: Statements on Their Art by Thirty Directors*, Indiana University Press, 1967.

Jean-Luc Godard, "Jean Renoir: La télévision m'a révélé un nouveau cinéma," *Arts*, no. 718, April 15, 1959.

Jacques Rivette and A. S. Labarthe, "Renoir le Patron: Propos de Jean Renoir," *Cahiers du cinéma*, no. 186, January 1967.

Jacques Rivette and François Truffaut, "Entretien avec Jean Renoir," *Cahiers du cinéma*, no. 34, April 1954, and no. 35, May 1954.

Jacques Rivette and François Truffaut, "Nouvel entretien avec Jean Renoir," *Cahiers du cinéma*, no. 78, Noël 1957.

Articles

Kees Bakker, "*The Spanish Earth*, the Spanish, and *Terre d'Espagne*," Catalogue of the Yamagata International Documentary Film Festival, "A Joris Ivens Retrospective," 1999.

Janet Bergstrom, "Généalogie du *Carrosse d'or* de Jean Renoir," *1895*, no. 62, December 2010.

Janet Bergstrom, "Jean Renoir's Return to France," in *Exile and Creativity: Signposts, Travellers, Outsiders, Backward Glances*, Duke University Press, 1998.

Janet Bergstrom, "Oneiric Cinema: *The Woman on the Beach*," *Film History* 11 (1999): 114–125.

William K. Everson, "Deanna Durbin and Jean Renoir, an Unravelled Mystery," *Films in Review*, October 1985.

Noël Herpe, "Les Cinéastes français à Hollywood," in *Les Européens dans le cinéma américain, Émigration et Exil*, under the direction of Irène Bessière and Roger Odin, Presses de la Sorbonne nouvelle, 2004.

Stéphane Launey, "Jean Renoir sous l'uniforme," *La Revue historique des armées*, no. 259, June 2010.

Jean Narboni (Introduced by), *Entretiens et propos*, with the collaboration of Janine Bazin and Claude Gauteur, Éditions de l'Étoile–Cahiers du cinéma, 1979; Ramsay Poche, 1986; Petite Bibliothèque des Cahiers du cinéma, 2005.

Pierre Philippe, "Entretien avec Catherine Hessling," *Cinéma 61*, no. 57, June 1961.

António Lopes Ribeiro, "O grande realizador francês Jean Renoir esta em Lisboa," *Animatògrafo*, December 2, 1940.

Alexander Sesonske, "Jean Renoir in Georgia: *Swamp Water*," *Georgia Review*, Spring 1982.

Charles Spaak, *Mes 31 mariages, Jean Renoir vu par Charles Spaak*, *Paris-Cinéma*, no. 10, December 12, 1945.

Jean Tedesco, "L'Artisan Jean Renoir," *Ciné-Club*, no. 6, April 1948.

Charles Tesson, *La production de Toni: la règle et l'esprit*, *Cinémathèque*, nos. 1, 2, and 3, 1992 and 1993.

Catherine Vialles, "Jean Renoir and *The Spanish Earth*," *European Foundation Joris Ivens Newsmagazine*, no. 10, November 2004.

Eyewitness Accounts

Françoise Arnoul, *Animal doué de bonheur,* Belfond, 1995.

Ingrid Bergman and Alan Burgess, *My Story,* Bantam Doubleday Dell, 1981.

Pierre Braunberger, *Cinémamémoire,* interviews collected by Jacques Gerber, Centre Georges Pompidou–CNC, 1987.

Jacques-Bernard Brunius, *En marge du cinéma français,* Arcanes, 1954.

Leslie Caron, *Thank Heaven,* JR Books, 2008.

Marcel Dalio, *Mes années folles,* Lattès, 1976.

Paulette Dubost, *C'est court, la vie,* Flammarion, 1992.

Pierre Fresnay and Pierre Possot, *Pierre Fresnay par Fresnay et Possot,* La Table Ronde, 1975.

Juliette Gréco, *Je suis faite comme ça, Mémoires,* Flammarion, 2012.

Jean-Paul Le Chanois, *Le Temps des cerises, entretiens avec Philippe Esnault,* Institut Lumière–Actes Sud, 1996.

Norman Lloyd, *Stages of Life in Theatre, Film and Television,* Limelight Editions, 1993.

Eugène Lourié, *My Work in Films,* Harcourt, Brace, Jovanovich, 1985.

Burgess Meredith, *So Far, So Good: A Memoir,* Little, Brown, 1994.

Paul Meurisse, *Les Éperons de la liberté,* Robert Laffont, 1979.

Eugene L. Miller and Edwin R. Arnold, *Robert Aldrich: Interviews,* University Press of Mississippi, 2003.

Jacques Morel, *Regards en coulisses,* Guy Authier, 1978.

Roger Richebé, *Au-delà de l'écran,* Pastorelly, 1977.

Jean Serge, *Le temps n'est plus de la bohème,* Stock-Kian, 1991.

Denise Tual, *Le Temps dévoré,* Fayard, 1980.

About the Renoirs

Jeanne Baudot, *Renoir, ses amis, ses modèles,* Éditions littéraires de France, 1949.

Pierre Chartrand and Bernard Pharisien, *Victor Charigot, son grand-père,* Némont, 2007.

Anne Distel, *Renoir,* Citadelles & Mazenod, 2009.

Jean-Claude Gélineau, *Jeanne Tréhot, la fille cachée de Pierre-Auguste Renoir,* Éditions du Cadratin, 2007.

Marc Le Cœur et Jean-Claude Gélineau, *Renoir, O Pintor da Vida,* Museu de Arte São Paolo, 2002.

Julie Manet, *Journal (1893–1899),* Klincksieck, 1979.

Henri Perruchot, *La Vie de Renoir,* Hachette, 1964.

Bernard Pharisien, *Renoir, de vigne en vin à Essoyes,* Némont, 2012.

Jacques Renoir, *Le Tableau amoureux,* Fayard, 2003.

Ambroise Vollard, *En écoutant Cézanne, Degas, Renoir,* Grasset, 1938.

Barbara Ehrlich White, *Renoir: His Life, Art, and Letters,* Abrams, 1984.

James Agee, *Agee on Film: Criticism and Comment on the Movies*, Modern Library Movies, new edition, 2000.

Jean-Pierre Aumont, *Le Soleil et les Ombres*, Opera Mundi, 1976.

Jean Aurenche, *La Suite à l'écran, Entretiens*, afterword by Bernard Chardère, Institut Lumière–Actes Sud, 1993.

Carole Aurouet, *Les Scénarios détournés de Jacques Prévert*, Dreamland, 2003.

Claude Autant-Lara, *La Rage dans le cœur*, Henri Veyrier, 1984.

Antoine de Baecque and Serge Toubiana, *François Truffaut*, Gallimard, 1996.

Rudy Behlmer, *Memo from Darryl F. Zanuck: The Golden Years at Twentieth Century Fox*, Grove Press, 1993.

Jean-Pierre Bertin-Maghit, *Le Cinéma sous l'Occupation*, Olivier Orban, 1989.

Pierre Billard, *L'Âge classique du cinéma français*, Flammarion, 1995.

Pierre Billard, *Le Mystère René Clair*, Plon, 1998.

Peter Biskind, *Star: How Warren Beatty Seduced America*, Simon & Schuster, 2010.

Éric Bonnefille, *Raymond Bernard: fresques et miniatures*, L'Harmattan, 2010.

Michel Boujut, *Conversations avec Claude Sautet*, Institut Lumière–Actes Sud, 1994.

Jean-Claude Brialy, *Le Ruisseau des singes*, Robert Laffont, 2000.

Patrick Brion, *Albert Lewin*, Bibliothèque du Film–Durante, 2002.

André G. Brunelin, *Jean Gabin*, Laffont, 1987.

Marcel Carné, *La Vie à belles dents*, Éditions Jean-Pierre Ollivier, 1975.

Collection, *American Film Institute Catalog: Within Our Gates: Ethnicity in American Feature Films, 1911–1960*, University of California Press, 1997.

Francis Courtade, *Les Malédictions du cinéma français*, Alain Moreau, 1978.

Tony Curtis with Barry Paris, *Tony Curtis: The Autobiography*, William Morrow, 1993.

Thomas Quinn Curtiss, *Von Stroheim*, Vintage Books, 1973.

Alain Desvignes, *Catherine Rouvel*, Autres Temps, 1997.

Jean Devaivre, *Action! Mémoires 1930–1970*, Nicolas Philippe, 2002.

Igor Devetak, *Nora Gregor, l'imperfezione della bellezza*, Kinoatelje Gorica, Amalthea Signum Verlag, 2005.

Michel Domange, *Ah ! Mes aïeux . . . (1830–1945)*, Les Éditions du Nant d'enfer, 1990.

Philip Dunne, *Take Two: A Life in Movies and Politics*, McGraw-Hill, 1980.

Susan Felleman, *Botticelli in Hollywood: The Films of Albert Lewin*, Twayne Publishers, 1997.

Syd Field, *Going to the Movies: A Personal Journey through Four Decades of Modern Film*, Bantam Dell, 2001.

Suzanne Finstad, *Warren Beatty: A Private Man*, Aurum, 2005.

Tag Gallagher, *The Adventures of Roberto Rossellini: His Life and Film*, Da Capo Press, 1998.

Maurizio Giammusso, *Vita di Rossellini*, Elleu multimedia, 2004.

Julie Gilbert, *Opposite Attraction: The Lives of Erich Maria Remarque and Paulette Goddard*, Pantheon, 1995.

Jean A. Gili, *Le Cinéma italien à l'ombre des faisceaux (1922–1945)*, Institut Jean Vigo, 1990.

Jean Gruault, *Ce que dit l'autre*, Julliard, 1992.

Jon Halliday, *Conversations avec Douglas Sirk*, Cahiers du cinéma, 1997.

Wes Herschensohn, *Resurrection in Cannes: The Making of* The Picasso Summer, A. S. Barnes and Company, Thomas Yoseloff, 1979.

Joris Ivens, *The Camera and I*, Seven Seas, 1969.

Jean-Pierre Jeancolas, *Quinze ans d'années trente*, Stock, 1983.

Henri Jeanson, *Soixante-dix ans d'adolescence*, Stock, 1971.

Brian Kellow, *The Bennetts: An Acting Family*, University Press of Kentucky, 2004.

Siegfried Kracauer, *Théorie du film, la rédemption de la réalité matérielle*, Flammarion, 2010.

Elsa Lanchester, *Herself*, Michael Joseph Limited, 1983.

Marcel Lapierre, *Les Cent Visages du cinéma*, Grasset, 1948.

Arthur Lennig, *Stroheim*, University Press of Kentucky, 2000.

Marcel L'Herbier, *La Tête qui tourne*, Belfond, 1979.

Sylvie Lindeperg, *Les Écrans de l'ombre, la Seconde Guerre mondiale dans le cinéma français (1944–1969)*, CNRS, 1997.

Vincent Lowy, *Guère à la guerre*, L'Harmattan, 2006.

Isabelle Marinone, *André Sauvage, un cinéaste oublié*, L'Harmattan, 2008.

Joseph McBride, *Searching for John Ford: A Life*, St. Martin's Press, 2001.

Patrick McGilligan, *Fritz Lang: The Nature of the Beast*, St. Martin's Press, 1997.

Liliane Meffre, *Carl Einstein, 1885–1940, Itinéraires d'une pensée moderne*, Presses de l'Université de Paris-Sorbonne, 2002.

James Morrison, *Passport to Hollywood: Hollywood Films, European Directors*, State University of New York Press, 1998.

Dileep Padgaonkar, *Under Her Spell: Roberto Rossellini in India*, Viking, 2008.

Bernard Pharisien, *Pierre Renoir*, Némont, 2003.

Pierre Philippe, *Maria Félix, la doña*, Assouline, 2006.

Jean Queval, *Jacques Becker*, Seghers, 1962.

Roberto Rossellini, *Fragments d'une autobiographie*, Ramsay, 1987.

Thomas Schatz, *The Genius of the System: Hollywood Filmmaking in the Studio Era*, Pantheon, 1989.

Laurence Schifano, *Visconti*, Perrin, 1987.

Marie Seton, *Portrait of a Director: Satyajit Ray*, Dobson, 1971.

Joel E. Siegel, *Val Lewton: The Reality of Terror*, Secker and Warburg–British Film Institute, 1972.

Walter Slezak, *What Time's the Next Swan?* Doubleday, 1962.

Janine Spaak, *Charles Spaak, mon mari*, France-Empire, 1977.

John Russell Taylor, *Strangers in Paradise: The Hollywood Émigrés 1933–1950*, Faber and Faber, 1983.

Jean-Paul Török, *Pour en finir avec le maccarthysme, Lumières sur la liste noire à Hollywood*, L'Harmattan, 1999.

King Vidor, *A Tree Is a Tree: An Autobiography*, Samuel French Edition, 1953.

Valérie Vignaux, *Jacques Becker ou l'exercice de la liberté*, Le Céfal, 2000.

Literary and Political History

Robert Aron, *Fragments d'une vie*, Plon, 1981.

Pierre Assouline, *Gaston Gallimard, Un demi-siècle d'édition française*, Gallimard, 2006.

Pierre Assouline, *Simenon*, Julliard, 1992.

Pierre Bertaux, *Un normalien à Berlin, lettres franco-allemandes 1927–1933*, Presses de la Sorbonne nouvelle, 2001.

André Beucler, *Plaisirs de mémoire, de Saint-Pétersbourg à Saint-Germain-des-Prés, Tome 2*, Gallimard, 1982.

Joseph Blotner, *Faulkner: A Biography*, Random House, 1974.

Brassaï, *Henry Miller, rocher heureux*, Gallimard, 1978.

Margaret Brenman-Gibson, *Clifford Odets: American Playwright: The Years from 1906–1940*, Atheneum, 1982.

Adry de Carbuccia, *Du tango à Lily Marlene, 1900–1940*, France-Empire, 1987.

Curtis Cate, *Antoine de Saint-Exupéry: His Life and Times*, Heinemann, 1970.

Larry Ceplair and Steven Englund, *The Inquisition in Hollywood: Politics in the Film Community, 1930–1960*, University of California Press, 1979.

Giulio Ceretti, *À l'ombre des deux T., quarante ans avec Maurice Thorez et Palmiro Togliatti*, Julliard, 1973.

Emmanuel Chadeau, *Saint-Exupéry*, Perrin, 2000.

Pierre Chevrier, *Antoine de Saint-Exupéry*, Gallimard, 1949.

Harold Clurman, *All People Are Famous (Instead of an Autobiography)*, Harcourt, Brace, Jovanovich, 1974.

Tom Dardis, *Some Time in the Sun: The Hollywood Years of Fitzgerald, Faulkner, Nathanael West, Aldous Huxley and James Agee*, Charles Scribner's Sons, 1976.

Christian Delporte, *Une histoire de la langue de bois*, Flammarion, 2009.

William W. Demastes, *Clifford Odets: A Research and Production Sourcebook*, Greenwood Press, 1991.

Simon Epstein, *Un paradoxe français: Antiracistes dans la Collaboration, anti-sémites dans la Résistance*, Albin Michel, 2008.

Philippe Erlanger, *La France sans étoile: Souvenirs de l'avant-guerre et de l'Occupation*, Plon, 1974.

Françoise Giroud, *Françoise Giroud vous présente le Tout-Paris*, Gallimard, 1952.

Françoise Giroud, *Leçons particulières*, Fayard, 1990.

Françoise Giroud, *Si je mens . . .*, Stock, 1972.

Henri Godard, *Céline*, Gallimard, 2011.

Rumer Godden, *A House with Four Rooms*, William Morrow, 1989.

Laurie B. Green, *Battling the Plantation Mentality: Memphis and the Black Freedom Struggle*, University of North Carolina Press, 2007.

Vittorio Mussolini, *Vita con mio padre*, Mondadori, 1957.

Lynn H. Nicholas, *The Rape of Europa: The Fate of Europe's Treasures in the Third Reich and the Second World War*, Knopf, 1994.

Henri Noguères, *La Vie quotidienne en France au temps du Front populaire, 1935–1938*, Hachette, 1977.

Pascal Ory, *La Belle Illusion, Culture et Politique sous le signe du Front populaire 1935–1938*, Plon, 1994.

Philippe Robrieux, *Maurice Thorez, vie secrète et vie publique*, Fayard, 1975.

Marie-Claude Roesch-Lalance, *Dans l'intimité de la communauté artistique de Bourron-Marlotte, si les maisons nous racontaient . . .*, edited by l'Association des Amis de Bourron-Marlotte, 1986.

Luc Van Dongen, *Un purgatoire très discret, la transition "helvétique" d'anciens nazis, fascistes et collaborateurs après 1945*, Perrin/Société d'histoire de la Suisse romande, 2008.

Novels, Journals, and Other Sources

Vereen Bell, *Swamp Water*, Little, Brown, 1941.

Bertolt Brecht, *Arbeitsjournal*, edited by Werner Hecht, Suhrkamp Verlag, 1973.

Bertolt Brecht, *La Vieille Dame indigne et autres histoires, 1928–1948*, translated by Bernard Lortholary, L'Arche, 1988.

Céline, *Bagatelles pour un massacre*, Denoël, 1937.

Jean des Vallières, *Kavalier Scharnhorst*, Albin Michel, 1931.

Jean Giraudoux, *Pleins Pouvoirs*, Gallimard, 1939.

Rumer Godden, *The River*, Little, Brown, 1946.

Roger Grenier, *Instantanés*, Gallimard, 2007.

Thomas Mann, *Journal 1940–1945*, text redacted by Peter de Mendelssohn and Inge Jens, French edition introduced and annotated by Christoph Schwerin, translated from the German by Robert Simon, Gallimard, 2000.

Prosper Mérimée, *Le Carrosse du Saint-Sacrement*, L'Arche, 1958.

Jacques Perret, *Le Caporal épinglé*, Gallimard, 1947.

George Sessions Perry, *Hold Autumn in Your Hand*, University of New Mexico Press, 1969.

Georges Simenon, *La Nuit du carrefour*, Fayard, 1931.

Mitchell Wilson, *None So Blind*, Simon & Schuster, 1945.

Index

Berthomieu, André, 174–175, 184

Besnard, René, 379–380

Bessie, Michael, 782

The Best Part. See La Meilleure Part

La Bête humaine, 43, 57–58, 292, 317

adaptation of, 330–333

American release of, 427

Carné's early involvement in, 328

cinematography and, 334

commercial success of, 346

critical reaction to, 343

director contract for, 330

fate in, 341

Gabin performance in, 339

locations in, 338–339

premiere screening of, 342

Le Quai des Brumes compared to, 342–343

realism and, 333

Renoir, Alain, working on, 339

Renoir, Jean, as actor in, 336–337

Renoir, Jean, offered, 328–329

screenplay of, 327, 331–333, 338

Simon, Simone, casting in, 337–339

Beucler, André, 379–380, 389, 392

Beylie, Claude, 697

Beysson, Constance, 645

Bézard, René, 707

Bickford, Charles, 528

The Big Knife (Odets), 669

The Big Sleep, 503

Billard, Pierre, 249, 661–662

Billiou, Olivier, 346

Billon, Pierre, 423

Binford, Lloyd T., 510–511

birth, 17–18

Birth of a Nation, 52

The Birth of Cinema. See Naissance du cinéma

Black Narcissus, 561

Blackbirds, 77–78

Blanchar, Pierre, 389, 698

Blasetti, Alessandro, 385

Blavette, Charles, 185, 187

Le Bled, 97, 99–101

Blier, Bernard, 340

Blondy, Raymond, 263–264, 270

Blood and Sand, 52

Blum, Léon, 276, 313

Blum, Ralph, 427

Blum-Byrnes agreements, 614

Bobone, Octávio, 421

Bodin, Richard-Pierre, 109–110, 128

Bogarde, Dirk, 762

Bogeaus, Benedict, 516

Boitel, Jeanne, 153

Le Bonheur (Renoir, Jean), 42

Bonin, Lou, 198

Bonne chance, 210

de Bonnemains, Céline, 652

Bonnie and Clyde, 747

Borradaile, Osmond, 571

Bossut, Louis, 258–259

Bost, Pierre, 595

Boudu sauvé des eaux (*Boudu Saved from Drowning*), 5, 137–138

adaptation of, 139–140

casting of, 140–141

critical reaction to, 145–148

directing style in, 144, 148

ingratitude in, 143–144

lack of recognition for, 149

locations in, 144–145

nonconformity and, 141

second editing of, 147–148

Simon, Michel, on, 142–144

Boulanger, Georges, 652–653

Boulay, Robert, 130

Bourdeau, Clément, 797

Bourneuf, Philip, 497

Boyer, Charles, 397, 446, 451–452

French Cancan and Gabin replacing, 625–626

Boyer, François, 476n

Les Braconniers. See Orvet

Bradbury, Ray, 744

Bradford, Ned, 741

Braque, Georges, 792

Le Brasier ardent, 53

Brasseur, Claude, 714

Brasseur, Pierre, 604

Braunberger, Pierre, 63–66, 102, 189, 595–596, 753–754

American film claims of, 59, 69

on authorship in cinema, 113

Bataille, Sylvia, and desire of, 225

La Chienne origination claims of, 113–114, 123

on Communist Party proposition, 211–212

directors hired by, 107–108

Doynel on faults of, 764

on editing of *La Chienne*, 119–120, 123

Les Établissements Braunberger-Richebé and, 105–107

as extra in *Diary of a Lost Girl*, 107

on financial needs of Renoir, Jean, 695

on Hitler assassination attempt, 155–156

on Hollywood and lack of options, 705–706

meeting, 59

Nana and, 67–68, 74–75

Partie de campagne and completion attempts of, 238–240, 545–546

Partie de campagne production halted by, 233, 235–236

assimilating to, 429

authorization to leave for, 400

Clair arriving in, 408

commitment to, 450, 541

Communism and ostracism from, 556–558

discontent with, 435

Duvivier offers from, 534

editing without directors in, 447–448

expectations for, 428

as factory, 442

failure and, 533, 538

finance struggles in, 556

France and preference for, 8

French exile community in, 451–453, 456–457, 487, 540

French press reaction to Renoir, Jean, in, 457–459

Godden's trip to, 572

homes in, 462, 533

HUAC and, 556–557

isolation away from, 717–718

journey to, 422–423

Lang, Fritz, struggling in, 481

offer from, 319

permission to leave for, 406–408

quality in, 538–539

reasons for fleeing to, 401–402

rejection from, 616

Renoir, Alain, arriving in, 454

Renoir, Alain, refusing exodus to, 414

Renoir, Dido, on opportunities in, 396–397

rustic existence in, 550

de Saint-Exupéry visiting, 216

Slade, Gabrielle, arriving in, 461–464

slowness of studios in, 526

studios downsizing in, 556

See also American films

Hollywood Museum, 616

Hollywood Reporter, 473, 483–484, 612

Holzki, Paul, 69

The Home and the World (Tagore), 568

Home to India (Rau), 563

L'Homme, 546

Les Hommes de bonne volonté (*Men of Good Will*) (Romains), 21

homosexuality, 172–173

of Carné, 326

of Laughton, 478–479

of Marais, 655

Honorary Oscar, 789–790

Hoover, Herbert, 15

Houllé, Marguerite, 11, 124, 132, 150–151, 196–197, 290, 625

appearance of, 173

Becker, Jacques, collaborating with, 537–538

on Becker, Jacques, as director, 310–311

Communism and, 174

falling out of love with, 345

letters from, 462–463

Mathieu killed by, 538

Partie de campagne and editing of, 239

reaction to breakup with, 549

La Règle du jeu and re-editing of, 365–366

relationship with, 10, 86, 100, 173–174

Renoir, Dido, compared to, 358

Renoir name taken by, 344

House Un-American Activities Committee (HUAC), 556–557, 560

How Green Was My Valley, 448

Howard, Cy, 651

Howard, Mary, 440, 458

HUAC. *See* House Un-American Activities

Committee

Hudgins, Johnny, 77–79

Hughes, Alice, 675

Hughes, Howard, 560

Hugon, André, 277

humanism, *The River* and, 590

L'Humanité, 118, 218–219, 234, 241–243, 291–292, 322, 723

Humberstone, H. Bruce, 435

The Hunchback of Notre Dame, 479

Hunger (Hamsun), 432, 704–705, 735

Hunt, Martita, 596

Las Hurdes (*Land without Bread*), 217

Huston, Virginia, 528, 531

Huston, Walter, 440, 558

I Wake Up Screaming, 433–435

Ibsen, Henrik, 618–619

identity

Durbin and promotion of adult, 471

French film struggles for, 175–176

La Grande Illusion and, 277

metamorphoses and, 14–15

Pierre-Auguste Renoir, mon père and, 727

IDHEC. *See* Institut des hautes écoles cinématographiques

Il y a encore des noisetiers (*There Are Still Hazelnut Trees*), 759

Illery, Paula, 184

Ilyin, Maximilian, 552–554

The Immortal Story, 768

improvisation, 108, 186

adaptation compared to, 629

Le Crime de monsieur Lange and, 202–204

La Grande Illusion and, 268–269

Julius Caesar and, 627

as rebellion, 632

Wattier, Lucienne, 673

Wayne, John, 13

We (Zamyatin), 243

Weaver, Randolph, 718

Webb, Mary, 494

Weill, Kurt, 156, 498

A Welcome to Britain, 496

Welles, Orson, 321, 486, 768

Wendt, Stefan, 435

Werner, Oskar, 705, 748

The Whirlpool of Fate, 48

  commercial failure of, 61

  distribution challenges of, 59–60

  dream sequence in, 58, 62

  enjoyment in creating, 58

  lessons learned from, 61–62

  locations of, 57

  production team formed for, 57–58

  special effects in, 58

White, Pearl, 43

Wiene, Robert, 66

Wilde, Oscar, 70

Wilder, Billy, 156, 731

Williams, Esther, 562

Wilson, Mitchell, 523–524

Wind, Sand and Stars. See Terre des hommes

Winfried, Winna, 130, 133

Woman of a Hundred Faces (treatment), 552–554

The Woman on the Bench

  adaptation of, 524

  bitterness towards, 529

  boredom with, 525

  casting of, 525, 528

  commercial and critical failure of, 531–532

  delay of, 526

  director vision for, 527

  genesis of, 523–524

  Rivette on, 532

  RKO's panic over, 530

  Rohmer on, 532

  second filming of, 531

  set atmosphere for, 528

  test screenings for, 529–530

The Woman Who Dared. See Le ciel est à vous

The Wonderful Country, 510

Woog, Roger, 233

Workers Leaving the Lumière Factory. See La Sortie des usines Lumière

World War I

  adventure of, 36

  American films rising in, 52

  aviation assignment in, 41

  early mobilization in, 34

  leg wounding in, 37–38

  length of, 36–37

  memories of, 42–43

  military transformation during, 35

  Renoir, Pierre's, injury in, 35

  See also military

World War II

  anti-Semitism in French films during, 404–405

  armistice and, 537

  departure reasons during, 401–402

  France postal communication with United States halted during, 487

  French films during, 399–401

  guilt and, 539

  Paris exodus and, 398–399

  Pearl Harbor attack and, 454, 471

  Renoir, Alain, serving in, 454–455, 522–523

Wyler, William, 744

xenophobia, Italy and, 391

You Ain't Seen Nothin' Yet. See Vous n'avez encore rien vu

The Youth of Maxim

  acting in, 241

  Communism and, 241–242

Yvette, 90

Zakrevskaya, Maria Ignatievna, 247–248

Zamyatin, Yevgeny, 243–244

Zanuck, Darryl F.

  on *The Diary of a Chambermaid*, 516

  on *Flight South*'s commercial prospects, 429–430

  on *La Grande Illusion*, 430

  incompatibility with, 445–446

  omnipotence of, 427–428

  screenplays sent from, 430–431, 433

  Swamp Water and crew change demands of, 445

  Swamp Water location battles with, 441

  Swamp Water shoot and criticism from, 444

  on *Swamp Water*'s budget, 437

Zay, Jean, 256

Zaza (monkey), 137

Zola, Émile, 69–71, 327, 343

Zuckmayer, Carl, 476–477

Zwobada, André, 174, 217, 346, 360, 605

Acknowledgments

Many thanks to Teresa Cremisi for having believed in this project and having made it possible.

Warm thanks to Christine, who supported me throughout all these years and who played an essential role in my research, especially in Los Angeles.

Claude Gauteur was there for me during the preparation and writing of this book from the first to the last day, and I'm infinitely grateful to him.

The help given me by the Institut Lumière for this book in the form of the first Prix Raymond Chirat turned out to be a decisive factor in its completion. I'd especially like to thank Bertrand Tavernier, its president, and Thierry Frémaux, its managing director.

Olivier Curchod was extremely attentive during the course of this project, and certain passages in this book are indebted to his work.

The research of Bernard Pharisien, great specialist on the history of the Renoir family, as well as the friendship he showed me, became an invaluable aid in the writing of this book.

Stéphane Launey revealed the secrets of Jean Renoir's military career to me.

The work and advice of several great Renoir scholars—Christopher Faulkner, Janet Bergstrom, Elizabeth Ann Vitanza, and William A. Gilcher—helped guide and illumine five years of research.

Raymond Chirat and Benoît Jacquot served as attentive and invaluable readers.

The portrait of Jean Renoir in this book was traced through conversations that the following individuals were kind enough to have with me:

Françoise Arnoul, Paolo Barzman, Jean Becker, Geneviève Boyard-Becker, Gisèle Braunberger, Laurence Braunberger, Leslie Caron, Aline Cézanne†, Isabelle d'Arnoux, Rosine Delamare, Nick Frankagis, Danièle Heymann, Dominique Labourier, Norman Lloyd, Eva Lothar, Walt Odets, Michel Piccoli, Alain Renoir†, Claude Rich, Marie-Claude Roesch-Lalance, Catherine Rouvel, Jacques Saulnier, Jo Siritzky, Jean Slade, and Christian Tual.

Thanks also to Sophie Renoir and Jacques Renoir.

Lauren Buisson was my guide through the twists and turns of the Jean Renoir Papers at UCLA, and she has become a friend. I'd also like to offer warm thanks to Amy Wong and the entire personnel of the Department of the Performing Arts, Special Collections, at the University of Southern California, Los Angeles.

My gratitude goes equally to the personnel of the research section of the Cinémathèque française, as well as to Marco Grifo, the Museo Nazionale del Cinema, Biblioteca Internazionale di Cinema e Fotogragia "Mario Gromo" of Turin, Odile Fuchs and *L'Est républicain,* Nebia Bendjebbour, and the research department of the *Nouvel Observateur.*

The Italian part of this book owes a great deal to the help and friendship of Marco Dell'Oro.

Bernard Lortholary, Christian Rozeboom, and Walter Salles made possible the translation of unpublished texts in German, Russian, and Portuguese.

This book was nourished by my conversations with friends in the film world who did or did not know Jean Renoir personally. I am thinking especially of Claude Chabrol,[†] Alain Corneau,[†] and Claude Miller,[†] as well as Alain Cavalier, Benoît Jacquot, Jean-Jacques Annaud, Bertrand Tavernier, and Gilles Bourdos.

Equally valuable to me was the help I received from Jean-Pierre Bertin-Maghit, N. T. Binh, Jean-Louis Blaisot, Jean-Pierre Bleys, Richard Boidin, Serge Bromberg, Freddy Buache, Lorenzo Codelli, Scott Foundas, Jacques Gerber, Gilles Grandmaire, Marie-Pierre Hauville, Philippe d'Hugues, Laure de La Tour, Dominique Lebrun, Gérard Lenne, Alain Liatard, Olivier Masclet, Pierre Murat, Jean Ollé-Laprune, Matthieu Orlean, Véronique Manniez-Rivette, Philippe Perebinossoff, Philippe Pochet, Jean-François Quemin, André-Paul Ricci, Pascal Rogard, Florence Roth, Jean-Pierre Saire, Jacques Siclier, Charles Silvestre, Alain Siritzky, Agnès Varda, and Régine Vial. Not to mention Marie Audet, Emma Saudin, and Anavril Wollman.

Thanks to Françoise Widhoff and Marie-Christine Damiens for their unending and discreet support.

Thanks also to Gilles Jacob for his friendship and collaborative spirit.

And thanks to Pierre Rissient, the "eminence grise" of world cinema.

Many thanks to Alice d'Andigné, an ideal editor.

My thoughts go to Patricia "Toupie" Renoir, in Esparto, California.

Brett Ratner's commitment and Scott Foundas's friendship have allowed this American edition to come into being. I offer them my warm thanks.

Cindy DeLaHoz was my attentive editor, and Cindi Rowell was a vigilant and expert copyeditor.

Throughout these long months, I've been able to evaluate my extraordinary good fortune in having Bruce Benderson as a translator who possesses expertise, intelligence, and a priceless sense of humor. The fact that a great writer such as he would devote himself to this essential task was a source of joy at every moment. I offer him my infinite gratitude and my friendship.